The Law of Journalism and Mass Communication

Fourth Edition

The Law of Journalism and Mass Communication

Fourth Edition

Robert Trager
University of Colorado

Joseph Russomanno
Arizona State University

Susan Dente Ross
Washington State University

Amy Reynolds
Louisiana State University

Los Angeles | London | New Delhi
Singapore | Washington DC

Los Angeles | London | New Delhi
Singapore | Washington DC

FOR INFORMATION:

CQ Press
An Imprint of SAGE Publications, Inc.
2455 Teller Road
Thousand Oaks, California 91320
E-mail: order@sagepub.com

SAGE Publications Ltd.
1 Oliver's Yard
55 City Road
London, EC1Y 1SP
United Kingdom

SAGE Publications India Pvt. Ltd.
B 1/I 1 Mohan Cooperative Industrial Area
Mathura Road, New Delhi 110 044
India

SAGE Publications Asia-Pacific Pte. Ltd.
3 Church Street
#10–04 Samsung Hub
Singapore 049483

Acquisitions Editor: Matthew Byrnie
Associate Editor: Nancy Loh
Assistant Editor: Allison Hughes
Editorial Assistant: Gabrielle Piccininni
Production Editor: David C. Felts
Copy Editor: Pam Suwinsky
Typesetter: C&M Digitals (P) Ltd.
Proofreader: Wendy Jo Dymond
Indexer: Joan Shapiro
Cover Designer: Rose Storey
Marketing Manager: Liz Thornton

Printed in the United States of America

Library of Congress Cataloging-in-Publication Data

Trager, Robert, author.

The law of journalism and mass communication / Robert Trager, University of Colorado Boulder; Joseph Russomanno, Arizona State University; Susan Dente Ross, Washington State University, Amy Reynolds, Louisiana State University.—Fourth Edition.

p. cm.
Includes bibliographical references and index.

ISBN 978-1-4522-3998-9 (alk. paper)

1. Mass media—Law and legislation—United States.
2. Press law—United States. 3. Freedom of the press—United States.
I. Russomanno, Joseph, author. II. Ross, Susan Dente, author.
III. Reynolds, Amy, 1967– author. IV. Title.

KF2750.T73 2015

343.7309'9—dc23   2013042662

Certified Chain of Custody
Promoting Sustainable Forestry
www.sfiprogram.org
SFI-01268
SFI label applies to text stock

13 14 15 16 17 10 9 8 7 6 5 4 3 2 1

For Our Families

About the Authors

Robert Trager is professor emeritus in journalism and mass communication at the University of Colorado. He taught courses in communication law, freedom of expression and media institutions. He is the founding editor of the law journal *Communication Law and Policy*. Before joining the University of Colorado faculty, he was an attorney with a major cable television company and practiced media law with a Washington, D.C., firm.

Joseph Russomanno is associate professor in the Walter Cronkite School of Journalism and Mass Communication at Arizona State University. His teaching and research focus on media law and First Amendment theory. He has a decade of experience as a broadcast journalist.

Susan Dente Ross is professor of English at Washington State University. A former newspaper owner and editor and head of the AEJMC Law Division, she is a Fulbright scholar whose international research, speaking and training focus on free speech and press for the disempowered and as a tool for global equity and justice. She publishes on law, policy and media's role in conflict transformation and reconciliation. She is a writer of creative nonfiction.

Amy Reynolds is the Thomas O. & Darlene Ryder II Distinguished Professor and Associate Dean for Graduate Studies and Research at the LSU Manship School of Mass Communication. She also co-directs the Press Law & Democracy Project at the Manship School. Her research focuses on dissent, First Amendment history, and breaking news. She has written or edited seven books. Prior to becoming a professor, she worked as a reporter at newspapers and television stations.

Brief Contents

Contents   x

Features   xx

Preface   xxvi

1. **The Rule of Law**
   Law in a Changing Communication Environment   2

2. **The First Amendment**
   Speech and Press Freedoms in Theory and Reality   50

3. **Speech Distinctions**
   Dangers, Fights, Threats and Educational Needs   100

4. **Libel**
   The Plaintiff's Case   142

5. **Libel**
   Defenses and Privileges   188

6. **Protecting Privacy**
   Conflicts between the Press, the Government
   and the Right to Privacy   226

7. **Emotional Distress and Physical Harm**
   When Words and Pictures Hurt   284

8. Newsgathering
Pitfalls and Protections   324

9. Reporter's Privilege
Protecting the Watchdogs   382

10. The Media and the Courts
Preserving Public Trials and Preventing Prejudice   418

11. Electronic Media Regulation
From Radio to the Internet   474

12. Obscenity, Indecency and Violence
Social Norms and Legal Standards   526

13. Intellectual Property
Protecting and Using Intangible Creations   576

14. Advertising
When Speech and Commerce Converge   636

Endnotes   675
Glossary   725
Recommended Readings   735
Photo Credits   741
Text Credits   745
Case Index   747
Subject Index   759

Contents

Features   xx
Preface   xxvi

Chapter 1 The Rule of Law
Law in a Changing Communication Environment   2

The Court System   8
   Jurisdiction   9
   Trial Courts   12
   Courts of Appeal   13
   The U.S. Supreme Court   15
   Judicial Review   18
Sources of the Law   20
   Constitutions   21
   Statutes   24
   Equity Law   26
   Common Law   26
   Administrative Rules   27
   Executive Orders   29
The Case Process   29
   Civil Suits   30
   Summary Judgment   33
Finding the Law   34
   Useful Legal Research Resources   35
Reading Case Law   35
   Briefing Cases   37
   Analyzing *Marbury v. Madison*   38

CASES FOR STUDY   40
  Citizens United v. Federal Election Commission   40
  Marbury v. Madison   46

Chapter 2 The First Amendment
Speech and Press Freedoms in Theory and Reality   50

Interpreting the First Amendment   53
The Origins of the First Amendment   56
  Foundations of First Amendment Theory   57
First Amendment Values   60
Media Emergence, Convergence and Consolidation   64
Contemporary Prior Restraints   65
Court Scrutiny of Laws That Affect First Amendment Rights 71
  Content-Based Laws   71
  Content-Neutral Laws   72
Political Speech   76
Elections and Campaign Finance   76
Anonymous Speech   78
Government Speakers   80
Public and Nonpublic Forums   81
  Private Property as a Public Forum   84
  Virtual Forums and Government Speakers   86
Compelled Speech   87
CASES FOR STUDY   89
  Near v. Minnesota   89
  New York Times Co. v. United States   97

Chapter 3 Speech Distinctions
Dangers, Fights, Threats and Educational Needs   100

National Security and Tranquility   102
  Threats to National Security   103

Court Tests to Protect Disruptive Speech   **108**

    The Clear and Present Danger Test   108

    The *Brandenburg* (or Incitement) Test   110

Speech Assaults   **111**

    Offensive Speech   112

    Fighting Words   112

    Hate Speech   114

    Current Standard   114

    Harmful Images   116

    Intimidation and Threats   117

Symbolic Speech   **120**

    Burning Speech   121

Speech in the Schools   **122**

    Protest in the Schools   123

    Offensive or Inappropriate Content   126

    Compelled Orthodoxy   128

    Campus Speech   129

    Speech Codes   134

CASES FOR STUDY   **136**

    Texas v. Johnson   136

    Tinker v. Des Moines Independent Community School District   138

Chapter 4 Libel
The Plaintiff's Case   142

A Brief History   **144**

Contemporary Issues   **149**

The Elements of Libel: The Plaintiff's Case   **150**

    Statement of Fact   150

    Publication   151

    Identification   157

    Defamation   158

    Falsity   162

    Fault   164

    Actual Malice   168

    Damages   178

CASES FOR STUDY   **180**

    New York Times Co. v. Sullivan   180

    Gertz v. Robert Welch, Inc.   182

Chapter 5 Libel
Defenses and Privileges

Defenses and Privileges | 188

Fair Report Privilege | **190**
Fair Comment and Criticism | **193**
Opinion | **195**
   Innocent Construction | 198
   Letters to the Editor | 200
   Rhetorical Hyperbole, Parody and Satire | 200
Neutral Reportage | **203**
Wire Service Defense | **204**
Single-Publication Rule | **204**
The Libel-Proof Plaintiff | **206**
Other Defense Issues | **208**
   Summary Judgment | 208
   Jurisdiction | 210
   Section 230 Immunity | 211
   Statute of Limitations | 212
   Length of Statutes of Limitation in Libel Actions | 212
   Retractions | 212
   Responsible Reporting | 214
CASES FOR STUDY | **216**
   Ollman v. Evans | 216
   Milkovich v. Lorain Journal Co | 221

Chapter 6 Protecting Privacy
Conflicts between the Press, the Government and the Right to Privacy

Conflicts between the Press, the Government and the Right to Privacy | 226

Privacy and the Supreme Court | **232**
Sources of Privacy Protection | **235**

Privacy Law's Development   **236**
False Light   **237**
   Plaintiff's Case   238
   Defenses   242
Appropriation   **243**
   Commercialization and Right of Publicity   244
   Plaintiff's Case   246
   Defenses   250
Intrusion   **259**
   Methods of Intruding   259
   Intrusion on Private Property   260
   Defenses   261
Private Facts   **264**
   Intimate Facts   265
   Legitimate Public Concern   267
   Publicity   268
   First Amendment Defense   269

CASES FOR STUDY   **273**
   City of Ontario v. Quon   273
   United States v. Jones   278

Chapter 7 Emotional Distress and Physical Harm
When Words and Pictures Hurt   284

Emotional Distress   **286**
   The Development of Emotional Distress Suits   286
Intentional Infliction of Emotional Distress   **288**
   Outrageousness   289
   Intentional or Reckless Action   292
   Actual Malice   293
   Cyberstalking   297
Negligent Infliction of Emotional Distress   **298**
Physical Harm   **301**
   Negligence   302
   Incitement   305
Communications Decency Act   **312**
Other Dangers   **313**
   Breach of Contract   313

Interference with Economic Advantage 314
Fraudulent Misrepresentation 315

CASES FOR STUDY **317**
Hustler Magazine Inc. v. Falwell 317
Snyder v. Phelps 319

Chapter 8 Newsgathering
Pitfalls and Protections 324

Access to Property **327**
Access to Public Property 327
Access to Quasi-Public Property 328
Newsgathering Pitfalls **334**
Harassment 334
Fraud and Misrepresentation 335
Using Social Media as Sources 338
Covert Recording **339**
Face-to-Face Recording 340
Recording "Wire" Conversations 341
Noncovert Recording 345
Denying Access to Records **346**
Privacy Act 347
Student Records 347
Medical Records 348
Driver's Information 348
Video Voyeurism 350
Newsgathering Protections **350**
Open-Government Laws 351
Access to Federal Records: The Freedom of Information Act 349
Access to Federal Meetings **367**
State Open-Records Laws 369
State Open-Meetings Laws 371

CASES FOR STUDY **373**
Wilson v. Layne 373
U.S. Department of Justice v. Reporters Committee for Freedom of the Press 376

Chapter 9 Reporter's Privilege
Protecting the Watchdogs

    382

Reporter's Privilege   **384**
   After *Branzburg*   388
Shield Laws   **391**
   Who Is Covered   394
   What Is Covered   394
   Shield Laws and Websites   395
   Other Sources of Protection   397
Breaking Promises of Confidentiality   **399**
Search Warrants   **401**
   Newsroom Searches   401
   The Privacy Protection Act   402
CASES FOR STUDY   **404**
   Branzburg v. Hayes   404
   Cohen v. Cowles Media Co.   416

Chapter 10 The Media and the Courts
Preserving Public Trials and Preventing Prejudice

    418

Fair Trials and Prejudicial Speech   **420**
   Media Effects   420
   Impartial Jurors   424
   Anonymous Juries   424
   Impartial Judges   426
Remedies to Prejudice   **426**
   Selecting the Jury   427
   Continuance   428
   Juror Admonition   428
   Juror Sequestration   428

Access to Trials   **429**
   Presumption of Open Trials   429
   Justifying Court Closure   432
   Closure to Protect Juveniles   435
   Closure to Protect Sexual Assault Victims   437
   Gags to Limit Extrajudicial Discussion   438
   Challenging Closure   441
Electronic Access to Trials   **441**
   Broadcasting and Recording   442
   Cameras and Courtrooms   444
   Newer Technologies   447
Bench-Bar-Press Guidelines   **450**
Access to Court Records   **452**
   Constitutional and Statutory Access   452
   Court Dockets   452
   State Secrets   453
   Court Access Rules   455
   Electronic Access to Court Records   456
CASES FOR STUDY   **459**
  Sheppard v. Maxwell   459
  Richmond Newspapers, Inc. v. Virginia   467

Chapter 11 Electronic Media Regulation
From Radio to the Internet   474

Federal Communications Commission   **478**
Broadcast Regulation   **481**
   Reasons to Regulate Broadcasting   481
   The Public Interest Standard   483
   Program and Advertising Regulations   483
   Broadcast Licensing   497
   Noncommercial Broadcasting   499
Cable Television Regulation   **500**
   Cable Regulation's Development   500
   Cable Franchising   504
   Cable Programming   506
Direct Broadcast Satellites   **511**
Internet Regulation   **512**
   FCC Internet Regulation   512

Net Neutrality 513
The Internet's First Amendment Status 514
CASES FOR STUDY **516**
Red Lion Broadcasting Co., Inc. v. Federal Communications Commission 516
Turner Broadcasting System, Inc. v. Federal Communications Commission 521

Chapter 12 Obscenity, Indecency and Violence
Social Norms and Legal Standards

526

Obscenity **529**
Comstock and *Hicklin* 529
Current Obscenity Definition 532
Enforcing Obscenity Laws 538
Indecency **544**
Broadcast Indecency 545
Cable Indecency 554
Internet Indecency 556
Video Games and Media Violence **560**
CASES FOR STUDY **566**
Miller v. California 566
FCC v. Fox Television Stations, Inc. 570

Chapter 13 Intellectual Property
Protecting and Using Intangible Creations

576

Copyright **578**
The Development of U.S. Copyright Law 579
The 1976 Copyright Act 580
Proving Copyright Infringement 599
Remedies for Copyright Infringement 602
Copyright Infringement Defense: Fair Use 603
Copyright, Computers and the Internet 609

Music Licensing 610
Music, the Internet and File Sharing 615
Trademarks 617
Distinctiveness Requirement 618
Registering a Trademark 622
Domain Names 623
Trademark Infringement 624
Trademark Infringement Defenses 626
CASES FOR STUDY 627
Golan v. Holder 627
Metro-Goldwyn-Mayer Studios, Inc. v. Grokster, Ltd. 631

Chapter 14 Advertising
When Speech and Commerce Converge 636

The Evolution of the Commercial Speech Doctrine 638
Controlled Substances and Activities 642
Corporate Speech Regulation 648
Legislative and Agency Advertising Regulation 649
The Federal Trade Commission 651
Other Administrative Regulation 658
Internet Advertising 658
CASES FOR STUDY 661
*Central Hudson Gas & Electric Corp. v. Public Service
Commission of New York* 661
Sorrell v. IMS Health Inc. 667

Endnotes 675
Glossary 725
Recommended Readings 735
Photo Credits 741
Text Credits 745
Case Index 747
Subject Index 759

Features

Chapter 1 The Rule of Law

Emerging Law
The People Flex to Change the Law   7
International Law
Transnational Rules of Justice   6
Points of Law
What's in a Face?   8
A Test for Court Jurisdiction of Internet Disputes   9
Six Sources of Law   20
The Three Branches of Federal Government   22
Real Word Law
U.S. Rule of Law Falls Behind   4
Ideological Leanings   13
A Bit Like Making Sausage?   19
Instant Petitions Online   22
Executive Order on Cybersecurity   28
Blogger Bests "Bullying" Subpoena   32

Chapter 2 The First Amendment

Emerging Law
What's Speech?   62
Nameless, Faceless and Powerful Online?   79
International Law
Internet Flavor-of-the-Month?   59
Cutting Off Online Access   66
Points of Law
What's the Value of Free Speech?   61
What Is a Prior Restraint?   67
When Are Prior Restraints Constitutional?   68
Strict Scrutiny   72

Intermediate-Level Scrutiny | 74
Where Does Intermediate Scrutiny Apply? | 75
Real World Law
First Amendment Protections for the Traveling Circus | 52
The Pentagon Papers of Our Time? | 69
The Politics of Election Finance | 78
Bimbos, Sleazebags and Bigots | 83
But Where Can I Speak? | 85

Chapter 3 Speech Distinctions

International Law
Does *This* Speech Pose an Imminent Threat? | 106
Points of Law
The *Brandenburg* Test | 111
Fighting Words | 113
Is That a Threat? | 118
Nonuniversity Student Speech | 123
Real World Law
Democracy's Unreasoned, Uncivil Promise | 104
Are These "Troublous" Times? | 107
Fighting Words, Hate or Free Speech? | 115
Text Threats | 119
Is Shouting Always "Shouting Fire"? | 131
A Conservative Take on Campus Speech? | 134

Chapter 4 Libel: The Plaintiff's Case

Emerging Law
Time for a Federal Anti-SLAPP Law? | 149
Anonymous Speech and Libel: Three Approaches | 155
Strict Liability: Is a Blogger a Journalist? | 176
International Law
The U.K. Abolishes Seditious Libel, Colorado Repeals Criminal Libel Law | 146
Points of Law
Slander vs. Libel | 144
States with Anti-SLAPP Protection | 148
The Plaintiff's Libel Case | 151
Libel Plaintiff's Case When Defendant Is Anonymous | 156
The Burden of Proof as Deterrent | 163
Actual Malice | 168
"Reckless Disregard" Criteria | 171
Limited-Purpose Public Figure | 174
Real World Law
Libel and the Online Publisher | 153
Twibel: Defamation in 140 Characters? | 154
Oprah and the Cattlemen | 161
The Impact of *New York Times Co. v. Sullivan*: The "Central Meaning of the First Amendment" | 167
Masson v. New Yorker Magazine, Inc. and Journalistic Responsibility | 169

Chapter 5 Libel: Defenses and Privileges

Emerging Law

The *Twombly* and *Iqbal* Standard: Motion to Dismiss for Actual Malice?   209

International Law

Libel Tourism and the U.K. Defamation Bill 2013   207

Points of Law

Fair Report Privilege   190

The *Ollman* Test for Opinion   196

Neutral Reportage   204

The Wire Service Defense   204

A Test for Jurisdiction   210

Real World Law

Consumer Reviews and Criticism Online   194

Defining Opinion: *Ollman v. Evans*   199

Best and Worst Lists: Rhetorical Hyperbole?   201

Edwards v. National Audubon Society: The Origin of Neutral Reportage   205

Chapter 6 Protecting Privacy

Emerging Law

Cloud Computing and "Going Dark"   234

Keyword Advertising and Commercial Use   245

Right of Publicity in Video Games   255

Points of Law

Constitutional Right to Privacy   235

The Four Privacy Torts   237

False Light   238

Appropriation   244

Commercialization   247

Intrusion by Trespass   261

Private Facts   264

Real World Law

Stuck in the 1980s?   231

Facebook's Sponsored Stories   248

The Naked Cowboy, Jimmy Kimmel and "Extreme Fast Food"   249

"Revenge Porn" Websites: Invasion of Privacy or Simply Unethical?   265

Chapter 7 Emotional Distress and Physical Harm

Emerging Law

Reality in Reality Programs   293

Media Incitement   307

Points of Law

Intentional Infliction of Emotional Distress   289

Parody or Satire?   295

Negligent Infliction of Emotional Distress   299

Proximate Cause   305

What Is a Contract?   314

Real World Law

Dateline, Texas: To Catch a Lawsuit?   290

The "Pornographer" and His Attorney 294
Cyberbullying 308
"Hit Man": Protected or Not? 310
Media Inspiring Violent Acts 311

Chapter 8 Newsgathering

International Law

Hacking into Arrest 338

Points of Law

The Media and Search Warrants 331
Wilson v. Layne: The State of Ride-Alongs 332
States That Forbid Unauthorized Use of Cameras in
 Private Places 340
Recording Calls 341
Freedom of Information Act: Some Basics 351
Freedom of Information Act: The Nine Exemptions 356
State Open-Meetings Laws: The New York Example 371

Real World Law

The Embarrassment of Ride-Alongs 333
"California v. Paparazzi" 335
Undercover at Work 336
Video of Public Places 345
Leaking to Reporters: Espionage? 349
How Responsive Is the U.S. Government to FOIA Requests? 355
NASA and FOIA 362
The Fight over Photos 365
E-Mail as a Public Record? 368
Access in the Digital Age 370

Chapter 9 Reporter's Privilege

Points of Law

The Reporter's Privilege Test 386
Contempt of Court 387
The U.S. Supreme Court Suggested Shield Laws 393
Potential Options for Journalist Protection of Confidential Sources 394

Real World Law

"An Act of Conscience" 389
Leakers and the Law 392
Reporters, Subpoenas and Contempt 395
Passing the First Test 396
Anonymous Posters on News Websites 398
Cohen v. Cowles Media Co.: A Reporter's Perspective 400

Chapter 10 The Media and the Courts

Emerging Law

Fair Trials and Facebook Friends 425
Tea Leaves, Cameras and Inevitability 446
Social Media Invasion 447

Points of Law

Open Courts   432

The *Press-Enterprise* Test for Court Closure   433

Closing Media Mouths: The *Nebraska Press* Standard   439

What Is Fair Coverage of Criminal Trials?   451

Real World Law

Crime Time News?   422

Media Target Their Battles for Open Courts   430

Open Your Mouth and Open Courts   440

Cameras or Coroners in the Court?   445

Managing New Media in Courts   449

A Reasonable Balance?   454

Chapter 11 Electronic Media Regulation

Emerging Law

Wi-Fi and the FCC   480

Violent Media Link to Mass Shootings?   491

Cutting the Cord?   507

International Law

Australian-American   498

Real World Law

The FCC and a Mega-merger   479

Political Advertising and the 2012 Elections   485

Reality TV and the First Amendment   492

Emergency Alert: Zombie Attack?   494

Chapter 12 Obscenity, Indecency and Violence

International Law

Obscenity in Canada   530

United Kingdom: No Online Sex for Minors   539

Games and Violence in Russia and China   561

Points of Law

Disgusting and Repugnant   528

The SLAPS Test   537

Censoring the Internet   556

Real World Law

Pornography from a Different Viewpoint   530

Comstock in Action   531

Sex and the Restaurant   533

Sex and the Internet   535

Comedian George Carlin   547

Pigs in Parlors   548

Dickens v. The House of the Dead   562

Video Game Ratings   564

Chapter 13 Intellectual Property

Emerging Law

Sell That Song? 592

Can Google Own Every Book Ever Printed? 607

International Law

It's Cool to Be Uncool 581

The Beatles' 1960s Recordings Are Safe for Another 20 Years 615

Sounds in Canada 621

Points of Law

The U.S. Constitution: Copyrights and Patents 578

Exclusive Rights in Copyrighted Works 591

The Public Domain 596

Infringing Copyright 600

Fair Use Defense 604

What Does "Perform" Mean? 611

Confusing? 619

Real World Law

Happy Money . . . er, Birthday 585

Oz the Copyrighted 587

The Sonny Bono Law 595

Use It for Free 597

Are These Photos Substantially Similar? 601

"South Park": Infringement or Parody? 605

Sports Trademarks 618

Apple and Its Trademarks 620

Diluting a Trademark 625

Chapter 14 Advertising

Emerging Law

Weed Control? 643

Piling on Unwanted Texts 659

International Law

New EU Tune on Misleading Advertising 641

Points of Law

The Free Flow of (Commercial) Information 640

The Commercial Speech Doctrine 640

False and Misleading 651

FTC Mechanisms 652

Real World Law

Smoke-Filled Rooms and Hazy Standards? 646

The Jury's Out: Does Advertising Increase Product Demand? 650

Cheat Death or Cease and Desist? 653

Advertisers Beware! 655

In the Amazon Jungle: Third-Party Liability 658

Preface

This fourth edition of "The Law of Journalism and Mass Communication" welcomes Amy Reynolds of Louisiana State University to the authors' circle. Although Joseph Russomanno did not participate in this new edition, much of his contribution remains in the book. And although this edition contains perhaps 40 percent new content, it is the progeny of earlier editions in which the authors strove to reconceive the nature of a media law text and to create a truly readable book focused sharply on the most significant aspects of the law situated within the social and political contexts that give them meaning.

If you plan to be a journalist or practitioner of new or old media, this book is intended and designed primarily to serve you, to help you understand the protections and constraints imposed by the law upon the practice of your future craft. At the same time, we suspect some of you may be interested in a career in the law, and we would be very pleased indeed if this book not only fueled that interest but also helped start you on your way.

Our goal is to make "The Law of Journalism and Mass Communication" as fresh and new as possible. To make it interesting and, yes, sometimes even fun or funny. To incorporate not only the latest court rulings and legislative enactments but also to present the trials and resolutions outside of court and beyond the judiciary that show how the law affects the ways mass communications work and how people perceive and receive that work. That means this edition deals with social media and occupations of public parks, it looks at limitations on student press freedom and cybersecurity, libel on the Internet and cigarette advertising and much more.

Our unique approach to "The Law of Journalism and Mass Communication" developed in response to the way we teach and the way we believe students learn best. We see the law as a product of specific decisions at a particular time and in a specific place. As such, the law is best understood when we see and feel its effects on real people, mundane conflicts and actions not only of our government but also of our friends, neighbors and families. Yet we recognize that time shifts rapidly, and decisions are both local and global. To widen the lens through which we view the law of mass communication and to emphasize that digital means local is global, this edition introduces two new features focused on **Emerging Law** and **International Law**. You'll find boxes in many chapters tying development in the U.S. courts to situations beyond our borders and beyond today. In addition, **realWorld Law** boxes point readers to the intersections among the law, media practitioners and the people and the world they cover each day. Boxes also reinforce essential **Points of Law** by pulling them out of the text and highlighting them.

Beyond that, we have fine-tuned a number of elements that you will not find in other textbooks on the law of journalism and mass communication. In each chapter, an initial quotation provides unique perspectives and real-life examples of the law at work. Timelines in each chapter remind us when the Web became our favorite public forum and when radio seemed like an alien intruder in our homes, the times when government regulation was welcomed as the last best hope of the people and when it was simply another weapon wielded by the powerful. We also offer definitions in the margins throughout the book as well as in a glossary at the back to make it easier to read and digest the often-unfamiliar terminology of the law. The **Suppose** . . . hypothetical that opens each chapter allows you to engage with a central issue of the law and to ponder its implications before it is resolved in one of the two excerpted cases at the chapter's end. And those excerpted **Cases for Study** transform this textbook from a discussion *about* to a presentation *of* the law. They provide the opportunity for you to engage directly and personally with the legal decisions that construct "The Law of Journalism and Mass Communication." Cases new to this edition include *Near v. Minnesota*, *United States v. Jones*, *Snyder v. Phelps*, *FCC v. Fox Television Stations, Inc.*, *Golan v. Holder* and *Sorrell v. IMS Healthcare, Inc.*

We incorporate ample photographs, color and break-out boxes to make the book more attractive and to reinforce significant points but also to respond to the need for a more dynamic reading environment that encourages critical evaluation. Beyond the innovations, though, "The Law of Journalism and Mass Communication" should feel familiar because it adopts the organization of traditional media law texts with sharper writing, bright descriptions and easy-to-navigate sections we believe you will read and, perhaps, enjoy. Oh, and there's a companion website, located at http://college.cqpress.com/medialaw, to help you as student or instructor with chapter summaries, learning objectives, practice quizzes, interactive flashcards and annotated Web links for further research. Instructors also will find test questions, PowerPoint lecture slides and sample classroom activities.

We make every effort to keep the contents of this book abreast of the most recent decisions of significance, of the cutting-edge research in the field and of the social, technological and economic shifts that transform how "dot-com" execs and reporters do their jobs. Just as Congress and the courts have altered the law in the two years since our last edition, updates and new information have reshaped every area of this edition of "The Law of Journalism and Mass Communication." Some of the more significant changes in this edition explore the following:

- Transnational rules of justice
- Website removals by federal agencies
- Sanctions on reporters for personal activities and expression
- Court ruling prohibiting public school discriminatory Internet filtering
- U.S. Supreme Court decision extending full First Amendment protection to violent video games
- Determination of who published material on the Internet as an element of libel
- Twitter libel or Twibel
- Protection of consumer criticism and reviews online
- New rulings on fair report privilege
- Court decisions on the opinion defense to libel
- U.S. Supreme Court ruling on the expectation of privacy from government surveillance
- Doxxing and the limits to privacy online
- U.S. Supreme Court decision on the right to picket military funerals
- Internet streaming, cyberstalking and emotional distress
- Limits on newsgathering through limited access to physical spaces
- Reporting leaked information, including WikiLeaks
- Reporter's privilege and nontraditional journalists
- West Virginia's shield law
- Social media in the courtroom
- Court orders as prior restraints
- Proposed changes in FCC ownership rules
- U.S. Supreme Court decision and other changes related to Net neutrality
- The Internet and child pornography
- U.S. Supreme Court ruling on broadcast indecency
- Government-mandated product labeling and its limits
- Cases involving the application of European Union copyright law
- Resale of digital music and books
- Regulation of unwanted texts, Tweets, e-mails and faxes

We hope the breadth and diversity of media law you will discover in this volume provide the framework for a dynamic, engaged experience with how the law is a tool both for empowerment and oppression. We also hope you find this text in good order, for, as Aristotle said, "Good law is good order."

Acknowledgments

As with our previous editions, this book is a collaborative effort not only among its authors but also between us and the community we serve. There is a large and expanding group of people whose knowledge, insights and comments have helped us create, update and improve this book. We offer our deep respect and abiding gratitude to all those who have helped shape our understanding of the field, gently pointed out our faults of commission or omission and reinforced the strengths of this edition of "The Law of Journalism and Mass Communication." You have been more generous than we deserve.

Beyond the friends, families, students and colleagues who have encouraged and supported us in uncounted ways, we extend special thanks to Jane Thompson and other faculty and staff at the University of Colorado Law Library; Washington, D.C., media attorney Jack Goodman; Don Zachary at the University of Southern California's Annenberg School for Communication and Journalism as well as the anonymous reviewers who provided valuable feedback or, perhaps, favored our text among other books in the field. We also express our gratitude to the talented editors, designers and staff at CQ Press who helped birth this newest edition.

Finally, and most important, we thank you, our readers.

The Law of Journalism
and Mass Communication

Chapter 1

Living under a written constitution, no branch or department of the government is supreme; and it is the province and duty of the judicial department to determine in cases regularly brought before them, whether the powers of any branch of the government, and even those of the legislature in the enactment of laws, have been exercised in conformity to the Constitution; and if they have not, to treat their acts as null and void.

U.S. Supreme Court Chief Justice Earl Warren[1]

Citizens assemble in Boston as part of a national "Occupy the Courts" event to protest the U.S. Supreme Court's *Citizens United* decision lifting restrictions on corporate contributions to political campaigns.

The Rule of Law

Law in a Changing Communication Environment

The Court System

Jurisdiction
Trial Courts
Courts of Appeal
The U.S. Supreme Court
Judicial Review

Sources of the Law

Constitutions
Statutes
Equity Law
Common Law
Administrative Rules
Executive Orders

The Case Process

Civil Suits
Summary Judgment

Finding the Law

Useful Legal Research
   Resources

Reading Case Law

Briefing Cases
Analyzing *Marbury v.
   Madison*

Cases for Study

➤ *Citizens United v.
   Federal Election
   Commission*
➤ *Marbury v. Madison*

Suppose . . .

. . . it now costs a lot to get elected, and people with money can distort elections. In response, the federal government adopts campaign finance laws that limit contributions to and spending by political candidates. The laws try to establish a balance between the right of individuals and groups to support candidates and the need to protect the integrity of elections from corruption. Big money challenges the campaign finance laws in court. In 1990 and 2003,[2] the U.S. Supreme Court upholds both state and federal restrictions on campaign funding by corporations and provides eloquent support for the need to regulate election spending. Then, in 2007, the Court finds a federal[3] ban on certain political advertisements unconstitutional. Writing in dissent, Justice David Souter argues that the Court's decision rejected more than a century of well-established law supporting limits on campaign spending and political advocacy. He writes, "The court (and, I think, the country) loses when important precedent is overruled without good reason."[4]

In the lead-up to the 2008 presidential election, a federal district court relied heavily on Supreme Court precedent to uphold campaign finance law and prohibit a nonprofit organization called Citizens United from running advertisements and airing a film about then-Sen. Hillary Clinton.[5] When appealed to the Supreme Court, one question posed by *Citizens United v. Federal Election Commission*[6] was whether precedent bound the Court's ruling. In this chapter and the case excerpts that follow, we explore how the rule of law remains stable and how it changes.

Some 2,500 years ago, the Greek philosopher Aristotle said people are basically self-interested; they pursue their own interests to the exclusion of the greater good or the cause of justice. However, self-interest is ultimately short-sighted and self-destructive. For example, a lumber company that seeks only to generate the greatest immediate profits ultimately deforests the timberlands it depends on, thereby eliminating its own future.[7] Far-sighted people therefore recognize that personal interests and short-term goals must sometimes give way to universal or long-term objectives. Aristotle observed that both individuals and the whole of society benefit when people adopt a mutually acceptable system of rules to promote a balance between gain and loss, cost and benefit, and between personal desires and universal concerns. Aristotle called this balance the "golden mean." Human interests are served and justice is achieved when a system of law applies equally and fairly to every individual—when people treat each other as they would like to be treated.

Belief in the power of laws to promote this balance and restrain human injustice is the foundation of the U.S. Constitution and the **rule of law**. The rule of law is intended to create a societal framework in which pre-established norms and procedures provide for consistent, neutral decision making. In essence, laws establish a contract that governs interactions among citizens, and between citizens and their government. The recognized system of laws binds both citizens and governors. A set of general, open and relatively stable legal rules determines the boundaries of acceptable individual and institutional behavior and empowers government to punish violations. The established rule of law limits the power of government because it prohibits government from infringing on the fundamental rights and liberties of the people. Another established set of procedures determines how government may enact, apply or alter the law. As a result, legal rules constrain the actions both of citizens and government to enhance liberty, freedom and justice for all.

The law functions best when citizens understand the boundary between legal and illegal behavior. Good laws must be sufficiently clear and precise to properly

rule of law The framework of a society in which pre-established norms and procedures provide for consistent, neutral decision making.

vague laws Laws that either fail to define their terms or use such general language that neither citizens nor judges know with certainty what the laws permit or punish.

realWorld Law

U.S. Rule of Law Falls Behind

A 2012 ranking by the World Justice Project, an initiative of the American Bar Association,[1] placed the United States below developing nations such as Botswana and Georgia in terms of adherence to the rule of law. Due primarily to low scores on scales of equal protection and civil justice, the United States ranked slightly above the bottom quarter of the 97 countries ranked and in the bottom 20 percent of wealthy nations. The report faulted the United States for insufficient mechanisms to assure legal access and equitable relief for minorities, foreigners and the poor.[2]

1. *Rule of Law Index* (Feb. 22, 2013), *available at* http://worldjusticeproject.org/who-we-are-0.
2. *See,* Dan Froomkin, *Rule of Law Index: U.S. Ranks Low in Access to Justice Compared to Other Wealthy Nations,* HUFFINGTON POST, Nov. 11, 2012, *available at* http://www.huffingtonpost.com/2012/11/28/rule-of-law-index-2012_n_2200765.html.

inform citizens of when and how the laws apply (as well as when they do not). **Vague laws** either fail to define their terms or use such general language that neither citizens nor judges know with certainty what the laws permit or punish. Vague laws relating to speech are unacceptable because they may chill or discourage speech by individuals who may choose not to speak rather than risk running afoul of a law that is unclear. In one recent example, a U.S. District Court judge in New York ruled that provisions of the 2012 National Defense Authorization Act were unconstitutionally vague.[8] Section 1021[9] of the act allows the indefinite detention of any "person who was a part of or substantially supported al-Qaeda, the Taliban, or associated forces." The judge agreed that the law had a chilling effect on the reporters and activists who argued that they might be subject to indefinite detention because U.S. authorities might decide that some of their sources fell under the law. With an appeal from the Obama administration pending, the Supreme Court in 2013 refused to vacate a stay that allowed the indefinite detention provision to stand without touching the issue of its vagueness.[10]

Clear laws define their terms and detail their application in order to limit government officials' **discretion.** In this way, clear laws enhance justice by reducing the likelihood that officials will apply legal rules differently to their friends as opposed to their foes.

Good laws accomplish their objectives with minimum infringement on the freedoms and liberties of the people. Carefully tailored laws advance specific government interests or prevent particular harms without punishing activities that pose no conceivable risk to society. A law that sought to limit noisy disturbances of residential areas at night, for example, would be poorly drawn and **overbroad** if it prohibited all discussion out of doors at any time even in a commercial district far from any homes. Well-crafted laws also must be sufficiently stable to adequately inform people of the legal limitations they impose. People will not long support a system that punishes them for infractions they did not know existed.

The rule of law thus requires the entire body of law to be internally consistent, logical and

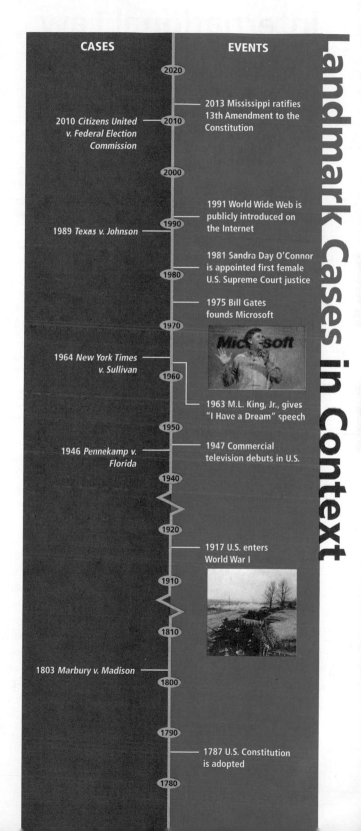

Landmark Cases in Context

CASES

EVENTS

2020

2013 Mississippi ratifies 13th Amendment to the Constitution

2010 *Citizens United v. Federal Election Commission* — 2010

2000

1991 World Wide Web is publicly introduced on the Internet

1989 *Texas v. Johnson* — 1990

1981 Sandra Day O'Connor is appointed first female U.S. Supreme Court justice — 1980

1975 Bill Gates founds Microsoft

1970

1964 *New York Times v. Sullivan* — 1960

1963 M.L. King, Jr., gives "I Have a Dream" speech

1950

1947 Commercial television debuts in U.S.

1946 *Pennekamp v. Florida* — 1940

1920

1917 U.S. enters World War I

1910

1810

1803 *Marbury v. Madison* — 1800

1790

1787 U.S. Constitution is adopted

1780

International Law

Transnational Rules of Justice

The United Nations views the rule of law as a cornerstone of international peace and justice.[1] In its 2011 report, the U.N. highlighted the special importance it places on rule of law efforts in conflict and post-conflict societies where such initiatives can be the foundation of a sustainable peace. The U.N. conducts initiatives to strengthen the rule of law in more than 150 countries, where it works to (1) promote transitional justice, (2) re-establish people's trust in public systems of justice and security, and (3) promote gender equality. U.N. activities also support the codification, development, promotion and implementation of international norms and standards in international law, according to the U.N. website.

Flags outside the United Nations headquarters in New York City represent some of the 150 countries that work together to craft transnational rules to structure the increasingly multinational reach of our activities.

Since 2007, the American Bar Association's Rule of Law Initiative also has employed more than 400 staffers in 40 countries to work with in-country partners to advance the rule of law by supporting sustainable institutions to advance economic opportunity and justice, and ensure respect for human dignity.[2]

1. United Nations, *Rule of Law* (Feb. 13, 2013), *available at* http://www.unrol.org/article.aspx?article_id=169.
2. American Bar Association Rule of Law Initiative (Feb. 22, 2013), *available at* http://www.americanbar.org/advocacy/rule_of_law/about/origin_principles.html.

---

discretion The authority to determine the proper outcome.

overbroad law Violates the principles of precision and specificity in legislation.

stare decisis Literally, "stand by the previous decision."

precedent Case judgment that establishes binding authority and guiding principles for cases to follow on closely analogous questions of law within the court's jurisdiction.

relatively stable. To ensure slow evolution rather than rapid revolution of legal rules, judges interpret and apply laws based upon the precedents established by other court rulings. Precedent, or **stare decisis**, is the legal principle that courts should stand by what has been decided. The principle holds that subsequent court decisions should adhere to the example and reasoning of earlier decisions on the same point. Reliance on **precedent** is the heart of the common law (discussed later) and encourages consistent, predictable application of the law. But precedent is not absolutely binding; it is not always followed; and sometimes precedents seem to conflict. As longtime Supreme Court reporter Linda Greenhouse wrote, "Continuity and change, the entwined spirals of a double helix, are the [law's] DNA."[11]

Laws are not inflexible. Even the U.S. Constitution—the foundational contract between the U.S. government and the citizens—can be changed through amendment. Other laws—the regulations, orders and rules that proliferate at the federal, state and local levels—may be repealed or amended by the bodies that adopted them, and they may be interpreted or invalidated by the courts. As the Supreme Court wrote in its landmark 1803 ruling in *Marbury v. Madison* (excerpted at the end of this chapter), "It is emphatically the province and duty of the judicial

Emerging Law

The People Flex to Change the Law

An "Occupy Wall Street" demonstrator displays displeasure with the U.S. Supreme Court's *Citizens United* decision that flooded the 2012 national elections with unprecedented corporate contributions.

The Supreme Court's decision in *Citizens United v. Federal Elections Commission*[1] angered the public and fueled initiatives to change the law through grassroots movements and congressional action. People marched in the streets and staged public protests outside federal court houses and state capitols across the country. One survey in 2012 found that almost half of U.S. voters strongly opposed the Court's decision.[2] Another found that nearly seven in ten registered voters believed that the super PACs *Citizens United* allowed to funnel corporate funding into campaigns should be illegal.[3] Public officials, including President Barack Obama, organized advisory reviews and called for campaign finance reform.

By early 2013, eight amendments to the U.S. Constitution designed to address various concerns with *Citizens United* were pending before the 113th Congress, according to the website United For The People.[4] The "We the People" amendment, proposed by Reps. Rick Nolan and Mark Pocan,[5] sought to establish that the rights extended by the U.S. Constitution "are the rights of natural persons only." The amendment also would empower local, state and federal governments to "regulate, limit, or prohibit [any] contributions and expenditures" intended to influence elections or ballot initiatives.[6] According to the website, other proposed constitutional amendments would impose limits on election expenditures and contributions, exclude corporations and businesses from the protections of the First Amendment, or regulate political contributions by corporations, for-profit organizations and labor unions.[7]

1. Citizens United v. Federal Elections Comm'n, 588 U.S. 50 (2010).
2. Press Release, Democracy Corps, Greenberg Quinlan Rosner Research, & Pub. Campaign Action Fund, *Two Years After Citizens United, Votes Fed Up with Money in Politics*, Jan. 19, 2012, *available at* http://campaignmoney.org/files/DemCorpPCA FmemoFINAL.pdf.
3. Chris Cillizza & Aaron Blake, *Poll: Voters Want Super PACs to Be Illegal*, Wash. Post, Mar. 13, 2012, *available at* http://www .washingtonpost.com/blogs/the-fix/post/poll-voters-want-super-pacs-to-be-illegal/2012/03/12/gIQA6skT8R_blog.html.
4. United For The People (Feb. 17, 2013), *available at* http://www.united4thepeople.org.
5. See *We the People, Not We the Corporations* (Feb. 11, 2013), *available at* https://movetoamend.org.
6. H.J.Res. 29, http://www.govtrack.us/congress/bills/113/hjres29/text, introduced Feb. 14, 2013.
7. United For The People (Feb. 17, 2013), *available at* http://www.united4thepeople.org/amendments113.html.

department to say what the law is. Those who apply the rule to particular cases must of necessity expound and interpret that rule."[12] All legislatures from the local city council to the U.S. Congress, all executives from the mayor to the U.S. president, and many administrative agencies have the power to enact laws. Thousands of individuals and agencies across the country freely exercise the authority to pass legal rules that define and restrict the rights of people and organizations. These laws respond to the changing expectations of citizens and the evolving needs of the nation in a rapidly changing global environment.

Points of Law

What's in a Face?

Some constitutional challenges to laws are raised before a law is applied. Such challenges, called **facial challenges**, claim that although the clear, plain and simple language of a law seems constitutional "on its face," it is nonetheless unconstitutional. For example, challenges for vagueness and overbreadth generally arise as facial First Amendment challenges to laws related to speech.

Laws are unconstitutionally vague if they are expressed in a way that is too unclear for a person to reasonably know whether or not the law applies to specific conduct. Vague laws do not provide fair notice to citizens about what actions are illegal and provide too much room for arbitrary or discriminatory enforcement. Vague laws also may have a "chilling" effect on individuals who will avoid activities the law was intended to proscribe as well as anything that might possibly fit under the law. In such a case, the law's vagueness leads to overbreadth.

Concerns with overbreadth sometimes arise over laws intended to regulate unprotected speech. The Supreme Court has ruled that certain types of speech (for example, obscenity and fighting words) may be regulated because they are not protected by the First Amendment. Such regulations must not harm protected speech. Thus, when a law designed to punish unprotected speech also infringes a substantial amount of protected speech, the law may be found unconstitutionally overbroad. For example, when the Supreme Court in 2010 struck down a law prohibiting the depiction of animal cruelty, the Court reiterated that a law is unconstitutionally overbroad if "'a substantial number of its applications are unconstitutional, judged in relation to the statute's plainly legitimate sweep.'"[1] The determination of overbreadth is based on a reasonable reading of the law's language.

1. United States v. Stevens, 559 U.S. 460 (2010) (mem.).

SUMMARY

facial challenges A broad legal claim based on the argument that the challenged law or government policy can never operate in compliance with the Constitution.

THROUGH THE RULE OF LAW, citizens establish a system for dealing with the innate human tendency toward injustice. The rule of law is designed to promote justice and to provide a relatively clear, neutral and stable mechanism for resolving conflicts. Legal rules bind both government and citizens by defining the boundaries of acceptable behavior, establishing the power and range of punishment and dictating procedures for creating, applying, interpreting and changing the law. Well-crafted laws are clear and well tailored to address identified harms or advance particular government or societal interests. Built-in procedures discourage rapid revolutionary change in the law while permitting legal flexibility in response to evolving needs and concerns. ∎

The Court System

A basic understanding of the structure of the court system in the United States is fundamental to an appreciation of the functioning of the law. Trial courts, or federal district courts, do fact finding, apply the law and adjudicate disputes. Courts of appeal, including federal circuit courts and supreme courts in each system, review the application of the law by the lower courts. The courts create equity and common law and apply and interpret constitutions, statutes and orders. Through their judgments, courts can apply the law, reshape the law and even throw out a statute as unconstitutional.

jurisdiction The geographic or topical area of responsibility and authority of a court.

Jurisdiction

An independent courts system operates in each of the states, the District of Columbia and the federal government. The military and the U.S. territories, such as Puerto Rico, also have separate court systems.

Each of these systems of courts operates under the authority of the relevant constitution. For example, the U.S. Constitution requires the establishment of the Supreme Court of the United States and authorizes Congress to establish other courts it deems necessary to the proper functioning of the federal judiciary. Jurisdiction refers to a court's authority to hear a case. Every court has its own jurisdiction—that is, its own geographic or topical area of responsibility and authority. In libel, for example, the traditional standard has been that any court in any locale where the statement in question could be seen or heard would have jurisdiction.[13] A court may dismiss a lawsuit outside of the court's jurisdiction.

Points of Law

A Test for Court Jurisdiction of Internet Disputes

To establish jurisdiction, the answer to all three of the following questions should be yes:

1. Did the defendant purposefully conduct activities in the jurisdiction of the court?

2. Did the plaintiff's claim arise out of the defendant's activities in this locale?

3. Is it constitutionally reasonable for the court to exercise jurisdiction?

The Federal Court System

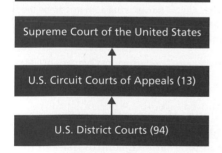

Supreme Court of the United States

U.S. Circuit Courts of Appeals (13)

U.S. District Courts (94)

The State Court System

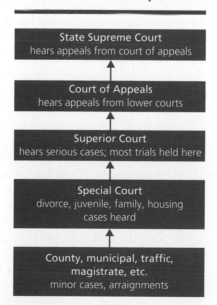

State Supreme Court
hears appeals from court of appeals

Court of Appeals
hears appeals from lower courts

Superior Court
hears serious cases; most trials held here

Special Court
divorce, juvenile, family, housing cases heard

County, municipal, traffic, magistrate, etc.
minor cases, arraignments

TABLE 1.1 Comparing State and Federal Courts

The federal government and each state government have their own court systems.

THE FEDERAL COURT SYSTEM
Structure
• Article III of the Constitution invests the judicial power of the United States in the federal court system. Article III, Section 1 specifically creates the U.S. Supreme Court and gives Congress the authority to create the lower federal courts. • Congress has used this power to establish the 13 U.S. Courts of Appeals, the 94 U.S. District Courts, the U.S. Court of Claims, and the U.S. Court of International Trade. U.S. Bankruptcy Courts handle bankruptcy cases. Magistrate Judges handle some District Court matters. • Parties dissatisfied with a decision of a U.S. District Court, the U.S. Court of Claims, and/or the U.S. Court of International Trade may appeal to a U.S. Court of Appeals. • A party may ask the U.S. Supreme Court to review a decision of the U.S. Court of Appeals, but the Supreme Court usually is under no obligation to do so. The U.S. Supreme Court is the final arbiter of federal constitutional questions.
Selection of Judges
The Constitution states that federal judges are to be nominated by the President and confirmed by the Senate. They hold office during good behavior, typically, for life. Through congressional impeachment proceedings, federal judges may be removed from office for misbehavior.
Types of Cases Heard
• Cases that deal with the constitutionality of a law; • Cases involving the laws and treaties of the U.S.; • Legal issues related to ambassadors and public ministers; • Disputes between two or more states; • Admiralty law, and • Bankruptcy.
Article I Courts
Congress has created several Article I or legislative courts that do not have full judicial power. Judicial power is the authority to be the final decider in all questions of constitutional law, all questions of federal law and to hear claims at the core of habeas corpus issues. • Article I courts are U.S. Court of Veterans' Appeals, the U.S. Court of Military Appeals, and the U.S. Tax Court.

Source: United States Courts. http://www.uscourts.gov/EducationalResources/FederalCourtBasics/CourtStructure/ComparingFederal AndStateCourts.aspx.

Article III, Section 1, of the U.S. Constitution spells out the areas of authority of the federal courts. Within their geographic regions, federal courts exercise authority over cases that relate to interstate or international controversies or that interpret and apply federal laws, treaties or the U.S. Constitution. Thus, federal courts hear cases involving copyright laws. The federal courts also decide cases in which the federal government is a party, such as when the news media ask the courts to hold open public proceedings when considering the deportation of aliens from the United States. Federal courts also have jurisdiction over whether a U.S. citizen captured in a war zone has the right to face his or her accusers in court. Cases involving controversies between states, between citizens of different

TABLE 1.1 (continued)

THE STATE COURT SYSTEM
Structure
• The Constitution and laws of each state establish the state courts. A court of last resort, often known as a Supreme Court, is usually the highest court. Some states also have an intermediate Court of Appeals. Below these appeals courts are the state trial courts. Some are referred to as Circuit or District Courts. • States also usually have courts that handle specific legal matters, e.g., probate court (wills and estates); juvenile court; family court; etc. • Parties dissatisfied with the decision of the trial court may take their case to the intermediate Court of Appeals. • Parties have the option to ask the highest state court to hear the case. • Only certain cases are eligible for review by the U.S. Supreme Court.
Selection of Judges
State court judges are selected in a variety of ways, including • election, • appointment for a given number of years, • appointment for life, and • combinations of these methods, e.g., appointment followed by election.
Types of Cases Heard
• Most criminal cases, probate (involving wills and estates), • Most contract cases, tort cases (personal injuries), family law (marriages, divorces, adoptions), etc. State courts are the final arbiters of state laws and constitutions. Their interpretation of federal law or the U.S. Constitution may be appealed to the U.S. Supreme Court. The Supreme Court may choose to hear or not to hear such cases.
Article I Courts
N/A

states or between a state and a citizen of another state also are heard in federal courts. Thus, a libel suit brought by a resident of Oregon against a newspaper in Washington would be heard in federal court.

New technologies present new challenges to the determination of jurisdiction. Consider online libel. Given that statements published online are potentially seen anywhere, any court could claim jurisdiction. More to the point, a plaintiff could initiate the lawsuit in any court, deciding to pursue the case in the court he or she thinks is most likely to render a favorable decision. Early in the 21st century, the U.S. Court of Appeals for the Fifth Circuit signaled significant limits to this practice, which is called **forum shopping.**[14]

In 2002, the court applied a three-pronged test to determine jurisdiction. The court said jurisdiction in a media libel case would be determined by whether (1) the media *purposefully conducted activities* in the locale of the court,

forum shopping A plaintiff choosing a court in which to sue because he or she believes the court will rule in the plaintiff's favor.

(2) the alleged libelous *harm* arose out of the media's activities *in that locale* and (3) the court's jurisdiction was constitutionally *reasonable*.[15] The decision, which establishes binding precedent only in the Fifth Circuit's south-central region, may create a test for jurisdiction only in libel cases, but it suggests the willingness of one court to limit the ability of litigants to freely choose the court in which to pursue online disputes.

Trial Courts

The separate court systems in the United States are organized similarly; most court systems have three tiers. Trial courts occupy the lowest level of courts. They are the only courts to use juries, and they are the courts where nearly all cases begin. Trial courts reach decisions by applying existing law to the specific facts of the case before them. They do not establish precedents. Each state contains at least one of the nation's 94 trial-level federal courts, which are called district courts. News reporters routinely cover legal actions taking place in trial courts, and some judges view media coverage as a threat to the fairness of trials (see Chapter 10). Some judges also fear that media coverage will cast their court in disrepute and reduce public trust in the judicial system.

U.S. Circuit Courts of Appeal

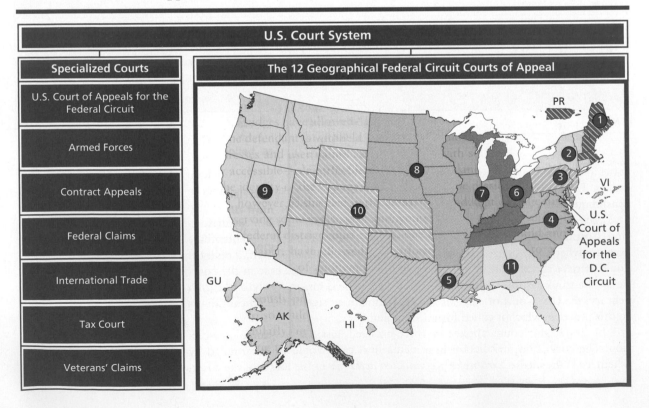

U.S. Court System

| Specialized Courts | The 12 Geographical Federal Circuit Courts of Appeal |

Specialized Courts:
- U.S. Court of Appeals for the Federal Circuit
- Armed Forces
- Contract Appeals
- Federal Claims
- International Trade
- Tax Court
- Veterans' Claims

realWorld Law

Ideological Leanings

Four of the five most conservative justices to serve on the U.S. Supreme Court since 1937, during the presidency of Franklin D. Roosevelt, sit on the bench today, according to a study by two legal experts.[1] The study ranks Clarence Thomas, the Court's second African-American justice who was appointed to the Court in 1991, as the most conservative justice of the past seven decades. Chief Justice John Roberts (ranked 4th) and Justice Samuel Alito (ranked 5th) join Justices Antonin Scalia (ranked 3rd) and Anthony Kennedy (ranked 10th) to build the conservative majority of the current Court. Justices Ruth Bader Ginsburg and Stephen Breyer are the only sitting justices ranked among the Court's *least* conservative justices. However, Justices Sonia Sotomayor and Elena Kagan were not members of the Court at the time of the study. All the members of today's Court studied law either at Yale or Harvard, although Justice Ginsburg graduated from the law school at Columbia University. All the justices also maintain active church affiliations. Two-thirds of the justices—as compared to fewer than one-fourth of Americans—are Roman Catholic, and one-third are Jewish, a religion claimed by fewer than 2 percent of Americans.[2]

1. William M. Landes & Richard A. Posner, *Rational Judicial Behavior: A Statistical Study,* 1:2 J. OF LEGAL ANALYSIS 775 (2009).
2. *Religious Affiliation of All U.S. Supreme Court Justices* (Feb. 23, 2012) *available at* http://www.adherents.com.

Courts of Appeal

Anyone who loses a case at trial may appeal the decision. However, courts of appeal generally do not make findings of fact or receive new evidence in the case. Instead, appellate courts defer to the factual assessment of the lower court and conduct an independent review of the legal process. In the main, courts of appeal examine the procedure of the lower court to determine whether **due process** was carried out—that is, whether the proper law was applied and whether the judicial process was fair and appropriate. In rare cases, courts of appeal may review the facts **de novo,** a phrase meaning "anew" or "over again." Decisions in appellate courts are based primarily on the written legal arguments, or briefs, of the parties and on short oral arguments from the attorneys representing each side of the case. Interested individuals and organizations who are not parties to the case may, with permission of the court, submit additional briefs for consideration. The interested person is called an **amicus curiae** ("friend of the court") and the filing is called an **amicus brief.**

Most court systems have two levels of appellate courts: the intermediate courts of appeal and the supreme court. In the federal court system, there are 13 intermediate-level appellate courts, called circuit courts. A panel of three judges hears all except the most important cases in the federal circuit courts of appeal. In rare cases, all the judges of the circuit court will sit **en banc** to hear an appeal. *En banc* literally means "on the bench" but now is used to mean "in full court." Twelve of the federal circuits represent geographic regions. For example, the U.S. Court of Appeals for the Ninth Circuit bears responsibility for the entire West Coast, Hawaii and Alaska, and the U.S. Court of Appeals for the D.C. Circuit covers the District of Columbia. The 13th circuit, the U.S. Court of Appeals

due process Fair legal proceedings. Due process is guaranteed by the Fifth and Fourteenth Amendments to the U.S. Constitution.

de novo Literally, "anew" or "over again." On appeal, the court may review the facts de novo rather than simply reviewing the legal posture and process of the case.

amicus brief A submission to the court from an **amicus curiae,** or "friend of the court," an interested individual or organization who is not a party in the case.

en banc Literally, "on the bench" but now meaning "in full court." The judges of a circuit court of appeals will sit en banc to decide important or controversial cases.

affirm To ratify, uphold or approve a lower court ruling.

for the Federal Circuit, handles specialized appeals. In addition, separate, specialized federal courts handle cases dealing with the armed forces, international trade or veterans' claims, among other things.

The U.S. Supreme Court at a Glance, 2014

Justice	Born	Nominating President	Year Appointed
Chief Justice John Roberts	1955	George W. Bush	2005
Associate Justice Antonin Scalia	1936	Ronald Reagan	1986
Associate Justice Anthony Kennedy	1936	Ronald Reagan	1988
Associate Justice Clarence Thomas	1948	George H. W. Bush	1991
Associate Justice Ruth Bader Ginsburg	1933	Bill Clinton	1993
Associate Justice Stephen Breyer	1938	Bill Clinton	1994
Associate Justice Samuel Alito	1950	George W. Bush	2006
Associate Justice Sonia Sotomayor	1954	Barack Obama	2009
Associate Justice Elena Kagan	1960	Barack Obama	2010

Courts of appeal may **affirm** the decision of the lower court with a majority opinion, which means they ratify or uphold the prior ruling and leave it intact. They may also **overrule** the lower court, reversing the previous decision. Any single judge or minority of the court may write a **concurring opinion** that agrees with the result reached in the majority opinion but that relies on different reasoning or legal principles or elaborates on significant issues not treated fully by the majority. When a judge disagrees with the opinion of the court, the judge may write a **dissenting opinion,** explaining the basis for the divergent conclusion. A dissenting opinion may challenge the majority's reasoning or the legal basis for its conclusion.

Majority decisions issued by courts of appeal establish precedent for lower courts within their jurisdiction. Their rulings also may be persuasive outside their jurisdiction. If a plurality rather than a majority of the judges hearing a case supports the opinion of the lower court, the decision does not establish binding precedent. Similarly, dissenting and concurring opinions do not have the force of law, but they often are highly influential to subsequent court decisions.

Courts of appeal also **remand,** or send back, decisions and require the lower court to reconsider the facts of the case. A decision to remand a case may not be appealed. Courts of appeal often remand cases when they believe that the lower court did not adequately explore the facts or issues in the case or that it needs to develop a more complete record of evidence as the basis for its decision.

A decision to affirm or reverse the lower court must be signed by at least two of the three sitting judges and is final. The losing party may ask the court to reconsider the case or may request a rehearing en banc. Such requests are rarely granted. The losing party also may appeal the verdict of an intermediate court of appeals to the highest court in the state or to the U.S. Supreme Court.

The U.S. Supreme Court

The Supreme Court of the United States was established in 1789. It functions primarily as an appellate court, although the Constitution establishes the Court's **original jurisdiction** in a few specific areas. In general, Congress has granted lower federal courts jurisdiction in these same areas, so almost no suits begin in the U.S. Supreme Court. Instead, the Court hears cases on appeal from all other federal courts, federal regulatory agencies and state supreme courts.

Cases come before the Court either on direct appeal or through the Court's grant of a **writ of certiorari.** Certain federal laws, such as the Bipartisan Campaign Reform Act,[16] guarantee a direct right of appeal to

How an Appeal Is Processed

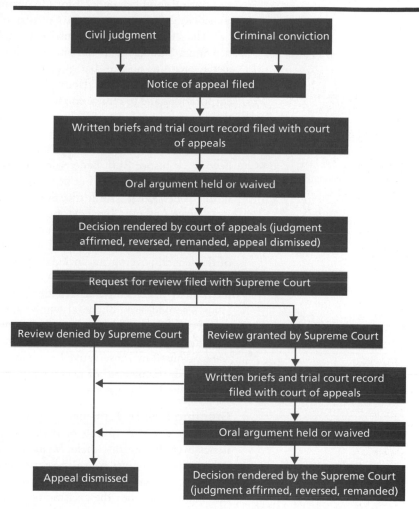

the U.S. Supreme Court. More often, the Court grants a writ of certiorari for compelling reasons, such as when a case poses a novel or pressing legal question. The Court often grants certiorari to cases in which different U.S. circuit courts of appeal have handed down conflicting opinions. The Court also may consider whether an issue is ripe for consideration, meaning that the case presents a real and present controversy rather than a hypothetical concern. In addition, the Court may reject some petitions as **moot** because the controversy is no longer "live." Mootness may be an issue, for example, when a student who has challenged school policy graduates before the case is resolved. The Court sometimes accepts cases that appear to be moot if it believes the problem is likely to arise again.

The Court's Makeup The chief justice of the United States and eight associate justices make up the Supreme Court. The president nominates and the Senate

overrule To reverse the ruling of a lower court.

concurring opinion A separate opinion of a minority of the court or a single judge or justice agreeing with the majority opinion but applying different reasoning or legal principles.

dissenting opinion A separate opinion of a minority of the court or a single judge or justice disagreeing with the result reached by the majority and challenging the majority's reasoning or the legal basis of the decision.

remand To send back to the lower court for further action.

original jurisdiction The authority to consider a case at its inception, as contrasted with appellate jurisdiction.

writ of certiorari A petition for review by the Supreme Court of the United States; *certiorari* means "to be informed of."

moot Term used to describe a case in which the issues presented are no longer "live" or in which the matter in dispute has already been resolved; a case is not moot if it is susceptible to repetition but evades review.

confirms the chief justice as well as the other eight members of the Court, who sit "during good behavior"[17] for life or until retirement. This gives the president considerable influence over the Court's political ideology.

The 2010 departure of Justice John Paul Stevens from the Court left Justice Sonia Sotomayor as the only true liberal among the sitting justices. Liberal justices tend to believe that government should play an active role in ensuring individual liberties. They also tend to support regulation of large businesses and corporations and to reduce emphasis on property rights. Although many expected the newest justice, Justice Elena Kagan, to serve the Court as "a center-left pragmatist" and swing vote,[18] her first three terms demonstrated her willingness to inject a "critical voice that could make the case for liberals within the court and beyond."[19] Justice Ruth Bader Ginsburg is sometimes viewed as the Court's only liberal-leaning moderate, but her voting patterns place her in the political center of the Court, along with Justice Stephen Breyer.

Justice Anthony Kennedy often joins Chief Justice John Roberts and Justices Antonin Scalia, Clarence Thomas and Samuel Alito to create a strong conservative bloc in the Roberts Court. Conservative justices, in general, want to reduce the role of the federal government, including the Supreme Court. They also tend to favor a narrow, or close, reading of the Constitution that relies more heavily on original intent than on contemporary realities or concerns. However, following the Roberts Court's second term, one legal scholar said, "The unifying element of the Court's conservative leanings is not a commitment to any particular conservative judicial doctrine (e.g., originalism) but a commitment to the political and ideological positions espoused by conservative Republicans in the 1980s. Further, the Court is not particularly 'minimalist' or restrained in its approach . . . [and] is quite willing to push a conservative agenda quite aggressively."[20]

Granting Review Petitioners may ask the Supreme Court for a writ of certiorari if the court of appeals or the highest state court denies them a hearing or issues a verdict against them. Writs are granted at the discretion of the Court. All nine justices must consider a writ, which is granted only if at least four justices vote to hear the case. This is called the rule of four. Officially, neither the decision to grant nor the decision to deny a writ of certiorari indicates anything about the Court's opinion regarding the merits of the lower court's ruling. Rather, denial of certiorari more likely means that the Court simply does not think the issue is sufficiently important or timely to decide. The numbers of petitions for certiorari increase each year at the same time the Court grants fewer petitions. Consequently, the vast majority of petitions for certiorari are denied. The Court consistently grants review to fewer than 5 percent of the paid petitions. In recent years, approximately 2,000 petitions accompanied by the required fee of $150 have been filed, and the Court has ruled in about 85 of them, or fewer than 4 percent. Some 6,000 unpaid petitions are filed each term—often by prisoners who cannot pay the required filing fee—and the court rules in only five or six of these.

Reaching Decisions Once the Court agrees to hear a case, the parties file written briefs outlining the facts and legal issues in the case and summarizing their legal arguments. The justices review the briefs prior to oral argument in the case, which generally lasts one hour. The justices may sit silent and implacable during oral argument, or, more often, they may pepper the attorneys with questions. Following oral argument, the justices meet in private in a closed conference session to discuss the case and to take an initial vote on the outcome. Discussion begins with the chief justice, who focuses on a few key issues. Discussion proceeds around the table with each associate justice speaking in turn, in order of descending seniority on the Court. When discussion is complete, voting begins with the most junior member of the Court and ends with the chief justice. A majority of the justices must agree on a point of law for the Court to establish binding precedent. The chief justice or the most senior justice in the majority determines who will draft the majority opinion. Draft opinions are circulated among the justices, and negotiations may attempt to shift votes. It may take months for the Court to achieve a final decision, which is then announced on decision day.

Two other options exist for the Supreme Court. It may issue a **per curiam opinion,** which is an unsigned opinion by the Court as a whole. Although a single justice may draft the opinion, that authorship is not made public. Per curiam opinions often do not include the same thorough discussion of the issues found in signed opinions. The Supreme Court also can resolve a case by issuing a **memorandum order.** A memorandum order simply announces the vote of the Court without providing an opinion. This quick and easy method to dispense with a case has become more common with the Court's tendency in the past decade to issue fewer and fewer signed opinions.

per curiam opinion An unsigned opinion by the court as a whole.

memorandum order An order announcing the vote of the Supreme Court without providing an opinion.

SUMMARY

A MULTITUDE OF COURT SYSTEMS exists in the United States: the federal system, one system for each state, the courts of the District of Columbia and the territories and the military court system. There are three levels of courts: trial courts, intermediate appellate courts and supreme courts. Trial courts review the evidence to determine the outcome of a case. Appellate courts review the legal basis for the decisions of lower courts.

State and federal courts function largely independently of each other. The federal Constitution establishes the U.S. Supreme Court and provides for other federal courts to oversee questions related to international, interstate and federal law. The U.S. Supreme Court has power to review the constitutionality of final rulings of the highest state courts. State courts are established by the relevant state constitution and have jurisdiction over issues arising within the state and relating to state law. New technologies raise challenges to the determination of court jurisdiction because the Internet, for example, transcends traditional jurisdictional boundaries.

Trial, or district, courts are the entry level for most legal disputes. Some disputes are heard first by an administrative agency, and, on very rare occasions, a case may originate in the U.S. Supreme Court. Trial courts are fact-finding forums and are the only courts to use juries. Appeals courts, including the 13 federal circuit courts of appeal, review the legal reasoning and process of the lower court. Three-judge panels generally decide cases in the federal courts of appeals, but en banc rulings sometimes come from the full court. Majority opinions of a court of appeals establish

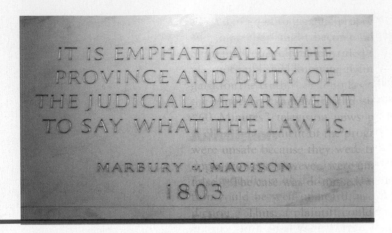

IT IS EMPHATICALLY THE PROVINCE AND DUTY OF THE JUDICIAL DEPARTMENT TO SAY WHAT THE LAW IS.

MARBURY v. MADISON

1803

The U.S. Supreme Court building displays a plaque bearing a quotation from *Marbury v. Madison* establishing its authority of judicial review.

binding precedent within the court's jurisdiction. Appeals courts can affirm, reverse or remand the decision of the lower court. Individual judges may join the opinion of the court, write a separate concurrence reaching the same decision but for different reasons or dissent from the court's opinion.

The Supreme Court is the court of last resort, and in most cases it has discretion to determine which cases to review. The nine justices of the Court are appointed for life. The Court tends to review cases it believes are "ripe" and raise significant legal questions. Most cases reach the Court through a petition for certiorari. Typically the Court grants fewer than 5 percent of the writs of certiorari it receives. Court decisions may be presented as relatively short memorandum orders, unsigned per curiam opinions or signed opinions of the Court. ∎

Judicial Review

judicial review The power of the courts to determine the meaning of the language of the Constitution and to assure that no laws violate constitutional dictates.

More than two centuries ago, in 1803, the U.S. Supreme Court essentially granted itself the power to strike down any laws it said conflicted with the U.S. Constitution. In *Marbury v. Madison*,[21] the Court said the Constitution's system of checks and balances provided the judicial branch with inherent authority to limit the power of the legislative branch and bar it from enacting unconstitutional laws. The Court decided that although the Constitution gave the legislative branch the power to make laws, the judicial branch was empowered to interpret laws and to discover what limits the Constitution placed on legislatures' lawmaking authority. In this controversial decision, the Court established its power of **judicial review.**

Judicial review allows all courts to examine government actions to determine whether they conform to the U.S. and state constitutions. However, courts other than the U.S. Supreme Court rarely use their power of judicial review. If a state supreme court determined that a statute was constitutional under its state constitution, the decision could be appealed to the U.S. Supreme Court, which could decide that the law did not meet the standards set by the U.S. Constitution. The Supreme Court tries to use its power of review sparingly and rarely strikes down laws as unconstitutional. As a general rule, the Court will defer to the lawmaking authority of the executive and legislative branches of government by interpreting laws in ways that do not conflict with the Constitution.

The ideological leanings of the individual justices, and of the Court as a whole, come into play in the choice of cases granted review and the ultimate decisions of the Court.[22] In 2010, for example, the Court was "bitterly divided" in its decision in *Citizens United v. Federal Elections Commission* (the case mentioned

realWorld Law

A Bit Like Making Sausage?

Observers disagree about how the Supreme Court makes decisions. Law professors generally say decision making follows the internal logic of jurisprudence; justices adhere to legal rules, principles and precedents. Political scientists argue that external factors and the political ideologies and preferences of individual justices determine votes that shape the law.

Favoring internal logic, Justice Antonin Scalia wrote in 1991,

The judicial power . . . must be . . . the power "to say what the law is," not the power to change it. . . . [Justices] make [the law] . . . as though they were "finding" it—discerning what the law is, rather than decreeing what it is today changed to, or what it will tomorrow be.[1]

Those who embrace the external view see the law, like *all* texts, as inherently ambiguous and subject to multiple interpretations. Thus, the interpretation of every law and its application necessarily reflects the unique situation of the interpreter. From this perspective,

there is a potentially never-ending debate about the best reading of a text. . . . As with other interpreters, the justices' expectations, interests and prejudices will shape their interpretive views. . . . Politics is always a part of the adjudicative process because legal interpretation is never mechanical.[2]

The difference between the two views of legal decision making is largely one of degree: How often and why does the Court turn to sources *outside* the body of the law to guide its decisions?

Despite the debate, research suggests the external view predicts Supreme Court decisions fairly effectively. This does not mean that politics, rather than precedent, dominate the Court's reasoning.[3] The largely secret process of Supreme Court debate obscures the specific ingredients in the justices' reasoning. Perhaps, like sausage, judicial decisions are more palatable when you don't see how they are made!

1. James B. Beam Distilling Co. v. Georgia, 501 U.S. 529, 549 (1991) (Scalia, J., concurring in judgment).
2. Stephen M. Feldman, *The Rule of Law or the Rule of Politics? Harmonizing the Internal and External Views of Supreme Court Decision Making*, 30 LAW & SOC. INQUIRY 89, 96, 101, 108 (2005).
3. *Id.* at 129.

at the beginning and excerpted at the end of this chapter) that declared some campaign finance regulations unconstitutional. Many agreed that the decision's "sweeping changes in federal election law"[23] "represented a sharp doctrinal shift"[24] that split the Court "five-to-four along typical ideological lines." The majority in *Citizens United* "cavalierly tossed aside decades of judicial opinions upholding the constitutionality of campaign finance restrictions," wrote one lawyer and columnist. However, "the central principle which critics of this ruling find most offensive—that corporations possess 'personhood' and are thus entitled to Constitutional and First Amendment rights—has also been affirmed by decades of Supreme Court jurisprudence."[25] Thus, the ideological conflict at the core of the decision centered more on *which* precedents to follow than on whether to apply precedent at all.

originalists Supreme Court justices who interpret the Constitution according to the perceived intent of its framers.

textualists Judges—in particular, Supreme Court justices—who rely exclusively on a careful reading of legal texts to determine the meaning of the law.

In determining the meaning of the Constitution and in deciding the constitutionality of statutes, the U.S. Supreme Court relies on a wide range of sources. **Originalists** and **textualists,** such as Justice Antonin Scalia, find the meaning of the Constitution primarily in the explicit text, the historical context in which the document developed and the recorded history of its deliberation, ratification and originally intended meaning. Originalists and textualists are relatively unmoved by arguments that neither the intent nor the meaning of the Constitution is clear. Other justices look beyond the original intent and the text itself to discern the appropriate contemporary application of the Constitution. Their interpretation of the Constitution relies more expressly on deep-seated personal and societal values, well-established ethical and legal concepts and the evolving interests of a shifting society. The Court's reasoning at times also builds on international standards, treaties or conventions, such as the Universal Declaration of Human Rights, or the decisions of courts outside the United States as well as state and other federal courts. On occasion, such as when the Court discovered a right to privacy embedded in the First Amendment, the justices refer to the views and insights of legal scholars.[26]

SUMMARY

MORE THAN 200 YEARS AGO, the U.S. Supreme Court granted itself the power to review the constitutionality of laws and government actions. The Court said the power of judicial review was embedded in the Constitution's balance of power as an essential means to maintain the rule of law and check abuse by the other two branches of government. Through judicial review, courts have the power to interpret constitutions and to determine when government actions are invalid because they fail to meet constitutional requirements. State courts rarely exercise their power of judicial review, and the U.S. Supreme Court prefers to use this power sparingly. Controversy surrounds the Court's exercise of judicial review because of the political appointment of justices and the argument that the justices' political philosophies inappropriately influence the Court's decisions. ■

Points of Law

Six Sources of Law

- Constitutions
- Statutes
- Equity law
- Common law
- Administrative law
- Executive orders

Sources of the Law

The body of law in the United States has grown in size and complexity as American society has become increasingly diverse and complicated. As people's ways of interacting and communicating have changed, so have the laws. Many laws that govern communication today did not exist in the 1800s; neither did the technologies they regulate. Indeed, technology has been a driving force for change in the law of journalism and mass communication. U.S. law also has developed in response to social, political, philosophical and economic changes. Legislatures create new laws to reflect evolving understandings of individual rights, liberties and responsibilities. Employment and advertising laws, for example, emerged and multiplied as the nation's workforce shifted and the power of corporations grew. Even well-established legal concepts, such as defamation, have evolved to reflect new realities of the role of communication in society and the power of mass media to harm individuals.

The laws of journalism and mass communication generally originate from six sources. **Constitutional law** establishes the nature, functions and limits of government. The U.S. Constitution, the fundamental law of the United States, was framed in 1787 and ratified in 1789. Each of the states also has its own constitution. City, county, state and federal legislative bodies enact **statutory law.** Like constitutions, statutes are written down; both types of law are part of what is called **black-letter law.**

Through their decisions, judges create law in the form of both **equity law** and **common law.** Equity law arises when judges apply general principles of ethics and fairness rather than specific legal rules to determine the proper remedy for a legal harm. Thus, restraining orders that prevent reporters from intimidating child celebrities are a form of equity law. Judges also craft the common law, but judges rely on custom, or precedent, to guide their common law decisions. Common law often arises in novel situations not covered expressly by statutes and involves the extension of the legal **doctrines** (which, essentially, are the principles or theories of law) from related areas of the law. For example, under common law, publishers and distributors of indecent communications have been treated differently from other publishers. This distinction may disappear as instant electronic communications convert millions of interconnected individuals into publishers in their own rights.[27]

Constitutions and legislatures grant authority to government executives and to specialized agencies to issue orders that form part of the law when published. Administrative agencies, such as the Federal Communications Commission (FCC) or the Federal Trade Commission (FTC), create the rules, regulations, orders and decisions that form **administrative law.** Government executives, such as the president, a governor or a mayor can issue **executive orders,** another source of law. In 2002, for example, President George W. Bush issued an executive order that initiated the development of the U.S. Department of Homeland Security.

These sources of law form a hierarchy, with the Constitution standing at the pinnacle of the body of law. The following sections explore each source in turn.

Constitutions

Constitutions at both the federal and state levels establish the structure of government and allocate and limit government's authority. The U.S. Constitution organizes government into three separate and coequal branches—the executive, the legislative and the judicial—and designates the functions and responsibilities of each. The separate branches of the federal government each serve distinct functions. The executive branch oversees government and administers, or executes, laws. The legislative branch enacts laws, and the judicial branch interprets laws and resolves legal conflicts. Separation of government into branches provides internal checks and balances within government that limit the power of any branch. For example, "restrictions derived from the separation of powers doctrine prevent the judicial branch from deciding **political questions,** controversies that revolve

constitutional law The set of laws that establish the nature, functions and limits of government.

statutory law Written law formally enacted by city, county, state and federal legislative bodies.

black-letter law Formally enacted, written law that is available in legal reporters or other documents.

equity law Law created by judges to apply general principles of ethics and fairness, rather than specific legal rules, to determine the proper remedy for legal harm.

common law Unwritten, judge-made law consisting of rules and principles developed through custom and precedent.

doctrines Principles or theories of law (e.g., the doctrine of content neutrality).

administrative law The orders, rules and regulations promulgated by executive branch administrative agencies to carry out their delegated duties.

executive orders Orders from a government executive, such as the president, a governor or a mayor, that have the force of law.

political questions Questions the courts will not review because they either fall outside the jurisdiction of the court or are incapable of judicial resolution; an issue that can and should be handled more appropriately by another branch of government.

realWorld Law

Instant Petitions Online

In 2013, the White House maintained a website dedicated to "[g]iving all Americans a way to engage their government on the issues that matter to them."[1] At the click of a button or two, the site enabled individuals to find and sign existing petitions, to initiate new petitions or to provide comments to the executive about issues of concern. The site assured visitors that petitions would not be swallowed by some Internet black hole. Instead, the administration promised to "issue a response" when petitions met a signature threshold.

---

1. White House, Petitions (Feb. 23, 2013), *available at* https://petitions.whitehouse.gov.

Online bots, such as those offered through the White House "We the People" site, enable instant participation in citizen-initiated petitions on a spectrum of issues.

Points of Law

The Three Branches of Federal Government

The Executive
> The president, the cabinet and the administrative agencies execute laws.

The Legislative
> The Senate and the House of Representatives pass laws.

The Judicial
> The three levels of courts review laws and adjudicate disputes.

federalism A principle according to which the states are related to yet independent of each other and are related to yet independent of the federal government.

around policy choices and value determinations," because the Constitution delegates responsibility for such political decisions to the legislative and executive branches.[28]

Although many state constitutions closely mirror the U.S. Constitution, they are distinct and independent. The U.S. Constitution establishes the basic character, concepts and principles of government; organizes the federal government; and provides a minimum level of individual rights and privileges throughout the country. Under the principle of **federalism,** states are related to, yet independent of, the federal government and each other. The independence of the state and federal constitutions is fundamental to federalism, which allows for and even encourages experimentation and variety in government. Each state, therefore, has the prerogative to structure its government in its own way and to craft state constitutional protections that exceed the rights granted by the U.S. Constitution. For example, the U.S. Constitution says nothing about municipalities; states create and determine the authority of cities or towns. Under this power, the Maine legislature amended the state constitution in 1970 to increase the independent authority of towns and to permit them to autonomously decide whether to abandon the traditional town meeting form of governance. In another example, Washington State's constitution contains an explicit privacy clause that protects individuals from disturbances of their private affairs. In contrast, the federal constitutional right to privacy exists only through

The Bill of Rights to the U.S. Constitution

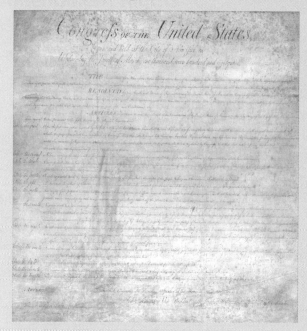

Amendment I

Congress shall make no law respecting an establishment of religion, or prohibiting the free exercise thereof; or abridging the freedom of speech, or of the press; or the right of the people peaceably to assemble, and to petition the government for a redress of grievances.

Amendment II

A well regulated militia, being necessary to the security of a free state, the right of the people to keep and bear arms, shall not be infringed.

Amendment III

No soldier shall, in time of peace be quartered in any house, without the consent of the owner, nor in time of war, but in a manner to be prescribed by law.

Amendment IV

The right of the people to be secure in their persons, houses, papers, and effects, against unreasonable searches and seizures, shall not be violated, and no warrants shall issue, but upon probable cause, supported by oath or affirmation, and particularly describing the place to be searched, and the persons or things to be seized.

Amendment V

No person shall be held to answer for a capital, or otherwise infamous crime, unless on a presentment or indictment of a grand jury, except in cases arising in the land or naval forces, or in the militia, when in actual service in time of war or public danger; nor shall any person be subject for the same offense to be twice put in jeopardy of life or limb; nor shall be compelled in any criminal case to be a witness against himself, nor be deprived of life, liberty, or property, without due process of law; nor shall private property be taken for public use, without just compensation.

Amendment VI

In all criminal prosecutions, the accused shall enjoy the right to a speedy and public trial, by an impartial jury of the state and district wherein the crime shall have been committed, which district shall have been previously ascertained by law, and to be informed of the nature and cause of the accusation; to be confronted with the witnesses against him; to have compulsory process for obtaining witnesses in his favor, and to have the assistance of counsel for his defense.

Amendment VII

In suits at common law, where the value in controversy shall exceed twenty dollars, the right of trial by jury shall be preserved, and no fact tried by a jury, shall be otherwise reexamined in any court of the United States, than according to the rules of the common law.

Amendment VIII

Excessive bail shall not be required, nor excessive fines imposed, nor cruel and unusual punishments inflicted.

Amendment IX

The enumeration in the Constitution, of certain rights, shall not be construed to deny or disparage others retained by the people.

Amendment X

The powers not delegated to the United States by the Constitution, nor prohibited by it to the states, are reserved to the states respectively, or to the people.

How a Bill Becomes a Law

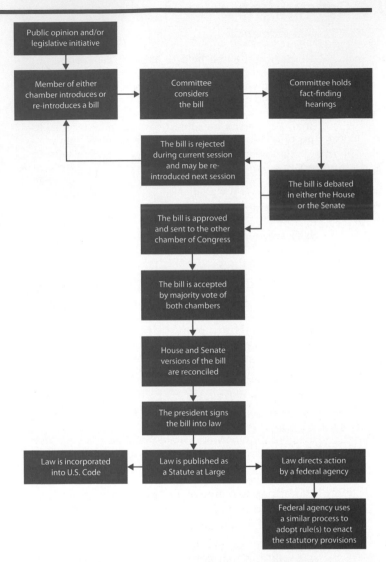

Public opinion and/or legislative initiative

Member of either chamber introduces or re-introduces a bill

Committee considers the bill

Committee holds fact-finding hearings

The bill is rejected during current session and may be re-introduced next session

The bill is debated in either the House or the Senate

The bill is approved and sent to the other chamber of Congress

The bill is accepted by majority vote of both chambers

House and Senate versions of the bill are reconciled

The president signs the bill into law

Law is incorporated into U.S. Code

Law is published as a Statute at Large

Law directs action by a federal agency

Federal agency uses a similar process to adopt rule(s) to enact the statutory provisions

the U.S. Supreme Court's interpretation of the protections afforded by the First Amendment.

The U.S. Constitution is the supreme law of the United States. It establishes the fundamental legal rules that dictate the proper actions of all divisions of government. As the foundation of government, the Constitution is relatively difficult to change. There are two ways to amend the Constitution. The first method, and the only one that actually has been used, is for a proposed constitutional amendment to pass both chambers of Congress by a two-thirds majority vote in each. The second method is for two-thirds of the state legislatures to vote for a Constitutional Convention, which then proposes one or more amendments. Regardless of the proposal method, all amendments to the Constitution also must be ratified by three-fourths of the state legislatures. It therefore was symbolically, not legally, important in 2013 when Mississippi became the last state to officially ratify the 13th Amendment to the Constitution, which banned slavery in 1865.[29] State constitutions can be amended only by a direct vote of the people.

Congress has approved only 33 of the thousands of proposed amendments to the U.S. Constitution, and the states have ratified only 27 of these. The first 10 amendments to the Constitution—generally known as the Bill of Rights—are of primary interest to students of journalism and mass communication law. In fewer than 500 words, the Bill of Rights guarantees the fundamental rights and freedoms of Americans and limits the power of government. The First Amendment, which is the focus of Chapter 2, specifically protects the people's freedoms of speech, press, assembly and petition. It also provides for the free exercise of religion and prohibits government from establishing an official national religion.

Statutes

The U.S. Constitution explicitly delegates the power to enact statutory laws to the popularly elected legislative branch of government: the U.S. Congress and the state, county and city legislatures. Through their power to make laws, legislatures respond to—or predict and attempt to prevent—social problems. Thus, statutory law sometimes is extremely fact specific and defines the legal limits of particular types of activities. All criminal laws are statutes, for example. Statutes also establish the rules of copyright, broadcasting, advertising and access to government meetings and information. Statutes are formally adopted through a public process and are meant to be clear and stable. They are written down in statute books and codified, which means they are collected by codes into related topics, and anyone can find and read them in public repository libraries.

The language of statutes, however, can be unclear, imprecise or ambiguous. In cases where a statute suggests more than one meaning, courts determine the proper meaning and application of the statute through a review process called **statutory construction**. In general, courts attempt to interpret laws in the way the legislature intended. Courts look to the preambles, or statements of purpose, incorporated into many laws as an indication of legislative intent. Committee reports, legislative debates and the public statements of legislators and sponsors of the bills all guide court interpretation of a statute. Problems arise when, for example, some state statutes fail to define key terms, such as the word *meeting* under their open-meetings law. As a consequence, it is unclear whether such laws apply to nonphysical meetings conducted over e-mail or convened in electronic chat rooms, for example.[30]

> **statutory construction** The review of statutes in which courts determine the meaning and application of statutes. Courts tend to engage in strict construction, which narrowly defines laws to their clear letter and intent.

Courts tend to interpret statutes narrowly and to confine a law's application to its clearly intended meaning. Courts prefer not to expand statutes by implication or inference beyond the statute's clear language. The effort to interpret laws according to the "plain meaning" of the words—the **facial meaning** of the law—limits any tendency courts might have to rewrite laws through creative or expansive interpretations. This policy reflects judicial awareness that the power to write laws rests with the publicly elected and responsible legislature. Moreover, because most judges are not elected, the power of courts to engage in judicial review is inherently nondemocratic.

> **facial meaning** The surface, apparent or obvious meaning of a legal text.

In its own text, the U.S. Constitution establishes its supremacy over all other laws of the land.[31] The Constitution's supremacy clause resolves conflicts among laws by stating that all state laws must give way to federal law, and state or federal laws that conflict with the Constitution are invalid. Statutory laws also form a hierarchy; some federal laws preempt state laws, which in turn may preempt city statutes. Courts may invalidate state statutes that conflict with federal laws or city statutes that conflict with either state or federal law. However, courts generally interpret the plain meaning of a statute in a way that avoids conflict with other laws, including the Constitution, when possible. Courts review the constitutionality of a statute only as a last resort. When engaging in constitutional review, courts generally will attempt to preserve any provisions of the law that can be upheld without violating the general intent or functioning of the statute. For example, the U.S. Supreme Court in 1997 struck down the Communications Decency Act, which was part of the comprehensive Telecommunications Act of 1996, without undermining the balance of the new telecommunications law.

Equity Law

Judges, not legislatures, make equity law in order to provide fair remedies and relief for various harms. Equity law is based on the presumption that fairness is not always achieved through the rigid application of strict rules. No specific, black-letter laws dictate equity. Rather, equity law allows judges to require or to prohibit certain actions in order to achieve justice in individual cases. Essentially, judges determine what is fair and issue decrees to ensure that justice is achieved. Thus, restraining orders that require paparazzi to stay a certain distance away from celebrities are a form of equity law. An injunction in 1971 that temporarily prevented The New York Times and The Washington Post from publishing stories based on the Pentagon Papers was another form of equity relief. While the law of equity is closely related to common law, the rules of equity law are more flexible and are not governed by precedent.

Common Law

The common law is another body of judge-made law. The common law consists of the rules and principles developed through custom and precedent. The common law is a vast and unwritten body of legal rules and doctrines established through hundreds of years of dispute resolution that reaches past the founding of this country and across the Atlantic to England. For centuries prior to the settlement of the U.S. colonies, English courts "discovered" the doctrines people traditionally had used to resolve disagreements. Judges then applied these "common" laws to guide court decisions. The resulting judicial decisions, and the reasoning that supported them, came to be known as English common law, which became the foundation of U.S. common law.

Eventually, common law grew to reflect more than the problem-solving principles of the common people. Today, U.S. common law rests on the presumption that prior court rulings, or precedent, should guide future decisions. The essence of precedent, stare decisis, is that courts should follow each other's guidance. Once a higher court has established a principle relevant to a certain set of facts, fairness requires lower courts to try to apply the same principle to similar facts. This establishes consistency and stability in the law.

Under the rule of stare decisis, the decision of a higher court, such as the U.S. Supreme Court, establishes a precedent that is binding on lower courts. A binding precedent of the U.S. Supreme Court constrains all lower federal courts throughout the country, and the decisions of each circuit court of appeals bind the district courts in that circuit. Similarly, lower state courts must follow the precedents of their own state appellate courts and the state supreme court. However, courts from different and co-equal jurisdictions do not establish binding precedent upon their peers. Courts in Rhode Island are not bound to follow precedents established in Wyoming, and federal district courts are not bound to apply precedents established by appellate courts in other federal circuits. In fact, different federal appellate courts sometimes hand down directly conflicting decisions. Courts prefer to avoid such conflicts, however, and often will look to other courts and consider their decisions as a guide when facing a novel question.

Even when the power of stare decisis is at its greatest, lower courts may choose not to adhere to precedent. Courts may, at the risk of the judges' credibility, simply ignore precedent. After all, the common law is not written down in one easily accessible volume. Instead, the common law must be discovered through research in the thousands of court decisions collected into centuries of volumes, called court reporters. Courts also may depart from precedent with good reason. Courts examining a new but similar question may decide to **modify precedent**—that is, to change or revise the precedent to adapt to changed realities and perceptions. Thus, the U.S. Supreme Court might find that contemporary attitudes and practices no longer support a 20-year-old precedent permitting government to maintain the secrecy of computer compilations of public records. Given the rapid disappearance of paper records in government, the Court might modify its precedent on application of the federal Freedom of Information Act FOIA; see Chapter 8) to find that computer compilations, like paper records, must be available unless disclosure clearly violates personal privacy.[32]

modify precedent To change or revise rather than follow or reject precedent.

Courts also may **distinguish from precedent** by asserting that differences between the current case and the precedent case outweigh any similarities. Thus, for example, the Supreme Court has distinguished between newspapers and broadcasters in terms of any right of public access.[33] The Court said the public has a right to demand that broadcasters provide diverse content on issues of public importance because broadcasters use the public airwaves. The Court did not apply that reasoning five years later when it considered virtually the same question as applied to newspapers. Newspaper owners, publishers and editors, the Court said, are private, independent members of the press who enjoy a virtually unabridgable right to control the content of their pages.

distinguish from precedent To justify an outcome in a case by asserting that differences between that case and preceding cases outweigh any similarities.

Finally, courts will occasionally, but only occasionally, **overturn precedent** outright and reject the fundamental premise of that decision. This is a rare and radical step and generally occurs only to remedy past injustices or to reflect a fundamental rethinking of the law. In one such instance, the Supreme Court in 1997 overruled a 12-year-old Court precedent that had prohibited public school teachers from providing remedial education in parochial schools.[34] The Court said the precedent had mistakenly confused government efforts to fulfill its mandate to educate all children with unconstitutional government establishment of religion.

overturn precedent To reject the fundamental premise of a precedent.

Administrative Rules

The legislative branch of government often delegates authority to expert administrative agencies in the executive branch to interpret, enable and implement statutory laws. Administrative law may constitute the largest proportion of contemporary law in the United States. A wide range of state and federal administrative agencies with specific areas of responsibility and expertise—such as the Federal Communications Commission (FCC), which oversees interstate electronic communication—incorporate both legislative and judicial functions. An alphabet soup of administrative agencies adopts orders, rules and regulations to carry out the agencies' delegated duties. Administrative agencies also enforce administrative

realWorld Law

Executive Order on Cybersecurity

Early in 2013, President Barack Obama signed an executive order[1] that gives federal agencies greater authority to make "cyber threat" information public, a step he had promised in his State of the Union address. The order calls for government recommendations on ways to protect critical infrastructure from cyberattacks and authorizes federal agencies to share "cyber threat information" with companies that run critical national infrastructures, such as the electrical grid, power stations, water supplies, air traffic control and financial institutions. "It is the policy of the United States Government to increase the volume, timeliness and quality of cyber threat information shared with U.S. private sector entities so that these entities may better protect and defend themselves against cyber threats," the order states.

Supported generally by privacy advocates as well as business groups, the most negative response to the executive order came from critics who argue that the president's use of such orders circumvents government checks and balances and violates the separation of power. In his first four years in office, President Obama issued a total of 144 executive orders, according to records of the National Archives.[2] In comparison, George W. Bush signed 170 executive orders during his first term.[3]

To protect the nation's cyberstructure from attack, President Barack Obama committed to improve national cyber security and asserted his power to initiate preemptive cyberattacks to ward of imminent threats.

1. Exec. Order—*Improving Critical Infrastructure Cybersecurity,* 78 Fed. Reg. 11,737 (Feb. 12, 2013), *available at* http://www.whitehouse.gov/the-press-office/2013/02/12/executive-order-improving-critical-infrastructure-cybersecurity.
2. Barack Obama Executive Order Disposition Tables, *available at* http://www.archives.gov/federal-register/executive-orders/obama.html.
3. *Presidential Documents, Executive Orders,* Federal Register, *available at* https://www.federalregister.gov/executive-orders.

law; they conduct hearings in which they grant relief, resolve disputes and levy fines or penalties. This body of rules has the force of law.

Courts generally have the power to hear challenges or appeals to the rules enacted and the decisions reached by administrative agencies after appeal procedures within the agency have been exhausted. Courts engage in regulatory construction and judicial review of administrative agency rules and decisions in much the same way that they review statutory laws. However, the power of courts to void agency rules and actions is limited to situations in which the agency has exceeded its authority, violated its own rules and procedures or provided no evidence to support its ruling. In other situations, courts are expected to show **deference** to the agency's decision, which means courts must give weight to the expert judgment of the agency.

The authority of administrative agencies, or even their existence, can change. Legislatures may adopt new statutes or amend preexisting laws to revise the responsibilities and power of administrative agencies. Thus, when Congress

deference A policy by which courts give weight to the judgment of expert administrative agencies or of legislative policies and strategies.

adopted the Telecommunications Act of 1996, it substantially revised the responsibilities of the FCC, originally authorized by the Communications Act of 1934.

Executive Orders

Heads of the executive branch of government—the president, governors and mayors—have limited power to issue executive orders, which have the force of law. For example, each president of the United States issues orders that determine what types of records will be classified as secret, how long they will remain secret and who has access to them. Recent executive orders from the president also have limited media access to military zones, excluded the public from meetings of groups advising the president on energy policy, and redefined access to presidential records. Similarly, mayors and governors have issued orders—particularly under perceived emergency conditions—that limit public freedom of movement. For example, mayors across the country have imposed city curfews that prohibit teenagers from being on the streets after a certain hour and have established no-protest zones around major, controversial events.

SUMMARY

LAWS, OR LEGAL RULES, in the United States come from six sources. Federal and state constitutions establish government structure, responsibilities and power. Constitutions are the highest law of the land. Congress and the legislatures of every state, city and county enact statutes. All statutes are codified. Courts determine the meaning of statutes through the process of statutory construction. Equity and common law are judge-made law and are not compiled into books. Judges create equity law when they issue orders or injunctions to solve a specific problem. The common law has developed through the body of judicial decisions that rely on precedent and tradition to determine the outcome of disputes. The authority of administrative agencies is established by statute to oversee complex areas that require special expertise. Thousands of executive branch administrative agencies establish legal rules that determine everything from the definition of false advertising to the number of different media a given corporation can control. Executives at each level of government issue orders that have the force of law. ∎

The Case Process

Although each court and each case follows a somewhat idiosyncratic path, general patterns can be traced through the judicial process. In a criminal matter, the case starts when a government agency investigates a possible crime. After gathering evidence, the government arrests someone for a crime, such as distributing obscene material through the Internet. The standard of evidence needed for an arrest or to issue a search warrant is known as **probable cause.** Probable cause involves more than mere suspicion; it is a showing based on reliable information

probable cause The standard of evidence needed for an arrest or to issue a search warrant. More than mere suspicion, it is a showing through reasonably trustworthy information that a crime has been or is being committed.

The Path of Civil Lawsuits

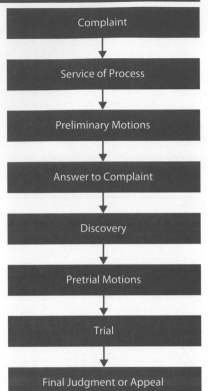

Complaint

↓

Service of Process

↓

Preliminary Motions

↓

Answer to Complaint

↓

Discovery

↓

Pretrial Motions

↓

Trial

↓

Final Judgment or Appeal

grand jury A group summoned to hear the state's evidence in criminal cases and decide whether a crime was committed and whether charges should be filed; grand juries do not determine guilt.

plaintiff The party who files a complaint; the one who sues.

defendant The party accused of violating a law, or the party being sued in a civil lawsuit.

tort A private or civil wrong for which a court can provide remedy in the form of damages.

strict liability Liability without fault; liability for any and all harms, foreseeable or unforeseen, which result from a product or an action.

that a crime was committed and that the accused individual is likely the person who committed it. The case then goes before a **grand jury** or a judge. Unlike trial juries (also called petit juries), grand juries do not determine guilt. Instead, grand juries are summoned on occasion to hear the state's evidence and determine whether that evidence establishes probable cause to believe that a crime has been committed. A grand jury may be convened on the county, state or federal level; with 12 to 23 members, grand juries are usually larger than trial juries. If the case proceeds without a grand jury, the judge is required to make a probable cause determination at a proceeding called a preliminary hearing. If the state fails to establish probable cause, the case may not proceed. If probable cause is found, the person is indicted.

Then the case moves to a court arraignment, where the defendant is formally charged and pleads guilty or not guilty. Often, a plea bargain may be arranged in which the defendant pleads guilty in exchange for a reduction in the charges or an agreed-upon sentence. In the absence of a guilty plea, the case ordinarily will proceed to trial. The judge may set bail. Proof beyond a reasonable doubt is required to establish guilt in a criminal trial. Upon a verdict of guilty, the judge normally requests a presentencing report from the probation department outlining the defendant's background and holds a sentencing hearing before pronouncing judgment. A criminal sentence may include time in a county jail, state or federal prison, and one or more fines.

Civil Suits

Civil cases generally involve two private individuals or organizations that cannot resolve a dispute. The government provides a neutral process through its judicial system to help settle the conflict. In a civil suit, the person who files a complaint or sues because she believes she has been harmed by an intrusion on her privacy or the inaccuracy of a news report, for example, is the **plaintiff.** The person responding to the suit is the **defendant.** The civil harm involved is called a **tort.** A tort is a private or civil injury one person or organization inflicts on another, and tort law provides a mechanism for the injured party to identify the person at fault and receive compensation through an award of damages.

Many communication lawsuits are civil suits in which the plaintiff must prove his or her case by the preponderance of evidence. This standard of proof is lower than in criminal cases. Plaintiffs often may choose among several courts in which to file their civil suits because the court system in the hometown of either party and every court system in which the harm occurred has jurisdiction to hear the suit.

Civil suits begin when the plaintiff files a civil complaint with the clerk of court. The civil pleading outlines the complaint and the result desired and requires the defendant to appear in court. Most plaintiffs seek money damages. To receive a damage award, a plaintiff generally must show that the harm occurred, that the defendant caused the harm and that the defendant was at fault, meaning the defendant acted either negligently or with malicious intent. Under a **strict liability** standard, the plaintiff does not need to demonstrate fault on the part of the defendant in order to win the suit. Under strict liability, the individual who produced a product or took an action is liable for any and all resulting harms.

Upon receiving a complaint, the court issues a summons to the defendant, notifying him or her of the complaint and requiring him or her to appear in court to respond. The court also schedules a hearing. The defendant may answer the complaint by filing a countersuit, by denying the charge, by filing a **motion to dismiss** or by filing a motion for summary judgment. A motion to dismiss, or **demurrer,** is a request to a court that a complaint be rejected because it is legally insufficient in some way. For example, a media defendant may admit that it published the news story that upset the plaintiff but argue that the story did not cause any legally actionable harm to the plaintiff. If the court grants the motion to dismiss, the plaintiff may appeal.

Before a case goes to trial, the disputing parties may agree to an out-of-court settlement. When this occurs, there is no public record of the outcome of the case. Out-of-court resolutions often prohibit the parties from discussing the terms of the settlement. Sometimes, as when Nike settled a lawsuit brought by attorney Mark Kasky in 2002,[35] some terms of the settlement are publicized. After a lengthy legal battle over Kasky's claim that Nike's statements about working conditions at its overseas factories amounted to false advertising, the parties settled out of court. Without admitting liability, Nike reported on its website that it had agreed to pay a total of $1.5 million toward independent oversight of its factories and additional worker training and development.[36]

If the issues in a civil suit are narrow or the parties are close to resolution, the judge may attempt to settle the case through a court conference. More often, the two sides do not agree on the facts and begin to gather evidence through a process called **discovery.** The discovery process can last for months, during which either side may file motions asking the court to take action on various issues or amend earlier complaints. In trying to build a case, one or both parties may issue a **subpoena,** which is a legal command for someone, sometimes a journalist, to testify in court. With few exceptions, citizens are legally obligated to comply with subpoenas. The judge may issue a contempt of court citation against individuals who refuse to comply with subpoenas. Contempt citations sometimes land journalists in jail. Throughout the pretrial period, both sides may attempt to "spin" their case in the media. Judges are sensitive to the potential harmful effects of pretrial publicity on the fairness of trials.

Finally, the dispute is heard in court. Most civil suits are resolved with a settlement between the parties before trial. If no settlement is reached, the case may then proceed to a jury trial, which is required if either party requests it. The court summons jurors to the courthouse from a local pool, usually from the voters' rolls. The locality of a lawsuit, where the original court hears the suit, is called the **venue.** The location from which a court draws its pool of jurors is the **venire.** The lawyers and judge select jurors through a process of questioning called **voir dire,** which literally means "to speak the truth." While the theoretical goal is to form an impartial jury to hear the evidence, attorneys on both sides hope to give themselves an advantage in the adversarial process. Today a large number of

motion to dismiss A request to a court for a complaint to be rejected because it does not state a claim that can be remedied by law or because it is legally lacking in some other way.

demurrer A request that a court dismiss a case on the grounds that although the claims are true they are insufficient to warrant a judgment against the defendant.

discovery The pretrial process of gathering evidence and facts. The word also may refer to the specific items of evidence that are uncovered.

subpoena A command for someone to testify in court.

venue The locality of a lawsuit and of the court hearing the suit. Thus, a change of venue means a relocation of a trial.

venire Literally, "to come" or "to appear"; the term used for the location from which a court draws its pool of potential jurors, who must then appear in court for voir dire; a change of venire means a change of the location from which potential jurors are drawn.

voir dire Literally, "to speak the truth"; the questioning of prospective jurors to assess their suitability.

realWorld Law

Blogger Bests "Bullying" Subpoena

In 2009, two days after the federal Department of Homeland Security (DHS) issued a subpoena to blogger Christopher Elliott in his home, the agency backed down.

The subpoena ordered Elliott to turn over "all documents, emails, and/or facsimile transmissions in your control possession or control (sic) concerning your receipt of TSA Security Directive 1544–09–06."[1] Federal law establishes penalties of a year in prison and a fine for failure to comply with a Transportation Security Administration (TSA) subpoena.

After Elliott's attorney said they would challenge the subpoena, DHS withdrew the subpoena and one to another blogger, Steve Frischling. Both bloggers had posted the controversial TSA directive requiring physical pat-downs of all passengers boarding planes in the United States.[3]

"These are just, sort of, bullying subpoenas," said Lucy Dalglish, former executive director of the Reporters Committee for Freedom of the Press (RCFP).[4]

1. Christopher Elliott, *Full Text of My Subpoena from the Department of Homeland Security,* Elliott Blog, Dec. 29, 2009, *available at* http://www.elliott.org/blog/full-text-of-my-subpoena-from-the-department-of-homeland-security/.
2. Christopher Elliott, *Department of Homeland Security: Your Subpoena "Is No Longer Necessary,"* Elliott Blog, Dec. 31, 2009, *available at* http://www.elliott.org/blog/department-of-homeland-security-withdraws-subpoena/.
3. Christopher Elliott, *Full Text of SD 1544–09–06 Authorizing Pat-Downs, Physical Inspections,* Elliott Blog, Dec. 27, 2009, *available at* http://www.elliott.org/blog/full-text-of-sd-1544–09–06-authorizing-pat-downs-physical-inspection/.
4. Cindy Cohn, *EFF Helps Blogger Subpoenaed by TSA, TSA Backs Down,* Electronic Frontier Foundation, Jan. 1, 2010, *available at* http://www.eff.org/deeplinks/2010/01/eff-helps-blogger-subpoenaed-tsa-tsa-backs-down.

peremptory challenge During jury selection, a challenge in which an attorney rejects a juror without showing a reason. Attorneys have the right to eliminate a limited number of jurors through peremptory challenges.

firms, such as Trial Behavior Consulting, provide expert consulting on jury selection, witness preparation, post-trial media interviews and the like. Either side's attorney may challenge potential jurors "for cause," such as when a prospective juror knows a party in the suit. Attorneys also may eliminate a limited number of potential jurors through **peremptory challenges,** in which they need not show a reason for the rejection.

After all the evidence is presented at trial, the judge issues instructions to the jury on how the law should be applied to the facts of the case. Then the jury deliberates. If the jury cannot reach a verdict, it may be necessary to hold a new trial with a new jury. More typically, a jury deliberates until it reaches a verdict. The judge generally accepts the verdict and enters it as the judgment of the court. However, the judge has the authority to overturn the verdict if he or she believes it is contrary to the law. If the plaintiff is successful, he or she will usually be awarded damages. After the judgment of the court is entered, either the plaintiff or the defendant may appeal. For example, having the jury properly instructed on the law is part of the right of due process, and improper instructions sometimes form the basis for appeal. The person who appeals, called the petitioner or **appellant,** challenges the decision of the court. The respondent to the appeal, or the **appellee,** wants the verdict to be affirmed. It can take years and cost hundreds of

appellant The party making the appeal; also called the petitioner.

appellee The party against whom an appeal is made.

thousands of dollars to appeal a case up to the Supreme Court. As noted previously, the chance the Court will agree to hear an appeal is slim.

Summary Judgment

When parties ask a court to dismiss a case, they file a motion for **summary judgment.** Parties moving for summary judgment seek to avoid the cost and risk of losing at trial by demonstrating to the judge that no material issues of fact remain in dispute. A motion for summary judgment must be filed with supporting evidence. A summary judgment is just what the name implies: a judge summarily decides the case and issues a judgment. Thus, a summary judgment results in a legal determination by a court *without* a full trial. A court's summary judgment may be issued based on the merits of the case as a whole or on specific issues critical to the case. If the judge determines there are no material issues of fact remaining for trial, the judge hands down a summary judgment in favor of one party. If there is no summary judgment or other form of pretrial dismissal, lawsuits generally proceed to trial.

A summary judgment can occur at any of several points in litigation, but usually prior to trial. In a libel case, this generally occurs when a plaintiff is clearly unable to meet one or more elements of the burden of proof (see Chapter 4). The U.S. Supreme Court has said that courts considering motions for summary judgment "must view the facts and inferences to be drawn from them in the light most favorable to the opposing party."[37] In libel cases, this means that courts must take into account the burden the plaintiff is required to meet at trial. The Court created this hurdle for individuals seeking summary judgment because the nonmoving party loses the opportunity to present his or her case when a judge grants summary judgment to the opposing side.[38] Nonetheless, one recent study found that the use of summary judgments increased markedly in the second half of the 20th century, with nearly 8 percent of civil cases in federal courts being concluded through this mechanism.[39] The frequency of summary judgments varied widely depending on the court and the type of dispute.

Summary judgments can be important tools for protecting free expression, particularly in an environment in which plaintiffs have harassed the media by filing frivolous lawsuits. One federal judge wrote that summary judgments are especially important in the First Amendment area.[40] Societal interest in free and open debate can be jeopardized when frivolous lawsuits go forward because the high cost of defending against such suits may discourage people from robustly exercising their First Amendment rights in the future.

summary judgment The quick resolution of a legal dispute in which a judge summarily decides certain points and issues a judgment dismissing the case.

SUMMARY

LAWSUITS ARE EITHER CRIMINAL OR CIVIL. In criminal cases, the government brings an action against an individual for violating a criminal statute. Crimes may be punished by fines and/or jail time. In a civil lawsuit, a private individual (the plaintiff) initiates the process by filing a complaint alleging the defendant caused some harm for which he or she should be held legally responsible. Civil suits generally seek damages to compensate the plaintiff and to penalize the individual responsible. Both criminal and civil suits involve a variety of pretrial processes, and juries hear both types of cases. Jurors are called and questioned through voir dire, which provides an opportunity for attorneys to remove jurors for cause or through peremptory challenge. Cases are decided either when a jury reaches a verdict or, in the case of a bench trial, the judge issues a judgment. Court decisions may be appealed. Judges also may have the power to end a case through dismissal or summary judgment. ∎

Finding the Law

This textbook provides an introduction and overview of key areas of the law of journalism and mass communication. Many students will wish, or their professors will require them, to supplement this text with research in primary legal sources. Primary sources are the actual documents that make up the law (e.g., statutes, case decisions and committee reports). Most students will want to begin legal research in secondary sources available in most government and academic libraries. Secondary sources analyze, interpret and discuss the primary documents. Perhaps the most useful secondary sources for beginning researchers in communication law are "American Jurisprudence 2d," "Corpus Juris Secundum" and "Media Law Reporter." The first two are legal encyclopedias. They provide summaries, indexed by subject, with citations to relevant cases and pertinent legal articles. "Media Law Reporter" provides both topical summaries and excerpts of key media law cases organized by subject. When using "Media Law Reporter," students must keep in mind that it is not comprehensive. It contains only the prominent cases selected by the editors to highlight central issues in media law.

To thoroughly research a topic in the law, students must turn to primary sources: the administrative, legislative and court documents that form the law. It is beyond the scope of this text to provide a detailed explanation of how to navigate through these complex and diverse legal materials. However, access to primary legal materials no longer requires extensive legal training and hours of research in intimidating legal libraries. Today a wealth of primary legal resources is available online and in databases such as Westlaw and LexisNexis. Law review articles provide invaluable scholarship and references to contemporary legal topics.

The notes at the end of this book contain the citations for many of the important cases in the law of journalism and mass communication. These legal citations provide the names of the parties in the case, the number of the volume in which the case is reported, the abbreviated name of the official legal reporter (or book) in which the case appears, the page of the reporter on which the case begins and the year in which the case was decided. For example, the citation in note 32 of this chapter looks like this: "Dept. of Justice v. Reporters Comm. for Freedom of the Press, 489 U.S. 749 (1989)." This citation shows that the first party, the

U.S. Department of Justice, filed an appeal from a decision in favor of the second party, The Reporters Committee for Freedom of the Press. The decision in this case dealing with the application of the federal Freedom of Information Act can be found in the United States Reporter (U.S.), which contains U.S. Supreme Court opinions. The case appears in volume 489 (the number *before* the name of the reporter), beginning on page 749 (the number *after* the name of the reporter). The case was decided in 1989 (the number in parentheses).

Useful Legal Research Resources

A huge number and variety of indexes, research tools and interpretive aids help those seeking to find and understand U.S. law. The following short list identifies some of the most useful databases and online resources to offer a starting point for the enterprising student.

- *Online search engines* helpful in legal research include Findlaw (http://www.findlaw.com), LawCrawler (http://www.lawcrawler.com) and Meta-Index for U.S. Legal Research (https://gsulaw.gsu.edu/metaindex).
- *LegalTrac* is an online index of articles in nearly 2,000 legal and nonlegal periodicals since 1981, searchable by keyword or subject. Many of the articles in LegalTrac are not full text.
- *LexisNexis,* available online at many universities through Academic Universe, is a full-text database of primary and secondary legal sources, business and financial information and news. It has multiple search options, including quick, keyword, case name, citation, and detailed Boolean searches.
- *Websites* helpful in finding and interpreting the law include: the Reporters Committee for Freedom of the Press (http://www.rcfp.org), the Student Press Law Center (http://www.splc.org), the Freedom Forum (http://www.freedomforum.org), the First Amendment Center (http://www.firstamendmentcenter.org), the Electronic Frontier Foundation (http://www.eff.org), First Amendment Law Review (falr.unc.edu), Cornell Legal Information Institute (http://www.law.cornell.edu) and many more.

Reading Case Law

This chapter shows that the law of journalism and mass communication contains many terms and concepts that may be unfamiliar to the general reader. At the beginning, reading the law is a bit like reading a foreign language; so many of the words are unfamiliar that it is difficult to grasp the underlying meaning and importance of the case. The difficulty arises because judges (who tend to use legal words and complex syntax) write opinions for lawyers, who are already trained in legal terminology and doctrines. With practice, however, people who are not judges or lawyers or even law students can learn the language and read case law with relative ease. It is a skill that empowers you, as a citizen, to learn your own rights and responsibilities and to oversee the actions of your government.

The following steps will help you read the law more quickly and with better comprehension. You will understand the law far better and more easily if you give yourself sufficient time to use these three steps:

1. *Pre-read the case.* Do not underline or highlight during pre-reading because only after pre-reading will you really understand which elements are important to the case. Pre-reading is designed to identify the *structure* of the decision; the various *rules or doctrines* that underlie the court's reasoning; and the *outcome* of the case. These three elements provide a context to help you highlight the most important elements of the court's reasoning. To pre-read, quickly read
   a. The topic sentence of each paragraph to get the gist of the case and identify the most important sections of the case
   b. The first few paragraphs of the case, which should establish the parties, the issues and the history of the case
   c. The last few paragraphs of the case to understand the **holding** (which is the legal principle taken from the decision of the court) or to get a summary of the outcome of the case

2. *Skim the entire case.* Skimming involves scanning lightly over the entire case. This provides more details to the pre-reading and further identifies the sections of the case that warrant careful reading. Again, do not highlight or underline. However, you will want to signal the start of key sections of the case for more careful reading.

3. *Read carefully the sections you have identified as important.* Underline or highlight as you go. You may want to identify different elements differently. In particular, take note of the following:
   a. *The issue.* Identifying the issue in the case helps you know which elements of the history and facts are significant. In this text, the chapter titles generally signal the issue on which the case excerpt will focus. The case itself also often includes language that identifies the issue. Such language includes, "The question before the Court is whether . . ." and "The issue in this case is . . ."
   b. *The facts.* Recognize that some facts are central to the issue whereas others are peripheral. To identify the important facts, ask yourself whether the dispute in the case is about a question of fact (e.g., what happened) or a question of law (e.g., which test, doctrine or category of speech is relevant). A libel decision that turns on the identity of the individual whose reputation was harmed would represent a question of fact.[41]
   c. *The case history.* The circumstances surrounding a decision often are pivotal to the issue before the Court. Sometimes the relevant history is one of shifting legal doctrine, as when the Court gradually affords

holding The decision or ruling of a court.

commercial speech greater constitutional protection.[42] Sometimes the important context is factual, as when the Court protects defamatory comments situated within a generally accurate portrayal of the violent oppression of blacks during the civil rights movement.[43]

    d. *The common law rule of law.* The rule is the heart of the decision; it is the common law developed in this case. To identify the rule, ask whether the Court has created a new test, engaged in balancing or applied an established doctrine in a new way. What are the elements of the rule and what are its exceptions? Under what conditions or to what type of communication does the rule apply?

    e. *The analysis.* To analyze the decision, compare the facts to the rule. In libel law, for example, public officials must prove actual malice to win their suit. In analyzing the decision, ask whether the individual involved is a public official. If so, did he or she prove actual malice? If not, what elements of the actual malice standard did he or she fail to establish and why?

If you follow this step-by-step process, you will be well on your way toward reading the law. That's the first stage in conducting legal research. This detailed reasoning also positions you well to write a case brief in response to a course assignment or as an excellent study tool.

Briefing Cases

Case briefs are a focused summary of a court decision. They simplify and clarify the court's language by selecting the five most important components of the decision. They sort through the court's detailed and complicated discussions to set aside content and comments that do not directly inform the court's decision.

An acronym for the five components of a case brief is FIRAC. FIRAC stands for Facts, Issue, Rule of Law, Analysis and Conclusion. In brief, the five components of a case brief are

1. *The Facts.* The facts summary should include all the information needed to understand the issue and the decision of the court. The facts statement consists of a brief but inclusive discussion of what happened in the legal dispute before it reached this court. The statement of facts should include not only who the parties are and what happened in the trial court but also an explanation of the basis for appeal. What happened between the parties that gave rise to the case? Who initiated the lawsuit? What was the substance of the complaint and what type of legal action was brought? What was the defense? What did other courts reviewing the case decide? What are the legal errors that provide the basis for the current appeal?

2. *The Issue.* Here, one sentence summarizes the specific question decided by the court in this case. The issue should be phrased as a single question that can be answered "yes" or "no."

3. *The Rule of Law.* The rule of law is the heart of the decision. It states, preferably in one sentence, the precedent established by this decision that will bind or guide lower courts.

4. *The Analysis.* This section, also called the *rationale,* details why the court reached its decision. In this section, it is important to discuss the details of the court's reasoning. What tests, logic, analysis, application of precedent, theory or evidence did the court use to justify and explain its decision? The analysis section needs to identify how and why the current decision creates new law. Consider whether it establishes a new test, clarifies existing legal distinctions, defines a new category or highlights changing realities that affect the law. A thorough analysis must describe the reasoning for all the opinions in the decision and highlight the specific points on which concurring and dissenting opinions diverge from the opinion of the court.

5. *The Conclusion.* This is a simple declarative statement of the holding reached by the present court. Did the court affirm, remand or reverse? Provide the vote of the court.

Analyzing *Marbury v. Madison*

The following case brief previews the second case excerpted at the end of this chapter.

FACTS: William Marbury was one of President John Adams' 42 "midnight appointments" on the eve of his departure from the White House. The necessary paperwork and procedures to secure his and several other appointments were completed, but Secretary of State John Marshall—himself a midnight appointee—failed to deliver Marbury's commission. Upon assuming the presidency, Thomas Jefferson ordered his secretary of state—James Madison—not to deliver the commission. Under authority of the Judiciary Act of 1789, Marbury sued to ask the Supreme Court to order Madison, through a writ of mandamus, to deliver the commission. A writ of mandamus is a court order requiring an individual or organization either to perform or to stop a particular action.

ISSUE: Does the Supreme Court have the power to review acts of Congress and declare them void if they violate the Constitution?

RULE: Under Article VI, Sec. 2 of the U.S. Constitution, the Supreme Court is implicitly given the power to review acts of Congress and to strike them down as void if they are "repugnant" to the Constitution.

ANALYSIS: A commission signed by the president and sealed by the secretary of state is complete and legally binding. Denial of Marbury's commission violates the law, creating a governmental obligation to remedy the violation. A writ of mandamus is such a remedy. The Constitution is the "supreme law of the land" (Art. VI). As such, it is "superior" and "fundamental and paramount." It establishes "certain limits" on the power of the government it creates, including the power of Congress. Accordingly, "a legislative act contrary to the Constitution is not law." The Constitution also establishes that "[it] is emphatically the province and duty of the judicial department to say what the law is." The Supreme Court, therefore, must determine the law that applies in a specific case and decide the case according to the law. If the Court finds that "ordinary" statutory law conflicts with the dictates of the Constitution, the "fundamental" constitutional law must govern. If Congress enacted legislation the Constitution forbids, the Court must strike it down to give the Constitution its due weight.

Under Article III of the Constitution, Congress has the power to regulate the appellate jurisdiction, but not the original jurisdiction, of the Supreme Court. The Court's original jurisdiction is defined completely and exclusively by Article III and cannot be altered except by amendment of the Constitution. Through the Judiciary Act of 1789, Congress *added* matters of mandamus to the original jurisdiction of the Court. Being outside the power given to Congress by the Constitution, this act is illegitimate. Neither was the power of mandamus granted to the Court by the Constitution. Following these principles, the Court does not have the power to order mandamus on behalf of Marbury.

The Court held the provision of the Judiciary Act unconstitutional and declared the mandamus void.

CONCLUSION: Marshall, C.J. 6–0. Yes. Relying heavily on the inherent "logical reasoning" of the Constitution, rather than on any explicit text, the Court dismissed the case for lack of jurisdiction but found that Congress' grant of original power of mandamus to the Court violated the division of power established in Article III of the Constitution.

SUMMARY

THE LAW IN ALL ITS FORMS is a rich topic for research. Many online sources and databases supplement and ease legal research once conducted exclusively in the numerous volumes held by legal, academic and government libraries. Law review articles are extremely valuable aids to legal research, as are legal encyclopedias. Legal researchers must be able to read and analyze case law. A three-step process of pre-reading, skimming and close reading helps those new to the law identify the important elements of case decisions. Creating case briefs, using the FIRAC method, helps clarify the key points of important court decisions. ■

Cases for Study

Thinking About It

Critics of campaign finance regulations designed to prevent corruption in elections won several legal decisions in 2010 in the wake of the Supreme Court's ruling in *Citizens United v. Federal Elections Commission*.[44] As one legal scholar noted, "The relevance of Citizens United has become an issue in every new campaign finance case" since the decision was handed down in January 2010.[45] This aspect of the Court's decision is developed in Chapter 3 when the First Amendment implications of campaign finance laws are discussed. Here we look instead at what *Citizens United* demonstrates about precedent and the rule of law. The debate raised in the Court's opinions has spawned vibrant public discussion about whether the doctrine of stare decisis serves "as an agent of stability" or "to destabilize the rule of law."[46]

The following case excerpts begin with Chief Justice John Roberts' concurring opinion in *Citizens United,* in which he "elaborated on when it *is* acceptable for the Court to overturn precedent."[47] Justice John Paul Stevens' rather acerbic dissent forms the second part of this contemporary Court debate on the role of precedent. Then an excerpt from *Marbury v. Madison,*[48] the decision in which the Supreme Court established its own power of judicial review, follows. A central question resolved by the Supreme Court in *Marbury v. Madison* was whether, under the Constitution, the Court had authority to void duly enacted laws that it deemed to violate the U.S. Constitution.

As you read these case excerpts, keep the following questions in mind:

- How do the sitting justices differ in their interpretation of the binding nature of Supreme Court precedent?
- In the case of *Citizens United,* which justices are exercising "restraint" or "activism"? Why?
- What are the legal foundations for the different opinions?
- What do these decisions suggest about the stability or "transformation" of the rule of law under judicial review and stare decisis?

Citizens United v. Federal Election Commission
Supreme Court of the United States
588 U.S. 50 (2010)

JUSTICE ANTHONY KENNEDY delivered the Court's opinion.

CHIEF JUSTICE ROBERTS, with whom JUSTICE SAMUEL ALITO joined, concurring:

The Government urges us in this case to uphold a direct prohibition on political speech. It asks us to embrace a theory of the First Amendment that would allow censorship not only of television and radio broadcasts, but of pamphlets, posters, the Internet, and virtually any other medium that corporations and unions might find useful in expressing their views on matters of public concern. Its theory, if accepted, would empower the Government to prohibit newspapers from running editorials or opinion pieces supporting or opposing candidates for office, so long as the newspapers were owned by corporations—as the major ones are. First Amendment rights could be confined to individuals, subverting the vibrant public discourse that is at the foundation of our democracy.

The Court properly rejects that theory, and I join its opinion in full. The First Amendment protects more than just the individual on a soapbox and the lonely pamphleteer. I write separately to address the important principles of judicial restraint and *stare decisis* implicated in this case.

Judging the constitutionality of an Act of Congress is "the gravest and most delicate duty that this Court is called upon to perform." Because the stakes are so high, our standard practice is to refrain from addressing constitutional questions except when necessary to rule on particular claims before us. This policy underlies both our willingness to construe ambiguous statutes to avoid constitutional problems and our practice "'never to formulate a rule of constitutional law broader than is required by the precise facts to which it is to be applied.'"

The majority and dissent are united in expressing allegiance to these principles. But I cannot agree with my dissenting colleagues on how these principles apply in this case.

The majority's step-by-step analysis accords with our standard practice of avoiding broad constitutional questions except when necessary to decide the case before us. The majority begins by addressing—and quite properly rejecting—Citizens United's statutory claim that [the Bipartisan Campaign Reform Act of 2002] does not actually cover its production and distribution of *Hillary: The Movie* (hereinafter *Hillary*). If there were a valid basis for deciding this statutory claim in Citizens United's favor (and thereby avoiding constitutional adjudication), it would be proper to do so. . . .

It is only because the majority rejects Citizens United's statutory claim that it proceeds to consider the group's various constitutional arguments, beginning with its narrowest claim (that *Hillary* is not the functional equivalent of express advocacy) and proceeding to its broadest claim (that *Austin v. Michigan Chamber of Commerce* (1990) should be overruled). . . .

The dissent advocates an approach to addressing Citizens United's claims that I find quite perplexing. It presumably agrees with the majority that Citizens United's narrower statutory and constitutional arguments lack merit—otherwise its conclusion that the group should lose this case would make no sense. Despite agreeing that these narrower arguments fail, however, the dissent argues that the majority should nonetheless latch on to one of them in order to avoid reaching the broader constitutional question of whether *Austin* remains good law. It even suggests that the Court's failure to adopt one of these concededly meritless arguments is a sign that the majority is not "serious about judicial restraint."

This approach is based on a false premise: that our practice of avoiding unnecessary (and unnecessarily broad) constitutional holdings somehow trumps our obligation faithfully to interpret the law. It should go without saying, however, that we cannot embrace a narrow ground of decision simply because it is narrow; it must also be right. Thus while it is true that "[i]f it is not necessary to decide more, it is necessary not to decide more," sometimes it is necessary to decide more. There is a difference between judicial restraint and judicial abdication. When constitutional questions are "indispensably necessary" to resolving the case at hand, "the court must meet and decide them." . . .

This is the first case in which we have been asked to overrule *Austin*, and thus it is also the first in which we have had reason to consider how much weight to give *stare decisis* in assessing its continued validity. The dissent erroneously declares that the Court "reaffirmed" *Austin*'s holding in subsequent cases. Not so. Not a single party in any of those cases asked us to overrule *Austin*, and as the dissent points out, the Court generally does not consider constitutional arguments that have not properly been raised. *Austin*'s validity was therefore not directly at issue in the cases the dissent cites. The Court's unwillingness to overturn *Austin* in those cases cannot be understood as a *reaffirmation* of that decision.

Fidelity to precedent—the policy of *stare decisis*—is vital to the proper exercise of the judicial function. "*Stare decisis* is the preferred course because it promotes the even-handed, predictable, and consistent development of legal principles, fosters reliance on judicial decisions, and contributes to the actual and perceived integrity of the judicial process." For these reasons, we have long recognized that departures from precedent are inappropriate in the absence of a "special justification."

At the same time, *stare decisis* is neither an "inexorable command," nor "a mechanical formula of adherence to the latest decision," especially in constitutional cases. If it were, segregation would be legal, minimum wage laws would be unconstitutional, and the Government could wiretap ordinary criminal suspects without first obtaining warrants. As the dissent properly notes, none of us has viewed *stare decisis* in such absolute terms.

Stare decisis is instead a "principle of policy." When considering whether to reexamine a prior erroneous holding, we must balance the importance of having constitutional questions *decided* against the importance of having them *decided right*. As Justice Jackson explained, this requires a "sober appraisal of the disadvantages of the innovation as well as those of the questioned case, a weighing of practical effects of one against the other."

In conducting this balancing, we must keep in mind that *stare decisis* is not an end in itself. It is instead "the means by which we ensure that the law will not merely change erratically, but will develop in a principled and intelligible fashion." Its greatest purpose is to serve a constitutional ideal—the rule of law. It follows that in the unusual circumstance when fidelity to any particular precedent does more to damage this constitutional ideal than to advance it, we must be more willing to depart from that precedent.

Thus, for example, if the precedent under consideration itself departed from the Court's jurisprudence, returning to the "'intrinsically sounder' doctrine established in prior cases" may "better serv[e] the values of *stare decisis* than would following [the] more recently decided case inconsistent with the decisions that came before it." Abrogating the errant precedent, rather than reaffirming or extending it, might better preserve the law's coherence and curtail the precedent's disruptive effects.

Likewise, if adherence to a precedent actually impedes the stable and orderly adjudication of future cases, its *stare decisis* effect is also diminished. This can happen in a number of circumstances, such as when the precedent's validity is so hotly contested that it cannot reliably function as a basis for decision in future cases, when its rationale threatens to upend our settled jurisprudence in related areas of law, and when the precedent's underlying reasoning has become so discredited that the Court cannot keep the precedent alive without jury-rigging new and different justifications to shore up the original mistake.

These considerations weigh against retaining our decision in *Austin*. First, as the majority explains, that decision was an "aberration" insofar as it departed from the robust protections we had granted political speech in our earlier cases . . . [and] does not explain why corporations may be subject to prohibitions on speech in candidate elections when individuals may not.

Second, the validity of *Austin*'s rationale—itself adopted over two "spirited dissents,"—has proved to be the consistent subject of dispute among Members of this Court ever since. The simple fact that one of our decisions remains controversial is, of course, insufficient to justify overruling it. But it does undermine the precedent's ability to contribute to the stable and orderly development of the law. In such circumstances, it is entirely appropriate for the Court—which in this case is squarely asked to reconsider *Austin*'s validity for the first time—to address the matter with a greater willingness to consider new approaches capable of restoring our doctrine to sounder footing.

Third, the *Austin* decision is uniquely destabilizing because it threatens to subvert our Court's decisions even outside the particular context of corporate express advocacy. The First Amendment theory underlying *Austin*'s holding is extraordinarily broad. *Austin*'s logic would authorize government prohibition of political speech by a category of speakers in the name of equality—a point that most scholars acknowledge (and many celebrate), but that the dissent denies.

It should not be surprising, then, that Members of the Court have relied on *Austin*'s expansive logic to justify greater incursions on the First Amendment, even outside the original context of corporate advocacy on behalf of candidates running for office. The dissent in this case succumbs to the same temptation, suggesting that *Austin* justifies prohibiting corporate speech because such speech might unduly influence "the market for legislation." The dissent reads *Austin* to permit restrictions on corporate speech based on nothing more than the fact that the corporate form may help individuals coordinate and present their views more effectively. A speaker's ability to persuade, however, provides no basis for government regulation of free and open public debate on what the laws should be.

If taken seriously, *Austin*'s logic would apply most directly to newspapers and other media corporations. They have a more profound impact on public discourse than most other speakers. These corporate entities are, for the time being, not subject to [the statute's] otherwise generally applicable prohibitions on corporate political speech. But this is simply a matter of legislative grace. The fact that the law currently grants a favored position to media corporations is no reason to overlook the danger inherent in accepting a theory that would allow government restrictions on their political speech.

These readings of *Austin* do no more than carry that decision's reasoning to its logical endpoint. In doing so, they highlight the threat *Austin* poses to First Amendment rights generally, even outside its specific factual context of corporate express advocacy. Because *Austin* is so difficult to confine to its facts—and because its logic threatens to undermine our First Amendment jurisprudence and the nature of public discourse more broadly—the costs of giving it *stare decisis* effect are unusually high.

Finally and most importantly, the Government's own effort to defend *Austin*—or, more accurately, to defend something that is not quite *Austin*—underscores its weakness as a precedent of the Court. The Government concedes that *Austin* "is not the most lucid opinion," yet asks us to reaffirm its holding. But while invoking *stare decisis* to support this position, the Government never once even mentions the compelling interest that *Austin* relied upon in the first place: the need to diminish "the corrosive and distorting effects of immense aggregations of wealth that are accumulated with the help of the corporate form and that have little or no correlation to the public's support for the corporation's political ideas." *Austin*'s specific holding on the basis of two new and potentially expansive interests—the need to prevent actual or apparent quid pro quo corruption, and the need to protect corporate shareholders. Those interests may or may not support the result in *Austin*, but they were plainly not part of the reasoning on which *Austin* relied. . . .

To its credit, the Government forthrightly concedes that *Austin* did not embrace either of the new rationales it now urges upon us. To be clear: The Court in *Austin* nowhere relied upon the only arguments the Government now raises to support that decision. . . .

To the extent that the Government's case for reaffirming *Austin* depends on radically reconceptualizing its reasoning, that argument is at odds with itself. *Stare decisis* is a doctrine of preservation, not transformation. It counsels deference to past mistakes, but provides no justification for making new ones. There is therefore no basis for the Court to give precedential sway to reasoning that it has never accepted, simply because that reasoning happens to support a conclusion reached on different grounds that have since been abandoned or discredited.

Doing so would undermine the rule-of-law values that justify *stare decisis* in the first place. It would effectively license the Court to invent and adopt new principles of constitutional law solely for the purpose of rationalizing its past errors, without a proper analysis of whether those principles have merit on their own. This approach would allow the Court's past missteps to spawn future mistakes, undercutting the very rule-of-law values that *stare decisis* is designed to protect.

None of this is to say that the Government is barred from making new arguments to support the outcome in *Austin*. On the contrary, it is free to do so. And of course the Court is free to accept them. But the Government's new arguments must stand or fall on their own; they are not entitled to receive the special deference we accord to precedent. They are, as grounds to support *Austin,* literally unprecedented. Moreover, to the extent the Government relies on new arguments—and declines to defend *Austin* on its own terms—we may reasonably infer that it lacks confidence in that decision's original justification.

Because continued adherence to *Austin* threatens to subvert the "principled and intelligible" development of our First Amendment jurisprudence, I support the Court's determination to overrule that decision. . . .

JUSTICE JOHN PAUL STEVENS, with whom JUSTICE RUTH BADER GINSBURG, JUSTICE STEPHEN BREYER and JUSTICE SONIA SOTOMAYOR join, concurring in part and dissenting in part:

. . . The majority's approach to corporate electioneering marks a dramatic break from our past. Congress has placed special limitations on campaign spending by corporations ever since the passage of the Tillman Act in 1907. We have unanimously concluded that this "reflects a permissible assessment of the dangers posed by those entities to the electoral process," and have accepted the "legislative judgment that the special characteristics of the corporate structure require particularly careful regulation." The Court today rejects a century of history when it treats the distinction between corporate and individual campaign spending as an invidious novelty born of *Austin v. Michigan Chamber of Commerce.* Relying largely on individual dissenting opinions, the majority blazes through our precedents, overruling or disavowing a body of case law.

In his landmark concurrence in *Ashwander v. TVA* (1936), Justice Brandeis stressed the importance of adhering to rules the Court has "developed . . . for its own governance" when deciding constitutional questions. Because departures from those rules always enhance the risk of error, . . . I emphatically dissent from its principal holding.

The Court's ruling threatens to undermine the integrity of elected institutions across the Nation. The path it has taken to reach its outcome will, I fear, do damage to this institution. Before turning to the question

whether to overrule *Austin* and part of *McConnell,* it is important to explain why the Court should not be deciding that question.

The first reason is that the question was not properly brought before us. . . . [T]he majority decides this case on a basis relinquished below, not included in the questions presented to us by the litigants, and argued here only in response to the Court's invitation. This procedure is unusual and inadvisable for a court. Our colleagues' suggestion that "we are asked to reconsider *Austin* and, in effect, *McConnell,*" would be more accurate if rephrased to state that "we have asked ourselves" to reconsider those cases. . . .

It is all the more distressing that our colleagues have manufactured a facial challenge, because the parties have advanced numerous ways to resolve the case that would facilitate electioneering by nonprofit advocacy corporations such as Citizens United, without toppling statutes and precedents. Which is to say, the majority has transgressed yet another "cardinal" principle of the judicial process: "[I]f it is not necessary to decide more, it is necessary not to decide more." . . .

The final principle of judicial process that the majority violates is the most transparent: *stare decisis.* I am not an absolutist when it comes to *stare decisis,* in the campaign finance area or in any other. No one is. But if this principle is to do any meaningful work in supporting the rule of law, it must at least demand a significant justification, beyond the preferences of five Justices, for overturning settled doctrine. "[A] decision to overrule should rest on some special reason over and above the belief that a prior case was wrongly decided." No such justification exists in this case, and to the contrary there are powerful prudential reasons to keep faith with our precedents.

The Court's central argument for why *stare decisis* ought to be trumped is that it does not like *Austin.* The opinion "was not well reasoned," our colleagues assert, and it conflicts with First Amendment principles. This, of course, is the Court's merits argument, the many defects in which we will soon consider. I am perfectly willing to concede that if one of our precedents were dead wrong in its reasoning or irreconcilable with the rest of our doctrine, there would be a compelling basis for revisiting it. But neither is true of *Austin,* and restating a merits argument with additional vigor does not give it extra weight in the *stare decisis* calculus.

Perhaps in recognition of this point, the Court supplements its merits case with a smattering of assertions. The Court proclaims that "*Austin* is undermined by experience since its announcement." This is a curious claim to make in a case that lacks a developed record. The majority has no empirical evidence with which to substantiate the claim; we just have its *ipse dixit* that the real world has not been kind to *Austin*. Nor does the majority bother to specify in what sense *Austin* has been "undermined." Instead it treats the reader to a string of non sequiturs: "Our Nation's speech dynamic is changing"; "[s]peakers have become adept at presenting citizens with sound bites, talking points, and scripted messages"; "[c]orporations . . . do not have monolithic views." How any of these ruminations weakens the force of *stare decisis,* escapes my comprehension.

The majority also contends that the Government's hesitation to rely on *Austin*'s antidistortion rationale "diminishe[s]" "the principle of adhering to that precedent." Why it diminishes the value of *stare decisis* is left unexplained. We have never thought fit to overrule a precedent because a litigant has taken any particular tack. Nor should we. Our decisions can often be defended on multiple grounds, and a litigant may have strategic or case-specific reasons for emphasizing only a subset of them. Members of the public, moreover, often rely on our bottom-line holdings far more than our precise legal arguments; surely this is true for the legislatures that have been regulating corporate electioneering since *Austin*. The task of evaluating the continued viability of precedents falls to this Court, not to the parties.

Although the majority opinion spends several pages making these surprising arguments, it says almost nothing about the standard considerations we have used to determine *stare decisis* value, such as the antiquity of the precedent, the workability of its legal rule, and the reliance interests at stake. It is also conspicuously silent about *McConnell,* even though the *McConnell* Court's decision to uphold [the Bipartisan Campaign Reform Act (BCRA)] relied not only on the antidistortion logic of *Austin* but also on the statute's historical pedigree, and the need to preserve the integrity of federal campaigns.

We have recognized that "[s]tare decisis has special force when legislators or citizens 'have acted in reliance on a previous decision, for in this instance overruling the decision would dislodge settled rights and expectations or require an extensive legislative response.'" *Stare decisis* protects not only personal rights involving property or contract but also the ability of the elected branches to shape their laws in an effective and coherent fashion. Today's decision takes away a power that we have long permitted these branches to exercise. State legislatures have relied on their authority to regulate corporate electioneering, confirmed in *Austin,* for more than a century. The Federal Congress has relied on this authority for a comparable stretch of time, and it specifically relied on *Austin* throughout the years it spent developing and debating BCRA. The total record it compiled was *100,000 pages* long. Pulling out the rug beneath Congress after affirming the constitutionality of [the statutory provision] six years ago shows great disrespect for a coequal branch.

By removing one of its central components, today's ruling makes a hash out of BCRA's "delicate and interconnected regulatory scheme." . . .

Beyond the reliance interests at stake, the other *stare decisis* factors also cut against the Court. Considerations of antiquity are significant for similar reasons. *McConnell* is only six years old, but *Austin* has been on the books for two decades, and many of the statutes called into question by today's opinion have been on the books for a half-century or more. The Court points to no intervening change in circumstances that warrants revisiting *Austin*. Certainly nothing relevant has changed since we decided WRTL [*Federal Election Commission v. Wisconsin Right to Life, Inc.*] two Terms ago. And the Court gives no reason to think that *Austin* and *McConnell* are unworkable.

In fact, no one has argued to us that *Austin*'s rule has proved impracticable, and not a single for-profit corporation, union, or State has asked us to overrule it. Quite to the contrary, leading groups representing the business community, organized labor and the nonprofit sector, together with more than half of the States, urge that we preserve *Austin*. As for *McConnell*, the portions of BCRA it upheld may be prolix, but all three branches of Government have worked to make §203 as user-friendly as possible. For instance, Congress established a special mechanism for expedited review of constitutional challenges; the FEC has established a standardized process, with clearly defined safe harbors, for corporations to claim that a particular electioneering communication is permissible under WRTL; and, as noted above, THE CHIEF JUSTICE crafted his controlling opinion in WRTL with the express goal of maximizing clarity and administrability. The case for *stare decisis* may be bolstered, we have said, when subsequent rulings "have reduced the impact" of a precedent "while reaffirming the decision's core ruling."

In the end, the Court's rejection of *Austin* and *McConnell* comes down to nothing more than its disagreement with their results. Virtually every one of its arguments was made and rejected in those cases, and the majority opinion is essentially an amalgamation of resuscitated dissents. The only relevant thing that has changed since *Austin* and *McConnell* is the composition of this Court. Today's ruling thus strikes at the vitals of *stare decisis,* "the means by which we ensure that the law will not merely change erratically, but will develop in a principled and intelligible fashion" that "permits society to presume that bedrock principles are founded in the law rather than in the proclivities of individuals." . . .

Marbury v. Madison
Supreme Court of the United States
5 U.S. 137 (1803)

CHIEF JUSTICE JOHN MARSHALL delivered the Court's opinion:

. . . The constitution vests the whole judicial power of the United States in one supreme court, and such inferior courts as congress shall, from time to time, ordain and establish. This power is expressly extended to all cases arising under the laws of the United States; and consequently, in some form, may be exercised over the present case; because the right claimed is given by a law of the United States.

In the distribution of this power it is declared that "the supreme court shall have original jurisdiction in all cases affecting ambassadors, other public ministers and consuls, and those in which a state shall be a party. In all other cases, the supreme court shall have appellate jurisdiction."

It has been insisted at the bar, that as the original grant of jurisdiction to the supreme and inferior courts is general, and the clause, assigning original jurisdiction to the supreme court, contains no negative or restrictive words; the power remains to the legislature, to assign original jurisdiction to that court in other cases than those specified in the article which has been recited; provided those cases belong to the judicial power of the United States.

If it had been intended to leave it to the discretion of the legislature to apportion the judicial power between the supreme and inferior courts according to the will of that body, it would certainly have been useless to have proceeded further than to have defined the judicial power, and the tribunals in which it should be vested. The subsequent part of the section is . . . entirely without meaning, if such is to be the construction. If congress remains at liberty to give this court appellate jurisdiction, where the constitution has declared their jurisdiction shall be original; and original jurisdiction where the constitution has declared it shall be appellate; the distribution of jurisdiction, made in the constitution, is form without substance. . . .

It cannot be presumed that any clause in the constitution is intended to be without effect; and therefore such a construction is inadmissible, unless the words require it. . . .

When an instrument organizing fundamentally a judicial system, divides it into one supreme, and so many inferior courts as the legislature may ordain and establish; then enumerates its powers, and proceeds so far to distribute them, as to define the jurisdiction of the supreme court by declaring the cases in which it shall take original jurisdiction, and that in others it shall take appellate jurisdiction, the plain import of the words seems to be, that in one class of cases its jurisdiction is original, and not appellate; in the other it is appellate, and not original. If any other construction would render the clause inoperative, that is an additional reason for rejecting such other construction, and for adhering to their obvious meaning.

To enable this court then to issue a mandamus, it must be shown to be an exercise of appellate jurisdiction, or to be necessary to enable them to exercise appellate jurisdiction.

It has been stated at the bar that the appellate jurisdiction may be exercised in a variety of forms, and that if it be the will of the legislature that a mandamus should be used for that purpose, that will must be obeyed. This is true; yet the jurisdiction must be appellate, not original.

It is the essential criterion of appellate jurisdiction, that it revises and corrects the proceedings in a cause already instituted, and does not create that case. Although, therefore, a mandamus may be directed to courts, yet to issue such a writ to an officer for the delivery of a paper, is in effect the same as to sustain an original action for that paper, and therefore seems not to belong to appellate, but to original jurisdiction. Neither is it necessary in such a case as this, to enable the court to exercise its appellate jurisdiction.

The authority, therefore, given to the supreme court, by the act establishing the judicial courts of the United States, to issue writs of mandamus to public officers, appears not to be warranted by the constitution; and it becomes necessary to enquire whether a jurisdiction, so conferred, can be exercised.

The question, whether an act, repugnant to the constitution, can become the law of the land, is a question deeply interesting to the United States; but, happily, not of an intricacy proportioned to its interest. It seems only necessary to recognise certain principles, supposed to have been long and well established, to decide it.

That the people have an original right to establish, for their future government, such principles as, in their opinion, shall most conduce to their own happiness, is the basis, on which the whole American fabric has been erected. The exercise of this original right is a very great exertion; nor can it, nor ought it to be frequently repeated. The principles, therefore, so established, are deemed fundamental. And as the authority, from which they proceed, is supreme, and can seldom act, they are designed to be permanent.

This original and supreme will organizes the government, and assigns to different departments their respective powers. It may either stop here; or establish certain limits not to be transcended by those departments.

The government of the United States is of the latter description. The powers of the legislature are defined, and limited; and that those limits may not be mistaken, or forgotten, the constitution is written. To what purpose are powers limited, and to what purpose is that limitation committed to writing; if these limits may, at any time, be passed by those intended to be restrained? The distinction between a government with limited and unlimited powers is abolished, if those limits do not confine the persons on whom they are imposed, and if acts prohibited and acts allowed are of equal obligation. It is a proposition too plain to be contested, that the constitution controls any legislative act repugnant to it; or, that the legislature may alter the constitution by an ordinary act.

Between these alternatives there is no middle ground. The constitution is either a superior, paramount law, unchangeable by ordinary means, or it is on a level with ordinary legislative acts, and like other acts, is alterable when the legislature shall please to alter it.

If the former part of the alternative be true, then a legislative act contrary to the constitution is not law: if the latter part be true, then written constitutions are absurd attempts, on the part of the people, to limit a power in its own nature illimitable.

Certainly all those who have framed written constitutions contemplate them as forming the fundamental and paramount law of the nation, and consequently the theory of every such government must be, that an act of the legislature repugnant to the constitution is void.

This theory is essentially attached to a written constitution, and is consequently to be considered by this court as one of the fundamental principles of our society. It is not therefore to be lost sight of in the further consideration of this subject.

If an act of the legislature, repugnant to the constitution, is void, does it, notwithstanding its invalidity, bind the courts, and oblige them to give it effect? Or, in other words, though it be not law, does it constitute a rule as operative as if it was a law? This would be to overthrow in fact what was established in theory; and would seem, at first view, an absurdity too gross to be insisted on. It shall, however, receive a more attentive consideration.

It is emphatically the province and duty of the judicial department to say what the law is. Those who apply the rule to particular cases, must of necessity expound and interpret that rule. If two laws conflict with each other, the courts must decide on the operation of each. So if a law be in opposition to the constitution; if both the law and the constitution apply to a particular case, so that the court must either decide that case conformably to the law, disregarding the constitution; or conformably to the constitution, disregarding the law; the court must determine which of these conflicting rules governs the case. This is of the very essence of judicial duty.

If then the courts are to regard the constitution; and the constitution is superior to any ordinary act of the legislature; the constitution, and not such ordinary act, must govern the case to which they both apply.

Those then who controvert the principle that the constitution is to be considered, in court, as a paramount law, are reduced to the necessity of maintaining that courts must close their eyes on the constitution, and see only the law.

This doctrine would subvert the very foundation of all written constitutions. It would declare that an act, which, according to the principles and theory of our government, is entirely void, is yet, in practice, completely obligatory. It would declare, that if the legislature shall do what is expressly forbidden, such act, notwithstanding the express prohibition, is in reality effectual. It would be giving to the legislature a practical and real omnipotence with the same breath which professes to restrict their powers within narrow limits. It is prescribing limits, and declaring that those limits may be passed at pleasure.

That it thus reduces to nothing what we have deemed the greatest improvement on political institutions—a written constitution, would of itself be sufficient, in America where written constitutions have been viewed with so much reverence, for rejecting the construction. But the peculiar expressions of the constitution of the United States furnish additional arguments in favour of its rejection.

The judicial power of the United States is extended to all cases arising under the constitution. Could it be the intention of those who gave this power, to say that, in using it, the constitution should not be looked into? That a case arising under the constitution should be decided without examining the instrument under which it arises?

This is too extravagant to be maintained. . . .

. . . [I]t is apparent, that the framers of the constitution contemplated that instrument, as a rule for the government of courts, as well as of the legislature.

Why otherwise does it direct the judges to take an oath to support it? This oath certainly applies, in an especial manner, to their conduct in their official character. How immoral to impose it on them, if they were to be used as the instruments, and the knowing instruments, for violating what they swear to support!

The oath of office, too, imposed by the legislature, is completely demonstrative of the legislative opinion on the subject. It is in these words, "I do solemnly swear that I will administer justice without respect to persons, and do equal right to the poor and to the rich; and that I will faithfully and impartially discharge all the duties incumbent on me as according to the best of my abilities and understanding, agreeably to the constitution, and laws of the United States."

Why does a judge swear to discharge his duties agreeably to the constitution of the United States, if that constitution forms no rule for his government?

if it is closed upon him, and cannot be inspected by him?

If such be the real state of things, this is worse than solemn mockery. To prescribe, or to take this oath, becomes equally a crime.

It is also not entirely unworthy of observation, that in declaring what shall be the supreme law of the land, the constitution itself is first mentioned; and not the laws of the United States generally, but those only which shall be made in pursuance of the constitution, have that rank.

Thus, the particular phraseology of the constitution of the United States confirms and strengthens the principle, supposed to be essential to all written constitutions, that a law repugnant to the constitution is void; and that courts, as well as other departments, are bound by that instrument.

The rule must be discharged.

Chapter 2

Without freedom of thought, there can be no such thing as wisdom; and no such thing as publick liberty, without freedom of speech: Which is the right of every man, as far as by it he does not hurt and control the right of another. . . .

Cato's Letters[1]

A New York City officer pushes a journalist away from the scene of an Occupy Wall Street protest in Manhattan.

The First Amendment

Speech and Press Freedoms in Theory and Reality

Suppose . . .

. . . that two leading national newspapers receive copies of classified federal government documents from an anonymous source. The documents show the government has been lying in public statements about the success of the U.S. war effort and the number of U.S. casualties. When newspapers begin publishing a series on the documents, the government obtains a court order to prohibit publication of the remaining stories on the grounds they will jeopardize the lives of U.S. soldiers, threaten ongoing military operations and undermine national security and foreign policy. The newspapers say they have a First Amendment right to publish the information and the public has a need to know the truth about the war.

Does the First Amendment permit the government to stop the media from accurately disclosing important information to the public? Does the government's authority to classify government records as secret also allow it to prevent public discussion of those records once legally obtained? Does it matter how the newspapers obtained the documents? Look for the answers to these questions in this chapter's discussion of *New York Times Co. v. United States* and its excerpt at the end of the chapter.

Interpreting the First Amendment

The Origins of the First Amendment

Foundations of First Amendment Theory

First Amendment Values

Media Emergence, Convergence and Consolidation

Contemporary Prior Restraints

Court Scrutiny of Laws That Affect First Amendment Rights

Content-Based Laws
Content-Neutral Laws

Political Speech

Elections and Campaign Finance

Anonymous Speech

Government Speakers

Public and Nonpublic Forums

Private Property as a Public Forum
Virtual Forums and Government Speakers

Compelled Speech

Cases for Study

➤ *Near v. Minnesota*
➤ *New York Times Co. v. United States*

The First Amendment to the U.S. Constitution includes only 45 words. It says, "Congress shall make no law respecting an establishment of religion, or prohibiting the free exercise thereof; or abridging the freedom of speech, or of the press; or the right of the people peaceably to assemble, and to petition the government for a redress of grievances." Since the adoption of the Bill of Rights in 1791, thousands of articles, books and legal cases have tried to explain the meaning of the First Amendment and to define the boundaries of the six freedoms it protects. A literal interpretation of the First Amendment would completely ban Congress, and only Congress, from "abridging" the freedom of speech or of the press in any way. However, in 1925, the U.S. Supreme Court said the First Amendment applied to state legislatures as well as to Congress.[2] The Supreme Court since has struck down both federal and state laws, court rulings, administrative agency actions and executive decisions because they violate the First Amendment.

Through its decisions, the Supreme Court has clarified the meaning of the First Amendment. Although the amendment says government "shall make no law," the Court fails to view the First Amendment as an absolute ban.[3] Instead, the justices interpret the meaning of the amendment in various ways. Some justices, the so-called textualists, believe a simple reading of the First Amendment's

realWorld Law

First Amendment Protections for the Traveling Circus

A supporter of WikiLeaks founder Julian Assange protests outside the Ecuadorian Embassy in London where he sought asylum to avoid criminal allegations in Sweden.

WikiLeaks says its mission is to provide the broadest possible dissemination of the news leaks and secret and classified information it receives from anonymous sources and whistleblowers. It has made headlines by disclosing U.S. military documents and diplomatic cables. But is WikiLeaks' founder, Julian Assange, a journalist, a First Amendment activist or a thief? One observer noted,

> The First Amendment doesn't much care whether WikiLeaks is a reputable news outlet, a gang of black-hat hackers, or a traveling circus. The group's free speech protections depend on what WikiLeaks publishes, not what it is. . . . To argue that the First Amendment would protect Assange and WikiLeaks only if they are part of the press is to assume that the speech clause would not protect them, and that there is a major difference between the speech and press clauses.[1]

There is not.

1. Jonathan Peters, *WikiLeaks, the First Amendment, and the Press*, Harv. L. and Pol'y Rev., Apr. 18, 2011, *available at* http:// hlpronline.com.

own words provides a full and clear explanation of the protections it guarantees. But the text offers little guidance on whether, for example, court orders requiring WikiLeaks to disclose its sources unconstitutionally "abridge" its freedom of "the press" or whether Facebook "Likes" are protected under the Constitution's "freedom of speech."[4]

The Supreme Court rarely has distinguished between free speech and a free press. In fact, the Court often interchanges the two terms or combines them under the label "free expression." Historians and Justice Potter Stewart, however, have argued that the free press clause was intended to provide special protections for journalists and the mass media in checking the power of government.[5]

Interpreting the First Amendment

Justice Stewart and others have looked to history or a variety of theories to help them decide what the First Amendment means. For example, members of the Court may try to discover the **original intent** of the framers of the Constitution to help them determine whether occupying Wall Street or burning a flag to protest government actions is a form of speech protected by the First Amendment.[6] Unfortunately, intent is a slippery thing, and the authors of the First Amendment did not leave many records to indicate what they meant by "the freedom of speech, or of the press."

Some justices argue that the Constitution should be a living document whose meaning evolves with societal changes. They insist that the flexibility of constitutional language is its greatest strength, not its failing. This strategy accepts that clear understanding of what the words of the First Amendment meant in 1791 rarely would be helpful or relevant nearly 225 years later. Others complain that such plasticity of meaning gives the Court complete power to change the protections of the First Amendment at whim. In fact, during the past 60 years, the Court consistently has decreased both the percentage

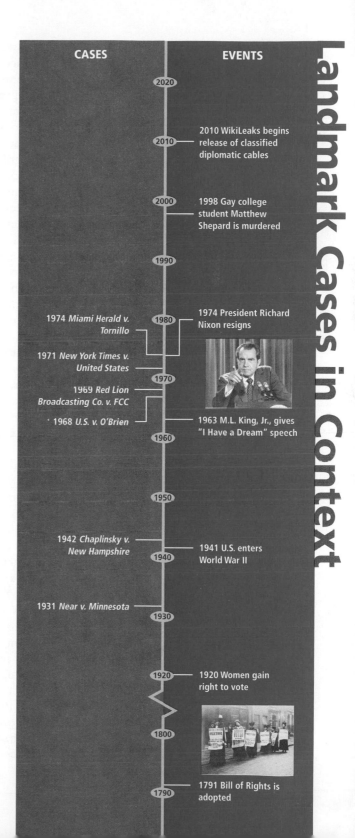

Landmark Cases in Context

CASES | EVENTS

2020

2010 — 2010 WikiLeaks begins release of classified diplomatic cables

2000 — 1998 Gay college student Matthew Shepard is murdered

1990

1974 *Miami Herald v. Tornillo* — 1980 — 1974 President Richard Nixon resigns

1971 *New York Times v. United States*

1970

1969 *Red Lion Broadcasting Co. v. FCC*

1968 *U.S. v. O'Brien* — 1963 M.L. King, Jr., gives "I Have a Dream" speech

1960

1950

1942 *Chaplinsky v. New Hampshire* — 1941 U.S. enters World War II

1940

1931 *Near v. Minnesota*

1930

1920 — 1920 Women gain right to vote

1800

1790 — 1791 Bill of Rights is adopted

original intent The perceived intent of the framers of the First Amendment that guides some contemporary First Amendment application and interpretation.

ad hoc balancing Making decisions according to the specific facts of the case under review rather than more general principles.

of First Amendment cases it reviews and its rulings in favor of First Amendment claims in those cases, according to a 2012 study.[7]

In practice, the Supreme Court tends to avoid broad statements about the First Amendment and generally decides what the First Amendment means on a case-by-case basis. To reach a decision, the Court often weighs the constitutional interests on one side of a case against the competing interests on the other side. This is an example of **ad hoc balancing,** in which courts make decisions according to the specific facts of the case under review rather than on the basis of more general principles. No clear rule dictates the Court's ad hoc balancing of interests. Instead, the justices carefully examine the competing rights and decide which side has the weightier constitutional merit. In 2013, when an apartment building owner tried to obtain information on the identity of a tenant anonymously posting criticism of the owner on Yelp!, for example, the Illinois court weighed the tenant's right to speak anonymously against the owner's right to seek payment for damages and decided in favor of the tenant.[8] In contrast, the Supreme Court in 2010 relied not on balancing but primarily on its own "historical and traditional" interpretation of the First Amendment to strike down a law prohibiting depictions of animal cruelty.[9]

Alternately, the Court may use a definitional or categorical approach to reach First Amendment decisions. Through decades of decisions, the Court has defined a variety of broad categories, such as political speech or commercial speech, and used them to determine the appropriate level of First Amendment protection. Simply put, the Court has decided that some types of speech deserve a lot of protection; some, less; others, none at all. Decades ago in *Chaplinsky v. New Hampshire,*[10] the Court first noted that "certain well-defined and narrowly limited classes of speech . . . are no essential part of any exposition of ideas, and are of such slight social value as a step to truth" that government may prevent and punish this speech without violating the First Amendment.

Courts have used this approach to rule that entire categories of speech are unprotected by the First Amendment. When speech falls into one of these narrow classes, the courts do not balance the value of the speech against society's interests—the Supreme Court determined the proper balance long ago. Using the categorical approach, then, the only question today is whether a specific act of expression falls within an unprotected class.

In *Chaplinsky,* the Court did not fully develop the different "narrow" categories of speech, but subsequent rulings make clear that political speech enjoys full constitutional protection, while seditious speech (criticism of government), fighting words, obscenity and defamation are unprotected categories. The First Amendment also poses no barrier to laws that punish blackmail, extortion, perjury, false advertising and disruptive speech in the public school classroom, for example. In addition, recent Court opinions suggest that child pornography, cross burning and true threats (particularly to national security) warrant little, if any, First Amendment protection.

Some categories of speech are neither well defined nor particularly narrow. But even loose categories serve as broad guidelines to the types of content that government may regulate with relative ease. In addition, the categories assist courts seeking to resolve cases involving similar speech. When cases involve loosely defined categories, however, courts generally use **categorical balancing** to determine the outcome; they look beyond the speech itself to consider the particular circumstances and the extent of harm caused to determine whether the expression is punishable. If the harm is likely to be cataclysmic, society's interest in preventing the crisis is more likely to outweigh concerns about protection of speech. Judges find it difficult to judge the gravity of harm caused by speech in advance or in the abstract.

The difficulty in determining whether false speech causes harm faced the Supreme Court squarely in 2012 when it considered whether the First Amendment prohibited Congress from enacting a law that made it a crime to lie about being awarded U.S. military honors.[11] In *United States v. Alvarez*, a majority of the Court struck down the Stolen Valor Act, but only four justices held that the Constitution absolutely protects such false statements as pure speech. Reasoning for this plurality, Justice Anthony Kennedy said there is no "general exception to the First Amendment for false statements." He argued that speech may be excluded from First Amendment protection only in the rare and extreme circumstances of the "historic categories" that pose a grave and imminent threat. False claims about military awards pose no such threat. Moreover, rebuttals, public disclosure and ridicule more than suffice to expose the lie and minimize any harm to public perceptions.

Two justices concurred but concluded that laws may punish false statements of easily determined facts in specific contexts with proof of the harm they cause. Justice Stephen Breyer reasoned that when laws punish lies made with intent to

categorical balancing A judge's or court's practice of deciding cases by weighing different broad categories, such as political speech, against other categories of interests, such as privacy, to create rules that may be applied in later cases with similar facts.

Is Journalism a "Conspiracy of Intellect"?

U.S. Supreme Court Justice Potter Stewart

Justice Potter Stewart believed the press had a particular, unique and special role under the Constitution. He said the framers of the Constitution intentionally singled out the press as the only business with a specific guarantee of freedom from government restraint because this protection was essential to the robust press vital to democratic self-governance. He wrote that, according to the framers,

> [A] free press was not just a neutral vehicle for the balanced discussion of diverse ideas. Instead, the free press meant organized, expert scrutiny of government. The press was a conspiracy of the intellect, with the courage of numbers. This formidable check on official power was what the British Crown had feared—and what the American Founders decided to risk.[1]

1. Potter Stewart, *Or of the Press*, 26 Hastings L.J. 631, 634 (1975).

deceive and knowledge of their falsity, "the dangers of suppressing valuable ideas are lower." But writing for a group of three dissenting justices, Justice Samuel Alito said flatly, "These lies have no value in and of themselves, and proscribing them does not chill any valuable speech." The three would have upheld the Stolen Valor Act as a constitutional means of preventing the substantial public harm caused by lying about military honors. In 2013, Congress amended the Stolen Valor Act making it illegal to profit from such lies.[12]

SUMMARY

DESPITE THE ABSOLUTIST LANGUAGE of the Constitution's First Amendment, the Supreme Court consistently has said the Constitution does not prevent government from regulating speech and press freedoms. While Justice Stewart believed the First Amendment provided explicit and special protection for the media, many justices do not distinguish between the speech and press guarantees and do not recognize any distinct press rights.

The Court tends to avoid sweeping declarations of the meaning of speech and press freedoms and to interpret the First Amendment only as applied to a particular set of facts. Many First Amendment decisions rely on ad hoc balancing of the competing rights. In addition, the Court has used categorical definitions of speech to place some types of speech beyond constitutional protection. At other times, speech categories assist the Court in its balancing of interests. ∎

The Origins of the First Amendment

Historians of the First Amendment generally agree that it was never meant to be an absolute ban on all government action involving freedom of speech or of the press. Instead, the First Amendment was intended to prevent the U.S. government from adopting the types of suppressive laws that flourished in England during the 300 years following the introduction of the printing press in 1450. Beginning in the early 1500s, the British Crown controlled all presses in England through its licensing power. King Henry VIII and the Roman Catholic Church feared that broad public distribution of printed materials would erode their control of information and their authority. The church and the crown sought to suppress challenges to their power by outlawing critical views as heresy (criticism of the church) or sedition. They jointly imposed a strict system of licensing of printers and prior review of all texts. The king's officers banned books and censored disfavored ideas.

The crown also provided favored printers with lucrative monopoly printing contracts for popular works like the Bible. In exchange, these printers became an extension of law enforcement, reporting suspicions of unlicensed publishing, attacking unlicensed printers and destroying their presses. Printers suspected of publishing or distributing unauthorized or outlawed texts faced fines, prison, torture or even execution. Despite the danger, unlicensed texts continued to appear in England.

Foundations of First Amendment Theory

In 1643, the power of prior review shifted from the king's officers to the British Parliament, with government censors reviewing all publications before they could be printed. Authors and publishers protested against government control of content and developed theories to justify press freedom. In 1644, for example, English poet John Milton's unlicensed "Areopagitica" argued that an open marketplace of ideas advanced the interests of society and humankind. Milton, who was angered by church and state condemnation and attempts to burn his earlier unlicensed pamphlet advocating divorce, said the free exchange of ideas was vital to the discovery of truth. He wrote, famously,

> Though all the winds of doctrine were let loose to play upon the earth, so Truth be in the field, we do injuriously by licensing and prohibiting to misdoubt her strength. Let her and Falsehood grapple; who ever knew Truth put to the worse in a free and open encounter?[13]

By the late 1600s, English philosopher and political theorist John Locke argued that government censorship was an improper exercise of power.[14] Locke first said that all people have fundamental natural rights, including life, personal liberty and self-fulfillment. Freedom of expression is central to these natural rights. In contrast, government has no innate rights or natural authority, Locke said. Government exists only through the grant of power from the people, and its actions are legitimate only within the sphere of granted power. Because the people do not grant government the power to limit their natural human rights, government censorship is always illegitimate.

Locke's vision of government was revolutionary. Nearly three-quarters of a century later, French political philosopher Jean-Jacques Rousseau advanced a similar view of a social contract between the people and their government.[15] Rousseau said all people are born free and equal but, unless constrained by morality and law, would become uncivilized and violent. Accordingly, people form a social contract in which they exchange some of their freedom for a limited government that advances the collective interest. Because the people remain sovereign and do not surrender their rights, government censorship violates the fundamental social contract and can never be justified. Many believe that Rousseau's ideas on the sovereignty of the people laid the foundation for the French Revolution.

In 1694, the British Parliament failed to renew the Licensing Act, which had authorized parliamentary **prior restraint** of publications. Still, for the next 100 years, the British government continued to enact and enforce laws that punished immoral, illegal or dangerous speech after the fact. Opinion leaders of the day generally accepted that punishment after the fact was a legitimate means

prior restraint Action taken by the government to prohibit publication of a specific document or text before it is distributed to the public; a policy that requires government approval before publication.

defamation A false communication that harms another's reputation and subjects him or her to ridicule and scorn; incorporates both libel and slander.

of minimizing the harms of sedition, **defamation** (criticism of individuals) and blasphemy (sacrilegious speech about God) and was not censorship because it merely held speakers responsible for their harmful or dangerous expression. In 1769, legal scholar Sir William Blackstone said that, under English common law, freedom of speech meant only that government could not censor speech prior to publication.[16] He wrote,

> The liberty of the press is indeed essential to the nature of a free state, but this consists in laying no previous restraints upon publications, and not in freedom from censure for criminal matter when published. Every freeman has an undoubted right to lay what sentiments he pleases before the public: to forbid this is to destroy the freedom of the press: but if he publishes what is improper, mischievous, or illegal, he must take the consequences of his own temerity.[17]

Blackstone's view of freedom of the press moved across the Atlantic with the British troops. The shadows of British licensing, taxation and common law restraints on speech and press were evident in the early years of American colonization.[18] Presses in the colonies were licensed, and government censors previewed publications until the 1720s. The crime of **seditious libel** made it illegal to publish anything harmful to the reputation of a colonial governor. Truth was not a defense because truthful criticism still harmed the governor's reputation, and the governor had a legal right to exact punishment for that harm.

seditious libel Communication meant to incite people to change the government; criticism of the government.

As the colonies became more independent, British common law traditions came under attack. The most renowned case is that of John Peter Zenger, the publisher of one of two newspapers in the colony of New York. Zenger clearly had broken the sedition law by printing criticism of colonial Gov. William Cosby. Cosby jailed Zenger to stop the attacks. In Zenger's defense, attorney Andrew Hamilton argued that no one should be jailed for publishing truthful and fair criticism of government. The jury agreed and acquitted Zenger in 1734.

Very few trials for seditious libel occurred after that ruling. However, the struggle to define the acceptable limits of free speech and a free press in the colonies continued. Colonial legislatures used their power of contempt to punish disfavored publishers. They had the power to question, convict, jail and fine publishers for breach of parliamentary privilege, which encompassed virtually any criticism of legislative performance.

The First Amendment freedoms of speech and of the press grew out of this mixed history of suppression and resistance. The Constitution's framers understood both the British tradition of punishment for sedition, blasphemy and libel, and the colonists' growing enthusiasm for increasingly wide-open debate. It seems clear the authors of the First Amendment intended to provide a ban on prior restraints. It is less clear whether they intended to eliminate the common law regarding sedition, blasphemy and libel.[19]

The passage of the Sedition Act seven years after the adoption of the First Amendment suggests that government leaders continued to support laws that

International Law

Internet Flavor-of-the-Month?

Swedish Foreign Minister Carl Bildt speaks to the press following an informal meeting of European Union representatives in Dublin in 2013.

With more than 80 nations co-sponsoring the resolution, the United Nations Human Rights Council in 2012 endorsed freedom of expression and information on the Internet as a cornerstone of development.[1] The U.N. resolution called on all countries to maintain the free flow of information on the Internet and improve global access. The membership voiced "near consensus" on the importance of preserving "a clean and open Internet."

In 2011, the Organisation for Economic Co-operation and Development (OECD), a group of 34 countries, similarly encouraged its members to protect the flow of information online, to invest in digital networks and to limit regulations that might hinder economic growth via the Internet.[2]

Nonetheless, Google reported that in 2012 it received a rapidly rising number—nearly 1,800 of government requests to remove information and political criticism from its search results.[3] The largest number of requests sought removal of allegedly defamatory content or related to privacy or security concerns.

Swedish foreign minister Carl Bildt called the U.N. resolution "truly important" and said, "We cannot accept that the Internet's content should be limited or manipulated depending on the flavor-of-the-month of political leaders."

1. Carl Bildt, *A Victory for the Internet*, N.Y. Times, July 5, 2012, *available at* http://www.nytimes.com.
2. Eric Pfanner, *O.E.C.D. Calls on Members to Defend Internet Freedoms*, N.Y. Times, Dec. 13, 2011, *available at* http://www.nytimes.com.
3. *Google Transparency Report, available at* http://www.google.com.

punished criticism of government. The law imposed heavy fines and jail time on individuals who stirred up public emotions or expressed malicious views against the government. As the 18th century ended, more than a dozen prosecutions and convictions under the Alien and Sedition Acts targeted outspoken publishers and political opponents of President John Adams.[20] The U.S. Supreme Court never reviewed the constitutionality of the federal Sedition Act, which expired in 1801. More than 150 years later, Justice William J. Brennan said that "the court of history" had clearly decided the Sedition Act was unconstitutional.[21]

SUMMARY

IN THE 1500s, BRITISH CHURCH AND STATE collaborated to license presses and strictly censor publications to limit the spread of information, retain power and suppress criticism of their power and authority. During the following century, the philosophic argument against government censorship was outlined. Milton attacked government's prior review as a form of thought control; Locke argued that government's authority should be limited to assuring people's natural rights; Rousseau said the sovereign people's contract with government did not grant government authority to censor expression.

A century after British Parliament failed to renew the Licensing Act, Blackstone defined freedom of speech in England as freedom from prior restraint by government. Punishment after the fact for harmful speech did not violate freedom of speech. Eventually, the American colonies largely rejected the British common law tradition of punishing truthful criticism of government. The American concept of freedom of speech and press developed from a mixture of government repression and public resistance. The framers of the First Amendment did not provide a clear definition of "the freedom of speech and of the press." ∎

First Amendment Values

The Supreme Court has interpreted the First Amendment as a means to achieve specific social functions or advance certain fundamental values. When the First Amendment is understood as an instrument, freedom of speech and freedom of the press receive protection only when they advance such social benefits as the search for truth or self-governance.[22] This instrumental, or functional, concept of the First Amendment lies beneath many Court decisions favoring broadcast regulation to increase the diversity of ideas reaching U.S. voters. Speech also deserves protection because it provides a check on government abuse of power, a safety valve for social discontent or a means of personal self-realization.[23] The Court endorsed the first of these purposes in *New York Times v. Sullivan,* saying that robust criticism of government is so vital to democracy that the First Amendment protects news media from punishment for unintentional defamation of government officials (see Chapter 4).[24] Some scholars argue that the most significant value of the First Amendment is to improve the ability of minority groups in society to be heard effectively[25] or to encourage the development of a tolerant society.[26]

Those who value free speech in and of itself—as an end rather than a means—see free speech as a natural right of individuals. Accordingly, freedom of speech is worthy of constitutional protection because it is fundamental to individual natural liberty.[27] Free speech is essential to what it means to be human.

Both the functional and the inherent-value perspectives on free speech are useful to the extent that they help courts determine what types of speech should be protected and what types of speech should be punished. Neither does a very good job of this, however. Neither provides strict guidelines or clear lines (what the law calls bright-line distinctions) to determine when speech deserves protection. For instance, the functional approach fails to establish a clear boundary between speech that helps democratic self-governance and speech that does not. For example, is a nonviolent march and occupation of Wall Street protected political expression? If speech is an essential element of what it means to be

Points of Law

What's the Value of Free Speech?

Many theories help explain why we should care about speech. Some, like some holy grail, try to define the single core value of free speech, but most people believe the First Amendment serves a number of important interests: individual and social, instrumental and inherent.[1] Values of free speech frequently identified in Supreme Court decisions include the following:

- *Individual liberty.* The freedom of speech is deeply intertwined with fundamental natural rights: human liberty, self-expression and personhood; the freedom to think and believe; the right to realize one's own nature and to explore one's intellect and imagination; the right to develop our intellectual and spiritual capacity and to delimit the boundaries of self.[2] In this sense, free speech is an inalienable right.

- *Self-government.*[3] The freedom to discuss the relative merits and demerits of candidates and policy options and to render judgments is an essential cornerstone of responsible self-governance. The freedom of speech enables each autonomous individual to join in discussion, participate in public deliberation and form associations of "the people" in pursuit of "democratic self-determination."[4]

- *Limited government power.* A closely related value of free speech is its role as an "invaluable bulwark against tyranny."[5] It is through free speech that "the people" exercise their right to judge the public officials whom they have entrusted to represent them. Here the freedoms of speech and press, and by extension the freedom of the vote, serve as a "check"[6] on authoritarian rule, a barrier to censorship or dictatorship and a limit to the abuse of power by the few.

- *Attainment of truth.* The oft-cited "marketplace of ideas" helps advance knowledge and the discovery of truth. Only by challenging "certain truth" and "received wisdom" through free and unfettered public discussion can a society test its accepted ideas and assure that they are not dead dogma.[7]

- *Safety valve.* Free speech is the means by which a society acknowledges and attends to problems and grievances before they escalate into violence. Free speech offers a necessary mechanism for "letting off steam" and defusing individual and societal pressures and helps achieve a balance between social stability and change, compromise and conflict, tolerance and hate.[8] This free speech value is most evident during "the worst of times," when societal tensions are high.[9]

- *Its own end.* Free speech may not be valued solely because of its beneficial functions for individuals and societies. Rather, free speech, like clean air, or beauty, or justice, may be an end in and of itself, a valuable good and a cherished right.[10]

---

1. Thomas I. Emerson, *Toward a General Theory of the First Amendment,* 72 Yale L.J. 877 (1963).
2. *See* John Locke, II Two Treatises of Government 4 (Peter Laslett ed., Cambridge Univ. Press 1988) (1698).
3. For detailed discussion, see Alexander Meiklejohn, Free Speech and Its Relation to Self-Government (1948).
4. Robert Post, *Managing Deliberation: The Quandary of Democratic Dialogue,* 103 Ethics 654, 672 (1993).
5. James Madison, Report on the Virginia Resolutions (Jan. 1800), *reprinted in* 5 The Founders' Constitution (Philip B. Kurland & Ralph Lerner eds., 1987).
6. Vincent Blasi, *The Checking Value in First Amendment Theory,* 1977 Am. B. Found. Res. J. 521, 523 (1977).
7. Zechariah Chafee, Jr., *Freedom of Speech in War Time,* 32 Harv. L. Rev. 932 (1919); Zechariah Chafee, Jr., Freedom of Speech 37 (1920).
8. C. Edwin Baker, *Scope of the First Amendment Freedom of Speech,* 25 UCLA L. Rev. 964 (1978).
9. Vincent Blasi, *The Pathological Perspective and the First Amendment,* 85 Colum. L. Rev. 449, 464 (1985).
10. Ronald Dworkin, A Moral Reading of the American Constitution (1996).

Emerging Law

What's Speech?

Despite what you may think based on this sign on the front door of Facebook headquarters in Menlo Park, Calif., one federal judge has ruled that clicking "Like" is not constitutionally protected speech.

Do computers have free speech?[1] When Google uses its algorithms to select and sort data from the Internet, is that speech? When an employee clicks "Like" on a Facebook post, is that speech? The answers may surprise you.

Constitutional scholar and lawyer Eugene Volokh says that because Google's search results and ordering are the result of independent judgments, Google results are comparable to "little opinion pieces" in a newspaper.[2] The search results reflect what information Google decides will be most valuable to the user, which is the essence of editorial judgment.[3] One U.S. district court said much the same thing when it ruled that "a page rank [on Google] is an opinion . . . entitled to First Amendment protection."[4] The court held that the First Amendment barred a claim for damages by a firm that said Google had harmed its business by intentionally lowering its placement in Google search results.

As for Facebook "Likes," in 2012 a U.S. district court in Virginia ruled that they are not speech.[5] In *Bland v. Roberts,* the district court reasoned that two sheriff's employees who clicked "Like" were not engaged in expression akin to writing or posting a message. The employees sought damages for retaliatory firing after they liked the page of their boss's election opponent. The trial court dismissed their First Amendment claim, but the ACLU and Facebook have filed amicus curiae briefs in the appeal to the Fourth Circuit. Many expect the case to reach the Supreme Court.

1. Tim Wu, *Free Speech for Computers?*, N.Y. Times, June 20, 2012, *available at* http://www.nytimes.com.
2. Eugene Volokh, *First Amendment Protection for Search Engine Search Results,* Apr. 20, 2012, *available at* http://www.volokh.com.
3. Adam Clark Estes, *362 Views,* May 9, 2012, *available at* http://www.theatlanticwire.com.
4. Search King. v. Google Technology, 2003 U.S. Dist. LEXIS 27193 (W.D. Okla., Jan. 13, 2003).
5. Bland v. Roberts, 857 F.Supp. 2d 599 (E.D. Va. 2012).

human, where is the logical limit to the right of self-expression? If individuals express themselves by shooting a gun in the middle of the city, by lying on the witness stand or by making harassing telephone calls, should all of these actions be protected?

The dilemmas presented by value-based adjudication are made clear in the Supreme Court's apparently contradictory rulings in two landmark cases exploring the right of the public to use the mass media as a means to distribute its own free speech. In the first of these, *Red Lion Broadcasting Co. v. FCC*, decided in 1969, the Court ruled unanimously that regulations requiring broadcasters to seek out and broadcast competing views on controversial public issues were constitutional.[28] Broadcasters had challenged Federal Communication Commission rules requiring them to notify and provide free broadcast time for political candidates to reply to editorials endorsing their opponents and for people attacked on the air. They argued that the rules violated broadcasters' First Amendment right to choose the information they broadcast. The Court disagreed and said,

> The right of free speech of a broadcaster, the user of a sound truck, or any other individual does not embrace a right to snuff out the free speech of others. . . . [The broadcaster] has no constitutional right to . . . monopolize a radio frequency to the exclusion of his fellow citizens.[29]

Here the Court held that *public* speech over the public airwaves was of paramount value. Five years later, a Supreme Court with three new members ruled in *Miami Herald v. Tornillo* that "compelling editors or publishers to publish that which 'reason tells them should not be published'" is unconstitutional.[30] The Court said the First Amendment barred government from requiring a newspaper to provide free reply space to political candidates attacked in the paper. Although the Court recognized the value of newspapers as a platform for public debate, it reasoned that "press responsibility is not mandated by the Constitution, and like many other virtues it cannot be legislated."[31] The Court lauded the autonomy of the printed press:

> A newspaper is more than a passive receptacle or conduit for news, comment and advertising. The choice of material to go into a newspaper, and the decisions made as to limitations on the size and content of the paper, and treatment of public issues and public officials—whether fair or unfair—constitute the exercise of editorial control and judgment. It has yet to be demonstrated how governmental regulation of this crucial process can be exercised consistent with First Amendment guarantees of a free press.

SUMMARY

THE SUPREME COURT HAS INTERPRETED the First Amendment through decisions that rest in part on British common law precedents. At a minimum, the First Amendment prohibits government prior restraints on speakers or the press. Court interpretation and application of the First Amendment rely upon different understandings of the purposes and values of free expression. Some believe free expression warrants protection because it is a fundamental natural right outside the reach of government. Others believe freedom of expression is protected only to the extent that it advances other extremely important interests, such as self-governance. The Supreme Court has not set down one clear, fixed definition of the freedoms of speech and press and allows the parameters of First Amendment freedoms to respond to the particulars of the cases it reviews. Today, the Constitution provides different degrees of protection to different speakers and to different types of speech. ■

Media Emergence, Convergence and Consolidation

In 1791, when the First Amendment was adopted, speaking to crowds in town squares was an important way to distribute a message broadly. Beyond that, individuals could print flyers, pamphlets, leaflets, posters, books and newspapers.

Although the printed word was *the* medium of mass communication, the masses reached were small. Thousands of American newspapers emerged in the 18th century; a few survived, and the largest had circulations of no more than 200 or so readers. Printed materials passed from hand to hand, with some people receiving newspapers months after they were published. Word of mouth remained a primary means of spreading timely information.

Today, the First Amendment faces a very different press. Mass communication has changed dramatically. The arrival of motion pictures, radio and television, telephones, cable and the Internet provided new communication and entertainment options. Citizens turned away from the discussions that had been a major source of news and entertainment, spent less time reading newspapers and devoted evenings to other media. Movies, broadcasts, cable and streamed content offered timely, active news and entertainment from the local community and around the globe.

Observers feared each new medium would dissolve families and disintegrate communities. Emerging media would divert citizens' attention from important issues, transform engaged community members into isolated media consumers[32] and alter both attitudes and behaviors. Newspaper owners feared the competition and sought legal protection from media they said threatened democracy. Representatives of the new media argued they offered new avenues for speech and increased diversity of the press.

Today the number of newspapers published in the United States has declined despite a significant growth in the number of households. The traditional press occupies a shrinking portion of the media reaching the U.S. audience, and wireless digital communications receive and transmit the full range of communications capabilities to the equivalent of portable personal broadcast stations instantly around the globe.

The Supreme Court has struggled to determine when and how the First Amendment protects these diverse media.[33] For a time, the Court generally treated each medium of communication differently on the basis that each presented unique First Amendment strengths and problems. In 1949, for example, one justice argued that "the moving picture screen, the radio, the newspaper, the handbill, the sound truck and the street corner orator have differing natures, values, abuses and dangers. Each, in my view, is a law unto itself."[34] The Court accepted regulatory differences "justified by some special characteristic of the press"[35] or by specific distinctions among the media, allowing government to regulate broadcasters differently from newspapers because broadcasters act as trustees of the scarce public airwaves.[36] Unique regulations on cable operators did not violate the First Amendment because cable systems threatened the economic survival of broadcasters.[37]

Significant changes and continuing developments in the ownership and operation of mass media also challenge the Court's carefully drawn distinctions. An ever-shrinking number of behemoth multimedia ownership conglomerates controls American media.[38] A single company's record labels and entertainment, books and video games reach around the globe. For example, Clear Channel Communications operated radio stations in nearly two-thirds of U.S. broadcast markets,[39] and 10 companies provided television programming to 85 percent of American households.[40] The top eight news media firms in New York ranked among the 300 largest companies in the world,[41] and General Electric alone—which owned NBC, USA Network and Universal Pictures, among other media holdings—reported revenue exceeding $100 billion.[42]

As rapid transformations of the communication environment stretch the traditional definition of "the press," they also challenge established understanding and application of First Amendment guarantees. Two out of three professional journalists said that increasing emphasis on media profits was seriously hurting the quality of news reporting in the United States.[43] With continued blurring of the once-discrete characteristics of content and media, consistent application of established First Amendment precedents becomes more difficult, and it is good to recall that hard cases make bad law.

SUMMARY

ISSUES OF MEDIA CONVERGENCE AND CONSOLIDATION present new challenges to the Supreme Court's interpretation and application of the First Amendment. The proliferation of new media suggests a growing abundance of avenues for free expression. However, control of an increasing number of media outlets by a very few corporations may limit the diversity of content reaching the public and reduce opportunities for citizens to send their messages to large audiences. The increasing overlap of once-distinct media also blurs once-clear distinctions under the First Amendment, posing new and difficult questions for the courts. ∎

Contemporary Prior Restraints

Although the Supreme Court has not settled on a single interpretation of the First Amendment, the Court has established one bedrock principle: freedom of the press cannot coexist with prior restraint. Prior restraint stops speech before it is expressed and halts presses before publication. It is the essence of censorship. The Court's modern understanding of prior restraint began with its 1931 decision in *Near v. Minnesota* (excerpted at the end of this chapter).[44]

International Law

Cutting Off Online Access

Jake Davis

In 2012, Jake Davis, a then 18-year-old from the Shetland Islands, Scotland, was among five men arrested in the United States and Europe for a variety of computer-based crimes.[1] Under the alias "Topiary," Davis was a leading member in Anonymous and LulzSec, recognized around the world for their hacktivism aimed at both business and government organizations. A London court said the five were among "the most sophisticated hackers in the world." For his part in cyberattacks on Sony, PBS, Fox Broadcasting, the Pentagon, the CIA and the U.S. Air Force, to name a few, Davis received house arrest and a curfew from 10 p.m. to 7 a.m. The court also banned him from accessing the Internet.

In a different case, however, London's Criminal Appeal Court ruled that Internet access is a public right and banning anyone from its use is "unreasonable" and "entirely excessive."[2] The court agreed with a convicted sex offender that a ban on Internet access unreasonably cut him off from the world. They instead imposed an order that the offender make his Internet use history available to police upon request.

1. Somini Sengupta, *Arrests Sow Mistrust Insides a Clan of Hackers,* N.Y. TIMES, Mar. 6, 2012, *available at* http://www.nytimes.com.
2. Owen Bowcott, *Internet Ban on Convicted Sex Offender "Unreasonable,"* TELEGRAPH (LONDON), Nov. 13, 2012, *available at* http://www.guardian.co.uk.

In *Near,* the Court said that prior restraint, especially any outright ban on expression, is the least tolerable form of government intervention in the speech marketplace.[45] The case began after Jay Near, publisher of The Saturday Press in Minneapolis, printed eight issues of his paper filled with charges that city government and police officials were doing nothing to stop Jewish gangsters from operating gambling, bootlegging and racketeering businesses all over the city. The paper was shut down under a state public nuisance law that allowed judges to stop publications of "scandalous or defamatory material" unless the publisher could convince a judge that the attacks were true and published with good intent.

When the Supreme Court reviewed the case, it ruled that the permanent ban on future issues of The Saturday Press was unconstitutional. The Court said the Minnesota law that allowed government to ban "nuisance" publications was a classic prior restraint, to which the First Amendment stands as a nearly absolute barrier. A classic prior restraint has three components: (1) It imposes government oversight of whole categories of speech, content or publication; (2) it allows the government to choose what content is acceptable;

and (3) it empowers government censors to ban content before it is distributed to the public.

In 1971, the Supreme Court created a legal landmark when it ruled in *New York Times Co. v. United States* that a court order preventing publication of news stories based on the Pentagon Papers was an unconstitutional prior restraint.[46] The Pentagon Papers, as they were commonly known, were the top-secret Department of Defense study of U.S. involvement in Vietnam between 1945 and 1967. Using classified information leaked to the newspaper, The New York Times started a series of news stories about the reality and history of the Vietnam War. The Nixon administration said the publication threatened national security and the safety of U.S. troops and asked for a court **injunction**. The court agreed and stopped the stories.

Acting with unusual speed, the Supreme Court said the injunction violated the Constitution because the federal government had not met its burden of showing that the ban was essential to prevent a real and immediate risk of harm to a compelling government interest. The Court said, "[A]ny system of prior restraints of expression comes to this Court bearing a heavy presumption against its constitutional validity."[47] However, the Court's decision left open the possibility that prior restraints may be constitutional if the government can show they are necessary to prevent serious harm to extremely important government interests.

The Court repeatedly has reasoned that prior restraints are generally unconstitutional because they pose too great a risk that government will censor ideas it disfavors and distort the marketplace of ideas. To emphasize this point, the Court has said that if "a threat of criminal or civil sanctions after publication 'chills' speech, prior restraint 'freezes' it."[48] The First Amendment poses its greatest obstacle to direct prior restraints on the news media because every moment of a ban on reporting causes direct harm to the First Amendment rights of both the media and the public.[49]

The Supreme Court has applied this understanding of "prior restraint" in a variety of different situations and to a range of government actions. Today,

Points of Law

What Is a Prior Restraint?

A prior restraint is what we think of as good old garden-variety censorship. When government prohibits publication or suppresses particular material, this is prior restraint. Prior restraint occurs when the following happen:

1. Any government body or representative.

2. Reviews speech or press prior to distribution.

3. Stops the dissemination of ideas *before* they reach the public.

According to the Supreme Court, prior restraint is "the most serious and the least tolerable infringement on First Amendment rights."[1]

---

1. Nebraska Press Ass'n v. Stuart, 427 U.S. 539, 559 (1976).

Dr. Daniel Ellsberg (left), the RAND Corporation employee and U.S. Defense Department consultant who leaked the Pentagon Papers to the media, speaks to reporters after his 1971 arraignment on charges of illegal possession of the classified documents.

Points of Law

When Are Prior Restraints Constitutional?

The Supreme Court suggested in *Near v. Minnesota*[1] that government prior restraints of speech may be found constitutional when they are necessary to prevent the following:

- Obstruction of military recruitment.
- Publication of troop locations, numbers and movements in time of war.
- Obscene publications.
- Incitements to violence.
- Forcible overthrow of government.
- Fighting words likely to promote imminent violence.

---

1. 283 U.S. 697 (1931).

injunction A court order prohibiting a person or organization from doing some specified act.

apparent prior restraints often arise in the form of court orders that stop speech or publication. For example, the Court affirmed the unconstitutionality of a state court injunction preventing the scheduled broadcast of an investigative news report two decades ago and said indefinite delay of news broadcasts is unacceptable under the First Amendment.[50] As another court noted elsewhere, "News delayed is news denied."[51] The Supreme Court decision involved CBS News' intended broadcast of footage of a South Dakota meatpacking plant obtained through "calculated misdeeds" involving an employee wearing a hidden camera. Although the broadcast might cause significant harm to the meatpacking company, the Court found the "most extraordinary remedy" of an injunction was unwarranted because it was not essential.

A prior restraint on the media can be justified only in exceptional situations. Prior restraints may be permitted either when there is clear and convincing evidence that the publication will cause great and certain harm that cannot be addressed by less intrusive measures or when the news media clearly engaged in criminal activity to obtain the information being restrained.[52]

The speed and breadth of distributing information through the Internet sometimes leads courts to impose injunctions. In 2010, for example, a district court in New Jersey imposed an injunction requiring TheFlyontheWall.com to delay distribution of stock tips it aggregated from more than five dozen investment firms.[53] The firms had sued the online publisher for "hot news" misappropriation, a form of unfair competition, for distributing their confidential stock recommendations before they were made public. On appeal, the Second Circuit Court quickly struck down the injunction and subsequently reversed the lower court, freeing TheFlyontheWall.com to continue rapid publication of the stock tips.[54]

State courts also struggle with the use of injunctions as a means to reduce the potentially severe and immediate harms of free speech on the Internet. In New Hampshire, for example, the state supreme court ruled that a lower court injunction forcing the website removal of a leaked document was an unlawful prior restraint.[55] The case involved a posted article on a mortgage lender with a link to a document leaked anonymously from the state banking authority. The lower court had granted the mortgage company request to order removal of the document and disclosure of its source.[56] A New Jersey court order shutting down several websites in response to allegations of hateful, racist and defamatory content about U.S. immigrants and requiring Internet service providers to disclose the identities of anonymous posters lasted six months and ended when the court granted a defense motion to dismiss the case.[57]

realWorld Law

The Pentagon Papers of Our Time?

Many compared WikiLeaks' 2010 posting of more than 90,000 classified U.S. military documents on the war in Afghanistan to the publication of the Pentagon Papers during the Vietnam War.[1]

Both leaks hinged on media providing greater transparency to an ongoing and controversial war involving U.S. troops. And both highlighted mainstream media's importance in establishing the credibility of the documents. "Transparency is moot without authority,"[2] according to one observer who noted WikiLeaks' use of The New York Times to vet the documents prior to release.

The comparisons obscure significant differences between the WikiLeaks and Pentagon Papers situations. The government imposed a prior restraint on the Pentagon Papers but not on WikiLeaks. The Pentagon Papers documents were at least three years old and were released as U.S. troops began to withdraw; some WikiLeaks material dated back only seven months, when the war in Afghanistan was ramping up.

Although the Obama White House condemned the WikiLeaks release, it did not seek an injunction to stop their publication,[5] perhaps because "it is technology, even more than law, that makes it nearly futile to pursue injunctions against publication of leaked documents. . . . Injunctions [do] not work once the cat is out of the bag or the genie out of the bottle"[6] or the information already available worldwide on the Web.

1. Janie Lorber, *Early Word: WikiLeaked*, N.Y. TIMES, July 30, 2010, *available at* http://thecaucus.blogs.nytimes.com.
2. Adam Kirsch, *Why Wikileaks Still Needs the New York Times*, NEW REPUBLIC, July 26, 2010, *available at* http://www.tnr.com/blog/foreign-policy.
4. WikiLeaks, *available at* http://wikileaks.org.
5. Alexandra Topping, *Wikileaks Condemned by White House over War Documents*, GUARDIAN, July 26, 2010, *available at* http://www.guardian.co.uk/world.
6. Lyrissa Lidsky, *Pentagon Papers II?: Wikileaks and Information Control in the Internet Era*, PRAWFSBLAWG, July 26, 2010, *available at* http://prawfsblawg.blogs.com.

The federal government, through its Immigrations and Customs Enforcement (ICE) bureau, also closes down websites it says are selling counterfeit goods and duping consumers.[58] Late in 2012, a coordinated international effort seized 132 domains in the third year of a program that "target[s] websites," according to customs information. In 2011, the program seized another150 websites "to mark the official beginning of the online holiday shopping season, known as Cyber Monday."[59] ICE is seeking forfeiture (permanent release) of many of these sites through a program the ACLU says "threaten[s] due process and First Amendment rights."[60] One technology blog reports that "multiple sites had been *trying* to challenge the seizures but had found the process to be incredibly difficult."[61]

ICE also pulled down 313 National Football League–related sites in January 2013 "without any adversarial hearings" on the grounds that they infringed copyright and broadcasting rights.[62] Rojadirecta.com has been under ICE's control since early 2011 for allegedly linking to unauthorized video streams of live sporting events. In response to Recording Industry of America claims that the site had linked to four prerelease music tracks in 2010, ICE removed the popular hip-hop blog called Dajaz1.com. Dajaz1.com regained its domain 13 months later without the government filing either civil or criminal charges.[63]

Many prior restraints on Internet content may be ineffective because of the ability to publish anonymously via a multiplicity of foreign and mirror sites. In one case, the court-ordered shutdown of the WikiLeaks website, in response to a suit from a Cayman Islands bank, lasted only one week. The case was dismissed after the material appeared elsewhere.[64] Yet in each of these situations, website information or the entire website was blocked for days or months.

Despite the Supreme Court's consistent opposition to prior restraints, many laws prevent or limit specific speakers from discussing particular topics, such as threats to national security. Judges' orders prohibiting trial participants from discussing the ongoing trial also generally are acceptable. Laws that limit use of copyrighted material are mandated by the Constitution, and laws that criminalize the production and distribution of obscenity are accepted. Police also may legally prevent the speech involved when individuals conspire to commit a crime or to incite others to violence.

In addition, some government actions that appear to restrain freedom of speech are permitted because the Court does not view them as prior restraints. These laws generally impose content-neutral restrictions on the time, place or manner of expression, which means they do not target or restrict particular messages because of their content. Accordingly, cities may require prior review and permitting for parades in the streets or meetings in public parks, as long as the permit process does not give uncontrolled authority to officials. Laws restricting anti-abortion protests and counseling outside family planning facilities are constitutional.[65] Laws that ban campaigning or distribution of election materials within a certain distance of the polls are acceptable, too.[66] More discussion of cases involving **content-neutral laws** follows.

content-neutral laws Laws that incidentally and unintentionally affect speech as they advance other important government interests.

SUMMARY

A FUNDAMENTAL PRINCIPLE OF THE First Amendment is that it stands as a nearly absolute barrier to government prior restraints on expression. A prior restraint involves government's official review and either permission or prohibition of certain content before it may be disseminated. In 1931, the Supreme Court said prior restraints may be constitutional under extremely narrow circumstances. Forty years later, the Supreme Court said the Constitution presumes prior restraints are unconstitutional and places an extremely heavy burden on government to justify prior restraint of news media. Courts struggle with issues of prior restraint related to Internet content but have not reviewed the constitutionality of a federal government program that removes Internet domains it believes violate federal laws. Content-neutral time, place and manner restrictions on speech generally are constitutional and are not considered prior restraints. ∎

Court Scrutiny of Laws That Affect First Amendment Rights

Some laws of journalism and mass communication do not involve speech at all. Minimum-wage regulations or laws that prevent monopolies are both laws that fall within the power of Congress to regulate commerce. Article I, Section 8, Clause 3, of the U.S. Constitution gives Congress authority "to regulate Commerce with foreign nations, and among the several states, and with the Indian Tribes." The Court generally presumes that **laws of general application**, such as wage and hour regulations, are constitutional and may be applied to media businesses. The Supreme Court reviews challenges to such laws of general application under minimum or **rational review.** Rational review presumes the constitutionality of legislative or administrative enactments that have a rational purpose. Laws reviewed under minimum scrutiny must be reasonable and serve a legitimate government purpose to be constitutional.

Many laws of journalism and mass communication do affect the freedom of speech and press protected by the Constitution. When asked to decide whether such laws violate the Constitution, the Supreme Court first determines whether the law targets the ideas expressed or aims at some goal unrelated to the content of the message. The Court calls the first type of law "content based" and the second "content neutral." **Content-based laws** regulate what is being said; they single out certain messages for punishment because of government disapproval of the ideas or subjects they present. Laws that prohibit the "desecration" of the U.S. flag are content based. Content-neutral laws restrict where, when and how ideas are expressed; they often advance public interests unrelated to speech. Laws that regulate the size and placement of billboards and ordinances that limit noise in hospital zones are content neutral and, generally, constitutional if they restrict speech as little as necessary to advance the related government interest.

laws of general application Laws such as tax and equal employment laws that fall within the express power of government. Laws of general application are generally reviewed under minimum scrutiny.

rational review A standard of judicial review that assumes the constitutionality of reasonable legislative or administrative enactments and applies minimum scrutiny to their review.

content-based laws Laws enacted because of the message, the subject matter or the ideas expressed in the regulated speech.

Content-Based Laws

The Supreme Court generally views content-based laws as presumptively invalid. Like prior restraints, laws that punish the expression of specific ideas after the fact pose a direct and serious threat of government censorship. To stop government censorship of disfavored ideas, the Supreme Court applies a very rigorous test to determine when content-based laws are constitutional. This most rigorous test, called **strict scrutiny**, finds laws that discriminate on the basis of content unconstitutional unless they use (1) the least restrictive means (2) to advance a compelling government interest. So few laws pass strict scrutiny review that people say strict scrutiny is strict in theory but fatal in fact.

Laws employ the least restrictive means only when they are extremely well tailored to their goals and restrict the smallest possible amount of protected speech. The Supreme Court generally finds that a law is least restrictive if no other

strict scrutiny A test for determining the constitutionality of laws restricting speech, under which the government must show it is using the least restrictive means available to directly advance a compelling interest.

compelling interest A government interest of the highest order, an interest the government is required to protect.

methods available to the government would achieve its goals and be less harmful to free speech rights. To pass strict scrutiny, laws also must directly advance a compelling or paramount government interest. The Court has said a **compelling interest** is an interest of the highest order. Compelling government interests relate to core constitutional concerns and to the most significant functions of government. Frequently cited compelling government interests are national security, the electoral process and the public health and welfare.

In *Simon & Schuster v. Crime Victims Board,* for example, the Supreme Court struck down a New York law that attempted to compensate crime victims and limit the rewards of crime.[67] Following a well-publicized series of killings by the "Son of Sam" in the mid-1970s, New York state passed a law that required criminal authors earning money from works describing their crimes or their thoughts related to their crimes to turn over the related income to the state. The money would compensate crime victims, with only the remaining balance paid to the author. The law applied to any authors who made even passing comments about actual crimes. The state said the law was intended to increase victim compensation and decrease the "fruits" of crime.

Simon & Schuster, which had published a true-crime autobiography of mafia figure Henry Hill, challenged the law as facially unconstitutional on the grounds that it targeted specific content for punitive treatment by the government. The Supreme Court concluded that although the content-based law advanced a compelling government interest, it unconstitutionally punished a substantial quantity of literature fully protected by the First Amendment.[68] It was overbroad.

Points of Law

Strict Scrutiny

The Supreme Court has said content-based laws are constitutional only if they pass strict scrutiny. To be constitutional, a content-based law must do the following:

1. Be necessary.
2. To advance a compelling government interest.
3. Harm First Amendment rights as little as possible.

Strict scrutiny is the most rigorous test used by the Court to determine whether a law is constitutional.

time/place/manner (TPM) laws A First Amendment concept that laws regulating the conditions of speech are more acceptable than those regulating content; also, the laws that regulate these conditions.

Content-Neutral Laws

The Supreme Court is much more willing to uphold the constitutionality of laws that affect speech but do not discriminate on the basis of content. Content-neutral laws generally regulate the nonspeech elements of a message, such as the time, the place or the manner (size or volume) in which the speech occurs. Thus, some content-neutral laws are called **time/place/manner (TPM) laws.** Content-neutral laws, such as noise ordinances, may reduce the overall quantity and diversity of speech or the ability of a speaker to reach a chosen audience but do not censor specific ideas and advance some legitimate government goal. In a case arising out of protests over the Vietnam War, the Court established its foundational First Amendment test for content-neutral laws. In 1968, the Court reviewed the conviction of David O'Brien for burning his draft card on the steps of the South Boston Courthouse to protest the Vietnam War. O'Brien had been convicted for violating a federal law that prohibited the knowing destruction of draft cards and required 18-year-old males to obtain and carry draft cards at all times to aid the smooth functioning of the draft and the U.S. military and to protect the national security.[69] O'Brien argued that the law was unconstitutional both facially (see Chapter 1) and as applied to the facts in his case because it infringed on freedom of speech. In *United States v. O'Brien*, the Supreme Court disagreed and affirmed O'Brien's conviction, focusing on why the government enacted the law and how the law operated.[70]

The Court's decision hinged neither on the government's intent nor the effect of the speech but rather on the purposes of the federal law. Looking at the actual words of the law—a type of review called statutory construction (see Chapter 1)—the Supreme Court said Congress had enacted the statute to ensure the efficient and orderly operation of the military draft. Any infringement the law caused to O'Brien's speech was minimal and incidental to the government's compelling interest in protecting the proper functioning of the military. The law did not target disfavored viewpoints and left O'Brien free to express his opposition to the draft in any number of ways. In addition, the Court said that when speech and action are intimately intertwined into **symbolic expression,** such as the burning of a draft card, the government's legitimate regulation of the actions may constitutionally place a small, incidental and content-neutral burden on protected speech.

Finding the law content neutral, the Court applied **intermediate scrutiny** by crafting a new test, now known as the ***O'Brien* test.** The O'Brien test's three substantive parts hold that a law is content neutral and will be constitutional if it (1) is not related to the suppression of speech, (2) advances an important government interest, and (3) is narrowly tailored to achieve that interest with only an incidental restriction of free expression. Generally, the *O'Brien* test does not have teeth. Most laws reviewed under intermediate scrutiny are upheld. If the Court says a law is content neutral because it does not target ideas disfavored by government, the law also generally is unrelated to suppression of speech. Laws said to serve government goals unrelated to content tend to meet this standard. Under the *O'Brien* test, a law also must serve an **important government interest.** A government interest is important when it is more than merely convenient or reasonable. Important interests are substantial, weighty or significant; they are not, however, compelling or of the highest order.

The third part of the *O'Brien* test, sometimes called the narrow-tailoring standard, requires a law to "fit" its purpose. A law "fits" when it advances the government interest without imposing an unnecessary burden on speech.[71] The calculation is not precise. To be narrowly tailored, laws must be clear and specific and may not vest officials with vague or unlimited discretion.[72] Complete bans are rarely constitutional because they are not well tailored. The Supreme Court often defers to the expertise of administrative agencies and legislatures to decide the best means to achieve content-neutral objectives.

symbolic expression Action that warrants First Amendment protection because its primary purpose is to express ideas.

intermediate scrutiny A standard applied by the courts to review laws that implicate core constitutional values; also called heightened review.

***O'Brien* test** A three-part test used to determine whether a content-neutral law is constitutional.

important government interest An interest of the government that is substantial or significant (i.e., more than merely convenient or reasonable) but not compelling.

Points of Law

Intermediate-Level Scrutiny

Protesters participating in Occupy DC sit in front of a barricade in front of the Supreme Court building in Washington, D.C.

The Supreme Court generally applies some form of intermediate scrutiny to content-neutral laws that affect the freedom of speech. To be constitutional under intermediate scrutiny, a law must do the following:

1. Fall within the power of government.
2. Advance an important or substantial government interest.
3. That is unrelated to suppression of speech.
4. Be narrowly tailored to impose only an incidental restriction on First Amendment freedoms.

The Court subsequently applied the *O'Brien* test to uphold a regulation requiring New York City employees to control the volume and sound mix of performers in Central Park.[1] Performers said the rule unconstitutionally allowed the city to control their expression even when the control served no important government interest because there was no threat of public disturbance. The Court, however, said the city's complete control of sound was a narrowly tailored means for the city to assure that park users did not disturb people living nearby. *Ward v. Rock Against Racism* established that a content-neutral law is narrowly tailored if it advances the government's interest reasonably well and the government interest would suffer in its absence.

Thus, when several states passed laws restricting access and speech around family planning clinics that were the sites of protests and violence, the Court said the protective zones generally were constitutional. In a representative decision, the Court ruled in *Hill v. Colorado* that a state law creating moving, non-protest zones around people entering abortion clinics was a valid, narrowly tailored, content-neutral, time, place and manner restriction that directly advanced the government's significant interest in protecting the public from confrontations and harassment.[2] The Court also has applied intermediate scrutiny review in cases related to election financing and advertising.

1. 491 U.S. 781 (1989).
2. 530 U.S. 703 (2000).

SUMMARY

THE SUPREME COURT HAS DESIGNED A VARIETY of tests to help determine when government actions or laws infringe on rights protected by the Constitution. When a government action falls within the delegated power of government, such as the power to levy taxes, the Court assumes the law is constitutional and examines it under its most lenient test, called minimum scrutiny or rational review. If a law

Points of Law

Where Does Intermediate Scrutiny Apply?

The Supreme Court applies intermediate scrutiny review to a wide array of laws with differing results. The scope of the Court's intermediate scrutiny review includes the following:

Symbolic conduct. The Court has held that activities from the destruction of draft cards to nude dancing are symbolic speech and has applied intermediate scrutiny to uphold regulations that banned or severely constrained these activities to avoid their undesirable "secondary effects."

Public forums. The Supreme Court has applied intermediate scrutiny to find flat bans on speech activities in traditional public forums unconstitutional. However, time, place and manner regulations that leave open alternate channels of speech or regulate speech outside a traditional public forum usually withstand intermediate scrutiny.

Government employees. Although the Supreme Court has not explicitly applied intermediate scrutiny review to laws or government actions that sanction employee speech, its balancing of interests approach in these cases "manifestly resembles the Court's approach to content-neutral speech regulations."[1] Under this balancing, the Court has upheld restrictions of employee speech.

Private media and property. Content-neutral regulations of the content of electronic media[2] generally survive intermediate scrutiny review. But the Court has employed a heightened version of intermediate scrutiny to strike down a ban on signs on private property,[3] limits on charitable solicitation,[4] and sanctions on media distribution of truthful information received from another party's illegal interception of electronic communications.[5]

---

1. Ashutosh Bhagwat, *The Test That Ate Everything: Intermediate Scrutiny in First Amendment Jurisprudence,* 2007 U. Ill. L. Rev. 783 (2007).
2. *See, e.g.,* Turner Broad. Sys. Inc. v. FCC, 512 U.S. 622 (1994); 520 U.S. 180 (1997).
3. City of Ladue v. Gilleo, 512 U.S. 43 (1994).
4. *See, e.g.,* Riley v. Nat'l Fed'n of the Blind of N.C., 487 U.S. 781 (1988).
5. Bartnicki v. Vopper, 532 U.S. 514 (2001).

affects constitutionally protected rights, such as speech and press, the Court uses a heightened form of review to assure that government is not overstepping its bounds. Many laws regulate the time, place and manner of expression and neither target particular messages nor are intended to limit speech that government disfavors. Such content-neutral laws must pass intermediate scrutiny, or the *O'Brien* test. Government actions that directly regulate or intentionally restrict particular messages are called content based. Because they distort the marketplace of ideas, the Court presumes these content-based laws are unconstitutional and reviews them under strict scrutiny, its most rigorous standard. ■

Political Speech

Political speech—or speech that favors or disfavors a particular public issue, policy position or candidate—lies at the "core of what the First Amendment is designed to protect."[73] The Supreme Court has said political speech involves any "interactive communication concerning political change,"[74] which encompasses ballots and voting, electioneering speeches and lobbying, campaign spending, contributions and yard signs, government speech and anonymous political advertisements, political cartoons and blogs, petitions and placards and buttons and more. Believing that political speech is integral to the functioning of the democratic government established by the Constitution, the Court generally has used strict scrutiny to review laws that seem to infringe on political speech.[75]

Although the Supreme Court has enshrined political speech at the highest level and at the core of protected speech, news organizations and government may sanction employees whose political expression violates established policies. In Colorado a reporter was placed on administrative leave in 2012 after he refused to remove a link to an article he had posted on his Facebook page.[76] Barrett Tryon posted the link to a Los Angeles Times report about Freedom Communications' sale of seven newspapers, including the Colorado Springs Gazette where he worked. In response, he was placed on leave. Rather than go to court, Tyron shared his story with other news outlets, some of which offered him a job.

Fifteen years earlier, Sandra Nelson's case reached the Washington State Supreme Court. The Tacoma News Tribune had removed Nelson from her reporting post after she refused to stop public activities for women's and gay rights. The paper said her activism violated its ethics code and raised public concerns about the newspaper's objectivity. Nelson sued under the state's Fair Campaign Practices Act, which prohibits employer discrimination on the basis of political activity. In *Nelson v. McClatchy,* the state high court ruled that the press clause of the First Amendment trumped the law.[77] First Amendment protection of editorial autonomy allows newspapers in Washington to prohibit reporters from engaging in political activity.

Elections and Campaign Finance

Increased focus on the role of money in the political process centers on whether campaign spending by individuals, corporations, unions, lobbyists and special interest groups is protected political speech or whether massive contributions distort and corrupt the democratic process and subvert the will of the citizens. A decade ago, Congress passed the Bipartisan Campaign Reform Act (BCRA), banning "soft money" contributions to national political parties and imposing limits on the amount and source of funds parties may accept and spend. The law specifically prohibited corporate (including nonprofit and union) funding of political messages during a certain period prior to an election.

In *Citizens United v. Federal Elections Commission,* the Supreme Court found the law's restrictions on corporate and union election spending facially unconstitutional.[78] The Court reasoned that the BCRA's reporting requirements adequately addressed the government's concern that unrestricted corporate election spending led to political corruption and the direct limits on how corporations and unions could fund "electioneering communications" violated the First Amendment. In dissent, Justice John Paul Stevens argued that corporations are not citizens (with equal rights of free speech) and government has a compelling interest to curb corporate influence on elections. Decades earlier the Court held in *Buckley v. Valeo*[79] that both campaign spending and contribution limits directly implicate significant fundamental First Amendment concerns.

Some $6 billion was spent on the 2012 election after the *Citizens United* decision opened the campaign spending floodgates, according to the Center for Responsive Politics (CRP).[80] More than a year after the election, little was publicly known about how much "soft money" organizations spent on election ads and on unreported "nonpolitical" activities. "One thing we can say for certain is that the transparency the Supreme Court relied upon to justify this new framework has been sorely lacking," said CRP executive director Sheila Krumholz.

In recent years, the Supreme Court also issued a two-sentence order upholding a federal ban on national political party use of unregulated, "soft money" contributions to fund election activities.[81] Federal district courts, reviewing the application of the BCRA's campaign contribution limits to a nonprofit organization designed to advance First Amendment freedoms[82] and to a "hybrid" nonprofit organization that engaged in both candidate support and get-out-the-vote drives,[83] found the restrictions unconstitutional. The lower courts reasoned that individuals have a First Amendment right to band together and pool their resources to express their political ideas.

The Supreme Court also has ruled that government may ban its own participation in employee political contributions.[84] Although the First Amendment is clearly implicated, the Court employed rational review to uphold an Idaho state ban on the use of government payroll deductions for political contributions. The majority reasoned that the Constitution imposed no affirmative obligation on government to facilitate such political activities and the ban reasonably advanced the state's interest in avoiding the appearance of partisan political activity.

The Supreme Court also has reviewed a number of constitutional challenges to state limits on campaign financing with differing results based often on the precise wording of the statutes. For example, a plurality of the Court struck down a Virginia state law imposing expenditure limits reasoning that it was not narrowly tailored.[85] But the Court upheld a Missouri law limiting campaign contributions to state political candidates because it said that law constitutionally furthered the government interest in fair elections without unduly inhibiting candidates' ability to gather the funds needed for effective advocacy.[86]

The influence of lobbyists on elections and government decision making was the target of two recent legal developments. First, the Federal Election Commission crafted new regulations requiring disclosure of the names of contributors

realWorld Law

The Politics of Election Finance

The Supreme Court's *Citizens United*[1] decision struck down limits on election spending by corporations and unions that the Court had upheld only seven years earlier.[2] This quick reversal of precedent struck many observers as imprudent, at best.

"Gosh," said Justice Sandra Day O'Connor, who penned the earlier decision. "I step away for a couple of years and there's no telling what's going to happen."[3]

Politics may be a major factor in the Court's about-face, legal observers suggest.

"Supreme Court justices do not acknowledge that any of their decisions are influenced by ideology rather than by neutral legal analysis," but knowing the political party of the president who appointed a given justice tells you a great deal about how the justice will vote in highly political cases such as those dealing with election finance, according to a recent law journal article.[4] Republican President Ronald Reagan appointed Justice O'Connor.

The William Rehnquist Court reached a liberal outcome 60 to 70 percent of the time, and the John Roberts Court reached a conservative result in all but one of the eight precedents it overruled and 60 percent of the time overall during its first five years, a recent study shows.[5] Both chief justices were Republican appointees, but the ideological positions of the other justices on their Courts differ dramatically.

---

1. Citizens United v. Federal Election Commission, 558 U.S. 50 (2010).
2. McConnell v. Federal Election Commission, 540 U.S. 93 (2003).
3. Adam Liptak, *Former Justice O'Connor Sees Ill in Election Finance Ruling*, N.Y. Times, Jan. 26, 2010, available at http://www.nytimes.com.
4. Adam Liptak, *Court Under Roberts Is Most Conservative in Decades*, N.Y. Times, July 24, 2010, *available at* http://www.nytimes.com.
5. Judicial Research Institute, *Supreme Court Data, available at* http://www.cas.sc.edu/poli/juri/sctdata.htm.

to "bundled" political contributions of more than $15,000. Second, an Obama administration memo prohibited lobbyists from speaking with—but not writing to—officials in the executive branch regarding specific allocations from the Recovery Act of 2009.[87]

Anonymous Speech

Two decades ago, the Supreme Court said anonymous political speech has an "honorable tradition" that "is a shield from the tyranny of the majority."[88] Finding a state ban on anonymous campaign literature unconstitutional, the Court said that although the state's interest in preventing fraud and informing the public about political influence was sufficiently important, the law was not narrowly tailored to advance that government interest. A line of cases dating back half a century protects anonymous political speech.[89]

However, in 2010 the Court suggested that citizens engaged in the political process do not have an absolute right to keep their identities secret.[90] The

Emerging Law

Nameless, Faceless and Powerful Online?

In a case that highlights disparate international legal standards, a French court in 2013 ordered Twitter to disclose the identities of pseudonymous posters of anti-Semitic and racist comments on Twitter's French site.[1] Twitter generally complies with such court orders and voluntarily removed some posts. Although French law prohibits hate speech, the U.S. First Amendment generally protects such speech unless it constitutes a true threat.[2]

The case also presents issues of jurisdiction over regulation of online speech. "The physical presence of a thing or a person have [sic] always been major factors in determining which government has the right to have its rules applied," said U.S. Attorney Chris Wolf.

In contrast to Twitter, Google in 2013 apparently became the first major online company to fight federal data collection efforts without a search warrant.[3] Citing a California court decision that aspects of the FBI's so-called national security letter policy were unconstitutional, Google argued that the FBI could no longer use the secret process to "obtain anything else from Google," according to reports on the sealed court proceedings.

U.S. courts disagree on when mandated disclosure is permissible. One Illinois appeals court ruled in 2013 that a building owner could not force Yelp! to release the identity of an anonymous blogger who badmouthed the company.[4] The court ruled that pseudonymous criticisms of the company were protected opinion. In another case, the Ninth Circuit Court of Appeals held that it is the "nature of the speech" involved that should determine the protection for online speakers.[5]

Some U.S. lawmakers, who see the "nature" of anonymous online messages as "a tool for the terrorists," are seeking federal bans on the use of social media by militant groups.[6]

---

1. Eric Pfanner & Somini Sengupta, *In a French Case, a Battle to Unmask Twitter Users,* N.Y. Times, Jan. 24, 2013, at B1, *available at* http://www.nytimes.com.
2. *See* RAV v. St. Paul, 505 U.S. 377 (1992); Virginia v. Black, 538 U.S. 343 (2003); Snyder v. Phelps, 131 S. Ct. 1207 (2011).
3. Declan McCullagh, *Google Fights FBI's Warrantless Data Requests in Federal Court,* Apr. 4, 2013, available at http://news.cnet.com.
4. Brompton Bldg., LLC v. Yelp!, 2013 Ill. App. Unpub. LEXIS 145 (Jan. 31, 2013).
5. *In re* Anonymous Online Speakers v. U.S. Dist. Ct., 661 F.3d 1168 (9th Cir. 2011).
6. Nick Bilton, *Disruptions: Silencing the Voices of Militants on Twitter,* N.Y. Times, Dec. 2, 2012, *available at* http://www.nytimes.com.

---

case involved a citizen referendum to repeal a Washington state law granting new rights to same-sex domestic partners. The state open records law (see more about these laws in Chapter 8) required release of the names of all those who had endorsed the referendum, but the referendum supporters, who feared harassment and reprisal, said disclosure violated the First Amendment. The Supreme Court applied strict scrutiny to find the ban constitutional on the grounds that public disclosure of referendum petitions as a general policy was substantially related to the important government interest in preserving the integrity of balloting and elections. The Court remanded on the question of whether the First Amendment protected anonymity in this case, where disclosure might facilitate harassment. The district court ruled that the names could be released.[91]

Government Speakers

The First Amendment limits government regulation of private speech but does not deal expressly with the issues raised when the government itself speaks. When government regulates communications, it is not always clear whether the government is clarifying its own policies or controlling the speech of its employees. In recent years, the Supreme Court has begun to craft a doctrine of government speech that supports the government's right to speak and, sometimes, to control or prevent the speech of others.

In its unanimous decision in *Pleasant Grove City v. Summum,* the Supreme Court established the power of government to select the monuments it chooses to display permanently in its public parks.[92] A religious group raised a First Amendment challenge to the city's decision not to display the group's "Seven Aphorisms" on a permanent monument in a city park alongside other monuments, including the Ten Commandments.[93] In reviewing the case, the Court declined to apply public forum doctrine (discussed later) on the grounds that space and other constraints implicit in public displays in parks make it impractical for government to accommodate unlimited speakers. Instead, the Court said, the selection of monuments was a form of government speech subject to government control of content. For the Court, Justice Samuel Alito concluded "that the City's decision to accept certain privately donated monuments while rejecting respondent's is best viewed as a form of government speech . . . not subject to the Free Speech Clause."[94] In concurrence, Justice David Souter offered a more limited perspective. He observed that "there are circumstances in which government maintenance of monuments does not look like government speech at all."

Although the Court recognized government authority to speak through its selection process, the Court generally has ruled that government has greater power to control the speech of its own workers than the expression of a private citizen. Although government employees do not lose their personal right to freedom of speech when they accept government work,[95] government may impose codes of silence and control the content of the speech and work product of its employees to advance government interests.[96] Government clearly has the authority to classify highly sensitive materials and control their distribution, especially in the name of national security. The Court also has said laws prohibiting political campaigning by federal employees pose no constitutional problem,[97] but government may not fire employees for their political statements.[98]

In 2012, many observers reacted strongly when a U.S. district court in Virginia ruled that two sheriff's employees could be fired for supporting their boss's opponent in the upcoming election. The district court dismissed the First Amendment claim in the case because it reasoned that clicking "Like" on the opponent's Facebook page was not speech. The ACLU and Facebook submitted briefs to the Fourth Circuit, where the appeal in *Bland v. Roberts* was heard in 2013.[99]

The Supreme Court ruling in *Garcetti v. Ceballos*[100] earlier distinguished work-related communications from independent government employee speech, particularly political speech, and said the First Amendment did not prohibit government from limiting or punishing employee work-related expression. The ruling came after Los Angeles County deputy district attorney Richard Ceballos wrote to his superiors recommending dismissal of criminal charges because of alleged inaccuracies in a sheriff's affidavit. Ceballos then was reassigned, transferred and denied a promotion. He filed suit claiming the actions unconstitutionally punished his protected expression in the memo. The government said the memo was an unprotected employee communication that was unrelated to "matters of public concern."[101] In a 5–4 ruling, the Supreme Court agreed with the government and said the government has authority "over what [expression] the employer itself has commissioned or created."[102]

In a similar case, a local police chief filed suit claiming the town council had retaliated against him for his successful challenge to their earlier attempt to fire him.[103] In *Borough of Duryea v. Guarnieri,* the Supreme Court called the chief's claim "an ordinary workplace grievance." The unanimous Court held that the right of the employee to petition for redress must be balanced "against the government's interest . . . in the effective and efficient management of its internal affairs." The Court said the government's need to manage its affairs "requires proper restraints on the invocation of rights by employees."

SUMMARY

POLITICAL SPEECH LIES AT THE CORE of the First Amendment and is accorded the highest degree of protection from government intrusion. The Supreme Court reviews most political speech cases using strict scrutiny. In recent years, federal courts have found several campaign finance restrictions to be unconstitutional restraints on free speech, and the Supreme Court reversed precedent to strike down bans on corporate funding of campaign communications.

The Court generally has recognized the right of individuals to speak anonymously about political issues and has identified a tradition of anonymous political speech. However, this right is not absolute. The government itself also enjoys a right, and often an obligation, to speak. Government control of the content of government speech is constitutional as long as it advances a central objective of the government program involved. Government may censor the speech of its workers when the workers speak for government or when employee speech presents a danger of real harm to the operation of government. ∎

Public and Nonpublic Forums

At a rock concert in Central Park and at thousands of other daily events in the United States, private citizens gather on public property or in government buildings to exchange ideas and associate freely. Local musicians practice in a conference room in town hall. The kennel club meets in the high school gym after hours.

public forum Government property held for use by the public, usually for purposes of exercising rights of speech and assembly.

Political organizers, grassroots groups, garage musicians and soapbox speakers all use the public parks and walkways to organize and to share information.

Each of these gatherings occurs in what the Supreme Court calls a **public forum**. The legal concept of public forums recognizes the long and central role of public oratory in the United States. The basic idea is that a lots of government property is essentially held in trust for use by the public; it is the public's space. In 1939, in a case involving a challenge to a city ordinance prohibiting the distribution of pamphlets on city streets and in city parks, the Supreme Court explained the idea as follows:

> Wherever the title of streets and parks may rest, they have immemorially been held in trust for the use of the public and, time out of mind, have been used for purposes of assembly, communicating thoughts between citizens, and discussing public questions. Such use of the streets and public places has, from ancient times, been a part of the privileges, immunities, rights, and liberties of citizens.[104]

The people have a First Amendment right to use such public property to express themselves freely. Access to public spaces without fear of government censorship or punishment has been critical to open public debate and dissent in the United States.[105] The Court has said the Constitution allows Nazis, Vietnam War protesters, civil rights activists and the homeless to march and assemble in public places.[106] In 2011 in *Snyder v. Phelps,* the Court ruled that even "outrageous" speech on a public sidewalk about a public issue cannot be sanctioned.[107] The father of a Marine killed in the Iraq War had sought damages from the Phelps family and Westboro Baptist Church for picketing his son's funeral with signs reading "Thank God for dead soldiers" and "Fag troops." The Court held that the First Amendment protects picketing on public matters in public locations even when the messages "fall short of refined social or political commentary."

While people have a right to speak and assemble in public forums, this right is balanced against other considerations. Public use of public forums must be compatible with the normal activity in that place. For example, a 10 a.m. meeting of the Girl Scouts in an elementary school classroom would disrupt educational activities; an evening meeting would not. A meeting at any time in the Pentagon is unlikely; a weekday meeting in the city park is far less likely to cause any problems.

The Supreme Court has defined three categories of public forums according to the nature of the place, the pattern of its primary activities and the history of public access.[108] In public forum analysis, the three categories of forums establish a hierarchy of public access rights in which the Court balances the public right to use a forum against other interests. First, lands designed for public use and historically used for public gathering, discussion and association—such as parks, streets and sidewalks adjacent to many public buildings—are **traditional public forums.**[109] The public has a general and presumed right to use these places for expression.

traditional public forum Lands designed for public use and historically used for public gathering, discussion and association (e.g., public streets, sidewalks and parks). Free speech is protected in these areas.

Government may set up rules, hours and policies to facilitate use of traditional public forums. In fact, many cities close parks after dark and coordinate use of park facilities by issuing permits. Such regulations are constitutional if they are fairly applied and content neutral, meaning they do not discriminate because of the official's degree of approval of the group's ideas or politics. The government must demonstrate a compelling interest to deny all public access or ban all expressive activities in a traditional public forum.

Second, some government spaces or buildings have never served primarily as places for public assembly or speech. Yet spaces such as public school and university classrooms, pages of high school newspapers and fairgrounds may provide ideal settings for public expression. These spaces are not automatically or presumptively available for public use. However, in many cases, government chooses to allow public use of these spaces as **designated public forums**.[110] Essentially, a designated public forum is a place that at government's discretion sometimes is, and sometimes is not, a public forum. This happens, for example, when a city school board says the public may use school buildings outside of school hours for activities that are suitable for the space.

In a designated public forum, the government may limit the times, places or manners of public use to ensure that public access does not conflict with the primary function of the property. Government may impose well-tailored, reasonable, content-neutral licensing and usage regulations. In general, the Supreme Court reviews regulations of limited public forums under intermediate scrutiny,

designated public forum
Government spaces or buildings that are available for public use (within limits).

realWorld Law

Bimbos, Sleazebags and Bigots

After a court found that New York City regulations used to ban anti-Islamic ads violated the Constitution, the ads appeared in city subway stations, and many were quickly defaced.

In 2012, a U.S. district court judge used these and other derogatory labels to illustrate that the First Amendment allows an open field day on abusive terms. The judge ruled the New York City Metropolitan Transportation Authority's (MTA) policy banning "images or information that demean[s] an individual or group of individuals" an unconstitutional content-based regulation that limited core political speech with "no good reason." The American Freedom Defense Initiative, a pro-Israel group, brought suit after the MTA refused to run its clearly anti-Muslim ad on city buses.[1] The ad labeled Muslims "savage" and urged readers to "Support Israel. Defeat Jihad." While admiring civility in public discourse, the judge said it could not justify content-based limits on protected speech on the public buses.

---

1. Am. Freedom Def. Initiative v. Metro. Transp. Auth., 889 F. Supp. 2d 606 (S.D.N.Y. 2012).

nonpublic forum Government-held property that is not available for public speech and assembly purposes.

balancing the citizen right of free expression against the primary role of the facility. When the government facility is operating as a public forum, government may not make content-based discriminations among users. Public access cannot be denied entirely without a compelling reason.

Third, some types of government property simply are not available for public use. The public has no right to hold a meeting in the secure areas of a federal penitentiary, for example. **Nonpublic forums** exist where public access, assembly and speech would conflict with the proper functioning of the government service and where there is no history of public access. Courts generally defer to the government to determine when government property is off limits. In nonpublic forums, government behaves more like a private property owner and controls the space to achieve government objectives. Military bases, prisons, post office walkways, utility poles, airport terminals and private mailboxes are all nonpublic forums.[111] Government may exclude the entire public or certain speakers or messages from nonpublic forums on the basis of a reasonable or rational, viewpoint-neutral interest.[112] Some scholars argue that the Court's imprecise terminology is collapsing the distinction between nonpublic and limited public forums.

The Supreme Court has said government may ban public picketing and protests from traditional public forums such as sidewalks and streets to protect core privacy, safety or health interests. Thus, the Court has upheld a ban on targeted picketing outside a doctor's residence and no-protest buffer zones outside abortion clinics.[113] The Court in 2012 did not speak to whether the First Amendment would have protected a protestor's right to comment directly to then-Vice President Dick Cheney at a public gathering when it ruled that Secret Service agents protecting Cheney were immune from suit.[114] In *Reichle v. Howards,* the protestor claimed his arrest for harassment after criticizing Cheney violated the First Amendment, but the Supreme Court said the agents were immune from suit because they acted "reasonably" under the established law at that time. The U.S. Court of Appeals for the Second Circuit also applied a "reasonable" standard when it affirmed the constitutionality of New York laws relocating protestors outside a "no-protest" zone. The Second Circuit said prohibiting protest directly outside the Republican National Convention was a reasonable restriction on the time, place and manner of protest.[115]

Private Property as a Public Forum

Public forums do not exist only on government property. When private property replaces or functions as a traditional public space, it may be treated as a public forum. When the open area of an enclosed shopping mall or a large private parking lot is used widely for public assembly and expression, the Supreme Court has said the private property owner sometimes may be required to allow public gatherings and free expression.[116] The law in this area is unclear. For example, the general public unquestionably is invited into shopping malls during the normal hours of business. It is not clear, though, whether working journalists enjoy the same degree of access to shopping mall spaces as the public does.

realWorld Law

But Where Can I Speak?

The Supreme Court long has held that "the freedom of speech and of the press guaranteed by the Constitution embraces at least the liberty to discuss *publicly* and truthfully all matters of public concern without prior restraint or fear of subsequent punishment."[1] The Court's public forum doctrine recognizes the concept that government property serves as a vital forum for the public exchange of ideas and information on important public issues.

The Court has established three categories of public forum in which it allows varying degrees of government restrictions on speech to protect the primary use of different types of public property.[2]

- *Traditional public forums.* In areas established for public gatherings or where expressive activity historically has occurred, the Court applies a heightened form of intermediate scrutiny to regulations.

- *Limited/designated public forum.* When government permits public use of its convention centers, theaters and off-hours public school rooms, use restrictions receive heightened intermediate scrutiny review. When government has *not expressly* provided public access to these spaces, the Court applies rational review to regulations of them.

- *Nonpublic forum.* On property where the government's primary purpose prevents public access and speech (e.g., inside the Pentagon or a prison), the Court subjects speech regulations to rational review.

Some argue that new communication technologies provide virtual space that reduces the need to protect physical places for public debate. Justice Anthony Kennedy, for example, has said,

Minds are not changed in the streets and parks as they once were. To an increasing degree, the more significant interchanges of ideas and shaping of public consciousness occur in mass and electronic media.[3]

Others disagree and decry the loss of the public sphere.[4] According to one law scholar, in the United States today "the simple regulation of place has made dissent effectively invisible, practically pointless, and criminally dangerous!"[5]

---

1. Thornhill v. Alabama, 310 U.S. 88, 101–2 (1940) (emphasis added).
2. *See, e.g.,* Madsen v. Women's Health Ctr., 512 U.S. 753 (1994); United States v. Kokinda, 497 U.S. 720 (1990); Frisby v. Schultz, 487 U.S. 474 (1988); United States v. Grace, 461 U.S. 171 (1983); Cox v. Louisiana, 379 U.S. 536 (1965); Schneider v. New Jersey, 308 U.S. 147 (1939).
3. Denver Area Educ. Telecomms. Consortium v. FCC, 518 U.S. 727, 802–03 (1996) (Kennedy, J., dissenting).
4. *See* Jürgen Habermas, The Structural Transformation of the Public Sphere: An Inquiry into a Category of Bourgeois Society (T. Burger trans., 1991) (1962); Cass R. Sunstein, *The Future of Free Speech,* in Eternally Vigilant: Free Speech in the Modern Era, 285–87 (Lee C. Bollinger & Geofrey R. Stone eds., 2002).
5. Thomas P. Crocker, *Displacing Dissent: The Role of "Place" in First Amendment Jurisprudence*, 75 Fordham L. Rev. 2587 (2007).

The U.S. Supreme Court has held that citizens' free speech and petition rights may remain intact in a privately owned shopping center.[117] The issue reached the Court after the owners of a California shopping center called Prune Yard attempted to exclude teenagers circulating a petition. The shopping center owners said that if the Court required the mall to permit the teens to use their space for

First Amendment purposes, the government would effectively be seizing part of their property for public use without payment.

"It is true," the Court acknowledged, "that one of the essential sticks in the bundle of property rights is the right to exclude others. . . . But it is well established that not every destruction or injury to property by governmental action has been held to be a 'taking' in the constitutional sense."[118] Instead, the Court said, the determination hinges on whether the "taking" of property forces some individuals to bear burdens that should be the responsibility of the public as a whole—responsibilities usually shouldered by government.[119]

In a very narrow ruling based in part on the expansive speech protections of the California Constitution, the Court in *Prune Yard Shopping Center v. Robins* reasoned that enforcing the free speech and petition rights of the teenagers did not unduly impose on the rights of the property owner. The large mall was a peculiarly public space, and the slight intrusion created by those circulating the petition did not infringe on the owner's own freedom of speech. The Supreme Court's *Prune Yard* ruling may suggest limits to the right of a property owner to exclude; all restrictions of the owner's rights are not automatically a "taking" of the property.[120] This may be especially true when the media's presence causes no harm, economically or otherwise.

Courts have shied away from a broad reading of *Prune Yard*. Some U.S. Supreme Court justices have suggested that its precedent allowing government to "coerce [the] creation of a speaker's forum" only applies in California.[121] Courts have struggled with this precedent and have not applied it directly to the question of news media access to shopping malls. Some believe that the First Amendment freedom of press should provide a right for news media to enter private property to gather information,[122] but most people agree that *Prune Yard* does not extend to newsgathering situations.

Virtual Forums and Government Speakers

Sometimes government funds that subsidize expression create a virtual public forum. When government funds support general speech and associational activities, the government may not discriminate on the basis of the ideas expressed.[123] Selection criteria must be neutral in terms of message content. The ban on discrimination also applies generally when government imposes taxes or provides tax exemptions on expression. Laws of general application that distribute tax obligations or benefits may not, for example, disfavor large newspapers, general interest magazines or commercial publications.[124]

Government collection and distribution of money does not always create a public forum. In fact, the Court has acknowledged that some government funding procedures have the express purpose of discriminating among applicants according to the ideas they express. The National Endowment for the Arts (NEA), for example, is a government agency that funds artists on the basis of its judgments about the value and quality of the artistic proposals it reviews. NEA grants are designed to fund the specific objectives of the NEA, not to create a public forum for art. So the NEA may choose not to fund art it disfavors or finds indecent or offensive.[125] The same is true of book purchases for public school libraries. School libraries are not public forums for all printed materials; they are funded specifically to provide curriculum- and age-appropriate materials to school students. Therefore, library discriminations based on the school-age appropriateness of books do not violate the Constitution; they are vital to the library's purpose.[126]

SUMMARY

THE SUPREME COURT RECOGNIZES that the right to speak freely means little if you cannot reach an audience. Accordingly, public property often provides a place for citizens to express themselves. Government spaces devoted to use by the public to accommodate free speech activities are called public forums. Sometimes government distribution of funds creates a public forum that prohibits government discrimination on the basis of the message. Traditional public forums are designed for public use and historically have been used by the people for the free exchange of ideas. Government has greater latitude to impose reasonable rules in designated public forums to eliminate uses that are incompatible with the primary function of these places. Nonpublic forums exist on government property where public access would undermine or endanger the government service conducted there. Private property owners generally control access to their property unless the property assumes a quasi-public function. ■

Compelled Speech

The First Amendment protects the right both to speak out publicly and to remain silent. In a case involving a New Hampshire law that made it a crime to remove or cover up the state slogan, "Live Free or Die," on a vehicle license plate, the Supreme Court protected an individual's right "to refrain from speaking."[127] George Maynard, a Jehovah's Witness, had been fined $50 and served six months in jail for covering up the slogan on his license plate. The Court ruled that Maynard had a constitutional right "not to be coerced by the state into advertising a slogan which [he found] morally, ethically, religiously, and politically abhorrent."

The Court also has ruled in a group of cases that private organizations cannot be forced to include individuals or to support messages with which they disagree.[128] In one case, organizers of the annual St. Patrick's Day parade in Boston, which includes a huge number and diversity of organizations, refused to allow an alliance of gay, lesbian and bisexual individuals to participate. The alliance sued, arguing that their exclusion from the parade violated their freedom of speech. The trial court agreed. Because the parade had no expressive purpose, the court said forced inclusion of alliance members in the event would cause no harm to the parade organizer's First Amendment rights.

A unanimous Supreme Court reversed. The Court said it was unnecessary to the alliance's message that it participate in the organizer's event. The alliance could reach the desired audience in a number of ways that would not infringe on the organizer's freedom of association and speech. The Court said, "Whatever the reason [for excluding the group], it boils down to the choice of a speaker not to propound a particular point of view, and that choice is presumed to lie beyond the government's power of control."[129]

SUMMARY

IN ADDITION TO PROTECTING an individual's right of expression, the Supreme Court says the First Amendment also contains a right to refrain from speaking. Laws that create compelled speech in city streets generally are unconstitutional. ∎

Cases for Study

The following excerpts of two cases examine the First Amendment protection from prior restraints on the press. The first case examines a state law that allegedly punished nuisance publications. In *Near v. Minnesota,* the Court established that the Constitution prevents government prior restraint in many guises, including the use of government sanctions after the fact to ban future publication. In *New York Times Co. v. United States,* the Supreme Court provided expedited review of a federal injunction against war reporting by the Times and The Washington Post based on leaked classified documents. The Court's careful delineation of the government's limited ability to exercise prior restraint on speech underscored the importance of the separation of powers and reaffirmed that the government has very limited authority over the press.

Thinking About It

The two case excerpts explore two Supreme Court decisions decades apart that establish the extent and limits of the First Amendment's protection from government prior restraint on the press. As you read these case excerpts, keep the following questions in mind:

- What are the justifications offered in the Court's two decisions for the First Amendment ban on prior restraints?
- What do these decisions indicate about the power of government to punish publication after the fact?
- What type or types of scrutiny do the justices use in these cases? How do you know?
- Do the tests and rationales used by the Court provide clear and solid guidance to lower courts facing similar issues? How?

Near v. Minnesota
Supreme Court of the United States
283 U.S. 697 (1931)

CHIEF JUSTICE CHARLES HUGHES delivered the Court's opinion:
Chapter 285 of the Session Laws of Minnesota for the year 1925 provides for the abatement, as a public nuisance, of a 'malicious, scandalous and defamatory newspaper, magazine or other periodical.' Section 1 of the act is as follows:

'Section 1. Any person who, as an individual, or as a member or employee of a firm, or association or organization, or as an officer, director, member or employee of a corporation, shall be engaged in the business of regularly or customarily producing, publishing or circulating, having in possession, selling or giving away.

'(a) an obscene, lewd and lascivious newspaper, magazine, or other periodical, or

'(b) a malicious, scandalous and defamatory newspaper, magazine or other periodical, is guilty of a nuisance, and all persons guilty of such nuisance may be enjoined, as hereinafter provided.

'Participation in such business shall constitute a commission of such nuisance and render the participant liable and subject to the proceedings, orders and judgments provided for in this Act. Ownership, in whole or in part, directly or indirectly, of any such periodical, or of any stock of interest in any corporation or organization which owns the same in whole or in part, or which publishes the same, shall constitute such participation.

'In actions brought under (b) above, there shall be available the defense that the truth was published with good motives and for justifiable ends and in such actions the plaintiff shall not have the right to report (sic) to issues or editions or periodicals taking place more than three months before the commencement of the action.'

Section 2 provides that, whenever any such nuisance is committed or exists, the county attorney of any county where any such periodical is published or circulated, or . . . a reputable citizen, the Attorney General, or . . . any citizen of the county, may maintain an action in the district court of the county in the name of the state to enjoin perpetually the persons committing or maintaining any such nuisance from further committing or maintaining it. Upon such evidence as the court shall deem sufficient, a temporary injunction may be granted. The defendants have the right to plead by demurrer or answer, and the plaintiff may demur or reply as in other cases.

The action, by section 3, is to be 'governed by the practice and procedure applicable to civil actions for injunctions,' and after trial the court may enter judgment permanently enjoining the defendants found guilty of violating the act from continuing the violation, and, 'in and by such judgment, such nuisance may be wholly abated.' The court is empowered, as in other cases of contempt, to punish disobedience to a temporary or permanent injunction by fine of not more than $1,000 or by imprisonment in the county jail for not more than twelve months.

Under this statute (section 1, clause (b), the county attorney of Hennepin county brought this action to enjoin the publication of what was described as a 'malicious, scandalous and defamatory newspaper, magazine or other periodical,' known as The Saturday Press. published by the defendants in the city of Minneapolis. The complaint alleged that the defendants, on September 24, 1927, and on eight subsequent dates in October and November, 1927, published and circulated editions of that periodical which were 'largely devoted to malicious, scandalous and defamatory articles' concerning Charles G. Davis, Frank W. Brunskill, the Minneapolis Tribune, the Minneapolis Journal, Melvin C. Passolt, George E. Leach, the Jewish Race, the members of the grand jury of Hennepin county impaneled in November, 1927, and then holding office, and other persons. . . . While the complaint did not so allege, it appears from the briefs of both parties that Charles G. Davis was a special law enforcement officer employed by a civic organization, that George E. Leach was mayor of Minneapolis, that Frank W. Brunskill was its chief of police, and that Floyd B. Olson, the relator in this action, was county attorney.

Without attempting to summarize the contents of the voluminous exhibits attached to the complaint, we deem it sufficient to say that the articles charged, in substance, that a Jewish gangster was in control of gambling, bootlegging, and racketeering in Minneapolis, and that law enforcing officers and agencies were not energetically performing their duties. Most of the charges were directed against the chief of police; he was charged with gross neglect of duty, illicit relations with gangsters, and with participation in graft. The county attorney was charged with knowing the existing conditions and with failure to take adequate measures to remedy them. The mayor was accused of inefficiency and dereliction. On member of the grand jury was stated to be in sympathy with the gangsters. A special grand jury and a special prosecutor were demanded to deal with the situation in general, and, in particular, to investigate an attempt to assassinate one Guilford, one of the original defendants, who, it appears from the articles, was shot by gangsters after the first issue of the periodical had been published. There is no question but that the articles made serious accusations against the public officers named and others in connection with the prevalence of crimes and the failure to expose and punish them.

At the beginning of the action on November 22, 1927, and upon the verified complaint, an order was made directing the defendants to show cause why a temporary injunction should not issue and meanwhile forbidding the defendants to publish, circulate, or have in their possession any editions of the periodical from September 24, 1927, to November 19, 1927, inclusive, and from publishing, circulating or having in their possession, 'any future editions of said The Saturday Press' and 'any publication, known by any other name whatsoever containing malicious, scandalous and defamatory matter of the kind alleged in plaintiff's complaint herein or otherwise.'

The defendants demurred to the complaint upon the ground that it did not state facts sufficient to constitute a cause of action, and on this demurrer challenged the constitutionality of the statute. The district court overruled the demurrer and certified the question of constitutionality to the Supreme Court of the state. The Supreme Court sustained the statute, and it is conceded by the appellee that the act was thus held to be valid over the objection that it violated not only the State Constitution, but also the Fourteenth Amendment of the Constitution of the United States.

Thereupon the defendant Near, the present appellant, answered the complaint. He averred that he was the sole owner and proprietor of the publication in question. He admitted the publication of the articles in the issues described in the complaint, but denied that they were malicious, scandalous, or defamatory as alleged. He expressly invoked the protection of the due process clause of the Fourteenth Amendment. The case then came on for trial. . . . The district court made findings of fact, which followed the allegations of the complaint and found in general terms that the editions in question were 'chiefly devoted to malicious, scandalous and defamatory articles' concerning the individuals named. The court further found that the defendants through these publications 'did engage in the business of regularly and customarily producing, publishing and circulating a malicious, scandalous and defamatory newspaper,' and that 'the said publication' 'under said name of The Saturday Press, or any other name, constitutes a public nuisance

under the laws of the State.' Judgment was thereupon entered adjudging that 'the newspaper, magazine and periodical known as The Saturday Press,' as a public nuisance, 'be and is hereby abated.' The judgment perpetually enjoined the defendants 'from producing, editing, publishing, circulating, having in their possession, selling or giving away any publication whatsoever which is a malicious, scandalous or defamatory newspaper, as defined by law,' and also 'from further conducting said nuisance under the name and title of said The Saturday Press or any other name or title.'

The defendant Near appealed from this judgment to the Supreme Court of the State, again asserting his right under the Federal Constitution, and the judgment was affirmed upon the authority of the former decision. With respect to the contention that the judgment went too far, and prevented the defendants from publishing any kind of a newspaper, the court observed . . . that it saw no reason 'for defendants to construe the judgment as restraining them from operating a newspaper in harmony with the public welfare, to which all must yield,' that the allegations of the complaint had been found to be true, and though this was an equitable action defendants had not indicated a desire 'to conduct their business in the usual and legitimate manner.'

From the judgment as thus affirmed, the defendant Near appeals to this Court.

This statute, for the suppression as a public nuisance of a newspaper or periodical, is unusual, if not unique, and raises questions of grave importance transcending the local interests involved in the particular action. It is no longer open to doubt that the liberty of the press and of speech is within the liberty safeguarded by the due process clause of the Fourteenth Amendment from invasion by state action. It was found impossible to conclude that this essential personal liberty of the citizen was left unprotected by the general guaranty of fundamental rights of person and property. In maintaining this guaranty, the authority of the state to enact laws to promote the health, safety, morals, and general welfare of its people is necessarily administered. The limits of this sovereign power must always be determined with appropriate regard to the particular subject of its exercise. Thus, while recognizing the broad discretion of the Legislature in fixing rates to be charged by those undertaking a public service, this Court has decided that the owner cannot constitutionally be deprived of his right to a fair return, because that is deemed to be of the essence of ownership. . . . Liberty of speech and of the press is also not an absolute right, and the state may punish its abuse. Liberty, in each of its phases, has its history and connotation, and, in the present instance, the inquiry is as to the historic conception of the liberty of the press and whether the statute under review violates the essential attributes of that liberty.

The appellee insists that the questions of the application of the statute to appellant's periodical, and of the construction of the judgment of the trial court, are not presented for review; that appellant's sold attack was upon the constitutionality of the statute, however it might be applied. The appellee contends that no question either of motive in the publication, or whether the decree goes beyond the direction of the statute, is before us. The appellant replies that, in his view, the plain terms of the statute were not departed from in this case, and that even if they were, the statute is nevertheless unconstitutional under any reasonable construction of its terms. The appellant states that he has not argued that the temporary and permanent injunctions were broader than were warranted by the statute; he insists that what was done was properly done if the statute is valid, and that the action taken under the statute is a fair indication of its scope.

With respect to these contentions it is enough to say that in passing upon constitutional questions the court has regard to substance and not to mere matters of form, and that, in accordance with familiar principles, the statute must be tested by its operation and effect. . . .

First. The statute is not aimed at the redress of individual or private wrongs. Remedies for libel remain available and unaffected. The Statute, said the state court, 'is not directed at threatened libel but at an existing business which, generally speaking, involves more than libel.' It is aimed at the distribution of scandalous matter as 'detrimental to public morals and to the general welfare,' tending 'to disturb the peace of the community' and 'the provoke assaults and the commission of crime.' In order to obtain an injunction to suppress the future publication of the newspaper or periodical, it is not necessary to prove the falsity of the charges that have been made in the publication condemned. In the present action there was no allegation that the matter published was not true. It is alleged, and the statute requires the allegation, that the publication was 'malicious.' But, as in prosecutions for libel, there is no requirement of proof by the state of malice in fact as distinguished from malice inferred from the mere publication of the defamatory matter.

The judgment in this case proceeded upon the mere proof of publication. The statute permits the defense, not of the truth alone, but only that the truth was published with good motives and for justifiable ends. It is apparent that under the statute the publication is to be regarded as defamatory if it injures reputation, and that it is scandalous if it circulates charges of reprehensible conduct, whether criminal or otherwise, and the publication is thus deemed to invite public reprobation and to constitute a public scandal. The court sharply defined the purpose of the statute, bringing out the precise point, in these words: 'There is no constitutional right to publish a fact merely because it is true. It is a matter of common knowledge that prosecutions under the criminal libel statutes do not result in efficient repression or suppression of the evils of scandal. Men who are the victims of such assaults seldom resort to the courts. This is especially true if their sins are exposed and the only question relates to whether it was done with good motive and for justifiable ends. This law is not for the protection of the person attacked nor to punish the wrongdoer. It is for the protection of the public welfare.'

Second. The statute is directed not simply at the circulation of scandalous and defamatory statements with regard to private citizens, but at the continued publication by newspapers and periodical of charges against public officers of corruption, malfeasance in office, or serious neglect of duty. Such charges by their very nature create a public scandal. They are scandalous and defamatory within the meaning of the statute, which has its normal operation in relation to publications dealing prominently and chiefly with the alleged derelictions of public officers.

Third. The object of the statute is not punishment, in the ordinary sense, but suppression of the offending newspaper or periodical. The reason for the enactment, as the state court has said, is that prosecutions to enforce penal statutes for libel do not result in 'efficient repression or suppression of the evils of scandal.' Describing the business of publication as a public nuisance does not obscure the substance of the proceeding which the statute authorizes. It is the continued publication of scandalous and defamatory matter that constitutes the business and the declared nuisance. In the case of public officers, it is the reiteration of charges of official misconduct, and the fact that the newspaper or periodical is principally devoted to that purpose, that exposes it to suppression. In the present instance, the proof was that nine editions of the newspaper or periodical in question were published on successive dates, and that they were chiefly devoted to charges against public officers and in relation to the prevalence and protection of crime. In such a case, these officers are not left to their ordinary remedy in a suit for libel, or the authorities to a prosecution for criminal libel. Under this statute, a publisher of a newspaper or periodical, undertaking to conduct a campaign to expose and to censure official derelictions, and devoting his publication principally to that purpose, must face not simply the possibility of a verdict against him in a suit or prosecution for libel, but a determination that his newspaper or periodical is a public nuisance to be abated, and that this abatement and suppression will follow unless he is prepared with legal evidence to prove the truth of the charges and also to satisfy the court that, in addition to being true, the matter was published with good motives and for justifiable ends.

This suppression is accomplished by enjoining publication, and that restraint is the object and effect of the statute.

Fourth. The statute not only operates to suppress the offending newspaper or periodical, but to put the publisher under an effective censorship. When a newspaper or periodical is found to be 'malicious, scandalous and defamatory,' and is suppressed as such, resumption of publication is punishable as a contempt of court by fine or imprisonment. Thus, where a newspaper or periodical has been suppressed because of the circulation of charges against public officers of official misconduct, it would seem to be clear that the renewal of the publication of such charges would constitute a contempt, and that the judgment would lay a permanent restraint upon the publisher, to escape which he must satisfy the court as to the character of a new publication. Whether he would be permitted again to publish matter deemed to be derogatory to the same or other public officers would depend upon the court's ruling. In the present instance the judgment restrained the defendants from 'publishing, circulating, having in their possession, selling or giving away any publication whatsoever which is a malicious, scandalous or defamatory newspaper, as defined by law.' The law gives no definition except that covered by the words 'scandalous and defamatory,' and publications charging official misconduct are of the class. While the court, answering the objection that the judgment was too broad, saw no reason for construing it as restraining the defendants 'from operating a newspaper in harmony with the public welfare to which all must yield,' and said that the defendants had not indicated 'any desire to conduct their business in the usual and legitimate manner,' the manifest inference is that, at least with respect to a new publication directed against official misconduct, the defendant would be held, under penalty of punishment for contempt as provided in the statute, to a manner of publication which the court considered to be 'usual and legitimate' and consistent with the public welfare.

. . . [T]he operation and effect of the statute in substance is that public authorities may bring the owner or publisher of a newspaper or periodical before a judge upon a charge of conducting a business of publishing scandalous and defamatory matter-in particular that the matter consists of charges against public officers of official dereliction-and, unless the owner or publisher is able and disposed to bring competent evidence to satisfy the judge that the charges are true and are published with good motives and for justifiable ends, his newspaper or periodical is suppressed and further publication is made punishable as a contempt. This is of the essence of censorship.

The question is whether a statute authorizing such proceedings in restraint of publication is consistent with the conception of the liberty of the press as historically conceived and guaranteed. In determining the extent of the constitutional protection, it has been generally, if not universally, considered that it is the chief purpose of the guaranty to prevent previous restraints upon publication. The struggle in England, directed against the legislative power of the licenser, resulted in renunciation of the censorship of the press. The liberty deemed to be established was thus described by Blackstone: 'The liberty of the press is indeed essential to the nature of a free state; but this consists in laying no previous restraints upon publications, and not in freedom from censure for criminal matter when published. Every freeman has an undoubted right to lay what sentiments he pleases before the public; to forbid this, is to destroy the freedom of the press; but if he publishes what is improper, mischievous or illegal, he must take the consequence of his own temerity.'

The distinction was early pointed out between the extent of the freedom with respect to censorship under our constitutional system and that enjoyed in England. Here, as Madison said, 'the great and essential rights of the people are secured against legislative as well as against executive ambition. They are secured, not by laws paramount to prerogative, but by constitutions paramount to laws. This security of the freedom of the press requires that it should be exempt not only from previous restraint by the Executive, as in Great Britain, but from legislative restraint also.' This Court said, in Patterson v. Colorado: 'In the first place, the main purpose of such constitutional provisions is 'to prevent all such previous restraints upon publications as had been practiced by other governments,' and they do not prevent the subsequent punishment of such as may be deemed contrary to the public welfare. The preliminary freedom extends as well to the false as to the true; the subsequent punishment may extend as well to the true as to the false. This was the law of criminal libel apart from statute in most cases, if not in all.

The criticism upon Blackstone's statement has not been because immunity from previous restraint upon publication has not been regarded as deserving of special emphasis, but chiefly because that immunity cannot be deemed to exhaust the conception of the liberty guaranteed by State and Federal Constitutions. The point of criticism has been 'that the mere exemption from restraints cannot be all that is secured by the constitutional provisions,' and that 'the liberty of the press might be rendered a mockery and a delusion, and the phrase itself a by-word, if, while every man was at liberty to publish what he pleased, the public authorities might nevertheless punish him for harmless publications.' But it is recognized that punishment for the abuse of the liberty accorded to the press is essential to the protection of the public, and that the common-law rules that subject the libeler to responsibility for the public offense, as well as for the private injury, are not abolished by the protection extended in our Constitutions. The law of criminal libel rests upon that secure foundation. There is also the conceded authority of courts to punish for contempt when publications directly tend to prevent the proper discharge of judicial functions.

In the present case, we have no occasion to inquire as to the permissible scope of subsequent punishment. For whatever wrong the appellant has committed or may commit, by his publications, the state appropriately affords both public and private redress by its libel laws. As has been noted, the statute in question does not deal with punishments; it provides for no punishment, except in case of contempt for violation of the court's order, but for suppression and injunction-that is, for restraint upon publication.

The objection has also been made that the principle as to immunity from previous restraint is stated too broadly, if every such restraint is deemed to be prohibited. That is undoubtedly true; the protection even as to previous restraint is not absolutely unlimited. But the limitation has been recognized only in exceptional cases. 'When a nation is at war many things that might be said in time of peace are such a hindrance to its effort that their utterance will not be endured so long as men fight and that no Court could regard them as protected by any constitutional right.' No one would question but that a government might prevent actual obstruction to its recruiting service or the publication of the sailing dates of transports or the number and location of troops. On similar grounds, the primary requirements of decency may be enforced against obscene publications. The security of the community life may be protected against incitements to acts of violence and the overthrow by force of orderly government. The constitutional guaranty of free speech does not 'protect a man from an injunction against uttering words that may have all the effect of force.' These limitations are not applicable here. Nor are we now concerned with questions as to the extent of authority to prevent publications in order to protect private rights according to the principles governing the exercise of the jurisdiction of courts of equity.

The exceptional nature of its limitations places in a strong light the general conception that liberty of the press, historically considered and taken up by the Federal Constitution, has meant, principally although not exclusively, immunity from previous restraints or censorship. . . . As was said by Chief Justice Parker . . . with respect to the Constitution of Massachusetts: 'Besides, it is well understood and received as a commentary on this provision for the liberty of the press, that it was intended to prevent all such previous restraints upon publications as had been practiced by other governments, and in early times here, to stifle the efforts of patriots towards enlightening their fellow subjects upon their rights and the duties of rulers. The liberty of the press was to be unrestrained, but he who used it was to be responsible in case of its abuse.' . . . Madison, who was the leading spirit in the preparation of the First Amendment of the Federal Constitution, thus described the practice and sentiment which led to the guaranties of liberty of the press in State Constitutions:

'In every State, probable, in the Union, the press has exerted a freedom in canvassing the merits and measures of public men of every description which has not been confined to the strict limits of the common law. On this footing the freedom of the press has stood; on this footing it yet stands. . . . Some degree of abuse is inseparable from the proper use of everything, and in no instance is this more true than in that of the press. It has accordingly been decided by the practice of the States, that it is better to leave a few of its noxious branches to their luxuriant growth, than,

by pruning them away, to injure the vigour of those yielding the proper fruits. And can the wisdom of this policy be doubted by any who reflect that to the press alone, chequered as it is with abuses, the world is indebted for all the triumphs which have been gained by reason and humanity over error and oppression; who reflect that to the same beneficent source the United States owe much of the lights which conducted them to the ranks of a free and independent nation, and which have improved their political system to a shape so auspicious to their happiness? Had 'Sedition Acts,' forbidding every publication that might bring the constituted agents into contempt or disrepute, or that might excite the hatred of the people against the authors of unjust or pernicious measures, been uniformly enforced against the press, might not the United States have been languishing at this day under the infirmities of a sickly Confederation? Might they not, possibly, be miserable colonies, growing under a foreign yoke?'

The fact that for approximately one hundred and fifty years there has been almost an entire absence of attempts to impose previous restraints upon publications relating to the malfeasance of public officers is significant of the deep-seated conviction that such restraints would violate constitutional right. Public officers, whose character and conduct remain open to debate and free discussion in the press, find their remedies for false accusations in actions under libel laws providing for redress and punishment, and not in proceedings to restrain the publication of newspapers and periodicals. The general principle that the constitutional guaranty of the liberty of the press gives immunity from previous restraints has been approved in many decisions under the provisions of state constitutions.

The importance of this immunity has not lessened. While reckless assaults upon public men, and efforts to bring obloquy upon those who are endeavoring faithfully to discharge official duties, exert a baleful influence and deserve the severest condemnation in public opinion, it cannot be said that this abuse is greater, and it is believed to be less, than that which characterized the period in which our institutions took shape. Meanwhile, the administration of government has become more complex, the opportunities for malfeasance and corruption have multiplied, crime has grown to most serious proportions, and the danger of its protection by unfaithful officials and of the impairment of the fundamental security of life and property by criminal alliances and official neglect, emphasizes the primary need of a vigilant and courageous press, especially in great cities. The fact that the liberty of the press may be abused by miscreant purveyors of scandal does not make any the less necessary the immunity of the press from previous restraint in dealing with official misconduct. Subsequent punishment for such abuses as may exist is the appropriate remedy, consistent with constitutional privilege.

In attempted justification of the statute, it is said that it deals not with publication per se, but with the 'business' of publishing defamation. If, however, the publisher has a constitutional right to publish, without previous restraint, an edition of his newspaper charging official derelictions, it cannot be denied that he may publish subsequent editions for the same purpose. He does not lose his right by exercising it. If his right exists, it may be exercised in publishing nine editions, as in this case, as well as in one edition. If previous restraint is permissible, it may be imposed at once; indeed, the wrong may be as serious in one publication as in several. Characterizing the publication as a business, and the business as a nuisance, does not permit an invasion of the constitutional immunity against restraint. Similarly, it does not matter that the newspaper or periodical is found to be 'largely' or 'chiefly' devoted to the publication of such derelictions. If the publisher has a right, without previous restraint, to publish them, his right cannot be deemed to be dependent upon his publishing something else, more or less, with the matter to which objection is made.

Nor can it be said that the constitutional freedom from previous restraint is lost because charges are made of derelictions which constitute crimes. With the multiplying provisions of penal codes, and of municipal charters and ordinances carrying penal sanctions, the conduct of public officers is very largely within the purview of criminal statutes. The freedom of the press from previous restraint has never been regarded as limited to such animadversions as lay outside the range of

renal enactments. Historically, there is no such limitation; it is inconsistent with the reason which underlies the privilege, as the privilege so limited would be of slight value for the purposes for which it came to be established.

The statute in question cannot be justified by reason of the fact that the publisher is permitted to show, before injunction issues, that the matter published is true and is published with good motives and for justifiable ends. If such a statute, authorizing suppression and injunction on such a basis, is constitutionally valid, it would be equally permissible for the Legislature to provide that at any time the publisher of any newspaper could be brought before a court, or even an administrative officer (as the constitutional protection may not be regarded as resting on mere procedural details), and required to produce proof of the truth of his publication, or of what he intended to publish and of his motives, or stand enjoined. If this can be done, the Legislature may provide machinery for determining in the complete exercise of its discretion what are justifiable ends and restrain publication accordingly. And it would be but a step to a complete system of censorship. The recognition of authority to impose previous restraint upon publication in order to protect the community against the circulation of charges of misconduct, and especially of official misconduct, necessarily would carry with it the admission of the authority of the censor against which the constitutional barrier was erected. The preliminary freedom, by virtue of the very reason for its existence, does not depend, as this court has said, on proof of truth.

Equally unavailing is the insistence that the statute is designed to prevent the circulation of scandal which tends to disturb the public peace and to provoke assaults and the commission of crime. Charges of reprehensible conduct, and in particular of official malfeasance, unquestionably create a public scandal, but the theory of the constitutional guaranty is that even a more serious public evil would be caused by authority to prevent publication. 'To prohibit the intent to excite those unfavorable sentiments against those who administer the Government, is equivalent to a prohibition of the actual excitement of them; and to prohibit the actual excitement of them is equivalent to a prohibition of discussions having that tendency and effect; which, again, is equivalent to a protection of those who administer the Government, if they should at any time deserve the contempt or hatred of the people, against being exposed to it by free animadversions on their characters and conduct.' There is nothing new in the fact that charges of reprehensible conduct may create resentment and the disposition to resort to violent means of redress, but this well-understood tendency did not alter the determination to protect the press against censorship and restrain upon publication. . . . The danger of violent reactions becomes greater with effective organization of defiant groups resenting exposure, and, if this consideration warranted legislative interference with the initial

freedom of publication, the constitutional protection would be reduced to a mere form of words.

For these reasons we hold the statute, so far as it authorized the proceedings in this action under clause (b) of section 1, to be an infringement of the liberty of the press guaranteed by the Fourteenth Amendment. We should add that this decision rests upon the operation and effect of the statute, without regard to the question of the truth of the charges contained in the particular periodical. The fact that the public officers named in this case, and those associated with the charges of official dereliction, may be deemed to be impeccable, cannot affect the conclusion that the statute imposes an unconstitutional restraint upon publication.

Judgment reversed.

New York Times Co. v. United States
SUPREME COURT OF THE UNITED STATES
403 U.S. 713 (1971)

PER CURIAM OPINION:
We granted certiorari in these cases in which the United States seeks to enjoin the New York Times and the Washington Post from publishing the contents of a classified study entitled "History of U.S. Decision-Making Process on Viet Nam Policy."

"Any system of prior restraints of expression comes to this Court bearing a heavy presumption against its constitutional validity." The Government "thus carries a heavy burden of showing justification for the imposition of such a restraint." The District Court for the Southern District of New York in the New York Times case and the District Court for the District of Columbia and the Court of Appeals for the District of Columbia Circuit in the Washington Post case held that the Government had not met that burden. We agree.

The judgment of the Court of Appeals for the District of Columbia Circuit is therefore affirmed. The order of the Court of Appeals or the Second Circuit is reversed, and the case is remanded with directions to enter a judgment affirming the judgment of the District Court for the Southern District of New York. The

stays entered June 25, 1971, by the Court are vacated. The judgments shall issue forthwith.

So ordered.

JUSTICE HUGO BLACK, with whom JUSTICE WILLIAM DOUGLAS joined, concurring:
I adhere to the view that the Government's case against the Washington Post should have been dismissed, and that the injunction against the New York Times should have been vacated without oral argument when the cases were first presented to this Court. I believe that every moment's continuance of the injunctions against these newspapers amounts to a flagrant, indefensible, and continuing violation of the First Amendment. . . .

In the First Amendment, the Founding Fathers gave the free press the protection it must have to fulfill its essential role in our democracy. The press was to serve the governed, not the governors. The Government's power to censor the press was abolished so that the press would remain forever free to censure the Government. The press was protected so that it could bare the secrets of government and inform the people.

Only a free and unrestrained press can effectively expose deception in government. And paramount among the responsibilities of a free press is the duty to prevent any part of the government from deceiving the people and sending them off to distant lands to die of foreign fevers and foreign shot and shell. In my view, far from deserving condemnation for their courageous reporting, the New York Times, the Washington Post, and other newspapers should be commended for serving the purpose that the Founding Fathers saw so clearly. In revealing the workings of government that led to the Vietnam war, the newspapers nobly did precisely that which the Founders hoped and trusted they would do. . . .

The word "security" is a broad, vague generality whose contours should not be invoked to abrogate the fundamental law embodied in the First Amendment. The guarding of military and diplomatic secrets at the expense of informed representative government provides no real security for our Republic. The Framers of the First Amendment, fully aware of both the need to defend a new nation and the abuses of the English and Colonial governments, sought to give this new society strength and security by providing that freedom of speech, press, religion, and assembly should not be abridged. . . .

JUSTICE WILLIAM DOUGLAS, with whom
JUSTICE HUGO BLACK joined, concurring:
. . . It should be noted at the outset that the First Amendment provides that "Congress shall make no law . . . abridging the freedom of speech, or of the press." That leaves, in my view, no room for governmental restraint on the press. . . .

The dominant purpose of the First Amendment was to prohibit the widespread practice of governmental suppression of embarrassing information. It is common knowledge that the First Amendment was adopted against the widespread use of the common law of seditious libel to punish the dissemination of material that is embarrassing to the powers-that-be. The present cases will, I think, go down in history as the most dramatic illustration of that principle. . . .

Secrecy in government is fundamentally anti-democratic, perpetuating bureaucratic errors. Open debate and discussion of public issues are vital to our national health. On public questions there should be "uninhibited, robust, and wide-open" debate. . . .

JUSTICE WILLIAM BRENNAN, concurring:
. . . The error that has pervaded these cases from the outset was the granting of any injunctive relief whatsoever, interim or otherwise. The entire thrust of the Government's claim throughout these cases has been that publication of the material sought to be enjoined "could," or "might," or "may" prejudice the national interest in various ways. But the First Amendment tolerates absolutely no prior judicial restraints of the press predicated upon surmise or conjecture that untoward consequences may result. Our cases, it is true, have indicated that there is a single, extremely narrow class of cases in which the First Amendment's ban on prior judicial restraint may be overridden. Our cases have thus far indicated that such cases may arise only when the Nation "is at war," during which times "[n]o one would question but that a government might prevent actual obstruction to its recruiting service or the publication of the dates of transports or the number and location of troops." Even if the present world situation were assumed to be tantamount to a time of war, or if the power of presently available armaments would justify even in peacetime the suppression of information that would set in motion a nuclear holocaust, in neither of these actions has the Government presented or even alleged that publication of items from or based upon the material at issue would cause the happening of an event of that nature. "[T]he chief purpose of [the First Amendment's] guaranty [is] to prevent previous restraints upon publication." Thus, only governmental allegation and proof that publication must inevitably, directly, and immediately cause the occurrence of an event kindred to imperiling the safety of a transport already at sea can support even the issuance of an interim restraining order. . . . Unless and until the Government has clearly made out its case, the First Amendment commands that no injunction may issue. . . .

JUSTICE POTTER STEWART, with whom JUSTICE BYRON WHITE joined, concurring:

. . . If the Constitution gives the Executive a large degree of unshared power in the conduct of foreign affairs and the maintenance of our national defense, then, under the Constitution, the Executive must have the largely unshared duty to determine and preserve the degree of internal security necessary to exercise that power successfully. It is an awesome responsibility, requiring judgment and wisdom of a high order. I should suppose that moral, political, and practical considerations would dictate that a very first principle of that wisdom would be an insistence upon avoiding secrecy for its own sake. For when everything is classified, then nothing is classified, and the system becomes one to be disregarded by the cynical or the careless, and to be manipulated by those intent on self-protection or self-promotion. I should suppose, in short, that the hallmark of a truly effective internal security system would be the maximum possible disclosure, recognizing that secrecy can best be preserved only when credibility is truly maintained. . . .

JUSTICE BYRON WHITE, with whom JUSTICE POTTER STEWART joined, concurring:

I concur in today's judgments, but only because of the concededly extraordinary protection against prior restraints enjoyed by the press under our constitutional system. I do not say that in no circumstances would the First Amendment permit an injunction against publishing information about government plans or operations. . . . But I nevertheless agree that the United States has not satisfied the very heavy burden that it must meet to warrant an injunction against publication in these cases, at least in the absence of express and appropriately limited congressional authorization for prior restraints in circumstances such as these. . . .

CHIEF JUSTICE WARREN BURGER, dissenting:

. . . As I see it, we have been forced to deal with litigation concerning rights of great magnitude without an adequate record, and surely without time for adequate treatment either in the prior proceedings or in this Court. . . .

. . . I agree generally with Mr. Justice Harlan and Mr. Justice Blackmun, but I am not prepared to reach the merits.

JUSTICE JOHN HARLAN, with whom CHIEF JUSTICE WARREN BURGER and JUSTICE HARRY BLACKMUN join, dissenting:

. . . The power to evaluate the "pernicious influence" of premature disclosure is not, however, lodged in the Executive alone. I agree that, in performance of its duty to protect the values of the First Amendment against political pressures, the judiciary must review the initial Executive determination to the point of satisfying itself that the subject matter of the dispute does lie within the proper compass of the President's foreign relations power. . . . Moreover, the judiciary may properly insist that the determination that disclosure of the subject matter would irreparably impair the national security be made by the head of the Executive Department concerned. . . .

But, in my judgment, the judiciary may not properly go beyond these two inquiries and re-determine for itself the probable impact of disclosure on the national security. . . .

JUSTICE HARRY BLACKMUN, dissenting:

. . . The First Amendment, after all, is only one part of an entire Constitution. . . . Each provision of the Constitution is important, and I cannot subscribe to a doctrine of unlimited absolutism for the First Amendment at the cost of downgrading other provisions. First Amendment absolutism has never commanded a majority of this Court. What is needed here is a weighing, upon properly developed standards, of the broad right of the press to print and of the very narrow right of the Government to prevent. Such standards are not yet developed. . . .

Chapter 3

The character of every act depends upon the circumstance in which it is done. The most stringent protection of free speech would not protect a man in falsely shouting fire in a theatre and causing a panic. It does not even protect a man from an injunction against uttering words that may have all the effect of force. The question in every case is whether the words used are used in such circumstances and are of such a nature as to create a clear and present danger that they will bring about the substantive evils that Congress has a right to prevent. It is a question of proximity and degree.

U.S. Supreme Court Justice Oliver Wendell Holmes[1]

A Federal Trade Commission report found that the movie, video game and music industries aggressively market adult-rated products to youths, who consume them alongside teen-rated products such as the two-shooter game Time Crisis II.

Speech Distinctions

Dangers, Fights, Threats and Educational Needs

National Security and Tranquility

Threats to National Security

Court Tests to Protect Disruptive Speech

The Clear and Present Danger Test
The *Brandenburg* (or Incitement) Test

Speech Assaults

Offensive Speech
Fighting Words
Hate Speech
Current Standard
Harmful Images
Intimidation and Threats

Symbolic Speech

Burning Speech

Speech in the Schools

Protest in the Schools
Offensive or Inappropriate Content
Compelled Orthodoxy
Campus Speech
Speech Codes

Cases for Study

➤ *Texas v. Johnson*
➤ *Tinker v. Des Moines Independent Community School District*

Suppose . . .

. . . that about 100 protesters outside the Republican National Convention chant, "America, the red, white, and blue, we spit on you!" and set ablaze an American flag they removed from a nearby flagpole. A state law prohibited the "desecration" or "physical mistreatment" of the flag in a manner intended to offend observers. Several onlookers said they were offended by the flag burning, and the protester, Gregory "Joey" Johnson, was sentenced to a year in prison and a $2,000 fine. Johnson appealed, arguing that the law violated his freedom of speech. But is burning a flag part of free speech? Is the American flag a unique symbol of national unity whose intentional destruction threatens the fabric of this country? Does intentionally burning a flag as part of an antigovernment protest actually incite illegal violence? Look for the answers to these questions when the case of *Texas v. Johnson*[2] is discussed later in this chapter and the Supreme Court's opinion in the case is excerpted at the chapter's end.

Chapter 2 established a foundation for First Amendment analysis. This chapter digs more deeply into the topic by looking at expression that resides at the fringes of constitutional protection, as well as expression that takes place in and around public educational institutions. It examines how courts determine the boundaries of protected speech.

Although the First Amendment says government may not abridge free speech, the prohibition is not absolute. Courts use a variety of methods to determine when expression is and is not protected—what speech the government is permitted to abridge. One method is for a court to balance the benefits of permitting the expression against the harm to competing values caused by the speech. As noted in Chapter 2, this method of determining whether speech is protected—weighing competing values case by case—is called ad hoc balancing. A drawback to ad hoc balancing is that it is difficult to generalize from such fact-specific decisions, and thus, the courts and society have difficulty applying them as a precedent to decide other similar controversies.

More often, then, courts use a method called categorical balancing. Using this method, a judge or a court develops rules by weighing different broad categories, such as political speech, against other categories of interest, such as privacy. The rules crafted then may be applied in later cases involving similar categories of speech. Under categorical balancing, some categories of speech—blackmail, extortion, perjury, false advertising and obscenity, for example—are unprotected by the First Amendment. Categorical balancing comes into play frequently when disruptive speech or school audiences are central to a case. In such cases, the central question is whether the speech is so disruptive to national security or educational interests that the interests in silencing it outweigh the benefits of its expression. If so, lawmakers may prohibit the speech.

Some categories of speech, such as hate speech, are not very well defined. In cases involving such categories, courts look at the specific circumstances and the level of offense or disruption to determine whether the speech falls into a punishable category. Under this approach, government's power to punish or ban a student newspaper article or a vitriolic speech before an armed and hostile audience depends on how much harm the speech is likely to cause. If the harm is likely to be cataclysmic, society's interest in preventing the crisis is more likely to outweigh concerns about protection of speech. One problem, though, is that the gravity of harm caused by speech cannot be known in advance.

National Security and Tranquility

Determining what speech threatens national security or how best to promote public peace and tranquility tends to reflect the national outlook and to shift with the historical context. Historically, during times of political conservatism, war or national turmoil, radical speech and organized protests are perceived to be more dangerous than during times of calm. Courts tend to restrict speech more readily when there is national unrest or the public is fearful. When the country moves from peace to war and back again, the nation alternately experiences waves of relative speech and press freedom followed by heightened suppression. These vacillations undermine the promised stability of the rule of law.[3] Despite one and a quarter centuries of trial and error, the Court has not created legal rules that consistently protect core First Amendment freedoms and counterbalance the urge to stifle speech during times of instability.[4] As Ann Beeson of the American Civil Liberties Union noted, "Sadly, our government has an ugly history of using its investigative powers to squelch dissent. We saw it during the Japanese internments of World War II, the Red Scare of the 1950s and the civil rights movement of the 1960s, and now we see it in the post–9/11 investigations and detention of Arabs and Muslims."[5]

Threats to National Security

Government efforts to punish speech that threatens its authority or undermines the security and stability of the nation did not end in 1801 when the Sedition Act (discussed in Chapter 2) expired. In the more than two centuries since, both federal and state governments have enacted laws to ensure that speakers do not provoke discontent or incite overthrow of government. Laws that target the speech related to conspiracies to commit crimes, advocacy of terrorism, treason, protest and intimidation also abound; these laws place limits on the types of speech protected in the United States.

Throughout U.S. history, threats to freedom of speech and of the press have occurred both when the nation is at war and when the national security appears vulnerable. In 2010, the U.S. Supreme Court ruled 6–3 that a 1996 federal ban on "material support" of terrorist groups did not violate the First Amendment, even when the law prevented support of legal activities by a designated terrorist organization.[6] In *Holder v. Humanitarian Law Project (HLP)*, a nonprofit organization established to protect human rights and promote peaceful conflict resolution sought a court injunction to prevent application of the ban to their proposed training of members of the Kurdistan Workers Party, also known as the PKK,

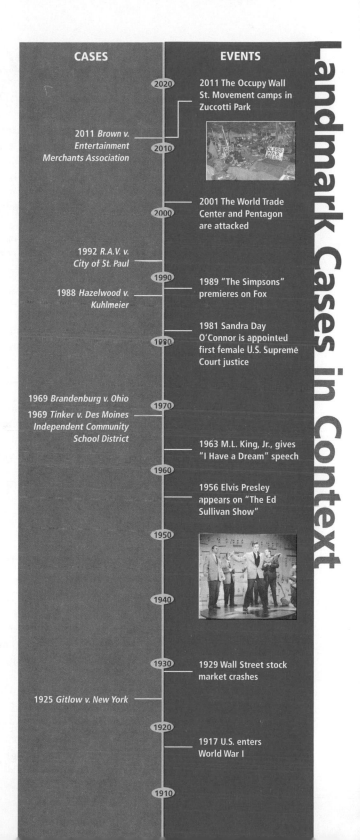

Landmark Cases in Context

CASES		EVENTS
	2020	2011 The Occupy Wall St. Movement camps in Zuccotti Park
2011 *Brown v. Entertainment Merchants Association*	2010	
	2000	2001 The World Trade Center and Pentagon are attacked
1992 *R.A.V. v. City of St. Paul*	1990	1989 "The Simpsons" premieres on Fox
1988 *Hazelwood v. Kuhlmeier*		
	1980	1981 Sandra Day O'Connor is appointed first female U.S. Supreme Court justice
1969 *Brandenburg v. Ohio*	1970	
1969 *Tinker v. Des Moines Independent Community School District*		1963 M.L. King, Jr., gives "I Have a Dream" speech
	1960	1956 Elvis Presley appears on "The Ed Sullivan Show"
	1950	
	1940	
	1930	1929 Wall Street stock market crashes
1925 *Gitlow v. New York*		
	1920	1917 U.S. enters World War I
	1910	

realWorld Law

Democracy's Unreasoned, Uncivil Promise

In a world where overconfidence in the correctness of one's own conclusions tends to inhibit truly open and informed deliberation, incivility may reign. When raucous name-calling, hate-filled signs and near-threats in the streets replace the reasoned exchange of ideas, free speech may seem pathological, undermining both civility and the core values many believe the First Amendment is intended to protect. Martin Redish suggests this type of speech "pathology pervades the flow of American political history," and the Supreme Court rules accordingly. "Virtually all periods of strong political dissent throughout the nation's history have been met with a corresponding rise in repress[ion]."[1]

A civility litmus test for free speech truncates public exchange. Rather than establish the range of useful democratic debate, "the labels 'civility' and 'incivility' . . . effectively function as exclusion instruments, although they create the appearance of inclusiveness and openness to contrarian views," according to one analyst.[2] And another argues, when court decisions

> locate the core of democratic legitimacy or authority in public processes of deliberation, [they] can seem to treat sharp or disruptive political activity as marginal, as unfortunate last resorts. This is unsatisfying since much of democracy's promise stems from our historical experience with brilliant and original forms of direct action.[3]

The vitriolic expression of opposing ideas, then, is not the antithesis of free speech or something to be sanctioned. Yet such free speech also will not presumptively produce deliberative consensus. "A fair resolution almost always requires not only acknowledging but also exploring conflicts, some of which cannot be simply subsumed into an overarching common good."[4]

If uncivil discord is a cost of democracy, sharply fractured Court decisions may be one price we pay.

1. Martin Redish, The Logic of Persecution: Free Expression and the McCarthy Era 54, 62 (2006).
2. Barak Y. Orbach, *On Hubris, Civility, and Incivility,* 54 Ariz. Law Rev. 443 (2012), *available at* http://ssrn.com/abstract=2046796.
3. David Estlund, *Democracy and the Real Speech Situation, in* Deliberative Democracy and Its Discontents 76 (Samantha Besson & Jose Luis Marti eds., 2006).
4. Samantha Besson & Jose Luis Marti, Deliberative Democracy and Its Discontents xxii (2006) (quoting Jane Mansbridge).

which the federal government designated a terrorist organization. HLP provided training on how to negotiate peace or seek help from the United Nations. But the law defined "prohibited material support" to include *any* service, training, expert advice or assistance, among other things. The State Department strongly supported the ban, saying it played "a critical role in our fight against terrorism."[7]

Ruling that the law's ban did not violate the group's freedom of speech, the Supreme Court said it reviewed the law, giving due "respect for the government's conclusions . . . given the sensitive interests in national security and foreign affairs at stake."[8] The Court said the law **as applied** to HLP was neither vague nor overbroad. Although "the scope of the material-support statute may not be

as applied as applied A phrase referring to interpretation of a statute on the basis of actual effects on the parties.

clear in every application, . . . the statutory terms are clear in their application to plaintiffs' proposed conduct," the Court wrote.[9] While the ban might not be constitutional in every situation, and while not every "statute relating to speech and terrorism would satisfy the First Amendment," the law's prevention of training to the PKK constitutionally advanced the government's compelling interest in "provid[ing] for the common defense," the Court concluded.[10]

Following the 2001 terrorist attacks on the World Trade Center and the Pentagon, government at all levels proposed new laws and strategies intended to better protect U.S. citizens and to punish terrorists and their supporters. One of the more visible and controversial actions of the federal government was the rapid enactment of the **USA**

The World Trade Center following the attacks in September 2001.

Patriot Act.[11] The Patriot Act, designed to identify suspicious activity and speed the interception and prosecution of terrorists, raised concerns among its critics that unclear definitions of "terrorism" and "support for terrorism" had a **chilling effect** on speech. A chilling effect arises from any practice that discourages the exercise of a constitutional right. In First Amendment law, it is brought about by any measure that deters freedom of expression.

The Patriot Act placed a broad array of radical political organizing, activism and speech within the category of support for terrorism and expanded the power of law enforcement and investigative authorities. The Free Expression Policy Project (FEPP) said the Patriot Act "contains more than 150 sections and amends over 15 federal statutes, including laws governing criminal procedure, computer fraud, foreign intelligence, wiretapping, and immigration."[12] Four provisions have specific First Amendment implications: Section 206 permits roving wiretaps and secret court orders to monitor electronic communications of people in the United States suspected of involvement with terrorists; Sections 214 and 216 expand the power to monitor Internet communications in criminal investigations; and Section 215 relaxes oversight of search warrants on business, medical, educational, library and bookstore records that might be related to an ongoing investigations or intelligence gathering. Section 215 also contains a gag order, making it illegal for anyone served with one of these search warrants to disclose what has taken place. Another federal law designed to enhance foreign intelligence gathering increased government surveillance of U.S. residents and provided legal immunity to telecommunication companies participating in secret government surveillance.[13]

Reporters said the laws' secrecy provisions hampered their ability to inform the nation about the state of the country's security.

USA Patriot Act The Uniting and Strengthening America by Providing Appropriate Tools Required to Intercept and Obstruct Terrorism Act of 2001. Passed in the wake of the Sept. 11, 2001, attacks, the act was designed to give law enforcement agencies greater authority to combat terrorism.

chilling effect The discouragement of a constitutional right, especially free speech, by any practice that creates uncertainty about the proper exercise of that right.

International Law

Does *This* Speech Pose an Imminent Threat?

Indians in Kashmir joined protesters worldwide responding in 2012 to the perceived insult to the Muslim Prophet Muhammed presented by the American-made film "Innocence of Muslims."

When is an online video equivalent to "a man falsely shouting fire in a theater and causing a panic," as Justice Oliver Wendell Holmes, Jr., once categorized the speech that does not warrant First Amendment protection?

When the online trailer for a mocking anti-Islamic video, "Innocence of Muslims," provoked international violence and controversy, Google denied a White House request to block access to it.[1] Google judged the video to be legal in the United States, but it blocked access in Egypt and Libya, where violence had broken out, and in India and Indonesia, where the video violated national law. Facebook blocked the video in Pakistan, removed an associated threat to a U.S. ambassador, and issued a statement that it "prohibits content that threatens or organizes violence, or praises violent organizations."

One law professor argued that "the only people who seem beyond a reasonable doubt to have intended imminent violence are those persons overseas who used the film to whip crowds into an angry frenzy."[2]

Clearly the decision of online providers about what to disseminate and what to delete involves a delicate balancing act on a swinging wire. It is not clear whether the Holmes standard is the proper test to be applied to private bans on speech such as these. Neither is it clear whether access to the video via Facebook or Google presents the proximity or degree of danger the Holmes test seeks to prevent. As national, local and personal standards shift, as citizens around the globe receive the same content but perceive it differently, as each individual gains new power to distribute and incite, the correct application of U.S. law becomes uncertain, especially when the connection between the speech and the deaths and injury of more than 100 people in Afghanistan is far from clear.

---

1. Somini Sengupta, *On Web, a Fine Line on Free Speech Across the Globe,* N.Y. TIMES, Sept. 17, 2012, *available at* http://query .nytimes.com/gst/fullpage.html?res=9A03E7DA1131F934A2575AC0A9649D8B63.
2. Sarah Chayes, *Does "Innocence of Muslims" Meet the Free-Speech Test?,* L.A. TIMES, Sept. 18, 2012, *available at* http://web2 .westlaw.com/result/default.wl?cfid=1&mt=208&origin=Search&sskey=CLID_SSSA93630572210198&query=SARAH+CHAYES +%26+da%2809%2f18%2f2012%29&db=LATIMES&rlt=CLID_QRYRLT98911572210198&method=TNC&service=Search&eq= search&rp=%2fsearch%2fdefault.wl&srch=TRUE&vr=2.0&action=Search&rltdb=CLID_DB9956372110198&sv=Split&fmqv=s &fn=_top&rs=WLW13.07.

Some observers have said laws enacted following the Sept. 11, 2001, attacks permitted government to persecute individuals who had spoken out against government policy or who were merely associated with members of unpopular groups or "suspect" religions. But the Department of Justice described the laws as essential restrictions of liberty necessary to ensure national security. As Chief Justice William H. Rehnquist once said, "It is neither desirable nor is it remotely likely that civil liberty will occupy as favored a position in wartime as it does in peacetime."[14]

realWorld Law

Are These "Troublous" Times?

Justice David Davis

During the Civil War, Lambden P. Milligan was sentenced to death for disloyalty by a military commission. Asked to determine whether the Constitution permitted civilians to be tried under military law, the Supreme Court held that military tribunals could not exist when the civil courts were operating. Justice David Davis, writing for the Court, noted that

Wicked men, ambitious of power, with hatred of liberty and contempt of law, may fill the place once occupied by Washington and Lincoln; and if this right [to open civilian trials] is conceded, and the calamities of war again befall us, the dangers to human liberty are frightful to contemplate.

. . . Time has proven the discernment of our ancestors. . . . Those great and good men foresaw that troublous times would arise, when . . . the principles of constitutional liberty would be in peril. . . . The Constitution of the United States is a law . . . equally in war and in peace, and covers with the shield of its protection all classes of men, at all times, and under all circumstances. No doctrine, involving more pernicious consequences, was ever invented by the wit of man than that any of its provisions can be suspended during any of the great exigencies of government. Such a doctrine leads directly to anarchy or despotism.[1]

1. Ex parte Milligan, 71 U.S. (4 Wall.) 2 (1866).

Some Supreme Court decisions support Rehnquist's view. For example, during the post–World War II "Red scare," the Court said the First Amendment did not stop government from requiring its employees to swear loyalty oaths and reject communism. Two decades later, the Court said the Constitution permitted the U.S. attorney general to exclude a foreign economist from visiting and speaking at U.S. universities simply because he was a Marxist.[15] Contemporary trials for espionage and treason, challenges to the secret proceedings of foreign intelligence courts and sweeping government authority to wiretap its own citizens raise new questions about the expanse and limits of government power under the ongoing "war on terror."

SUMMARY

FIRST AMENDMENT PROTECTIONS ARE NOT ABSOLUTE. History shows that expression tends to be more susceptible to government restraints during wartime. The government may restrict the freedom of expression when it establishes a sufficiently important interest in doing so. Protecting the national security is a sufficiently important concern to outweigh speech protection under certain conditions. In evaluating laws that limit speech, courts tend to balance the interests at stake, usually categorically. ∎

Court Tests to Protect Disruptive Speech

The Supreme Court has developed several tests to help it decide when speech must be protected in order to encourage robust discussion and debate and when speech may be punished. The Court has said speech and press content are not protected if they would cause imminent harm or play "no essential part of any exposition of ideas, and are of such slight social value as a step to truth that any benefit that may be derived from them is clearly outweighed by the social interest in order and morality."[16] However, the lines drawn around this category are not clear. The boundary between protected and unprotected speech is not fixed. The Court's tests afford leeway for different interpretations in response to changing circumstances.

The Clear and Present Danger Test

clear and present danger
Doctrine establishing that restrictions on First Amendment rights will be upheld if they are necessary to prevent an extremely serious and imminent harm.

In 1919, Justice Oliver Wendell Holmes wrote for a unanimous Supreme Court that government had a right and a duty to prevent speech that presented a "**clear and present danger**" to the nation.[17] The case of *Schenck v. United States* began when Charles Schenck, a member of the Socialist Party, mailed some 15,000 antidraft pamphlets to men in Philadelphia. The pamphlets encouraged recipients to reject the pro-war philosophy of the U.S. government and oppose U.S. participation in World War I. Schenck was convicted of violating the Espionage Act of 1917, which was one of several federal laws enacted to unify the nation behind the war effort.

In affirming Schenck's conviction, the Court said the mailing had a "bad tendency" and posed a clear and present danger to national security. Justice Holmes said ordinarily harmless words may become criminal during times of war because of the heightened danger they pose: "It is a question of proximity and degree."[18] Common sense indicates that "the most stringent protection of free speech would not protect a man in falsely shouting fire in a theatre and causing a panic."[19] Nor would it protect an individual in a military recruitment office falsely shouting, "I have a bomb."

In other cases involving the Espionage Act, Justice Holmes continued to write for a unanimous Court and affirmed the conviction of antiwar protesters for speeches and pamphlets the Court said might tend to endanger the nation. In one case, the Court upheld Jacob Frohwerk's fine and 10-year prison sentence for published writings that questioned the constitutionality of the draft and the merits of the war.[20] The Court said the publications presented "a little breath [that] would be enough to kindle a flame" of unrest.[21] In another, Socialist Party leader Eugene Debs was convicted of an attempt to cause military insubordination and to obstruct the draft for giving a speech at a Socialist Party convention opposing the government's war policy.[22] Debs' most direct comment was to tell listeners, "You are fit for something better than slavery and cannon fodder." In court, Debs said he abhorred war, and the jury used this statement as evidence that there was both intent and likelihood that his speech would harm the war effort.

Yet that same year, when the Court used its so-called bad-tendency standard to uphold the Sedition Act conviction of Jacob Abrams and four friends for pamphlets critical of U.S. interference in the Russian Revolution and encouraging strikes at U.S. munitions factories,[23] Justice Holmes dissented. The five men had dropped leaflets from a New York City skyscraper urging workers to unite to oppose "the hypocrisy of the United States and her allies." In dissent, Justice Holmes said the "surreptitious publishing of a silly leaflet by an unknown man" did not pose a sufficiently grave and imminent danger to permit punishment.[24] The First Amendment requires government to protect diverse and loathsome opinions, he wrote, "unless they so imminently threaten immediate interference with the lawful and pressing purposes of the law that an immediate check is required to save the country."[25] This 1919 dissent by Holmes in *Abrams v. United States* marked a transformation in his interpretation of the First Amendment.

Still, the Court relied on various forms of the clear and present danger test for 50 years to affirm punishment of communists during the Red scares of the 1920s and 1950s.[26] During the 1920s, the Court affirmed the conviction of an immigrant arrested as a threat to the U.S. government. Benjamin Gitlow, the business manager of a branch of the Socialist Party, oversaw publication and distribution of party literature urging class action to establish socialism in the United States.[27] Without evidence that the pamphlets caused any harm or disruption, the trial court convicted Gitlow of criminal anarchy and sentenced him to prison for advocating the overthrow of government. In *Gitlow v. New York*, the Supreme Court upheld the conviction, finding that the pamphlets "endanger[ed] the foundations of organized government and threaten[ed] its overthrow by unlawful means."[28] The Court said the writings constituted a "revolutionary spark" that might incite a "sweeping and destructive conflagration."[29] In dissent, Justice Holmes declared, "Every idea is an incitement."[30] He said most ideas "should be given their chance and have their way" in the dialogue of a free and democratic society, and radical political advocacy should be protected by the First Amendment because the mere dissemination of ideas would not endanger the nation.

The Court did not embrace Holmes' view, but it used *Gitlow* to expand free speech protection by establishing the doctrine of **incorporation**. The incorporation doctrine applies the Fourteenth Amendment's due process clause to limit the power of state and local governments to abridge the guarantees of the Bill of Rights.[31] In other words, incorporation prevents the states, as well as the federal government, from abridging protected First Amendment rights.

In the years leading up to U.S. involvement in World War II, the Court continued to use the clear and present danger test. In 1927, it upheld the

Incorporation doctrine The Fourteenth Amendment concept that most of the Bill of Rights applies equally to the states.

Jerry Karnas, center, and about 30 others protested the Keystone XL oil pipeline when President Obama visited Miami in 2013.

conviction of a 64-year-old female labor activist who participated in meetings of the Communist Labor Party.[32] The majority of the Court ruled that the First Amendment did not prevent California from making it a crime for Anita Whitney merely to belong to a group—the Communist Labor Party— that advocated violence as a means to bring about political change.

The Court accepted, without evidence, that the Communist Labor Party was violent. Whitney's membership in the party was sufficient to pose a danger that was imminent and constituted a threat that was "relatively serious."[33] In his concurrence in *Whitney v. California*, Justice Louis Brandeis said a clear and present danger existed and punishment was constitutional when previous conduct suggested a group *might contemplate* advocacy of immediate serious violence.[34]

During the wave of anti-communist frenzy in the 1950s, the Court upheld a federal law that required labor union officers to swear they were not communists. In dissent, Justice Hugo Black argued that the clear and present danger test did not sufficiently protect unpopular or radical political speech and association: "Too often it is fear which inspires such passions, and nothing is more reckless or contagious. In the resulting hysteria, popular indignation tars with the same brush all those who have ever been associated with any member of the group under attack."[35] Members of the Court increasingly questioned the application of the clear and present danger test, and ruled that regulation of speech is unconstitutional if it is not narrowly tailored to avoid infringing on protected speech and does not punish more than mere expression of the abstract concept of citizen revolt.[36] While it is constitutional to regulate speech that advocates illegal action, government may not punish speech that simply expresses a radical political idea. This doctrine is established fully by the Court in a case involving incitement.

The *Brandenburg* (or Incitement) Test

The clear and present danger test was too flexible, too subjective and too easily swayed by political realities or social concerns to consistently protect innocuous speech.[37] In 1969, the Court attempted to resolve this problem by adopting a new test that drew a bright-line distinction between advocating violence as an abstract concept and inciting imminent illegal or violent activity. In *Brandenburg v. Ohio,* the Supreme Court ruled that the First Amendment protects the right to advocate but not to incite violence.[38] The First Amendment does not protect speech that incites, prompts or provokes immediate violence.

The case involved Clarence Brandenburg, a television repairman and Ku Klux Klan (KKK) leader, who spoke to a rally of a dozen KKK members in the woods of rural Ohio. In his speech, Brandenburg made nonspecific threats to take "revengeance" against various leaders in government. The rally was covered by a television news crew. After Brandenburg's comments were broadcast, he was convicted under a state law that made it a crime to conspire to violently overthrow government. He appealed, arguing that the conviction violated his right of free speech.

The Supreme Court readily acknowledged that Brandenburg's anti-Semitic and racist comments were highly offensive. However, the Court ruled that the First Amendment protects people's right to advocate abhorrent ideas about social, political and economic change: "Mere advocacy of the use of force or violence does not remove speech from the protection of the First Amendment."[39] The teaching and expression of abstract philosophies, even those that embrace or advise the necessity of violence, are protected free speech. To ensure that government did not intrude upon this protected speech, the Court said government could forbid or punish the advocacy of force only when the advocacy (1) was directed to and (2) was likely to (3) incite or produce imminent lawless action.[40]

Points of Law

The *Brandenburg* Test

In 1969, the Supreme Court replaced the rather vague "clear and present danger" standard with the *Brandenburg* test to determine when speech is sufficiently likely to prompt illegal action that it no longer warrants First Amendment protection. The *Brandenburg* incitement test allows punishment of "advocacy of illegal action" if the speech is

1. Directed toward inciting,

2. Immediate violence or illegal action, and

3. Is likely to produce that action.

The *Brandenburg* decision established that government may punish criticism of government or advocacy of radical ideas only when speakers intentionally incite immediate illegal activity. That remains the rule today.

SUMMARY

FOR YEARS, COURTS USED THE "clear and present danger" test developed early in the 20th century to determine the proper balance between freedom of speech and harmful incitement of lawless activity. Under this loose test, courts asked whether the words used had a tendency to create the kind of danger lawmakers might constitutionally prevent. In early 20th-century rulings, the Supreme Court used the test in several First Amendment cases and frequently upheld the constitutionality of laws that overtly constrained unpopular political speech. The test was fine-tuned over the years and eventually evolved into the current *Brandenburg* test. Under *Brandenburg,* the Constitution prohibits government punishment of advocacy of an idea unless the speech is meant to and likely to produce imminent illegal action. ∎

Speech Assaults

Words can cause harm unrelated to the security or stability of government. Speakers—sometimes intentionally, sometimes not—insult, denigrate and degrade others. People call each other names; they throw hateful insults and hurtful epithets in each other's faces. They threaten, they harass and they offend. They fill the streets with dissent and discontent, disturbing the tranquility with messages and symbols that challenge society's mores and values. The words and images they use alienate others, cause fear and generate conflict.

Offensive Speech

In 1971, the Supreme Court ruled directly on whether profanity was protected under the First Amendment. The case of *Cohen v. California*[41] involved an antiwar protest by Paul Robert Cohen, who wore a jacket in the Los Angeles Courthouse bearing the phrase "Fuck the Draft." Convicted of disturbing the peace for "offensive conduct," Cohen appealed on First Amendment grounds, arguing that the conviction targeted his pure political speech. The Supreme Court acknowledged that court officials, like school administrators, have broad authority to maintain order and decorum. Nevertheless, if the speech did not disturb the court's functioning, government could not ban particular words it found offensive unless the words fell into an unprotected category, such as obscenity, incitement or fighting words.

The Court went further. In *Cohen*, the Court said the First Amendment protected both the content and the emotional value of a message. Information would have been lost, and Cohen's message would have been diluted, if he were forced to express his opposition to the war by declaring, "Please do not support the war." Meaningful protection for free speech went beyond the "cognitive content" of expression to protect its "emotive function" as well, the Court said. In other words, it is not simply *what* you say but *how* you say it that enjoys constitutional protection.

Fighting Words

The First Amendment protects people's right to say offensive, unkind and even ugly things to each other. Some argue that the ability to vent anger in words rather than in physical violence is a primary value of free speech. Free speech serves as a societal safety valve; it helps maintain social stability because it provides catharsis to discontented individuals and allows them to blow off steam.[42] But the Supreme Court also recognizes that words used to vent anger may inflame tempers and "set fire to reason."[43] They do not inform; they assail. They hurt like a slap in the face.

The Supreme Court's 1942 ruling in *Chaplinsky v. New Hampshire*[44] first articulated the logic that violent listener reaction may provide the basis for limits on the freedom of speech. In response to a complaint that Walter Chaplinsky was distributing Jehovah's Witness pamphlets on the streets of Rochester, N.H., a police officer warned him to stop because he was disturbing the peace and the residents. Later in the day, as a group of people became increasingly restless in response to Chaplinsky's continuing pamphlet distribution, another officer detained Chaplinsky. On the way to the police station, they encountered the first officer, who repeated his earlier warning. Angered, Chaplinsky called the officer a "goddamned racketeer" and a "damned Fascist," for which he was convicted under a state law that made calling someone "any offensive, derisive or annoying word . . . or name, [or] mak[ing] any noise or exclamation in his presence and hearing with intent to deride, offend or annoy" while in public punishable as a disturbance of the peace.

On appeal, the U.S. Supreme Court upheld the conviction, reasoning that the First Amendment did not protect narrow categories of speech that made no contribution to the discussion of ideas or the search for truth. While today Chaplinsky's speech may seem routine or harmless, the Court said his comments were unprotected **fighting words** that "by their very utterance inflict injury or tend to incite immediate breach of peace."[45]

In 1949, the Supreme Court heard the case of a priest whose anti-Semitic and pro-Fascist comments to a sympathetic audience riled a group gathered outside the assembly hall. When the crowd outside became increasingly violent, the police arrested the speaker for disorderly conduct. Illinois courts upheld his conviction, ruling that the law punished only fighting words, which it defined as any behavior that "stirs the public to anger, invites dispute, brings about a condition of unrest . . . creates a disturbance or . . . molests the inhabitants in the enjoyment of peace and quiet by arousing alarm."

But the Supreme Court reversed. It reasoned that "a function of free speech under our system of government is to *invite* dispute."[46] The Court in *Terminiello v. Chicago* said speech "may indeed best serve its high purpose when it induces a condition of unrest, creates dissatisfaction with conditions as they are, or even stirs people to anger."[47] The First Amendment protects such speech "unless shown likely to produce a clear and present danger of a serious substantive evil that rises far above public inconvenience, annoyance or unrest."[48] Subsequent Supreme Court rulings[49] have confirmed that the Constitution permits government to prohibit only those face-to-face comments—including hate speech—that are inherently likely to trigger a group reaction of disorder and violence.

In 2012, for example, the U.S. Court of Appeals for the Eighth Circuit ruled that the Constitution prevented government from prohibiting the display of controversial signs on a highway overpass.[50] Donald Stahl displayed a sign that said, "911 was an inside job," above a St. Louis, Mo., highway during rush hour. After a driver reported the "offensive sign," an officer arrested Stahl on the belief that his sign might create a driving hazard. Stahl was convicted under a city ordinance prohibiting criminal obstruction of traffic. But the Eighth Circuit overturned the conviction. It called the law "especially problematic" because it imposed an "excessive chill" on protected speech and criminalized conduct on the basis of third-party reactions.[51]

fighting words Words not protected by the First Amendment because they cause immediate harm or illegal acts.

Points of Law

Fighting Words

Under the Supreme Court's fighting words doctrine, the First Amendment does not protect words that

> . . . are directed at an individual.

> . . . that automatically inflict emotional harm or trigger violence.

Hate Speech

hate speech A category of speech that includes name-calling and pointed criticism that demeans others on the basis of race, color, gender, ethnicity, religion, national origin, disability, intellect or the like.

Contemporary concerns about the harms caused by intolerance, racism and bigotry have generated state and local speech codes to regulate so-called **hate speech,** but courts generally find these laws unconstitutional. Courts have not defined hate speech, but it is commonly understood to involve name-calling and pointed criticism that demeans others on the basis of race, color, gender, ethnicity, sexual preference, religion, national origin, disability, intellect or the like. Few cases dealing squarely with hate speech have reached the Supreme Court, but lower courts consistently have found anti-bias and anti-hate-speech laws unconstitutional.

The primary Supreme Court decision dealing with hate speech, *R.A.V. v. City of St. Paul,* involved several white teenage boys who, late one night, made a crude wooden cross from a broken chair and set it ablaze in the yard of a black family living in the neighborhood of one of the boys.[52] They were convicted of violating a St. Paul, Minn., statute that punished the display of symbols or objects—such as a burning cross—that arouse "anger, alarm or resentment in others on the basis of race, color, creed, religion or gender." The Minnesota Supreme Court upheld the conviction, reasoning that the bias-motivated crime statute punished only unprotected fighting words. The U.S. Supreme Court reversed.

underinclusive A First Amendment doctrine that disfavors narrow laws that target a subset of a recognized category for discriminatory treatment.

viewpoint-based discrimination Government censorship or punishment of expression based on the ideas or attitudes expressed. Courts will apply a strict scrutiny test to determine whether the government acted constitutionally.

While the members of the Court voted unanimously in *R.A.V.* that the ordinance was unconstitutional, the justices did not agree on why. Five justices said the law was too narrow, or **underinclusive,** because it punished only a specific subset of fighting words that the government found particularly objectionable. Thus, the law imposed unconstitutional **viewpoint-based discrimination** because it censored expression on the basis of the message expressed. It punished certain forms of racist speech (cross burnings) but not others, such as homophobic or sexist speech, for example. In contrast, the remaining four justices said the law was overbroad; it punished too much speech, not too little. They said the law unconstitutionally went beyond fighting words to punish speech that did not arise in face-to-face encounters and whose only harm was to prompt "generalized reactions" of hurt feelings, resentment or offense. Since *R.A.V.,* most efforts to tailor a constitutional hate speech ordinance have failed.

Current Standard

In the past 60 years, the Supreme Court has shied away from directly applying the fighting words category to determine the expanse of constitutional protection for free speech. Instead, the Court has tended to judge the constitutionality of laws that attempt to regulate highly volatile speech directed at specific individuals on the basis of the reach of the law. The Court has struck down a variety of laws that attempt to punish specific categories of extremely offensive speech on the grounds that the laws are not sufficiently narrowly tailored to prevent intrusion on protected speech. In one such ruling, the Court rearticulated the category of

realWorld Law

Fighting Words, Hate or Free Speech?

Some observers criticize the lone-wolf stance of the United States regarding hate speech. They argue that "Americans [need] to take more seriously the damage such speech does and [ ] overcome the 'knee-jerk,' impulsive and thoughtless" arguments against punishing speech that assaults.[1] Others say we need to protect hate speech "not because we doubt the speech inflicts harm, but because we fear the censorship more."

Similar disagreement is evident in Denmark, where legislators who recently considered repealing anti-hate speech legislation watched as the law was applied to their own Jesper Langballe, who was convicted of "hate speech" and "racial discrimination" for talking about incestual rape in Muslim families.[2]

In the United States, the National Religious Broadcasters (NRB) initiated a campaign against what they call "hate-speech censorship" by major social media and Internet Service Providers (ISP).[3] An NRB study of seven ISPs and Web companies found they consistently engage in "censorship" of conservative Christian speech on issues of public concern. Calling Apple, AT&T, Comcast, Facebook, Google, MySpace and Verizon "arbiter[s] of truth," one NRB spokesman said they routinely strike content that, for example, promotes orthodox Christianity, is deemed antigay or calls abortion murder. Twitter was the only leading company whose content policy did not allow it arbitrarily to screen content from its sites, the study found.

Ex-FCC Commissioner Harold Furchtgott-Roth called the findings "deeply troubling." While they show no "systematic effort by these companies to block content based on religion," he said the collective result is an environment where companies stifle religious speech and truncate public debate.[4]

Rather than support government regulation to address their concerns, the NRB recommended that Internet companies voluntarily and collectively agree to a charter limiting their content removals to traditionally unprotected speech—obscenity, incitement, fraud and unlawful conduct.

1. Michael W. McConnell, *You Can't Say That,* N.Y. Times Book Rev., June 24, 2012, at BR14, *available at* http:// www.nytimes.com (quoting Jeremy Waldron, The Harm in Hate Speech (2012)).
2. Lawrence Auster, *Danish Government Is Prosecuting Individuals for Hate Speech,* View from the Right, Jan. 10, 2011, *available at* http://www.amnation.com.
3. John Eggerton, *National Religious Broadcasters Promote New Media Speech Charter,* Broadcasting & Cable, Sept. 18, 2012, *available at* http://www.broadcastingcable.com.
4. *Id.*

fighting words and said this type of speech sometimes does warrant protection by the First Amendment. In 1992, the Court wrote,

> Our cases [on fighting words] surely do not establish the proposition that the First Amendment imposes no obstacle whatsoever to regulation of particular instances of such proscribable expression, so that the government "may regulate [them] freely." . . . Such a simplistic, all-or-nothing-at-all approach to First Amendment protection is at odds with common sense and with our jurisprudence as well. It is not true that "fighting words" have at most a "di minimus" expressive content, or that their content is in all respects "worthless and undeserving of constitutional

protection"; sometimes they are quite expressive indeed. We have not said that they constitute "no part of the expression of ideas," but only that they constitute "no essential part of any expression of ideas." . . . [T]he unprotected features of [fighting] words are, despite their verbal character, essentially a "nonspeech" element of communication.

Given this and other similar Supreme Court decisions, the precise level of protection the Constitution affords fighting words is unclear. The most relevant decisions suggest that speech loses its constitutional protection when the speaker intends to provoke violence or incite unrest in a targeted individual or group.

Retired U.S. Supreme Court Justice Sandra Day O'Connor

Harmful Images

In two recent cases, the Supreme Court reaffirmed its sole power to determine what categories of speech are, and are not, fully protected by the First Amendment. In reviewing one federal and one state statute, the Court reiterated its position that the Constitution fully protects even violent and deeply disturbing expression.

In the first of these, *United States v. Stevens*, the Supreme Court denied Congress the power to exclude images of animal cruelty from First Amendment protection.[53] Robert J. Stevens had been convicted and given a 37-month sentence under the federal Animal Crush Video Prohibition Act for trafficking in "depictions of animal cruelty." He had compiled and sold videotapes of dogfights, though he had not arranged or participated in the fights.

In an 8–1 ruling written by Chief Justice John Roberts, with Justice Samuel Alito alone in dissent, the Court struck down the law as substantially overbroad because it penalized speech that did not fit within a historically recognized First Amendment exception. Neither Congress nor the Supreme Court has "freewheeling authority to declare new categories of speech outside the scope of the First Amendment," the Court concluded.

In the second case, the Entertainment Merchants Association (EMA) raised a facial challenge to a California state law prohibiting the sale of violent video games to minors.[54] The law attempted to narrowly target only violent video games that, like obscenity, (1) appeal to deviant or morbid interests, (2) are patently offensive to contemporary community standards and (3) lack serious artistic or other value (see related discussion in Chapter 12). The state said the law was designed to advance the important government interest in preventing psychological harm to minors.

But the Supreme Court in *Brown v. EMA* rejected California's effort to distinguish video games from other media because of their interactivity and refused to carve out a new category of disfavored speech for violent expression. The Court called California's attempt to create a whole new category of unprotected speech directed at children both "unprecedented and mistaken." It held that violent video games deserve full First Amendment protection and accordingly applied strict scrutiny review to strike down the law. "It is difficult to distinguish politics from entertainment," Justice Antonin Scalia wrote for the Court, "and dangerous to try."[55]

Intimidation and Threats

But what happens when speech is more than merely disturbing, offensive or violent? At what point can government punish speakers because the message they convey is sufficiently detrimental to important competing interests?

In 2003, the Supreme Court helped answer some of the questions regarding offensive speech in another case involving cross burning. In *Virginia v. Black,* the Court ruled that states may punish Ku Klux Klansmen and others who set crosses ablaze if the intent is to intimidate someone.[56] The Court said the First Amendment permits states to target a specific set of fighting words, such as cross burnings, when the speech constitutes a **true threat** because it is "inextricably intertwined" with a clear and pervasive history of violence. The Court said a burning cross is such a powerful and threatening instrument of racial terror and impending violence that its ability to intimidate overshadows free speech concerns. Justice Clarence Thomas dissented to argue that the law punished only illegal acts and therefore was unrelated to First Amendment concerns: "Those who hate cannot terrorize and intimidate to make their point."[57]

true threat Speech directed toward one or more specific individuals with the intent of causing listeners to fear for their safety.

Writing for a slim majority of the Court, Justice Sandra Day O'Connor reasoned that despite the inextricable connection between cross burnings and the KKK's "reign of terror in the South," history alone does not transform merely offensive speech into unprotected threats or intimidation. For speech to become punishable as a true threat, a speaker must (1) direct the threat toward one or more individuals (2) with the intent of causing the listener(s) (3) to fear bodily harm or death.[58] In this case, the majority reasoned that cross burning was constitutionally punishable because the virulent intimidation of a burning cross is intended to create pervasive fear of violence in the targeted individual or group. It is not clear whether *Black* redefines and reinvigorates the category of fighting words by tying this unprotected form of speech to historic oppression and violence or whether it establishes a new category of punishable expression: true threats that intimidate.

The concept of true threat had been tested earlier in a federal trial court when a University of Michigan student posted an allegedly fictional story on the Internet. The story graphically described the torture, rape and murder of a woman. The woman had the same name as one of the author's female classmates. The student was charged under federal law criminalizing the interstate communication of threats of personal injury, but the trial court found that the Internet story did

Points of Law

Is That a Threat?

Common sense holds that a threat is a message a reasonable speaker would expect the listener to interpret as a sincere expression of the intent to do serious harm.

Some 60 years ago the U.S. Supreme Court defined a threat as an "utterance in a context of violence [that] can lose its significance as an appeal to reason and become part of an instrument of force." Such speech, the Court held, is "not meant to be sheltered by the Constitution."[1] In *Virginia v. Black,*[2] the most recent in a series of decisions,[3] the Court concluded that punishment of true threats is acceptable under the Constitution. The Court said a punishable threat if the following exist:

- The speaker intended the statement to be a threat.

- The statement, taken in context, conveys the speaker's intention to do bodily harm to the target.

Court rationales for a true threat exception to the First Amendment's protection of speech include the following:

- Protecting individuals from the fear of violence.

- Protecting society from the disruptive effects of violent threats.

- Preempting the violence threatened by the speaker.[4]

- Preventing coercion of the target of threats.

---

1. Milk Wagon Drivers Union of Chicago v. Meadowmoor Dairies, 312 U.S. 287, 293 (1941) (emphasis added).
2. 538 U.S. 343 (2003).
3. *See, e.g.,* Schenck v. Pro-Choice Network of Western New York, 519 U.S. 357, 373 (1997); Madsen v. Women's Health Center, 512 U.S. 753, 773 (1994); R.A.V. v. St. Paul, 505 U.S. 377 (1992); NAACP v. Claiborne Hardware, 458 U.S. 886 (1982); Watts v. United States, 394 U.S. 705, 708 (1969). *See also* Chaplinsky v. New Hampshire, 315 U.S. 568 (1942) (providing concept of words that "by their very utterance inflict injury").
4. R.A.V. v. St. Paul, 505 U.S. 377, 388 (1992).

not constitute a true threat and dismissed the charges.[59] The court reasoned that a punishable threat must be unequivocal, unconditional, immediate and specific.

In this case, nothing suggested any imminent prospect that the author intended to carry out the "threat"[60] nothing in the story suggested the "threatened" violence would even occur.[61] While the ability of the Internet to communicate potentially harmful ideas to a vast and varied audience "may complicate analysis, and may sometimes require new or modified laws, it does not in this instance qualitatively change the analysis under the statute or under the First Amendment," the court reasoned.[62]

The Internet was involved in another court ruling on true threats that began after several abortion clinics in the United States were bombed and several doctors associated with clinics were murdered in the 1990s. At least three of the murdered doctors previously had been identified on "unWANTED" posters produced by the American Coalition of Life Activists (ACLA). The posters said the

realWorld Law

Text Threats

In 2010, a Maryland Court of Appeals ruled that comments posted by Walter C. Abbott, Jr., on a state website soliciting feedback to the governor might be punishable under state law making it a crime to threaten state officials.[1] In an e-mail to the governor laced with obscenities and typing errors, Abbott provided his real name and address and identified himself as "president" of an organization called "FUCKING SOLD OUT AMERICAN." Abbott wrote, among other things, "If I ever get close enough to you, I will rap [sic] my hands around your throat and strangle the life from you. This will solve many problems for true AMERICANS."

Convicted for "knowingly and willfully mak[ing] a threat to take the life of, kidnap, or cause physical injury to a State official or local official," Abbott appealed and argued that he "meant no harm" with what he called "political hyperbole." The appeals court found that Abbott's e-mail met the law's target of a "threat in any written form" but remanded the case for clearer instructions to the jury on "how to determine whether [Abbott's] communication amounted to a threat."

In 2011, the Supreme Court of Iowa reversed the conviction and remanded the case of Jeffrey Soboroff, who had been convicted under state law for illegal "threats" after he posted a slideshow titled "Targets for Tonight" containing photographs of a city's water tower, some local residents and references to putting Thorazine into the water supply because some people "could use some medication."[2] The state high court concluded, "While there was evidence that Soboroff's threats were real, there was also evidence from which a jury could have concluded his statements were not real threats, and this issue should have been squarely presented to the jury."

1. Abbott v. State, 989 A.2d 795 (Md. App. 2010).
2. State v. Soboroff, 798 N.W.2d 1 (Ia. 2011).

doctors were "extremely dangerous to women and children" and were "guilty" of "crimes against humanity." They offered $5,000 rewards to people who helped the doctors "leave" their professions. ACLA's printed materials suggested that a mafia-type "contract" should be taken out on abortion providers whose "crimes" were compared to the Nazi extermination of Jews during World War II. The ACLA website used color coding to identify 200 "abortionists" and approximately 200 other supporters of abortion as "working," "wounded" or "fatality." The three murdered doctors were listed, with their names struck through to identify them as fatalities.

Four doctors, whose names, addresses and family member information appeared on the website, sued under a federal law that made it a crime to intentionally intimidate abortion providers with a threat of force. They said they feared for their lives and were afraid to continue practicing medicine. A jury found the ACLA guilty of intentionally threatening to harm the doctors as a means to stop them from providing legal medical services. On appeal, a federal court of appeals initially upheld both the decision and a permanent injunction preventing ACLA from publishing or posting threats against abortion doctors.[63] Sitting en banc, the U.S. Court of Appeals for the Ninth Circuit subsequently upheld the conviction. It said true threats arise not from the use of specific words but from the meaning of a message interpreted in context. When speech such as this, taken in context, is intended and likely to convey a threat of serious harm to a reasonable person, it is not protected by the First Amendment.

SUMMARY

THE CONSTITUTION PROTECTS THE RIGHT TO express ideas in an offensive manner because effective speech has both cognitive and emotional content, but the Supreme Court has established fighting words as a disfavored category of speech. Efforts to regulate such disfavored speech must be well tailored to the government's objectives. The Court has suggested that laws that target highly offensive speech are constitutional only if they are extremely narrowly tailored to address real and demonstrable harms. The Supreme Court has not established hate speech as a specific category of speech. The Court's most relevant decisions suggest that attempts to prohibit unpopular or racist speech as a subset of fighting words will rarely be constitutional. The Supreme Court generally has said the Constitution prohibits punishment for vague statements with distant or speculative harms, but in recent years the Court has developed the concept of true threats. When speech becomes an overt act of threat or intimidation it may be regulated and punished, but merely violent or disturbing images deserve full First Amendment protection. ■

Symbolic Speech

Much expression that might anger or upset people does not cross the line into hate speech, fighting words, threats or incitement. Sometimes it doesn't even take the form of words. Nonverbal expression, in the form of burning flags, wearing armbands or marching through the public streets, is very much a part of what the Supreme Court has called symbolic speech. The Court has said symbolic speech deserves First Amendment protection in some cases, but it has rejected "the view that an apparently limitless variety of conduct can be labeled speech whenever the person engaging in the conduct intends thereby to express his idea."[64] Only actions that are "closely akin to 'pure speech'" are viewed as symbolic speech.[65]

Some of the most vehement and heated debate in recent memory involved symbolic speech during the 1960s, at the height of the civil rights movement and protests against the Vietnam War. In general, the Constitution protected the right of members of protest groups to express the most radical and unpopular political ideas. However, there were limits, and the line between protected political protest and illegal activity, incitement or fighting words was not always obvious.

Burning Speech

In the first of these cases (which is discussed and excerpted in Chapter 2), the Supreme Court affirmed the power of government to punish David Paul O'Brien for burning his draft card in violation of a federal law intended to facilitate the military draft and the ongoing war effort. The *O'Brien* ruling established intermediate scrutiny as the proper review of content-neutral laws that incidentally infringe on protected speech. In affirming O'Brien's conviction, the Court focused on why the government had enacted the law and how the law operated while acknowledging the expressive content of the public destruction of a draft card.[66]

Some 15 years later, the Court reviewed another case of political protest involving symbolic speech. Gregory Lee Johnson had been convicted, sentenced to a year in prison and fined $2,000 for desecration of a venerated object, for burning the American flag during a protest at the 1984 Republican National Convention in Dallas. In *Texas v. Johnson,* the Supreme Court employed strict scrutiny to strike down a Texas law that made it a crime to desecrate the flag.[67] The state of Texas said its ban on flag desecration preserved an important symbol of national unity and helped prevent breaches of the peace. Johnson challenged the law and argued that it violated his right to free speech. After establishing flag burning as a form of symbolic speech, the Supreme Court ruled that the Texas law prohibiting flag desecration was unconstitutional.

A sharply divided Supreme Court held that the law failed to pass strict scrutiny because it served no compelling interest. The state's interest was insufficient to justify the law's content-based suppression of speech. In fact, the government interest in preserving the sanctity of the flag represented an unconstitutional attempt to punish ideas the government disliked. The law's sole purpose was to prohibit expression the state found offensive. "If there is a bedrock principle underlying the First Amendment," Justice William Brennan wrote for the Court, "it is that the government may not prohibit the expression of an idea simply because society finds the idea itself offensive or disagreeable."[68] The law was unconstitutional because it failed to serve a compelling interest and it did not use the least intrusive means to advance its goals.

The Constitution also protects exaggeration, hyperbole and excess in speech by considering the context of the speech to determine whether government may punish protest. For example, the Court said an antiwar protester's comment to fellow marchers that "we'll take the fucking street later" did not present the clear and present danger of violence required under the *Brandenburg* test because it was unlikely to prompt any immediate action.[69]

SUMMARY

THE COURT HAS RECOGNIZED THAT CERTAIN symbolic acts are a form of speech that implicates the First Amendment. Rulings on speech acts suggest that nondisruptive political protest is generally protected from government regulation. One exception was a draft-card-burning case in which the Supreme Court upheld criminal punishment on the grounds that the cards were vital to the efficient operation of the draft and the military. ■

Speech in the Schools

There is nothing in the wording of the First Amendment itself to suggest that it protects the rights of minors, public school students or campus media differently from the rights of other speakers and members of the press. However, society does have unique interests in protecting and educating its youth. Sometimes courts have accepted the idea that the nation's interest in raising its young people outweighs the free speech rights of public school students.

Courts have struggled for nearly a century to determine both how and where to draw the line between advancing the important concerns of parents and educators and protecting the freedom of speech and association of children, students or others in the public educational system. In fact, the courts have not developed a consistent approach to decide when, or whether, student press and speech are protected. The Supreme Court generally has viewed public schools and universities—including school-sponsored events, publications, funding and physical spaces—as limited public forums. Under public forum doctrine, discussed in Chapter 2, schools may impose reasonable content-neutral time, place and manner regulations on student speech activities to advance educational objectives. What this means in practice is that schools and universities may adopt regulations to achieve their educational goals even if the rules incidentally limit the freedom of speech of students and teachers. However, school officials generally may not dictate the content of student speech except to prevent speech that would directly undermine the educational missions of the school.

The standards for what speech may and may not be regulated by schools depend upon the age, impressionability and maturity of the students; the place in which the expression occurs; and the specific educational goals of the institution. As a result, the standards applied to primary schools, high schools and universities differ. The standards also differ, for example, between a school-run high school newspaper and a university student's speech during an open public debate.

Court distinctions based on differences among student speakers and types of speech are not always clear-cut. The political unrest and security of the nation also play a part. In recent years one Court observer noted that "the very concept of academic freedom is under fire."[70] Public schools may regulate, among other things, the clothing of students, the hours facilities may be used by outsiders, the school-related expression of teachers and the content of school-sponsored student speech and publications. Rules affecting expression in public schools generally are constitutional as long as the policies neither (1) limit expressive content that is compatible with the school's educational priorities nor (2) target specific content without a strong educational justification.

Points of Law

Nonuniversity Student Speech

Recent Supreme Court decisions on student expression generally approach nonuniversity student speech cases in one of three ways:

1. Is the speech disruptive? If the speech disrupts the functioning of the public school or violates the rights and interests of other students, it may be regulated.[1]

2. Is the speech of low value? If the speech is lewd or if it conflicts with the school's pedagogical goals or public values, it may be regulated.[2]

3. Is the speech sponsored by the school and therefore perceived to reflect the school's official position and attitude? If the speech occurs in a school-sponsored forum or event, if it is part of the school's official curriculum, or if it appears to entangle the school with a particular religious viewpoint, it may be regulated.[3]

---

1. *See, e.g.,* Tinker v. Des Moines Indep. Cmty. Sch. Dist., 393 U.S. 503, 509 (1969).
2. *See, e.g.,* Bethel Sch. Dist. v. Fraser, 478 U.S. 675 (1986); Hazelwood v. Kuhlmeier, 484 U.S. 260 (1988).
3. *See, e.g.,* Hazelwood v. Kuhlmeier, 484 U.S. 260 (1988); Lemon v. Kurtzman, 403 U.S. 602 (1971); Bd. of Regents of the Univ. of Wis. v. Southworth, 529 U.S. 217 (2000).

The Court tends to protect the free speech and free press rights of university students as an essential part of the educational experience. The university and, to a lesser degree, its faculty control the content of the curriculum. Otherwise, university policies and procedures generally must provide a neutral platform for broad student discussion of issues.[71] The Court has refused to grant university administrators "the same degree of deference" it grants to high school administrators to regulate student expression[72] because college students are "less impressionable than younger students"[73] and because the free speech rights of public school students are "not automatically coextensive with the rights of adults in other settings."[74] Although courts tend to defer to the expertise of school authorities to determine the proper boundaries of speech in the public school environment, they generally require universities to justify speech-intrusive rules.

Protest in the Schools

In 1969, the Court reviewed a case involving symbolic antiwar protest and issued its foundational decision establishing the school classroom as a location that is "peculiarly the marketplace of ideas." The case of *Tinker v. Des Moines Independent Community School District*[75] began with junior and senior high school students silently wearing black armbands to school to protest the Vietnam War. The three students did not act out or disrupt classes, but the school suspended them

The Tinkers (Lorena, Paul and Mary Beth, left to right) speak with the press in 1969 after learning the U.S. Supreme Court upheld the youngsters' right to wear anti-war armbands in school.

for violating a new school policy prohibiting the wearing of black armbands, which was a common means of opposing the war. The students sued, claiming the suspensions violated their right to free speech.

In what has been called "the most important Supreme Court case in history protecting the constitutional rights of students,"[76] the Court in *Tinker* agreed with the students. The Court said the symbolic expression of the armbands was "akin to pure speech" and was protected under the First Amendment.[77] When novel or deviant issues are expressed, the First Amendment must weigh heavily in favor of the expression and against the bureaucratic urge to suppress, the Court said. Without evidence that the armbands disrupted education, the school lacked a sufficient justification for the rule. Officials could not suppress student expression simply to avoid unpleasantness or discomfort or because of some vague fear that disruption might occur. School administrators did not have authority to control the students' silent political expression unless that expression materially or substantially disrupted the school's educational activities, which it did not.[78]

In addition, the school's decision to ban only the armbands but not other potentially disruptive expressive symbols suggested that the administration was attempting to exclude disfavored viewpoints. This was patently unconstitutional, the Court said. Although school administrators have broad authority to establish rules of conduct, the Constitution prohibits them from limiting free speech to "only that which the State chooses to communicate."[79] The Constitution makes it "unmistakable" that individuals do not "shed their constitutional rights to freedom of speech or expression at the schoolhouse gate."[80]

For nearly four decades, the rule was clear: Only when protests inside or adjacent to the school during school hours disrupt school activities may they be punished. While the Supreme Court had upheld content-neutral regulations intended to prevent disruptive protests on school grounds during school hours,[81] the Court's ruling in *Morse v. Frederick* crafted a new standard for student speech law. In *Morse,* the Court held that the "substantial disruption" rule established in *Tinker* was not the only acceptable basis for restricting student speech.[82]

The case began when high school senior Joseph Frederick and several others displayed a 14-foot-long banner reading "Bong Hits 4 Jesus" during a school field trip to watch the Olympic torch pass through Juneau, Alaska. Frederick said he did it for a laugh and to get himself on TV. The school's principal, Deborah

Morse, apparently was not laughing when she told him to take the banner down. He refused. She tore down the sign and suspended him for 10 days for violating a school policy that banned the advocacy of illegal drug use. Frederick sued, alleging that the principal had violated his right to free speech. The district court sided with the principal, but the U.S. Court of Appeals for the Ninth Circuit reversed, ruling that school officials may not "punish and censor non-disruptive" speech by students at school-sponsored events simply because they object to the message.

In a 5–4 ruling, the Supreme Court again reversed. The Court held that school officials may prohibit messages that advocate illegal drug use without running afoul of the First Amendment. Writing for the majority, Chief Justice John Roberts confirmed that students do not lose their right to freedom of speech inside schools but said the freedom of student speech does not extend to speech that directly contravenes an important school anti-drug policy. The majority flatly rejected the dissent's contention that the case implicated political speech. Instead, the Court reasoned that the "special environment" and the educational mandate of the schools permitted officials to prohibit student speech that raises a "palpable" danger to established school policy. "The First Amendment does not require schools to tolerate at school events student expression that contributes to [the] dangers" of illegal drug use, Justice Roberts wrote for the majority.[83] In dissent, Justice John Paul Stevens argued that "the Court's ham-handed, categorical approach is deaf to the constitutional imperative to permit unfettered debate, even among high-school students."[84] He said it condoned content-based discrimination.

The decision granted school officials new latitude to sanction nondisruptive speech. Subsequent rulings from four U.S. Circuit courts further increase uncertainty about when the Supreme Court's ruling in *Tinker*[85] permits public schools to punish student off-campus speech via new media.

In the most recent of these, the Eighth Circuit ruled that a school could expel a Hannibal (Mo.) High School student for sending threatening text messages.[86] Then 10th grader Dylan J. Mardis sent off-campus instant messages to a friend saying "he wanted Hannibal to be known for something" and he wanted to kill at least five classmates. He told the friend he knew someone who had a .357 Magnum revolver. Mardis said he was joking, but school officials expelled him for the school year, police put him in juvenile detention, and he received a psychiatric evaluation. He later graduated from high school. He also sued, arguing that the school violated his First Amendment rights. The federal appeals court ruled that his online messages were sufficiently threatening and disruptive to warrant discipline because school officials have a paramount responsibility to protect students. However, the three-judge panel noted, "School officials cannot constitutionally reach out to discover, monitor, or punish [just] any type of out-of-school speech."[87]

The previous week, a decision from the Fourth Circuit held that a West Virginia high school could punish a student's off-campus, non-school-related speech via a MySpace group webpage because it harassed another student and substantially interfered with school functions.[88] The disruption at issue was the harassed student's decision to miss one day of school. The court said the First Amendment permits schools to punish speech that it is "reasonably foreseeable" would reach school and impact school functioning. This standard had been used by the U.S. Court of Appeals for the Second Circuit (which then included Judge Sonia Sotomayor).[89] In 2008, the Second Circuit upheld a Connecticut high school's punishment of a student for off-campus blog posts denigrating school officials and encouraging students to call an administrator and "piss her off." The court reasoned that such postings, which "foreseeably create[d] a risk of substantial disruption," were not entitled to First Amendment protection.

But in two decisions in 2010 and 2011, the Third Circuit held that neither middle nor high school students could be suspended for insulting online social media parodies of their principals even though the parodies likely were disruptive.[90] The court said that *Tinker* did not explicitly grant schools authority to punish vulgar speech that reached inside the schoolhouse gate.

Without deciding the "metaphysical question of where [the] speech occurred when [the student] used the Internet as the medium," the Third Circuit held in its more recent decision that the school had failed to establish a sufficiently close connection between the after-hours, off-campus speech and school functions. Although online communications may have moved the schoolhouse gate beyond the brick-and-mortar buildings, the court said schools carry a heavier burden to justify regulating off-campus speech. One legal observer argued that off-campus speech should not be subject to on-campus punishment even under the *Tinker* standard.[91] The U.S. Supreme Court declined to review any of these cases, and the death of the plaintiff in a case involving a university student's offensive Facebook posts means the much-awaited Supreme Court review of *Tatro v. University of Minnesota*[92] (discussed later) will not occur.[93]

Offensive or Inappropriate Content

Some 40 years ago, the Supreme Court said students' free speech rights prevented schools from removing books from the school library simply because someone might find them offensive.[94] On its own initiative, a school board in New York state removed 10 books from the school libraries contrary to the recommendation of a library review committee, which said the volumes were appropriate and educationally suitable. Some board members said the books, which they had not reviewed, were "objectionable," "anti-American, anti-Christian, anti-[Semitic], and just plain filthy."[95] Several students sued.

The Supreme Court said the book removal violated the First Amendment. Although schools must exercise oversight of curriculum to assure an age-appropriate, quality education for students, school authority does not extend to the summary removal of books from the school library simply to placate a few hypersensitive individuals. The Court distinguished between required classroom reading and optional readings available in the school's library for selection by individual students. If students are compelled to read a specific book, schools may exercise greater sensitivity and responsiveness. However, when—as in this case—students voluntarily choose to read particular books, the Court said that "access [to controversial materials] prepares students for active and effective participation in the pluralistic, often contentious society in which they will soon be adult members."[96]

The Court did not suggest, however, that public schools must purchase highly controversial books for inclusion in their libraries. Nor did it say schools cannot remove books for good reason. Rather, the Court said decisions to remove books must not be made "in a narrowly partisan or political manner."[97] Such decisions were more likely to be constitutional if they advanced a curricular purpose, responded to a real educational disruption and did not unduly limit or bias student access to ideas.

The issue of mandatory exposure to offensive speech in public schools reached the Court in *Bethel School District v. Fraser*.[98] In a speech nominating one of his classmates for student government, Matthew Fraser used rather clever metaphors for male sexual virility. Nearly 600 high school students, including some 14-year-olds, attended the required, school-sponsored assembly. The assistant principal said the speech violated a school policy forbidding profanity and obscenity that "materially and substantially interferes with the educational process." She suspended Fraser for three days and said he could not be a candidate for graduation speaker.

Fraser challenged the action as a violation of his First Amendment rights. On review, the Supreme Court affirmed the punishment. The Court said that when student speech occurs during a school-sponsored event, the student's liberty of speech may be curtailed to protect the school's educational purpose, especially when young students are in the audience. This was particularly true if the forum for the student speech suggested that the student were speaking for the school.

In *Fraser,* the Court said eliminating vulgarity and profanity from school events advanced the obligation of schools to "inculcate . . . habits and manners of civility."[99] Rather than view student First Amendment rights as paramount, the Court said it was "perfectly appropriate" for a school to impose student sanctions to disassociate the school from speech that threatened its core purpose.

A case involving students in the journalism class at Hazelwood East High School presented related issues. The class published a student newspaper, Spectrum, under the supervision of a faculty adviser who reviewed the content. The principal also reviewed each issue before publication, but school policy said students enjoyed freedom of "responsible" speech.

In 1983, the principal removed two pages of the newspaper that contained a story about teen pregnancy at Hazelwood and another about the impact of divorce on students at the school. Pregnant students and children of divorced parents were interviewed for the stories. The principal said the stories invaded the privacy of the students and their parents, contained material inappropriate for younger students in the school and were biased and poorly researched. Other stories that appeared on the same pages as the articles in question were also cut from the paper to expedite printing of the newspaper before the school year ended.

Student staffers challenged the removal as an unconstitutional violation of their freedom of speech and press. The trial court rejected their challenge, but the court of appeals sided with the students, saying the school could edit the newspaper's content only to avoid legal liability, not to advance grammatical, journalistic or social values.

In *Hazelwood v. Kuhlmeier,* the Supreme Court reversed and said school administrators, not student reporters and editors, have authority to determine the appropriate content of a school-sponsored student newspaper.[100] When a school creates and supervises a forum for student speech, such as a student assembly or a teacher-supervised student newspaper, the school endorses that speech and is not only permitted but required to control the content to achieve educational goals, the Court said.[101] Schools are not only free from any obligation to "promote particular student speech"[102] but must exercise their supervisory function to promote a positive educational environment in all "school-sponsored publications, theatrical productions and other expressive activities that students, parents and members of the public might reasonably perceive to bear the imprimatur of the school."[103] In a footnote, however, the Court made clear that the decision did not apply to the university student press.[104]

In 2012, a U.S. district court judge in Missouri required Camdenton High School to stop using an Internet filtering system that discriminated against websites that expressed pro-LGBT concepts and values.[105] "These filters are a new version of book-banning or pulling books off the shelf," a spokesperson for the American Library Association said. "The difference is, this is much more subtle and harder to identify."[106] The school's filter tagged anti-gay sites under "religion," which allowed access to sites such as People Can Change, an organization that counsels how to become heterosexual. It tagged pro-gay sites with "sex," the category used to block pornography, which prevented access to websites like the Gay-Straight Alliance Network and even the 2003 Supreme Court ruling protecting the constitutional privacy of gay adults.[107]

Compelled Orthodoxy

The U.S. Supreme Court has said, "The right to speak and the right to refrain from speaking are complementary components of the broader concept of individual freedom of mind."[108] Accordingly, government may not force citizens to express ideas with which they disagree.

More than 70 years ago, students who were Jehovah's Witnesses used this rationale to challenge a policy mandating the daily flag salute and pledge of allegiance in school as a violation of their religious beliefs. The Court agreed.[109] Despite the important role of public schools in teaching students civic values and responsibilities,[110] schools may not indoctrinate students into particular ideologies or silence teachers who wish to speak out on issues of public concern, the Court said.[111] Compulsory saluting of the American flag is unconstitutional because the requirement enables government to dictate a particular belief and a certain attitude of mind.[112]

"If there is any fixed star in our constitutional constellation," the Court wrote, "it is that no official, high or petty, can prescribe what shall be orthodox in politics, nationalism, religion or other matters of opinion or force citizens to confess by word or act their faith therein."[113] Unless schools demonstrate that failure to salute the flag (or to engage in other compelled speech) presents a grave threat to the functioning of the school, forced speech violates the students' First Amendment freedom of belief and association and "invade[s] the sphere of intellect and spirit" vital to self-expression and self-fulfillment.[114] The ban on most government-enforced slogans and indoctrination applies both inside and outside the schools.[115]

Campus Speech

The Supreme Court has established that universities have a greater obligation to create and maintain forums for broad public discussion than do the public schools. As mentioned in Chapter 2, when a university's funding "program [is] designed to facilitate private speech," the funding creates a public forum that prohibits government control of the content of the speech.[116] Consequently, neither the students who contribute the fees nor the university administrators who oversee their allocation may discriminate among student groups because of the ideas they express.[117] Public universities must fund all student groups on the basis of the same content-neutral policies.

Thus, the Supreme Court upheld a University of Wisconsin policy to use mandatory student fees to fund an array of student organizations, including organizations with political or ideological objectives opposed by some students who paid the fees. The Court said the fees established a public forum, and the university was obliged to support all student expression without consideration of content. Writing in concurrence, Justice David Souter said the power of school authorities "to limit expressive freedom of students . . . is confined to high schools, whose students and their schools' relation to them are different and at least arguably distinguishable from their counterparts in college education."[118]

Many years earlier in its per curiam decision in *Papish v. Board of Curators of the University of Missouri,* the U.S. Supreme Court established that "the mere dissemination of ideas—no matter how offensive to good taste—on a state university campus may not be shut off in the name alone of 'conventions of decency.'"[119] The Court said the university violated the First Amendment rights of 32-year-old journalism graduate student Barbara Papish when it expelled her for distributing a campus newspaper containing what university officials labeled "indecent speech." Papish had distributed an issue of the Free Press Underground that contained a political cartoon depicting policemen raping the Statue of Liberty and the Goddess of Justice, and an article under the title, "M—f— Acquitted."

The Court distinguished colleges from public schools and held that a university's "mission is well served if students have the means to engage in dynamic discussions of philosophical, religious, scientific, social and political subjects in their extracurricular campus life outside the lecture hall."[120] As a consequence,[121] public universities not only may but must support all messages without regard to content to enhance wide-open extracurricular debate and free speech interests.[122]

But the Court recently reshaped this concept when it ruled in *Christian Legal Society v. Martinez* that a California law school could deny funding and other benefits to an explicitly religious student group whose members were required to sign a statement of faith.[123] The Court said the law school's requirement that official student groups be open to "all comers" was a reasonable, viewpoint-neutral policy and advanced school interests in nondiscriminatory access for students. Through failure to recognize Christian Legal Society (CLS) status as an official student group, the university denied CLS the ability to maintain tables at university recruitment fairs, to send bulk e-mails to all registered law students or to post messages on law school bulletin boards—benefits that clearly implicate First Amendment rights. Yet Justice Ruth Bader Ginsburg argued for the majority that alternative, nonuniversity means of communication available to CLS "reduce[d] the importance of those [university] channels" as an essential means of reaching law school students and adequately protected the group's speech interests.[124] The decision blurred or erased the established distinction between adult and younger students by relying on *Tinker* and deferring to the judgment of law school administrators "in light of the special characteristics of the school environment."[125]

In dissent, Justice Samuel Alito wrote that the decision meant that there is "no freedom for expression that offends prevailing standards of political correctness in our country's institutions of higher learning."[126]

Despite the fact that student fees, or even university allocations, support student newspapers and yearbooks, the Supreme Court generally has viewed campus publications as forums for student expression in which universities may not control content. "Colleges and universities are supposed to be bastions of unbridled inquiry and expression," as one writer put it, "but they probably do as much to repress speech as any other institution in young people's lives."[127] The author referenced a recent study that found that only about one-third of students and fewer than one in five faculty members strongly agreed that it is "safe to hold unpopular positions on campus."

Two recent cases suggest the range of problems facing college speakers and publications. In a widely watched decision, the Minnesota Supreme Court ruled in favor of the University of Minnesota's sanctions of the "satirical commentary and violent fantasy" about a school cadaver posted on Facebook by a student. Amanda Tatro, then enrolled in an anatomy lab in the university's mortuary science program, signed a mandatory course agreement that prohibited blogging and limited students to "respectful and discreet" comments about cadavers. The penalty for violation was "eviction" from the course.

Tatro was sent to the Campus Committee on Student Behavior after she posted Facebook comments that referred to a cadaver as "Bernie" (the title character in a 1989 comedy film), said she liked working with cadavers because it provided opportunity for "lots of aggression to be taken out" with an embalming tool and said she wanted to "stab a certain someone in the throat" with the embalming knife. At the committee's direction, Tatro received an F in the lab,

realWorld Law

Is Shouting Always "Shouting Fire"?

Nearly a dozen members of a Muslim student association at the University of California, Irvine, were arrested after they disrupted a speech by shouting repeatedly, so the audience could not hear Israeli Ambassador to the United States Michael Oren's comments. One person after another would shout until escorted out of the auditorium. Afterward, some argued that members of the "Irvine 11" were simply exercising their own right to speak. Others said the students should be expelled from the university.

"Both of these views are wrong," legal scholar and professor Erwin Chemerinsky said.[1] "Freedom of speech never has been regarded as an absolute right to speak out at any time and in any manner." There is no right to falsely shout "Fire" in a crowded theater.

Although the students did not shout falsehoods or incite panic, Professor Chemerinsky argued that "the government, including public universities, always can impose time, place and manner restrictions on speech." The offense did not rise to a level justifying expulsion, but the government can and should protect a speaker's rights by preventing a heckler's veto that effectively silences the speaker.

In 2011, Muslim students from the University of California, Irvine, hear the jury announce their convictions for illegally disrupting the Israeli ambassador's campus speech the previous year.

1. Erwin Chemerinsky, *UC Irvine's Free Speech Debate*, L.A. Times, Feb. 18, 2010, *available at* http://articles.latimes.com/2010/feb/18/opinion/la-oe-chemerinsky18–2010feb18/2.

was required to have an ethics class and a psychiatric evaluation and was placed on probation for the remainder of her undergraduate program. Tatro sued and later appealed to the Minnesota Supreme Court, arguing that the sanctions violated her freedom of speech, which she said were "the same . . . as members of the general public."[128] The university countered that it should be permitted to regulate any student speech "reasonably related to legitimate pedagogical concerns."

The court disagreed with both but upheld the university's sanctions. It reasoned that although the university could "constitutionally regulate off-campus conduct that violate[s] specific professional obligations," it could not "regulate a student's personal expression at any time, in any place, for any claimed curriculum-based reason" or "reach into a university student's personal life outside of and unrelated" to professional school programs.[129] The court found no precedent for its decision either in *Tinker*, which it said applied only when speech caused actual disruptions on campus,[130] or in *Hazelwood*, which it limited to school-sponsored rather than private speech.[131] Instead, it focused on the breadth of the university's professed ability to regulate student speech and limited that power to narrowly tailored restrictions "directly related" to speech "that violates established professional conduct standards" and is widely distributed to thousands via Facebook posts. Emphasizing the narrowness of its ruling and the uniqueness of the facts of the case, the court upheld the university's punishment of Tatro's speech as falling within this narrow regulatory capacity. Tatro died in 2012 at age 31, only weeks after the court ruling.

In another 2012 decision, the U.S. Court of Appeals for the Ninth Circuit ruled that Oregon State University (OSU) violated the First Amendment by allowing the removal from campus of distribution boxes for a conservative student newspaper.[132] The case involved Liberty, an independent conservative newspaper published by the OSU Student Alliance and distributed across campus via newspaper boxes. Under a new unwritten policy to clean up campus by limiting the location of distribution boxes for "off-campus" publications, university employees removed all of Liberty's outdoor distribution boxes. They did not remove the boxes for national papers, such as U.S.A. Today.

The editors and publishers of Liberty sued. In reaching its decision, the Ninth Circuit held that written policy designated most of the OSU campus a public forum and, therefore, university constraints on free speech on campus were subject to the most stringent scrutiny. The court concluded that OSU had used a "standardless policy" to arbitrarily deprive the newspaper of its ability to circulate in a public forum, which is expressive conduct protected by the First Amendment. The court reasoned that university officials purposefully engaged in content discrimination when they denied Liberty editors' requests to allow them to replace the boxes in high traffic areas adjacent to other publications. Although the university officials named in the suit did not personally remove the boxes, they "oversaw" and "knowingly acquiesced" in the action and, therefore, were liable, the court said. The sole dissenting judge argued that the ruling "muddles and obscures" clear precedent that officials "may not be held accountable for the misdeeds of their agents."

In an earlier highly publicized case, the U.S. Court of Appeals for the Sixth Circuit said Kentucky State University could not constitutionally refuse to distribute the student yearbook because of content and aesthetic concerns.[133] The court said the yearbook constituted a limited public forum that must be free from university censorship. The court said the university had neither the need nor the authority to control the content of speech in this student publication.

Despite the Supreme Court's clear signals, a ruling that establishes precedent only in the Seventh Circuit applied *Hazelwood* to a university publication to allow administrators to review school-sponsored publications before they are printed and distributed.[134] The case began when the dean of student affairs at Governors State University, a public college, said she would have to approve each issue of the student newspaper before it could be published. Three students sued, claiming the dean and other administrators violated their First Amendment rights. The U.S. Court of Appeals for the Seventh Circuit rejected that claim, saying that *Hazelwood* established that administrators may edit student newspapers that are not designated a public forum. The court said that even when, as in the case before it, the newspaper in question is neither part of the university's curriculum nor published as part of a class, the Constitution does not require a university to financially support publication of views its administrators reject.

Some university administrators also continue to try to influence the content of student media by pressuring faculty or staff advisers. In an example from 2012, the top editors of the University of Georgia's student newspaper resigned en masse, claiming nonstudent managers hired to oversee The Red and Black had

A crowd gathers for a press conference in Athens, Ga., following the 2012 walkout of staff from the University of Georgia's student newspaper.

interfered with their editorial autonomy.[135] One editor said the newly hired managers of the independent student paper had veto power on editorial content and had pressured editors to assign "grip-and-grin" photos and positive fluff stories. The student staff also obtained a copy of a memo on content guidelines circulated among the paper's publishing board that questioned the journalistic value of "content that catches people or organizations doing bad things." Within days of the walkout, the university reiterated its support of student control of content and reinstated the student editors.[136]

In a previous fight over content of a university student newspaper, a federal district court reversed itself to rule that the First Amendment did not prohibit Kansas State University from removing and reassigning the adviser of the Collegian.[137] The adviser was dismissed amid controversy over the newspaper's coverage of campus diversity issues and events, both court records and published reports show.[138] Complaints surfaced and adviser Ron Johnson was reassigned after the newspaper failed to cover the university-hosted annual Big 12 Conference on Black Student Government.[139] The Collegian's editors joined Johnson's lawsuit, claiming that the removal amounted to censorship. Although a letter from the head of the journalism school and university's publications said a content analysis of the newspaper supported the adviser's removal,[140] university administrators and members of the student publications board said budget concerns drove the decision.[141] The Society of Professional Journalists and the Student Press Law Center both officially condemned Johnson's removal, criticized administrators who recommended the move and urged the university to reinstate the former newspaper adviser.[142]

Speech Codes

In what some called a concession to political correctness[143] and others saw as an important step toward a more tolerant and inclusive society,[144] universities across the United States began adopting and strengthening campus speech codes in the 1980s.[145] The codes varied widely but generally prohibited verbal harassment of minorities, hate-filled invective, bigotry and offensive speech on campus. Courts consistently and resoundingly found these codes unconstitutional because they targeted disfavored speech and reduced the flow of information and ideas.[146] As one federal district court wrote, "The Supreme Court has consistently held that statutes punishing speech or conduct solely on the grounds that they are unseemly or offensive are unconstitutionally overbroad."[147]

Yet campus hate speech codes continue to be adopted.[148] One recent study found that although restrictions are declining, nearly 60 percent of the 400 universities examined maintained policies that "seriously infringe upon the free speech rights of students."[149] The universities argue that the codes are essential to the protection of informed discourse and serve the core educational mission of universities. Courts have not accepted the notion that limiting hateful speech enhances the diversity of ideas discussed in the university environment.

realWorld Law

A Conservative Take on Campus Speech?

Even before the Supreme Court's 2010 ruling in *Christian Legal Society v. Martinez,* observers argued that the Roberts Court has "moved the law sharply to the right on a number of constitutional fronts" and "limited free speech in ways that could adversely affect higher education."[1] They expressed concern over the Supreme Court's 5–4 decision in *Morse v. Frederick* that affirmed the power of high school administrators to discipline an 18-year-old's "Bong Hits 4 Jesus" sign.[2] The Court said the school's need "to protect those entrusted to their care from . . . celebrating illegal drug use" outweighed the student's right to nondisruptively display a sign at an off-campus school-sponsored event. They also decried the Court's decision that a university's freedoms of association and speech were not touched by rules requiring it to open campus to U.S. military recruiters who discriminated on the basis of sexual orientation.[3] Recruitment is conduct, not speech, the Court said.

By extension, these decisions "support punishing student speech that conflicts with important institutional values . . . and punishing the university itself if it fails to comply with external commands regarding the conduct of its auxiliary activities," one legal scholar warned.[4]

1. *See* David Kairys, *Searching for the Rule of Law,* 36 Suffolk U.L. Rev. 307, 325 (2003); Mark C. Rahdert, *Point of View: The Roberts Court and Academic Freedom,* Chron. Higher educ., July 27, 2007, *available at* http://chronicle.com/forums/index.
2. 551 U.S. 393 (2007).
3. 547 U.S. 47 (2006).
4. Rahdert, *supra* note 1.

SUMMARY

SUPREME COURT PRECEDENTS ESTABLISHING the constitutional limits to regulation of threats and objectionable speech inside schools and universities draw fine distinctions and turn on specific facts. Case outcomes hinge on statutory language, the intensity of the threat or offense and the societal interest involved. Few bright lines or broad precedents exist in this evolving area of First Amendment law. Government generally may curb the language reaching schoolchildren to advance educational goals, but universities have a greater obligation to afford forums for wide-ranging expression of opinion on campus. ∎

Cases for Study

Thinking About It

The two case excerpts that follow highlight the Supreme Court's attempts to balance the First Amendment freedom of speech with concerns for personal safety and educational goals. Both cases help identify the parameters of First Amendment protection: The first helps define when actions have sufficient expressive content and intent that they warrant constitutional protection; the second clarifies the extent to which important competing values—in this case, education of the young—may limit the freedom of speakers.

- Consider what each decision, as well as the two taken together, demonstrate about the different categories of speech in the Court's jurisprudence.

- In these two decisions defining the extent of First Amendment freedoms, does the Court focus on the nature of the speech, the intent of the law, the impact of the regulation or on something else to reach its conclusion?

- Does *Texas v. Johnson* provide a workable definition of symbolic speech and a clear test to determine when it is protected under the First Amendment?

- To what extent does the Court's decision in *Tinker* turn on the category of speech, the type of speaker, the location of speech or other factors involved?

Texas v. Johnson
SUPREME COURT OF THE UNITED STATES
491 U.S. 397 (1989)

JUSTICE WILLIAM BRENNAN delivered the Court's opinion:

. . . The First Amendment literally forbids the abridgment only of "speech," but we have long . . . acknowledged that conduct may be "sufficiently imbued with elements of communication to fall within the scope of the First and Fourteenth Amendments" . . . [when] "[a]n intent to convey a particularized message was present, and [whether] the likelihood was great that the message would be understood by those who viewed it." . . .

. . . Johnson burned an American flag as part—indeed, as the culmination—of a political demonstration. . . . The expressive, overtly political nature of this conduct was both intentional and overwhelmingly apparent. . . .

The government generally has a freer hand in restricting expressive conduct than it has in restricting the written or spoken word. . . .

[However,] the governmental interest in question [must] be unconnected to expression in order to come under *O'Brien*'s less demanding rule. . . .

. . . The State, apparently, is concerned that [flag desecration] will lead people to believe either that the flag does not stand for nationhood and national unity, but instead reflects other, less positive concepts, or that the concepts reflected in the flag do not in fact exist, that is, that we do not enjoy unity as a Nation. These concerns blossom only when a person's treatment of the flag communicates some message, and thus are related "to the suppression of free expression." . . .

. . . Johnson was not, we add, prosecuted for the expression of just any idea; he was prosecuted for his expression of dissatisfaction with the policies of this country, expression situated at the core of our First Amendment values.

Moreover, Johnson was prosecuted because he knew that his politically charged expression would cause "serious offense." . . . The Texas law is thus not aimed at protecting the physical integrity of the flag in all circumstances, but is designed instead to protect it only against impairments that would cause serious offense to others. . . .

. . . Johnson's political expression was restricted because of the content of the message he conveyed. We must therefore subject the State's asserted interest in preserving the special symbolic character of the flag to "the most exacting scrutiny." . . .

If there is a bedrock principle underlying the First Amendment, it is that the government may not prohibit the expression of an idea simply because society finds the idea itself offensive or disagreeable.

We have not recognized an exception to this principle even where our flag has been involved. . . .

. . . [N]othing in our precedents suggests that a State may foster its own view of the flag by prohibiting expressive conduct relating to it. . . .

. . . [T]heir enduring lesson, that the government may not prohibit expression simply because it disagrees with its message, is not dependent on the particular mode in which one chooses to express an idea. If we were to hold that a State may forbid flag burning wherever it is likely to endanger the flag's symbolic role, but allow it wherever burning a flag promotes that role . . . [w]e would be permitting a State to "prescribe what shall be orthodox" by saying that one may burn the flag to convey one's attitude toward it and its referents only if one does not endanger the flag's representation of nationhood and national unity. . . .

There is, moreover, no indication—either in the text of the Constitution or in our cases interpreting it—that a separate juridical category exists for the American flag alone. Indeed, we would not be surprised to learn that the persons who framed our Constitution and wrote the Amendment that we now construe were not known for their reverence for the Union Jack. The First Amendment does not guarantee that other concepts virtually sacred to our Nation as a whole—such as the principle that discrimination on the basis of race is odious and destructive—will go unquestioned in the marketplace of ideas. We decline, therefore, to create for the flag an exception to the joust of principles protected by the First Amendment.

. . . We are tempted to say, in fact, that the flag's deservedly cherished place in our community will be strengthened, not weakened, by our holding today. Our decision is a reaffirmation of the principles of freedom and inclusiveness that the flag best reflects, and of the conviction that our toleration of criticism such as Johnson's is a sign and source of our strength. . . . It is the Nation's resilience, not its rigidity, that Texas sees reflected in the flag—and it is that resilience that we reassert today.

The way to preserve the flag's special role is not to punish those who feel differently about these matters. It is to persuade them that they are wrong. . . .

. . . We do not consecrate the flag by punishing its desecration, for in doing so we dilute the freedom that this cherished emblem represents. . . . Affirmed.

JUSTICE ANTHONY KENNEDY, concurring:
. . . The hard fact is that sometimes we must make decisions we do not like. We make them because they are right, right in the sense that the law and the Constitution, as we see them, compel the result. And so great is our commitment to the process that, except in the rare case, we do not pause to express distaste for the result, perhaps for fear of undermining a valued principle that dictates the decision. This is one of those rare cases. . . .

. . . It is poignant but fundamental that the flag protects those who hold it in contempt. . . .

CHIEF JUSTICE WILLIAM REHNQUIST, with whom JUSTICE BYRON WHITE and JUSTICE SANDRA DAY O'CONNOR join, dissenting:
. . . The American flag, then, throughout more than 200 years of our history, has come to be the visible

symbol embodying our Nation. It does not represent the views of any particular political party, and it does not represent any particular political philosophy. The flag is not simply another "idea" or "point of view" competing for recognition in the marketplace of ideas. Millions and millions of Americans regard it with an almost mystical reverence regardless of what sort of social, political, or philosophical beliefs they may have. I cannot agree that the First Amendment invalidates the Act of Congress, and the laws of 48 of the 50 States, which make criminal the public burning of the flag. . . .

. . . As with "fighting words," so with flag burning, for purposes of the First Amendment: It is "no essential part of any exposition of ideas, and [is] of such slight social value as a step to truth that any benefit that may be derived from [it] is clearly outweighed" by the public interest in avoiding a probable breach of the peace. . . .

. . . The Texas statute deprived Johnson of only one rather inarticulate symbolic form of protest—a form of protest that was profoundly offensive to many—and left him with a full panoply of other symbols and every conceivable form of verbal expression to express his deep disapproval of national policy. Thus, in no way can it be said that Texas is punishing him because his hearers—or any other group of people—were profoundly opposed to the message that he sought to convey. Such opposition is no proper basis for restricting speech or expression under the First Amendment. It was Johnson's use of this particular symbol, and not the idea that he sought to convey by it or by his many other expressions, for which he was punished. . . .

. . . Surely one of the high purposes of a democratic society is to legislate against conduct that is regarded as evil and profoundly offensive to the majority of people—whether it be murder, embezzlement, pollution, or flag burning. . . .

. . . I would uphold the Texas statute as applied in this case.

JUSTICE JOHN PAUL STEVENS, dissenting:

. . . The value of the flag as a symbol cannot be measured. Even so, I have no doubt that the interest in preserving that value for the future is both significant and legitimate. . . . [S]anctioning the public desecration of the flag will tarnish its value—both for those who cherish the ideas for which it waves and for those who desire to don the robes of martyrdom by burning it. That tarnish is not justified by the trivial burden on free expression occasioned by requiring that an available, alternative mode of expression—including uttering words critical of the flag—be employed. . . .

The Court is . . . quite wrong in blandly asserting that respondent "was prosecuted for his expression of dissatisfaction with the policies of this country, expression situated at the core of our First Amendment values." Respondent was prosecuted because of the method he chose to express his dissatisfaction with those policies. Had he chosen to spray paint—or perhaps convey with a motion picture projector—his message of dissatisfaction on the facade of the Lincoln Memorial, there would be no question about the power of the Government to prohibit his means of expression. The prohibition would be supported by the legitimate interest in preserving the quality of an important national asset. Though the asset at stake in this case is intangible, given its unique value, the same interest supports a prohibition on the desecration of the American flag. . . .

I respectfully dissent.

Tinker v. Des Moines Independent Community School District
SUPREME COURT OF THE UNITED STATES
393 U.S. 503 (1969)

JUSTICE ABE FORTAS delivered the Court's opinion:

. . . The District Court recognized that the wearing of an armband for the purpose of expressing certain views is the type of symbolic act that is within the Free Speech Clause of the First Amendment. As we shall discuss, the wearing of armbands in the circumstances of this case was entirely divorced from actually or potentially disruptive conduct by those participating in it. It was closely akin to "pure speech" which, we have repeatedly held, is entitled to comprehensive protection under the First Amendment.

First Amendment rights, applied in light of the special characteristics of the school environment, are available to teachers and students. It can hardly be argued that either students or teachers shed their constitutional rights to freedom of speech or expression at the schoolhouse gate. This has been the unmistakable holding of this Court for almost 50 years. . . .

. . . On the other hand, the Court has repeatedly emphasized the need for affirming the comprehensive authority of the States and of school officials, consistent with fundamental constitutional safeguards, to prescribe and control conduct in the schools. . . . Our problem lies in the area where students in the exercise of First Amendment rights collide with the rules of the school authorities.

The problem posed by the present case . . . does not concern aggressive, disruptive action or even group demonstrations. Our problem involves direct, primary First Amendment rights akin to "pure speech."

The school officials banned and sought to punish petitioners for a silent, passive expression of opinion, unaccompanied by any disorder or disturbance on the part of petitioners. There is here no evidence whatever of petitioners' interference, actual or nascent, with the school's work or of collision with the rights of other students to be secure and to be let alone. Accordingly, this case does not concern speech or action that intrudes upon the work of the schools or the rights of other students. . . .

. . . Outside the classrooms, a few students made hostile remarks to the children wearing armbands, but there were no threats or acts of violence on school premises.

The District Court concluded that the action of the school authorities was reasonable because it was based upon their fear of a disturbance from the wearing of the armbands. But, in our system, undifferentiated fear or apprehension of disturbance is not enough to overcome the right to freedom of expression. Any departure from absolute regimentation may cause trouble. Any variation from the majority's opinion may inspire fear. Any word spoken, in class, in the lunchroom, or on the campus, that deviates from the views of another person may start an argument or cause a disturbance. But our Constitution says we must take this risk; and our history says that it is this sort of hazardous freedom—this kind of openness—that is the basis of our national strength and of the independence and vigor of Americans who grow up and live in this relatively permissive, often disputatious, society.

In order for the State in the person of school officials to justify prohibition of a particular expression of opinion, it must be able to show that its action was caused by something more than a mere desire to avoid the discomfort and unpleasantness that always accompany an unpopular viewpoint. Certainly where there is no finding and no showing that engaging in the forbidden conduct would "materially and substantially interfere with the requirements of appropriate discipline in the operation of the school," the prohibition cannot be sustained.

. . . [T]he record fails to yield evidence that the school authorities had reason to anticipate that the wearing of the armbands would substantially interfere with the work of the school or impinge upon the rights of other students. . . .

On the contrary, the action of the school authorities appears to have been based upon an urgent wish to avoid the controversy which might result from the expression, even by the silent symbol of armbands, of opposition to this Nation's part in the conflagration in Vietnam. It is revealing, in this respect, that the meeting at which the school principals decided to issue the contested regulation was called in response to a student's statement to the journalism teacher in one of the schools that he wanted to write an article on Vietnam and have it published in the school paper. (The student was dissuaded.)

It is also relevant that the school authorities did not purport to prohibit the wearing of all symbols of political or controversial significance. The record shows that students in some of the schools wore buttons relating to national political campaigns, and some even wore the Iron Cross, traditionally a symbol of Nazism. . . . Instead, a particular symbol—black armbands worn to exhibit opposition to this Nation's involvement in Vietnam—was singled out for prohibition. Clearly, the prohibition of expression of one particular opinion, at least without evidence that it is necessary to avoid material and substantial interference with schoolwork or discipline, is not constitutionally permissible.

In our system, state-operated schools may not be enclaves of totalitarianism. School officials do not possess absolute authority over their students. Students in school as well as out of school are "persons" under our Constitution. They are possessed of fundamental rights, which the State must respect, just as they themselves must respect their obligations to the State. In our system, students may not be regarded as closed-circuit recipients of only that which the State chooses to communicate. They may not be confined to the expression of those sentiments that are officially approved. In the absence of a specific showing of constitutionally valid reasons to regulate their speech, students are entitled to freedom of expression of their views. . . .

. . . A student's rights, therefore, do not embrace merely the classroom hours. When he is in the cafeteria, or on the playing field, or on the campus during the authorized hours, he may express his opinions, even on controversial subjects like the conflict in Vietnam, if he does so without "materially and substantially interfer[ing] with the requirements of appropriate discipline in the operation of the school" and without colliding with the rights of others. But conduct by the student, in class or out of it, which for any reason—whether it stems from time, place, or type of behavior—materially disrupts class work or involves substantial disorder or invasion of the rights of others is, of course, not immunized by the constitutional guarantee of freedom of speech.

Under our Constitution, free speech is not a right that is given only to be so circumscribed that it exists in principle but not in fact. Freedom of expression would not truly exist if the right could be exercised only in an area that a benevolent government has provided as a safe haven for crackpots. . . . [W]e do not confine the permissible exercise of First Amendment rights to a telephone booth or the four corners of a pamphlet, or to supervised and ordained discussion in a school classroom.

If a regulation were adopted by school officials forbidding discussion of the Vietnam conflict, or the expression by any student of opposition to it anywhere on school property except as part of a prescribed classroom exercise, it would be obvious that the regulation would violate the constitutional rights of students, at least if it could not be justified by a showing that the students' activities would materially and substantially disrupt the work and discipline of the school. In the circumstances of the present case, the prohibition of the silent, passive "witness of the armbands," as one of the children called it, is no less offensive to the Constitution's guarantees. . . .

JUSTICE POTTER STEWART, concurring:
Although I agree with much of what is said in the Court's opinion, and with its judgment in this case, I cannot share the Court's uncritical assumption that, school discipline aside, the First Amendment rights of children are coextensive with those of adults. . . . I continue to hold the view [that] . . . [A] State may permissibly determine that, at least in some precisely delineated areas, a child—like someone in a captive audience—is not possessed of that full capacity for individual choice which is the presupposition of First Amendment guarantees.

JUSTICE BYRON WHITE, concurring:
While I join the Court's opinion, I deem it appropriate to note, first, that the Court continues to recognize a distinction between communicating by words and communicating by acts or conduct which sufficiently impinges on some valid state interest. . . .

JUSTICE HUGO BLACK, dissenting:
The Court's holding in this case ushers in what I deem to be an entirely new era in which the power to control pupils by the elected "officials of state supported public schools . . ." in the United States is in ultimate effect transferred to the Supreme Court. The Court brought this particular case here on a petition for certiorari urging that the First and Fourteenth Amendments protect the right of school pupils to express their political views all the way "from kindergarten through high school." Here, the constitutional right

to "political expression" asserted was a right to wear black armbands during school hours and at classes in order to demonstrate to the other students that the petitioners were mourning because of the death of United States soldiers in Vietnam and to protest that war which they were against. . . .

. . . [T]he crucial . . . questions are whether students and teachers may use the schools at their whim as a platform for the exercise of free speech—"symbolic" or "pure"—and whether the courts will allocate to themselves the function of deciding how the pupils' school day will be spent. While I have always believed that, under the First and Fourteenth Amendments, neither the State nor the Federal Government has any authority to regulate or censor the content of speech, I have never believed that any person has a right to give speeches or engage in demonstrations where he pleases and when he pleases. . . .

I think the record overwhelmingly shows that the armbands did exactly what the elected school officials and principals foresaw they would, that is, took the students' minds off their class work and diverted them to thoughts about the highly emotional subject of the Vietnam War. And I repeat that, if the time has come when pupils of state-supported schools, kindergartens, grammar schools, or high schools, can defy and flout orders of school officials to keep their minds on their own schoolwork, it is the beginning of a new revolutionary era of permissiveness in this country fostered by the judiciary. . . .

It may be that the Nation has outworn the old-fashioned slogan that "children are to be seen, not heard," but one may, I hope, be permitted to harbor the thought that taxpayers send children to school on the premise that at their age they need to learn, not teach. . . . Iowa's public schools . . . are operated to give students an opportunity to learn, not to talk politics by actual speech, or by "symbolic" speech. And,

as I have pointed out before, the record amply shows that public protest in the school classes against the Vietnam War "distracted from that singleness of purpose which the State [here Iowa] desired to exist in its public educational institutions." . . .

This case, therefore, wholly without constitutional reasons, in my judgment, subjects all the public schools in the country to the whims and caprices of their loudest-mouthed, but maybe not their brightest, students. I, for one, am not fully persuaded that school pupils are wise enough. . . . I wish, therefore, wholly to disclaim any purpose on my part to hold that the Federal Constitution compels the teachers, parents, and elected school officials to surrender control of the American public school system to public school students. I dissent.

JUSTICE JOHN HARLAN, dissenting:
I certainly agree that state public school authorities in the discharge of their responsibilities are not wholly exempt from the requirements of the Fourteenth Amendment respecting the freedoms of expression and association. At the same time I am reluctant to believe that there is any disagreement between the majority and myself on the proposition that school officials should be accorded the widest authority in maintaining discipline and good order in their institutions. To translate that proposition into a workable constitutional rule, I would, in cases like this, cast upon those complaining the burden of showing that a particular school measure was motivated by other than legitimate school concerns—for example, a desire to prohibit the expression of an unpopular point of view, while permitting expression of the dominant opinion.

Finding nothing in this record which impugns the good faith of respondents in promulgating the armband regulation, I would affirm the judgment below.

Chapter 4

[D]ebate on public issues should be uninhibited, robust, and wide open, and [ ] it may well include vehement, caustic, and sometimes unpleasantly sharp attacks on government and public officials. . . . [E]rroneous statement is inevitable in free debate, and [ ] it must be protected if the freedoms of expression are to have the breathing space that they need to survive.

U.S. Supreme Court Justice William Brennan[1]

Montgomery, Ala., police commissioner L.B. Sullivan (second from right) celebrates with his attorneys after an Alabama jury found in his favor in his libel lawsuit against The New York Times. The verdict would eventually be appealed to the U.S. Supreme Court, resulting in a landmark case on libel law.

Libel
The Plaintiff's Case

A Brief History

Contemporary Issues

**The Elements of Libel:
The Plaintiff's Case**

Statement of Fact
Publication
Identification
Defamation
Falsity
Fault
Actual Malice
Damages

Cases for Study

➤ *New York Times Co. v.
  Sullivan*
➤ *Gertz v. Robert Welch,
  Inc.*

Suppose . . .

. . . that a civil rights group buys space in a major national newspaper. Within its full-page editorial, attention is called to the plight of many individuals who are engaged in nonviolent demonstrations. Some recent events are described. The overall thrust of the text is accurate, but it also contains some minor errors. In addition, it is critical of how some public officials—police officers, in particular—handled one demonstration. Several public officials, including the police commissioner, believe this piece has damaged their reputations; they sue for defamation. Especially given the false statements contained in the text, should the plaintiffs be able to win their lawsuit? Should it make any difference that they are public officials? Look for the answers to these questions when the case of *New York Times Co. v. Sullivan* is discussed later in this chapter and in an excerpt at the end of this chapter.

Libel law is meant to protect an individual's reputation. It allows a person who believes his or her reputation has been injured to file a claim against the party responsible, asking for damages in an effort to obtain monetary compensation and to restore his or her reputation.

The idea that a person's reputation is something of value that is worth protecting is a centuries-old concept. Throughout the course of Western civilization, reputation has been closely associated with one's ability to participate in a community's social and economic life.[2] It is a concept rooted in civilized society. Former Chief Justice William Rehnquist said, "The right of a man to the protection of his own reputation from unjustified invasion and wrongful hurt reflects no more than our basic concept of the essential dignity and worth of every human being—a concept at the root of any decent system of ordered liberty."[3]

As stated by the U.S. Supreme Court, the common law of slander and libel is designed to achieve society's "pervasive and strong interest in preventing and redressing attacks upon reputation."[4] The challenge becomes "balanc[ing] the State's interest in compensating private individuals for injury to their reputation against the First Amendment interest in protecting this type of expression."[5]

Of course, one who damages an individual's reputation through the spoken or written word has not necessarily committed libel. One important consideration is truth. Should one who makes a truthful statement that happens to damage a person's reputation be subject to penalty under the law? There was a time when truthful statements that damaged reputation were seen as serious violations of the law. That is no longer the case.

The word "defamation" refers generally to false communications about another person that damage that person's reputation or bring her into disrepute. Both slander and libel are forms of defamation. The general purpose of libel laws is to allow people who have been defamed to restore their reputations. Libel laws also serve as a deterrent to prevent similar defamations in the future. When a successful plaintiff—the party initiating the lawsuit—is awarded damages, three objectives are served: The plaintiff is compensated for his or her reputational and other losses, the defendant is punished, and the defendant and others are discouraged from committing the same kind of libelous conduct in the future. Thus, a societal benefit may result, particularly if as much attention is given to setting the record straight as was given to the reputation-damaging remarks.

Points of Law

Slander vs. Libel

Historically, "slander" has been associated with spoken words that damage reputation and "libel" with written defamation. The laws governing each were similar but distinct, with the damages awarded for libel usually being higher than for slander. The idea was that a written communication likely caused more harm because it lasted longer and its audience was larger. But with the development of mass communication technology, that distinction has been blurred. Defamatory motion picture content may be grounds for a libel suit. Defamatory content in broadcasting is deemed libel in most states, slander in some others. Some states say that if broadcast defamation is from scripted (i.e., written) material, it is libel. Otherwise, it is slander.

Why does it matter? What the plaintiff must prove to win his or her case may vary depending on whether the defamation is categorized as slander or libel. Perhaps more than anything, however, the distinction is simply a leftover from another time.

A Brief History

Western civilization's earliest recorded prosecution for reputation-damaging remarks is arguably the trial and execution of Socrates in 399 BCE. In response to charges of slandering Greek gods and corrupting the youth of Athens, the philosopher was brought before a Heliastic court (a public court unique to ancient Athens). He admitted his "slanderous" teachings and, by a vote of 277 to 224, was found guilty. Socrates accepted his execution to dramatize the primacy of the life of the mind and the need for freedom of thought.[6]

Although ancient Greece may have contributed to the development of libel law in Western societies, it is the English common law—itself a descendant of Roman law—where American libel law finds its most significant roots. In a general sense, English defamation law tells us slander is a false accusation that results in the humiliation of its victims. The law tries to suppress such language, "which is seen to pose various threats to the social order."[7]

Many people believe that laws against defamation help to maintain the status quo, particularly when libel laws are enforced to punish criticism of those in positions of power.[8] Consequently, the development of libel law depends a great deal on the social and political forces at play in a given historical period.

In 15th-century England, complaints against defamation were heard in one of two courts: the court of common law or the infamous court of the Star Chamber. In the early 1600s, the court of the Star Chamber declared libel a criminal offense because it tended to cause breach of the peace. If the libel was "against a magistrate, or other public person, it [was] a greater offence."[9] The court of the Star Chamber tended to view written defamation as a more serious offense than the spoken version. Penalties for defamation included the possibility that the defamer "may be punished by fine and imprisonment, and if the case be exorbitant, by pillory and loss of his ears."[10] To the dismay of very few English citizens, the Star Chamber was disbanded in 1641, and common law courts resumed their jurisdiction over defamation cases. It was not until about 1660 that the common law courts consistently began to distinguish between libel and slander.[11]

Libel

The word "libel" comes from the Latin *libellus,* or "little book." The legal term derives from the practice in ancient Rome of publishing little books or booklets that one Roman used to defame another. The history of valuing and protecting reputation is centuries old.

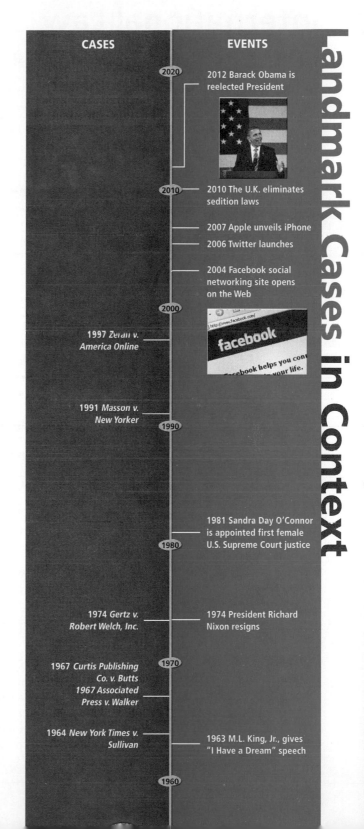

Landmark Cases in Context

CASES

EVENTS

- 2012 Barack Obama is reelected President
- 2020
- 2010 The U.K. eliminates sedition laws
- 2010
- 2007 Apple unveils iPhone
- 2006 Twitter launches
- 2004 Facebook social networking site opens on the Web
- 2000
- 1997 Zeran v. America Online
- 1991 Masson v. New Yorker
- 1990
- 1981 Sandra Day O'Connor is appointed first female U.S. Supreme Court justice
- 1980
- 1974 Gertz v. Robert Welch, Inc.
- 1974 President Richard Nixon resigns
- 1970
- 1967 Curtis Publishing Co. v. Butts
- 1967 Associated Press v. Walker
- 1964 New York Times v. Sullivan
- 1963 M.L. King, Jr., gives "I Have a Dream" speech
- 1960

International Law

The U.K. Abolishes Seditious Libel, Colorado Repeals Criminal Libel Law

United Kingdom Ministry of Justice headquarters

After years of pressure from free speech advocates, in 2009 the Ministry of Justice in the United Kingdom abolished the common law offenses of sedition, seditious libel, defamatory libel and obscene libel. Section 73 of the Coroners and Justice 2009 took effect in 2010 and eliminated the laws that dated back to 1275. U.K. sedition laws made it a criminal offense to criticize the monarch or the government. Courts could punish sedition and seditious libel offenses with unlimited fines or imprisonment. Defamatory libel is a criminal counterpart to civil libel.

"Abolishing these offenses will allow the U.K. to take a lead in challenging similar laws in other countries where they are used to suppress free speech," said U.K. Justice Minister Claire Ward.[1]

Human rights group Article 19 noted that the shift in U.K. law "will send a very strong and clear signal globally that democracies do not have criminal defamation laws."[2]

In the United States, while seditious libel is an historical artifact, some states do have criminal libel statues. Those guilty of criminal libel can be fined or jailed just as those guilty of most crimes. They are rarely enforced. In 2012, the Colorado legislature repealed its 100-year-old criminal libel statute after it became the subject of extensive litigation. A University of Northern Colorado college student was threatened under the statute after he published a derogatory, web-based satire of one of his professors.[3]

Criminal libel laws in the United States are subject to the same constitutional requirements as their civil counterparts discussed in this chapter. However, in criminal libel suits, the burden of proof is higher and the alleged libel must be proven beyond a reasonable doubt rather than a preponderance of the evidence.

1. *PA Media Lawyer, Criminal Libel and Sedition Offences Abolished,* Press Gazette, Jan. 13, 2010, *available at* http://www.pressgazette.co.uk/node/44884.
2. Afua Hirsch, *House of Lords to Back Libel Law Changes,* Guardian (London), Oct. 25, 2009, *available at* http://www.guardian.co.uk/uk/2009/oct/25/house-of-lords-libel-laws.
3. Mink v. Knox, 613 F.3d 995 (10th Cir. 2010).

As noted in Chapter 1, the role of Sir William Blackstone and his "Commentaries on the Law of England" played a major role in the development of law in the United States. Libel law is no exception. Punishment for defamation, Blackstone believed, was not inconsistent with the concept of freedom of the press. A free press, he wrote, "consists in laying no previous restraints upon publications, and not in freedom from censure for criminal matter when published."[12] Anyone can express his sentiments to the public, he added, "but if he publishes what is improper, mischievous, or illegal, he must take the consequences of his own temerity."[13]

Those consequences were to take the form of monetary **damages** sought by a plaintiff in compensation for a tarnished reputation. As a chief justice of the United States later described its evolution, "Defamation law developed not only as a means of allowing an individual to vindicate his good name, but also for the purpose of obtaining redress for harm caused by such statements. As the common law developed in this country, apart from the issue of damages, one usually needed only allege an unprivileged publication of false and defamatory matter to state a cause of action for defamation."[14]

That legal principle was brought to the American colonies and later followed in the states after independence. But England also provided America with legal theories that were less desirable in a republic committed to individual freedoms. Among them was the concept of **seditious libel**. At various times throughout American history the authorities have been especially sensitive to criticism of the government. In response, laws have been passed criminalizing such expression. One of those eras was the post–Revolutionary War period. The **Sedition Act of 1798** made it a crime to write "any false, scandalous and malicious" statements against either the president or Congress.[15] While the act permitted a defendant to escape penalty by proving the truth of the writing, and juries were permitted to decide critical questions of law and fact, there was no doubt that it was intended to silence critics of the entrenched political powers.

Echoing Blackstone, John Marshall—a public official of the same era who would become Chief Justice of the United States—defended the Sedition Act as being consistent with the First Amendment because it did not impose a prior restraint.[16] "It is known to all," he wrote, that those who publish libels or who "libel the government of the state" may "be both sued and indicted."[17] Among the act's opponents was James Madison, the principal author of the First Amendment, who said, "It would seem a mockery to say that no laws should be passed preventing publications from being made, but that laws might be passed punishing them in case they should be made."[18] Madison and his supporters ultimately prevailed, with the act expiring in 1801.

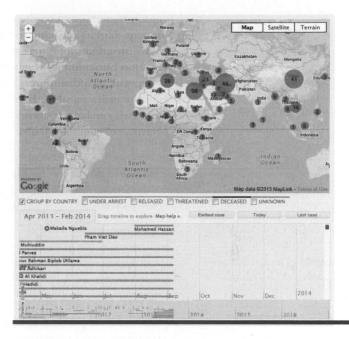

Threatened Voices and Google Maps track suppression of online free speech across the globe. In some cases, citizens and journalists who take to social media or blogs to express their political opinions are arrested and charged with seditious libel by governments who hope to silence them. The larger the dot on the map, the greater the number of censorship cases (although not all cases involve accusations of seditious libel).

damages Monetary compensation that may be recovered in court by any person who has suffered loss or injury. Damages may be compensatory for actual loss or punitive as punishment for outrageous conduct.

Sedition Act of 1798 Federal legislation under which anyone "opposing or resisting any law of the United States, or any act of the President of the United States" could be imprisoned for up to two years. The act also made it illegal to "write, print, utter, or publish" anything that criticized the president or Congress. The act ultimately was seen as a direct violation of the First Amendment and expired in 1801.

The Star Chamber

The court of the Star Chamber evolved from the meetings of the king's royal council. It was established in 1487 and was named after the star painted on the ceiling of the room in which it met. Over time, its powers expanded to include issues of public disorder, land disputes and sedition against royal policies. It was disbanded in 1641 by Parliament, though its name survives still to designate arbitrary, secretive proceedings in opposition to personal rights and liberty.

SLAPP (strategic lawsuits against public participation) Lawsuits whose purpose is to harass critics into silence, often to suppress those critics' First Amendment rights.

Points of Law

States with Anti-SLAPP Protection

Arizona	Nebraska
Arkansas	Nevada
California	New Mexico
Colorado	New York
Delaware	Oklahoma
Florida	Oregon
Georgia	Pennsylvania
Hawaii	Rhode Island
Illinois	Tennessee
Indiana	Texas
Louisiana	Utah
Maine	Vermont
Maryland	Washington
Massachusetts	West Virginia
Minnesota	(+Washington, D.C.)
Missouri	

In tracts opposing the Sedition Act, one finds the earliest musings on the notion of the "chilling effect," a form of prior restraint that recognizes that laws punishing behavior after it takes place will also likely deter, or chill, that behavior from occurring in the first place. While it is certainly desirable to deter people from committing crimes, discouraging relatively innocuous activities like speaking and writing because of the threat of a libel lawsuit threatens to make speakers and writers less inclined to communicate in the first place. Many people believe that is itself an infringement on the freedom of expression guaranteed by the First Amendment.

Chilling speech is precisely the goal of some defamation lawsuits. In those cases libel law is used not as a shield against threatened harms or as a means of correcting them, but as a weapon to prevent speech from occurring in the first place. These are called **SLAPP (strategic lawsuits against public participation)** suits.[19] They are meant to silence critics. The plaintiffs who file them are sometimes under investigation for possible wrongdoing or people whose questionable business motives are being probed. Plaintiffs rarely win these cases. Instead, their purpose is to harass their critics into silence. Noting that SLAPPs are often used to suppress a party's First Amendment rights, some states have enacted anti-SLAPP legislation.[20] The constitutionality of these laws has been upheld. Twenty-eight states, the District of Columbia and one U.S. territory (Guam) have enacted anti-SLAPP statutes. In Colorado and West Virginia, courts recognize anti-SLAPP protections as a matter of case law. In 2012, Michigan and North Carolina introduced anti-SLAPP legislation.

As an example, in June 2010 a strengthened anti-SLAPP law took effect in the state of Washington. The enhanced law covered more kinds of speech and allowed judges to dismiss meritless lawsuits quickly and to award attorney's fees in cases that had been dismissed. A Seattle attorney who helped draft the new law said that after three decades of defamation defense, "I was tired of defending meritless libel lawsuits, and then telling clients that they had no basis for getting reimbursed for the expenses incurred in getting rid of the case."[21] Anti-SLAPP laws can address meritless claims of all kinds, not just libel.

State courts are considering new anti-SLAPP statutes as they emerge. Recently, the Illinois Supreme Court narrowed the application of that state's anti-SLAPP law. The court placed a substantial burden on defendants who seek to dismiss a case when it held that the law was not intended to give absolute immunity for defamation and applied only

Emerging Law

Time for a Federal Anti-SLAPP Law?

As more states adopted or considered enacting laws to protect against SLAPP suits, called anti-SLAPP statutes, Congress considered a federal anti-SLAPP bill. Arizona Sen. John Kyl introduced the Free Press Act of 2012 with the purpose of protecting the First Amendment rights of journalists and Internet Service Providers (ISPs). It would allow them to file a special motion to dismiss a SLAPP lawsuit if "the claim arises in whole or in part from . . . expression that is on a matter of public concern or that relates to a public official or figure."[1] The bill would not apply to SLAPP suits filed by the federal government or state attorneys general, or to commercial speech claims.

Organizations such as the Reporter's Committee for Freedom of the Press (RCFP) support anti-SLAPP efforts and have published a guide (available on the RCFP.org website) to help journalists on the receiving end of a SLAPP suit. RCFP's legal defense director told the First Amendment Center, "We have long been a supporter of this effort to enact a federal anti-SLAPP law. Reporters—and particularly the newer breed of journalists who are reporting on their own blog or web site and do not have the backing of big publishing or broadcasting companies—are constantly the target of lawsuits that really are designed to do nothing more than shut them up."[2]

Former Sen. Jon Kyl (R-Ariz.) appears on "Meet The Press."

The online directory Yelp and the California Anti-SLAPP Project are among others calling for passage of federal legislation. Similar federal anti-SLAPP legislation was introduced in the House in 2009 but never left the House Judiciary Committee.[3] The Free Press Act of 2012 seems headed for the same fate—it was referred to the Senate Judiciary Committee, but that committee has not acted on the legislation.

1. Free Press Act of 2012, S. 3493, 113th Cong. (2012).
2. David Hudson, *Bill to Counter Lawsuits vs. Journalists Introduced,* First Amendment Center, Aug. 17, 2012, *available at* http://www.firstamendmentcenter.org/bill-to-counter-lawsuits-vs-journalists-introduced.
3. Eliza Krugman, *Yelp Pushes for Federal Anti-SLAPP Laws,* Politico.com, Jan. 4, 2013, *available at* http://dyn.politico.com/printstory.cfm?uuid=B0511A56–54EE-4142-A4D6-AA2C7CEFE759.

to claims that are "solely based on protected speech and with no other basis than to chill speech."[22]

Contemporary Issues

Many of the issues involving libel that existed in previous eras have surfaced again in the 20th and 21st centuries. Just as defamation was recognized first as a harm committed by the spoken word and later as one that could also be committed through writing, the opportunities for libelous speech have increased exponentially with the development of communications technology. Each new communicative medium increases the volume of communication in the world and, accordingly, the opportunities for defamatory statements increase. In the digital age—complete with blogs and social media with global reach—and because of the ease and speed of communicating, the possibilities for libel are on the rise. Add to this a media preoccupation with sensational events and a public fixation on celebrities and other renowned people, the potential for libel has never been greater.

Libel law serves to check the power of the media by opening its newsgathering and decision-making processes to public scrutiny and accountability. Although the best cure for bad speech may be more speech,[23] contemporary American society is often unwilling to rely only on corrective speech as a remedy for false and damaging statements to reputations. Libel law is one of the checks and balances in that process. The right of individuals to be secure in their reputations is weighed against the rights of others to be heard on issues of importance.

SUMMARY

THE VALUE OF INDIVIDUAL REPUTATION, the importance of protecting it and the ability to restore it once it is damaged are centuries-old concepts. Libel law is meant to help with those processes. As with much of law in the United States, libel stems in large part from the English common law. The threat of a libel suit can create a chilling effect in the media—a reluctance to publish freely and pursue stories aggressively. For those who either file or defend libel claims, it is an expensive process, taking a toll both financially and emotionally. Many claims are settled out of court. The purpose of a SLAPP is to harass critics into silence. Noting that SLAPPs are often used to suppress a party's First Amendment rights, some states have enacted anti-SLAPP legislation. The constitutionality of these laws has been upheld. ∎

The Elements of Libel: The Plaintiff's Case

burden of proof The requirement for a party to a case to demonstrate one or more claims by the presentation of evidence. In libel law, for example, the plaintiff has the burden of proof.

Unlike in the era of common law libel, when the defendant was required to prove that a defamatory statement was true, the entire initial **burden of proof** is now on the plaintiff in libel cases. To win, the plaintiff must prove that all of the required elements apply to the allegedly libelous material. Each of these elements requires definition and explanation.

Statement of Fact

In order to be libelous, a statement must make an assertion of fact. An expression of opinion cannot be libelous. For example, if you write that food in a specific restaurant tastes awful, that is opinion. If you write that food in a specific restaurant gave someone food poisoning you are offering an assertion of fact that can be proved. Legitimate opinion cannot be considered libelous because an opinion cannot be false—falsity being another requirement for libelous material. (The opinion defense is considered in detail in Chapter 5.) For now, it is enough to understand that whether material can be considered an expression of opinion requires a rigorous analysis.

Publication

In order for a statement to be libelous, the plaintiff must show that the statement was made public. To satisfy this standard, only one person in addition to the source and subject of the allegedly defamatory statement must have seen or heard the information in question. When information is presented through the mass media, publication is presumed. Under the law of libel, material is considered published any time it is printed in a periodical, broadcast over the airwaves or posted on the Internet. Again, publication simply means making material public, and that can mean to only one person other than the plaintiff and defendant in a libel suit.

Republication Repeating libelous information is as potentially harmful to someone's reputation as publishing it in the first place. Thus, the republisher can be held just as responsible as the originator. For example, if someone falsely tells a reporter that another person robbed a bank, it is publication. If the reporter includes that false information in a story the newspaper publishes on the Web, it is republication. Republishing libelous information is seen as a new publication in the eyes of the law. This is true even when careful attribution occurs. The law's rationale here is to prevent individuals or the media from freely committing defamation simply by attributing the libelous material to another source.

Particularly in an age of advancing communications technology, the republication rule would seem at odds with the wish to promote the free flow of ideas—clearly a tenet of the First Amendment. In fact, even in a slightly less technological age, some courts began to allow for some degree of protection for publication of otherwise libelous information. Section 230 of the Communications Decency Act, the neutral reportage defense and the wire service defense, discussed in Chapter 5, confront this issue.

An online version of republication illustrates how new technologies open the door to refinements in the law. New comments made to older messages in order to return them to prominent positions on a website to keep a conversation alive—"bump messages"—do not count as republication in the libel context. A New York judge wrote, "One of the unique characteristics of the Internet is that it allows for the dissemination of information and ideas on a global scale," adding that considering bump messages as republication would have "a serious inhibitory effect" on this form of communication.[24] In a different case, a New York trial court held that adding a "share button" to online archived articles is

Points of Law

The Plaintiff's Libel Case

1. A statement of fact
2. That is published,
3. That is of and concerning the plaintiff,
4. That is defamatory,
5. That is false and
6. That causes damage (or harm) and
7. For which the defendant is at fault.

not republication, even though the buttons facilitate content sharing. The court based its decision on the idea that the target audience, newspaper readers, did not change with the addition of the button. Moreover, readers always had the option to share even without the button; they could print, e-mail or distribute articles in other ways. The court said the use of a share button was "akin to a delayed circulation of the original rather than republication."[25]

Vendors and Distributors Publisher liability in libel is predicated on the notion that publishers are or should be aware of the material they disseminate, possibly including a presumption that they have read and edited the content. To prove publication, a libel plaintiff must show not just that libelous material was published; the plaintiff must also identify a specific person, group or business responsible for the publication. Simply making information available to the public is not the same as publishing it. Among those who are granted a sort of republication exception are vendors and distributors of information. For example, bookstores, libraries and newsstands are not publishers of the works they stock. They cannot be sued for libel based on the works they make available because they do not control the content of those products.

Given this "vendor exception," how should the law treat information providers on the Internet? Information appears on the Internet in a variety of ways. One way is through an Internet Service Provider that stores and facilitates access to material, for example, in a database. If the ISP originates any part of this information, then it is considered the publisher and can be held responsible for its content. More commonly, the ISP simply makes information posted by users available to subscribers. In that situation, the ISP is like the newsstand vendor—a provider of information but not a publisher and therefore not responsible for it. One court likened ISPs to a telephone company, "which one neither wants nor expects to superintend the content of its subscribers' conversations."[26]

Communications Decency Act (CDA) The part of the 1996 Telecommunications Act that largely attempted to regulate Internet content. The CDA was successfully challenged in *Reno v. ACLU (1997)*.

This protection of ISPs did not exist until one section of the **Communications Decency Act (CDA)** was put to the test. Before Congress passed the CDA in 1996 as part of the Telecommunications Act, court rulings in this area had been mixed. Some judges ruled that ISPs should be regarded as publishers,[27] while others said that they were only distributors of information that others had published.[28] The discrepancy was resolved when Section 230 of the CDA was tested by a libel claim against America Online (AOL).[29]

Not all online defamation takes place in a liability-free zone, however. In fact, defamatory material posted on an ISP site can be the subject of a libel action, provided that the publisher is identified. For example, when a former aide to President Bill Clinton claimed political columnist Matt Drudge defamed him by writing about his alleged history of spousal abuse, the ex-aide tried to sue AOL, the ISP that posted "The Drudge Report" where the comments appeared. The court refused to allow the suit to go forward against AOL, saying that AOL was not responsible for information it had transmitted but not originated. However, the court permitted the lawsuit to proceed against "The Drudge Report."[30] That case was ultimately settled out of court.

realWorld Law

Libel and the Online Publisher

Given that determining who published material is important as an element of the libel plaintiff's case, burgeoning online communication has raised the question about how courts should treat Internet Service Providers. Congress addressed this question in the Communications Decency Act. Section 230 of the law is sometimes referred to as the "Online Defamation Limited Liability Act." The law gives ISPs immunity from libel claims.[1]

Within a year, the new law was tested when a Seattle man sued America Online. Kenneth Zeran claimed AOL injured his reputation by not quickly removing false information about him. His claim arose after an anonymous AOL user posted an advertisement for T-shirts with images and a slogan glorifying the 1995 Oklahoma City bombing. The ad included Zeran's telephone number, although he claimed no role in or knowledge of the ad. Ultimately, a federal appeals court ruled, "By its plain language, Section 230 creates a federal immunity to any cause of action that would make service providers liable for information originating with a third-party user of that service." The court said Section 230 prevents courts from even considering claims that place a computer service provider in the role of publisher[2] because Congress recognized that a law requiring ISPs to restrict or eliminate speech to avoid liability would create an "obvious chilling effect" on speech.[3]

More recently, the First Circuit ruled that the definition of "provider of an interactive computer service" includes service providers who do not directly connect their users to the Internet.[4] Unlike AOL in the *Zeran* case, the defendant here did not provide users with access to the Internet but operated a series of websites. The court reasoned that narrowing protection only to services that provide Internet access would undermine congressional intent in passing the CDA.[5] The First Circuit said that Section 230 immunity should be broadly construed.[6]

1. Communications Decency Act, 47 U.S.C. § 230 (c)(1).
2. Zeran v. America Online, Inc., 129 F.3d 327, 330 (4th Cir. 1997).
3. *Id.* at 331.
4. Universal Communication Systems, Inc. v. Lycos, Inc., 478 F.3d 413 (1st Cir. 2007).
5. *Id.* at 418–19.
6. *Id.* at 419.

Blogs provide another example of "publishers." A blogger is responsible for the material he or she posts. But is the blogger legally responsible for items others may post on his or her site? What if the postings are anonymous? In a ruling that also relied on Section 230, a federal judge dismissed a libel claim against a website operator whose site included anonymous postings that the plaintiff claimed damaged his reputation.[31] The judge relied on what he said was the intention of Section 230: to promote the free flow of information, a goal that was especially well served in a medium where citizens from all walks of life could have a voice. Otherwise, he wrote, the specter of liability "in an area of such prolific speech would have an obvious chilling effect."[32]

Unknown Publisher/Anonymous Speech Sometimes material is published, but the speaker is unknown. A hallmark of cyberspace is anonymous communication. The ability to speak anonymously serves several interests, including

realWorld Law

Twibel: Defamation in 140 Characters?

The most notorious Twitter libel case, sometimes called Twibel cases, involved rocker Courtney Love. Love took to Twitter, MySpace and Etsy in 2009 to rant about designer Dawn Simorangkir, calling her a "drug-pushing prostitute," suggesting she had a history of assault and had lost custody of her child. The trigger for the series of tweets and posts was Simorangkir's demand that Love pay her for a few thousand dollars' worth of her clothing. Simorangkir sued for libel, claiming that Love's tweets damaged her career. The case settled in 2011, with Simorangkir receiving $430,000 from Love.[1]

Also in 2011, National Basketball Association (NBA) Referee Bill Spooner settled a libel lawsuit he brought against The Associated Press (AP) sportswriter John Krawczynski after he tweeted about Spooner's officiating during a game between the Houston Rockets and the Minnesota Timberwolves. Krawczynski tweeted, "Ref Bill Spooner told [Timberwolves coach Kurt] Rambis he'd 'get it back' after a bad call. Then he made an even worse call on Rockets. That's NBA officiating folks." According to the NBA, what Krawczynski actually overheard was Spooner telling the coach that he would "get back to him" after reviewing a videotape replay during halftime. AP settled the case by issuing a statement of clarification about the tweet and paying Spooner $20,000 to cover his legal fees.[2]

NBA Referee William Spooner argued that a Twitter message damaged his professional reputation and led to a disciplinary investigation by the NBA.

Questions about Twitter and libel also arose in an action brought in the U.K. by British politician Alistair McAlpine. McAlpine sued the British Broadcasting Company (BBC) after the BBC falsely accused him of child sexual abuse. The suit settled out of court, but McAlpine is pursuing defamation claims against high-profile tweeters who discussed the BBC story at the time of publication. The London newspaper, The Guardian, reported that McAlpine targeted at least 20 high-profile tweeters and planned to pursue action against thousands of other Twitter users who retweeted some of the comments. His law firm has said that Twitter users with fewer than 500 followers can settle their cases if they will apologize.[3]

The situation in the U.K. would play out differently in the United States. Many legal experts say Section 230 of the Communication Decency Act protects journalists' retweets as long as they simply retweet without adding new defamatory remarks.

1. Matthew Perpetua, *Courtney Love Settles Twitter Defamation Suit for $430,000,* Rolling Stone, Mar. 3, 2011, *available at* http://www.rollingstone.com/music/news/courtney-love-settles-twitter-defamation-suit-for-430–000–20110303.
2. Ed Stych, *NBA Ref and AP Settle Suit over Reporter's Tweet,* Minneapolis St. Paul B.J., Dec. 7, 2011, *available at* http://www.bizjournals.com/twincities/blog/law/2011/12/nba-ref-ap-reporter-settle-over-tweet.html?page=all.
3. Jeff Sonderman, *Twitter Users Face Libel Claims for Spreading False Accusations,* Poytner.org, Nov. 26, 2012, *available at* http://www.poynter.org/latest-news/mediawire/196241/twitter-users-face-libel-claims-fear-chilling-effect.

Emerging Law

Anonymous Speech and Libel: Three Approaches

For more than a decade, state courts have explored the tension between the First Amendment rights of a speaker to remain anonymous and the rights of other parties seeking relief for alleged harms. The federal appellate courts are taking a look at anonymous speech and libel. So far no decisions have yielded clear standards. The Supreme Court has yet to weigh in on the conflicting rights of anonymous online speakers and those who wish to unmask them for the purposes of a libel lawsuit. Generally speaking, the courts have taken three approaches to "unmasking" anonymous posters on the Internet in libel cases.

Good Faith. When a court applies good faith, plaintiffs must show they have a legitimate, good faith basis to claim an actionable offense within the court's jurisdiction, and that the identity of the anonymous speaker is central to advancing their case. Most courts have rejected this standard because it does not offer sufficient protection for the First Amendment rights of the speaker. Currently, only the state of Virginia—the home of America Online's corporate headquarters—uses a good faith test.[1]

Withstand Motion to Dismiss. In *Dendrite v. John Doe #3,* the court held that the plaintiff must present the court with prima facie ("on its face") evidence—evidence that is sufficient to prove the plaintiff has a case—that can withstand a motion to dismiss. If a plaintiff can withstand a motion to dismiss, then the court should balance the First Amendment rights of the anonymous speaker against the strength of the prima facie case and the need to disclose the anonymous identity for the case to proceed.[2]

Withstand Summary Judgment Motion. The Delaware Supreme Court has rejected good faith as the proper standard in these cases and held that a defamation plaintiff must "satisfy a 'summary judgment' standard before obtaining the identity of an anonymous defender."[3] Summary judgment is the quick resolution of a legal dispute in which a judge summarily decides certain points and issues a judgment to resolve a case. This approach is the most protective of anonymous speech. The Delaware Supreme Court wrote, "We are concerned that setting the standard too low will chill potential posters from exercising their First Amendment rights to speak anonymously. . . . Indeed, there is reason to believe that many defamation plaintiffs bring suit merely to unmask the identities of anonymous critics. . . . The goals of this new breed of libel action are largely symbolic, the primary goal being to silence John Doe and others like him."[4]

Some basic legal principles involving anonymous speech and libel have taken root in the state courts. "Courts have almost uniformly granted expressive speech by anonymous speakers the highest level of protection."[5] Still, some First Amendment lawyers consider anonymous online speech one of the fastest-growing areas of communication law, and until the Supreme Court weighs in, state courts will likely continue to take different approaches.[6]

---

1. Ashley I. Kissinger, Katharine Larsen & Matthew E. Kelley, *Protections for Anonymous Online Speech,* 2 COMM. L. IN THE DIGITAL AGE 532 (2012).
2. Dendrite International, Inc. v. Doe No. 3, 775 A.2d 756, 760–61 (2001).
3. Doe v. Cahill, 884 A. 2d 451, 457 (Del. 2005).
4. *Id.*
5. Kissinger, Larsen & Kelley, *supra* note 1, at 543.
6. *Id.*

Points of Law

Libel Plaintiff's Case When Defendant Is Anonymous

The *Dendrite* test requires the plaintiff to do the following:

- Undertake efforts to notify the anonymous party that they are the subject of a subpoena or order of disclosure.

- Identify the precise, alleged actionable speech made by each anonymous poster.

- Show prima facie evidence that the case is strong enough to withstand a motion to dismiss.

- If the case is strong enough to withstand the motion to dismiss, the court must then balance the defendant's First Amendment right to anonymous speech against the strength of the case presented by the plaintiff and the need to identify the defendant for the case to proceed.[1]

---

1. Dendrite International, Inc. v. Doe No. 3, 775 A.2d 756, 760–61 (2001).

allowing ideas and viewpoints that otherwise might remain unexpressed to enter the marketplace of ideas because the fear of reprisal is reduced. U.S. Supreme Court Justice Antonin Scalia once noted the historical significance of anonymous speech. He wrote: "Under our constitution, anonymous pamphleteering is not a pernicious, fraudulent practice, but an honorable tradition of advocacy and of dissent. Anonymity is a shield from the tyranny of the majority."[33] Many famous writers and political figures in American history wrote under fictitious names—Benjamin Franklin and Mark Twain, to name just a couple. And, as Chapter 2 notes, the Supreme Court has recognized a First Amendment right to anonymous speech. But what happens when the wish to protect anonymous speech collides with the imperative of holding people accountable for libelous expression?

Some judges have allowed "John Doe" lawsuits to proceed in which the identity of the defendant is withheld by the court. Knowing that Internet Protocol (or IP) addresses and user names can be traced—with some providers, identities are readily accessible—plaintiffs file John Doe claims and then compel the ISP to disclose the identity of the "anonymous" poster to the presiding court. The person's identity, however, is shielded in the courtroom and kept out of court documents, thus preserving some measure of anonymity.

Two federal district court rulings, one involving an ISP and another involving a newspaper, have allowed both to act as a third party to assert the First Amendment rights of anonymous speakers. In a 2003 case, the District Court for the District of Columbia held that Verizon, as an ISP, had a vested interest in "vigorously protecting its subscribers' First Amendment rights, because a failure to do so could affect Verizon's ability to maintain and broaden its client base."[34] Similarly, in 2008 a U.S. District Court in Pennsylvania extended the Verizon ruling to a newspaper that was trying to protect the identity of anonymous readers posting in the newspaper's online forums. The court reasoned that the relationship between the newspaper and its online forum readers "is the type of relationship that allows [the newspaper] to assert the First Amendment rights of the anonymous commentators."[35]

Identification

A libel plaintiff is required to show that he or she was specifically the person whose reputation was harmed or, possibly, was a member of a small group that was defamed. Early common law asked whether the statement was "of and concerning" the plaintiff—a standard still employed. This test asks whether the statement reasonably refers to the plaintiff. There are several ways a person can be identified. The most obvious is by name, but people can be identified in other ways—for instance, by title, through photographic images or within a context in which their identity can be inferred. As long as someone other than the plaintiff and the defendant recognize that the content is about the plaintiff, identification has taken place. In addition, the intention of the publisher is not critical to this determination; a publisher may not have intended to implicate the plaintiff, but identification could have occurred nonetheless.

Group Identification In some circumstances, libel law allows any member of a group to sue when the entire group has been libeled. The key is whether in libeling the group, the information is also "of and concerning" the specific individual bringing the lawsuit. In general, the smaller the group, the more likely it is that its individual members have been identified. For example, writing "all members of our town's city council are taking bribes" when there are only five members of the council would make it possible for any one of them to sue for libel. A claim that "all politicians are on the take" would not allow any single politician to sue because the group being libeled is so large that no single politician has been identified. How many members must a group include before it crosses the threshold from small enough to too big? Like so much in the law, there is no definitive answer. According to one authority, "It is not possible to set definite limits as to the size of the group or class, but the cases in which recovery [of damages] has been allowed usually have involved numbers of 25 or fewer."[36]

A court will evaluate each situation on its specific facts. Some rulings in this category indicate that if a group has fewer than 100 members, any one of them could file a successful libel claim, depending on the libelous material in question. As a group grows in size, the inclusiveness of the language that allegedly libeled its members becomes a factor. For example, a book titled "USA: Confidential" disparaged various groups of employees of the Neiman-Marcus department store in Dallas, Tex., including "some" of the models, the saleswomen and "most" of the salesmen. All nine models, 30 of 382 saleswomen and 15 of the 25 salesmen filed lawsuits. The libel claims of the models and the salesmen were allowed to go forward, but a federal trial judge dismissed the saleswomen's case. The trial court said that the large size of the saleswomen group made it impossible for a reader to conclude anything about any of its individual members. But the court conceded that even with large groups, if a particular member is identified in some manner, that individual would have a legitimate complaint.[37]

Identification in Fiction A somewhat recent permutation of libel law has been libel claims based on works of fiction. One key to the sustainability of the claim is whether the work identifies the plaintiff. Is it "of and concerning" him or her? Generally, the plaintiff must prove that a reasonable reader would perceive the writing as intending to portray a real person and that the plaintiff is that person. The level of recognition must rise to a portrayal of the fictional character as the plaintiff—a standard that is rarely met in fiction. A notable example revolves around "Primary Colors," a novel whose characters strongly resemble Bill Clinton and those around him. A libel lawsuit by a person who claimed that she was identified and defamed through a character in the book was dismissed. "For a depiction of a fictional character to constitute actionable defamation," the judge wrote, "the description of the fictional character must be so closely akin to the real person claiming to be defamed that a reader of the book, knowing the real person, would have no difficulty linking the two. Superficial similarities are insufficient."[38] In this case, the court said, any similarities between the plaintiff and the fictional character were insufficient for a reader, even one who knew the plaintiff, to reasonably believe the characterizations were about her.

Similarly, various forms of "new journalism" that blend fact and fiction to create compelling narratives about real-life events can present challenges when applying the rules of libel law. For example, the author of a nonfiction book may imagine conversations between various real-life people that convey the essence of what transpired but do so through largely invented dialogue. These unorthodox forms of journalistic storytelling straddle the line between fact and fiction—they are neither one nor the other, but both—and categorizing them for libel law purposes poses unique challenges.

Works of fiction, parody, satire and rhetorical hyperbole—in short, works that are unbelievable and could not be construed as statements of fact—are explored in Chapter 5.

Defamation

Another element in the plaintiff's case involves the allegedly libelous content itself. In order for the plaintiff to win, the material at issue must be defamatory. The challenge is defining and establishing a standard of defamation. The standard begins with the premise that when reputation is damaged, defamation occurs.

Some words by themselves may qualify as defamatory. Some kinds of statements convey such defamatory meaning that they are considered to be defamatory as a matter of law; on its face and without further proof, the content is defamatory. This is referred to as **libel per se**. Libel per se typically involves accusations of criminal activity, unethical activity or practice, unprofessional behavior

libel per se A statement whose injurious nature is apparent and requires no further proof.

and/or immoral actions (sometimes called "moral turpitude, which is conduct contrary to community standards).

Distinguishing defamatory from nondefamatory statements is more art than science. Within various contexts, the following definitions of "defamatory" have been offered:

- Words that are false and injurious to another
- Words that expose another person to hatred, contempt or ridicule
- Words that tend to harm the reputation of another so as to lower him or her in the estimation of the community or deter third persons from associating or dealing with him[39]
- Words that subject a person to the loss of goodwill or confidence from others[40]
- Words that subject a person to scorn or ridicule
- Words that tend to expose a person to hatred, contempt or aversion, or tend to induce an evil or unsavory opinion of him or her in the minds of a substantial number in the community
- Words that tend to prejudice someone in the eyes of a substantial and respectable minority of the community[41]

Whatever the standard, courts have traditionally said that the matter must be viewed from the perspective of "right-thinking" people.[42] Some examples of recent cases that explored the meaning of defamation include a New York appellate court's decision that a false allegation of homosexuality is no longer defamatory per se. The court cited New York's Marriage Equality Act as evidence of changing attitudes toward homosexuality.[43] Rhode Island's Supreme Court held that deliberately and falsely stating that a political event is "off the record" is not defamatory. A plaintiff argued that a newspaper portrayed him falsely as "someone to be disliked because he is a political insider who attacks the First Amendment."[44] Similarly, in Massachusetts an appellate court held that when a newspaper wrote that it could not reach a person for comment such a statement isn't defamatory even if it is false, and, in Florida a state court said that reporting that a plaintiff refused to cooperate or comment in a televised news story is not defamatory.[45]

In contrast with libel per se is **libel per quod**. It arises when the matter by itself does not appear to be defamatory, but knowledge of additional information would damage the plaintiff's reputation. An example of libel per quod would be a news report that the plaintiff was seen visiting 123 Main Street. By itself, that report would not seem defamatory. But if many readers are aware there is a drug-manufacturing lab at that address, then the report would have accused the plaintiff of involvement in illegal activity. Both kinds of libel lawsuits proceed along similar paths through the courts once it has been determined that the statement at issue was defamatory.

Article headlines can occasionally be the source of successful libel claims. As with captions and teasers, their abbreviated nature and shortened message can

libel per quod A statement whose injurious nature requires proof.

be interpreted in a defamatory way, as with the published headline "Red Tape Holds Up Bridge." Courts often deny recovery, however, perhaps in deference to the space demands of journalism. Whether the headline is "of and concerning" the plaintiff becomes material—as, of course, do the other elements of the plaintiff's case. In a lawsuit spawned by the murder trial of O.J. Simpson, the National Examiner was found liable for the headline "Cops Think Kato Did It." The implication regarding Brian "Kato" Kaelin was clear: The "it" being referred to was the murder of Nicole Brown Simpson and Ronald Goldman. The article itself clarified that the "it" mentioned in the front-page headline was actually perjury related to his trial testimony. Kaelin sued, claiming his reputation was damaged.[46] A defense witness who admitted that "the front page of the tabloid paper is what we sell the paper on, not what's inside it"[47] only served to strengthen the plaintiff's case.

Article illustrations and photographs can also result in libel if they are juxtaposed in a way that creates a defamatory impression. Recently, a New York court held that an archived crime scene photo used as a visual with an article about gang violence was capable of defamatory meaning. The photo of a 10-year-old African-American boy looking over yellow police tape at a crime scene was placed underneath the headline "Call to Get Tougher on Gang Activities." The appeals court said that the juxtaposition of the photo and the text could create a defamatory impression and that connecting a person to a serious crime like gang activity constitutes libel per se.[48]

Among the challenges for a court is deciding what the words or images at issue in a libel case mean and whether they can be considered defamatory. Whether they are actionable cannot simply be determined according to whether they harmed the plaintiff's reputation. The allegedly libelous matter may conceivably harm reputation without rising to the level of defamation. Thus, another element of defamation that plaintiffs must show is that the material "is reasonably capable of sustaining defamatory meaning."[49] A judge decides whether the words constituting the statement at issue are capable of conveying defamatory meaning. If so, the case may move to trial to determine whether, in fact, the words did convey a defamatory meaning.

Business Reputation While businesses and corporations do not have reputations in the same sense that individuals do, they can suffer a kind of reputational harm that can impair their ability to conduct business. Consequently, they may sue, particularly if their business depends on the goodwill of the public. In addition, individuals within businesses and corporations may have a legitimate libel claim when criticism of the business falsely implies wrongdoing on their part.

Trade Libel Trade libel pertains to criticism of products rather than criticism of people or businesses. For example, the Bose Corporation sued the publisher of Consumer Reports magazine for negative remarks in a review of audio speakers. In part, the review said "[I]ndividual instruments heard through the Bose system

realWorld Law

Oprah and the Cattlemen

Oprah Winfrey

In an example of a defamation claim originating from criticism of a product, talk show host Oprah Winfrey was sued by a group of Texas cattlemen for remarks made about "Mad Cow" disease. In 1996, diseased beef was a topic explored on an episode of "The Oprah Winfrey Show" titled "Dangerous Food."

Although neither Texas nor any of the plaintiffs was mentioned, the Texas Beef Group and several other Texas-based cattle companies filed suit. They claimed the producers "intentionally edited from the taped show much of the factual and scientific information that would have calmed the hysteria it knew one guest's false exaggerations would create."[1] The plaintiffs added that this "malicious" treatment "caused markets to immediately" crash and that they suffered damages as a result.[2]

Adding to the plaintiffs' anguish was Winfrey's well-documented influence on her millions of viewers—she could turn a book into a best-seller merely by mentioning it or start a diet craze by extolling a diet's virtues.[3] When Winfrey commented during the show that the information about tainted beef had "just stopped me cold from eating another burger,"[4] the flames were fanned. The plaintiffs sought $100 million in damages.

During the trial, Winfrey established a temporary residence in Texas and sought assistance on her testimony from Courtroom Sciences' founder Phil McGraw. McGraw told Winfrey, "There's a huge difference between telling the truth and telling the truth effectively."[5] After Winfrey won at trial[6] and on appeal,[7] she attributed much of her success to "Dr. Phil." She began inviting him regularly to appear on her show. His popularity led to his own daily television program.

---

1. Texas Beef Group v. Oprah Winfrey, 11 F. Supp. 2d 858, 862 (N.D. Tex. 1998). The program had been tape recorded on Apr. 11, 1996.
2. *Id.*
3. *See, e.g.,* Richard Roeper, *Oprah's Sheep Ready to Follow Every Whim,* CHI. SUN-TIMES, Jan. 22, 1998, at 11 ("If Oprah Winfrey appeared on her show tomorrow morning wearing a bucket on her head while extolling the virtues of yodeling, by this weekend you'd see millions of Americans walking around with buckets on their heads as they warbled to the sky: 'Yo-da-lay-dee-yo-da-lay-dee-yo-da-lay-hee-hoo. . . . ' Such is Winfrey's power to sway her flock to do her bidding. Sometimes I think she couldn't have any more influence on her viewers if she had them hypnotized. That's why there's a trial going on in Amarillo, Texas."). *See also* David McLemore, *Oprah's Talk Shows Why She's Daytime Queen,* DAILY TELEGRAPH (London), Feb. 5, 1998, at 20 ("On Tuesday, she acknowledged her show, seen by 20 million people daily, had the power to influence her viewers.").
4. Texas Beef Group v. Oprah Winfrey, 11 F. Supp. 2d at 869 (1998).
5. CNN Business Unusual, (Sept. 10, 2000), *available at* http://transcripts.cnn.com/TRANSCRIPTS/0009/10/bun.00.html.
6. Texas Beef Group, 11 F. Supp. 2d 858. The ruling was also based on the failure of the plaintiffs to prove that cattle are perishable food, a requirement under the Texas False Disparagement of Perishable Food Products Act. The plaintiffs sued for the alleged violation of this provision of the act.
7. Texas Beef Group v. Oprah Winfrey, 201 F.3d 680 (9th Cir. 2000).

seemed to grow to gigantic proportions and tended to wander about the room. . . . We think they might become annoying when listening to soloists."[50] The U.S. Supreme Court ultimately ruled that no libel had taken place because the review was not published knowing it contained false information or with reckless disregard for the truth.

Another example is the successful defense presented by CBS when its "60 Minutes" television news program was sued for product disparagement. A claim in a segment of the program suggested that apples grown in Washington were unsafe because they were treated with the chemical Alar. The Washington apple growers, however, were unable to prove that the "60 Minutes" claims were false.[51] The case was dismissed, and the ruling was upheld on appeal.[52]

Falsity

For a statement to be libelous, it must be false. The plaintiff is responsible for demonstrating that the statement at issue is false rather than the defendant proving the statement is true.

Historically this was reversed: The burden of proof to show a statement is true was placed on the defendant. This was the case in English common law. Moreover, when the English government used libel law in an effort to silence critics, truth was rejected as a defense. True but defamatory statements about the government, it was believed, were even more harmful than false criticism. Later, the common law recognized truth as a defense in civil libel cases.

Libel law in the United States now clearly places the burden of proof regarding falsity on the plaintiff. The U.S. Supreme Court has emphatically reinforced this aspect of libel law. Justice Sandra Day O'Connor, writing for the Court in a case involving a Philadelphia newspaper, emphasized the importance of protecting and encouraging the free flow of information and ideas:

> We believe that the Constitution requires us to tip [the scales] in favor of protecting free speech. . . . The burden of proving truth upon media defendants who publish speech of public concern deters such speech because of the fear that liability will unjustifiably result. . . . Because such a "chilling" effect would be antithetical to the First Amendment's protection of true speech on matters of public concern . . . a plaintiff must bear the burden of showing that the speech at issue is false before recovering damages for defamation from a media defendant. To do otherwise could only result in a deterrence of the speech which the Constitution makes free.[53]

Substantial **Truth** Libel law provides some latitude with regard to falsity. Minor error or discrepancy does not necessarily make a statement false. As long as the statement is substantially true, it cannot meet the standard for falsity and therefore cannot be libelous. The Supreme Court said that substantial truth "would absolve a defendant even if she cannot justify every word of the alleged defamatory matter; it is sufficient if the substance of the charge is proved true, irrespective of the slight inaccuracy in the details. . . . Minor inaccuracies do not amount to falsity so long as the substance, the gist, the sting of the libelous charge can be justified."[54]

One appellate court has used a test to determine whether a published statement is substantially true by considering both the gist of the statement and "whether the alleged defamatory statement was more damaging to the plaintiff's reputation, in the mind of the average listener, than a truthful statement would have been."[55] The nonlibelous nature of substantially true statements would mean, for example, that if a newspaper reports that an individual was in police custody when, in fact, the individual had been released on bail, the story would likely be substantially true because the individual had been in custody and it was only an error in timing that had caused the mistake. If, however, a newspaper publishes a story saying that a person has been charged with a crime when in fact he or she has only been investigated by the police, it is unlikely the story would be judged to be substantially true. If something is not at least substantially true, then it is false.

Implication and Innuendo While individual statements within an article or report may be factually accurate, taken together they may paint a different picture. Through implication or innuendo, libelous messages may be created. In a case dismissed by a Washington appeals court, for example, a crane operator sued a newspaper for what he said was implied in headlines. After an accident, Seattle Post-Intelligencer headlines read "Operator in crane wreck has history of drug abuse" and "Man completed mandated rehab program after his last arrest in 2000." The crane operator's tests for drugs after the accident were negative. He filed several claims including libel, though he admitted that there were no false statements in the newspaper. Still, he claimed "defamation by implication" due to the juxtaposing of true statements in a way that created a false impression. Although the Washington court said it did recognize libel by implication (some states do not), it is only when a false implication occurs through the omission of facts. There was nothing to indicate, the court ruled, that the Seattle newspaper omitted any facts.[56] This case followed an Iowa Supreme Court ruling that public plaintiffs there can sue for "defamation by implication." The court said that if a true fact is not properly and thoroughly explained, it can become defamatory if, when read in a particular way, it carries false implications.[57]

And, those in the electronic media face another pitfall: The meaning of a story may be altered, sometimes

Points of Law

The Burden of Proof as Deterrent

The burden of proof of falsity occasionally serves as a deterrent to potential plaintiffs. The requirement to delve deeply into the allegedly libelous statement and refute its veracity is sometimes so distasteful that would-be plaintiffs choose not to file libel claims in the first place. The information revealed in the process may be more embarrassing and damaging to reputation than the allegedly libelous statement. In addition, this proof of falsity requirement leads targets of some news media investigations to conclude that a libel claim is not their best course of action. That is, under some circumstances plaintiffs may not want the truth or falsity of a news report's claims analyzed. The possibility that the allegations could be proved true or substantially true can be discouraging to a potential plaintiff. (See, e.g., the examination of the *Food Lion* case in Chapter 8.)

dramatically, through voice inflections. Given the informal style that is a hallmark of broadcast writing, the effect can be devastating. Imagine, for example, a newscaster saying in a cynical tone, "Well, the mayor was at it again last night." The juxtaposition of visual images and accompanying "voice over," although each may be factually correct, can combine to create a false statement.

SUMMARY

THE LIBEL PLAINTIFF'S CASE HAS SEVERAL ELEMENTS, all of which must be proved in court to win. The material in question must be (1) a statement of fact (2) that is published, (3) that is of and concerning the plaintiff, (4) that is defamatory, (5) that is false, (6) that causes damage (or harm), and (7) that is the result of fault by the defendant. The first five elements are examined in the preceding sections. No matter where libel occurs or in what communicative medium, the plaintiff must prove the same elements. ■

Fault

To support a libel claim, a plaintiff must show that the defendant was at fault in making public the allegedly false and defamatory statement of fact. Prior to *New York Times Co. v. Sullivan,* fault was not an element of common law libel. The landmark case did away with the concept of libel as a no-fault tort, and subsequent Supreme Court cases addressed next explain what level of fault is used in libel suits. As a general rule, public officials and public figures must prove actual malice as a standard of fault, and private individuals must prove negligence.

New York Times Co. v. Sullivan One of the most important legal cases in the history of American constitutional law is a libel case, *New York Times Co. v. Sullivan.*[58] The U.S. Supreme Court's ruling in that case has had a monumental impact not just on journalism but on society as a whole.

The circumstances of *New York Times Co. v. Sullivan* arose within the context of the civil rights movement of the 1960s. African-American groups seeking racial equality under the law frequently engaged in nonviolent marches in southern states. These events were minimized or ignored by the local southern press but were covered elsewhere, including frequently in The New York Times. Many southern leaders resented the Times and other northern newspapers that covered the marches.

Against that backdrop, a coalition of civil rights leaders purchased space in The New York Times for a full-page statement. Carrying the headline "Heed Their Rising Voices," the "advertorial" made charges against officials in southern states who, the statement claimed, had used violent and illegal methods to suppress the marches. Although the gist of the statements was factually accurate, there were some errors of fact. Asserting he had been defamed, L.B. Sullivan, the police commissioner of Montgomery, Ala., filed a libel claim against the Times and some of the civil rights leaders who had purchased the newspaper space. He sought $500,000 in damages from the Times, which was at the time far from financially invulnerable.

Although Sullivan was not identified by name in the statement, he maintained that it was nevertheless "of and concerning" him. The ad criticized public officials who, it said, used illegal tactics and violence to counter peaceful demonstrations. Sullivan maintained that the statements implicated him. He and his attorneys were able to file a libel claim in Alabama because several copies of the paper had been circulated in Montgomery County. A trial court there quickly ruled in Sullivan's favor, awarding him $500,000 in damages. The Alabama Supreme Court upheld both the verdict and the award.

The New York Times appealed the case to the U.S. Supreme Court, arguing that because Sullivan was a public official, a higher standard should be applied to his claim that a news story had libeled him. The case came at a critical time both in the history of the civil rights movement and for The New York Times, which could have suffered crippling financial damage if the judgment against it was affirmed. In a landmark ruling that rewrote the law of libel in the United States, the Court ruled 9–0 in favor of the Times, reversing the judgment of the Alabama Supreme Court.

The Court's decision in *Sullivan* was based on the premise that to readily punish a media organization for publishing criticism of government officials was contrary to "the central meaning of the First Amendment," an argument that for the first time applied the protections of the First Amendment to the law of libel. The Court's decision rested on the principle that media defendants did not have sufficient protection from libel suits. Awarding victories to libel plaintiffs too easily, the Court reasoned, threatened to choke off the free flow of information that is essential to the maintenance of a democratic society. Fear of making even minor errors would result in a chilling effect on the media, unduly restricting press freedom. Moreover, this freedom was especially important when it came to criticism of the government and government officials. This kind of political speech is a core First Amendment value.[59] To allow libel plaintiffs who are government officials to be successful without a showing of fault would be tantamount to reinstituting seditious libel—prohibiting criticism of the government.

For Sullivan to win his case, Justice William Brennan wrote, the police commissioner would have to prove that The New York Times published the editorial-advertisement knowing it contained false information or with reckless disregard for its truth. This new standard of fault, Brennan wrote, was called "**actual malice.**" Media defendants must have some room for error—"breathing space."[60] After this ruling, plaintiffs who are public officials had to prove that the content was published with actual malice—a new level of fault.

Justice Brennan explained that the Court's ruling was based on the importance in a free society of unfettered debate on public issues: "We consider this case against the background of a profound national commitment to the principle that debate on public issues should be uninhibited, robust, and wide-open."[61]

actual malice In libel law, a statement made knowing it is false or with reckless disregard for its truth.

THE NEW YORK TIMES, TUESDAY, MARCH 29, 1960

> "*The growing movement of peaceful mass demonstrations by Negroes is something new in the South, something understandable. . . . Let Congress heed their rising voices, for they will be heard.*"
> —New York Times editorial
> Saturday, March 19, 1960

Heed Their Rising Voices

As the whole world knows by now, thousands of Southern Negro students are engaged in widespread non-violent demonstrations in positive affirmation of the right to live in human dignity as guaranteed by the U. S. Constitution and the Bill of Rights. In their efforts to uphold these guarantees, they are being met by an unprecedented wave of terror by those who would deny and negate that document which the whole world looks upon as setting the pattern for modern freedom...

In Orangeburg, South Carolina, when 400 students peacefully sought to buy doughnuts and coffee at lunch counters in the business district, they were forcibly ejected, tear-gassed, soaked to the skin in freezing weather with fire hoses, arrested en masse and herded into an open barbed-wire stockade to stand for hours in the bitter cold.

In Montgomery, Alabama, after students sang "My Country, 'Tis of Thee" on the State Capitol steps, their leaders were expelled from school, and truckloads of police armed with shotguns and tear-gas ringed the Alabama State College Campus. When the entire student body protested to state authorities by refusing to re-register, their dining hall was padlocked in an attempt to starve them into submission.

In Tallahassee, Atlanta, Nashville, Savannah, Greensboro, Memphis, Richmond, Charlotte, and a host of other cities in the South, young American teenagers, in face of the entire weight of official state apparatus and police power, have boldly stepped forth as protagonists of democracy. Their courage and amazing restraint have inspired millions and given a new dignity to the cause of freedom.

Small wonder that the Southern violators of the Constitution fear this new, non-violent brand of freedom fighter... even as they fear the upwelling right-to-vote movement. Small wonder that they are determined to destroy the one man who, more than any other, symbolizes the new spirit now sweeping the South—the Rev. Dr. Martin Luther King, Jr., world-famous leader of the Montgomery Bus Protest. For it is his doctrine of non-violence which has inspired and guided the students in their widening wave of sit-ins; and it is this same Dr. King who founded and is president of the Southern Christian Leadership Conference—the organization which is spearheading the surging right-to-vote movement. Under Dr. King's direction the Leadership Conference conducts Student Workshops and Seminars in the philosophy and techniques of non-violent resistance.

Again and again the Southern violators have answered Dr. King's peaceful protests with intimidation and violence. They have bombed his home almost killing his wife and child. They have assaulted his person. They have arrested him seven times—for "speeding," "loitering" and similar "offenses." And now they have charged him with "perjury"—a *felony* under which they could imprison him for *ten years*. Obviously, their real purpose is to remove him physically as the leader to whom the students and millions

of others—look for guidance and support, and thereby to intimidate *all* leaders who may rise in the South. Their strategy is to behead this affirmative movement, and thus to demoralize Negro Americans and weaken their will to struggle. The defense of Martin Luther King, spiritual leader of the student sit-in movement, clearly, therefore, is an integral part of the total struggle for freedom in the South.

Decent-minded Americans cannot help but applaud the creative daring of the students and the quiet heroism of Dr. King. But this is one of those moments in the stormy history of Freedom when men and women of good will must do more than applaud the rising-to-glory of others. The America whose good name hangs in the balance before a watchful world, the America whose heritage of Liberty these Southern Upholders of the Constitution are defending, is *our* America as well as theirs...

We must heed their rising voices—yes—but we must add our own.

We must extend ourselves above and beyond moral support and render the material help so urgently needed by those who are taking the risks, facing jail, and *even death* in a glorious re-affirmation of our Constitution and its Bill of Rights.

We urge you to join hands with our fellow Americans in the South by supporting, with your dollars, this combined appeal for all three needs—the defense of Martin Luther King—the support of the embattled students—and the struggle for the right-to-vote.

Your Help Is Urgently Needed . . . NOW!!

Stella Adler	Dr. Alan Knight Chalmers	Anthony Franciosa	John Killens	L. Joseph Overton	Maureen Stapleton
Raymond Pace Alexander	Richard Coe	Lorraine Hansbury	Eartha Kitt	Clarence Pickett	Frank Silvera
Harry Van Arsdale	Nat King Cole	Rev. Donald Harrington	Rabbi Edward Klein	Shad Polier	Hope Stevens
Harry Belafonte	Cheryl Crawford	Nat Hentoff	Hope Lange	Sidney Poitier	George Tabor
Julie Belafonte	Dorothy Dandridge	James Hicks	John Lewis	A. Philip Randolph	Rev. Gardner C.
Dr. Algernon Black	Ossie Davis	Mary Hinkson	Viveca Lindfors	John Raitt	Taylor
Marc Blitzstein	Sammy Davis, Jr.	Van Heflin	Carl Murphy	Elmer Rice	Norman Thomas
William Branch	Ruby Dee	Langston Hughes	Don Murray	Jackie Robinson	Kenneth Tynan
Marlon Brando	Dr. Philip Elliott	Morris Iushewitz	John Murray	Mrs. Eleanor Roosevelt	Charles White
Mrs. Ralph Bunche	Dr. Harry Emerson	Mahalia Jackson	A. J. Muste	Bayard Rustin	Shelley Winters
Diahann Carroll	Fosdick	Mordecai Johnson	Frederick O'Neal	Robert Ryan	Max Youngstein

We in the south who are struggling daily for dignity and freedom warmly endorse this appeal

Rev. Ralph D. Abernathy *(Montgomery, Ala.)*	Rev. Matthew D. McCollom *(Orangeburg, S.C.)*	Rev. Walter L. Hamilton *(Norfolk, Va.)*	Rev. A. L. Davis *(New Orleans, La.)*
Rev. Fred L. Shuttlesworth *(Birmingham, Ala.)*	Rev. William Holmes Borders *(Atlanta, Ga.)*	I. S. Levy *(Columbia, S.C.)*	Mrs. Katie E. Whickham *(New Orleans, La.)*
Rev. Kelley Miller Smith *(Nashville, Tenn.)*	Rev. Douglas Moore *(Durham, N.C.)*	Rev. Martin Luther King, Sr. *(Atlanta, Ga.)*	Rev. W. H. Hall *(Hattiesburg, Miss.)*
Rev. W. A. Dennis *(Chattanooga, Tenn.)*	Rev. Wyatt Tee Walker *(Petersburg, Va.)*	Rev. Henry C. Bunton *(Memphis, Tenn.)*	Rev. J. E. Lowery *(Mobile, Ala.)*
Rev. C. K. Steele *(Tallahassee, Fla.)*		Rev. S.S. Seay, Sr. *(Montgomery, Ala.)*	Rev. T. J. Jemison *(Baton Rouge, La.)*
		Rev. Samuel W. Williams *(Atlanta, Ga.)*	

COMMITTEE TO DEFEND MARTIN LUTHER KING AND THE STRUGGLE FOR FREEDOM IN THE SOUTH

312 West 125th Street, New York 27, N.Y. UNiversity 6-1700

Chairmen: A. Philip Randolph, Dr. Gardner C. Taylor; *Chairmen of Cultural Division:* Harry Belafonte, Sidney Poitier; *Treasurer:* Nat King Cole; *Executive Director:* Bayard Rustin; *Chairmen of Church Division:* Father George B. Ford, Rev. Harry Emerson Fosdick, Rev. Thomas Kilgore, Jr., Rabbi Edward E. Klein; *Chairman of Labor Division:* Morris Iushewitz

Please mail this coupon TODAY!

Committee To Defend Martin Luther King
and
The Struggle For Freedom in The South
312 West 125th Street, New York 27, N.Y.
UNiversity 6-1700

I am enclosing my contribution of $
for the work of the Committee.

Name _____

Address _____

City _____ Zone ___ State ___

☐ I want to help   ☐ Please send further information

Please make checks payable to:
Committee to Defend Martin Luther King

The New York Times "advertorial" that prompted L.B. Sullivan's libel lawsuit against the newspaper.

realWorld Law

The Impact of *New York Times Co. v. Sullivan*: The "Central Meaning of the First Amendment"

New York Times Co. v. Sullivan "revolutionized the law of libel and, equally importantly, it signaled a critical shift in our general First Amendment jurisprudence."[1] The ruling went beyond determining whether particular material was protected or unprotected. It embraced principles that decry chilling effects and include a speech-protective approach, what one scholar suggested was the central meaning of the First Amendment. Harry Kalven, Jr., wrote that for the first time, the *Sullivan* ruling put seditious libel—criticism of government or government officials—in its proper place. "The concept of seditious libel strikes at the very heart of democracy," Kalven wrote. "Political freedom ends when government can use its powers and its courts to silence its critics."[2] Defamation of the government, he continued, is an impossible notion for a democracy.

Kalven believed that *New York Times Co. v. Sullivan* squarely addressed the concept of seditious libel, punishment for which was first legalized in the United States by the Sedition Act of 1798. In turn, that law made possible two early 20th-century laws that, in Kalven's words, "oddly echoed the idiom of seditious libel."[3] By doing so, the Supreme Court reaffirmed the core meaning of the First Amendment initially outlined by James Madison.

1. Kermit L. Hall (ed.), The Oxford Guide to United States Supreme Court Decisions 216 (1999).
2. Harry Kalven, Jr., *The New York Times Case: A Note on "The Central Meaning of the First Amendment,"* 1964 Sup. Ct. Rev. 191, 205.
3. *Id.* at 207.

This debate should be open not just to members of the press but also to members of the public, who otherwise may not have access to the press.[62] If libel plaintiffs were not required to show actual malice by news organizations before they could win libel suits, he wrote, such debate would be unduly limited, because of self-censorship by both public and press.[63] His opinion for the Court emphasized that when people enter government service, they assume roles in which their job performance is rightly scrutinized and often criticized by the public and press. Thus, the open debate the Court sought to protect, he acknowledged, "may well include vehement, caustic, and sometimes unpleasantly sharp attacks on government and public officials."[64]

Furthermore, because public officials have easy access to the news media, they have an avenue by which to correct any reputational harm they may have suffered. Thus, they must meet a more difficult standard than the one applied to cases involving private plaintiffs.

One major impact of the Court's decision in *New York Times Co. v. Sullivan* was to embolden the U.S. news media. The opinion emphasized that the First Amendment permitted—even encouraged—an aggressive press. This was especially true with regard to the media's role as a "watchdog" in democratic society, keeping an eye on those in government. Allowing libel suits to proceed too easily against this vital organ of democratic society would be damaging to our form of government. Referring to the consequences of large damage awards against

Points of Law

Actual Malice

- Knowledge of falsity or
- Reckless disregard for the truth

newspapers, Brennan wrote, "Whether or not a newspaper can survive a succession of such judgments, the pall of fear and timidity imposed upon those who would give voice to public criticism is an atmosphere in which the First Amendment freedoms cannot survive."[65]

Enjoying added protection from lawsuits in public official libel cases, the news media were more aggressive in the wake of the *Sullivan* case. In the years immediately following the ruling, aggressive coverage of events such as the civil rights movement, the Vietnam War and the Watergate scandal followed. That same protection was later used by the media in public figure cases.[66]

Thus, with *New York Times Co. v. Sullivan,* libel law was "constitutionalized." The phrase "freedom of the press" was given new meaning. Restricting the flow of information, as the Court observed was possible under prior libel standards, is antithetical to the philosophy and spirit of the First Amendment.

Actual Malice

"Actual malice" is defined as knowledge of falsity or reckless disregard for the truth. Although the examination of this concept began within the discussion of *New York Times Co. v. Sullivan,* additional scrutiny is required given the developments that followed the landmark ruling.

Knowledge of Falsity Knowledge of falsity is nothing more than lying—publishing information knowing it is false. Knowledge of falsity is uncommon in the news media, where truth and accuracy are universal standards. Nonetheless, a news report in which the publisher "stacks the deck" to produce an intentionally distorted representation may rise to the level of knowledge of falsity. During the 1964 presidential campaign, for example, some people questioned the fitness for office of the Republican Party nominee, Sen. Barry Goldwater. The publisher of Fact magazine, Ralph Ginsburg, sent a questionnaire to hundreds of psychiatrists that asked them to analyze Goldwater's mental condition. Ginsburg received a variety of responses but published in a "psychobiographical" article only those that reflected poorly on the senator. When Goldwater sued for libel, the court concluded Ginsburg's conduct qualified as knowledge of falsity.[67]

Does knowingly changing the statements of an interview subject also qualify as knowledge of falsity, especially when those words are enclosed by quotation marks in print? Not necessarily. Reporter Janet Malcolm did just that in articles published in The New Yorker in 1983. The articles were based on more than 40 hours of taped interviews with psychoanalyst Jeffrey Masson. When Masson sued for libel, a decade-long journey through the courts began. At one stop along the way, the U.S. Supreme Court noted that in those hours of recorded interviews, no statements identical to the challenged passages appeared. In its decision, the Court ruled that while readers presume that words within quotation marks are verbatim reproductions of what the interviewee said, it would be unrealistic for

realWorld Law

Masson v. New Yorker Magazine, Inc. and Journalistic Responsibility

Jeffrey Masson

The U.S. Supreme Court's handling of *Masson v. New Yorker Magazine, Inc.* led to disillusionment in some circles over a ruling that some say is inconsistent with any semblance of journalistic responsibility. Given that public trust is at the foundation of journalistic ethics—and that deliberately altering the words of someone who has granted an interview violates that trust—the approval of a practice that undermines that trust has attracted criticism.[1] Justice Byron White's dissenting opinion expressed the idea that because reporter Janet Malcolm wrote that Jeffrey Masson said certain things that Malcolm knew Masson did not say, she acted with "knowing falsehood,"[2] thus satisfying the actual malice standard. According to this view, the sort of quotation alteration in which Malcolm engaged would not be permitted, and Masson's libel suit ultimately could have been successful. In the end, *Masson* may serve as a classic example of a case that represents a clash between legal and ethical standards.

1. *See, e.g.,* Neil J. Kinkopf, *Malice in Wonderland: Fictionalized Quotations and the Constitutionally Compelled Substantial Truth Doctrine,* 41 CASE W. RES. 1271 (1991).
2. Masson v. New Yorker Magazine, Inc., 501 U.S. 496, 526 (1991) ("By any definition of the term, this was "knowing falsehood.").

the law to require the press to meet such a standard. Justice Anthony Kennedy wrote, "A deliberate alteration of the words uttered by a plaintiff does not equate with knowledge of falsity . . . unless the alteration results in a material change in the meaning conveyed by the statement."[68] Absent an alteration that changes the meaning, the words remain substantially true.

Reckless Disregard for the Truth Reckless disregard for the truth may be thought of as very sloppy journalism. The sloppiness must be both careless and irresponsible. In its *New York Times Co. v. Sullivan* ruling, the U.S. Supreme Court made it clear that the failure by the newspaper in that case to check the advertisement against its own records did not rise to the level of reckless disregard. A few years later, the Court considered two cases simultaneously that began to add to the understanding of this prong of actual malice. In the first, a weekly magazine, The Saturday Evening Post, published an article in 1963 about an attempt to fix a 1962 college football game. The magazine's source claimed he had been "patched" into a telephone conversation between the athletic director at the University of Georgia, Wally Butts, and the head football coach at the University of Alabama, Paul "Bear" Bryant. Moreover, the source claimed that in the call he heard the two men arranging the fix. The source, George Burnett, said he took careful notes of the conversation. The Saturday Evening Post based its article on Burnett's recollection but never asked to see his notes. No effort was made by the magazine to corroborate the information with other sources, nor were other potential sources of information consulted, such as football experts, game films or witnesses. Burnett's credibility also went unchecked. It turned out he had a criminal record. The magazine's editors—and Burnett—failed to do their jobs adequately. As Justice John Harlan wrote in his opinion for the Court, "In short, the evidence is ample to support a finding of highly unreasonable conduct constituting an extreme departure from the standards of investigation and reporting ordinarily adhered to by responsible publishers."[69] The Court indicated that the omissions of responsibility by The Saturday Evening Post clearly qualified as the kind of conduct that rises to the level of reckless disregard for the truth.

In the second case, a retired major general, Edwin Walker, sued the Associated Press (AP) for its reports on his role in incidents surrounding efforts to keep the peace at the University of Mississippi when that institution was attempting to enroll its first African-American student in 1962. The AP reported that Walker had taken command of a violent crowd of protestors and had personally led a charge against federal marshals sent there to enforce a court decree and to assist in preserving order. The report also described Walker as encouraging rioters to use violence and giving them technical advice on combating the effects of tear gas.[70] These false statements were distributed to several other media outlets.

In distinguishing the two cases, the Court cited one significant factor: "The evidence showed that the Butts story was in no sense 'hot news' and the editors of the magazine recognized the need for a thorough investigation of the serious charges. . . . In contrast to the Butts article, the dispatch which concerns us in Walker was news which required immediate dissemination. . . . Considering the necessity for rapid dissemination, nothing in this series of events gives the slightest hint of a severe departure from accepted publishing standards."[71]

Thus, the urgency of a story has a significant bearing on whether the methods used by the news media defendant exhibit reckless disregard for the truth. The Court is willing to allow the news media some "wiggle room" when there is deadline pressure. In addition, the reliability of a story's source and the believability of the information are also factors in the judgment.

The following year, the Supreme Court further developed its reckless disregard standard. First, the Court admitted that "reckless disregard" cannot be summarized in a single, infallible definition. But it went on to say that reckless conduct is not measured merely by whether a reasonably prudent person would have published or would have investigated before publishing. "There must be sufficient evidence to permit the conclusion that the defendant in fact entertained serious doubts as to the truth of his publication. Publishing with such doubts shows reckless disregard for the truth or falsity and demonstrates actual malice."[72] Thus, the Supreme Court had now infused the reckless disregard standard with an element of subjectivity. It was no longer enough to merely examine the evidence related to the publisher's actions; now it was also necessary to determine the publisher's state of mind. But does this standard place a premium on ignorance? Does it reward a publisher who has doubts about the information but does nothing prior to publication to investigate? Evidence of investigation could be used against the publisher in court. The Supreme Court admitted that this possibility existed but said the purpose of the actual malice standard was to emphasize free expression. If it was going to err in its definition of reckless disregard, the Court said it would do so on the side that enhanced rather than chilled expression.

Points of Law

"Reckless Disregard" Criteria

- *Urgency of the story.* Is there time to check the information?

- *Source reliability.* Is the source trustworthy?

- *Story believability.* Is further examination necessary?

More than a decade later, the Supreme Court considered whether evidence could be used to help make judgments about a libel defendant's state of mind. During a **deposition** a "60 Minutes" segment producer had refused to answer certain questions related to his editorial decisions concerning a 1973 broadcast about a government cover-up of atrocities during the Vietnam War, claiming the First Amendment protected them from being disclosed. The Supreme Court disagreed and ruled that the plaintiff could look into the defendant's mental processes.[73]

deposition Testimony by a witness conducted outside a courtroom and intended to be used in preparation for trial.

A decade later, in 1989, the Court further indicated that a judgment concerning reckless disregard need not necessarily focus on any single lapse by the defendant but may rest on an evaluation of the record as a whole. In other words, the more mistakes are made, the more readily a court may conclude that a defendant acted with reckless disregard.

The Court ruled that an Ohio newspaper acted with actual malice when it failed to interview the one witness who could have verified its story about alleged corruption in a local election for a judgeship; the newspaper did not listen to a tape it had been told would exonerate the plaintiff, a tape that the plaintiff delivered to the newspaper at the newspaper's request; an editorial the newspaper published prior to the libelous report indicated the editor had already decided to publish the allegations at issue regardless of evidence to the contrary; and discrepancies in the testimony of the defendant's own witnesses that supported the idea that the defendant had failed to conduct a complete investigation with the deliberate intent of avoiding the truth.[74]

Public Officials *New York Times Co. v. Sullivan* also established that not only is the content of the allegedly libelous material important, so is the nature of the plaintiff. The ruling said public official plaintiffs must show that fault on the part of the defendant is at the level of actual malice. Private figures, on the other hand, are usually required to show some lesser, easier-to-prove level of fault, typically negligence.

But who qualifies as a public official? There is a temptation to answer by saying, "All government employees." But this is not quite accurate. The U.S. Supreme Court, again through Justice Brennan, has said, "It is clear that the 'public official' designation applies at the very least to those among the hierarchy of government employees who have or appear to have to the public substantial responsibility for or control over the conduct of governmental affairs."[75] The idea is that people who meet that definition are people whom the public is justified in wanting to know about because they serve the public. Information about them may relate to the officials' qualifications, conduct and character. But not all those paid by government for their work meet the criteria.

Conversely, one can meet the public official standard without being a government employee. For example, a libel plaintiff in New Hampshire who was hired by three elected county commissioners to supervise a public recreation facility owned by the county was deemed to be a public official by the Supreme Court in 1966. The Court explained the standard as follows: "Where a position in government has such apparent importance that the public has an independent interest in the qualifications and performance of the person who holds it, beyond the general public interest in the qualifications, conduct and performance of all government employees, both elements we identified in New York Times are present and the New York Times malice standards apply."[76]

A person usually remains a public official even after leaving a position that includes substantial responsibility for or control over the conduct of governmental affairs as long as the allegedly libelous material pertains to the person's conduct while in that post. However, the U.S. Supreme Court has said that it is possible, though rare, for the passage of time to erode the public's interest in the official's conduct in office so much that the actual malice standard would no longer apply.[77]

Public Figures After *New York Times Co. v. Sullivan,* the question arose whether the actual malice standard should be limited only to public officials. Is there another category of people whose public status ought to require them to also prove the defendant acted with actual malice when they sue for libel? The U.S. Supreme Court answered this question in the affirmative in *Curtis Publishing Co. v. Butts* and *Associated Press v. Walker,* the two cases described previously and considered simultaneously by the Court. Chief Justice Earl Warren wrote, "To me, differentiation between 'public figures' and 'public officials' and the adoption of separate standards of proof for each has no basis in law, logic, or First Amendment policy. Increasingly in this country, the distinctions between governmental and private sectors are blurred."[78] One reason that a higher level of fault is required of public officials is that they typically have access to the media to correct damage to their reputation. **Public figures,** Warren claimed, are no different:

> "Public figures," like "public officials," often play an influential role in ordering society. And surely as a class these "public figures" have as ready access as "public officials" to the mass media of communication, both to influence policy and to counter criticism of their views and activities. Our citizenry has a legitimate and substantial interest in the conduct of such persons, and freedom of the press to engage in uninhibited debate about their involvement in public issues and events is as crucial as it is in the case of "public officials." The fact that they are not amenable to the restraints of the political process only underscores the legitimate and substantial nature of the interest, since it means that public opinion may be the only instrument by which society can attempt to influence their conduct.[79]

public figure In libel law, a plaintiff who is in the public spotlight, usually voluntarily, and must prove the defendant acted with actual malice in order to win damages.

Thus, the opportunity to "set the record straight" because of access to the media justified expanding the actual malice standard to any public figure. Private figures typically have no such access to the media. One question remained, however: Who qualifies as a public figure?

All-Purpose Public Figures The U.S. Supreme Court has defined two categories of public figures. Both must prove that a defendant acted with actual malice. In *Gertz v. Robert Welch, Inc.* (excerpted at the end of this chapter), the Court said that some people "occupy positions of such persuasive power and influence that they are deemed public figures for all purposes."[80] An **all-purpose public figure** is anyone whom a court labels to be "public" under all circumstances. That is, no matter the context, the individual's name is widely recognizable to at least some segments of the public. However, some courts demand that an additional requirement be met for all-purpose public figure status: The person must also have written or spoken about a broad range of issues. These are people who have acquired some degree of fame outside the public official sphere— "celebrities," for example. This could include not only those in the entertainment field but also some athletes, activists, religious leaders and business leaders.

Lawyer Elmer Gertz was well known beyond *Gertz v. Robert Welch, Inc.* He successfully represented author Henry Miller against claims his 1934 novel "Tropic of Cancer" was obscene, and he managed to get Jack Ruby's murder conviction for the assassination of Lee Harvey Oswald overturned because of excessive trial publicity. Oswald assassinated President John F. Kennedy in 1963. Gertz died in 2000 at the age of 93.

Limited-Purpose Public Figures More common than all-purpose public figures are those people who have attained public status but only within a narrow set of circumstances. These people, in the words of the Court, "have thrust themselves to the forefront of particular public controversies in order to influence the resolution of the issues involved."[81] Like an all-purpose public figure, a **limited-purpose public figure** invites attention and comment. An individual may be a limited-purpose public figure within a particular community or a particular field. In the *Gertz* ruling, Justice Lewis Powell echoed Justice Brennan's *New York Times Co. v. Sullivan* rationale, noting that an individual who seeks government office must accept "certain necessary consequences of that involvement in public affairs. He runs the risk of closer public scrutiny than might otherwise be the case."[82] He then added the key declaration: "Those classed as public figures stand in a similar position."[83]

Although the groundwork had already been established,[84] another series of rulings by the Court more precisely articulated a definition of who qualifies as a public figure. In one case, a man had been in the news 16 years prior to a false characterization in a book, but he had not voluntarily thrust himself into the

all-purpose public figure In libel law, a person who occupies a position of such persuasive power and influence as to be deemed a public figure for all purposes. Public figure libel plaintiffs are required to prove actual malice.

limited-purpose public figure In libel law, those plaintiffs who have attained public figure status within a narrow set of circumstances by thrusting themselves to the forefront of particular public controversies in order to influence the resolution of the issues involved; this kind of public figure is more common than the all-purpose public figure.

Points of Law

Limited-Purpose Public Figure

- A public controversy must exist before the publication of the allegedly libelous statement.

- The plaintiff must have in some way participated voluntarily in trying to resolve this controversy.

- The plaintiff's participation actively sought to influence public opinion regarding the controversy.

bootstrapping In libel law, the forbidden practice of a defendant claiming that the plaintiff is a public figure solely on the basis of the statement that is the reason for the lawsuit.

public eye. The Supreme Court ruled he was not a public figure.[85] In another case, when a wealthy and well-known socialite sued for libel over a report about her behavior that led to divorce, the Court said she was private because her involvement in the divorce was not voluntary.[86] In yet another case, the Court held that a scientist who had received federal grants and who had published papers in scientific journals was nevertheless a private figure. The defendant tried to claim the scientist had become a public figure through the notoriety of his libel suit. The Court ruled that libel defendants cannot, in effect, create a public figure through the defamation claim itself or media coverage of it.[87]

This and similar cases illustrate what is described as **bootstrapping**. Bootstrapping occurs when media defendants "attach" themselves to the protection of the actual malice standard by citing media coverage—including the very media coverage they generate—of the plaintiff as evidence that the plaintiff is a public figure. Courts have noted that the public controversy at issue must have existed prior to the publication upon which the defamation claim is based in order for the plaintiff to be categorized as a public figure. As the Supreme Court said, "Clearly, those charged with defamation cannot, by their own conduct, create their own defense by making the claimant a public figure."[88] However, a possible side effect can occur when a court rigidly applies the pre-existing controversy requirement. Such an approach may punish legitimate reporting that uncovers specific acts of wrongdoing. Courts therefore attempt to carefully decide which came first: the controversy or the allegedly libelous story about the controversy.

Just as media are not permitted to bootstrap themselves onto their own material to strengthen their defense, a plaintiff may not avoid the actual malice standard by claiming that the attention was unwanted. The proper question for a court is not whether the plaintiff volunteered for the publicity but whether the plaintiff volunteered for an activity from which publicity would foreseeably arise.

Even if an individual is not active in a particular field of endeavor, mere presence within that field may satisfy a court's public figure requirements. One court explains that where a person has "chosen to engage in a profession which draws him regularly into regional and national view and leads to fame and notoriety in the community . . . he invites general public discussion. . . . If society chooses to direct massive public attention to a particular sphere of activity, those who enter that sphere inviting such attention overcome the *Times* standard."[89] Thus, voluntary entry into a sphere of activity is sufficient to satisfy this element of the public figure inquiry.

Because the Supreme Court has said that a public figure is someone with widespread fame or notoriety, the individual's prominence is important in determining public figure status. Moreover, that prominence may apply to a narrowly drawn context. Merely being an executive within a prominent and influential company does not by itself make one a public figure. Professionals are typically not public figures, but under certain circumstances they can be. For example, voluntary use of controversial or unorthodox techniques may be enough to confer public figure status. Publicly defending such methods or adopting other controversial stands also tends to bring about public figure status, a doctor who had written extensively on health issues as a newspaper columnist, who had authored several journal articles on the subject and who had appeared on at least one nationally broadcast television program discussing health and nutrition issues was held to be a public figure for a limited range of issues—those pertaining to health and nutrition.[90]

An individual may assume public figure status within small publics but may revert to being a private figure in larger spheres. For example, a university professor may be a public figure on campus and in the adjacent academic community but a private person beyond those boundaries. The professor therefore may be a public figure for purposes of an article in the university newspaper but not if featured in a regional newspaper or a national magazine. Thus, the professor's public figure status is limited. Similarly, an individual may attain the status of an all-purpose public figure within a particular geographical area.[91]

Involuntary Public Figures In the same ruling that categorized public figures as all-purpose and limited-purpose, the U.S. Supreme Court also suggested that there may be a third category: **involuntary public figures**. These are people who do not necessarily thrust themselves into public controversies voluntarily but who are drawn into specific issues.[92] An individual could be drawn into a matter of public controversy through unforeseen or unintended circumstances, becoming a public figure through no purposeful action. The Court added, however, that the occurrence of such public figures is "exceedingly rare."[93]

Nevertheless, cases surface occasionally where plaintiffs are declared involuntarily public figures. For example, a Connecticut court ruled that a plaintiff who had served time in prison for a crime he did not commit was just such an involuntary public figure. "There are . . . individuals who have not sought publicity or consented to it, but through their own conduct or otherwise have become a legitimate subject of public interest. They have, in other words, become 'news,'" the court decided.[94]

Losing Public Figure Status It is theoretically possible for one-time public figures to revert to private status with the passage of time. However, the courts have been inconsistent in their application of this concept. How much time must pass before a person loses his public status is difficult to pin down. One consideration is whether the person's role in a particular matter remains in the public consciousness or is of public concern. To return to private status, it is likely that a plaintiff would need to demonstrate not only that he or she is no longer a subject of public concern but also that his or her libel claim is not connected to events or controversies of which the public remains aware.

Private Figures A libel plaintiff who does not qualify as a public official or public figure is considered a **private figure.** Private figures usually do not have to prove actual malice as the level of fault in their cases. Typically, they need to show only that the libel defendant acted with **negligence,** although this is not universally true.

involuntary public figure In libel law, a person who does not necessarily thrust himself or herself into public controversies voluntarily but is drawn into a given issue.

private figure In libel law, a plaintiff who cannot be categorized as either a public figure or public official. Generally, in order to recover damages a private figure is not required to prove actual malice but merely negligence on the part of the defendant.

negligence Generally, the failure to exercise reasonable or ordinary care. In libel law, negligence is usually the minimum level of fault a plaintiff must prove in order to receive damages.

Emerging Law

Strict Liability: Is a Blogger a Journalist?

Most legal scholars celebrated the death of strict liability as applied to libel cases when the Supreme Court handed down its decisions in *New York Times Co. v. Sullivan* and *Gertz v. Robert Welch, Inc.* Strict liability means that a defendant is automatically held responsible for damages when an inherently dangerous or wrongful act occurs. Fault is not required to recover damages. When a court applies strict liability, the person injured doesn't have to prove negligence to receive monetary damages.

Generally speaking, a majority of lower court decisions involving libel in the private person–private information context have concluded that states can impose liability without fault. But, in a U.S. District Court in Oregon in 2011, the application of strict liability to a libel case raised new concerns about bloggers and their status as journalists. It also raises concerns about how courts determine matters of public concern.[1]

Kevin Padrick, a senior executive with Obsidian Finance Group, sued blogger Crystal Cox for criticisms she posted about him and Obsidian on her personal, issue-specific website www.obsidianfinancesucks.com, as well as on some third-party websites. Cox suggested, among other things, that Padrick and Obsidian committed fraud, were corrupt, paid off the media and politicians and suggested Padrick had hired a hitman to kill her.[2]

Prior to the case going to trial, a U.S. District Court judge held that most of Cox's posts were protected opinion. Only one post proceeded to trial. During the trial, the judge instructed the jury to treat the case as a strict liability tort. The court rejected Cox's claim that it should treat her as a media defendant—this meant the plaintiff did not have to show fault. The court made its determination of Cox's status as a private figure because she provided no evidence of education in journalism, no connections with established news organizations and no adherence to basic journalistic standards. The court also held that her post about Obsidian Financial did not involve matters of public concern.[3]

In November 2011 a jury awarded damages of $1 million to Obsidian Financial and $1.5 million to Padrick. In 2012 Cox filed a motion for a new trial, arguing that the jury instructions misstated the law and that the verdict was excessive. That motion was denied. Subsequently, both Cox and Obsidian appealed to the 9th Circuit, where the case is still pending.

Cox's motion for a new trial came from noted First Amendment scholar and law professor Eugene Volokh. In arguing for a new trial, Volokh noted that Cox is entitled to the same protection afforded media defendants in the *Gertz* case: that the court must apply a standard of fault of at least negligence. He also argued that the speech at issue was a matter of public concern. Further, he suggested that even if the speech was truly private, the court still must require some level of fault—negligence or actual malice—to uphold a finding of liability.

New York Times media columnist David Carr pointed out that Cox is far from a sympathetic figure in this case. He wrote, "As it turned out, all of the allegations [against Obsidian and Padrick] were coming from Ms. Cox, who churned URLs and cut-and-pasted documents to portray Mr. Padrick as a 'thug,' and a 'thief" who 'committed tax fraud,' and who may have 'hired a hit man' to kill her while engaging in 'illegal and fraudulent activity.' Here's the problem. None of that was ever proved, nor was it picked up by other mainstream media outlets."[4]

Some media and First Amendment groups support Cox's appeal, though, because they say the implications of denying her status as "media" has broad implications for blogs that provide information-based public services. The best example is Scotusblog, which offers comprehensive coverage of the Supreme Court but would not qualify for protection as media under the criteria put forth in the Cox case because it is not affiliated with an established media organization.

---

1. Michael K. Cantwell, *Exploring the Issue of "Strict Liability" for Defamation*, MLRC Bᴜʟʟᴇᴛɪɴ, Dec. 2012, at 3.
2. *Id.*
3. Obsidian Finance Group, LLC v. Cox, 812 F. Supp. 2d 1220 (D. Ore. 2011).
4. David Carr, *When Truth Survives Free Speech*, N.Y. Tɪᴍᴇs, Dec. 11, 2011, *available at* http://www.nytimes.com/2011/12/12/business/media/when-truth-survives-free-speech.html?pagewanted=1.

While the definition of negligence varies from state to state, it is in all cases easier to prove than actual malice. Negligence is the failure to exercise reasonable or ordinary care. What constitutes negligence, however, can vary from one professional setting to another. When establishing what constitutes negligence in the field of journalism, it can be difficult to arrive at a single definition, because news media operate according to a variety of professional standards. What is "acceptable" in television news reporting may not be so in a daily newspaper or online. In other words, unlike professions such as medicine and law, journalism has no single authoritative code of conduct.

That said, some common examples of negligent behavior in the news media have emerged. These include, but are not limited to, the following:

- Relying on a single or anonymous source
- Relying on other media reports without independent investigation
- Careless misstatements of the contents of documents
- Possessing ill will toward the plaintiff
- Conclusions or inferences unreasonably deduced
- Failure to follow established internal practices and policies
- Errors in taking notes and quoting sources

In sum, journalistic negligence may be viewed as the failure to take reasonable care to ensure that a report is accurate and that its subjects are treated fairly.

The Nature of the Statement Whether a plaintiff is considered a public figure for purposes of a libel suit can depend on the nature of the material being published—specifically whether it relates to a matter of public concern. In one case that reached the U.S. Supreme Court, a credit reporting agency issued a credit report that erroneously reported the bankruptcy filing of a Vermont construction contractor. The credit report had been sent to five subscribers who, by agreement, could not repeat the information. The contractor sued for libel. The U.S. Supreme Court upheld a lower court ruling that the contractor was a private figure, making it easier for the company to make a case that it had been libeled. The reason: The statement about its supposed bankruptcy was not a matter of public concern.[95] The Court's opinion stated that the purpose of the speaker and the nature and size of the audience are relevant in determining when speech involves matters of public concern.[96] In determining whether a statement is libelous, therefore, the Court identified the importance of both the status of the plaintiff and the nature of the statement in question.

There was some concern in the media that this ruling might dilute libel protections if plaintiffs were no longer required to prove fault on the part of media outlets who reported on matters that were not of public concern. But that has not occurred. In this same case, the question surfaced as to whether plaintiffs could be required to prove actual malice even when suing a non-media defendant. The Court stated that since its inception, the standard had been applied to non-media defendants.[97] That application, however, is facilitated when the statement is a matter of public concern.

SUMMARY

LIBEL PLAINTIFFS must show that the defendant is at fault for publishing the defamatory material. The level of fault that must be proved varies according to the plaintiff's status. Public officials and public figures must show the defendant acted with actual malice, meaning with knowledge of falsity or reckless disregard for the truth. Private figures usually must prove negligence on the part of the defendant, a much less difficult standard to meet. This distinction in fault standards began with the landmark 1964 U.S. Supreme Court ruling in *New York Times Co. v. Sullivan*. Justice Brennan's opinion for the Court transformed the law and journalism. By affording the media more "breathing space" for error, the ruling reduces the possible chilling effect of libel suits and encourages the journalistic tradition of close scrutiny and criticism of government. ■

Damages

Damages are an essential element to all torts, including libel. In addition to restoring a damaged reputation, a typical goal of libel plaintiffs is to extract financial damages from the defendant to compensate for the harm they suffered. In libel per se cases, damages are presumed. In other libel suits, the plaintiff must prove damages. Damages in libel have generated controversy, particularly when excessive awards produce a chilling effect in the news media.[98] There are several different kinds of civil damages a plaintiff may seek.

Actual Actual damages are the most common kind of libel damages. They represent the quantity of the harm actually suffered by the plaintiff due to the libel. The plaintiff is required to produce evidence showing the monetary loss attributable to the harm suffered. This may include compensation for loss of standing in the community, humiliation and mental suffering—all harms for which it is admittedly difficult to assign a specific dollar amount. Thus, the awarding of actual damages, whether by the court or a jury, tends to be imprecise.

Special Special damages are those for which there is an exact monetary figure specifically related to the material loss suffered because of the libel. These could include extra costs incurred by the plaintiff, lost earnings and other economic losses resulting from the libelous statement. This may lead one to wonder whether the names of actual and special damages should be reversed. Plaintiffs typically do not seek special damages, although there are some circumstances in which they are the only kind of damages a plaintiff may seek.

Presumed Unlike actual or special damages, presumed damages do not require the plaintiff to produce evidence of harm. Some degree of harm is presumed even absent proof. There are limitations, however, with regard to the kind of plaintiff who is entitled to presumed damages and under what circumstances. Public officials, public figures and private figures suing over matters of public concern can be awarded presumed damages only where the defendant acted with actual malice.[99] Private figures suing over matters not of public concern are required to prove the defendant's negligence to obtain presumed damages.

Punitive Punitive damages are intended to punish libel defendants with a monetary penalty and to make an example of them as a means of discouraging both the defendant and others from committing similar acts in the future. A survey of libel plaintiffs showed that nearly one-third were motivated to bring lawsuits in order to punish the defendants.[100] In defamation cases, state law determines punitive damages. According to the 2012–13 Media Libel Survey, seven states and Puerto Rico do not permit punitive damages in defamation suits, and 32 states limit punitive damages by imposing statutory limits, through retraction laws or both. South Carolina's tort reform statute is an example—it became effective in 2012 and "limits punitive damages to the greater of three times the amount of actual damages or $500,000."[101] When they are awarded, punitive damages are often the biggest monetary part of a judgment. Punitive damages (also sometimes called "exemplary damages") are also controversial, and efforts to eliminate or reduce them through legal reforms—both in libel and other areas of law—have proliferated.[102] Especially in an era when news media organizations tend to be owned by multibillion-dollar corporations, plaintiffs typically target these "deep pockets," or what defense attorneys sometimes refer to as the "smart money." In this environment, the plaintiff's attorney may benefit from portraying the case as a David-versus-Goliath battle. Jurors may be sympathetic to such rhetorical appeals and are frequently willing to grant large damage requests. Many believe this to be an unfair situation, leading several states to prohibit punitive damages altogether, while others have limited them.

The courts themselves have also addressed excessive punitive damage awards. In some cases the trial judge has authority to reduce punitive damages awarded by a jury. Appeals courts may also reduce the monetary amount of a punitive damages award. Courts sometimes weigh a punitive damages award against the defendant's ability to pay, as judged by net worth.[103] Under this model, wealthy corporations are more likely to have large punitive damage awards assessed against them. Does this mean their libelous conduct was more egregious than one committed by a small media organization with fewer resources? Not necessarily; hence, another rationale for reform.

SUMMARY

LIBEL PLAINTIFFS TYPICALLY SEEK FINANCIAL COMPENSATION, CALLED DAMAGES. Damages are an essential element of a libel tort. There are four categories of damages: actual, special, presumed and punitive. Excessive awards, especially in the latter category, have prompted some critics to call for reform of the laws and standards that govern damages. ∎

Cases for Study

Thinking About It

The two case excerpts that follow are considered landmark libel cases. The U.S. Supreme Court issued its rulings in these cases at a time when libel law was being dramatically transformed. As you read these case excerpts, keep the following questions in mind:

- How do the two decisions help define the meaning of libel and the contours of libel law?

- How do these rulings balance the freedoms of speech and press protected by the First Amendment against the right of individuals to protect their reputations?

- What are the important concepts that each of these decisions adds to libel law?

- How, according to the Supreme Court in *New York Times Co. v. Sullivan,* does libel law implicate the First Amendment?

New York Times Co. v. Sullivan
SUPREME COURT OF THE UNITED STATES
376 U.S. 254 (1964)

JUSTICE WILLIAM BRENNAN delivered the Court's opinion:

We are required in this case to determine for the first time the extent to which the constitutional protections for speech and press limit a State's power to award damages in a libel action brought by a public official against critics of his official conduct.

Respondent L.B. Sullivan is one of the three elected Commissioners of the City of Montgomery, Alabama. He testified that he was "Commissioner of Public Affairs and the duties are supervision of the Police Department, Fire Department, Department of Cemetery and Department of Scales." He brought this civil libel action against the four individual petitioners, who are Negroes and Alabama clergymen, and against petitioner the New York Times Company, a New York corporation which publishes the New York Times, a daily newspaper. A jury in the Circuit Court of Montgomery County awarded him damages of $500,000, the full amount claimed, against all the petitioners, and the Supreme Court of Alabama affirmed....

Of the 10 paragraphs of text in the advertisement, the third and a portion of the sixth were the basis of respondent's claim of libel....

It is uncontroverted that some of the statements contained in the two paragraphs were not accurate descriptions of events which occurred in Montgomery. Although Negro students staged a demonstration on the State Capitol steps, they sang the National Anthem and not "My Country, 'Tis of Thee." Although nine students were expelled by the State Board of Education, this was not for leading the demonstration at the Capitol, but for demanding service at a lunch counter in the Montgomery County Courthouse on another day. Not the entire student body, but most of it, had protested the expulsion, not by refusing to register, but by boycotting classes on a single day; virtually all the students did register for the ensuing semester....

Because of the importance of the constitutional issues involved, we granted the separate petitions for certiorari of the individual petitioners and of the Times. We reverse the judgment. We hold that the rule of law applied by the Alabama courts is constitutionally deficient for failure to provide the safeguards for freedom of speech and of the press that are required by the First and Fourteenth Amendments in a libel action brought by a public official against critics of his official conduct. We further hold that under the proper safeguards the evidence presented in this case is constitutionally insufficient to support the judgment for respondent. . . .

The publication here was not a "commercial" advertisement in the sense in which the word was used in Chrestensen. It communicated information, expressed opinion, recited grievances, protested claimed abuses, and sought financial support on behalf of a movement whose existence and objectives are matters of the highest public interest and concern. That the Times was paid for publishing the advertisement is as immaterial in this connection as is the fact that newspapers and books are sold. . . . Any other conclusion would discourage newspapers from carrying "editorial advertisements" of this type, and so might shut off an important outlet for the promulgation of information and ideas by persons who do not themselves have access to publishing facilities—who wish to exercise their freedom of speech even though they are not members of the press. . . . To avoid placing such a handicap upon the freedoms of expression, we hold that, if the allegedly libelous statements would otherwise be constitutionally protected from the present judgment, they do not forfeit that protection because they were published in the form of a paid advertisement. . . .

The general proposition that freedom of expression upon public questions is secured by the First Amendment has long been settled by our decisions. The constitutional safeguard, we have said, "was fashioned to assure unfettered interchange of ideas for the bringing about of political and social changes desired by the people. . . ."

. . . The First Amendment, said Judge Learned Hand, "presupposes that right conclusions are more likely to be gathered out of a multitude of tongues, than through any kind of authoritative selection. To many this is, and always will be, folly; but we have staked upon it our all." . . .

Thus we consider this case against the background of a profound national commitment to the principle that debate on public issues should be uninhibited, robust, and wide-open, and that it may well include vehement, caustic, and sometimes unpleasantly sharp attacks on government and public officials. The present advertisement, as an expression of grievance and protest on one of the major public issues of our time, would seem clearly to qualify for the constitutional protection. The question is whether it forfeits that protection by the falsity of some of its factual statements and by its alleged defamation of respondent. . . .

That erroneous statement is inevitable in free debate, and that it must be protected if the freedoms of expression are to have the "breathing space" that they "need . . . to survive. . . ."

Injury to official reputation affords no more warrant for repressing speech that would otherwise be free than does factual error. . . .

If neither factual error nor defamatory content suffices to remove the constitutional shield from criticism of official conduct, the combination of the two elements is no less inadequate. . . .

. . . A rule compelling the critic of official conduct to guarantee the truth of all his factual assertions—and to do so on pain of libel judgments virtually unlimited in amount—leads to a comparable "self-censorship." Allowance of the defense of truth, with the burden of proving it on the defendant, does not mean that only false speech will be deterred. . . . The constitutional guarantees require, we think, a federal rule that prohibits a public official from recovering damages for a defamatory falsehood relating to his official conduct unless he proves that the statement was made with "actual malice"—that is, with knowledge that it was false or with reckless disregard of whether it was false or not. . . .

. . . As Madison said, "the censorial power is in the people over the Government, and not in the Government over the people." It would give public servants an unjustified preference over the public they serve, if critics of official conduct did not have a fair equivalent of the immunity granted to the officials themselves. . . .

We hold today that the Constitution delimits a State's power to award damages for libel in actions brought by public officials against critics of their official conduct. Since this is such an action, the rule requiring proof of actual malice is applicable. . . .

Applying these standards, we consider that the proof presented to show actual malice lacks the convincing clarity which the constitutional standard demands, and hence that it would not constitutionally sustain the judgment for respondent under the proper rule of law. . . .

Finally, there is evidence that the Times published the advertisement without checking its accuracy against the news stories in the Times' own files. The mere presence of the stories in the files does not, of course, establish that the Times "knew" the advertisement was false, since the state of mind required for actual malice would have to be brought home to the persons in the Times' organization having responsibility for the publication of the advertisement. . . .

The judgment of the Supreme Court of Alabama is reversed and the case is remanded to that court for further proceedings not inconsistent with this opinion.

Reversed and remanded.

Gertz v. Robert Welch, Inc.
SUPREME COURT OF THE UNITED STATES
418 U.S. 323 (1974)

JUSTICE LEWIS POWELL delivered the Court's opinion:

This Court has struggled for nearly a decade to define the proper accommodation between the law of defamation and the freedoms of speech and press protected by the First Amendment. With this decision we return to that effort. We granted certiorari to reconsider the extent of a publisher's constitutional privilege against liability for defamation of a private citizen.

In 1968, a Chicago policeman named Nuccio shot and killed a youth named Nelson. The state authorities prosecuted Nuccio for the homicide and ultimately obtained a conviction for murder in the second degree. The Nelson family retained petitioner Elmer Gertz, a reputable attorney, to represent them in civil litigation against Nuccio.

Respondent publishes American Opinion, a monthly outlet for the views of the John Birch Society. Early in the 1960's, the magazine began to warn of a nationwide conspiracy to discredit local law enforcement agencies and create in their stead a national police force capable of supporting a Communist dictatorship. As part of the continuing effort to alert the public to this assumed danger, the managing editor of American Opinion commissioned an article on the murder trial of Officer Nuccio. For this purpose, he engaged a regular contributor to the magazine. In March, 1969, respondent published the resulting article under the title "FRAME-UP: Richard Nuccio And The War On Police." The article purports to demonstrate that the testimony against Nuccio at his criminal trial was false, and that his prosecution was part of the Communist campaign against the police.

In his capacity as counsel for the Nelson family in the civil litigation, petitioner attended the coroner's inquest into the boy's death and initiated actions for damages, but he neither discussed Officer Nuccio with the press nor played any part in the criminal proceeding. Notwithstanding petitioner's remote connection with the prosecution of Nuccio, respondent's magazine portrayed him as an architect of the "frame-up." According to the article, the police file on petitioner took "a big, Irish cop to lift." The article stated that petitioner had been an official of the "Marxist League for Industrial Democracy, originally known as the Intercollegiate Socialist Society, which has advocated the violent seizure of our government." It labeled Gertz a "Leninist" and a "Communist-fronter." It also stated that Gertz had been an officer of the National

Lawyers Guild, described as a Communist organization that "probably did more than any other outfit to plan the Communist attack on the Chicago police during the 1968 Democratic Convention."

These statements contained serious inaccuracies. The implication that petitioner had a criminal record was false. Petitioner had been a member and officer of the National Lawyers Guild some 15 years earlier, but there was no evidence that he or that organization had taken any part in planning the 1968 demonstrations in Chicago. There was also no basis for the charge that petitioner was a "Leninist" or a "Communist-fronter." And he had never been a member of the "Marxist League for Industrial Democracy" or the "Intercollegiate Socialist Society."

The managing editor of American Opinion made no effort to verify or substantiate the charges against petitioner. Instead, he appended an editorial introduction stating that the author had "conducted extensive research into the Richard Nuccio Case." And he included in the article a photograph of petitioner and wrote the caption that appeared under it: "Elmer Gertz of Red Guild harasses Nuccio." Respondent placed the issue of American Opinion containing the article on sale at newsstands throughout the country and distributed reprints of the article on the streets of Chicago.

Petitioner filed a diversity action for libel in the United States District Court for the Northern District of Illinois. He claimed that the falsehoods published by respondent injured his reputation as a lawyer and a citizen. Before filing an answer, respondent moved to dismiss the complaint for failure to state a claim upon which relief could be granted, apparently on the ground that petitioner failed to allege special damages. But the court ruled that statements contained in the article constituted libel *per se* under Illinois law, and that consequently petitioner need not plead special damages. . . .

After answering the complaint, respondent filed a pretrial motion for summary judgment, claiming a constitutional privilege against liability for defamation.

It asserted that petitioner was a public official or a public figure, and that the article concerned an issue of public interest and concern. For these reasons, respondent argued, it was entitled to invoke the privilege enunciated in *New York Times Co. v. Sullivan*. Under this rule, respondent would escape liability unless petitioner could prove publication of defamatory falsehood "with 'actual malice'—that is, with knowledge that it was false or with reckless disregard of whether it was false or not." Respondent claimed that petitioner could not make such a showing, and submitted a supporting affidavit by the magazine's managing editor. The editor denied any knowledge of the falsity of the statements concerning petitioner, and stated that he had relied on the author's reputation and on his prior experience with the accuracy and authenticity of the author's contributions to American Opinion.

The District Court denied respondent's motion for summary judgment in a memorandum opinion of September 16, 1970. The court did not dispute respondent's claim to the protection of the *New York Times* standard. Rather, it concluded that petitioner might overcome the constitutional privilege by making a factual showing sufficient to prove publication of defamatory falsehood in reckless disregard of the truth. During the course of the trial, however, it became clear that the trial court had not accepted all of respondent's asserted grounds for applying the *New York Times* rule to this case. It thought that respondent's claim to the protection of the constitutional privilege depended on the contention that petitioner was either a public official under the *New York Times* decision or a public figure under *Curtis Publishing Co. v. Butts* (1967), apparently discounting the argument that a privilege would arise from the presence of a public issue. After all the evidence had been presented but before submission of the case to the jury, the court ruled in effect that petitioner was neither a public official nor a public figure. It added that, if he were, the resulting application of the *New York Times* standard would require a directed verdict for respondent. Because some statements in the article constituted libel *per se* under Illinois law, the court submitted the case to the jury under instructions that withdrew from its consideration all issues save the measure of damages. The jury awarded $50,000 to petitioner.

Following the jury verdict and on further reflection, the District Court concluded that the *New York Times* standard should govern this case even though petitioner was not a public official or public figure. It accepted respondent's contention that that privilege protected discussion of any public issue without regard to the status of a person defamed therein. Accordingly, the court entered judgment for respondent notwithstanding the jury's verdict. . . .

Petitioner appealed to contest the applicability of the *New York Times* standard to this case. . . . After reviewing the record, the Court of Appeals endorsed the District Court's conclusion that petitioner had failed to show by clear and convincing evidence that respondent had acted with "actual malice" as defined by *New York Times*. There was no evidence that the managing editor of American Opinion knew of the falsity of the accusations made in the article. In fact, he knew nothing about petitioner except what he learned from the article. The court correctly noted that mere proof of failure to investigate, without more, cannot establish reckless disregard for the truth. Rather, the publisher must act with a " 'high degree of awareness of . . . probable falsity.' " The evidence in this case did not reveal that respondent had cause for such an awareness. The Court of Appeals therefore affirmed. For the reasons stated below, we reverse.

The principal issue in this case is whether a newspaper or broadcaster that publishes defamatory falsehoods about an individual who is neither a public official nor a public figure may claim a constitutional privilege against liability for the injury inflicted by those statements. . . .

Three years after *New York Times,* a majority of the Court agreed to extend the constitutional privilege to defamatory criticism of "public figures." This extension was announced in *Curtis Publishing Co. v. Butts* and its companion, *Associated Press v. Walker* (1967). . . .

We begin with the common ground. Under the First Amendment, there is no such thing as a false idea. However pernicious an opinion may seem, we depend for its correction not on the conscience of judges and juries but on the competition of other ideas. But there is no constitutional value in false statements of fact. Neither the intentional lie nor the careless error materially advances society's interest in "uninhibited, robust, and wide-open" debate on public issues. They belong to that category of utterances which "are no essential part of any exposition of ideas, and are of such slight social value as a step to truth that any benefit that may be derived from them is clearly outweighed by the social interest in order and morality."

Although the erroneous statement of fact is not worthy of constitutional protection, it is nevertheless inevitable in free debate. As James Madison pointed out in the Report on the Virginia Resolutions of 1798: "Some degree of abuse is inseparable from the proper use of every thing; and in no instance is this more true than in that of the press." And punishment of error runs the risk of inducing a cautious and restrictive exercise of the constitutionally guaranteed freedoms of speech and press. Our decisions recognize that a rule of strict liability that compels a publisher or broadcaster to guarantee the accuracy of his factual assertions may lead to intolerable self-censorship. Allowing the media to avoid liability only by proving the truth of all injurious statements does not accord adequate protection to First Amendment liberties. As the Court stated in *New York Times Co. v. Sullivan*: "Allowance of the defense of truth, with the burden of proving it on the defendant, does not mean that only false speech will be deterred." The First Amendment requires that we protect some falsehood in order to protect speech that matters.

The need to avoid self-censorship by the news media is, however, not the only societal value at issue. If it were, this Court would have embraced long ago the view that publishers and broadcasters enjoy an unconditional and indefeasible immunity from liability for defamation. Such a rule would, indeed, obviate the fear that the prospect of civil liability for injurious falsehood might dissuade a timorous press from the effective exercise of First Amendment freedoms. Yet absolute protection for the communications media requires a total sacrifice of the competing value served by the law of defamation.

The legitimate state interest underlying the law of libel is the compensation of individuals for the harm inflicted on them by defamatory falsehood. . . .

Some tension necessarily exists between the need for a vigorous and uninhibited press and the legitimate interest in redressing wrongful injury. . . . In our continuing effort to define the proper accommodation between these competing concerns, we have been especially anxious to assure to the freedoms of speech and press that "breathing space" essential to their fruitful exercise. To that end, this Court has extended a measure of strategic protection to defamatory falsehood.

The *New York Times* standard defines the level of constitutional protection appropriate to the context of defamation of a public person. Those who, by reason of the notoriety of their achievements or the vigor and success with which they seek the public's attention, are properly classed as public figures and those who hold governmental office may recover for injury to reputation only on clear and convincing proof that the defamatory falsehood was made with knowledge of its falsity or with reckless disregard for the truth. This standard administers an extremely powerful antidote to the inducement to media self-censorship of the common-law rule of strict liability for libel and slander. And it exacts a correspondingly high price from the victims of defamatory falsehood. . . .

Theoretically, of course, the balance between the needs of the press and the individual's claim to compensation for wrongful injury might be struck on a case-by-case basis. . . . But this approach would lead to unpredictable results and uncertain expectations, and it could render our duty to supervise the lower courts unmanageable. Because an *ad hoc* resolution of the competing interests at stake in each particular case is not feasible, we must lay down broad rules of general application. . . .

With that caveat, we have no difficulty in distinguishing among defamation plaintiffs. The first remedy of any victim of defamation is self-help—using available opportunities to contradict the lie or correct the error and thereby to minimize its adverse impact on reputation. Public officials and public figures usually enjoy significantly greater access to the channels of effective communication, and hence have a more realistic opportunity to counteract false statements than private individuals normally enjoy. Private individuals are therefore more vulnerable to injury, and the state interest in protecting them is correspondingly greater.

More important than the likelihood that private individuals will lack effective opportunities for rebuttal, there is a compelling normative consideration underlying the distinction between public and private defamation plaintiffs. An individual who decides to seek governmental office must accept certain necessary consequences of that involvement in public affairs. He runs the risk of closer public scrutiny than might otherwise be the case. And society's interest in the officers of government is not strictly limited to the formal discharge of official duties. . . .

Those classed as public figures stand in a similar position. Hypothetically, it may be possible for someone to become a public figure through no purposeful action of his own, but the instances of truly involuntary public figures must be exceedingly rare. For the most part those who attain this status have assumed roles of special prominence in the affairs of society. Some occupy positions of such persuasive power and influence that they are deemed public figures for all purposes. More commonly, those classed as public figures have thrust themselves to the forefront of particular public controversies in order to influence the resolution of the issues involved. In either event, they invite attention and comment.

Even if the foregoing generalities do not obtain in every instance, the communications media are entitled to act on the assumption that public officials and public figures have voluntarily exposed themselves to increased risk of injury from defamatory falsehood concerning them. No such assumption is justified with respect to a private individual. . . .

For these reasons, we conclude that the States should retain substantial latitude in their efforts to enforce a legal remedy for defamatory falsehood injurious to the reputation of a private individual. . . .

We hold that, so long as they do not impose liability without fault, the States may define for themselves the appropriate standard of liability for a publisher or broadcaster of defamatory falsehood injurious to a private individual. This approach provides a more equitable boundary between the competing concerns involved here. It recognizes the strength of the legitimate state interest in compensating private individuals for wrongful injury to reputation, yet shields the press and broadcast media from the rigors of strict liability for defamation. . . .

Our accommodation of the competing values at stake in defamation suits by private individuals allows the States to impose liability on the publisher or broadcaster of defamatory falsehood on a less demanding showing than that required by *New York Times*. This conclusion is not based on a belief that the considerations which prompted the adoption of the *New York Times* privilege for defamation of public officials and its extension to public figures are wholly inapplicable to the context of private individuals. Rather, we endorse this approach in recognition of the strong and legitimate state interest in compensating private individuals for injury to reputation. . . . [T]he States may not permit recovery of presumed or punitive damages, at least when liability is not based on a showing of knowledge of falsity or reckless disregard for the truth. . . .

We would not, of course, invalidate state law simply because we doubt its wisdom, but here we are attempting to reconcile state law with a competing interest grounded in the constitutional command of the First Amendment. It is therefore appropriate to require that state remedies for defamatory falsehood reach no farther than is necessary to protect the legitimate interest involved. It is necessary to restrict defamation plaintiffs who do not prove knowledge of falsity or reckless disregard for the truth to compensation for actual injury. . . .

We also find no justification for allowing awards of punitive damages against publishers and broadcasters held liable under state-defined standards of liability for defamation. In most jurisdictions jury discretion over the amounts awarded is limited only by the gentle rule that they not be excessive. Consequently, juries assess punitive damages in wholly unpredictable amounts bearing no necessary relation to the actual harm caused. . . .

Notwithstanding our refusal to extend the *New York Times* privilege to defamation of private individuals, respondent contends that we should affirm the judgment below on the ground that petitioner is either a public official or a public figure. There is little basis for the former assertion. Several years prior to the present incident, petitioner had served briefly on housing committees appointed by the mayor of Chicago, but at the time of publication, he had never held any remunerative governmental position. Respondent admits this, but argues that petitioner's appearance at the coroner's inquest rendered him a *"de facto* public official." Our cases recognize no such concept. Respondent's suggestion would sweep all lawyers under the *New York Times* rule as officers of the court, and distort the plain meaning of the "public official" category beyond all recognition. We decline to follow it.

Respondent's characterization of petitioner as a public figure raises a different question. That designation may rest on either of two alternative bases. In some instances an individual may achieve such pervasive fame or notoriety that he becomes a public figure for all purposes and in all contexts. More commonly, an individual voluntarily injects himself or is drawn into a particular public controversy, and thereby becomes a public figure for a limited range of issues. In either case such persons assume special prominence in the resolution of public questions.

Petitioner has long been active in community and professional affairs. He has served as an officer of local civic groups and of various professional organizations, and he has published several books and articles on legal subjects. Although petitioner was consequently well known in some circles, he had achieved no general fame or notoriety in the community. None of the prospective jurors called at the trial had ever heard of petitioner prior to this litigation, and respondent offered no proof that this response was atypical of the local population. We would not lightly assume that a citizen's participation in community and professional affairs rendered him a public figure for all purposes. Absent clear evidence of general fame or notoriety in the community, and pervasive involvement in the affairs of society, an individual should not be deemed a public personality for all aspects of his life. It is preferable to reduce the public-figure question to a more meaningful context by looking to the nature and extent of an individual's participation in the particular controversy giving rise to the defamation.

In this context it is plain that petitioner was not a public figure. He played a minimal role at the coroner's inquest, and his participation related solely to his representation of a private client. He took no part in the criminal prosecution of Officer Nuccio. Moreover, he never discussed either the criminal or civil litigation with the press and was never quoted as having done so. He plainly did not thrust himself into the vortex of this public issue, nor did he engage the public's attention in an attempt to influence its outcome. We are persuaded that the trial court did not err in refusing to characterize petitioner as a public figure for the purpose of this litigation.

We therefore conclude that the *New York Times* standard is inapplicable to this case, and that the trial court erred in entering judgment for respondent. Because the jury was allowed to impose liability without fault and was permitted to presume damages without proof of injury, a new trial is necessary. We reverse and remand for further proceedings in accord with this opinion.

It is so ordered.

Chapter 5

Under the First Amendment there is no such thing as a false idea. However pernicious an opinion may seem, we depend for its correction not on the conscience of judges and juries but on the competition of other ideas. But there is no constitutional value in false statements of fact.

U.S. Supreme Court Justice Lewis Powell[1]

With the rise in popularity of use created reviews on websites like Yelp and Angie's List, opportunitie[s] for lawsuits about criticism are increasing. Especially notable are a steady strea[m] of defamation lawsuits brought by businesses tha[t] argue they are sustaining damag[e] in the form of los[t] future customers

Libel
Defenses and Privileges

Fair Report Privilege

Fair Comment and Criticism

Opinion

Innocent Construction
Letters to the Editor
Rhetorical Hyperbole,
  Parody and Satire

Neutral Reportage

Wire Service Defense

Single-Publication Rule

The Libel-Proof Plaintiff

Other Defense Issues

Summary Judgment
Jurisdiction
Section 230 Immunity
Statute of Limitations
Length of Statutes of
  Limitation in Libel
  Actions
Retractions
Responsible Reporting

Cases for Study

➤ *Ollman v. Evans*
➤ *Milkovich v. Lorain
  Journal Co.*

Suppose . . .

. . . that a newspaper columnist writes about a school board hearing that is investigating possible neglect or wrongdoing on the part of school employees. The column contains accusations that some people lied at the hearing. One of the accused, believing that the statement was false and damaged his reputation, sues the columnist and his newspaper for libel. The defendants claim the column is an expression of opinion and they are protected by the First Amendment. These were the circumstances in *Milkovich v. Lorain Journal Co.,* discussed in this chapter and excerpted at the end.

Parties sued for libel can use many defenses, any of which has the potential to be successful, depending on the circumstances of the case. There is one important difference between the plaintiff's case and the defendant's challenges: Although the plaintiff must prove every element of her case, a successful defendant needs only one suitable defense. The libel defense attorney is like a carpenter who must choose the right tool for a given job. A carpenter has many tools to choose from, yet it is crucial to choose the proper one to get the job done. The libel defense attorney is no different.

Defending a libel suit may consist of merely turning the plaintiff's case inside out. That is, by taking those elements of the plaintiff's case explained in Chapter 4 and proving their inverse, a libel defendant may be able to demonstrate that there is no liability for publishing the statement at issue. For example, truth or substantial truth is the appropriate counterargument to the plaintiff's claim that the material at issue is false. Truth is sometimes viewed as the most basic and iron-clad of all libel defenses. Those accused of libel have several defenses at their disposal that may not directly correspond with any element of the plaintiff's case.

Fair Report Privilege

Imagine that you, a journalist, get a telephone call from someone who says that a fight involving two local celebrities is taking place at a nearby watering hole. By the time you get there, order has been restored and the celebrities are gone. But you interview witnesses, and some of them tell you the fight began when one man made some disparaging remarks about the other's girlfriend. You write the story, including details about the accusations that started the dispute, and it is published in the next day's newspaper.

You are distressed to see that the competing newspaper in town also has a story about the fight that includes the same details you used in your story, even though it had no reporter on the scene. The writer of that story cobbled together some facts strictly from the official police report. Then, a week later, you are shocked to learn that the celebrity's girlfriend is suing you and your newspaper for libel, accurately claiming the accusations reported about her are false. On top of that, her attorney knows libel law well enough not to sue the other reporter and his paper.

The other paper's reporter is protected by the **fair report privilege** because his story is based on a police report, but it is unlikely that you have that same defense. Why? The fair report privilege is based on the idea that keeping citizens informed about matters of public concern is sometimes more important than avoiding occasional damage to individual reputations. It gives reporters some breathing room to report on official governmental conduct without having to first prove the truth of what the government says. How does the privilege apply to this situation? By relying only on the police report, the other reporter satisfied the conditions to maintain the privilege. Your story came from sources that were not official government records or proceedings. Even if a contributor to an official proceeding makes a statement that is false and defamatory—or if an official government record does the same—a news organization whose report is based exclusively on the statement will not be liable for defamation as long as the story accurately and fairly reflects the content of the report or proceeding.

In addition, some question has been raised about whether a reporter's intent to harm a person's reputation may terminate the fair report privilege. This question surfaced in a Minnesota

fair report privilege A privilege claimed by journalists who report events on the basis of official records. The report must fairly and accurately reflect the content of the records; this is the condition that sometimes leads to this privilege being called "conditional privilege."

Points of Law

Fair Report Privilege

1. The information must be obtained from a record or proceeding recognized as "official."

2. The news report must fairly and accurately reflect what is in the public record or what was said during the official proceeding.

3. The source of the statement should be clearly noted in the news report.

4. Not all states recognize the fair report privilege.

case in which a citizen mentioned the name of a police officer during a city council meeting. The citizen accused the officer of dealing drugs. The reporter who covered the meeting did not report the accusation immediately but instead investigated the situation. When the reporter published several articles, the officer sued, claiming that the articles were inaccurate and were written with malice, or ill will. (This is not the same as actual malice, discussed in Chapter 4.) Lower courts said the fair report privilege could be lost if the defendants are motivated by ill will. But ultimately courts ruled that the reporter in this case had no intent to injure the plaintiff.[2] Nevertheless, the question of whether malice could possibly eliminate the privilege in some jurisdictions remains.

The fair report privilege covers officials and proceedings in the executive, judicial and legislative branches of state, local and federal governments and, often, private individuals communicating with the government. Law enforcement agencies are also covered, including reports of police activity. For example, a former Belleville, Ill., police chief sued the local newspaper for libel after the newspaper reported that he was the subject of a rape investigation. A three-judge panel of the state appellate court unanimously dismissed the case, ruling that the newspaper was protected by the fair report privilege because its article was a fair and accurate report based on a local prosecutor's comments.[3]

Not every statement by a police officer is privileged, however. This generally is determined on a case-by-case fact basis with different outcomes in different states. One state supreme court, for example, refused to apply the fair report privilege to statements made by a police officer to a reporter during an interview.[4] The court ruled that the officer's participation in the interview and his remarks were not considered to be part of his official duties—a key determinant in deciding whether the privilege applies. More recent decisions have taken a different approach. In South Carolina, a court held that the fair report privilege applied to an e-mail the sheriff's department sent to a newspaper and was not limited to official records and press releases. In Michigan, a U.S. District Court applied the privilege to unofficial statements made to

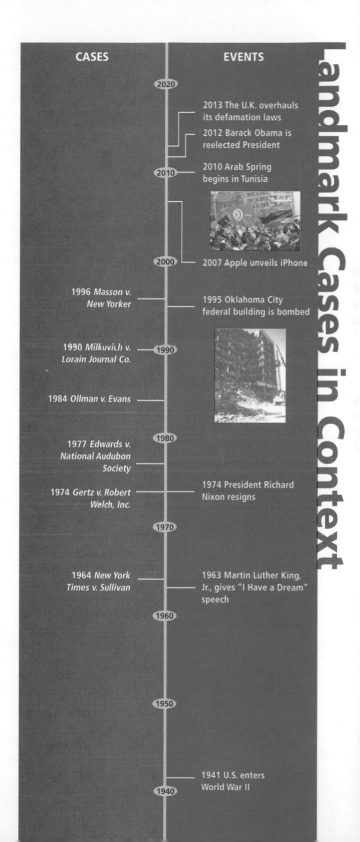

Landmark Cases in Context

CASES

EVENTS

2020

2013 The U.K. overhauls its defamation laws

2012 Barack Obama is reelected President

2010 Arab Spring begins in Tunisia

2010

2007 Apple unveils iPhone

2000

1996 *Masson v. New Yorker*

1995 Oklahoma City federal building is bombed

1990 *Milkovich v. Lorain Journal Co.*

1990

1984 *Ollman v. Evans*

1980

1977 *Edwards v. National Audubon Society*

1974 *Gertz v. Robert Welch, Inc.*

1974 President Richard Nixon resigns

1970

1964 *New York Times v. Sullivan*

1963 Martin Luther King, Jr., gives "I Have a Dream" speech

1960

1950

1941 U.S. enters World War II

1940

the press by police officers.[5] The Sixth Circuit, applying Tennessee law, upheld a summary judgment in favor of a local TV news station that videotaped a story based on a ride-along with the U.S. Marshals Service during which the marshals erroneously arrested an individual with the same name as the fugitive. A day after the ride-along, the station aired its report of the arrest. Although the arrest itself was in error, the court held that the television report was a fair and accurate account of an official government action. Because the station didn't know the marshals had arrested the wrong person, the court found no evidence of actual malice to overcome the privilege.[6] Journalists should note that different outcomes, including failure to recognize privilege, occur in different states and court systems. This happened recently when a federal court in Maine noted that the state does not recognize the fair report privilege.[7]

The justification for the fair report privilege is that it stems from another kind of privileged situation. Within some spheres of society, it is so vitally important that people be allowed to speak and communicate information without fear of being sued for libel that they are granted immunity from liability. The rationale is that citizens in a participatory democracy are entitled to such information.[8] As a Massachusetts judge, Oliver Wendell Holmes, Jr., was among those who reasoned that the public should be provided with information about judicial proceedings because "those who administer justice should act under a sense of public responsibility."[9] Nearly a century later, another Massachusetts court echoed Holmes and held that the value of granting privilege to media reports about the courts is "the security which publicity gives for the proper administration of justice."[10]

This privilege—called **absolute privilege**—typically occurs within the context of carrying out the business of government. An open society demands that members of the public have access to information relating to government proceedings. It logically follows that people reporting on these proceedings or information related to these proceedings also have some protection. That protection, though, is only available when the news report is fair and accurate. Thus, in addition to this protection sometimes being referred to as the fair report privilege, it also is called **conditional privilege** or **qualified privilege**.

Reports about judicial activities—the courts—are conditionally privileged. Therefore, media accounts of testimony, depositions, attorney arguments, trials, verdicts, opinions and orders—those aspects that are typically open or available to the public—are among the proceedings covered. Also, documents that relate to the judicial branch are typically privileged. For example, the New Jersey Supreme Court ruled that journalists who report accurately from court filings, including pretrial documents, are protected from libel claims.[11] In Maryland a state court in 2012 applied the fair report privilege to a newspaper's coverage of a murder trial that included reporting based on a discovery memo in the case file that was not offered as evidence at trial.[12]

The fair report privilege is important to the news media given that much of what they do is report on the activities, people, records and documents of the various levels of government. The privilege can be forfeited if the allegedly

absolute privilege A complete exemption from liability for the speaking or publishing of defamatory words of and concerning another because the statement was made within the performance of duty such as in judicial or political contexts.

conditional (or qualified) privilege An exemption from liability for repeating defamatory words of and concerning another because the original statement was made within the performance of duty such as in judicial or political contexts; usually claimed by journalists who report statements made in absolutely privileged situations; this privilege is conditional (or qualified) on the premise that the reporting is fair and accurate.

defamatory material is published with inaccuracies or if reported unfairly. This unfair reporting can include ill will toward the plaintiff, if the gist of the article is not substantially true or if the author draws conclusions or adds comments to the official report. The fair report privilege protects media reports of official government actions, regardless of possible defamatory elements within those reports and proceedings.

The Detroit News, for example, successfully used the fair report privilege when it was sued for libel for printing the names of convicted felons working in Detroit public schools. The newspaper had obtained the names from state records. One of the people named sued for libel, claiming the felony charges against her would soon be dismissed. "The privilege precludes damages in a libel suit," the Michigan Court of Appeals ruled, "where a defendant engages in the publication of the contents of a public record, provided the defendant presents a 'fair and true' report of the public record."[13]

Fair Comment and Criticism

Reviews of books and other works subject to public scrutiny are at the root of another libel defense: fair comment and criticism. **Fair comment and criticism** is a common law privilege that protects critics from lawsuits brought by individuals in the public eye. A critic can be anyone who comments on these individuals and their work. Being in the public eye is not the same as being a public figure for purposes of actual malice. A person in the public eye is anyone who enters a public sphere: artists, entertainers, dramatists, writers, members of the clergy, teachers—anyone who moves in and out of the public eye, either professionally or as an amateur. By placing their work products or services into the public sphere, they invite criticism. The privilege also protects commentary on institutions whose activities are of interest to the public or where matters of public interest are concerned. Thus, not only are written works subject to fair comment and criticism, but so are works of art and other products of businesses such as restaurants that implicitly invite reviews of their offerings.

A libel suit involving a book review is instructive: An author sued The New York Times for a reviewer's criticisms of his book. Among other things, the reviewer wrote that the book contained "too much sloppy journalism to trust the bulk of [its] 512 pages including its whopping 64 pages of footnotes."[14] A federal appeals court held that the review was not defamatory, ruling that the genre of

In 1898, a well-known stage act, the Cherry Sisters, sued for libel after a bad review from an Iowa newspaper. They lost, and the ruling in that case is regarded as partly responsible for acceptance of the fair comment and criticism privilege.

fair comment and criticism A common law privilege that protects critics from lawsuits brought by individuals in the public eye.

realWorld Law

Consumer Reviews and Criticism Online

With the rise in popularity of user-created reviews on websites like Yelp and Angie's List, opportunities for lawsuits about criticism are increasing. Especially notable are a steady stream of defamation lawsuits brought by businesses that argue they are sustaining damages in the form of lost future customers. One example that received national attention is a case involving Jane Perez, who wrote a Yelp and an Angie's List review criticizing a contractor whom she said failed to deliver promised services. Perez also implied he might be responsible for jewelry missing from her home. The contractor filed a defamation lawsuit seeking $750,000. In 2012 a county circuit court in Virginia ordered a preliminary injunction, instructing Perez to remove portions of her negative review, including references she had made to an earlier lawsuit in which she won a judgment against the contractor for unpaid bills. The court also barred her from repeating her accusations in future posts.[1]

The Virginia Supreme Court quickly overturned the injunction saying it amounted to an unreasonable prior restraint of Perez's right to free speech. The court noted that the contractor also had adequate remedy by suing Perez for damages. Public Citizen, which filed the appeal of the preliminary injunction, said the court's decision "confirms the importance of not shutting down public discussion on the Internet just because someone doesn't like what's being talked about."[2]

The defamation suit against Perez is pending. But Public Citizen's attorney said, "This ruling means if you have a sound case for defamation, by all means, you can bring it, but you shouldn't expect to have (comments) taken off-line at first blush. You have to show to the satisfaction of a jury that false statements have been made about you with malice or negligence."[3]

---

1. Justin Jouvenal, *Injunction Over Negative Yelp Review Overturned by Virginia Supreme Court,* Wash. Post (Jan. 2, 2013), *available at* http://articles.washingtonpost.com/2013–01–02/local/36212098_1_yelp-online-reviews-injunction.
2. Bob Sullivan, *Court Overturns Ruling That Required "Copy Editing" of Yelp Criticism,* NBC News (Jan. 2, 2013), *available at* http://redtape.nbcnews.com/_news/2013/01/02/16306557-court-overturns-ruling-that-required-copy-editing-of-yelp-criticism?lite.
3. *Id.*

the writing and the context within which it appeared must be considered: "The statements at issue in the instant case are assessments of a book, rather than direct assaults on [the author's] character, reputation, or competence as a journalist. . . . While a critic's latitude is not unlimited, he or she must be given the constitutional 'breathing space' appropriate to the genre."[15]

Historically, the fair comment and criticism privilege was incorporated into the common law to afford legal immunity for the honest expression of opinion on matters of legitimate public interest based on a true or privileged statement of fact.[16] Comment was generally privileged when it concerned a matter of public concern, was based on true or privileged facts, represented the actual opinion of the speaker and was not made solely for the purpose of causing harm.[17] The privilege of fair comment applied only to an expression of opinion and not to a false statement of fact, whether it was expressly stated or implied from an expression of opinion.[18] As the U.S. Supreme Court has stated, "The privilege of 'fair comment' was the device employed to strike the appropriate balance between the need for vigorous public discourse and the need to redress injury to citizens wrought by invidious or irresponsible speech."[19]

Opinion

Although similar to fair comment and criticism, the libel defense of opinion is distinct. The primary difference is that fair comment and criticism is rooted in the common law. Opinion stems from the First Amendment and is therefore a constitutional defense and thus stronger and more effective. It is considered to be an unqualified defense in that once proved, it cannot be lost. The question, however, becomes whether specific case circumstances permit the application of the opinion defense.

Holding and expressing opinions is a right guaranteed by the First Amendment. U.S. Supreme Court Justice Lewis Powell laid this out explicitly: "Under the First Amendment there is no such thing as a false idea. However pernicious an opinion may seem, we depend for its correction not on the conscience of judges and juries but on the competition of other ideas."[20] The First Amendment "rests on the assumption that the widest possible dissemination of information from diverse and antagonistic sources is essential to the welfare of the public."[21] Moreover, as Justice Louis Brandeis wrote early in the 20th century, "[F]reedom to think as you will and speak as you think are means indispensable to the discovery and spread of political truth."[22] Thus, a libel defendant may put forth an argument that, in part, echoes Justice William Brennan's opinion in *New York Times Co. v. Sullivan*.[23] The question becomes, "Does the speech contribute to the 'profound national commitment to the principle that debate on public issues should be uninhibited, robust, and wide-open'?"[24] At a fundamental level, a libel defense may be constructed on constitutional grounds—a claim that limiting ability to convey information is an abridgment of the First Amendment guarantees of free speech and press. Denying an individual the opportunity to express an opinion would be such an abridgment.

The challenge comes in attempting to distinguish statements of fact from statements of opinion. To attempt to separate statements of fact from statements of opinion is to venture onto one of the law's slipperiest of slopes. Yet to do so is vital in establishing the boundaries of the opinion defense's protection. Stating an opinion involves far more than attaching "In my opinion," "I believe" or similar qualifiers to a statement.

The distinguishing attributes of opinion were developed and ultimately solidified by a federal appeals court. That court articulated a four-part test to determine whether a statement was one of fact or an expression of opinion.[25] Not all of the test's elements need to be satisfied; rather, the answers to its questions are to be evaluated in total.

The *Ollman* test (named for the case from which it stems, *Ollman v. Evans*,[26] excerpted at the end of this chapter) appeared to provide a sound and relatively straightforward instrument to assess opinion. The following are four parts:

1. Is the statement verifiable—objectively capable of proof or disproof? In other words, can the statement be proved either true or false? Opinion is indirectly linked to the falsity/truth element of libel. That is, if a statement cannot be proved true or false, then it may satisfy the legal definition of an expression of opinion.

2. What is the common usage or meaning of the words?

3. What is the journalistic context in which the statement occurs? This element is especially important for the media. It provides added weight for an opinion defense when the material in question appears in a part of a publication (or, e.g., a broadcast or website) traditionally reserved for opinions—for example, the op-ed pages, personal columns or a blog. The entire article or column must be considered as a whole. The language of the entire column may signal that a specific statement, standing alone, which would appear to be factual, is in fact an expression of opinion.

4. What is the broader social context into which the statement fits? For example, was the statement at issue made within a context or in a place where the expression of opinions is not only common but expected? Or was it made within a context in which opinion is not commonplace and, instead, statements are presumed to be statements of fact?

Over time, opinion was granted a wide berth of protection. Newsweek magazine, for example, was vindicated in publishing a reference to a false accusation that a former South Dakota governor had sexually assaulted a teenage girl. The words appeared to some people to constitute a statement of fact, but the court found them to be "imprecise, unverifiable" and "presented in a forum where spirited writing is expected and involves criticism of the motives and intentions of a public official."[27] Other plaintiffs who sued because they were called unscrupulous charlatans, neo-Nazis, sleazebags and ignorant and spineless politicians lost their cases because these charges were determined to be expressions of opinion rather than statements of fact.[28]

The latitude afforded to opinion was extensive, but then came a case that put the "no such thing as a false idea"[29] doctrine to the test. Six years after the *Ollman* test was created, the U.S. Supreme Court reframed what had appeared to be a nearly absolute opinion defense. The case involved a high school wrestling team

Points of Law

The *Ollman* Test for Opinion

1. Verifiability
2. Common meaning
3. Journalistic context
4. Social context

that brawled with a competing team during a match. Several people were injured. After a hearing, the coach of one team was censured and his team was placed on probation. A lawsuit was filed in an attempt to prevent the team probation. At a hearing, the coach, Michael Milkovich, denied that he had incited the brawl. In the next day's newspaper, a local sports columnist wrote that Milkovich, along with a school superintendent, misrepresented the truth in an effort to keep the team from being placed on probation. "Anyone who attended the meet . . . knows in his heart that [they] lied at the hearing after each having given his solemn oath to tell the truth," the column read. "But they got away with it." The columnist added that the entire episode provided a lesson for the student body: "If you get in a jam, lie your way out."[30]

The coach sued for libel. After 15 years and several appeals, the Ohio Court of Appeals held that the column was constitutionally protected opinion, but the U.S. Supreme Court reversed.[31] The Court rejected the broad application of the concept that there is "no such thing as a false idea." "[T]his passage has become the opening salvo in all arguments for protection from defamation actions on the ground of opinion," wrote Chief Justice William Rehnquist, "even though [the original] case did not remotely concern the question."[32] The passage was not intended to create a wholesale defamation exemption for anything that might be labeled "opinion," he continued. "Not only would such an interpretation be contrary to the tenor and context of the passage, but it would also ignore the fact that expressions of 'opinion' may often imply an assertion of objective fact."[33] Rehnquist wrote that facts can disguise themselves as opinions, and, when they do, they imply knowledge of hidden facts that led to the opinion. Merely embedding statements of fact in a column does not transform those statements into expressions of opinion. They remain statements of fact and, if false, may be the basis of a libel suit. Whether the material is verifiable—whether it can be proved true or false—is paramount. The Supreme Court said the key question in this case was whether a reasonable reader could conclude that the statements in the column implied that Milkovich had lied in the judicial proceeding. The Court believed that such an implication had been made and ruled for Milkovich. Even though the material was in a column and thus satisfied the "journalistic context" part of the *Ollman* test, the Court said it was not opinion.[34]

Now more than two decades since the *Milkovich* ruling, court decisions involving the opinion defense continue to distinguish fact from opinion. In 2012, a New York trial court dismissed a libel case on the grounds that criticism published on an online review website amounted to pure opinion and did not include provable defamatory facts. In that case, a medical doctor sued over comments that claimed she was "a terrible doctor" and was "mentally unstable and has poor skills."[35] The court held that the comments were opinion in the context of the Internet and said that anonymous comments on the Web "can be understood as a platform for 'unsupported and often baseless assertions of opinion' rather than fact."[36] That same year an appellate court in California affirmed the dismissal of a libel case against the Gizmodo tech blog. In that case the plaintiff challenged an article that criticized him for overhyping his startups and new tech products. Gizmodo's use of the word "scam" was central to the plaintiff's argument, but the court looked at the article as a whole and said it was opinion that had "the tone and style of a sarcastic product or movie review."[37] The court also noted that Gizmodo allowed readers to draw their own conclusions about the plaintiff's products through links to product source materials.[38]

Innocent Construction

innocent construction Allegedly libelous words that are capable of being interpreted, or construed, to have an innocent meaning are not libelous, so long as that interpretation is a reasonable one.

Libel cases often hinge on what words mean. Determining meaning in a specific circumstance, in turn, may depend on context. In most states, if a statement has two possible meanings—and one is defamatory and one is not—a jury decides how the words are understood for that case. But this situation is treated differently in Illinois. Under the **innocent construction** rule, as long as the words at issue have one nondefamatory (or innocent) meaning, the defendant wins. In establishing the rule, the Illinois Supreme Court said that allegedly libelous words capable of being read innocently "must be so read and declared nonactionable as a matter of law."[39]

A federal appeals court affirmed the ruling of a lower federal court in Illinois that deferred to the innocent construction rule. The case centered on a book written by a former police officer. In it, she mentions a man who advised her after she left the police department. The two had disagreements and later parted ways. The book was nonfiction but contained "fantasy sequences" in which the author created fictional scenes to symbolically describe her experiences. This included a story that she had been beaten. Though her former adviser was mentioned in the book, it was never by name within these sequences. Still, he believed he had been identified in the sequences and sued for libel. The Seventh Circuit ruled that these sequences could be read in a way that did not call into question the plaintiff's integrity or reputation. The court added, "Statements that cannot reasonably be interpreted as stating actual facts are protected under the First Amendment."[40]

Courts can be tough, however, in deciding whether to apply the rule. In another case originating in Illinois, a court ruled that a press release that accused the plaintiff of filing false documents was not eligible for innocent construction protection. In other words, the court believed that the statement at issue could be read only in a way that damaged the plaintiff's reputation.[41]

There is also some evidence that the innocent construction rule exists in Ohio, Missouri, New Mexico and Montana. In addition, a few states hold that statements susceptible to the application of the rule are actionable only when special damages can be proved. They are Alabama, Mississippi, Iowa, Montana and Oklahoma.[42]

The mention of this rule brings up the matter of state libel law. As noted in Chapter 4, the federal Constitution affects libel law. *New York Times Co. v. Sullivan* recognized that the First Amendment affords some protection to libel defendants. Most libel lawsuits are brought in state, not federal, courts. Many nuances of libel law vary from state to state. As long as states are consistent with the First Amendment, they may structure libel laws as they choose.

realWorld Law

Defining Opinion: *Ollman v. Evans*

Robert Novak

The University of Maryland wanted to hire a chair of its Department of Government and Politics. They contacted a political science professor at New York University (NYU), Bertell Ollman, and invited him to apply. After the job interview, Ollman was offered the position, and he accepted.

Soon, news that Ollman was a Marxist began to spread, first across the University of Maryland campus and the community at large, then to nearby Washington, D.C. Maryland's acting governor was among those who denounced Ollman's appointment. The news media took an interest, and columnists began expressing their views. Among those were Rowland Evans, Jr., and Robert Novak, whose jointly written syndicated column was published in newspapers nationwide. "It struck me as an interesting column of why in the world this state university would hire a Marxist, and what kind of Marxist he was. I didn't know anything about him until I started doing some research on him," Novak said.[1]

The column—included as the Appendix to the court opinion at the end of this chapter—was authored primarily by Novak and was published by a number of newspapers, including The Washington Post, on May 4, 1978. It questioned whether Ollman was qualified to assume his new role at the University of Maryland. But Ollman thought the column did more than that. He believed it damaged his reputation and contributed to the ultimate withdrawal of the job offer. In February 1979, Ollman filed a $6 million libel suit against Evans and Novak.

The case began what proved to be a circuitous path in which a battle was waged over what constitutes a statement of fact as opposed to an expression of opinion. The case is also noteworthy for those judges at the U.S. Court of Appeals in Washington, D.C., who participated in the 6–5 ruling against Ollman.

Judge Kenneth Starr (who acquired perhaps his greatest notoriety in the late 1990s as the independent counsel in the Whitewater investigation of the Clinton administration) wrote the court's majority opinion in favor of Evans and Novak. Starr outlined the most noteworthy element to stem from this case: the *Ollman* test, a four-part test to distinguish fact from opinion. Judge Robert Bork, whose 1987 nomination to the U.S. Supreme Court was rejected by the Senate amid a storm of political controversy, wrote a concurring opinion.

Judge Antonin Scalia wrote a dissenting opinion in *Ollman*. He was appointed to the Supreme Court two years later. He referred to the Evans and Novak column as "classic and cooly crafted libel."[2]

"I think what was really at issue was whether a columnist could give a fair opinion, using sources and giving justification, on someone who is a private citizen or a public figure,"[3] said Novak. "Certainly a columnist has a wide berth of freedom to render judgments about public people who are in controversial positions. I think that there is no dividing line between the column and the news story."[4]

Ollman believed the decision was a product of a system that protects the powerful: "They . . . have to find legal reasons to justify what they want because of their personal biases."[5] Ollman returned to NYU.

---

1. Joseph Russomanno, Speaking Our Minds: Conversations with the People Behind Landmark First Amendment Cases 92 (Mahwah, N.J.: Lawrence Erlbaum Associates/Taylor & Francis, 2002).
2. Ollman v. Evans, 750 F.2d 970, 1036 (D.C. Cir. 1984).
3. Russomanno, *supra* note 1, at 115.
4. *Id.* at 112.
5. *Id.* at 108–9.

Letters to the Editor

Letters to the editor are typically viewed as expressions of opinions rather than statements of fact. For that reason, newspapers and magazines have won most cases based on the publication of such letters. Courts have sought to provide protection for the publication of letters, often viewing them as part of an open forum for the general public. Today, based on the same rationale, courts generally offer the same protection for opinions published as opinion blogs or as comments on review or comment-based websites.

Where a letter appears within a publication is likely to have a significant bearing in determining whether it qualifies as opinion. This stems directly from the "journalistic context" element of the *Ollman* test. That is, by appearing within a section of a publication that is clearly set aside for the expression of opinions—including opinions from readers—a letter (versus an article) is much more likely to be viewed by a court as an expression of opinion. The same is true in the context of publication on specific websites. For example, a court in New York recently held that two women who called an ex-boyfriend a liar and a cheater were expressing opinion because their words appeared in the context of a website whose sole purpose is to air complaints about dishonest romantic partners.[43]

In cases in which letters were not protected as opinion, courts have held that those letters combined opinion and facts. Often cases based on such expressions are resolved in favor of libel plaintiffs. For example, a Florida appellate court ruled that a letter questioning a child psychologist's qualifications was defamatory because it was just such a mixed expression and therefore not privileged.[44]

An example of the idea that authors of letters to the editor enjoy the same constitutional protection for their opinions as newspaper reporters was provided by an early 21st-century case. In the ruling on this case, a state court said, "The robust exchange of ideas that occurs each day on the editorial pages of our state's newspapers could indeed suffer if the nonmedia authors of letters to the editor published in these forums were denied the same constitutional protections enjoyed by the editors themselves."[45] Thus, the authors of letters that the news media publish are as shielded as the media themselves.

Rhetorical Hyperbole, Parody and Satire

The history of successful libel defenses includes this premise: If the material on which a libel claim is based is so outrageous that no reasonable person could believe it, damage to the plaintiff's reputation could not have happened. The most infamous example lies within the circumstances of *Hustler Magazine v. Falwell*,[46] discussed in Chapter 7.

As with other libel defenses, context can be a critical element when it comes to the defense of rhetorical hyperbole, parody and satire. The context of the material in question can play a big role in determining whether a reasonable person would believe it to be a statement of fact.

realWorld Law

Best and Worst Lists: Rhetorical Hyperbole?

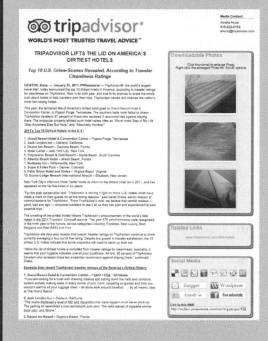

Would you stay a hotel labeled the #1 Dirtiest Hotel of the year by online reviewers? When the Grand Resort and Convention Center in Pigeon Forge, Tenn., nabbed this top spot on a 2011 list, major television news outlets and websites reported the distinction. The list on TripAdvisor.com's website included a link to the hotel with a photograph of a ripped bedspread and a user quote that read, "There was dirt at least ½ inch thick in the bathtub which was filled with lots of dark hair."[1]

The Grand Resort took issue with a system of online reviews that resulted in this ranking. It argued that such a distinction "maliciously" caused customers to lose confidence in the resort and the TripAdvisor rating caused "great injury and irreparable damage to . . . destroy [its] business and reputation by false and misleading means."[2] The hotel sued TripAdvisor for libel and said the numerical ranking system the site used to determine each year's top 10 dirtiest hotels was based solely on customer reviews.

A federal district court in Tennessee dismissed the hotel's libel suit, holding that the online ranking was clearly rhetorical hyperbole, even though it offered a numerical ranking system based on user reviews. "TripAdvisor's list is of the genre of hyperbole that is omnipresent. From law schools to restaurants, from judges to hospitals, everything is ranked, graded, ordered and critiqued. Undoubtedly, some will accept the array of 'Best' and 'Worst' rankings as impenetrable maxims," the court wrote. "[T]he standard, fortunately, is what a 'reasonable person' would believe. A reasonable person would not confuse a ranking system, which uses consumer reviews as its litmus, for an objective assertion of fact."[3]

1. Seaton d/b/a Grand Resort Hotel & Convention Cntr. v. TripAdvisor, 2012 U.S. Dist. LEXIS 118584 (E.D. Tenn. Aug. 22, 2012).
2. *Id.*
3. *Id.* at 277.

The U.S. Supreme Court first recognized rhetorical hyperbole as protected speech—and therefore a libel defense—when a developer sued the publisher of a newspaper after the newspaper printed articles reporting that some people characterized the developer's negotiating tactics as blackmail.[47] The developer argued that the word "blackmail" implied that the developer had committed the crime of blackmail. The Supreme Court rejected the developer's argument, holding that the word "blackmail" was not slander when spoken and not libel when reported because "even the most careless reader must have perceived that the word was no more than rhetorical hyperbole, a vigorous epithet used by those who considered [the developer's] negotiating position extremely unreasonable."[48]

That case was mentioned in another ruling a few years later, this one involving a labor dispute.[49] In its monthly newsletter, a local union published under the headline "List of Scabs" the names of those who had not joined the union. This was followed up by union literature that contained writer Jack London's definition of "scab," which read in part: "After God had finished the rattlesnake, the toad, and the vampire, He had some awful substance left with which He made a scab. A scab is a two-legged animal with a corkscrew soul, a water brain, a combination backbone of jelly and glue. Where others have hearts, he carries a tumor of rotten principles."[50] The definition also described a scab as a "traitor."

The Court noted that the use of "scab" is common in labor disputes and is entitled to protection, and that words such as "traitor" cannot be construed as representations of fact: "It is similarly impossible to believe that any reader of the [newsletter] would have understood [it] to be charging [those listed] with committing the criminal offense of treason. . . . Jack London's 'definition of a scab' is merely rhetorical hyperbole. . . ."[51] As one court has said, "The specific context of a statement shades its meaning. Language that is 'loose, figurative and hyperbolic . . . tends to negate the impression that a statement contains an assertion of verifiable fact.'"[52]

Similar to rhetorical hyperbole, satire or parody meant to be humorous or offer social commentary is often not libelous. For example, an artist was sued for libel because one of his paintings portrayed the plaintiffs holding knives and attacking a young woman. The artist knew the plaintiffs, also artists, but had become embroiled in a spat with them over their views on art. The painting was meant to satirize the views of those depicted. An appellate court considered the context and identified it as symbolic expression with no accusation of criminal conduct.[53]

Compare that to a situation in which a newspaper published a fictional article describing a Texas juvenile court judge who ordered the detention of a first grader for making a threat in a book report. The fictional student was described as appearing before the judge in handcuffs and ankle shackles.[54] The problem arose because the judge named in this otherwise made-up story was real. The satirical article came out after a real court case in which that same judge had ordered the detention of a 13-year-old student who wrote a Halloween horror story depicting the shooting death of a teacher and two students. The newspaper did not dispute that its article on the first grader was completely made up. It was meant to be a commentary on the judge and his heavy-handed justice. But the judge and a district attorney sued for libel, claiming that the article could be understood by a reasonable reader as making false statements of fact about them and that they were made with actual malice. The newspaper defended itself by claiming the article was satire and parody and therefore protected by the First Amendment. Ultimately, the Texas Supreme Court ruled for the newspaper.[55] The court cited clues in the article that would alert a reasonable reader that the article was not a statement of fact but instead a criticism or opinion. Though the article did have a superficial degree of plausibility, the court said, that is the hallmark of satire.

SUMMARY

THOSE SUED FOR LIBEL HAVE SEVERAL DEFENSE OPTIONS from which to choose, any one of which can lead to success. Truth is one of the most straightforward defenses, given that material must be false to be libelous. Even material that is less than completely accurate may be regarded as substantially true.

Journalists are able to report on certain events without fear of libel as long as their reporting is fair and accurate. The fair report privilege generally applies to reporting on official government proceedings (e.g., hearings, trials) or records, but not all states recognize this privilege. Another defense, fair comment and criticism, pertains to honest evaluation of works or series of legitimate public interest.

Expressing an opinion is regarded as a basic First Amendment right. Opinion is protected speech, not susceptible to a libel claim. However, for material to qualify as protected opinion, it must satisfy the four-part *Ollman* test. Published letters to the editor and websites or blogs purely used to express opinions are typically viewed as protected opinion because of context. If a statement is unbelievable, then it cannot be libelous. Thus, parody, satire and rhetorical hyperbole can be used as libel defenses when it is clear to a reasonable person that their use is not to be taken seriously. ■

Neutral Reportage

As explained in Chapter 4, someone who repeats libelous information is as potentially responsible as the originator of that same information. Republication is not a valid libel defense. But that longtime rule of libel law was loosened somewhat by the doctrine of neutral reportage. **Neutral reportage** recognizes that the First Amendment principle of the free flow of information and ideas is important. Among the kinds of information that should be free to reach people, the doctrine suggests, are accusations made by one party about another. In some circumstances, the news value lies not in whether the accusation is true but simply in the fact that the accusation was made or who made it. According to neutral reportage, the news media should not be restrained from merely reporting an accusation as long as the reporting is done in a fair, objective and balanced (i.e., neutral) manner. Even if the publisher of the reported accusations has serious doubts about their veracity, the neutral reportage doctrine could provide a successful defense.

The neutral reportage defense was established in 1977[56] and only applied to cases involving public figures. Since then, the scope of that application has sometimes expanded beyond public figures; but, the nation's courts have not

neutral reportage In libel law, a defense accepted in some jurisdictions that says that when an accusation is made by a responsible and prominent organization, reporting that accusation is protected by the First Amendment even when it turns out the accusation was false and libelous.

Points of Law

Neutral Reportage

The First Amendment is a defense in a libel case if the following apply:

- The story is newsworthy and related to a public controversy.
- The accusation is made by a responsible person or group.
- The charge is about a public official, public figure or public organization.
- The story is accurate, containing denials or other views.
- The reporting is neutral.

Points of Law

The Wire Service Defense

The wire service defense may be applied as long as the following are present:

1. The defendant received material containing the defamatory statements from a reputable news-gathering agency.
2. The defendant did not know the story was false.
3. Nothing on the face of the story reasonably could have alerted the defendant that it may have been incorrect.
4. The original wire service story was republished without substantial change.

embraced neutral reportage. Its recognition, in fact, has been spotty. One obstacle to more widespread acceptance is that the U.S. Supreme Court has had virtually nothing to say about neutral reportage. Because it has been left to individual state and federal districts to determine how to handle it, the legal landscape is uncertain.[57] Thus, while neutral reportage remains an option in the libel defendant's arsenal, the inconsistent manner in which courts have accepted it makes its application in a specific case questionable. Much depends on how a court in a given jurisdiction may have ruled on neutral reportage previously.

Wire Service Defense

The wire service defense is related to the neutral reportage doctrine. It is similar to neutral reportage in that it provides a defense for republication on the condition that the reporting meets certain standards. The wire service defense reflects and acknowledges the extent to which news media are dependent on news services, particularly for nonlocal news. To expect verification of every report is unreasonable. This defense holds that the accurate republication of a story provided by a reputable news agency does not constitute fault as a matter of law. The wire defense is available to libel defendants if four factors are met: (1) The defendant received material containing the defamatory statements from a reputable news-gathering agency, (2) the defendant did not know the story was false, (3) nothing on the face of the story reasonably could have alerted the defendant that it may have been incorrect, and (4) the original wire service story was republished without substantial change.

The wire service defense has succeeded even when a newspaper published a story that relied on past wire service articles[58] and when a network affiliate broadcast news reports of its parent network.[59] Also, like the neutral reportage privilege, the wire service defense has been accepted in a limited number of jurisdictions.

Single-Publication Rule

Another issue related to republication is the availability of an article subsequent to its initial publication. Does the republication of a work weeks, months or years after its

realWorld Law

Edwards v. National Audubon Society: The Origin of Neutral Reportage

When a group of scientists sued the National Audubon Society and The New York Times for libel, they raised the question of how safe a journalist is in reporting accusations made by one party against another.[1] An article in the Times had reported that the scientists were paid liars for their support of DDT as a chemical pesticide. A National Audubon Society publication, American Birds, contained an article critical of DDT and claiming that bird counts were down. "Any time you hear a 'scientist' say the opposite, you are in the presence of someone who is being paid to lie."[2]

The accusation came to the attention of The New York Times' nature reporter. He contacted the writer of the article to ask for names of people who qualified as the "paid liars" for DDT. After some research, the American Birds writer provided the names of five scientists who had distorted Audubon statistics. The Times reporter then attempted to contact each of the five individuals. He succeeded in reaching three of them. All denied the charges, with one of them referring to the charges as "almost libelous."

The nature reporter's article in The New York Time identified the five scientists by name and accused them of being paid liars by the Audubon publication. Three of the scientists sued the National Audubon Society, The New York Times and both writers—the Times reporter and the American Birds writer.

After a federal trial court jury found in favor of the scientists, the ruling was reversed on appeal. The appeals court emphasized that The New York Times article accurately reported the facts of the story, and thus a libel judgment against the newspaper would be constitutionally impermissible. "When a responsible, prominent organization . . . makes serious charges against a public figure, the First Amendment protects the accurate and disinterested reporting of those charges," the court wrote. "What is newsworthy about such accusations is that they were made."[3]

The court's rationale for its finding was the public interest in being fully informed about controversial and sometimes sensitive issues. Literal accuracy is not a prerequisite, the court said, for the press' right of neutral reportage, especially when the journalist believes reasonably and in good faith that the report accurately conveys the charges made.

1. Edwards v. National Audubon Society, 556 F.2d 113 (2d Cir. 1977).
2. *Id.* at 116.
3. *Id.* at 120.

original publication constitute a publication, therefore to additional, separate libel claims? According to the **single-publication rule,** no. According to the rule, the entire edition of a newspaper or magazine is a single publication. Subsequent sales or reissues are not new publications. Courts across the United States also apply the single publication rule to Internet publications and to emerging online publishing platforms.[60] Thus, a new libel suit with merit is not possible in any of these circumstances. However, if in the republication process, content changes in a way that creates a new libel, the single-publication rule is unlikely to apply.

single-publication rule A rule that limits libel victims to only one cause of action even with multiple publications of the libel, common in the mass media and on websites.

The Libel-Proof Plaintiff

libel-proof plaintiff A plaintiff whose reputation is deemed to be so damaged already that additional false statements of and concerning him or her cannot cause further harm.

When an individual's reputation is already so bad that additional false accusations could not harm it further, the individual may be without the ability to win a defamation suit. In other words, it may be argued that the individual's reputation cannot be harmed any further by a new libelous publication. Under these circumstances, a libel defendant may be able to invoke the concept of the **libel-proof plaintiff**. Since the concept was first articulated as a libel defense,[61] two different ways to implement it have emerged.

One way stipulates that any reputational harm to the plaintiff caused by a false accusation only incrementally injures the reputation beyond its already damaged condition. Suppose, for example, that an individual is identified in an article as a thief, child molester and tax evader. If all of those charges are true, does it make any difference if the article also falsely identifies the individual as a kidnapper? No—in such a case, the publisher could probably win, arguing that the single false statement causes harm that is negligible (or incremental) beyond what already exists and therefore is not grounds for a libel suit. The plaintiff is libel-proof. In short, under these kinds of circumstances the false statement causes very little harm to the plaintiff's reputation beyond where it stood prior to the most recent publication.

Like other common law libel privileges, the acceptance of this part of the doctrine has not been universal. For example, a federal appeals court rejected the libel-proof plaintiff doctrine in 1984.[62] A journalist described the founder of an organization as a racist, fascist, anti-Semitic neo-Nazi and wrote that he had founded the organization to pursue his goals. The defense argued that previous publications had already so irreparably tarnished the plaintiff's reputation that the libel-proof doctrine should apply. In an opinion written by then judge Antonin Scalia, an appellate court rejected the claim, ruling that "we cannot envision how a court would go about determining that someone's reputation had already been 'irreparably' damaged—i.e., that no new reader could be reached by the freshest libel."[63] In writing that no matter how bad one's reputation is, it can always be worsened, Scalia offered an analogy: "It is shameful that Benedict Arnold was a traitor; but he was not a shoplifter to boot, and one should not have been able to make that charge while knowing its falsity with impunity."[64]

Courts may also recognize the second aspect of the libel-proof doctrine, which says that libel plaintiffs with tarnished reputations with regard to a particular issue are libel-proof only with respect to that issue. Libel claims pursued in this context present the question of whether previous publicity and the issue before the court are within the same framework.

For example, a plaintiff challenged a newspaper report that he had tested positive for drug use. The court found that although the report was incorrect, the plaintiff was libel-proof regarding this specific issue because he had previously admitted using drugs.[65] Had the new report falsely damaged his reputation regarding a topic unrelated to drug use, the libel-proof plaintiff doctrine could not have been invoked. The plaintiff still had a positive reputation to protect in those other areas.

International Law

Libel Tourism and the U.K. Defamation Bill 2013

Rachel Ehrenfeld

Because U.S. libel law is more protective of defendants than are laws in other countries, U.S. citizens have historically been more susceptible to libel verdicts against them in foreign courts. International plaintiffs have been known to engage in "libel tourism," shopping for a country other than the United States in which to file a libel claim. Their claims are often filed in England, where libel laws are historically plaintiff-friendly, even in cases that have little or no connection to British courts. In 2008, the United Nations Human Rights Committee noted that U.K. defamation laws chilled free speech and encouraged the country to pass reforms.

The U.S. Congress passed a libel tourism bill in 2010. The law prevents federal courts from enforcing a foreign libel judgment against an American journalist, author or publisher if it is inconsistent with the protections afforded by the First Amendment. It also allows individuals who have a foreign judgment levied against them to demonstrate that it is not enforceable in the United States.[1]

Rachel Ehrenfeld, now director of the American Center for Democracy, was instrumental in bringing attention to the phenomenon of libel tourism. A Saudi Arabian sued her for libel in England over her book, "Funding Evil." Though the book was marketed and sold exclusively in the United States, he showed that 23 copies had entered England through online sales. "English libel law originated to protect thin-skinned lords from 19th-century gossips," Ehrenfeld said in 2010. "Today it makes London the libel capital of the world, an international destination of 'libel tourists' who, because of the Internet, can sue anyone for spreading alleged mistruths in England."[2]

All three of the main political parties in the U.K. as well as Queen Elizabeth II supported the overhaul of British defamation laws, and Parliament proposed reforms in 2012.[3] The Defamation Bill 2012–13, which became law in 2013, seeks to find a better balance "between the right to freedom of expression and the protection of reputation." The bill includes a requirement that plaintiffs prove serious harm; it removes presumption in favor of a jury trial; it introduces the defenses of "responsible publication on matters of public interest," truth and opinion; and, it provides more protection for websites that host user-generated content. It also adopts the single-publication rule.[4]

---

1. *U.S. Passes Historic SPEECH Act,* EUROPENEWS (July 28, 2010), *available at* http://europenews.dk en/node/34081.
2. Rachel Ehrenfeld, *A Legal Thriller in London,* NEWSWEEK, June 7, 2010, at 12.
3. Eric Pfanner, *Britain to Seek Curbs to "Libel Tourism,"* N. Y. TIMES (May 9, 2012), *available at* http://www.nytimes.com/2012/05/10/business/media/britain-to-seek-curbs-to-libel-tourism.html?_r=0.
4. Defamation Bill 2012–13, *available at* http://services.parliament.uk/bills/2012–13/defamation.html.

Thus, the doctrine of the libel-proof plaintiff may serve a defendant who has published otherwise defamatory statements about an individual whose reputation is already so sullied as to render additional accusations moot, regardless of their falsity. Depending on the circumstances, the doctrine may apply to accusations of any nature or to those that relate only to a specific issue.

The libel-proof plaintiff doctrine remains a valuable defense weapon, particularly against frivolous libel suits and especially given the U.S. Supreme Court's opinion that states are free to adopt the doctrine as they see fit.[66]

SUMMARY

SOME LIBEL DEFENSES ALLOW FOR A KIND OF REPUBLICATION. These include neutral reportage and the wire service defense. Under the single-publication rule, multiple issues of the same publication do not make the defendant vulnerable to multiple libel claims. Courts across the United States also apply the single-publication rule to Internet publications and to emerging online publishing platforms.

Sometimes false, defamatory material is published about someone whose reputation cannot be lowered beyond its current level. Under those circumstances, a defendant may argue the plaintiff is libel-proof. ■

Other Defense Issues

Summary Judgment

A libel defendant can ask a court to dismiss a lawsuit by filing a motion for summary judgment. As noted in Chapter 1, a summary judgment is just what the name implies: A judge promptly decides certain points of a case and grants the motion to dismiss the case. It can occur at any of several points in litigation but usually occurs prior to trial.

A judge may issue a summary judgment on grounds that there is no genuine dispute about any material fact. With libel, this generally means a plaintiff is clearly unable to meet at least one element in his or her burden of proof. On numerous occasions, the U.S. Supreme Court said that when considering motions for summary judgment, courts "must view the facts and inferences to be drawn from them in the light most favorable to the opposing party."[67] Particularly in libel cases, this means that courts must take into account the burden the plaintiff must meet at trial. The rationale behind this view is that if the summary judgment is granted, the plaintiff's opportunity to prove a case ends, but if a defendant's motion for summary judgment is denied, the defendant still has an opportunity to prove his or her case at trial.[68]

Summary judgments can be important tools for protecting free expression, particularly in an environment in which plaintiffs have harassed the media by filing frivolous lawsuits (e.g., see the description of SLAPPs in Chapter 4). One federal judge wrote that in the First Amendment area, summary procedures are even more essential. Free debate is at stake if the harassment succeeds. One purpose of the *New York Times Co. v. Sullivan* actual malice principle, the judge wrote, is to prevent people from being discouraged in the full and free exercise of First Amendment rights with respect to the conduct of their government.[69]

Until 1979, summary judgment was a preferred method of dealing with libel cases involving actual malice. When the defense submitted a motion for summary judgment—based on the contention that the plaintiff could not prove actual malice—the judge would either grant or deny it. If granted, the case was over. In 1979,

Emerging Law

The *Twombly* and *Iqbal* Standard: Motion to Dismiss for Actual Malice?

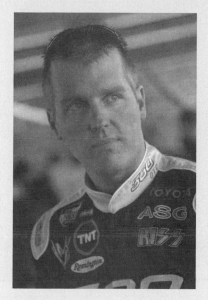

NASCAR driver Jeremy Mayfield

In 2007, the U.S. Supreme Court significantly changed the standard for the motion to dismiss in *Bell Atlantic Corp. v. Twombly*.[1] Two years later, it affirmed its decision in *Ashcroft v. Iqbal*.[2] Since then, legal experts argue that a new standard has emerged—called the *Twombly* and *Iqbal* standard—that has, in essence, made a motion to dismiss equivalent to a motion for summary judgment. Under *Twombly* and *Iqbal,* judges should use "judicial common sense" to determine the plausibility of a claim and the sufficiency of the evidence. The Supreme Court justified the change by noting the increasing legal costs to defendants. One study suggests that, since the decision, more motions to dismiss have succeeded in courts across the country in many different areas of the law.[3]

In 2012, two federal appeals courts applied the *Twombly* and *Iqbal* standard to actual malice proceedings. The First Circuit became the first to apply the standard to actual malice and granted a motion to dismiss in a case involving a political candidate's complaint that a political attack ad defamed him. The court said that the use of "actual malice buzzwords" was not sufficient to make a claim and that the candidate must "lay out enough facts from which malice might reasonably be inferred."[4]

In the Fourth Circuit, the court granted a motion to dismiss a case involving NASCAR driver Jeremy Mayfield, who sued NASCAR for reporting that he tested positive for recreational or performance-enhancing drugs. Mayfield said NASCAR knew the test result was a false positive because he was taking prescription medication at the time. The court said Mayfield's evidence was insufficient.[5]

Many legal experts are calling the application of the *Twombly* and *Iqbal* standard to actual malice claims another form of defense: "This emerging line of authority represents a promising trend toward the disposition of infirm speech claims on preliminary motions—a trend that bears close attention by First Amendment and media litigators."[6]

1. Bell Atlantic Corp. v. Twombly, 550 U.S. 544 (2007).
2. Ashcroft v. Iqbal, 556 U.S. 662 (2009).
3. Suja A. Thomas, *The New Summary Judgment Motion: The Motion to Dismiss Under Iqbal and Twombly*, ILLINOIS PUBLIC LAW AND LEGAL THEORY RESEARCH PAPERS SERIES (Oct. 27, 2009), *available at* http://www.parker-international.com/public/2009_Public/SSRN-id1494683.pdf.
4. Schatz v. Republican State Leadership Committee, 669 F. 3d. 57 (1st Cir., 2012).
5. Mayfield v. National Association for Stock Car Auto Racing, 674 F. 3d 369 (4th Cir., 2012).
6. Chad R. Bowman & Shaina D. Jones, *Courts Extend Twombly and Iqbal Standard to Actual Malice Proceeding*, 17 FIRST AMENDMENT & MEDIA LITIGATION 5 (2012/ 2013).

the U.S. Supreme Court cast doubt on the appropriateness of summary judgment in libel cases because any examination of actual malice "calls a defendant's state of mind into question." Such a circumstance "does not readily lend itself to summary disposition."[70] Although some lower courts took the admonition to heart—using it as a basis for denying summary judgment—motions for summary judgment are still granted more often than not. In 1986, the Court ruled that in deciding whether to grant motions for summary judgment, trial judges should decide whether public plaintiffs who file lawsuits claiming they have been libeled can meet the actual malice standard by "clear and convincing evidence." If not, summary judgment for the party they have sued should be granted.[71]

Jurisdiction

A court may dismiss a lawsuit on the ground that the court lacks jurisdiction. Traditionally in libel, the standard has been that wherever the material in question could be seen or heard, a court in any of those locales would have jurisdiction.[72] Thus, a plaintiff could go "forum shopping" in an attempt to find a jurisdiction most favorable to his or her case.

Given that statements published on the Internet can potentially be seen anywhere, any court could claim jurisdiction. A plaintiff could initiate the lawsuit in any court, including those that might be most favorable. But early in the 21st century, significant restrictions were placed on this practice. The U.S. Court of Appeals for the Fourth Circuit applied a three-pronged test for determining the exercise of jurisdiction: (1) whether the defendant purposefully conducted activities in the state, (2) whether the plaintiff's claim arises out of the defendant's activities there, and (3) whether the exercise of jurisdiction would be constitutionally reasonable.[73]

Points of Law

A Test for Jurisdiction

1. Whether the defendant purposefully conducted activities in the state

2. Whether the plaintiff's claim arises out of the defendant's activities there, and

3. Whether the exercise of jurisdiction would be constitutionally reasonable

To understand the test, it may be helpful to examine the circumstances surrounding the case in which it was first applied. Two Connecticut newspapers were investigating conditions of confinement at a Virginia prison. The story was relevant in Connecticut because some of the overflow prison population in Connecticut was being transferred to a Virginia facility. Articles that included content critical of the Virginia prison and its management appeared in the newspaper in both its print and online editions. The Virginia prison warden sued in federal court in Virginia, claiming that the online content was seen in Virginia and had defamed him there. The appeals court ruled that because the newspapers did not direct their website content to a Virginia audience, courts there had no jurisdiction. The court carefully reviewed the articles and determined they were aimed at a local (Connecticut) audience.[74] Placing content online, the court ruled, is not sufficient by itself to subject a person to the jurisdiction in another state just because the information could be accessed there.[75] Otherwise, a person who places information on the Internet could be sued anywhere the information could be accessed. The bottom line, according to this ruling, is that jurisdiction rests where the publication's intended audience is located.

Section 230 Immunity

Section 230 of the federal Communications Decency Act (CDA) of 1996,[76] mentioned in Chapter 4, offers immunity to websites in libel claims, although the protection is not absolute. Section 230 generally provides legal protection to website operators and Internet Service Providers (ISPs) when issues arise from the content created by others. For 20 years, courts have rejected attempts to limit the application of Section 230 to only "traditional" ISPs like Verizon or America Online. Instead, they have extended protection to the many diverse entities commonly called "interactive computer service providers."[77] Under this broader definition, blog sites and other interactive services like YouTube, Facebook or Twitter that rely on user-generated content, information provided from third-party RSS feeds or reader comments also may receive immunity from libel claims under Section 230.

The key to determining whether Section 230 protects against a libel claim is to identify the source of the content and the extent to which the ISP interacted directly with the content. For example, courts have ruled that when bloggers allow third parties to add readers' comments or other materials to their blogs, then Section 230 protects them. What is less clear is whether those who edit comments or selectively publish reader comments also would fall under Section 230 immunity.[78] One Ninth Circuit decision held that a service provider or user is immune from liability when a third person or content creator furnished content under circumstances in which a reasonable person would conclude the information was intended for publication.[79]

In 2011, a California state court considered whether Facebook qualified for immunity under Section 230 for its "Sponsored Story" advertising system. Five plaintiffs sued Facebook for placing their user names and profile pictures into Sponsored Stories on friends' Facebook pages. For example, plaintiff Angel Fraley "liked" Rosetta Stone's Facebook profile in order to receive a free software demonstration. Subsequently, Fraley's friends' Facebook pages showed a Sponsored Story advertisement with the Rosetta Stone logo and her "Like" for Rosetta Stone.[80] Facebook argued that it is protected under Section 230 because it is an "interactive computer service" with content provided by third parties. But, the court disagreed, saying that because Facebook creates and develops the Sponsored Story feature as commercial content without user consent, Facebook is not immune. "Although Facebook meets the definition of an interactive computer service under the CDA . . . it also meets the statutory definition of an information content provider. . . . Furthermore, '[the fact that members] are information content providers does not preclude [Facebook] from also being an information content provider by helping 'develop' at least 'in part' the information" posted in the form of Sponsored Stories."[81] In this case, the court is making a clear distinction between content creation and distribution.

Another case further establishes the limits to Section 230 protection if the operator of a website creates or adds content to a post that is potentially libelous. A Kentucky federal court ruled that when the operator of a gossip website called thedirty.com endorsed defamatory statements with his own online comments he forfeited Section 230 protection."[82]

Statute of Limitations

Statute of limitations apply for virtually all crimes and civil actions. Charges of most criminal activity and civil actions can be filed only during a limited time after the alleged violation of the law. Courts do not like old claims. While not a defense per se, delay in filing a libel lawsuit can work to the benefit of a defendant, sometimes requiring dismissal where the lawsuit is barred by the statute of limitations.

Length of Statutes of Limitation in Libel Actions

In libel, the length of the statute of limitations is one, two or three years, depending on the state. The clock begins ticking on the date the material was made available to the public. With some printed publications, this can be prior to the date of publication on the cover. Many monthly magazines, for example, are mailed to subscribers and appear on newsstands or online well before the official publication date.

On a related note, the single-publication rule also applies to statutes of limitation. The reissue of a publication does not restart the statute of limitation calendar as a truly new publication would. This standard now also applies to Internet publications. A modification to a website—when the modification is unrelated to the allegedly defamatory statement—does not amount to a new publication. For purposes of libel claims and the statute of limitations, the date of publication remains the date on which the material was originally posted.

Retractions

While not a libel defense per se, retractions and corrections published to correct content can play a role in helping libel defendants by mitigating the damage to the plaintiff that resulted from the libelous publication. The degree to which a retraction is offered promptly, is displayed prominently and is plainly stated will likely help the defendant's cause. The rationale for this is that a retraction can help reduce the damage to the plaintiff's reputation; the defendant therefore should be required to pay less in damages.

Note one pitfall of issuing retractions or apologies: While issuing one is certainly the responsible action to undertake, doing so may actually work against the defendant if the offended party files a lawsuit. Depending on their wording, retractions may be viewed as an admission of guilt. Consequently, libel defense attorneys may advise against issuing them in the first place. In part as a response to this paradox, a majority of states have adopted **retraction statutes.** Increasingly,

retraction statutes In libel law, state laws that limit the damages a plaintiff may receive if the defendant had issued a retraction of the material at issue. Retraction statutes are meant to discourage the punishment of any good-faith effort of admitting a mistake.

Length of Statutes of Limitation in Libel Actions

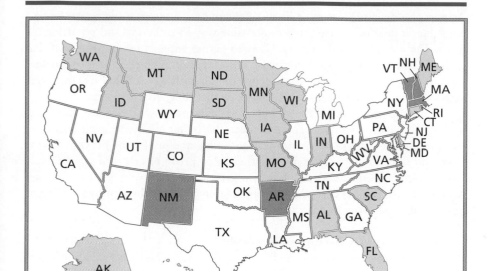

One year
Two years
Three years

these laws prevent plaintiffs from recovering some damages after publication of a retraction.[83] Retraction statutes vary in their strength and coverage.[84] The protection they offer differs in many ways, from prohibitions on punitive damages to restricting damages to out-of-pocket losses.[85] Most of these statutes look favorably on media defendants who issue retractions. Rather than penalizing media organizations that indirectly acknowledge some degree of negligence, these statutes offer a kind of compensation by reducing their obligation to pay damages.

Retraction statutes do not always fare well under judicial review in their respective states. Some have been ruled unconstitutional. The Arizona Supreme Court, for example, ruled that the retraction statute in that state violated the state constitution.[86] The law limited plaintiffs to recovering only special damages when retractions were published.[87] But the Arizona Constitution holds that "[t]he right of action to recover damages for injuries shall never be abrogated, and the amount recovered shall not be subject to any statutory limitation."[88] Because the law conflicted with the Arizona Constitution, it did not survive judicial scrutiny. However, although a retraction or correction of a news report in Arizona may no longer immunize a libel defendant from all punitive damage claims, it may serve to reduce those damages.

Responsible Reporting

As part of a defense strategy, a libel defendant may attempt to demonstrate to a court that it conducted itself in a responsible way in gathering and reporting the news. The defendant is then more likely to garner support for its argument that it should not be found legally responsible for committing libel. The media defendant, for example, may need to disprove the plaintiff's claim that its employees acted with reckless disregard for the truth or that they were negligent.

In attempting to prove that a libel defendant acted with reckless disregard, a plaintiff is likely to attempt to build a case bit by bit, demonstrating a series of irresponsible or careless acts in the newsgathering and publishing process. Courts have said that no single element is sufficient to prove clearly and convincingly that a defendant acted with reckless disregard, but each can be used as evidence to build a case. A libel defendant wants to strengthen its position by showing as many of the following as possible:

- The story was investigated thoroughly.
- Interviews were conducted with people who had knowledge of facts related to the story, including the subject of the report.
- Previously published material was not relied on.
- Biased stories were not relied on.
- The reporting was careful, systematic and painstaking.
- Multiple viewpoints were sought and, when possible, included in the report.
- There was a willingness to retract or correct if facts warranted such action.
- If applicable, there was a demonstrable deadline.
- There was no ill will or hatred toward the plaintiff.

Even if media defendants are unable to escape liability altogether, they are likely to mitigate damages by substantiating these points and demonstrating responsible reporting.

Two situations illustrate how courts may consider one or more of the elements of responsible reporting. Within the context of a libel suit, a state appellate court once concluded that a reporter's failure to interview one of the police officers accused of brutality in a series of reports could be regarded as negligent behavior. The court ruled, however, that such irresponsibility alone did not support the officer's claim that the reporter had acted with actual malice.[89] In another case, a television journalist argued that his reporting methods were responsible, noting that he spent four days interviewing 30 people and reviewing 500 pages of court records in preparing the story. This argument contributed to an appellate court decision overturning a libel judgment against him.[90]

SUMMARY

A LIBEL DEFENDANT OFTEN FILES A MOTION to dismiss the lawsuit when it is clear that the plaintiff cannot prove his case. Courts granting such a motion issue a summary judgment.

Questions about jurisdiction can also work in the defendant's favor. Whether the court has authority over a certain defendant and whether the applicable statute of limitations has expired can affect the court's authority to act at all in a particular case.

Section 230 of the Communications Decency Act offers immunity to websites and ISPs in libel claims, although the protection is not absolute. The key to determining whether Section 230 protects against a libel claim is to identify the source of the content and the extent to which the service provider or website interacted directly with the content.

Libel defendants should know about retractions, corrections and apologies. These may help to reduce damage awards. Media defendants want to be viewed as reliable and trustworthy organizations that conduct themselves responsibly. While it is not technically a defense, demonstrating basic journalistic responsibility can enhance the defendant's standing with the court and provide either a defense in the lawsuit or a solid basis for the court to minimize monetary damages assessed against a media defendant. Moreover, journalistic integrity is simply the proper way to conduct business and often tends to be the best way to avoid libel suits in the first place. ∎

Cases for Study

Thinking About It

The two case excerpts that follow are very important libel cases. Note that only one of them is from the U.S. Supreme Court. The other is from the D.C. Circuit Court of Appeals. At the center of each is the libel defense of opinion. As you read these case excerpts, keep the following questions in mind:

- How do the two decisions help define the meaning of opinion?
- Does either ruling outline any kind of test or standard to help judge opinion? If so, what is that?
- Do these rulings expand or narrow the definition of opinion?

Ollman v. Evans
UNITED STATES COURT OF APPEALS FOR THE DISTRICT OF COLUMBIA CIRCUIT
750 F.2d 970 (1984)

JUDGE KENNETH STARR delivered the court's opinion:

This defamation action arises out of the publication of a syndicated column by Rowland Evans and Robert Novak in May 1978. The question before us is whether the allegedly defamatory statements set forth in the column are constitutionally protected expressions of opinion or, as appellant contends, actionable assertions of fact. We conclude, as did the District Court, that the challenged statements are entitled to absolute First Amendment protection as expressions of opinion. . . .

The plaintiff, Bertell Ollman, is a professor of political science at New York University. . . . In March 1978, Mr. Ollman was nominated by a departmental search committee to head the Department of Government and Politics at the University of Maryland. The committee's recommendation was "duly approved by the Provost of the University and the Chancellor of the College Park campus."

With this professional move from Washington Square to College Park, Maryland thus in the offing, the Evans and Novak article appeared. . . .

This case presents us with the delicate and sensitive task of accommodating the First Amendment's protection of free expression of ideas with the common law's protection of an individual's interest in reputation. It is a truism that the free flow of ideas and opinions is integral to our democratic system of government. Thomas Jefferson well expressed this principle in his First Inaugural Address, when the Nation's memory was fresh with the passage of the notorious Alien and Sedition Acts:

If there be any among us who would wish to dissolve this Union or to change its republican form, let them stand undisturbed as monuments of the safety with which error of opinion may be tolerated where reason is left free to combat it.

At the same time, an individual's interest in his or her reputation is of the highest order. Its protection is an eloquent expression of the respect historically afforded the dignity of the individual in Anglo-American legal culture. A defamatory statement may destroy an individual's livelihood, wreck his standing in the community, and seriously impair his sense of dignity and self-esteem. . . .

. . . In *Gertz,* the Supreme Court in *dicta* seemed to provide absolute immunity from defamation actions for all opinions and to discern the basis for this immunity in the First Amendment. The Court began its analysis of the case by stating:

Under the First Amendment there is no such thing as a false idea. However pernicious an opinion may seem, we depend for its correction not on the conscience of judges and juries but on the competition of other ideas. But there is no constitutional value in false statements of fact. Neither the intentional lie nor the careless error materially advances society's interest in "uninhibited, robust, and wide-open debate on the public issues." . . .

. . . *Gertz*'s implicit command thus imposes upon both state and federal courts the duty as a matter of constitutional adjudication to distinguish facts from opinions in order to provide opinions with the requisite, absolute First Amendment protection. At the same time, however, the Supreme Court provided little guidance in *Gertz* itself as to the manner in which the distinction between fact and opinion is to be discerned. . . .

. . . With largely uncharted seas having been left in *Gertz's* wake, the lower federal courts and state courts have, not surprisingly, fashioned various approaches in attempting to articulate the *Gertz*-mandated distinction between fact and opinion. . . .

In formulating a test to distinguish between fact and opinion, courts are admittedly faced with a dilemma. Because of the richness and diversity of language, as evidenced by the capacity of the same words to convey different meanings in different contexts, it is quite impossible to lay down a bright-line or mechanical distinction. . . . While this dilemma admits of no easy resolution, we think it obliges us to state plainly the factors that guide us in distinguishing fact from opinion and to demonstrate how these factors lead to a proper accommodation between the competing interests in free expression of opinion and in an individual's reputation. . . .

While courts are divided in their methods of distinguishing between assertions of fact and expressions of opinion, they are universally agreed that the task is a difficult one. . . .

The degree to which such kinds of statements have real factual content can, of course, vary greatly. We believe, in consequence, that courts should analyze the totality of the circumstances in which the statements are made to decide whether they merit the absolute First Amendment protection enjoyed by opinion. To evaluate the totality of the circumstances of an allegedly defamatory statement, we will consider four factors in assessing whether the average reader would view the statement as fact or, conversely, opinion. . . .

First, we will analyze the common usage or meaning of the specific language of the challenged statement itself. Our analysis of the specific language under scrutiny will be aimed at determining whether the statement has a precise core of meaning for which a consensus of understanding exists or, conversely, whether the statement is indefinite and ambiguous. . . .

Second, we will consider the statement's verifiability—is the statement capable of being objectively characterized as true or false? . . . Third, moving from the challenged language itself, we will consider the full context of the statement—the entire article or column, for example—inasmuch as other, unchallenged language surrounding the allegedly defamatory statement will influence the average reader's readiness to infer that a particular statement has factual content. . . . Finally, we will consider the broader context or setting in which the statement appears. Different types of writing have, as we shall more fully see, widely varying social conventions which signal to the reader the likelihood of a statement's being either fact or opinion. . . .

. . . [O]nce our inquiry into whether the statement is an assertion of fact or expression of opinion has concluded, the factors militating either in favor of or against the drawing of factual implications from any statement have already been identified. A separate inquiry into whether a statement, already classified in this painstaking way as opinion, implies allegedly defamatory facts would, in our view, be superfluous. In short, we believe that the application of the four-factor analysis set forth above, and drawn from the considerable judicial teaching on the subject, will identify those statements so "factually laden" that they should not receive the benefit of the opinion privilege. . . .

Now we turn to the case at hand to apply the foregoing analysis. As we have seen, Mr. Ollman alleges various instances of defamation in the Evans and Novak column. Before analyzing each such instance, we will first examine the context (the third and fourth factors in our approach) in which the alleged defamations arise. We will then assess the manner in which this context would influence the average reader in interpreting the alleged defamations as an assertion of fact or an expression of opinion.

From the earliest days of the Republic, individuals have published and circulated short, frequently sharp and biting writings on issues of social and political interest. From the pamphleteers urging revolution to abolitionists condemning the evils of slavery, American authors have sought through pamphlets and tracts both to stimulate debate and to persuade. Today among the inheritors of this lively tradition are the columnists and opinion writers whose works appear on the editorial and Op-Ed pages of the Nation's newspapers. The column at issue here is plainly part and parcel of this tradition of social and political criticism.

The reasonable reader who peruses an Evans and Novak column on the editorial or Op-Ed page is fully aware that the statements found there are not "hard" news like those printed on the front page or elsewhere in the news sections of the newspaper. Readers expect that columnists will make strong statements, sometimes phrased in a polemical manner that would hardly be considered balanced or fair elsewhere in the newspaper. That proposition is inherent in the very notion of an "Op-Ed page." Because of obvious space limitations, it is also manifest that columnists or commentators will express themselves in condensed fashion without providing what might be considered the full picture. Columnists are, after all, writing a column, not a full-length scholarly article or a book. This broad understanding of the traditional function of a

column like Evans and Novak will therefore predispose the average reader to regard what is found there to be opinion. . . .

. . . Evans and Novak made it clear that they were not purporting to set forth definitive conclusions, but instead meant to ventilate what in their view constituted the central questions raised by Mr. Ollman's prospective appointment. . . . Prominently displayed in the Evans and Novak column, therefore, is interrogatory or cautionary language that militates in favor of treating statements as opinion. . . .

Nor is the statement that "[Mr. Ollman] is widely viewed in his profession as a political activist" a representation or assertion of fact. . . . While Mr. Ollman argues that this assertion is defamatory since it *implies* that he has no reputation as a scholar, we are rather skeptical of the strength of that implication, particularly in the context of this column. . . .

Next we turn to Mr. Ollman's complaints about the column's quotations from and remarks about his writings. . . . When a critic is commenting about a book, the reader is on notice that the critic is engaging in interpretation, an inherently subjective enterprise, and therefore realizes that others, including the author, may utterly disagree with the critic's interpretation. . . . The reader is thus predisposed to view what the critic writes as opinion. . . .

Evans' and Novak's statements about Mr. Ollman's article clearly do not fall into the category of misquotation or misrepresentation. . . .

Professor Ollman also objects to the column's posing the question, prompted in Evans' and Novak's view by Mr. Ollman's article, of whether he intended to use the classroom for indoctrination. As we noted previously, the column in no wise affirmatively stated that Mr. Ollman was indoctrinating his students. Moreover, indoctrination is not, at least as used here in the setting of academia, a word with a well-defined meaning. . . .

Finally, we turn to the most troublesome statement in the column. In the third-to-last paragraph, an anonymous political science professor is quoted as saying: "Ollman has no status within the profession but is a pure and simple activist." . . .

Certainly a scholar's academic reputation among his peers is crucial to his or her career. . . .

We are of the view, however, that under the constitutionally based opinion privilege announced in *Gertz,* this quotation, under the circumstances before us, is protected. . . . [H]ere we deal with statements by well-known, nationally syndicated columnists on the Op-Ed page of a newspaper, the well-recognized home of opinion and comment. In addition, the thrust of the column, taken as a whole, is to raise questions about Mr. Ollman's scholarship and intentions, not to state conclusively from Evans' and Novak's first-hand knowledge that Professor Ollman is not a scholar or that his colleagues do not regard him as such. . . .

. . . [W]e are reminded that in the accommodation of the conflicting concerns reflected in the First Amendment and the law of defamation, the deep-seated constitutional values embodied in the Bill of Rights require that we not engage, without bearing clearly in mind the context before us, in a Talmudic parsing of a single sentence or two, as if we were occupied with a philosophical enterprise or linguistic analysis. Ours is a practical task, with elemental constitutional values of freedom looming large as we go about our work. And in that undertaking, we are reminded by *Gertz* itself of our duty "to assure to the freedoms of speech and press that 'breathing space' essential to their fruitful exercise." For the contraction of liberty's "breathing space" can only mean inhibition of the scope of public discussion on matters of general interest and concern. The provision of breathing space counsels strongly against straining to squeeze factual content from a single sentence in a column that is otherwise clearly opinion. . . .

The judgment of the District Court is therefore *Affirmed.*

JUDGE ROBERT BORK, concurring:

. . . [T]he statement challenged in this lawsuit, in terms of the policies of the first amendment, is functionally more like an "opinion" than a "fact" and should not be actionable. It thus falls within the category the Supreme Court calls "rhetorical hyperbole." . . .

. . . Ollman, by his own actions, entered a political arena in which heated discourse was to be expected and must be protected; the "fact" proposed to be tried is in truth wholly unsuitable for trial, which further imperils free discussion; the statement is not of the kind that would usually be accepted as one of hard fact and appeared in a context that further indicated it was rhetorical hyperbole.

Plaintiff Ollman, as will be shown, placed himself in the political arena and became the subject of heated political debate. . . .

. . . [I]n order to protect a vigorous marketplace in political ideas and contentions, we ought to accept the proposition that those who place themselves in a political arena must accept a degree of derogation that others need not. . . .

. . . [T]he core function of the first amendment is the preservation of that freedom to think and speak as one please which is the "means indispensable to the discovery and spread of political truth." Necessary to the preservation of that freedom, of course, is the willingness of those who would speak to be spoken to and, as in this case, to be spoken about. . . .

. . . Ollman has, as is his undoubted right, gone well beyond the role of the cloistered scholar, and he did so before Evans and Novak wrote about him. . . . Professor Ollman was an active proponent not just of Marxist scholarship but of Marxist politics. . . . It was plain that Ollman was a political activist and that he saw his academic post as, among other things, a means of advancing his political goals. . . .

. . . Ollman was not simply a scholar who was suddenly singled out by the press or by Evans and Novak. . . . He had entered the political arena before he put himself forward for the department chairmanship. . . . [H]e must accept the banging and jostling of political debate, in ways that a private person need not, in order to keep the political arena free and vital. . . .

. . . Ollman entered a first amendment arena and had to accept the rough treatment that arena affords. . . .

. . . [I]t is indisputable that this swirling public debate provided a strong context in which charges and countercharges should be assessed. In my view, that context made it much less likely that what Evans and Novak said would be regarded as an assertion of plain fact rather than as part of the judgments expressed by each side on the merits of the proposed appointment. . . .

When we come to the context in which this statement occurred, it becomes even more apparent that few people were likely to perceive it as a direct assertion of fact, to be taken at face value. That context was one of controversy and opinion, and it is known to be such by readers. It is significant, in the first place, that the column appeared on the Op-Ed pages of newspapers. These are pages reserved for the expression of opinion, much of it highly controversial opinion. That does not convert every assertion of fact on the Op-Ed pages into an expression of opinion merely by its placement there. It does alert the reader that he is in the context of controversy and politics, and that what he reads does not even purport to be as balanced, objective, and fair-minded as he has a right to hope to be the case with what is contained in the news columns of the paper. . . .

. . . I am persuaded that Ollman may not rest a libel action on the statement contained in the Evans and Novak column.

JUDGE ANTONIN SCALIA, dissenting:

More plaintiffs should bear in mind that it is a normal human reaction, after painstakingly examining and rejecting thirty invalid and almost absurd contentions, to reject the thirty-first contention as well, and make a clean sweep of the matter. I have no other explanation for the majority's affirmance of summary judgment dismissing what seems to me a classic and coolly crafted libel, Evans and Novak's disparagement of Ollman's professional reputation. . . .

. . . [T]o say, as the concurrence does, that hyperbole excuses not merely the exaggeration but *the fact sought to be vividly conveyed by the exaggeration* is to mistake a freedom to enliven discourse for a freedom to destroy reputation. The libel that "Smith is an incompetent carpenter" is not converted into harmless and nonactionable word-play by merely embellishing

it into the statement that "Smith is the worst carpenter this side of the Mississippi." . . .

APPENDIX

"The Marxist Professor's Intentions"
by Rowland Evans & Robert Novak

The Washington Post
May 4, 1978

What is in danger of becoming a frivolous public debate over the appointment of a Marxist to head the University of Maryland's department of politics and government has so far ignored this unspoken concern within the academic community: the avowed desire of many political activists to use higher education for indoctrination.

The proposal to name Bertell Ollman, professor at New York University, as department head has generated wrong-headed debate. Politicians who jumped in to oppose Ollman simply for his Marxist philosophy have received a justifiable going-over from defenders of academic freedom in the press and the university. Academic Prince Valiants seem arrayed against McCarythite [sic] know-nothings.

But neither side approaches the central question: not Ollman's beliefs, but his intentions. His candid writings avow his desire to use the classroom as an instrument for preparing what he calls "the revolution." Whether this is a form of indoctrination that could transform the real function of a university and transcend limits of academic freedom is a concern to academicians who are neither McCarthyite nor know-nothing.

To protect academic freedom, that question should be posed not by politicians but by professors. But professors throughout the country troubled by the nomination, clearly a minority, dare not say a word in today's campus climate.

While Ollman is described in news accounts as a "respected Marxist scholar," he is widely viewed in his profession as a political activist. Amid the increasingly popular Marxist movement in university life, he is distinct from philosophical Marxists. Rather, he is an outspoken proponent of "political Marxism."

He twice sought election to the council of the American Political Science Association as a candidate of the "Caucus for a New Political Science" and finished last out of 16 candidates each time. Whether or not that represents a professional judgment by his colleagues, as some critics contend, the verdict clearly rejected his campaign pledge: "If elected . . . I shall use every means at my disposal to promote the study of Marxism and Marxist approaches to politics throughout the profession."

Ollman's intentions become explicit in "On Teaching Marxism and Building the Movement," his article in the Winter 1978 issue of New Political Science. Most students, he claims, conclude his course with a "Marxist outlook." Ollman concedes that will be seen "as an admission that the purpose of my course is to convert students to socialism."

That bothers him not at all because "a correct understanding of Marxism (as indeed of any body of scientific truths) lead automatically to its acceptance." Non-Marxists students are defined as those "who do not yet understand Marxism." The "classroom" is a place where the students' "bourgeois ideology is being dismantled." "Our prior task" before the revolution, he writes, "is to make more revolutionaries. The revolution will only occur when there are enough of us to make it."

He concludes by stressing the importance to "the movement" of "radical professors." If approved for his new post, Ollman will have a major voice in filling a new professorship promised him. A leading prospect is fellow Marxist Alan Wolfe; he is notorious for his book "The Seamy Side of Democracy," whose celebration of communist China extols the beneficial nature of "brainwashing."

Ollman's principal scholarly work, "Alienation: Marx's Conception of Man in Capitalist Society," is a ponderous tome in adoration of the master (Marxism "is like a magnificently rich tapestry"). Published in 1971, it does not abandon hope for the revolution forecast by Karl Marx in 1848. "The present youth rebellion," he writes, by "helping to change the workers of tomorrow" will, along with other factors, make possible "a socialist revolution."

Such pamphleteering is hooted at by one political scientist in a major eastern university, whose scholarship and reputation as a liberal are well known. "Ollman has no status within the profession, but is a pure and simple activist," he said. Would he say that publicly? "No chance of it. Our academic culture does not permit the raising of such questions."

"Such questions" would include these: What is the true measurement of Ollman's scholarship? Does he intend to use the classroom for indoctrination? Will he indeed be followed by other Marxist professors? Could the department in time be closed to non-Marxists, following the tendency at several English universities?

Even if "such questions" cannot be raised by the faculty, they certainly should not be raised by politicians. While dissatisfaction with pragmatism by many liberal professors has renewed interest in the comprehensive dogma of the Marxists, there is little tolerance for confronting the value of that dogma. Here are the makings of a crisis that, to protect its integrity and true academic freedom, academia itself must resolve.

Milkovich v. Lorain Journal Co.
SUPREME COURT OF THE UNITED STATES
497 U.S. 1 (1990)

CHIEF JUSTICE WILLIAM REHNQUIST delivered the Court's opinion:
Respondent J. Theodore Diadiun authored an article in an Ohio newspaper implying that petitioner

Michael Milkovich, a local high school wrestling coach, lied under oath in a judicial proceeding about an incident involving petitioner and his team which occurred at a wrestling match. Petitioner sued Diadiun and the newspaper for libel, and the Ohio Court of Appeals affirmed a lower court entry of summary judgment against petitioner. This judgment was based in part on the grounds that the article constituted an "opinion" protected from the reach of state defamation law by the First Amendment to the United States Constitution. We hold that the First Amendment does not prohibit the application of Ohio's libel laws to the alleged defamations contained in the article.

This case is before us for the third time in an odyssey of litigation spanning nearly 15 years. Petitioner Milkovich, now retired, was the wrestling coach at Maple Heights High School in Maple Heights, Ohio. In 1974, his team was involved in an altercation at a home wrestling match with a team from Mentor High School. Several people were injured. In response to the incident, the Ohio High School Athletic Association (OHSAA) held a hearing at which Milkovich and H. Don Scott, the Superintendent of Maple Heights Public Schools, testified. Following the hearing, OHSAA placed the Maple Heights team on probation for a year and declared the team ineligible for the 1975 state tournament. OHSAA also censured Milkovich for his actions during the altercation. Thereafter, several parents and wrestlers sued OHSAA in the Court of Common Pleas of Franklin County, Ohio, seeking a restraining order against OHSAA's ruling on the grounds that they had been denied due process in the OHSAA proceeding. Both Milkovich and Scott testified in that proceeding. The court overturned OHSAA's probation and ineligibility orders on due process grounds.

The day after the court rendered its decision, respondent Diadiun's column appeared in the News-Herald, a newspaper which circulates in Lake County, Ohio, and is owned by respondent Lorain Journal Co. The column bore the heading "Maple beat the law with the 'big lie,'" beneath which appeared Diadiun's photograph and the words "TD Says." The carryover page headline announced ". . . Diadiun says Maple told a lie." The column contained the following passages:

> . . . [A] lesson was learned (or relearned) yesterday by the student body of Maple Heights High School, and by anyone who attended the Maple-Mentor wrestling meet of last Feb. 8.

> A lesson which, sadly, in view of the events of the past year, is well they learned early.

> It is simply this: If you get in a jam, lie your way out.

> If you're successful enough, and powerful enough, and can sound sincere enough, you stand an excellent chance of making the lie stand up, regardless of what really happened.

> The teachers responsible were mainly head Maple wrestling coach, Mike Milkovich, and former superintendent of schools H. Donald Scott.

> . . .

> Anyone who attended the meet, whether he be from Maple Heights, Mentor, or impartial observer, knows in his heart that Milkovich and Scott lied at the hearing after each having given his solemn oath to tell the truth.

> But they got away with it.

> Is that the kind of lesson we want our young people learning from their high school administrators and coaches?

> I think not.[91]

Petitioner commenced a defamation action against respondents in the Court of Common Pleas of Lake County, Ohio, alleging that the headline of Diadiun's article and the nine passages quoted above "accused plaintiff of committing the crime of perjury, an indictable offense in the State of Ohio, and damaged plaintiff directly in his life-time occupation of coach and teacher, and constituted libel *per se*." The action proceeded to trial, and the court granted a directed verdict to respondents on the ground that the evidence failed to establish the article was published with "actual malice" as required by *New York Times Co. v. Sullivan*. The Ohio Court of Appeals for the Eleventh Appellate District reversed and remanded, holding that there was sufficient evidence of actual malice to go to the jury. The Ohio Supreme Court dismissed the ensuing appeal for want of a substantial constitutional question, and this Court denied certiorari.

On remand, relying in part on our decision in *Gertz v. Robert Welch, Inc.,* (1974), the trial court granted summary judgment to respondents on the grounds that the article was an opinion protected from a libel action by "constitutional law," and alternatively, as a public figure, petitioner had failed to make out a *prima facie* case of actual malice. The Ohio Court of Appeals affirmed both determinations. On appeal, the Supreme Court of Ohio reversed and remanded. The court first decided that petitioner was neither a public figure nor a public official under the relevant decisions of this Court. The court then found that "the statements in issue are factual assertions as a matter of law, and are not constitutionally protected as the opinions of the writer. . . . The plain import of the author's assertions is that Milkovich, *inter alia,* committed the crime of perjury in a court of law." This Court again denied certiorari.

Meanwhile, Superintendent Scott had been pursuing a separate defamation action through the Ohio courts. Two years after its Milkovich decision, in considering Scott's appeal, the Ohio Supreme Court reversed its position on Diadiun's article, concluding that the column was "constitutionally protected opinion." Consequently, the court upheld a lower court's grant of summary judgment against Scott.

The *Scott* court decided that the proper analysis for determining whether utterances are fact or opinion was set forth in the decision of the United States Court of Appeals for the District of Columbia Circuit in *Ollman v. Evans* (1984). Under that analysis, four factors are considered to ascertain whether, under the "totality of circumstances," a statement is fact or opinion. These factors are: (1) "the specific language used"; (2) "whether the statement is verifiable"; (3) "the general context of the statement"; and (4) "the broader context in which the statement appeared." The court found that application of the first two factors to the column militated in favor of deeming the challenged passages actionable assertions of fact. That potential outcome was trumped, however, by the court's consideration of the third and fourth factors. With respect to the third factor, the general context, the court explained that "the large caption 'TD Says' . . . would indicate to even the most gullible reader that the article was, in fact, opinion." As for the fourth factor, the "broader context," the court reasoned that because the article appeared on a sports page—"a traditional haven for cajoling, invective, and hyperbole"—the article would probably be construed as opinion.

Subsequently, considering itself bound by the Ohio Supreme Court's decision in *Scott,* the Ohio Court of Appeals in the instant proceedings affirmed a trial court's grant of summary judgment in favor of respondents, concluding that "it has been decided, as a matter of law, that the article in question was constitutionally protected opinion." The Supreme Court of Ohio dismissed petitioner's ensuing appeal for want of a substantial constitutional question. We granted certiorari, to consider the important questions raised by the Ohio courts' recognition of a constitutionally required "opinion" exception to the application of its defamation laws. We now reverse. . . .

Respondents would have us recognize, in addition to the established safeguards discussed above, still another First-Amendment-based protection for defamatory statements which are categorized as "opinion" as opposed to "fact." For this proposition they rely principally on the following dictum from our opinion in *Gertz:*

"Under the First Amendment there is no such thing as a false idea. However pernicious an opinion may seem, we depend for its correction not on the conscience of judges and juries but on the competition of other ideas. But there is no constitutional value in false statements of fact." Judge Friendly appropriately observed that this passage "has become the opening salvo in all arguments for protection from defamation actions on the ground of opinion, even though the case did not remotely concern the question." Read in context, though, the fair meaning of the passage is to equate the word "opinion" in the second sentence with the word "idea" in the first sentence. Under this view, the language was merely a reiteration of Justice Holmes' classic "marketplace of ideas" concept. ("[T]he ultimate good desired is better reached by free trade in ideas . . . the best test of truth is the power of the thought to get itself accepted in the competition of the market"). Thus, we do not think this passage from *Gertz* was intended to create a wholesale defamation exemption for anything that might be labeled "opinion." (The "marketplace of ideas" origin of this passage "points strongly to the view that the 'opinions' held to be constitutionally protected were the sort of thing that could be corrected by discussion"). Not only would such an interpretation be contrary to the tenor and context of the passage, but it would also ignore the fact that expressions of "opinion" may often imply an assertion of objective fact.

If a speaker says, "In my opinion John Jones is a liar," he implies a knowledge of facts which lead to the conclusion that Jones told an untruth. Even if the speaker states the facts upon which he bases his opinion, if those facts are either incorrect or incomplete, or if his assessment of them is erroneous, the statement may still imply a false assertion of fact. Simply couching such statements in terms of opinion does not dispel these implications; and the statement, "In my opinion Jones is a liar," can cause as much damage to reputation as the statement, "Jones is a liar." As Judge Friendly aptly stated: "[It] would be destructive of the law of libel if a writer could escape liability for accusations of [defamatory conduct] simply by using, explicitly or implicitly, the words 'I think.'" It is worthy of note that, at common law, even the privilege of fair comment did not extend to "a false statement of fact, whether it was expressly stated or implied from an expression of opinion."

. . . [R]espondents do not really contend that a statement such as, "In my opinion John Jones is a liar," should be protected by a separate privilege for "opinion" under the First Amendment. But they do contend that in every defamation case the First Amendment mandates an inquiry into whether a statement is "opinion" or "fact," and that only the latter statements may be actionable. They propose that a number of factors developed by the lower courts (in what we hold was a mistaken reliance on the *Gertz* dictum) be considered in deciding which is which. But we think the "'breathing space'" which "'freedoms of expression require in order to survive,'" is adequately secured by existing constitutional doctrine without the creation of an artificial dichotomy between "opinion" and fact.

Foremost, we think [precedent] stands for the proposition that a statement on matters of public concern must be provable as false before there can be liability under state defamation law, at least in situations, like the present, where a media defendant is involved. Thus, unlike the statement, "In my opinion Mayor Jones is a liar," the statement, "In my opinion Mayor Jones shows his abysmal ignorance by accepting the teachings of Marx and Lenin," would not be actionable. [Precedent] ensures that a statement of opinion relating to matters of public concern which does not contain a provably false factual connotation will receive full constitutional protection. . . .

We are not persuaded that, in addition to these protections, an additional separate constitutional privilege for "opinion" is required to ensure the freedom of expression guaranteed by the First Amendment. The dispositive question in the present case then becomes whether a reasonable factfinder could conclude that the statements in the Diadiun column imply an assertion that petitioner Milkovich perjured himself in a judicial proceeding. We think this question must be answered in the affirmative. As the Ohio Supreme Court itself observed, "The clear impact in some nine sentences and a caption is that [Milkovich] 'lied at the hearing after . . . having given his solemn oath to tell the truth.'" This is not the sort of loose, figurative, or hyperbolic language which would negate the impression that the writer was seriously maintaining that petitioner committed the crime of perjury. Nor does the general tenor of the article negate this impression.

We also think the connotation that petitioner committed perjury is sufficiently factual to be susceptible of being proved true or false. A determination whether petitioner lied in this instance can be made on a core of objective evidence by comparing, *inter alia,* petitioner's testimony before the OHSAA board with his subsequent testimony before the trial court. As the *Scott* court noted regarding the plaintiff in that case, "Whether or not H. Don Scott did indeed perjure himself is certainly verifiable by a perjury action with evidence adduced from the transcripts and witnesses present at the hearing. Unlike a subjective assertion, the averred defamatory language is an articulation of an objectively verifiable event." So too with petitioner Milkovich.

[Previous] decisions [ ] establishing First Amendment protection for defendants in defamation actions surely demonstrate the Court's recognition of the Amendment's vital guarantee of free and uninhibited discussion of public issues. But there is also another side to the equation; we have regularly acknowledged the "important social values which underlie the law of defamation," and recognized that "[s]ociety has a pervasive and strong interest in preventing and redressing attacks upon reputation." . . .

We believe our decision in the present case holds the balance true. The judgment of the Ohio Court of Appeals is reversed, and the case is remanded for further proceedings not inconsistent with this opinion.

Reversed.

Chapter 6

There is a huge disconnect between what consumers think happens to their data [online] and what really happens.

Jonathan Leibowitz, chair, Federal Trade Commission[1]

Awareness that the Government may be watching chills associational and expressive freedoms. And the Government's unrestrained power to assemble data that reveal private aspects of identity is susceptible to abuse . . . [and] may alter the relationship between citizen and government in a way that is inimical to democratic society.

Supreme Court Justice Sonya Sotomayor[2]

As technology advances, so does the potential to create new ways to compromise personal privacy.

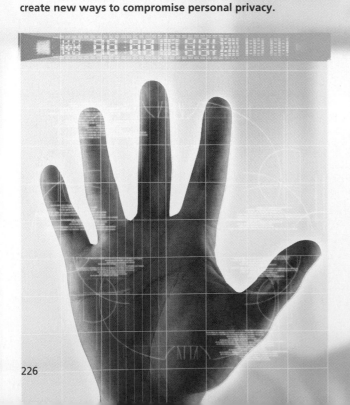

Protecting Privacy

Conflicts Between the Press, the Government and the Right to Privacy

**Privacy and the
   Supreme Court**

**Sources of Privacy
   Protection**

**Privacy Law's
   Development**

False Light
Plaintiff's Case
Defenses

Appropriation
Commercialization and
   Right of Publicity
Plaintiff's Case
Defenses

Intrusion
Methods of Intruding
Intrusion on Private
   Property
Defenses

Private Facts
Intimate Facts
Legitimate Public Concern
Publicity
First Amendment Defense

Cases for Study
➤ *City of Ontario v.
   Quon*
➤ *United States v. Jones*

Suppose . . .

. . . that police install a Global Positioning System (GPS) on the car of a woman whose husband is suspected of dealing drugs. Police attach the GPS device to the outside of the car while it is parked in a public parking lot. Based on evidence collected by the GPS tracking device, police arrest the man and he is subsequently charged with multiple counts of distributing and possessing cocaine. He is later indicted by a grand jury, based largely on evidence from the GPS that connected the man to a co-conspirator's stash house. Upon conviction at trial, the man is sentenced to life imprisonment. He appeals his conviction on the grounds that the evidence collected by the GPS device violated his Fourth Amendment rights because it amounted to a warrantless search. The Fourth Amendment protects against "unreasonable searches and seizures" and is one of the amendments on which a constitutional right to privacy is based. Is the installation of a GPS device defined as a search under the Fourth Amendment? If so, did the police violate the man's privacy in this case? Does a person have a reasonable expectation of privacy in his car, even though the car drives on public roads and is visible to the public? How has technology changed our societal understanding of a "reasonable expectation of privacy"? Look for the answers to these questions when you read the discussion of *United States v. Jones* in this chapter and excerpted at the end of the chapter.

Americans have been concerned about their privacy since the United States' inception. The U.S. Constitution reflects this, as the framers, for example, adopted the Fourth Amendment, protecting "the right of the people to be secure in their persons, houses, papers, and effects, against unreasonable searches and seizures."[3] The Third Amendment ensures that the government cannot force residents to have soldiers living in their homes, except perhaps during wartime.[4] More than a century later, in 1890, reporters prying into private affairs of the rich and elite prompted two prominent Boston lawyers to write a law review article arguing that the courts should protect people's privacy.

In the 21st century, people are less concerned with soldiers in their homes and snooping reporters asking personal questions than with technology allowing other individuals, the government, the press and corporations to learn about their innermost secrets. There is substantial reason for these concerns.

In the summer of 2013, the public learned that United States and British intelligence agencies reportedly mined data from nine United States Internet companies as part of its PRISM program, which is designed to secretly gather information to fight terrorism. The Washington Post and London's Guardian newspaper reported that the National Security Agency and the Federal Bureau of Investigation (FBI) tapped directly into the central servers of companies such as Google, Facebook, YouTube, Apple, Microsoft and others to extract video and audio chats, photos, e-mails, documents and connection logs to allow them to track foreign targets. The privacy implications of such actions by the government are significant and will likely be a hot topic for discussion for the next few years.[5]

Today, Google, Microsoft and many popular websites install tracking devices on users' computers, some able to "record a person's keystrokes online and then transmit the text to a data-gathering company that analyzes it for content, tone and clues to a person's social connections." A Wall Street Journal study found the devices "enabled data-gathering companies to build personal profiles that could include age, gender, race, zip code, income, marital status and health concerns, along with recent purchases and favorite TV shows and movies." One company alone sells more than 50 million pieces of this information each day to advertisers and others.[6] Courts have allowed websites and advertisers to put cookies—technology that tracks what websites people visit—on computers.[7]

Many smartphone applications send users' sensitive information to advertisers and companies compiling data about individuals.[8] In 2013, 38 states reached a privacy settlement with Google for $7 million after a privacy breach with the Google's Street View car fleet. For two years, the cars collected passwords, messages and other private data from unsecured Wi-Fi networks as they drove past homes and businesses. Following the settlement, Google said it had secured the information and would destroy it without using it. Google also agreed to initiate a new consumer privacy employee-training program and a national advertising campaign to educate users on how to protect their privacy.[9]

Recently, a "doxxing" website exposed the Social Security numbers, credit reports, mortgage information, addresses, phone numbers and other sensitive information of celebrities and prominent government officials. Doxxing is the practice of finding information about a person from limited, publicly available data. The word is derived from the phrase "document tracing." The doxxing website posted the credit report of the FBI director, other personal information about former Secretary of State Hillary Clinton and Vice President Joe Biden, and the Social Security numbers of Jay-Z, Beyonce, Kim Kardashian, Ashton Kutcher, Paris Hilton and Mel Gibson among other A-list celebrities.[10]

Digital privacy invasions are serious matters when they lead to identity theft, a possibility if someone discovers another person's Social Security number, bank account number or passwords for various websites. For example, counties in the state of Virginia have more than 200 million land records, such as home sales and home foreclosures, online. Many of these records have individuals' Social Security numbers attached despite state laws requiring that the numbers be removed. A woman advocating that counties be certain Social Security numbers are removed from land records posted some of those numbers on her own website to show how easily accessible they are. Virginia then adopted a law making it illegal to post other people's Social Security numbers. The U.S. Court of Appeals for the Fourth Circuit held that the law violated the woman's First Amendment rights.[11] The state argued posting Social Security numbers did not express ideas so should not have First Amendment protection. The court said posting the numbers was "integral to her message."

Another important privacy concern is protecting minors. The Federal Trade Commission (FTC) says 90 percent of U.S. minors between 12 and 17 years old spend time online. Although they consider themselves skilled at online activities, the FTC says young people often inadvertently or deliberately disclose personal information and other sensitive details that could lead to identity theft, online stalking and more serious attacks.[12]

Current federal and state privacy laws do not sufficiently protect American consumers, according to the FTC. Rather, today the burden of understanding websites' privacy policies is with online users who must affirmatively try to ensure their own privacy.[13] Is it possible for individuals to do that? The social

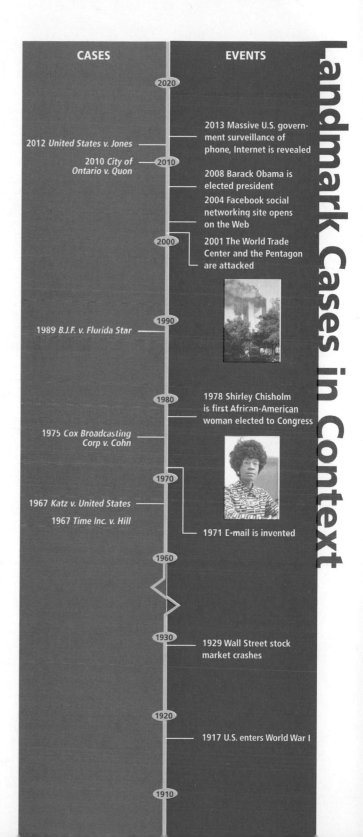

Landmark Cases in Context

CASES

2012 *United States v. Jones*
2010 *City of Ontario v. Quon*

1989 *B.J.F. v. Florida Star*

1975 *Cox Broadcasting Corp v. Cohn*

1967 *Katz v. United States*
1967 *Time Inc. v. Hill*

EVENTS

2020

2013 Massive U.S. government surveillance of phone, Internet is revealed

2010

2008 Barack Obama is elected president
2004 Facebook social networking site opens on the Web

2000

2001 The World Trade Center and the Pentagon are attacked

1990

1980

1978 Shirley Chisholm is first African-American woman elected to Congress

1970

1971 E-mail is invented

1960

1930

1929 Wall Street stock market crashes

1920

1917 U.S. enters World War I

1910

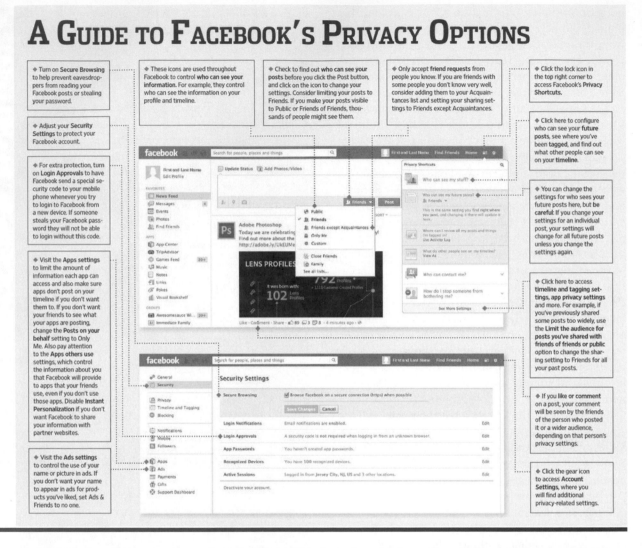

A Guide to Facebook's Privacy Options

◆ Turn on **Secure Browsing** to help prevent eavesdroppers from reading your Facebook posts or stealing your password.

◆ Adjust your **Security Settings** to protect your Facebook account.

◆ For extra protection, turn on **Login Approvals** to have Facebook send a special security code to your mobile phone whenever you try to login to Facebook from a new device. If someone steals your Facebook password they will not be able to login without this code.

◆ Visit the **Apps settings** to limit the amount of information each app can access and also make sure apps don't post on your timeline if you don't want them to. If you don't want your friends to see what your apps are posting, change the **Posts on your behalf** setting to Only Me. Also pay attention to the **Apps others use** settings, which control the information about you that Facebook will provide to apps that your friends use, even if you don't use those apps. Disable **Instant Personalization** if you don't want Facebook to share your information with partner websites.

◆ Visit the **Ads settings** to control the use of your name or picture in ads. If you don't want your name to appear in ads for products you've liked, set Ads & Friends to no one.

◆ These icons are used throughout Facebook to control **who can see your information.** For example, they control who can see the information on your profile and timeline.

◆ Check to find out **who can see your posts** before you click the Post button, and click on the icon to change your settings. Consider limiting your posts to Friends. If you make your posts visible to Public or Friends of Friends, thousands of people might see them.

◆ Only accept **friend requests** from people you know. If you are friends with some people you don't know very well, consider adding them to your Acquaintances list and setting your sharing settings to Friends except Acquaintances.

◆ Click the lock icon in the top right corner to access Facebook's **Privacy Shortcuts.**

◆ Click here to configure who can see your **future posts**, see where you've been **tagged**, and find out what other people can see on your **timeline**.

◆ You can change the settings for who sees your future posts here, but be **careful!** If you change your settings for an individual post, your settings will change for all future posts unless you change the settings again.

◆ Click here to access **timeline and tagging settings, app privacy settings** and more. For example, if you've previously shared some posts too widely, use the **Limit the audience for posts you've shared** with friends of friends or public option to change the sharing setting to Friends for all your past posts.

◆ If you like or comment on a post, your comment will be seen by the friends of the person who posted it or a wider audience, depending on that person's privacy settings.

◆ Click the gear icon to access **Account Settings**, where you will find additional privacy-related settings.

Facebook's privacy options are complicated—this graphic from the Wall Street Journal breaks down the different ways a user can protect her privacy when using the social media site.

networking site Facebook's privacy policy is thousands of words long, nearly 1,300 words longer than the U.S. Constitution. Facebook's policy requires users to opt out if they want privacy. That is, users' posted information is publicly available and becomes private only if a user clicks on the appropriate settings. As one technology security expert notes, "It isn't always easy to figure out, or to keep up with the changes the company makes over time."[14] Facebook continually updates its privacy and information security policies, even relocating where a user

realWorld Law

Stuck in the 1980s?

Sen. Patrick Leahy

In 1986, Congress passed the Electronic Communications Privacy Act (ECPA)[1] in an effort to limit government wiretaps of transmissions of electronic data by computers and to deal with stored electronic communications and records held by third-party Internet service providers (ISPs). Technology has rapidly evolved since then, and Congress has struggled to keep pace. For years, privacy advocates have complained that ECPA's out-of-date standards allow law enforcement agencies to obtain e-mail older than six months without a warrant. They say this gives them easy access to personal information.[2] In 2013, Senator Patrick Leahy led an effort to amend the ECPA to require a court-approved search warrant before police can review e-mail or any other electronic content. Under Leahy's amendment, the government must also notify a person about the warrant and provide a copy. When Leahy introduced the Electronic Communication Privacy Act Amendments Act of 2013, he noted that 27 years ago he led the effort to write the ECPA and "email was a novelty. No one could have imagined the way the Internet and mobile technologies would transform how we communicate and exchange information today."[3]

Leahy's effort has bipartisan support in both the Senate and the House, and if it is signed into law it could take effect in 2014.

---

1. Pub. L. No. 99 1508, 100 Stat. 1848 (1986), codified at 18 U.S.C. §§ 2510–2522. Title II of the ECPA is called the Stored Communications Act, codified at 18 U.S.C., ch. 121 §§ 2701–2712.
2. Ellen Nakashima, *Senate Panel Backs E-mail Privacy Bill*, WASH. POST (Nov. 29, 2012), *available at* http://articles.washingtonpost.com/2012–11–29/world/35586082_1_law-enforcement-privacy-law-e-mail-content.
3. 159 Cong. Rec. S1951–S1955 (daily ed. Mar. 19, 2013), *available at* http://www.fas.org/irp/congress/2013_cr/s607.html.

can find the privacy and security icons as it changes its basic design. How many of Facebook's more than 1 billion members who "like" 2.7 billion posts every day read the policy and opt for privacy?

In 2012, the FTC issued a substantive commission report titled "Protecting Consumer Privacy in an Era of Rapid Change" and called on companies to adopt its recommended best practices. The report suggested that companies build in consumer privacy protections at all stages of product development. Those protections should include consumer data security, limited data collection and retention, and procedures to promote data accuracy. The report also recommended giving consumers the option to control how they share their information and the ability to choose a "Do-Not-Track" mechanism, and the FTC encouraged companies to strive toward transparency in how they collect and use consumer information.[15]

There is little privacy in the workplace and only somewhat more privacy protection for personal health information. Despite a federal law protecting the privacy of health care information possessed by health care providers and health plans, the law does not cover health information in school records, employment files or financial records. Courts allow an employer to inspect employees' e-mail, including personal messages, and listen to their telephone conversations.

Privacy and the Supreme Court

The U.S. Supreme Court in 2010 held that government employers may see public employees' text messages sent and received on government-issued equipment if the searches have a legitimate work-related purpose and the public employees have been told not to expect privacy.[16] The case, *City of Ontario v. Quon*, involved an Ontario, Calif., police officer who used a department-issued pager to communicate with fellow officers. The city gave permission to use the pagers for a limited number of personal messages. When the city audited officers' pagers, it found one officer had sent text messages to and received them from both his wife and mistress. The Court said the messages were sexually explicit. The officer claimed the city violated his reasonable expectation of privacy. The Court said even if the office did have a reasonable expectation of privacy, the city's search of his pager did not violate it. The Court cited the city's written policy that public employees had no privacy expectation when using city equipment. Also, the city had a reasonable purpose in auditing police officers' pagers. The city wanted to know if it needed to increase the limit it had set on pager messages. Although the Court stressed its ruling was narrowly applied to the case facts, it could relate to government-issued cell phones, computers and other communication technologies. The decision affects the country's more than 20 million public employees.

The *Quon* decision is not the first time the Supreme Court ruled that employees have limited privacy rights. The Court in 1987 said a search of a public employee's desk and filing cabinet did not violate his Fourth Amendment rights.[17] May a private employer look at an e-mail message on an employee's computer? Courts have said the First Amendment does not bar companies from doing so.[18] "By intercepting [e-mail] communications, the company is not . . . requiring the employee to disclose any personal information about himself or invading the employee's person or personal effects. Moreover, the company's interest in preventing inappropriate and unprofessional comments or even illegal activity over its e-mail system outweighs any privacy interest the employee may have . . . ," one federal court said.[19]

Privacy protection diminished after Sept. 11, 2001. At airports, employees of the Transportation Safety Administration, a federal government agency, may open and look through travelers' luggage. The USA Patriot Act allows the government to obtain information about anyone from public libraries, businesses, hospitals and Internet service providers. The government only has to say the information is being sought for a terrorism investigation. The person revealing the information is not allowed to tell anyone else that the government asked for it.[20]

Although the *Quon* decision and the USA Patriot Act diminish privacy expectations, two recent Supreme Court cases expand privacy protection as it relates to "unreasonable searches and seizures" under the Fourth Amendment. In *United States v. Jones,* excerpted at the end of this chapter, the Supreme Court unanimously held that physically mounting a GPS transmitter on a car amounts to a search and violates the Fourth Amendment.[21] In *Jones* the Court relied partially on its 1967 decision in *Katz v. United States.* Katz had been convicted of illegal betting over a telephone line in a public phone booth. The government recorded his phone conversations without a warrant, and those recordings led to his conviction. The Supreme Court threw out that evidence, calling it a Fourth Amendment violation. In his concurrence, Justice John Marshall Harlan II wrote, "[A] person has a constitutionally protected reasonable expectation of privacy," and "electronic as well as physical intrusion into a place that is in this sense private may constitute a violation of the Fourth Amendment."[22]

Subsequent courts have recognized Justice Harlan's concurrence in *Katz* as the Harlan "reasonable expectation of privacy test." The test requires that an individual exhibit an actual expectation of privacy and that this expectation is one that society is prepared to recognize as reasonable.[23] Referencing *Katz,* the *Jones* Court said that "a violation occurs when government officers violated a person's 'reasonable expectation of privacy.'"[24]

In *Florida v. Jardines* (2013), the Supreme Court held that the use of drug-sniffing dogs to search an area around a house after a tip that the homeowner was growing marijuana amounts to a Fourth Amendment violation. Police obtained a search warrant after the dog found the drugs, but the Supreme Court said the warrant was not valid because it was based on the illegal search by the K-9 officer and his dog. The majority reasoned that "while law enforcement officers need not 'shield their eyes' when passing by the home 'on public thoroughfares,' an officer's leave to gather information is sharply circumscribed when he steps off those thoroughfares and enters the Fourth Amendment's protect areas."[25]

Legal scholars note that since the *Katz* case offered the reasonable expectation of privacy test in 1967, the Supreme Court has decided very few Fourth Amendment cases dealing with advanced technology. But the decisions in *Jones* and *Jardines* show that the Court has decided in the 21st century to both reaffirm the traditional privacy expectation near the home (*Jardines*) and to extend protection to newer technologies that have given rise to public concern (*Jones*). One legal scholar notes that the subject matter in *Jones* involves

> the most advanced surveillance technology the Court has dealt with [and] . . . all nine justices voted to protect citizens' Fourth Amendment rights. . . . [Five justices] are prepared to apply the reasonable expectation of privacy test in a manner that recognizes society's reasonable expectation that it will not be continuously monitored by GPS technology. This . . . strongly indicates that the reasonable expectation of privacy test can be applied in a way that protects citizens' Fourth Amendment rights from the advancement of modern technology.[26]

Should they choose, the Supreme Court justices will have many future opportunities to rule on questions of privacy and the use of technology, specifically as

Emerging Law

Cloud Computing and "Going Dark"

In another example of technology outpacing the law, the FBI has argued that it needs Congress to update the Communications Assistance for Law Enforcement Act (CALEA)[1] passed in 1994. CALEA allows the FBI, with a warrant, to monitor citizens' digital phone conversations and Internet traffic. The FBI's general counsel said the advent of cloud computing has thwarted law enforcement's ability to monitor real-time conversations in cloud-based applications. He calls the phenomenon "going dark" because cloud computing allows users to store communications in a location different than their personal computers, and often cloud storage is encrypted, which means law enforcement cannot easily access it. A recent top priority of the FBI has been to propose new laws that will give law enforcement real-time access to cloud-based online communications, including services such as Gmail, Dropbox, Skype and the chat feature in some online games, which he said "are being used for criminal conversations."[2]

Privacy advocates argue that the expansion of FBI power is unnecessary because Title III of the Wiretap Act[3] requires Internet service providers (ISPs) to provide them with "technical assistance" to solve problems like this one. They also complain that public debate about the issue has been limited. Privacy groups also are challenging the Cyber Intelligence Sharing and Protection Act (CISPA), which was reintroduced in the House of Representatives in 2013. If passed, CISPA will allow technology companies and law enforcement to share Internet traffic information with the goal of protecting the country against a cyberattack. Privacy advocates like the Electronic Frontier Foundation criticize CISPA because it offers broad immunities to companies that share private data with any federal agency, including military intelligence and the National Security Agency.[4]

According to one blogger who follows technology and privacy issues, "Online privacy is undoubtedly shaping up to be one of the most crucial issues of the year."[5]

---

1. 47 U.S.C. §§ 1001–1010.
2. Alex Fitzpatrick, *FBI: Expanding Internet Snooping Powers a "Top Priority,"* MASHABLE.COM (Mar. 27, 2013), *available at* http://mashable.com/2013/03/27/internet-snooping-fbi/.
3. 18 U.S.C. §§ 2510–2522.
4. *CISPA, the Privacy-Invading Cybersecurity Spying Bill Is Back in Congress,* EFF.ORG (Feb. 13, 2013), *available at* https://www.eff.org/deeplinks/2013/02/cispa-privacy-invading-cybersecurity-spying-bill-back-congress.
5. Fitzpatrick, *supra* note 2.

it relates to cell phones and their geolocation abilities, their stored information and the ability of police to search a seized cell phone without a warrant. Many state and federal courts have come to different conclusions, leaving numerous questions about privacy and cell phone technology in flux. For example, in 2012 the Fifth Circuit ruled that data stored on a cell phone or other personal devices are not protected by the Stored Communications Act,[27] and the Seventh Circuit decided that a warrantless search of a suspect's cell phone in order to get his phone number is not a violation of the Fourth Amendment.[28]

In 2013 judges in California raised concerns about the use of cell phone tracking devices called "stingrays." These devices simulate a cell phone tower and can locate a cell phone even if it is not making a call. The threshold for a federal officer to obtain a stingray is not as high as a search warrant.[29] But, in New York, a judge wrote in a recent decision, "A person necessarily has no reasonable expectation of privacy with respect to the phone's location." He argues that technology and consumer sophistication have progressed to the point that people understand a satellite can track their cell phone's location without their knowledge.[30] In 2013, a bipartisan group in the House of Representatives introduced the Geolocation Privacy and Surveillance Act (GPSA) that would require police to obtain a warrant to collect location data from a cell phone, tablet or other portable electronic device.[31] The GPSA was introduced in part to counteract a Sixth Circuit ruling that held police do not need a warrant to track the location of a suspect's phone. The Sixth Circuit's decision came after the Supreme Court issued its ruling in *United States v. Jones*.[32]

Points of Law

Constitutional Right to Privacy

- Protection comes from the Third, Fourth, Fifth and Fourteenth Amendments.

- The Constitution protects from governmental invasion of privacy.

- Harlan's "reasonable expectation of privacy" test from *Katz* establishes a Fourth Amendment right to privacy when:

  1. A person exhibits an actual expectation of privacy, and

  2. Society is prepared to recognize this expectation as reasonable.

Is personal privacy more at risk from the press than from the government? Journalists often are accused of delving into people's private lives, using new technologies to uncover their deepest secrets. Of course, journalists need access to information, sometimes including private facts, to write their stories, as discussed in Chapter 8. This chapter treats the privacy torts for which the media often are sued.

SUMMARY

SOME PRIVACY PROTECTION DIMINISHED after Sept. 11, 2001. The USA Patriot Act allows the government to obtain information about anyone from public libraries, businesses, hospitals and ISPs. The U.S. Supreme Court in 2010 held that government employers may see public employees' text messages sent and received on government-issued equipment if the searches have a legitimate work-related purpose and the public employees have been told not to expect privacy. Two Supreme Court decisions in 2012 and 2013 that explored privacy and the Fourth Amendment reaffirmed the traditional privacy expectation near the home and unanimously held that physically mounting a GPS transmitter on a car amounts to a search and violates the Fourth Amendment. ∎

Sources of Privacy Protection

The U.S. Constitution, state and federal laws and court decisions offer some limited privacy protection. Although the word "privacy" is not in the federal Constitution, the U.S. Supreme Court has said the Constitution protects certain privacy rights.[33]

The Court said the word "liberty" in the 14th Amendment—"[N]or shall any State deprive any person of life, liberty, or property, without due process of law"— includes personal privacy.[34] Additionally, the Constitution includes the Third and Fourth Amendments, mentioned earlier in this chapter, and the Fifth Amendment, protecting people from having to incriminate themselves.[35] Based on these constitutional provisions, the Court has overturned laws prohibiting use of contraceptives,[36] distributing contraceptives to unmarried couples,[37] providing abortions[38] and same-sex intimate contact.[39] Beyond the bedroom, however, the U.S. Constitution does not protect against government, media or private snooping into people's personal lives.

State and federal governments have adopted statutes protecting privacy. Most of these laws stop government agencies from giving out confidential information without the individual's permission. As discussed in Chapter 8, state public records laws make certain government documents obtainable for distribution but categorize others—usually those containing private information—as not accessible to the public.

Privacy Law's Development

Using tort law—in civil law, a tort is an injury one person or entity inflicts on another—to sue the media for invading privacy is a relatively new idea. Although libel has been recognized for four centuries, the notion that courts or legislatures should protect privacy rights is only about 120 years old. Concerns about the press delving into individuals' private lives date back at least to the 19th century in the United States, but it took two Boston lawyers to put privacy on the legal map.[40] Samuel Warren and his law partner, future Supreme Court justice Louis Brandeis, wrote an article for the Harvard Law Review—perhaps the country's most prestigious academic law journal—titled "The Right to Privacy."[41] Published in 1890, the article argued that human dignity required protecting individual privacy. Warren and Brandeis knew that no statutes shielded people's private lives from prying journalists, but the lawyers contended that the common law should recognize privacy rights.[42] The article elaborated for the first time a legal theory as to why the courts should recognize a right to privacy, and it proved influential when the Supreme Court eventually recognized a right to privacy based in the U.S. Constitution and its underlying principles.

During the seven decades after Warren and Brandeis' article, courts in a few states accepted a common-law right of privacy, and several other states adopted laws protecting privacy.[43] But courts were unclear about what was being protected. Some decisions conflicted with others, state statutes differed from each other and privacy law became a jumble. In 1960, William Prosser, a torts expert and law school dean, published an article trying to clarify matters.[44] Prosser suggested privacy law be divided into four categories: false light, appropriation, intrusion and private facts. Courts and state legislatures adopted and continue to use Prosser's categories, but not all states allow plaintiffs to sue for each of the four privacy torts.

In 2013, 34 states recognized the false light tort and 10 had rejected it; 41 states recognized private facts and four have rejected that doctrine; 42 states recognized the intrusion tort, while two have rejected it; and 44 states recognized appropriation/right of publicity torts and six states have not had the opportunity to rule on the issue. The District of Columbia and the U.S. Virgin Islands both recognized all four privacy torts, while Puerto Rico only recognized appropriation.[45]

Only living individuals may sue for three of the privacy torts: intrusion, private facts and false light.[46] Like a person's reputation in a libel case, privacy is considered a personal right. The dead do not have personal rights. Also, businesses, associations, unions and other groups do not have personal rights, and most often cannot sue for a privacy tort.[47] Only individuals may sue for appropriation in many states. But a few states allow businesses, nonprofit organizations and associations to bring appropriation lawsuits.

Points of Law

The Four Privacy Torts

1. *False light:* Intentionally or recklessly publicizing false information a reasonable person would find highly offensive

2. *Appropriation:* Using another's name or likeness for advertising or other commercial purposes without permission

3. *Intrusion:* Intentionally intruding on another's solitude or seclusion

4. *Private facts:* Publicizing private, embarrassing information

SUMMARY

PROTECTING PERSONAL PRIVACY HAS BEEN a concern since the country's founding. There is some protection found in the U.S. Constitution and in federal and state laws. However, for the media, privacy questions usually arise in tort suits. Legal attention to privacy began with Samuel Warren and Louis Brandeis' 1890 Harvard Law Review article suggesting the law recognize the right to be let alone as a way to recognize human dignity. In 1960, Prosser divided privacy law into four torts: false light, appropriation, intrusion and private facts.

Privacy law among states is inconsistent; some states even refuse to recognize one or more of the privacy torts. Only living individuals may bring privacy lawsuits, although a few suits allow businesses to sue for appropriation. ∎

False Light

False light is a first cousin to libel. It is so close to libel, some state courts say, that it should not exist as a separate tort. If someone publishes a false statement, sue that person for libel, not false light, such courts maintain. But not all false statements are defamatory, other courts say. Some false statements make a person appear better than they really are . . . but the statement still is false. The false light tort, then, includes statements both disparaging and flattering.

False light and libel both punish publishing false information. Libel protects reputation—a person's good name. In contrast, false light compensates for

false light A privacy tort that involves making a person seem in the public eye to be someone he or she is not. Several states do not allow false light suits.

the emotional distress a false report causes. An article making a person appear to be someone he or she is not but not injuring the person's reputation may be grounds for a false light suit, but not libel. For example, a poetry magazine publishes a poem and attributes it to a famous poet, but the poet did not write it. The poem is not so bad that it injures the poet's reputation; however, the magazine says the poet wrote something the poet did not, putting the poet in a false light. If the poem was very badly written, the poet might sue for libel because his or her reputation would be injured.[48]

For example, an unauthorized biography said that a former baseball player was a war hero, but he was not. The book said the player won a medal for outstanding heroism, but he did not. If the player sued the author and the publisher, would he sue for libel? To win a libel suit, the player must prove the book injured his reputation. But the community likely would not be contemptuous of a person called a war hero, making a successful libel suit impossible. Instead, the player might sue for false light, based on making a person appear to be someone he or she is not. Warren Spahn, a Hall of Fame pitcher, did just that and won the case.[49] The book's author did not speak to Spahn but instead obtained information from news reports. The author also invented conversations and events. Winning a lawsuit because you were called a war hero? Confusing? Foolish? Some state courts say the false light tort is both, and therefore, they refuse to recognize it. Courts in these states argue that false light should not be a separate tort because it is similar to defamation. They also say false light is so vague it encroaches on First Amendment rights. Some courts do not want to consider lawsuits based on articles that make people appear better than they really are.

Although 34 states allow false light suits, 10 states explicitly reject them.[50] California sees false light and libel as such close relatives that a false light plaintiff must prove reputational injury.[51] A number of courts allow a plaintiff to sue for both defamation and false light based on the same facts.

Points of Law

False Light

Plaintiff's Case

- Publicizing

- False facts

- About someone who is identified

- That would be highly offensive to a reasonable person

- Acting intentionally or recklessly (according to the Supreme Court), or negligently if the plaintiff is a private person (according to some courts)

Defense

- Libel defenses

Plaintiff's Case

Most states recognizing false light require a plaintiff to prove (1) the material was published, (2) the plaintiff was identified, (3) the published material was false or created a false impression, (4) the statements or pictures put the plaintiff in a false light that would be highly offensive to a reasonable person and (5) the defendant knew the material was false or recklessly disregarded its falsity.[52] Corporations, other businesses, unions, associations and other groups cannot sue for false light. Only individuals can bring a false light suit because only individuals can be highly offended.[53]

Publication Like the private facts tort, false light requires material to have been widely distributed to the public generally or to a large segment of the community.[54] An oral comment to a few people does not amount to publicity for the false light tort. Courts in a few states disagree and allow publication to be proved by dissemination to just one person or a few people.[55] For these courts, that smaller group must have a special relationship with the plaintiff so the plaintiff would be highly offended if the group saw or heard the publication.[56] Anything published in a mass medium likely will meet the publicity test.

Identification The plaintiff must prove the offensive material was about her or him. The courts of some states, such as California, define identification for false light as they do for libel. It is sufficient if one or more persons say the article identified the plaintiff.[57] Most courts hold that because the publication requirement means many people must be exposed to the story, a large segment of the public must reasonably believe the offensive material refers to the plaintiff. For example, a young boy's photograph accompanied an article about retarded children. The boy was not retarded. The boy's face was not visible because of the angle from which the picture was taken. Only a few people were able to recognize the boy. Although that might prove identification in a libel case, it was not sufficient for a false light claim.[58]

Falsity The tort's name makes it clear: Published material supporting a false light suit must be false or imply false information. If the publication is true, it cannot be grounds for a false light suit even if the material emotionally upsets the plaintiff. Minor errors ordinarily do not make a story sufficiently incorrect to meet the falsity standard.

Some courts hold that true facts can lead to false implications if the defendant intended that result. For example, The New York Times published a story implying that a businessman named Robert Howard might be using an alias and really was another person, Howard Finkelstein, a convicted felon. The story included only true statements: Records showed that Finkelstein used the name Robert Howard; Howard denied he was Finkelstein, yet rumors circulated saying he might be. A jury found that the reporter did not libel Howard because the story did not absolutely say he was Finkelstein. A federal appellate court said the story's implication that the businessman might be the felon could sustain a false light suit.[59]

However, there must be a clear connection between the statements leading to a false light suit and the implied falsehood the plaintiff claims. For example, best-selling author John Grisham's book, "The Innocent Man," described two men who were wrongly convicted of rape and murder, jailed for more

John Grisham

than a decade and then exonerated. Several people involved with the conviction sued Grisham for false light. In 2010, the U.S. Court of Appeals for the 10th Circuit held that nothing in Grisham's book accused the plaintiffs of a crime or, despite the plaintiff's contentions, could be construed as implying a crime.[60]

fact finder In a trial, a judge or the jury determining which facts presented in evidence are accurate.

Highly Offensive At a false light trial, the **fact finder**—the jury, if there is one, or the judge—must determine whether the published material would be highly offensive to a reasonable person. There are no definite standards. Defining "highly offensive" is a very subjective task. It is made even more difficult because a publication may be highly offensive even though it is positive, such as making a person appear to be a superhero, as did the unauthorized biography of pitcher Warren Spahn.

Some legal scholars try to clarify the term "highly offensive" by putting false light cases into three categories: embellishment, distortion and fictionalization. Categorizing may highlight the false statements' offensive nature.

A story is embellished when false material is added to otherwise true facts. For example, a series of newspaper columns told a true story of a mother giving up a baby for adoption, the baby being adopted, a court giving the natural father custody four years later and the father hiring a psychologist to help the child adjust to a new home. One column falsely said the psychologist "has readily admitted that she sees her job as doing whatever the natural parents instruct her to do." A jury could find it highly offensive to a reasonable person to suggest a psychologist would ignore her professional commitments, a court ruled.[61]

Distortion occurs when facts are omitted or the context in which material is published makes an otherwise accurate story appear false. In one case, police arrested four people at a chop shop, a garage where, authorities alleged, stolen cars were reduced to parts and then sold. The local newspaper ran a story about the arrest. Three of those arrested were convicted, but the fourth was found not guilty. Police located the chop shop by using a LoJack, a device attached to a car that emits a signal when the car is stolen. The LoJack Corporation used the newspaper story in its advertising but did not include information that one of those arrested was acquitted. A federal district court allowed a suit for defamation and false light to continue. The court said a jury could conclude that the advertising material implied the plaintiff was a car thief.[62]

Context, as well as omitted facts, can cause distortion and lead to a false light suit. For example, a young woman consented to having a photographer take her picture. The photographer said it was for his portfolio. A magazine later used the picture to illustrate a story headlined "In Cold Blood—An Exposé of the Baltimore Teen Murders." The accompanying article said the high murder rate among the city's African-American teenagers was due to drug abuse and poor economic conditions. Used in other circumstances, the photo might not have led to a lawsuit. This context, however, implied that the young woman was poor, abused drugs or perhaps even was connected with a murder. A federal district court allowed the young woman's false light suit against the photographer and magazine to go to a jury.[63]

Fictionalization in false light occurs when some truth, such as a person's name or identifying characteristics, is part of a largely fictional piece. In one case, The Sun, a supermarket tabloid newspaper, published a picture of 97-year-old Arkansas resident Nellie Mitchell to illustrate a story carrying the headline, "Pregnancy Forced Granny to Quit Work at Age 101." The story was a fictional account of an Australian woman who left her paper route at the age of 101 because she became pregnant during an extramarital affair with a rich client on her route. Mitchell, in fact, delivered newspapers in her hometown for nearly 50 years. Mitchell won her false light suit and, after the newspaper's appeals, was awarded $1 million in damages.[64]

Fault The U.S. Supreme Court has decided only two false light cases: *Time, Inc. v. Hill* in 1967, and *Cantrell v. Forest City Publishing Co.* in 1974. Despite the plaintiffs in both cases being private individuals, not public officials or public figures, the Court held that they had to prove actual malice to win their false light cases.

The seven Hill family members sued Time, Inc., publisher of Life magazine, for a story based on the family's experience of being held hostage by escaped convicts. News stories across the country had reported that three prison escapees had held the Hills hostage for 19 hours. The Hills were not harmed, and the family later said they were treated with respect. The family moved from their Philadelphia suburban home to Connecticut, trying to return to a private life. But within a year of the incident, a novel appeared: "The Desperate Hours" was about the fictional Hilliard family of four held hostage by escaped convicts. In the novel, the convicts beat the fictional father and son and subjected the daughter to verbal sexual insults. The novel was turned into a play of the same name, portraying the same fictional family and violent convicts. Life published an article about the play, including pictures of actors staging scenes in the Hills' Philadelphia house. The Hills claimed that the text and accompanying photographs suggested the convicts had treated the real Hill family as ruthlessly as the convicts treated the fictional hostages. The Hills said that did not happen; the convicts had treated them well. Implying they had been treated badly put the family in a false light. The Hills sued and won in the New York state courts. Richard Nixon, who was elected U.S. president in 1968, represented Time, Inc., in its appeal to the U.S. Supreme Court.

The Court reversed, saying the jury should have been told that the Hills could win only if they proved actual malice.[65] The First Amendment protects the press from being sued for negligent misstatements when reporting stories of public interest, the Court reasoned. After pursuing their case for more than 10 years, the Hills decided not to return to trial court. At trial, they would have to show that Life either knew the article and photographs were false or recklessly disregarded whether they were false.

In the *Cantrell* case, decided seven years after *Hill*, the Court again said a private plaintiff had to prove actual malice to win a false light case. A bridge in West Virginia collapsed, killing 43 people, including Margaret Cantrell's husband, Melvin. Five months later, Cleveland Plain Dealer reporter Joe Eszterhas went with a photographer to the Cantrell home. Eszterhas talked with the Cantrell children, and the photographer took dozens of pictures. Margaret Cantrell was not at home while Eszterhas was at her residence. According to the Supreme Court, Eszterhas' article in the Plain Dealer stressed the family's abject poverty. The children's old, ill-fitting clothes and the deteriorating condition of their home were detailed in both the text and the accompanying photographs. As he had done in his original, prize-winning article on the Silver Bridge disaster, Eszterhas used the Cantrell family to illustrate the impact of the bridge collapse on the lives of the people in the Point Pleasant area.

The Supreme Court upheld a jury verdict in the Cantrells' favor because the trial judge had told the jury actual malice was part of the plaintiff's false light case. The Court said there was sufficient evidence to show that portions of the article were false and were published with knowing falsity or reckless disregard for the truth.

Cantrell and the Hills were not public officials, limited-purpose public figures or universal public figures. They were private people who, the Court said, had to prove in their false light suits that the media defendants had acted with actual malice.

Lower courts are supposed to follow U.S. Supreme Court rulings. But when requiring private persons to prove actual malice in false light cases, some courts do not agree with the Supreme Court. State courts are divided regarding this question. Courts in at least five states and the District of Columbia have applied *Gertz v. Robert Welch, Inc.* (see case excerpt in Chapter 4) to false light cases, as they suggest the Supreme Court would if it heard another false light appeal.[66] These courts would require only that a private individual prove negligence in a false light suit, not malice. Courts in at least 11 other states follow the Supreme Court dictates in *Hill* and *Cantrell,* requiring all false light plaintiffs to show actual malice.[67]

Defenses

Because false light is a relatively new tort and not all courts recognize it, parts of it remain in flux. However, many courts say that if a false light plaintiff proves all elements of his case, a media defendant may use the libel defenses to defeat the claim.[68]

People with an absolute privilege if sued for libel—those involved in judicial proceedings or government meetings, certain public officials and others discussed in Chapter 5—also are absolutely privileged in false light suits. The press has a conditional privilege to report what people with absolute privilege and in absolutely privileged documents say. It also is likely in false light cases that the media may use a privilege of fair and accurate reporting about government meetings and activities.[69]

Truth is a defense to a false light suit. A defendant can prove truth by showing that the story is substantially true. If a person agrees to an interview in which she reveals highly offensive false facts or agrees to an article containing those false facts being published, consent will be an effective defense. The few courts deciding the issue disagree about whether opinion is a defense for a false light suit.[70]

States disagree about the appropriate statute of limitations for false light suits. A state may apply the general statute of limitations for torts, the same one used for battery or trespass, for example. Or the statute of limitations for privacy suits may be based on the time period for filing a libel suit. The statute of limitations period for libel suits usually is shorter than the general torts limitation period.[71]

SUMMARY

NOT ALL STATES ALLOW FALSE LIGHT SUITS. Most that do require a plaintiff to prove (1) publicity, (2) identification, (3) the published material was false or created a false impression, (4) the statements or pictures put the plaintiff in a false light that would be highly offensive to a reasonable person and (5) the defendant knew the material was false or recklessly disregarded its falsity. A story need not be derogatory to put a person in a false light. Publishing false information praising a person may be grounds for a false light suit. In the only two false light cases the U.S. Supreme Court has decided, it said all plaintiffs must prove actual malice. Some lower courts also require all false light plaintiffs to prove actual malice. Other courts require public officials and public figures, but not private persons, to prove actual malice.

Courts recognize most libel defenses as defenses in false light cases, including conditional privilege, fair reporting and truth. States may use the shorter statute of limitations applied to libel cases, or the longer limitations period used for other torts, in false light cases. ■

Appropriation

If a celebrity's picture is used on a greeting card without her permission, can the celebrity sue the greeting card company? Yes, a court said. This is **appropriation**—generally, using a person's name, picture or voice without permission for commercial or trade purposes. Hallmark Cards used Paris Hilton's "picture above a caption that reads, 'Paris's First Day as a Waitress.' The picture depicts a cartoon waitress, complete with apron, serving a plate of food to a restaurant patron. An oversized photograph of Hilton's head is super-imposed on the cartoon waitress's body."[72] Hilton said the card was based on an episode of Fox Television's "The Simple Life," in which she starred. In a program called "Sonic Burger Shenanigans," Hilton works in a fast food restaurant. The Ninth Circuit said, "[W]e see Paris Hilton, born to privilege, working as a waitress." The program and card were similar, the court said, and Hilton could sue for right of publicity, a celebrity's version of appropriation.

appropriation Using a person's name, picture, likeness, voice or identity for commercial or trade purposes without permission.

Points of Law

Appropriation

The appropriation tort may be divided into two torts:

1. *Commercialization:* Applying to someone who wants to remain private and unknown except to family and friends. Using this person's name, picture, likeness or voice for advertising or other commercial purposes without permission is commercialization. It is invading this person's privacy, causing emotional distress.

2. *Right of publicity:* Applying to someone who wants to be known far and wide, to be a celebrity—a musician, athlete, movie star, television personality. Using this person's name, picture, likeness, voice, identity—or a look-alike or sound-alike—for advertising or other commercial purposes without permission invades this person's right of publicity. It diminishes the person's economic value.

commercialization The appropriation tort used to protect people who want privacy.

right of publicity The appropriation tort protecting a celebrity's right to have his or her name, picture, likeness, voice and identity used for commercial or trade purposes only with permission.

Commercialization and Right of Publicity

Appropriation includes two different torts: **commercialization** and the **right of publicity.** Most people do not want their names or pictures to be in advertisements because they want to remain private. Despite all the contestants clamoring to be on televised reality programs, most people prefer to remain anonymous. The appropriation tort used to protect people who want privacy is called "commercialization" or "misappropriation." Commercialization, the word this chapter uses, prohibits using another person's name or likeness for advertising purposes without permission. No state has refused to allow appropriation suits, though courts in some have not yet ruled on the issue.[73]

Some people, however, want their names and pictures to be publicized. They make their living by being famous. Movie stars, television personalities, recording artists and professional athletes, for example, would be disappointed if they were not well known. But they want to control when and where their names and pictures will be used for advertising and other commercial purposes. They also want to be paid for giving their permission. Courts often refer to this part of the appropriation tort as the "right of publicity."[74]

Although both commercialization and the right of publicity prevent the use of someone's name, picture, likeness, voice or identity for advertising or other commercial purposes without permission, they differ in two important ways. One difference is that commercialization protects an individual's dignity connected with personal privacy, while the right of publicity protects the monetary value of using well-known individuals' names and pictures.

A second difference is that courts generally consider commercialization to be a personal right, one that does not survive a person's death. However, the right of publicity may be considered a property right, not a personal right. Just as a person may say who gets his or her car after he or she dies—through a will or by state law—a person may choose who will control her right of publicity after death.[75] In a majority of states the right of publicity survives after a person's death.[76] The right may last for a specific number of years (from 20 to 100 years, depending on the state), as long as the right is used or, in at least one state, forever.[77] Recently, a handful of state legislatures have explored efforts to extend or alter the right of publicity after death. Maryland, Massachusetts and New Hampshire failed to extend the application of their statutes to 70 years beyond death, but Indiana lawmakers passed an amendment to the state's existing statute and applied

Emerging Law

Keyword Advertising and Commercial Use

Does using a person's name as a keyword search term in an Internet search engine like Google or Bing violate the right of publicity? No, according to a 2013 Wisconsin appeals court decision. In one of the first cases of its kind, a high-profile personal injury law firm in Wisconsin bought keyword advertising on the names of a second high-profile personal injury law firm so that when searchers typed in the name of the second law firm an ad for the first firm would appear. The second firm sued for violation of the right of publicity instead of trademark (See Chapter 13, which covers trademark law) but lost because the judge found that employing names as "invisible" ad triggers did not amount to "use." The court used a physical space analogy in its decision and noted that if the first law firm bought billboard advertising right outside the offices of the second law firm, it would not constitute "use," and keyword advertising is basically the same concept in the online world.[1]

---

1. Habush v. Cannon, 828 N.W.2d 876 (Wis. App. Ct. 2013).

post-mortem publicity rights retroactively.[78] The law exempts people who became famous as a result of a criminal charge or conviction.

Some federal courts have resolved issues of jurisdiction in post-mortem right of publicity cases. For example, the Ninth Circuit ruled in 2012 that Marilyn Monroe's publicity rights died with her more than 50 years ago because she lived in New York at the time of her death and New York does not recognize a right of publicity after death. Her estate argued that because she died in California that state's post-mortem right of publicity statute should apply.[79] Similarly, a federal court in California also dismissed a right of publicity suit about the use of Albert Einstein's image in a car ad. The court applied New Jersey law because that's where Einstein lived when he died, and it held that the state would recognize a common law post-mortem right of publicity that would last for only 50 years beyond death. The court concluded that Einstein's identity had entered the public domain by the time the advertisement was published, and it rejected an argument that a common law post-mortem right of publicity should be linked to the post-mortem time frame of copyright law, which is 70 years (Chapter 13 discusses copyright law). The trend in these cases is to apply the law of the state in which the celebrity had his primary residence at the time of death.[80]

New York state adopted the country's first appropriation law in 1903.[81] Two years later, Georgia became the first state to recognize appropriation as a common law privacy tort. A federal appeals court judge, Jerome Frank, first used the phrase "right of publicity" nearly 60 years ago.[82] The court ruled that professional baseball players had a right to earn money when their names were used on baseball cards. The players' goal was to control when their names were used publicly—and to be paid when that happened. Courts generally find that everyone has both a right to protect his or her privacy and a right to decide when his or her name or picture may or may not be used commercially by others.[83]

Kareem Abdul-Jabbar successfully sued for appropriation when an Oldsmobile advertisement used his birth name, Lew Alcindor, without his permission.

The commercial value of a celebrity's name or picture, though, will be much greater than that of a relatively unknown individual. Also, the court said a right of publicity could be transferred, as a car can be sold. But the right of privacy cannot be transferred.

Plaintiff's Case

To win a commercialization or right of publicity case, a plaintiff must prove her or his name or likeness was used in an advertisement without permission. The plaintiff also must show the ad was of and concerning him or her and was widely distributed.

Name or Likeness Appropriation occurs most obviously when a person's name, picture or likeness—clearly identifying the person—is used in an advertisement without permission. Having the same name that is used in an advertisement is not enough to show identification. Something in the ad must show the ad was of and concerning that plaintiff. However, identification may be proved despite the defendant's not intending to identify the plaintiff. For example, a name and hometown used in an ad may have been meant to be fictitious. But if a real person with that name living in that town can show a number of people assumed the ad referred to that person, identification may be established.[84]

Although individual faces of the 1969 New York Mets World Series–winning team were very small when printed on jerseys without the players' permission, a court said "legions of baseball fans" could recognize them.[85] However, it is not sufficient that the ad only hints at the plaintiff's identity or may remind some people of the plaintiff.[86] Rather, there must be reasonable grounds for identifying the plaintiff as the person in the advertisement.

What if the name used is not a person's real name? In one case, an Oldsmobile commercial used the name Lew Alcindor. Kareem Abdul-Jabbar sued because he had not given permission. Oldsmobile said Alcindor no longer was Abdul-Jabbar's name, so he had no right to protect it. A federal appellate court disagreed. Abdul-Jabbar was named Ferdinand Lewis ("Lew") Alcindor at birth. He played college and several years of professional basketball under that name. When he converted to Islam, he took the name Kareem Abdul-Jabbar, later legally adopting that as his name. The court said the name Lew Alcindor still identified Abdul-Jabbar.[87]

When an advertisement uses a person who looks like a celebrity, can the celebrity prove identification? An actor looking very much like New Orleans chef

Paul Prudhomme urged television viewers to buy Folgers coffee. A federal district court said people could be confused, justifiably believing the real Prudhomme endorsed Folgers.[88] In another case, three singers who looked like members of a rap group called The Fat Boys appeared in a Miller beer commercial. A federal court allowed members of the group to sue, in part because they had declined to appear in the commercial when asked.[89]

Voice Individuals' voices are protected against use for commercial or trade purposes. Further, advertisers may not use **sound-alikes,** just as they may not use look-alikes, without permission or a disclaimer. Singer and actress Bette Midler refused to allow Ford Motor Co. to use her hit recording "Do You Want to Dance?" in a commercial. Ford's advertising agency then hired a member of Midler's backup singing group. The singer was told to imitate Midler's rendition of the song. After the radio commercial aired, a number of people told Midler they thought she had performed in the ad. The commercial failed to say Midler was not the singer. Midler sued Ford and its advertising agency. The defendants had appropriated part of Midler's identity, a federal appellate court said.[90] The court said a "voice is as distinctive and personal as a face" and "is one of the most palpable ways identity is manifested."

Identity Do people have characteristics beyond their face or voice that the appropriation tort should protect? Can a robot wearing a blond wig standing in front of a letterboard bring to mind a well-known person? Game-show hostess Vanna White thought so and sued Samsung Electronics for appropriation. The company ran a series of magazine ads showing its products in futuristic settings. The ads intended to show that the products were stylish and long lasting. One ad pictured a Samsung videocassette recorder in a game show set. A robot standing by a letterboard wore an evening gown, jewelry and a long blond wig. The advertising agency wanted the scene to look like the set from "Wheel of Fortune."

A federal appellate court agreed that it did, and said the ad appropriated White's identity.[91] Although the ad did not use White's name, picture, likeness or voice, it nonetheless used White, the court said. The court cited Dean Prosser's 1960 law review article suggesting that invasion of privacy be thought of as four individual torts. In discussing appropriation, Prosser said, "It is not impossible that there might be appropriation of the plaintiff's identity, as by impersonation, without the use of either [the plaintiff's] name or . . . likeness."[92]

Two actors from the television show "Cheers" brought a lawsuit that extended the rule from the Vanna White court decision even further. A company wanted to install in airport bars a set looking like the scene from the television

Points of Law

Commercialization

Plaintiff's Case

- Using a person's name, picture, likeness (such as a drawing), voice or identity
- For advertising or other commercial uses
- Without permission

Defenses

- News
- Incidental use
- Advertising for a mass medium
- Consent

sound-alike Someone whose voice sounds like another person's voice. Sound-alikes may not be used for commercial or trade purposes without permission or a disclaimer.

realWorld Law

Facebook's Sponsored Stories

In 2013, Facebook settled a class action lawsuit tied to its "Sponsored Story" advertising system. Five plaintiffs sued Facebook for misappropriation in a California state court. They argued that placing their user names and profile pictures into Sponsored Stories on friends' Facebook pages violated their right of publicity because Facebook did not obtain their consent. For example, plaintiff Angel Fraley "liked" Rosetta Stone's Facebook profile in order to receive a free software demonstration. Subsequently, Fraley's friends' Facebook pages showed a Sponsored Story advertisement with the Rosetta Stone logo and her "like" for Rosetta Stone.[1]

The terms of the settlement include no acknowledgement of wrongdoing on the part of Facebook, which denies wrongdoing or liability. Facebook agreed to pay $20 million into a fund that will pay out up to $10 per person for claims from people who appeared in a Sponsored Story.[2]

1. Kashmir Hill, *Facebook Sends Most of America an Offer to Settle a Class Action Lawsuit for $10,* ABOVE THE LAW (Jan. 22, 2013), *available at* http://abovethelaw.com/tag/fraley-v-facebook/.
2. GCG, *Fraley v. Facebook, Inc.: Overview of the Proposed Settlement* (Mar. 28, 2013), *available at* http://www.fraleyfacebook settlement.com.

program "Cheers." Two animatronic figures named Hank and Bob were to sit at the bar, and customers could have a drink sitting next to the figures. Paramount, which owned the "Cheers" copyright, granted permission. However, George Wendt, who played Norm on "Cheers," and John Ratzenberger, who played Cliff, refused to give consent. Wendt and Ratzenberger sued, claiming the company would appropriate their identities without permission.

The animatronic figures resembled Wendt's and Ratzenberger's characters in their size, clothing and sitting positions at the bar. But the figures' faces were different from the actors'. That difference, however, was not enough. Ruling in Wendt's and Ratzenberger's favor, a federal appellate court said the figures sufficiently resembled the actors that Wendt and Ratzenberger could bring a suit claiming appropriation of their identities.[93] It would be for a jury to decide whether the figures looked sufficiently like the actors, the court said. The parties settled the case out of court before a trial was held.[94]

Vanna White was able to sue because the robot in the Samsung advertisement looked like Vanna White. Wendt and Ratzenberger were able to sue because the robots might look like characters the actors played. Actors do not lose the right to exploit their likenesses, or to prevent others from such exploitation, just because they portrayed fictional characters, the court said in the "Cheers" case.

Actors impersonating celebrities in nonadvertising situations, such as in a satire or parody, are not appropriating the celebrities' likenesses or voices. The

realWorld Law

The Naked Cowboy, Jimmy Kimmel and "Extreme Fast Food"

Street performer Robert John Burck, better known as the Naked Cowboy, thinks his persona deserves right of publicity protection.

Several recent state court decisions illustrate the range of cases that come before courts as appropriation claims. In New York, a local street performer known as "the Naked Cowboy" sued CBS in federal court for using his "persona" on the soap opera The Bold and Beautiful. A trial court dismissed his claim noting that the right to privacy does not extend to fictitious characters.[1] A New York state court dismissed an appropriation claim against the Jimmy Kimmel show for using a YouTube clip without compensation. The court held that the use of the video qualified for the newsworthiness exception.[2] And an Illinois court dismissed a right of publicity lawsuit over an episode of the Travel Channel's "Extreme Fast Food." A woman made the claim after the show filmed her without consent as she ate at a popular hot dog stand. The court said the woman's appearance in the show was noncommercial and noted, "Exposure of the self to others in varying degrees is a concomitant of life in a civilized community."[3]

1. Naked Cowboy v. CBS, 844 F. Supp. 2d 510 (S.D.N.Y. 2012).
2. Sondik v. Kimmel, 941 N.Y.S.2d 541 (Sup. Ct. 2011).
3. *New Developments 2012*, MLRC BULLETIN, Dec. 2012, at 74.

First Amendment protects such expression.[95] But the Vanna White case shows that protection does not extend to impersonations in advertisements or other commercial situations. The appellate court specifically rejected Samsung's contention that the robot ad was meant as a satire.

Although a celebrity himself is not in an advertisement, that person's identity may be implied in a number of ways. The public may think of the well-known person based on "a unique vocal style, body movement, costume, makeup or distinguishing setting."[96] One or more of these elements could lead to a right of publicity lawsuit based on using someone's identity for commercial purposes without permission. Some courts do not so easily find a plaintiff's identity when the plaintiff is not identified. A singing group, the Romantics, claimed "What I Like About You" so reminded listeners of that group that the video game, "Guitar Hero Encore: Rock the '80s," abridged the group's right of publicity by using the song in the game. The Romantics did not claim a copyright in the song (see Chapter 13 for a discussion of music licensing), but they said the song and the group's identity were intertwined. A federal district court disagreed. The court held that because the game did not refer to the Romantics in its advertising and said the Romantics made the song famous but were not performing the song in the game, the group could not show the game used the Romantics' identity for commercial purposes.[97]

Damages Plaintiffs may be awarded monetary damages based on two injuries. First, they may be compensated for injured feelings caused by their names or pictures being distributed widely in connection with a commercial product or service. Second, they may receive damages for unwillingly helping another gain financially.[98] The value of this latter injury naturally will be greater for well-known individuals than for others.

SUMMARY

APPROPRIATION IS ONE OF THE FOUR PRIVACY TORTS, together with intrusion, private facts and false light. Appropriation is divided into commercialization and right of publicity. Commercialization protects individuals from having their names, pictures, likenesses, voices and identities used for commercial or trade purposes without their permission. Commercialization applies to famous and ordinary people alike. Courts recently have recognized a right of publicity that protects celebrities from being exploited for commercial or trade reasons.

A successful appropriation plaintiff must prove her name, picture, likeness, voice or identity was used for commercial or trade purposes without her permission. Even a pseudonym or stage name is protected. An advertisement may use a model who looks like another person only if a disclaimer explains the person not pictured in the ad is not endorsing the product or service. Similarly, a person who sounds like another when talking or singing may be used in an advertisement if accompanied by a disclaimer. Some courts also allow a plaintiff to sue for appropriation if his or her identity is used for commercial or trade purposes without permission. Some individuals are so well known for what they do—a game show hostess, in one case—they are identified with that role. An advertisement showing someone with those characteristics might be grounds for an appropriation suit. ∎

Defenses

Even if a plaintiff can prove that his or her name or likeness was used for commercial purposes without permission, there may be a defense to the appropriation allegation.

Newsworthiness Newsworthiness is the defense most often used against appropriation suits. If a newspaper article about an automobile accident used the driver's name, the driver cannot successfully bring an appropriation suit. The article is newsworthy. Newspapers and other media publish newsworthy material despite having a commercial purpose. As one federal court said, "Speech is protected even though it is carried in a form that is sold for profit."[99]

Courts have defined the word "newsworthy" broadly. Courts see a bright line between commercial use (advertising) and trade use on one side, and nearly everything else on the other side of the line. Judges do not carefully analyze an article to determine whether it is newsworthy. Rather, if it is not on the commercial/trade use side of the bright line, it will be found newsworthy.

For example, a magazine, Young and Modern, took pictures of a 14-year-old girl who hoped to be a model. The girl's mother had not consented to the photo session. The magazine used the photos to illustrate a "Love Crisis" column that printed a letter from an underage girl identified only as "Mortified." The letter said the girl had attended a party, had too much to drink and had sex with her boyfriend and two of his friends. Responding to the letter, the magazine advised the writer to avoid similar situations in the future and to be tested for pregnancy and sexually transmitted diseases. Neither the girl nor her mother had approved using the pictures with the letter. The girl sued, saying the magazine used her pictures for commercial purposes without permission. Basing its decision on New York's appropriation statute, the state's highest court said articles about matters of public interest are newsworthy.[100] A story remains newsworthy even if it includes a person's name or picture used to boost the mass medium's audience. The court ruled that "the 'Love Crisis' column was newsworthy, since it is informative and educational regarding teenage sex, alcohol abuse and pregnancy—plainly matters of public concern." The magazine's newsworthiness defense defeated the girl's appropriation claim.

Some courts find the line between newsworthy material and advertising not so bright. Hustler magazine could not use the newsworthiness defense when publishing 20-year-old nude photographs of a murdered woman, the U.S. Court of Appeals for the 11th Circuit held. The victim was a model and female wrestler. Her husband, also a professional wrestler, murdered his wife and child and committed suicide. Hustler published a brief story about the events but surrounded the article with nude pictures of the victim taken 20 years before her death. When the victim's family sued Hustler for violating the woman's right of publicity, the appellate court held that Hustler used the pictures for economic gain—increasing magazine sales—and not news reporting. The pictures did not accompany the article, the court said; rather, the article accompanied the pictures. The nude pictures were not newsworthy, the court said.[101]

The U.S. Supreme Court has heard only one appropriation case. The Court's decision, applied to a unique set of facts, rejected a television station's claim that it had a newsworthy defense to a right of publicity suit. Hugo Zacchini was a human cannonball. A television station recorded 15 seconds of Zacchini's act, including his flight from the cannon to the net, and showed the recording on its news program. A public event shown on a news program would seem newsworthy.

People seeing the entire act on television are less likely to attend the performance in person, according to the Court. *Zacchini* is a right of publicity case. The Court focused on the economic value of his act, not on his desire to be private. The television station's First Amendment rights were not more important than protecting Zacchini's financial interest in his performance, the Court said.

Public Domain Courts have held that names and associated information may be widely available to the public and therefore cannot be protected by right of

The U.S. Supreme Court said human cannonball Hugo Zacchini could win an appropriation lawsuit against a television station that aired only 15 seconds of his performance. The station claimed the newsworthiness defense, but the Court rejected it. The station showed Zacchini's entire act, the Court said, threatening the performance's economic value.

publicity. An online fantasy baseball league operator could use Major League Baseball (MLB) players' names and statistics without MLB's permission, the U.S. Court of Appeals for the Eighth Circuit ruled.[102] The court said that information is widely available in the public domain. That is, many print, electronic and digital sources provide players' names and statistics, making that information factual rather than personal to the players.

First Amendment Does the First Amendment protect using a celebrity's name or picture if the use is not in an advertisement? What if the use is for parody or satirical purposes or is in a fictional or artistic work? Or if the use is for a commercial product such as a poster or bobble-head doll?

Courts have considered whether the merchandise—such as posters, dolls, T-shirts and games—that is the focus of many right of publicity cases has First Amendment protection.[103] The first case in which a court used the term "right of publicity" involved baseball cards included in bubble gum packages. Players could give a company an exclusive right to use their pictures because a baseball player has a right to exploit the value of his name or likeness, a federal appellate court said.[104]

The First Amendment may protect the satirical use of personal information. The Major League Baseball Players Association sued a company selling baseball cards with recognizable caricatures of baseball players accompanied by satiric comments. For example, the player on one card is named Treasury Bonds, a spoof of Barry Bonds' name. The card includes such statements as "Having Bonds on your team is like having money in the bank" and "He plays so hard he gives 110 percent, compounded daily."[105] A federal appellate court said the First Amendment fully protects the baseball cards. The cards "provide social commentary on public figures, major league baseball players, who are involved in a significant commercial enterprise, major league baseball," the court said.[106] The cards are "an important form of entertainment and social commentary that deserve First Amendment protection," the court concluded.[107]

Posters are not like satirical baseball cards. Courts most often have decided posters do not have First Amendment protection. Courts found appropriation when posters of singer Elvis Presley, model Christie Brinkley and professional wrestlers were distributed without permission.[108]

But courts have said the First Amendment protects selling posters with pictures of newsworthy individuals or events, such as a poster with a picture of comedian Pat Paulson when he ran for president and one showing former San Francisco 49ers quarterback Joe Montana celebrating the team's 1990 Super Bowl victory.[109] Courts drew a distinction between merchandise exploiting celebrities' names or likenesses and posters conveying newsworthy information of public interest.

The question of First Amendment protection versus right of publicity arises when a well-known person is used in an artistic work. For example, in 2013 a federal judge in New York ruled that hip hop star Pitbull did not violate actress Lindsay Lohan's right of publicity by including the line, "I'm toptoein', to keep flowin', I got it locked up, like Lindsay Lohan" in his hit song "Give Me Everything." Rather, the song is a work of art protected by the First Amendment.[110] One approach used to resolve this kind of conflict is the artistic relevance test. This test asks whether using a celebrity's name or picture is relevant to a work's artistic purpose. If it is, the First Amendment, which applies to artistic as well as journalistic works, may allow using the celebrity's name without permission. However, consent is needed if the name or a celebrity's likeness is used primarily to give the work commercial appeal. For example, Italian movie director Federico Fellini made a film titled "Ginger and Fred." To movie fans, the obvious reference is to the Fred Astaire and Ginger Rogers films. The Fellini movie was about two cabaret dancers who were given the nicknames Ginger and Fred because they imitated Rogers and Astaire. Ginger Rogers sued, claiming the movie title infringed on her right to use her name for commercial purposes. In *Rogers v. Grimaldi,* a federal appellate court applied the **artistic relevance test**.[111] The court said Rogers could not win unless the movie title had no artistic relevance to the film itself or misled consumers about the film's contents. The movie's title and contents were artistically related, the court held.

Similarly, Mattel, the manufacturer of Barbie dolls, sued the band Aqua. The group's song "Barbie Girl" parodied Barbie dolls and the lifestyle the band said Barbie represented. Using the *Rogers* test, a federal appellate court held that the song title had an artistic relevance to the song lyrics.[112]

Not all song titles clearly relate to the song's lyrics. For example, the rap duo Outkast recorded a song titled "Rosa Parks." Parks was a major figure during the civil rights struggles of the 1950s and 1960s. In 1955, riding in the middle of a racially segregated Montgomery, Ala., bus, Parks refused to give her seat to a white person and move to the back of the bus, as city law required. Her defiant act spurred a 381-day bus boycott by Montgomery blacks and touched off other boycotts, sit-ins and demonstrations throughout the South.[113]

Applying the *Rogers* test, a federal appellate court concluded that a jury could find the title "Rosa Parks" had no artistic relevance to the lyrics, despite the phrase "move to the back of the bus" being used repeatedly in the chorus. The lyrics, containing profanity and explicit sexual references, only meant that Outkast had recorded a new album, the court concluded. Using Rosa Parks' name in the title also was misleading, the court held. It could make potential consumers

artistic relevance test A test to determine whether the use of a celebrity's name, picture, likeness, voice or identity is relevant to a disputed work's artistic purpose. It is used in cases regarding the infringement of a celebrity's right of publicity.

Rosa Parks won a right of publicity suit against the rap group Outkast when she convinced a court that a song's title, "Rosa Parks," was not artistically relevant to the song's lyrics.

transformativeness test A test to determine whether a creator has transformed a person's name, picture, likeness, voice or identity for artistic purposes. If so, the person cannot win a right-of-publicity suit against the creator.

believe the song in fact was about Parks, although the lyrics in no way referred to her.

Instead of the *Rogers* artistic relevance test, some courts have used a **transformative test** to decide whether a challenged work has First Amendment protection against a right of publicity suit.[114] These courts ask whether the new work only copies the original—an artist makes an exact drawing of a celebrity and sells copies of that picture— or instead transforms the original by adding new creative elements. If an artist drawing a caricature exaggerates a person's facial or body features, perhaps for comic effect, the caricature transforms the original, that is—changes the person's actual physical features. The First Amendment protects caricatures that have enough originality.

The California Supreme Court developed the transformative test in a case involving the Three Stooges.[115] An artist created a charcoal sketch of the Three Stooges, transferred the sketch to T-shirts and lithographs and sold thousands of the items. A company owning the Three Stooges' publicity rights sued.[116] The California court acknowledged the conflict between the artist's First Amendment right to express himself, particularly about public personalities, and the right of celebrities to protect their property and financial interests in their images. The sketch was an expressive work, the court said. Commentary about celebrities is part of a public discussion about public matters. The court also said that a right of publicity suit could stifle discourse about a celebrity even if a libel or privacy action would not be successful.

But many celebrities work hard to achieve their fame, the California court said. These efforts justify protecting celebrities' rights to exploit their renown. The court proposed the transformative test to distinguish protected artistic expression about celebrities from expression that encroaches on a personality's right of publicity. The First Amendment protects a work that adds enough new elements to the original to transform it. Changing the original by giving it a new meaning or a different message justifies First Amendment protection. Transformative works may be satires, news reports or works of fiction or social criticism, the court said. However, the court concluded, "When artistic expression takes the form of a literal depiction or imitation of a celebrity for commercial gain, directly trespassing on the right of publicity without adding significant expression beyond that trespass," the celebrity's rights outweigh First Amendment protections.[117] The court found that the Three Stooges' drawing was a "literal, conventional" depiction of the three men, with no discernible transformative elements. Because the drawing did not transform the Three Stooges' pictures, it had no First Amendment protection.

Emerging Law

Right of Publicity in Video Games

In his final season at UCLA, Ed O'Bannon won the John Wooden Award, given to the best player of the year in men's college basketball.

Two federal court cases could have tremendous impact on the future of the video game industry and the publicity rights of individuals, particularly athletes. The key question: Do the First Amendment rights of video game producers trump an individual's right to publicity?

The cases involve three college athletes who sued the video game company Electronic Arts (EA). In 2009 Ed O'Bannon, the star of UCLA's 1995 championship basketball team, and Sam Keller, former quarterback from Arizona State University and the University of Nebraska, argued in a U.S. District Court in California that EA's National Collegiate Athletic Association (NCAA)–themed games violated their right to publicity because their likenesses were used without compensation.[1] The players noted that the video games depicted every distinctive characteristic of them except their names. At the same time, former Rutgers quarterback Ryan Hart made the same claim in a U.S. District Court in New Jersey.[2]

In both cases, EA argued that its First Amendment rights trumped the players' right of publicity. Although the facts in both cases are nearly identical, the lower courts came to different decisions. In California, the court applied the transformative use test and held that EA's use of Keller was not transformative and did not deserve First Amendment protection. In New Jersey, the court also applied the transformative use test but came to the opposite conclusion and ruled in favor of EA. The N.J. decision also referenced the Keller decision, critically noting that "it is logically inconsistent to consider the setting in which the character sits . . . yet ignore the remainder of the game."[3] In 2013, the Hart and Keller cases remained under appeal in the Third and Ninth Circuits respectively, while EA petitioned the U.S. Supreme Court to hear the cases together. In Sept. 2013 O'Bannon and EA settled out of court. EA says it will not produce a college football video game in 2014.[4]

One media and technology lawyer notes that these cases raise practical concerns:

In the event the athletes prevail . . . to what extent are the NCAA, the (Collegiate Licensing Company) and each athlete's individual colleges . . . liable for those damages? Alternatively, if EA prevails . . . it may cast doubt on the need for EA to continue to secure costly licenses for its depiction of professional players in games, such as NBA Live, Madden and Tiger Woods PGA Tour. Either way, the future of the video game industry as well as the rights of collegiate athletes remain in the balance.[5]

1. Keller v. Electronic Arts, Inc., 2010 U.S. Dist. LEXIS 10719 (N.D. Calif. Feb. 8, 2010).
2. Hart v. Electronic Arts, Inc. 808 F. Supp. 2d. 757 (D.N.J. 2011).
3. *Id.* at 787.
4. Hart v. Electronic Arts, 717 F.3d 141 (3d Cir. 2013); Michael McCann, *O'Bannon Settles with EA and CLC in Class Action, NCAA Still Remaining,* Sᴘᴏʀᴛs Iʟʟᴜsᴛʀᴀᴛᴇᴅ (Sept. 26, 2013), *available at* http://sportsillustrated.cnn.com/college-football/news/20130926/mccann-obannon-ea-clc-settlement.
5. Gina Reif Ilardi, *First Amendment v. The Right of Publicity: The Game Is On!,* Mᴇᴛʀᴏᴘᴏʟɪᴛᴀɴ Cᴏʀᴘ. Cᴏᴜɴs. (Aug. 20, 2012), *available at* http://www.metrocorpcounsel.com/articles/20189/first-amendment-v-right-publicity-game#_edn4.

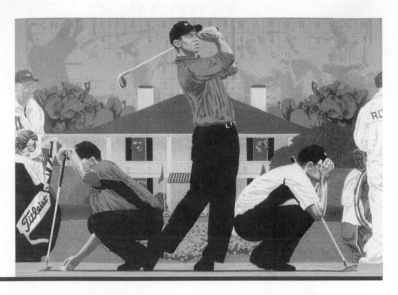

A court found Rick Rush's painting, "The Masters of Augusta," transformed Tiger Woods' image into an artistic work, preventing Woods from winning his right-of-publicity lawsuit.

Image reprinted by permission of Jireh Publishing and Rick Rush, www.RickRushArt.com

The transformative test may result in First Amendment protection for artists. The California Supreme Court used the test to rule that a comic book artist transformed images of two musicians, Johnny and Edgar Winter.[118] One issue of the Jonah Hex series showed the Winter brothers as half-human, half-worm creatures named Edgar and Johnny Autumn. But the characters had the Winters' long white hair and albino skin. The court said the drawings were not "conventional depictions" but rather had "significant expressive content." That is, the comic book artist has transformed the brothers into cartoon characters as part of a story that itself had expressive content.

When does an artist transform someone's image into art? The California Supreme Court said "an artist depicting a celebrity must contribute something more than a 'merely trivial' variation" of the celebrity's image. The artist "must create something recognizably 'his own'" for a court to find "significant transformative elements" in the artist's work.[119]

Similarly, the artist Rick Rush sold prints of his painting portraying the golfer Tiger Woods' win at the Professional Golfers' Association's 1997 Masters Tournament. The painting shows Woods in several poses and includes his caddy and six other famous golfers. Woods sued, claiming that the artist's sales of the prints violated Woods' right of publicity. Applying the transformative test, a federal appellate court held for the artist.[120] The painting and prints used Woods' image to comment on sports' place in American culture, according to the court. The court also used the *Rogers* test and said that Woods' picture had artistic relevance to the painting.

Another way to balance the First Amendment and the right of publicity is the **predominant use test.** The question is whether a person's name or picture is used more for commercial purposes or substantive expression. The Missouri Supreme Court applied this test in ruling that a comic book creator named a character "Anthony 'Tony Twist' Twistelli" more to sell the comics than for free speech purposes. In the comic, Twistelli was portrayed as an organized crime leader. A real Tony Twist, a former professional hockey player, sued for misuse of his name. A jury awarded $15 million in damages.[121]

Courts long have held that the First Amendment protects using celebrities' names in biographies and fiction, including movies and television programs.

predominant use test In a right-of-publicity lawsuit, a test to determine whether the defendant used the plaintiff's name or picture more for commercial purposes or protected expression.

Although this was part of appropriation law long before the California Supreme Court used the transformative test, the reasons are similar. Books, news stories, movies and television programs add transformative elements by putting the names in a context. For example, a movie called "Panther," combining fact and fiction, portrayed several members of the Black Panther Party, a political group active in the 1960s and 1970s that promoted black power and social activism. Bobby Seale, a prominent member of the Black Panthers, sued. A federal district court rejected Seale's appropriation claim, saying the First Amendment protected using his name in the film.[122]

Some celebrities, such as the now-deceased wealthy recluse Howard Hughes, have tried to limit who may write their biographies.[123] But no person, or deceased person's relative, has the right to prevent anyone from writing about another's life.[124]

The First Amendment usually protects even fictionalized biographies from right of publicity suits. Courts found that somewhat fictionalized televised biographies of the silent screen star Rudolph Valentino and the actress Elizabeth Taylor were as protected as factual biographies.[125] Even fiction including the names of real people is protected. However, if an author claims that a work is a biography, but the work is much more fiction than fact, the First Amendment may not protect it.

Ads for the Media Another First Amendment–based appropriation defense says mass media may run advertisements for themselves that use names and likenesses they have included in their coverage. They may do this without being granted permission by those whose names and likenesses were used. Courts recognized this defense when a magazine, Holiday, ran ads for itself in two other publications. One ad urged people to subscribe to Holiday. The other ad suggested advertising agencies place their clients' ads in Holiday. Both ads included pictures of actress Shirley Booth that Holiday had published in one of its issues. Booth sued under New York's appropriation law. The state's highest court said that in order to stay in business and to use its First Amendment rights, the magazine had to attract subscribers and advertisers. Illustrating the magazine's contents and quality by showing what it publishes does not violate Booth's rights, the court concluded.[126]

Holiday magazine won the suit in part because it did not suggest Booth endorsed the magazine. However, a men's magazine's advertisement for itself used a picture of the actress and singer Cher that had accompanied a published interview with her. A cartoon balloon over Cher's head included the words, "So join Cher and FORUM's hundreds of thousands of other adventurous readers today." Cher sued, saying the magazine had implied her endorsement of the magazine without permission, which is impermissible under the California appropriation statute. A federal appellate court agreed with her.[127]

Consent The best appropriation defense is having the person's consent to use his or her name or likeness. That is why professional photographers use model releases—contracts prepared by lawyers and signed by all parties involved—when taking pictures for advertisements. Oral consent can be a defense, but proving it can be difficult if the plaintiff claims she or he did not give permission. Also, the law does not allow certain people to give consent, such as minors and those who are not mentally or emotionally capable of agreeing. And consent is limited to the agreement's terms. Consent to use a picture in an ad during 2014, for example, does not allow its use in 2016. Similarly, if a person gives consent to use a picture in a shampoo ad, the picture cannot be used to advertise bedsheets. If a person gives sweeping consent—to use a picture at any time in the future in any advertisement—a court likely will hold that the agreement is more limited than its words, or lack of words, indicate.

Consent most often is explicit. A person agrees to allow his or her name to be used in an advertisement. But consent may be implied. In one case, two people sat on a bench at a dog-racing track. Track personnel announced that a picture would be taken of the area where the people sat, and the camera was within their view. The two people did not move from the bench. When the track used the picture in an advertising brochure, the two people sued for appropriation. A court ruled that the plaintiffs gave implied consent by not moving when they knew their picture would be taken.[128]

Incidental Use The use of a person's name or likeness may be incidental to a work's primary purpose. A court could rule that a person's name or likeness was used so briefly that the purpose was not to make a profit or gain commercial benefit. For example, a name applied to a fictional terrorist in a comic book appeared in 1 of 116 panels spanning 24 pages. A person who said the comic book applied his name to the terrorist sued under New York's appropriation law. A federal district court said the name's use was incidental to the comic book's primary purpose and could not sustain a privacy suit.[129] Similarly, if a photograph of a large crowd of people is used in an advertisement, it is unlikely one person in the group could claim successfully that her picture is being used for commercial purposes.

Incidental use is not measured in time or space only. An organization sponsored a hole-in-one contest. Dan Pooley, a professional golfer, made a hole-in-one to win $1 million, half going to a charity. The organization made an eight-minute promotional videotape to help sell its products and promote the contest. Six seconds of the tape included Pooley's name and his winning shot. Pooley, who had not given his permission, sued. A federal district court did not accept the incidental use defense. Pooley's name and picture, although a very small part of the tape, were significantly related to the tape's purpose, the court said, and the organization needed Pooley's permission.[130]

SUMMARY

COURTS RECOGNIZE SEVERAL DEFENSES TO an appropriation suit. The press most often uses the newsworthiness defense. Courts consider media content to be newsworthy if it is not used in an advertisement. The Supreme Court has held that the media lose the newsworthiness defense if they show a performer's entire act in a news program.

Courts recognize a First Amendment defense in cases celebrities bring for right of publicity. Courts use several tests in balancing celebrities' rights to earn money from their names and likenesses against the media's free speech rights. One is to determine whether a celebrity's name or likeness is used in conveying information of public concern. Another is to assess whether using a celebrity's name or likeness is artistically relevant to the work. A third is to decide whether the disputed work transformed the celebrity's likeness, making it into something new.

Courts allow the media to use someone's name or likeness in an advertisement for the mass medium itself if the ad does not suggest the person is endorsing the mass medium. Also, if a person consents to a commercial use of his or her name or likeness, the person cannot sue successfully for appropriation unless the use goes beyond the consent given. Finally, an incidental use of a person's name or likeness is not appropriation. ■

Intrusion

Critics say the press is obsessed with publishing the sensational, the lurid, the most confidential secrets. Some argue this obsession prompts journalists to intrude into personal privacy through whatever means necessary—planting microphones (bugs), using telescopic camera lenses and infrared heat-sensing film, trespassing on private property, lying. But, unconventional newsgathering techniques may be necessary in order to provide information about the targets of investigative reporting, who often have the most to hide, journalists claim. Whose rights should be dominant: those who want privacy or journalists who want to report on matters of public interest?

Invasive newsgathering techniques may amount to intrusion or, as courts say, **intrusion upon seclusion**.[131] A journalist may be sued for intrusion if he intentionally interferes with another person's solitude or meddles in the person's private concerns, and if the intrusion would highly offend a **reasonable person** (the law's version of an average person). The intrusion may be physical, such as entering someone's house without permission, or technological, such as using a miniature camera. The intrusion tort is intended to ensure people retain their dignity by preventing unwanted encroachment into their physical space and their private affairs. Only New York state and Virginia have refused to recognize the intrusion tort.[132] (Newsgathering techniques that may be classified as intrusion are discussed further in Chapter 8.)

intrusion upon seclusion Physically or technologically disturbing another's reasonable expectation of privacy.

reasonable person The law's version of an average person.

Methods of Intruding

The more technology develops, the more ways intrusion can occur. But even older technology, such as a camera's telephoto lens, can be a means of intruding. In one case, a woman mysteriously disappeared from her home. The woman's sister-in-law, husband and children visited the woman's home. They were in bathing suits at the home's swimming pool, surrounded by a seven-foot-high fence, when a CBS television network cameraman stood on a neighbor's porch and, using a telephoto lens, videotaped the family. A federal district court permitted the family to sue CBS for intrusion, saying, "We find that the plaintiffs' allegations that they were swimming in the backyard pool of a private home surrounded by a seven foot privacy fence are sufficient to allege both that they believed they were in a secluded place and that the activity was private."[133]

Intrusion suits have been brought based on news reporters finding information in public records. Courts hold that there is no reasonable expectation of privacy in public records.[134]

Intrusion on Private Property

Journalists might obtain information by intentionally entering private property without permission. A reporter who does so has committed intrusion, an act similar to trespass (discussed in Chapter 8). Trespass is both a crime and a tort. A trespasser may be sued for intrusion.

A plaintiff suing for intrusion must prove that the defendant acted intentionally to intrude into private matters in a way a reasonable person would find highly offensive. A highly offensive and intrusive act is one the community thinks is beyond the limits of decency.

Intrusion may occur only if a person has a reasonable expectation of privacy. For instance, there is a reasonable expectation others will not enter into private property, such as a house or apartment, without consent. A person who controls the property, such as the homeowner or renter, must give permission for entry. Without consent, a journalist entering a private residence is intruding. Simply entering private land, however, may not be intruding. In a lawsuit involving Google's Street View feature, which provides panoramic views of streets in metropolitan areas, a couple sued Google for intrusion. Street View showed the couple's house and swimming pool. The couple claimed the pictures could be obtained only by driving up the private street on which their home is located, a street marked as "Private Road, No Trespassing." However, no reasonable person would be highly offended by Google's entry onto the road, the Third Circuit said, because guests and delivery trucks entered the road and saw what Street View's pictures showed.[135] Ordinarily, there is not a reasonable expectation of privacy on public streets and sidewalks and in public parks where people can be seen or overheard. However, there may be circumstances when people do have a reasonable expectation of privacy in public places.

For example, the U.S. Supreme Court upheld a Colorado law that created an eight-foot bubble around individuals entering a health care facility.[136] The statute made it illegal to approach within eight feet of a person going into an abortion clinic—the law's primary focus—to hand her a leaflet, show her a sign or talk with her without her consent. The law applied within a 100-foot radius around a health care facility's entrance. In *Hill v. Colorado,* the Court said the law was neither content based nor viewpoint based. Therefore, the Court did not apply a strict scrutiny standard. The state needed to show only a substantial interest. The Court said Colorado's interests in public health and in protecting the rights of individuals to avoid unwanted communication met the intermediate scrutiny test. Colorado's law implies that people entering health clinics have a reasonable expectation of privacy.

Courts may not permit journalists to exceed acceptable means of obtaining information. Following Princess Diana's death, California passed an anti-paparazzi law.[137] The California law says that offensively trespassing to photograph or record a person's personal or family activities is an invasion of privacy. A plaintiff may receive three times the damages a jury awards and may receive punitive damages under the California statute.

These cases show that reporters are wrong if they assume people involved in a news event occurring on public property do not have a reasonable expectation of privacy. In another example, an automobile accident victim reasonably expected discussions with emergency personnel to be private even if medical treatment took place on the side of a public road, a court held.[138]

It is not always easy to determine whether property is private or public. Taxpayers own government land, but they may not always be permitted on the property. Reporters entering a naval base without permission to cover protests could be arrested, a federal district court ruled.[139] Businesses invite the public to enter to buy their products or services. However, reporters entering for other reasons may be intruding. A television news crew burst into a New York City restaurant with cameras on and bright lights blazing to report on a health code violation at the establishment. The court said the journalists had trespassed in this instance, because the restaurant only allowed the public to enter for the purpose of dining, not to take pictures and generate news reports.[140]

Points of Law

Intrusion by Trespass

Plaintiff's Case

- A reasonable expectation of privacy
- Intentional intrusion on the privacy
- The intrusion would be highly offensive to a reasonable person

Defense

- Consent

Defenses

Consent is the only defense for an intrusion suit based on trespass in nearly all cases. Newsworthiness is not a defense because publishing is not an element of the tort. The intrusion happens in the news-gathering process, not when the material is published. However, the U.S. Court of Appeals for the Ninth Circuit said a story's newsworthiness may reduce the intrusion's offensiveness.[141] This is important because a plaintiff must prove the intrusion was highly offensive.

Consent A person cannot claim a reasonable expectation of privacy if he or she gave consent for someone to be on his or her private property. For example, a restaurant owner allowed a television news crew to videotape a health inspector evaluating the restaurant. After the station ran an unflattering story, the restaurant sued for intrusion. Because a trial jury found that the restaurant owner had given the television crew consent to enter the premises, an appeals court rejected the restaurant's claim.[142]

Consent can be implied. For example, if a journalist enters private property and the property owner responds to the reporter's questions, there is implied consent to remain and continue the interview.[143]

False Pretenses A journalist who cannot get permission to be on private property might lie to obtain consent. Using false pretenses to enter private property is a long-standing reporting technique. Courts are not in agreement, but generally they say reporters may use deceit to gain entry. At least two federal courts have reached that conclusion. In one case, a producer for the ABC television network program "Primetime Live" sent seven people to eye clinics owned by Dr. J.H. Desnick. The seven posed as patients, each equipped with hidden cameras used to record the eye surgeons who examined them. "Primetime Live" aired a story, using portions of the video, that said the Desnick clinics "may be doing unnecessary cataract surgery for the money." Desnick sued ABC for intrusion and other torts. The clinics were open to anyone who wanted an eye examination, a federal appellate court said. The people posing as patients were allowed into the clinics, just as anyone else would have been. That the "patients" meant to deceive did not invalidate the consent to enter, the court held.[144]

The U.S. Court of Appeals for the Seventh Circuit observed that many people use deception to enter private or semi-private premises. For example, a restaurant owner might refuse entry to a food critic known to write harsh reviews. But restaurant critics usually do not identify themselves to the owner. They enter and eat anonymously. That is, they pretend to be ordinary patrons. The court said this deception does not negate the restaurant owner's consent that the unknown critic enter. The court indicated, however, that this analysis might not apply to someone using false pretenses to enter with no substantive reason to be there, citing as an example someone who pretends to be a utilities meter reader to enter a private home. In contrast, the hypothetical restaurant critic—and the eye clinic "patients"—did have valid reasons to be on private property, the court said.

What if the context involves medical treatment? In one case, a photographer recorded video of emergency room personnel treating a man who had a bad reaction to a drug. The photographer, dressed in hospital apparel, asked the man to sign a release form allowing the recording. The photographer said the video would be used to help train hospital personnel. The patient signed the form, thinking the photographer was a doctor. After a portion of the video ran on a cable program, "Trauma: Life in the ER," the patient sued for intrusion and other claims. A court agreed with the patient's argument that he was in a "zone of physical and sensory privacy and he had a reasonable expectation of seclusion" in a hospital emergency room. The court said the photographer's deception invalidated the patient's consent.[145]

The fact that someone gained entry to a home using false pretenses may not provide grounds for an intrusion suit in most circumstances. But at least one court said that combining false pretenses with surreptitious image and audio recording after entering the home was intrusive. To investigate a person practicing medicine without a license, a Life magazine reporter and a photographer claimed to be patients and were admitted to the man's home. The reporter had a microphone in her purse, and the photographer used a small, concealed camera to take pictures. A federal appellate court ignored the false pretenses question and focused on the surreptitious reporting. The court said people have a reasonable expectation of privacy in their homes. Even though a person might expect a visitor to repeat what is said in the house and describe the scene, it is not expected that "what is heard and seen will be transmitted by photograph or recording, or in our modern world, in full living color and [high fidelity] to the public at large or to any segment of it that the visitor may select."[146] The court said, "the First Amendment has never been construed to accord newsmen immunity from torts or crimes committed during the course of newsgathering. The First Amendment is not a license to trespass, to steal, or to intrude by electronic means into the precincts of another's home or office."[147]

Most states have laws making it illegal to pretend to be a law enforcement officer. In some states it is unlawful to pretend to be any public official.

Newsworthiness Newsworthiness rarely is a defense to an intrusion suit based on trespass or surreptitious surveillance.[148] This is because a plaintiff can win an intrusion lawsuit without proving that the defendant published the information or pictures obtained through the intrusion. Publication is not part of the plaintiff's burden of proof in an intrusion case. Whether a journalist has committed intrusion is determined on the basis of the techniques used to gather information. Publishing that information may lead to other torts, such as libel. But publication alone does not prove that the journalist committed intrusion. Therefore, the story's newsworthiness is not an intrusion defense.

Newsworthiness may be a defense in rare circumstances, however. One court held that reporters using false pretenses to enter a medical laboratory and then secretly recording activities in that lab was not highly offensive because the journalists were investigating laboratory errors in testing for certain cancers. The public's interest in important health issues prevailed over privacy interests, the court said.[149] Another court said that "the legitimate motive of gathering the news" could "negate the offensiveness element of the intrusion tort."[150]

SUMMARY

INTRUSION OCCURS IF A PERSON INTENTIONALLY interferes with another's solitude or private concerns through physical or technological means. Physical intrusion is also trespass. Trespass is both a crime and a tort.

To win an intrusion suit, a plaintiff must prove the defendant acted intentionally to intrude into private matters in a way a reasonable person would find highly offensive. A highly offensive and intrusive act is one the community thinks is beyond the limits of decency. If highly offensive intrusion occurs, a plaintiff is able to show he had a reasonable expectation of privacy that the defendant violated.

Intrusion concerns how information is gathered. Publication is not part of the intrusion tort.

Intrusion by trespass occurs when entering private property where a person has a reasonable expectation of privacy. Generally, people on public property have no reasonable expectation of privacy, but particularly aggressive news gathering even on public property can be considered intrusion. Also, some publicly owned property, such as military bases, is not open to the public. Consent is the defense for intrusion by trespass. The person who owns or is using the property must give consent. Courts have ruled that law enforcement officials may not give journalists consent to enter private property. Courts generally, but not unanimously, hold that consent is valid even if obtained by using false pretenses.

Journalists may use visible equipment to photograph or record on public property. However, secret recording is intrusion if the circumstances suggest a person should have a reasonable expectation of privacy in public, such as during a medical emergency. People talking so passersby can hear do not have a reasonable expectation of privacy in the workplace or other private locations. Secretly videotaping on private property is intrusion.

Consent is a defense in an intrusion suit. Newsworthiness rarely is an effective defense against an intrusion suit. ■

private facts The tort under which media are sued for publishing highly embarrassing private information that is not newsworthy or lawfully obtained from a public record.

Private Facts

Journalists do not expect to be sued for publishing the truth—but they can be. Journalists can be sued for a tort called **private facts** if they publish truthful private information that is not of legitimate public concern and if publicizing the facts would be highly offensive to a reasonable person.[151] The private facts tort is intended to protect a person's dignity and peace of mind by discouraging the publication of intimate facts. If intimate private facts are publicized, a jury may award monetary damages to compensate for the resulting emotional injury.[152] Of course, the egg cannot be put back into the shell: Once intimate facts are revealed to the public, money cannot make the facts private again.

A court first recognized the private facts tort in 1927, holding that placing a large sign in the window of a car repair business correctly stating that a local veterinarian owed $49.67 could violate the veterinarian's right of privacy.[153] Today, a plaintiff must show that the facts were private, dealt with intimate or highly personal matters, were not of legitimate public concern and were published. Courts recognize a First Amendment defense to a private facts lawsuit. Forty-one states and the District of Columbia allow private facts lawsuits.[154]

Points of Law

Private Facts

Plaintiff's Case

- Publicizing
- Private, intimate facts
- That would be highly embarrassing to a reasonable person
- And are not of legitimate concern to the public

Defenses

- First Amendment: Truthful information lawfully obtained from public records

realWorld Law

"Revenge Porn" Websites: Invasion of Privacy or Simply Unethical?

The news media recently drew attention to a growing trend commonly called "revenge porn" or involuntary porn. Involuntary porn websites allow scorned exes and others to post nude pictures of people without their consent, including their real names, hometowns and even phone numbers. But in 2013 two victims of the practice sued in Texas, claiming the website Texxxan.com violated their privacy rights when it allowed users to post private, nude pictures of them. Soon after the lawsuit was filed, the site closed to the public and became members-only. When one of the victims e-mailed the website owners and demanded they remove the pictures, "they said they would be happy to remove the pictures for me if I would enter my credit card information."[1]

The Texas lawsuit not only targets Texxxan.com but also the site's host, GoDaddy, even though the host is likely protected by Section 230 of the Communications Decency Act.[2] An attorney for the plaintiff said, "GoDaddy is profiting off of it. The reality of it is at some level this issue of revenge porn has to become a public discussion and a legislative discussion, and it raises issues of corporate responsibility."[3]

The owner of the pioneering "revenge porn" site IsAnybodyUp said at the site's peak he was earning $10,000 a month in advertising revenue based on 30 million reported page views. That site is no longer active, but the owner of a different site modeled after it says he makes $3,000 a month, with some of that money coming from the $250 it charges people to remove pictures from the site. "We don't want anyone shamed or hurt," the site owner said. "We just want the pictures there for entertainment purposes and business."[4]

Local law enforcers say federal officials need to deal with these websites because they reach across state lines. The FBI says the issue is best dealt with in the civil court system. The Texas lawsuit and the website EndRevengePorn.com both intend to counteract this phenomenon. EndRevengePorn.com encourages people to lobby state legislatures to make "revenge porn" a criminal act.[5]

---

1. Joe Mullin, *New Lawsuit Against "Revenge Porn" Site Also Targets GoDaddy,* ARSTECHNICA.COM (Jan. 21, 2013), *available at* http://arstechnica.com/tech-policy/2013/01/new-lawsuit-against-revenge-porn-site-also-targets-godaddy.
2. 47 U.S.C. §§ 230 (c)(1), (e)(3).
3. Mullin, *supra* note 1.
4. Joe Mullin, *Revenge Porn Is "Just Entertainment," Says Owner of IsAnybodyDown,* ARSTECHNICA.COM (Feb. 4, 2013), *available at* http://arstechnica.com/tech-policy/2013/02/revenge-porn-is-just-entertainment-says-owner-of-isanybodydown.
5. Mullin, *supra* note 1.

Intimate Facts

Private facts cases involve a person's most intimate or personal information. Intimate facts are those that a person would not want the community to know. This information must be more than just embarrassing. A plaintiff will not win a private facts case if the media reveal she or he chews bubble gum or slipped on a patch of ice. But intimate facts do not have to concern illegal or reprehensible matters. There are many facts a person might want to keep private simply because they are not for public knowledge. Private facts suits can relate to a person's financial condition,[155] medical information,[156] domestic difficulties[157] and similar intimate facts. Often, private facts suits concern sexual activities.[158]

It is not always clear why a court does or does not find publishing a fact offensive. In 2002 a federal court said showing on television a woman kissing drummer Dominic Weir in a women's bathroom stall in a bar was not offensive and objectionable.[159] However, a state court in 2004 ruled that it was reasonable for a jury to find objectionable television commercials showing a man having hair replacement treatments.[160]

Private facts cases focus on the community's reaction to disseminating the intimate information.[161] The question before a court hearing a private facts case is, Would it outrage the community's notions of decency if the intimate information were published?[162]

Not all facts about a person are private; not even all intimate facts about a person are private. Information in a public record, such as a court filing or an arrest record, by definition is public information, not private. Nor are facts private if the person himself or herself made them public. Courts hold that information told to a few close relatives or friends remains private. A person may define her or his own circle of intimacy.[163] But if a person reveals intimate facts publicly, the private facts tort does not limit the media from also publishing the information.

One illustrative case involves a friendship between two high school girls that deteriorated into a bitter feud. The first girl accused the second of being pregnant, and that girl teased the first about her Jewish heritage, seeking psychological counseling and having plastic surgery. The feud also involved swastikas painted on road signs and culminated in the second girl's family self-publishing a book about the feud. The book included school, police and legal documents connected with the situation. The first girl sued for private facts, among other torts. She claimed the book included "1) excerpts and summaries from her myspace.com webpage; 2) three statements related to her Jewish ancestry; 3) her enrolment at [a university]; 4) two statements regarding Plaintiff's decision to seek professional psychological care or counseling; 5) Plaintiff's transfer from one high school to another under a superintendent's agreement; and 6) two statements regarding plastic surgery on Plaintiff's nose."[164] The court held categories 1, 2, 3 and 5 were not private, noting the plaintiff agreed she could not conceal what she posted on her MySpace webpage. She also wrote on her MySpace page that she sought psychological help. As to plastic surgery, the court said it "questions whether this matter is truly private: cosmetic surgery on one's face is by its nature exposed to the public eye."

SUMMARY

A PRIVATE FACTS PLAINTIFF MUST SHOW THE WIDELY disseminated facts were private, dealt with intimate or highly personal matters and were not of legitimate public concern. A plaintiff also must prove that publication would be highly offensive to a reasonable person. It is not the published facts that must be highly offensive, but that the facts were published. Facts are not private if they are from public records or are generally known. ∎

Legitimate Public Concern

Even if intimate facts were private before being published, a plaintiff cannot win a private facts lawsuit if the information is newsworthy or of legitimate public concern. The mass media help determine what is newsworthy by reporting on some stories and not others, partly by considering community standards. The media often publish reports including intimate facts. Stories about crimes, suicides, divorces, catastrophes, diseases and other topics may include intimate information the people involved do not want published. Also, once people are part of a newsworthy event, their lives are open books. The media often reveal intimate facts about them.[165] If newsworthy, these private facts cannot be the basis of a successful private facts suit.

Courts give the media considerable freedom to determine what is newsworthy. Judges do not want to infringe on journalists' First Amendment rights to report the news. Nor do judges want to become journalists by deciding what is of public concern. But courts do draw lines, finding that very intimate facts are not newsworthy if publishing the information would outrage the community.

Many courts have adopted a test to determine newsworthiness, first used by a federal appeals court in a case in which a Southern California surfer sued Sports Illustrated magazine.[166] A Sports Illustrated story included information about Mike Virgil, who bodysurfed at the Wedge, a public beach near Newport Beach, Calif. The Wedge is reputed to be the world's most dangerous place to bodysurf. To illustrate the surfers' daredevil attitudes, the story said Virgil put out a cigarette on his tongue, burned holes through a dollar bill that rested on the back of his hand, dove headfirst down a flight of stairs to impress women, ate spiders and jumped off billboards. Virgil spoke with the Sports Illustrated reporter but withdrew his consent to the story before publication. The surfer sued the magazine for publishing private facts.

The court said the First Amendment did not protect publicity of highly intimate facts unless they were of public concern. Defining newsworthiness, the court distinguished between information the public is entitled to know and facts published for a morbid and sensational reason, prying into private lives for no justifiable purpose. If a reasonable person would have no interest in knowing the information, a court could find it was published for morbid and sensational reasons, the court said. Surfing at the Wedge could be of public concern, the court grudgingly admitted. But did that justify revealing intimate details of Mike Virgil's life? The court sent the case back to the trial court to decide that question.[167] The trial court held that the information in the article about eating spiders, diving down stairs and other private facts in the article was embarrassing but not morbid and sensational. The facts helped describe people who bodysurfed at the Wedge, the court said in ruling for Sports Illustrated.[168]

Several courts have taken a slightly different approach to defining what is newsworthy when stories concern people involuntarily put in the public eye. These courts determine whether there is a logical connection between the news event and the private facts revealed. Well-known persons such as actors, athletes, politicians and musicians are inherently more newsworthy than others. The public wants to know about them, and they have chosen to be in the public eye. Even celebrities, though, have a right to keep private those facts that would be highly embarrassing if publicized. For example, in part based on a private facts claim, actress Pamela Anderson Lee and rock musician Bret Michaels successfully prevented distribution of a videotape showing them having sex.[169]

At one time, newsworthiness was a defense to a private facts suit. A media defendant had the burden of showing that the facts were of legitimate public interest. Some courts continue to put the newsworthiness burden on the defendant. Many courts instead now require the plaintiff in a private facts suit to prove the intimate facts were not newsworthy. This change came when a newspaper reported that a student body president was a transsexual.[170] Toni Diaz, born Antonio Diaz, underwent sex reassignment surgery before entering a community college. Elected student body president, she charged school administrators with mishandling student funds. A local newspaper columnist wrote of Diaz, "Now I realize, that in these times, such a matter is no big deal, but I suspect his female classmates in P.E. 97 may wish to make other showering arrangements." Diaz, who had told only close relatives and friends of her operation, sued the paper and columnist.

A court ruled that Diaz, as plaintiff, had to prove the private facts were not newsworthy. The special role of the press in society must be protected, the court said. Putting the burden on the media could lead to self-censorship. The press might be concerned that it could not prove newsworthiness no matter how much in the public interest it thought the story to be. The court ruled that Diaz could show it was not newsworthy to publish remarks about her gender and that her gender had no connection with her ability to be student body president. Nor, the court said, did her being the college's first female student body president open her entire life to examination.

Publicity

A private facts plaintiff must prove that the defendant gave publicity to the intimate information. Publicity in the private facts tort is not the same as publication in a libel suit. In libel, publication to a third party, someone other than the plaintiff and defendant, is sufficient. For the private facts tort, most courts require widespread publicity.[171] These courts hold that telling one other person or a small group of people will not show publicity in a private facts suit. Revealing intimate information in the mass media will meet the definition of giving publicity to private facts.[172]

Some courts hold that revealing private facts to small groups of people who have a special relationship with the plaintiff is sufficient to show there was publicity. This could include the plaintiff's fellow workers, church members, colleagues in a social organization or neighbors.[173] For instance, Kmart hired private investigators to pose as employees in the company's distribution warehouse to check on reports of theft and drug sales. Through the undercover investigators' reports, Kmart managers learned private facts about their employees, including facts regarding family matters, sexual conduct and health. Several employees sued Kmart for revealing private facts. A court said that telling private facts to a few people with whom a plaintiff has close ties may prove the publicity element.[174]

Publishing private facts is permissible if the information is newsworthy or of legitimate public concern. Judges or juries determine newsworthiness in private facts cases. The criteria many courts use is that private facts are newsworthy if the publication was not intended to be sensational and morbid. Courts also consider whether there is a logical connection between the news event and the published private facts. Most courts require a private facts plaintiff to prove the article was not newsworthy. Some courts regard newsworthiness as a defense to a private facts lawsuit. Most courts require a private facts plaintiff to prove the information was widely published.

First Amendment Defense

When the press faces a private facts lawsuit, it often argues the First Amendment protects publishing truthful information. One way to balance privacy interests against free speech interests is to focus on the source of the information. Should the press lose a private facts suit if the intimate information came from a **public record**—that is, a government document, particularly one publicly available?

public record A government record, particularly one that is publicly available.

The U.S. Supreme Court has said the First Amendment protects publishing truthful information of public significance lawfully obtained from public records, unless punishing the media would serve a compelling state interest. Court decisions have not held that the First Amendment always will protect publishing truthful information taken from public records.[175] However, in each of the cases it has decided involving private facts obtained from public records, the Supreme Court has ruled for the press. The Court has not yet found a compelling state interest that overrides the press's First Amendment rights.

Public Significance In determining whether a publication is about a matter of public significance, the Supreme Court focuses on the story's subject, not on individuals named in the article.[176] Whether a person mentioned in the story is of public interest is not the important factor. Rather, the question is whether the story's topic is of public importance.

In *B.J.F. v. Florida Star,* for example, the Supreme Court held that the First Amendment protected a newspaper that published the name of a rape victim, reasoning that violent crime is a publicly significant topic.[177] In October 1983, a woman identified as B.J.F. reported to a Florida sheriff's department that she had been robbed and sexually assaulted. The sheriff's department prepared an incident report that identified B.J.F. by her full name and placed the report in its pressroom, which was open to the public. A beginning reporter for the Florida Star saw the report and the paper published a story on the case in a section containing brief articles describing local criminal incidents, including B.J.F.'s full name. This was contrary to the paper's policy of not naming rape victims. B.J.F. sued the sheriff's department and the Florida Star under a state law making it illegal for media to publish the name of a sexual assault victim. The sheriff's department settled before trial, and B.J.F. won her case against the newspaper, a result that was upheld by a Florida appellate court.

The newspaper, however, appealed the case to the U.S. Supreme Court, which reversed, holding that the First Amendment protects a newspaper that publishes truthful information lawfully obtained from public records, provided no compelling state interest requires otherwise. If the government had wanted to shield B.J.F.'s identity, it should not have put the report where a journalist could see it, the Court suggested. Because the government made the information available, it could not punish the press for publishing it. Although protecting the identity of a sexual assault victim could in principle be a compelling state interest, the Court said, three factors worked against that conclusion in this case: First, the government itself supplied the information. Second, the state law forbidding names from being published had no exceptions, not even if the community already knew the victim's name. Third, the state law applied only to the media, allowing individuals or non-media groups to disseminate a victim's name. Under these circumstances, the Court said, the right to a free press outweighed the state's interest in preventing publication of B.J.F.'s name.

Lawfully Obtained In three other decisions underscoring the primacy of press freedoms over individual privacy, the Court ruled that where the press had legally obtained truthful information from public records it was not liable for publishing private facts. In *Cox Broadcasting Corp. v. Cohn,* the Court said for the first time that truthful information lawfully obtained from a public record could not be the basis of a private facts lawsuit.[178] The case had its genesis in a 1971 rape and murder of a 17-year-old girl in Georgia. Although there was substantial press coverage of the crime, the identity of the victim was not disclosed pending trial. At a court proceeding some months later, though, a reporter covering the incident learned the name of the victim from an examination of indictments filed against six defendants that were made available for inspection in the courtroom. Her name was published in a television newscast later that day. The victim's father sued the television station for broadcasting the name of his daughter. He won at trial and again on the television station's appeal to the Georgia Supreme Court. But the U.S. Supreme Court reversed, holding in favor of the television station that the First Amendment protects the press against a private facts tort if the information is obtained from generally available public records. It would impinge on the press's obligation to accurately report judicial proceedings, the Court said, if reporters had access to information but were not allowed to publish it.

In a separate case originating in Oklahoma in 1976, news media violated a juvenile court judge's order by publishing the name and picture of an 11-year-old boy who was charged with second-degree murder for shooting a railroad employee. Reporters were in the courtroom when the juvenile appeared, and the court put his name on the public record. Photographers took pictures as the minor left the courthouse. The Supreme Court said the press had lawfully obtained information available to the public and held that the First Amendment prohibits punishing the press for revealing information taken from public records.[179]

In a third case affirming the importance of press freedoms, newspaper reporters who had been monitoring a police scanner in West Virginia in 1978 responded to a crime scene and learned from witnesses and investigators the name of a 14-year-old boy charged with killing a classmate at a junior high school. State prosecutors obtained an indictment against the press for publishing the boy's name in violation of a state law making it illegal to publish, without prior court approval, the name of a juvenile offender. The Supreme Court, however, ruled in favor of the newspaper, reasoning that the First Amendment protects news reports where journalists have lawfully obtained truthful information from publicly available sources. The Court said protecting the minor's privacy was not a compelling reason to restrict the freedom of the press.[180]

These cases show that sensitive personal information legally obtained from law enforcement officials, from generally available records, or by what a journalist sees or hears will not support a private facts lawsuit. The Supreme Court has also held that the First Amendment sometimes protects publication of private information even where it was not lawfully obtained—so long as the media were not involved in illegally acquiring the information. In *Bartnicki v. Vopper* (discussed further in Chapter 8), the Court said the media were not liable for intercepting a cell phone conversation between two labor negotiators. Punishing the media for publishing information they obtained without acting illegally would not further a compelling government interest, the Court said.[181]

Public Record Publicly available facts are not private. Names, addresses and telephone numbers are available in phone books, so they are not confidential.[182] Information in government records available to the public cannot be considered private. Facts presented in public meetings also are not secret. Unless a judge seals a record, making it unavailable, court records are public. A private facts suit cannot be based on intimate information contained in publicly accessible records.

Some government records are not publicly accessible and may not be considered public records in a private facts lawsuit. For example, grand jury proceedings are closed and not available to the public or press.[183] Also, information about individuals' medical conditions, tax filings and other personal data may not be considered a public record.[184]

Similarly, not all publicly accessible places are "public." Publishing a picture and a conversation obtained by entering a private hospital room may not be protected even if the hospital generally is open to the public.[185]

Passage of Time Some private facts plaintiffs have argued that the passage of time may mean that information is no longer of legitimate concern to the public. Either the plaintiff was newsworthy many years before the media published the intimate information, or the private facts relate to events that happened long ago. Courts have rejected this contention, saying that newsworthiness does not disappear over time. In a well-known case, a child prodigy who, at age 11, lectured on complex mathematical concepts and graduated from Harvard at age 16 dropped out of the public eye. Many years later, a magazine published a "Where Are They Now?" feature about him. The story accurately said the former prodigy worked as a store clerk and lived in a small apartment. He sued the magazine, in part claiming that his public fame had disappeared long ago. A federal appellate court said he remained newsworthy, the public being interested in what he did after he was no longer well known.[186]

SUMMARY

THE FIRST AMENDMENT PROTECTS PUBLISHING truthful information of public significance lawfully obtained from public records. However, this would not be a defense to a private facts lawsuit if a court determined that punishing the media would serve a compelling state interest. The U.S. Supreme Court, though, has never found a state interest compelling enough to allow such punishment, even where the media has revealed the name of a rape victim.

The topic of a news story, rather than the individual people discussed in the story, determines whether the story is of public significance. Information is lawfully obtained as long as a journalist does nothing illegal to obtain it. Information is public if it is in government records or otherwise available to the public.

Newsworthiness does not diminish over time. Facts and people once newsworthy remain newsworthy. ■

Cases for Study

Thinking About It

The two case excerpts that follow are recent landmark privacy cases. As you read these case excerpts, keep the following questions in mind:

- Think back to chapter 1 and the discussion of originalism (interpretation of the Constitution according to the perceived intent of its framers). Can you spot originalist ideas in a modern-day decision about how advances in technology impact the right to privacy as protected by the Fourth Amendment?

- How do the decisions try to balance right to privacy against other important rights?

- How has technology changed our societal understanding of a "reasonable expectation of privacy"?

- Why did the justices come to different conclusions in these two cases, both of which explore the right to privacy in a Fourth Amendment context?

City of Ontario v. Quon
SUPREME COURT OF THE UNITED STATES
560 U.S. 746 (2010)

JUSTICE KENNEDY delivered the Court's opinion:
This case involves the assertion by a government employer of the right, in circumstances to be described, to read text messages sent and received on a pager the employer owned and issued to an employee. The employee contends that the privacy of the messages is protected by the ban on "unreasonable searches and seizures" found in the Fourth Amendment to the United States Constitution, made applicable to the States by the Due Process Clause of the Fourteenth Amendment. Though the case touches issues of far-reaching significance, the Court concludes it can be resolved by settled principles determining when a search is reasonable.

The City of Ontario (City) is a political subdivision of the State of California. The case arose out of incidents in 2001 and 2002 when respondent Jeff Quon was employed by the Ontario Police Department

(OPD). He was a police sergeant and member of OPD's Special Weapons and Tactics (SWAT) Team. The City, OPD, and OPD's Chief, Lloyd Scharf, are petitioners here. As will be discussed, two respondents share the last name Quon. In this opinion "Quon" refers to Jeff Quon, for the relevant events mostly revolve around him.

In October 2001, the City acquired 20 alphanumeric pagers capable of sending and receiving text messages. Arch Wireless Operating Company provided wireless service for the pagers. Under the City's service contract with Arch Wireless, each pager was allotted a limited number of characters sent or received each month. Usage in excess of that amount would result in an additional fee. The City issued pagers to Quon and other SWAT Team members in order to help the SWAT Team mobilize and respond to emergency situations.

Before acquiring the pagers, the City announced a "Computer Usage, Internet and E-Mail Policy" (Computer Policy) that applied to all employees. Among other provisions, it specified that the City "reserves the right to monitor and log all network activity including e-mail and Internet use, with or without notice. Users should have no expectation of privacy or confidentiality when using these resources." In March 2000, Quon signed a statement acknowledging that he had read and understood the Computer Policy.

The Computer Policy did not apply, on its face, to text messaging. Text messages share similarities with e-mails, but the two differ in an important way. In this case, for instance, an e-mail sent on a City computer was transmitted through the City's own data servers, but a text message sent on one of the City's pagers was transmitted using wireless radio frequencies from an individual pager to a receiving station owned by Arch Wireless. It was routed through Arch Wireless' computer network, where it remained until the recipient's pager or cellular telephone was ready to receive the message, at which point Arch Wireless transmitted the message from the transmitting station nearest to the recipient. After delivery, Arch Wireless retained a copy on its computer servers. The message did not pass through computers owned by the City.

Although the Computer Policy did not cover text messages by its explicit terms, the City made clear to employees, including Quon, that the City would treat text messages the same way as it treated e-mails. At an April 18, 2002, staff meeting at which Quon was present, Lieutenant Steven Duke, the OPD officer responsible for the City's contract with Arch Wireless, told officers that messages sent on the pagers "are considered e-mail messages. This means that [text] messages would fall under the City's policy as public information and [would be] eligible for auditing." Duke's comments were put in writing in a memorandum sent on April 29, 2002, by Chief Scharf to Quon and other City personnel.

Within the first or second billing cycle after the pagers were distributed, Quon exceeded his monthly text message character allotment. Duke told Quon about the overage, and reminded him that messages sent on the pagers were "considered e-mail and could be audited." Duke said, however, that "it was not his intent to audit [an] employee's text messages to see if the overage [was] due to work related transmissions." Duke suggested that Quon could reimburse the City for the overage fee rather than have Duke audit the messages. Quon wrote a check to the City for the overage. Duke offered the same arrangement to other employees who incurred overage fees.

Over the next few months, Quon exceeded his character limit three or four times. Each time he reimbursed the City. Quon and another officer again incurred overage fees for their pager usage in August 2002. At a meeting in October, Duke told Scharf that he had become "'tired of being a bill collector.'" Scharf decided to determine whether the existing character limit was too low—that is, whether officers such as Quon were having to pay fees for sending work-related messages—or if the overages were for personal messages. Scharf told Duke to request transcripts of text messages sent in August and September by Quon and the other employee who had exceeded the character allowance.

At Duke's request, an administrative assistant employed by OPD contacted Arch Wireless. After verifying that the City was the subscriber on the accounts, Arch Wireless provided the desired transcripts. Duke reviewed the transcripts and discovered that many of the messages sent and received on Quon's pager were not work related, and some were sexually explicit. Duke reported his findings to Scharf, who, along with Quon's immediate supervisor, reviewed the transcripts himself. After his review, Scharf referred the matter to OPD's internal affairs division for an investigation into whether Quon was violating OPD rules by pursuing personal matters while on duty.

The officer in charge of the internal affairs review was Sergeant Patrick McMahon. Before conducting a review, McMahon used Quon's work schedule to redact the transcripts in order to eliminate any messages Quon sent while off duty. He then reviewed the content of the messages Quon sent during work hours. McMahon's report noted that Quon sent or received

456 messages during work hours in the month of August 2002, of which no more than 57 were work related; he sent as many as 80 messages during a single day at work; and on an average workday, Quon sent or received 28 messages, of which only 3 were related to police business. The report concluded that Quon had violated OPD rules. Quon was allegedly disciplined.

. . .

The Fourth Amendment states: "The right of the people to be secure in their persons, houses, papers, and effects, against unreasonable searches and seizures, shall not be violated. . . ." It is well settled that the Fourth Amendment's protection extends beyond the sphere of criminal investigations. "The Amendment guarantees the privacy, dignity, and security of persons against certain arbitrary and invasive acts by officers of the Government," without regard to whether the government actor is investigating crime or performing another function. The Fourth Amendment applies as well when the Government acts in its capacity as an employer.

The Court discussed this principle in *O'Connor v. Ortega* (1987). There a physician employed by a state hospital alleged that hospital officials investigating workplace misconduct had violated his Fourth Amendment rights by searching his office and seizing personal items from his desk and filing cabinet. All Members of the Court agreed with the general principle that "[i]ndividuals do not lose Fourth Amendment rights merely because they work for the government instead of a private employer." A majority of the Court further agreed that "'special needs, beyond the normal need for law enforcement,'" make the warrant and probable-cause requirement impracticable for government employers.

[In *O'Connor* a] . . . four-Justice plurality concluded that the correct analysis has two steps. First, because "some government offices may be so open to fellow employees or the public that no expectation of privacy is reasonable," a court must consider "[t]he operational realities of the workplace" in order to determine whether an employee's Fourth Amendment rights are implicated. On this view, "the question whether an employee has a reasonable expectation of privacy must be addressed on a case-by-case basis." Next, where an employee has a legitimate privacy expectation, an employer's intrusion on that expectation "for noninvestigatory, work-related purposes, as well as for investigations of work-related misconduct, should be judged by the standard of reasonableness under all the circumstances."

. . .

Later, in the [*Treasury Employees* v.] *Von Raab* (1985) decision, the Court explained that "operational realities" could diminish an employee's privacy expectations, and that this diminution could be taken into consideration when assessing the reasonableness of a workplace search. In the two decades since *O'Connor*, however, the threshold test for determining the scope of an employee's Fourth Amendment rights has not been clarified further. . . .

Before turning to the reasonableness of the search, it is instructive to note the parties' disagreement over whether Quon had a reasonable expectation of privacy. The record docs establish that OPD, at the outset, made it clear that pager messages were not considered private. The City's Computer Policy stated that "[u]sers should have no expectation of privacy or confidentiality when using" City computers. Chief Scharf's memo and Duke's statements made clear that this official policy extended to text messaging. The disagreement, at least as respondents see the case, is over whether Duke's later statements overrode the official policy. Respondents contend that because Duke told Quon that an audit would be unnecessary if Quon paid for the overage, Quon reasonably could expect that the contents of his messages would remain private.

At this point, were we to assume that inquiry into "operational realities" were called for, it would be necessary to ask whether Duke's statements could be taken as announcing a change in OPD policy, and if so, whether he had, in fact or appearance, the authority to make such a change and to guarantee the privacy of text messaging. It would also be necessary to consider whether a review of messages sent on police pagers, particularly those sent while officers are on duty, might be justified for other reasons, including performance evaluations, litigation concerning the lawfulness of police actions, and perhaps compliance with state open records laws. These matters would all bear on the legitimacy of an employee's privacy expectation.

The Court must proceed with care when considering the whole concept of privacy expectations in communications made on electronic equipment owned by a government employer. The judiciary risks error by elaborating too fully on the Fourth Amendment implications of emerging technology before its role in society has become clear. In *Katz* [*v. United States* (1967)], the Court relied on its own knowledge and experience to conclude that there is a reasonable expectation of privacy in a telephone booth. It is not so clear that courts at present are on so sure a ground. Prudence counsels caution before the facts in the instant case are used to establish far-reaching premises that define the existence, and extent, of privacy expectations enjoyed by employees when using employer-provided communication devices.

Rapid changes in the dynamics of communication and information transmission are evident not just in the technology itself but in what society accepts as proper behavior. As one *amici* brief notes, many employers expect or at least tolerate personal use of such equipment by employees because it often increases worker efficiency. Another *amicus* points out that the law is beginning to respond to these developments, as some States have recently passed statutes requiring employers to notify employees when monitoring their electronic communications. At present, it is uncertain how workplace norms, and the law's treatment of them, will evolve.

Even if the Court were certain that the *O'Connor* plurality's approach were the right one, the Court would have difficulty predicting how employees' privacy expectations will be shaped by those changes or the degree to which society will be prepared to recognize those expectations as reasonable. Cell phone and text message communications are so pervasive that some persons may consider them to be essential means or necessary instruments for self-expression, even self-identification. That might strengthen the case for an expectation of privacy. On the other hand, the ubiquity of those devices has made them generally affordable, so one could counter that employees who need cell phones or similar devices for personal matters can purchase and pay for their own. And employer policies concerning communications will of course shape the reasonable expectations of their employees, especially to the extent that such policies are clearly communicated.

A broad holding concerning employees' privacy expectations vis-à-vis employer-provided technological equipment might have implications for future cases that cannot be predicted. It is preferable to dispose of this case on narrower grounds. For present purposes we assume several propositions *arguendo*: First, Quon had a reasonable expectation of privacy in the text messages sent on the pager provided to him by the City; second, petitioners' review of the transcript constituted a search within the meaning of the Fourth Amendment; and third, the principles applicable to a government employer's search of an employee's physical office apply with at least the same force when the employer intrudes on the employee's privacy in the electronic sphere.

Even if Quon had a reasonable expectation of privacy in his text messages, petitioners did not necessarily violate the Fourth Amendment by obtaining and reviewing the transcripts. Although as a general matter, warrantless searches "are *per se* unreasonable under the Fourth Amendment," there are "a few specifically established and well-delineated exceptions" to that general rule. The Court has held that the "'special needs'" of the workplace justify one such exception.

Under the approach of the *O'Connor* plurality, when conducted for a "noninvestigatory, work-related purpos[e]" or for the "investigatio[n] of work-related misconduct," a government employer's warrantless search is reasonable if it is "'justified at its inception'" and if "'the measures adopted are reasonably related to the objectives of the search and not excessively intrusive in light of'" the circumstances giving rise to the search. The search here satisfied the standard of the *O'Connor* plurality and was reasonable under that approach.

The search was justified at its inception because there were "reasonable grounds for suspecting that the search [was] necessary for a noninvestigatory work-related purpose." As a jury found, Chief Scharf ordered the search in order to determine whether the character limit on the City's contract with Arch Wireless was sufficient to meet the City's needs. This was, as the Ninth Circuit noted, a "legitimate work-related rationale." The City and OPD had a legitimate interest in ensuring that employees were not being forced to pay out of their own pockets for work-related expenses, or on the other hand that the City was not paying for extensive personal communications.

As for the scope of the search, reviewing the transcripts was reasonable because it was an efficient and expedient way to determine whether Quon's overages were the result of work-related messaging or personal use. The review was also not "'excessively intrusive.'" Although Quon had gone over his monthly allotment a number of times, OPD requested transcripts for only the months of August and September 2002. While it may have been reasonable as well for OPD to review transcripts of all the months in which Quon exceeded his allowance, it was certainly reasonable for OPD to review messages for just two months in order to obtain a large enough sample to decide whether the character limits were efficacious. And it is worth noting that during his internal affairs investigation, McMahon redacted all messages Quon sent while off duty, a measure which reduced the intrusiveness of any further review of the transcripts.

Furthermore, and again on the assumption that Quon had a reasonable expectation of privacy in the contents of his messages, the extent of an expectation is relevant to assessing whether the search was too intrusive. Even if he could assume some level of privacy would inhere in his messages, it would not have been reasonable for Quon to conclude that his messages were in all circumstances immune from scrutiny. Quon was told that his messages were subject to auditing. As a law enforcement officer, he would

or should have known that his actions were likely to come under legal scrutiny, and that this might entail an analysis of his on-the-job communications. Under the circumstances, a reasonable employee would be aware that sound management principles might require the audit of messages to determine whether the pager was being appropriately used. Given that the City issued the pagers to Quon and other SWAT Team members in order to help them more quickly respond to crises—and given that Quon had received no assurances of privacy—Quon could have anticipated that it might be necessary for the City to audit pager messages to assess the SWAT Team's performance in particular emergency situations.

From OPD's perspective, the fact that Quon likely had only a limited privacy expectation, with boundaries that we need not here explore, lessened the risk that the review would intrude on highly private details of Quon's life. OPD's audit of messages on Quon's employer-provided pager was not nearly as intrusive as a search of his personal e-mail account or pager, or a wiretap on his home phone line, would have been. That the search did reveal intimate details of Quon's life does not make it unreasonable, for under the circumstances a reasonable employer would not expect that such a review would intrude on such matters. The search was permissible in its scope.

. . .

Because the search was motivated by a legitimate work-related purpose, and because it was not excessive in scope, the search was reasonable under the approach of the *O'Connor* plurality. For these same reasons—that the employer had a legitimate reason for the search, and that the search was not excessively intrusive in light of that justification—the Court also concludes that the search would be "regarded as reasonable and normal in the private-employer context." . . . The search was reasonable, and the Court of Appeals erred by holding to the contrary. Petitioners did not violate Quon's Fourth Amendment rights.

. . .

It is so ordered.

United States v. Jones
SUPREME COURT OF THE UNITED STATES
132 S. Ct. 945 (2012)

JUSTICE ANTONIN SCALIA delivered the Court's opinion:

We decide whether the attachment of a Global-Positioning-System (GPS) tracking device to an individual's vehicle, and subsequent use of that device to monitor the vehicle's movements on public streets, constitutes a search or seizure within the meaning of the Fourth Amendment.

In 2004 respondent Antoine Jones, owner and operator of a nightclub in the District of Columbia, came under suspicion of trafficking in narcotics and was made the target of an investigation by a joint FBI and Metropolitan Police Department task force. Officers employed various investigative techniques, including visual surveillance of the nightclub, installation of a camera focused on the front door of the club, and a pen register and wiretap covering Jones's cellular phone.

Based in part on information gathered from these sources, in 2005 the Government applied to the United States District Court for the District of Columbia for a warrant authorizing the use of an electronic tracking device on the Jeep Grand Cherokee registered to Jones's wife. A warrant issued, authorizing installation of the device in the District of Columbia and within 10 days.

On the 11th day, and not in the District of Columbia but in Maryland, agents installed a GPS tracking device on the undercarriage of the Jeep while it was parked in a public parking lot. Over the next 28 days, the Government used the device to track the vehicle's movements, and once had to replace the device's battery when the vehicle was parked in a different public lot in Maryland. By means of signals from multiple satellites, the device established the vehicle's location within 50 to 100 feet, and communicated that location by cellular phone to a Government computer. It relayed more than 2,000 pages of data over the 4-week period.

The Government ultimately obtained a multiple-count indictment charging Jones and several alleged co-conspirators with, as relevant here, conspiracy to distribute and possess with intent to distribute five kilograms or more of cocaine and 50 grams or more of cocaine base, in violation of 21 U.S. C. ßß 841 and 846. Before trial, Jones filed a motion to suppress evidence obtained through the GPS device. The District Court granted the motion only in part, suppressing the data obtained while the vehicle was parked in the garage adjoining Jones's residence. It held the remaining data admissible, because " '[a] person traveling in an automobile on public thoroughfares has no reasonable expectation of privacy in his movements from one place to another.' " Jones's trial in October 2006 produced a hung jury on the conspiracy count.

In March 2007, a grand jury returned another indictment, charging Jones and others with the same conspiracy. The Government introduced at trial the same GPS-derived locational data admitted in the first trial, which connected Jones to the alleged conspirators' stash house that contained $850,000 in cash, 97 kilograms of cocaine, and 1 kilogram of cocaine base. The jury returned a guilty verdict, and the District Court sentenced Jones to life imprisonment.

The United States Court of Appeals for the District of Columbia Circuit reversed the conviction because of admission of the evidence obtained by warrantless use of the GPS device which, it said, violated the Fourth Amendment. The D. C. Circuit denied the Government's petition for rehearing en banc, with four judges dissenting. . . .

The Fourth Amendment provides in relevant part that "[t]he right of the people to be secure in their persons, houses, papers, and effects, against unreasonable searches and seizures, shall not be violated." It is beyond dispute that a vehicle is an "effect" as that term is used in the Amendment. We hold that the Government's installation of a GPS device on a target's vehicle, and its use of that device to monitor the vehicle's movements, constitutes a "search."

It is important to be clear about what occurred in this case: The Government physically occupied private property for the purpose of obtaining information. We have no doubt that such a physical intrusion would have been considered a "search" within the meaning of the Fourth Amendment when it was adopted. . . .

The text of the Fourth Amendment reflects its close connection to property, since otherwise it would have referred simply to "the right of the people to be secure against unreasonable searches and seizures"; the phrase "in their persons, houses, papers, and effects" would have been superfluous.

Consistent with this understanding, our Fourth Amendment jurisprudence was tied to common-law trespass, at least until the latter half of the 20th century. Thus, in *Olmstead v. United States,* we held that wiretaps attached to telephone wires on the public streets did not constitute a Fourth Amendment search because "[t]here was no entry of the houses or offices of the defendants."

Our later cases, of course, have deviated from that exclusively property-based approach. In *Katz v. United States,* we said that "the Fourth Amendment protects people, not places," and found a violation in attachment of an eavesdropping device to a public telephone booth. Our later cases have applied the analysis of Justice Harlan's concurrence in that case, which said that a violation occurs when government officers violate a person's "reasonable expectation of privacy."

The Government contends that the Harlan standard shows that no search occurred here, since Jones had no "reasonable expectation of privacy" in the area of the Jeep accessed by Government agents (its underbody) and in the locations of the Jeep on the public roads, which were visible to all. But we need not address the Government's contentions, because Jones's Fourth Amendment rights do not rise or fall with the *Katz* formulation.

At bottom, we must "assur[e] preservation of that degree of privacy against government that existed when the Fourth Amendment was adopted." . . .

More recently . . . the Court unanimously rejected the argument that although a "seizure" had occurred "in a 'technical' sense" when a trailer home was forcibly removed, no Fourth Amendment violation occurred because law enforcement had not "invade[d]

the [individuals'] privacy." *Katz,* the Court explained, established that "property rights are not the sole measure of Fourth Amendment violations," but did not "snuf[f] out the previously recognized protection for property." . . . *Katz* did not erode the principle "that, when the Government *does* engage in physical intrusion of a constitutionally protected area in order to obtain information, that intrusion may constitute a violation of the Fourth Amendment." We have embodied that preservation of past rights in our very definition of "reasonable expectation of privacy" which we have said to be an expectation "that has a source outside of the Fourth Amendment, either by reference to concepts of real or personal property law or to understandings that are recognized and permitted by society." *Katz* did not narrow the Fourth Amendment's scope. . . .

The concurrence [by Justice Alito, joined by Justices Ginsburg, Breyer and Kagan] begins by accusing us of applying "18th-century tort law." That is a distortion. What we apply is an 18th-century guarantee against unreasonable searches, which we believe must provide at *a minimum* the degree of protection it afforded when it was adopted. The concurrence does not share that belief. It would apply *exclusively Katz*'s reasonable-expectation-of-privacy test, even when that eliminates rights that previously existed. . . .

This Court has to date not deviated from the understanding that mere visual observation does not constitute a search. . . . Thus, even assuming that the concurrence is correct to say that "[t]raditional surveillance" of Jones for a 4-week period "would have required a large team of agents, multiple vehicles, and perhaps aerial assistance," our cases suggest that such visual observation is constitutionally permissible. It may be that achieving the same result through electronic means, without an accompanying trespass, is an unconstitutional invasion of privacy, but the present case does not require us to answer that question.

And answering it affirmatively leads us needlessly into additional thorny problems. The concurrence posits that "relatively short-term monitoring of a person's movements on public streets" is okay, but that "the use of longer term GPS monitoring in investigations *of most offenses* is no good. (emphasis added). That introduces yet another novelty into our jurisprudence. There is no precedent for the proposition that whether a search has occurred depends on the nature of the crime being investigated. And even accepting that novelty, it remains unexplained why a 4-week investigation is "surely" too long and why a drug-trafficking conspiracy involving substantial amounts of cash and narcotics is not an "extraordinary offens[e]" which may permit longer observation. What of a 2-day monitoring of a suspected purveyor of stolen electronics? Or of a 6-month monitoring of a suspected terrorist? We may have to grapple with these "vexing problems" in some future case where a classic trespassory search is not involved and resort must be had to *Katz* analysis; but there is no reason for rushing forward to resolve them here.

The Government argues in the alternative that even if the attachment and use of the device was a search, it was reasonable—and thus lawful—under the Fourth Amendment because "officers had reasonable suspicion, and indeed probable cause, to believe that [Jones] was a leader in a large-scale cocaine distribution conspiracy." We have no occasion to consider this argument. The Government did not raise it below, and the D. C. Circuit therefore did not address it. We consider the argument forfeited.

The judgment of the Court of Appeals for the D. C. Circuit is affirmed.

It is so ordered.

JUSTICE SONIA SOTOMAYOR, concurring:

I join the Court's opinion because I agree that a search within the meaning of the Fourth Amendment occurs, at a minimum, "[w]here, as here, the Government obtains information by physically intruding on a constitutionally protected area." In this case, the Government installed a Global Positioning System (GPS) tracking device on respondent Antoine Jones' Jeep without a valid warrant and without Jones' consent, then used that device to monitor the Jeep's movements over the course of four weeks. The Government usurped Jones' property for the purpose of conducting surveillance on him, thereby invading privacy interests long afforded, and undoubtedly entitled to, Fourth Amendment protection.

Of course, the Fourth Amendment is not concerned only with trespassory intrusions on property. Rather, even in the absence of a trespass, "a Fourth Amendment search occurs when the government violates a subjective expectation of privacy that society recognizes as reasonable." . . . As the majority's opinion makes clear, however, *Katz*'s reasonable-expectation-of-privacy test augmented, but did not displace or diminish, the common-law trespassory test that preceded it. . . .

With increasing regularity, the Government will be capable of duplicating the monitoring undertaken in this case by enlisting factory- or owner-installed vehicle tracking devices or GPS-enabled smartphones. In cases of electronic or other novel modes of surveillance that do not depend upon a physical invasion on property, the majority opinion's trespassory test may provide little guidance. But "[s]ituations involving merely the transmission of electronic signals without trespass would *remain* subject to *Katz* analysis." As Justice Alito incisively observes [in his concurrence], the same technological advances that have made possible nontrespassory surveillance techniques will also affect the *Katz* test by shaping the evolution of societal privacy expectations. Under that rubric, I agree with Justice Alito that, at the very least, "longer term GPS monitoring in investigations of most offenses impinges on expectations of privacy."

In cases involving even short-term monitoring, some unique attributes of GPS surveillance relevant to the *Katz* analysis will require particular attention. GPS monitoring generates a precise, comprehensive record of a person's public movements that reflects a wealth of detail about her familial, political, professional, religious, and sexual associations. ("Disclosed in [GPS] data . . . will be trips the indisputably private nature of which takes little imagination to conjure: trips to the psychiatrist, the plastic surgeon, the abortion clinic, the AIDS treatment center, the strip club, the criminal defense attorney, the by-the-hour motel, the union meeting, the mosque, synagogue or church, the gay bar and on and on"). The Government can store such records and efficiently mine them for information years into the future. And because GPS monitoring is cheap in comparison to conventional surveillance techniques and, by design, proceeds surreptitiously, it evades the ordinary checks that constrain abusive law enforcement practices: "limited police resources and community hostility."

Awareness that the Government may be watching chills associational and expressive freedoms. And the Government's unrestrained power to assemble data that reveal private aspects of identity is susceptible to abuse. The net result is that GPS monitoring—by making available at a relatively low cost such a substantial quantum of intimate information about any person whom the Government, in its unfettered discretion, chooses to track—may "alter the relationship between citizen and government in a way that is inimical to democratic society."

I would take these attributes of GPS monitoring into account when considering the existence of a reasonable societal expectation of privacy in the sum of one's public movements. I would ask whether people reasonably expect that their movements will be recorded and aggregated in a manner that enables the Government to ascertain, more or less at will, their political and religious beliefs, sexual habits, and so on. . . .

More fundamentally, it may be necessary to reconsider the premise that an individual has no reasonable expectation of privacy in information voluntarily disclosed to third parties. This approach is ill suited to the digital age, in which people reveal a great deal of information about themselves to third parties in the course of carrying out mundane tasks. People disclose the phone numbers that they dial or text to their cellular providers; the URLs that they visit and the e-mail addresses with which they correspond to their Internet service providers; and the books, groceries, and medications they purchase to online retailers. Perhaps, as Justice Alito notes, some people may find the "tradeoff" of privacy for convenience "worthwhile," or come to accept this "diminution of privacy" as "inevitable," and perhaps not. I for one doubt that people would accept without complaint the warrantless disclosure to the Government of a list of every Web site they had visited in the last week, or month, or year.

But whatever the societal expectations, they can attain constitutionally protected status only if our Fourth Amendment jurisprudence ceases to treat secrecy as a prerequisite for privacy. . . .

Resolution of these difficult questions in this case is unnecessary, however, because the Government's physical intrusion on Jones' Jeep supplies a narrower basis for decision. I therefore join the majority's opinion.

JUSTICE SAMUEL ALITO, with whom JUSTICE RUTH BADER GINSBURG, JUSTICE STEPHEN BREYER and JUSTICE ELENA KAGAN join, concurring in the judgment.

This case requires us to apply the Fourth Amendment's prohibition of unreasonable searches and seizures to a 21st-century surveillance technique, the use of a Global Positioning System (GPS) device to monitor a vehicle's movements for an extended period of time. Ironically, the Court has chosen to decide this case based on 18th-century tort law. By attaching a small GPS device to the underside of the vehicle that respondent drove, the law enforcement officers in this case engaged in conduct that might have provided grounds in 1791 for a suit for trespass to chattels. And for this reason, the Court concludes, the installation and use of the GPS device constituted a search.

This holding, in my judgment, is unwise. It strains the language of the Fourth Amendment; it has little if any support in current Fourth Amendment case law; and it is highly artificial.

I would analyze the question presented in this case by asking whether respondent's reasonable expectations of privacy were violated by the long-term monitoring of the movements of the vehicle he drove.

The Fourth Amendment prohibits "unreasonable searches and seizures," and the Court makes very little effort to explain how the attachment or use of the GPS device fits within these terms. The Court does not contend that there was a seizure. A seizure of property occurs when there is "some meaningful interference with an individual's possessory interests in that property," and here there was none. Indeed, the success of the surveillance technique that the officers employed was dependent on the fact that the GPS did not interfere in any way with the operation of the vehicle, for if any such interference had been detected, the device might have been discovered.

The Court does claim that the installation and use of the GPS constituted a search, but this conclusion is dependent on the questionable proposition that these two procedures cannot be separated for purposes of Fourth Amendment analysis. If these two procedures are analyzed separately, it is not at all clear from the Court's opinion why either should be regarded as a search. It is clear that the attachment of the GPS device was not itself a search; if the device had not functioned or if the officers had not used it, no information would have been obtained. And the Court does not contend that the use of the device constituted a search either. . . .

The Court argues—and I agree—that "we must 'assur[e] preservation of that degree of privacy against government that existed when the Fourth Amendment was adopted.' " But it is almost impossible to think of late-18th-century situations that are analogous to what took place in this case. (Is it possible to imagine a case in which a constable secreted himself somewhere in a coach and remained there for a period of time in order to monitor the movements of the coach's owner?) The Court's theory seems to be that the concept of a search, as originally understood, comprehended any technical trespass that led to the gathering of evidence, but we know that this is incorrect. At common law, any unauthorized intrusion on private property was actionable.

. . .

The Katz expectation-of-privacy test . . . is not without its own difficulties. It involves a degree of circularity, and judges are apt to confuse their own expectations of privacy with those of the hypothetical reasonable person to which the *Katz* test looks. In addition, the *Katz* test rests on the assumption that this hypothetical reasonable person has a well-developed and stable set of privacy expectations. But technology can change those expectations. Dramatic technological change may lead to periods in which popular expectations are in flux and may ultimately produce significant changes in popular attitudes. New technology may provide increased convenience or security at the expense of privacy, and many people may find the tradeoff worthwhile. And even if the public does not welcome the diminution of privacy that new technology entails, they may eventually reconcile themselves to this development as inevitable.

On the other hand, concern about new intrusions on privacy may spur the enactment of legislation to protect against these intrusions. This is what ultimately happened with respect to wiretapping. . . .

Recent years have seen the emergence of many new devices that permit the monitoring of a person's movements. . . .

Perhaps most significant, cell phones and other wireless devices now permit wireless carriers to track and record the location of users—and as of June 2011, it has been reported, there were more than 322 million wireless devices in use in the United States. For older phones, the accuracy of the location information depends on the density of the tower network, but new "smart phones," which are equipped with a GPS device, permit more precise tracking. . . . The availability and use of these and other new devices will continue to shape the average person's expectations about the privacy of his or her daily movements.

In the pre-computer age, the greatest protections of privacy were neither constitutional nor statutory, but practical. Traditional surveillance for any extended period of time was difficult and costly and therefore rarely undertaken. The surveillance at issue in this case—constant monitoring of the location of a vehicle for four weeks—would have required a large team of agents, multiple vehicles, and perhaps aerial assistance. Only an investigation of unusual importance could have justified such an expenditure of law enforcement resources. Devices like the one used in the present case, however, make long-term monitoring relatively easy and cheap. In circumstances involving dramatic technological change, the best solution to privacy concerns may be legislative. A legislative body is well situated to gauge changing public attitudes, to draw detailed lines, and to balance privacy and public safety in a comprehensive way.

To date, however, Congress and most States have not enacted statutes regulating the use of GPS tracking technology for law enforcement purposes. The best that we can do in this case is to apply existing Fourth Amendment doctrine and to ask whether the use of GPS tracking in a particular case involved a degree of intrusion that a reasonable person would not have anticipated.

Under this approach, relatively short-term monitoring of a person's movements on public streets accords with expectations of privacy that our society has recognized as reasonable. But the use of longer term GPS monitoring in investigations of most offenses impinges on expectations of privacy. For such offenses, society's expectation has been that law enforcement agents and others would not—and indeed, in the main, simply could not secretly monitor and catalogue every single movement of an individual's car for a very long period. . . . We also need not consider whether prolonged GPS monitoring in the context of investigations involving extraordinary offenses would similarly intrude on a constitutionally protected sphere of privacy. In such cases, long-term tracking might have been mounted using previously available techniques.

For these reasons, I conclude that the lengthy monitoring that occurred in this case constituted a search under the Fourth Amendment. I therefore agree with the majority that the decision of the Court of Appeals must be affirmed.

Chapter 7

When school shootings and other random acts of terror occasionally invade our communities, the media look like a pretty good target, for lawmakers and litigants alike. . . .

Bruce Sanford, First Amendment lawyer[1]

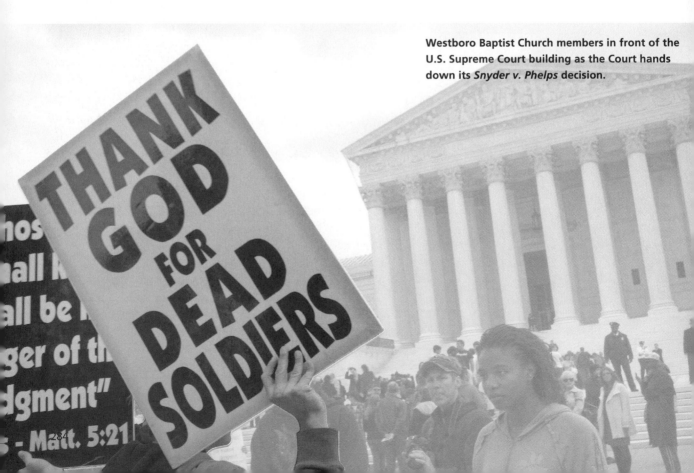

Westboro Baptist Church members in front of the U.S. Supreme Court building as the Court hands down its *Snyder v. Phelps* decision.

THANK GOD FOR DEAD SOLDIERS

- Matt. 5:21

284

Emotional Distress and Physical Harm

When Words and Pictures Hurt

Emotional Distress

The Development of
  Emotional Distress Suits

**Intentional Infliction
  of Emotional
  Distress**

Outrageousness
Intentional or Reckless
  Action
Actual Malice
Cyberstalking

**Negligent Infliction of
  Emotional Distress**

Physical Harm

Negligence
Incitement

**Communications
  Decency Act**

Other Dangers

Breach of Contract
Interference with Economic
  Advantage
Fraudulent
  Misrepresentation

Cases for Study

➤ *Hustler Magazine Inc.
  v. Falwell*
➤ *Snyder v. Phelps*

Suppose . . .

. . . a U.S. Marine is killed in action in Iraq. The soldier's family is attending his funeral at a Catholic church in their hometown. A group gathers nearby holding signs saying, "God Hates the USA/Thank God for 9/11," "God Hates You," "Don't Pray for the USA," "Thank God for Dead Soldiers," "Priests Rape Boys," "Semper fi fags" and "You're Going to Hell." The protesters say they believe God hates the United States for tolerating homosexuality, particularly homosexuality in the military. The deceased Marine was not gay, but the protesters use his funeral to express their views. Should the Marine's family be able to successfully sue the protesters, claiming the signs caused the family severe emotional harm and the protesters deliberately intended for that harm to occur? Look for the answer to this question when the case of *Snyder v. Phelps* is discussed later in this chapter, and the case is excerpted at the end of the chapter.

America is a litigious society. Americans sue for imagined slights or real harms, from spilling McDonald's hot coffee on themselves to medical malpractice.[2] They sue neighbors, businesses, lawyers, doctors and the media. News sources, people named in stories, people who believe articles or entertainment programs harmed them sue the media. Although libel and invasion of privacy claims are the most commonly filed suits based on media content and news gathering, the media are sued for a variety of other legal claims as well.

Emotional Distress

emotional distress Serious mental anguish.

Mass media content might harm a plaintiff in several ways. For example, a story could cause **emotional distress** even though it is not defamatory. Or a libelous story injuring a plaintiff's reputation also will upset him or her emotionally. Plaintiffs increasingly have difficulty winning libel and privacy suits. First Amendment principles—such as public plaintiffs having to prove actual malice, as discussed in Chapter 4—mean fewer plaintiffs will prevail in defamation suits. Plaintiffs usually do not win embarrassing facts and false light privacy cases. Several states have refused to allow plaintiffs to sue for false light, as noted in Chapter 6. Plaintiffs' lawyers searching for alternatives to libel and privacy claims may turn to the emotional distress tort.

intentional infliction of emotional distress Extreme and outrageous intentional or reckless conduct causing plaintiffs severe emotional harm; public official and public figure plaintiff also must show actual malice on defendant's part.

negligent infliction of emotional distress Owing a duty to a plaintiff, breaching that duty and causing the plaintiff severe emotional harm.

reckless Word used to describe actions taken with no consideration of the legal harms that might result.

There are two categories of emotional distress suits: **intentional infliction of emotional distress** and **negligent infliction of emotional distress.** Just as a libel defendant may act with actual malice—that is, intentionally or recklessly publishing false material—so may an intentional or **reckless** act or statement cause emotional distress. Acting recklessly is not caring what the result of an action will be. Also, being negligent—an act or statement made by mistake or without anticipating the possible harm the act or statement could cause—may inflict emotional distress, just as a negligently published article may defame someone. Emotional distress cases sometimes are called "emotional injury" or "mental distress" suits.

The law defines "emotional distress" as being frightened or extremely anxious. A plaintiff must show the emotional injury is very serious or severe, that she or he experienced considerable mental pain or anguish.[3] Merely being upset, angry, embarrassed or resentful is not enough to win a lawsuit based on infliction of emotional distress.[4] However, emotions such as severe disappointment or an intense feeling of shame or humiliation may cause the extreme mental pain that the emotional distress tort requires.[5]

The Development of Emotional Distress Suits

The media can emotionally upset people in many ways, but only rarely will a person be able to sue successfully for emotional distress.[6] For example, a man saw a newspaper article mentioning the funeral home that buried his wife. Looking at the accompanying photograph, he recognized his deceased wife lying in an open casket. He became emotionally upset because he had told the funeral home not to open his wife's casket for any reason. In another case, the head of a police and military training company claimed to be emotionally injured when a newspaper headline called him a militant. The widower and the company manager both sued, claiming the media caused them mental distress. Neither suit was successful. One court said the widower did not have a special relationship with the newspaper, which was required in that state to win a negligent infliction of emotional distress case. The other court said it was not outrageous to use the word "militant" in a headline.[7] In fact, that court said it would be nearly impossible for a plaintiff to win an intentional infliction of emotional distress case in New York state, where the plaintiff filed suit.

When plaintiffs began bringing emotional distress cases more than a century ago courts denied all mental suffering claims. Today American law still severely limits a plaintiff's chances of winning damages for emotional injury. Plaintiffs do not often win emotional distress suits because mental suffering is difficult to prove. Tort law traditionally compensated plaintiffs for physical injuries to themselves or damage to their property caused by another person. A judge can see a broken arm caused by a traffic accident, but it is more difficult to measure the emotional trauma the accident caused. Judges feared plaintiffs would pretend to have emotional pain or would concoct emotional injuries. Because internal anguish cannot be seen, judges were concerned juries could be fooled into awarding damages for fictitious grievances. Even if a plaintiff could prove emotional injury, courts did not know what it was worth. How could a jury put a monetary value on emotional suffering? Judges also believed people should be able to overcome mental pain, not be compensated for infliction of emotional distress.

It is understandable that early 20th-century courts had doubts about compensating mental distress. Medical science then knew little about diagnosing or treating emotional injury.[8] In the 1920s and 1930s, some jurisdictions began allowing plaintiffs to recover for emotional distress, but only if the mental pain directly resulted from a physical injury. A jury could find a defendant had to pay damages for hitting the plaintiff and could add more for the plaintiff's emotional suffering caused by being hit. As emotional distress law progressed, a few jurisdictions allowed compensation for emotional injuries even if the accompanying physical harm was slight,

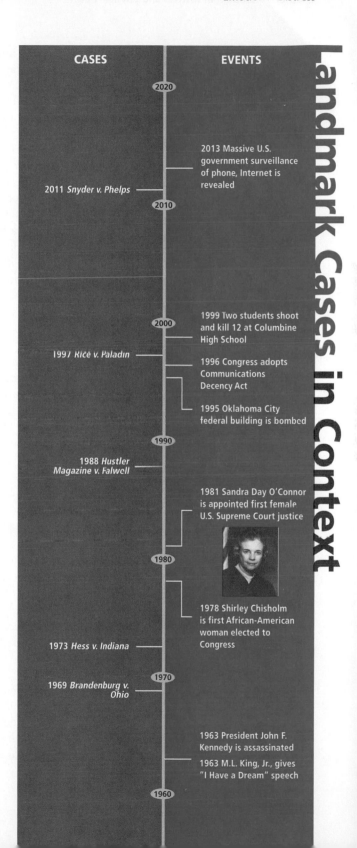

CASES

2011 *Snyder v. Phelps*

1997 *Rice v. Paladin*

1988 *Hustler Magazine v. Falwell*

1973 *Hess v. Indiana*

1969 *Brandenburg v. Ohio*

EVENTS

2020

2013 Massive U.S. government surveillance of phone, Internet is revealed

2010

2000

1999 Two students shoot and kill 12 at Columbine High School

1996 Congress adopts Communications Decency Act

1995 Oklahoma City federal building is bombed

1990

1981 Sandra Day O'Connor is appointed first female U.S. Supreme Court justice

1980

1978 Shirley Chisholm is first African-American woman elected to Congress

1970

1963 President John F. Kennedy is assassinated

1963 M.L. King, Jr., gives "I Have a Dream" speech

1960

Landmark Cases in Context

such as the defendant brushing against the plaintiff. By the 1950s, courts realized advances in psychiatry's understanding of emotional injuries allowed mental distress to be identified and treated. An increasing number of state courts began allowing plaintiffs to recover for emotional distress and its physical manifestations, such as severe headaches or stomach disorders.[9]

In the past few decades, some jurisdictions have stopped requiring emotional distress to be connected with physical harm.[10] Currently, some jurisdictions recognize legal actions for intentional infliction of emotional distress alone—without accompanying physical injury or other offensive conduct—if the defendant's actions causing the emotional injury were outrageous and deliberate or reckless.

Some states also now permit negligent infliction of emotional distress suits if the defendant violates a plaintiff's legal rights, such as defaming the plaintiff or invading his privacy.[11] In these cases, the plaintiff must show the defendant acted negligently rather than intentionally or recklessly. However, some states, such as Mississippi, do not allow negligent infliction of emotional distress lawsuits based on news coverage.[12]

SUMMARY

AT ONE TIME COURTS DID NOT ALLOW RECOVERY for emotional distress. Over time, courts began requiring physical injury to accompany emotional distress. Then judges allowed emotional distress suits if they arose from an invasion of a person's legal rights, such as libel or privacy. However, the requirements for a successful emotional distress lawsuit continue to differ among the states. There are two categories of emotional distress tort claims: intentional and negligent. Emotional distress is defined as severe mental anguish. ∎

Intentional Infliction of Emotional Distress

Intentional or reckless conduct that is extreme and outrageous and causes severe emotional harm can be grounds for a successful lawsuit.[13] The key to intentional infliction of emotional distress (IIED) is that the defendant's actions must have been outrageous—that is, actions a civilized society considers intolerable and beyond all bounds of decency.[14] Because this element of the tort is so important, some courts call the tort "outrage" instead of intentional infliction of emotional distress.

Usually insults do not amount to outrageous conduct, nor do words that annoy, or even statements that are mild threats. Courts understand the verbal jousting people experience in 21st-century America can cause hurt feelings. People are not always polite and considerate. The law expects people to ignore unpleasant comments. The high standard plaintiffs must meet—the defendant's conduct must be beyond all possible bounds of decency—is meant to prevent lawsuits being filed over mere insults, annoying comments and other remarks that are aggravating but not outrageous.[15] That some harms suffered in life do not rise to the level of legally actionable claims is captured in the Latin phrase *de minimus non curat lex,* "the law does not concern itself with trifles."

In addition to outrageousness, an IIED plaintiff must prove severe emotional distress caused by the defendant's action or expression. This requires more than mild annoyance or embarrassment.

Outrageousness

Media defendants win most intentional infliction of emotional distress cases primarily because courts do not find the media acted in an outrageous manner. As one federal district judge put it, "In order to make out an IIED claim the 'recitation of the facts to an average member of the community [should] arouse his resentment against the [defendant], and lead him to exclaim, 'Outrageous!'"[16]

Points of Law

Intentional Infliction of Emotional Distress

Plaintiff's Case

Defendant's intentional or reckless conduct

- Was extreme and outrageous—beyond the bounds of decency tolerated in civilized society,

- Involved actual malice, if plaintiff is a public official or public figure, and

- Caused plaintiff's severe emotional distress.

Defenses

There is no defense if plaintiff proves his or her case.

For example, there was nothing extreme or outrageous when a photographer on assignment for Harper's Magazine took a picture of a soldier's body lying in an open casket at the soldier's funeral. The soldier, who died while serving in Iraq, was the first member of the Oklahoma National Guard to be killed in action in more than 50 years. Harper's published the photograph along with others showing Americans and Iraqis mourning those killed in the war. A federal appellate court rejected a lawsuit for intentional infliction of emotional distress brought by the soldier's family, ruling that the photograph was not "so extreme and outrageous as to go beyond all possible bounds of decency."[17]

Broadcasting the identity of undercover narcotics police officers has not been found outrageous. A federal appellate court said publishing "upsetting but true news reports" is not "so extreme and outrageous as to permit recovery" in an intentional infliction of emotional distress lawsuit.[18]

Not even incorrectly suggesting a scientist sent anthrax-laced letters was deemed outrageous. In a series of newspaper columns, New York Times columnist Nicholas Kristof wrote that the Federal Bureau of Investigation (FBI) should focus on a Mr. Z in the investigation into the mailing of letters containing anthrax that caused five deaths. The columnist later identified Mr. Z as Dr. Steven J. Hatfill, a research scientist employed by the U.S. Department of Defense. Hatfill sued the Times for intentional infliction of emotional distress and other torts. A federal appellate court found Hatfill could not show that publishing the columns constituted extreme and outrageous conduct.[19] The U.S. government exonerated Hatfill in 2008 and awarded him $4.6 million to settle a lawsuit he brought against the government.[20]

realWorld Law

Dateline, Texas: To Catch a Lawsuit?

Chris Hansen

An NBC television series worked with local police departments and an online watchdog group called Perverted Justice to identify and arrest sexual predators. The program, "Dateline," used decoys posing as teenagers online to lure individuals suspected of being sexual predators to a "sting house."[1]

One target was an assistant district attorney in Texas, Louis Conradt. Conradt had been in contact with a decoy and agreed to appear at a house. But when he did not show up, the host of the television series, Chris Hansen, insisted the local police obtain arrest and search warrants on Conradt's home.[2] The police chief agreed and the warrants were ready the next day.

When the warrants were ready to be served, 10 members of the program's crew were at the home, including some who trespassed onto Conradt's property.[3] At least a dozen police officers were also present, including a SWAT team. They entered the home and announced their presence. Conradt emerged from a room holding a handgun, said he was not going to hurt anyone, then shot himself in the head. He died an hour later in a hospital.

A former detective with the local police department said, "I understand he took his own life, but I have a feeling that he took his own life when he looked out the door and saw there was a bunch of television cameras outside."[4]

Conradt's sister filed several claims against NBC, maintaining the network was responsible for her brother's death. NBC filed a motion requesting that all claims be dismissed. A U.S. district court granted the request in part but ruled the intentional infliction of emotional distress and civil rights claims could proceed to trial.[7] The court said "Dateline" "seeks to sensationalize and enhance the entertainment value" of confrontations with its targets,[5] and the "mainstay of the show is public humiliation."[6] NBC reached a settlement of the $105 million lawsuit. Terms were not disclosed.

1. Conradt v. NBC Universal, 536 F. Supp. 2d 380, 384 (S.D.N.Y. 2008).
2. *Id.* at 386.
3. *Id.*
4. Brian Stelter, *NBC Settles with Family That Blamed a TV Investigation for a Man's Suicide,* N.Y. TIMES, June 26, 2008, at C3.
5. *Conradt,* 536 F. Supp. 2d at 385.
6. *Id.*

However, plaintiffs have proved outrageousness in several intentional infliction of emotional distress cases brought against the media. Eran Best sued for intentional infliction of emotional distress based on an episode of the A&E network reality program "Female Forces." The program follows female police officers through their workday. An episode focused on the Naperville, Ill., police department. A male Naperville officer stopped Best and called for a female officer, who arrived with a "Female Forces" camera crew. The officers gave Best a field sobriety test and arrested her for driving on a suspended driver's license. They handcuffed Best, searched her car and took her to the police station, all recorded by the camera crew. In the police car, the male officer told Best her arrest would not be on "Female Forces" if she did not sign a consent form. At the police station, a "Female Forces" producer urged Best to sign. Best repeatedly refused and did not sign a consent form. Despite that, footage of her arrest appeared on "Female Forces," including the sobriety test and her being handcuffed. Best's face is visible and her voice heard. The program also included a scene in which the two officers kidded about Best's "expensive taste" while searching her car. One officer said Best "likes Coach purses, bags, and shoes." The other commented on Best's driving a Jaguar. The court held Best could show outrageousness based on the program's airing footage that included the mocking comments, knowing Best objected and ignoring the assurances given her that the footage would not be televised.[21]

Also, a Florida court ruled that showing a murdered child's skull on television was outrageous.[22] Police in Florida had determined that an unearthed skull and dress belonged to a 6-year-old child abducted three years earlier. The police chief agreed to show the skull to a television news reporter, who videotaped the chief lifting the skull from a box. Some station personnel objected to airing the tape, but the news director overruled them. The child's unsuspecting family, who had attended the child's memorial service that day, happened to be watching when the tape aired. "The close-up of the skull was intentionally included to create sensationalism for the report. The close-up was gruesome and macabre," the court said.[23] No doubt the station's conduct "was outrageous in character and exceeded the bounds of decency so as to be intolerable in a civilized community," the court said.[24] Indeed, if these facts "do not constitute the tort of outrage, then there is no such tort," the court concluded.[25]

Courts have ruled that some newsgathering techniques by themselves are outrageous. For instance, a television news reporter and cameraman approached a house next door to one where earlier in the day a woman had murdered her two small children and then committed suicide. The reporter talked with a 5 year old child, her 7-year-old sister and their 11-year-old babysitter, who were home without an adult present. The reporter asked the children what had happened next door. After the children said they knew nothing about it, the reporter said, "Well, the mom has killed the two little kids and herself." With the camera continuing to film, the reporter asked about the family next door. Although the station did not show the videotape, the children's parents sued for intentional infliction of emotional distress. Ruling in favor of the plaintiff, a California appellate court noted that the reporter approached the children suddenly and with no warning; a cameraman pointed bright lights at the children; the reporter pushed the door open; the reporter blurted out "information with emotionally devastating potential"; the children were not allowed to object to being interviewed on videotape and were too young to understand they could refuse.[26] The court said these actions could be seen as extreme and outrageous, especially because they involved children under 12 years old.

Entertainment programs as well as news reports may be the basis of intentional infliction of emotional distress cases. For example, a visitor to Howard

Nancy Grace, television host and former prosecutor, is known for her victim's rights advocacy and outspoken style.

Stern's radio program brought to the studio the cremated remains of a woman who had been a regular guest on Stern's show. Stern held up bone fragments, guessing aloud whether they came from the deceased's skull or ribs. Stern also told the guest to "chew on it," said he would "glue her together," remarked that one of the larger pieces of bone "looks like a piece of her head" and said another bone piece "looks like her ribs." The videotaped program also ran on Stern's cable television show. The woman's family sued Stern for intentional infliction of emotional distress. A New York state appellate court said the remarks were "crude" and ruled that a jury could decide that Stern's comments, combined with his handling the woman's remains for entertainment purposes, went beyond the bounds of decent behavior.[27]

A court may find remarks are extreme and outrageous if the person who made the statements knew or should have known that the plaintiff was particularly susceptible to emotional distress. For instance, after Melinda Duckett's 2-year-old son disappeared, CNN's Nancy Grace recorded a telephone conversation with Duckett. The recording was for Grace's show the following day. Just before the program aired, Duckett committed suicide. CNN ran the recording as scheduled and several times after that. Duckett's estate, her parents and her sister sued CNN and Grace for intentional infliction of emotional distress. A federal district court allowed the suit to go forward. The court said if the defendants knew Duckett already suffered emotional and psychological stress because her son had disappeared, as the plaintiffs alleged, "'the potential for severe emotional distress is enormously increased.'"[28]

Intentional or Reckless Action

In addition to proving that the defendant's actions or statements were outrageous, a plaintiff suing for intentional infliction of emotional distress must prove the defendant acted intentionally or recklessly.[29] If the defendant knew his or her actions or speech would cause emotional harm, a plaintiff can show the defendant acted intentionally. But the plaintiff does not have to show the plaintiff acted intentionally. A defendant only needed to act in a reckless way—a way that a reasonable person should have known could cause severe emotional distress.

For example, an 18-year-old girl was decapitated in an automobile accident. On Halloween, two California Highway Patrol (CHP) officers e-mailed to their friends and family nine pictures of the victim. Subsequently, the pictures went viral on the Internet. The family sued the CHP for intentional infliction of emotional distress. A California appellate court said that because the girl's father identified himself to officers at the accident scene and some people who saw the pictures on the Internet sent them, along with hateful comments, to the girl's family, the officers must have included information about the family with the

Emerging Law

Reality in Reality Programs

Ashton Kutcher

Reality programs draw large television audiences. Program participants and those who expected to be participants sometimes react in unexpected ways. One contestant committed suicide after being eliminated from "Expedition Robinson," a Swedish television show similar to "Survivor."[1] And a woman whose appearance on "Extreme Makeover" was canceled sued the program's producers, saying they had convinced her sister to make cruel remarks about the woman's appearance and the cancellation then caused her sister to commit suicide.[2]

Some reality shows trick unknowing people into dangerous or frightening situations. Most often the unwary participants get the joke and are happy to be on television. But not always. On Ashton Kutcher's MTV program "Punk'd" an unknowing couple found what appeared to be a bloody corpse on their hotel room floor. The couple sued for $10 million for intentional infliction of emotional distress and other torts.[3] A Los Angeles teacher sued for IIED after being chased by an actor in an alien costume for Sci-Fi Channel's program "Scare Tactics."[4] In another incident, an unemployed woman answered a call for an opening as a waitress. The call was from a reality program, "The Jamie Kennedy Experiment," and the restaurant was "staffed by Kennedy and his accomplices, who proceeded to engage in a mock confrontation complete with feigned injuries." The woman said she suffered severe emotional distress and sued the program producers for IIED and other torts.[5]

None of these suits went to trial; they were settled out of court. But as reality program producers use new measures to attract viewers, an outraged participant may file and win a claim for IIED. Or perhaps producers have learned caution. In 2012 NBC cancelled an episode of "Fear Factor" in which contestants were to drink glasses of donkey urine and semen to win a cash prize.[6]

1. Melody Hsiou, *Harsh Reality: When Producers and Networks Should Be Liable for Negligence and Intentional Infliction of Emotional Distress,* 23 Seton Hall J. Sports & Ent. L. 187, 213 (2013).
2. *Id.* at 194.
3. *Couple Sue over TV Corpse "Prank"* (June 13, 2002), *available at* news.bbc.co.uk.
4. Joel Michael Ugolini, *So You Want To Create the Next Survivor: What Legal Issues Networks Should Consider Before Producing a Reality Television Program,* 4 Va. Sports & Ent. L.J. 68, 83–84 (2004).
5. *Id.* at 84.
6. Hsiou, *supra* note 1, at 211–12.

photos. The plaintiffs could show, then, that the officers intentionally "directed their conduct toward" the family, causing them "severe emotional distress."[30]

Actual Malice

Public officials and public figures have an additional hurdle to overcome to win an intentional infliction of emotional distress case. The U.S. Supreme Court requires public people to prove actual malice in addition to the tort's other elements. As

realWorld Law

The "Pornographer" and His Attorney

Allan Isaacman (the attorney representing Hustler at the Supreme Court in *Hustler Magazine v. Falwell*):

Losing the intentional infliction of emotional distress [at trial] was easy to explain because Flynt, in his deposition, said he intended to assassinate the character of Falwell—tried to hurt him in his profession and that was his whole purpose. He also said in his deposition testimony that he meant it as a factual statement, and it wasn't intended to be a parody. He said he had witnesses to Falwell having sex with his mother in an outhouse. [Flynt] did everything he could to make it tough for us to win the case.

Larry Flynt (Hustler publisher):

I actually thought I was going to lose the case, and I'm not just saying that. I saw it was the preacher versus the pornographer, and I felt that there was no way I would win that case. But after being able to analyze it since, I realized what happened. First of all, had they come down on the side of Jerry Falwell, the mainstream press would have been in chaos. That means that in order to collect damages, you didn't have to prove libel, you only had to prove intentional infliction of emotional distress. So what would that do to Jay Leno's monologue or David Letterman or "Saturday Night Live"? I think that the justices could see far enough ahead to realize what a ruling the other way would have meant.[1]

1. Joseph Russomanno, Speaking Our Minds: Conversations with People Behind Landmark First Amendment Cases 179, 188 (Mahwah, N.J.: Lawrence Erlbaum Associates, 2002).

discussed in Chapter 4, in *New York Times Co. v. Sullivan* the Court defined "actual malice" as publishing with knowledge of falsity or a reckless disregard for the truth.[31] The Court's intentional infliction of emotional distress decision, in *Hustler Magazine v. Falwell*, prevented the Rev. Jerry Falwell from winning his suit against Hustler magazine's publisher, Larry Flynt.[32] Flynt published what he claimed was a parody of a Campari advertising campaign. Campari, a liquor manufacturer, published ads in which celebrities discussed their "first time," an obvious double entendre about tasting Campari and having sex.

In Flynt's satire, Falwell, the leader of a national organization named the Moral Majority, described his "first time" as being with his mother in an outhouse. The magazine portrayed Falwell, who was known for speaking out against immorality, as a hypocrite for engaging in immoral activities. Hustler included a disclaimer saying "ad parody—not to be taken seriously," and the magazine's table of contents cited the page as "Fiction—Ad and Personality Parody."

Falwell sued Flynt for libel, appropriation and intentional infliction of emotional distress. A federal district court jury rejected the libel claim because the satire was so outlandish no one would believe it was a statement of fact. And while the court also ruled that Falwell could not win on the appropriation part of his lawsuit, it allowed the emotional distress claim to proceed. At trial on that issue, a jury said Flynt intentionally inflicted emotional distress, and it awarded Falwell $100,000 in compensatory damages and $100,000 in punitive damages.[33] A federal appellate court affirmed, saying the satire was outrageous and intentionally published.[34]

But the Supreme Court reversed that decision, holding that as a public figure Falwell had to present proof of actual malice.[35] The Court found that, as satire, the magazine's Campari ad was protected by the First Amendment, just as political cartoons are. Biting, even hurtful, humor is the stock-in-trade of satirical works, the Court found, and it was simply not possible to create a constitutionally valid distinction between political cartoons and satires and the arguably tasteless Campari ad spoof. If juries were permitted to award damages for such satires, the Court warned, jurors could decide what was outrageous based on their political leanings, which would violate the First Amendment.

However, not all parodies and satires were protected, the *Falwell* Court said. A public figure or public official who could prove that a satire included a false statement of fact published with actual malice could win a lawsuit for intentional infliction of emotional distress. Because the jury in this case had found there were no factual statements in the piece—it was just a parody—Falwell could not successfully sue for intentional infliction of emotional distress.

The Court also suggested Falwell may have used intentional infliction of emotional distress as an expedient replacement for his rejected libel claim. If public figures had to prove actual malice to win libel cases, they should carry that burden for intentional infliction as well, the Court implied. In both torts, actual malice served to protect the press's First Amendment right to make caustic comments about public people.

Twenty-three years after issuing the *Falwell* decision, the U.S. Supreme Court again ruled that an IIED claim infringed the First Amendment. The Court said in 2011 that speech about matters of public concern, even if "particularly hurtful" expression, is protected against an IIED lawsuit.[36] In *Snyder v. Phelps,* protesters from Westboro Baptist Church of Topeka, Kansas, picketed the funeral of a Marine killed in action in Iraq. Westboro's 75 congregants, most of whom are church founder Fred Phelps' family members, believe "God hates and punishes the United States for its tolerance of homosexuality, particularly in America's military," according to the Court.[37] The group expresses its views by picketing, frequently near military funerals. Phelps and six of his family picketed 1,000 feet from the hometown Catholic church for 30 minutes before the Marine's funeral. They displayed signs saying, for example, "God Hates the USA/Thank God for 9/11," "America is Doomed," "Don't Pray for the USA," "Thank God for

Points of Law

Parody or Satire?

The Supreme Court has explained that there is a difference between "parody" (in which the copyrighted work is the target) and "satire" (in which the copyrighted work is merely used to poke fun at another target): "Parody needs to mimic an original to make its point, and so has some claim to use the creation of its victim's (or collective victims') imagination, whereas satire can stand on its own two feet and so requires justification for the very act of borrowing."[1]

1. Campbell v. Acuff-Rose Music, 510 U.S. 569, 580–81 (1994).

Jerry Falwell talks about his first time.*

FALWELL: My first time was in an outhouse outside Lynchburg, Virginia.

INTERVIEWER: Wasn't it a little cramped?

FALWELL: Not after I kicked the goat out.

INTERVIEWER: I see. You must tell me all about it.

FALWELL: I never *really* expected to make it with Mom, but then after she showed all the other guys in town such a good time, I figured, "What the hell!"

INTERVIEWER: But your mom? Isn't that a bit odd?

FALWELL: I don't think so. Looks don't mean that much to me in a woman.

INTERVIEWER: Go on.

FALWELL: Well, we were drunk off our God-fearing asses on Campari, ginger ale and soda—that's called a Fire and Brimstone—at the time. And Mom looked better than a Baptist whore with a $100 donation.

INTERVIEWER: Campari in the crapper with Mom . . . how interesting. Well, how was it?

FALWELL: The Campari was great, but Mom passed out before I could come.

INTERVIEWER: Did you ever try it again?

FALWELL: Sure . . .

lots of times. But not in the outhouse. Between Mom and the shit, the flies were too much to bear.

INTERVIEWER: We meant the Campari.

FALWELL: Oh, yeah. I always get sloshed before I go out to the pulpit. You don't think I could lay down all that bullshit *sober*, do you?

© 1983 – Imported by Campari U.S.A., New York, NY 48°proof Spirit Aperitif (Liqueur)

Campari, like all liquor, was made to mix you up. It's a light, 48-proof, refreshing spirit, just mild enough to make you drink too much before you know you're schnockered. For your first time, mix it with orange juice. Or maybe some white wine. Then you won't remember anything the next morning. **Campari. The mixable that smarts.**

CAMPARI® **You'll never forget your first time.**

*AD PARODY—NOT TO BE TAKEN SERIOUSLY

The satire that prompted Jerry Falwell to sue Larry Flynt and Hustler magazine.

IEDs," "Thank God for Dead Soldiers," "Pope in Hell" and "Priests Rape Boys." Another sign said "God Hates Fags," although the Marine was not gay. Only the tops of the signs were visible to those in the funeral procession as it passed close to the protesters. Later that evening, while watching a televised news report about the demonstration, the Marine's father, Albert Snyder, saw what the signs said.

Snyder sued for IIED and other torts. He said several of the signs, such as those saying "You're Going to Hell" and "God Hates You," were directed at him. The trial court dismissed the libel and private facts claims, saying Snyder could not prove the required elements. Westboro appealed the multimillion-dollar jury award for the IIED and other claims. The U.S. Court of Appeals for the Fourth Circuit reversed, holding that the First Amendment protected Westboro's statements because they dealt with matters of public concern, could not be proven false and were hyperbole.[38]

The U.S. Supreme Court agreed with the appellate court. Westboro's signs related to matters of public concern and, as *New York Times v. Sullivan* emphasized, the First Amendment stands for "a profound national commitment to the principle that debate on public issues should be uninhibited, robust, and wide-open," the Court ruled.[39] "Speech deals with matters of public concern when it can 'be fairly considered as relating to any matter of political, social, or other concern to the community,'" according to the Court.[40] Also how, where and when the speech was delivered must be examined to determine whether the expression involves matters of public concern, the Court said. Westboro's signs dealt with homosexuals' rights, homosexuality in the military and priests abusing children. These are public issues, the Court said. The context was not targeted picketing aimed at, for example, someone's residence. Rather, the demonstrators were 1,000 feet from the funeral standing on public property adjacent to a public street, consequently expressing themselves in a public forum. Nor did Westboro use threatening language, fighting words or other unprotected language. Citing *Hustler Magazine v. Falwell,* the Court said the First Amendment may be a defense against an intentional infliction of emotional distress claim.

In response to the *Snyder* decision, Congress adopted a law forbidding protests two hours before or after a military funeral and demonstrations closer than 300 feet from such funerals with a possible award of $50,000 in statutory damages.[41]

The Court did not decide whether expression directed to a private individual or disorderly demonstrations would be protected against an IIED claim even if the content addressed matters of public concern. The *Snyder* Court said it did not consider whether the Marine's father was a public or private figure. Had he been found a public figure he would have had to prove actual malice, as the Court said in *Falwell.* But in *Snyder* the Court said the Westboro picketers were aiming their expression at the general public, not at Albert Snyder or his family in particular. Because the expression was about matters of public concern and was directed toward a broad audience, the speech was protected regardless of what elements Snyder had to prove to win an IIED lawsuit.

Cyberstalking

Physically stalking a person may violate criminal law but also may cause the victim severe emotional distress. New technologies provide new ways of stalking. As one legal commentator wrote, "With access to . . . interactive communication tools, stalkers can easily find an individual's personal information and use it to harass, annoy, or threaten people online—cyberstalking. . . . [R]ecent statistics suggest that nearly a quarter of all stalking victims report some form of cyberstalking, which means that roughly 850,000 people are cyberstalked each year."[42]

To combat this, Congress amended a federal law to make it illegal to intentionally cause someone substantial emotional distress through online means.[43] The Interstate Stalking Statute criminalizes expression that could cause emotional distress. The statute thus curbs speech, which might abridge First Amendment rights. Courts agree the law is constitutional as written, but not always as applied. In one case, a man used nearly 8,000 tweets on Twitter and a number of blog entries directed at the plaintiff, a Buddhist leader. A federal district court ruled the victim was a public figure and the tweets and blogs related to her religious role, challenging her qualifications to be a religious leader. Although the statements may have caused severe emotional distress, the court ruled the First Amendment protected the online entries.[44]

The facts differed, however, when a victim's former boyfriend "created fictitious internet advertisements and social media profiles using [the victim's] name and other identifying information, . . . and invited men to come to her home for sexual encounters [and] posted video clips to several adult pornography websites depicting sexual acts [the victim] had consensually performed with him during their relationship."[45] Many men came to the victim's home seeking sexual encounters, "terrifying her and causing her to fear that she would be raped or assaulted."[46] The various posts, the court said, "involve no political or religious speech or the promotion of ideas of any sort. Instead, [the online speech was] integral to [the accused's] criminal conduct seeking to injure, harass or cause substantial emotional distress to the victim."[47] The court concluded that the Interstate Stalking Statute is not unconstitutional when applied to this type of speech.[48]

Twenty-nine states have laws making cyberstalking illegal.[49] All but seven states make cyberharassment a crime.[50]

SUMMARY

EXTREME OR OUTRAGEOUS CONDUCT THAT IS DONE either intentionally or recklessly and results in severe emotional harm may amount to intentional infliction of emotional distress. The most important element is the defendant's actions. Outrageous actions, defined as being beyond all bounds of decency, may lead to successful intentional infliction of emotional distress suits. A plaintiff who is especially susceptible to emotional harm may successfully sue if the defendant knew of the plaintiff's vulnerability. In addition to proving outrageous intentional or reckless conduct and severe emotional harm, public officials and public figures must show the defendant acted with actual malice to win an intentional infliction of emotional distress case. The First Amendment protects speech on matters of public concern from a successful intentional infliction of emotional distress suit. Also, the First Amendment likely will not allow successful IIED suits based on satires and parodies. In a few instances, journalists and media personalities have lost intentional infliction of emotional distress lawsuits in cases not involving public plaintiffs. The Federal Interstate Stalking Statute makes it a criminal act to intentionally cause another person severe emotional distress using interactive communication media. The statute does not apply if the First Amendment protects the expression. ■

Negligent Infliction of Emotional Distress

If one person accidentally causes another emotional harm, the injured person may sue using a tort called "negligent infliction of emotional distress." The law asks whether the defendant should have anticipated that her or his careless action would injure the plaintiff. More formally, a plaintiff suing for negligent infliction of emotional distress must prove (1) the defendant had a duty to use due care, (2) the defendant negligently breached that duty, (3) the breach caused the plaintiff's injury, and (4) the breach was the proximate cause of the plaintiff's severe emotional distress.[51]

A "duty of due care" means the defendant should have foreseen that negligence could cause harm to the person or people to whom he or she owed a duty. Breaching the duty means the defendant did not act as a reasonable person would. Causing the plaintiff's emotional distress means the defendant's actions were the direct reason the plaintiff was emotionally harmed. This may be called "cause-in-fact." Proximate cause is the law's way of asking if it is reasonable to conclude the defendant caused the plaintiff's injury. Negligent infliction of emotional distress suits against the media often turn on the proximate cause question. Courts usually find that actions taken by a media organization are only tangentially related to the plaintiff's injury. If the connection between what the organization did and how the plaintiff was injured is too indirect to find the mass medium responsible, the plaintiff cannot prove proximate cause.

Courts in some states also require plaintiffs to show a degree of physical harm.[52] The harm may be that the defendant physically injured (or even just touched) the plaintiff, causing emotional harm, or that the defendant caused emotional harm resulting in physical symptoms.[53] The plaintiff's problem is convincing courts that an emotional distress claim is real. Courts agree the negligent infliction of emotional distress tort is caught between two important concerns. First, the law wants to compensate people whose emotional injuries are caused by others' negligence. But second, judges want to avoid suits for trivial, de minimus, harms or fraudulent emotional harm claims.[54] These competing interests have "caused inconsistency and incoherence in the law," one court said.[55]

The competing interests are reflected in two approaches applicable to suits against the media for negligent infliction of emotional distress. Some jurisdictions require proof that physical harm caused emotional injury, or vice versa. Examples include not being able to sleep, having an upset stomach, experiencing weight loss or not being able to work.[56] Either way, to be sure the emotional injury is real, courts in these jurisdictions want proof of a physical injury connected with emotional distress.

Other jurisdictions require proof that the defendant acted negligently and that it was reasonably foreseeable such conduct would cause the plaintiff severe emotional distress. These courts do not require a physical injury or a subsequent

Points of Law

Negligent Infliction of Emotional Distress

Plaintiff's Case

- The defendant had a duty to use due care
- Negligently breached that duty
- Causing the plaintiff's severe emotional distress, and
- The breach was the proximate cause of the plaintiff's emotional distress.

Defense

There is no defense if plaintiff proves the case.

physical manifestation of emotional distress.[57] Under this scheme, plaintiffs can allege negligent infliction of emotional distress if it accompanies another tort, such as defamation or invasion of privacy.[58]

Negligent infliction of emotional distress suits against the media usually fail. However, two cases show plaintiffs can be successful if the court does not require a physical injury to be connected with emotional harm. In one instance, a television station produced a report about rape. Station employees asked two rape victims if they would consent to interviews, promising to disguise the women's faces and voices. The women agreed to participate, but after seeing a promotional ad about the program the employer of one of the rape victims recognized her face and voice. After the first interview ran, friends of the second rape victim said they recognized her, particularly through her voice. One of the women complained to the station and the producers assured her that future broadcasts would better disguise the interviewees. Nevertheless, both women were again recognized in the next program, which failed to disguise their voices and included a brief shot of one victim's face. The women said they were emotionally distraught. A New York state appellate court allowed them to sue for negligent infliction of emotional distress.[59]

In a second case, in preparing a directory for the 15-year reunion of a Yale University class, the school's Alumni Records Office mailed questionnaires to the graduates. One returned questionnaire included a graduate's name along with the statement "I have come to terms with my homosexuality and the reality of AIDS in my life. I am at peace." The questionnaire response was a hoax; it was not completed by the person named on the questionnaire. However, the directory mailed to the graduates included the plaintiff's name along with the incorrect information. The person named on the hoax questionnaire sued Yale for negligent infliction of emotional distress. A federal district court held that a jury could find Yale had a duty to carefully review personal statements and to confirm whether unusual statements were valid.[60] A jury could find Yale acted negligently by not checking the questionnaires, the court said. A reasonable person could foresee that someone might submit a false questionnaire that would cause severe emotional injury. The court allowed the graduate to proceed with a suit for negligent infliction of emotional distress.

Plaintiffs also have successfully sued for negligent infliction of emotional distress when the media have put them in harm's way. For example, after a woman had been physically attacked, but before the assailant was apprehended by police, a newspaper published the woman's name and address. After the newspaper published the article, the assailant terrorized his victim several more times. A Missouri appellate court upheld the victim's negligent infliction of emotional distress suit.[61]

Similarly, a woman witnessed a murder. A newspaper published her name while the murderer remained at large. A California appellate court ruled that the First Amendment did not protect the newspaper against the witness's negligent infliction of emotional distress lawsuit.[62]

SUMMARY

A PLAINTIFF MAY SUCCESSFULLY SUE FOR INFLICTION of emotional distress, even if caused accidentally, if the defendant acted negligently. A plaintiff suing for negligent infliction of emotional distress must prove the defendant had a duty of due care and breached that duty, causing the plaintiff's severe emotional distress, and that there is proximate cause to find the defendant liable for the tort. Some states require that physical harm accompany emotional trauma. In some jurisdictions even slight touching of the plaintiff will be enough. In some other states it is sufficient that another tort, such as libel or privacy, cause the emotional harm. Most jurisdictions find the media do not owe a duty to individuals because the media cannot know what particular individuals will hear or see the mass medium. ∎

Physical Harm

Americans have been concerned for 90 years about media violence causing real-life violence. Movies were the focus in the 1920s, comic books in the 1950s, music lyrics in the 1990s and video games in the early 21st century.[63] A Federal Trade Commission (FTC) report concluded the video game, music recording and movie industries market and advertise products with violent content to children. The report said researchers "generally have agreed that exposure to violence in entertainment media alone does not cause a child to commit a violent act and that it is not the sole, or even necessarily the most important, factor contributing to youth aggression." But the report recognized that studies show "a high correlation between exposure to media violence and aggressive and, at times, violent behavior."[64] A recent follow-up to this study found the movie and video game industries showed progress in limiting marketing of violent products to children, but the music recording industry's marketing practices had not changed significantly.[65] The American Academy of Pediatrics (AAP), a physicians group, said in 2011, "When it comes to teen violence . . . there is sufficient research to establish that TV influences youthful behavior. Since 1955, more than one thousand studies have substantiated that for some adolescents, frequent exposure to television violence contributes to overly aggressive behavior."[66]

Despite the AAP's view, there is little agreement on how much television, video games, recordings and movies influence children and teenagers to be violent.[67] Faced with inconclusive research results, courts nonetheless are asked to make a connection between media content and physical violence. The media have been blamed—and sued—for encouraging people to injure or kill others.[68] For example, a mother claimed a role-playing game had caused a young person to kill her son, and a family contended a movie had inspired two young people to engage in a killing spree. Lawsuits also claim people injure or kill themselves because of media content. Media violence cases may arise from copycat situations—the plaintiff arguing that injury resulted from imitating media content such as that in the movies "Natural Born Killers" and "The Basketball Diaries," and video games such as "Doom" and "Mortal Kombat." No suit has been brought against a video game manufacturer or movie, recording or television producer claiming they caused Jared Loughner in Tucson, James Holmes in Aurora, Colo., or Adam Lanza in Newtown, Conn., to commit multiple murders. However, commentators have suggested connections between an obsession with one or more of these media and the mass murders.[69]

A pattern of lawsuits began 35 years ago. When he was 13 years old, Ronny Zamora shot and killed his 83-year-old neighbor. Zamora's parents sued the major television networks—ABC, CBS and NBC. The parents claimed their son "became involuntarily addicted to and 'completely subliminally intoxicated' by the extensive viewing of television violence." They said the networks failed to exercise "ordinary care to prevent Ronny Zamora from being 'impermissibly stimulated, incited and instigated' to duplicate the atrocities he viewed on television."[70] In 1979 a federal district court said the networks could not be held responsible for Zamora's actions.

Media violence lawsuits often are not successful. Courts usually find the media did not act negligently or did not intend to cause harm. However, recently some jurisdictions have refused to dismiss suits alleging that the media caused injury or death.

Negligence

Plaintiffs suing the media for causing physical harm most often argue the defendants negligently distributed material leading to injury or death. These suits are based on the tort of negligence, discussed earlier in this chapter. The plaintiff must show the media defendant had a duty of due care, negligently breached that duty, caused the plaintiff's physical injury and proximately caused the injury.

For example, the *Zamora* court rejected the argument that television networks had a duty to stop making violent programs available to the public. The court said it would be against public policy to require networks to determine what would be too violent and against the networks' First Amendment rights to limit their ability to provide their audiences a breadth of programming.[71]

Leonardo DiCaprio starred as Jim Carroll in "The Basketball Diaries," a movie alleged to have inspired illegal acts. Lawsuits against the movie's producers have not been successful.

Similarly, a court did not find a television network negligent when a young girl was raped after a television film showed a rape scene. NBC aired the film "Born Innocent." Set in a girls' reformatory, the film implied that four inmates used a toilet plunger to rape another girl. Four days later a 9-year-old girl suffered a similar attack, being raped with a bottle, at a San Francisco beach. The girl's parents sued NBC and the San Francisco station that broadcast the movie, claiming the defendants were negligent in showing the movie when children could watch it. A state appellate court said the First Amendment did not allow the argument that NBC had a duty to the raped girl.[72] Finding NBC negligent would cause television networks to engage in self-censorship, the court said.

Foreseeability To determine whether a defendant had a duty to the plaintiff, courts often ask whether the defendant should have foreseen the plaintiff's injury. This means that if the person should have anticipated an action would cause harm, the person had a duty to protect others. But if a reasonable person could not have foreseen the harm, there is no duty. In a case arising from the 1999 shooting deaths of 12 students and one teacher at Columbine High School in Littleton, Colo., the family of the murdered teacher, William Sanders, sued video game and movie producers. The Sanders family said the student shooters, Eric Harris and Dylan Klebold, copied what they had seen in the movie "The Basketball Diaries," which includes a dream sequence of a high school student killing his teacher and several classmates. The family said Harris and Klebold also played a number of video games, such as "Mortal Kombat," "Mech Warrior," "Nightmare Creatures," "Doom," "Quake" and "Redneck Rampage." A federal district court rejected the suit, saying the media defendants did not have an obligation to protect Sanders.[73] The movie producers and game manufacturers could not have foreseen Harris and Klebold would commit illegal acts, the court ruled. The movie and video game producers, then, did not have a duty and so were not negligent. In a similar case, a federal appellate court held there was insufficient proof that video game, movie production and Internet companies should have foreseen that their products could lead a 14-year-old boy to shoot several of his fellow high school students.[74] After arresting Michael Carneal for killing three people and wounding several more, police found that Carneal regularly had played violent interactive computer games, visited pornographic Internet sites and owned a videotape of the movie "The Basketball Diaries." The dead students' families and the wounded students sued the media companies, contending that Carneal's actions were a reaction to the violent media representations. The court said even if the contention were true, the defendants could not have foreseen Carneal's response to the violent images. It is "simply too far a leap from shooting characters on a video screen . . . to shooting people in a classroom," the court said.[75] The defendants did not owe the students a duty of care because Carneal's actions were unforeseeable.

Three cases, all tied to classified advertisements in the magazine Soldier of Fortune, show how courts use the foreseeability element to determine whether the defendant had a duty. Soldier of Fortune publishes stories about hunting, war and guns. The magazine appeals to "a male who owns camouflage clothing and more than one gun."[76] In each decision, a court considered whether it was foreseeable that the ad would lead to physical injury. The magazine won the case in which a judge ruled criminal activity was not foreseeable. Plaintiffs won the two cases in which courts said physical harm was foreseeable.

In the first case, *Norwood v. Soldier of Fortune Magazine,* two people each published an advertisement. Michael Savage's ad said, "GUN FOR HIRE: 37 year old professional mercenary desires jobs. Vietnam Veteran. Discreet and very private. Bodyguard, courier, and other special skills. All jobs considered." The second ad said, "GUN FOR HIRE. NAM sniper instructor. SWAT. Pistol, rifle, security specialist, body guard, courier plus. All jobs considered, Privacy guaranteed." Norman Norwood claimed Larry Gray, and others Gray contacted through Savage's ad, conspired to kill Norwood. Several unsuccessful attempts on Norwood's life resulted in physical injuries, he said. A federal district court rejected the magazine's argument that its First Amendment rights protected publishing the ads.[77] The court said free speech is not absolute. Plaintiffs may recover damages if speech causes injuries. In refusing to throw out Norwood's suit, as Soldier of Fortune requested, the court said a jury could find the ads "had a substantial probability of ultimately causing harm to some individuals."[78] The magazine had a duty of due care because it was foreseeable that the ads could lead to physical injury.

In the second case, *Eimann v. Soldier of Fortune Magazine,* a federal appellate court took a different view of an advertisement.[79] John Wayne Hearn's Soldier of Fortune ad said, "EX-MARINES—67–69 'Nam Vets, Ex-DI, weapons specialist—jungle warfare, pilot, M.E., high risk assignments, U.S. or overseas." Hearn testified that he hoped the ad would bring an offer to train troops in South America. However, when Robert Black saw the ad and offered Hearn $10,000 to kill Black's wife, Hearn accepted and murdered Sandra Black. Sandra Black's mother and son sued the magazine. A jury found that Soldier of Fortune breached its duty, resulting in Sandra Black's death. The jury awarded $9.4 million in damages. The appellate court reversed. The magazine had "no duty to refrain from publishing a facially innocuous classified advertisement when the ad's context— at most—made its message ambiguous," the court held.[80] The magazine's burden in investigating all its advertisers and their ads to prevent criminal solicitation would be much greater than the unlikely possibility that an ad may result in physical harm. A reasonable person would not have foreseen that the ad might cause physical harm, the court ruled.

Finally, *Braun v. Soldier of Fortune* involved another Michael Savage ad, one identical to the ad in the *Norwood* case.[81] In this instance, a man contacted Savage through the ad and arranged to have Savage kill the man's business partner. Savage and others committed the murder. The murdered man's family sued the magazine. A jury awarded $12.4 million, which the trial judge reduced to $4.4 million. The jury properly found that "the advertisement on its face would have alerted a reasonably prudent publisher to the clearly identifiable risk of harm to the public" the ad posed, a federal appellate court held.[82] The court said that while Soldier of Fortune did not have a duty to investigate every ad submitted for publication, it was obligated to determine whether, based on the ad's language, publishing the ad would create an unreasonable risk of causing violent crime.

Plaintiffs rarely are successful when suing the media for injury caused by false information. For example, a book publisher had no obligation to confirm the accuracy of all information in a book about mushrooms, a federal appellate court held, although people became seriously ill after eating mushrooms the book said were edible.[83]

Proximate Cause A plaintiff bringing a negligence suit must prove it is reasonable to find that the defendant caused the plaintiff's harm. A court decides if there is a direct relationship between the defendant's action and the plaintiff's injury. This direct relationship is called **proximate cause.** In one case, a teenager committed suicide while listening to an Ozzy Osbourne album that includes the song "Suicide Solution." The song's lyrics say, in part, "Suicide is the only way out." The teenager's parents sued Osbourne and his record company. A California appellate court said there was not a close connection between the recording and the suicide.[84] The court noted that Osbourne had composed and recorded the song years before the teenager's death. That made the connection between the recording and the suicide too tenuous to show proximate cause.[85] It was not reasonable to blame Osbourne for the teenager's death.

A connection between a defendant's actions and a plaintiff's injuries can be broken by unanticipated incidents. Courts often refuse to find proximate cause if there is an unforeseeable event intervening between the defendant's act and the plaintiff's later physical injury. In one case a mother whose son committed suicide sued the manufacturer of "Dungeons & Dragons," a game in which players assume roles in adventures illustrated in booklets.[86] The mother said her son lost touch with reality because of his devotion to the game. However, the child's suicide was an independent action, a federal appellate court said, not caused by playing the game. That is, the child's decision to commit suicide was an intervening cause between playing the games and the child's taking his life.

proximate cause Determining whether it is reasonable to conclude the defendant's actions led to the plaintiff's injury.

Points of Law

Proximate Cause

In a negligence case, the plaintiff must prove both "cause" and "proximate cause." Cause is straightforward. If the defendant's actions led to the plaintiff's injury, the defendant caused the injury. But courts do not say every defendant who caused an injury is liable. That is because the plaintiff may not be able to prove the second element: proximate cause.

SUMMARY

PLAINTIFFS SUING THE MEDIA FOR CAUSING PHYSICAL injury or death may claim the media were negligent. To establish liability, the plaintiff must prove the defendant had a duty of care that was breached and that the breach was the proximate cause of physical harm. Courts may decide whether the defendant had a duty of care by determining whether a reasonable person would have foreseen the resulting harm. Courts also must be convinced the defendant caused the plaintiff's harm. Proximate cause is the most difficult element to prove. Proximate cause means it is reasonable to find the defendant responsible for causing the plaintiff's harm. ■

Incitement

An alternative to showing that a media defendant acted negligently is to prove the defendant incited harm. First Amendment scholar David Anderson suggests that the two legal concepts—negligence and incitement—are related rather than separate.[87] Anderson says courts first should determine whether a plaintiff is able to prove that a mass medium's negligence caused physical injury. If the plaintiff cannot prove negligence, the defendant wins and the case is over. But if the plaintiff can prove all elements of the negligence tort, the defendant then will claim First Amendment protection. To counter the defendant's argument, the plaintiff will insist that the incitement test removes the First Amendment shield, Anderson says. That is, the First Amendment does not protect communication that incites harm.

However, jurisdictions using the incitement test often skip the negligence analysis. Many courts go straight to deciding if the mass medium intentionally meant for harm to happen and whether imminent harm likely would result from the defendant's actions.

As discussed in Chapter 3, the U.S. Supreme Court established the incitement test in its *Brandenburg v. Ohio* and *Hess v. Indiana* decisions. In *Brandenburg,* a Ku Klux Klan leader was arrested and convicted for declaring at a Klan rally that "revengeance" might have to be taken against politicians and for making a number of derogatory remarks about African-Americans and Jews. The U.S. Supreme Court overturned the conviction. The Court said the government may not punish advocacy unless it is "directed to inciting or producing imminent lawless action and is likely to incite or produce such action."[88]

In the second case, at an anti–Vietnam War rally Gregory Hess used profane language in saying that the crowd should wait until a later time to take over a public street. Hess made his remark after sheriff's officers moved demonstrators from the street to the sidewalks. The sheriff overheard Hess, who was not talking to the gathering generally or to anyone in particular, and arrested him for disorderly conduct. A jury convicted Hess. The U.S. Supreme Court overturned the verdict, holding that the First Amendment protected Hess' comments because his words were not intended to, and not likely to, provoke an imminent violation of the law.[89]

If a court uses the incitement test when a mass medium is sued for causing physical harm, a plaintiff likely will not win. With rare exceptions, such as the "Hit Man" case discussed later in this chapter, courts have not found that a mass media defendant incited physical injury.[90] Plaintiffs generally have not convinced courts that media companies intentionally encourage people to harm themselves or others after being exposed to media content.

Emerging Law

Media Incitement

Cases in which media producers were sued on the grounds that content caused consumers to harm themselves or others all involved older technologies: audiotapes, movies shown in theaters, television programs, video games using joy sticks and push buttons. Technology has changed very quickly since those court decisions with the advent of digitization and the Internet. Now music and video are streamed, and "controllerless gaming systems . . . allow the gamer to engage in a full-body simulation within the game." A player's movements "are mirrored by her avatar on the screen," allowing direct interaction with the "gaming environment."[1]

Will these technological changes convince courts to find that video game and other media producers meet the *Brandenburg* test for incitement (see Chapter 3)? One legal commentator thinks it is possible. First, does the media content producer intend to incite others to illegal action? It is likely the content producer did not intend to incite anyone considering the bad publicity and possible lawsuits that would follow. But could a court or jury find that the content and context implied incitement? Second, did the content cause immediate violence or illegal action? Ubiquitous access to digitized content means people can engage with material that might incite them anywhere, anytime on a smartphone, tablet or laptop computer and imminent action can follow. Third, is it likely illegal action will occur? Perhaps it is likely as content becomes more graphic, more abrasive, violent, controversial and immersive. Although it also may be that the more a person consumes such content, the less it affects a person.[2]

No court yet has considered a lawsuit involving digital media, the Internet and/or streaming in which a content producer is said to have incited violence. But such a case is certain to arise, likely sooner than later.

---

1. Jennifer Jones, *Evolving Entertainment Technology: Can New Types of Fun Lead to New Types of Liability?* 13 Yale J. L. & Tech. 188, 205 (2011).
2. *Id.* at 210–12.

Intending to Incite The *Brandenburg/Hess* incitement test requires a plaintiff to show that the media defendant intentionally meant to cause harm. Courts consistently reject this notion. For example, two people robbed a convenience store. During the robbery the store clerk was shot and seriously wounded. The clerk claimed the movie "Natural Born Killers" inspired her assailants. The woman who shot the store clerk admitted the movie motivated her and her boyfriend to commit violence. The film portrays a man and a woman engaging in a crime spree, killing people they do not know, and being glorified by the media after they are apprehended. The film's characters then foment a prison riot during which they escape from prison.[91] A state appellate court dismissed the store clerk's lawsuit.[92] The movie may exalt and glamorize violence, the court said, but the movie's fantasy violence did not urge or encourage viewers to engage in unlawful or violent activity. Nor did the movie order or command anyone to immediately commit a crime. The incitement test cannot be met without proving that the movie producers intentionally urged immediate unlawful activity, the court held.

In another case, Hustler magazine published an article titled "Orgasm of Death," describing autoerotic asphyxiation. A 14-year-old boy accidentally hanged himself in his closet with a copy of Hustler on the floor open to the story.

realWorld Law

Cyberbullying

Sarah Drew (left) and mother, Lori Drew (right), leave the US Federal Courthouse in Los Angeles after the MySpace suicide trial. The case ended with three guilty verdicts against the Missouri mother who created a fake MySpace account, which she used to torment 13-year old Megan Meier, who committed suicide.

Megan Meier, 13 years old, and Sarah Drew were classmates in 2006. Sarah's mother, Lori, used MySpace to establish a profile for a nonexistent 16-year-old boy whom Lori Drew called Josh Evans. The profile included a photograph of a boy posted without that boy's knowledge or approval. Using Josh's MySpace, Drew contacted Megan, flirted with her, then said he was moving away, no longer liked her and that "the world would be a better place without her in it." The day those comments were posted, Megan committed suicide by hanging herself with a belt. Federal prosecutors charged Drew with violating the Computer Fraud and Abuse Act (CFAA)[1] that makes it illegal to use a computer in excess of authorization to commit a crime or tort. The prosecutors said Drew violated MySpace's rules prohibiting posting of anything that "harasses or advocates harassment of another person, solicits personal information from anyone under 18, provides information that you know is false or misleading, or includes a photograph of another person that you have posted without that person's consent." At trial, the jury cleared Drew of the most serious charges but found her guilty of three misdemeanors. The trial judge, however, found the CFAA vague and dismissed all charges against Drew.[2]

In response to Megan's suicide, nine states have made cyberbullying criminal.[3] Texas' 2009 statute makes it illegal (1) to use another's name without permission, (2) to create a website, open a profile on a social networking site or send a digital communication, such as an e-mail message, (3) intending to harm, defraud, intimidate or threaten another person. The law also forbids sending a digital communication that includes, without permission, another's name, domain address, phone number or other identifying information.[4]

---

1. 18 U.S.C. § 1030.
2. United States v. Drew, 259 F.R.D. 449 (C.D. Calif. 2009).
3. Alabama, Alaska, Arkansas, Georgia, Idaho, Louisiana, Nevada, North Carolina and Texas have adopted statutes making cyberbullying a criminal activity. RonNell Anderson Jones & Lyrissa Barnett Lidslay, *Recent Developments in the Law of Social Media Communications,* 3 COMM. L. IN THE DIGITAL AGE 2012, at 17, 121–50 (2012).
4. Tex. Penal Code § 33.07.

The boy's parents sued Hustler, but a federal appellate court held that the article did not incite the boy's actions.[93] The court said not only did the magazine not urge readers to perform the act described but repeatedly warned not to attempt autoerotic asphyxiation.

Courts have not found incitement even when the media knew criminal activity might be related to media content. For example, Paramount Pictures continued distributing the movie "The Warriors" despite knowing about two killings near California theaters that showed the film. The movie includes many scenes of young people fighting with guns, knives and other weapons. Two days after the California murders, a teenager was stabbed and killed by another youth after leaving a showing of "The Warriors" in Boston. The murdered boy's father sued Paramount, claiming the movie producer incited violence by keeping the movie in circulation despite knowing it caused criminal activity. Massachusetts' highest court held that the film's fictional portrayal of gang warfare did not constitute incitement.[94] The movie did not advocate violent or unlawful acts, the court said, and therefore it retained its First Amendment protection.

In the only decision of its kind, a court said a book publisher encouraged a murderer.[95] The publisher said it intended for criminals to purchase and use a book, "Hit Man: A Technical Manual for Independent Contractors," to plan and carry out real murders. When a contract killer did just that, a federal appellate court said the book publisher had aided and abetted murder. The court said the First Amendment did not protect media that aid in the commission of a crime. In this case, after Paladin Press published "Hit Man," James Perry bought and read it. Acting as a contract killer, Perry mimicked the book's detailed, graphic instructions almost to the letter in brutally murdering a woman, her 8-year-old quadriplegic son and the son's nurse. The victims' relatives sued Paladin Press.

Paladin Press argued that because the First Amendment completely protected it, the publisher could not be responsible for any crimes connected to "Hit Man." The appellate court rejected Paladin's argument, saying that "every court that has addressed the issue" agrees the First Amendment does not necessarily prevent finding a mass medium liable for assisting a crime, even if that aid "takes the form of the spoken or written word."[96] After the court's ruling and before the trial began, Paladin Press settled the case for $5 million.[97]

Imminent Lawless Action The incitement test requires a plaintiff to show that media content would result in violent or unlawful activity immediately after the criminal was exposed to it. That is nearly impossible to prove in court. The *Brandenburg* and *Hess* decisions were meant to protect speech unless a speaker so inflamed a crowd that people responded to their emotions and immediately committed illegal acts. Media content does not ordinarily provoke such a rapid response. After seeing, reading or hearing media material, there is time to think before taking action, even time to have someone else prevent a person from committing violent acts.

For example, after a young friend stabbed to death a 13-year-old boy, the murdered child's mother sued the manufacturers of "Mortal Kombat," a video game. The mother claimed the murderer's addiction to the game made him believe he was one of the game's characters, causing him to stab her son. Using the incitement test, a federal district court said even if the game caused the boy's death, the game's advocacy of violence was no more than urging illegal action at some indefinite future time.[98] The incitement test requires that the media content cause "imminent" lawless action—a crime directly and immediately connected with the content. The court said the murdered boy's mother could not show a connection between "Mortal Kombat" and her son's death, so she could not win her case.

realWorld Law

"Hit Man": Protected or Not?

James Edward Perry forced his way into Mildred Horn's home and killed her, her 8-year-old quadriplegic son and the son's nurse. Horn's former husband, Lawrence, had hired Perry to commit the murders so that Lawrence Horn would inherit the $1.7 million the son had received to settle a medical malpractice lawsuit. Perry, sentenced to death for committing the murders, said he followed instructions in a book, "Hit Man: A Technical Manual for Independent Contractors." The book clearly explains how to commit a murder. The U.S. Court of Appeals for the Fourth Circuit said the First Amendment did not protect the book's publisher from a lawsuit for aiding and abetting the murders.[1]

One view is that the Fourth Circuit's decision was wrong. The court should have applied the *Brandenburg v. Ohio* test: Speech that advocates committing an unlawful act is protected unless it is "directed to inciting or producing imminent lawless action and was likely to incite or produce such action."[2] As one law review article noted, of the 13,000 copies of "Hit Man" sold, only one is known to be a guidebook for an actual murder. "This correlates to less than a one-ten-thousandth of a percent (.0001%) chance that the book actually incited imminent lawless activity and strongly suggests that such activity was not likely to occur from reading this book."[3] Also, Perry committed the murders a year after reading the book, hardly the "*imminent* lawless activity" required by the *Brandenburg* test.[4]

Alternatively, "Hit Man" may be called a recipe book with clearly defined instructions that provide "otherwise missing information needed to commit a crime," combining "description with details that amount to instructions" with "a detailed road map for violence."[5] How could such a book be anything but incitement? The Fourth Circuit was correct, according to this view.

Which is the better analysis? The decision is excerpted at the end of this chapter.

---

1. *See* Gregory Akselrun, Note: *Hit Man: The Fourth Circuit's Mistake in* Rice v. Paladin Enters., Inc., 19 Loy. L.A. Ent. L.J. 375, 375 (1999).
2. 395 U.S. 444, 447 (1969) (per curiam).
3. Akselrun, *supra* note 1.
4. *Id.*
5. David Crump, *Camouflaged Incitement: Freedom of Speech, Communicative Torts, and the Borderland of the Brandenburg Test*, 29 Ga. L. Rev. 1, 33–37 (1994); see also Lise Vansen, Comment: *Incitement by Any Other Name: Dodging a First Amendment Misfire in* Rice v. Paladin Enters., Inc., 25 Hastings Const. L.Q. 605 (1998).

Likelihood of Lawless Acts The incitement test also requires proof that it is likely media content would cause violence. This is not the same as foreseeability. For example, it may be foreseeable that a movie with violent scenes would cause a deranged person to commit unlawful acts. But courts say the determining factor is whether the movie is likely to cause a reasonable person to act illegally. Rarely will a court find it likely that a reasonable person would commit violence in response to media content.

One court held that a radio station advertising campaign did inspire reasonable people to commit illegal acts. A Los Angeles Top 40 station with a large teenage audience devised a promotional campaign. It gave a bright red car to one of its well-known disc jockeys. The DJ drove to several locations in the

realWorld Law

Media Inspiring Violent Acts

Zazi Pope, Warner Brothers' senior vice president and deputy general counsel, commenting on the effects of media content, said the Book of Revelations inspired the Branch Davidians in Waco, Texas; the Beatles inspired Charles Manson, convicted of organizing Sharon Tate's murder; the novel "The Catcher in the Rye" inspired Mark David Chapman, John Lennon's killer; the movie "Taxi Driver" inspired John W. Hinckley, who shot President Ronald Reagan. Pope said, "If you're going to say that anything that could inspire some crazy person to commit a violent act is going to be subject to liability, our culture would cease to have any meaning." Rather, Pope said, courts have ruled that these "random violent acts, even if somehow linked to a movie, song, or other work of art" do not justify holding responsible those who create and distribute mass media content.[1]

1. F. Jay Dougherty et al., *Potential Liability Arising from the Dissemination of Violent Music*, 22 Loy. L.A. Ent. L. Rev. 237, 249 (2002).

Los Angeles area, periodically calling the station and broadcasting his intended destination. Anyone finding the DJ would win a cash prize and be interviewed on the air. Two teenagers independently saw the DJ's car on a Los Angeles freeway and raced to catch him. As the DJ took an off-ramp to exit the freeway, the two cars followed. One of the teenagers forced a third car off the highway, killing the driver. The dead driver's relatives sued the station. The family won at trial, and the jury awarded $300,000 in damages.

On appeal, the California Supreme Court ruled that it was foreseeable the station's promotion could lead to physical injury or death.[99] The station staged the promotion in the summer, when many teenagers with cars were at home and bored. The promotion offered money and a bit of fame. The disc jockey testified he had seen certain cars following him from one location to another. The court took this admission to mean the station should have foreseen that a teenager who missed winning the money at one location would speed to the next. It is foreseeable that speeding and reckless driving are likely to result in death or serious injury. The station is not relieved of liability because a third party, the teenagers, caused the harm, the court said. The station's action in broadcasting the promotion created the circumstances leading to the harm.

SUMMARY

THE INCITEMENT TEST IS AN ALTERNATIVE to the negligence test when a plaintiff contends a media defendant caused physical harm: Did the defendant intentionally or recklessly intend to cause harm, and was imminent harm likely to result from the defendant's actions? There is no free speech protection if the media defendant intended harm to result. ∎

Communications Decency Act

The Communications Decency Act (CDA) shields Web-based service providers from legal claims based on their carriage of material that third parties create.[100] For example, this protects Internet service providers against libel, as discussed in Chapter 5, privacy and emotional distress suits, as long as the provider did not create the disputed content. Congress adopted the CDA as part of the Telecommunications Act of 1996 primarily to limit minors' access to indecent and obscene material on the Internet. As discussed in Chapter 11, the U.S. Supreme Court found most of the CDA abridged Internet users' First Amendment rights. However, courts have upheld the part of the CDA protecting Web-based service providers. This allows interactive computer service providers, when sued for allegedly causing physical harm, to defend themselves by asserting protection under the CDA.

The CDA applied, for example, when a 13-year-old girl created a MySpace profile and chose to represent herself as 18 years old. A year later she met a 19-year-old man through her MySpace profile. The two spoke by phone. He then sexually assaulted her when they met in person. The girl and her mother sued MySpace, claiming it failed to institute reasonable safety measures that would prevent older users from communicating with minors. The U.S. Court of Appeals for the Fifth Circuit read the CDA as giving broad immunity to Web services that carry information third parties provide and rejected the suit against MySpace.[101] The court said MySpace did not publish the material on the girl's profile; it merely transmitted information the girl placed there. The CDA protects Web services that transmit but do not create material, the court said.

When other girls aged 13 to 15 years old were assaulted by adults they met through MySpace, the minors and their families sued the social networking site. A California appellate court said the CDA protects Web service providers against civil suits when the providers do not create the disputed material.[102] Similarly, a federal district court held that the CDA protected MySpace when a minor, not MySpace, provided the information that led to an assault.[103] Plaintiffs in these suits argue the social networking sites do not merely transmit material; they create it because they process users' information. For example, after a user entered his or her date of birth, MySpace automatically displayed the user's zodiac sign. MySpace also prompted the user to enter additional information about background and lifestyle, schools and preferred music. Courts have determined when a site requires users to provide specific information, as did a site allowing users to search for a roommate, it could be an information content provider, not just an information transmitter, and would not come under the CDA's protection.[104] But courts have determined sites only prompting a user to provide information, such as MySpace, do not create content and therefore enjoy CDA's safeguards.[105]

Craigslist is a Web service that does not create content itself. A person bought a gun though a Craigslist ad and shot and wounded Calvin Gibson. Gibson sued Craigslist for not ensuring that "inherently hazardous objects, such as handguns, did not come into the hands of individuals" who would use them to physically injure others. A federal district court said Craigslist provided an interactive computer service, did not itself post the handgun ad and acted only as a transmitter of third-party content. Those three factors, the court held, meant the CDA protected Craigslist.[106]

Although some courts have interpreted the CDA broadly to cover many claims against Web service providers, others have not. For example, Cynthia Barnes' ex-boyfriend posted profiles on Yahoo! that included nude pictures of Barnes and implications that she was seeking casual sex with men. The profiles contained Barnes' work contact information. Men began contacting Barnes, even coming to her workplace. Several times she unsuccessfully asked Yahoo to remove the profiles. A local television reporter learned of Barnes' situation and alerted Yahoo. A Yahoo employee contacted Barnes and said the profiles would be removed. Barnes conveyed that information to the reporter, but the profiles remained on Yahoo. Barnes sued Yahoo, claiming she relied on its promise to take down the profiles, yet Yahoo did not comply with its promise, a legal concept called "promissory estoppel." That is, Yahoo promised to remove the profiles, did not do so and Barnes continued to hear from men who wanted to have sex with her. Federal courts ruled the CDA did not prevent Barnes from suing Yahoo for promissory estoppel.[107]

SUMMARY

THE COMMUNICATIONS DECENCY ACT protects interactive computer service providers that did not create the disputed content from liability when plaintiffs seek damages for information originating with a third-party user of the computer service. Courts generally, though not always, read the CDA broadly, shielding interactive computer service providers from defamation, privacy, emotional distress and physical harm civil lawsuits. ∎

Other Dangers

Reporters, editors, photographers, newspapers, television stations, Internet sites—any person and company involved with preparing and publishing news, entertainment and advertising—may be sued for any number of legal claims. In addition to those already discussed in this and previous chapters, the following are samples of other lawsuits media have faced.

Breach of Contract

Media personnel often make contractual agreements. They sign employment contracts, contracts to buy new computers for the newsroom and contracts to buy advertising time on a television station. They also may contract with a news source—agreeing to keep a source's name secret in exchange for the source's information.

Media personnel may be sued for breaching a contract. For example, a British documentary producer planned a film about American censorship of art. A British television channel financially supported the production and would air the film when completed. The producer wanted to include an interview with Donald Wildmon, a prominent critic of government arts funding. Wildmon agreed, but only if the producer signed a contract stating that the interview would not be made available to any other media outlet besides the British channel without Wildmon's permission. The producer agreed. The film, "Damned in the U.S.A.," won many awards after it aired in Britain. When Wildmon learned that the film was selected to open a prestigious documentary festival in New York City, he sued. Wildmon objected to his picture and words being juxtaposed in the film with images of art Wildmon considered obscene. Wildmon asked a federal district court to declare that the contract prevented showing the film in America. The film producers argued that the contract referred only to the complete interview, not the brief portions used in the film.

The court said neither the contract's wording nor the parties' intentions were clear.[108] However, the court read the contract to mean that the raw interview footage could not be used by the British producer or anyone else to make a new film. The original documentary, including the interview excerpts, could be exhibited wherever the producer wanted, the court held.

The *Cohen v. Cowles Media Co.* decision, discussed in Chapter 9, in which newspapers revealed the name of a source to whom confidentiality was promised, also is a breach of contract case.

Interference with Economic Advantage

A person who has an opportunity to gain financially but believes another person interfered with that opportunity may file a tort suit. The tort goes by different names in different states. No matter what the tort is called, the complaint remains

Points of Law

What Is a Contract?

A contract is an agreement, an exchange of promises between the contracting parties. A court can enforce a legal contract against a party who has breached—violated in some way—the terms or conditions of the agreement. Most contracts are written documents. However, an oral agreement may be as legally binding as a contract. To form a contract, there must be both a valid offer and a valid acceptance. There also must be "consideration," or payment for the obligation. "I want to buy your car." "OK, I agree to sell it to you." The first statement is an offer. The second is an acceptance. But there is no contract because there is no consideration. "I want to buy your car for $5,000." "OK, I agree to sell it to you for $5,000." This constitutes a contract: offer, acceptance and consideration of $5,000 to pay for the obligation to sell the car.

the same: The defendant interfered with the plaintiff's prospective business relationship that promised economic rewards. For example, a utility company executive pressured a newspaper that reported on energy matters not to use articles by a freelance writer whom the executive thought was biased. The writer sued the utility company for interfering with her economic relationship with the paper. A California appellate court said the utility executive might have acted improperly in influencing the paper.[109] The writer could pursue her economic interference claim, the court ruled.

The First Amendment can be a defense against an economic interference claim. A software company owner wrote a letter to the editor disagreeing with certain statements in an article a computer magazine published. The magazine printed the letter together with a response from the article's author. The company owner thought the response made him appear uninformed about important aspects of computer software. He complained that the response caused his company to lose business and he sued for interference with prospective economic gain. A federal district court said the First Amendment protected the article author's response.[110] Because the response was constitutionally protected, it could not be the basis of any tort suit, the court said.

Section 230 of the Communications Decency Act offers protection against economic interference lawsuits, as it does against other torts such as libel and invasion of privacy. If a website does not create content, but only hosts material created by third-parties, the website cannot be held liable for the content. For instance, a website that invited users to post complaints about businesses carried negative reviews of a car dealership. The auto company sued for libel and interference with business expectations. Although the website posted a comment saying the "complaints pretty well cover the territory—everything from prices engraved in sand to advertising that overlooks certain crucial elements," the U.S. Court of Appeals for the Fourth Circuit ruled the car dealer could not offer plausible proof the website created the allegedly false postings.[111] The court therefore upheld dismissal of the lawsuit against the website.

Fraudulent Misrepresentation

Some relationships require full disclosure. A **fiduciary relationship** is a legal duty or responsibility one party owes to another when the parties are in certain relationships with each other. For example, when a person agrees to act primarily for another's benefit, he or she must reveal pertinent facts to the other person. A financial consultant investing a person's savings is in a fiduciary relationship with the client and must give the client important information about the investments. It is fraudulent misrepresentation if the fiduciary fails to disclose information. What does this have to do with the media? In one case, a teacher was convicted of sexually molesting some of his former students. One of those students appeared at the teacher's sentencing hearing. The judge ordered reporters in the courtroom not to identify any of the sexual assault victims who testified. Thinking the media

fiduciary relationship A legal duty or responsibility one party owes to another when the parties are in certain relationships with each other.

would not reveal his name, the former student testified. An Associated Press (AP) reporter wrote a story using the victim's name, the only journalist to do so. The victim sued the AP for fraudulent misrepresentation. A federal appellate court said the AP did not have a fiduciary relationship with the victim.[112] In fact, the court said, the AP and the victim had no relationship at all. Without a fiduciary relationship, the AP was not required to tell the victim it planned to ignore the judge's order and publish his name, the court ruled.

SUMMARY

PLAINTIFFS SUE THE MASS MEDIA FOR MANY DIFFERENT TORTS. For example, breach of contract means media personnel agree to do something but fail to meet their commitment. A contract may be an oral as well as written agreement. Interfering with prospective economic gain may occur when an advertiser, for example, pressures a mass medium to fire a journalist. The journalist may sue his or her former employer. ∎

Cases for Study

Thinking About It

The two case excerpts that follow deal with unusual sets of facts. As you read these case excerpts, keep the following questions in mind:

- Do the decisions do more to protect free speech or individuals' emotional well being?

- What approaches do the courts take in trying to balance First Amendment rights against the right not to be emotionally harmed?

- Do the two cases show that sometimes judges know in advance what decisions they want to reach and then go about finding justifications for those decisions?

Hustler Magazine Inc. v. Falwell
SUPREME COURT OF THE UNITED STATES
485 U.S. 46 (1988)

CHIEF JUSTICE WILLIAM REHNQUIST delivered the Court's opinion:

Petitioner Hustler Magazine, Inc., is a magazine of nationwide circulation. Respondent Jerry Falwell, a nationally known minister who has been active as a commentator on politics and public affairs, sued petitioner and its publisher, petitioner Larry Flynt, to recover damages for invasion of privacy, libel, and intentional infliction of emotional distress. . . .

The inside front cover of the November 1983 issue of Hustler Magazine featured a "parody" of an advertisement for Campari Liqueur that contained the name and picture of respondent and was entitled "Jerry Falwell talks about his first time." This parody was modeled after actual Campari ads that included interviews with various celebrities about their "first times." Although it was apparent by the end of each interview that this meant the first time they sampled Campari, the ads clearly played on the sexual double entendre of the general subject of "first times." Copying the form and layout of these Campari ads, Hustler's editors chose respondent as the featured celebrity and drafted an alleged "interview" with him in which he

states that his "first time" was during a drunken incestuous rendezvous with his mother in an outhouse. The Hustler parody portrays respondent and his mother as drunk and immoral, and suggests that respondent is a hypocrite who preaches only when he is drunk. In small print at the bottom of the page, the ad contains the disclaimer, "ad parody—not to be taken seriously." The magazine's table of contents also lists the ad as "Fiction; Ad and Personality Parody."

[Falwell sued. He failed on the libel and privacy claims.] The jury ruled for respondent on the intentional infliction of emotional distress claim, however, and stated that he should be awarded $100,000 in compensatory damages, as well as $50,000 each in punitive damages. . . .

On appeal, the United States Court of Appeals for the Fourth Circuit affirmed the judgment against petitioners. . . .

At the heart of the First Amendment is the recognition of the fundamental importance of the free flow of ideas and opinions on matters of public interest and concern. . . . We have therefore been particularly vigilant to ensure that individual expressions of ideas remain free from governmentally imposed sanctions. . . .

The sort of robust political debate encouraged by the First Amendment is bound to produce speech that is critical of those who hold public office or those public figures who are "intimately involved in the resolution of important public questions or, by reason of their fame, shape events in areas of concern to society at large." . . . Such criticism, inevitably, will not always be reasoned or moderate; public figures as well as public officials will be subject to "vehement, caustic, and sometimes unpleasantly sharp attacks." . . .

Of course, this does not mean that any speech about a public figure is immune from sanction in the form of damages. Since *New York Times Co. v. Sullivan,* we have consistently ruled that a public figure may hold a speaker liable for the damage to reputation caused by publication of a defamatory falsehood, but only if the statement was made "with knowledge that it was false or with reckless disregard of whether it was false or not." False statements of fact are particularly valueless; they interfere with the truth-seeking function of the marketplace of ideas, and they cause damage to an individual's reputation that cannot easily be repaired by counterspeech, however persuasive or effective. But even though falsehoods have little value in and of themselves, they are "nevertheless inevitable in free debate," and a rule that would impose strict liability on a publisher for false factual assertions would have an undoubted "chilling" effect on speech relating to public figures that does have constitutional value. "Freedoms of expression require 'breathing space.'" This breathing space is provided by a constitutional rule that allows public figures to recover for libel or defamation only when they can prove both that the statement was false and that the statement was made with the requisite level of culpability. . . .

Generally speaking, the law does not regard the intent to inflict emotional distress as one which should receive much solicitude, and it is quite understandable that most if not all jurisdictions have chosen to make it civilly culpable where the conduct in question is sufficiently "outrageous." But in the world of debate about public affairs, many things done with motives

that are less than admirable are protected by the First Amendment. . . .

[Although] a bad motive may be deemed controlling for purposes of tort liability in other areas of the law, we think the First Amendment prohibits such a result in the area of public debate about public figures.

Were we to hold otherwise, there can be little doubt that political cartoonists and satirists would be subjected to damages awards without any showing that their work falsely defamed its subject. . . .

. . . Several famous examples of this type of intentionally injurious speech were drawn by Thomas Nast, probably the greatest American cartoonist to date, who was associated for many years during the post–Civil War era with Harper's Weekly. In the pages of that publication Nast conducted a graphic vendetta against William M. "Boss" Tweed and his corrupt associates in New York City's "Tweed Ring." It has been described by one historian of the subject as "a sustained attack which in its passion and effectiveness stands alone in the history of American graphic art." . . .

Despite their sometimes caustic nature, from the early cartoon portraying George Washington as an ass down to the present day, graphic depictions and satirical cartoons have played a prominent role in public and political debate. . . .

Respondent contends, however, that the caricature in question here was so "outrageous" as to distinguish it from more traditional political cartoons. There is no doubt that the caricature of respondent and his mother published in Hustler is at best a distant cousin of the political cartoons described above, and a rather poor relation at that. If it were possible by laying down a principled standard to separate the one from the other, public discourse would probably suffer little or no harm. But we doubt that there is any such standard, and we are quite sure that the pejorative description "outrageous" does not supply one. "Outrageousness" in the area of political and social discourse has an inherent subjectiveness about it which would allow a jury to impose liability on the basis of the jurors' tastes or views, or perhaps on the basis of their dislike of a particular expression. An "outrageousness" standard thus runs afoul of our longstanding refusal to allow damages to be awarded because the speech in question may have an adverse emotional impact on the audience. . . .

We conclude that public figures and public officials may not recover for the tort of intentional infliction of emotional distress by reason of publications such as the one here at issue without showing in addition that the publication contains a false statement of fact which was made with "actual malice," *i.e.,* with knowledge that the statement was false or with reckless disregard as to whether or not it was true. This is not merely a "blind application" of the *New York Times* standard, it reflects our considered judgment that such a standard is necessary to give adequate "breathing space" to the freedoms protected by the First Amendment.

Here it is clear that respondent Falwell is a "public figure" for purposes of First Amendment law.

The jury found against respondent on his libel claim when it decided that the Hustler ad parody could not "reasonably be understood as describing actual facts about [respondent] or actual events in which [he] participated." The Court of Appeals interpreted the jury's finding to be that the ad parody "was not reasonably believable," and in accordance with our custom we accept this finding. Respondent is thus relegated to his claim for damages awarded by the jury for the intentional infliction of emotional distress by "outrageous" conduct. But, for reasons heretofore stated, this claim cannot, consistently with the First Amendment, form a basis for the award of damages when the conduct in question is the publication of a caricature such as the ad parody involved here. The judgment of the Court of Appeals is accordingly

Reversed.

Snyder v. Phelps
SUPREME COURT OF THE UNITED STATES
131 S. Ct. 1207 (2011)

CHIEF JUSTICE JOHN ROBERTS delivered the Court's opinion:

A jury held members of the Westboro Baptist Church liable for millions of dollars in damages for picketing near a soldier's funeral service. The picket signs reflected the church's view that the United States is overly tolerant of sin and that God kills American soldiers as punishment. The question presented is whether the First Amendment shields the church members from tort liability for their speech in this case.

Fred Phelps founded the Westboro Baptist Church in Topeka, Kansas, in 1955. The church's congregation believes that God hates and punishes the United States for its tolerance of homosexuality, particularly in America's military. The church frequently communicates its views by picketing, often at military funerals. In the more than 20 years that the members of Westboro Baptist have publicized their message, they have picketed nearly 600 funerals.

Marine Lance Corporal Matthew Snyder was killed in Iraq in the line of duty. Lance Corporal

Snyder's father selected the Catholic church in the Snyders' hometown of Westminster, Maryland, as the site for his son's funeral. Local newspapers provided notice of the time and location of the service.

Phelps became aware of Matthew Snyder's funeral and decided to travel to Maryland with six other Westboro Baptist parishioners (two of his daughters and four of his grandchildren) to picket. On the day of the memorial service, the Westboro congregation members picketed on public land adjacent to public streets near the Maryland State House, the United States Naval Academy, and Matthew Snyder's funeral. The Westboro picketers carried signs that were largely the same at all three locations. They stated, for instance: "God Hates the USA/Thank God for 9/11," "America is Doomed," "Don't Pray for the USA," "Thank God for IEDs," "Thank God for Dead Soldiers," "Pope in Hell," "Priests Rape Boys," "God Hates Fags," "You're Going to Hell," and "God Hates You."

The church had notified the authorities in advance of its intent to picket at the time of the funeral, and the picketers complied with police instructions in staging their demonstration. The picketing took place within a 10- by 25-foot plot of public land adjacent to a public street, behind a temporary fence. That plot was approximately 1,000 feet from the church where the funeral was held. Several buildings separated the picket site from the church. The Westboro picketers displayed their signs for about 30 minutes before the funeral began and sang hymns and recited Bible verses. None of the picketers entered church property or went to the cemetery. They did not yell or use profanity, and there was no violence associated with the picketing.

The funeral procession passed within 200 to 300 feet of the picket site. Although Snyder testified that he could see the tops of the picket signs as he drove to the funeral, he did not see what was written on the signs until later that night, while watching a news broadcast covering the event.[1]

Snyder filed suit against Phelps, Phelps's daughters, and the Westboro Baptist Church (collectively Westboro or the church) in the United States District Court for the District of Maryland under that court's diversity jurisdiction. Snyder alleged five state tort law claims: defamation, publicity given to private life, intentional infliction of emotional distress, intrusion upon seclusion, and civil conspiracy. Westboro moved for summary judgment contending, in part, that the church's speech was insulated from liability by the *First Amendment.*

The District Court awarded Westboro summary judgment on Snyder's claims for defamation and publicity given to private life, concluding that Snyder could not prove the necessary elements of those torts. A trial was held on the remaining claims. At trial, Snyder described the severity of his emotional injuries. He testified that he is unable to separate the thought of his dead son from his thoughts of Westboro's picketing, and that he often becomes tearful, angry, and physically ill when he thinks about it. Expert witnesses testified that Snyder's emotional anguish had resulted in severe depression and had exacerbated pre-existing health conditions.

A jury found for Snyder on the intentional infliction of emotional distress, intrusion upon seclusion, and civil conspiracy claims, and held Westboro liable for $2.9 million in compensatory damages and $8 million in punitive damages. Westboro filed several post-trial motions, including a motion contending that the jury verdict was grossly excessive and a motion seeking judgment as a matter of law on all claims on First Amendment grounds. The District Court remitted the punitive damages award to $2.1 million, but left the jury verdict otherwise intact.

In the Court of Appeals, Westboro's primary argument was that the church was entitled to judgment as a matter of law because the First Amendment fully protected Westboro's speech. The Court of Appeals agreed. The court reviewed the picket signs and concluded that Westboro's statements were entitled to First Amendment protection because those statements were on matters of public concern, were not provably false, and were expressed solely through hyperbolic rhetoric.

We granted certiorari.

To succeed on a claim for intentional infliction of emotional distress in Maryland, a plaintiff must demonstrate that the defendant intentionally or recklessly engaged in extreme and outrageous conduct that caused the plaintiff to suffer severe emotional distress. The Free Speech Clause of the First Amendment—"Congress shall make no law . . . abridging the freedom of speech"—can serve as a defense in state tort suits, including suits for intentional infliction of emotional distress.

---

1. A few weeks after the funeral, one of the picketers posted a message on Westboro's Web site discussing the picketing and containing religiously oriented denunciations of the Snyders, interspersed among lengthy Bible quotations. Snyder discovered the posting, referred to by the parties as the "epic," during an Internet search for his son's name. The epic is not properly before us and does not factor in our analysis. Although the epic was submitted to the jury and discussed in the courts below, Snyder never mentioned it in his petition for certiorari. Nor did Snyder respond to the statement in the opposition to certiorari that "[t]hough the epic was asserted as a basis for the claims at trial, the petition . . . appears to be addressing only claims based on the picketing." Snyder devoted only one paragraph in the argument section of his opening merits brief to the epic. Given the foregoing and the fact that an Internet posting may raise distinct issues in this context, we decline to consider the epic in deciding this case.

Whether the First Amendment prohibits holding Westboro liable for its speech in this case turns largely on whether that speech is of public or private concern, as determined by all the circumstances of the case. "[S]peech on 'matters of public concern' . . . is 'at the heart of the First Amendment's protection.'" The First Amendment reflects "a profound national commitment to the principle that debate on public issues should be uninhibited, robust, and wide-open." That is because "speech concerning public affairs is more than self-expression; it is the essence of self-government." Accordingly, "speech on public issues occupies the highest rung of the hierarchy of *First Amendment* values, and is entitled to special protection."

"'[N]ot all speech is of equal First Amendment importance,'" however, and where matters of purely private significance are at issue, First Amendment protections are often less rigorous. That is because restricting speech on purely private matters does not implicate the same constitutional concerns as limiting speech on matters of public interest: "[T]here is no threat to the free and robust debate of public issues; there is no potential interference with a meaningful dialogue of ideas"; and the "threat of liability" does not pose the risk of "a reaction of self-censorship" on matters of public import.

We noted a short time ago, in considering whether public employee speech addressed a matter of public concern, that "the boundaries of the public concern test are not well defined." Although that remains true today, we have articulated some guiding principles, principles that accord broad protection to speech to ensure that courts themselves do not become inadvertent censors.

Speech deals with matters of public concern when it can "be fairly considered as relating to any matter of political, social, or other concern to the community," or when it "is a subject of legitimate news interest; that is, a subject of general interest and of value and concern to the public." The arguably "inappropriate or controversial character of a statement is irrelevant to the question whether it deals with a matter of public concern."

Our opinion in *Dun & Bradstreet,* on the other hand, provides an example of speech of only private concern. In that case we held, as a general matter, that information about a particular individual's credit report "concerns no public issue." The content of the report, we explained, "was speech solely in the individual interest of the speaker and its specific business audience." *Ibid.* That was confirmed by the fact that the particular report was sent to only five subscribers to the reporting service, who were bound not to disseminate it further. *Ibid.* To cite another example, we concluded in *San Diego* v. *Roe* that, in the context of a government employer regulating the speech of its employees, videos of an employee engaging in sexually explicit acts did not address a public concern; the videos "did nothing to inform the public about any aspect of the [employing agency's] functioning or operation." *543 U.S., at 84, 125 S. Ct. 521, 160 L. Ed. 2d 410.*

Deciding whether speech is of public or private concern requires us to examine the "'content, form, and context'" of that speech, "'as revealed by the whole record.'" As in other First Amendment cases, the court is obligated "to 'make an independent examination of the whole record' in order to make sure that 'the judgment does not constitute a forbidden intrusion on the field of free expression.'" In considering content, form, and context, no factor is dispositive, and it is necessary to evaluate all the circumstances of the speech, including what was said, where it was said, and how it was said.

The "content" of Westboro's signs plainly relates to broad issues of interest to society at large, rather than matters of "purely private concern." The placards read "God Hates the USA/Thank God for 9/11," "America is Doomed," "Don't Pray for the USA," "Thank God for IEDs," "Fag Troops," "Semper Fi Fags," "God Hates Fags," "Maryland Taliban," "Fags Doom Nations," "Not Blessed Just Cursed," "Thank God for Dead Soldiers," "Pope in Hell," "Priests Rape Boys," "You're Going to Hell," and "God Hates You." While these messages may fall short of refined social or political commentary, the issues they highlight—the political and moral conduct of the United States and its citizens, the fate of our Nation, homosexuality in the military, and scandals involving the Catholic clergy—are matters of public import. The signs certainly convey Westboro's position on those issues, in a manner designed, unlike the private speech in *Dun & Bradstreet,* to reach as broad a public audience as possible. And even if a few of the signs—such as "You're Going to Hell" and "God Hates You"—were viewed as containing messages related to Matthew Snyder or the Snyders specifically, that would not change the fact that the overall thrust and dominant theme of Westboro's demonstration spoke to broader public issues.

Apart from the content of Westboro's signs, Snyder contends that the "context" of the speech—its connection with his son's funeral—makes the speech a matter of private rather than public concern. The fact that Westboro spoke in connection with a funeral, however, cannot by itself transform the nature of Westboro's speech. Westboro's signs, displayed on public land next to a public street, reflect the fact that the church finds much to condemn in modern society. Its speech is "fairly characterized as constituting speech on a matter of public concern," and the funeral setting does not alter that conclusion.

Snyder argues that the church members in fact mounted a personal attack on Snyder and his family, and then attempted to "immunize their conduct by claiming that they were actually protesting the United States' tolerance of homosexuality or the supposed evils of the Catholic Church." We are not concerned in this case that Westboro's speech on public matters was in any way contrived to insulate speech on a private matter from liability. Westboro had been actively engaged in speaking on the subjects addressed in its picketing long before it became aware of Matthew Snyder, and there can be no serious claim that Westboro's picketing did not represent its "honestly believed" views on public issues. There was no preexisting relationship or conflict between Westboro and Snyder that might suggest Westboro's speech on public matters was intended to mask an attack on Snyder over a private matter.

Snyder goes on to argue that Westboro's speech should be afforded less than full First Amendment protection "not only because of the words" but also because the church members exploited the funeral "as a platform to bring their message to a broader audience." There is no doubt that Westboro chose to stage its picketing at the Naval Academy, the Maryland State House, and Matthew Snyder's funeral to increase publicity for its views and because of the relation between those sites and its views—in the case of the military funeral, because Westboro believes that God is killing American soldiers as punishment for the Nation's sinful policies.

Westboro's choice to convey its views in conjunction with Matthew Snyder's funeral made the expression of those views particularly hurtful to many, especially to Matthew's father. The record makes clear that the applicable legal term—"emotional distress"—fails to capture fully the anguish Westboro's choice added to Mr. Snyder's already incalculable grief. But Westboro conducted its picketing peacefully on matters of public concern at a public place adjacent to a public street. Such space occupies a "special position in terms of First Amendment protection." "[W]e have repeatedly referred to public streets as the archetype of a traditional public forum," noting that "'[t]ime out of mind' public streets and sidewalks have been used for public assembly and debate."

That said, "[e]ven protected speech is not equally permissible in all places and at all times." Westboro's choice of where and when to conduct its picketing is not beyond the Government's regulatory reach—it is "subject to reasonable time, place, or manner restrictions" that are consistent with the standards announced in this Court's precedents. Maryland now has a law imposing restrictions on funeral picketing, as do 43 other States and the Federal Government. To the extent these laws are content neutral, they raise very different questions from the tort verdict at issue in this case. Maryland's law, however, was not in effect at the time of the events at issue here, so we have no occasion to consider how it might apply to facts such as those before us, or whether it or other similar regulations are constitutional.

We have identified a few limited situations where the location of targeted picketing can be regulated under provisions that the Court has determined to be content neutral. In *Frisby* [*v. Schultz*], for example, we upheld a ban on such picketing "before or about" a particular residence. In *Madsen* v. *Women's Health*

Center, Inc., we approved an injunction requiring a buffer zone between protesters and an abortion clinic entrance. The facts here are obviously quite different, both with respect to the activity being regulated and the means of restricting those activities.

Simply put, the church members had the right to be where they were. Westboro alerted local authorities to its funeral protest and fully complied with police guidance on where the picketing could be staged. The picketing was conducted under police supervision some 1,000 feet from the church, out of the sight of those at the church. The protest was not unruly; there was no shouting, profanity, or violence.

The record confirms that any distress occasioned by Westboro's picketing turned on the content and viewpoint of the message conveyed, rather than any interference with the funeral itself. A group of parishioners standing at the very spot where Westboro stood, holding signs that said "God Bless America" and "God Loves You," would not have been subjected to liability. It was what Westboro said that exposed it to tort damages.

Given that Westboro's speech was at a public place on a matter of public concern, that speech is entitled to "special protection" under the First Amendment. Such speech cannot be restricted simply because it is upsetting or arouses contempt. "If there is a bedrock principle underlying the First Amendment, it is that the government may not prohibit the expression of an idea simply because society finds the idea itself offensive or disagreeable." Indeed, "the point of all speech protection . . . is to shield just those choices of content that in someone's eyes are misguided, or even hurtful."

The jury here was instructed that it could hold Westboro liable for intentional infliction of emotional distress based on a finding that Westboro's picketing was "outrageous." "Outrageousness," however, is a highly malleable standard with "an inherent subjectiveness about it which would allow a jury to impose liability on the basis of the jurors' tastes or views, or perhaps on the basis of their dislike of a particular expression." In a case such as this, a jury is "unlikely to be neutral with respect to the content of [the] speech," posing "a real danger of becoming an instrument for the suppression of . . . 'vehement, caustic, and sometimes unpleasan[t]'" expression. Such a risk is unacceptable; "in public debate [we] must tolerate insulting, and even outrageous, speech in order to provide adequate 'breathing space' to the freedoms protected by the First Amendment." What Westboro said, in the whole context of how and where it chose to say it, is entitled to "special protection" under the First Amendment, and that protection cannot be overcome by a jury finding that the picketing was outrageous.

For all these reasons, the jury verdict imposing tort liability on Westboro for intentional infliction of emotional distress must be set aside.

. . .

Our holding today is narrow. We are required in First Amendment cases to carefully review the record, and the reach of our opinion here is limited by the particular facts before us. As we have noted, "the sensitivity and significance of the interests presented in clashes between First Amendment and [state law] rights counsel relying on limited principles that sweep no more broadly than the appropriate context of the instant case."

Westboro believes that America is morally flawed; many Americans might feel the same about Westboro. Westboro's funeral picketing is certainly hurtful and its contribution to public discourse may be negligible. But Westboro addressed matters of public import on public property, in a peaceful manner, in full compliance with the guidance of local officials. The speech was indeed planned to coincide with Matthew Snyder's funeral, but did not itself disrupt that funeral, and Westboro's choice to conduct its picketing at that time and place did not alter the nature of its speech.

Speech is powerful. It can stir people to action, move them to tears of both joy and sorrow, and—as it did here—inflict great pain. On the facts before us, we cannot react to that pain by punishing the speaker. As a Nation we have chosen a different course—to protect even hurtful speech on public issues to ensure that we do not stifle public debate. That choice requires that we shield Westboro from tort liability for its picketing in this case.

The judgment of the United States Court of Appeals for the Fourth Circuit is affirmed.

It is so ordered.

Chapter 8

News must not be unnecessarily cut off at its source, for without freedom to acquire information the right to publish would be impermissibly compromised. Accordingly, a right to gather news, of some dimensions, must exist.

U.S. Supreme Court Justice Lewis Powell, 1972–1987[1]

When The New York Times sought cockpit voice recordings after the space shuttle Challenger exploded, a court ruled against the Times, holding that privacy rights outweighed the public interest in hearing the recordings.

Newsgathering
Pitfalls and Protections

Access to Property

Access to Public Property
Access to Quasi-Public
    Property

Newsgathering Pitfalls

Harassment
Fraud and
    Misrepresentation
Using Social Media as
    Sources

Covert Recording

Face-to-Face Recording
Recording "Wire"
    Conversations
Noncovert Recording

**Denying Access to
    Records**

Privacy Act
Student Records
Medical Records
Driver's Information
Video Voyeurism

**Newsgathering
    Protections**

Open-Government Laws
Access to Federal Records:
    The Freedom of
    Information Act

**Access to Federal
    Meetings**

State Open-Records Laws
State Open-Meetings Laws

Cases for Study

➤ *Wilson v. Layne*
➤ *U.S. Department of
    Justice v. Reporters
    Committee for
    Freedom of the Press*

Suppose . . .

. . . that a team of law enforcement officers executes a search warrant on what they believe is the home of a suspect. A newspaper reporter and photographer accompany the officers, who forcibly enter the home in the early morning, awakening two residents, who are the suspect's parents. The couple assures the officers their son is not there. The photographer takes several pictures, though none are published. After a search of the home to confirm, the officers and journalists leave. Was the journalists' presence illegal? If so, who is responsible—the journalists or the law enforcement agency? Look for the answers to these questions when the case of *Wilson v. Layne* is discussed later in this chapter and excerpted at the end of the chapter.

This chapter deals with how journalists obtain information. Newsgathering largely revolves around access—whether journalists have access to information—to potentially newsworthy documents, records, people and places.

As Justice Lewis Powell's statement at the beginning of the chapter asserts, unless journalists have some ability to obtain information, the First Amendment's freedom of the press clause would seem toothless. After all, what purpose does the freedom to distribute news serve unless there is also freedom to acquire that news in the first place? Information is the lifeblood of the news media, and the ability to obtain it should be an integral element of freedom of the press. An explicit newsgathering privilege is required because providing freedom to publish information matters little without the protection to obtain it in the first place.[2]

Though logical, this argument falls largely on deaf ears within the judiciary. In fact, the Supreme Court said that while some newsgathering protection may exist, "the First Amendment does not guarantee the press a constitutional right of special access to information not available to the public generally."[3] Although the Supreme Court has proclaimed that "without some protection for seeking out the news, freedom of the press could be eviscerated,"[4] one source calls this proclamation "empty rhetoric."[5] Some argue that because newsgathering serves core purposes of the First Amendment, it should be regarded as a First Amendment–protected activity.[6]

But those core purposes of the First Amendment also provide support for the contention that there neither is, nor should be, specific protection for newsgathering. That argument—one the courts seem to accept—relies, in part, on an "originalist" interpretation of the Constitution and, specifically, the First Amendment. In other words, because the framers of the Bill of Rights did not view newsgathering as a major function of the press of their time, the freedom of press clause in the First Amendment could not have been intended to protect newsgathering. It merely protected the publication of information once it was obtained.

A clear articulation of this judicial perspective came from a 1975 article by Justice Potter Stewart:

> So far as the Constitution goes, the autonomous press may publish what it knows, and may seek to learn what it can. But this autonomy cuts both ways. The press is free to do battle against secrecy and deception in government. But the press cannot expect from the Constitution any guarantee that it will succeed. There is no constitutional right to have access to particular government information, or to require openness from the bureaucracy. The public's interest in knowing about its government is protected by the guarantee of a Free Press, but the protection is indirect. The Constitution itself is neither a Freedom of Information Act nor an Official Secrets Act.[7]

Generally, the courts have held that journalists have the same degree of access as any person. No more. No less. What newsgathering protection the media have simply is no different than the rights and privileges of every citizen. The concept of general applicability comes into play here. As long as laws do not specifically target or single out the press, they may be applied to the press. Laws are not unconstitutional merely because they incidentally or unintentionally infringe on the news media's First Amendment rights.[8] One observer says this "simplistic 'general law' approach is not so much a solution as a judicial abdication of responsibility in this area of the law."[9]

The doctrine that news media have the same access as other citizens was reinforced by a series of U.S. Supreme Court rulings involving the right to gather news in jails and prisons. In each of three cases, the media claims were rejected. The Court ruled that "[n]ewsmen have no constitutional right of access to prisons or their inmates *beyond that afforded the general public.*"[10] This doctrine was highlighted when a San Francisco television station challenged limitations placed on its crew and lost.[11] The crew could view parts of a county jail by taking part in one of the regular tours of the facility but could not have unregulated access to the jail. Similar challenges brought by the press against policies barring interviews with selected inmates also were rejected.[12]

Access to Property

Although journalists and bloggers may find information online and conduct interviews by phone and e-mail, being where news events occur remains a crucial part of reporting. Absent a First Amendment right to gather news, journalists may not be allowed to enter public, quasi-public or private land or buildings.

Access to Public Property

Generally journalists have the same right as anyone to be on public land or in public buildings. Police and other public safety officials may order individuals, including the press, to stay away from a crime scene or other event if their presence could make it difficult for officials to carry out their duties. Those who disobey a lawful order may be arrested for interfering with police functions.

Public safety officials do not have an unlimited right to prevent journalists and others from observing a crime scene, however. When a television news photographer, standing on public property, used a bright light to film police taking suspects from a robbery scene, the officers demanded the camera. A federal district court said the police violated the photographer's First Amendment rights by not proving the light or camera interfered with the officers' duties.[13] Similarly, the U.S. Court of Appeals for the First Circuit said the police violated the First Amendment rights of a man arrested when he used his cell phone's video camera to film police officers arresting a young man in a public park. The police could not prove the filming hindered the arrest.[14] In 2013 the

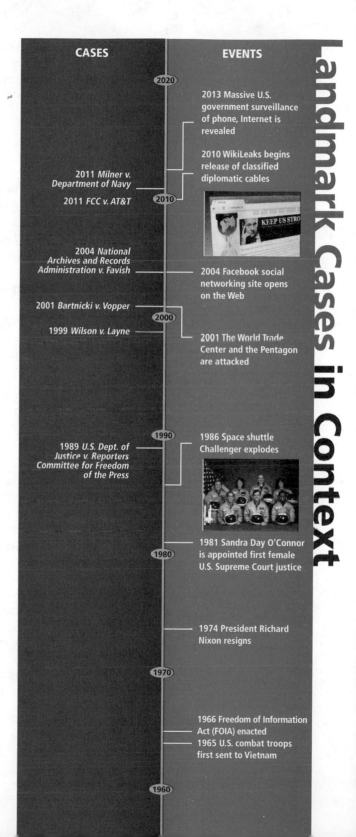

CASES

2011 *Milner v. Department of Navy*

2011 *FCC v. AT&T*

2004 *National Archives and Records Administration v. Favish*

2001 *Bartnicki v. Vopper*

1999 *Wilson v. Layne*

1989 *U.S. Dept. of Justice v. Reporters Committee for Freedom of the Press*

EVENTS

2013 Massive U.S. government surveillance of phone, Internet is revealed

2010 WikiLeaks begins release of classified diplomatic cables

2004 Facebook social networking site opens on the Web

2001 The World Trade Center and the Pentagon are attacked

1986 Space shuttle Challenger explodes

1981 Sandra Day O'Connor is appointed first female U.S. Supreme Court justice

1974 President Richard Nixon resigns

1966 Freedom of Information Act (FOIA) enacted

1965 U.S. combat troops first sent to Vietnam

2020
2010
2000
1990
1980
1970
1960

Landmark Cases in Context

U.S. Department of Justice supported a photojournalist's lawsuit against police officers who arrested him when he took pictures of their arrest of two men. Police later dropped the charges, but the Department of Justice said the First Amendment protects journalists and others who peacefully photograph police on duty in public places.[15]

The Seventh Circuit joined other courts in holding the First Amendment protects audio recording of police officers.[16] Illinois law requires the consent of all parties to audio record any conversation. The American Civil Liberties Union of Illinois sued to prevent enforcement of the law to its monitoring of police activities. A law forbidding the recording of public officials performing their duties in a traditional public forum violates the First Amendment even when the law targets a technology rather than a speaker, the Seventh Circuit ruled. The burden on speech rights outweighs any substantial state interest in prohibiting audio recording of police officers when other witnesses can overhear what would be recorded.

Access to Quasi-Public Property

Some land and buildings, such as military bases and prisons, are government owned or controlled but generally not open to the public or journalists. As noted earlier, the U.S. Supreme Court ruled that reporters do not have a First Amendment right to enter jails or prisons.

Access to Polling Places Polling places should be open to the press, the U.S. Court of Appeals for the Sixth Circuit ruled.[17] The court reviewed an Ohio law allowing only voters to be in a polling place and requiring nonvoters to stay well away from the polls. Applying the strict scrutiny test, the court found the law violated the press's First Amendment rights. The state had a compelling interest in ensuring orderly elections, but the law was not narrowly drawn to achieve that end, the court said.

The Third Circuit disagreed in 2013.[18] A newspaper company challenged Pennsylvania's law requiring people to remain 10 feet away from the polls. The Third Circuit said the Sixth Circuit approached the Ohio statute as a speech limitation. But it was not and neither is the Pennsylvania law, the court said. Both are limits on newsgathering, and that is not a First Amendment protected right. Instead, the Third Circuit said, the test to be used is one the U.S. Supreme Court uses for access to courtrooms (discussed in Chapter 10).[19] That two-pronged test first asks if the quasi-public place traditionally was open to the public. The court said voting might have started that way but progressively has become a secret ballot. Second, the test asks whether requiring openness will benefit the process. The court said openness might help limit voter fraud and voter intimidation, but it also has a downside. Who qualifies as a journalist if reporters have a right to enter polling places, the court asked? And will potential voters decide not to vote because reporters might learn voters' personal information during the voting process? Both prongs of the test required upholding the Pennsylvania law, the court concluded.

Access to Government Land The two-pronged test also applies to reporters being on government land, the Ninth Circuit concluded in 2012.[20] A photojournalist asked for access to holding facilities where wild horses are kept after being rounded up by the Bureau of Land Management (BLM). The photojournalist filed suit after BLM refused her request. Saying the two-pronged test may be used "to evaluate attempts to access a wide range of civil and administrative government activities," the Ninth Circuit found the BLM may have infringed the photojournalist's First Amendment rights. The appellate court remanded the case to the district court.

Access to Military Sites In 2010, Defense Secretary Robert Gates issued a memo on "Interaction with the Media" to all of those under his command. It emphasized the importance of news media access to many aspects of Department of Defense (DOD) activities and operations. "[W]e are obliged to ensure that the information provided to [the media] is timely, accurate, credible and consistent," Gates wrote. "I have said many times that we must strive to be as open, accessible and transparent as possible."[21] Gates also expressed concern about laxity with department rules and procedures, including individuals talking to the media outside of channels or providing unauthorized information. He said media interactions needed to be coordinated through proper channels to maintain the integrity of the government decision-making processes. Gates' memo followed fast on the heels of a Rolling Stone article that profiled Gen. Stanley McChrystal, led to the general's forced resignation and may have prompted reassessment of media access policies.[22]

News media coverage from the battlefield dates back to the U.S. Civil War in the mid-19th century. As the media and technology evolved, so did the scope and immediacy of coverage as well as government concern about the effects of this reporting. The Vietnam War was sometimes referred to as "the living room war" because of the vivid television images broadcast nightly into American homes. Television coverage that included images of body bags of U.S. casualties was blamed by many for the demise of U.S. public support for the war. As a result, government officials resolved to assume greater control over media in future military operations; while technology eased the making and transmission of timely war coverage, the struggle over access to the battlefield and control of media coverage grew.

Protests over the denial of media access to the 1983 U.S. invasion of the Caribbean nation of Grenada led to a congressional study that recommended "pool reporting"—reporting by a small, select group of journalists who would accompany military operations and share their information and video with other members of the media. Pool reporting was used in Panama in 1989 and in the Persian Gulf War in 1991 as well as in some high-profile trials. In Panama, military rules also delayed the formation, transportation and deployment of the reporting pool and confined pool reporters to a military base during most of the fighting. In the Gulf War, military personnel selected the members of the press pool, dictated terms of coverage (including imposition of the stringent press standards of the

Points of Law

The Media and Search Warrants

"We hold that police violate the Fourth Amendment rights of homeowners when they allow members of the media to accompany them during the execution of a warrant in their home."[1]

---

1. Hanlon v. Berger, 526 U.S. 808, 810 (1999).

Saudi Arabian government), required full-time military escorts of pool reporters and reviewed material before it could be transmitted.

Although the media accepted standard military restrictions, such as barring the reporting of troop locations and movements, they protested the pool plan as overly restrictive. In one lawsuit, veterans joined news photographers to protest DOD rules prohibiting pictures of flag-draped caskets at Dover Air Force Base, the main military mortuary for American soldiers killed abroad. In 2009, the federal government reversed the policy, allowing news media to photograph those coffins with family consent.

Prior to the 2003 invasion of Iraq, the DOD developed a plan in conjunction with news media to embed journalists within military units. Participating journalists had to undergo extensive training and sign a contract agreeing to comply with military directions and rules that focused on prohibiting reporting of the locations, tactics, strategies and numbers of U.S. forces. The embedding provided reporters greater access and some of the most immediate and direct war coverage ever but raised questions about the potential lack of objectivity of reporters who identified too closely with the military units on whom their relied and reported and on limitations on the coverage of American casualties. One journalist noted, "Whether reporters and photographers in Iraq could maintain their independence while accompanying the troops has been the subject of ongoing debate."[23]

Access to Private Property Trespass is entering another's property, particularly private property, without permission.[24] Journalists have no greater right than any other citizen to enter the property of others. This includes entering property in the course of newsgathering, no matter how important or how much in the public interest the resulting information would be. The prohibition against trespassing is generally applicable; no one, journalists included, may trespass.

Certain properties may be protected by laws limiting journalists and others from gaining access. For example, Iowa, Kansas, Montana, North Dakota and Utah have statutes prohibiting anyone from entering places where animals are commercially raised or slaughtered to take still or video pictures. Several other states are considering these so-called ag-gag laws,[25] intended, it appears, to prevent journalists and animal rights proponents from obtaining evidence of animal mistreatment.

Permission to enter the property may be given or denied only by the owner or the resident, who may not be the owner. When law enforcement officials obtain a search warrant or have emergency control of property, they have the legal authority to enter without permission.

The tradition of the **ride-along**—in which journalists accompany law enforcement or emergency personnel on rounds or to various scenes—was deep-seated in both journalism and law enforcement. The practice provided media representatives with the material for stories or program segments and gave officers

ride-along A term given to the practice of journalists and other private citizens accompanying government officials—usually those in law enforcement or other emergency response personnel—as they carry out their duties.

greater public visibility. However, when homes and other private properties were visited, the residents' Fourth Amendment protection against unreasonable searches of their dwellings and unreasonable intrusion or trespass came into play. A series of rulings weighing the media's First Amendment rights against the residents' has significantly limited news media access.

Three decades ago, the tide began to turn in state court cases. In one, a television crew accompanied Los Angeles Fire Department paramedics into the home of a heart attack victim. The unsuccessful resuscitation efforts were videotaped and broadcast on a local newscast that night and later as part of a documentary on paramedics. The victim's widow and daughter sued. Among their claims was trespassing. In ruling for the plaintiffs, a California appeals court said, "Personal security in a society saturated daily with

Embedded journalist Jill Carroll of the Christian Science Monitor (right) drives through Iraq with the U.S. Marines. She later was kidnapped and held hostage for 82 days before being released unharmed.

publicity about its members requires protection not only from governmental intrusion, but some basic bulwark of defense against private commercial enterprises which derive profits from gathering and disseminating information."[26] The court's analysis included the following points:

- There was no evidence the television crew considered entering the home to be improper.
- Because the entry was intentional, the crew members were liable.
- The defense claim that calling for paramedics implied consent for the television crew to enter the home was, the court said, "devoid of merit."[27]

The court acknowledged the importance of newsgathering but noted that the "First Amendment has never been construed to accord newsmen immunity from torts or crimes committed during the course of newsgathering. The First Amendment is not a license to trespass, to steal, or to intrude by electronic means into the precincts of another's home or office."[28] Holding the television crew liable for trespass does not impermissibly burden the First Amendment rights of newsgatherers. "To hold otherwise," the court said, "might have extraordinarily chilling implications for all of us."[29] This and similar rulings began to establish that government permission for media to enter a private residence is not equivalent to obtaining the consent of the resident, nor is it adequate for legal entry.

The U.S. Supreme Court reinforced that doctrine. In one case, a CNN crew accompanied federal agents to a Montana ranch. U.S. Fish and Wildlife Service (FWS) agents obtained a warrant to search the 75,000-acre ranch. Officials suspected the residents, the Berger family, had shot or poisoned eagles, violating federal wildlife laws.[30] The Bergers did not know until later that the lead FWS officer was wearing a CNN microphone and the officers were using CNN video cameras. CNN agreed to air the videotape only if the case was resolved or a jury had been chosen if charges were brought.[31] When the Bergers learned of the FWS–CNN agreement, they claimed the FWS officers violated their Fourth Amendment rights to be free from unreasonable searches and seizures. In *Hanlon v. Berger* the Supreme Court said a jury should consider the Bergers' Fourth Amendment claim.[32] The Court sidestepped the First Amendment and analyzed the case as a Fourth Amendment search matter. The raid violated the Fourth Amendment largely because it was intended to serve a purpose other than law enforcement, purposes the Court characterized as "entertainment."[33] CNN and the Bergers settled out of court.[34]

The Supreme Court dealt another blow to ride-alongs in *Wilson v. Layne*. This decision, excerpted at the end of this chapter, involved the search of a private home. Armed with a search warrant, deputy federal marshals and local police officers had invited a Washington Post reporter and photographer to accompany them when they conducted an early morning raid to arrest a fugitive. Once inside, officers were confronted by a man who awoke and demanded an explanation. The photographer took pictures as police wrestled him to the floor and his wife emerged from the bedroom. None of the photos was published. The couple in the home were the parents of the fugitive, who was not at home. Believing the raid and the presence of journalists violated their Fourth Amendment protection from unreasonable search, the couple sued.[35]

Ruling in favor of the couple, the U.S. Supreme Court in *Wilson v. Layne* cited a number of reasons why the news media were not lawfully in the home and established several legal points that apply to the day-to-day work of journalists. First, because the officers had a warrant, they were clearly entitled to enter the home. But a warrant neither implies nor provides the authority for officers to invite journalists to accompany them.[36] Second, the presence of reporters inside the home was not related to the objectives authorized by the warrant. The journalists did not engage in the execution of the warrant and did not assist the police in their task. The reporters' presence, therefore, was not related to the purpose of the law enforcement intrusion.[37]

The assertion that the journalists' presence served a number of legitimate law enforcement purposes did not outweigh the residential privacy rights protected by the Fourth Amendment. Even if media ride-alongs further general police

Points of Law

Wilson v. Layne: The State of Ride-Alongs

- A search warrant entitles officers, but not reporters, to enter a home.

- The presence of reporters is unrelated to the authorized intrusion.

- The presence of reporters serves no legitimate law enforcement purposes.

- Inviting reporters for the execution of a search warrant violates the Fourth Amendment.

realWorld Law

The Embarrassment of Ride-Alongs

From the news media's perspective, the benefits of ride-alongs are apparent: the opportunity to observe and record law enforcement or emergency personnel at work. But the practice is also highly questionable. First Amendment scholar Rodney Smolla cautions journalists to be careful about ride-alongs. If nothing else, ride-alongs place the media and government officials "dangerously close" to working together. While that may seem innocent, it endangers press autonomy and the adversarial relationship necessary to hold those in government accountable. At the very least, Smolla says, journalists should make the distinction between public and private spaces. Cruising neighborhoods is one thing; being part of warrant execution, especially on private property, is another. While ride-alongs in public spheres may provide journalists unique and valuable access, it is vital to maintain stay away from any quid pro quo relationship. Journalists should find it an embarrassment when law enforcement officials defend themselves by claiming journalists were working with them, as happened in *Wilson v. Layne,* Smolla says.[1]

1. Rodney A. Smolla, *Privacy and the Law: The Media's Intrusion on Privacy: Privacy and the First Amendment Right to Gather News,* 67 Geo. Wash. L. Rev. 1097 (1999).

objectives, that does not mean they further the purposes of the search. While ride-alongs might advance government anti-crime and law enforcement activities through greater and more accurate news reporting, the Court said these benefits do not overcome the Fourth Amendment, which protects fundamental individual rights.[38] Neither good public relations for the police nor the need for accurate reporting on police activities furnishes an adequate constitutional justification for media to accompany police into a home during execution of an arrest warrant.[39]

The Court also rejected the argument that third parties could help minimize police abuses and protect suspects. Although police may take videos to preserve evidence and document an arrest, the intent of the journalists in this case was to gather news, not to serve officers or residents. Although the presence of third parties during the execution of a warrant may be constitutionally permissible in some circumstances, the Court said, in this case it was not.[40] The rule that emerged, then, is that it generally is a violation of the Fourth Amendment for police to bring members of the media or other third parties into a home during the execution of a warrant unless that third party is there to help execute the warrant.[41]

In neither of the two relevant U.S. Supreme Court rulings were either media organizations or journalists the defendants. Instead, law enforcement officials were held accountable. Nevertheless, the implications for news media are clear. The law is now clearly on the side of residents. Media ride-alongs on public property are safer for journalists, but reporters are not immune from liability even in those circumstances.[42]

Although some thought the Court's ruling in *Wilson v. Layne* would end television programs, such as "COPS," once on Fox and now on Spike TV, that depend on cameras accompanying law enforcement officers onto private property, they continued to be financially successful. "While we do not necessarily agree with that decision," said "COPS" executive producer John Langley, "we are obligated to point out that, as a so-called 'ride-along' show, we are unaffected by the decision because we obtain releases from everyone involved in our program."[43]

Newsgathering Pitfalls

tortious newsgathering The use of reporting techniques that are wrongful and unlawful and for which the victim may obtain damages in court.

During the late 20th and early 21st centuries, the intrusiveness of some newsgathering methods raised concerns. As newsgathering technologies evolved to make surveillance and the recording easier and more covert, and as television news magazines and reality programs multiplied, so did the legal complaints about newsgathering.

Jacqueline Kennedy Onassis in 1968 with her children, Caroline and John, Jr.

Harassment

Some aggressive newsgathering efforts cross a line and become harassment. Perhaps the most notable examples occur when celebrities are pursued by photographers known as "paparazzi." One infamous case involved a photographer who repeatedly stalked former first lady Jacqueline Kennedy Onassis and her children.[44] The photographer, Ron Galella, was sued not only by Onassis but also by the Secret Service, which claimed that Galella continually interfered with agents assigned to protect Onassis and her children. The court flatly rejected Galella's claim that the First Amendment was a complete defense to his behavior. The court ordered Galella to remain 150 feet from Onassis, 225 feet from her children, and 300 feet from their homes and schools. The distances were significantly reduced on appeal.[45]

As the sort of "ambush-and-surveillance" journalism practiced by Galella became more commonplace, the label **tortious newsgathering** arose. Tortious newsgathering encompasses the various problematic practices examined in this chapter. One case symbolizes the evolution of the law—and the media—in this area. Employees of the syndicated television program "Inside Edition" were working on a story on the insurance firm U.S. Healthcare. The CEO denied them an interview, so they targeted his daughter and son-in-law,

realWorld Law

"California v. Paparazzi"

California lawmakers targeted newsgathering practices typically associated with paparazzi in 2010. The law adds a misdemeanor charge to photographers charged with driving recklessly in pursuit of celebrity photos or who block sidewalks to create a sort of "false imprisonment."[1] It adds extra penalties if children have been endangered as a result. Those who trespass or invade a celebrity's privacy to obtain a good picture will face triple the normal penalties and up to three times the damages that applied prior to 2010.[2] Critics, including the California Newspaper Publishers Association, say previous laws against reckless driving and trespassing adequately address public concerns without implicating the First Amendment.

First Amendment advocates also criticized Malibu and other Los Angeles–area cities when they moved to regulate paparazzi conduct to increase the comfort of their celebrity residents and guests.[3]

1. Patrick McGreevy & Jack Dolan, *Pay Reforms Inspired by Bell OKd*, L.A. TIMES, Sept. 1, 2010, at AA1.
2. Dennis Romero, *Stiff Penalties for Aggressive Paparazzi in California Likely*, L.A. WEEKLY (Sept. 1, 2010), *available at* http://blogs.laweekly.com informer/hollywood/paparazzi-bill-passes/.
3. Harriet Ryan, *Plan Would Protect Stars from Paparazzi*, L.A. TIMES, Nov. 20, 2008, at B4.

also executives in the company. The "Inside Edition" tactics included staking out the executives' home, following them and their 3-year-old, and using hidden cameras, powerful microphones and extreme telephoto lenses. To escape, the family vacationed in Florida. The "Inside Edition" crew followed them and set up in a boat about 50 yards offshore from the family house.

Back in Philadelphia, a federal district court granted the family an injunction.[46] The judge ruled the "*legal* newsgathering activities" of the "Inside Edition" crew would not be "irreparably harmed by an injunction narrowly tailored to preclude them from continuing their harassing conduct" toward the family. Such newsgathering tactics are not only illegal but also breach ethical standards.

Anti-paparazzi legislation grew in popularity after incidents like these—and especially after the 1997 car accident that killed England's Princess Diana as photographers pursued her. Celebrity-populated California enacted a law that imposes liability for trespass with the intent to capture any visual image or sound recording.[47] A similar federal measure was explored but not enacted.[48]

Fraud and Misrepresentation

Journalists are not immune to prosecution for illegal activities. The issue arose when producers of an ABC News television magazine program decided to infiltrate the Food Lion grocery chain to investigate accusations of unsanitary practices. With the approval of many within ABC, two female news reporters used false names and invented work histories to obtain jobs at Food Lion, one in North

realWorld Law

Undercover at Work

The practice of journalists working for the very company or industry the reporter wants to expose has a long history. From Upton Sinclair writing about the terrible conditions in the meat-packing business to ABC reporters working in Food Lion grocery stores, going undercover long has been a journalistic technique. When ABC journalists lied on their job applications to Food Lion, the U.S. Court of Appeals for the Fourth Circuit ruled that the journalists were not liable for lying to get jobs but were liable for trespass. How was it trespass when Food Lion gave them access to the nonpublic parts of the stores? It was because Food Lion did not know the reporters were filming a story. This suggests "a reporter or producer can be liable for trespass if, while working undercover, he works for the company he is reporting on."[1]

---

1. Shelly Rosenfeld, *Note: Lights, Camera, Sanction? Whether a Proposed Anti-Paparazzi Ordinance Would Limit Investigative Journalism in the News Business,* 6 Hastings Bus. L.J. 483, 493 (2010).

Carolina and the other in South Carolina. They wore hidden miniature cameras and microphones to work.[49] Food Lion sharply criticized their story when it aired and documented allegedly unsanitary meat-handling practices at the stores.

Food Lion denied the accusations and sued ABC. The high-profile case, *Food Lion, Inc. v. Capital Cities, Inc./ABC,* initially went well for the plaintiff grocery chain and sent a chill through the media industry. Although a federal appellate court eventually reversed the verdict against ABC, the case remains a cautionary tale for the press.[50] First, it was a milestone in the trend of plaintiffs veering away from libel claims. Rather than suing ABC for libel, where the truth or falsity of ABC's claims would be examined, Food Lion waged its legal battle on the newsgathering and business fronts, alleging fraud, trespass, unfair trade practices and breach of duty of loyalty.[51] The trial court's published opinion on the case said that because Food Lion chose not to sue for libel, it could be assumed the content of the story was true.[52] Rather than claim its reputation had been unfairly damaged, the court said, "Food Lion attacked the methods used by defendants to gather the information ultimately aired on 'PrimeTime Live.'"[53] At trial, the jury found for Food Lion, awarding the grocery chain negligible amounts of money for its actual damages but more than $5.5 million in punitive damages. However, the trial court judge ruled that the punitive damages award was excessive and reduced it to $315,000. ABC appealed.

A three-judge panel of the federal appeals court reversed the verdict for Food Lion on all but the trespass and breach of loyalty claims. In the end, Food Lion was awarded a total of $2. But the effects of this case remain.[54] Not only had the lower court called some newsgathering techniques illegal; the reporters had initially been hit hard with a punitive damages award. In addition, the dissenting judge on the federal appeals court would have sustained the fraud claim and the punitive damages against ABC.[55] At least one federal appeals court judge believes the conduct of the ABC producers merits stiff punishment.

This case also forced one media organization to explain at length why the behavior of some of its employees was not criminal. While the news organization ultimately paid less than pocket change in damages, a few factors should not be overlooked:

- First, the attorney fees were costly.[56]
- Second, those costs had a chilling effect on the sort of newsgathering techniques used in the Food Lion story.
- Third, the jury's verdict and subsequent interviews of jury members revealed a deep-seated animosity toward the news media, particularly toward an organization perceived as big, powerful, and possessing an above-the-law attitude and deep pockets. After the verdict, several jurors expressed delight in reaching into those pockets with their punitive damage award.[57]

The success of ABC's appeal hinged largely on interpretation of the laws in North and South Carolina, where the alleged transgressions took place. It is conceivable a different result could have occurred in a different state. In fact, a Minnesota court ruled against a local television station in Minneapolis when a station employee said she was unemployed when she volunteered to work in a facility for the mentally disabled. During her volunteer work, she was armed with a hidden camera that recorded video later used in broadcasts critical of the ministry's care facility. The ministry sued for fraud and trespass and claimed it was forced to relocate as a result of the reports. The Minnesota appeals court ruled against the station's effort to dismiss the suit, saying that the station misrepresented itself and entered private property without the consent of its owner—that is, it had trespassed.[58] The parties reached a confidential settlement.

Misrepresentation can occur not only when individuals completely mask their identities and intent but also when journalists honestly disclose who they are but disguise the nature of the story they are seeking. For example, when truckers were unwilling to cooperate with producers of NBC newsmagazine "Dateline" on a story about the trucking industry, NBC gained the participation of a truck driver with a Maine company by promising that the report would be positive. NBC also promised the driver the story would not include comments from anyone from Parents Against Tired Truckers (PATT). The driver's boss, Raymond Veilleux, received the same promises and also eventually agreed. The segment "Dateline" aired was not positive about the trucking industry or the driver. A representative statement from the segment said, "American highways are a trucker's killing field."[59] The report also contained interviews with PATT members.

Veilleux and the driver sued NBC for fraud and misrepresentation. Although the federal appeals court favored NBC on nearly every point and ruled that the network's promises to produce a "positive portrayal" were too vague to sustain a claim against it,[60] it said damages could be awarded based on NBC's specific and unequivocal promise not to include anyone from PATT. The parties settled

International Law

Hacking into Arrest

London's The Guardian features the hacking scandal faced by its competitor, The News of the World.

One illegal way to gather information is by hacking into another's computer or phone messages. England's News of the World newspaper, owned by Rupert Murdoch, hacked into kidnapped and murdered schoolgirl Milly Dowler's cellphone and perhaps as many as 600 other people's cellphones, including those of many celebrities.[1] The hacking "scandal has led to civil suits, criminal investigations [and] a parliamentary inquiry . . . scrutiny that coursed through British public life, exposing previously hidden relationships between the press, the police and politicians. . . . More than 100 reporters, editors, investigators, executives and public officials have been implicated in wrongdoing by police units investigating accusations of criminal activity, including phone intercepts and bribery."[2] Arrests and convictions of Murdoch U.K. executives, News of the World editors and other employees have cost Murdoch's newspapers hundreds of millions of dollars and caused Murdoch to shut down the News of the World, a very profitable Sunday tabloid.[3]

Prompted in part by a 2,000-page report on the hacking scandal, the British Parliament in 2013 adopted a press code that establishes an independent regulator to oversee Britain's press. Any paper refusing to participate in the new regulatory process will face punitive damages if it loses a lawsuit. British editors claim this is the first press regulation in more than three centuries and violates the country's long history of press freedom.

U.S. investigators have not filed charges related to allegations that Murdoch's News Corporation employees hacked into phones of some Sept. 11, 2001 victims' families.[4]

---

1. *See* Alan Cowell & John F. Burns, *Britain: 7 Appear in Court in Phone Hacking Case,* N.Y. Times, Aug. 17, 2012, at A6.
2. Stephen Castle & Alan Cowell, *Britain: Newspapers Protest New Press Rules,* N.Y. Times, March 20, 2013, at A6.
3. Thomas S. Leatherbury & Travis R. Wimberly, *2012 Update: Developments in the Law of Newsgathering Liability,* in 3 Comm. L. in the Digital Age 2012, at 595–96; John F. Burns, *Six More Journalists Held in British Hacking Case,* N.Y. Times, Feb. 14, 2013, at A6.
4. *Id.*

for an undisclosed amount.[61] Media defendants may settle in part because the U.S. Supreme Court has held that media promises—at least promises of source confidentiality—are legally binding.[62] After the Supreme Court said media organizations may be responsible for damages if they break a promise of confidentiality, the Minnesota Supreme Court affirmed a judgment of $200,000 against the media for breaking that promise.[63]

Using Social Media as Sources

Using material from social media may be perilous. A Washington Post columnist based a column on a tweet saying "Bush fought 2 wars without costing taxpayers a dime." The purported tweeter did not exist. When a Washington Post book critic wanted to see how quickly the misinformation would go viral, he tweeted that the weekly magazine The New Yorker would switch to biweekly or monthly. The critic said it took 10 minutes for the story without any named source to be picked up by newspapers and bloggers. When another Washington Post writer tweeted that a National Football League quarterback would be suspended for five games, many websites and major news outlets picked up the false story. The sportswriter sent the tweet to see how incorrect claims become news stories.

Many news organizations warn reporters to be cautious about using social media accounts as sources. The Associated Press, for example, says, "Fake accounts are rampant in the social media world and can appear online within minutes of a new name appearing in the news. . . . [N]ever lift quotes, photos or video from social networking sites and attribute them to the name on the profile or feed where you found the material."[64]

SUMMARY

REPORTERS' EXUBERANCE IN PURSUING A STORY MAY be legally punishable when it constitutes harassment. Courts make a factual determination case by case on whether tortious interference has occurred. Persistence that resembles stalking or that frightens the subjects may result in court restraining orders or fines. Assault, with or without a reporter's pad, is illegal.

When reporters use deceit to gather news, they clearly violate ethical standards and sometimes violate the law. Courts generally look carefully at the specific facts of each case to determine when fraud or misrepresentation is legally punishable. Reporters promises may be legally binding. ∎

Covert Recording

Journalists often record conversations and behavior, sometimes without the knowledge of those being recorded. It may be the only way to gather evidence of possible wrongdoing and images or sound recordings aid resolution of disputes about what happened or what was said, which otherwise may come down to one person's word against another's.

Ethical questions arise because some degree of deception is necessarily involved; hidden recording devices are, by definition, unknown to some parties. Technological developments that miniaturize devices increase the ability to record communication without the knowledge of one or more of the recorded parties. The ubiquity of communications technologies from smartphones to e-mail to computer-based voice messaging systems provides multiple platforms for recording conversations either by a participant in the conversation or by someone who is eavesdropping.

Some media organizations enforce policies about the use of hidden recordings or recordings without consent and regard them as a last resort. In addition,

Points of Law

States That Forbid Unauthorized Use of Cameras in Private Places[1]

- Alabama*
- Arkansas
- California
- Delaware*
- Georgia*
- Hawaii*
- Kansas*
- Maine*
- Michigan*
- Minnesota*
- New Hampshire
- South Dakota*
- Utah*

1. Reporters Committee for Freedom of the Press, *The First Amendment Handbook* (n.d.), *available at* http://www.rcfp.org/handbook/c03p02.html.

*States that also prohibit trespassing on private property to conduct surveillance of people.

various state and federal laws come into play. Laws and court decisions may or may not permit surreptitious recording. Recording may be acceptable in one state but not another.[65] Covert recording also may violate federal laws.

The use of hidden cameras by the news media does not typically in and of itself constitute an illegal intrusion. However, 13 states specifically prohibit the unauthorized use or installation of cameras in private places.

Face-to-Face Recording

Reporters often record interviews. Recording audio or video in an interview with plainly visible equipment does not violate any state or federal law. There is nothing secret about recording this way.

If a reporter records an interview without the interviewee's knowledge, over the phone or with a recorder hidden in his or her pocket, circumstances change and laws may be triggered. Thirty-seven states and the District of Columbia allow the use of a hidden recorder for a face-to-face interview. These are called "one-party" states because only one party must know the recording is happening—and that party can be the reporter. The one-party approach protects against an electronic eavesdropper or illegal wiretap when no one in the conversation is aware of the recording.

Twelve states are not so lenient. These all-party states require all participants in an interview or conversation to give consent or recording is not permitted. (Vermont remains the one state without a law specifically addressing audio recording of interviews.)

California is an all-party state[66] that makes it illegal to record a "confidential communication" unless all parties in the conversation give consent.[67] This was central to a political incident that led the Association of Community Organizations for Reform Now (ACORN), a community service organization, to close down. Some politically conservative organizations accused ACORN, which engaged in voter registration drives in poor neighborhoods, of violating voting laws or federal financing rules.[68] But the California case involved two people who entered an ACORN office claiming they wanted help obtaining a home mortgage. One "was wearing a hidden recording device on his tie and also used his cell phone to record the audio," according to a federal district court.[69] The two told the ACORN worker "they intended to fill the house with underage girls working as prostitutes. Additionally, they told [him] they needed help filling out tax forms so the income from this illegal operation would appear legitimate," the court said. They asked whether the conversation was confidential and were told it was. There was discussion about the possibility of the ACORN employee helping smuggle the underage girls into the country.

The reporters later posted an edited videotape of the conversation on the Internet showing the ACORN employee "conspiring to promote an underage prostitution business by agreeing to help [them] file fraudulent tax forms and smuggle underage girls from Mexico," according to the court. The ACORN employee sued, claiming the recording violated California law.

The key question, the court said in 2012, was whether the ACORN employee had a reasonable expectation that the conversation would be confidential and not recorded. The discussion was inside the employee's office, ACORN dealt with personal client matters and the two said they wanted help with tax forms and with establishing an illegal business. Under those circumstances, according to the court, the ACORN employee could reasonably believe the conversation was sensitive and would remain confidential. Therefore, it could not be assumed the employee gave implicit consent to the recording. The court set the case for trial.

Points of Law

Recording Calls

State Laws

- Thirty-seven states require one-party consent.
- Twelve states require all-party consent.

Federal Laws

- Federal laws allow one-party consent but not if to commit a crime or tort.
- Federal Communications Commission (FCC) rules require all-party consent, notification to all parties or repeating beep.
- FCC rules require notifying all parties if a phone conversation will be recorded and broadcast or if it will be aired live.

Recording "Wire" Conversations

Federal laws cover "wire communication," which includes technologies that may not be wired but transfer voice communications from a point of origin to a point of reception.[70] Landline telephones, cellphones and computer-based voice messaging services, sometimes called "Voice over Internet Protocol" (VoIP),[71] such as Skype, Google Talk and iChat, all fall under the same regulatory umbrella. The federal **Wiretap Act**[72] applies to the interception (and recording) of a call or voice communication via any of these means.

One limitation of the Wiretap Act is that it only protects communications that are intercepted in transit, not those that are stored after transmission. VoIP calls create data packets that are stored after transmission and are subject to the Stored Communications Act,[73] which offers "considerably less protection" than the Wiretap Act.[74] The data are accessible through warrants and subpoenas.

Recording In-State Calls State laws regulating telephone calls that originate and end within that state may present problems for reporters who want to record an interview (or other conversation) conducted over telephone or VoIP. Some state courts insist on applying that state's laws even if the case involves an interstate phone call.[75] As with face-to-face recording, 12 states' laws (the same all-party states for face-to-face interviews) make it illegal to record a telephone conversation without all parties consenting.[76] Some of these all-party state laws apply only to confidential conversations. Thirty-seven states, the District of Columbia and federal law allow recording a phone call if only one party to the conversation agrees. That one party could be the reporter conducting a phone interview. In

Wiretap Act A federal law to protect the privacy of phone calls and other oral communications that makes it illegal to intercept, record, disseminate or use a private communication without a participant's permission. The law allows the government to bring criminal charges and those whose privacy was violated to sue for civil damages.

Recording Laws by State

Criminal penalties, Statute allows for civil suits, Specific hidden camera law

Criminal penalties, Specific hidden camera law

Consent of all parties required, Criminal penalties, Statute allows for civil suits, Specific hidden camera law, Additional penalties for disclosing or publishing information

Criminal penalties, Additional penalties for disclosing or publishing information

Consent of all parties required, Criminal penalties, Criminal penalties

Criminal penalties, Statute allows for civil suits, Specific hidden camera law, Additional penalties for disclosing or publishing information

Criminal penalties, Statute allows for civil suits, Additional penalties for disclosing or publishing information

Criminal penalties, Statute allows for civil suits, Specific hidden camera law

Consent of all parties required, Criminal penalties, Statute allows for civil suits

Consent of all parties required, Criminal penalties, Additional penalties for disclosing or publishing information

No law

Source: Reporters Committee for Freedom of the Press, *Can We Tape?* (n.d.), *available at* http://rcfp.org/taping/quick.html.

these states, the reporter would not need to ask the other person's permission to record the call.

Several organizations urge journalists to err on the side of caution when recording calls, due in part to the varying state laws. The safest strategy is to assume that the stricter law will apply and request permission to record from all parties.[77]

Recording Interstate Calls Both federal law and the FCC have authority over calls that cross state lines. Federal law allows recording if only one party consents.[78] An FCC rule requires obtaining all parties' consent and notifying all parties at the beginning of a call that it will be recorded, or using a regularly repeating beep tone so all parties will be aware the call is being recorded.[79] The FCC says the federal law is meant to help law enforcement officers listen to calls as part of their duties but the commission rule is meant to dissuade the public from recording calls without permission.[80] Journalism organizations generally recommend obtaining permission to record from all parties.

Broadcasting Recorded Calls The FCC requires radio and television stations to notify parties to a phone conversation if the station intends to broadcast the call live or record the call for later broadcast. Consent is not necessary, only notification. There is an exception for programs that customarily air calls live or broadcast recorded calls, such as radio call-in shows. Callers have a reasonable expectation that their conversations will be aired or recorded.[81]

The federal Electronic Communications Privacy Act (ECPA) also addresses eavesdropping, wiretapping and intercepting electronic communication. This law prohibits the unauthorized interception of electronic communication while it is in transit or in storage. One party's consent authorizes interception.

The U.S. Supreme Court in *Bartnicki v. Vopper* ruled that the First Amendment allows media use of an unauthorized recording as long as the user did not make the illegal recording. In this case, an unknown person intercepted and recorded a cell phone conversation between two teachers' union negotiators and sent it to local media. The union and school board were in heated negotiations over a collective bargaining agreement. On the tape, one negotiator says to the other, "[W]e're gonna have to go to their, their homes . . . [t]o blow off their front porches, we'll have to do some work on some of those guys."[82] Two local radio stations played the tape, and newspapers printed its contents.

The negotiator who made the remarks sued the media. Although the media did not illegally intercept the conversation, they did intentionally "disclose" the exchange when they had reason to know it was obtained illegally. That violates the federal wiretap law, the negotiator charged.[83] The media claimed the First Amendment allowed the use of the tape if they did not engage in wiretapping.

The Supreme Court agreed with the media. The First Amendment protects a journalist who reports illegally intercepted private conversations only if the conversation is newsworthy and the journalist was not involved in the interception. The Court said the federal wiretap statute was content neutral and applied no matter what the private conversation was about, but the ban on disclosing illegally intercepted communications is a prohibition on speech content. So, rather than apply the intermediate scrutiny courts usually use in deciding whether a content-neutral statute is constitutional (see Chapter 2), the Court applied the higher strict scrutiny standard it applies to regulations of content.

The Court said the law failed the strict scrutiny test because there was little evidence the law served the government's alleged compelling interest of dissuading people from intercepting private communications. More importantly, the Court said, the media in *Bartnicki* did not intercept the conversation. While the Court acknowledged that the government's second compelling interest—to minimize harm to the people whose conversations were intercepted by discouraging distribution of illegally obtained information—was important, it said informing people about matters of public interest can be more important. The Court referenced its 1971 Pentagon Papers decision affirming "the right of the press to publish information of great public concern obtained from documents stolen by a third party."[84] Noting that publication of information of public interest is one of the "core purposes of the First Amendment," the Court concluded that "a stranger's illegal conduct does not suffice to remove the First Amendment shield from speech about a matter of public concern."[85] The Court's rationale in ruling for the broadcaster was threefold: (1) media played no part in the illegal interception, (2) media access to the information on the tapes was lawful (the unlawful interception was by someone else) and (3) the conversation was on a matter of public concern.[86] Justice Stephen Breyer concurred in the result but said its application should be limited to instances concerning personal safety, as in this case.

The ECPA also prohibits accessing a computer facility without permission to obtain and disclose information. Thus, Internet messages intended for private use are not legally accessible—unless the Internal Revenue Service (IRS) wants them. The American Civil Liberties Union said in 2013 it had obtained documents in which IRS attorneys claimed that once e-mails are sent from a computer they lose Fourth Amendment protection against unreasonable search and seizure.[87] This assertion is contrary to the U.S. Court of Appeals for the Sixth Circuit's ruling in 2010 that personal e-mail messages are private.[88]

Alleged violation of the ECPA has been among the claims in suits against Internet service providers (ISPs) when they reveal the identity of a message poster. Courts generally have favored ISPs that disclose identities according to the standards outlined in the act. In one case, for example, the plaintiff posted a message on America Online (AOL) that harassed the soon-to-be ex-wife of the plaintiff's lover. When advised of the posting, AOL investigated and terminated the poster's contract for violating AOL's "Rules of the Road." Under subpoena and in compliance with an exception provided by ECPA, AOL provided the identity of the poster to the subject of the post. A federal court ruled that such disclosure did not violate the poster's privacy.[89]

Under federal and many state laws, a recording made to commit a crime or a tort is illegal regardless of who consents. For example, rap artists Andre Young, Snoop Dogg, Ice Cube and Eminem were scheduled to perform in Detroit as part

realWorld Law

Video of Public Places

A New Jersey man was arrested for recording video outside a federal courthouse in New York City. Antonio Musumeci shot video of a man handing out pamphlets in a plaza area, then interviewed that man. During the interview, the interviewee was approached and arrested by a member of the Federal Protective Service. After that, Musumeci also was arrested, the memory card from his camera was confiscated and he was charged with violating a federal regulation that governs photography on federal property.[1]

The regulation requires advance permission to photograph certain agency-occupied areas, with some exceptions for news photography. In 2010, Musumeci alleged that the law and its enforcement violated his First and Fourteenth Amendment rights.[2]

In a settlement, the federal government agreed that no federal statutes or regulations bar photography of federal courthouses from publicly accessible property. The settlement also required all federal employees who monitor federal buildings to be informed about the rights of photographers.[3]

1. 41 C.F.R. § 102–74.420.
2. Musumeci v. U.S. Dep't of Homeland Security, S.D.N.Y., Index No. 10 CIV 3370 (2010); *see also* Heicklen v. U.S. Dept. of Homeland Security, 2011 WL 3841543 (S.D.N.Y.).
3. *Id., available at* http://www.nyclu.org/files/releases/Final_Stip_and_Order_10.18.10.pdf.

of a nationwide tour. In each of 10 cities before Detroit, a short video introduced Andre Young and Snoop Dogg. But Detroit police and other city officials told tour producers the video violated obscenity laws and could not be shown. People connected with the tour secretly recorded the meeting and included parts of the recording in a music video called "Gangster Rap Concert DVD" that was marketed and sold internationally. City officials sued under the federal wiretap law that makes it illegal to record any private conversation.[90] However, it is not illegal if one party gives consent. Tour representatives said their commercial use of the recording was legal because they gave themselves permission. The court said one-party consent is not sufficient if recording is for an illegal purpose or to commit a tort.[91] Here the tour representatives made the video intending to use it to commit the tort of appropriation—taking the material without consent for commercial purposes (see Chapter 6). By using an excerpt in a commercial DVD, the court said, one-party consent would not be effective.

Noncovert Recording

Even where public access is permitted, recording of certain events may be restricted. The Maryland Legislature, for example, prohibits reporters with recording devices from attending its sessions. When reporters who claimed the speed and accuracy of recording justified the practice challenged the restriction, a Maryland appeals court said that while newsgathering is entitled to some First Amendment protection, banning recorders does not infringe on that right.[92] It called the ban "a mere inconvenience."[93] Similar reasoning guides the federal court system and the few state judiciaries that continue to limit cameras in courtrooms, as explained in Chapter 10.[94]

Recording may also be limited simply by preventing access to events. Obtaining access through trespass, harassment or fraud and misrepresentation is illegal. Access to public property is generally permitted to any member of the public. Moreover, whatever can be seen from public property can generally be recorded. If access to a specific area of public property is restricted by law enforcement officials, however, individuals must comply. This could apply to disaster sites. For example, when an airliner crashed at a publicly owned airport, the crash site was secured with officers positioned to keep unauthorized people away. When a television photojournalist followed an emergency vehicle through a roadblock, a city detective ordered the photographer to leave. The photographer then jumped a fence, ran to the top of a hill and began taking pictures of the site. The officer again ordered the photojournalist to leave the restricted area. The photojournalist said he would not stop taking pictures unless he was arrested. The officer arrested him. When the photojournalist appealed his conviction for disorderly conduct, the Wisconsin Supreme Court upheld the conviction. It rejected the argument that the First Amendment demands news media access to emergency sites and pointed out that media access was not denied in this situation. While the photojournalist was arguing with the detective, other journalists followed the airport's media guidelines and were taken to the crash site.[95]

SUMMARY

REPORTERS' USE OF HIDDEN AUDIO AND VIDEO recording equipment can raise serious legal and ethical questions. Many state laws forbid covert recording and require informed consent from the parties being recorded. In addition, federal law prohibits electronic eavesdropping and wiretapping and protects the privacy of electronic communications via telephone or the Internet. The U.S. Supreme Court, however, ruled that journalists who do not illegally record intercepted newsworthy telephone conversation are not liable for its broadcast. Under some conditions, Internet service providers may also disclose the identity of senders and the content of private Internet communications without liability.

Reporters allowed into a particular place may not always record there. Some government proceedings may ban recordings. Overt recording to document news events also may be limited by constraints on physical access to emergency scenes and private property. ∎

Denying Access to Records

Some federal laws allow or mandate agencies to withhold records, usually in an effort to protect individual privacy. While Chapter 6 discusses privacy torts whose violation may result in civil lawsuits, the privacy violations described here may result in criminal prosecution. These laws meant to protect privacy also limit the ability to gather news.

Privacy Act

The federal Privacy Act gives individuals the right to examine government files that contain information about them. Just as important, the act also allows government agencies to use the information in these files only for the reason it was collected. Federal government agencies cannot disclose such information without the written consent of the person involved except that the law may not be used to deny access to information that should be available under the Freedom of Information Act (FOIA). Whenever the two statutes are in opposition, the FOIA prevails. In reality, federal agencies have been very careful about violating personal privacy. Some observers, however, are concerned about invasions of privacy that may result from increased sharing of information among government agencies. The USA Patriot Act allows agencies to exchange information that they previously were required to keep only for internal use.

Student Records

The **Family Educational Rights and Privacy Act (FERPA)**, sometimes referred to as the Buckley Act,[96] forbids federally funded institutions of education from releasing students' school records unless they, as adults, or their parents provide consent. The adult students and the parents of minor children are permitted access to the records. The protected records are those containing personally identifiable information. The U.S. Department of Education (DOE) defines "personally identifiable information" as including a family member's name, personal information such as the student's Social Security number or student number, and personal characteristics or other information that would make it easy to determine the student's identity.[97] Government-supported schools also are forbidden from releasing grades or information related to a student's health, although they can disclose "directory" information such as a student's name, address, telephone number, date and place of birth, major field of study, dates of attendance and degrees and awards received. Violating the law puts an institution's government funding at risk.

Schools often tell journalists that FERPA prevents release of information about disciplinary actions involving students. University officials have cited FERPA as preventing them from releasing information such as campus police records or student disciplinary records. While nondisclosure may protect individuals, the news media argue that the public has a right to know information related to possible crimes and justice systems on the campuses of public institutions. The federal Campus Security Act, or the Clery Act as it is now known, requires universities to compile and publish statistics on campus crime each year.

Family Educational Rights and Privacy Act (FERPA) A federal law that protects the privacy of student education records. The law applies to all schools that receive funds under an applicable program of the U.S. Department of Education; FFRPA gives parents certain rights with respect to their children's school records; these rights transfer to the student when he or she reaches the age of 18 or attends a school beyond the high school level.

Reporting using these statistics has unveiled significant problems on campuses, such as the excesses in fraternity hazing and gay bashing at the University of Georgia that were uncovered when student journalists obtained records of university disciplinary hearings.[98] The Georgia Supreme Court held that universities could release student disciplinary records without violating FERPA.[99] The Georgia court said disciplinary records were not student records under FERPA because they were not concerned with student academic performance, financial aid or academic probation.

Such campus information is more difficult to obtain in the wake of a federal district court ruling in response to a DOE argument that student disciplinary records are student records that may not be released under FERPA without permission, however. The Chronicle of Higher Education, a weekly newspaper, and a student newspaper at Miami University of Ohio sought the records of internal discipline committees to look at crime trends on the campus. A federal appellate court supported the DOE's interpretation.[100] The court said the law's language made clear that disciplinary proceedings were part of student records and could not be released without a student's consent.

Although student media enjoy the same First Amendment rights as non-campus media to publish legally obtained information and a full range of ideas, privacy and campus security laws permit a variety of campus records to be kept confidential. Legal as well as institutional barriers impede journalists' access to information about individual university students. Laws that protect interests in personal privacy and the integrity of educational files pose obstacles to campus reporters.

Medical Records

Health Insurance Portability and Accountability Act (HIPAA)
is a federal law protecting against health professionals and institutions revealing individuals' private medical records.

The **Health Insurance Portability and Accountability Act (HIPAA)** prevents health professionals and institutions from revealing individuals' medical records. When Congress passed HIPAA in 1996, it started efforts to fashion rules designed to protect patients' medical privacy. The act eventually led the Department of Health and Human Services to offer the first federal medical privacy regulations, called the Standards for Privacy of Individually Identifiable Health Information. These rules were designed to give patients more control over their health information and to limit the use and release of health records to third parties. Generally, the privacy standards established a federal requirement that most doctors, hospitals and other health care providers obtain a patient's written consent before using or disclosing the patient's personal health information. The rules restrict the use of such records for marketing and research purposes.

Driver's Information

Driver's Privacy Protection Act
Federal legislation that prohibits states from disclosing personal information that drivers submit in order to obtain drivers' licenses.

The federal **Driver's Privacy Protection Act** of 1994 prohibits states from releasing information obtained from driver's license and vehicle registration records without permission.[101] The law allows disclosure under certain circumstances.

realWorld Law

Leaking to Reporters: Espionage?

Bradley Manning

Journalists develop sources for information. Sometimes those sources provide inside information, commonly called "leaks." At other times, leaks—perhaps top secret—come from unexpected informants. New York Times reporters scarcely had heard of Daniel Ellsberg when he gave them documents that became known as the Pentagon Papers (see Chapter 2). And the world did not know Pfc. Bradley Manning when he gave WikiLeaks 700,000 confidential U.S. government diplomatic and military documents. WikiLeaks posted those documents, and many newspapers developed stories from them. A military judge found Manning not guilty of the most serious charge against him, "aiding the enemy," carrying a possible death sentence under the Uniform Code of Military Justice. However, the court found Manning guilty of violating the Espionage Act of 1917 and sentenced him to 35 years in prison.[1]

Just months before Manning's conviction, Edward J. Snowden released National Security Agency documents. Snowden, employed by an NSA (National Security Agency) contractor, leaked the documents to The Guardian, a British newspaper. The United States filed criminal charges against Snowden for leaking classified documents.[2] The documents Snowden released showed the NSA has extensively logged information about American residents' phone calls and e-mails. Snowden fled the United States, and Russia granted him temporary asylum.

Charges against Snowden are the seventh time under President Barak Obama that a government official has faced criminal charges for leaking classified documents to the press. There were only three such cases under all previous presidents. For example, Espionage Act charges were brought against former Central Intelligence Agency (CIA) officer John Kiriakou for disclosing to journalists classified information about the waterboarding of al-Qaida suspects. Kiriakou is serving a 30-month prison sentence.[3]

Spurred by its concern about leaks, the U.S. Department of Justice acquired Associated Press phone records during a two-month period in 2012. The department admitted in mid-2013 that a top Justice official agreed to subpoena the records to investigate a leak to a reporter about the CIA's involvement in a sting operation involving al-Qaida. Responding to an uproar over the subpoenas, the Obama administration said it did not favor pursuing reporters who publish leaked information but that it is necessary to discover what government official gave secret information to the press.[4] Nevertheless, The Washington Post revealed in 2013 that the Justice Department accused a Fox News reporter of being "at the very least, either . . . an aider, abettor and/or co-conspirator" for receiving information about North Korea possibly intending to launch a nuclear missile in 2009. The Department of Justice searched the "reporter's personal e-mails and attempted to track his movements," according to The New York Times.[5]

Is Manning equivalent to Ellsberg although he released secret documents to WikiLeaks rather than to The New York Times? If Ellsberg was not tried for violating the Espionage Act of 1917, should Manning have been tried?

1. Charlie Savage & Emmarie Huetteman, *Manning Sentenced to 35 Years for a Pivotal Leak of U.S. Files*, N.Y. TIMES, Aug. 22, 2013, at A1; Charlie Savage, *Manning Is Acquitted of Aiding the Enemy*, N.Y. TIMES, July 31, 2013, at A1.
2. Scott Shane, *Ex-Contractor Is Charged in Leaks on N.S.A. Surveillance*, N.Y. TIMES (June 21, 2013), *available at* http://www.nytimes.com/2013/06/22/us/snowden-espionage-act.html?pagewanted=all.
3. Michael S. Schmidt, *Ex-C.I.A. Officer Sentenced to 30 Months in Leak*, N.Y. TIMES (Jan. 25, 2013), *available at* http://www.nytimes.com/2013/01/26/us/ex-officer-for-cia-is-sentenced-in-leak-case.html.
4. Charlie Savage, *Proposals May Rein in Prosecutors on Leaks*, N.Y. TIMES, May 31, 2013, at A10.
5. Brian Stelter & Michael Shear, *Justice Dept. Investigated Fox Reporter over Leaks*, N.Y. TIMES, May 21, 2013, at A15.

Driver's license and motor vehicle records may include an individual's name, address, picture, telephone number, vehicle description, Social Security number, medical information and other personal data. At one time, many states sold this information to individuals and companies, earning millions of dollars annually. Congress stopped this practice in part to prevent stalkers from obtaining information about potential targets. However, the law also prevents journalists from using these records to find information for stories. The U.S. Supreme Court upheld the law against a constitutional challenge, finding that Congress' power over interstate commerce allowed it to adopt the statute.[102]

Video Voyeurism

Advancements in technology often drive developments in the law. Miniaturized cameras and cellular phones equipped with cameras were the catalyst for laws meant to protect against video voyeurism. Described in various ways, video voyeurism includes photography in private areas and the practice of covertly taking low-angle photos up a woman's skirt, often with the intent of posting them online. The federal Video Voyeurism Prevention Act[103] prohibits unauthorized photography of an individual's private areas. In addition, 23 states have laws that specifically address this issue, while another 26 states have general "antivoyeurism" or "peeping" laws, New Mexico being the only state without either a specific or general law in the area.

SUMMARY

LIKE ACCESS TO FEDERAL RECORDS, OBTAINING ACCESS to U.S. military operations can be challenging. The history in this area is one of give-and-take, with the government attempting to exert more control in recent decades.

Many federal and state laws limit access to records held by government that contain individually identifiable information. The federal Privacy Act permits individuals to access their own records—but not the records of others—to verify their accuracy. Federal laws protect the privacy of educational, medical and driver's license records from disclosure. ■

Newsgathering Protections

Although courts have repeatedly and consistently ruled that no explicit newsgathering right exists under the First Amendment, there are various protections that can enhance access to information. Some of these protections take the form of statutes or other enacted legislation; others stem from court rulings. Either way, it was only in the latter part of the 20th century that the concept of a truly open government—open to all citizens—was codified to any meaningful extent.

Open-Government Laws

"Knowledge will forever govern ignorance; and a people who mean to be their own governors must arm themselves with the power which knowledge gives."[104] The words are James Madison's. They epitomize both the spirit of, and the need for, openness in a democratic government. Absent information, the electorate is blind. Liberal democratic theory maintains that an obligation exists on the part of those in authority to open the blinds and allow in the sunshine by providing access to the information necessary to self-govern. Fulfillment of the obligation results in accountability. The governed—that is, the people—cannot maintain control of their government absent knowledge of its inner workings. This responsibility of government to open its processes to citizens, however, did not emerge in a significant and material way until almost a century and a half after Madison's proclamation.

Points of Law

Freedom of Information Act: Some Basics

- It applies to all executive federal government agencies but not to the U.S. Congress, federal courts and courts-martial or the military during wartime.

- It requires each federal agency to publish in the Federal Register a description of its organization and a list of its personnel who can be contacted for records.

- It requires each agency to publish the procedures by which records can be obtained.

- It requires that all records be segregated so that an entire record cannot be classified as exempt, only part(s) of it.

Access to Federal Records: The Freedom of Information Act

The ability of citizens to hold their governments accountable, as Madison noted, depends on knowledge. That knowledge stems from two primary sources to which laws can enhance access: government records and government meetings. The section that follows focuses on the law that helps to provide access to records kept by the federal government. (Access to court records is addressed in Chapter 10.)

Growing secrecy in the federal government during and after World War II led to a movement for greater transparency. The press, along with some congressional support, pushed for creating a law to allow greater access to information. Organizations such as the American Society of Newspaper Editors and the Society of Professional Journalists played key roles in the late 1940s.[105] Still, momentum was slow to build.

The growth of the federal government through the mid-20th century saw the creation of agency after agency. This added to the criticism that government was a closed system. The sheer size and complexity of the rapidly expanding government gave rise to concerns about the ability of citizens to understand it and oversee its workings. The Congressional Record was no longer enough to report on federal government business because government business was being conducted on multiple levels outside the U.S. Capitol. After much debate, Congress responded to critics by passing the **Freedom of Information Act (FOIA)** in 1966. It was intended to permit any person access to records held by federal executive branch agencies. The act was amended in 1974, with additional revisions in 1976, 1986, and 1996 and, with the Open Government Act, in 2007.

Freedom of Information Act (FOIA) The 1966 act that requires records held by federal government agencies to be made available to the public, provided that the information sought does not fall within one of nine exempted categories.

The U.S. Supreme Court has stated that the basic policy is that "disclosure, not secrecy, is the dominant objective of the act."[106] Under the FOIA, government records are presumed to be open. Exemptions that enable government to withhold information from citizens must be interpreted narrowly to afford the greatest possibility of a fully informed citizenry. To that end, the FOIA is available to anyone, not just to members of the news media. In fact, some argue that journalists do not use the act's provisions enough. Still, it has been a valuable tool in the pursuit of information for many reporters, including journalists seeking and obtaining information related to NASA mishaps,[107] design deficiencies in both the Ford Pinto's gas tank and the Hubble space telescope, dangers to local communities from nuclear weapons plants and hazardous lead levels in imported wine.

The FOIA specifies that records held by federal agencies may be requested. That raises two questions:

1. *What is an agency?* "Agency" is defined as "any executive department, military department, Government corporation, Government controlled corporation, or other establishment in the executive branch of the Government, including the Executive Office of the President, or any independent regulatory agency."[108] By specifically including the Executive Office of the President, which encompasses offices such as the Office of Management and Budget, the Office of Policy Development and the Office of Science and Technology Policy, Congress implicitly excluded the White House Office, which includes the president's closest advisers and their staffs.[109] Also excluded are Congress and the federal courts. Organizations that receive federal funding but are not under the direct control of the federal government—for example, the Corporation for Public Broadcasting—are also outside the FOIA's coverage.

    Among the covered agencies are federal agencies, departments, commissions and government-controlled corporations at the federal level only. This includes cabinet-level departments such as Defense, Homeland Security, State, Treasury and Justice. Regulatory agencies such as the Federal Communications Commission, the Securities and Exchange Commission, and the Federal Trade Commission are also included under the FOIA, as are NASA and the U.S. Postal Service.

2. *What is a record?* The FOIA does not define a record, but the act has been interpreted to apply to all tangible or fixed items that (a) document government actions and (b) may be reproduced. Thus, computer files, paper reports, films, videotapes, photographs and audio recordings are considered to be records under the law. A record is something that already exists, not something that government could compile from the diverse information it holds.

But are all records in the possession of a federal government agency records under the law? There is no precise answer to that question. Neither the text of the FOIA nor its **legislative history** defines "agency record."[110] Congress largely has resolved the question of what an agency is and courts generally have agreed on the necessary properties of a record. However, the criteria satisfying the link between an agency and a record necessary to have the document defined as an agency record remains in dispute.

legislative history Congressional reports and records containing discussions about proposed legislation.

The U.S. Supreme Court, while noting that "Congress has supplied no definition of 'agency records in the FOIA,'"[111] observed that "[t]he use of the word 'agency' as a modifier demonstrates that Congress contemplated some relationship between an 'agency' and the 'record' requested."[112] In that same ruling, the Court noted that during the FOIA Senate hearings, the term "agency record" was assumed to include "all papers which an agency preserves in the performance of its functions."[113]

A federal appeals court noted the congressional failure to identify the link between an agency and a record: "[T]he Freedom of Information Act, for all its attention to the treatment of 'agency records,' never defines that crucial phrase."[114] Some observers believe that such "statutory silence"[115] permits courts to construe the phrase too narrowly, diminishing the FOIA's policy of broad disclosure.[116]

A federal appellate court provided one of the first judicial interpretations of the term in 1978.[117] A party requesting an agency record sought a congressional hearing transcript that was located in Central Intelligence Agency files. The CIA argued that the transcript was not an agency record but was instead a congressional document exempt from FOIA coverage. The court agreed with the CIA and held that the agency's possession of a document, by itself, was not sufficient to create an agency record. Under the circumstances, the court concluded, the decision to disclose should be made by the originating body—in this case, Congress—not the recipient agency.[118]

In spite of the ambiguity in establishing what an agency record is under the FOIA, the following criteria have developed:

- A record is anything in documentary form. This now includes computer-stored records, and the Electronic Freedom of Information Act of 1996 mandates disclosure of records in the format chosen by the requester if that format is available as part of the agency's normal business procedures.
- An agency record likely includes any document created and possessed by the agency.
- A record possessed but not created by an agency may not qualify as an agency record.
- An agency is not required either to create a record if the record does not exist or obtain the requested record if it is not in the control of the agency at the time the request is made.
- The requested record must be part of the legitimate conduct of the agency's official duties.

Using the FOIA to Obtain Records Requesting a record from a federal government agency is relatively easy. (Obtaining the record may be another matter.)

Familiarity with the FOIA and the preferred procedures is extremely helpful and enhances the likelihood that the request will be granted. Useful information is provided by the Reporters Committee for Freedom of the Press and its online guide, "How to Use the Federal FOI Act."[119] This includes an online FOIA letter generator[120] that provides step-by-step guidance on letter preparation. Contacting the agency is the next step. This can be done by telephone, e-mail or mail. It is sometimes best to begin with a friendly telephone call to clarify the nature of the request, identify the record holder and perhaps obtain the records without further effort. However, a written request allows keeping track of the date of the request, the records requested and the agency's responses, all of which are essential if the agency must be taken to court for noncompliance with the law.

Because agencies exert a certain amount of discretion on whether they release records, understanding the elements of human interaction is also helpful in the records request process. Sometimes agencies will ignore friendly requests, so reminders of the law can be useful in getting their attention. Two studies conducted by a FOIA researcher show that a threatening letter resulted in faster responses, lower copy fees and more compliance with the law than a friendly or neutral letter.[121] That same researcher, together with another FOIA expert, has outlined strategies for working with record custodians to acquire records without having to go to court. They suggest that the records request process is not like barging through a door to get information; rather, it is like winding through a maze, turning different corners, going around roadblocks and eventually getting where you need to be.[122]

Federal agencies now have links within their own websites that guide the FOIA user. Federal agencies and departments have websites that include instructions on how to file FOIA requests to that specific agency or department. It is important that requests be as detailed and specific as possible. Otherwise, the exchange needed to clarify the request wastes valuable time. Sweeping searches for all the records related to a given property transaction, for example, also increase response time. The FOIA permits agencies to charge search and/or duplicating fees at cost, but fee waivers may be granted upon request. In fact, there is a specific FOIA provision that allows news media members to obtain fee waivers. Fee reductions are also available to nonprofit organizations. But other users of the FOIA have sometimes found that requests for fee waivers can trigger lengthy delays as agency personnel attempt to classify the requester's appropriate fee status. If the budget permits, a record requester may simply want to pay the costs.

Agencies have 20 working days to respond to FOIA requests. "Respond" does not mean comply, but in 2013 the U.S. Court of Appeals for the District of Columbia Circuit held that an agency must do more within 20 days than just say sometime in the future it will produce documents or refuse to do so under an exemption.[123] The agency "must at least indicate within the relevant time period the scope of the documents it will produce and the exemptions it will claim with respect to any withheld documents," the court said. If a wait seems unreasonable, written appeals may be made. If the agency refuses the request, a claim may be

realWorld Law

How Responsive Is the U.S. Government to FOIA Requests?

The Coalition of Journalists for Open Government (CJOG) released its most recent study in 2008 showing how 25 federal departments and agencies responded to Freedom of Information Act requests.[1] The report was not encouraging for those who believe their government should be open and responsive to its citizens' requests for information. These are some excerpts from that report:

[F]ederal departments and agencies have made little if any progress in responding to Freedom of Information Act requests, despite a two-year-old presidential order to improve service. . . .

The CJOG review of performance reports shows agencies did cut their record backlog but more because of a steep decline in requests than stepped up processing of requests. It also indicated scant improvement and some regression in traditional measures of response, including the amount of time requesters have to wait for an answer and whether a request or an appeal is granted. . . .

The CJOG study looked at 25 departments and agencies that handle the bulk of the third-party information requests. . . .

The 25 agencies blew an opportunity to make a significant dent in their huge backlog of requests. Those agencies received the fewest requests since reporting began in 1998—63,000 fewer than 2006. But they processed only 2,100 more requests than they did in 2006 when the backlog soared to a record 39%. . . .

Agencies got even stingier in granting requests. Fewer people got all the information they sought than at any time since agency reporting began in 1998. The percent of requesters getting either a full or a partial grant fell to 60%, also a record low.

Those who did get information still had to endure lengthy delays. Fifteen of the agencies reported slower processing times than the year before in the handling of "Simple" requests, and 13 showed slower times in dealing with "Complex" requests. And all 21 agencies that processed requests in the "Complex" category said they missed the 20-day statutory response deadline for at least half of the requests processed.

Those who file administrative appeals are usually out of luck—even more so in 2007. However, a majority of the agencies did say "no" more quickly. In 2007, the percentage of appeals granted dropped to the lowest level in 10 years. Only 13% of those who appealed got any satisfaction. Of those who appealed, only 3% got all the records requested; another 10% received a partial grant. . . .

1. Coalition of Journalists for Open Government, *An Opportunity Lost: An In-Depth Analysis of FOIA Performance from 1998 to 2007* (July 3, 2008), *available at* http://www.cjog.net/documents//Part_1_2007_FOIA_Report.pdf.

filed in a federal district court. The burden of proof lies with the government; it must show why the delay or nondisclosure is valid. The agency must cite the specific exemption that justifies nondisclosure and must withhold only those portions of the requested records that qualify for the exemption. For example, a federal judge ruled the National Nuclear Security Administration (NNSA) unnecessarily delayed responding to numerous records requests from a citizens' group regarding documents on nuclear waste sites in New Mexico. The judge said NNSA's reliance on the complexity and sensitive nature of the records being sought was inconsistent with the agency's obligations under the FOIA.[124]

Courts have allowed federal agencies essentially to say, "We don't have to tell you if we have the documents you requested under the FOIA." This response is permitted when an agency can prove revealing that it does or does not have the documents will cause the same harm an FOIA exemption is meant to prevent—a national security breach under Exemption 1, for example. This "We're not telling you" reply is called a "Glomar response," taken from the name of Howard Hughes' Glomar Explorer, a ship disguised as a private craft used in an attempt to recover a lost Soviet submarine. The ship was involved in an FOIA lawsuit seeking information about the incident from the Central Intelligence Agency. In that case, the CIA refused to say whether it had the requested documents. The D.C. Circuit in 2013 refused to allow the CIA to use the Glomar response to reject the American Civil Liberties Union's FOIA request for documents about drones used for targeted killings. The court said national security would not be harmed by the CIA's revealing whether it had such documents because several public officials, including President Obama and a former CIA director, already had publicly revealed the CIA's involvement in the drone program.[125]

FOIA Exemptions Federal agencies are not compelled to hand over any and every record requested. There are nine specifically enumerated FOIA exemptions to disclosure. Information within requested records that falls into one or more of those categories does not have to be provided. It is important to note, however, that the wording of the FOIA permits agencies to reject a request for information. The law does not make nondisclosure mandatory; the decision is at the agency's discretion. Nevertheless, that discretion is often exercised in favor of nondisclosure.

If an agency chooses to deny all or part of a FOIA request, the law requires that the agency show that the request falls under one of the nine exemptions. The exemptions to disclosure are permissive, and the law requires agencies to interpret the exemptions narrowly. Thus, record keepers are required to cover up, or redact, only the specific portions of records covered by the law's exemptions. The physical process of redacting records line by line is painstaking, and delays in accomplishing the task can result in backlogs of weeks, months or even years. In addition, even if a portion of a record may be exempted, the agency may still choose to release it. Agency administrators, though, may take a dim view of such a practice.

Among the major sticking points of the FOIA since its enactment have been agency interpretations of its nine exemptions. A very narrow reading of them results in agencies releasing more information more often; a broad interpretation reduces the likelihood of disclosure. In the

Points of Law

Freedom of Information Act: The Nine Exemptions

1. National security
2. Internal agency rules and procedures
3. Disclosures forbidden by other statutes
4. Trade secrets
5. Agency memoranda
6. Personal privacy
7. Law enforcement records
8. Financial records
9. Geological information

confinement box. The other inquiry involved claims that the SERE training caused two individuals to engage in criminal behavior, namely, felony shoplifting and downloading child pornography onto a military computer. According to this official, these claims were found to be baseless. Moreover, he has indicated that during the three and a half years he spent as ██████ ██████ of the SERE program, he trained 10,000 students. Of those students, only two dropped out of the training following the use of these techniques. Although on rare occasions some students temporarily postponed the remainder of their training and received psychological counseling, those students were able to finish the program without any indication of subsequent mental health effects.

You have informed us that you have consulted with ██████████ who has ten years of experience with SERE training ███████████████████████████████████ ██ He stated that, during those ten years, insofar as he is aware, none of the individuals who completed the program suffered any adverse mental health effects. He informed you that there was one person who did not complete the training. That person experienced an adverse mental health reaction that lasted only two hours. After those two hours, the individual's symptoms spontaneously dissipated without requiring treatment or counseling and no other symptoms were ever reported by this individual. According to the information you have provided to us, this assessment of the use of these procedures includes the use of the waterboard.

Additionally, you received a memorandum from the ████████████████████ ███████████████████████████ which you supplied to us. ████████████ has experience with the use of all of these procedures in a course of conduct, with the exception of the insect in the confinement box and the waterboard. This memorandum confirms that the use of these procedures has not resulted in any reported instances of prolonged mental harm, and very few instances of immediate and temporary adverse psychological responses to the training. ████████████ reported that a small minority of students have had temporary adverse psychological reactions during training. Of the 26,829 students trained from 1992 through 2001 in the Air Force SERE training, 4.3 percent of those students had contact with psychology services. Of those 4.3 percent, only 3.2 percent were pulled from the program for psychological reasons. Thus, out of the students trained overall, only 0.14 percent were pulled from the program for psychological reasons. Furthermore, although █████████ indicated that surveys of students having completed this training are not done, he expressed confidence that the training did not cause any long-term psychological impact. He based his conclusion on the debriefing of students that is done after the training. More importantly, he based this assessment on the fact that although training is required to be extremely stressful in order to be effective, very few complaints have been made regarding the training. During his tenure, in which 10,000 students were trained, no congressional complaints have been made. While there was one Inspector General complaint, it was not due to psychological concerns. Moreover, he was aware of only one letter inquiring about the long-term impact of these techniques from an individual trained

An example of a redacted document that was released under FOIA. This is one page from a memo to the CIA's general counsel written by the assistant attorney general in 2002.

aftermath of the Sept. 11, 2001, terrorist attacks, for example, U.S. Attorney General John Ashcroft issued a memorandum to the heads of all federal departments and agencies urging restraint with any discretionary granting of records when it could fall under one or more exemptions.[126] The memo instructed federal agencies to withhold information sought through FOIA requests whenever a "sound legal basis" might justify secrecy. It also required record keepers to review all applicable FOIA exemptions and disclose information "only after full and deliberate consideration of the institutional, commercial and personal privacy interests that could be implicated."[127] This represented an about-face to established policy that had advised agencies to grant more liberal public access to federal government records in response to FOIA requests. An audit of federal agencies that receive the vast majority of FOIA requests found that, after the Ashcroft memo, the system was in "extreme disarray," with slow response times, lackadaisical document searches, lost requests and no accountability.[128]

Another post–Sept. 11 development was the passage of the Homeland Security Act of 2002. Many regard it as weakening the Freedom of Information Act by providing broad exemptions under the FOIA for information related to the security of critical infrastructure or protected systems, including computer systems and information.[129] Thus, a broad interpretation of the Homeland Security Act expands the categories under which records may be withheld. As a result, fewer FOIA requests were granted after Sept. 11, 2001, than before.

Many believed that trend would likely change under the administration of President Obama. On his first day in office, Obama issued a memo to the heads of federal agencies. In words that echoed Madison, he noted that a "democracy requires accountability, and accountability requires transparency." In our democracy, he continued, the Freedom of Information Act "is the most prominent expression of a profound national commitment to ensuring an open Government."[130] Although the principle may stand in theory, some government watchdog groups believe that, in practice, the record is unquestionably mixed. Some say the Obama administration took as many steps to shield government information as it did to make it accessible.[131] In part, this perception may have been driven by high expectations. Moreover, many critics acknowledge that openness is a matter of degree, with the Obama administration being transparent in ways that previous presidencies were not. A 2010 study found that some of the problem lies in agencies that are not following Obama's directive: that is, to release any information whose disclosure was not prohibited by law or would not cause foreseeable harm. The study by the National Security Archive concludes that the Obama administration "clearly stated a new policy direction for open government but has not conquered the challenge of communicating and enforcing that message throughout the executive branch."[132] A point remains that open-government laws and policies are subject to interpretation, including by the officials who decide during any given period how to implement them. This especially applies to FOIA and its exemptions. When there is disagreement between a requester and an agency over whether one or more of the exemptions applies to a particular request, a federal court may ultimately settle the dispute.

Exemption 1: National Security

Records fall under the exemption of national security if they are classified as confidential, secret or top secret. Each classification reflects a greater sensitivity of the information and its potential for harm if released. The authority to classify information, and thus use the national security exemption, is ripe for abuse. Members of the executive branch reinterpret the standards for classification of government secrets in ways that may radically increase or decrease the amount of information unavailable to the public.[133] A 1974 FOIA amendment addressed this by empowering judges to assess whether information was properly classified. Federal judges have the authority to privately examine the requested materials to determine whether they could damage national security or foreign policy if released.

Despite announcing a commitment to FOIA and transparency in government, President Barack Obama and his administration have disappointed many.

Records requests denied on the basis of this exemption have proved to be the most difficult to overturn. Typically, judges rule in favor of classification. The U.S. Supreme Court, for example, in suggesting that Exemption 1 should have been used by the CIA to prevent disclosure of records related to research about brainwashing techniques, referred to the exemption as the "keystone of a congressional scheme that balances deference to the Executive's interest in maintaining secrecy with continued judicial and congressional oversight."[134] The CIA's refusal to disclose the names of some institutions and all individual researchers related to the project was affirmed. Similarly, even when information is widely known, such as the CIA's use of waterboarding and other "enhanced interrogation techniques, an agency may refuse an FOIA request on the basis of national security," the Second Circuit ruled in 2012.[135]

Exemption 2: Internal Agency Rules and Procedures

The exemption related to internal agency rules and procedures is sometimes known as the "housekeeping" exemption. It pertains to matters related exclusively to the practices of the agency itself: vacation policies, lunch break rules, parking space assignments and so on. The rationale is not so much that any harm could result in the disclosure of such information but that keeping the records and then retrieving them when requests are made is not worth the expense. An exception to this no-harm aspect—but still justifying nondisclosure—is any internal policy that could be used inappropriately. For example, break or shift change procedures used by federal prison guards could conceivably be used to breach the security of a particular facility.

It is generally accepted that the spirit of open government is not violated by the enforcement of this exemption. Nevertheless, the exemption cannot be used to conceal all agency practices. If a matter is of public concern and its disclosure would not circumvent agency regulations or statutes, a court could rule that related records do not qualify for Exemption 2 and order their release. The U.S. Supreme Court addressed this issue in a case in which the records related to Air Force Academy honor and ethics hearings were sought. Where the situation is not one where disclosure would compromise agency regulation, Exemption 2 is not applicable to subjects that are genuinely in the public interest, the Court ruled. "[T]he general thrust of the exemption is simply to relieve agencies of the burden of assembling and maintaining for public inspection matter in which the public could not reasonably be expected to have an interest," said the Court.[136] The Court also ruled that Exemption 2 applies only to human resource and "employee relations" records, not to other records an agency might possess.[137] In this case the Court said the U.S. Navy could not use Exemption 2 to reject an FOIA request for information about explosives at a naval base in Puget Sound, Wash., because the location of munitions is not related to employee records.

Exemption 3: Statutory Exemptions The FOIA provision regarding statutory exemptions stipulates that the act cannot override other laws that forbid the disclosure of certain information. This exemption increasingly comes into play as Congress continues to enact laws that prohibit disclosure of information. Still, litigation surfaces related to this exemption. Courts usually require the government to show that (1) the information being sought falls within the scope of the statute being cited, and (2) the statute grants no discretionary authority to the government agency holding the information (i.e., the nondisclosure is mandatory). If those standards are met, the decision of nondisclosure is generally upheld.

Exemption 4: Trade Secrets In compliance with federal law, the Chrysler Corporation had turned over to a government agency documents related to its affirmative action program and the general composition of its workforce. Afterward, the agency received a FOIA request that targeted those records. The agency was inclined to grant the request, but Chrysler objected and challenged it on the basis of Exemption 4.

This situation illustrates that private businesses generate a lot of information that is provided to various government agencies. That includes profit-and-loss statements, market-share information and secret formulas. No government agency or its personnel has created the information; agencies merely collect and keep it to assist other government objectives, such as enforcement of copyright law or regulation of broadcasters. Often, other businesses could use to their competitive advantage information that government requires businesses to disclose. And that is why the FOIA exempts such information from mandatory disclosure. When an agency's nondisclosure decision under Exemption 4 is challenged, the agency is expected to show that the information sought is, in fact, a trade secret. In other words, it has to prove that the information is confidential and that its release would cause considerable competitive harm or loss to a business or make it more difficult to collect similar information in the future.

As for the *Chrysler* case, the U.S. Supreme Court ruled that the automaker had no claim to prevent disclosure. The FOIA, it said, "is an attempt to meet the demand for open government while preserving workable confidentiality in governmental decisionmaking."[138]

Exemption 5: Agency Memos Sometimes referred to as the "working papers" or "discovery" exemption, the exemption regarding agency memos protects two kinds of information from disclosure. First, internal agency memoranda, studies or drafts that are prepared and used to create final reports or policies are exempted from disclosure. One court ruled that this exemption helps both to protect the integrity of the decision-making process and to avoid confusing the public if preliminary policy decisions were to be disclosed.[139] Opponents argue that this exemption hides the processes that lead up to final policies and obscures the true decision-making process.

In one situation, Exemption 5 was at the center of a request to disclose documents related to water allocation that had been transmitted by various Native American tribes to the Department of the Interior and the Bureau of Indian Affairs. The association seeking those documents challenged the rejection of its FOIA request. Ultimately, the Supreme Court ruled in favor of full disclosure. The Court emphasized that Exemption 5 is not intended to protect government secrets, noting that the exemptions collectively "do not obscure the basic policy that disclosure, not secrecy, is the dominant objective of the Act."[140] The key here was whether the transmission of the documents from tribes to the Interior Department qualified as "inter-agency or intra-agency memoranda or letters." The Court said they did not.

Second, this exemption protects information exchanged between an agency and its attorney(s). This is directly related to the traditional attorney-client privilege. Exemption 5 recognizes that the privilege is not waived merely because the client is a federal agency. Nothing that is considered discovery material—the evidence gathered by both sides in a civil trial that both sides may examine—must be disclosed under FOIA.

Exemption 6: Personal Privacy Privacy is at the heart of Exemptions 6 and 7. Under Exemption 6, "personnel and medical files and similar files the disclosure of which would constitute a clearly unwarranted invasion of personal privacy" may be withheld. The phrase "similar files" has been the source of much dispute. It has generally been interpreted broadly to include lists, files, records and letters.

Courts attempt to balance privacy concerns against the purpose of the FOIA—informing the public about government activities. It is a delicate balance. Sometimes courts consider the purpose of the request. How will the information be used? Is there a legitimate public interest in its disclosure? If so, the scales of justice sometimes tip in favor of disclosure. "Exemption Six overwhelmingly

realWorld Law

NASA and FOIA

An illustration of FOIA Exemption 6 at work occurred when The New York Times sued NASA. Several months after the 1986 explosion of the space shuttle Challenger that killed all seven astronauts aboard, The New York Times filed a FOIA request with NASA for cockpit voice recordings and their accompanying transcripts. NASA provided the transcripts but refused to release any recordings, citing Exemption 6. After unsuccessfully appealing to the Office of the Administrator of NASA, the Times sued.

The newspaper claimed there was a public interest in the cockpit recording because there was substantial interest in the disaster and in NASA's conduct before, during and after the tragedy. NASA maintained that the privacy that Exemption 6 protects extends to the families of the astronauts. Moreover, NASA claimed that voice recordings would shed no additional light on the tragedy and the space administration's conduct beyond what was revealed in the transcript.

After an appeal and re-hearing, the U.S. District Court for the District of Columbia provided the final word. It determined that the privacy interests clearly outweighed the public interest and ruled against The New York Times.[1]

1. New York Times Co. v. Nat'l Aeronautics and Space Admin., 783 F. Supp. 628 (D.D.C. 1991).

favors the disclosure of information relating to a violation of the public trust by a government official," a federal appeals court once ruled.[141] However, the balance sometimes tilts toward privacy interests. The U.S. Supreme Court recognized that the FOIA's purpose is allowing government activity—not that of private citizens—to be open for public scrutiny.[142] The Court clarified that Exemption 6 applies to individuals and not corporations, holding that the ordinary meaning of the word "personal" refers to human beings.[143] Federal agencies, then, cannot use this exemption to reject FOIA requests for information about corporations and other businesses.

Exemption 7: Law Enforcement Records Records compiled within the context of law enforcement investigations may be exempt from FOIA disclosure. There are limits, however, to the exemption. For the government to deny disclosure, release of a record must reasonably be expected to do the following:

a. Interfere with enforcement proceedings, or

b. Deprive a person of the right to a fair trial with an impartial jury, or

c. Constitute an unwarranted invasion of privacy, or

d. Disclose the identity of a confidential source, or

e. Disclose law enforcement techniques and procedures, or

f. Endanger the life or physical safety of any individual.

The government needs to show only that one of these circumstances would occur if the requested record is released.

At one time, items such as rap sheets, arrest records, convictions records and department manuals were not exempt. More recently, however, nondisclosure is the norm. One of the more noteworthy FOIA-related cases is *U.S. Department of Justice v. Reporters Committee for Freedom of the Press,* excerpted at the end of this chapter. A journalist filed a FOIA request with the Federal Bureau of Investigation (FBI) for its criminal records on four members of a family suspected of criminal activity. The FBI complied with the requests pertaining to the three family members who were deceased but not to the remaining living member of the family. That decision was challenged but upheld on the basis of Exemption 7. With regard to the surviving family member, the journalist and the Reporters Committee argued that there was a public interest in learning about his past arrests or convictions. First, the survivor allegedly had improper dealings with a corrupt congressman and, second, he was an officer of a corporation with defense contracts. But as is clear in its ruling, the Supreme Court was of a mind to safeguard personal privacy. "Disclosure of records regarding private citizens, identifiable by name, is not what the framers of the FOIA had in mind,"[144] wrote Justice John Paul Stevens, upholding the FBI's decision against disclosure.

There has been a tendency toward nondisclosure when personal privacy is at stake. In 2004, the U.S. Supreme Court affirmed the authority of several federal agencies and organizations to withhold death scene photographs of Vincent Foster. At the time of his death, Foster was legal counsel to President Bill Clinton.[145] The U.S. Park Police conducted an investigation into Foster's death and took color photographs of the death scene, including 10 pictures of Foster's body. The investigation concluded that Foster committed suicide by shooting himself with a revolver. Subsequent investigations by the FBI, Congress and independent counsels reached the same conclusion. Still, several people remained skeptical, among them attorney Allan Favish. He believed disclosure of the pictures was vital to public understanding about whether Foster was a victim of a murder that had been disguised as a suicide. Favish filed FOIA requests with two different

Skepticism about the 1993 death of Vincent Foster, Jr. (left), former deputy counsel to President Bill Clinton, led to a FOIA request for photos. Foster is seen here in 1988 with his wife, Lisa, and Hillary and Bill Clinton.

federal agencies. Both were denied. Lawsuits followed, with appeals culminating at the U.S Supreme Court.

In ruling against Favish, the Court explicitly recognized that surviving family members enjoy a right of privacy under FOIA regarding pictures of their deceased relative. In addition, the Supreme Court refused to accept Favish's conspiracy theory as sufficient grounds to overcome the family's right to privacy. The Court said that when people seek information that implicates personal privacy interests, they must demonstrate a clear connection between the information sought and a significant public interest. More important, the Court said when

> the public interest being asserted is to show that responsible officials acted negligently or otherwise improperly in the performance of their duties, the requester must establish more than a bare suspicion in order to obtain disclosure. Rather, the requester must produce evidence that would warrant a belief by a reasonable person that the alleged Government impropriety might have occurred.[146]

Thus, rather than requiring broad disclosure of records that might shed some light on possible government malfeasance, the Court said Favish could overcome the family's privacy interest only if he provided substantial evidence to demonstrate the public interest in the records. The Court relied on an earlier decision in which it had said the FOIA is intended to provide access to "official information that sheds light on an agency's performance of its statutory duties. . . . That purpose, however, is not fostered by disclosure of information about private citizens that is accumulated in various governmental files but that reveals little or nothing about an agency's own conduct."[147]

In 2011, the U.S. Supreme Court narrowed and clarified this privacy exemption. AT&T's records revealed it overbilled the federal government for telephone and other services. The company said Exemption 7 should keep those records secret. A group had submitted a FOIA request for records that AT&T had forwarded to the FCC. The FCC thought the records could be released, believing that AT&T did not qualify for the personal privacy exemption. Ultimately, the Supreme Court agreed that the exemption is for individuals, not corporations. Chief Justice John Roberts concluded the Court's opinion by writing, "We trust that AT&T will not take it personally."[148]

Exemption 8: Financial Records This exemption is meant to deny disclosure of sensitive financial reports or audits. The burden on the government agency is to show that the disclosure of certain reports would undermine public confidence in banks and other financial institutions. Although seldom used, this exemption assumes greater significance during periods when financial scandals take place. Information about institutions that federal agencies possess is in greater demand. This is a sweeping exemption that left many questions unanswered during the massive financial crisis of savings and loan organizations during the 1980s.

realWorld Law

The Fight over Photos

One of the photographs from the Abu Ghraib prison. The Second Circuit ruled that the FOIA permitted the photographs' distribution, but Congress adopted a law forbidding release. However, the AP permits publication of Abu Ghraib photographs for "editorial use only," such as in this book.

Freedom of Information Act Exemptions 6 and 7 were at the heart of a battle over whether the Defense Department should release photos of U.S. detainees in Afghanistan and Iraq, including the Abu Ghraib prison. The Defense Department initially claimed the FOIA exemptions protecting privacy applied—claiming the privacy of those in the pictures was at stake—relieving the department of any obligation to release the photos. Later, the Pentagon added another part of Exemption 7 to its argument, claiming that disclosure of the photos could reasonably endanger the life or physical safety of any individual. It was referring to U.S. troops abroad.

The Second Circuit Court of Appeals said that "FOIA's purpose is to encourage public disclosure of information in the possession of federal agencies so that the people may know what their government is up to," adding that the release of information of this sort represents FOIA's basic purpose: to ensure an informed citizenry, vital to the functioning of a democratic society, needed to check against corruption and to hold the governors accountable to the governed."[1] In its ruling in favor of releasing the photos, the court concluded that the exemption required a specific anticipated danger to a particular individual rather than diffuse risks to "any" members of the U.S. forces.

The case was far from over, however. A new law was passed allowing the secretary of defense to block the pictures' release. At the urging of his national security advisers, President Obama was convinced that releasing the photos would inflame anti-American sentiment abroad and endanger U.S. troops. The Justice Department brought the case to the U.S. Supreme Court. Without comment, the Court vacated the lower court ruling in light of the new law.[2]

1. ACLU v. Dep't of Defense, 543 F.3d 59, 66 (2nd Cir. 2008) (internal quotations omitted).
2. Dep't of Defense v. ACLU, 558 U.S. 1042 (2009).

Exemption 9: Geological Data Like Exemption 8, Exemption 9 rarely comes into play within a news media context and is equally broad. It is designed to prevent oil and gas exploration companies from obtaining information from federal agencies that can provide them a competitive advantage. In other words, because those companies must file information about their exploration and the location of discovered natural gas or oil deposits with federal agencies, profitable information could be obtained through the FOIA were it not for this exemption.

Electronic Freedom of Information Act (EFOIA) A 1996 amendment to the Freedom of Information Act that updates the act by including electronically stored information and subjecting it to the FOIA's provisions.

Computer Records As more government records and information are kept and transferred to electronic storage, the demand for access to computerized formats grows. Access advocates wanted to make sure that records were not concealed or buried merely because of their non-paper format. The FOIA now applies to computer records. Congress passed an amendment to the FOIA in 1996 known as the **Electronic Freedom of Information Act (EFOIA)**.[149] It provides access to electronic federal records. Among other things, the law clearly established that records in electronic format are records subject to disclosure under the FOIA. The law also stipulates that computer searches to retrieve records do not constitute creation of a new record, a justification some agency record keepers had used previously to deny access to electronic records.

To aid public access to government records, the EFOIA mandates that publicly accessible electronic records be posted in a readily reproducible format, generally in the format of choice of the requester. The law also requires federal agencies to create a FOIA section on their websites and to provide "electronic reading rooms" filled with online copies of records, policy statements, administrative opinions and indexes of frequently sought documents. This provision applies only to records created after Nov. 1, 1996.

When Congress examined the effects of the law in 2000, it found that the number of public records requests had been stable or even declined at most agencies. Nonetheless, most agencies reported an increasing number of unprocessed requests for records.[150] The law does not permit agencies to extend the response deadline of 20 days simply because of routine backlogs. Moreover, the EFOIA encourages agencies to provide expedited access to records when the requester can demonstrate a compelling need for rapid access based on personal safety or heightened public concern.

Despite the promise of electronic access, the General Accounting Office (GAO), which monitors compliance with the law, reported in 2002 that agencies had not put enough resources into providing and maintaining electronic access to public records. The report concluded, in part, that many agencies had not begun to implement electronic access options. The GAO recommended that noncompliant agencies be held accountable for their failure to improve citizen access to government records.

Because federal agencies are not obligated to create records that do not already exist, that provision sometimes creates a way out for agencies reluctant to part with electronic-based information. They may claim that the computer programming required to retrieve a record amounts to record "creation," thereby relieving them of any duty to disclose. The EFOIA is designed to prevent such evasion. It requires agencies to deliver documents in "any form or format requested" that is "readily reproducible by the agency." A federal appeals court said this required the Department of Defense to provide files in zipped format because the agency used such files as part of its "business as usual."[151] Another obstacle for seekers of computer-based records can be agencies that subcontract with private companies to computerize their hard-copy records. During those periods, because a record is not in the agency's possession, access likely is difficult.

While the EFOIA applies only to federal records, many states followed the federal example and adopted specific provisions to ensure and improve electronic access to state records.[152]

Following Sept. 11, 2001, and the start of the war on terrorism, government agencies hesitated to release defense-related data and a wide array of other information potentially related to national security. Some government agencies also argued that they must move slowly in providing public online access to their records for fear that such access would violate personal privacy rights. In 2003, the GAO also reported that the huge proliferation of electronic records was creating an increasing nightmare for archivists and record keepers.[153] The sheer volume of records, some record keepers argue, was impeding electronic access.

SUMMARY

THE FEDERAL FREEDOM OF INFORMATION ACT was intended to shed light on the inner workings of government. Its goals were to better inform citizens about the actions of their governors and to protect against government malfeasance. The FOIA applies to federal executive branch agencies and departments. It does not regulate access to federal courts or Congress. The act mandates public access to agency records in any format. Although the law presumes the public should have access to most agency records, courts have struggled to determine which records are covered by the act. Requests under the FOIA may be written or oral, and requesters do not need to provide information about themselves or the purpose of their request.

The FOIA includes nine categories of exemptions that permit government to maintain the secrecy of records. Some of the exemptions are narrow and pose little difficulty for reporters. Others, including the protection of investigative records, statutory exemptions or personal privacy rights, are more sweeping and often pose barriers to newsgathering. Statutes specifically exempting federal records from disclosure have multiplied since the adoption of the FOIA. Concerns over privacy have swelled. Nevertheless, the language of the act makes clear that exemptions should be read narrowly to permit the greatest level of access. The exemptions are permissive; they allow but do not require government to withhold the identified records. ∎

Access to Federal Meetings

The protections and limits described so far in this chapter relate largely to access to records. Another source of valuable information to journalists and other members of the public is meetings. Important information about topics of great public interest arises and is discussed in a myriad of meetings held by various governing and policymaking bodies at all levels of government. Moreover,

realWorld Law

E-Mail as a Public Record?

Whether the e-mail of public employees is a public record was an issue handled by the Wisconsin Supreme Court in 2010. Using that state's open-records law, a citizen had requested records of schoolteachers' e-mail, both work related and private. The teachers did not object to revealing their work-related e-mail, but they resisted releasing their personal e-mails, even those that had been sent and received on their work computers.

A circuit court first ruled that all the e-mails should be released. But the state supreme court reversed, ruling that because the teachers' personal e-mail could not be considered "records" under Wisconsin law, it was not subject to the public records request. "To be a record . . . the content of the document must have a connection to a government function. In the instant case, the contents of the teachers' personal e-mails have no connection to a government function and therefore are not records," the court held. The Wisconsin law exempts "materials which are purely the personal property of the custodian and have no relation to his or her office."[1] The court also cited the intent of lawmakers who passed the open-records bill. They said for a document to be considered a record, it must have a connection to a government function.[2]

The Wisconsin ruling followed similar decisions made by courts in West Virginia,[3] Michigan[4] and the District of Columbia[5] in which private e-mails, even those sent or received on government workplace computers, were determined not to be subject to open-records or FOIA requests. Like other state and District of Columbia rulings, these rulings are not binding in other states.

1. Wis. Stat. §§ 19.31–19.39.
2. Schill v. Wisconsin Rapids School Dist., 786 N.W.2d 177 (Wis. 2010).
3. Associated Press v. Canterbury, 688 S.E.2d 317 (W. Va. 2009).
4. Howell Education Association v. Howell Board of Education, 789 N.W.2d 495 (Mich. App. 2010).
5. Convertino v. United States Dept. of Justice, 674 F. Supp. 2d 97 (D.D.C. 2009).

Government in the Sunshine Act Sometimes referred to as the Federal Open Meetings Law, an act passed in 1976 that mandates that meetings of federal government agencies be open to the public unless all or some part of a meeting is exempted according to exceptions outlined in the law.

because the public's business is being conducted, the processes involved and not merely the results are of legitimate interest. This philosophy was adopted into law when the **Government in the Sunshine Act**—also known as the "Federal Open Meetings Law"—was passed in 1976. It applies to the 50 or so federal agencies, commissions and boards whose members are appointed by the president and that have some independent authority. These groups are required to conduct their business in public and to give public notice of their meetings. Ten exemptions allow the closing of these meetings. Exemptions 1 through 9 are similar to those of the FOIA. Exemption 10 applies to agency litigation or arbitration. An often-invoked reason for closing meetings is that the board will discuss matters related to personnel, and closure is needed to protect the privacy of those involved.

Some observers estimate that nearly 1,000 advisory boards provide expert guidance to the federal government. Neither the FOIA nor the Government in the Sunshine Act covers these boards because the boards have no independent decision-making authority. Yet they play a major, and often definitive, role in the development of government policy. In 1972, the Federal Advisory Committee Act

(FACA) opened the meetings and records of these advisory groups to the public unless the committee is "composed wholly of full-time officers or employees of the federal government."

State Open-Records Laws

As important as the federal Freedom of Information Act is, most journalists' work occurs on the local level. As a result, they are more likely to rely on the open-records laws in the state in which they live.[154] Every state and the District of Columbia have some version of an access-to-information statute. Some follow the model of the FOIA, while others look very different. Those differences may be in the form of requiring more or less disclosure than the FOIA or in the enforcement mechanisms. In Texas, for example, a state agency has 10 days either to comply with a request or seek the state attorney general's judgment on whether access can be denied.

State laws that facilitate access to records have a tradition whose roots are much deeper than the federal version. In 1849, Wisconsin provided for inspection of public records. Only eight states—Arkansas, Delaware, Maryland, Mississippi, New Hampshire, New York, South Carolina and Virginia—did not have some kind of open-records law when the FOIA was passed in 1966. The explicit purposes of state open-records laws tend to be consistent: government accountability. Some go further. Hawaii's statute, for example, echoing James Madison, says that opening government to public scrutiny "is the only viable and reasonable method of protecting the public's interest."[155] The Delaware law asserts that "It is vital that citizens have easy access to public records in order that the society remain free and democratic."[156] Illinois links the right of access with enabling "people to fulfill their duties of discussing public issues fully and freely" and making "informed political judgments."[157]

Because there is so much state-to-state variation in these laws, characterizing them broadly is virtually impossible. Even those that appear similar may, in reality, differ in how states implement and interpret them. Generally speaking, however, some observations are helpful:

- Like federal agencies, those on the state level are not required to create or acquire records in response to a request.
- Some state open-records laws cover the legislature, executive branch and courts.
- Few states require record indexes to be produced by agencies.
- Some states require that requesters be state residents.
- Many states have exemptions similar to those of the FOIA.
- Most states' open-records laws cover electronic and computer-stored records, but some states do not require that these records be transformed into a user-friendly format. Some charge extra for electronic manipulation.
- Some states' open-records laws do not specify response time limits. Delays can be lengthy.
- Some states do not specify penalties for agencies violating the law.

realWorld Law

Access in the Digital Age

Social media websites such as Facebook allow government officials to post and exchange information in ways not considered when most open-records and open-meetings laws were adopted.

As with FOIA on the federal level, states grapple with how to apply open-records laws to computerized records, including information that appears in social media. In one recent case, the issue was whether metadata were part of a public record or separate from it. Metadata is information that is embedded in an electronic record that may not be readily readable. This embedded data may include the creation and edit dates of a file, its authorship and edit history. In the case, as part of an administrative complaint, a Phoenix police officer filed a public records request. After examining the records, he suspected that some information had been altered, such as backdating when the files had been created. His request for the metadata to confirm his suspicions was denied. The city claimed the metadata was not part of the record, but something separate, and therefore not subject to the state open-records law. The Arizona Supreme Court disagreed, ruling that metadata in an electronic document is "part of the underlying document; it does not stand on its own."[1] In 2010, the Washington Supreme Court ruled similarly, holding that metadata is subject to disclosure because it may contain information that relates to the conduct of government and is important for the public to know.[2]

Electronic mail, text messages and social media websites such as Facebook represent not only a shift in how people communicate and share information but also in how records are created and meetings held. It makes sense for lawmakers and other officials to use technology and its platforms and applications to communicate with citizens and one another. In doing so, records are created that are often subject to state access laws. Just because some people can view some information online does not relieve a government entity from the obligation to provide the information to other citizens on request.[3] Moreover, "Internet exchanges that create virtual records can also create virtual meetings," write two lawyers who analyzed how to apply open-records and open-meeting laws in their native Texas.[4] That is, while technology permits online meetings, it is also forcing an expanded definition of "meeting" and how laws permitting access may apply.

1. Lake v. City of Phoenix, 218 P.3d 1004, 1007 (Ariz. 2009).
2. O'Neill v. City of Shoreline, 240 P.3d 1149 (Wash. 2010).
3. *See* Alan J. Bojorquez & Damien Shores, *Open Government and the Net: Bringing Social Media into the Light,* 11 Tex. Tech. Admin. L. J. 45, 59 (2009).
4. *Id.*

State open-records laws apply to not only state government agencies and departments, but also to cities, school districts and other governing authorities within a given state. These laws are utilized frequently—much more than the U.S. FOIA. Like the FOIA, state laws have been amended to apply to the digital age. The law in Tennessee, for example, covers "all documents, papers, letters,

Points of Law

State Open-Meetings Laws: The New York Example

The following is excerpted from the New York State Opening Meeting Law's section on opening meetings and executive sessions:

(a) Every meeting of a public body shall be open to the general public, except that an executive session of such body may be called and business transacted thereat in accordance with section one hundred five of this article. (b) Public bodies shall make or cause to be made all reasonable efforts to ensure that meetings are held in facilities that permit barrier-free physical access to the physically handicapped, as defined in subdivision five of section fifty of the public buildings law. (c) A public body that uses videoconferencing to conduct its meetings shall provide an opportunity to attend, listen and observe at any site at which a member participates. (d) Public bodies shall make or cause to be made all reasonable efforts to ensure that meetings are held in an appropriate facility which can adequately accommodate members of the public who wish to attend such meetings.[1]

1. Committee on Open Government, New York Dept. of State (n.d.), *available at* http://www.dos.state.ny.us/coog/openmeetlaw .html.

maps, books, photographs, microfilms, electronic data processing files and output, sound recordings, or other materials regardless of physical form made or received pursuant to law or ordinance or in connection with the transaction of official business by a governmental agency."[158] Like many states and the federal government, Tennessee emphasizes that only records are covered by its law. A requester cannot demand that a government agency provide information.[159]

Enforcement is an issue within the context of newsgathering access. That is, while laws demand compliance, what happens when government agencies refuse to cooperate as laws require? Thirty-four states and the District of Columbia have civil and/or criminal sanctions for first-time government official violators who do not properly comply with records requests.[160] In fact, several states have recently revised enforcement provisions in their open-records laws. For example, in 2009 Illinois added a provision to its law stating that "it is the public policy of the State of Illinois that access by all persons to public records promotes the transparency and accountability of public bodies at all levels of government," adding that openness is a "fundamental obligation of government to operate openly."[161]

State Open-Meetings Laws

Although seven states combine public records and open-meetings access into one law,[162] the vast majority of states—and the federal government—find it best to address these areas of access separately. All states and the District of Columbia have open-meetings laws or constitutional provisions ensuring some degree of access to public meetings. These laws vary widely from state to state, as do the penalties for violating them. In general, open-meetings laws trigger public access whenever a quorum of a decision-making body deliberates public business. By law, a meeting generally means either a physical gathering or videoconferencing that allows members to interact in real time. Applying this same logic, some observers believe open-meetings laws should apply to online chat rooms. Boards may accommodate citizens' right to attend meetings either by providing space in their meeting room or by providing electronic access. Most state laws require agencies to provide public notice in advance of meetings and to keep minutes of their business. A few states also require boards to keep minutes of their executive sessions, which become available to the public if closure is improper or once the need for closure has passed.

Several states outline those provisions for the enforcement of open-meetings laws. In Michigan, for example, any citizen may challenge in court a decision made by a public body to deny access. If it is determined by the court that the decision was in violation of the law, the court can invalidate that decision. In addition, a public official who intentionally breaks the law is subject to a fine up to $1,000. A second deliberate violation can result in a fine up to $2,000, a jail term of up to one year, or both.[163]

SUMMARY

THE COMPUTER AGE HAS NOT CIRCUMVENTED freedom of information. The Electronic Freedom of Information Act provides access to digitally recorded and stored information in the hands of the federal government.

Just as federal records laws help provide access to federal records, similar laws exist on the state level. In fact, the states have overwhelmingly been ahead of the federal government in advancing the idea of open records. Similarly, access to meetings is provided for by law on both the federal and state levels. ■

Cases for Study

Thinking About It

The two case excerpts that follow cover different subsets in the broad area of news gathering. The first case addresses the concept of the ride-along. The second is a case related to the Freedom of Information Act. As you read these case excerpts, keep the following questions in mind:

- Note that in the *Wilson* ride-along case, a media organization is not a party to the case. Nevertheless, it is a ruling that affects the media significantly. How and why?

- In *Wilson,* why were members of the news media on the scene? Did their presence help in the execution of the warrant?

- Just how much information does the Freedom of Information Act provide? Are the limits that have been established fair?

- In the *Reporters Committee* case, what factor does the Supreme Court identify as critical in deciding whether to disclose a private document?

- The *Reporters Committee* case was decided in 1989. Has the nature of privacy changed in such a way that the ruling would be different today?

Wilson v. Layne
SUPREME COURT OF THE UNITED STATES
526 U.S. 603 (1999)

CHIEF JUSTICE WILLIAM REHNQUIST delivered the Court's opinion:

While executing an arrest warrant in a private home, police officers invited representatives of the media to accompany them. We hold that such a "media ride along" does violate the Fourth Amendment, but that because the state of the law was not clearly established at the time the search in this case took place, the officers are entitled to the defense of qualified immunity.

In early 1992, the Attorney General of the United States approved "Operation Gunsmoke," a special national fugitive apprehension program in which United States Marshals worked with state and local police to apprehend dangerous criminals. The "Operation Gunsmoke" policy statement explained that the operation was to concentrate on "armed individuals wanted on federal and/or state and local warrants for serious drug and other violent felonies." This effective program ultimately resulted in over 3,000 arrests in 40 metropolitan areas.

One of the dangerous fugitives identified as a target of "Operation Gunsmoke" was Dominic Wilson, the son of petitioners Charles and Geraldine Wilson. Dominic Wilson had violated his probation on previous felony charges of robbery, theft, and assault with intent to rob, and the police computer listed "caution indicators" that he was likely to be armed, to resist arrest, and to "assault police." The computer also listed his address as 909 North Stone Street Avenue in Rockville, Maryland. Unknown to the police, this was actually the home of petitioners, Dominic Wilson's parents. Thus, in April 1992, the Circuit Court for Montgomery County issued three arrest warrants for Dominic Wilson, one for each of his probation violations. The warrants were each addressed to "any duly authorized peace officer," and commanded such officers to arrest him and bring him "immediately" before the Circuit Court to answer an indictment as to his probation violation. The warrants made no mention of media presence or assistance.

In the early morning hours of April 16, 1992, a Gunsmoke team of Deputy United States Marshals and Montgomery County Police officers assembled to execute the Dominic Wilson warrants. The team was accompanied by a reporter and a photographer from the Washington Post, who had been invited by the Marshals to accompany them on their mission as part of a Marshal's Service ride-along policy.

At around 6:45 a.m., the officers, with media representatives in tow, entered the dwelling at 909 North Stone Street Avenue in the Lincoln Park neighborhood of Rockville. Petitioners Charles and Geraldine Wilson were still in bed when they heard the officers enter the home. Petitioner Charles Wilson, dressed only in a pair of briefs, ran into the living room to investigate. Discovering at least five men in street clothes with guns in his living room, he angrily demanded that they state their business, and repeatedly cursed the officers. Believing him to be an angry Dominic Wilson, the officers quickly subdued him on the floor. Geraldine Wilson next entered the living room to investigate, wearing only a nightgown. She observed her husband being restrained by the armed officers.

When their protective sweep was completed, the officers learned that Dominic Wilson was not in the house, and they departed. During the time that the officers were in the home, the Washington Post photographer took numerous pictures. The print reporter was also apparently in the living room observing the confrontation between the police and Charles Wilson. At no time, however, were the reporters involved in the execution of the arrest warrant. The Washington Post never published its photographs of the incident.

Petitioners sued the law enforcement officials in their personal capacities for money damages. . . . They contended that the officers' actions in bringing members of the media to observe and record the attempted execution of the arrest warrant violated their Fourth Amendment rights. . . .

. . . [G]overnment officials performing discretionary functions generally are granted a qualified immunity and are "shielded from liability for civil damages insofar as their conduct does not violate clearly established statutory or constitutional rights of which a reasonable person would have known."

. . . A court evaluating a claim of qualified immunity "must first determine whether the plaintiff has alleged the deprivation of an actual constitutional right at all, and if so, proceed to determine whether that right was clearly established at the time of the alleged violation." This order of procedure is designed to "spare a defendant not only unwarranted liability, but unwarranted demands customarily imposed upon those defending a long drawn-out lawsuit." Deciding the constitutional question before addressing the qualified immunity question also promotes clarity in the legal standards for official conduct, to the benefit of both the officers and the general public. We now turn to the Fourth Amendment question.

In 1604, an English court made the now-famous observation that "the house of every one is to him as his castle and fortress, as well for his defence against injury and violence, as for his repose." In his Commentaries on the Laws of England, William Blackstone noted that

> the law of England has so particular and tender a regard to the immunity of a man's house, that it stiles it his castle, and will never suffer it to be violated with impunity: agreeing herein with the sentiments of antient Rome. . . . For this reason no doors can in general be broken open to execute any civil process; though, in criminal causes, the public safety supersedes the private.

The Fourth Amendment embodies this centuries-old principle of respect for the privacy of the home: "The right of the people to be secure in their persons, houses, papers, and effects, against unreasonable searches and seizures, shall not be violated, and no Warrants shall issue, but upon probable cause, supported by Oath or affirmation, and particularly describing the place to be searched, and the persons or things to be seized."

Our decisions have applied these basic principles of the Fourth Amendment to situations, like those in this case, in which police enter a home under the authority of an arrest warrant in order to take into custody the suspect named in the warrant. In *Payton v. New York* (1980), we noted that although clear in its protection of the home, the common-law tradition at the time of the drafting of the Fourth Amendment was ambivalent on the question of whether police could enter a home without a warrant. We were ultimately persuaded that the "overriding respect for the sanctity of the home that has been embedded in our traditions since the origins of the Republic" meant that absent a warrant or exigent circumstances, police could not enter a home to make an arrest. We decided that "an arrest warrant founded on probable cause implicitly carries with it the limited authority to enter a dwelling in which the suspect lives when there is reason to believe the suspect is within."

Here, of course, the officers had such a warrant, and they were undoubtedly entitled to enter the Wilson home in order to execute the arrest warrant for Dominic Wilson. But it does not necessarily follow that they were entitled to bring a newspaper reporter and a photographer with them. . . .

Certainly the presence of reporters inside the home was not related to the objectives of the authorized intrusion. Respondents concede that the reporters did not engage in the execution of the warrant, and did not assist the police in their task. The reporters therefore were not present for any reason related to the justification for police entry into the home—the apprehension of Dominic Wilson.

This is not a case in which the presence of the third parties directly aided in the execution of the warrant. Where the police enter a home under the authority of a warrant to search for stolen property, the presence of third parties for the purpose of identifying the stolen property has long been approved by this Court and our common-law tradition.

Respondents argue that the presence of the Washington Post reporters in the Wilsons' home nonetheless served a number of legitimate law enforcement purposes. They first assert that officers should be able to exercise reasonable discretion about when it would "further their law enforcement mission to permit members of the news media to accompany them in executing a warrant." But this claim ignores the importance of the right of residential privacy at the core of the Fourth Amendment. It may well be that

media ride-alongs further the law enforcement objectives of the police in a general sense, but that is not the same as furthering the purposes of the search. Were such generalized "law enforcement objectives" themselves sufficient to trump the Fourth Amendment, the protections guaranteed by that Amendment's text would be significantly watered down.

Respondents next argue that the presence of third parties could serve the law enforcement purpose of publicizing the government's efforts to combat crime, and facilitate accurate reporting on law enforcement activities. There is certainly language in our opinions interpreting the First Amendment which points to the importance of "the press" in informing the general public about the administration of criminal justice. . . . But the Fourth Amendment also protects a very important right, and in the present case it is in terms of that right that the media ride-alongs must be judged.

Surely the possibility of good public relations for the police is simply not enough, standing alone, to justify the ride-along intrusion into a private home. And even the need for accurate reporting on police issues in general bears no direct relation to the constitutional justification for the police intrusion into a home in order to execute a felony arrest warrant.

Finally, respondents argue that the presence of third parties could serve in some situations to minimize police abuses and protect suspects, and also to protect the safety of the officers. While it might be reasonable for police officers to themselves videotape home entries as part of a "quality control" effort to ensure that the rights of homeowners are being respected, or even to preserve evidence, such a situation is significantly different from the media presence in this case. The Washington Post reporters in the Wilsons' home were working on a story for their own purposes. They were not present for the purpose of protecting the officers, much less the Wilsons. A private photographer was acting for private purposes, as evidenced in part by the fact that the newspaper and not the police retained the photographs. Thus, although the presence of third parties during the execution of a warrant may in some circumstances be constitutionally permissible, the presence of these third parties was not.

The reasons advanced by respondents, taken in their entirety, fall short of justifying the presence of media inside a home. We hold that it is a violation of the Fourth Amendment for police to bring members of the media or other third parties into a home during the execution of a warrant when the presence of the third parties in the home was not in aid of the execution of the warrant.

Since the police action in this case violated the petitioners' Fourth Amendment right, we now must decide whether this right was clearly established at the time of the search. As noted above, government officials performing discretionary functions generally are granted a qualified immunity and are "shielded from liability for civil damages insofar as their conduct does not violate clearly established statutory or constitutional rights of which a reasonable person would have known." What this means in practice is that "whether an official protected by qualified immunity may be held personally liable for an allegedly unlawful official action generally turns on the 'objective legal reasonableness' of the action, assessed in light of the legal rules that were 'clearly established' at the time it was taken." . . .

We hold that it was not unreasonable for a police officer in April 1992 to have believed that bringing media observers along during the execution of an arrest warrant (even in a home) was lawful. First, the constitutional question presented by this case is by no means open and shut. The Fourth Amendment protects the rights of homeowners from entry without a warrant, but there was a warrant here. The question is whether the invitation to the media exceeded the scope of the search authorized by the warrant. Accurate media coverage of police activities serves an important public purpose, and it is not obvious from the general principles of the Fourth Amendment that

the conduct of the officers in this case violated the Amendment.

Second, although media ride-alongs of one sort or another had apparently become a common police practice, in 1992 there were no judicial opinions holding that this practice became unlawful when it entered a home. . . .

Finally, important to our conclusion was the reliance by the United States marshals in this case on a Marshal's Service ride-along policy which explicitly contemplated that media who engaged in ride-alongs might enter private homes with their cameras as part of fugitive apprehension arrests. The Montgomery County Sheriff's Department also at this time had a ride-along program that did not expressly prohibit media entry into private homes. Such a policy, of course, could not make reasonable a belief that was contrary to a decided body of case law. But here the state of the law as to third parties accompanying police on home entries was at best undeveloped, and it was not unreasonable for law enforcement officers to look and rely on their formal ride-along policies.

Given such an undeveloped state of the law, the officers in this case cannot have been "expected to predict the future course of constitutional law." Between the time of the events of this case and today's decision, a split among the Federal Circuits in fact developed on the question whether media ride-alongs that enter homes subject the police to money damages. If judges thus disagree on a constitutional question, it is unfair to subject police to money damages for picking the losing side of the controversy.

For the foregoing reasons, the judgment of the Court of Appeals is affirmed.

It is so ordered.

U.S. Department of Justice v. Reporters Committee for Freedom of the Press
SUPREME COURT OF THE UNITED STATES
489 U.S. 749 (1989)

JUSTICE JOHN PAUL STEVENS delivered the Court's opinion:
The Federal Bureau of Investigation (FBI) has accumulated and maintains criminal identification records,

sometimes referred to as "rap sheets," on over 24 million persons. The question presented by this case is whether the disclosure of the contents of such a file to a third party "could reasonably be expected to constitute an unwarranted invasion of personal privacy" within the meaning of the Freedom of Information Act (FOIA).

In 1924 Congress appropriated funds to enable the Department of Justice (Department) to establish a program to collect and preserve fingerprints and other criminal identification records. That statute authorized the Department to exchange such information with "officials of States, cities and other institutions." . . . Congress created the FBI's identification division, and gave it responsibility for "acquiring, collecting, classifying, and preserving criminal identification and other crime records and the exchanging of said criminal identification records with the duly authorized officials of governmental agencies, of States, cities, and penal institutions." Rap sheets compiled pursuant to such authority contain certain descriptive information, such as date of birth and physical characteristics, as well as a history of arrests, charges, convictions, and incarcerations of the subject. Normally a rap sheet is preserved until its subject attains age 80. Because of the volume of rap sheets, they are sometimes incorrect or incomplete and sometimes contain information about other persons with similar names.

The local, state, and federal law enforcement agencies throughout the Nation that exchange rap-sheet data with the FBI do so on a voluntary basis. The principal use of the information is to assist in the detection and prosecution of offenders; it is also used by courts and corrections officials in connection with sentencing and parole decisions. As a matter of executive policy, the Department has generally treated rap sheets as confidential and, with certain exceptions, has restricted their use to governmental purposes. Consistent with the Department's basic policy of treating these records as confidential, Congress in 1957 amended the basic statute to provide that the FBI's exchange of rap-sheet information with any other agency is subject to cancellation "if dissemination is made outside the receiving departments or related agencies."

As a matter of Department policy, the FBI has made two exceptions to its general practice of prohibiting unofficial access to rap sheets. First, it allows the subject of a rap sheet to obtain a copy, and second, it occasionally allows rap sheets to be used in the preparation of press releases and publicity designed to assist in the apprehension of wanted persons or fugitives. . . .

Although much rap-sheet information is a matter of public record, the availability and dissemination of the actual rap sheet to the public is limited. Arrests, indictments, convictions, and sentences are public events that are usually documented in court records. In addition, if a person's entire criminal history transpired in a single jurisdiction, all of the contents of his or her rap sheet may be available upon request in that jurisdiction. That possibility, however, is present in only three States. All of the other 47 States place substantial restrictions on the availability of criminal-history summaries even though individual events in those summaries are matters of public record. Moreover, even in Florida, Wisconsin, and Oklahoma, the publicly available summaries may not include information about out-of-state arrests or convictions.

The statute known as the FOIA is actually a part of the Administrative Procedure Act (APA). Section 3 of the APA as enacted in 1946 gave agencies broad discretion concerning the publication of governmental records. In 1966 Congress amended that section to implement "'a general philosophy of full agency disclosure.'" The amendment required agencies to publish their rules of procedure in the Federal Register, and to make available for public inspection and copying their opinions, statements of policy, interpretations, and staff manuals and instructions that are not published in the Federal Register . . . requires every agency "upon any request for records which . . . reasonably describes such records" to make such records "promptly available to any person." If an agency improperly withholds any documents, the district court has jurisdiction to order their production. Unlike the review of other agency action that must be upheld if supported by substantial evidence and not arbitrary or capricious, the FOIA expressly places the burden "on the agency to sustain its action" and directs the district courts to "determine the matter de novo."

Congress exempted nine categories of documents from the FOIA's broad disclosure requirements. Three of those exemptions are arguably relevant to this case. Exemption 3 applies to documents that are specifically exempted from disclosure by another statute. Exemption 6 protects "personnel and medical files and similar files the disclosure of which would constitute a clearly unwarranted invasion of personal privacy." Exemption 7(C) excludes records or information compiled for law enforcement purposes, "but only to the extent that the production of such [materials] . . . could reasonably be expected to constitute an unwarranted invasion of personal privacy."

Exemption 7(C)'s privacy language is broader than the comparable language in Exemption 6 in two respects. First, whereas Exemption 6 requires that the invasion of privacy be "clearly unwarranted," the adverb "clearly" is omitted from Exemption 7(C). This omission is the product of a 1974 amendment adopted in response to concerns expressed by the President. Second, whereas Exemption 6 refers to disclosures that "would constitute" an invasion of privacy, Exemption 7(C) encompasses any disclosure that "could reasonably be expected to constitute" such an invasion. This difference is also the product of a specific amendment. Thus, the standard for evaluating a threatened invasion of privacy interests resulting from the disclosure of records compiled for law enforcement purposes is somewhat broader than the standard applicable to personnel, medical, and similar files.

This case arises out of requests made by a CBS news correspondent and the Reporters Committee for Freedom of the Press (respondents) for information concerning the criminal records of four members of the Medico family. The Pennsylvania Crime Commission had identified the family's company, Medico Industries, as a legitimate business dominated by organized crime figures. Moreover, the company allegedly had obtained a number of defense contracts as a result of an improper arrangement with a corrupt Congressman.

The FOIA requests sought disclosure of any arrests, indictments, acquittals, convictions, and sentences of any of the four Medicos. Although the FBI originally denied the requests, it provided the requested data concerning three of the Medicos after their deaths.

In their complaint in the District Court, respondents sought the rap sheet for the fourth, Charles Medico (Medico), insofar as it contained "matters of public record." . . .

Exemption 7(C) requires us to balance the privacy interest in maintaining, as the government puts it, the "practical obscurity" of the rap sheets against the public interest in their release.

The preliminary question is whether Medico's interest in the nondisclosure of any rap sheet the FBI might have on him is the sort of "personal privacy" interest that Congress intended Exemption 7(C) to protect. As we have pointed out before, "[t]he cases sometimes characterized as protecting 'privacy' have in fact involved at least two different kinds of interests. One is the individual interest in avoiding disclosure of personal matters, and another is the interest in independence in making certain kinds of important decisions." Here, the former interest, "in avoiding disclosure of personal matters," is implicated. Because events summarized in a rap sheet have been previously disclosed to the public, respondents contend that Medico's privacy interest in avoiding disclosure of a federal compilation of these events approaches zero. We reject respondents' cramped notion of personal privacy.

To begin with, both the common law and the literal understandings of privacy encompass the individual's control of information concerning his or her person. In an organized society, there are few facts that are not at one time or another divulged to another. Thus the extent of the protection accorded a privacy right at common law rested in part on the degree of dissemination of the allegedly private fact and the extent to which the passage of time rendered it private. According to Webster's initial definition, information may be classified as "private" if it is "intended for or restricted to the use of a particular person or group or class of persons: not freely available to the public." Recognition of this attribute of a privacy interest supports the distinction, in terms of personal privacy, between scattered disclosure of the bits of information contained in a rap sheet and revelation of the rap sheet as a whole. The very fact that federal funds have been spent to prepare, index, and maintain these criminal-history files demonstrates that the individual items of information in the summaries would not otherwise be "freely available" either to the officials who have access to the underlying files or to the general public. Indeed, if the summaries were "freely available," there would be no reason to invoke the FOIA to obtain access to the information they contain. Granted, in many contexts the fact that information is not freely available is no reason to exempt that information from a statute generally requiring its dissemination. But the issue here is whether the compilation of otherwise hard-to-obtain information alters the privacy interest implicated by disclosure of that information. Plainly there is a vast difference between the public records that might be found after a diligent search of courthouse files, county archives, and local police stations throughout the country and a computerized summary located in a single clearinghouse of information.

This conclusion is supported by the web of federal statutory and regulatory provisions that limits the disclosure of rap-sheet information. That is, Congress has authorized rap-sheet dissemination to banks, local licensing officials, the securities industry, the nuclear-power industry, and other law enforcement agencies. Further, the FBI has permitted such disclosure to the subject of the rap sheet and, more generally, to assist in the apprehension of wanted persons or fugitives. Finally, the FBI's exchange of rap-sheet information "is subject to cancellation if dissemination is made outside the receiving departments or related agencies." This careful and limited pattern of authorized rap-sheet disclosure fits the dictionary definition of privacy as involving a restriction of information "to the use of a particular person or group or class of persons." Moreover, although perhaps not specific enough to constitute a statutory exemption under FOIA Exemption 3, these statutes and regulations, taken as a whole, evidence a congressional intent to protect the privacy of rap-sheet subjects, and a concomitant recognition of the power of compilations to affect personal privacy that outstrips the combined power of the bits of information contained within.

Other portions of the FOIA itself bolster the conclusion that disclosure of records regarding private citizens, identifiable by name, is not what the framers of the FOIA had in mind. Specifically, the FOIA provides that "[t]o the extent required to prevent a clearly unwarranted invasion of personal privacy, an agency may delete identifying details when it makes available or publishes an opinion, statement of policy, interpretation, or staff manual or instruction." Additionally, the FOIA assures that "[a]ny reasonably segregable portion of a record shall be provided to any person requesting such record after deletion of the portions which are exempt under Section (b)." These provisions, for deletion of identifying references and disclosure of segregable portions of records with exempt information deleted, reflect a congressional understanding that disclosure of records containing personal details about private citizens can infringe significant privacy interests.

Also supporting our conclusion that a strong privacy interest inheres in the nondisclosure of compiled computerized information is the Privacy Act of 1974. The Privacy Act was passed largely out of concern over "the impact of computer data banks on individual privacy." The Privacy Act provides generally that "[n]o agency shall disclose any record which is contained in a system of records . . . except pursuant to a written request by, or with the prior written consent of, the individual to whom the record pertains." Although the Privacy Act contains a variety of exceptions to this rule, including an exemption for information required to be disclosed under the FOIA, Congress' basic policy concern regarding the implications of computerized data banks for personal privacy is certainly relevant in our consideration of the privacy interest affected by dissemination of rap sheets from the FBI computer.

Given this level of federal concern over centralized data bases, the fact that most States deny the general public access to their criminal-history summaries should not be surprising. As we have pointed out, in 47 States nonconviction data from criminal-history summaries are not available at all, and even conviction data are "generally unavailable to the public." State policies, of course, do not determine the meaning of a federal statute, but they provide evidence that the law enforcement profession generally assumes—as has the Department of Justice—that individual subjects have a significant privacy interest in their criminal histories. It is reasonable to presume that Congress legislated with an understanding of this professional point of view.

In addition to the common-law and dictionary understandings, the basic difference between scattered bits of criminal history and a federal compilation, federal statutory provisions, and state policies, our cases have also recognized the privacy interest inherent in the nondisclosure of certain information even where the information may have been at one time public. . . .

In sum, the fact that "an event is not wholly 'private' does not mean that an individual has no interest in limiting disclosure or dissemination of the information." The privacy interest in a rap sheet is substantial. The substantial character of that interest is affected by the fact that in today's society the computer can accumulate and store information that would otherwise have surely been forgotten long before a person attains age 80, when the FBI's rap sheets are discarded.

Exemption 7(C), by its terms, permits an agency to withhold a document only when revelation "could reasonably be expected to constitute an unwarranted invasion of personal privacy." We must next address what factors might warrant an invasion of the interest described in Part IV.

Our previous decisions establish that whether an invasion of privacy is warranted cannot turn on the purposes for which the request for information is made. Except for cases in which the objection to disclosure is based on a claim of privilege and the person requesting disclosure is the party protected by the privilege, the identity of the requesting party has no bearing on the merits of his or her FOIA request. Thus, although the subject of a presentence report can waive a privilege that might defeat a third party's access to that report, and although the FBI's policy of granting the subject of a rap sheet access to his own criminal history is consistent with its policy of denying access to all other members of the general public, the rights of the two press respondents in this case are no different from those that might be asserted by any other third party, such as a neighbor or prospective employer. As

we have repeatedly stated, Congress "clearly intended" the FOIA "to give any member of the public as much right to disclosure as one with a special interest [in a particular document]." . . . "The Act's sole concern is with what must be made public or not made public."

Thus whether disclosure of a private document under Exemption 7(C) is warranted must turn on the nature of the requested document and its relationship to "the basic purpose of the Freedom of Information Act 'to open agency action to the light of public scrutiny'" . . . rather than on the particular purpose for which the document is being requested. In our leading case on the FOIA, we declared that the Act was designed to create a broad right of access to "official information." . . .

This basic policy of "'full agency disclosure unless information is exempted under clearly delineated statutory language'" indeed focuses on the citizens' right to be informed about "what their government is up to." Official information that sheds light on an agency's performance of its statutory duties falls squarely within that statutory purpose. That purpose, however, is not fostered by disclosure of information about private citizens that is accumulated in various governmental files but that reveals little or nothing about an agency's own conduct. In this case—and presumably in the typical case in which one private citizen is seeking information about another—the requester does not intend to discover anything about the conduct of the agency that has possession of the requested records. Indeed, response to this request would not shed any light on the conduct of any Government agency or official. . . .

Respondents argue that there is a twofold public interest in learning about Medico's past arrests or convictions: He allegedly had improper dealings with a corrupt Congressman, and he is an officer of a corporation with defense contracts. But if Medico has, in fact, been arrested or convicted of certain crimes, that information would neither aggravate nor mitigate his allegedly improper relationship with the Congressman; more specifically, it would tell us nothing directly about the character of the Congressman's behavior. Nor would it tell us anything about the conduct of the Department of Defense (DOD) in awarding one or more contracts to the Medico Company. Arguably a FOIA request to the DOD for records relating to those contracts, or for documents describing the agency's procedures, if any, for determining whether officers of a prospective contractor have criminal records, would constitute an appropriate request for "official information." Conceivably Medico's rap sheet would provide details to include in a news story, but, in itself, this is not the kind of public interest for which Congress enacted the FOIA. In other words, although there is undoubtedly some public interest in anyone's criminal history, especially if the history is in some way related to the subject's dealing with a public official or agency, the FOIA's central purpose is to ensure that the Government's activities be opened to the sharp eye of public scrutiny, not that information about private citizens that happens to be in the warehouse of the Government be so disclosed. Thus, it should come as no surprise that in none of our cases construing the FOIA have we found it appropriate to order a Government agency to honor a FOIA request for information about a particular private citizen.

What we have said should make clear that the public interest in the release of any rap sheet on Medico that may exist is not the type of interest protected by the FOIA. Medico may or may not be one of the 24 million persons for whom the FBI has a rap sheet. If respondents are entitled to have the FBI tell them what it knows about Medico's criminal history, any other member of the public is entitled to the same disclosure—whether for writing a news story, for deciding whether to employ Medico, to rent a house to him, to extend credit to him, or simply to confirm or deny a suspicion. There is, unquestionably, some public interest in providing interested citizens with answers to their questions about Medico. But that interest falls outside the ambit of the public interest that the FOIA was enacted to serve.

Finally, we note that Congress has provided that the standard fees for production of documents under the FOIA shall be waived or reduced "if disclosure of the information is in the public interest because it is likely to contribute significantly to public understanding of the operations or activities of the government and is not primarily in the commercial interest of the requester." Although such a provision obviously implies that there will be requests that do not meet such a "public interest" standard, we think it relevant to today's inquiry regarding the public interest in release of rap sheets on private citizens that Congress once again expressed the core purpose of the FOIA as "contribut[ing] significantly to public understanding of the operations or activities of the government."

Both the general requirement that a court "shall determine the matter de novo" and the specific reference to an "unwarranted" invasion of privacy in Exemption 7(C) indicate that a court must balance the public interest in disclosure against the interest Congress intended the Exemption to protect. Although both sides agree that such a balance must be undertaken, how such a balance should be done is in dispute. The Court of Appeals majority expressed concern about assigning federal judges the task of striking a proper case-by-case, or ad hoc, balance between individual privacy interests and the public interest in the disclosure of criminal-history information without providing those judges standards to assist in performing that task. Our cases provide support for the proposition that categorical decisions may be appropriate and individual circumstances disregarded when a case fits into a genus in which the balance characteristically tips in one direction. . . .

. . . [W]e hold as a categorical matter that a third party's request for law enforcement records or information about a private citizen can reasonably be expected to invade that citizen's privacy, and that when the request seeks no "official information" about a Government agency, but merely records that the Government happens to be storing, the invasion of privacy is "unwarranted." The judgment of the Court of Appeals is reversed.

It is so ordered.

Chapter 9

[N]o harassment of newsmen will be tolerated. . . . [I]f the newsman is called upon to give information bearing only a remote and tenuous relationship to the subject of the investigation, or if he has some other reason to believe that his testimony implicates confidential source relationships without a legitimate need of law enforcement, he will have access to the court on a motion to quash and an appropriate protective order may be entered. The asserted claim to privilege should be judged on its facts by the striking of a proper balance between freedom of the press and the obligation of all citizens to give relevant testimony with respect to criminal conduct.

U.S. Supreme Court Justice Lewis Powell[1]

Freelance photojournalist Josh Wolf served 226 days in jail—a record—for refusing to give a grand jury his videotape of a San Francisco demonstration in which a police officer was injured.

Reporter's Privilege
Protecting the Watchdogs

Reporter's Privilege

After *Branzburg*

Shield Laws

Who Is Covered
What Is Covered
Shield Laws and Websites
Other Sources of Protection

Breaking Promises of Confidentiality

Search Warrants

Newsroom Searches
The Privacy Protection Act

Cases for Study

➤ *Branzburg v. Hayes*
➤ *Cohen v. Cowles Media Co.*

Suppose . . .

. . . that a reporter promises a source anonymity in exchange for sensitive information that relates to criminal activity. When the article is published, law enforcement officials learn the reporter has information that could help their investigation. The reporter receives a subpoena to appear before a grand jury. When asked questions that would force him to reveal his source's identity, he refuses. He says to do so would infringe his and his newspaper's First Amendment rights.

Is refusing to disclose a source a First Amendment right for journalists, even when it involves an investigation of criminal activity? Why or why not?

Should a journalist who refuses to cooperate with criminal investigations go to jail? Look for the answers to these questions when the case of *Branzburg v. Hayes* is discussed later in this chapter and excerpted at the end of the chapter.

In the course of doing their work, journalists can come across a lot of information. Some of that information may be sensitive and potentially useful to criminal investigations. That same information may have been revealed to a reporter on the condition that its source or specific elements of it not be revealed. The reporter may agree, granting the source confidentiality in exchange for information that will contribute to a story.

383

What if a judge orders a journalist to reveal a source or information not yet published? This chapter explores whether reporters can be forced to reveal information in their possession, particularly the identities of confidential sources. The use of confidential sources is a long-standing practice in journalism.[2] One estimate claims that at least 33 percent of newspaper stories and up to 85 percent of all newsmagazine sources contain veiled attribution.[3] The use of confidential sources has been referred to as "one form of currency that journalists use to get something they want and need, which is information."[4]

A promise of anonymity may be the only way a reporter can convince a source to talk. In return, reporters and their news organizations typically keep those promises, even when compelled by courts to break them. Keeping such promises is not only ethical but also practical. "Burned" sources tend to become former sources. Moreover, reporters and news organizations that break promises develop a reputation for being untrustworthy. Sources vanish. A chilling effect ensues. A source may successfully sue a reporter for breaking a confidentiality promise.

For these reasons, many argue that a reporter's privilege that protects journalists from being forced to reveal source identity should exist. If the First Amendment guarantees freedom of the press, according to this rationale, it also must protect against any infringement on the free flow of ideas. Divulging information can act as just such an infringement. But balanced against reporter's privilege is the deep-rooted judicial philosophy that justice is best served by requiring anyone who has information relevant to a criminal case or civil lawsuit to reveal it. More than 60 years ago, the U.S. Supreme Court wrote, "For more than three centuries it has now been recognized as a fundamental maxim that the public has a right to every man's evidence."[5] Later, the Court noted, "The obligation of all citizens [is] to give relevant testimony with respect to criminal conduct."[6]

Anyone may receive a subpoena—an order to appear in court to, for example, testify or produce evidence. As professional recorders of news and information, journalists have an enhanced possibility of being subpoenaed. Those who receive subpoenas are expected to comply. However, recipients may file a motion to quash the subpoena. A motion to **quash** is simply a request to a court to annul or vacate the order to appear. Journalists may rely on one of two legal concepts to quash a subpoena. In most federal courts and courts in certain states, reporter's privilege may allow a journalist to refuse to reveal sources or information. In other states a shield law may protect the journalist.

quash To nullify or annul, as in quashing a subpoena.

Reporter's Privilege

Whether reporters can keep the identities of their sources confidential, even when that information is sought through a court order, revolves around the concept of **reporter's privilege,** sometimes called "journalist's privilege." The privilege is tenuous and depends on several conditions being met. Thus, it is a qualified privilege.

reporter's privilege The concept that reporters can keep information such as source identity confidential. The idea is that the reporter–source relationship is similar to doctor–patient and lawyer–client relationships.

Courts long have granted certain privileges not to testify against those with whom they have a special relationship—lawyer–client, doctor–patient, husband–wife or clergy–parishioner, for example. Journalists maintain that they have similar relationships with their sources and should not be forced to testify against them by revealing their identities. Moreover, they believe reporter's privilege has the protection of the First Amendment. Compelling a journalist to violate an agreement with a source for confidentiality, according to this view, impinges on freedom of the press by interfering with the free flow of information. Although arguments drawing parallels between lawyer–client and reporter–source privileges have been made,[7] some maintain there is a vital distinction: A client may release an attorney from the agreement—thus removing the lawyer's privilege. However, even if a source releases a journalist, the journalist may still want to maintain the confidentiality. According to this view, reporter's privilege belongs to the reporter, someone who is protecting not only a source, but also the integrity of the process.[8]

Reporter's privilege developed from the landmark U.S. Supreme Court case *Branzburg v. Hayes.*[9] *Branzburg* involved four consolidated cases the Court heard together, two involving Paul Branzburg, a reporter with the Louisville Courier-Journal. In the course of his reporting, Branzburg had uncovered and written about illegal drug use and sales in the Louisville, Ky., area. He promised his sources that he would not identify them. When he was issued a subpoena to appear before a grand jury to answer questions about the published stories and his sources, he kept his promises. The other two cases involved journalists who refused to provide information to grand juries about militant organizations they had covered. A grand jury is a group of citizens charged with deciding whether enough evidence exists to indict a suspect for committing a serious crime.

All three reporters claimed the First Amendment and its free press clause meant they should not be required to reveal confidential information given the circumstances of their cases. If forced to do so, their ability to report news would be irreparably harmed. Not only would those specific sources be betrayed

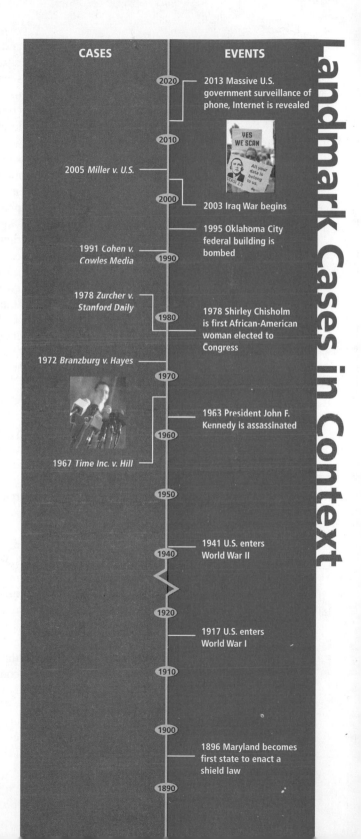

Landmark Cases in Context

CASES | **EVENTS**

2020

2013 Massive U.S. government surveillance of phone, Internet is revealed

2010

2005 *Miller v. U.S.*

2003 Iraq War begins

2000

1995 Oklahoma City federal building is bombed

1991 *Cohen v. Cowles Media*

1990

1978 *Zurcher v. Stanford Daily*

1980

1978 Shirley Chisholm is first African-American woman elected to Congress

1972 *Branzburg v. Hayes*

1970

1963 President John F. Kennedy is assassinated

1960

1967 *Time Inc. v. Hill*

1950

1941 U.S. enters World War II

1940

1920

1917 U.S. enters World War I

1910

1900

1896 Maryland becomes first state to enact a shield law

1890

The dissenting opinion by Justice Potter Stewart in *Branzburg v. Hayes* proposed a qualified reporter's privilege.

Points of Law

The Reporter's Privilege Test

A reporter's privilege to withhold information may exist unless the government can demonstrate the following:

1. Probable cause to believe that the reporter has information clearly relevant to a specific violation of law, and

2. That the information sought cannot be obtained by alternative means less destructive of First Amendment values, and

3. That there is a compelling and overriding interest in the information.

and less likely to cooperate with the news media in the future, but many potential future sources would also go silent. The reporters argued that even if they refused to name sources, their mere appearance before a grand jury could cause this harm because their sources would never know what the reporter had revealed during the closed grand jury process. As a result, less information would be available, both to the public and the press. The reporters maintained this disruption of the journalistic process constituted a violation of the First Amendment's guarantee of press freedom.

A 5–4 majority of the Supreme Court rejected the idea that there is a First Amendment privilege protecting journalists from testifying before grand juries. In balancing the possibility of such a privilege against the public interest in law enforcement, the Court favored the latter. The importance of obtaining evidence is critical to that effort. That a reporter may be in possession of the evidence is immaterial. Grand juries, Justice Byron White wrote for the Court, are entitled to "every man's evidence."[10] Journalists are not exempted.

The concurring and dissenting opinions written in the case were also significant. Writing in concurrence, Justice Lewis Powell emphasized "the limited nature" of the Court's holding.[11] He suggested that any journalist's privilege to withhold information should be evaluated case by case. In addition, he wrote that a refusal to provide information might be permitted if the information was not relevant to an investigation or failed to serve "a legitimate need of law enforcement."[12]

Justice Potter Stewart led the dissenters, criticizing the "Court's crabbed view of the First Amendment."[13] He stated that reporters have a limited First Amendment right to refuse to reveal sources, a right that stems from "the broad societal interest in a full and free flow of information to the public."[14] That basic concern, he wrote, underlies the First Amendment's protection for a free press—a guarantee "not for the benefit of the press so much as for the benefit of all of us."[15] Justice William Douglas' dissent contended journalists have an absolute privilege to withhold information, including sources' names.[16]

Justice Stewart did not minimize the importance of either the grand jury process or the need for "every man's evidence." However, he believed those interests ought to be balanced against the critical role of the press. A First

Points of Law

Contempt of Court

Judges have broad power to issue contempt of court orders. In general, any willful disobedience of a court order, any misconduct in court or any action that interferes with the judge's administration of justice might result in a contempt of court citation and may be punishable by a fine, imprisonment or both. Each judge has discretion to determine what types of conduct constitute contempt, to cite someone for contempt, to find the person guilty and to decide the penalty. The judge's decision to issue a contempt citation may be appealed. Contempt citations must be obeyed even if they may be found unconstitutional upon appeal. There is both civil and criminal contempt, and the distinction between the two often is unclear.

Civil Contempt

Civil contempt citations usually compel an individual to do something, such as name a source or turn over interview notes or outtakes of a broadcast program. They also arise when someone intentionally disobeys a court order. For example, if attorneys speak to the media in violation of a court order not to discuss the trial in public, they may be cited for contempt. Civil contempt sometimes is called "indirect contempt" because the action that prompts the citation generally occurs outside the direct supervision of the judge. Civil contempt orders most often are lifted as soon as the individual performs the required action or the trial ends.

Criminal Contempt

Criminal contempt is any conduct in or near the court that willfully disobeys a court order or obstructs court proceedings. Because much criminal contempt directly interferes with the proceedings of the court, some forms of criminal contempt are also called "direct contempt." It is often unclear whether a particular action is a form of criminal or civil contempt or both. For example, if journalists under oath refuse to answer questions about confidential sources, they may be cited for both civil and criminal contempt.

Although judges enjoy sweeping authority to issue contempt citations, their power is not unlimited. Some states limit judges' contempt power to punishment of actions committed by the officers of the court, actions in the court or acts that directly disobey court mandates, orders or rules. The First Amendment prevents judges from using their contempt power to silence criticism of themselves or court proceedings unless the criticism poses a clear and present danger to justice.[1] Thus, even when newspapers publish caustic attacks on the court that are, at best, partially accurate, judges may not cite them for contempt unless the comments reach the level of intimidating jurors or undermining the fairness of the trial. The Supreme Court has ruled that individuals charged with contempt who could be sentenced to more than six months in jail if convicted have a right to a jury trial.[2]

1. Pennekamp v. Florida, 328 U.S. 331 (1946).
2. *See, e.g.,* Bloom v. Illinois, 391 U.S. 194, 203 n.6 (1968).

Amendment privilege to withhold information should exist, he said, unless officials could meet "a heavy burden of justification" to overcome the privilege.[17] He outlined the conditions under which that burden could be met: (1) There is probable cause to believe the reporter has information clearly relevant to a specific violation of law, (2) the information being sought cannot be obtained by other means that are less intrusive of First Amendment values, and (3) there is a compelling and overriding interest in the information.[18] This was adopted by many courts nationwide and is now commonly referred to as the "reporter's privilege test."

All but one of the circuits of the U.S. Courts of Appeals have recognized a journalist's privilege to protect confidential sources.[19] The exception is the Sixth Circuit. Nearly 30 years ago it rejected reporter's privilege as a protection for journalists called to testify at trial.[20]

After *Branzburg*

Because the *Branzburg* decision was narrow, speaking only to a journalist being called before a grand jury, its direct application has been relatively limited. The Court's 5–4 decision was unequivocal about no reporter's privilege with regard to grand juries.

The various *Branzburg* opinions did not make clear how to interpret the decision in cases not pertaining to grand juries. Part of the ambiguity lay in Justice Powell's opinion. Although listed as a concurrence and therefore giving Justice White's opinion a 5–4 majority, Powell's concurrence seemed to have more in common with the dissenters. That included his willingness to consider a reporter's privilege under certain conditions. Thus, a sort of "unofficial majority" of the Court said that a qualified reporter's privilege should at least be contemplated outside of grand jury circumstances.

Some lower courts adopted the three-part test to determine whether the privilege survives. It is therefore most accurate to characterize reporter's privilege as limited or qualified. That is, a court using the test will balance the three factors against the likelihood the journalist's information will help ensure a fair trial. If one factor clearly favors the journalist, the journalist very likely will have reporter's privilege protection.

For example, a federal district court ruled reporter's privilege shielded a journalist from being questioned because there were other ways to obtain the information. After the Boston police imposed strict limits on where street performers could appear around Faneuil Hall, a popular tourist attraction, one performer sued the city for abridging his First Amendment rights. He subpoenaed a reporter who had written an article about the situation, seeking confirmation of the space restrictions the police enforced. The court said the performer failed to determine whether sources other than the reporter could supply the information. The court suggested business owners, street vendors, local residents and individuals who often walk through the Faneuil Hall area should be questioned rather than subpoenaing the reporter.[21]

A federal district court applied the privilege test's relevancy factor to protect a journalist from testifying. A Minneapolis, Minn., policeman sued his chief and others claiming they conspired to harass him. As part of the lawsuit, a newspaper reporter received a subpoena seeking names of city employees who allegedly gave the journalist confidential information about the policeman. The reporter's

realWorld Law

"An Act of Conscience"

Former New York Times reporter Judith Miller was a target of a probe into a White House leak that led to the outing of a Central Intelligence Agency agent. She refused to comply with a court order to reveal what she knew, including the identity of her source. She was ultimately cited for contempt of court by a federal appellate judge.[1] Any sentence was delayed until all possible appeals were exhausted.

The U.S. Supreme Court rejected her appeal,[2] allowing the lower appeals court decision to stand and leaving it to the judge there whether Miller would be sentenced to prison. The New York Times did not waver in its support of Judith Miller, who claimed never to have published anything based on information she received from the undisclosed source.

The prosecutor in the case maintained that Miller's testimony was necessary, writing that "journalists are not entitled to promised complete confidentiality—no one in America is."[3] "Special treatment" for journalists, in the prosecutor's words, may counteract the coercive effect of jail and enable, rather than deter, defiance of the court's authority.

Miller chose to protect her source's identify and refused to testify. The judge ordered Miller to prison until she agreed to testify or the grand jury's term expired. In response, New York Times Company chairman Arthur Sulzberger, Jr., said, "There are times when the greater good of democracy demands an act of conscience. Judy has chosen such an act in honoring her promise of confidentiality to her sources. She believes, as do we, that the free flow of information is critical to an informed citizenry."[4]

In announcing his decision to jail Miller, however, the judge disputed Miller's claims that jailing her would bring good reporting to an end. "*Branzburg* has been the law for 33 years," he said, "and it hasn't stopped anything."[5] After spending 85 days in jail, Miller testified before the federal grand jury when her source relieved her of any confidentiality obligation. She had spent more time in jail than any other full-time reporter for refusing to identify a source.

After being released from jail, Miller and The New York Times reached an agreement for her to leave the newspaper.

---

1. *In re* Grand Jury Subpoena, (Miller), 397 F.3d 964 (D.C. Cir. 2005).
2. Miller v. U.S., 545 U.S. 1150 (2005).
3. *New York Times Reporter Jailed* (Oct. 28, 2005), *available at* http://www.cnn.com/2005/LAW/07/06/reporters.contempt.
4. Adam Liptak, *Reporter Jailed After Refusing to Name Source,* N.Y. TIMES, July 7, 2005, at A1.
5. Carol D. Leonnig, *N.Y. Times Reporter Jailed,* WASH. POST, July 7, 2005, at A1.

privilege protected the journalist, the court ruled in 2012, because the information sought was not relevant to the case. It related "only to two supposed instances of wrongdoing within a larger scheme that allegedly spanned at least two years," the court said. Even if the policeman did not have the reporter's sources, his case would not be "critically harmed," according to the court.[22]

Some courts apply reporter's privilege narrowly. In one case, the federal government accused a former Central Intelligence Agency (CIA) employee of revealing classified information to James Risen, a book author and New York Times reporter. The U.S. Court of Appeals for the Fourth Circuit said Risen did not have

First Amendment protection against testifying in the trial of the former employee. Risen had "direct, firsthand account of the [alleged] criminal conduct . . . [that] cannot be obtained by alternative means, as [Risen] is without dispute the only witness who can offer this critical testimony," the court said in 2013.[23]

Even when required to relinquish the privilege and comply with a subpoena, some journalists still refuse to testify, as Risen said he would not. They remain steadfast in their belief that their primary obligation is upholding a journalist's creed not to expose sources when promises of confidentiality are made. Taking this stance risks being found in contempt of court.[24] A finding of criminal contempt results in a specific jail term and/or fine. More common is a sanction of civil contempt, in which the journalist is jailed until he or she complies with the order to disclose. Reporters have remained in jail until a judge allows their release, usually when their information is no longer necessary in resolving the case.

Recently, journalists and news organizations witnessed renewed government efforts to demand source information, with courts increasingly holding uncooperative reporters in contempt. The situation that attracted considerable attention ended with the jailing of Judith Miller, then a New York Times reporter.

Reporter's privilege does not necessarily protect freelance journalists. For example, the U.S. Court of Appeals for the Second Circuit ruled that a documentary filmmaker could not use reporter's privilege because attorneys representing the film's subjects helped with the movie's production. That meant the filmmaker was not a journalist because he did not function with journalistic independence, the court said.[25]

However, in a 2013 decision involving the documentary filmmaker Ken Burns, a federal district court refused to rule Burns had become an advocate, causing him to lose his reporter's privilege protection.[26] Burns, his daughter and his son-in-law produced "The Central Park Five," a film about the five men convicted for raping a jogger in New York's Central Park. After serving prison terms, the men's convictions were vacated based on DNA evidence and another man's confession. The five then sued New York City, the city's police department, the district attorney's office and certain employees of those offices contending they conspired to use false evidence in securing the convictions. The defendants in that lawsuit subpoenaed the filmmakers, asking for outtakes and other materials used to produce the film. The court quashed the subpoena. "If the filmmaker is independent at the beginning of the process, and not influenced inappropriately by the subject, the fact that the filmmaker develops an opinion or additional motivations will not remove the protections of the privilege," the court said.[27] The filmmakers' developing a point of view as film production did not mean they lost the reporter's privilege, the court ruled.

Two freelancers have served lengthy jail terms for refusing to name sources. Josh Wolf, a freelance photojournalist, refused to give a grand jury videotape he made of a San Francisco demonstration in which a police officer was injured and a police car set on fire.[28] He was jailed for 226 days before striking an agreement to be released. As part of the agreement, he uploaded all of his demonstration footage.[29]

In another case, English teacher Vanessa Leggett conducted numerous interviews with the hope of publishing a book about a murder case.[30] A federal grand jury, investigating possible illegal activities of a millionaire bookie from Houston, Tex., subpoenaed Leggett. She failed to comply with the demand to turn over her notes. A federal district court cited her for civil contempt and ordered her jailed until she furnished the materials.[31] Finding no governmental harassment or oppression, a federal appeals court held that the district court did not abuse its discretion in ordering Leggett incarcerated.[32] She served 168 days and was released only after the grand jury's term expired.

Book authors may—or may not—have shield law protection depending on a judge's interpretation of the law's language. In Arizona, Dary Matera conducted research for a book about how an ex-mobster exposed political corruption in the state. An indicted lawmaker subpoenaed Matera, demanding his notes. An Arizona appellate court refused to quash the subpoena.[33] The Arizona shield law protected those who regularly gather and disseminate news, the court said. Book authors do not report news or regularly report information, according to the court.

SUMMARY

JOURNALISTS MAY RECEIVE SUBPOENAS THAT REQUIRE them to reveal information in judicial proceedings. That information may include divulging sources of information. A qualified reporter's privilege to keep that information confidential may be invoked if the proceeding is something other than a grand jury inquiry. Courts typically use the three-part *Branzburg* test to determine whether the privilege stands. That standard demands that the information being sought is essential to an investigation and that there is no other way of obtaining it. Anyone who does not comply with a subpoena, including journalists who are denied reporter's privilege, are subject to contempt of court citations, which can result in time in jail and/or fines. ■

Shield Laws

The U.S. Supreme Court's opinion in *Branzburg* essentially invited legislatures—both federal and state—to address whether "a statutory newsman's privilege is necessary and desirable."[34] Although 17 states had already dealt with the issue by enacting laws prior to *Branzburg,* many other state legislatures answered in the affirmative by passing **shield laws** that protect journalists from being found in contempt of court for refusing to reveal a source. To date, 40 states, the District of Columbia and the U.S. territory of Guam have laws that recognize and protect reporter's privilege to one extent or another. The states without a shield law are Idaho, Iowa, Massachusetts, Mississippi, Missouri, New Hampshire, South Dakota, Vermont, Virginia and Wyoming. Courts in these states, except Wyoming, have recognized some kind of reporter's privilege. There is no federal shield law, although in 2013 President Barack Obama said he favored one. Journalists

shield laws State laws that protect journalists from being found in contempt of court for refusing to reveal sources.

realWorld Law

Leakers and the Law

Julian Assange, Wikileaks Editor-in-Chief

An illustration of how real-world events can influence laws and law-making occurred in 2010 when attempts to pass a federal shield law were derailed in the U.S. Senate. Shortly after the website WikiLeaks published tens of thousands of Afghanistan war documents, some senators concluded that any shield law should exclude from protection websites like WikiLeaks that are based outside the United States. There is doubt, however, whether a non-U.S. entity even could be subject to a subpoena.

Some senators repeatedly had expressed reservations about how the legislation's provisions applied to leakers of classified information. The WikiLeaks situation played into their hands. Sen. Charles Schumer (D-N.Y.) was among those seeking to amend the bill "to remove even a scintilla of doubt"[1] that a shield law would *not* protect a site like WikiLeaks from prosecution. "WikiLeaks should not be spared in any way from the fullest prosecution possible under the law," Sen. Schumer added.[2] A particular concern was publishing raw data without editorial oversight.

Although some people claimed the WikiLeaks situation highlighted the dangers of a federal shield law, others claimed the opposite. Paul Boyle, Newspaper Association of America senior vice president, said WikiLeaks publishing the documents demonstrated the need for the law. Absent the bill's protections, journalists would become "the first stop rather than the last" in efforts to obtain information in legal cases. This could create a potential chilling effect on investigative reporting, he said, as whistleblowers would stay silent and news organizations would pull back in fear of legal penalties.[3]

Boyle argued that the absence of a shield law encouraged would-be leakers to take material to groups like WikiLeaks that could not be forced to give up their sources. A shield law, however, would give whistleblowers greater confidence that their identities would not become public, increasing the chance they would work with news organizations that exercise editorial control.

1. Charlie Savage, *After Afghan War Leaks, Revisions in a Shield Bill,* N.Y. TIMES, Aug. 3, 2010, at A12.
2. *Id.*
3. Paul Farhi, *WikiLeaks Is Barrier to Shield Arguments,* WASH. POST, Aug. 21, 2010, at C1.

involved in federal court cases are left to use only the qualified reporter's privilege in situations where it is warranted.

Reasons vary for the absence of shield laws in those states without such statutes. In Massachusetts, for example, the Supreme Judicial Court ruled that journalists' First Amendment interests do not warrant any kind of comprehensive privilege: "News reporters do not have a constitutionally based testimonial privilege that other citizens do not have. There is no such statutory privilege, nor is there any rule of court providing such a privilege."[35] That court, though, did acknowledge that courts may refuse to enforce a subpoena based on common law principles—in other words, on a case-by-case basis.

Points of Law

The U.S. Supreme Court Suggested Shield Laws

In *Branzburg* the Court said states should consider adopting shield laws or finding protection in state constitution: "There is . . . merit in leaving state legislatures free . . . to fashion their own standards . . . [regarding] relations between law enforcement officials and press. . . . [State courts could construe] their own constitutions so as to recognize a newsman's privilege, either qualified or absolute."[1]

The following is excerpted from the newest state shield law, West Virginia's, enacted in 2011.[2] Note that student journalists are included in the definition of "reporter."

§ 57–3-10. Reporters' Privilege.

(a) "Reporter" means a person who regularly gathers, prepares, collects, photographs, records, writes, edits, reports, or publishes news or information that concerns matters of public interest for dissemination to the public for a substantial portion of the person's livelihood, or a supervisor, or employer of that person in that capacity: Provided, That a student reporter at an accredited educational institution who meets all of the requirements of this definition, except that his or her reporting may not provide a portion of his or her livelihood, meets the definition of reporter for purposes of this section.

(b) No reporter may be compelled to:

(1) Testify in any civil, criminal, administrative or grand jury proceeding in any court in this state concerning the confidential source of any published or unpublished information obtained by the reporter in the course of the above described activities without the consent of the confidential source, unless such testimony is necessary to prevent imminent death, serious bodily injury or unjust incarceration; or

(2) Produce any information or testimony that would identify a confidential source, without the consent of the confidential source, unless such testimony or information is necessary to prevent imminent death, serious bodily injury or unjust incarceration.

1. Branzburg v. Hayes, 408 U.S. 665, 706 (1972).
2. W. Va. Code § 57 -3-10.

The details of shield laws vary from state to state, sometimes widely. To one extent or another, these laws grant some degree of reporter's privilege, and some people believe they are preferable to relying on the privilege in the abstract. With a concrete law on the books, a journalist does not have to rely on the subjective judgment of a court in evaluating whether a constitutionally based privilege exists within a given case. The shortcoming, however, may lie in the wording of a state shield law and just what and whom it protects. That is, some journalists and certain material may be excluded from protection.

Historically, any suggestion that a shield law offered journalists protection from grand jury subpoenas was rejected. In part, courts took their cue from the *Branzburg* Court's affirmation of the grand jury's importance to reject the notion that any qualified reporter's privilege would apply there. But the Pennsylvania Supreme Court modified a decades-long practice, at least in that state. A newspaper reporter used a confidential source to report about a grand jury proceeding. The high court ruled that the state shield law grants an absolute privilege to journalists and protects their

Points of Law

Potential Options for Journalist Protection of Confidential Sources

In Federal Courts

1. Qualified reporter's privilege*

In State, D.C. and Guam Courts

1. Shield law, but if none, then

2. State constitution, either explicitly stated or a court-recognized interpretation, but if none, then

3. Qualified reporter's privilege*

*But not in grand jury situations. The U.S. Court of Appeals for the Sixth Circuit has not recognized a qualified reporter's privilege.

*But not in most grand jury situations. Pennsylvania is the exception.

sources' identities from compelled disclosure in all cases—civil, criminal and grand jury proceedings.[36] It is worth noting that the reporter was not the subject of a grand jury subpoena but merely reported on a grand jury. Nevertheless, based on her articles, she and her newspaper employer were named as defendants in a libel lawsuit and within that context were issued subpoenas seeking the identity of her confidential source.

Who Is Covered

U.S. Supreme Court Justice Byron White was among those who recognized the challenge in creating a privilege and determining precisely who would be protected. Indeed, this challenge has materialized. How can the words "journalist" or "reporter" be defined, especially when the First Amendment freedom of the press implicitly allows anyone to assume those roles, including independent bloggers? Unlike doctors and lawyers, for example, journalists are not licensed and do not have to meet any particular qualifications to practice their trade.

Some shield law statutes recognize this difficulty by applying protection to several categories of people. For example, the Minnesota shield law broadly defines those eligible for protection: anyone "directly engaged in the gathering, procuring, compiling, editing, or publishing of information . . . to the public."[37] Many other shield laws define "journalist" in ways that protect only those who work full-time for a newspaper or broadcast station. Some use the term "news media" to specify those who are covered. A few states even shield those engaged in reporting or editorial activities for motion picture news. Freelance writers, book authors, Internet journalists and many others are left out of many shield laws. Some states also exclude magazine writers.

Like other privileges, reporter's privilege can be waived—another way in which it is qualified. Particularly when a journalist is on the verge of going to court, the source granted anonymity may waive the reporter's obligation of confidentiality. In other words, the source may grant permission to the reporter to disclose his or her identity. Although the reporter then may feel comfortable disclosing the source, it is still not necessary for the journalist to do so. The privilege of not disclosing the source belongs to the journalist. However, a court is likely to consider the privilege weak when the reporter has been released and thus order disclosure.

What Is Covered

The specific kind of information protected by shield laws also varies from state to state. At stake are not only sources of information but also items such as

realWorld Law

Reporters, Subpoenas and Contempt

Toni Locy, a former USA Today reporter who covered the investigation into anthrax mailings that killed five people, became embroiled in a source confidentiality situation and risked having to pay $5,000 a day out of her own pocket. When former Army scientist Stephen Hatfill was identified as a "person of interest," he sought the identities of reporters' sources. A federal judge ordered six journalists, including Locy, to reveal their sources. Locy declined, and the judge found her in contempt of court, ruling that until she disclosed all of her sources she would face fines rising from $500 to $1,000 to $5,000 after 14 days. In addition, the judge did not suspend those fines pending Locy's appeal and said Locy could not receive any assistance in paying the fines because he believed she was unlikely to prevail in her appeal.[1]

A federal appeals court subsequently stayed Locy's contempt fines pending her appeal. Several months later, Hatfill reached a settlement with the government that might logically have led to the dismissal of Locy's case, but Hatfill then sought to collect attorney's fees from her—fees that could have totaled hundreds of thousands of dollars. A federal appeals court set aside the contempt order on grounds that Hatfill's settlement left the order moot, effectively dismissing the request for fees, a lawyer at the Reporters Committee for Freedom of the Press explained. Winning attorney's fees requires first winning the lawsuit, "and there's no order finding [Hatfill] prevailed. If every time reporters stood up for constitutional rights they're hit with huge attorneys' fees, that would be a huge chilling effect. It would be a novel way of harassing reporters," the attorney said.[2] Some experts claimed this situation was further evidence of the need for a federal shield law.

1. *See, e.g.,* Kevin Johnson, *Anthrax Settlement Doesn't Address Reporters' Issue,* USA Today, June 30, 2008, at 6A; Kevin Johnson, *Reporter's Fines Blocked in Anthrax Case,* USA Today, Mar. 12, 2008, at 3A.
2. *Judge Tosses Contempt Order Against ex-USA Today Reporter,* USA Today (Nov. 17, 2008), available at http://www.usatoday.com/news/washington/2008-11-17-locy-contempt_N.htm.

notes and outtakes. A shield law such as Tennessee's is broad in scope, applying to any information and the source of information obtained for publication or broadcast, but other shield laws are not so generous. For example, when called to testify about events reporters witnessed, such as crimes, most statutes do not protect journalists. Also, when journalists and/or news organizations are defendants—for example, in a libel case—protecting source identity is likely to be rejected. To prove the defendant acted with negligence or actual malice, the plaintiff may require access to the reporter's knowledge, notes and other work materials. Finally, courts may be more likely to protect source confidentiality in civil cases in which journalists are not parties to the litigation. Not only are such cases usually less serious than criminal cases, but there are often alternative sources for the information that do not implicate the First Amendment.

Shield Laws and Websites

Bloggers and others transmitting through the Internet, just as traditional media journalists, may be served with subpoenas demanding sources' names, notes and

realWorld Law

Passing the First Test

In 2010, just five months after being enacted, the Kansas shield law passed its first test. The Wichita Eagle had reported on a 5-year-old boy who had fallen to his death from a ride at an indoor playground. Two former employees of the playground were quoted anonymously in an article, saying the way they had been taught to operate the ride caused the boy's death. The boy's mother subpoenaed the reporter for the sources' names. A county judge ruled the new state shield law protected the reporter because no effort had been made to seek that information elsewhere. The judge said all other means must be exhausted before going to the media. Even then, the law requires that the information being sought is relevant to a case and that a compelling interest exists in providing it.[1]

1. *See* Daniel Skallman, *Judge Upholds Reporter's Right in First Test of Kansas Shield Law,* Reporter's Committee for Freedom of the Press News (Oct. 27, 2010), *available at* http://www.rcfp.org/newsitems/index.php?i=11614.

other materials. Many states adopted shield laws in the pre-Internet era, leaving unanswered the question whether bloggers qualify as journalists and have shield law protection.

Several state courts have ruled bloggers do not qualify as journalists for shield law purposes. A self-identified investigative blogger who was a defendant in a libel suit did not qualify for protection under Oregon's shield law, a federal district court ruled.[38] The blog was not a "medium of communication," the court said, because it was not "affiliated with any newspaper, magazine, periodical, book, pamphlet, news service, wire service, news or feature syndicate, broadcast station or network, or cable, television system." The court also said the blogger was not a journalist because she presented no evidence of

> (1) any education in journalism; (2) any credentials or proof of any affiliation with any recognized news entity; (3) proof of adherence to journalistic standards such as editing, fact-checking, or disclosures of conflicts of interest; (4) keeping notes of conversations and interviews conducted; (5) mutual understanding or agreement of confidentiality between the [blogger] and her sources; (6) creation of an independent product rather than assembling writings and postings of others; or (7) contacting "the other side" to get both sides of a story.[39]

The court did not explain the origin of these criteria or hold that any criterion would be more important than others in deciding whether a blogger was a journalist. In a later decision related to the lawsuit, the same judge defended his narrow reading of the Oregon shield law. He said he did not "state that a person who 'blogs' could never be considered 'media,' . . . [nor] that to be considered 'media' one had to possess all or most of the [criteria]."[40] Rather, this blogger presented no evidence concerning even one of the criteria that might categorize her as a journalist.

A New Jersey court took a similar approach in finding that state's shield law did not protect an online bulletin-board poster. The court said the poster did not comply with customary journalistic practices such as fact checking, seeking comments from those with differing views or promising sources confidentiality.[41] The New Jersey Supreme Court agreed the shield law did not apply to the blogger and said the law did not require journalistic credentials or "adhering to professional standards of journalism."[42] Instead the court decided the issue on different grounds. Reviewing the law's language, which protects those engaged in, connected with or employed by "news media," defined as "newspapers, magazines, press associations, news agencies, wire services, radio, television or other similar printed, photographic, mechanical or electronic means of disseminating news to the general public," the state supreme court said electronic bulletin boards do not meet this definition. They are, rather, "little more than forums for discussion."

A Texas court said the state's shield law did not apply to someone who blogged about oil and gas drilling's impact on the environment. The blogger was an activist, not a journalist, because she had no journalism background, was not objective and did not adhere to journalistic ethics, the court said.[43]

But judges are not always certain about websites and shield laws. One judge initially said the Illinois shield law did not protect bloggers on a website containing technology news and commentary. The court then reversed that decision when it determined the website also included reviews and undertook fact checking. This made it more like traditional media, the court said. When a blog contributes to information flow by reporting recent events, it can be considered a news medium, according to the court.[44]

Other Sources of Protection

If a court decides reporter's privilege or a state shield law does not protect a journalist from revealing sources or materials, there are other possible defenses. Any subpoena in a federal criminal case, including one for a reporter, must comply with Rule 17(c) of the Federal Rules of Criminal Procedure. The rule says a subpoena may be issued only for materials "admissible as evidence." The U.S. Supreme Court said the materials sought must be relevant, not otherwise available and necessary for the trial, and the subpoena must not be for a "fishing expedition."[45] The same is true in federal civil trials where Rule 26 of the Federal Rules of Civil Procedure prohibits a judge from granting a subpoena if the materials can be obtained elsewhere or if the burden to get the materials outweighs any benefit.

Also, the U.S. Department of Justice places limits on its attorneys asking for a subpoena compelling journalists to reveal sources or provide notes and other materials. The department's guidelines require, in part: (1) balancing First Amendment interests against effective law enforcement; (2) using reasonable attempts to obtain the information or material elsewhere; (3) negotiating with the media before a subpoena is requested; and (4) in criminal cases, establishing

realWorld Law

Anonymous Posters on News Websites

Can a shield law protect a newspaper from having to reveal the identity of someone who made comments anonymously on a newspaper's website? Courts in at least six states have used shield laws to prevent the names of anonymous posters from being revealed. Courts reached these decisions because information protected by laws in those states—Colorado, Florida, Illinois, Montana, Oregon and North Carolina—is defined broadly.

But courts in Indiana and Kentucky ruled their states' shield laws inapplicable to anonymous posters. Idaho also rejected applying the qualified reporter's privilege to anonymous speakers.[1] The Indiana case involved someone anonymously posting a comment on a newspaper website. The plaintiff in a libel suit based on the posting sought the poster's name. The anonymous poster was not "the source of any information," a state appellate court said in 2012.[2] Nor was the posting used in any way to gather information or further investigate the story to which the poster responded. The poster, then, was neither a journalist nor involved in journalism, and the state shield law did not offer protection.

However, in a 2010 North Carolina case, an attorney for an accused murderer wanted to force the Gaston Gazette to unmask an anonymous poster. The poster's comments included information that had not yet been made public, raising suspicion about the poster's identity. But the judge said the First Amendment and the state shield law protected the information.[3]

That ruling followed one in which a Montana district court said that state's shield law protects anonymous bloggers. The Billings Gazette had been issued a subpoena demanding the identities of two bloggers who had posted comments anonymously on the newspaper's website. Although Montana's shield law does not specifically protect bloggers or online commenters, the judge agreed with the Gazette that online commenters are sufficiently connected to the newspaper to warrant protection.[4]

---

1. Ashley I. Kissinger, Katharine Larsen & Matthew E. Kelley, *Protections for Anonymous Online Speech, in* 2 COMM. L. IN THE DIGITAL AGE 2012, at 534 (2012).
2. Indiana Newspapers Inc. v. Junior Achievement of Central Indiana, Inc., 963 N.E.2d 534, 548 (Ind. Ct. App. 2012), *aff'd on rehearing*, 980 N.E.2d 852 (Ind. Ct. App. 2013).
3. Kevin Ellis, *Judge Gives Online Commenters First Amendment Protection,* GASTON GAZETTE (July 28, 2010), *available at* http://www.gastongazette.com/waptest/news/judge-49409-online-amendment.html.
4. Reporters Committee for Freedom of the Press, *Anonymous Bloggers Protected by Shield Law, Judge Finds* (n.d.), *available at* http://www.rcfp.org/newsitems/index.php?i=6964.

there are reasonable grounds for believing a crime occurred and the information is vital to proving guilt or innocence.[46]

In 2013 the U.S. Court of Appeals for the Ninth Circuit ruled that Homeland Security's border agents do not have unlimited power to search laptops, mobile phones and other electronic devices.[47] Although that case involved a search revealing child pornography on a laptop, the decision could protect journalists' electronic devices from being examined. The Fourth Amendment requires border agents to have a "reasonable suspicion" before undertaking a search, the court said. However, "a quick look" or "unintrusive search of a laptop," such as asking that the computer be turned on, is acceptable, according to the Ninth Circuit.

BECAUSE JOURNALISTS ARE OFTEN GOOD RECORDERS of information, they and their notes are sometimes subject to subpoenas that require them to reveal what they know. This is usually information regarding criminal conduct. But journalists sometimes claim they have reporter's privilege—a right to keep information confidential. Courts have not ruled clearly whether such a privilege exists and, if so, under what circumstances. The U.S. Supreme Court has established a three-part test to determine under what circumstances the qualified privilege may exist. In addition, 38 states and the District of Columbia have shield laws that grant some journalists some degree of privilege. State constitutions may also establish reporter's privilege. In all, 49 states and Washington, D.C., recognize the privilege in one way or another. Wyoming is the exception. ■

Breaking Promises of Confidentiality

Reporter's privilege and shield laws protect journalists who do not want to reveal sources of information. But what happens when a news organization voluntarily decides to reveal the identity of a source after making a promise of confidentiality? Can the source successfully sue for damages? Or does the First Amendment protect a news organization's freedom to include its sources in its reports even when it promised not to do so?

The U.S. Supreme Court faced these questions in *Cohen v. Cowles Media Co.*, excerpted at the conclusion of this chapter. Dan Cohen had been associated with the campaign of a Minnesota gubernatorial candidate. As Election Day neared, he contacted four Minneapolis and St. Paul reporters and offered them information about a political opponent, informing them that she had been arrested for unlawful assembly and for petty theft more than 10 years earlier. Cohen stipulated, however, that the information could be used only if he were not identified as its source. Two newspaper reporters accepted the offer.

Before publication, debate ensued in both newsrooms whether to keep the promises to Cohen. Editors believed that Cohen had engaged in "dirty tricks" politics. They concluded that identifying him was essential so readers could completely evaluate the stories. In spite of the promises made to the contrary, the articles were published with Cohen clearly identified.

As a result, Cohen was fired from his job. He sued the newspapers, claiming breach of a contractual agreement. A trial court agreed, awarding Cohen $200,000 in compensatory damages and $500,000 in punitive damages. An appeals court threw out the punitive damages award, and the Minnesota Supreme Court reversed the ruling against the newspapers entirely. At the Minnesota Supreme Court, an alternative to breach of contract arose, a concept called **promissory estoppel**. The doctrine of promissory estoppel requires courts to enforce a

promissory estoppel A legal doctrine requiring liability when a clear and unambiguous promise is made and is relied on and injury results from the breaking of the promise.

realWorld Law

Cohen v. Cowles Media Co.: A Reporter's Perspective

One reporter who agreed to accept Dan Cohen's information in exchange for his anonymity was Bill Salisbury of the St. Paul Pioneer Press. Salisbury felt Cohen's offer was not unusual: Promises of anonymity are "fairly widely used in politics and in covering government." He wrote his article after he contacted the gubernatorial candidate, who confirmed her arrest and conviction several years earlier.

The newspaper's top editor subsequently ordered Salisbury to include Cohen's name in the article. "We had an argument about that," Salisbury said. "I told him that I made a promise and that I strenuously objected to breaking the promise."

When Cohen's case went to trial, Salisbury testified against the Pioneer Press. He agreed with the U.S. Supreme Court ruling. He said, "I'm not a lawyer—I'm not that familiar with the law, but it seemed to me that I had made a contract with Dan Cohen and we broke that contract."

Many of Salisbury's colleagues agreed: "No matter whether we broke the law or not, it was a bad practice because it raised suspicion about the newspaper by our sources. By burning a source we made a lot of potential sources worried about coming to us and giving us information. I think it was important for us in journalism to learn the lesson from this case. Our credibility was really at stake. I think the bottom line is that we've learned that we can't burn our sources. We have to keep our promises. If we don't, we're liable. I think perhaps the most important ramification is that our sources are aware of [the Court's ruling.] . . . I think the decision has helped us in the practice of journalism. I think sources trust us more knowing that we have to keep our promises or we risk being sued."[1]

1. JOSEPH RUSSOMANNO, SPEAKING OUR MINDS: CONVERSATIONS WITH THE PEOPLE BEHIND LANDMARK FIRST AMENDMENT CASES 204–05, 220, 239 (Mahwah, N.J.: Lawrence Erlbaum Associates/Taylor & Francis, 2002).

promise if it is relied on and its breach creates an injustice that should be remedied by law. The state supreme court, however, said it was unnecessary to consider this concept because enforcing it against the press would violate the First Amendment. Cohen appealed to the U.S. Supreme Court. The Court ruled in Cohen's favor that the First Amendment did not shield the press from the requirements of promissory estoppel.

generally applicable law A law that is enforced evenly, across the board. Within First Amendment contexts, it is the idea that the freedom of the press clause does not exempt journalists and news organizations from obeying laws.

Promissory estoppel is a **generally applicable law,** meaning that it is one of many that are enforced against journalists and everyone else. The First Amendment does not insulate news organizations or those employed by them from generally applicable laws. "Generally applicable laws do not offend the First Amendment simply because their enforcement against the press has incidental effects on its ability to gather and report the news," wrote Justice White in *Cohen.* The case was sent back to Minnesota, and the Minnesota Supreme Court awarded Cohen $200,000 (plus interest) in damages. The ruling means promises of confidentiality must be kept. It has also resulted in news organizations instituting and clarifying policies that address whether and how to grant sources anonymity.

Search Warrants

No matter the source of a reporter's protection—the common law, a court decree, a state constitution or a shield law—the privilege can, in effect, be wiped out by a search warrant. A **search warrant** is a court order directing law enforcement officers to conduct a search of specified premises for particular items or people. The Fourth Amendment to the U.S. Constitution requires that searches be conducted reasonably. Warrants are issued by judges only when there is probable cause to believe that items or people vital to a criminal investigation are on the premises to be searched. Some believe that an exception to the search warrant requirement exists when national security is at stake—that is, such searches do not need to be approved by a court. The U.S. Supreme Court has never recognized such an exception.

Although search warrants have some similarity to subpoenas in that both are court orders requiring cooperation with the justice system, they differ in very important ways. Search warrants demand immediate cooperation and compliance. When law enforcement officials arrive with a search warrant, they are fully authorized to immediately enter and conduct a search of the premises. There is no legal way to delay, resist or prevent the search. Subpoenas, however, do not require on-the-spot compliance. They order the named person to appear on some future date for a judicial proceeding. In the interim, the recipient can file a motion to quash the subpoena. For journalists, that motion may contain a request to invoke reporter's privilege. A search warrant implies greater urgency and may be justified where evidence could imminently be lost or destroyed. In fact, concern that important evidence could be destroyed during the period between serving a subpoena and the date of the required court appearance is one of the justifications for search warrants.

search warrant A written order issued by a judge, directed to a law enforcement officer, authorizing the search and seizure of any property for which there is reason to believe it will serve as evidence in a criminal investigation.

Newsroom Searches

What happens when a newsroom is the location targeted by a search warrant? Does the First Amendment protect news organizations from government searches? Should freedom of the press protections bar execution of search warrants that might reveal confidential sources or otherwise infringe on press freedoms?

These questions were put to the test in a U.S. Supreme Court case. After a demonstration on Stanford University's campus, investigators wanted to look at unpublished photographs taken by staff members of the campus newspaper, the Stanford Daily. Police hoped the photos would help identify people who took part in the demonstration, including some who assaulted police officers. A search warrant was obtained and served on the Daily. There was no indication as to why the situation required the warrant rather than a subpoena.

After the search, the Daily brought action against the chief of police and other local officials claiming the search violated the newspaper's First, Fourth and Fourteenth Amendment rights. A district judge concluded that because no one at the Daily was suspected of a crime, a search warrant should not have been issued unless it could be shown that a subpoena was impractical. In addition, the judge said that when a newspaper is the object of a search, a warrant may be issued only when there is a clear showing that important materials would be destroyed or removed and that a restraining order would be useless. An intermediate appellate court upheld this decision, but the police chief appealed to the U.S. Supreme Court.

The Supreme Court overturned the lower court decision and delivered a blow to media organizations across the country, ruling that newsrooms are entitled to no special treatment beyond that afforded any citizen by the Fourth Amendment's prohibition of unreasonable searches and seizures. The Daily had argued that searches of newspaper offices for crime evidence threatens the ability of the press to gather, analyze and disseminate news. As summarized by Justice White, the argument was based on five points:

1. Searches will be physically disruptive to such an extent that timely publication will be impeded.

2. Confidential sources of information will dry up, and the press will also lose opportunities to cover various events because of the fears of participants that press files will be readily available to authorities.

3. Reporters will be deterred from recording and preserving their recollections for future use if such information is subject to seizure.

4. The processing and dissemination of news will be chilled by the prospect of searches that would disclose internal editorial deliberations.

5. The press will resort to self-censorship to conceal its possession of information of potential interest to the police.[48]

The Court rejected these arguments, saying the Fourth Amendment's prohibition of unreasonable searches and seizures sufficiently guarded against the identified harms. Perhaps most important, the Court ruled that nothing in the Fourth Amendment restricted searches of newsrooms. Implicitly, the ruling also suggested that there is nothing in the First Amendment that prevented newsroom searches.

Criticism, particularly from the news media, followed swiftly in the wake of the *Stanford Daily* ruling. Compared with search warrants, subpoenas suddenly appeared a rather mild intrusion. At least reporters could see them coming and challenge them legally. Not surprisingly, another result of the ruling was an increase in search warrant applications by law enforcement organizations targeting newsrooms. As one report of a search noted, police swept through the desks and files of a newsroom "with the authority of the Supreme Court."[49]

The Privacy Protection Act

After the *Stanford Daily* case, the media lobbied for legislative relief. Incidents in which law enforcement officials were accused of abusing the search warrant right underscored their arguments. Congress ultimately obliged, passing a law that applies to both state and federal searches. The Privacy Protection Act of 1980 significantly limits the use of search warrants against public communicators. The act states that, "notwithstanding any other law," federal and state officers and employees are prohibited from searching or seizing a journalist's work product or documentary materials in the journalist's possession, as part of a criminal investigation. A journalist's work product includes notes and drafts of news stories. Documentary materials include videotapes, audiotapes and computer disks.[50] The law provides much more protection for outtakes—the raw materials of the journalistic process that are not included in the final published or broadcast product.

Some limited exceptions under the Privacy Protection Act allow the government to search for or seize certain types of national security information, child pornography, evidence that a journalist has committed a crime or documentary materials that must be immediately seized to prevent death or serious bodily injury. Documentary materials also may be seized if there is reason to believe that they would be destroyed in the time it took government officers to seek a subpoena. Those materials also can be seized if a court has ordered disclosure, the news organization has refused and all other remedies have been exhausted. The Privacy Protection Act gives journalists the right to sue the United States or a state government, or federal and state employees, for damages for violating the law. The law also allows journalists to recover attorney's fees and court costs.

In short, the Privacy Protection Act significantly mitigates the effect of the *Stanford Daily* ruling by restricting the use of search warrants on newsrooms, forcing law enforcement officials to rely on subpoenas instead. The U.S. Department of Justice, however, has accused at least one reporter of being a co-conspirator, a criminal charge, in an attempt to circumvent the Privacy Protection limits on obtaining search warrants. The department claimed a Fox News reporter conspired with a State Department analyst to obtain classified documents. The department said it did not intend to criminally charge the reporter, but only to search the reporter's e-mails.[51] In 2013 U.S. Atty. Gen. Eric Holder issued rules preventing the department, including the Federal Bureau of Investigation (FBI), from using a co-conspirator accusation to obtain a search warrant for a reporter's materials.[52]

SUMMARY

WHEN JOURNALISTS PROMISE SOURCES that their identities will be kept confidential in exchange for information, the journalists and their employers are legally bound to keep their word. Freedom of the press is not freedom to break the law. Laws that are generally applicable pertain to the media.

The concept of general applicability also applies to legally issued search warrants on newsrooms. The First Amendment does not grant freedom from such searches. ■

Cases for Study

Thinking About It

The two case excerpts that follow address very different aspects of source confidentiality. The first is the U.S. Supreme Court ruling that established a test for a qualified reporter's privilege. The second ruling, also from the U.S. Supreme Court, dealt with news organizations that not only did not want to protect a source but consciously decided to expose him. As you read these case excerpts, keep the following questions in mind:

- How did the reporters in each case behave? What actions did they take to precipitate the lawsuits that eventually reached the Supreme Court?

- Does the Court seem to understand the purpose of journalism and the inner workings of a newsroom in each case?

- In *Branzburg,* from whose opinion does the *Branzburg* test emerge? What kind of opinion is that?

- In *Cohen,* the Court mentions "generally applicable laws." What does it say about them and the First Amendment? Do you agree with the Court's position?

- Aside from the ruling in *Cohen,* do you agree with how the newspapers handled their source's identity? If not, what should they have done differently?

Branzburg v. Hayes
SUPREME COURT OF THE UNITED STATES
408 U.S. 665 (1972)

JUSTICE BYRON WHITE delivered the Court's opinion:

The issue in these cases is whether requiring newsmen to appear and testify before state or federal grand juries abridges the freedom of speech and press guaranteed by the First Amendment. We hold that it does not. . . .

On November 15, 1969, the Courier-Journal carried a story under petitioner's by-line describing in detail his observations of two young residents of Jefferson County synthesizing hashish from marihuana, an activity which, they asserted, earned them about $5,000 in three weeks. The article included a photograph of a pair of hands working above a laboratory table on which was a substance identified by the caption as hashish. The article stated that petitioner had promised not to reveal the identity of the two hashish makers. Petitioner was shortly subpoenaed by the Jefferson County grand jury; he appeared but refused to identify the individuals he had seen possessing marihuana or the persons he had seen making hashish from marihuana. A state trial court judge ordered petitioner to answer these questions and rejected his contention that the Kentucky reporters' privilege statute, Ky.

Rev. Stat. § 421.100 (1962), the First Amendment of the United States Constitution, or §§ 1, 2, and 8 of the Kentucky Constitution authorized his refusal to answer. Petitioner then sought prohibition and mandamus in the Kentucky Court of Appeals on the same grounds, but the Court of Appeals denied the petition. It held that petitioner had abandoned his First Amendment argument in a supplemental memorandum he had filed and tacitly rejected his argument based on the Kentucky Constitution. It also construed Ky. Rev. Stat. § 421.100 as affording a newsman the privilege of refusing to divulge the identity of an informant who supplied him with information, but held that the statute did not permit a reporter to refuse to testify about events he had observed personally, including the identities of those persons he had observed.

The second case involving petitioner Branzburg arose out of his later story published on January 10, 1971, which described in detail the use of drugs in Frankfort, Kentucky. The article reported that in order to provide a comprehensive survey of the "drug scene" in Frankfort, petitioner had "spent two weeks interviewing several dozen drug users in the capital city" and had seen some of them smoking marihuana. A number of conversations with and observations of several unnamed drug users were recounted. Subpoenaed to appear before a Franklin County grand jury "to testify in the matter of violation of statutes concerning use and sale of drugs," petitioner Branzburg moved to quash the summons; the motion was denied, although an order was issued protecting Branzburg from revealing "confidential associations, sources or information" but requiring that he "answer any questions which concern or pertain to any criminal act, the commission of which was actually observed by [him]." Prior to the time he was slated to appear before the grand jury, petitioner sought mandamus and prohibition from the Kentucky Court of Appeals, arguing that if he were forced to go before the grand jury or to answer questions regarding the identity of informants or disclose information given to him in confidence, his effectiveness as a reporter would be greatly damaged. The Court of Appeals once again denied the requested writs, reaf-

firming its construction of Ky. Rev. Stat. § 421.100, and rejecting petitioner's claim of a First Amendment privilege. It distinguished *Caldwell v. United States,* 434 F.2d 1081 (1970), and it also announced its "misgivings" about that decision, asserting that it represented "a drastic departure from the generally recognized rule that the sources of information of a newspaper reporter are not privileged under the First Amendment." It characterized petitioner's fear that his ability to obtain news would be destroyed as "so tenuous that it does not, in the opinion of this court, present an issue of abridgement of the freedom of the press within the meaning of that term as used in the Constitution of the United States." . . .

Petitioners Branzburg and Pappas and respondent Caldwell press First Amendment claims that may be simply put: that to gather news it is often necessary to agree either not to identify the source of information published or to publish only part of the facts revealed, or both; that if the reporter is nevertheless forced to reveal these confidences to a grand jury, the source so identified and other confidential sources of other reporters will be measurably deterred from furnishing publishable information, all to the detriment of the free flow of information protected by the First Amendment. Although the newsmen in these cases do not claim an absolute privilege against official interrogation in all circumstances, they assert that the reporter should not be forced either to appear or to testify before a grand jury or at trial until and unless sufficient grounds are shown for believing that the reporter possesses information relevant to a crime the grand jury is investigating, that the information the reporter has is unavailable from other sources, and that the need for the information is sufficiently compelling to override the claimed invasion of First Amendment interests occasioned by the disclosure. Principally relied upon are prior cases emphasizing the importance of the First Amendment guarantees to individual development and to our system of representative government, decisions requiring that official action with adverse impact on First Amendment rights be justified by a public interest that is "compelling" or "paramount," and those precedents establishing the principle that justifiable governmental goals may not be achieved by unduly broad means having an unnecessary impact on protected rights of speech, press, or association. The heart of the claim is that the burden on news gathering resulting from compelling reporters to disclose confidential information outweighs any public interest in obtaining the information.

We do not question the significance of free speech, press, or assembly to the country's welfare. Nor is it suggested that news gathering does not qualify for First Amendment protection; without some protection for seeking out the news, freedom of the press could be eviscerated. But these cases involve no intrusions upon speech or assembly, no prior restraint or restriction on what the press may publish, and no express or implied command that the press publish what it prefers to withhold. No exaction or tax for the privilege of publishing, and no penalty, civil or criminal, related to the content of published material is at issue here. The use of confidential sources by the press is not forbidden or restricted; reporters remain free to seek news from any source by means within the law. No attempt is made to require the press to publish its sources of information or indiscriminately to disclose them on request.

The sole issue before us is the obligation of reporters to respond to grand jury subpoenas as other citizens do and to answer questions relevant to an investigation into the commission of crime. Citizens generally are not constitutionally immune from grand jury subpoenas; and neither the First Amendment nor any other constitutional provision protects the average citizen from disclosing to a grand jury information that he has received in confidence. The claim is, however, that reporters are exempt from these obligations because if forced to respond to subpoenas and identify their sources or disclose other confidences, their informants will refuse or be reluctant to furnish newsworthy information in the future. This asserted burden on news gathering is said to make compelled testimony from newsmen constitutionally suspect and to require a privileged position for them.

It is clear that the First Amendment does not invalidate every incidental burdening of the press that may result from the enforcement of civil or criminal statutes of general applicability. Under prior cases, otherwise valid laws serving substantial public interests may be enforced against the press as against others, despite the possible burden that may be imposed. The Court has emphasized that "the publisher of a newspaper has no special immunity from the application of general laws. He has no special privilege to invade the rights and liberties of others." It was there held that the Associated Press, a news-gathering and disseminating organization, was not exempt from the requirements of the National Labor Relations Act. . . .

The prevailing view is that the press is not free to publish with impunity everything and anything it desires to publish. Although it may deter or regulate what is said or published, the press may not circulate knowing or reckless falsehoods damaging to private reputation without subjecting itself to liability for damages, including punitive damages, or even criminal prosecution.

It has generally been held that the First Amendment does not guarantee the press a constitutional right of special access to information not available to the public generally. . . .

Despite the fact that news gathering may be hampered, the press is regularly excluded from grand jury proceedings, our own conferences, the meetings of other official bodies gathered in executive session, and the meetings of private organizations. Newsmen have no constitutional right of access to the scenes of crime or disaster when the general public is excluded, and they may be prohibited from attending or publishing information about trials if such restrictions are necessary to assure a defendant a fair trial before an impartial tribunal. . . .

It is thus not surprising that the great weight of authority is that newsmen are not exempt from the normal duty of appearing before a grand jury and answering questions relevant to a criminal investigation. At common law, courts consistently refused to recognize the existence of any privilege authorizing a newsman to refuse to reveal confidential information to a grand jury. . . .

The prevailing constitutional view of the newsman's privilege is very much rooted in the ancient role of the grand jury that has the dual function of determining if there is probable cause to believe that a crime has been committed and of protecting citizens against unfounded criminal prosecutions. Grand jury proceedings are constitutionally mandated for the institution of federal criminal prosecutions for capital or other serious crimes, and "its constitutional prerogatives are rooted in long centuries of Anglo-American history." The Fifth Amendment provides that "no person shall be held to answer for a capital, or otherwise infamous crime, unless on a resentment or indictment of a Grand Jury." The adoption of the grand jury "in our Constitution as the sole method for preferring charges in serious criminal cases shows the high place it held as an instrument of justice." Although state systems of criminal procedure differ greatly among themselves, the grand jury is similarly guaranteed by many state constitutions and plays an important role in fair and effective law enforcement in the overwhelming majority of the States. Because its task is to inquire into the existence of possible criminal conduct and to return only well-founded indictments, its investigative powers are necessarily broad. "It is a grand inquest, a body with powers of investigation and inquisition, the scope of whose inquiries is not to be limited narrowly by questions of propriety or forecasts of the probable result of the investigation, or by doubts whether any particular individual will be found properly subject to an accusation of crime." Hence, the grand jury's authority to subpoena witnesses is not only historic, but essential to its task. Although the powers of the grand jury are not unlimited and are subject to the supervision of a judge, the longstanding principle that "the public . . . has a right to every man's evidence," except for those persons protected by a constitutional, common-law, or statutory privilege. . . .

A number of States have provided newsmen a statutory privilege of varying breadth, but the majority have not done so, and none has been provided by federal statute. Until now the only testimonial privilege for unofficial witnesses that is rooted in the Federal Constitution is the Fifth Amendment privilege against compelled self-incrimination. We are asked to create another by interpreting the First Amendment to grant newsmen a testimonial privilege that other citizens do not enjoy. This we decline to do. . . .

This conclusion itself involves no restraint on what newspapers may publish or on the type or quality of information reporters may seek to acquire, nor does it threaten the vast bulk of confidential relationships between reporters and their sources. Grand juries address themselves to the issues of whether crimes have been committed and who committed them. Only where news sources themselves are implicated in crime or possess information relevant to the grand jury's task need they or the reporter be concerned about grand jury subpoenas. Nothing before us indicates that a large number or percentage of all confidential news sources falls into either category and would in any way be deterred by our holding that the Constitution does not, as it never has, exempt the newsman from performing the citizen's normal duty of appearing and furnishing information relevant to the grand jury's task.

The preference for anonymity of those confidential informants involved in actual criminal conduct is presumably a product of their desire to escape criminal prosecution, and this preference, while understandable, is hardly deserving of constitutional protection. It would be frivolous to assert—and no one does in these cases—that the First Amendment, in the interest of securing news or otherwise, confers a license on either the reporter or his news sources to violate valid criminal laws. Although stealing documents or private wiretapping could provide newsworthy information, neither reporter nor source is immune from conviction for such conduct, whatever the impact on the flow of news. Neither is immune, on First Amendment grounds, from testifying against the other, before the grand jury or at a criminal trial. The Amendment does not reach so far as to override the interest of the public in ensuring that neither reporter nor source is invading the rights of other citizens through reprehensible conduct forbidden to all other persons. To assert the contrary proposition "is to answer it, since it involves in its very statement the contention that the freedom of the press is the freedom to do wrong with impunity and implies the right to frustrate and defeat the discharge of those governmental duties upon the performance of which the freedom of all, including that of the press, depends. . . . It suffices to say that, however complete is the right of the press to state public things and discuss them, that right, as every other right enjoyed in human society, is subject to the restraints which separate right from wrong-doing." Thus, we cannot seriously entertain the notion that the First Amendment protects a newsman's agreement to conceal the criminal conduct of his source, or evidence thereof, on the theory that it is better to write about crime than to do something about it. Insofar as any reporter in these cases undertook not to reveal or testify about the crime he witnessed, his claim of privilege under the First Amendment presents no substantial question. The crimes of news sources are no less reprehensible and threatening to the public interest when witnessed by a reporter than when they are not.

There remain those situations where a source is not engaged in criminal conduct but has information suggesting illegal conduct by others. Newsmen frequently receive information from such sources pursuant to a tacit or express agreement to withhold the source's name and suppress any information that the source wishes not published. Such informants presumably desire anonymity in order to avoid being entangled as a witness in a criminal trial or grand jury investigation. They may fear that disclosure will threaten their job security or personal safety or that it will simply result in dishonor or embarrassment.

The argument that the flow of news will be diminished by compelling reporters to aid the grand jury in a criminal investigation is not irrational, nor are the records before us silent on the matter. But we remain unclear how often and to what extent informers are actually deterred from furnishing information when newsmen are forced to testify before a grand jury. The available data indicate that some newsmen rely a great deal on confidential sources and that some informants are particularly sensitive to the threat of exposure and may be silenced if it is held by this Court that, ordinarily, newsmen must testify pursuant to subpoenas, but the evidence fails to demonstrate that there would be a significant constriction of the flow of news to the public if this Court reaffirms the prior common-law and constitutional rule regarding the testimonial obligations of newsmen. Estimates of the inhibiting effect of such subpoenas on the willingness of informants to make disclosures to newsmen are widely divergent and to a great extent speculative. It would be difficult to canvass the views of the informants themselves; surveys of reporters on this topic are chiefly opinions of

predicted informant behavior and must be viewed in the light of the professional self-interest of the interviewees. Reliance by the press on confidential informants does not mean that all such sources will in fact dry up because of the later possible appearance of the newsman before a grand jury. The reporter may never be called and if he objects to testifying, the prosecution may not insist. Also, the relationship of many informants to the press is a symbiotic one which is unlikely to be greatly inhibited by the threat of subpoena: quite often, such informants are members of a minority political or cultural group that relies heavily on the media to propagate its views, publicize its aims, and magnify its exposure to the public. Moreover, grand juries characteristically conduct secret proceedings, and law enforcement officers are themselves experienced in dealing with informers, and have their own methods for protecting them without interference with the effective administration of justice. There is little before us indicating that informants whose interest in avoiding exposure is that it may threaten job security, personal safety, or peace of mind, would in fact be in a worse position, or would think they would be, if they risked placing their trust in public officials as well as reporters. We doubt if the informer who prefers anonymity but is sincerely interested in furnishing evidence of crime will always or very often be deterred by the prospect of dealing with those public authorities characteristically charged with the duty to protect the public interest as well as his. . . .

We note first that the privilege claimed is that of the reporter, not the informant, and that if the authorities independently identify the informant, neither his own reluctance to testify nor the objection of the newsman would shield him from grand jury inquiry, whatever the impact on the flow of news or on his future usefulness as a secret source of information. More important, it is obvious that agreements to conceal information relevant to commission of crime have very little to recommend them from the standpoint of public policy. . . .

Of course, the press has the right to abide by its agreement not to publish all the information it has, but the right to withhold news is not equivalent to a First Amendment exemption from the ordinary duty of all other citizens to furnish relevant information to a grand jury performing an important public function. Private restraints on the flow of information are not so favored by the First Amendment that they override all other public interests. . . .

Neither are we now convinced that a virtually impenetrable constitutional shield, beyond legislative or judicial control, should be forged to protect a private system of informers operated by the press to report on criminal conduct, a system that would be unaccountable to the public, would pose a threat to the citizen's justifiable expectations of privacy, and would equally protect well-intentioned informants and those who for pay or otherwise betray their trust to their employer or associates. . . .

We are admonished that refusal to provide a First Amendment reporter's privilege will undermine the freedom of the press to collect and disseminate news. But this is not the lesson history teaches us. As noted previously, the common law recognized no such privilege, and the constitutional argument was not even asserted until 1958. From the beginning of our country the press has operated without constitutional protection for press informants, and the press has flourished. The existing constitutional rules have not been a serious obstacle to either the development or retention of confidential news sources by the press.

It is said that currently press subpoenas have multiplied, that mutual distrust and tension between press and officialdom have increased, that reporting styles have changed, and that there is now more need for confidential sources, particularly where the press seeks news about minority cultural and political groups or dissident organizations suspicious of the law and public officials. These developments, even if true, are treacherous grounds for a far-reaching interpretation of the First Amendment fastening a nationwide rule on courts, grand juries, and prosecuting officials everywhere. The obligation to testify in response to grand jury subpoenas will not threaten these sources not involved with criminal conduct and without information relevant to grand jury investigations, and we cannot hold that the Constitution places the sources in these two categories either above the law or beyond its reach.

The argument for such a constitutional privilege rests heavily on those cases holding that the infringement of protected First Amendment rights must be

no broader than necessary to achieve a permissible governmental purpose. We do not deal, however, with a governmental institution that has abused its proper function, as a legislative committee does when it "expose[s] for the sake of exposure." Nothing in the record indicates that these grand juries were "prob[ing] at will and without relation to existing need." Nor did the grand juries attempt to invade protected First Amendment rights by forcing wholesale disclosure of names and organizational affiliations for a purpose that was not germane to the determination of whether crime has been committed. . . . The investigative power of the grand jury is necessarily broad if its public responsibility is to be adequately discharged. . . .

Similar considerations dispose of the reporters' claims that preliminary to requiring their grand jury appearance, the State must show that a crime has been committed and that they possess relevant information not available from other sources, for only the grand jury itself can make this determination. The role of the grand jury as an important instrument of effective law enforcement necessarily includes an investigatory function with respect to determining whether a crime has been committed and who committed it. To this end it must call witnesses, in the manner best suited to perform its task. "When the grand jury is performing its investigatory function into a general problem area . . . society's interest is best served by a thorough and extensive investigation." A grand jury investigation "is not fully carried out until every available clue has been run down and all witnesses examined in every proper way to find if a crime has been committed." Such an investigation may be triggered by tips, rumors, evidence proffered by the prosecutor, or the personal knowledge of the grand jurors. It is only after the grand jury has examined the evidence that a determination of whether the proceeding will result in an indictment can be made. . . .

The privilege claimed here is conditional, not absolute; given the suggested preliminary showings and compelling need, the reporter would be required to testify. Presumably, such a rule would reduce the instances in which reporters could be required to appear, but predicting in advance when and in what circumstances they could be compelled to do so would be difficult. Such a rule would also have implications for the issuance of compulsory process to reporters at civil and criminal trials and at legislative hearings. If newsmen's confidential sources are as sensitive as they are claimed to be, the prospect of being unmasked whenever a judge determines the situation justifies it is hardly a satisfactory solution to the problem. For them, it would appear that only an absolute privilege would suffice.

We are unwilling to embark the judiciary on a long and difficult journey to such an uncertain destination. The administration of a constitutional newsman's privilege would present practical and conceptual difficulties of a high order. Sooner or later, it would be necessary to define those categories of newsmen who qualified for the privilege, a questionable procedure in light of the traditional doctrine that liberty of the press is the right of the lonely pamphleteer who uses carbon paper or a mimeograph just as much as of the large metropolitan publisher who utilizes the latest photocomposition methods. Freedom of the press is a "fundamental personal right" which "is not confined to newspapers and periodicals. It necessarily embraces pamphlets and leaflets. . . . The press in its historic connotation comprehends every sort of publication which affords a vehicle of information and opinion." The informative function asserted by representatives of the organized press in the present cases is also performed by lecturers, political pollsters, novelists, academic researchers, and dramatists. Almost any author may quite accurately assert that he is contributing to the flow of information to the public, that he relies on confidential sources of information, and that these sources will be silenced if he is forced to make disclosures before a grand jury.

In each instance where a reporter is subpoenaed to testify, the courts would also be embroiled in preliminary factual and legal determinations with respect to whether the proper predicate had been laid for the reporter's appearance: Is there probable cause to believe a crime has been committed? Is it likely that the reporter has useful information gained in confidence? Could the grand jury obtain the information elsewhere? Is the official interest sufficient to outweigh the claimed privilege?

Thus, in the end, by considering whether enforcement of a particular law served a "compelling" governmental interest, the courts would be inextricably involved in distinguishing between the value of enforcing different criminal laws. By requiring testimony from a reporter in investigations involving some crimes but not in others, they would be making a value judgment that a legislature had declined to make, since in each case the criminal law involved would represent a considered legislative judgment, not constitutionally suspect, of what conduct is liable to criminal prosecution. The task of judges, like other officials outside the legislative branch, is not to make the law but to uphold it in accordance with their oaths.

At the federal level, Congress has freedom to determine whether a statutory newsman's privilege is necessary and desirable and to fashion standards and rules as narrow or broad as deemed necessary to deal with the evil discerned and, equally important, to refashion those rules as experience from time to time may dictate. There is also merit in leaving state legislatures free, within First Amendment limits, to fashion their own standards in light of the conditions and problems with respect to the relations between law enforcement officials and press in their own areas. It goes without saying, of course, that we are powerless to bar state courts from responding in their own way and construing their own constitutions so as to recognize a newsman's privilege, either qualified or absolute.

In addition, there is much force in the pragmatic view that the press has at its disposal powerful mechanisms of communication, and is far from helpless to protect itself from harassment or substantial harm. Furthermore, if what the newsmen urged in these cases is true—that law enforcement cannot hope to gain and may suffer from subpoenaing newsmen before grand juries—prosecutors will be loath to risk so much for so little. Thus, at the federal level the Attorney General has already fashioned a set of rules for federal officials in connection with subpoenaing members of the press to testify before grand juries or at criminal trials. These rules are a major step in the direction the reporters herein desire to move. They may prove wholly sufficient to resolve the bulk of disagreements and controversies between press and federal officials.

Finally, as we have earlier indicated, news gathering is not without its First Amendment protections, and grand jury investigations if instituted or conducted other than in good faith, would pose wholly different issues for resolution under the First Amendment. Official harassment of the press undertaken not for purposes of law enforcement but to disrupt a reporter's relationship with his news sources would have no justification. Grand juries are subject to judicial control and subpoenas to motions to quash. We do not expect courts will forget that grand juries must operate within the limits of the First Amendment as well as the Fifth. . . .

JUSTICE LEWIS POWELL, concurring:
I add this brief statement to emphasize what seems to me to be the limited nature of the Court's holding. The Court does not hold that newsmen, subpoenaed to testify before a grand jury, are without constitutional rights with respect to the gathering of news or in safeguarding their sources. . . .

As indicated in the concluding portion of the opinion, the Court states that no harassment of newsmen will be tolerated. If a newsman believes that the grand jury investigation is not being conducted in good faith, he is not without remedy. Indeed, if the newsman is called upon to give information bearing only a remote and tenuous relationship to the subject of the investigation, or if he has some other reason to believe that his testimony implicates confidential source relationships without a legitimate need of law enforcement, he will have access to the court on a motion to quash, and an appropriate protective order may be entered. The asserted claim to privilege should be judged on its facts by the striking of a proper balance between freedom of the press and the obligation of all citizens to give relevant testimony with respect to criminal conduct. The balance of these vital constitutional and societal interests on a case-by-case basis accords with the tried and traditional way of adjudicating such questions.

In short, the courts will be available to newsmen under circumstances where legitimate First Amendment interests require protection.

JUSTICE POTTER STEWART, with whom JUSTICE WILLIAM BRENNAN and JUSTICE THURGOOD MARSHALL join, dissenting:
The Court's crabbed view of the First Amendment reflects a disturbing insensitivity to the critical role of an independent press in our society. The question whether a reporter has a constitutional right to a confidential relationship with his source is of first impression here, but the principles that should guide our decision are as basic as any to be found in the Constitution. While Mr. Justice Powell's enigmatic concurring opinion gives some hope of a more flexible view in the future, the Court in these cases holds that a newsman has no First Amendment right to protect his sources when called before a grand jury. The Court thus invites state and federal authorities to undermine the historic independence of the press by attempting to annex the journalistic profession as an investigative arm of government. Not only will this decision impair performance of the press' constitutionally protected functions, but it will, I am convinced, in the long run harm rather than help the administration of justice.

I respectfully dissent.

The reporter's constitutional right to a confidential relationship with his source stems from the broad societal interest in a full and free flow of information to the public. It is this basic concern that underlies the Constitution's protection of a free press, because the guarantee is "not for the benefit of the press so much as for the benefit of all of us." Enlightened choice by an informed citizenry is the basic ideal upon which an open society is premised, and a free press is thus indispensable to a free society. Not only does the press enhance personal self-fulfillment by providing the people with the widest possible range of fact and opinion, but it also is an incontestable precondition of self-government. The press "has been a mighty catalyst in awakening public interest in governmental affairs, exposing corruption among public officers and employees and generally informing the citizenry of public events and occurrences. . . ." As private and public aggregations of power burgeon in size and the pressures for conformity necessarily mount, there is obviously a continuing need for an independent press to disseminate a robust variety of information and opinion through reportage, investigation, and criticism, if we are to preserve our constitutional tradition of maximizing freedom of choice by encouraging diversity of expression.

In keeping with this tradition, we have held that the right to publish is central to the First Amendment and basic to the existence of constitutional democracy.

A corollary of the right to publish must be the right to gather news. The full flow of information to the public protected by the free-press guarantee would be severely curtailed if no protection whatever were afforded to the process by which news is assembled and disseminated. We have, therefore, recognized that there is a right to publish without prior governmental approval, a right to distribute information, and a right to receive printed matter.

No less important to the news dissemination process is the gathering of information. News must not be unnecessarily cut off at its source, for without freedom to acquire information the right to publish would be impermissibly compromised. Accordingly, a right to gather news, of some dimensions, must exist. As Madison wrote: "A popular Government, without popular information, or the means of acquiring it, is but a Prologue to a Farce or a Tragedy, or perhaps both."

The right to gather news implies, in turn, a right to a confidential relationship between a reporter and his source. This proposition follows as a matter of simple logic once three factual predicates are recognized: (1) newsmen require informants to gather news; (2) confidentiality—the promise or understanding that names or certain aspects of communications will be kept off the record—is essential to the creation and maintenance of a news gathering relationship with informants; and (3) an unbridled subpoena power—the absence of a constitutional right protecting, in any way, a confidential relationship from compulsory process—will either deter sources from divulging information or deter reporters from gathering and publishing information.

It is obvious that informants are necessary to the news-gathering process as we know it today. If it is to perform its constitutional mission, the press must do far more than merely print public statements or publish prepared handouts. Familiarity with the people and circumstances involved in the myriad background activities that result in the final product called "news" is vital to complete and responsible journalism, unless the press is to be a captive mouthpiece of "newsmakers."

It is equally obvious that the promise of confidentiality may be a necessary prerequisite to a productive relationship between a newsman and his informants. An officeholder may fear his superior; a member of the bureaucracy, his associates; a dissident, the scorn of majority opinion. All may have information valuable to the public discourse, yet each may be willing to relate that information only in confidence to a reporter whom he trusts, either because of excessive caution or because of a reasonable fear of reprisals or censure for unorthodox views. The First Amendment concern must not be with the motives of any particular news source, but rather with the conditions in which informants of all shades of the spectrum may make information available through the press to the public. . . .

Finally, and most important, when governmental officials possess an unchecked power to compel newsmen to disclose information received in confidence, sources will clearly be deterred from giving information, and reporters will clearly be deterred from publishing it, because uncertainty about exercise of the power will lead to "self-censorship." The uncertainty arises, of course, because the judiciary has traditionally imposed virtually no limitations on the grand jury's broad investigatory powers.

After today's decision, the potential informant can never be sure that his identity or off-the-record communications will not subsequently be revealed through the compelled testimony of a newsman. A public-spirited person inside government, who is not implicated in any crime, will now be fearful of revealing corruption or other governmental wrongdoing, because he will now know he can subsequently be identified by use of compulsory process. The potential source must, therefore, choose between risking exposure by giving information or avoiding the risk by remaining silent.

The reporter must speculate about whether contact with a controversial source or publication of controversial material will lead to a subpoena. In the event of a subpoena, under today's decision, the newsman will know that he must choose between being punished for contempt if he refuses to testify, or violating his profession's ethics and impairing his resourcefulness as a reporter if he discloses confidential information.

Again, the commonsense understanding that such deterrence will occur is buttressed by concrete evidence. The existence of deterrent effects through fear and self-censorship was impressively developed in the District Court in *Caldwell*. Individual reporters and commentators have noted such effects. Surveys have verified that an unbridled subpoena power will substantially impair the flow of news to the public, especially in sensitive areas involving governmental officials, financial affairs, political figures, dissidents, or minority groups that require in-depth, investigative reporting. And the Justice Department has recognized that "compulsory process in some circumstances may have a limiting effect on the exercise of First Amendment rights." No evidence contradicting the existence of such deterrent effects was offered at the trials or in the briefs here by the petitioner in *Caldwell* or by the respondents in *Branzburg* and *Pappas*.

The impairment of the flow of news cannot, of course, be proved with scientific precision, as the Court seems to demand. Obviously, not every news-gathering relationship requires confidentiality. And it is difficult to pinpoint precisely how many relationships do require a promise or understanding of non-disclosure. But we have never before demanded that First Amendment rights rest on elaborate empirical studies demonstrating beyond any conceivable doubt that deterrent effects exist; we have never before required proof of the exact number of people potentially affected by governmental action, who would actually be dissuaded from engaging in First Amendment activity.

Rather, on the basis of common sense and available information, we have asked, often implicitly, (1) whether there was a rational connection between the cause (the governmental action) and the effect (the deterrence or impairment of First Amendment activity), and (2) whether the effect would occur with some regularity, *i.e.,* would not be *de minimis*. And, in making this determination, we have shown a special solicitude towards the "indispensable liberties" protected by the First Amendment, for "[f]reedoms such as these are protected not only against heavy-handed frontal attack, but also from being stifled by more subtle governmental interference." Once this threshold inquiry has been satisfied, we have then examined the competing interests in determining whether there is an unconstitutional infringement of First Amendment freedoms. . . .

. . . We cannot await an unequivocal—and therefore unattainable—imprimatur from empirical studies. We can and must accept the evidence developed in the record, and elsewhere, that overwhelmingly supports the premise that deterrence will occur with regularity in important types of news-gathering relationships.

Thus, we cannot escape the conclusion that when neither the reporter nor his source can rely on the shield of confidentiality against unrestrained use of the grand jury's subpoena power, valuable information will not be published and the public dialogue will inevitably be impoverished.

Posed against the First Amendment's protection of the newsman's confidential relationships in these cases is society's interest in the use of the grand jury to administer justice fairly and effectively. The grand jury serves two important functions: "to examine into the commission of crimes" and "to stand between the prosecutor and the accused, and to determine whether the charge was founded upon credible testimony or was dictated by malice or personal ill will." And to perform these functions, the grand jury must have available to it every man's relevant evidence.

Yet the longstanding rule making every person's evidence available to the grand jury is not absolute. The rule has been limited by the Fifth Amendment, the Fourth Amendment, and the evidentiary privileges of the common law. So it was that in *Blair, supra*, after recognizing that the right against compulsory self-incrimination prohibited certain inquiries, the Court noted that "some confidential matters are shielded from considerations of policy, and perhaps in other cases for special reasons a witness may be excused from telling all that he knows." And in *United States v. Bryan*, the Court observed that any exemption from the duty to testify before the grand jury "presupposes a very real interest to be protected."

Such an interest must surely be the First Amendment protection of a confidential relationship that I have discussed above in Part I. As noted there, this protection does not exist for the purely private interests of the newsman or his informant, nor even, at bottom, for the First Amendment interests of either partner in the newsgathering relationship. Rather, it functions to insure nothing less than democratic decisionmaking through the free flow of information to the public, and it serves, thereby, to honor the "profound national commitment to the principle that debate on public issues should be uninhibited, robust, and wide-open."

In striking the proper balance between the public interest in the efficient administration of justice and the First Amendment guarantee of the fullest flow of information, we must begin with the basic proposition that because of their "delicate and vulnerable" nature, and their transcendent importance for the just functioning of our society, First Amendment rights require special safeguards.

This Court has erected such safeguards when government, by legislative investigation or other investigative means, has attempted to pierce the shield of privacy inherent in freedom of association. In no previous case have we considered the extent to which the First Amendment limits the grand jury subpoena power. But the Court has said that "the Bill of Rights is applicable to investigations as to all forms of governmental action. Witnesses cannot be compelled to give evidence against themselves. They cannot be subjected to unreasonable search and seizure. Nor can the First Amendment freedoms of speech, press . . . or political belief and association be abridged." And, in *Sweezy v. New Hampshire,* it was stated: "It is particularly important that the exercise of the power of compulsory process be carefully circumscribed when the investigative process tends to impinge upon such highly sensitive areas as freedom of speech or press, freedom of political association, and freedom of communication of ideas."

The established method of "carefully" circumscribing investigative powers is to place a heavy burden of justification on government officials when First Amendment rights are impaired. The decisions of this Court have "consistently held that only a compelling state interest in the regulation of a subject within the State's constitutional power to regulate can justify limiting First Amendment freedoms." And "it is an essential prerequisite to the validity of an investigation which intrudes into the area of constitutionally protected rights of speech, press, association and petition that the State convincingly show a substantial relation between the information sought and a subject of overriding and compelling state interest."

Thus, when an investigation impinges on First Amendment rights, the government must not only show that the inquiry is of "compelling and overriding importance," but it must also "convincingly" demonstrate that the investigation is "substantially related" to the information sought.

Governmental officials must, therefore, demonstrate that the information sought is clearly relevant to a precisely defined subject of governmental inquiry. They must demonstrate that it is reasonable to think the witness in question has that information. And they must show that there is not any means of obtaining the information less destructive of First Amendment liberties.

These requirements, which we have recognized in decisions involving legislative and executive investigations, serve established policies reflected in numerous First Amendment decisions arising in other contexts. The requirements militate against vague investigations that, like vague laws, create uncertainty and needlessly discourage First Amendment activity. They also insure that a legitimate governmental purpose will not be pursued by means that "broadly stifle fundamental personal liberties when the end can be more narrowly achieved." . . .

I believe the safeguards developed in our decisions involving governmental investigations must apply to the grand jury inquiries in these cases. Surely the function of the grand jury to aid in the enforcement of the law is no more important than the function of the legislature, and its committees, to make the law. We have long recognized the value of the role played by legislative investigations, for the "power of the Congress to conduct investigations is inherent . . . [encompassing] surveys of defects in our social, economic or political system for the purpose of enabling the Congress to remedy them." Similarly, the associational rights of private individuals, which have been the prime focus of our First Amendment decisions in the investigative sphere, are hardly more important than the First Amendment rights of mass circulation newspapers and electronic media to disseminate ideas and information, and of the general public to receive them. Moreover, the vices of vagueness and overbreadth that legislative investigations may manifest are also exhibited by grand jury inquiries, since grand jury investigations are not limited in scope to specific criminal acts, and since standards of materiality and relevance are greatly relaxed. For, as the United States notes in its brief in *Caldwell,* the grand jury "need establish no factual basis for commencing an investigation, and can pursue rumors which further investigation may prove groundless."

Accordingly, when a reporter is asked to appear before a grand jury and reveal confidences, I would hold that the government must (1) show that there is probable cause to believe that the newsman has information that is clearly relevant to a specific probable violation of law; (2) demonstrate that the information sought cannot be obtained by alternative means less destructive of First Amendment rights; and (3) demonstrate a compelling and overriding interest in the information.

This is not to say that a grand jury could not issue a subpoena until such a showing were made, and it is not to say that a newsman would be in any way privileged to ignore any subpoena that was issued. Obviously, before the government's burden to make such a showing were triggered, the reporter would have to move to quash the subpoena, asserting the basis on which he considered the particular relationship a confidential one.

The crux of the Court's rejection of any newsman's privilege is its observation that only "where news sources themselves are implicated in crime or possess information relevant to the grand jury's task need they or the reporter be concerned about grand jury subpoenas." But this is a most misleading construct. For it is obviously not true that the only persons about whom reporters will be forced to testify will be those "confidential informants involved in actual criminal conduct" and those having "information suggesting illegal conduct by others." As noted above, given the grand jury's extraordinarily broad investigative powers and the weak standards of relevance and materiality that apply during such inquiries, reporters, if they have no testimonial privilege, will be called to give information about informants who have neither committed crimes nor have information about crime. It is to avoid deterrence of such sources and thus to prevent needless injury to First Amendment values that I think the government must be required to show probable cause that the newsman has information that is clearly relevant to a specific probable violation of criminal law.

Similarly, a reporter may have information from a confidential source that is "related" to the commission of crime, but the government may be able to obtain an indictment or otherwise achieve its purposes by subpoenaing persons other than the reporter. It is an obvious but important truism that when government aims have been fully served, there can be no legitimate reason to disrupt a confidential relationship between a reporter and his source. To do so would not aid the administration of justice and would only impair the flow of information to the public. Thus, it is to avoid deterrence of such sources that I think the government must show that there are no alternative means for the grand jury to obtain the information sought. . . .

The error in the Court's absolute rejection of First Amendment interests in these cases seems to me to be most profound. For in the name of advancing the administration of justice, the Court's decision, I think, will only impair the achievement of that goal. People entrusted with law enforcement responsibility, no less than private citizens, need general information relating to controversial social problems. Obviously, press reports have great value to government, even when the newsman cannot be compelled to testify before a grand jury. The sad paradox of the Court's position is that when a grand jury may exercise an unbridled subpoena power, and sources involved in sensitive matters become fearful of disclosing information, the newsman will not only cease to be a useful grand jury witness; he will cease to investigate and publish information about issues of public import. I cannot subscribe to such an anomalous result, for, in my view, the interests protected by the First Amendment are not antagonistic to the administration of justice. Rather, they can, in the long run, only be complementary, and for that reason must be given great "breathing space." . . .

Cohen v. Cowles Media Co.
SUPREME COURT OF THE UNITED STATES
501 U.S. 663 (1991)

JUSTICE BYRON WHITE delivered the Court's opinion:

The question before us is whether the First Amendment prohibits a plaintiff from recovering damages, under state promissory estoppel law, for a newspaper's breach of a promise of confidentiality given to the plaintiff in exchange for information. We hold that it does not.

During the closing days of the 1982 Minnesota gubernatorial race, Dan Cohen, an active Republican associated with Wheelock Whitney's Independent-Republican gubernatorial campaign, approached reporters from the St. Paul Pioneer Press Dispatch (Pioneer Press) and the Minneapolis Star and Tribune (Star Tribune) and offered to provide documents relating to a candidate in the upcoming election. Cohen made clear to the reporters that he would provide the information only if he was given a promise of confidentiality. Reporters from both papers promised to keep Cohen's identity anonymous and Cohen turned over copies of two public court records concerning Marlene Johnson, the Democratic-Farmer-Labor candidate for Lieutenant Governor. The first record indicated that Johnson had been charged in 1969 with three counts of unlawful assembly, and the second that she had been convicted in 1970 of petit theft. Both newspapers interviewed Johnson for her explanation, and one reporter tracked down the person who had found the records for Cohen. As it turned out, the unlawful assembly charges arose out of Johnson's participation in a protest of an alleged failure to hire minority workers on municipal construction projects, and the charges were eventually dismissed. The petit theft conviction was for leaving a store without paying for $6 worth of sewing materials. The incident apparently occurred at a time during which Johnson was emotionally distraught, and the conviction was later vacated.

After consultation and debate, the editorial staffs of the two newspapers independently decided to publish Cohen's name as part of their stories concerning Johnson. In their stories, both papers identified Cohen as the source of the court records, indicated his connection to the Whitney campaign, and included denials by Whitney campaign officials of any role in the matter. The same day the stories appeared, Cohen was fired by his employer.

Cohen sued respondents, the publishers of the Pioneer Press and Star Tribune, in Minnesota state court, alleging fraudulent misrepresentation and breach of contract. The trial court rejected respondents' argument that the First Amendment barred Cohen's lawsuit. A jury returned a verdict in Cohen's favor, awarding him $200,000 in compensatory damages. . . .

A divided Minnesota Supreme Court reversed the compensatory damages award. . . . The court then went on to address the question whether Cohen could establish a cause of action under Minnesota law on a promissory estoppel theory. Apparently, a promissory estoppel theory was never tried to the jury, nor briefed nor argued by the parties; it first arose during oral argument in the Minnesota Supreme Court when one of the justices asked a question about equitable estoppel. . . .

We granted certiorari to consider the First Amendment implications of this case. . . .

. . . We proceed to consider whether that Amendment bars a promissory estoppel cause of action against respondents. . . .

Respondents rely on the proposition that, "if a newspaper lawfully obtains truthful information about a matter of public significance, then state officials may not constitutionally punish publication of the information, absent a need to further a state interest of the highest order." That proposition is unexceptionable, and it has been applied in various cases that have found insufficient the asserted state interests in preventing publication of truthful, lawfully obtained information.

This case, however, is not controlled by this line of cases but rather by the equally well-established line of decisions holding that generally applicable laws do not offend the First Amendment simply because their enforcement against the press has incidental effects on its ability to gather and report the news. As the cases relied on by respondents recognize, the truthful information sought to be published must have been lawfully acquired. The press may not with impunity break and enter an office or dwelling to gather news. Neither does the First Amendment relieve a newspaper reporter of the obligation shared by all citizens to respond to a grand jury subpoena and answer questions relevant to a criminal investigation, even though the reporter might be required to reveal a confidential source. The press, like others interested in publishing, may not publish copyrighted material without obeying the copyright laws. . . .

There can be little doubt that the Minnesota doctrine of promissory estoppel is a law of general applicability. It does not target or single out the press. Rather, insofar as we are advised, the doctrine is generally applicable to the daily transactions of all the citizens of Minnesota. The First Amendment does not forbid its application to the press. . . .

Also, it is not at all clear that Respondents obtained Cohen's name "lawfully" in this case, at least for purposes of publishing it. . . . [R]espondents obtained Cohen's name only by making a promise that they did not honor. The dissenting opinions suggest that the press should not be subject to any law, including copyright law for example, which in any fashion or to any degree limits or restricts the press' right to report truthful information. The First Amendment does not grant the press such limitless protection.

Nor is Cohen attempting to use a promissory estoppel cause of action to avoid the strict requirements for establishing a libel or defamation claim. As the Minnesota Supreme Court observed here, "Cohen could not sue for defamation because the information disclosed [his name] was true." Cohen is not seeking damages for injury to his reputation or his state of mind. He sought damages in excess of $50,000 for breach of a promise that caused him to lose his job and lowered his earning capacity. . . .

Respondents and *amici* argue that permitting Cohen to maintain a cause of action for promissory estoppel will inhibit truthful reporting because news organizations will have legal incentives not to disclose a confidential source's identity even when that person's identity is itself newsworthy. . . . But if this is the case, it is no more than the incidental, and constitutionally insignificant, consequence of applying to the press a generally applicable law that requires those who make certain kinds of promises to keep them. . . . The Minnesota Supreme Court's incorrect conclusion that the First Amendment barred Cohen's claim may well have truncated its consideration of whether a promissory estoppel claim had otherwise been established under Minnesota law, and whether Cohen's jury verdict could be upheld on a promissory estoppel basis. Or perhaps the State Constitution may be construed to shield the press from a promissory estoppel cause of action such as this one. These are matters for the Minnesota Supreme Court to address and resolve in the first instance on remand. Accordingly, the judgment of the Minnesota Supreme Court is reversed, and the case is remanded for further proceedings not inconsistent with this opinion.

Chapter 10

[W]e note that unfair and prejudicial news comment on pending trials has become increasingly prevalent. Due process requires that the accused receive a trial by an impartial jury free from outside influences. Given the pervasiveness of modern communications and the difficulty of effacing prejudicial publicity from the minds of the jurors, the trial courts must take strong measures to ensure that the balance is never weighed against the accused. . . . The cure lies in those remedial measures that will prevent the prejudice at its inception.

U.S. Supreme Court Justice Tom Clark[2]

In a new twist on the media and the courts, CNN faced particular criticism for its coverage of the Steubenville rape trial, which many said was focused on the plight of the rapists rather than the victim.[1]

The Media and the Courts
Preserving Public Trials and Preventing Prejudice

Fair Trials and Prejudicial Speech

Media Effects
Impartial Jurors
Anonymous Juries
Impartial Judges

Remedies to Prejudice

Selecting the Jury
Continuance
Juror Admonition
Juror Sequestration

Access to Trials

Presumption of Open Trials
Justifying Court Closure
Closure to Protect Juveniles
Closure to Protect Sexual
    Assault Victims
Gags to Limit Extrajudicial
    Discussion
Challenging Closure

Electronic Access to Trials

Broadcasting and Recording
Cameras and Courtrooms
Newer Technologies

Bench-Bar-Press Guidelines

Access to Court Records

Constitutional and Statutory
    Access
Court Dockets
State Secrets
Court Access Rules
Electronic Access to Court
    Records

Cases for Study

➤ *Sheppard v. Maxwell*
➤ *Richmond
    Newspapers, Inc. v.
    Virginia*

Suppose . . .

. . . that a well-known local professional in a quiet community is accused of bludgeoning his wife to death in their home while she and their son slept. Local and national media swarm to the town, converging on the home, the police and every aspect of the investigation. Investigative and pretrial proceedings are open to the media, with one grand jury process held in a raucous, public session in the school gym. Daily news screams the husband's guilt, urges investigators to put him behind bars, and publish rumors and inaccuracies about the defendant and the crime.

After the husband is charged with second-degree murder, the media dominate the trial court. They are so close to the defendant that he and his attorney cannot converse privately. The jurors, drawn from the local community, are allowed to follow the inflammatory coverage and literally rub elbows with the press. They become media celebrities and are allowed to make unsupervised telephone calls at night.

After his conviction, the husband appeals on the grounds that media coverage damaged his constitutional right to a fair trial. Is that true? If so, what may a judge do to reduce media's adverse impact without violating the right to public trials and a free press? Look for the answers to these questions when the case of *Sheppard v. Maxwell* is discussed later and excerpted at the end of the chapter.

M any people may argue that little has changed for the better in the decades since U.S. Supreme Court Justice Tom Clark suggested that courts must remedy the inherent conflict between a free and robust press and fair trials. Today, news media cover crimes when they occur, often in lurid detail and with exuberant fascination. Reporters seek access to crime scenes and provide the public with descriptions of the evidence. Interviews with neighbors, police and victims follow the progress of investigations, shedding light or creating rumors about the suspects, methods and victims. Media post, broadcast and publish gory photographs and subject celebrities such as Randy Travis, who was associated twice in 2012 with driving while under the influence (DWI), to intensive scrutiny even before charges are filed.[3] Travis pleaded guilty and received probation for DWI in 2013.[4]

Studies show that people who rely on media coverage to understand crime—a majority of people—misunderstand the frequency and nature of criminal activity and increasingly view crimes and trials as entertainment.[5] For example, heavy news consumers mistakenly believed that crime in schools skyrocketed following the shootings at Columbine High School in Littleton, Colo. Details that flood both entertainment and news on and offline, such as reports of Travis being found naked in the road beside his crushed truck and threatening to kill the officers on the scene, may affect both a celebrity's income and any charges filed. Travis was charged with DWI early in 2013.

Fair Trials and Prejudicial Speech

The Sixth Amendment to the U.S. Constitution gives criminal defendants the right to a speedy public trial by an impartial jury of his or her peers. An impartial juror is *not* someone who has no information about the defendant or the crime before he or she steps into the courtroom. An impartial juror is anyone who will give the facts full and unbiased consideration and render a verdict solely on the basis of evidence presented in court. The problem is, as the news makes clear daily, criminal trials do not exist in a vacuum.

Billie Sol Estes arrives at a creditors' hearing in the federal court house in El Paso, Texas, in 1962.

Media Effects

Citizens engrossed by media crime coverage may be called to sit on a jury. Nearly five decades ago, in the early days of America's romance with television, the U.S. Supreme Court handed down two decisions recognizing the potential harms media publicity might cause to fair trials. In

Estes v. Texas, the Court in 1965 ruled that televised coverage of the criminal trial of Texas financier Billie Sol Estes was inherently prejudicial.[6]

The defendant was charged with a multimillion-dollar con involving government officials, improper federal loans, a phony storage business and fraudulent fertilizer sales to Texas farmers. Congress launched a high-profile investigation of Estes, more than six dozen FBI agents dug into the case and the press across the country covered developments almost daily. The May 25, 1962, cover of Time magazine bore Estes' image beneath the banner "The Billie Sol Estes Scandal," and a Texas newspaper editor won the 1963 Pulitzer Prize for local reporting for bringing the fraud "to national attention with resultant investigation, prosecution and conviction of Estes."[7] Prior to his state trial, defense lawyers requested that the judge ban photographs and broadcasts, but dozens of reporters with yards of cable snaking through the courtroom were allowed to attend the proceedings. With his state trial underway, Estes was convicted on federal charges of conspiracy and fraud.

In reviewing Estes' state conviction, the U.S. Supreme Court held that intensive pretrial broadcast coverage automatically altered juror perceptions of the case and constituted a form of harassment of the defendant. Given the significant potential harms of publicity, the Court said judges must take steps to reduce the impact of media on trials. The Court later rejected the assumption that all broadcast coverage of trials is inherently prejudicial,[8] but it imposed additional burdens on judges to assure that media did not undermine fairness and decorum in their courts. Judges must protect trials from the effects of publicity.

In the second case, *Sheppard v. Maxwell,* the Supreme Court severely criticized a judge who had allowed extensive pretrial and trial publicity to turn the high-profile murder trial into a "Roman holiday."[9] The Court said that limited press coverage may be consistent with a fair trial, but "massive and pervasive" coverage that reaches the jurors and permeates the trial may be presumed to prejudice the fairness of the process.

The *Sheppard* case involved the 1954 beating death of the wife of a well-respected physician in a

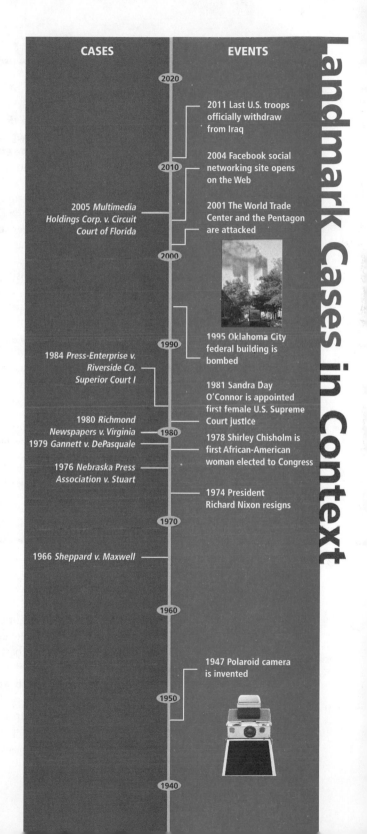

Landmark Cases in Context

CASES

2005 *Multimedia Holdings Corp. v. Circuit Court of Florida*

1984 *Press-Enterprise v. Riverside Co. Superior Court I*

1980 *Richmond Newspapers v. Virginia*
1979 *Gannett v. DePasquale*

1976 *Nebraska Press Association v. Stuart*

1966 *Sheppard v. Maxwell*

EVENTS

2020

2011 Last U.S. troops officially withdraw from Iraq

2010

2004 Facebook social networking site opens on the Web

2001 The World Trade Center and the Pentagon are attacked

2000

1995 Oklahoma City federal building is bombed

1990

1981 Sandra Day O'Connor is appointed first female U.S. Supreme Court justice

1978 Shirley Chisholm is first African-American woman elected to Congress

1980

1974 President Richard Nixon resigns

1970

1960

1947 Polaroid camera is invented

1950

1940

realWorld Law

Crime Time News?

High-profile, real-time media coverage of criminal investigations, such as the FBI pursuit of Tamerlan Tsarnaev following the 2013 Boston Marathon bombing, raise concerns about the ability to seat a jury that will reach a verdict based solely on the evidence presented in court.

For at least a decade, researchers have said skewed crime reporting may lead Americans to believe incorrectly that crime rates are soaring and anti-crime efforts are failing because the quantity of crime coverage is not tied to real rates of crime. One study found that more than three-fourths of network television news stories about rural America focused on crime.[1] Given the nature of TV crime reporting, blogger Don Campagna coined the phrase "crime time news."

Such over-reporting may lead misinformed jurors to inaccurately assess evidence in a trial. Some studies contend that what is known as the "CSI effect" leads jurors to expect more and more convincing forensic evidence than is generally available in a real criminal trial.[2] Surveys suggest growing concern about the nature of televised crime reporting. Respondents fear that sensational, repetitive coverage of crimes makes it more difficult to catch criminals, harms a suspect's right to a fair trial, neglects victims and may prompt "copycat" crimes. These viewers want more "meaningful" crime reporting that focuses more on the apprehension of criminals than on the crimes they commit, coverage that emphasizes punishment rather than crime.[3]

1. The Center for Media and Public Affairs (results based on analysis of all morning and evening newscasts on ABC, NBC and CBS). See summary of the 2002 study at 17 Media Monitor (2003), *available at* http://www.cmpa.com/files/media_monitor/03janfeb.pdf.
2. Young S. Kim, Gregg Barak & Donald E. Shelton, *Examining the "CSI-Effect" in the Cases of Circumstantial Evidence and Eyewitness Testimony: Multivariate and Path Analyses,* 37 J. Crim. Just. 22 (2009); Tamara F. Lawson, *Before the Verdict and Beyond the Verdict: The CSI Infection Within Modern Criminal Jury Trials,* 41 Loy. U. Chic. L.J. 132 (2009).
3. *The Right to More Meaningful Crime Coverage,* Insite Media Research (2000), *available at* http:www.tvsurveys.com/billofrites/crime.htm.

wealthy suburb of Cleveland. In his defense, Dr. Sam Sheppard said he struggled with and was knocked unconscious by a "bushy-haired stranger" who entered the family home the night of the murder. The doctor said he woke to find his wife dead and called the police.

The media frenzy began the day of the crime and pervaded every aspect of what was called "the trial of the century." Media swarmed the coroner's inquest into the cause of death and "emphasized evidence that tended to incriminate Sheppard."[10] Although no hard evidence tied him to crime, Sheppard was charged with second-degree murder. During the trial, media filled the courtroom, broadcast live coverage and printed verbatim transcripts of the proceedings almost every day. Sheppard was convicted, sentenced to life imprisonment and spent

10 years in prison before the U.S. Supreme Court overturned his conviction on the grounds that the intense and prejudicial press coverage prevented a fair trial. Retried in 1966, Sheppard was found not guilty.

In overturning his conviction, the Supreme Court said judges must protect the fair trial rights of a defendant by controlling the participants and the process of the trial, including the media. In its 8–1 decision, the Court acknowledged the importance of free press in a democracy and its role in the administration of justice. However, the Court said the press does not have the right to inflame the minds of jurors, jeopardize the fairness of trials or make a mockery of the solemn judicial process.

The Court said judges should use any of a variety of narrowly tailored measures to preserve the fairness of criminal trials. These measures, which are discussed in more detail later in the chapter, include the following:

1. **Continuance,** or delay, of the trial until publicity has subsided

2. Change of the trial venue, or location, to relocate it outside the area of intense media attention

3. **Sequestration,** or isolation, of the jury from the public

4. Extensive voir dire, or questioning, to identify juror prejudice

5. **Gag orders** on participants to limit discussion of the case outside the courtroom

6. Protection of potential witnesses from outside influences

7. Instructions, or **admonitions,** to the jury to avoid media coverage of the trial and to set aside any prejudices or preconceptions they may have

8. Retrial if the jury or the judicial process has been contaminated by media coverage

9. Limitations on press attendance, through measures such as pool reporting, to reduce the impact of their presence on jurors and witnesses

Although the *Sheppard v. Maxwell* ruling has been applauded as a watershed in protecting the rights of defendants, it also has been criticized for prompting judges to move away from open judicial proceedings.[11] In a recent example, media were barred from a 2011 pretrial hearing in Miami in the case against four men accused of the shooting murder of Washington Redskins star Sean Taylor.[12] The judge agreed with defense attorneys who said media coverage of the hearing on whether to allow purported confessions and incriminating statements at trial might skew the views of prospective jurors and affect the outcome of the high-profile case. Attorneys for The Miami Herald and Post-Newsweek unsuccessfully argued that the hearing should be open because Miami's juror pool was sufficiently large to enable the seating of unbiased jurors and any harm to the trial was speculative.

continuance Postponement of a trial to a later time.

sequestration The isolation of jurors to avoid prejudice from publicity in a sensational trial.

gag orders A nonlegal term used to describe court orders that prohibit publication or discussion of specific materials

admonitions Judges' instructions to jurors warning them to avoid potentially prejudicial communications.

Contrary to the assumptions of many, including the Supreme Court itself, the effects of media coverage may be highly specific and somewhat inconsistent.[13] One recent study of civil awards in state courts found that when there is little media coverage, elected judges in liberal jurisdictions oversee far larger damage awards than do judges in conservative areas. However, frequent newspaper coverage of the courts reduces disparities in the amount of damages awarded and "may enhance fairness in the civil justice system," the study found. In contrast, another study found that while media coverage does not appear to affect the verdict in high-profile cases, it does affect the punishment.[14] Defendants in highly publicized cases get longer sentences.[15]

Impartial Jurors

An impartial juror is not ignorant of the case. Rather impartial jurors must have no fixed opinion of the guilt or innocence of the defendant.[16] And they must be capable of rendering a verdict based purely on the evidence presented in court. A potential juror is not disqualified simply because he or she has seen or read news accounts about the crime or the defendant. Similarly, prejudice may not be assumed simply because of a juror's race or gender.[17] Instead courts are required to engage in close questioning of the jury pool during voir dire to determine when media exposure results in prejudice toward the defendant.

Courts generally do not rely on social science research to determine when, or whether, news coverage affects jurors. If they did, they would find conflicting results. However, courts generally accept the commonsense notion that media coverage has an effect on the fairness of a trial.[18] Members of the legal community tend to believe that when officials of the court—police and attorneys, for example—publicly discuss ongoing trials, their speech influences jurors' perceptions of witnesses and may potentially alter their determination of guilt or innocence. Courts also believe other government officials may affect the impartiality of jurors. For example, a federal judge rebuked former U.S. Atty. Gen. John Ashcroft for comments about a pending trial. The court said the attorney general's highly publicized comments about the credibility of key witnesses in the first public terrorism trail in the United States following the Sept. 11 attacks "exhibited a distressing lack of care [about] potentially prejudicial statements about this case."[19]

Anonymous Juries

Criminal defense attorneys often argue that shielding a juror's identity increases his or her anxiety and perception that the crime is especially severe and the defendant is guilty. Courts, however, have said anonymous juries are not inherently prejudicial to defendants. Some courts refuse to release the names and identities of jurors in high-profile cases or in cases where jurors may legitimately be concerned for their personal safety.[20] In fact, the Texas criminal code requires

Emerging Law

Fair Trials and Facebook Friends

An appeals court in Florida decided that the judge in a criminal case, who was a Facebook friend of the prosecutor, should have disqualified himself because the "friendship" posed a sufficient risk to the impartiality of the trial.[1]

In presenting the question to the state's high court, one appeals court judge said,

> Judges do not have the unfettered social freedom of teenagers. . . . Maintenance of the appearance of impartiality requires the avoidance of entanglements and relationships that compromise that appearance. . . . The existence of a judge's Facebook page might exert pressure on lawyers or litigants to take direct or indirect action to curry favor with the judge. . . . [A] person who accepts the responsibility of being a judge must also accept limitations on personal freedom.[2]

A federal district court in Pennsylvania earlier refused to put any weight on such electronic relationships:

> [T]he court assigns no significance to the Facebook "friends" reference. Facebook reportedly has more than 200 million active users, and the average user has 120 "friends" on the site. . . . Indeed, "friendships" on Facebook may be as fleeting as the flick of a delete button.[3]

It remains to be seen, however, whether or when social media connections present a challenge to the workings of the courts.

---

1. Eric Goldman, *Social Media Law Roundup*, Tech. & Marketing L. Blog (Jan. 18, 2013), *available at* http://blog.ericgoldman.org/archives/2013/01/social_media_ev_2.htm.
2. Domville v. State, 103 So. 3d 184 (Fla. Ct. App. 2012).
3. Quigley Corp. v. Karkus, 2009 U.S. Dist. LEXIS 41296 at *16 (E.D. Pa., May 19, 2009).

anonymous juries unless there is a showing that access serves the public good.[21] Elsewhere courts justify their refusal to release information about jurors by claiming that the release would violate the jurors' personal privacy interests.

Recent rulings in the Courts of Appeals for the Third and Seventh Circuits suggest that the issue of public access to juror information remains unsettled. Although both courts held that the public has a constitutional right to contemporaneous access to juror names in a criminal proceeding,[22] one member of the Seventh Circuit panel requested a full review of its decision.[23] Judge Richard Posner argued that judges may base their decisions about access on experience and common sense and need not rely on admissible evidence. Court bans on press photographs of jurors outside the courtroom, however, generally must pass strict scrutiny because they constitute a form of prior restraint on a free press.

Impartial Judges

Sometimes the fairness of the judge is also cast into doubt. Many judges run for election, and the Supreme Court has ruled that the due process clause of the Constitution requires judges to disqualify themselves from hearing a "pending or imminent" case in which "a risk of actual bias or prejudgment" arises because "a person with a personal stake . . . had a significant and disproportionate influence" in getting the judge elected or appointed to the bench.[24] When spending on the election campaign of a judge by one of the parties presents "a serious, objective risk of actual bias," the judge must step off the case, according to the 5–4 majority.[25] Among the range of prejudicial influences the U.S. Supreme Court noted in its decision in *Sheppard v. Maxwell,* the Court said the judge was running for reelection and the lead prosecutor was a candidate for a judgeship in an election that took place two weeks after the trial began.[26]

In some states where judges stand for election, laws have been passed to protect the appearance of judicial fairness and impartiality by prohibiting judges from campaigning on disputed issues that might come before them in court. But in 2002 the U.S. Supreme Court ruled that such laws violate the First Amendment rights of judicial candidates.[27] The Court said the laws directly limit speech vital to elections, "place . . . most subjects of interest to voters off limits" and undermine the ability of citizens to inform themselves effectively about the candidates.[28]

SUMMARY

MEDIA COVERAGE OF CRIME OFTEN INCLUDES details that may be incorrect or may be inadmissible in court. Although the media have a First Amendment right to publish this information, such pretrial publicity may undermine the defendant's Sixth Amendment right to a fair trial. A fair trial requires impartial jurors and an impartial judge. Media exposure may cause potential jurors to form fixed ideas about the guilt or innocence of the defendant before a trial begins. While studies disagree on whether publicity harms juror deliberations and verdicts, courts struggle with the effect of media on court processes. The U.S. Supreme Court has said that judges must take steps to reduce the risk of bias in court proceedings. State laws designed to protect the appearance of judicial impartiality by prohibiting judges from taking public stands on issues that may come before them in court are unconstitutional. ∎

Remedies to Prejudice

Courts have ruled that media coverage may prejudice a fair trial in numerous ways, and judges apply a range of measures suggested by the Supreme Court's guidelines set out in *Sheppard v. Maxwell* to prevent or correct prejudice in the jury. Judges specifically determine where and how the jury is chosen, where and when the trial takes place and the amount of speech freedom jury members and other trial participants will have during the ongoing trial.

Selecting the Jury

When a court needs to select a jury for a trial, the clerk of court chooses names at random from a list of adult licensed drivers, registered voters or other source in the county where the trial will be held. The geographic location from which the pool of jurors is drawn is known as the "venire." Each potential juror receives a **summons,** a notice asking him or her to appear at the court. Attorneys for each side and/or the judge question those in the jury pool about their backgrounds, life experiences and opinions to determine whether each individual will be able to weigh the evidence presented during trial objectively. This process is called "voir dire," which literally means "to speak the truth."

Either the defense or the prosecution in a criminal trial may pose a **for-cause challenge** against a potential juror if the individual's response to questioning suggests a prejudice relevant to the case. The person's life experiences, attitudes, employment or association with the defendant may justify for-cause challenges. Each attorney also has a limited number of peremptory challenges with which to remove potential jurors without offering any reason to disqualify the person to sit as a juror.

The process is designed to ensure that overtly biased individuals do not sit on a jury, but both the defense and the prosecution work to eliminate not only biased jurors but also anyone they believe will be hostile to their sides of the case. In major criminal or civil cases, a party may hire consultants on jury selection to profile a model juror as a tool for jury selection. Consultants rely on trial experience, psychology, expertise in nonverbal cues, computer modeling and private investigations of potential jurors to improve the chances of obtaining a sympathetic jury. Once both sides accept the jury, jurors are **impaneled** (selected and seated). Then the jury is sworn in.

Changing Venue A trial may be transferred from one venue, or location, to another to protect fairness if pretrial publicity or other conditions in the initial location are substantially likely to endanger a fair trial. Either side in a criminal trial may request a change of venue, which requires the relocation of the trial and all its participants. A change of venue also shifts the location from which the jury pool will be selected away from locales believed to be tainted by prejudicial publicity. Sometimes this evasive maneuver fails because media coverage follows the trial. Changing a trial's venue is expensive.

New Venire Another means to avoid prejudicial publicity is to bring in a pool of jurors from an adjoining county. The trial stays in its original location, providing easier access to witnesses but requiring transporting the jury back and forth each day of the trial or housing them in the town where the trial is held. Changes of venire are expensive, and some defense attorneys believe they impose inconveniences on jurors that make the jury hostile to the defendant.

summons A notice asking an individual to appear at a court. Potential jurors receive such a summons.

for-cause challenge In the context of jury selection, the ability of attorneys to remove a potential juror for a reason the law finds sufficient, as opposed to a peremptory challenge.

impanel To select and seat a jury.

Continuance

The Sixth Amendment protects the right of criminal defendants to a speedy trial. However, defendants may waive this right if they, and their attorneys, believe that a delay, or continuance, will reduce the prejudicial impact of publicity. Parties to the trial may oppose a continuance because postponements often reduce the availability and recall of witnesses.

Juror Admonition

Judges routinely issue admonitions, or warnings, to jurors, telling them to avoid potentially prejudicial communications, including media coverage of the trial. Judges also instruct jurors not to discuss the case among themselves or with others or to express any opinion about the case until they begin deliberations. Experts disagree on whether such admonitions are effective. Judges also give instructions on the law to the jury prior to deliberation. These instructions generally advise jurors about the applicable law and inform them of their duty to reach a verdict in the case on the basis only of the evidence presented in court, not on speculation, sympathy or prejudice.

Juror Sequestration

Sometimes, though rarely, a judge will sequester, or isolate, a jury during a trial. Sequestration generally houses jurors in a hotel near the courthouse and prohibits them from having contact with people outside of court. Sequestered jurors generally have only limited and supervised opportunities to communicate with their families. Sequestration also may be used to protect jurors who face threats to their safety or to keep them away from media during highly publicized cases. Jurors do not like to be sequestered, and some people believe that sequestration affects juror attitudes, the quality of their deliberations and the outcome of the trial.

As discussed in Chapter 9, judges may use their discretionary power of contempt of court to sanction reporters or others who disobey a court order or interfere with court proceedings. In extraordinary situations, a judge also may call for a retrial to ensure a trial free from prejudice.

SUMMARY

THE SIXTH AMENDMENT TO THE CONSTITUTION guarantees criminal defendants the right to a speedy and public trial before an impartial jury to be held in the district where the crime was committed. To protect justice, courts take care in composing juries and in protecting the court's process from external influences, including media. The safeguards of a fair trial encompass voir dire, judges' admonitions, instructions, sequestrations and even contempt citations. On occasion, judges will delay or relocate a trial to overcome impediments to fairness. These remedies are rare, as are retrials. ∎

Access to Trials

Although the Sixth Amendment to the U.S. Constitution provides a right to public trials in criminal cases, the U.S. Supreme Court considered whether a defendant may waive his right to a public trial and exclude the public. The Court also examined the question of whether the public, including the media, has a Sixth Amendment right of access to criminal court proceedings. If the public has a right of access, the defendant would not have a right to a private trial because it would infringe on the right of others to participate in and oversee the process of the courts.

Presumption of Open Trials

For nearly four decades, the U.S. Supreme Court has said the Sixth Amendment creates a personal right for criminal defendants to be tried in an open court by their peers to ensure they receive a fair trial and due process.[29] The Court also said the public maintains its long-standing common-law right to view public trials. The Court said the two rights must be balanced. The landmark ruling in *Gannett v. DePasquale* arose after Judge Daniel DePasquale granted pretrial motions to exclude the public and the press from the trial of three individuals charged with the murder of an off-duty police officer. At the same hearing, he also granted pretrial motions to suppress evidence and confessions by the defendants. No one present during the pretrial hearing, including a Gannett reporter, objected to the motions or the court's rulings.

After Gannett reporter Carol Ritter later objected to the closure, the judge reviewed the pretrial motions and said the defendant's right to a fair trial outweighed the right of the press to cover the pretrial suppression hearing. On subsequent review, Justice Potter Stewart, writing for the Supreme Court, agreed that publicity could prejudice the defendant's right to a fair trial and affirmed the right of a judge to use means that "are not strictly and inescapably necessary" to protect a fair trial.[30] Justice Stewart observed that

> There can be no blinking the fact that there is a strong societal interest in public trials. Openness in court proceedings may improve the quality of testimony, induce unknown witnesses to come forward with relevant testimony, cause all trial participants to perform their duties more conscientiously, and generally give the public an opportunity to observe the judicial system. But there is a strong societal interest in other constitutional guarantees extended to the accused as well.[31]

realWorld Law

Media Target Their Battles for Open Courts

Without news photographers in the courtroom, an artist provides the only images of a pretrial military hearing for five Guantanamo Bay prisoners accused in the Sept. 11, 2001, attacks.

The media may be abdicating their traditional role as champions of open courts. "The days of powerful newspapers with ample legal budgets appear to be numbered," according to one Georgia public defender, who questions whether "underfunded bloggers [will] be able to carry the financial burdens of opening our courtrooms."[1]

A shrinking number of media-spearheaded battles for access to courtrooms and court records worries some who believe controversial rulings denying public access too often go unchallenged. Given their financial straits, news media have "shifted our emphasis from principle to survival," according to access advocate Jane Kirtley.[2]

But early in 2013, 14 media organizations and the American Civil Liberties Union signaled that they will fight for access to court proceedings if the stakes are high enough.[3] The group appealed the military court ruling that classifies as a threat to national security and, thereby automatically seals, all defendants' discussion in the Guantanamo Bay war court of government torture of abuse.

Central to the appeal is whether the public will hear accused 9/11 organizer Khalid Sheik Mohammed and his alleged co-conspirators testify in their death-penalty trial about their treatment by the CIA during their years of secret custody prior to their arrival at Guantanamo. Government officials have disclosed that agents waterboarded Mohammed 183 times.

The order closes the court during all discussion of harsh interrogation techniques and imposes a time-delay on the audio feed to court spectators that enables government to mute or delete select court testimony. The media/ACLU appeal argues that the closures are insufficiently tailored to address any national security risk, fail to provide evidence of such risk and mandate closure of entire categories of testimony in violation of the First Amendment.

---

1. Adam Liptak, *Shrinking Newsrooms Wage Fewer Battles for Public Access to Courtrooms,* N.Y. Times, Aug. 31, 2009, at A10.
2. *Id.*
3. S. Carol Rosenberg, *Media, ACLU Challenge Guantanamo War-Court Closure Policy* (Feb. 25, 2013), available at http://www .miamiherald.com.

In a concurring opinion joined by three other justices, however, Justice Harry Blackmun suggested that court closure "may implicate interests beyond those of the accused . . . [including] important social interests relating to the integrity of the trial process."[32] He said judges must weigh those competing interests fully even if neither the prosecution nor the defense objects to closure. To do so, judges should presume that court processes should be open and require the party seeking closure to demonstrate (1) the probability that publicity would infringe on the right to a fair trial, (2) the inadequacy of alternatives to closure and (3) the effectiveness of closure.

More than a decade after its *Gannett v. DePasquale* decision, a majority of the U.S. Supreme Court moved toward Justice Blackmun's position to find that the Sixth Amendment right to a public trial does not belong exclusively to the defendant. In *Richmond Newspapers, Inc. v. Virginia*,[33] the Court in 1980 held that criminal trials are presumptively open and the First Amendment prohibits judges from closing courtrooms without a full exploration of alternatives. The Court reasoned that the Constitution protects the people's right to assemble and petition government for redress of grievances through the courts. It also provides some presumptive right for the press, as members of the public, to cover criminal trials because court processes have been open to the public throughout history.[34] Chief Justice Warren Burger wrote that "absent an overriding interest articulated in findings, the trial of a criminal case must be open to the public."[35]

The Court said open criminal trials serve the public interest in a variety of ways, including advancement of the core First Amendment goal of protecting "freedom of communications on matters relating to the functioning of government."[36] Information about the criminal process enables citizens to evaluate government performance, to maintain faith in the judicial system and to seek catharsis for the trauma of crimes. In 2011, the Supreme Court of South Dakota applied this reasoning to recognize a qualified First Amendment right of access to civil trials in that state.[37] The state high court found that the presumption of openness outweighed the agreement of all trial parties and the judge to close the trial involving the finances of a popular tourist attraction. The court also held that the justification for gag orders, as a means to reduce prejudicial publicity and protect a criminal defendant's right to a fair trial, did not apply in civil cases tried by the court rather than a jury.

In a separate ruling that quickly followed *Richmond Newspapers, Inc.*, the Supreme Court said that because courts are presumptively open, states may not require closure of certain portions of criminal trials.[38] In *Globe Newspaper Co. v. Superior Court,* the Supreme Court struck down a Virginia law that closed courtrooms during all testimony of any minor who was a victim of sexual assault. The Court said some parts of a trial might need to be closed, but the Constitution requires judges to demonstrate the need for such closures: "The institutional value of the open criminal trial is recognized in both logic and experience."[39]

In a pair of cases involving the Press-Enterprise, the Supreme Court established the public's right of access to both jury selection and preliminary hearings, reasoning that these are integral parts of the judicial process.[40] Preliminary hearings generally determine whether there is sufficient evidence to proceed to trial. The Court said two interrelated factors—experience and logic—determine whether a court proceeding is presumptively open.[41] According to the **experience and logic test,** if the proceeding has historically been open and if openness contributes to the proper functioning of the process itself, the proceeding is presumptively open. In recent years, Courts of Appeal in the Second, Third, Sixth and Ninth Circuits have applied the experience and logic test to find a right of access

experience and logic test A doctrine that evaluates both the history and the role openness plays in assuring the credibility of a process to determine whether it is presumptively open.

Points of Law

Open Courts

According to the U.S. Supreme Court's rulings in the two *Press-Enterprise* cases, court proceedings are presumptively open to the public and the press if logic and experience dictate openness. Accordingly, court processes are presumed to be open if the following apply:

1. This type of proceeding has a largely uninterrupted history of openness, and

2. Openness contributes to the proper functioning of the proceeding itself.

to government proceedings and activities beyond the courts.[42] These rulings found a right of access to administration hearings on city transit rules, executive branch deportation hearings and Bureau of Land Management horse roundups.

In the second of the 1980s rulings, *Press Enterprise II v. Superior Court,* the Supreme Court said access to the hearings themselves, not merely to proceeding transcripts released after the fact, is vital to assure public confidence in the functioning of the process.

The Court in *Press-Enterprise II* emphasized that jury selection historically had been open to the public, but it acknowledged that the responses of some jurors to some particularly sensitive questions during voir dire might raise privacy concerns sufficient to warrant protection from public disclosure. Thus, courts constitutionally may develop narrowly tailored measures to close only those portions of voir dire that raise serious concerns. Some courts have expanded beyond this individual juror's right to personal privacy to rule that juror privacy in general justifies closed voir dire and anonymous juries. They reason that access to jury selection and juror identity erodes the willingness of potential jurors to speak candidly and harms effective juror selection.

In 2010, the Supreme Court again held that the Sixth Amendment right to a public trial applies to the voir dire of prospective jurors.[43] In *Presley v. Georgia,* the Court's 8–2 decision reiterated that "the public has a right to be present whether or not any party has asserted the right,"[44] and "courts are obligated to take every reasonable measure to accommodate public attendance at criminal trials."[45] A "generic risk of jurors overhearing prejudicial remarks, unsubstantiated by any specific threat or incident" is insufficient basis for closing voir dire, the Court said.[46]

Justifying Court Closure

The *Press-Enterprise* and *Presley* decisions should make clear that generalized privacy interests are insufficient to justify closing a courtroom or voir dire. Anyone seeking to close a presumptively public judicial hearing must meet a high standard, which the court articulated through a two-part test. First, the individual seeking to close records or proceedings must show that openness has a "substantial probability" of significantly threatening the fair trial process. Second, the evidence must prove that closure is a last resort and is "essential" in order to preserve fair trial rights.

Generally, courts must demonstrate that the interests of justice require withholding information, including the names and addresses of jurors, from the public.[47] A request to close a courtroom should be granted only if closure meets the standards of strict scrutiny and if the party seeking closure makes a specific showing of serious harm that would result from an open proceeding. "The presumption of openness may be overcome only by an overriding interest based on findings that closure is essential to preserve higher values and is narrowly tailored to serve that interest," the Court said.[48] Thus, before closing a courtroom, judges are required to determine that facts demonstrate *all* of the following:

- Openness poses a substantial threat to a fair proceeding.
- No alternative exists that would effectively eliminate the threat to fairness.
- Closure will effectively eliminate the threat to fairness.
- Closure will be narrowly tailored to eliminate the threat while protecting the greatest public access to the judicial process.

The Court also has said judges may not close any part of a trial unless they first allow interested parties and the public to raise objections to the proposed closure.

Despite this high standard, courts continue to close their doors and seal their records. When media mogul and home décor guru Martha Stewart was tried for securities fraud a decade ago, the trial court barred the media from attending jury selection and from contacting potential jurors. In response to a media challenge to the closure, the federal court of appeals found the trial judge's actions unconstitutional, writing that

> No right is more sacred in our constitutional firmament than that of the accused to a fair trial. Our national experience instructs us that except in rare circumstances openness preserves, indeed, is essential to, the realization of that right and to public confidence in the administration of justice. The burden is heavy on those who seek to restrict access to the media, a vital means to open justice. . . . The mere fact of intense media coverage of a celebrity defendant, without further compelling justification, is simply not enough to justify closure.[49]

In a second 2010 ruling on access to courts, the U.S. Supreme Court issued an emergency stay to prevent the broadcast of a federal district court trial on California's ballot measure banning same-sex marriage.[50] The Court barred cameras on the grounds that the lower court failed to "follow the appropriate procedures set forth in federal law" for allowing broadcasts and because camera coverage might increase the potential harassment of trial participants. The trial judge subsequently ruled that the ban violated the civil rights of gay Californians, and the state declined to pursue an appeal to defend the ballot measure.[51]

Points of Law

The *Press-Enterprise* Test for Court Closure

Under the Supreme Court test developed in the mid-1980s in *Press-Enterprise (II) v. Superior Court*, an individual seeking to close open court records or proceedings, including pretrial hearings, must provide the following:

1. Specific, on-the-record findings that there is a "substantial probability" that openness will jeopardize the defendant's right to a fair trial, and

2. Convincing evidence that closure is "essential" to preserve the trial's fairness.[1]

---

1. 478 U.S. 1 (1986).

Does Publicity Bias Jurors?

Some experts argue that court strategies to ensure the fairness of trials are more than adequate to counteract any harmful effects of media coverage on the fair trial rights of defendants. "We believe pretrial publicity does not usually bias decisions in actual cases because of the care courts take to apply remedies," two legal scholars concluded.[1]

They say pretrial publicity alters the outcome of a trial only in very narrow and rare circumstances. Those rare conditions occur only when the following apply:

- Jurors are exposed to pretrial publicity.

- The evidence in court does not point convincingly to a clear verdict.

- The information provided by the media seems better—more convincing, more likely or more reliable—than the evidence presented in court.

- The media consistently lean toward one verdict.

- All the remedies available to the court fail at the same time.

1. Jon Bruschke & William E. Loges, Free Press vs. Fair Trials: Examining Publicity's Role in Trial Outcomes 134–37 (2004).

A number of courts have closed their doors and sealed their files in cases related to new media and the computer industry. In what has been called the "landmark monopolization case of the 21st Century"[52] between computer industry giant Intel and its chief competitor, Advanced Micro Devices (AMD), a virtual who's who of elite media in the United States filed a motion to unseal records.[53] The media coalition argued that the court's sweeping closure order improperly shielded Intel business practices from public scrutiny. Although the parties settled, with Intel agreeing to new business practices and payment of $1.25 billion to AMD, the court proceedings included sealing "hundreds of millions of pages of documentation" to safeguard the companies' trade secrets and facilitate discovery as well as a ruling that opened Intel international business documents to discovery and Intel's "loss" of substantial internal company communication related to the case and sought under discovery.[54] In an earlier related case brought before the European Union's antitrust tribunal, AMD had sought some 600,000 pages of discovery records through the U.S. courts. Although the lower courts denied the request, the U.S. Supreme Court ordered disclosure on the grounds that nothing in the relevant federal statute limited disclosure to proceedings in U.S. courts.[55]

In a case involving social media, one federal judge closed the courtroom and sealed documents to protect the business secrets of Facebook and ConnectU. Another federal judge sealed the courtroom and records to shield trade secrets in a lawsuit brought by the Motion Picture Association of America (MPAA) to prevent RealDVD from selling decryption software.[56] The case settled in 2010, with RealDVD agreeing not to sell its software and to pay MPAA's court costs.[57]

The Supreme Court has not ruled directly on whether hearings to consider the suppression of evidence or plea bargains must be open. The American Bar Association argues that these hearings also are presumptively open, but at least one federal appeals court has upheld the authority of judges to hold conferences in closed chambers or conduct whispered bench conferences in the courtroom with the lawyers during the trial. Courts also recognize and protect the secrecy of jury deliberations. Narrowly drawn orders to protect jury deliberation by preventing jurors from discussing key aspects of other jurors' comments in a specific case—particularly when the case may be appealed or reheard—may be constitutional.

Although the broad right of public access extends to virtually all criminal trial proceedings, some related procedures generally are closed. Thus, grand jury hearings, which determine whether an individual should be indicted and prosecuted for a crime, generally are closed. The long-standing tradition of secret grand jury proceedings also generally seals all grand jury documents. However, the Supreme Court said a state may not punish grand jury witnesses who discuss their own testimony after the conclusion of a grand jury investigation.[58]

A solo-authored "in chambers" opinion denying certiorari to a press appeal challenging two Florida court orders related to publication of leaked grand jury transcripts is the Supreme Court's most recent word on access to grand jury testimony.[59] The initial Florida court order directed that "no party shall further disclose the contents of the transcript of testimony before the grand jury." When the press appealed, however, the court said its order applied only to "the parties to this action" and the appellants were neither "precluded or restrained from publishing matters which are public record, nor . . . enjoined or restrained from broadcasting matters in this case."[60]

In his opinion, Justice Anthony Kennedy denied review of the order "despite indications that a prior restraint may have been imposed" because the record did not sufficiently establish either that the order enjoined the appellant or imposed a real harm. Nonetheless, his analysis noted that

> [a] threat of prosecution or criminal contempt against a specific publication raises special First Amendment concerns, for it may chill protected speech much like an injunction against speech by putting that party at an added risk of liability. The court's first order was not accompanied by notice or hearing or any other of the usual safeguards of the judicial process. It bears many of the marks of a prior restraint. . . . The first order is of further concern because it singles out this applicant and could be interpreted to place it on notice that publication of grant jury testimony in the underlying case could subject it to prosecution or place it in contempt of court.[61]

Closure to Protect Juveniles

Courts generally recognize that different public interests may apply to legal proceedings involving juveniles. On one hand, the public has a legitimate interest in access to juvenile proceedings, and open proceedings may provide all the benefits that accrue in open judicial processes for adults. On the other, government also has a substantial interest in restricting exposure of juvenile defendants and witnesses to reduce potential trauma and stigma to the juvenile and to facilitate his or her rehabilitation.

As far back as 1966, the Supreme Court expressed concern that individuals in the juvenile justice system do not necessarily receive either the due process protections provided to adults or the care and rehabilitation intended for children. The Court said juvenile court procedures must assure that minors receive the full "reach of constitutional guarantees applicable to adults."[62] The next year, the Supreme Court decided that the rights of juvenile defendants include the right to counsel and notice, but the Court failed to determine whether juvenile proceedings must be open to the public.[63] Elsewhere the Court has reasoned that confidential juvenile processes, particularly to shield them from media scrutiny, has played an important historical role in reducing the stigmatization of minors.[64]

Today, most federal courts do not consider juvenile proceedings to be presumptively open. Instead, federal law permits but does not require closure of juvenile proceedings. As a result, federal judges may close juvenile proceedings and records on a case-by-case basis. This is true in some states as well. Although most states bar cameras from juvenile courts[65] and about a third of the states, including Alaska and South Carolina, presume that juvenile proceedings are closed,[66] juvenile court judges are propelling a growing movement to open juvenile proceedings.[67] As Minnesota was considering broader access to its juvenile records, a juvenile advocacy group challenged a California judge's decision to open Los Angeles juvenile courts.[68]

Some states provide a broad right of public access to juvenile courts.[69] Washington state law, for example, presumes that juvenile proceedings will be open: "The general public and press shall be permitted to attend any hearing unless the court, for good cause, orders a particular hearing to be closed."[70] Juvenile courts in Colorado, Florida and New Mexico also operate with a presumption of openness, but an Ohio Supreme Court ruling established that the openness of juvenile proceedings is determined through balancing of the public and private interests involved.[71]

All states allow certain juveniles to be treated as adults within the justice system, but Maryland, New Jersey and Wisconsin may prohibit the media from revealing the identity of a juvenile.[72] News reporters who legally obtain information about the juvenile or the proceeding from sources outside the juvenile court process generally may publish the information without fear of punishment. A recent Massachusetts Supreme Court decision confirmed that courts in that state cannot ban media from releasing the name of a minor obtained legally through reporting on the courts.[73] The state's high court said that although it was "probably unwise" for the court in question to allow a live-streaming broadcaster to record a juvenile hearing, "the prior restraint doctrine" prevented the court from "restrain[ing] the publication of the recording" without

Access to Juvenile Delinquency Hearings

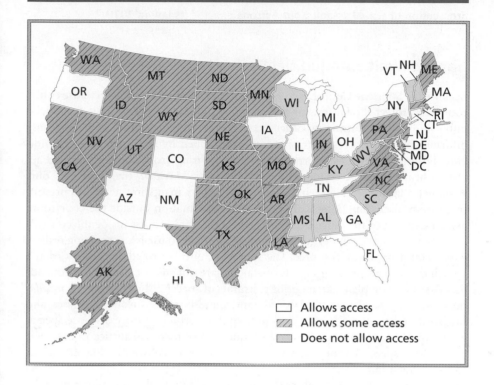

Allows access
Allows some access
Does not allow access

"detailed findings of fact" demonstrating that no less restrictive alternative means was available.

Reporters should consult the specific laws of their states to determine their right of access, and those interested in multistate comparisons may turn to a 2012 report on juvenile justice produced by the Reporters Committee for Freedom of the Press and regular reports from the National Center for Juvenile Justice.[74]

Closure to Protect Sexual Assault Victims

Related issues arise frequently in cases of sexual assault, where open courts and press coverage are widely perceived to aggravate the injury to the victim. Every state and the District of Columbia has a rape shield law intended to protect the alleged victim from questions about sexual history and other topics likely to prejudice jurors against the victim.[75] With the exception of Mississippi, every state has a statute making evidence of the complaining witness's past sexual activity generally inadmissible in court.[76] A few states also exclude opinion or evidence of the complainant's chastity, past relations with the defendant and manner of dress. Some of these laws also shield the victim's identity and other personal information in much the same way courts protect children's legal rights to privacy.[77] Most states enacted the statutes in the 1970s in order to encourage women to report and support the prosecution of sexual assaults, but Arizona enacted its law in 2010.[78]

Gags to Limit Extrajudicial Discussion

restraining order A court order forbidding an individual or group of individuals from doing a specified act until a hearing can be conducted.

Because the Supreme Court has found it generally unconstitutional to close courtrooms to protect the fairness of a trial, many judges attempt to limit prejudicial publicity by using **restraining orders** to prevent trial participants from disclosing information to the press. A restraining order issued by a court forbids an individual or group (such as attorneys engaged in a trial) from doing a specified act until a hearing can be conducted. In *Sheppard v. Maxwell,* the Supreme Court suggested that judges use their authority over participants in the trial to prevent them from discussing potentially prejudicial information outside the courtroom as an extension of the judge's duty to protect the trial process inside the court.

Gag orders, the non-legal term journalists prefer to use for restraining orders, control information at its source. The Supreme Court has ruled that court-ordered speech restrictions on attorneys during a trial are not subject to the First Amendment's nearly complete ban on prior restraints of speech.[79] In *Mu'Min v. Virginia,* the Court reasoned that the lawyers, and quite possibly jurors, witnesses and other trial participants, are insiders to a vital government process whose special access to sensitive information and unique power to derail justice opens their trial-related speech to court control when it poses a "substantial likelihood" of jeopardizing a fair trial.[80]

Gags may ban some or all of the participants in a trial from talking with the media about the trial. They also may target specific individuals or limit discussion of particular topics or information. Gag orders on trial participants generally are upheld on appeal if the judge has considered alternatives, narrowly drawn the restrictions and demonstrated through evidence that media coverage poses a substantial likelihood of jeopardizing a fair trial. Narrowly drawn restraining orders generally end as soon as the threat to the trial process passes. Thus, the Supreme Court has struck down a state ban on grand jury witnesses discussing their testimony even after the grand jury proceeding has ended.[81]

In high-profile cases such as the trial of suspected Aurora, Colo., theater shooter James Egan Holmes, judges concerned about the potential damaging influence of pretrial publicity may issue gag orders on all parties to the trial. Thus, in 2012, after both the prosecutor and the attorneys for the defense sought to keep evidence in the *Holmes* case secret to protect a fair trial, Circuit Judge William Sylvester issued a sweeping gag order prohibiting all parties and the University of Colorado, where Holmes was a student, from disseminating any information on the case.[82] The Reporters Committee for Freedom of the Press called the order "very broad," "highly unorthodox" and "overly aggressive" and argued that the result of the information blackout was not silence but "strategic, anonymous leaks of information designed to benefit one side or the other." [83]

Gag orders on media prohibit publication or discussion of specific materials. Court orders that directly bar the media from publicizing legally obtained information about ongoing trials are rarely constitutional because they are seen as prior restraints on speech.[84] The Supreme Court's 1976 decision in *Nebraska Press Association v. Stuart* called gags on the press an extraordinary remedy and held such gags to be presumptively unconstitutional.[85] The case involved the murders of six family members in a tiny rural town in Nebraska. The day after the murders, a 30-year-old neighbor turned himself in to police and confessed to the crime. National news media converged on the town, and the judge ordered the media not to publish information obtained during the pretrial proceedings.

The judge then issued an order barring publication of the confession or of lab test results relating to a sexual assault of one of the victims. Moreover, the judge required the media to observe the voluntary Nebraska Bar/Press Guidelines. The guidelines, endorsed by the state bar (attorney's group) and media, encouraged the press not to publish information about confessions, opinions of guilt or innocence, the results of lab tests, comments on witness credibility or other statements that reasonably would be expected to influence the outcome of the trial. The state press association appealed the restraining order, which the Nebraska Supreme Court upheld.

The U.S. Supreme Court reversed. The Court classified gag orders on the media as the type of prior restraint that is the most serious and least tolerable infringement on First Amendment freedoms. Consequently, judges who impose restraining orders directly on the press bear a heavy burden of showing that media coverage is likely to pose a substantial threat to the fair trial. Courts must consider three things when determining whether a press gag may be constitutional: (1) the quantity and content of media coverage, (2) the potential effectiveness of alternatives to a gag, and (3) the likelihood that a gag would remedy the harmful publicity.

Before issuing an order that prohibits media from disclosing information obtained in open court, judges must show with compelling evidence that the gag narrowly targets information that poses a clear and present danger to a fair trial. The gag must also be a last resort intended to protect the fair trial. Only the most narrowly tailored gags on media are constitutional. This test is very difficult to meet, and constitutionally valid gag orders against news media are rare.

In one such rare example, a federal appeals court upheld a temporary gag order after then Panamanian ruler Gen. Manuel Noriega was overthrown, seized and transferred to the United States to face trial on federal trafficking and racketeering charges.[86] CNN had obtained copies of tape recordings of conversations between Noriega and his defense attorneys while in U.S. custody and intended to

Points of Law

Closing Media Mouths: The *Nebraska Press* Standard

In the wake of *Nebraska Press Association v. Stuart*, a judge must justify orders that prevent media disclosure of information produced in court with convincing evidence of the following:

1. Disclosure of the protected information would present a substantial threat to a fair trial.

2. There is no effective alternative to a gag on the press.

3. The gag will effectively eliminate the danger to the fair trial, and

4. The gag is narrowly tailored to restrict only the information that must be kept secret.

realWorld Law

Open Your Mouth and Open Courts

The Federal Judicial Center provides information to enable citizens and reporters alike to help maintain the openness of judicial proceedings by attending court processes and objecting to any improper attempts at closure.[1] If you wish to object to the closing of records or court processes, the Society of Professional Journalists (SPJ) recommends you stand, receive the judge's recognition and permission to speak, and say the following:

> I respectfully protest closure of [this record or this proceeding]. The U.S. Supreme Court has ruled that the First Amendment forbids exclusion of the public from pretrial and trial proceedings without findings of fact identifying the overriding interest to be protected and the necessity of closure to protect that interest.
>
> The Court has also ruled openness is a constitutional presumption. More than speculation or conclusory assertion of harm is required to justify closure. I ask the court to follow the rulings of the U.S. Supreme Court.

Or, if you plan to involve an attorney, then you might say,

> I request that the court delay further proceedings to allow time for counsel to appear and file a motion in opposition to closure.

Finally, if you actually are barred from entering the courtroom, you may write a note using one of the two statements above and give it to the bailiff or clerk to provide to the judge. As a reporter, you likely will want to file a story on the closure as well!

---

1. SEALING COURT RECORDS AND PROCEEDINGS: A POCKET GUIDE (2010), *available at* http://www.fjc.gov/public/pdf.nsf/lookup/sealing_guide .pdf/$file/sealing_guide.pdf.

broadcast them. The defense successfully argued that disclosure of the privileged communications would have serious adverse effects on the fairness of the trial. When, despite the court's gag, CNN aired portions of the tapes, it was convicted of criminal contempt[87] even though the court, upon review, found the tapes prejudiced neither the fair trial nor Noriega's right to effective counsel.[88] Rather than pay an undetermined but hefty fine, CNN agreed to the trial judge's alternative sentence; it broadcast an admission of guilt and apology for violating the court's order.[89]

A few years earlier, the Supreme Court upheld a restraining order that prevented two newspapers from publicizing a confidential membership and donor list of a religious group that was disclosed through the discovery in a libel lawsuit.[90] After the lawsuit, the newspapers sought to use the donor and membership information in news reports. But the Court refused to allow that, ruling that because the information was made available to the newspapers through a trial proceeding, it could not be used beyond the context of the trial. The Court unanimously ruled that the restraining order was constitutional, in part because it did not prohibit the newspapers from publishing the same information if they could obtain it in another way. The Court said the order simply prevented the newspapers from improperly using the legal discovery process as a reporting tool.

Challenging Closure

The media, like all members of the public, have a right to challenge court closures. They may ask a judge not to seal records or not to close any proceeding during the criminal process. Such requests should be made in open court. In general, individuals should stand and request recognition by the presiding judge and then simply state an objection to the closure. As an alternative, anyone may request that the court delay proceedings so they can seek the advice of an attorney in order to file an objection to the closure.

SUMMARY

THE U.S. SUPREME COURT HAS DETERMINED that the right to an open public trial belongs to the public as well as the defendant. Three decades ago, the Supreme Court established that the First Amendment and common law provide a public right to attend criminal trials and many of the hearings integral to trial proceedings. The presumption of open proceedings extends to pretrial hearings and voir dire. It may also include other historically open proceedings. An individual seeking to close a criminal trial must show with clear evidence that closure is vital to serve a compelling government interest, such as the fairness of the trial. Closures must be limited in scope and duration to provide the broadest possible public access. Grand jury proceedings are closed, as are some juvenile proceedings. Laws that automatically close parts of trials are not constitutional. Court restraining orders that limit public discussion of trials to reduce prejudicial publicity generally are constitutional if a substantial likelihood exists that publicity would harm the fair trial rights of the defendants. Direct gags on the media rarely are constitutional. Trial observers may challenge the closure of court sessions as individuals or through attorneys. ■

Electronic Access to Trials

The Supreme Court has said the Sixth Amendment prevents judges from imposing outright bans on media coverage of trials because the media, like the public, have a right to access and scrutinize the judicial system. Open courtrooms are essential to the fairness of the courts and to the public's faith in the judicial system. But openness and access are not absolute. Judges may limit the number of media representatives in the courtroom, and they may exclude cameras and recording devices to prevent disruptions and distractions, protect the fairness of the trial and ensure the solemnity of the proceedings.

Broadcasting and Recording

In 1981, the U.S. Supreme Court said the right of access to public trials did not include a promise of access for cameras.[91] In *Chandler v. Florida,* the Court even then recognized that technological advances had decreased (and likely would continue to decrease) the intrusiveness of cameras so that they were no longer inherently prejudicial, but the Court said individual states should determine whether to permit cameras in courtrooms. The Court reasoned that coverage by print alone sufficiently protected the interests of the media and the public in open trials. The Court raised concerns that are voiced even today that electronic media subtly alter the trial process and influence participants in unpredictable ways.

Debate over the costs and benefits of covering courts with cameras and other new technologies continues, with Supreme Court justices voicing the most virulent objection to broadcast of their proceedings. Studies of the effects on courts of accelerating news cycles, 24-hour news coverage, citizen blogs, live audio and webcasts and other "new media" mechanisms abound. Some have found that such media do not fulfill their potential to serve the public. Another reported that rather than inform and educate the public, cameras in courts sensationalize, focus selectively and present fleeting, dramatic images of the most accessible portions of trials with little or no context.[92]

Cameras in Federal Courts

U.S. Supreme Court	no cameras
U.S. Circuit Courts	civil trials at judges' discretion; barred from criminal proceedings by the Federal Rule of Criminal Procedure 53
U.S. District Courts	three-year pilot project begun in 2011 in 14 districts to assess impact of cameras on civil trials
The Participating Courts are	Middle District of Alabama Northern District of California Southern District of Florida District of Guam Northern District of Illinois Southern District of Iowa District of Kansas District of Massachusetts Eastern District of Missouri District of Nebraska Northern District of Ohio Southern District of Ohio Western District of Tennessee Western District of Washington

Source: Cameras and Electronic Devices in the Federal Courtroom, FED. EVIDENCE REV. (n.d.), available at http://federalevidence.com/node/1345.

Nonetheless, pressures to broadcast federal court proceedings continue to increase. In response, the U.S. Judicial Conference launched a three-year pilot project in fourteen districts[93] to assess the impact of cameras in civil proceedings in federal courts.[94] Amid prolonged contention over the proper implementation of this pilot project in California, the Ninth Circuit Court of Appeals said court recordings should remain sealed because the judge in charge of the recording had made "express assurances" that they would not be released to the public.[95] Despite assuming both a common-law and First Amendment right of access to the court recordings, the Ninth Circuit said the judge's promise provided a sufficiently compelling reason to overcome the public's right to access.

In most state courts and federal courts of appeals, judges generally do permit cameras in the courtroom at least some of the time. Camera access to state courts generally is determined at the discretion of the presiding judge, with court rules determining the conditions under which cameras may be allowed. Many states limit the number and location of cameras. Florida courts, however, for years have assumed that access for recording equipment is essential to reporting by television and radio journalists and serves both the courts and the public.

In 2012, Massachusetts issued new rules establishing access for journalists with still, audio and video recording and transmitting devices and laptop computers with some limitations, including exclusion given evidence of a "substantial likelihood of harm" or a necessity to protect fair trial rights.[96] South Dakota modified its rules allowing extended broadcast coverage of trials with the consent of the judge and all parties, except that no recording is allowed of jurors or proceedings when the jury is excluded.[97] In contrast, the Illinois code of judicial conduct limits broadcasting or television of court proceedings to "the extent authorized by order of the Supreme Court"[98] and prohibits broadcasting or recording of any compelled witness testimony.[99]

Federal Rule of Criminal Procedure 53 generally prohibits cameras in federal criminal trial courts, and federal policy bans televised civil proceedings. However, the 13 federal circuit courts of appeal each may decide whether to allow televised or other news media coverage of oral arguments. The circuits vary in their policies, with the Fifth Circuit Court of Appeals forbidding broadcasts and the Second Circuit Court of Appeals allowing cameras during oral arguments that do not involve criminal matters. Congress has considered, but not passed, bills that would give judges in federal courts discretion to permit the photographing, electronic recording, broadcasting or televising of court proceedings.

Despite experience and studies indicating that unobtrusive cameras in courtrooms have only a minimal effect upon jurors, some judges believe that cameras influence the testimony of witnesses, discourage some witnesses from testifying, encourage theatrics in the courtroom and change the attitudes and behavior of jurors and other trial participants. The U.S. Supreme Court is famous for its dislike of cameras. Neither still nor video cameras are permitted in the U.S. Supreme Court.

State-by-State Media Access to Juvenile Offender Identities

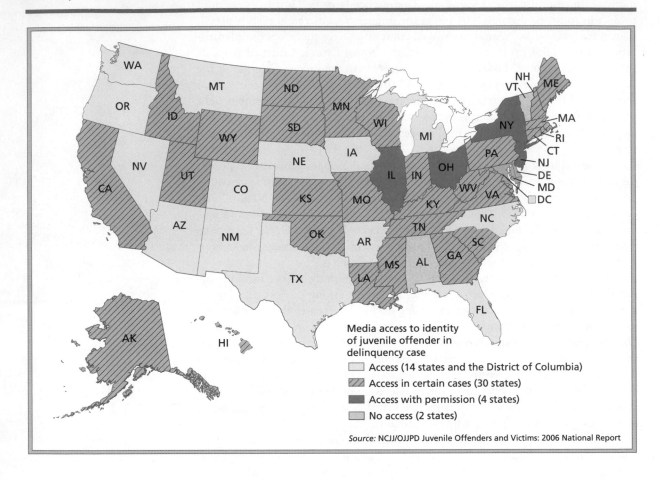

Media access to identity of juvenile offender in delinquency case

- Access (14 states and the District of Columbia)
- Access in certain cases (30 states)
- Access with permission (4 states)
- No access (2 states)

Source: NCJJ/OJJPD Juvenile Offenders and Victims: 2006 National Report

Cameras and Courtrooms

C-SPAN's request to broadcast the oral arguments before the Supreme Court in the case that effectively determined the outcome of the 2000 U.S. presidential election was denied. In rejecting the request, then Chief Justice William Rehnquist said the ban on cameras reflected the view of a majority of the Court's nine justices. Immediately after oral arguments, however, the Court took the unprecedented step of releasing an audiotape of the arguments that permitted media to broadcast audio of the hearings the same day they occurred. During its 2010–11 term, the U.S. Supreme Court began releasing audio recordings of the oral arguments for every case heard the previous week on each Friday of the term.

Cameras are allowed in some courtrooms some of the time in all 50 states. Some of this access is long-standing, some is experimental, some is broad and

realWorld Law

Cameras or Coroners in the Court?

As long as one or more sitting justices remains adamantly opposed to cameras in the U.S. Supreme Court, lower court judges feel secure in banning electronic media coverage of their proceedings. Former Justice David Souter is famous for his 1996 statement to Congress opposing cameras in the high court: "The day you see a camera coming into our courtroom, it's going to roll over my dead body."[1] A decade later, after his first term on the Court, Chief Justice John Roberts told a conference of judges that the Supreme Court might never allow cameras into its proceedings. "We don't have oral arguments to show people, the public, how we function," he said. We are "trustees of an extremely valuable institution, . . . [and] we're going to be very careful before we do anything that will have an adverse impact on that."[2]

1. Marcia Coyle, *Justices Voice Extralegal Musings,* Nat'l L.J., Apr. 22, 1996, at A16; *see also* Tim O'Brien, *High Court TV,* N.Y. Times, Jan. 6, 1997, at A17.
2. Associated Press, *Chief Justice Says Court Not Interested in Allowing Cameras* (July 16, 2006), *available at* http://www.first amendmentcenter.org/news.aspx?id=17161.

U.S. Supreme Court Justice David Souter

some is extremely limited. Roughly 20 states are extremely permissive when it comes to television cameras in the courtroom. In Florida, for example, a judicially created presumption permits camera coverage of virtually all cases.[100] In Mississippi, the law generally allows cameras that do not disrupt the proceedings. Applying this standard in a 2005 case, the Mississippi Supreme Court overturned a circuit judge's ruling prohibiting television coverage of the sentencing phase of a conspiracy case.

In overturning the ban, Mississippi's highest court noted that exclusion of cameras restricts public access and should be a last resort. The court wrote that

> The proper standard for restricting press coverage is that there is a "substantial probability" that the accused will be deprived of a fair trial. . . . The decision to restrict press access, whether by closing proceedings or by eliminating the use of the tools of the trade must be supported by specific, on the record findings of fact which show in what manner the coverage will cause a party to lose the right to a fair trial.[101]

States from Alabama to Utah limit camera coverage of trials based on the type of case or the ages of the witnesses involved. In nine states, judges who permit cameras in the courtroom may limit their number and location, prohibit recording of jurors or especially vulnerable witnesses, such as children, or require broadcast reporters to pool cameras. Pool reporting may be used in extremely high-profile cases to limit the media swarm in the courtroom. In another six states, including Delaware and Illinois, courts are virtually closed

Emerging Law

Tea Leaves, Cameras and Inevitability

In 2012, Supreme Court Justice Sonia Sotomayor publicly reversed her position supporting cameras in the courtroom. "I think the process could be more misleading than helpful," she said. "It's like reading tea leaves."[1] In contrast, Justice Stephen G. Breyer has said increased media coverage could be "helpful" and offers "tremendous potential in getting across the message [about the justice system] that might be oppressed."[2]

Despite bipartisan support in Congress and the media, and public and legislative requests that the Court allow cameras, the Supreme Court camera ban continues, with only 50 seats set aside for public viewing of Court sessions.[3] Early in 2013, Congress reintroduced the Cameras in the Courtroom Act of 2011 to require the Supreme Court to allow television coverage of all open Court sessions unless a majority of the justices voted to close the Court to protect specific due process interests.[4]

U.S. Supreme Court Justice Sonia Sotomayor

One observer said the Court's exclusion of cameras is anachronistic and motivated by "fear of change, nostalgia, a self-interested desire for anonymity, but most of all exceptionalism: the Court's view of itself as a unique institution that can and should resist the demands of the information age."[5] He argued that Congress has the power to mandate camera access. But several observers, including Justice Anthony Kennedy, said congressional action would violate established "etiquette" if not the letter of the law mandating separation of power between the two branches.

"It is inevitable that television will be in the Supreme Court," another attorney said, "and I would not provoke the constitutional controversy of requiring them to do it."[6]

---

1. Sam Baker, *Justice Sotomayor No Longer Backs Television Cameras in Supreme Court* (Feb. 7, 2013), *available at* http://thehill.com/homenews/news/281765-sotomayor-no-longer-backs-cameras-in-supreme-court.
2. La Monica Everett-Haynes, *Experts Evaluate the "New Media" and Courts,* Univ. of Ariz. News, Sept. 9, 2008, *available at* http://uanews.org/node/21471.
3. *Battles to Gain Camera/Audio Access to State And Federal Courtrooms Continue,* Silha Bull., Fall 2011.
4. *Connolly Sponsors Bill to Allow Cameras in U.S. Supreme Court Proceedings* (Jan. 4, 2013), *available at* http://connolly.house.gov/news/connolly-sponsors-bill-to-allow-cameras-in-us-supreme-court-proceedings/.
5. Anthony E. Mauro, *Let the Cameras Roll: Cameras in the Court and the Myth of Supreme Court Exceptionalism,* 1 Reynolds Cts. & Media L.J. 259 (2011).
6. *Id.*

---

to cameras. Because state laws vary widely on their standards for cameras in courtrooms, reporters must be familiar with the details of the laws in the states where they report.

In addition to their variety, state laws on cameras in courtrooms are a moving target. Several state legislatures have formed judicial committees to review the effects of current state laws on access and to recommend modifications if needed. For example, a Maryland committee recently recommended that the state retain its ban on cameras in criminal trials. The committee reported that "the putative benefits of electronic media coverage are illusory, while the adverse impacts on the criminal justice process are real."[102]

Emerging Law

Social Media Invasion

"Has the jury tweeted a verdict?"

© www.CartoonStock.com

The defense in the Trayvon Martin murder case embraced social media to counter an "avalanche of misinformation" disseminated through the media about defendant George Zimmerman.[1] The trial court judge twice refused to bar defense attorney Mark O'Mara from using a website, a Twitter page and a Facebook account to rebuff negative coverage of Zimmerman,[2] and the court provided the defense with access to Martin's school and social media records.[3]

Martin's family had used Twitter first to bring attention to the 17-year-old's death, and social media galvanized the public after it learned Martin was unarmed when he was killed in Florida in 2012. But as the case progressed, both the prosecution and the defense "agree[d] that social media [were] playing a highly invasive role in the court proceedings and [might] even affect the outcome."[4]

O'Mara suggested that, absent social media, his client "may never have been charged" with second-degree murder. In contrast, the prosecution said social media had focused the whole world on the case to see whether U.S. law provides equal justice for all. When Zimmerman was found not guilty in 2013, public response to the verdict focused on the influence of race rather than on the impact of new media coverage.[5]

In other cases, judges have confiscated juror cellphones and laptops to stop sitting jurors from posting comments on Facebook and Twitter.[5] Future decisions will need to determine how best to assess and deal with the effects of social media on ongoing trials.

1. Lizette Alvarez, *Social Media, Growing in Legal Circles, Find a Role in Florida Murder Case* (Nov. 7, 2012), *available at* http://www.nytimes.com/2012/11/07/us/social-media-finds-a-role-in-case-against-zimmerman.html?pagewanted=all&_r=0.
2. Lizette Alvarez, *Judge in Trayvon Martin Case Denies Request for Silence* (Oct. 30, 2012), A-16, *available at* http://www.nytimes.com/2012/10/30/us/judge-in-trayvon-martin-case-denies-request-for-silence.html.
3. Yamiche Alcindor, *Trayvon Martin's Postings, Records Spark Court Debate* (Oct. 19, 2012), *available at* http://www.usatoday.com/story/news/nation/2012/10/19/trayvon-zimmerman-sanford-racial/1644403/.
4. Heather Manes, *Lawyers of Trayvon Martin Case Lament Social Media Engagement* (Apr. 28, 2013), *available at* http://www.opposingviews.com/i/money/jobs-and-careers/lawyers-trayvon-martin-case-lament-social-media-engagement.
5. *See, e.g.,* Tom Foreman, Analysis: *The Race Factor in George Zimmerman's Trial* (July 15, 2013), *available at* http://www.cnn.com/2013/07/14/justice/zimmerman-race-factor.

Newer Technologies

Although the executive and legislative branches of government have run willingly toward new technologies to transform their ways of doing business, the courts have lagged behind. Claims that "social media is the new norm" in courts still struggling to adapt to cameras overstate the slow evolution of U.S. courts.[103] However, new media are making inroads and offering both new opportunities and new challenges to the administration of justice, and a variety of judicial and extrajudicial groups, including journalists, have begun exploring how to leverage the opportunities and minimize the risks of new media in the courts.

Video, Audio and Webcasts of State Courtrooms[104]

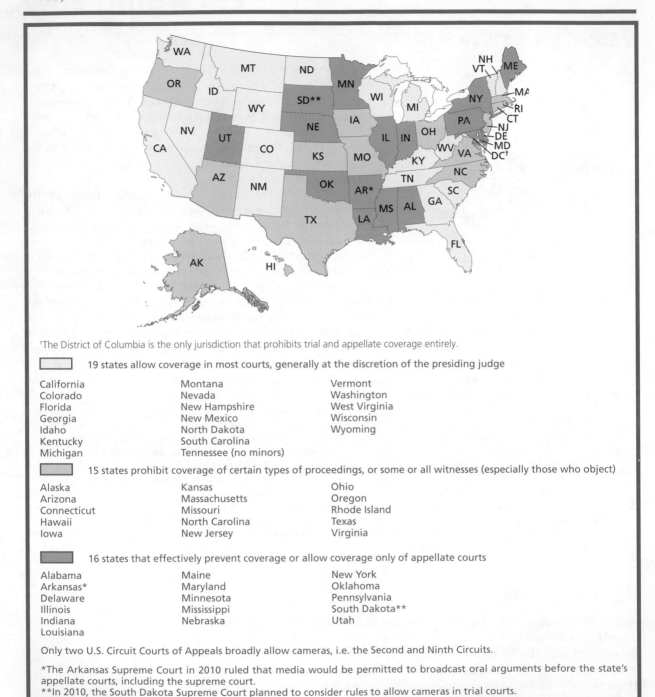

†The District of Columbia is the only jurisdiction that prohibits trial and appellate coverage entirely.

19 states allow coverage in most courts, generally at the discretion of the presiding judge

California	Montana	Vermont
Colorado	Nevada	Washington
Florida	New Hampshire	West Virginia
Georgia	New Mexico	Wisconsin
Idaho	North Dakota	Wyoming
Kentucky	South Carolina	
Michigan	Tennessee (no minors)	

15 states prohibit coverage of certain types of proceedings, or some or all witnesses (especially those who object)

Alaska	Kansas	Ohio
Arizona	Massachusetts	Oregon
Connecticut	Missouri	Rhode Island
Hawaii	North Carolina	Texas
Iowa	New Jersey	Virginia

16 states that effectively prevent coverage or allow coverage only of appellate courts

Alabama	Maine	New York
Arkansas*	Maryland	Oklahoma
Delaware	Minnesota	Pennsylvania
Illinois	Mississippi	South Dakota**
Indiana	Nebraska	Utah
Louisiana		

Only two U.S. Circuit Courts of Appeals broadly allow cameras, i.e. the Second and Ninth Circuits.

*The Arkansas Supreme Court in 2010 ruled that media would be permitted to broadcast oral arguments before the state's appellate courts, including the supreme court.
**In 2010, the South Dakota Supreme Court planned to consider rules to allow cameras in trial courts.

Source: Cameras in the Court: A State-By-State Guide (Nov. 15–26, 2012), available at http://rtdna.org/article/cameras_in_the_court_a_state_by_state_guide_updated#.Uielybx1Ets.

realWorld Law

Managing New Media in Courts

From left, Ramzi Binalshibh, Walid bin Attash and the self-proclaimed terrorist mastermind Khalid Sheikh Mohammed, sit with laptops at hand while attending a hearing on pretrial motions in their death penalty case at the Guantanamo Bay U.S. Naval Base in Cuba in 2013.

Amid broad disagreement and growing trends both in favor of and against the use of new media in courts, the Media Law Resource Center in 2010 proposed a model policy for court use of electronic media. The first portion of the policy deals with new technologies in the administrative and public areas of the courts. The second section dealing with new media in courtrooms reads as follows:

1. Inside courtrooms, persons may use an electronic device to silently take notes and/or transmit and receive data communications in the form of text, only, without need for obtaining prior authorization from the presiding judge or judicial officer.

2. A judge or other judicial officer may prohibit or further restrict use of electronic devices if they interfere with the administration of justice, pose any threat to safety or security, or compromise the integrity of the proceeding.

3. It should be anticipated that reporters, bloggers and other observers seated in the courtroom may use electronic devices to prepare and post online news accounts and commentary during the proceedings. Absent any of the circumstances identified above in paragraph [2], such use is presumptively permitted.[1]

1. Media Law Resource Center, Newsgathering Committee Defense Counsel Section (2010), *available at* http://www.medialaw .org/Content/NavigationMenu/Member_Resources/Litigation_Resources/Litigation_Resources.htm.

Courts across the country, led by California and Massachusetts, are developing strategies to integrate new communication technologies into their administrative offices and courtrooms and beginning to establish a presence on Facebook, Twitter, YouTube and other social media sites as a component of their efforts to reach and educate the public. Courts use blogs, embedded video, closed-circuit coverage of sensitive witnesses and other media techniques to facilitate operations and connect with a public that increasingly expects instant access. Some state and federal courts allow reporters to webcast and use social media posts to provide play-by-play coverage of unfolding trials.[105] One judge—overseeing a $1 million recording industry lawsuit against a Boston University student for copyright infringement by intentional unauthorized downloading and sharing of songs through KaZaA—said nothing in local rules or in "life or logic" prevents live-streamed access to court proceedings, especially in a case with implications for digital access.[106] However, when the U.S. Court of Appeals for the First Circuit heard the student's appeal of a $675,000 penalty for the illegal downloading and sharing of 30 songs, that court refused to allow webcasting of the appeal.[107] The fine later was reduced to $67,500.[108]

At the same time, courts were struggling to determine the boundaries of appropriate use of new media records as evidence at trial. In 2009, responding to worries that texting and "tweets" threatened the sanctity of the judicial process, the Michigan Supreme Court became the first to ban all electronic communication by jurors during trials, and a number of courts declared mistrials because of juror use of new media during trial.[109] In the second decade of the 21st century, such bans were spreading across the country.[110]

SUMMARY

ALTHOUGH THE SUPREME COURT HAS RULED THAT CAMERAS are not inherently prejudicial to fair trials, judges in many courts have discretion to permit, deny or delineate the ability of cameras and other electronic technologies to cover court proceedings. Electronic access to courts varies widely based on distinct court rules and policies established at either the federal or state level. Most courts allow some electronic coverage during some of their proceedings, but federal trial courts generally are closed to cameras. Judges, attorneys and scholars continue to debate the costs and benefits of real-time coverage of trials, with some jurisdictions expanding experiments with cameras and Web coverage, others moving away, and still others waiting to see the effects of ongoing experiments. ∎

Bench-Bar-Press Guidelines

In the years following *Sheppard v. Maxwell,* state media groups, bar associations and members of the judiciary developed cooperative agreements to guide reporting on the courts. In general, the guidelines aimed to limit the prejudicial impact of media coverage of the courts by restricting both the content and the tone of media coverage of upcoming and ongoing trials. The guidelines attempted to balance the sometimes competing interests of the media and the courts by recognizing the needs of both privacy and openness, robust debate and solemn deliberation. Some of these agreements include voluntary adjudication boards that review media practices and issue statements of disapproval when media transgress appropriate coverage rules.

Starting in the 1980s, some courts tried to impose the voluntary bench-bar-press guidelines as enforceable contracts on media practice. In Washington, for example, one state court excluded the press from a suppression hearing after it ruled that press pretrial publication of incriminating ballistics information violated the guidelines and justified exclusion of reporters.[111] Another trial judge

Points of Law

What Is Fair Coverage of Criminal Trials?

Agreements between media and the judiciary—as well as independent media standards of professional and ethical performance—provide guidelines for fair reporting on ongoing criminal proceedings. Many of the guidelines say that without some overwhelming justification to do otherwise, media coverage should not include any of the following:

- The existence of a confession
- The content of a confession
- Statements or opinions of guilt or innocence
- The results of lab tests
- Statements or opinions on witness credibility
- Statements or opinions on the credibility of the evidence or the investigative process or personnel, and
- Other information or statements reasonably likely to affect the trial verdict.

made press adherence to the guidelines a necessary condition for media to attend a pretrial hearing, even though the general public was admitted without limitation. The Washington Supreme Court upheld this procedure,[112] and the U.S. Supreme Court denied review.

The U.S. Supreme Court has never adopted the position of the Washington state court: that the guidelines are legally binding on media. Although Justice Harry Blackmun implicitly accepted the guidelines endorsed by Nebraska's bar-press guidelines when he granted a temporary injunction in the case of *Nebraska Press Association v. Stuart,* the full Court said decisions about appropriate news content are the domain of editors, not judges. While that remains the law today, some media organizations are reluctant to officially endorse bench-bar-press agreements for fear the courts may subsequently use the guidelines to punish press practices.

SUMMARY

MANY STATES HAVE ADOPTED VOLUNTARY bench-bar-press guidelines to delimit the appropriate bounds of media coverage of courts and the proper conduct of trial participants in interactions with the media. Some media organizations choose not to endorse the guidelines out of fear that courts will attempt to enforce them as binding contracts, limiting their editorial discretion in covering judicial proceedings. ∎

Access to Court Records

The public and the media have a right to access court records that is grounded in common law, the U.S. and state constitutions and numerous public records laws. This right is not unlimited; it must be balanced against competing interests within the judicial system as well as external interests, such as national security, privacy and trade secrets. Court rules that vary by jurisdiction also shape the specific character of access to records.

Constitutional and Statutory Access

The Supreme Court made clear in 1978 that the common-law right of access to court records is not unlimited. The decision stemmed from the criminal trial of some of the people involved in the Watergate conspiracy in which tape recordings of former President Richard Nixon were used as evidence. A federal law establishes procedures to retain and provide public access to presidential records of historic interest, including the Nixon tapes. Finding that public rebroadcast of the tapes might prejudice the appeals of the defendants, the district court denied media requests to make copies of the tapes. In *Nixon v. Warner Communications,* the court of appeals reversed, but the U.S. Supreme Court held that courts are not required to provide access to all records in their custody, particularly when—as in this case—the records are available through alternative means.[113] In addition, the Court rejected the idea that the press had a First Amendment right to inspect and copy the tapes, holding instead that the media have no rights of access superior to those of the general public.[114]

Similarly, one U.S. district court in 2012 ruled that the constitutional right of access to trials encompassed only the right to attend judicial proceedings.[115] The court held that it had no constitutional obligation to allow media access to copies of trial exhibits in the possession of various parties and not in court files. However, based on a common-law right of access and using a categorical analysis, the court permitted release of categories of records whose release would advance the public interest without unduly harming due process or privacy rights of various parties.

Court Dockets

For the past decade, growing concerns over global terrorism have produced new issues and strategies for prosecuting criminal conspirators and terrorists while protecting the secrecy of national counterterrorism practices and personnel. Virtually all of the actions of the Foreign Intelligence Surveillance Court are kept secret, for example. But within hours of his inauguration, President Barack Obama signed an executive order that promised to reduce the secrecy surrounding the apprehension, detention and prosecution of accused terrorists.[116] Some observers argue that he has failed to make good on this promise.

Particularly since Sept. 11, 2001, courts across the United States have cited national security and other concerns and taken cases off the docket or "super-sealed" them to remove the proceedings from the public eye. Super-sealed cases are never listed on the public dockets, or schedules, of cases appearing in the courts. In comparison, sealed cases generally appear in court records but are referenced only by docket numbers. Because super-sealed cases never appear in the filing systems of the courts, the public—and the media—have virtually no way to learn that the cases exist as a necessary prerequisite to challenging their secrecy. Some observers fear that the use of super-sealed and secret dockets is spreading. A study by the Tulsa World newspaper reported that during one five-year period judges sealed all or part of more than 2,300 court cases in Oklahoma, including divorce documents, wrongful death settlements, name changes and probate cases involving the deceased person's will.[117]

In one case reviewing a motion to unseal records in a case that raised neither state secrets nor national security issues, the Court of Appeals for the Third Circuit refused to open the sealed docket or files in the underlying abortion case.[118] In *Doe v. C.A.R.S. Protection Plus, Inc.*, a woman suing anonymously claimed she was wrongfully fired for ending her pregnancy. The case had been super-sealed, and it became public when the Third Circuit reversed the lower court's dismissal of the motion but upheld the court's discretion to seal the entire case file and docket. The Supreme Court declined to review the ruling of the Third Circuit,[119] although the court of appeals said, "The issue of the propriety of the continued sealing of the case . . . is an important one."[120]

One study by the Federal Judicial Center cited a lack of judicial standards as the foundation for wide disparities in court practices of sealing cases.[121] The study found that despite requirements that access restrictions be narrowly tailored to meet a compelling interest, few courts provided a public record of evidence justifying closure. Public access is further jeopardized by failure of some courts to include sealed cases in their electronic case management systems, making the cases effectively invisible to the public and preventing public challenges to closure.

State Secrets

In 1953, the Supreme Court gave the executive branch the power to keep secret—with little judicial review—information that it said would present a "reasonable danger" to national security.[122] Despite pledging increased transparency during his 2008 campaign for president, President Barack Obama "has continued to deploy [state secrets privilege] to block litigation over the so-called warrantless wiretapping program, renditions of terrorism suspects by the Central Intelligence Agency and other matters," according to one report.[123] Another noted that since 9/11, both the Bush and Obama administrations have "aggressively used the 'state secrets' privilege, insisting that entire cases could be exempt from judicial review at the outset if they touch on national security."[124] One study found the federal executive branch was increasingly using its power to declare "state

realWorld Law

A Reasonable Balance?

Co-founder of Reddit, Aaron Swartz

Congress was investigating possible overreach by federal prosecutors who had charged a 26-year-old programming wunderkind with 13 felonies for using Massachusetts Institute of Technology (MIT) computers to hack into the JSTOR database and download millions of academic articles.[2] Although Swartz did not profit from the JSTOR download, he faced a maximum prison sentence of 35 years at the time he hanged himself.

The court ordered release of the documents after redaction of any information on weaknesses in the MIT and JSTOR computer networks. A spokesperson for the prosecution said the ruling achieved "a reasonable balance between providing the public access to relevant information and protecting the privacy and safety interests of witnesses and victims in this matter."[3]

1. Larraine Bailey, *Aaron Swartz Records to Be Unsealed for Congress,* Courthouse News Serv. (May 16, 2013), *available at* http://www.courthousenews.com/2013/05/16/57710.htm.
2. *Documents in Case Against Internet Activist Swartz to Be Released* (May 13, 2013), *available at* http://www.reuters.com/article/2013/05/13/us-swartz-idUSBRE94C11Q20130513.
3. *Id.*

secrets" to thwart open judicial proceedings.[125] "The trend is toward the government claiming this privilege earlier in civil litigation, to block discovery. The end result is often the complete dismissal of cases," according to the organization Open the Government.

In 2013, a federal district court judge in Los Angeles challenged the government's secrecy surrounding its "no fly" list and its long-standing position that only the executive branch can authorize access to classified information.[126] The judge ordered the government to disclose dozens of unclassified documents it claimed were protected by various statutes and to "show cause" why at least nine documents it had classified should not be released. In another recent case involving state secrets, the U.S. Court of Appeals for the Ninth Circuit upheld the Obama administration's claim that details of the Bush administration's rendition program should be protected and kept outside the authority of the courts.[127] The case had sought criminal punishment of the Boeing subsidiary that removed alleged terrorists from the country.[128]

In an earlier, non-terrorism-related case brought before the U.S. Court of Appeals for the D.C. Circuit, however, the court reinstated a lawsuit that had been dismissed after the government had claimed state secrets privilege.[129] The lawsuit was filed by former Drug Enforcement Administration official who claimed the

State Department and the CIA had illegally wiretapped his communications while he was overseas. When the federal government invoked state secrets privilege, the federal district court dismissed the case. But the circuit court of appeals reversed without challenging the government's state secrets privilege. The court ruled that sufficient unprivileged evidence existed on the record to allow the case to proceed.

Court Access Rules

Access to court records in many states is not dictated by the legislature. Instead, state courts generally develop their own rules and policies for the handling and release of court records. Access to records of the courts raises concerns about invasion of privacy and fair trial because many court files contain information litigants are required to disclose under filing requirements or rules of discovery (such as personal financial information), and some of this information will not become public until and unless it is presented in the open courtroom. To protect these interests, states generally limit the release of information from the courts and impose penalties on state employees who violate these rules.

While state courts control many aspects of access to their records, the Supreme Court has ruled that states may not punish media for publishing legally obtained truthful information obtained from court files.[130] In *Florida Star v. B.J.F.,* the Supreme Court said states may not impose penalties on the press for the publication of legally obtained truthful information unless they demonstrate that the penalty is "narrowly tailored to a state interest of the highest order."[131] (See Chapter 6 for a discussion of this case.) In general, decisions to seal court records are subject to the same constitutional limits as court closure, are strongly disfavored under the First Amendment and must pass the stringent *Press-Enterprise* test.

State or federal open-records laws (also discussed in Chapter 8) that recognize the strong public interest in information about criminal prosecutions do not apply to court records in at the federal level and in more than half the states. Where state open-records laws do apply, at least to some extent, the rules vary widely. The Indiana Open Records Law, for example, covers all court records unless there is a specific exemption or a protective order to constrain their release.[132] The Kansas Open Records Act applies broadly to court records but explicitly excludes judges from its purview.[133]

Other states generally provide more limited rights of access. In Washington, state courts have interpreted the broad provisions of its Public Disclosure Act to exclude the courts.[134] In Ohio, the state supreme court ruled that neither the constitutional right to open courts nor the state's open-records law prevented a judge from sealing an entire court record five weeks after the conclusion of a criminal trial in which the defendant was acquitted.[135] The court said that "limit[ing] the life of a particular record" did not harm the public's right to know about criminal proceedings because it did not diminish the ability of the press or the public to attend or report on the trial. In contrast, the Louisiana Supreme Court struck down a judge's order to seal the entire record of a divorce proceeding.[136] The court said the blanket order sealing the record violated the state constitution's strong presumption in favor of open public access to court proceedings.

Electronic Access to Court Records

During the past decade, many courts around the country have reviewed and upgraded their records access rules and implemented new forms of electronic access. Two court organizations—the Conference of Chief Justices and the Conference of State Court Administrators—led a nationwide effort to set guidelines to facilitate online public access while protecting personal privacy, among other interests.[137] The report called for generous, remote electronic access to civil case files as well as electronic access to criminal case files on the same terms as is provided in the courthouse.[138]

Both the National Center for State Courts and the Justice Management Institute have advocated that court records be posted online and be presumptively open. Electronic access to federal court records is provided through the Public Access to Court Electronic Records (PACER) site (http://www.pacer.gov), but online access to state court records is "remarkably disparate."[139] Some states provide centralized statewide access while others offer distinct, single jurisdiction links to partial or complete civil and/or criminal court records. Some states treat electronic records and their access exactly as they do paper files, while others restrict access according to the identity or purpose of the user or prohibit access to records that may contain sensitive personal information, including trial court records. While some states extend free comprehensive access to their court records, many others charge fees. Reporters who need detailed information on these variations may find an online compilation of links providing specific information on state laws on access to court records through the National Center for State Courts.[140]

Electronic access to public records—either online or as compiled databases used by journalists or commercial information providers—has prompted fears and challenges that the databases alter the amount of access in different states or courts. Access advocates and journalists who argue the benefits of electronic access to court records must grapple with studies suggesting that media fail to deliver on their promises to the public. One study, for example, found that the media sensationalize rather than educate, fail to provide adequate context in reporting on courtroom proceedings and generally seek to entertain rather than inform.[141] Some privacy advocates also argue that online access increases the likelihood that identity thieves will find Social Security numbers in court records. They point out that Internet distribution of court records also propels worldwide dissemination of false allegations made in divorce and civil disputes.[142]

Such concerns are not new. In 1890 noted jurists Louis Brandeis and Samuel Warren argued that the people have a "right to be let alone."[143] State committees reviewing access have suggested prohibiting access to records containing sensitive information, such as Social Security numbers, financial account numbers and street addresses of litigants, or deleting the information before the records are posted online.[144] Although the redaction of records is both time-consuming and costly, one state committee recommended that some information accessible in paper records, such as health data or identification of people involved in some family law cases, not be put online.[145]

Fee systems in some states distinguish among users and may limit access. For example, some jurisdictions use high fees to prevent identity thieves from fishing through online records. Others require the media, attorneys and other bulk users to subscribe to online court access for hundreds or thousands of dollars a year. Such subscriptions generally are not available to non-bulk users, and the costs inhibit widespread public access.

Courts also differ on whether to create and/or share databases of aggregated information that can help journalists examine societal trends. For example, some journalists have combined databases of court conviction records with databases of school bus drivers, finding drivers who have extensive drunken driving records. Yet government agencies and the courts have been reluctant to provide aggregated information to the public, fearful of people piecing together personal information. In its foundational decision in this area, the Supreme Court ruled in *Department of Justice v. Reporters Committee for Freedom of the Press* that federal law did not allow journalists access to a Federal Bureau of Investigation (FBI) electronic compilation of rap sheets.[146] The reporter intended to piece together the background of a suspected mobster, but the Court said access to the compiled information represented an unacceptable threat to individual privacy.

The *Reporters Committee* case involved the federal Freedom of Information Act, not court rules, but courts have applied similar reasoning to electronic access. For example, a court rule approved in Washington requires people who request criminal conviction data to sign a contract agreeing to allow court officials to examine the person's computer that houses the data—even in the newsroom—to make sure the information is being used responsibly.[147] The Minnesota court records committee suggests that large fees be charged for court databases in order to make money.

The checkered pattern of electronic access to court records is unlikely to change in the near term as each state pursues its own policies and practices.

SUMMARY

THE U.S. SUPREME COURT long has recognized a common-law right of public access to court records. This right is not unlimited, and it is shaped by the specific access rules established in each court jurisdiction. State constitutions, public records laws and court rules vary widely on whether and how they treat public access to court records. Restrictions that apply to some information held in courthouse files may be overcome when records are presented in an open courtroom, but those limitations may expand when records go online. Most records presented in court are presumptively open, but may not remain open permanently.

Courts generally must exhaust all reasonable alternatives before sealing presumptively open court records. National security concerns and state secrets privilege sometimes close court records, including any mention of some cases in progress. The U.S. Supreme Court has said media cannot be punished for accurately publishing information legally obtained from court records even when state law prohibits dissemination of the information. The media have no extraordinary right of access to court records that exceeds the right of the public. ■

Cases for Study

Thinking About It

The two case excerpts that follow examine the constitutional right of public—and media—access to criminal trials as well as the limits to press freedoms within the confines of the courtroom. The two cases exemplify the threats that exist to the U.S. justice system from media running amok and from closed proceedings that eliminate public checks and balances on the courts. When reading these excerpts, keep these questions in mind:

- What are the assumptions and evidence used by the Supreme Court in assessing the prejudicial impact of media coverage?

- In *Sheppard v. Maxwell,* does the Court distinguish between the media and trial participants when it establishes judicial remedies to threats to fair trials? If so, why?

- What are the foundations the Court draws upon in *Richmond Newspapers v. Virginia* to conclude that the public has a right of access to criminal trials?

- To what extent do these two cases provide a judicial foundation for a right of electronic access to trials and court records?

Sheppard v. Maxwell
SUPREME COURT OF THE UNITED STATES
384 U.S. 333 (1966)

JUSTICE TOM CLARK delivered the Court's opinion:

This federal habeas corpus application involves the question whether Sheppard was deprived of a fair trial in his state conviction for the second-degree murder of his wife because of the trial judge's failure to protect Sheppard sufficiently from the massive, pervasive and prejudicial publicity that attended his prosecution. The United States District Court held that he was not afforded a fair trial. . . . The Court of Appeals for the Sixth Circuit reversed. . . . We granted certiorari [and] have concluded that Sheppard did not receive a fair trial consistent with the Due Process Clause of the Fourteenth Amendment and, therefore, reverse the judgment.

Marilyn Sheppard, petitioner's pregnant wife, was bludgeoned to death in the upstairs bedroom of their lakeshore home in Bay Village, Ohio, a suburb of Cleveland. . . .

From the outset officials focused suspicion on Sheppard. After a search of the house and premises on the morning of the tragedy, Dr. Gerber, the Coroner, is reported—and it is undenied—to have told his men, "Well, it is evident the doctor did this, so let's go get the confession out of him." He proceeded to interrogate and examine Sheppard while the latter was under sedation in his hospital room. On the same occasion, the Coroner was given the clothes Sheppard wore at the time of the tragedy together with the personal items in them. Later that afternoon Chief Eaton and two Cleveland police officers interrogated Sheppard at some length, confronting him with evidence and demanding explanations. Asked by Officer Shotke to take a lie detector test, Sheppard said he would if it were reliable. Shotke replied that it was "infallible" and "you might as well tell us all about it now." At the end of the interrogation, Shotke told Sheppard: "I think you killed your wife." Still later in the same afternoon, a physician sent by the Coroner was permitted to make a detailed examination of Sheppard. Until the Coroner's inquest on July 22, at which time he was subpoenaed, Sheppard made himself available for frequent and extended questioning without the presence of an attorney.

On July 7, the day of Marilyn Sheppard's funeral, a newspaper story appeared in which Assistant County Attorney Mahon—later the chief prosecutor of Sheppard—sharply criticized the refusal of the Sheppard family to permit his immediate questioning. From there on headline stories repeatedly stressed Sheppard's lack of cooperation with the police and other officials. Under the headline "Testify Now In Death, Bay Doctor Is Ordered," one story described a visit by Coroner Gerber and four police officers to the hospital on July 8. When Sheppard insisted that his lawyer be present, the Coroner wrote out a subpoena and served it on him. Sheppard then agreed to submit to questioning without counsel and the subpoena was torn up. The officers questioned him for several hours. On July 9, Sheppard, at the request of the Coroner, re-enacted the tragedy at his home before the Coroner, police officers, and a group of newsmen, who apparently were invited by the Coroner. The home was locked so that Sheppard was obliged to wait outside until the Coroner arrived. Sheppard's performance was reported in detail by the news media along with photographs.

The newspapers also played up Sheppard's refusal to take a lie detector test and "the protective ring" thrown up by his family. Front-page newspaper headlines announced on the same day that "Doctor Balks At Lie Test; Retells Story." A column opposite that story contained an "exclusive" interview with Sheppard headlined: "'Loved My Wife, She Loved Me,' Sheppard Tells News Reporter." The next day,

another headline story disclosed that Sheppard had "again late yesterday refused to take a lie detector test" and quoted an Assistant County Attorney as saying that "at the end of a nine hour questioning of Dr. Sheppard, I felt he was now ruling [a test] out completely." But subsequent newspaper articles reported that the Coroner was still pushing Sheppard for a lie detector test. More stories appeared when Sheppard would not allow authorities to inject him with "truth serum."

On the 20th, the "editorial artillery" opened fire with a front-page charge that somebody is "getting away with murder." The editorial attributed the ineptness of the investigation to "friendships, relationships, hired lawyers, a husband who ought to have been subjected instantly to the same third-degree to which any other person under similar circumstances is subjected. . . ." The following day, July 21, another page-one editorial was headed: "Why No Inquest? Do It Now, Dr. Gerber." The Coroner called an inquest the same day and subpoenaed Sheppard. It was staged the next day in a school gymnasium; the Coroner presided with the County Prosecutor as his advisor and two detectives as bailiffs. In the front of the room was a long table occupied by reporters, television and radio personnel, and broadcasting equipment. The hearing was broadcast with live microphones placed at the Coroner's seat and the witness stand. A swarm of reporters and photographers attended. Sheppard was brought into the room by police who searched him in full view of several hundred spectators. Sheppard's counsel were present during the three-day inquest but were not permitted to participate. When Sheppard's chief counsel attempted to place some documents in the record, he was forcibly ejected from the room by the Coroner, who received cheers, hugs, and kisses from ladies in the audience. Sheppard was questioned for five and one-half hours about his actions on the night of the murder, his married life, and a love affair with Susan Hayes. At the end of the hearing the Coroner announced that he "could" order Sheppard held for the grand jury, but did not do so.

Throughout this period the newspapers emphasized evidence that tended to incriminate Sheppard and pointed out discrepancies in his statements to authorities. At the same time, Sheppard made many public statements to the press and wrote feature articles asserting his innocence. During the inquest on July 26, a headline in large type stated: "Kerr [Captain of the Cleveland Police] Urges Sheppard's Arrest." In the story, Detective McArthur "disclosed that scientific tests at the Sheppard home have definitely established that the killer washed off a trail of blood from the murder bedroom to the downstairs section," a circumstance casting doubt on Sheppard's accounts of the murder. No such evidence was produced at trial. The newspapers also delved into Sheppard's personal life. Articles stressed his extramarital love affairs as a motive for the crime. The newspapers portrayed Sheppard as a Lothario, fully explored his relationship with Susan Hayes, and named a number of other women who were allegedly involved with him. The testimony at trial never showed that Sheppard had any illicit relationships besides the one with Susan Hayes.

On July 28, an editorial entitled "Why Don't Police Quiz Top Suspect" demanded that Sheppard be taken to police headquarters. It described him in the following language: "Now proved under oath to be a liar, still free to go about his business, shielded by his family, protected by a smart lawyer who has made monkeys of the police and authorities, carrying a gun part of the time, left free to do whatever he pleases. . . ."

A front-page editorial on July 30 asked: "Why Isn't Sam Sheppard in Jail?" It was later titled "Quit Stalling—Bring Him In." After calling Sheppard "the most unusual murder suspect ever seen around these parts," the article said that "except for some superficial questioning during Coroner Sam Gerber's inquest, he has been scot-free of any official grilling. . . ." It asserted that he was "surrounded by an iron curtain of protection [and] concealment."

That night at 10 o'clock, Sheppard was arrested at his father's home on a charge of murder. He was taken to the Bay Village City Hall, where hundreds of people, newscasters, photographers and reporters were awaiting his arrival. He was immediately arraigned—having been denied a temporary delay to secure the presence of counsel—and bound over to the grand jury.

The publicity then grew in intensity until his indictment on August 17. Typical of the coverage during this period is a front-page interview entitled: "DR. SAM: 'I Wish There Was Something I Could Get Off My Chest—but There Isn't.'" Unfavorable publicity included items such as a cartoon of the body of a sphinx with Sheppard's head and the legend below: "'I Will Do Everything In My Power to Help Solve This Terrible Murder.'—Dr. Sam Sheppard." Headlines announced, *inter alia,* that: "Doctor Evidence is Ready for Jury," "Corrigan Tactics Stall Quizzing," "Sheppard 'Gay Set' Is Revealed By Houk," "Blood Is Found In Garage," "New Murder Evidence Is Found, Police Claim," "Dr. Sam Faces Quiz At Jail On Marilyn's Fear Of Him." On August 18, an article appeared under the headline "Dr. Sam Writes His Own Story." And reproduced across the entire front page was a portion of the typed statement signed by Sheppard: "I am not guilty of the murder of my wife, Marilyn. How could I, who have been trained to help people and devoted my life to saving life, commit such a terrible and revolting crime?"

We do not detail the coverage further. There are five volumes filled with similar clippings from each of the three Cleveland newspapers covering the period from the murder until Sheppard's conviction in December 1954. The record includes no excerpts from newscasts on radio and television, but, since space was reserved in the courtroom for these media, we assume that their coverage was equally large.

With this background the case came on for trial two weeks before the November general election at which the chief prosecutor was a candidate for common pleas judge and the trial judge, Judge Blythin, was a candidate to succeed himself. Twenty-five days before the case was set, 75 veniremen were called as prospective jurors. All three Cleveland newspapers published the names and addresses of the veniremen. As a consequence, anonymous letters and telephone calls, as well as calls from friends, regarding the impending prosecution were received by all of the prospective jurors. . . .

The courtroom in which the trial was held measured 26 by 48 feet. A long temporary table was set up inside the bar, in back of the single counsel table.

It ran the width of the courtroom, parallel to the bar railing, with one end less than three feet from the jury box. Approximately 20 representatives of newspapers and wire services were assigned seats at this table by the court. Behind the bar railing there were four rows of benches. These seats were likewise assigned by the court for the entire trial. The first row was occupied by representatives of television and radio stations, and the second and third rows by reporters from out-of-town newspapers and magazines. One side of the last row, which accommodated 14 people, was assigned to Sheppard's family, and the other to Marilyn's. The public was permitted to fill vacancies in this row on special passes only. Representatives of the news media also used all the rooms on the courtroom floor, including the room where cases were ordinarily called and assigned for trial. Private telephone lines and telegraphic equipment were installed in these rooms so that reports from the trial could be speeded to the papers. Station WSRS was permitted to set up broadcasting facilities on the third floor of the courthouse next door to the jury room, where the jury rested during recesses in the trial and deliberated. Newscasts were made from this room throughout the trial, and while the jury reached its verdict.

On the sidewalk and steps in front of the courthouse, television and newsreel cameras were occasionally used to take motion pictures of the participants in the trial, including the jury and the judge. Indeed, one television broadcast carried a staged interview of the judge as he entered the courthouse. In the corridors outside the courtroom, there was a host of photographers and television personnel with flash cameras, portable lights and motion picture cameras. This group photographed the prospective jurors during selection of the jury. After the trial opened, the witnesses, counsel, and jurors were photographed and televised whenever they entered or left the courtroom. Sheppard was brought to the courtroom about 10 minutes before each session began; he was surrounded by reporters and extensively photographed for the newspapers and television. A rule of court prohibited picture-taking in the courtroom during the actual sessions of the court, but no restraints were put on photographers during recesses, which were taken once each morning and afternoon, with a longer period for lunch.

All of these arrangements with the news media and their massive coverage of the trial continued during the entire nine weeks of the trial. The courtroom remained crowded to capacity with representatives of news media. Their movement in and out of the courtroom often caused so much confusion that, despite the loud-speaker system installed in the courtroom, it was difficult for the witnesses and counsel to be heard. Furthermore, the reporters clustered within the bar of the small courtroom made confidential talk among Sheppard and his counsel almost impossible during the proceedings. . . .

The daily record of the proceedings was made available to the newspapers, and the testimony of each witness was printed verbatim in the local editions, along with objections of counsel, and rulings by the judge. Pictures of Sheppard, the judge, counsel, pertinent witnesses, and the jury often accompanied the daily newspaper and television accounts. At times the newspapers published photographs of exhibits introduced at the trial, and the rooms of Sheppard's house were featured along with relevant testimony.

The jurors themselves were constantly exposed to the news media. Every juror, except one, testified at *voir dire* to reading about the case in the Cleveland papers or to having heard broadcasts about it. Seven of the 12 jurors who rendered the verdict had one or more Cleveland papers delivered in their home; the remaining jurors were not interrogated on the point. Nor were there questions as to radios or television sets in the jurors' homes, but we must assume that most of them owned such conveniences. . . .

. . . While the intense publicity continued unabated, it is sufficient to relate only the more flagrant episodes:

On October 9, 1954, nine days before the case went to trial, an editorial in one of the newspapers criticized defense counsel's random poll of people on the streets as to their opinion of Sheppard's guilt or innocence in an effort to use the resulting statistics to show the necessity for change of venue. The article said the survey "smacks of mass jury tampering," . . . The article was called to the attention of the court but no action was taken.

On the second day of *voir dire* examination, a debate was staged and broadcast live over WHK radio. The participants, newspaper reporters, accused Sheppard's counsel of throwing roadblocks in the way of the prosecution and asserted that Sheppard conceded his guilt by hiring a prominent criminal lawyer. Sheppard's counsel objected to this broadcast and requested a continuance, but the judge denied the motion. . . .

On November 19, a Cleveland police officer gave testimony that tended to contradict details in the written statement Sheppard made to the Cleveland police. Two days later, in a broadcast heard over Station WHK in Cleveland, Robert Considine likened Sheppard to a perjurer and compared the episode to Alger Hiss' confrontation with Whittaker Chambers. Though defense counsel asked the judge to question the jury to ascertain how many heard the broadcast, the court refused to do so. The judge also overruled the motion for continuance based on the same ground, saying:

"Well, I don't know, we can't stop people, in any event, listening to it. It is a matter of free speech, and the court can't control everybody. . . . We are not going to harass the jury every morning. . . . It is getting to the point where if we do it every morning, we are suspecting the jury. I have confidence in this jury. . . ."

On November 24, a story appeared under an eight-column headline: "Sam Called A 'Jekyll-Hyde' By Marilyn, Cousin To Testify." It related that Marilyn had recently told friends that Sheppard was a "Dr. Jekyll and Mr. Hyde" character. No such testimony was ever produced at the trial. . . . Defense counsel made motions for change of venue, continuance and mistrial, but they were denied. No action was taken by the court.

When the trial was in its seventh week, Walter Winchell broadcast over WXEL television and WJW radio that Carole Beasley, who was under arrest in New York City for robbery, had stated that, as Sheppard's mistress, she had borne him a child. The defense asked that the jury be queried on the broadcast. Two jurors admitted in open court that they had heard it. The judge asked each: "Would that have any effect upon your judgment?" Both replied, "No." This was

accepted by the judge as sufficient; he merely asked the jury to "pay no attention whatever to that type of scavenging. . . . Let's confine ourselves to this courtroom, if you please." . . .

On December 9, while Sheppard was on the witness stand, he testified that he had been mistreated by Cleveland detectives after his arrest. Although he was not at the trial, Captain Kerr of the Homicide Bureau issued a press statement denying Sheppard's allegations which appeared under the headline: "'Bare-faced Liar,' Kerr Says of Sam." Captain Kerr never appeared as a witness at the trial. . . .

. . . After the verdict, defense counsel ascertained that the jurors had been allowed to make telephone calls to their homes every day while they were sequestered at the hotel. . . . By a subsequent motion, defense counsel urged that this ground alone warranted a new trial, but the motion was overruled and no evidence was taken on the question.

The principle that justice cannot survive behind walls of silence has long been reflected in the "Anglo-American distrust for secret trials." A responsible press has always been regarded as the handmaiden of effective judicial administration, especially in the criminal field. . . . The press does not simply publish information about trials, but guards against the miscarriage of justice by subjecting the police, prosecutors, and judicial processes to extensive public scrutiny and criticism. This Court has, therefore, been unwilling to place any direct limitations on the freedom traditionally exercised by the news media for "[w]hat transpires in the court room is public property." . . . And where there was "no threat or menace to the integrity of the trial," we have consistently required that the press have a free hand, even though we sometimes deplored its sensationalism.

But the Court has also pointed out that "legal trials are not like elections, to be won through the use of the meeting-hall, the radio, and the newspaper." And the Court has insisted that no one be punished for a crime without "a charge fairly made and fairly tried in a public tribunal free of prejudice, passion, excitement, and tyrannical power." "Freedom of discussion should be given the widest range compatible with the essential requirement of the fair and orderly administration of justice." But it must not be allowed to divert the trial from the "very purpose of a court system . . . to adjudicate controversies, both criminal and civil, in the calmness and solemnity of the courtroom according to legal procedures." Among these "legal procedures" is the requirement that the jury's verdict be based on evidence received in open court, not from outside sources. Thus, we set aside a federal conviction where the jurors were exposed "through news accounts" to information that was not admitted at trial. . . . At the same time, we did not consider dispositive the statement of each juror "that he would not be influenced by the news articles, that he could decide the case only on the evidence of record, and that he felt no prejudice against petitioner as a result of the articles." Likewise, even though each juror indicated that he could render an impartial verdict despite exposure to prejudicial newspaper articles, we set aside the conviction holding: "With his life at stake, it is not requiring too much that petitioner be tried in an atmosphere undisturbed by so huge a wave of public passion. . . ."

The undeviating rule of this Court was expressed by Mr. Justice Holmes over half a century ago . . . : "The theory of our system is that the conclusions to be reached in a case will be induced only by evidence and argument in open court, and not by any outside influence, whether of private talk or public print." Moreover, "the burden of showing essential unfairness . . . as a demonstrable reality," need not be undertaken when television has exposed the community "repeatedly and in depth to the spectacle of [the accused] personally confessing in detail to the crimes with which he was later to be charged." . . .

Only last Term we set aside a conviction despite the absence of any showing of prejudice. We said there: "It is true that in most cases involving claims of due process deprivations, we require a showing of identifiable prejudice to the accused. Nevertheless, at times a procedure employed by the State involves such a probability that prejudice will result that it is deemed inherently lacking in due process." . . .

It is clear that the totality of circumstances in this case also warrants such an approach. . . . Sheppard was not granted a change of venue to a locale away from where the publicity originated; nor was his jury sequestered. . . . [T]he Sheppard jurors were subjected to newspaper, radio, and television coverage of the trial while not taking part in the proceedings. They were allowed to go their separate ways outside of the courtroom, without adequate directions not to read or listen to anything concerning the case. The judge's "admonitions" at the beginning of the trial are representative:

"I would suggest to you and caution you that you do not read any newspapers during the progress of this trial, that you do not listen to radio comments nor watch or listen to television comments, insofar as this case is concerned. You will feel very much better as the trial proceeds. . . . I am sure that we shall all feel very much better if we do not indulge in any newspaper reading or listening to any comments whatever about the matter while the case is in progress. After it is all over, you can read it all to your heart's content. . . ."

At intervals during the trial, the judge simply repeated his "suggestions" and "requests" that the jurors not expose themselves to comment upon the case. Moreover, the jurors were thrust into the role of celebrities by the judge's failure to insulate them from reporters and photographers. . . . For months, the virulent publicity about Sheppard and the murder had made the case notorious. Charges and countercharges were aired in the news media besides those for which Sheppard was called to trial. In addition, only three months before trial, Sheppard was examined for more than five hours without counsel during a three-day inquest which ended in a public brawl. The inquest was televised live from a high school gymnasium seating hundreds of people. . . .

While we cannot say that Sheppard was denied due process by the judge's refusal to take precautions against the influence of pretrial publicity alone, the court's later rulings must be considered against the setting in which the trial was held. In light of this background, we believe that the arrangements made by the judge with the news media caused Sheppard to be deprived of that "judicial serenity and calm to which [he] was entitled." The fact is that bedlam reigned at the courthouse during the trial and newsmen took over practically the entire courtroom, hounding most of the participants in the trial, especially Sheppard. . . . Having assigned almost all of the available seats in the courtroom to the news media, the judge lost his ability to supervise that environment. The movement of the reporters in and out of the courtroom caused frequent confusion and disruption of the trial. And the record reveals constant commotion within the bar. Moreover, the judge gave the throng of newsmen gathered in the corridors of the courthouse absolute free rein. Participants in the trial, including the jury, were forced to run a gantlet of reporters and photographers each time they entered or left the courtroom. . . .

There can be no question about the nature of the publicity which surrounded Sheppard's trial. We agree, as did the Court of Appeals, with the findings in Judge Bell's opinion for the Ohio Supreme Court: "Murder and mystery, society, sex and suspense were combined in this case in such a manner as to intrigue and captivate the public fancy to a degree perhaps unparalleled in recent annals. Throughout the pre-indictment investigation, the subsequent legal skirmishes and the nine-week trial, circulation-conscious editors catered to the insatiable interest of the American public in the bizarre. . . . In this atmosphere of a 'Roman holiday' for the news media, Sam Sheppard stood trial for his life." Indeed, every court that has considered this case, save the court that tried it, has deplored the manner in which the news media inflamed and prejudiced the public.

Much of the material printed or broadcast during the trial was never heard from the witness stand, such as the charges that Sheppard had purposely impeded the murder investigation and must be guilty since he had hired a prominent criminal lawyer; that Sheppard was a perjurer; that he had sexual relations with numerous women; that his slain wife had characterized him as a "Jekyll-Hyde"; that he was "a bare-faced liar" because of his testimony as to police treatment; and, finally, that a woman convict claimed Sheppard to be the father of her illegitimate child. As the trial progressed, the newspapers summarized and interpreted the evidence, devoting particular attention to the material that incriminated Sheppard, and often drew unwarranted inferences from testimony. At one point, a front-page picture of Mrs. Sheppard's blood-stained pillow was published after being "doctored" to show more clearly an alleged imprint of a surgical instrument.

Nor is there doubt that this deluge of publicity reached at least some of the jury. On the only occasion that the jury was queried, two jurors admitted in open court to hearing the highly inflammatory charge that a prison inmate claimed Sheppard as the father of her illegitimate child. . . .

The court's fundamental error is compounded by the holding that it lacked power to control the publicity about the trial. From the very inception of the proceedings, the judge announced that neither he nor anyone else could restrict prejudicial news accounts. And he reiterated this view on numerous occasions. Since he viewed the news media as his target, the judge never considered other means that are often utilized to reduce the appearance of prejudicial material and to protect the jury from outside influence. We conclude that these procedures would have been sufficient to guarantee Sheppard a fair trial, and so do not consider what sanctions might be available against a recalcitrant press, nor the charges of bias now made against the state trial judge.

The carnival atmosphere at trial could easily have been avoided, since the courtroom and courthouse premises are subject to the control of the court. . . . [T]he presence of the press at judicial proceedings must be limited when it is apparent that the accused might otherwise be prejudiced or disadvantaged. Bearing in mind the massive pretrial publicity, the judge should have adopted stricter rules governing the use of the courtroom by newsmen. . . . They certainly should not have been placed inside the bar. Furthermore, the judge should have more closely regulated the conduct of newsmen in the courtroom. . . .

Secondly, the court should have insulated the witnesses. All of the newspapers and radio stations apparently interviewed prospective witnesses at will, and in many instances disclosed their testimony. . . . Although the witnesses were barred from the courtroom during the trial, the full verbatim testimony was available to them in the press. This completely nullified the judge's imposition of the rule.

Thirdly, the court should have made some effort to control the release of leads, information, and gossip to the press by police officers, witnesses, and the counsel for both sides. Much of the information thus disclosed was inaccurate, leading to groundless rumors and confusion. . . .

Defense counsel immediately brought to the court's attention the tremendous amount of publicity in the Cleveland press that "misrepresented entirely the testimony" in the case. Under such circumstances, the judge should have at least warned the newspapers to check the accuracy of their accounts. And it is obvious that the judge should have further sought to alleviate this problem by imposing control over the statements made to the news media by counsel, witnesses, and especially the Coroner and police officers. The prosecution repeatedly made evidence available to the news media which was never offered in the trial. Much of the "evidence" disseminated in this fashion was clearly inadmissible. The exclusion of such evidence in court is rendered meaningless when news media make it available to the public. . . .

The fact that many of the prejudicial news items can be traced to the prosecution as well as the defense aggravates the judge's failure to take any action. Effective control of these sources—concededly within the court's power—might well have prevented the divulgence of inaccurate information, rumors, and accusations that made up much of the inflammatory publicity, at least after Sheppard's indictment.

More specifically, the trial court might well have proscribed extrajudicial statements by any lawyer, party, witness, or court official which divulged prejudicial matters, such as the refusal of Sheppard to submit to interrogation or take any lie detector tests; any statement made by Sheppard to officials; the identity of prospective witnesses or their probable testimony; any belief in guilt or innocence; or like statements concerning the merits of the case.

Being advised of the great public interest in the case, the mass coverage of the press, and the potential prejudicial impact of publicity, the court could also have requested the appropriate city and county officials to promulgate a regulation with respect to dissemination of information about the case by their employees. In addition, reporters who wrote or broadcast prejudicial stories could have been warned as to the impropriety of publishing material not introduced in the proceedings. . . . Had the judge, the other officers of the court, and the police placed the interest of justice first, the news media would have soon learned to be content with the task of reporting the case as it unfolded in the courtroom—not pieced together from extrajudicial statements.

. . . Due process requires that the accused receive a trial by an impartial jury free from outside influences. Given the pervasiveness of modern communications and the difficulty of effacing prejudicial publicity from the minds of the jurors, the trial courts must take strong measures to ensure that the balance is never weighed against the accused. . . . Of course, there is nothing that proscribes the press from reporting events that transpire in the courtroom. But where there is a reasonable likelihood that prejudicial news prior to trial will prevent a fair trial, the judge should continue the case until the threat abates, or transfer it to another county not so permeated with publicity. In addition, sequestration of the jury was something the judge should have raised *sua sponte* with counsel. If publicity during the proceedings threatens the fairness of the trial, a new trial should be ordered. But we must remember that reversals are but palliatives; the cure lies in those remedial measures that will prevent the prejudice at its inception. The courts must take such steps by rule and regulation that will protect their processes from prejudicial outside interferences. Neither prosecutors, counsel for defense, the accused, witnesses, court staff nor enforcement officers coming under the jurisdiction of the court should be permitted to frustrate its function. Collaboration between counsel and the press as to information affecting the fairness of a criminal trial is not only subject to regulation, but is highly censurable and worthy of disciplinary measures.

Since the state trial judge did not fulfill his duty to protect Sheppard from the inherently prejudicial publicity which saturated the community and to control disruptive influences in the courtroom, we must reverse the denial of the habeas petition. . . .

Richmond Newspapers, Inc. v. Virginia
SUPREME COURT OF THE UNITED STATES
448 U.S. 555 (1980)

Chief JUSTICE WARREN BURGER delivered the Court's opinion:

The narrow question presented in this case is whether the right of the public and press to attend criminal trials is guaranteed under the United States Constitution.

In March, 1976, one Stevenson was indicted for the murder of a hotel manager who had been found stabbed to death on December 2, 1975. Tried promptly in July, 1976, Stevenson was convicted of second-degree murder in the Circuit Court of Hanover County, Va. The Virginia Supreme Court reversed the conviction in October, 1977, holding that a blood-stained shirt purportedly belonging to Stevenson had been improperly admitted into evidence.

Stevenson was retried in the same court. This second trial ended in a mistrial on May 30, 1978, when a juror asked to be excused after trial had begun and no alternate was available.

A third trial, which began in the same court on June 6, 1978, also ended in a mistrial. It appears that the mistrial may have been declared because a prospective juror had read about Stevenson's previous trials in a newspaper and had told other prospective jurors about the case before the retrial began.

Stevenson was tried in the same court for a fourth time beginning on September 11, 1978. Present in the courtroom when the case was called were . . . reporters for appellant Richmond Newspapers, Inc. Before the trial began, counsel for the defendant moved that it be closed to the public:

"[T]here was this woman that was with the family of the deceased when we were here before. She had sat in the Courtroom. I would like to ask that everybody be excluded from the Courtroom because I don't want any information being shuffled back and forth when we have a recess as to what—who testified to what."

The trial judge, who had presided over two of the three previous trials, asked if the prosecution had any objection to clearing the courtroom. The prosecutor stated he had no objection and . . . the trial judge . . . ordered "that the Courtroom be kept clear of all parties except the witnesses when they testify." The record does not show that any objections to the closure order were made by anyone present at the time. . . .

Later that same day, however, appellants sought a hearing on a motion to vacate the closure order. The trial judge granted the request and scheduled a hearing to follow the close of the day's proceedings. When the hearing began, the court ruled that the hearing was to be treated as part of the trial; accordingly, he again ordered the reporters to leave the courtroom, and they complied.

At the closed hearing, counsel for appellants observed that no evidentiary findings had been made by the court prior to the entry of its closure order, and pointed out that the court had failed to consider any other, less drastic measures within its power to ensure a fair trial. Counsel for appellants argued that constitutional considerations mandated that before ordering closure, the court should first decide that the rights of the defendant could be protected in no other way.

Counsel for defendant Stevenson pointed out that this was the fourth time he was standing trial. He also referred to "difficulty with information between the jurors," and stated that he "didn't want information to leak out," be published by the media, perhaps inaccurately, and then be seen by the jurors. Defense counsel argued that these things, plus the fact that "this is a small community," made this a proper case for closure.

The trial judge noted that counsel for the defendant had made similar statements at the morning hearing. The court also stated: "One of the other points that we take into consideration in this particular Courtroom is layout of the Courtroom. I think that having people in the Courtroom is distracting to the jury. Now, we have to have certain people in here and maybe that's not a very good reason. When we get into our new Court Building, people can sit in the audience so the jury can't see them. The rule of the Court may be different under those circumstances. . . ."

The prosecutor again declined comment, and the court summed up by saying: "I'm inclined to agree with [defense counsel] that, if I feel that the rights of the defendant are infringed in any way, [when] he makes the motion to do something and it doesn't completely override all rights of everyone else, then I'm inclined to go along with the defendant's motion."

The court denied the motion to vacate and ordered the trial to continue the following morning "with the press and public excluded."

What transpired when the closed trial resumed the next day was disclosed in the following manner by an order of the court entered September 12, 1978: "[In] the absence of the jury, the defendant, by counsel, made a Motion that a mistrial be declared, which motion was taken under advisement.

"At the conclusion of the Commonwealth's evidence, the attorney for the defendant moved the Court to strike the Commonwealth's evidence on grounds stated to the record, which Motion was sustained by the Court.

"And the jury having been excused, the Court doth find the accused NOT GUILTY of Murder, as charged in the Indictment, and he was allowed to depart." . . .

. . . The Virginia Supreme Court . . . finding no reversible error, denied the petition for appeal. . . .

The criminal trial which appellants sought to attend has long since ended, and there is thus some suggestion that the case is moot. This Court has frequently recognized, however, that its jurisdiction is not necessarily defeated by the practical termination of a contest which is short-lived by nature. If the underlying dispute is "capable of repetition, yet evading review," it is not moot. . . .

. . . More often than not, criminal trials will be of sufficiently short duration that a closure order will evade review. . . . Accordingly, we turn to the merits. . . .

In prior cases the Court has treated questions involving conflicts between publicity and a defendant's right to a fair trial. . . . But here for the first time the Court is asked to decide whether a criminal trial itself may be closed to the public upon the unopposed request of a defendant, without any demonstration

that closure is required to protect the defendant's superior right to a fair trial, or that some other overriding consideration requires closure.

The origins of the proceeding which has become the modern criminal trial in Anglo-American justice can be traced back beyond reliable historical records. . . . What is significant for present purposes is that, throughout its evolution, the trial has been open to all who cared to observe. . . .

From these early times, although great changes in courts and procedure took place, one thing remained constant: the public character of the trial at which guilt or innocence was decided. . . .

We have found nothing to suggest that the presumptive openness of the trial, which English courts were later to call "one of the essential qualities of a court of justice," was not also an attribute of the judicial systems of colonial America. . . .

In some instances, the openness of trials was explicitly recognized as part of the fundamental law of the Colony. . . .

Other contemporary writings confirm the recognition that part of the very nature of a criminal trial was its openness to those who wished to attend. . . .

As we have shown, . . . the historical evidence demonstrates conclusively that, at the time when our organic laws were adopted, criminal trials both here and in England had long been presumptively open. This is no quirk of history; rather, it has long been recognized as an indispensable attribute of an Anglo-American trial. . . . Jeremy Bentham not only recognized the therapeutic value of open justice but regarded it as the keystone:

"Without publicity, all other checks are insufficient: in comparison of publicity, all other checks are of small account. Recordation, appeal, whatever other institutions might present themselves in the character of checks, would be found to operate rather as cloaks than checks; as cloaks in reality, as checks only in appearance." . . .

. . . The early history of open trials in part reflects the widespread acknowledgment, long before there were behavioral scientists, that public trials had significant community therapeutic value. Even without such experts to frame the consent in words, people sensed from experience and observation that, especially in the administration of criminal justice, the means used to achieve justice must have the support derived from public acceptance of both the process and its results.

When a shocking crime occurs, a community reaction of outrage and public protest often follows. Thereafter the open processes of justice serve an important prophylactic purpose, providing an outlet for community concern, hostility, and emotion. Without an awareness that society's responses to criminal conduct are underway, natural human reactions of outrage and protest are frustrated and may manifest themselves in some form of vengeful "self-help," as indeed they did regularly in the activities of vigilante "committees" on our frontiers. . . .

Civilized societies withdraw both from the victim and the vigilante the enforcement of criminal laws, but they cannot erase from people's consciousness the fundamental, natural yearning to see justice done—or even the urge for retribution. The crucial prophylactic aspects of the administration of justice cannot function in the dark; no community catharsis can occur if justice is "done in a corner [or] in any covert manner." It is not enough to say that results alone will satiate the natural community desire for "satisfaction." A result considered untoward may undermine public confidence, and where the trial has been concealed from public view, an unexpected outcome can cause a reaction that the system at best has failed and at worst has been corrupted. To work effectively, it is important that society's criminal process "satisfy the appearance of justice," and the appearance of justice can best be provided by allowing people to observe it. . . .

People in an open society do not demand infallibility from their institutions, but it is difficult for them to accept what they are prohibited from observing. When a criminal trial is conducted in the open, there is at least an opportunity both for understanding the system in general and its workings in a particular case: "The educative effect of public attendance is a material advantage. Not only is respect for the law increased and intelligent acquaintance acquired with the methods of government, but a strong confidence in judicial remedies is secured which could never be inspired by a system of secrecy." . . .

. . . Instead of acquiring information about trials by firsthand observation or by word of mouth from those who attended, people now acquire it chiefly through the print and electronic media. In a sense, this validates the media claim of functioning as surrogates for the public. While media representatives enjoy the same right of access as the public, they often are provided special seating and priority of entry so that they may report what people in attendance have seen and heard. This "[contributes] to public understanding of the rule of law and to comprehension of the functioning of the entire criminal justice system. . . ."

From this unbroken, uncontradicted history, supported by reasons as valid today as in centuries past, we are bound to conclude that a presumption of openness inheres in the very nature of a criminal trial under our system of justice. . . .

Despite the history of criminal trials being presumptively open since long before the Constitution, the State presses its contention that neither the Constitution nor the Bill of Rights contains any provision which, by its terms, guarantees to the public the right to attend criminal trials. Standing alone, this is correct, but there remains the question whether, absent an explicit provision, the Constitution affords protection against exclusion of the public from criminal trials.

The First Amendment, in conjunction with the fourteenth, prohibits governments from "abridging the freedom of speech, or of the press; or the right of the people peaceably to assemble, and to petition the Government for a redress of grievances." These expressly guaranteed freedoms share a common core purpose of assuring freedom of communication on matters relating to the functioning of government. Plainly it would be difficult to single out any aspect of government of higher concern and importance to the people than the manner in which criminal trials are conducted; as we have shown, recognition of this pervades the centuries-old history of open trials and the opinions of this Court.

The Bill of Rights was enacted against the backdrop of the long history of trials being presumptively open. Public access to trials was then regarded as an important aspect of the process itself; . . . In guaranteeing freedoms such as those of speech and press, the

First Amendment can be read as protecting the right of everyone to attend trials so as to give meaning to those explicit guarantees. "The First Amendment goes beyond protection of the press and the self-expression of individuals to prohibit government from limiting the stock of information from which members of the public may draw." Free speech carries with it some freedom to listen. . . . What this means in the context of trials is that the First Amendment guarantees of speech and press, standing alone, prohibit government from summarily closing courtroom doors which had long been open to the public at the time that Amendment was adopted. . . .

. . . It is not crucial whether we describe this right to attend criminal trials to hear, see, and communicate observations concerning them as a "right of access," or a "right to gather information," for we have recognized that "without some protection for seeking out the news, freedom of the press could be eviscerated." The explicit, guaranteed rights to speak and to publish concerning what takes place at a trial would lose much meaning if access to observe the trial could, as it was here, be foreclosed arbitrarily.

The right of access to places traditionally open to the public, as criminal trials have long been, may be seen as assured by the amalgam of the First Amendment guarantees of speech and press; and their affinity to the right of assembly is not without relevance. . . . [A] trial courtroom also is a public place where the people generally—and representatives of the media—have a right to be present, and where their presence historically has been thought to enhance the integrity and quality of what takes place.

The State argues that the Constitution nowhere spells out a guarantee for the right of the public to attend trials, and that, accordingly, no such right is protected. . . .

But arguments such as the State makes have not precluded recognition of important rights not enumerated. . . .

We hold that the right to attend criminal trials is implicit in the guarantees of the First Amendment; without the freedom to attend such trials, which people have exercised for centuries, important aspects of freedom of speech and "of the press could be eviscerated."

Having concluded there was a guaranteed right of the public under the First and Fourteenth Amendments to attend the trial of Stevenson's case, we return to the closure order challenged by appellants. . . . Despite the fact that this was the fourth trial of the accused, the trial judge made no findings to support closure; no inquiry was made as to whether alternative solutions would have met the need to ensure fairness; there was no recognition of any right under the Constitution for the public or press to attend the trial. There exist in the context of the trial itself various tested alternatives to satisfy the constitutional demands of fairness. . . . There was no suggestion that any problems with witnesses could not have been dealt with by their exclusion from the courtroom or their sequestration during the trial. Nor is there anything to indicate that sequestration of the jurors would not have guarded against their being subjected to any improper information. All of the alternatives admittedly present difficulties for trial courts, but none of the factors relied on here was beyond the realm of the manageable. Absent an overriding interest articulated in findings, the trial of a criminal case must be open to the public. Accordingly, the judgment under review is

Reversed. . . .

JUSTICE JOHN PAUL STEVENS concurring:
This is a watershed case. Until today, the Court has accorded virtually absolute protection to the dissemination of information or ideas, but never before has it squarely held that the acquisition of newsworthy matter is entitled to any constitutional protection whatsoever. . . .

Today, however, for the first time, the Court unequivocally holds that an arbitrary interference with access to important information is an abridgment of the freedoms of speech and of the press protected by the First Amendment. . . .

. . . I agree that the First Amendment protects the public and the press from abridgment of their rights of access to information about the operation of their government, including the Judicial Branch; given the total absence of any record justification for the closure order entered in this case, that order violated the First Amendment.

JUSTICE WILLIAM BRENNAN, with whom
JUSTICE THURGOOD MARSHALL joined,
concurring:

. . . I agree with those of my Brethren who hold that,
without more, agreement of the trial judge and the
parties cannot constitutionally close a trial to the
public.

While freedom of expression is made inviolate by
the First Amendment, and, with only rare and stringent exceptions, may not be suppressed, the First
Amendment has not been viewed by the Court in all
settings as providing an equally categorical assurance
of the correlative freedom of access to information.
Yet the Court has not ruled out a public access component to the First Amendment in every circumstance.
Read with care and in context, our decisions must
therefore be understood as holding only that any privilege of access to governmental information is subject
to a degree of restraint dictated by the nature of the
information and countervailing interests in security or
confidentiality. These cases neither comprehensively
nor absolutely deny that public access to information
may at times be implied by the First Amendment and
the principles which animate it.

The Court's approach in right-of-access cases
simply reflects the special nature of a claim of First
Amendment right to gather information. . . . [T]he
First Amendment . . . has a structural role to play in
securing and fostering our republican system of self-
government. Implicit in this structural role is not only
"the principle that debate on public issues should be
uninhibited, robust, and wide-open," but also the
antecedent assumption that valuable public debate—
as well as other civic behavior—must be informed.
The structural model links the First Amendment to
that process of communication necessary for a democracy to survive, and thus entails solicitude not only for
communication itself, but also for the indispensable
conditions of meaningful communication. . . .

This judicial task is as much a matter of sensitivity to practical necessities as it is of abstract reasoning.
But at least two helpful principles may be sketched.
First, the case for a right of access has special force
when drawn from an enduring and vital tradition of
public entree to particular proceedings or information.

Such a tradition commands respect, in part, because
the Constitution carries the gloss of history. More
importantly, a tradition of accessibility implies the
favorable judgment of experience. Second, the value
of access must be measured in specifics. Analysis is not
advanced by rhetorical statements that all information
bears upon public issues; what is crucial in individual
cases is whether access to a particular government
process is important in terms of that very process.

To resolve the case before us, therefore, we must
consult historical and current practice with respect to
open trials, and weigh the importance of public access
to the trial process itself. . . .

. . . [S]ignificantly for our present purpose, [the
Court has] recognized that open trials are bulwarks of
our free and democratic government: public access to
court proceedings is one of the numerous "checks and
balances" of our system, because "contemporaneous
review in the forum of public opinion is an effective
restraint on possible abuse of judicial power." Indeed,
the Court focused with particularity upon the public
trial guarantee "as a safeguard against any attempt
to employ our courts as instruments of persecution,"
or "for the suppression of political and religious her-
esies." Thus, . . . open trials are indispensable to First
Amendment political and religious freedoms. . . .

Publicity serves to advance several of the particular purposes of the trial (and, indeed, the judicial)
process. . . . But, as a feature of our governing system of justice, the trial process serves other, broadly
political, interests, and public access advances these
objectives as well. To that extent, trial access possesses
specific structural significance. . . .

Secrecy is profoundly inimical to this demonstrative purpose of the trial process. . . .

But the trial is more than a demonstrably just
method of adjudicating disputes and protecting rights.
It plays a pivotal role in the entire judicial process,
and, by extension, in our form of government. Under
our system, judges are not mere umpires, but, in
their own sphere, lawmakers—a coordinate branch
of government. While individual cases turn upon the
controversies between parties, or involve particular
prosecutions, court rulings impose official and practical consequences upon members of society at large.

Moreover, judges bear responsibility for the vitally important task of construing and securing constitutional rights. Thus, so far as the trial is the mechanism for judicial fact finding, as well as the initial forum for legal decision making, it is a genuine governmental proceeding.

It follows that the conduct of the trial is preeminently a matter of public interest. . . .

. . . [R]esolution of First Amendment public access claims in individual cases must be strongly influenced by the weight of historical practice and by an assessment of the specific structural value of public access in the circumstances. With regard to the case at hand, our ingrained tradition of public trials and the importance of public access to the broader purposes of the trial process, tip the balance strongly toward the rule that trials be open. What countervailing interests might be sufficiently compelling to reverse this presumption of openness need not concern us now, for the statute at stake here authorizes trial closures at the unfettered discretion of the judge and parties. Accordingly, [the law] violates the First and Fourteenth Amendments, and the decision of the Virginia Supreme Court to the contrary should be reversed.

JUSTICE POTTER STEWART concurring:

. . . [The presumption of open criminal proceedings] does not mean that the First Amendment fight of members of the public and representatives of the press to attend civil and criminal trials is absolute. Just as a legislature may impose reasonable time, place, and manner restrictions upon the exercise of First Amendment freedoms, so may a trial judge impose reasonable limitations upon the unrestricted occupation of a courtroom by representatives of the press and members of the public. Much more than a city street, a trial courtroom must be a quiet and orderly place. Moreover, every courtroom has a finite physical capacity, and there may be occasions when not all who wish to attend a trial may do so. And while there exist many alternative ways to satisfy the constitutional demands of a fair trial, those demands may also sometimes justify limitations upon the unrestricted presence of spectators in the courtroom.

Since, in the present case, the trial judge appears to have given no recognition to the right of representatives of the press and members of the public to be present at the Virginia murder trial over which he was presiding, the judgment under review must be reversed.

JUSTICE HARRY BLACKMUN concurring:

. . . I remain convinced that the right to a public trial is to be found where the Constitution explicitly placed it—in the Sixth Amendment.

The Court, however, has eschewed the Sixth Amendment route. The plurality turns to other possible constitutional sources and invokes a veritable potpourri of them—the Speech Clause of the First Amendment, the Press Clause, the Assembly Clause, the Ninth Amendment, and a cluster of penumbral guarantees recognized in past decisions. This course is troublesome, but it is the route that has been selected and, at least for now, we must live with it. . . .

. . . [W]ith the Sixth Amendment set to one side in this case, I am driven to conclude, as a secondary position, that the First Amendment must provide some measure of protection for public access to the trial. . . . It is clear and obvious to me, on the approach the Court has chosen to take, that, by closing this criminal trial, the trial judge abridged these First Amendment interests of the public.

I also would reverse, and I join the judgment of the Court.

JUSTICE WILLIAM REHNQUIST dissenting:

. . . I do not believe that either the First or Sixth Amendment, as made applicable to the States by the Fourteenth, requires that a State's reasons for denying public access to a trial, where both the prosecuting attorney and the defendant have consented to an order of closure approved by the judge, are subject to any additional constitutional review at our hands. . . .

. . . [T]o gradually rein in, as this Court has done over the past generation, all of the ultimate decision making power over how justice shall be administered, not merely in the federal system but in each of the 50 States, is a task that no Court consisting of nine persons, however gifted, is equal to. Nor is it desirable that such authority be exercised by such a tiny numerical fragment of the 220 million people who compose the population of this country. . . .

. . . [I]t is basically unhealthy to have so much authority concentrated in a small group of lawyers who have been appointed to the Supreme Court and enjoy virtual life tenure. . . .

The issue here is not whether the "right" to freedom of the press conferred by the First Amendment to the Constitution overrides the defendant's "right" to a fair trial conferred by other Amendments to the Constitution; it is, instead, whether any provision in the Constitution may fairly be read to prohibit what the trial judge in the Virginia state-court system did in this case. Being unable to find any such prohibition in the First, Sixth, Ninth, or any other Amendment to the United States Constitution, or in the Constitution itself, I dissent.

Chapter 11

The concept of universal access to modern communications is at the heart of our consumer mission and our founding statute, and access to broadband is this generation's universal service imperative. Wired and wireless broadband have become an indispensable platform for innovation, commerce and civic engagement.

FCC chairman Julius Genachowski[1]

In 2013, the FCC implemented a section of the 21st Century Communications and Video Accessibility Act of 2010 that requires all mobile phone service providers and manufacturers to ensure that people with visual or hearing impairments have access to innovative and emerging communication technologies, including Internet browsers on mobile phones.

Electronic Media Regulation
From Radio to the Internet

Federal Communications Commission

Broadcast Regulation

Reasons to Regulate Broadcasting
The Public Interest Standard
Program and Advertising Regulations
Broadcast Licensing
Noncommercial Broadcasting

Cable Television Regulation

Cable Regulation's Development
Cable Franchising
Cable Programming

Direct Broadcast Satellites

Internet Regulation

FCC Internet Regulation
Net Neutrality
The Internet's First Amendment Status

Cases for Study

➤ Red Lion Broadcasting Co., Inc. v. Federal Communications Commission
➤ Turner Broadcasting System, Inc. v. Federal Communications Commission

Suppose . . .

. . . an author publishes a book that criticizes a politically conservative presidential candidate. In reviewing the book, a newspaper columnist says the author must be sympathetic to terrorist groups. Could the newspaper be forced to give the author space to reply to the columnist? No, the First Amendment protects the paper from being required to grant a reply. But if a radio or television station airs similar criticism of the author, could the author force the station to allow a reply? If so, what would the rationale be for the courts to uphold that requirement despite the First Amendment? What differentiates broadcast stations from other forms of media? Look for a discussion of these questions when the case of *Red Lion Broadcasting Co., Inc. v. Federal Communications Commission* is discussed later in this chapter and the case is excerpted at the end of the chapter.

Broadcasters can be sued for libel, invasion of privacy, intentional infliction of emotional distress and other torts discussed in previous chapters. So can Internet bloggers and producers of programs transmitted by satellite, cable and broadband. A judge may order a television reporter to reveal his or her story's sources, just as a judge may demand sources from a newspaper journalist. Legal issues discussed in this book apply to the electronic media just as they apply to the print media. However, the electronic media, particularly radio and television,

Guglielmo Marconi, an Italian physicist, shared a Nobel Prize in 1909 for developing wireless telegraphy, one of the inventions leading to broadcast radio and television and ultimately to new technologies like the Internet.

must comply with regulations that are not applicable to print. For example, it is illegal to broadcast without first obtaining a license from the Federal Communications Commission (FCC), a federal government agency. Newspaper, magazine and book publishers do not need a government license to print and distribute materials.

Electronic media developed long after the United States adopted the First Amendment. Guglielmo Marconi invented the means of sending radio signals without using wires. Many ships used Marconi's equipment for ship-to-shore communication. To protect his patents, Marconi ordered his employees not to accept messages from ships using other manufacturers' radios. Fearing that ships' distress signals would be ignored, Congress passed the Wireless Ship Act of 1910, requiring oceangoing vessels to carry radio equipment and radio operators.[2] The law also made it illegal for companies to disregard ships' radio transmissions.

Because all large ships had radios, countless radio messages went from ships to shore and ship to ship. Also, amateur radio fans sent many transmissions. All these messages clogged the spectrum, the range of electromagnetic radio frequencies used to transmit radio and television signals and data. Congress had not considered the law's impact on the spectrum. Congress required ships to have radios but had not specified what ships could use which portions of the spectrum. Signals carrying ships' messages interfered with each other, preventing messages from reaching their destinations.

Not only American ships but ships all over the world were also affected. Countries pressured Congress to establish standards allowing messages to reach their destinations without other messages interfering. Many nations said they would cooperate in setting international norms.

Then tragedy struck. In 1912 the Titanic hit an Atlantic Ocean iceberg, plunging thousands to their deaths. Many passengers could have been saved if a rescue ship had arrived. The Titanic sent a distress signal, but there were two problems. The signal, received in Newfoundland, Canada, could not be sent to authorities because ordinary messages from other ships and amateur radio users' messages interfered with the Titanic's signal.[3] Also, the radio operator on the ship closest to the Titanic was off duty and did not hear the message.

Federal Radio Commission (FRC)
A federal agency established by the Federal Radio Act in 1927 to oversee radio broadcasting. The Federal Communications Commission succeeded the FRC in 1934.

The Titanic disaster prompted Congress to regulate wireless communication. This led to the Radio Act of 1912, the first statute directly regulating commercial radio.[4] The 1912 law required oceangoing ships to have radio operators on duty around the clock. It also gave the U.S. secretary of commerce power to grant radio station licenses, stipulating what frequency each licensee would use. The intent was to prevent message interference.

However, the law did not give the secretary power to refuse a license or to regulate radio in any substantial way. Any person applying for a license would get one, as long as no two licenses were for the same frequency. The commerce secretary also had no authority to limit the power stations used to broadcast. A powerful station could drown out stations broadcasting at lower power even though they were not on the same frequency. Amateur radio operators began ignoring the law, changing the frequencies they used and even relocating to other cities without the secretary's permission. A federal court tied the secretary's hands, saying the 1912 law allowed moving a station without approval.[5]

During the early and mid-1920s a number of commercial radio stations went on the air. These stations experienced signal degradation from other commercial stations and amateur users who clogged the spectrum with their broadcasts. A federal appellate court said the secretary of commerce could not refuse to grant a radio license even when there was no frequency space available.[6] The decision also said the secretary could not limit the power level stations used to broadcast their signals, allowing some stations to drown out other stations' signals. The situation was chaotic.

Congress finally realized that many Americans listened to radio and that radio was playing an increasingly important role in American commerce, so it adopted the Radio Act of 1927.[7] The law established the **Federal Radio Commission (FRC)**, a federal agency charged with issuing or denying radio licenses and assigning frequencies to prevent stations from interfering with each other. The law gave the FRC the power to regulate stations as necessary to allow radio's development.

The 1927 law included several provisions that are in effect today. First, the act specifically said the FRC could not censor radio content. Second, it said the public, not station licensees, owned the spectrum. Third, the law required the FRC to make decisions based on the "public interest, convenience and necessity." Also, a federal court interpreted the 1927 act to say the federal government had exclusive control over radio broadcasting, and states were not to make their own broadcasting laws.[8]

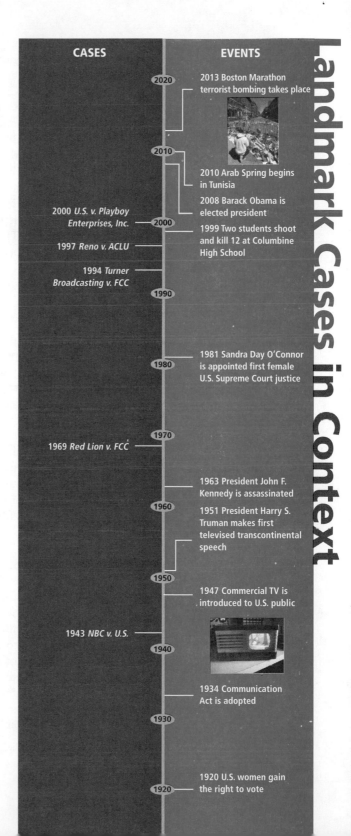

Landmark Cases in Context

CASES

EVENTS

2020

2013 Boston Marathon terrorist bombing takes place

2010

2010 Arab Spring begins in Tunisia

2008 Barack Obama is elected president

2000 *U.S. v. Playboy Enterprises, Inc.* — 2000

1999 Two students shoot and kill 12 at Columbine High School

1997 *Reno v. ACLU*

1994 *Turner Broadcasting v. FCC*

1990

1981 Sandra Day O'Connor is appointed first female U.S. Supreme Court justice

1980

1970

1969 *Red Lion v. FCC*

1963 President John F. Kennedy is assassinated

1960

1951 President Harry S. Truman makes first televised transcontinental speech

1950

1947 Commercial TV is introduced to U.S. public

1943 *NBC v. U.S.*

1940

1934 Communication Act is adopted

1930

1920 U.S. women gain the right to vote

1920

Congress intended the FRC to put the radio industry on firm footing and then have the secretary of commerce oversee radio stations. But Congress soon realized that plan would not work. Radio needed continued oversight. Also, in addition to the FRC, a number of different federal agencies had authority over various aspects of the radio industry. To resolve these problems, Congress rescinded the 1927 act and adopted the Communications Act of 1934.[9] Although often amended, the 1934 law still is in place, giving the **Federal Communications Commission (FCC)** authority to regulate over-the-air radio and television. States still may not regulate broadcasting. The 1934 act also allows the commission to oversee long-distance telephone companies and other industries providing interstate communication services by wire. In 1984, Congress gave the FCC power to regulate cable television.[10] The FCC also has jurisdiction over direct broadcast satellites.[11] The Internet is largely unregulated by either the FCC or other government agencies.

Federal Communications Commission (FCC) An independent U.S. government agency, directly responsible to Congress, charged with regulating interstate and international communications by radio, television, wire, satellite and cable. The Communications Act of 1934 established the FCC; its jurisdiction covers the 50 states, the District of Columbia and U.S. possessions.

Federal Communications Commission

The 1934 act established the FCC as an independent federal agency; however, it is not completely independent. Politics envelop the commission. The U.S. president selects the five commissioners, who are appointed to five-year terms. The president also designates one of the commissioners to be FCC chair. The chair is the commission's chief executive officer. The U.S. Senate must approve people nominated to be commissioners, including the chair. No more than three commissioners may be from the same political party at any one time. Commissioners may not have financial interests in any company or industry the FCC oversees and must be U.S. citizens. The FCC operates under the Administrative Procedure Act, a law telling federal agencies how they may propose and adopt regulations and giving federal courts power to rule on challenges to those decisions. Congress gives the FCC its funding, increasing or decreasing the budget each year as Congress chooses.

The commission's responsibilities include regulating all technologies using the electromagnetic spectrum, such as radio, television, cable, satellite and broadband communications. The FCC also regulates wireline and wireless telephone companies offering long-distance services. Day-to-day commission work includes enforcing the Communications Act of 1934 and the FCC's rules, granting licenses for various communications services, resolving disputes, ensuring that spectrum users comply with the commission's regulations. FCC rules cover a wide range of issues such as the sale of stolen cell phones and global positioning system (GPS) devices, deceptive practices by telemarketers and even the loudness of television commercials.[12]

The commissioners adopt rules and regulations affecting entire industries—every radio or television station, for example. The process starts when commissioners identify an issue they want to examine. FCC staff members prepare a

realWorld Law

The FCC and a Mega-merger

Under FCC chair Julius Genachowski, who served from 2009 to 2013, the FCC played a more active role in scrutinizing proposed mergers of communication companies. In 2011, the FCC blocked AT&T's move to acquire T-Mobile for $39 billion. This was the first FCC block of a communication merger in more than a decade. Genachowski's FCC sought extensive data to evaluate whether or not the merger could lead to a duopoly in the wireless broadband market, with a post-merger AT&T and Verizon controlling as much as 80 percent of the nation's market. While the United States Department of Justice sued to block the merger and that case continued on in court, AT&T continued to press for approval from the FCC. After the FCC's Wireless Telecommunication Bureau's Staff Report found that the merger would cost jobs and not serve the public interest, Genachowski blocked the transaction.[1]

Julius Genachowski

1. Aaron George, *Seven Legacies of the Genachowski Era: Part One of Two,* HOGAN LOVELLS: FOCUS ON REGULATION, Feb. 20, 2013, *available at:* http://www.hlregulation.com/2013/02/20/seven-legacies-of-the-genachowski-era-part-one-of-two.

Notice of Proposed Rule Making explaining what the commissioners plan to do and why. Members of the public and companies that will be affected by the proposed regulations submit comments to the commission, saying why they like or dislike the proposal. There is an opportunity to submit reply comments responding to the original submissions. The FCC staff considers all the submissions and drafts a Report and Order. The commissioners discuss the draft, suggest changes and vote on a final version in a public meeting. Companies and individuals who object to the commission's final decision may ask the commissioners to reconsider. Sometimes the FCC will reconsider its decision, but usually it does not. The final regulations then become part of the FCC's rules.

A company, an industry association or an individual affected by a commission decision may challenge it in a federal appellate court. Usually the appeal is to the U.S. Court of Appeals for the District of Columbia Circuit, although other circuits also may hear an appeal of a commission decision. A federal court ruling takes precedence over an FCC decision. The FCC cannot enforce a regulation that a court rejected.

Companies, industries and individuals must comply with the FCC's rules or face sanctions. The commission's rules have the effect of a law. The commission has a range of possible punishments, from a letter of reprimand in a licensee's file, to a fine, to revoking or not renewing a license. Commonly, the FCC punishes by issuing a fine, called a "forfeiture." If the FCC merely considers regulating, an

Notice of Proposed Rule Making
A notice issued by the FCC announcing that the commission is considering changing certain of its regulations or adopting new rules.

Emerging Law

Wi-Fi and the FCC

In 2013, the FCC proposed several initiatives to improve the nation's Wi-Fi networks. Wi-Fi is the technology that allows electronic devices to wirelessly exchange data using radio waves over a computer network, including high-speed Internet connections. The FCC received unanimous support from the cable industry when it proposed freeing up additional spectrum space in the band that cable operators already use to provide more than 100,000 Wi-Fi hot spots across the country. The additional spectrum space would expand spectrum allocation in that band by 35 percent, speeding up existing Wi-Fi networks and relieving congestion.[1]

In addition, the FCC set up an auction of broadcaster airwaves that would boost 4G networks, and it proposed creating a super, public Wi-Fi network so powerful that consumers could use the new network to make calls or surf the Internet without paying a cellphone bill.[2] Not surprisingly, tech companies support the move while the wireless industry opposes it. If approved, the free network, which would come from freeing up unlicensed spectrum, would take a few years to set up. It would be more powerful than existing networks and would have farther reach. But, one of the challenges with a public Wi-Fi network harks back to the early days of radio—with no one actively managing new public Wi-Fi networks, connections in larger cities could easily become jammed because of the high volume of traffic. Still, outgoing FCC chairman Julius Genachowski, who led the effort to crate the public Wi-Fi network, said it "is a vibrantly free-market approach that offers low barriers to entry to innovators developing the technologies of the future and benefits consumers."[3]

1. John Eggerton, *FCC Votes to Free up More Wi-Fi Spectrum,* BROADCASTING & CABLE, Feb. 20, 2013, *available at:* http://www.broadcastingcable.com/article/491940-FCC_Votes_to_Free_Up_More_Wi_Fi_Spectrum.php
2. Cecilia King, *Tech, Telecom Giants Take Sides as FCC Proposes Large Public Wi-Fi Networks,* WASHINGTON POST, Feb. 3, 2013, *available at:* http://articles.washingtonpost.com/2013–02–03/business/36728627_1_wifi-networks-wireless-industry-wireless-networks.
3. *Id.*

industry may take action on its own. When the FCC suggested in 1971 that radio stations played songs glorifying and encouraging drug use, a number of stations self-censored their playlists.

SUMMARY

FEDERAL LAW FIRST REGULATED ELECTRONIC MEDIA—radio—in 1910, requiring oceangoing ships to have radios and radio operators. The 1912 law, prompted by the Titanic's sinking, gave the U.S. secretary of commerce power to license radio stations. Despite licensing, amateur and commercial radio stations continually interfered with each other's signals. National conferences urging cooperation among radio broadcasters were unsuccessful. In 1927, Congress established the Federal

Radio Commission and gave it extensive power over radio broadcasting. The Federal Communications Commission replaced the FRC in 1934. Today, the FCC uses its powers to adopt regulations affecting large segments of the electronic media, as well as licensing spectrum users and enforcing the commission's regulations. ∎

Broadcast Regulation

Over-the-air radio and television broadcasters use the electromagnetic spectrum to send signals to many listeners and viewers simultaneously. This is the Communication Act's definition of "broadcasting."[13] It is not a broadcast when the CBS television network sends a signal to the CBS station in Des Moines, Iowa. That is a private transmission from the network to the station, and it is illegal for anyone else to intercept the signal.[14] It is a broadcast when the Des Moines station sends the signal through its transmitter to thousands of television sets and to the local cable system. CBS, then, does not broadcast; rather, the stations owned by or affiliated with CBS broadcast. The FCC's broadcast regulations apply to radio and television stations.

Reasons to Regulate Broadcasting

Radio and television station licensees often tell courts there is no valid reason to regulate broadcasting. Stations are mass media, just like print media and the Internet, they say. The First Amendment should apply equally to all mass media, so broadcast stations should not be regulated any more than newspapers or magazines.

The U.S. Supreme Court has rejected this argument in two ways. First, the Court's decisions say all mass media need not be treated the same way under the First Amendment. The court has held that movies, for example, do not have the same First Amendment rights that print media have.[15] Each mass medium has its own peculiarities, although each has basic free speech protection, the Court said.

Second, broadcasting uses the spectrum, a publicly owned natural resource only a select few companies may use. Unlike the print media—anyone with enough money can start a newspaper—the spectrum limits the number of stations in a geographical area. In 1943, the Supreme Court for the first time said this is the principal reason broadcasters can be regulated.[16] In that case, the Court upheld the FCC's jurisdiction of broadcast networks. After the Communications Act of 1934 created the commission, radio station owners expected the FCC to prevent interference by carefully choosing licensees and controlling the power that stations used to broadcast. Owners wanted the FCC to do no more than that. But the commission took more control over the radio industry than expected. Among other decisions, the FCC adopted rules regulating the relationship between the emerging radio networks and local stations. The commission was concerned that networks exerted too much control over stations, requiring the stations to carry all network programs, for example. The networks sued the FCC, claiming that it overstepped its statutory responsibilities.

The U.S. Supreme Court supported the commission. The Court said radio's "facilities are limited; they are not available to all who may wish to use them; the radio spectrum simply is not large enough to accommodate everybody. There is a fixed natural limitation upon the number of stations that can operate without interfering with one another." The few companies using the spectrum have a special privilege, making it reasonable to regulate them, the Court said.

Twenty-six years later the Court reinforced this rationale for regulating the broadcast media. In *Red Lion Broadcasting Co. v. FCC,* the Court upheld the FCC's rule requiring that a station offer free time to an individual personally attacked by comments made on the station.[17] The audience's right to hear both sides of the issue was more important than the licensee's First Amendment rights, according to the Court. The Court justified this conclusion by saying the spectrum prevents everyone who wants to broadcast from doing so. Print media do not have the same right-of-reply requirement, the Court said. In fact, in *Miami Herald Publishing Co. v. Tornillo,* discussed in Chapter 1, the Court said a Florida statute requiring a newspaper that had printed a critical editorial about a candidate for public office to allow the candidate to publish a reply was unconstitutional.[18] The First Amendment prohibited government from forcing newspapers to publish anything, the Court said.

spectrum scarcity The limitation that arises because only a certain number of broadcast radio and television stations in a geographical area may use the spectrum without causing interference with other stations' signals. Spectrum scarcity is the primary reason courts give for allowing Congress and the FCC to regulate broadcasters.

Spectrum scarcity remains the reason courts most often give for allowing broadcast regulation. Not everyone who wants a license to operate a television or radio station may have one, because there is only enough room in the spectrum to accommodate a limited number of stations. The U.S. Supreme Court used this rationale in *National Broadcasting Co. v. FCC* in 1943 to justify the Federal Communications Commission adopting regulations affecting the broadcast industry.[19] Again, in the *Red Lion* case the Court emphasized that spectrum scarcity justifies limiting broadcasters' First Amendment rights.

In taking this position, courts seem to ignore the development of direct broadcast satellite (DBS) service, satellite radio, low-power radio and television stations (broadcasting signals available within a few miles of the transmitter), the Internet and other new technologies. The Supreme Court has recognized the advent of cable and satellite television technology and the Internet but said it would not alter its spectrum scarcity rationale "without some signal from Congress or the FCC that technological developments have advanced so far that some revision of the system of broadcast regulation may be required."[20] Outside of Congress and the FCC, some leaders in the technology sector are vigorously arguing for change. In 2013 at its annual conference, Google CEO Larry Page criticized government regulations that impact the Internet and said, "the law can't be right when it's 50 years old. It's before the Internet—that's a pretty major change."[21]

In addition to spectrum scarcity, courts use two other rationales to justify regulating radio and television. One is that the broadcast media are pervasive. Radio and television sets are turned on and available nearly everywhere. Without regulation, children in particular could be exposed to inappropriate content.[22]

A second reason is that broadcast media have a greater influence on audiences—a "special impact"—than do print media.[23] Again, this rationale is especially concerned with children.

Although broadcasting remains the most regulated mass medium, during the past two decades the FCC, with the courts' approval, has rescinded many broadcasting regulations. However, the Supreme Court has yet clearly to state that spectrum scarcity no longer is a valid rationale for regulating over-the-air radio and television.

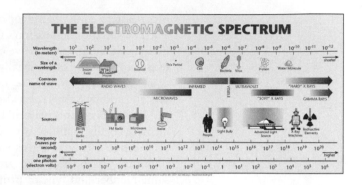

The Public Interest Standard

In the 1927 Radio Act and again in the 1934 Communications Act, Congress said it wanted the public interest to come before the stations' interests. Both laws say federal regulation is to be guided by the "public interest, convenience and necessity."[24] But the law does not define the term "public interest." The FCC can say it is in the public interest to adopt a specific regulation, and a different group of commissioners later can say the public interest requires rescinding the regulation. Courts over the years have not agreed how to define "public interest."

Radio stations, over-the-air television stations and direct broadcast satellites (DBS) transmit signals using radio frequencies, all a part of the electromagnetic spectrum. The "electromagnetic spectrum" is the name for the range of radiation making up what may be thought of as a seamless band. Electromagnetic radiation is a stream of photons, massless particles traveling at the speed of light in a pattern looking like a wave.

Through its first 50 years overseeing broadcasters, the FCC justified adopting regulations by citing the public interest. Then in the 1980s, the commission said the public interest required deregulating the broadcast industry. The FCC's focus turned more to letting the market rather than the commission regulate broadcasting. This became the commission's definition of regulating in the public interest. Mark Fowler, FCC chairman from 1981 to 1987, led the charge against regulation. He thought the marketplace could substitute for government regulation. Under Fowler and subsequent commission chairs, the FCC eliminated many program requirements, including rules obliging stations to survey their communities to determine programming preferences and limits on how many minutes per hour could be used for commercials and other regulations.

Program and Advertising Regulations

The FCC is not allowed to censor broadcast content.[25] But the FCC may set certain general programming rules, such as prohibiting hoaxes, requiring children's programming and regulating politicians' radio and television appearances.

Political Broadcasting Politicians want to be certain of reelection. It is not surprising, then, that in both the 1927 and 1934 laws Congress ensured that broadcasters could not favor one candidate for an elective office over another. The law and the commission's implementing rules say that when one legally qualified candidate for an elective office uses a radio or television station, the station must provide any other legally qualified candidate for the same office with an equal opportunity to use the station if the candidate asks for an opportunity. The law and commission's rules also apply to cable television systems. Section 315 of the 1934 act controls political broadcasting and is in effect any time there are two or more legally qualified candidates for the same office.[26]

Section 315 guarantees equal opportunity rather than equal time. "Equal opportunity" means being given the opportunity to reach approximately the same number and type of people as a candidate's opponent did. Being allowed to purchase a minute of time at midnight is not equal opportunity if the candidate's opponent purchased a minute at 9 p.m. Nor is being given one minute an equal opportunity if the candidate's opponent has been given 30 minutes. Also, equal opportunity means getting free time if a candidate's opponent appeared on a station or cable system without paying, or paying for time if a candidate's opponent pays.

Legally Qualified Candidate A legally qualified candidate can be voted for and elected under applicable rules. FCC regulations explain that a legally qualified candidate is someone who has publicly announced a bid for office, has her or his name on the ballot or is a serious write-in candidate. The candidate also must be legally qualified to hold the office.[27] For example, a 25-year-old cannot be a legally qualified candidate for president, because the Constitution requires the president to be at least 35 years old. Independent candidates and those running on a third-party ticket are legally qualified candidates if they meet the criteria.

Candidates in a primary election for, say, mayor would seem to be running against each other. But that is not the case in applying Section 315. In a primary, Democrats oppose other Democrats for their party's nomination and Republicans oppose other Republicans. But neither party's candidates oppose the other's, nor do they oppose independents or third-party candidates. Therefore, if a Democrat buys 60 seconds of advertising time on a radio station during a primary election period, a Republican running in the primary cannot invoke Section 315 to require the station to sell him or her a minute. Not until the general election does a Democrat oppose a Republican as well as all other legally qualified candidates for the office. During the general election every legally qualified candidate may use the equal opportunity rule if another candidate for the office uses a broadcast station or cable system.

Use of a Station or Cable System Section 315's equal opportunity requirement applies when a legally qualified candidate uses a broadcast station or cable system. "Use" is defined as the candidate or the candidate's picture being seen or the candidate's voice being heard on a broadcast station or cable system. The broadcasting of a candidate's name without the candidate's picture or voice is not a use.

realWorld Law

Political Advertising and the 2012 Elections

The $3.1 billion spent on political advertising in 2012 was 38 percent more than was spent in 2010 and almost double the amount spent during the 2008 presidential election year.[1] Almost all of the $3.1 billion went to local television stations, and those in the hotly contested battleground states of Colorado, Florida, Ohio and Virginia made the most money. Some stations in those states extended their commercial breaks and even pre-empted network programming to air more ads in the final days leading up to the election.[2]

In an effort to add more transparency to the source of political ads, the FCC in 2012 passed a rule that required TV stations to post political ad buying information online, but many watchdog groups complained that compliance with the rule was spotty. ProPublica reported that some of the stations' files contained "illegible writing, duplicate contracts, opaque revisions and obscure internal filing practices."[3]

Although the new FCC website that hosted the information is an improvement over the previous paper file system, the FCC acknowledged that it would need to develop a standard format for submission and create searchable and sortable functions. In 2014 the online system will expand to include all TV stations. In 2012 it only covered the four major network affiliate stations in the Top 50 broadcast markets. In 2014 the D.C. Circuit Court of Appeals is also expected to rule on a lawsuit filed by the National Association of Broadcasters that challenged the new FCC rule.[4]

1. Deborah Potter, Katerina-Eva Matsa and Amy Mitchell, *The State of the News Media 2013—Local TV: Audience Declines as Revenue Bounces Back,* PROJECT FOR EXCELLENCE IN JOURNALISM, *available at:* http://stateofthemedia.org/2013/local-tv-audience-declines-as-revenue-bounces-back/
2. *Id.*
3. Justin Elliott, *FCC's Plan for Fixing its Political Ads Transparency Site? It Won't Say,* PROPUBLICA, Dec. 6, 2012, *available at:* http://www.propublica.org/article/fcc-clams-up-on-its-own-transparency-initiative-free-the-files
4. *Id.*

Whenever a candidate, her picture or her voice is on a station or cable system, there is a use. This does not apply only to a candidate's commercials. If a candidate appears on a television station's outdoor recreation program to give a fly-fishing demonstration, the candidate has used the station. This is true even if the candidate does not mention that she is a candidate, discuss her platform or refer to politics in any way. Potential voters might have a more favorable impression of the candidate when she proves herself a fly-fishing expert instead of discussing her political platform in a commercial. Her legally qualified opponents, then, may request equal opportunity.

Exceptions to the Use Rule Many years ago, independent and minor party candidates saw a loophole in the law. If a local news program interviews the Republican and Democratic candidates for mayor, those candidates have used the station. Numerous mayoral candidates could demand equal opportunity, even if the station did not want to interview them. Realizing this, the station could decide to interview none of the candidates.

Not wanting to discourage broadcast reporting, Congress in 1959 adopted four exceptions to the use rule. First, regularly scheduled news programs are exempt. A candidate's appearance on these programs will not trigger Section 315 for opposing candidates. This exemption was meant for the 11 p.m. news and similar local news programs. But when the commission defined this category as including "programs reporting about some area of current events, in a manner similar to more traditional newscasts,"[28] it also included such programs as "Entertainment Tonight"[29] and "Celebrity Justice."[30] If an anchor or reporter on a regularly scheduled news program is a legally qualified candidate for an elective office, equal opportunity will apply. Why doesn't the news program qualify as an exception to the use rule? It is because the reporter, for example, is not the subject of a news report giving voters more information about the reporter's candidacy, the reason Congress adopted the news program exception. Rather, the reporter is conveying news about others. If the reporter stays on the air in that role while running for office, all her opponents would be entitled to free air time.

Second, regularly scheduled news interview programs are exempt. These must have been regularly scheduled for some time before the election. For example, scheduling four interview shows, one each week for a month before an election, does not qualify a program as "regularly scheduled." Although this exemption initially was for programs such as "Meet the Press" and "Face the Nation," the FCC has included "Jerry Springer"[31] and even "The Howard Stern Show."[32]

Third, live coverage of bona fide news events is exempt. If a candidate's campaign speech is covered live, the candidate's on-air appearance will not be considered a use. Nor is it a use if candidates participate in a televised debate, no matter who sponsors the debate. Because debates are exempt from the use rule, the debate organizers may include and exclude any candidates they want. Even debates on noncommercial stations are exempt from the Section 315 use rule.[33]

Fourth, candidates' appearances on documentaries do not trigger Section 315 if the appearance is incidental to the program's topic. For example, if a mayoral candidate is an expert on the state's tourist industry and appears in a documentary about that topic, it will not be considered a use. Of course, if the documentary is about the candidate's childhood in a housing project, his appearance would not be incidental to the program's topic and would be a use.

Invoking Section 315 A candidate wanting equal opportunity must request time from the station or cable system within seven days of his opponent's appearance. If the candidate fails to make a request within the seven-day period, the station or system need not honor a request for equal opportunity. The station or cable system is under no obligation to notify opponents of a political candidate who uses the station.

Lowest Unit Rate If one candidate uses the station or system without paying—for example, making a pot roast as a guest on the station's cooking program—his opponents do not have to pay for their uses. Making one candidate pay while another gets free time is not equal opportunity. But if the first candidate pays for time—buying a minute to show a commercial, for instance—opponents also have to pay.

Congress ensured that politicians had to pay as little as possible to buy advertising time on broadcast stations and cable systems. Section 315 requires a station or system to charge politicians the **lowest unit rate,** equivalent to the rate the very best commercial advertiser pays. The advertiser buying the most time on the station gets the lowest per-minute advertising rate; a political candidate will pay no more than that. It does not matter if a candidate purchases only one minute of time during a campaign or 1,000 minutes of time. Each minute will cost what the station's biggest advertiser pays per minute. Of course, the biggest advertiser will pay less for a minute at 3 a.m. than at 8 p.m. So will political candidates.

To reduce negative political advertising, a 2002 federal law requires candidates to promise stations they will not refer to their opponents in a commercial. A candidate may refer to an opponent only under certain conditions: For a radio commercial, the ad must include the candidate's voice approving the commercial's contents. For a television commercial, the ad must show the candidate or the candidate's picture with a printed statement approving the commercial. If a candidate mentions an opponent and these requirements are not met, the lowest unit rate will not apply.[34]

The lowest unit rate is in effect during the 45 days before any primary election and the 60 days before any general election. Outside those periods, political candidates are charged a rate comparable to other advertisers. If a candidate and a car dealer both buy 50 minutes of advertising time, they will pay the same per-minute amount when the lowest unit rate requirement does not apply.

lowest unit rate The maximum rate a broadcaster or cable system may charge a politician for advertising time during the 45 days before primary elections and the 60 days before general elections.

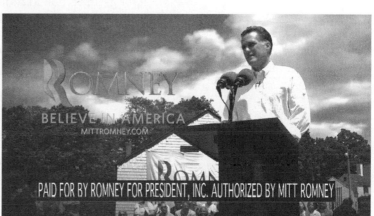

This Mitt Romney ad from the 2012 U.S. presidential election prominently displays the sponsorship identification required by the FCC.

Sponsorship Identification FCC regulations require any commercial on a broadcast station to identify who paid for the ad.[35] This rule applies to political advertisements as well. A candidate's ad, then, must say on radio or show in print for a televised ad something like "This advertisement paid for by the Pat Smith for Congress Committee."

Censoring Not Permitted Broadcast stations and cable systems may not edit or censor political appearances. For example, if one candidate appears for 30 minutes showing how to fly-fish, the candidate's opponent must be given 30 minutes if he asks the station for that time. During his 30 minutes, he need not show his fly-fishing technique. He may discuss his candidacy and platform, say why voters should favor him and not his opponent or do anything else he wants with his time. Even if a station knows that a candidate will make racist or homophobic remarks, or say anything else the community does not want to hear, the station may not censor the candidate's presentation or refuse to put the candidate on the air. Similarly, if a station manager believes that a political ad is inappropriate for children, the manager may not air the commercial late at night, for example.[36] The ad must be broadcast when the candidate paid for it to be aired.

Because stations are not permitted to edit or censor, they also are not responsible for what candidates say. If a candidate libels his opponent, the opponent may sue the candidate but not the station.[37]

Reasonable Time for Federal Candidates It is possible for a station to avoid all the complications of political broadcasting by never putting candidates on the air. If the first legally qualified candidate running for an office does not appear on a station, Section 315 would not be triggered for other candidates. Although this is legal under Section 315, the FCC has suggested stations should not refuse candidates air time. The commission believes a station that does not allow its listeners to hear from candidates is not acting in the public interest.

However, Congress recognized this Section 315 loophole and decided to close it—at least for itself. Section 312(a)(7) of the Communications Act requires radio and television stations to provide federal candidates with reasonable access.[38] This means even the first candidate for a federal office asking to buy commercial time must be sold the advertising spot.[39] The federal elective offices are senator, representative and president. Although the law does not specifically state that it applies to cable systems, the FCC assumes it does. Section 312(a)(7) exempts noncommercial stations from complying with the section's requirements.

Section 312(a)(7)'s requirement that commercial stations provide candidates for federal office with "reasonable access" is not clear. The U.S. Supreme Court, rejecting CBS Television Network's decision not to sell President Jimmy Carter 30 minutes of prime time, gave only limited direction in interpreting the statute. Broadcasters must consider each federal candidate's request "on an individualized basis, and broadcasters are required to tailor their responses to accommodate, as much as reasonably possible, a candidate's stated purposes in seeking air time." However, broadcasters also may "give weight to such factors as the amount of time previously sold to the candidate, the disruptive impact on regular programming, and the likelihood of requests for time by rival candidates." But broadcasters may not use these criteria as an excuse to deny federal candidates the time requested. Rather, "broadcasters must cite a realistic danger of substantial program disruption" or the likelihood of too many requests.[40]

Aside from being assured they can get on the air, federal candidates are treated under Section 315 just as candidates for state and local offices are.

Candidates' Supporters If a candidate's campaign manager appears in an ad saying, "Vote for my person," is Section 315 in effect? Not unless the candidate, the candidate's picture or the candidate's voice is in the ad. Realizing that this situation would be unfair to others running for the same office, the FCC said opposing candidates' supporters could ask for equal opportunity under the same standards that Section 315 requires. This means the candidate him- or herself cannot ask for equal opportunity if his or her opponent's supporters use a station, but the candidate's supporters can ask for time. This is called the **Zapple rule,** named after a congressional staff attorney who first asked the FCC about these circumstances.

Zapple rule A political broadcasting rule that allows a candidate's supporters equal opportunity to use broadcast stations if the candidate's opponents' supporters use the stations.

Broadcast Editorials If a station airs an editorial supporting one candidate, opposing candidates cannot request equal opportunity under Section 315. A federal appellate court said commercial radio and television stations have a First Amendment right to support candidates.[41] A federal law forbids noncommercial stations from supporting political candidates.[42] However, noncommercial stations may air editorials supporting or opposing public issues.[43]

Ballot Issues Section 315 does not apply to ballot issues, such as referendums, state constitutional amendments, initiatives and recalls of elected officials. These may be very controversial questions and broadcast stations may carry many commercials on both sides of these issues, but the equal opportunity rules are not applicable to ballot issues. Section 315 and Section 312(a)(7) apply only to legally qualified candidates for elective offices.

Recordkeeping Radio and television stations must keep records of requests they receive to broadcast political messages by or about candidates or to broadcast messages about "national legislative issues of public importance" or "a political matter of national importance."[44] The records must be available to the public upon request. The Supreme Court upheld the constitutionality of these requirements, adopted as part of the Bipartisan Campaign Reform Act of 2002.[45]

527 Groups A 527 group may purchase advertisements focusing on political issues but may not support or oppose individual candidates for elective office. It could urge people to vote, for example. The term "527 group" comes from a section of the federal tax code exempting the organizations from paying taxes on contributions they receive.[46] There are no limits on the amount of contributions an individual or business may give to a 527 group, unlike political action committees, which are subject to limits. For example, in 2012 Fred Eshelmann, founder of Pharmaceutical Product Development, Inc., contributed more than $4 million to the conservative 572 group RightChange.com.[47] The Federal Election Commission (FEC) and state election commissions do not oversee 527 groups unless a group supports or opposes a candidate. In 2006 and 2007, the FEC fined several 527 groups for violating the tax code rules during the 2004 presidential election. For example, Swift Boat Veterans for Truth spent $22.6 million on television ads opposing John Kerry, the Democratic presidential candidate, and MoveOn.org, a politically liberal group, opposed Republican George W. Bush's reelection. The FEC said that, as 527 groups, neither should have attempted to influence the presidential election.[48]

FCC rules require commercial television stations to broadcast programs meeting children's intellectual/cognitive and social/emotional needs. The commission has ruled that "telenovelas" on Spanish-language stations, such as "Cuidado con el Angel," shown here, and "The Jetsons" cartoon program do not meet these requirements.

Children's Programming Despite several decades of deregulating radio and television, the political broadcast rules demonstrate that Congress and the FCC still are concerned about stations operating in the public interest. Children's programming rules also show that broadcasters must respond to the public's concern about radio and television content.

The clash over children's programming on broadcast television has continued for more than half a century. Parents and public advocacy groups representing children demand more and better quality programming meant for young people. Broadcast networks and stations say they carry good quality children's programming responsive to audience preferences. There have been congressional hearings, court cases and FCC proceedings about this issue. But there was little agreement or resolution until Congress acted in 1990, adopting the Children's Television Act.[49] The law sets general requirements for children's programming on broadcast television stations. This portion of the law does not apply to noncommercial stations or cable networks. The law also limits commercial time before, during and after children's programs on broadcast and cable television.

The statute requires broadcast television stations to provide programming intended for children up to 17 years old that meets their "educational and informational needs."[50] Before, during and after programming specifically meant for children 12 years old and younger, advertising is limited to 12 minutes per hour during the week and 10 1/2 minutes per hour on the weekends. These limits are prorated—a half-hour program may have six minutes of commercials on a weekday afternoon, for example. The FCC also has ruled that characters in children's programs cannot appear in commercials before, during or after those programs.[51]

The 1990 law does not state how much children's programming stations must carry. The FCC allowed individual stations to decide.[52] The broadcasting industry's attempts to comply with the law did not please the commission. For example, one industry executive said the cartoon "The Jetsons" was an educational program because it taught children about the future.

By 1996, the FCC lost patience and adopted standards for complying with the 1990 law.[53] The commission ruled that broadcast television stations must carry three hours per week, averaged over a six-month period, of programming

Emerging Law

Violent Media Link to Mass Shootings?

On the heels of the 2012 Aurora, Colo., movie theater mass shooting that left 12 dead and 58 injured, and the Sandy Hook Elementary School massacre that killed 20 children and 8 adults, many people called for regulations on violent content in video games and on television. In 2013, Rep. Frank Wolf of Va. highlighted a National Science Foundation advisory committee report that suggested exposure to violent media is one of three risk factors associated with mass shootings.[1] Other factors included access to guns and mental illness.

According to the report, "aggressive youth often consume violent media because it allows them to justify their own behavior as being normal."[2] While most of the focus is on curbing violence in video games, the advisory committee report suggests further research that explores the role played by the Internet and social media. The issue of mass shootings and media violence is political and often connected to the debates on gun control. Immediately following the Sandy Hook mass shooting in 2012, Sen. Jay Rockefeller introduced a bill to study the impact of violent video games on children. In 2013, several lawmakers called for legislation to limit violence in video games and on television.[3]

1. John Eggerton, *NSF Subcommittee Report Includes Violent Media as Mass Shooting Risk Factor*, BROADCASTING & CABLE, Feb. 19, 2013, *available at* http://www.broadcastingcable.com/article/491925-NSF_Subcommittee_Report_Includes_Violent_Media_as_Mass_Shooting_Risk_Factor.php.
2. Penny Starr, *Gov't Report on Mass Shootings: Violent Media, Mental Health, Access to Guns All Play Role*, CNSNEWS.COM, Feb. 19, 2013, *available at* http://cnsnews.com/news/article/govt-report-mass-shootings-violent-media-mental-health-access-guns-all-play-role.
3. Will Wrigley, *Dianne: Feinstein: Congress May Take Action on Video Game Violence*, THE HUFFINGTON POST, April 4, 2013, *available at* http://www.huffingtonpost.com/2013/04/04/dianne-feinstein-video-games_n_3016703.html.

specifically intended to meet children's intellectual/cognitive and social/emotional needs. The programs must be at least 30 minutes long, regularly scheduled weekly and broadcast between 7 a.m. and 10 p.m. local time. The commission identifies this as "core programming." A station not meeting the core programming standard may substitute shorter programs, public service announcements for children and programs not scheduled weekly. The FCC may choose not to renew a station's license if the station does not use one of these two methods to meet the requirements or otherwise convince the commission the station's programming meets the law's intent.

The FCC requires all television broadcasters to include an on-screen symbol, E/I (for programming designed to educate and inform children), throughout all core programming.[54] The commission updated the children's television rules as television stations shifted to digital transmission, a transition discussed later in this chapter.[55] Stations using their spectrum allocation to provide several signals have to offer three hours of core programming on each of their channels.

Internet website addresses may be displayed during children's programming only if the website (1) offers a substantial amount of program-related or other noncommercial content, (2) is not primarily intended for commercial purposes, (3) has pages clearly labeled to distinguish noncommercial from commercial

realWorld Law

Reality TV and the First Amendment

David Hester

Is reality television real? Is it required to be? Reality TV has steadily grown in popularity since the late 1990s and accounts for some of the highest-rated shows that currently air—in 2012, "American Idol," "Dancing with the Stars" and "The Voice" all landed on Nielsen's Top 10 Primetime Programs.[1] And while many suggest that the premises of reality TV programs are often contrived, it wasn't until 2012 that a reality TV star sued a network and suggested his reality show was actually rigged. David Hester, star of A&E's "Storage Wars," claimed that the cable network wrongfully terminated him, breached his contract and participated in unfair business practices when it fired him. He says the dismissal came after he confronted the show's producers for allegedly planting valuable items or memorabilia on the show.[2]

Hester asked a judge to issue an injunction to prevent A&E from continuing to produce "Storage Wars," but a judge denied his request in 2013, saying it would amount to a violation of the network's First Amendment rights. The judge also threw out Hester's claim of unfair business practices and asked for more specific information about his wrongful termination claim.[3]

Hester's lawsuit compares his allegations to those that arose in the 1950s when producers secretly helped some contestants on popular TV quiz shows in order to arrange the outcomes of what was supposed to be a fair competition. The quiz show scandals led Congress to amend the Communications Act of 1934 to prevent anyone from fixing a televised competition. Hester alleges A&E violated that law, which prohibits "influencing, prearranging, or predetermining outcomes in contests of knowledge, skill or chance." A&E has filed an anti-SLAPP motion (see Chapter 4) to Hester's claim.[4]

1. *Nielsen Tops of 2012: Television,* NIELSEN.COM, Dec. 11, 2012, *available at* http://www.nielsen.com/us/en/newswire/2012/nielsen-tops-of-2012-television.html.
2. Natalie Finn, *Storage Wars Victory: Suing Ex-Star David Hester Is No Match for First Amendment,* EONLINE.COM, Mar. 12, 2013, *available at* http://www.eonline.com/news/397042/storage-wars-victory-suing-ex-star-david-hester-is-no-match-for-first-amendment.
3. Eriq Gardner, *A&E Wins First Round of Lawsuit Alleging 'Storage Wars' Is Rigged,* THE HOLLYWOOD REPORTER, March 12, 2013, *available at:* http://www.hollywoodreporter.com/thr-esq/a-e-wins-first-round-428079.
4. Eriq Gardner, *'Storage Wars' Rigging Lawsuit: David Hester Says A&E Can't Plead First Amendment,* THE HOLLYWOOD REPORTER, Feb. 18, 2013, *available at* http://www.hollywoodreporter.com/thr-esq/storage-wars-rigging-lawsuit-david-422093.

sections and (4) does not immediately display a page used for commercial purposes. This restriction applies to cable television operators as well as all commercial television stations.

The FCC prohibits cartoon or live action characters in children's programs or children's program hosts from selling products in commercials during or adjacent to shows in which the character or host appears.[56] In the context of digital television, the commission's rules prevent displaying a website address during a children's show if the website uses the show's characters to sell products or the site offers products featuring the show's characters.

It might seem the law forbidding FCC broadcast censorship would preclude the commission's children's programming regulations. However, the FCC said the rules are "reasonable, viewpoint-neutral" requirements for licensees who must operate in the public interest. Because the commission does not "tell licensees what topics they must address," the FCC is not acting as a censor, the commission said.[57]

Hoaxes FCC rules forbid stations to broadcast a hoax. Under current commission regulations a hoax occurs when a licensee knowingly broadcasts false reports of crimes or catastrophes that "directly cause" foreseeable, "immediate, substantial and actual public harm."[58] However, the definition of "hoax" has changed during the last 95 years. The Radio Act of 1912 made it illegal to transmit a false distress signal or fraudulent signal of any kind.[59] The Radio Act of 1927[60] and the Communications Act of 1934[61] were more limited, prohibiting false distress signals. Although that regulation remains in place today, the FCC adopted the current ban on broadcast hoaxes in 1992.

The most famous broadcast hoax was not a false distress signal, nor was it intended to be a hoax, merely a radio drama. Orson Welles directed and starred in a radio broadcast based on H.G. Wells' novel "The War of the Worlds." The drama aired nationwide on Oct. 30, 1938—the night before Halloween—and depicted Martian monsters emerging from a meteor that landed in New Jersey. Despite Welles breaking in four times to say the broadcast was fictional, the program sounded very real to many listeners. People ran from their homes, cars jammed streets, hospitals treated hysterical listeners and police station telephones were clogged with calls.[62] Some writers argue that newspaper stories exaggerated the public panic,[63] yet the FCC was sufficiently concerned to promise an inquiry. However, because the drama was not a false signal, the commissioners had no grounds to take any action other than making public statements that broadcasters should consider the public interest in choosing their programs.[64]

Almost 45 years after the "War of the Worlds" broadcast, the FCC adopted a regulation attempting to prohibit false broadcasts. In 1992 the commission adopted a rule prohibiting the broadcast of false information concerning a crime or catastrophe if the station knows the story is false, it is foreseeable the broadcast will cause substantial public harm and harm does result. Public harm includes police and other public safety officials being diverted from their duties in reaction to a false broadcast.[65]

The FCC has heard of very few incidents since 1992 that could be considered hoaxes and has not punished a single station under the new rule. For example, a San Diego radio station falsely reported the Discovery space shuttle would be diverted from its usual landing area to set down at an airfield surrounded by houses and industry. More than a thousand people showed up, blocking roads and causing police to direct traffic. The commission said the false story was not about a crime or catastrophe, so the station had not violated the rule.[66]

realWorld Law

Emergency Alert: Zombie Attack?

"Civil authorities in your area have reported that the bodies of the dead are rising from the grave and attacking the living."[1] This is what viewers of some television stations in Michigan and Montana heard over the Emergency Alert System (EAS) in 2013 after hackers broke into vulnerable EAS equipment with unsecured passwords. Following the attack on a handful of stations, the FCC ordered all broadcasters to inspect their systems, change their EAS passwords, and properly secure equipment behind firewalls. A hardware security analyst told the Chicago Tribune that he found at least 30 systems vulnerable to a similar attack. Another cybersecurity expert said that undermining the EAS would compromise the government's ability to communicate with the public in times of crisis. "While EAS may not control nuclear power or hydroelectric dams or air traffic control, it can be used to cause widespread panic," he said.[2]

1. *Zombie Hack Blamed on Easy Passwords*, Chi. Trib., Feb. 14, 2013, *available at* http://articles.chicagotribune.com/2013–02–14/business/chi-zombie-hack-blamed-on-easy-passwords-20130214_1_karole-white-ioactive-labs-passwords.
2. *Id.*

Fairness Doctrine Eighty years ago the Federal Radio Commission, the FCC's predecessor, said radio stations should broadcast various views about public issues.[67] The FCC adopted regulations in 1949 stating how that policy, called the "fairness doctrine," should be put into effect. Forty years later, in 1989, a federal appellate court allowed the doctrine to expire.

The FCC's 1949 rule said that television and radio stations had to (1) air programs discussing public issues and (2) include a variety of views about controversial issues of public importance.[68] Different views did not have to be presented in one program, but rather the station's overall programming had to reflect important opinions about controversial topics. The commission justified the fairness doctrine by pointing to licensees' responsibilities to the public.[69] The U.S. Supreme Court upheld the doctrine in the 1969 *Red Lion* decision, saying that spectrum scarcity allowed the FCC to require broadcasters to present a variety of opinions.[70] However, the Court has held that the First Amendment protects the print media from being subjected to rules similar to the fairness doctrine.[71]

The FCC changed its rules in 1987, finding that the fairness doctrine violated broadcasters' First Amendment rights.[72] The commission said that broadcasters censored themselves under the fairness doctrine, choosing not to present discussions about important public issues rather than be forced to air a variety of opinions about those issues. In 1989, a federal appellate court upheld challenges to the FCC's decision to eliminate the fairness doctrine.[73]

Two features of the fairness doctrine remained even after 1989. First, the commission's personal attack rule, the *Red Lion* decision's focus, required broadcast stations to provide free reply time to any person or group whose integrity, honesty or character was attacked on the air. The rule did not apply to public officials. Second, the political editorial rule required broadcasters to give free time for a legally qualified candidate to respond to an editorial opposing the candidate or promoting any of the candidate's rivals. But in 2000, a federal appellate court said the FCC had not justified keeping these two rules after it eliminated the fairness doctrine.[74] Public stations still may not endorse or oppose a political candidate, although they may air editorials about public issues.[75]

Sponsorship Identification The FCC requires broadcasters to disclose when they are paid to air material, whether a car advertisement, stories in news programs or a recording.[76] Product placement in programs comes under this regulation, as do video news releases. If the furnished program is political or involves discussion of a controversial issue, broadcasters must tell the material's source even if there was little or no payment. This seemingly innocent rule caused many radio stations enormous problems when the so-called payola scandal broke in the 1960s and once more recently when some stations again were found to have accepted payola. And some television stations ran afoul of the rule recently when they broadcast video news releases (VNR).

Paying a radio station or station employees to play recordings—payola—spread through the industry in the 1950s and 1960s. On-air personalities took money and other gifts from recording companies to play rock records and promote artists. Congress investigated and adopted an anti-payola law in 1960.[77] The commission's own rules require stations to inform listeners when someone pays to air programming.[78] Although the law made clear that a station's employees taking money to play records violated FCC regulations and could lead to criminal punishment, payola did not stop.[79] Recording companies used intermediaries to pay radio stations, putting the stations one step removed from the record companies. By the 1990s, some larger station owners were directly paid by recording companies, no longer using intermediaries. For example, in 2000 the FCC fined Clear Channel Communications $8,000. A company Clear Channel purchased had not revealed it received money to play a Bryan Adams recording.[80] That slap-on-the-wrist punishment paled compared with the $36 million in fines the state of New York imposed on four major record companies—Universal Music, Warner, EMI and Sony BMG—for offering radio station personnel trips, concert tickets and other gifts if they would air certain recordings.[81] The New York investigation spurred the FCC to undertake its own payola inquiry, resulting in four large radio station owners—CBS Radio, Citadel Broadcasting, Clear Channel and Entercom—paying fines of $12.5 million in 2007.[82] The FCC, together with the U.S. Department of Justice and Univision Radio agreed to a $1 million fine to settle a payola investigation in 2010.[83]

Video news releases (VNR), essentially public relations stories used to promote a product or even a political agenda, are not new, having been produced since the early 1980s.[84] They first attracted public attention when the newspaper USA Today broke a story in 2005. USA Today reported that commentator Armstrong Williams took $240,000 from the U.S. Department of Education to advance the agency's plans on Williams' syndicated television show. In 2007 the FCC fined 10 stations for playing Williams' programs pushing the No Child Left Behind initiative in 2003. The stations did not tell viewers that Williams had been paid to offer positive commentary.[85] That same year the commission twice fined Comcast Corporation for showing VNRs on its cable channel without disclosing sponsorship identification.[86] The commission reminded broadcast stations and cable systems that government-sponsored VNRs must state their source.[87]

The FCC also is concerned with product placement and what it calls "product integration." Product placement occurs when a program producer is paid to use as a prop, for example, a can of a particular brand of cola shown on a kitchen counter. Product integration occurs when a program's dialogue or plot focuses on a product.[88]

SUMMARY

THE FIRST AMENDMENT RIGHTS OF BROADCASTERS are not equal to those enjoyed by the print media. Spectrum scarcity limits broadcasting to a select few who obtain FCC licenses. Courts say this justifies limiting broadcasters' free speech rights. Courts also point to broadcasting's pervasiveness and impact on audiences, particularly children. The FCC regulates broadcasting to ensure it operates in the public interest, but the FCC is not allowed to censor broadcasting content.

Section 315 of the Communications Act of 1934 requires broadcasters and cable systems to give equal opportunity to use the airwaves to legally qualified candidates running for the same office. Federal candidates may obtain time even if their opponents have not appeared in a broadcast. A political "candidate" is someone who has announced he or she is running for office and has his or her name on the ballot or is a write-in candidate. "Use" of a station or cable system occurs whenever a candidate's image or voice appears on radio or television. A candidate appearing on a regularly scheduled news or interview program, however, is not deemed to have engaged in use, and the same goes for his or her appearance at a news event or in a documentary. Candidates must ask for equal opportunity within seven days of their opponents' broadcast appearances. Starting 45 days before a primary election and 60 days before a general election, stations and systems may charge candidates no more than the lowest unit rate to purchase time.

A federal law and FCC rules require broadcast television stations to show at least three hours per week of programming that meets children's intellectual/cognitive and social/emotional needs. FCC rules prohibit broadcasting hoaxes.

The FCC rescinded the Fairness Doctrine, requiring stations to cover all major views of important public issues. FCC rules require that sponsorship identification accompany all material a station did not create itself. ∎

Broadcast Licensing

Although pirate (unlicensed) radio stations sometimes can be heard, it is unlawful to operate any broadcast station in the United States without an FCC license. A license allows the station to use part of the broadcast spectrum.[89] A broadcast license is granted for an eight-year period and may be renewed for subsequent eight-year periods. Renewal is assured unless the licensee has not operated in the public interest, has regularly violated FCC rules or has shown a pattern of abusing the law. There is no limit on the number of renewals a station owner may receive; a corporate owner can retain a station license as long as the corporation exists. An FCC license is not transferable: A licensee wanting to sell a broadcast station may sell the building, equipment, transmitter and trucks—but not the license. The FCC acts for the public in allowing a licensee to use the spectrum for the license period.

If a frequency is not already used for broadcasting and two or more competing applicants want a license for the frequency, the FCC holds an auction.[90] The bidder offering to pay the government the most money is awarded the station license. Auctions are not used for noncommercial stations.

To obtain a license, a company or individual must meet certain criteria specified in the 1934 law and the FCC regulations.[91] The criteria apply to a company or an individual purchasing a station. One requirement is that a broadcast licensee must be an American citizen. A foreign corporation may not hold a license, nor may a corporation with more than 20 percent foreign ownership. A foreign government may not be a licensee, nor may a corporation controlled by another corporation with more than 25 percent foreign ownership.[92] These foreign ownership restrictions, first adopted in the 1927 law and continued in the 1934 act, were justified by national security concerns. Congress did not want American media used for foreign propaganda.

A licensee must have good character.[93] The commission does not want licensees who are convicted felons, have committed antitrust violations or have defrauded the FCC.[94] A licensee also must show that she or he has technical expertise and sufficient funds available to operate a station.[95]

For decades, the commission also limited the number of stations a single licensee could own, both in one metropolitan area and nationally. Over time, the FCC removed some and changed other ownership restrictions. For example, there now is no limit on how many radio stations one licensee may own nationally. A single company may own from five to eight radio stations in one metropolitan area, depending on the number of radio stations in that area.[96] One company may own television stations reaching a maximum of 39 percent of the country's television households[97] and may own two television stations in the same community if (1) no more than one of the stations is among the four highest-rated stations in the city and (2) at least eight independently owned commercial or noncommercial television stations remain in the community.[98] Also, one owner may have licenses for up to two television stations in a community and, at the same time, from one to six radio stations in the same area, depending

International Law

Australian-American

Rupert Murdoch controls newspapers from Australia to England to America, including the Wall Street Journal, the Fox broadcast television network, several Fox news and entertainment cable networks, a direct broadcast satellite company and many other media businesses throughout the world. Murdoch was born in Australia. Before purchasing several American television stations, Murdoch renounced his Australian citizenship and became a U.S. citizen. However, that did not meet the rule requiring licensees to be American citizens because Murdoch's Australian company, News Corporation, owned the stations. Murdoch asked the FCC to waive its rule so that a foreign company could own television

Rupert Murdoch

stations in the United States. The FCC ruled that a waiver would be in the public interest. The commission said forcing News Corporation to sell the stations might have prevented the Fox network from effectively competing with ABC, CBS and NBC. The FCC also said Murdoch controlled News Corporation. Effectively, then, an American citizen owned the company.[1]

1. Fox Television Stations, Inc., 78 Rad. Reg. 2d (P & F) 1294 (1995).

on how many independent media voices (primarily local broadcast stations and local newspapers) remain in the community.[99] FCC rules forbid a company from owning more than one of the top four broadcast television networks—that is, ABC, CBS, Fox and NBC.[100]

A commission rule applying only to the country's 20 largest metropolitan areas allows a radio station licensee also to own a newspaper in the same city.[101] The rule also permits one owner to have a television station license and a newspaper in the same community if (1) the station is not one of the four most popular television stations in the city and (2) at least eight independent "major media voices" remain in the metropolitan area after the television station and newspaper are joined under one owner. Major media voices include commercial and public full-power television stations and major newspapers. Before this rule was adopted, one owner could not control both a newspaper and a broadcast station in the same city.

The FCC periodically reviews its media ownership rules. The last review was slated for 2011, but was officially put on hold until 2014. In 2013, then FCC chairman Julius Genachowski decided to wait on a report that would explore how a draft order to lift the ban on owning a newspaper and radio station in the same market (not limited only in the Top 20 markets) would impact minority ownership. Additionally, the draft order called for keeping the cross-ownership ban on owning a newspaper and TV station outside the Top 20 markets, and keeping the ownership cap on the number of TV and radio stations.[102]

The FCC has attempted to increase the number of minority- and female-owned broadcast stations.[103] Courts struck down the commission's rules specifically favoring these groups.[104] The commission then decided to give special consideration in awarding new broadcast licenses to those who own few or no other radio or television stations or daily newspapers. This is done by giving such applicants a financial discount in bidding for station licenses through the FCC's auction process.[105]

FCC rules also encourage stations to recruit members of minority groups and women as employees, particularly in positions of responsibility.[106] The rules require careful recordkeeping to show the FCC how well stations are doing with such recruiting efforts.[107] The FCC's most recent study of minority ownership in 2010 showed that white men own 69 percent of commercial broadcast stations—women owned only 6.8 percent of all commercial stations.[108]

Noncommercial Broadcasting

The FCC oversees public broadcasting stations, which must comply with most of the same rules commercial broadcasters follow. Public stations do not carry advertising.[109] However, corporations and individuals make financial contributions to noncommercial stations and may receive on-air acknowledgments of those contributions. The Communications Act bans advertisements on noncommercial stations that "promote any service, facility, or product" of a for-profit company.[110] The FCC interprets this as prohibiting announcements containing comparative or qualitative descriptions; price information; or exhortations to buy, rent or lease products or services.[111] The commission fines noncommercial stations violating this rule when they broadcast announcements more like an advertisement than an acknowledgment that a company gave the station a contribution.[112]

Public stations receive funding from the Corporation for Public Broadcasting (CPB). Congress allocates money to the CPB, which also receives funds from other sources. The CPB helps support National Public Radio (NPR) and the Public Broadcasting Service (PBS), which provides programming to public television stations.

The Public Broadcasting Act established the CPB. The act says public stations must strictly adhere to "objectivity and balance in all programs or series of programs of a controversial nature."[113] The Public Broadcasting Act did not give the FCC specific powers to enforce that requirement.[114] Despite the Public Broadcasting Act's "objectivity" language, the Supreme Court has allowed public stations to air editorials favoring or opposing public and political issues.[115] Public stations have "important journalistic freedoms which the First Amendment jealously protects," the Court said.[116] Public station personnel may use their best judgments in selecting programming, courts have held.

Noncommercial stations may identify businesses and individuals contributing to the stations but may not air commercials. The difference is not always clear, but the FCC says announcements "may not contain comparative or qualitative descriptions, price information . . . or inducements to buy, sell, rent or lease."[117]

The FCC awards licenses to operate noncommercial stations by using a point system. The commission gives two points for ownership diversity, favoring license applicants without other stations near the community for which the license is being awarded. One to two points are awarded to applicants with technical proposals allowing the station's signal to cover large parts of the metropolitan area. Three points may be awarded if the applicant is based within the community for which the license is being awarded. The FCC awards the license to the applicant with the highest number of points.[118]

SUMMARY

EVERY BROADCAST STATION MUST HAVE AN **FCC** LICENSE. If there is an available frequency, or if a station is being sold, the commission grants licenses to applicants who meet certain criteria. An applicant must be an American citizen or a corporation not controlled by foreign interests. An applicant also must be of good character and have the technical and financial ability to operate a station. The commission has a complex, ever-changing set of rules limiting broadcast ownership. Although the Public Broadcasting Act requires noncommercial stations to be objective, the FCC has no power to enforce the law, and the Supreme Court allowed public stations to air editorials supporting political candidates. ■

Cable Television Regulation

Turn on a television set and a picture appears. Viewers do not care if the picture comes from an over-the-air signal sent by a broadcast station or a signal sent through a wire by a cable system. But to regulators there is a world of difference. Broadcast television stations use the spectrum to transmit signals. The Communications Act of 1934 gives the FCC jurisdiction over spectrum users. The FCC—not states, not cities—regulates broadcasting. Cable systems send signals through a wire—coaxial cable or fiber optic lines—and do not use the spectrum. However, cable systems do use public land, running their wires over or under city streets, sidewalks, alleys and other property. Does this mean local governments regulate cable systems and the FCC does not? The answer is not that simple.

Cable Regulation's Development

Cable television began because some people could not use the spectrum—they could not get a television signal. Programs began coming into television-owning homes in the late 1940s, but rural area residents could not receive them. Either they were too far away from the station's transmitter or the signal could not get through mountains or other barriers. Seeing an opportunity, a power company employee built a large antenna in the Appalachian Mountains of Pennsylvania.

The antenna received signals from Philadelphia television stations. A wire ran from the antenna to a building, and other wires from there to houses with television sets, giving birth to cable television.[119] For decades, it was called "community antenna television" (CATV).

During the 1950s the FCC considered whether it had jurisdiction over CATV and decided not to become involved.[120] But broadcast television station owners became wary of CATV. They thought CATV could take away broadcast viewers and stations' advertisers. Station owners urged the FCC to look again at cable.

In 1962, the FCC said some CATV operators used microwave transmissions to get signals from stations' transmitters to the cable systems' antennas. Microwave transmissions use the spectrum. That was enough for the FCC to say it had jurisdiction over at least part of the CATV business.[121] With that jurisdiction, the commission adopted several CATV rules. Cable operators challenged the commission's authority to control CATV, but the U.S. Supreme Court upheld the FCC's cable jurisdiction.[122] The Court said CATV had the potential to affect broadcast television. Because the commission was responsible for protecting the public's interest in broadcasting, it had the right to oversee CATV as ancillary to its responsibility toward broadcasting, the Court held.

Initially, cable had little impact on broadcast television, except to allow viewing in homes that could not receive stations' signals over the air. But commission rule changes in the mid-1970s allowed cable systems to carry signals of stations not in the local community. For example, cable systems picked up Channel 17 in Atlanta, making WTBS the first superstation. Significantly, Home Box Office (HBO) began a pay cable service in 1975. With distant station signals and HBO, cable television could offer programming not available on local television stations.

Pole Rules Cable's wires started to attract considerable attention. Cable systems needed to string their wires across public streets, sidewalks and alleys. These are called public rights-of-way, and local governments control them. Telephone companies and power companies controlled poles that cable systems needed to use to string their wires down the streets. Cable was becoming a major factor in the home entertainment business, and others wanted to benefit. Cities charged high fees for cable to use rights-of-way. Pole owners charged high rents to allow cable systems to attach their wires. Trying to resolve disputes surrounding the industry, Congress allowed the FCC to take control of pole attachment agreements, limiting the rates pole owners could charge cable companies.[123] In 2013, the D.C. Circuit Court unanimously rejected an appeal filed by a coalition of electric utilities who argued that the FCC does not have authority or reasonable justification to lower pole attachment rates. That decision upheld a 2011 FCC order to reduce the rates electric utilities charged telecom service providers to attach wires.[124]

Federal Cable Laws Controversy surrounded cable television by the early 1980s. Communities wanted to regulate cable, arguing that systems' wires ran over public streets and sidewalks. Telephone companies wanted to offer cable services throughout the country. Cable operators did not want their monthly

U.S. Supreme Court Justice Stephen Breyer said fast-changing technology made it difficult to determine what cable television's First Amendment rights should be.

customer charges regulated. Trying to strike a compromise among these and other competing interests, Congress adopted the Cable Communications Policy Act of 1984.[125] Somewhat deregulating the cable industry, the law gave local and state governments and the federal government shared authority over cable.

A few years later, critics said the 1984 law gave the cable industry monopoly power in communities and allowed cable companies to raise rates without limit, offer poor customer service and prevent any competition. Congress responded by re-regulating cable in the Cable Television Consumer Protection and Competition Act of 1992.[126] The 1992 law responded to cable customer complaints by allowing the government to regulate rates cable systems charged subscribers. To foster competition, Congress required the cable industry to offer competitors, such as direct broadcast satellite companies, the programming cable companies had developed, such as ESPN and MTV. The 1992 law also barred local governments from letting only one cable system provide service if others wanted to compete and required cable systems to carry local broadcast television stations.

Just four years after the 1992 law took effect, Congress adopted the Telecommunications Act of 1996, loosening many of the cable regulations imposed in 1992.[127] Designed primarily to foster competition in the telephone industry, the 1996 law also affected cable. It deregulated cable subscriber rates, again allowing cable companies to raise most prices without government permission. The basic, lowest-level programming package remains rate regulated for most cable systems. The law also allows cable companies to offer local telephone service.

Cable's First Amendment Rights The 1984, 1992 and 1996 laws did not define cable's First Amendment status. Should content-based regulations imposed on cable television be subject to strict scrutiny analysis of their constitutionality, as required for print media? Or should an intermediate scrutiny standard of judicial review be used, giving cable limited First Amendment rights similar to broadcasting's restricted First Amendment protection? The Supreme Court has vacillated. It once decided the cable industry had protection similar to the print media,[128] then suggested it was not certain what First Amendment analysis applied to cable television[129] and finally applied strict scrutiny to cable content regulations.[130]

In ruling on cable's challenge to must-carry rules—regulations requiring cable systems to transmit local broadcast television stations—the Supreme Court said cable sends signals by wire, not through the air. Therefore, the spectrum scarcity rationale does not apply to cable. In 1994 in *Turner Broadcasting System, Inc. v. FCC*, the Court applied to cable the First Amendment test it uses for print media:

If the regulation affects speech because of its content, apply strict scrutiny; if the regulation is content neutral, apply an intermediate standard.[131] (Strict scrutiny and intermediate scrutiny are discussed in Chapter 2.) The 1994 *Turner* decision is excerpted at the end of this chapter. In a subsequent 1997 *Turner* decision the Court upheld the must-carry rules, saying they are content neutral, further a substantial governmental interest that is not related to suppressing speech and are no more restrictive than necessary.[132] These rules are discussed more fully later in this chapter.

However, two years later in *Denver Area Educational Telecommunications Consortium, Inc. v. FCC,* the Supreme Court overturned a law allowing cable companies to reject sexually offensive material on certain channels.[133] The justices could not agree on what First Amendment test to use for cable, despite having the *Turner* decision as precedent. Justice Stephen Breyer, writing only for himself and three other justices, said technology changed too fast to definitively apply a single standard to cable television. Instead, the four justices applied "close judicial scrutiny," a standard the Court never had used before for any mass medium. Justice Breyer said the test meant the statute was constitutional if "it properly addresses an extremely important problem, without imposing, in light of the relevant interests, an unnecessarily great restriction on speech."[134]

In its next try, the Court seemed to get it right. In 2000, the Court said that content-specific cable regulations are to be judged by the strict scrutiny test. The *United States v. Playboy Entertainment Enterprises, Inc.* case involved Congress' concern about adult programming on cable.[135] Even if a cable customer does not subscribe to an adult channel, the channel's signal could bleed into an adjacent channel and be seen. To protect children from seeing adult programming, Congress said cable systems had to take one of two steps. First, they could fully scramble adult channels' signals so programming could not be seen even if the signals bled. Alternatively, they could choose to carry adult programming only late at night when most children were not watching.[136] Hearing a challenge to the law, all nine Supreme Court justices said the restriction was content based, not content neutral, because it applied only to certain programming. To be constitutional, a content-based regulation must pass the strict scrutiny test, meeting two criteria. First, the regulation has to be narrowly tailored to further a compelling governmental interest. Second, there can be no alternative means of achieving Congress' goal that restricts First Amendment rights less than the adopted law does. The Court said although shielding children from adult programming is a compelling governmental interest, an alternative exists: subscribers can tell their cable company to block the adult channel's signal before it reaches their home. On that basis, the Court overturned the law.

The Court, then, held that strict scrutiny is the proper test for content-based regulations applied to cable television, and the intermediate test is to be used for content-neutral regulations. This approach still leaves much room for regulating cable.

Cable Franchising

Just as broadcast stations may not operate without an FCC license, cable systems may not provide service without permission from a local government. Usually, permission is obtained from the city where service will be offered. Alternatively, a few state governments, such as Hawaii and Connecticut, regulate cable companies. Some states, such as New York, give authority over cable to both the state and local governments. In areas not incorporated as cities, a county government oversees cable. The FCC requires cable systems to register with the commission before providing service, but the commission does not license cable systems.

A **franchise** is a contract or agreement between a government, usually a city, and a cable system operator. A cable system must obtain a franchise from the **franchising authority** where the system will offer service. Because franchises are contracts, they are negotiated between the cable company and the franchising authority—the city, county or state. The 1984, 1992 and 1996 federal laws establish certain franchise limits and requirements. Beyond that, the two sides must reach agreement. In general, the franchising authority is offering permission to use public rights-of-way for the system's wires to be placed over (on telephone and power poles) and under (in underground conduits) the city's streets and sidewalks. In return the cable company is offering to provide service to the community.

Franchises contain many provisions. For example, franchises are for definite periods of time. Once granted for as long as 20 or 25 years, franchises now usually are granted for 10 or fewer years. They may be renewed if the cable company and franchising authority agree.

Franchise fees—the charges cable system companies pay to franchising authorities to use public rights-of-way—once were a contentious point in negotiating a franchise. Early in cable's history, authorities charged as much as 35 percent of a cable system's income for the right to provide cable service in the community. The 1984 act set a maximum of 5 percent of a system's gross annual revenues.[137] Cable systems pass the franchise fees on to subscribers. If a cable system pays a 5 percent franchise fee, its subscribers will be charged 5 percent more than the rate for services.

The 1984 cable act limits franchising authorities' control of programming.[138] A franchise may require the cable system to offer subscribers certain categories of programming, such as children's programming, news and public affairs and sports. But the franchise may not require or prevent carrying particular cable networks, such as Nickelodeon, CNN or ESPN. Congress saw this provision as allowing communities to insist that certain kinds of programming be available without giving cities the right to censor cable operators' programming choices.

A cable company and its franchising authority can agree to renew the franchise and can renegotiate terms. However, if the franchising authority is unwilling to negotiate a renewal, the 1984 law specifies the process a cable operator may use to require the franchising authority to consider renewal.[139]

franchise A contract or agreement between a government, usually a city, and a cable system operator.

franchising authority The governmental unit granting a franchise to a cable system operator; usually a city, but may also be a state or county.

franchise fees The charges cable companies pay to franchising authorities for the right to use public rights-of-way.

A cable operator may sell a system. Selling a cable system is similar to selling a broadcast station. The cable operator sells the equipment, the subscriber list, the trucks—everything but the franchise. The franchise belongs to the franchising authority, just as a broadcast license belongs to the FCC. A franchising authority may agree to allow the transfer of a franchise from one cable operator to another or may refuse to allow the transfer. A franchising authority also may ask to renegotiate the franchise before approving a transfer. If a franchising authority does not decide to approve or refuse a transfer request within three months of being asked, the 1992 act says, then approval is assumed.[140]

Franchising authorities may not grant an exclusive cable franchise. If they request one, other qualified cable operators, including telephone companies, must be given a franchise to compete with an existing cable system in a community.[141] Similarly, the FCC in 2007 ruled that cable and satellite systems may not have exclusive contracts with owners of apartment buildings and other multiple-dwelling units. Building owners must allow their residents a choice of video service providers, whether the local cable system, a satellite system or other programming supplier.[142]

In 2007 the FCC stepped into the franchising process to ensure existing cable companies faced competition, particularly from telephone companies.[143] The commission required franchising authorities to speed up franchise negotiations with companies seeking to offer cable service, restricted cities' requests for certain payments and limited franchising authorities' demands for how quickly new cable providers have to offer service to the entire city. The FCC said it adopted these regulations to prevent franchising authorities from unreasonably preventing new cable providers from offering service.

Cable System Ownership Attempting to prevent any cable system operator from monopolizing cable service or programming, Congress in the 1992 cable act allowed the FCC to limit the number of subscribers one cable operator could serve. The commission twice set the maximum at 30 percent of all cable subscribers and twice, most recently in 2009, the U.S. Court of Appeals for the D.C. Circuit said the FCC did not justify that cap.[144] In the 2009 decision the court said the commission had not considered the growth of other multichannel video services (MVS), particularly direct broadcast satellites, as alternatives to cable. Other MVS could prevent a cable operator from dominating the field, the court said.

Federal statutes additionally prevent the owner of a cable system from also controlling any other MVS in the city or country where the cable system provides service.[145] This restriction is waived when a cable system faces effective competition from, for example, a telephone company offering service comparable to that which the cable system provides.

Although once telephone companies were not allowed to own cable systems due to fears they simply would swallow the cable industry, today telephone companies may be cable system owners. They may operate cable systems under four different regulatory schemes, some requiring a franchise, others not.[146]

SUMMARY

THE FCC INITIALLY DECLINED TO REGULATE CABLE TELEVISION. In 1984, a federal law spread cable television jurisdiction between local governments and the FCC. After some vacillating, the Supreme Court said the strict scrutiny test should be applied to regulations affecting cable content, and the intermediate scrutiny test should be applied to content-neutral regulations imposed on cable.

Cable systems must have a franchise to offer service. Franchising authorities and cable operators negotiate terms of franchises. Franchises include provisions, for example, specifying the franchise fee and categories of programming the system will provide. Franchises may be renewed. If the franchising authority balks at renewing, the cable system may initiate a formal renewal process. Franchising authorities must approve sales of cable systems to new owners.

Congress has allowed the FCC to impose certain limits on cable system ownership, but courts have rejected the commission's cap forbidding any cable system owner to reach more than 30 percent of households that receive television programming by cable or satellite. ∎

Cable Programming

Congress has tried to balance several factors in regulating cable programming. Congress knows that the First Amendment protects operators' choice of cable networks and other programs. But Congress also wants to ensure competition, such as from direct broadcast satellite systems, to help hold down customer rates. And Congress believes that cable systems have sufficient numbers of channels to allow the public, schools and local governments to use some cable system capacity as well as permit individuals or companies to purchase time on cable channels. Congress also wants cable systems to carry most local broadcasting stations to protect over-the-air television's future.

Cable Must-Carry and Retransmission Consent Rules Currently, nearly 90 percent of television viewers do not receive programming through antennas.[147] Most subscribe to cable, and others subscribe to direct broadcast satellite or other delivery systems. Broadcast television stations, then, must be on cable systems or most viewers will not watch them. Congress knew that subscribers would demand their cable systems carry the most popular local stations, but Congress was concerned about less popular stations. Cable systems would have no reason to use channel capacity for these marginal stations. Congress argued that stations not carried would go out of business because they would have no audience and therefore no advertisers. To prevent this problem, Congress adopted the must-carry rules.

The number of local stations a cable system must carry depends on how many channels the system has. The largest systems must devote up to one-third of their channels to local stations plus carry all local noncommercial stations that

Emerging Law

Cutting the Cord?

More than five million homes "cut the cord" in 2013 and began to receive their television programs from Internet streaming or through DVD or video game consoles, according to a Nielsen study. In New York City, upstart tech company Aereo emerged to capture some of these viewers.[1]

Barry Diller, the man who launched the Fox network in 1986, created Aereo to retransmit over-the-air TV signals to consumers via the Internet for a fee. Aereo uses hundreds of individual, dime-sized antennas to do this. In 2013, the major broadcast networks in New York City sued Aereo for copyright infringement (see Chapter 14 for a discussion of copyright law) and lost their bid to immediately shut down the service. What's at stake? The nearly $3 billion in retransmission fees that broadcasters collect from cable and satellite systems. Aereo and systems like it do not pay retransmission fees.[2]

Both a District Court in New York and a panel of the Second Circuit refused to grant a preliminary injunction in the Aereo case. In upholding the lower court's ruling, the Second Circuit panel relied heavily on the 2008 Cablevision case.[3] In that case, the Second Circuit concluded that a cable system's Remote Storage Digital Video Recorder (RS-DVR) did not amount to copyright infringement by providing an unauthorized "public performance," even though the RS-DVR made a new copy of a program. The court said that copying streamed content for buffering purposes and to allow for time shifting so a viewer can watch a program later does not constitute a public performance.[4]

In its Aereo decision, the Second Circuit panel applied the Cablevision precedent and said that Aereo's "unique copies of broadcast television programs created at its users' requests and transmitted while the programs are still airing on broadcast television are not 'public performances.'"[5] Meanwhile, an Aereo knockoff in California—Aereokiller, LLC—lost its bid to stave off an injunction from West coast broadcast networks when it faced the same challenge in the Ninth Circuit.[6]

After the Second Circuit panel ruling, Aereo expanded its service to 22 cities across the United States in 2013, and major broadcasters began investing in their own Internet streaming technology to offer their own content. All of this leaves the door open to continued appeals and new lawsuits in different jurisdictions—and, it invites the U.S. Supreme Court to weigh in on the issue.[7]

1. Liana B. Baker and Ronald Grover, *Tech Upstarts Threaten TV Broadcast Model,* Reuters, Apr. 7, 2013, *available at* http://www.reuters.com/article/2013/04/07/us-broadcaster-threats-idUSBRE9360E220130407.
2. *Id.*
3. Cartoon Network, LP v. CSC Holdings, Inc., 536 F.3d 121 (2d. Cir. 2008).
4. *Id.*
5. WNET, Thirteen v. Aereo, Inc.; Am. Broad. Cos. Inc. v Aereo, Inc., 12–2786-cv; 12–2807-cv (2d. Cir., April 1, 2013).
6. Shalini Ramachandran, *Aereo to Expand TV Streaming Service,* The Wall Street Journal, May 14, 2013, *available at* http://online.wsj.com/article/SB10001424127887324715704578483152335201648.html.
7. *Id.*

do not duplicate another station's programming. A cable system must carry all of a station's programming, not just a few hours per day. A system is required to carry the station on the cable channel number that is the same as a station's on-air channel number—broadcast channel 4 is carried on cable channel 4—unless the station agrees otherwise. The must-carry rules were applied to digital television signals beginning in 2009, when stations switched from analog to digital transmission.

retransmission consent Part of the federal cable television law allowing broadcast television stations to negotiate.

A local station does not have to require carriage on a cable system. Instead, the station may choose to negotiate with the system for carriage.[148] The law calls this **retransmission consent.** Cable operators need to carry network-affiliated and popular independent television stations. These remain among the most watched programming on cable systems. Because they are so popular, these stations have negotiating power. The stations may demand that cable systems pay to carry the stations under the retransmission consent provision. Also, television networks such as ABC, CBS, NBC and Fox own many television stations. These station groups use the retransmission consent provision to negotiate carriage with large cable system owners such as Comcast and Time Warner. Unless a television station has chosen must-carry status, it will be dropped from a cable system's channel lineup if the station and system cannot agree on retransmission compensation.

The 1992 law said cable systems could carry broadcast television stations only with the stations' consent or under the law's must-carry provision. Every three years commercial television stations choose between must-carry and retransmission consent. Noncommercial stations may not choose retransmission consent; they are carried under the must-carry provision.

The cable industry fought the must-carry rule in court. Cable companies argued that a system can carry only a limited number of networks. Finding room to carry a local station's signal could force a cable system to eliminate programming it already was carrying—the Food Channel, for example. Cable companies also argued the must-carry rules therefore were content-specific regulations, forcing cable to choose a local station over some other programming. Congress would have to show it had a compelling interest to justify imposing a content-specific rule, cable companies argued, and no such compelling interest existed.

In the second *Turner Broadcasting System, Inc. v. FCC decision,* in 1997, the Supreme Court refused to accept the cable industry's argument that the must-carry rules were content specific.[149] The must-carry rules are content neutral because they do not dictate specific programming, the Court said. To determine the rules' constitutionality, the Court applied the test it established in *United States v. O'Brien,* discussed in Chapter 2.[150] The *O'Brien* test applies to regulations incidentally affecting speech when that is not the regulation's primary purpose. Protecting broadcast stations is an important objective, the Court said, and in doing so Congress did not intend to directly affect cable systems' speech. Rather, Congress needed to adopt the rules to achieve its purpose of ensuring that local stations could be seen on cable television, which approximately two-thirds of viewers use to watch television.

The cable industry again challenged the must-carry rules in 2009. The FCC ruled that Cablevision Systems, the New York City cable provider, must carry a Kingston, N.Y., television station. Kingston is 80 miles from New York City. The U.S. Court of Appeals for the Second Circuit rejected Cablevision's argument that must-carry rules violate cable operators' First Amendment rights.[151] In 2010 the U.S. Supreme Court refused to hear the case.

Cable Access Requirements By the time Congress adopted the Cable Communications Policy Act of 1984, most cable franchises already included provisions for public, educational or governmental (PEG) access channels. The 1984 statute made that reality into law. Congress saw **PEG access channels** as a way to allow the public, various educational institutions and local governments to have access to cable systems in ways they do not have for newspapers, magazines, radio and television stations, and other mass media. The 1984 law permits a franchising authority and cable company to negotiate, as part of the franchising process, to set aside channels for public, educational or governmental use.[152] Although the law does not require cable system operators to agree, they usually do.

> **PEG access channels** Channels that cable systems set aside for public, educational and government use.

Public access channels generally allow local citizens, on a first-come basis, to put on programming they choose. Many municipalities have a government official or nonprofit organization oversee public channel programming.[153] Local school boards and colleges use educational channels. Government channels often carry city council and county board meetings.

A federal appellate court applying intermediate scrutiny found the law's PEG provisions constitutional.[154] However, the court said a cable system's First Amendment rights might be infringed upon if a franchising authority demanded a very large number of PEG channels. The 1984 law also requires cable systems to make channels available for lease.[155] The 1984 cable act prohibits cable system operators from exercising any editorial control over PEG or leased access programming.[156]

Nonduplication Rules To protect local broadcasters, the FCC's rules require a cable system to delete certain programming on distant stations the system carries. The network **nonduplication rules** allow a station carrying network programming to insist that a cable system block duplicate network programs on another station the system carries—even if the programs do not run at the same time.[157] The FCC adopted the rule when there were only three networks—ABC, CBS and NBC. The rule still applies only to those networks' programs.[158]

> **nonduplication rules** FCC regulations requiring cable systems not to carry certain programming that is available through local broadcast stations.

Syndicated exclusivity rules apply to specific programs stations purchase on a market-by-market basis rather than programs provided by a network. A local station that has a contract to show a syndicated program may require a cable system to delete that program from any other station the system carries.[159]

Another FCC rule benefits professional sports team owners. A team may prohibit a local cable system from carrying the team's home game.[160] The blackout rule does not apply if a local television station is broadcasting the game. National Football League team owners have an internal agreement not to prohibit carriage if a home game is sold out at least 72 hours before it is to be played.

Sharing Programs and Channel Capacity To prevent cable companies from developing programming and keeping it to themselves, the 1992 law requires them to sell the programs to competitors.[161] For example, Time Warner owns cable systems throughout the United States. It also owns HBO. The 1992 statute and FCC rules require Time Warner to sell HBO programming, for reasonable rates, to direct broadcast satellite services and other cable competitors.[162] More generally, the FCC says companies owning cable systems and cable networks cannot unreasonably refuse to sell programming to competitors.[163] This provision was to expire in 2002, but the FCC has extended it twice.[164]

The 1992 law also limits the number of channels a cable system may use to show programming that the system's owner controls.[165] By adopting this provision, Congress tried to increase the number of different programmers cable systems would carry. Commission rules say a cable operator may not use more than 40 percent of its channels or 30 channels, whichever is fewer, to carry programming in which the operator's owner has a financial interest. This limit applies to a cable system's first 75 channels.[166]

Cable Subscribers' Privacy When Congress adopted the first federal law regulating cable television, it was concerned about subscribers' privacy because cable operators would have access to bank-from-home and shop-from-home records as well as customers' programming choices. That was 1984. More than 25 years later, these concerns may have some basis in reality. Cable systems offer Internet connections that their customers use for banking and shopping from home. To protect cable subscribers Congress limited the information cable systems were allowed to collect and distribute.[167]

A cable company may obtain information such as a customer's name, address, phone number and programming services without the subscriber's permission, but it may use the information only to provide programming and to ensure that subscribers pay for the services they order. Also, a cable company may not share that information with others without the customer's permission, unless the sharing is necessary to provide requested programming and other services or for the cable operator's own business reasons. Cable companies may distribute aggregate information without their subscribers' permission if the information does not identify individual customers. Cable systems are required to give customers an annual written notice explaining their privacy rights.

SUMMARY

CABLE SYSTEMS ARE REQUIRED TO USE A PORTION of their channels to carry local broadcast television stations. Every three years, stations choose to require their carriage or to negotiate with cable systems for carriage. The Supreme Court ruled the must-carry rules are constitutional. A cable operator and franchising authority may negotiate to include public, educational and governmental access channels on the system. Federal law requires cable systems to set aside several channels for lease.

Broadcasters may require cable systems to delete duplicative network and syndicated programming. Professional sports team owners may require blacking out home games, unless a local television station is carrying the game. Federal law prohibits the cable industry from unreasonably refusing to sell programming to competitors, such as direct broadcast satellite operators. The law also limits the number of channels a cable system may devote to programming in which the system's owner has a financial interest. ∎

Direct Broadcast Satellites

More than 33 million American households receive their television programming by subscribing to a direct broadcast satellite (DBS) service.[168] DBS was not entirely successful in the mid-1980s, when several companies offering the service failed financially. For many years, DBS used a large backyard antenna, called a dish, for receiving satellite signals. Currently, a small dish attached to a roof or the side of a house can receive signals from a high-powered satellite.

To encourage DBS service as a cable competitor, the FCC did not classify satellite service as broadcasting. The commission's decision relieved DBS of the regulatory burdens that broadcasters face. The commission instead categorized DBS as a point-to-multipoint nonbroadcast service, a ruling upheld in court.[169] Dissatisfied with the FCC's decision not to impose regulations on DBS, Congress, in the Cable Television Consumer Protection and Competition Act of 1992, required DBS providers to abide by the political broadcasting rules in Sections 315 and 312(a)(7). The law also required DBS operators to offer leased access channels for noncommercial educational purposes.[170] A federal appellate court rejected the PEG and leased access requirements as infringing on DBS providers' First Amendment rights.[171]

As DBS became a more prominent multichannel video provider, the FCC imposed additional regulations. The commission said DBS operators must abide by the syndicated exclusivity, network nonduplication and sports blackout rules.[172] In 1998, the FCC returned to its objective of having DBS operators use some of their capacity for educational programming. The commission required satellite operators to set aside 4 percent of their channel capacity for educational or informational programming.[173] The commission said carrying noncommercial broadcast stations would not satisfy this requirement. The FCC also required DBS systems to comply with the same advertising limits during children's programming the commission applied to broadcast television stations.[174]

Sirius, which combined with XM Radio in 2008, offers subscription satellite radio services. The FCC has regulatory power over Sirius because the company uses radio frequencies to transmit its programming.

DBS emerged as a challenger to cable's dominance when Congress allowed satellite services to offer subscribers their local television stations as well as satellite programming.[175] In 2010 Congress renewed legislation requiring a DBS operator to offer all local stations if the operator offers one or more local stations to subscribers.[176] If the satellite service offers one or more local stations carried in high definition, by no later than 2012 it must offer all high-definition signals from all stations in that city, the FCC ruled.[177] The commission also said commercial television stations may choose must-carry status or retransmission consent, as the stations may do for cable carriage.[178]

Internet Regulation

The Internet began as a computer network ensuring there would be a military communications network in the event of a nuclear attack. The goal was to set up a series of computers that could continue to receive and relay data even if one or more links in the communication chain were broken.[179] This network grew into the Internet, a series of computers linked together almost randomly. The Internet is redundant, meaning there are many ways for a message to get from its origin to its intended recipient. The computers comprising this network are in universities, government installations, public and private companies and other locations. There is no central focus, no international regulating agency. The Internet Corporation for Assigned Names and Numbers (ICANN) is a nonprofit organization responsible for standardizing the technology and computer codes needed to allow the simultaneous, instantaneous exchange of billions of messages. In particular, ICANN oversees the domain name system. Domain names are website addresses, such as www.fcc.gov. But ICANN does not regulate the Internet as, say, the FCC regulates broadcasting.[180]

FCC Internet Regulation

The FCC has considered its role in Internet regulation since 2005. Acknowledging Congress had not given the commission statutory authority over the Internet, the FCC said it had ancillary jurisdiction.[181] The notion of ancillary jurisdiction comes from the 1934 Communications Act. That law provides the FCC with the power to act "as may be necessary in the execution of its functions."[182] Years before Congress adopted the first cable television law in 1984, the U.S. Supreme Court held that the 1934 act's language gave the FCC jurisdiction over cable as "ancillary" to its statutory right to regulate broadcasting.[183] Because cable could have an adverse effect on broadcasters' business, the FCC said, the commission could regulate cable to protect local broadcast stations.

Although initially the FCC took a "hands off the Internet" approach, more recently it claimed it has ancillary jurisdiction over broadband. The FCC's claimed ancillary jurisdiction over the Internet has been upheld and rejected by courts. For example, one way to gain high-speed Internet access is through a cable modem offered by a cable television system. An Internet service provider (ISP) provides the Internet connection. In mid-2005 the Supreme Court held that cable television systems do not have to give their customers a choice of ISPs.[184] Many cable systems wanted their customers to use only an ISP the system owned or with which the system had an agreement. But other ISPs might want to use a cable system to provide high-speed Internet access through cable modems. Must cable systems allow these other ISPs to offer access?

The case turned on deciding into what legal category cable Internet access falls. The Telecommunications Act of 1996 says providers of telecommunications service can be regulated, which includes requiring them to sell access to their networks to anyone wanting it.[185] However, information service providers are not regulated and therefore can prevent anyone they want from using their networks. The FCC had decided each cable Internet access is an information service, not a telecommunications service.[186] The Supreme Court said the 1996 law was ambiguous on this point. Therefore, the FCC had a right to interpret that part of the law and courts should abide by the commission's decision, the Court said. The Court's ruling, allowing the FCC to categorize cable modem service as an information service, permits cable system operators to choose what ISPs may offer high-speed Internet access through cable modems. The ruling also prevents local cable television franchising authorities from regulating high-speed Internet access through cable modems.

Net Neutrality

As the volume of Internet traffic increased, particularly with the exchange of video files, some ISPs blocked or delayed certain Internet transmissions, allowing other messages to be sent more quickly. The FCC attempted to deal with this issue, called "network (or net) neutrality," but the U.S. Court of Appeals for the D.C. Circuit ruled the commission had no authority over the matter. Pitting the Internet's traditional free nature against ISPs' business interests, net neutrality would treat all Internet traffic equally. Alternatively, may an ISP favor certain messages over others? Perhaps the ISP charges more to carry some messages or the ISP needs to treat messages differently to allow its network to function most efficiently. In 2008, the FCC ruled that Comcast, a cable company also providing broadband Internet access, could not "selectively target and interfere with connections of peer-to-peer (P2P) applications." Comcast claimed it needed to divert and delay some Internet traffic that used particular peer-to-peer applications so Comcast could prevent network congestion. The commission said "the company's discriminatory and arbitrary practice unduly squelches the dynamic benefits of an open and accessible Internet."[187] However, the D.C. Circuit ruled that Congress had not given the FCC explicit statutory "authority to regulate an Internet service provider's network management practices."[188]

A few months after that court defeat, the commission made another attempt to regulate net neutrality. In December 2010 the FCC adopted rules forbidding Internet providers from blocking lawful content and applications that computers use. Nor may these providers unreasonably discriminate in transmitting content.

The FCC could interpret this to prevent Internet providers from charging more to speed transmission of certain content while moving other content more slowly. Providers of mobile Internet services, such as for cell phones, may not block lawful websites or voice or video applications that compete with the provider's services. The commission based these rules on its ancillary jurisdiction over the Internet and on various other communications act provisions.[189] Soon after the Open Internet Report and Order became effective Verizon challenged the order's validity in court, relying on the decision in the Comcast case. On appeal in the D.C. Circuit Court, Verizon argued that the FCC does not have the authority to create net neutrality rules and that the rules are arbitrary and capricious. The court was expected to hear arguments in the case in spring 2013, but deferred to fall 2013.[190] Many legal experts speculated that the D.C. Circuit first wanted to know the outcome of the Supreme Court's decision in *Arlington v. FCC*, which was handed down in May 2013. In the Arlington case, some state and local governments questioned the FCC's authority in requiring zoning authorities to process requests for wireless facilities within 90 days. The FCC rule emerged after many requesters complained that "unreasonable delays" were "obstruct[ing] the provision of wireless services."[191] While the case is not about net neutrality per se, its central question—does the FCC have the authority to regulate in instances when Congress has left the agency's jurisdiction ambiguous?—is directly relevant to the pending Verizon case. In Arlington, a 6–3 majority of justices noted that "Congress has unambiguously vested the FCC with general authority to administer the Communications Act through rulemaking and adjudication," and that in situations in which Congress has left the agency's jurisdiction ambiguous the courts must defer to the agency's construction of a permissible statute. In other words, the Supreme Court gave deference to the FCC to interpret its own jurisdiction.[192]

The Internet's First Amendment Status

In overturning a congressional attempt to limit online sexual expression, the Supreme Court held in *Reno v. ACLU* that the Internet has complete First Amendment protection.[193] *Reno v. ACLU* decided a challenge to the Communications Decency Act (CDA), a provision of the Telecommunications Act of 1996.[194] The CDA prohibited using the Internet to transmit indecent, patently offensive or obscene material to minors.

To determine the CDA's constitutionality, the Court had to decide what First Amendment protections apply to the Internet. The starting assumption is that the First Amendment protects expression communicated by any means. But the Court has said each mass medium has its own peculiarities, so there may need to be adjustments to a medium's First Amendment rights. Broadcasting, for example, uses a scarce spectrum, justifying its limited First Amendment protection. The Internet does not use the spectrum. Nor is the Internet as invasive as broadcasting, the Court said in *Reno*. Families not wanting their children to have Internet access do not need to subscribe to an Internet service. There are reasons to regulate broadcasting, the Court said, but the Internet has not been "subject to the type of government supervision and regulation that has attended the broadcast industry."[195] Unlike broadcasting, the Internet does not have any special characteristics that require decreasing its First Amendment rights, the *Reno* Court held.

Justice John Paul Stevens, writing for the Court majority, emphasized the "wide variety of communication" taking place on the Internet and the number of places—homes and universities and cafés—where Internet access is available. Stevens characterized the Internet as "a unique medium" that is "located in no particular geographical location but available to anyone, anywhere in the world." The Internet is "a vast platform from which to address and hear from a worldwide audience of millions of readers, viewers, researchers, and buyers. Any person or organization with a computer connected to the Internet can 'publish' information," the Court said.[196]

Further emphasizing its unique nature as a communications medium, Justice Stevens said the Internet

> includes not only traditional print and news services, but also audio, video, and still images, as well as interactive, real-time dialogue. Through the use of chat rooms, any person with a phone line can become a town crier with a voice that resonates farther than it could from any soapbox. Through the use of Web pages, mail exploders, and newsgroups, the same individual can become a pamphleteer. . . . [O]ur cases provide no basis for qualifying the level of First Amendment scrutiny that should be applied to this medium.[197]

Having held that Internet content has full First Amendment protection, the Court overturned congressional restrictions on transmitting indecent and patently offensive material through the Internet. The Court did uphold the ban on obscene content sent over the Internet. The First Amendment does not protect obscene material on the Internet or in any medium (see Chapter 12).[198] The *Reno* Court rejected the Communications Decency Act's limit on patently offensive material. Patent offensiveness is only one of the three factors defining obscenity. Patently offensive material may be protected if the other two obscenity elements are not present. (Additional Supreme Court decisions about indecency and the Internet are discussed in Chapter 12.)

SUMMARY

AT FIRST, THE FCC CHOSE TO REGULATE DIRECT broadcast satellites minimally. As DBS developed into a cable competitor, Congress required the commission to impose on satellite operators some cable and broadcast regulations. Congress allowed DBS to provide its subscribers their local television stations.

The Supreme Court said the Internet has full First Amendment protection. Although Congress has not given the FCC complete authorization to regulate the Internet, the commission has claimed it has ancillary jurisdiction over broadband providers. ∎

Cases for Study

Thinking About It

The two case excerpts that follow deal with an older mass medium, broadcasting, and a newer one, cable television. As you read these case excerpts, keep the following questions in mind:

- How does the U.S. Supreme Court treat each medium under the First Amendment?
- What reasons does the Court give for the way it applies the First Amendment to broadcasting and cable?
- Do these two decisions logically lead to the Court's ruling in *Reno v. ACLU* that the Internet should have full First Amendment protection?

Red Lion Broadcasting Co., Inc. v. Federal Communications Commission
SUPREME COURT OF THE UNITED STATES
395 U.S. 367 (1969)

[In the years after the U.S. Supreme Court ruled in *Red Lion,* the fairness doctrine and its corollary regulations, the personal attack and political editorial rules, have been found unconstitutional by the courts or rescinded by the FCC. However, the *Red Lion* decision remains important precedent for the spectrum scarcity rationale that still underlies broadcast regulation.]

JUSTICE BYRON WHITE delivered the Court's opinion:

The Federal Communications Commission has for many years imposed on radio and television broadcasters the requirement that discussion of public issues be presented on broadcast stations, and that each side of those issues must be given fair coverage. This is known as the fairness doctrine, which originated very early in the history of broadcasting and has maintained its present outlines for some time. It is an obligation whose content has been defined in a long series of FCC rulings in particular cases, and which is distinct from the statutory requirement of Section 315 of the

Communications Act that equal time be allotted all qualified candidates for public office. Two aspects of the fairness doctrine, relating to personal attacks in the context of controversial public issues and to political editorializing, were codified more precisely in the form of FCC regulations in 1967. The two cases before us now, which were decided separately below, challenge the constitutional and statutory bases of the doctrine and component rules. *Red Lion* involves the application of the fairness doctrine to a particular broadcast, and *RTNDA* arises as an action to review the FCC's 1967 promulgation of the personal attack and political editorializing regulations, which were laid down after the *Red Lion* litigation had begun.

The Red Lion Broadcasting Company is licensed to operate a Pennsylvania radio station, WGCB. On November 27, 1964, WGCB carried a 15-minute broadcast by the Reverend Billy James Hargis as part of a "Christian Crusade" series. A book by Fred J. Cook entitled "Goldwater—Extremist on the Right" was discussed by Hargis, who said that Cook had been fired by a newspaper for making false charges against city officials; that Cook had then worked for a Communist-affiliated publication; that he had defended Alger Hiss and attacked J. Edgar Hoover and the Central Intelligence Agency; and that he had now written a "book to smear and destroy Barry Goldwater." When Cook heard of the broadcast he concluded that he had been personally attacked and demanded free reply time, which the station refused. After an exchange of letters among Cook, Red Lion, and the FCC, the FCC declared that the Hargis broadcast constituted a personal attack on Cook; that Red Lion had failed to meet its obligation under the fairness doctrine . . . to send a tape, transcript, or summary of the broadcast to Cook and offer him reply time; and that the station must provide reply time whether or not Cook would pay for it. On review in the Court of Appeals for the District of Columbia Circuit, the FCC's position was upheld as constitutional and otherwise proper. . . .

Believing that the specific application of the fairness doctrine in *Red Lion,* and the promulgation of the regulations in *RTNDA,* are both authorized by Congress and enhance rather than abridge the freedoms of speech and press protected by the First Amendment, we hold them valid and constitutional, reversing the judgment below in *RTNDA* and affirming the judgment below in *Red Lion.*

The history of the emergence of the fairness doctrine and of the related legislation shows that the Commission's action in the *Red Lion* case did not exceed its authority, and that in adopting the new regulations the Commission was implementing congressional policy rather than embarking on a frolic of its own.

Before 1927, the allocation of frequencies was left entirely to the private sector, and the result was chaos. It quickly became apparent that broadcast frequencies constituted a scarce resource whose use could be regulated and rationalized only by the Government. Without government control, the medium would be of little use because of the cacophony of competing voices, none of which could be clearly and predictably heard. Consequently, the Federal Radio Commission was established to allocate frequencies among competing applicants in a manner responsive to the public "convenience, interest, or necessity."

Very shortly thereafter the Commission expressed its view that the "public interest requires ample play for the free and fair competition of opposing views, and the commission believes that the principle applies . . . to all discussions of issues of importance to the public." This doctrine was applied through denial of license renewals or construction permits, both by the FRC, and its successor FCC. After an extended period during which the licensee was obliged not only to cover and to cover fairly the views of others, but also to refrain from expressing his own personal views, the latter limitation on the licensee was abandoned and the doctrine developed into its present form.

There is a twofold duty laid down by the FCC's decisions and described by the 1949 Report on Editorializing by Broadcast Licensees. The broadcaster must give adequate coverage to public issues, and coverage must be fair in that it accurately reflects the opposing views. This must be done at the broadcaster's own expense if sponsorship is unavailable. Moreover, the duty must be met by programming obtained at the licensee's own initiative if available from no other source. . . .

When a personal attack has been made on a figure involved in a public issue, . . . [it is required] that the individual attacked himself be offered an opportunity to respond. Likewise, where one candidate is endorsed in a political editorial, the other candidates must themselves be offered reply time to use personally or through a spokesman. These obligations differ from the general fairness requirement that issues be presented, and presented with coverage of competing views, in that the broadcaster does not have the option of presenting the attacked party's side himself or choosing a third party to represent that side. But insofar as there is an obligation of the broadcaster to see that both sides are presented, and insofar as that is an affirmative obligation, the personal attack doctrine and regulations do not differ from the preceding fairness doctrine. The simple fact that the attacked men or unendorsed candidates may respond themselves or through agents is not a critical distinction, and indeed, it is not unreasonable for the FCC to conclude that the objective of adequate presentation of all sides may best be served by allowing those most closely affected to make the response, rather than leaving the response in the hands of the station which has attacked their candidacies, endorsed their opponents, or carried a personal attack upon them. . . .

The broadcasters challenge the fairness doctrine and its specific manifestations in the personal attack and political editorial rules on conventional First Amendment grounds, alleging that the rules abridge their freedom of speech and press. Their contention is that the First Amendment protects their desire to use their allotted frequencies continuously to broadcast whatever they choose, and to exclude whomever they choose from ever using that frequency. No man may be prevented from saying or publishing what he thinks, or from refusing in his speech or other utterances to give equal weight to the views of his opponents. This right, they say, applies equally to broadcasters.

Although broadcasting is clearly a medium affected by a First Amendment interest, differences in the characteristics of new media justify differences in the standards applied to them. For example, the ability of new technology to produce sounds more raucous than those of the human voice justifies restrictions on the sound level, and on the hours and places of use, of sound trucks so long as the restrictions are reasonable and applied without discrimination.

Just as the Government may limit the use of sound-amplifying equipment potentially so noisy that it drowns out civilized private speech, so may the Government limit the use of broadcast equipment. The right of free speech of a broadcaster, the user of a sound truck, or any other individual does not embrace a right to snuff out the free speech of others. . . .

It was . . . the chaos which ensued from permitting anyone to use any frequency at whatever power level he wished, which made necessary the enactment of the Radio Act of 1927 and the Communications Act of 1934. It was this reality which at the very least necessitated first the division of the radio spectrum into portions reserved respectively for public broadcasting and for other important radio uses such as amateur operation, aircraft, police, defense, and navigation; and then the subdivision of each portion, and assignment of specific frequencies to individual users or groups of users. Beyond this, however, because the frequencies reserved for public broadcasting were limited in number, it was essential for the Government to tell some applicants that they could not broadcast at all because there was room for only a few.

Where there are substantially more individuals who want to broadcast than there are frequencies to allocate, it is idle to posit an unabridgeable First Amendment right to broadcast comparable to the right of every individual to speak, write, or publish. If 100 persons want broadcast licenses but there are only 10 frequencies to allocate, all of them may have the same "right" to a license; but if there is to be any effective communication by radio, only a few can be licensed and the rest must be barred from the airwaves. It would be strange if the First Amendment, aimed at protecting and furthering communications, prevented the Government from making radio communication possible by requiring licenses to broadcast and by limiting the number of licenses so as not to overcrowd the spectrum.

This has been the consistent view of the Court. Congress unquestionably has the power to grant and deny licenses and to eliminate existing stations. No one has a First Amendment right to a license or to monopolize a radio frequency; to deny a station license because "the public interest" requires it "is not a denial of free speech."

By the same token, as far as the First Amendment is concerned those who are licensed stand no better than those to whom licenses are refused. A license permits broadcasting, but the licensee has no constitutional right to be the one who holds the license or to monopolize a radio frequency to the exclusion of his fellow citizens. There is nothing in the First Amendment which prevents the Government from requiring a licensee to share his frequency with others and to conduct himself as a proxy or fiduciary with obligations to present those views and voices which are representative of his community and which would otherwise, by necessity, be barred from the airwaves.

This is not to say that the First Amendment is irrelevant to public broadcasting. On the contrary, it has a major role to play as the Congress itself recognized in forbidding FCC interference with "the right of free speech by means of radio communication."

Because of the scarcity of radio frequencies, the Government is permitted to put restraints on licensees in favor of others whose views should be expressed on this unique medium. But the people as a whole retain their interest in free speech by radio and their collective right to have the medium function consistently with the ends and purposes of the First Amendment. It is the right of the viewers and listeners, not the right of the broadcasters, which is paramount. It is the purpose of the First Amendment to preserve an uninhibited marketplace of ideas in which truth will ultimately prevail, rather than to countenance monopolization of that market, whether it be by the Government itself or a private licensee. "Speech concerning public affairs is more than self-expression; it is the essence of self-government." It is the right of the public to receive suitable access to social, political, esthetic, moral, and other ideas and experiences which is crucial here. That right may not constitutionally be abridged either by Congress or by the FCC.

Rather than confer frequency monopolies on a relatively small number of licensees, in a Nation of 200,000,000, the Government could surely have decreed that each frequency should be shared among all or some of those who wish to use it, each being assigned a portion of the broadcast day or the broadcast week. The ruling and regulations at issue here do not go quite so far. They assert that under specified circumstances, a licensee must offer to make available a reasonable amount of broadcast time to those who have a view different from that which has already been expressed on his station. The expression of a political endorsement, or of a personal attack while dealing with a controversial public issue, simply triggers this time sharing. As we have said, the *First Amendment* confers no right on licensees to prevent others from broadcasting on "their" frequencies and no right to an unconditional monopoly of a scarce resource which the Government has denied others the right to use.

In terms of constitutional principle, and as enforced sharing of a scarce resource, the personal attack and political editorial rules are indistinguishable from the equal-time provision of Section 315, a specific enactment of Congress requiring stations to set aside reply time under specified circumstances and to which the fairness doctrine and these constituent regulations are important complements. That provision, which has been part of the law since 1927, has been held valid by this Court as an obligation of the licensee relieving him of any power in any way to prevent or censor the broadcast, and thus insulating him from liability for defamation. The constitutionality of the statute under the First Amendment was unquestioned.

Nor can we say that it is inconsistent with the First Amendment goal of producing an informed public capable of conducting its own affairs to require a broadcaster to permit answers to personal attacks occurring in the course of discussing controversial issues, or to require that the political opponents of those endorsed by the station be given a chance to communicate with the public. Otherwise, station owners and a few networks would have unfettered power to make time available only to the highest bidders, to communicate only their own views on public issues, people and candidates, and to permit on the air only those with whom they agreed. There is no sanctuary in the First Amendment for unlimited private censorship operating in a medium not open to all. "Freedom of the press from governmental interference under the First Amendment does not sanction repression of that freedom by private interests."

It is strenuously argued, however, that if political editorials or personal attacks will trigger an obligation in broadcasters to afford the opportunity for expression to speakers who need not pay for time and whose views are unpalatable to the licensees, then broadcasters will be irresistibly forced to self-censorship and their coverage of controversial public issues will be eliminated or at least rendered wholly ineffective. Such a result would indeed be a serious matter, for should licensees actually eliminate their coverage of controversial issues, the purposes of the doctrine would be stifled.

At this point, however, as the Federal Communications Commission has indicated, that possibility is at best speculative. The communications industry, and in particular the networks, have taken pains to present controversial issues in the past, and even now they do not assert that they intend to abandon their efforts in this regard. It would be better if the FCC's encouragement were never necessary to induce the broadcasters to meet their responsibility. And if experience with the administration of these doctrines indicates that they have the net effect of reducing rather than enhancing the volume and quality of coverage, there will be time enough to reconsider the constitutional implications. The fairness doctrine in the past has had no such overall effect.

That this will occur now seems unlikely, however, since if present licensees should suddenly prove timorous, the Commission is not powerless to insist that they give adequate and fair attention to public issues. It does not violate the First Amendment to treat licensees given the privilege of using scarce radio frequencies as proxies for the entire community, obligated to give suitable time and attention to matters of great public concern. To condition the granting or renewal of licenses on a willingness to present representative community views on controversial issues is consistent with the ends and purposes of those constitutional provisions forbidding the abridgment of freedom of speech and freedom of the press. Congress need not stand idly by and permit those with licenses to ignore the problems which beset the people or to exclude from the airways anything but their own views of fundamental questions. The statute, long administrative practice, and cases are to this effect.

Licenses to broadcast do not confer ownership of designated frequencies, but only the temporary privilege of using them. . . . The statute mandates the issuance of licenses if the "public convenience, interest, or necessity will be served thereby." . . . [In 1943] the Court considered the validity of the Commission's chain broadcasting regulations, which among other things forbade stations from devoting too much time to network programs in order that there be suitable opportunity for local programs serving local needs. The Court upheld the regulations, unequivocally recognizing that the Commission was more than a traffic policeman concerned with the technical aspects of broadcasting and that it neither exceeded its powers under the statute nor transgressed the First Amendment in interesting itself in general program format and the kinds of programs broadcast by licensees. . . .

It is argued that even if at one time the lack of available frequencies for all who wished to use them justified the Government's choice of those who would best serve the public interest by acting as proxy for those who would present differing views, or by giving the latter access directly to broadcast facilities, this condition no longer prevails so that continuing control is not justified. To this there are several answers.

Scarcity is not entirely a thing of the past. Advances in technology . . . have led to more efficient utilization of the frequency spectrum, but uses for that spectrum have also grown apace. Portions of the spectrum must be reserved for vital uses unconnected with human communication, such as radio-navigational aids used by aircraft and vessels. Conflicts have even emerged between such vital functions as defense preparedness and experimentation in methods of averting midair collisions through radio warning devices. . . .

The rapidity with which technological advances succeed one another to create more efficient use of spectrum space on the one hand, and to create new uses for that space by ever growing numbers of people on the other, makes it unwise to speculate on the future allocation of that space. It is enough to say that the resource is one of considerable and growing importance whose scarcity impelled its regulation by an agency authorized by Congress. . . .

Even where there are gaps in spectrum utilization, the fact remains that existing broadcasters have often attained their present position because of their initial government selection in competition with others before new technological advances opened new opportunities for further uses. Long experience in broadcasting, confirmed habits of listeners and viewers, network affiliation, and other advantages in program procurement give existing broadcasters a substantial advantage over new entrants, even where new entry is technologically possible. These advantages are the fruit of a preferred position conferred by the Government. Some present possibility for new entry by competing stations is not enough, in itself, to render unconstitutional the Government's effort to assure that a broadcaster's programming ranges widely enough to serve the public interest.

In view of the scarcity of broadcast frequencies, the Government's role in allocating those frequencies, and the legitimate claims of those unable without governmental assistance to gain access to those frequencies for expression of their views, we hold the regulations and ruling at issue here are both authorized by statute and constitutional. . . .

Turner Broadcasting System, Inc. v. Federal Communications Commission
SUPREME COURT OF THE UNITED STATES
512 U.S. 622 (1994)

JUSTICE ANTHONY KENNEDY delivered the opinion of the Court:

. . . [T]he Cable Television Consumer Protection and Competition Act of 1992 requires cable television systems to devote a portion of their channels to the transmission of local broadcast television stations. This case presents the question whether these provisions abridge the freedom of speech or of the press, in violation of the First Amendment. . . .

The role of cable television in the Nation's communications system has undergone dramatic change over the past 45 years. Given the pace of technological advancement and the increasing convergence between cable and other electronic media, the cable industry today stands at the center of an ongoing telecommunications revolution with still undefined potential to affect the way we communicate and develop our intellectual resources.

The earliest cable systems were built in the late 1940's to bring clear broadcast television signals to remote or mountainous communities. The purpose was not to replace broadcast television but to enhance it. Modern cable systems do much more than enhance the reception of nearby broadcast television stations. With the capacity to carry dozens of channels and import distant programming signals via satellite or microwave relay, today's cable systems are in direct competition with over-the-air broadcasters as an independent source of television programming.

Broadcast and cable television are distinguished by the different technologies through which they reach viewers. Broadcast stations radiate electromagnetic signals from a central transmitting antenna. These signals can be captured, in turn, by any television set within the antenna's range. Cable systems, by contrast, rely upon a physical, point-to-point connection between a transmission facility and the television sets of individual subscribers. Cable systems make this connection much like telephone companies, using cable or optical fibers strung above ground or buried in ducts to reach the homes or businesses of subscribers. The construction of this physical infrastructure entails the use of public rights-of-way and easements and often results in the disruption of traffic on streets and other public property. As a result, the cable medium may depend for its very existence upon express permission from local governing authorities.

Cable technology affords two principal benefits over broadcast. First, it eliminates the signal interference sometimes encountered in over-the-air broadcasting and thus gives viewers undistorted reception of broadcast stations. Second, it is capable of transmitting many more channels than are available through broadcasting, giving subscribers access to far greater programming variety. . . .

The cable television industry includes both cable operators (those who own the physical cable network and transmit the cable signal to the viewer) and cable programmers (those who produce television programs and sell or license them to cable operators). In some cases, cable operators have acquired ownership of cable programmers, and vice versa. Although cable operators may create some of their own programming, most of their programming is drawn from outside sources. These outside sources include not only local or distant broadcast stations, but also the many national and regional cable programming networks that have emerged in recent years, such as CNN, MTV, ESPN, TNT, C-SPAN, The Family Channel, Nickelodeon, Arts and Entertainment, Black Entertainment

Television, CourtTV, The Discovery Channel, American Movie Classics, Comedy Central, The Learning Channel, and The Weather Channel. Once the cable operator has selected the programming sources, the cable system functions, in essence, as a conduit for the speech of others, transmitting it on a continuous and unedited basis to subscribers.

In contrast to commercial broadcast stations, which transmit signals at no charge to viewers and generate revenues by selling time to advertisers, cable systems charge subscribers a monthly fee for the right to receive cable programming and rely to a lesser extent on advertising. In most instances, cable subscribers choose the stations they will receive by selecting among various plans, or "tiers," of cable service. In a typical offering, the basic tier consists of local broadcast stations plus a number of cable programming networks selected by the cable operator. For an additional cost, subscribers can obtain channels devoted to particular subjects or interests, such as recent-release feature movies, sports, children's programming, sexually explicit programming, and the like. Many cable systems also offer pay-per-view service, which allows an individual subscriber to order and pay a one-time fee to see a single movie or program at a set time of the day.

On October 5, 1992, Congress overrode a Presidential veto to enact the Cable Television Consumer Protection and Competition Act of 1992. Among other things, the Act subjects the cable industry to rate regulation by the Federal Communications Commission (FCC) and by municipal franchising authorities; prohibits municipalities from awarding exclusive franchises to cable operators; imposes various restrictions on cable programmers that are affiliated with cable operators; and directs the FCC to develop and promulgate regulations imposing minimum technical standards for cable operators. At issue in this case is the constitutionality of the so-called must-carry provisions, which require cable operators to carry the signals of a specified number of local broadcast television stations. . . .

Congress enacted the 1992 Cable Act after conducting three years of hearings on the structure and operation of the cable television industry. . . .

Congress found that the physical characteristics of cable transmission, compounded by the increasing concentration of economic power in the cable industry, are endangering the ability of over-the-air broadcast television stations to compete for a viewing audience and thus for necessary operating revenues. Congress determined that regulation of the market for video programming was necessary to correct this competitive imbalance.

In particular, Congress found that over 60 percent of the households with television sets subscribe to cable, and for these households cable has replaced over-the-air broadcast television as the primary provider of video programming. This is so, Congress found, because "most subscribers to cable television systems do not or cannot maintain antennas to receive broadcast television services, do not have input selector switches to convert from a cable to antenna reception system, or cannot otherwise receive broadcast television services." In addition, Congress concluded that due to "local franchising requirements and the extraordinary expense of constructing more than one cable television system to serve a particular geographic area," the overwhelming majority of cable operators exercise a monopoly over cable service. "The result," Congress determined, "is undue market power for the cable operator as compared to that of consumers and video programmers."

According to Congress, this market position gives cable operators the power and the incentive to harm broadcast competitors. The power derives from the cable operator's ability, as owner of the transmission facility, to "terminate the retransmission of the broadcast signal, refuse to carry new signals, or reposition a broadcast signal to a disadvantageous channel position." The incentive derives from the economic reality that "cable television systems and broadcast television stations increasingly compete for television advertising revenues." By refusing carriage of broadcasters' signals, cable operators, as a practical matter, can reduce the number of households that have access to the broadcasters' programming, and thereby capture advertising dollars that would otherwise go to broadcast stations. . . .

In light of these technological and economic conditions, Congress concluded that unless cable operators are required to carry local broadcast stations, "[t]here is a substantial likelihood that . . . additional local broadcast signals will be deleted, repositioned, or not carried"; the "marked shift in market share" from broadcast to cable will continue to erode the advertising revenue base which sustains free local broadcast television; and that, as a consequence, "the economic viability of free local broadcast television and its ability to originate quality local programming will be seriously jeopardized." . . .

There can be no disagreement on an initial premise: Cable programmers and cable operators engage in and transmit speech, and they are entitled to the protection of the speech and press provisions of the First Amendment. Through "original programming or by exercising editorial discretion over which stations or programs to include in its repertoire," cable programmers and operators "seek to communicate messages on a wide variety of topics and in a wide variety of formats." By requiring cable systems to set aside a portion of their channels for local broadcasters, the must-carry rules regulate cable speech in two respects: The rules reduce the number of channels over which cable operators exercise unfettered control, and they render it more difficult for cable programmers to compete for carriage on the limited channels remaining. Nevertheless, because not every interference with speech triggers the same degree of scrutiny under the First Amendment, we must decide at the outset the level of scrutiny applicable to the must-carry provisions.

We address first the Government's contention that regulation of cable television should be analyzed under the same First Amendment standard that applies to regulation of broadcast television. It is true that our cases have permitted more intrusive regulation of broadcast speakers than of speakers in other media. . . . But the rationale for applying a less rigorous standard of First Amendment scrutiny to broadcast regulation, whatever its validity in the cases elaborating it, does not apply in the context of cable regulation.

The justification for our distinct approach to broadcast regulation rests upon the unique physical limitations of the broadcast medium. As a general matter, there are more would-be broadcasters than frequencies available in the electromagnetic spectrum.

And if two broadcasters were to attempt to transmit over the same frequency in the same locale, they would interfere with one another's signals, so that neither could be heard at all. The scarcity of broadcast frequencies thus required the establishment of some regulatory mechanism to divide the electromagnetic spectrum and assign specific frequencies to particular broadcasters. In addition, the inherent physical limitation on the number of speakers who may use the broadcast medium has been thought to require some adjustment in traditional First Amendment analysis to permit the Government to place limited content restraints, and impose certain affirmative obligations, on broadcast licensees. As we said in *Red Lion*, "where there are substantially more individuals who want to broadcast than there are frequencies to allocate, it is idle to posit an unabridgeable First Amendment right to broadcast comparable to the right of every individual to speak, write, or publish." . . .

. . . The broadcast cases are inapposite in the present context because cable television does not suffer from the inherent limitations that characterize the broadcast medium. Indeed, given the rapid advances in fiber optics and digital compression technology, soon there may be no practical limitation on the number of speakers who may use the cable medium. Nor is there any danger of physical interference between two cable speakers attempting to share the same channel. . . .

This is not to say that the unique physical characteristics of cable transmission should be ignored when determining the constitutionality of regulations affecting cable speech. They should not. But whatever relevance these physical characteristics may have in the evaluation of particular cable regulations, they do not require the alteration of settled principles of our First Amendment jurisprudence. . . .

. . . Our precedents thus apply the most exacting scrutiny to regulations that suppress, disadvantage, or impose differential burdens upon speech because of its content. Laws that compel speakers to utter or distribute speech bearing a particular message are subject to the same rigorous scrutiny. In contrast, regulations that are unrelated to the content of speech are subject to an intermediate level of scrutiny, because in most cases they pose a less substantial risk of excising certain ideas or viewpoints from the public dialogue. . . .

As a general rule, laws that by their terms distinguish favored speech from disfavored speech on the basis of the ideas or views expressed are content-based. By contrast, laws that confer benefits or impose burdens on speech without reference to the ideas or views expressed are in most instances content-neutral.

Insofar as they pertain to the carriage of full-power broadcasters, the must-carry rules, on their face, impose burdens and confer benefits without reference to the content of speech. Although the provisions interfere with cable operators' editorial discretion by compelling them to offer carriage to a certain minimum number of broadcast stations, the extent of the interference does not depend upon the content of the cable operators' programming. The rules impose obligations upon all operators, save those with fewer than 300 subscribers, regardless of the programs or stations they now offer or have offered in the past. Nothing in the Act imposes a restriction, penalty, or burden by reason of the views, programs, or stations the cable operator has selected or will select. The number of channels a cable operator must set aside depends only on the operator's channel capacity; hence, an operator cannot avoid or mitigate its obligations under the Act by altering the programming it offers to subscribers.

The must-carry provisions also burden cable programmers by reducing the number of channels for which they can compete. But, again, this burden is unrelated to content, for it extends to all cable programmers irrespective of the programming they choose to offer viewers. And finally, the privileges conferred by the must-carry provisions are also unrelated to content. The rules benefit all full power broadcasters who request carriage—be they commercial or noncommercial, independent or network-affiliated, English or Spanish language, religious or secular. The aggregate effect of the rules is thus to make every full power commercial and noncommercial broadcaster eligible for must-carry, provided only that the broadcaster operates within the same television market as a cable system. . . .

That the must-carry provisions, on their face, do not burden or benefit speech of a particular content does not end the inquiry. Our cases have recognized that even a regulation neutral on its face may be content-based if its manifest purpose is to regulate speech because of the message it conveys.

Appellants contend, in this regard, that the must-carry regulations are content-based because Congress' purpose in enacting them was to promote speech of a favored content. We do not agree. Our review of the Act and its various findings persuades us that Congress' overriding objective in enacting must-carry was not to favor programming of a particular subject matter, viewpoint, or format, but rather to preserve access to free television programming for the 40 percent of Americans without cable. . . .

In short, Congress' acknowledgment that broadcast television stations make a valuable contribution to the Nation's communications system does not render the must-carry scheme content-based. The scope and operation of the challenged provisions make clear, in our view, that Congress designed the must-carry provisions not to promote speech of a particular content, but to prevent cable operators from exploiting their economic power to the detriment of broadcasters, and thereby to ensure that all Americans, especially those unable to subscribe to cable, have access to free television programming—whatever its content. . . .

JUSTICE SANDRA DAY O'CONNOR, with whom JUSTICE ANTONIN SCALIA AND JUSTICE RUTH BADER GINSBURG joined, and with whom JUSTICE CLARENCE THOMAS joined in part, concurring in part and dissenting in part:
There are only so many channels that any cable system can carry. If there are fewer channels than programmers who want to use the system, some programmers will have to be dropped. In the must-carry provisions of the Cable Television Consumer Protection and Competition Act of 1992, Congress made a choice: By reserving a little over one-third of the channels on a cable system for broadcasters, it ensured that in most cases it will be a cable programmer who is dropped and a broadcaster who is retained. The question presented in this case is whether this choice comports with the commands of the First Amendment.

The 1992 Cable Act implicates the First Amendment rights of two classes of speakers. First, it tells cable operators which programmers they must carry, and keeps cable operators from carrying others that they might prefer. Though cable operators do not actually originate most of the programming they show, the Court correctly holds that they are, for First Amendment purposes, speakers. Selecting which speech to retransmit is, as we know from the example of publishing houses, movie theaters, bookstores, and Reader's Digest, no less communication than is creating the speech in the first place.

Second, the Act deprives a certain class of video programmers—those who operate cable channels rather than broadcast stations—of access to over one-third of an entire medium. Cable programmers may compete only for those channels that are not set aside by the must-carry provisions. A cable programmer that might otherwise have been carried may well be denied access in favor of a broadcaster that is less appealing to the viewers but is favored by the must-carry rules. It is as if the Government ordered all movie theaters to reserve at least one-third of their screening for films made by American production companies, or required all bookstores to devote one-third of their shelf space to nonprofit publishers. As the Court explains, cable programmers and operators stand in the same position under the First Amendment as do the more traditional media. . . .

I agree with the Court that some speaker-based restrictions—those genuinely justified without reference to content—need not be subject to strict scrutiny. But looking at the statute at issue, I cannot avoid the conclusion that its preference for broadcasters over cable programmers is justified with reference to content. . . .

Preferences for diversity of viewpoints, for localism, for educational programming, and for news and public affairs all make reference to content. They may not reflect hostility to particular points of view, or a desire to suppress certain subjects because they are controversial or offensive. They may be quite benignly motivated. But benign motivation, we have consistently held, is not enough to avoid the need for strict scrutiny of content-based justifications. The First Amendment does more than just bar government from intentionally suppressing speech of which it disapproves. It also generally prohibits the government from excepting certain kinds of speech from regulation because it thinks the speech is especially valuable.

This is why the Court is mistaken in concluding that the interest in diversity—in "access to a multiplicity" of "diverse and antagonistic sources"—is content neutral. Indeed, the interest is not "related to the *suppression* of free expression," but that is not enough for content neutrality. The interest in giving a tax break to religious, sports, or professional magazines, is not related to the suppression of speech; the interest in giving labor picketers an exemption from a general picketing ban, is not related to the suppression of speech. But they are both related to the *content* of speech-to its communicative impact. The interest in ensuring access to a multiplicity of diverse and antagonistic sources of information, no matter how praiseworthy, is directly tied to the content of what the speakers will likely say. . . .

Having said all this, it is important to acknowledge one basic fact: The question is not whether there will be control over who gets to speak over cable—the question is who will have this control. Under the FCC's view, the answer is Congress, acting within relatively broad limits. Under my view, the answer is the cable operator. Most of the time, the cable operator's decision will be largely dictated by the preferences of the viewers; but because many cable operators are indeed monopolists, the viewers' preferences will not always prevail. Our recognition that cable operators are speakers is bottomed in large part on the very fact that the cable operator has editorial discretion. . . .

But the First Amendment as we understand it today rests on the premise that it is government power, rather than private power, that is the main threat to free expression; and as a consequence, the Amendment imposes substantial limitations on the Government even when it is trying to serve concededly praiseworthy goals. Perhaps Congress can to some extent restrict, even in a content-based manner, the speech of cable operators and cable programmers. But it must do so in compliance with the constitutional requirements, requirements that were not complied with here. Accordingly, I would reverse the judgment below.

Chapter 12

I have reached the conclusion . . . that under the First and Fourteenth Amendments criminal laws in this area are constitutionally limited to hard-core pornography. I shall not today attempt further to define the kinds of material I understand to be embraced within that shorthand description; and perhaps I could never succeed in intelligibly doing so. But I know it when I see it.

U.S. Supreme Court Justice Potter Stewart[1]

Cher's saying "fuck" on a television program led to a U.S. Supreme Court decision about the Federal Communications Commission's indecency rules.

Obscenity, Indecency and Violence

Social Norms and Legal Standards

Obscenity

Comstock and *Hicklin*
Current Obscenity Definition
Enforcing Obscenity Laws

Indecency

Broadcast Indecency
Cable Indecency
Internet Indecency

Video Games and Media Violence

Cases for Study

➤ *Miller v. California*
➤ *FCC v. Fox Television Stations, Inc.*

Suppose . . .

. . . that a singer-actress and a television personality say four-letter words on live television broadcasts and a TV cop program shows brief female nudity. On one hand, these are words most people have heard from the time they were small children on the playground and images most teenagers and adults have seen. On the other hand, for 85 years federal law has banned broadcasting such words and pictures. Should the Federal Communications Commission (FCC) find the broadcasts indecent? Should the FCC punish stations for airing them? Look for the answers to these questions when the case of *Federal Communications Commission* v. *Fox Television Stations, Inc.* is discussed later in this chapter and the case is excerpted at the end of the chapter.

Michelangelo's "David"—a 13-foot statue on display at the Galleria dell'Accademia in Florence, Italy—depicts a fully nude young man. The "Venus de Milo," a sculpture in Paris' Louvre Museum, is a bare-breasted woman. Would Justice Potter Stewart, quoted in the introduction to this

527

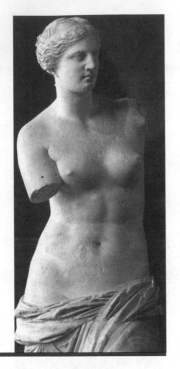

The famous "Venus de Milo" statue is not obscene—is it?

chapter, call these famous artistic creations "hard-core pornography"? Or to use the word courts apply today, would he call them "obscene"? Likely he would not, and neither would the Supreme Court. If the depiction of nudity is not obscene, what is? Who decides? Using what definition? (*A note:* There are words in this chapter that may be offensive to some, but part of everyday conversation to others. The words are taken from court and FCC decisions.)

Sexual expression is ubiquitous in contemporary societies—as it has been for centuries. It can be found in art, in beer commercials, on Internet sites and in television programs and movies. There is little agreement—aside from the Supreme Court's definition of "obscenity"—about what sexual expression should be protected and what should be illegal. The argument has two sides, each based on a different set of moral values. Some believe sexually explicit material does not deserve First Amendment protection. Others argue sexual expression is just that—expression. The First Amendment protects depictions of violence because the depictions are not real. Why not protect sexual expression that is not real sex but is only expression?

Current federal and state laws have stripped obscene material—meeting the U.S. Supreme Court's definition—of all First Amendment protection. Making, selling, distributing and exhibiting obscene material, and possessing child pornography, are illegal activities. People can be jailed and fined for violating federal and state obscenity statutes.

Sex and "dirty" words that may refer to sex upset many people. For example, when passersby could see a bare buttock on a Jacksonville, Fla., outdoor movie screen, authorities prosecuted the theater owner. A local ordinance prohibited nudity on screens visible from outside the theater area. However, the U.S. Supreme

Points of Law

Disgusting and Repugnant

The U.S. Supreme Court wrote,

> Derived from the Latin *obscaenus, ob* to, plus *caenum,* filth, "obscene" is defined in the Webster's Third New International Dictionary as "1a: disgusting to the senses . . . b: grossly repugnant to the generally accepted notions of what is appropriate . . . 2: offensive or revolting as countering or violating some ideal or principle."
>
> The material we are discussing in [Miller v. California] is more accurately defined as "pornography" or "pornographic material." "Pornography" derives from the Greek (*porne,* harlot, and *graphos,* writing). The word now means "a depiction (as in writing or painting) of licentiousness or lewdness: a portrayal of erotic behavior designed to cause sexual excitement." . . . The words "obscene material," as used in this case, have a specific judicial meaning . . . , i.e., obscene material "which deals with sex."[1]

1. Miller v. California, 413 U.S. 15, 19 n.2 (1973).

Court said the image on the screen was not obscene.[2] The law abridged the First Amendment, the Court said, because it prohibited all nudity, obscene or not. Those offended by nudity on the screen could choose not to look, the Court said. Similarly, a Vietnam War protester walked into the Los Angeles County courthouse, where women and children were present, with the words "Fuck the draft" printed on the back of his jacket.[3] As discussed in Chapter 3, he was arrested for disturbing the peace. The words may have been offensive, the Supreme Court said in overturning his conviction, but the words were not obscene. People not wanting to see the words may "avert their eyes," the Court said.

There is not even agreement on what word to use in describing offensive sexual expression. The word **pornography** is vague—not legally precise—because it encompasses both protected and unprotected sexual material. The term **indecency** has only a narrow legal meaning, referring to sexual expression and expletives inappropriate for children on broadcast radio and television. A precise definition of indecency remains in abeyance while the Federal Communications Commission responds to recent court decisions, discussed later in this chapter, calling into question the FCC's indecency regulations. The obscenity definition the Supreme Court adopted more than three decades ago still is in use and is discussed later in this chapter.

Obscenity

In the late 18th century and through most of the 19th century, Americans paid no attention to regulating sexual expression. During those years American society considered religious blasphemy and heresy to be more troublesome than sexual expression. With few exceptions, governments—state and federal—did not adopt laws or bring criminal charges concerning sexual material.

Comstock and *Hicklin*

After the Civil War some people claimed that U.S. citizens, particularly indigent men, lacked morality.

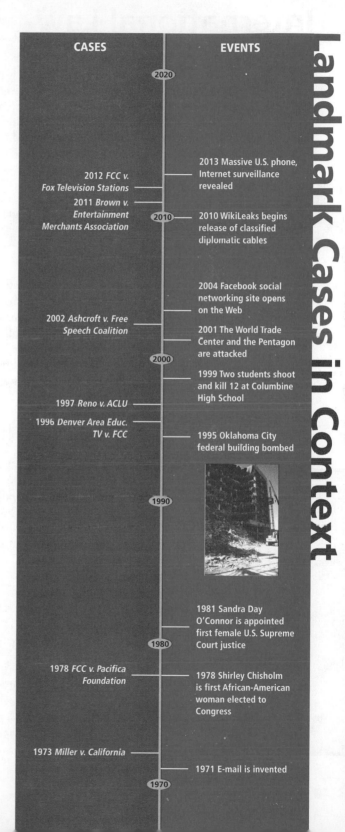

Landmark Cases in Context

CASES	EVENTS
	2020
	2013 Massive U.S. phone, Internet surveillance revealed
2012 *FCC v. Fox Television Stations*	
2011 *Brown v. Entertainment Merchants Association*	*2010*
	2010 WikiLeaks begins release of classified diplomatic cables
	2004 Facebook social networking site opens on the Web
2002 *Ashcroft v. Free Speech Coalition*	2001 The World Trade Center and the Pentagon are attacked
	2000
	1999 Two students shoot and kill 12 at Columbine High School
1997 *Reno v. ACLU*	
1996 *Denver Area Educ. TV v. FCC*	1995 Oklahoma City federal building bombed
	1990
	1981 Sandra Day O'Connor is appointed first female U.S. Supreme Court justice
	1980
1978 *FCC v. Pacifica Foundation*	1978 Shirley Chisholm is first African-American woman elected to Congress
1973 *Miller v. California*	
	1971 E-mail is invented
	1970

International Law

Obscenity in Canada

The Canadian Parliament's law making obscenity illegal defined obscenity as material that unduly exploits sex or combines sex with crime, horror, cruelty or violence. The Canadian Supreme Court upheld the statute despite its apparent conflict with the Canadian Charter of Rights and Freedoms. The charter, Canada's guiding legal document, protects "freedom of thought, belief, opinion and expression, including freedom of the press." The Court said Parliament was justified in limiting this right because obscenity "reinforces male-female stereotypes to the detriment of both sexes. It attempts to make degradation, humiliation, victimization and violence in human relationships appear normal and acceptable."[1]

---

1. Regina v. Butler, [1992] 89 D.L.R. 4th 449 (Canada); *see also* Little Sisters Book and Art Emporium v. Canada (Minister of Justice), [2000] 193 D.L.R. (4th) 193 (Canada).

---

pornography A vague—not legally precise—term for sexually oriented material.

indecency A narrow legal term referring to sexual expression and expletives inappropriate for children on broadcast radio and television.

Anthony Comstock, a store clerk, became the unlikely champion of young men's decency.[4] In 1872, Comstock convinced the Young Men's Christian Association (YMCA) to support his campaign against sexual content in art, newspapers, books, magazines and other media. Comstock became secretary of the Society for the Suppression of Vice, funded in part by financier J.P. Morgan, mining tycoon William Dodge, Jr., and business magnate Samuel Colgate. Although federal laws already banned importing and mailing obscene material, Comstock vigorously lobbied Congress to further tighten mailing restrictions. His campaign culminated

realWorld Law

Pornography from a Different Viewpoint

Nadine Strossen, former American Civil Liberties Union national president and a law professor at New York Law School, says there are important reasons for women that pornography not be censored. These are some of her reasons:

- Censoring pornography perpetuates the myth that sex is bad.
- Censoring pornography perpetuates the myth that women are victims and need help to protect themselves.
- Censoring pornography hinders the use of constructive approaches to counter discrimination and violence against women.
- Women who voluntarily work in the sex industry would be harmed by censoring pornography.
- Sexual freedom and freedom to publish sexually explicit material are important aspects of a free society.[1]

---

1. Nadine Strossen, *A Feminist Critique of "The" Feminist Critique of Pornography*, 79 Va. L. Rev. 1099, 1111–12 (1993).

realWorld Law

Comstock in Action

Anthony Comstock

Former grocer Anthony Comstock became a prominent crusader against all he considered immoral. He believed that "anything remotely touching upon sex was . . . obscene."[1] His Society for the Suppression of Vice, starting as an anti-obscenity movement in the late 1800s, lasted for more than 60 years. During that time, the society convinced schools and libraries to ban works by such prominent authors as D.H. Lawrence, Theodore Dreiser, Edmund Wilson, James Joyce, Leo Tolstoy and Honore de Balzac.[2] During the last three decades of the 19th century, Comstock and his society were involved in destroying more than 36 tons of books they said were obscene.[3] As a U.S. postal service special agent, Comstock prosecuted many people for selling and mailing material he considered obscene. He would order through the mail material he said was obscene. With the illicit item as evidence, he took the seller to court.[4] He successfully used these prosecutions to urge that courts adopt the *Hicklin* definition of obscenity.[5] He also effectively pushed all states to pass obscenity laws.

1. HEYWOOD BROUN & MARGARET LEECH, ANTHONY COMSTOCK 265 (1927).
2. Robert Corn-Revere, *New Age Comstockery,* 4 COMMLAW CONSPECTUS 173, 173 (1996).
3. Donna I. Dennis, *Obscenity Law and Its Consequences in Mid-Nineteenth-Century America,* 16 COLUM. J. GENDER & L. 43, 53 (2007).
4. Margaret A. Blanchard, *The American Urge to Censor,* 33 WM. & MARY L. REV. 741, 749 (1992).
5. David Greene, Book Review: *Not in Front of the Children: "Indecency," Censorship, and the Innocence of Youth,* 10 B.U. PUB. INT. L.J. 360, 362 (2001).

in the Comstock Act, a federal law adopted in 1873 prohibiting the mailing of "obscene, lewd, or lascivious" material.[5] Initially used only to stop mailings concerning contraception and abortion, the law was amended in 1876 to ensure that it banned the mailing of pornographic materials.[6] After the law's adoption, Congress appointed Comstock as a special postal inspector to help enforce the statute bearing his name. He held the post for 42 years. The law remains in effect today, although now it applies only to obscene content.

When courts in post–Civil War America began hearing cases involving sexually explicit material, it became clear that any publication found obscene would not have First Amendment protection. The question simply was how to define obscenity. Beginning in the late 19th century and continuing for more than 60 years, federal courts applied the *Hicklin* **rule** in deciding obscenity cases. The rule came from an 1868 English case, *Regina v. Hicklin,* stating that "the test of obscenity is this, whether the tendency of the matter charged as obscenity is to deprave and corrupt those whose minds are open to such immoral influences and into whose hands a publication of this sort may fall."[7] Whose minds are open to immoral influences? Children's minds. The *Hicklin* rule meant adults could be exposed only to material acceptable for the young. U.S. courts commonly held

Hicklin **rule** A rule taken from a mid-19th-century English case and used in the United States until the mid-20th century that defines material as obscene if it tends to corrupt children.

531

that if even a portion of a publication met the *Hicklin* test, the entire publication was obscene. The *Hicklin* rule remained dominant in America into the 1930s.

Deciding whether U.S. customs officials could prevent James Joyce's novel "Ulysses" from being imported, a federal district court in 1933 rejected the *Hicklin* test. The court said the test for obscenity should be the entire work's impact on an "average person." The court said "Ulysses" was literary art and was not obscene.[8] Some federal and state courts continued to apply *Hicklin* into the 1950s. However, the "Ulysses" decision effectively showed courts they should determine what is obscene by reviewing the material in its entirety instead of assessing isolated passages or pictures. The decision also suggested the test should ascertain a work's effect on an average person instead of on children.

Federal laws prohibit mailing or importing obscene material and producing, transporting and selling obscene material across state lines.[9] Additionally, the U.S. Congress has adopted criminal laws prohibiting Internet obscenity, particularly when addressed to minors.[10] States also have adopted obscenity laws.

SUMMARY

Sᴇxᴜᴀʟ ᴇxᴘʀᴇssɪᴏɴ ɪs ꜰᴏᴜɴᴅ ᴛʜʀᴏᴜɢʜᴏᴜᴛ American society, as it has been in many countries for centuries. Obscene material has no First Amendment protection. But not all sexually oriented content is obscene. The First Amendment protects most merely offensive sexual expression. The Supreme Court suggests those who are offended can turn their heads and refuse to look at offensive material. Even if sexual portrayals are protected, however, are they harmful to society, particularly to women? Sexual expression did not concern most Americans until the late 19th century when Anthony Comstock made it a public issue. Congress adopted the Comstock Act making it illegal to mail obscene or lewd material. That and other federal laws ban obscenity production and distribution, including on the Internet. States also have obscenity laws. Until the mid-20th century, American courts used a broad definition of obscenity, allowing government officials to ban a wide range of materials. ∎

Current Obscenity Definition

The U.S. Supreme Court handed down its first major obscenity decision in 1957, 167 years after the First Amendment took effect. In *Roth v. United States,* the Court said the First Amendment does not protect obscene material. At the same time it definitively rejected *Hicklin* and narrowed the obscenity definition to give sexual expression more freedom. The Court said material was obscene if, first, an "average person, applying contemporary community standards" found the work taken as a whole appealed to **prurient interest,** meaning that it "excites lustful thoughts." Second, obscene material was "utterly without redeeming social importance." Third, even if a work did appeal to the prurient interest, the *Roth* test said it was not obscene if it had even a small amount of social value.[11]

prurient interest Lustful thoughts or sexual desires.

realWorld Law

Sex and the Restaurant

Marvin Miller sent brochures in a mass mailing to advertise four "adult" books and a film. The brochures included pictures, drawings and text "very explicitly depicting men and women in groups of two or more engaging in a variety of sexual activities, with genitals often prominently displayed," the Supreme Court said. Many of the brochures were mailed to people who had not requested the information. The manager of a Newport Beach, Calif., restaurant opened the mail one morning with his mother standing at his side. Five brochures slipped out of an unmarked envelope for all to see. The manager called the police. A jury convicted Miller of violating a California statute forbidding knowingly distributing obscene materials. Miller appealed to the U.S. Supreme Court. Before the Court could decide if Miller's brochures were obscene, it had to define obscenity.[1]

1. Miller v. California, 413 U.S. 15, 18 (1973).

The Court refined the *Roth* test several times between 1957 and 1973. The test remained difficult for government prosecutors to meet, however, and there were relatively few obscenity convictions after *Roth*.

Finally, the Court decided it needed to reconsider obscenity law. In 1973, the Court in *Miller v. California* set down a definition of obscenity unchanged to this day.[12] A defendant convicted under California's obscenity statute appealed to the Supreme Court. The justices used the case to establish a complex, three-part definition of obscenity. Under the *Miller* test, to find material obscene a court must consider whether (1) "the average person, applying contemporary community standards" would find that the work, taken as a whole, appeals to prurient interests; (2) the work depicts or describes, in a patently offensive way, sexual conduct specifically defined by the applicable state law; and (3) the work, taken as a whole, lacks serious literary, artistic, political or scientific value.[13]

A work must meet each part of the test to be obscene. That is, the government must show a work, considered in its entirety, (1) arouses sexual lust, (2) is hard-core pornography and (3) has no serious social value. If the government cannot prove any part of this test, the work is not obscene and the First Amendment protects it.

Prurient Interest and Local Standards The first part of the *Miller* test to determine whether material is obscene requires showing that an average person would find the work, taken in its entirety, appeals to prurient interests, in other words, "lustful thoughts." The Court said "prurient" refers to "morbid or lascivious longings."[14] Material arousing morbid or shameful sexual thoughts meets this part of the *Miller* test.

The *Miller* case confirmed what the U.S. Supreme Court held in earlier cases: To determine whether material appeals to prurient interests, the content must be considered as a whole, not as discrete pictures or words. A photograph that might be found obscene on its own may be protected in a magazine by surrounding it with fiction and nonfiction articles by leading authors.

An assessment of whether the material appeals to prurient interests must be based on conclusions drawn by an average person, not a child or a particularly sensitive person. Jurors are not to use their own personal standards but instead those of an average person in the community.[15] The Court has not explained how a juror can know the standards of an average person. Some courts allow survey results to help jurors understand community attitudes, but not all courts permit social science data as evidence.

The standards are to be community-wide. Legislatures and courts decide what geographic area will be the community for setting obscenity standards. Although the Court once approved using the entire country as the community,[16] in *Miller* it ruled that jurors may not use national standards. The Supreme Court has said the community may be the city or county where the jurors live. In the *Miller* decision, the Court allowed California to use statewide standards. Other states, such as Illinois, also have permitted statewide obscenity standards.[17] Even a "deviant sexual group, rather than the public at large," may be a community for determining appropriate standards, the Court has said.[18]

It is easy to apply local, not national, standards when a movie theater shows a film. Local authorities charge the theater owner with showing an obscene film, and a local jury decides whether the film meets the *Miller* obscenity definition. It is far more difficult to apply local standards when an Internet site in San Jose, Calif., sends sexually explicit photographs to Memphis, Tenn. Which is the local community—San Jose or Memphis or one of the hundreds of cities the Internet images passed through on their way to Tennessee?

In one case, a U.S. postal inspector in Memphis using an assumed name gained access to a bulletin board operating on a website physically located in Milpitas, Calif., a city north of San Jose. The postal inspector downloaded sexually explicit images and ordered videotapes delivered to him in Memphis by a freight service. Robert and Carleen Thomas, the bulletin board operators, were charged with sending obscene material across state lines and other obscenity-related crimes. The charges were filed in Memphis, and a Memphis jury convicted the defendants. Appealing their conviction, the bulletin board operators said a local community standard cannot apply to the Internet, a geographically limitless communication medium. The U.S. Court of Appeals for the Sixth Circuit disagreed, declining to use a national standard for determining obscenity.[19] The court also rejected the defendants' suggestion to use an "Internet community." The court said it was appropriate to use the local Memphis standards. Sellers of sexually explicit material should make certain they do not have customers in communities with inhospitable standards, the court said.

The Thomases' proposed Internet community would be the entire country. Websites may be viewed and their material downloaded in any U.S. city. Even an e-mail message sent to one person can be read wherever the recipient is, not necessarily in the person's home community. Under the *Miller* standard, then,

realWorld Law

Sex and the Internet

The U.S. Court of Appeals for the Ninth Circuit held that applying "contemporary community standards" to the Internet requires defining "community" as the entire country:

> Because persons utilizing email to distribute possibly obscene works cannot control which geographic community their works will enter, [defendants argue the] definition of contemporary community standards to works distributed via email unavoidably subjects such works to the standards of the least tolerant community in the country. . . . To avoid this constitutional problem, defendants argue, obscenity disseminated via email must be defined according to a national community standard. [The U.S. Court of Appeals for the Ninth Circuit] agree[s] with defendants that the district court should have instructed the jury to apply a national community standard. . . . [The court holds] that application of local community standards [when allegedly obscene material is sent via the Internet] raises grave constitutional doubts on its face and application of a national community standard does not, thereby persuading us to adopt a national community standard to alleviate the former doubts.[1]

1. United States v. Kilbride, 584 F.3d 1240, 1250, 1254 n.8 (9th Cir. 2009).

which community's standard determines whether the material appeals to prurient interests—where the message was sent, where it was received, any community it passed through or a national standard? How can an online publisher avoid sending content to communities that would find the material appeals to prurient interests while also sending it to communities that would not? U.S. Supreme Court Justice Anthony Kennedy, joined by Justices Ruth Bader Ginsburg and David Souter, recognized that the "national variation in community standards constitutes a particular burden on Internet speech."[20] Similarly, Justice Stephen Breyer said applying "the community standards of every locality in the United States would provide the most puritan of communities with a heckler's Internet veto affecting the rest of the Nation."[21] Former Justice Sandra Day O'Connor also favored a national community for judging Internet communications.[22]

Despite several current and former Supreme Court justices suggesting a nationwide standard be used in Internet obscenity cases, the Court has not yet chosen to adopt that approach. That leaves lower courts to decide, and courts disagree about whether an Internet community is local or national. For example, in 2009 the U.S. Court of Appeals for the Ninth Circuit ruled that a jury must use a national community standard when deciding if material transmitted on the Internet is obscene.[23] However, in 2010 the U.S. Court of Appeals for the 11th Circuit disagreed. Paul Little, also known as Max Hardcore, was convicted of using the Internet to market obscene videos. Hearing Little's appeal, the 11th Circuit held that the *Miller* contemporary community requirement means a local or statewide standard "on the Internet or elsewhere."[24]

patently offensive Term
describing material with hard-core
sexual conduct.

Patently Offensive The second part of the *Miller* test requires the government to show the material is **patently offensive** according to state law. In *Miller* the U.S. Supreme Court provided examples of patent offensiveness: (1) "patently offensive representations or descriptions of ultimate sexual acts, normal or perverted, actual or simulated" or (2) "patently offensive representations or descriptions of masturbation, excretory functions and lewd exhibition of the genitals."[25] As in the first part of the *Miller* test, patent offensiveness is to be determined by contemporary community standards, the Court said.

The Supreme Court's examples of patent offensiveness mean that state definitions must meet a certain standard. Patently offensive material at least has to include hard-core sexual conduct, as the Court said. The Court made this clear when it rejected a jury's finding that the movie "Carnal Knowledge" was obscene.[26] The movie, directed by a leading Broadway and Hollywood director, Mike Nichols, contained some partial nudity but had no sex scenes. Starring Candice Bergen, Jack Nicholson and Ann-Margret, who received an Oscar nomination for her role, it had made several critics' Top 10 lists. An Albany, Ga., jury convicted a theater operator for showing the film, finding the movie to be obscene. The Supreme Court said the jury had the right to use local community standards in deciding whether the film appealed to prurient interests. However, the jury could not find the movie was patently offensive unless at a minimum it met the Court's understanding of that term, as illustrated by the Court's examples.

An Albany, Ga., jury found the 1971 movie "Carnal Knowledge" obscene, but the U.S. Supreme Court disagreed. Candice Bergen and Jack Nicholson starred in the film.

The Court has said the *Miller* examples of patently offensive material were just that—examples—not an exhaustive list. Sexually explicit material not included in the Court's list of sexual acts could be patently offensive.[27] Deciding whether material appeals to prurient interests, then, largely is in a jury's hands. But the Court said "it would be a serious misreading of *Miller* to conclude that juries have unbridled discretion in determining what is 'patently offensive.'"[28] A jury could decide that local community standards set a higher level for patent offensiveness than the Court required. Jurors in San Francisco or New York, for example, might determine that in those communities patently offensive material depicts scenes even more offensive than the Court's examples. However, jurors in Albany, Ga., cannot decide that scenes of partly nude actors make a film patently offensive. Partial nudity is not the equivalent of the Court's criteria for finding patent offensiveness.

The second part of the *Miller* obscenity test requires states to specifically define the sexual acts forbidden by state law. Courts require criminal laws to be clear and specific, allowing people to know what they must do or not do in order to obey the laws. The Supreme Court's language in *Miller* says that is how states must write obscenity laws—clearly and definitively. In practice, the court has not held to that standard. For example, the Court upheld a conviction under Illinois' very broad obscenity statute.[29] Illinois defined obscenity as material predominantly appealing to prurient interest "if it goes substantially beyond customary limits of candor in description or representation" of sexual matters. The Supreme Court said it was sufficient that Illinois courts interpreted the state law to include the *Miller* examples of patently offensive material.

Points of Law

The SLAPS Test

To show a book, movie, magazine or other material is obscene, the government must prove all three parts of the *Miller v. California* test. The third part of the test says the material, taken as a whole, must lack any serious literary, artistic, political or scientific value. This often is called the SLAPS test.

Serious Social Value The third part of the *Miller* obscenity test says material cannot be found obscene if it has serious literary, artistic, political or social value. In the *Roth* decision, the Court had said a work could be found obscene only if it were "utterly without redeeming social value."[30] This meant material with any redeeming social value at all could not be obscene. The *Miller* test is not so restrictive. Under *Miller,* the work has to lack serious social value to be considered obscene. There is a wide gap between any social value and serious social value. Material falling in the space between "any social value" and "serious social value" could be found obscene if it also meets the first two parts of the *Miller* test. *Miller,* then, does not protect as much sexual expression as some earlier Court decisions did.

In *Pope v. Illinois,* decided after *Miller,* the Court said serious social value should be decided using national standards, not local criteria.[31] The *Pope* decision also said a determination of **serious social value** should be based on what a reasonable person would decide. Because this suggests an objective, rather than a subjective, analysis of a work's social value, juries may consider testimony of expert witnesses who express their opinions about a work's social value. For example, at the request of a county sheriff in Florida, a federal district court found a 2 Live Crew album, "As Nasty as They Wanna Be," to be obscene. However, a federal appellate court observed that 2 Live Crew presented several expert witnesses at trial who testified the album had serious social value. The sheriff played the album at trial but offered no expert witnesses to support his contention that the recording was obscene. The appellate court said simply listening to a recording was not enough to determine whether the recording possessed serious social value. Expert witnesses' testimony was required.[32]

serious social value Material cannot be found obscene if it has serious literary, artistic, political or scientific value determined using national, not local, standards.

SUMMARY

THE U.S. SUPREME COURT IN 1973 ADOPTED the definition of obscenity courts still use today. For the government to prove material is obscene and therefore without First Amendment protection, it must show the work considered in its entirety

(1) arouses sexual lust, (2) is hard-core pornography and (3) has no serious social value. If the government is unable to prove any one of these elements, the material cannot be found obscene. Prurient interest, or arousing sexual lust, is determined using contemporary community standards. These may be citywide or statewide standards. The Supreme Court has provided examples of the kind of content that would be patently offensive or hard-core pornography. Jurors may not find material patently offensive if it does not at least meet the Court's standards. Whether material has serious literary, artistic, political or scientific value is determined using national criteria based on expert testimony. ∎

Enforcing Obscenity Laws

The *Miller v. California* decision did not answer all questions about obscenity. For example, is *Miller* the correct test to determine whether sexual material should be made available to minors? Even if it is illegal to produce, distribute, sell and exhibit obscene material, is it illegal to possess it? What is child pornography? The Supreme Court has worked its way through these and other matters concerning obscene material.

Variable Obscenity Long ago, the Supreme Court held that government officials may not limit adults to seeing only material acceptable for children. In 1957 the Court struck down a Michigan law making it illegal to distribute sexual material "tending to incite minors to violent or depraved or immoral acts."[33] The Court said the law violated the First Amendment because its effect "is to reduce the adult population of Michigan to reading only what is fit for children."[34]

However, the opposite is not true. That is, the First Amendment does not protect giving minors sexually explicit material that is protected for adults. For example, a restaurant owner appealed his conviction for selling minors magazines containing pictures of nude women. State law prohibited distributing to young people sexual material that would be harmful to minors. The magazines' content did not meet the Supreme Court's obscenity definition. However, in *Ginsberg v. New York* the Court said minors do not have a First Amendment right to sexual material acceptable for adults. Under its power to protect minors' well-being, the Court said, a state may "adjust the definition of obscenity to social realities" by considering minors' sexual interests.[35] Restricting minors' access to sexual material has been called **variable obscenity**: Material not obscene for adults may be obscene if the same material is given to minors.

variable obscenity The concept that sexually oriented material would not meet the definition of obscenity if distributed to adults but would be found obscene if distributed to minors.

child pornography Any image showing children in sexual or sexually explicit situations.

Child Pornography Making, selling, distributing or possessing child pornography is illegal. Federal law defines **child pornography** as "any visual depiction . . . involving the use of a minor engaging in sexually explicit conduct . . . or such visual depiction has been created . . . to appear that an identifiable minor is engaging in sexually explicit conduct."[36] The question is not whether children are appearing in videos, films or photographs that would be obscene under the

International Law

United Kingdom: No Online Sex for Minors

The United Kingdom's Office of Communication (Ofcom) fined Playboy £100,000 (approximately $155,000) in 2013 because it did not prevent minors from accessing online hard-core sexual content. Playboy could have confirmed website users were at least 18 years old by requiring payment by credit card. Cards are not available to minors, Ofcom said. Debit cards are available to minors, and some Playboy websites could be accessed with a debit card. Ofcom said, "Playboy's failure to protect children from potentially accessing these sites was serious, repeated and reckless."[1]

Ofcom fined the online adult website Strictly Broadband £60,000 (approximately $93,000) in 2012 for not verifying site users were at least 18 years old.

The British government established Ofcom to regulate broadcasting, telecommunications and postal services in the United Kingdom. Among other responsibilities, Ofcom regulates companies providing on-demand programs through the Internet. Ofcom coordinates with an independent regulator, the Authority for Television On Demand (ATVOD), responsible for editorial content. An ATVOD rule states, "If an on-demand programme service contains material which might seriously impair the physical, mental or moral development of persons under the age of eighteen, the material must be made available in a manner which secures that such persons will not normally see or hear it." The rule applies to sexually explicit videos.

In the United States, courts generally have found unconstitutional congressional attempts to prevent children from seeing sexual material on the Internet (discussed later in this chapter). Obscene material is not permitted on the Internet.

1. Office of Communication, *Playboy Fined £100,000 for Failing to Protect Children* (Jan. 16, 2013), *available at* http://media .ofcom.org.uk/2013/01/16/playboy-fined-100000-for-failing-to-protect-children/.

Miller v. California test. Rather, the question is whether minors are being sexually exploited. In addition to the federal law, all states and the District of Columbia have child pornography laws.

Courts, Congress and child welfare organizations have recognized the harm child pornography does to young people. Not only is there harm from the initial sexual act or depiction, but also from the presence of the images on the Internet. As one legal scholar wrote: "[D]istribution and possession of pornographic images may further traumatize a victim because of the victim's knowledge that her 'pictures are circulating globally on the Internet with no hope of permanent removal.' . . . [T]he continued distribution of pornographic images on the Internet results in revictimization, a lack of control, and further shame and humiliation."[37]

In *Ferber v. New York* the Supreme Court upheld New York's child pornography law, one of the nation's strictest.[38] Ferber sold pornographic films of young boys to an undercover officer. Hearing Ferber's appeal of his conviction, the Court said child pornography laws are essential to protecting minors. Using children in sexual material harms minors' "physiological, emotional, and mental health" in several ways, the Court said.[39] First, there is the psychological harm the child endures, knowing there is a permanent record of his participation in sexual activity. Second, making, selling and obtaining pornography showing children in sexual situations helps to perpetuate the sexual exploitation of children and encourages pedophilia.

Federal law is applied to visual depictions and defines child pornography as any image showing minors in "sexually explicit conduct."[40] The conduct may be actual or simulated "sexual intercourse," "masturbation" or lewd "exhibition of the genitals or pubic area."[41]

Courts strictly interpret child pornography laws. "Unlike the Court's obscenity standards, child pornography laws involve no fuzzy facts like 'community standards' or 'artistic value,' and prosecutors can make a case with little more than proof that the defendant possessed or made a visual depiction of sexual conduct by a minor," wrote a First Amendment scholar.[42] For example, a film showed preteen and teenaged girls younger than 17 years old wearing bikinis, leotards or underwear (but not nude) and gyrating to music. The "photographer would zoom in on the children's pubic and genital area and display a close-up view for an extended period of time," a federal appellate court said.[43] The film was child pornography, the court found. The federal child pornography law does not require nudity, the court said. Non-nude child models in pictures and films "can qualify as lascivious exhibitions."[44] This broad interpretation of the federal law does not make the law unconstitutionally overbroad, the court held.

An award-winning radio and television journalist could not convince courts that the First Amendment allowed him to violate the federal child pornography law. The journalist attempted to create his own chat room; logged on to other chat rooms; used the Internet to be in touch with persons he thought were female minors, some of whom were FBI agents pretending to be minors; and sent or received 160 photographs that law enforcement officials said showed child pornography. All this was done to research a story he planned to write and sell, the journalist claimed. He entered a guilty plea based on sending or receiving 15 pictures but reserved the right to appeal. A federal appellate court would not accept the journalist's First Amendment argument, saying that "any literary, artistic, political, scientific (or journalistic) value of child pornography does nothing to ameliorate its harm to children."[45] The Supreme Court emphasized the importance of protecting children from being involved in the sex trade, the appellate court said. Reporting about child pornography is not more important than prohibiting it, according to the court.

At least one court has taken to the extreme concern about child pornography's role in entangling minors in the sex trade. A Florida circuit court judge sentenced a 26-year-old man to life in prison without possibility of parole when he was found guilty of having hundreds of pornographic images of children on his computer.[46]

Congress adopted the Child Pornography Protection Act (CPPA) in 1996, criminalizing the sending or possessing of digital images of children in sexual poses or activities, even if the images were not of real children or were of adults who looked young. The Supreme Court found the law unconstitutional because children were not being involved in the sex trade.[47]

A minor's face morphed (by digitally altering a photograph) onto the body of an adult who is in a sexual pose is child pornography, the U.S. Court of Appeals for the Second Circuit ruled.[48] The court focused on the defendant storing the pictures on his hard drive, using Hypertext Markup Language (HTML) to encode folders containing the altered pictures, labeling the folders with an Internet uniform resource locator (URL) and identifying each picture with the minor's real name. These factors suggested the defendant could distribute the pictures on the Internet. The court distinguished the case from one in which a defendant morphed minors' faces onto naked adult bodies but stored the pictures on a CD-ROM rather than a hard disk. In this second case the New Hampshire Supreme Court said the pictures did not constitute child pornography and were protected by the First Amendment.[49] Criminalizing the possession of pictures showing heads of identifiable minors superimposed on naked female bodies does not promote the state's compelling interest in protecting children from the sex trade, the court said.

United States law allows child pornography victims to seek restitution not only from the person who created the images but also those who possess the pictures.[50] The victim may recover for physical and psychological medical services, temporary housing, child care, lost income, attorney's fees and other expenses. The person who created the images will be liable for these damages.[51] However, restitution from a person who did not make but only possessed the child pornography must be based on proof of harm. Ten U.S. courts of appeals have ruled the victim must show a person who only has, or perhaps also transmitted, the illegal images caused specific harms.[52] The Fifth Circuit is the only federal appellate court to disagree.[53] It decided in 2012 that the victim need show only that he was harmed by the image being in circulation and anyone found guilty of possessing that image may be liable for damages.

Sexting is an aspect of child pornography made possible by cellphones and the Internet.[54] Using cellphones, computers or other digital technologies, minors take pictures of themselves or others scantily dressed, nude or semi-nude, or engaging in sexual activities. The pictures then are transmitted to others, with or without permission of those pictured, and are perhaps posted on sites such as Facebook or MySpace. One survey found 20 percent of those between 13 and 19 years old have sent or posted nude or semi-nude pictures of themselves.[55] Also called "autopornography"[56] or "self-produced child pornography,"[57] sexting is classified as child pornography by some prosecutors. For example, two Florida teens took more than 100 pictures of themselves engaging in what a state appellate court did not deny was "legal sexual behavior." The 16-year-old girl and 17-year-old boy did not show the pictures to anyone else, although they did send the pictures from the girl's computer to the boy's computer. They were charged as juveniles with violating Florida's child pornography laws. The court upheld the girl's conviction, ruling that the state had a right to prevent sexual exploitation of children.[58]

In another sexting case, a 15-year-old girl used her cellphone to send nude pictures of herself. A prosecutor charged her under a state law the U.S. Supreme Court had previously upheld.[59] The Court ruled the state law was constitutional

SEX AND TECH

RESULTS FROM A SURVEY OF TEENS AND YOUNG ADULTS

This report includes a survey that found 20 percent of those between 13 and 19 years old have used cellphones or other means to send or post nude or semi-nude pictures of themselves.

only if limited to "lewd exhibition or graphic focus on a minor's genitals," a standard the girl's pictures did not meet. The girl could have been required to register as a sex offender for 20 years. Instead, she pleaded guilty to a lesser felony but violated a plea bargain condition (she was forbidden from using a cellphone) and was sentenced.[60]

If sexting pictures are child pornography, those who receive and retain those pictures can be charged with possessing child pornography, a felony under state and federal laws. Pictures of two teenage girls wearing opaque bras and another of a teenage girl with a towel wrapped around her bare breasts appeared on confiscated student cellphones in a Pennsylvania school district. Claiming the pictures showed provocative poses, the district attorney threatened to bring child pornography charges against the pictured girls and students whose phones contained the photographs. Alternatively, the district attorney said, the students could complete a months-long counseling and education class, including writing an essay about what they did wrong. In 2010 the U.S. Court of Appeals for the Third Circuit held that the district attorney's compelling a student to write an essay to avoid prosecution violated the student's First Amendment rights.[61]

Some state legislatures—including those in Arizona, Connecticut, Louisiana and Illinois—have adopted laws imposing lighter sentences on teenage sexters than on adults convicted of making or possessing child pornography. In Louisiana, for example, a first offense for sexting warrants 10 days in jail and a second offense could lead to 30 days in jail. The Arizona law categorizes sexting by those 8 to 18 years old as a petty offense if pictures are sent only to one other person.[62]

Possessing Obscene Material Although courts have upheld laws against making, distributing, selling and exhibiting obscene material, the Supreme Court said the First Amendment protects having obscene material in the privacy of one's home. This does not apply to child pornography, however.

In the case establishing protection for possessing obscene material at home, police officers searched a suspected bookmaker's house for gambling evidence. Police found three films in a desk drawer, viewed the movies, decided they were obscene and arrested the suspect. Overturning a conviction for possessing obscene films, the Supreme Court in *Stanley v. Georgia* said merely categorizing the films as obscene did not justify "such a drastic invasion of personal liberties guaranteed by the First Amendment."[63] The Court said there are reasons to have obscenity statutes, but the reasons do not allow authorities to "reach into the privacy of one's own home."[64] Government may not tell people what books they may read or films they may watch, the Court said.

But the government may limit possession of child pornography.[65] The U.S. Supreme Court has said the underlying interests prohibiting the possession of child pornography are so vital that they support a ban on possession.[66] The justifications for punishing possession of child pornography—protecting children's physical and psychological well-being and ending the sexual exploitation of children—are sufficiently important to overcome First Amendment rights, the Court said.

Procedural Protections The First Amendment protects filmmakers, according to the Supreme Court.[67] Nonetheless, the Court has allowed government censorship boards to license films for exhibition. That is, in some states and communities a theater had to obtain board approval before it could show a film.[68] When they were active, some censorship boards assumed a given film was obscene and required the movie producer to prove it was not. This violated the movie producer's rights, the Supreme Court said.[69] Additionally, a censorship board had to follow careful procedures complying with First Amendment standards, the Court held, including making a quick decision as to whether a movie met the board's standards.

There are no more government movie censors. The last movie censorship board, the Maryland State Board of Censors, stopped functioning in 1981. But the procedural safeguards the Supreme Court required of those committees set the standard for all obscenity prosecutions. For example, government officials must prove in court that a work is obscene. Officials cannot merely claim material is obscene and then ban it. Also, any prior restraint on allegedly obscene material must be for as short a time as possible until a court decides whether the work meets the obscenity definition.

Authorities have tried to control obscenity using a law with more bite than censorship boards had. In 1970 Congress adopted the Racketeer Influenced and Corrupt Organizations Act, popularly known as RICO.[70] Thirty-two states also have RICO acts, many similar to the federal statute. The RICO laws forbid using money earned from illegal activities—racketeering—to finance legal or illegal businesses or nonprofit enterprises engaged in interstate commerce. Violators can be imprisoned and fined.[71]

RICO prosecutions implicate the First Amendment because the laws allow the government to seize all assets acquired through racketeering activity. This means the government may try to seize an adult bookstore's contents, for example. In one case, the owner of a dozen adult theaters and bookstores was convicted of violating obscenity laws. Under the state's RICO law, authorities seized the contents of the defendant's theaters and bookstores. The defendant claimed the seizure violated his First Amendment rights. In part, he said the seizure amounted to a prior restraint because not all his store's books and his theater's films were obscene. Nevertheless, he was not allowed to sell the store's books or show films in his theaters. The seizure was for past criminal acts—selling obscene material, the Supreme Court said.[72] If the defendant wanted to open a new adult bookstore that sold sexually explicit but not obscene material, he could do so in the future. Therefore, there was no prior restraint. The theater and bookstore owner also argued the seizure chilled his First Amendment rights, since he would be hesitant to operate another adult theater or bookstore. The Court said the RICO seizure penalty no more chilled free speech rights than does the possibility of a fine or imprisonment for racketeering activities.

SUMMARY

It is illegal to provide minors with sexually explicit material that would not be obscene if given to an adult. Courts call this variable obscenity. The federal government and all states have laws making it illegal to make, distribute or possess material showing children in sexual situations. This is child pornography. However, the First Amendment protects possessing obscene material if it is not child pornography. The government must act expeditiously if it wants to censor material on the basis that it is obscene. The government may use laws originally aimed at organized crime to seize the assets of people found guilty of creating or distributing obscene material. ∎

Indecency

Consider obscene sexual expression on one side of an imaginary line and non-obscene sexual expression on the other side. Take the non-obscene sexual expression, add excretory functions and filthy words, and it all adds up to indecent speech. The Supreme Court has made clear that the First Amendment does not protect obscenity. Does the First Amendment protect indecency? The answer is both yes and no. Indecent speech is protected in print media, movies, recordings and the Internet. It is protected on most cable television programming. Indecent speech is not protected if broadcast by radio or television between 6 a.m. and 10 p.m. or if directed to children over the telephone.[73] As with obscenity, the problem is defining "indecency."

Arguments about how to define indecency, when, if ever, it should be protected in broadcasting and what penalties should be imposed for broadcasting indecent material have raged for years among the courts, Congress, broadcasters and the public. One example is that the Communications Act of 1934 makes it illegal to broadcast indecent material.[74] However, the courts and the FCC allow broadcast radio and television stations to air indecent material when it is likely that few children will be in the audience.

Many individuals and members of federal administrative agencies and Congress want to limit children's exposure to indecency. The anti-indecency campaign has become more fervent as courts have reduced the range of material found to be obscene. If sexually oriented material cannot be banned as obscene, perhaps it can be limited as indecent, critics contend.

What is indecent speech? According to the U.S. Supreme Court, "The normal definition of 'indecent' merely refers to nonconformance with accepted standards of morality."[75] "Indecency" is not a synonym for "obscenity," the Court said.[76] Material that is patently offensive but does not have prurient appeal is not obscene but may be indecent.[77] Also, material may be indecent even if it has serious social value. The FCC once defined indecency as "language or material that, in context, depicts or describes in terms patently offensive as measured by contemporary community standards for the broadcast medium, sexual or excretory activities or organs."[78] However, this definition is flexible. During the past 35 years the commission variously has expanded, contracted and again expanded its interpretation of indecency.

Broadcast Indecency

Indecent images or language are not the same as obscene material. Obscenity meets the *Miller v. California* definition.[79] Indecency does not; rather, indecency is content some people find offensive. The U.S. Supreme Court has said people can turn their heads and not look at offensive material.[80] But that is not easy with broadcast radio or television because their content comes upon people unexpectedly, for example, walking into someone's house, going into a restaurant, entering a store, getting into a car. An adult exposed to offensive broadcast material may be annoyed but can ignore it. The Supreme Court says children are a different matter, however.

The Federal Communications Commission, the courts and Congress agree and disagree about indecent material on broadcast radio and television. They agree that the law forbids it. In the past, they disagreed whether broadcasters could air indecent programming during certain times of the day, although that now is a settled issue. Most important, they disagree about how to define indecency. In 2012 the U.S. Supreme Court had an opportunity to clarify what indecency means in the broadcasting context.[81] It also could have agreed—or disagreed—with lower courts that the FCC's indecency policy, including its definition of indecency, was so vague that broadcasters could not know how to comply with the commission's regulations and avoid being fined.[82] A vague policy affecting expression would abridge broadcasters' First Amendment rights. However, the Court did not accept either challenge, leaving broadcast indecency in a gray area.

What is indecency? Is it the repetition of certain four-letter and other unacceptable words? Is it patently offensive material that describes or shows sexual or excretory organs or activities? Is it the single utterance of an expletive? At various times the FCC has said one or all of these definitions describe indecency.

In both the 1927 Federal Radio Act and the Communications Act of 1934, Congress prohibited broadcasting "any obscene, indecent, or profane language."[83] Congress later eliminated the 1934 act's provision but inserted the ban on indecent broadcasts into the federal criminal code.[84] In 1960 Congress gave the FCC power to impose civil fines on broadcasters who violate the commission's indecency regulations.[85]

The law seems clear: no indecent material on broadcast radio or television. But the First Amendment protects indecent speech unless the government has a compelling interest in regulating it and chooses the least restrictive regulatory method.[86] Also, the law forbids the FCC from censoring radio or television broadcasts.[87] And among all media, only broadcasting is forbidden from carrying indecent material. How, then, can banning broadcast indecency be justified?

The FCC and the courts, with Congress' acquiescence, found the answer to this conundrum by saying the reason for limiting indecent programs is to protect children.[88] For example, in fining a radio station for discussing oral sex during an afternoon program, the commission emphasized "the presence of children in the broadcast audience."[89] Also, the First Amendment protects indecent material in nonbroadcast media because these media can separate children from adults in their audiences. Minors can be prevented from having access to indecent books, magazines and movies, for example. But broadcast radio and television are too pervasive; they are available everywhere and children continually are exposed to them. Banning indecency, then, had to balance concerns for children against broadcasters' First Amendment rights.

Defining Broadcast Indecency The commission's statutory duty to limit indecent broadcasts lay dormant for many years. Despite the 1934 Communications Act's forbidding broadcast indecency, and later the federal criminal code doing the same, the FCC did not act against indecency until 1975. The commission responded to a father's complaint that in 1973 he and his young son heard a New York City radio station playing comedian George Carlin's "Filthy Words" monologue at 2 p.m. The 12-minute live performance on the recording "George Carlin, Occupation: FOOLE" contained the seven "words you couldn't say on the public airwaves" according to Carlin. He then said them repeatedly.[90] Defining indecency as "language that describes, in terms patently offensive as measured by contemporary community standards for the broadcast medium, sexual or excretory activities and organs, at times of the day when there is a reasonable risk that children may be in the audience," the FCC fined the station's operator, Pacifica Foundation.[91]

When the case reached the U.S. Supreme Court, it said indecent broadcast speech is material in "nonconformance with accepted standards of morality." Broadcasters have First Amendment protection, the Court noted, but the protection is limited because of spectrum scarcity. This allows courts to restrict indecency in broadcasting but not in other media, the Court said.

In determining whether the Carlin recording was indecent, the Court said the context of the challenged material is "all-important" and that an "occasional expletive" need not lead to sanctioning a broadcaster.[92] The Court focused on the "repetitive, deliberate use" of words that refer to "excretory or sexual activities

realWorld Law

Comedian George Carlin

George Carlin

The late George Carlin's comedy routine, "Seven Words You Can Never Say on Television," from his third album, "Class Clown," was the focus of the U.S. Supreme Court's *FCC v. Pacifica Foundation* broadcast indecency decision. Carlin performed on stage, recordings, radio and television for 50 years, until a few weeks before his death in 2008. He also wrote three books.

Carlin grew up in New York City, did not finish high school and joined the Air Force. After his military service he worked as a disc jockey. He teamed with Jack Burns, another comedian, as a comedy act, appearing on radio, in nightclubs and on "The Tonight Show." Carlin and Burns split in the 1960s. Carlin continued television appearances but became best known for his comedy albums. His second album, "FM & AM," won a Grammy Award, one of four awarded to Carlin, and three albums sold more than a million copies each.

In the 1970s, Carlin used the "Seven Words" routine in his stage and nightclub appearances and was arrested several times on charges of public obscenity, though he was never convicted. He was host of the first "Saturday Night Live" show. But cable television, without indecency restrictions, was a better forum for Carlin. He did 14 HBO comedy shows in 30 years.[1]

---

1. See Mel Watkins & Bruce Weber, *George Carlin, Comic Who Chafed at Society and Its Constraints, Dies at 71*, N.Y. Times, June 24, 2008, at C12.

or organs" in a "patently offensive" but non-obscene manner.[93] This suggested that indecency applied only to a Carlin-like monologue—defining indecency as "filthy words." Double-entendre and sly suggestions about sex seemed not to be included in the Court's definition of indecent speech. The Court stressed radio and television's "uniquely pervasive presence in the lives of all Americans" but focused on children. The nature of broadcasting made it "uniquely accessible to children, even those too young to read." That concern and the unique facts of the case—Carlin's repeatedly saying the seven words—justified the FCC's fining the radio station, the Court said.[94]

For a decade after *Pacifica* the FCC defined indecency as it did in that case—repeated dirty words—and took no action against broadcasters for violating the commission's indecency standard. In 1987 the commission decided to return to the indecency definition it offered in *Pacifica*. However, words not describing sexual activities or organs, and therefore not patently offensive, were not indecent unless they were Carlin-type words constantly repeated. When the words were only expletives, that is, swear words, the commission said, "[D]eliberate and repetitive use in a patently offensive manner is a requisite to a finding of indecency."[95] At that time, a single expletive was not indecent.

realWorld Law

Pigs in Parlors

The FCC's decision finding George Carlin's monologue was indecent for the broadcast media involved

a host of variables. The time of day was emphasized by the Commission. The content of the program in which the language is used will also affect the composition of the audience, and differences between radio, television, and perhaps closed-circuit transmissions, may also be relevant. As Mr. Justice Sutherland wrote, a "nuisance may be merely a right thing in the wrong place—like a pig in the parlor instead of the barnyard." We simply hold that when the Commission finds that a pig has entered the parlor, the exercise of its regulatory power does not depend on proof that the pig is obscene.[1]

1. FCC v. Pacific Found., 438 U.S. 726, 750–51 (1978), *quoting* Euclid v. Ambler Realty Co., 272 U.S. 365, 388 (1926).

The calm ended in 1987. The FCC expressed a concern that the "filthy words" indecency definition did not sufficiently protect children. Instead, the commission adopted a broader generic standard to define indecency.[96] The commission said it would consider a broadcast's context and tone as well as its language. This allowed the FCC to expand its indecency definition beyond Carlin's seven words. The FCC justified this change by referring to the Supreme Court's *Pacifica* decision.[97] The Court had said indecency includes all "language or material that depicts or describes, in terms patently offensive as measured by contemporary community standards for the broadcast medium, sexual or excretory activities or organs."[98] The *Pacifica* Court did not say what it meant by "patently offensive" as measured by "community standards for the broadcast medium," leaving broadcasters with little guidance beyond knowing what seven words George Carlin used in his monologue.

The FCC tried to clarify its standards in 2001 by adopting broadcast industry indecency guidelines. The commission again said material is indecent if it meets the generic *Pacifica* test. That is, the material must (1) describe or depict sexual or excretory organs or activities and (2) be patently offensive as measured by contemporary community standards for broadcasting. The commission said it would consider several factors in determining whether broadcast material was patently offensive: (1) how explicitly or graphically the material describes sexual activities, (2) whether the material dwells on sexual activities and (3) whether the material is meant to shock or sexually excite the audience. The FCC said it would consider the full context in which the material appeared.[99]

But the commission's clarified definition of indecency did not last long. U2 band member Bono received a Golden Globe prize and, during the 2003 awards ceremony telecast, said, "This is really, really, fucking brilliant. Really, really, great." Complaints poured in to the FCC, and the commission asserted, for the first time, that a "fleeting expletive"—a single, nonliteral use of a curse word—could be indecent.[100] The "'F-Word' is one of the most vulgar, graphic, and explicit descriptions of sexual activity in the English language," and therefore "inherently has a sexual connotation," the commission said. This conclusion overruled previous FCC decisions that found a fleeting expletive not indecent. The commission also found Bono's comment "profane," discarding its earlier definitions limiting that word to meaning blasphemy.

Similarly, the FCC found singer and actress Cher's unscripted exclamation on the 2002 Billboard Music Awards program—"People have been telling me I'm on the way out every year, right? So fuck 'em,"—and television personality Nicole Richie's remark on the 2003 Billboard Music Awards program—"Have you ever tried to get cow shit out of a Prada purse? It's not so fucking simple"—to be indecent and profane.[101] The FCC also said the two programs were patently offensive because the material was explicit, shocking and gratuitous.

The U.S. Court of Appeals for the Second Circuit rejected the FCC's decision, saying the commission "failed to adequately explain why it had changed its nearly-30-year policy on fleeting expletives . . . [and] that the FCC's justification for the policy—that children could be harmed by hearing even one fleeting expletive . . .—bore 'no rational connection to the Commission's actual policy,' because the FCC had not instituted a blanket ban on expletives."[102]

The U.S. Supreme Court overturned the Second Circuit's Cher and Nicole Richie decision. The Court in 2009 said the FCC did not act arbitrarily or capriciously when it ruled that a single use of an expletive is indecent. The FCC supplied sufficient reasons for its new policy, the Court said. The FCC admitted it overturned a long-standing regulation that a single use was not indecent. But the commission said the "F-word" has a sexual meaning no matter how it is used, a meaning that insults and offends. That was enough justification for the Court, in a 5–4 decision, to uphold the FCC's new rule.[103]

The Supreme Court did not discuss the constitutional issue beyond instructing the Second Circuit to consider whether the FCC's "fleeting obscenity" rule abridged broadcasters' First Amendment rights. In 2010, the Second Circuit said the rule did infringe broadcasters' free speech. The appellate court held that the commission's fleeting-expletive policy violated the First Amendment because it was vague, not allowing broadcasters to know what content would be found indecent and thus creating a chilling effect. The court said the chilling effect went beyond the fleeting-expletive regulation, forcing broadcasters not to take risks but rather self-censor content that might be found indecent under the FCC's

The FCC ruled indecent U2 lead singer Bono's uttering the "F-word" on broadcast television. The U.S. Supreme Court held that Fox television network did not have warning that the FCC's indecency rule applied to fleeting expletives.

definition. Also, some words might be indecent in entertainment shows but not necessarily in a news program or if used for educational or artistic purposes. For example, the commission rejected complaints that swear words in the movie "Saving Private Ryan" were indecent when a broadcast television network showed the film.[104]

The FCC appealed the Second Circuit's decision to the Supreme Court. And the Court once again chose not to give clear guidance how indecency should be defined or determine if indecency regulations violate broadcasters' First Amendment rights. Instead in 2012 the Court told the FCC it could not fine broadcasters for carrying the Bono, Cher and Richie utterances because the FCC adopted the fleeting-expletive rule after those programs were aired.[105] Broadcasters could not be held liable for violating a rule they did not know would change, the Court said. In its 2012 indecency decision the Supreme Court did not define, or give the FCC guidance in defining, indecency. Nor did the Court determine whether indecency regulations infringe broadcasters' First Amendment rights. Aside from telling the FCC it could not apply new rules retroactively, the Court did no more than say the commission may modify its indecency regulations, considering the public interest and legal requirements, and courts may review the current or modified indecency rules when appropriate cases arise.

While the Bono, Cher and Richie questions were bouncing back and forth in the courts, Justin Timberlake ever-so-briefly exposed (for 9/16 of one second) Janet Jackson's breast during the 2004 Super Bowl halftime show, and an anti-indecency frenzy ensued. Congress increased the maximum fine the FCC could impose for broadcasting indecent material "by a factor of 10—from $32,500 to $325,000—meaning that the fine for a single expletive uttered during a broadcast could easily run into the tens of millions of dollars."[106] Reacting to public and congressional outrage, the FCC said Jackson's partial nudity violated its indecency standard and imposed $550,000 in fines against Viacom-owned television stations that aired the Super Bowl.[107] Viacom Inc. owns CBS, the network that carried the Super Bowl.

The U.S. Court of Appeals for the Third Circuit overturned the commission's decision, saying that for three decades the FCC punished broadcasters for indecent programming only when the material was "so pervasive as to amount to 'shock treatment' for the audience. . . . [T]he Commission consistently explained that isolated or fleeting material did not fall within the scope of actionable indecency."[108]

The U.S. Supreme Court told the Third Circuit to reconsider its decision.[109] The Court said its 2009 ruling concerning Bono and Cher could mean the FCC did not act arbitrarily and capriciously in finding that CBS aired indecent material. In 2011 the Third Circuit issued a new ruling in the Super Bowl case. It said the 2009 *Fox* decision supported its conclusion in the Super Bowl case.[110] First, both the FCC and the Supreme Court acknowledged the commission changed the definition of indecency in its fleeting-expletive ruling, applying to both words and images. Second, as the Supreme Court said about the Bono and Cher broadcasts, the Janet Jackson incident occurred before the commission announced its new approach, so the CBS network and stations could not have anticipated the change. On this basis, then, the Third Circuit affirmed its previous ruling that the FCC could not impose fines for airing a fleeting image of Jackson's breast. The Supreme Court refused to hear an appeal of the Third Circuit's 2011 decision.

The Supreme Court's 2012 *Fox Television* decision and the Court's refusal to take the Third Circuit's Super Bowl ruling leave broadcasters with little guidance. The Court gave the FCC a strong suggestion, however. In *Fox Television* it said, "[T]his opinion leaves the Commission free to modify its current indecency policy in light of its determination of the public interest and applicable legal requirements."[111] The commission accepted the offer and in 2013 began reconsidering its indecency regulations. And it needed to reconsider. In January 2012 there were 1.5 million indecency complaints pending at the FCC; the number was reduced to 465,000 by January 2013. The reduction resulted in part from dismissing complaints more than five years old—the statute of limitations—and from focusing only on the most flagrant violations.[112]

Channeling Broadcast Indecency Balancing the U.S. Supreme Court's expressed concern for children against broadcasters' free speech rights, and complying with a congressional mandate, the FCC adopted a **safe harbor policy** in 1993. The commission would not punish any station that broadcasts indecent programming in a certain time period, a scheduling practice called "channeling." An FCC rule says stations may air indecent—but not obscene—material from 10 p.m. to 6 a.m. local time.[113] Strictly speaking, broadcasting indecent material at any time violates federal law. But the commission, with court approval, agreed not to take action against indecent broadcasts aired at times when few children are expected to be in the audience.[114] The 10 p.m. to 6 a.m. period is a safe harbor, a time when stations safely may broadcast material that does not fully comply with the law's indecency ban.

Congress, the courts and the FCC took a circuitous route to reaching the current 10 p.m. to 6 a.m. safe harbor. As part of its 1987 decision to use a generic indecency definition, the commission suggested that broadcasters could air indecent material between midnight and 6 a.m.[115] But a federal appellate court found the rule arbitrary.[116] The court said the FCC could not justify picking midnight rather than 10 p.m., for example. However, two months after the appellate court's decision, Congress adopted a law ordering the FCC to enforce the law as written—no obscene, indecent or profane broadcasts anytime.[117] The commission did as it was told. At the same time, the FCC defined the children who should not be exposed to indecent material as those 17 years old and younger.[118] The appellate court rejected the FCC's ruling.[119] The court held that the First Amendment does not allow broadcast indecency to be banned completely. The court told the FCC to try again.

Congress once more stepped in, telling the FCC to allow indecent broadcasts only between midnight and 6 a.m.[120] However, public radio and television stations going off the air at midnight or earlier also could broadcast indecent material between 10 p.m. and midnight. The FCC adopted that regulation.[121]

safe harbor policy An FCC policy designating 10 p.m. to 6 a.m. as a time when broadcast radio and television stations may air indecent material without violating federal law or FCC regulations.

Television Program Ratings

Following is a list of television parental guidelines. The first two ratings are for programs designed solely for children. The rest are for programs designed for general audiences.

- TV-Y (All children—This program is designed to be appropriate for all children.) Whether animated or live-action, the themes and elements in this program are specifically designed for a very young audience, including children from ages 2–6. This program is not expected to frighten younger children.

- TV-Y7 (Directed to older children—This program is designed for children age 7 and older.) It may be more appropriate for children who have acquired the developmental skills needed to distinguish between make-believe and reality. Themes and elements in this program may include mild fantasy or comedic violence or may frighten children under the age of 7. Therefore, parents may wish to consider the suitability of this program for their very young children. *Note:* For those programs where fantasy violence may be more intense or more combative than other programs in this category, such programs will be designated TV-Y7-FV.

- TV-G (General audience—Most parents would find this program suitable for all ages.) Although this rating does not signify a program designed specifically for children, most parents may let younger children watch this program unattended. It contains little or no violence, no strong language and little or no sexual dialogue or situations.

- TV-PG (Parental guidance suggested—This program contains material that parents may find unsuitable for younger children.) Many parents may want to watch it with their younger children. The theme itself may call for parental guidance and/or the program contains one or more of the following: moderate violence (V), some sexual situations (S), infrequent coarse language (L) or some suggestive dialogue (D).

- TV-14 (Parents strongly cautioned—This program contains some material that many parents would find unsuitable for children under 14 years of age.) Parents are strongly urged to exercise greater care in monitoring this program and are cautioned against letting children under the age of 14 watch unattended. This program contains one or more of the following: intense violence (V), intense sexual situations (S), strong coarse language (L), or intensely suggestive dialogue (D).

- TV-MA (Mature audience only—This program is specifically designed to be viewed by adults and therefore may be unsuitable for children under 17.) This program contains one or more of the following: graphic violence (V), explicit sexual activity (S) or crude indecent language (L).[1]

---

1. Federal Communications Commission, *V-Chip: Viewing Television Responsibly* (n.d.), *available at* http://www.fcc.gov/vchip.

The appellate court said Congress offered no justification for establishing two categories of broadcasters.[122] A 10 p.m. to 6 a.m. safe harbor for all stations met constitutional standards, the court ruled.

Television Program Ratings and the V-Chip In the mid-1990s some members of Congress expressed a concern about the impact on children not only of televised sexual content but also of violent programming. Realizing that the First Amendment prevented government censorship of television programs, Congress considered other alternatives. After an acrimonious fight, Congress required television set manufacturers to include an electronic chip, the V-chip, enabling parents to block reception of certain programs. Congress also encouraged the FCC or the television industry to establish a program rating system.

Preferring to adopt its own program ratings system rather than have the FCC recommend or require one, the National Association of Broadcasters, representing broadcast stations and networks; the National Cable Television Association, representing cable system owners; and the Motion Picture Association of America (MPAA), representing television program producers, created the TV Parental Guidelines. The guidelines are a voluntary ratings system. All broadcast and basic cable networks have chosen to rate their programs, as have premium cable networks such as Home Box Office (HBO) and the major distributors of syndicated television programs such as "Oprah" and "Wheel of Fortune."[123]

The broadcast television, cable and program production industries also established an Oversight Monitoring Board to review ratings applied to television programs.[124] The board has no legal authority. It can only encourage the television, cable and production industries to apply the ratings accurately and consistently. Neither the V-chip requirement nor the ratings system has been challenged in court.

The television rating system is similar to that adopted by the Motion Picture Association of America for movies. The MPAA system, also supported by the National Association of Theater Owners, is voluntary for film producers and movie theaters, but the film industry generally follows it.[125]

SUMMARY

THE FIRST AMENDMENT PROTECTS INDECENT material—except on broadcast television and radio. The FCC and the Supreme Court define broadcast indecency as patently offensive material describing or depicting sexual or excretory activities and organs. The FCC's rules consider whether the material explicitly or graphically describes and dwells on sexual activities and whether the material is meant to shock or sexually excite the audience. The FCC recently adopted new rules categorizing fleeting expletives as indecent. The Supreme Court did not determine whether this violated broadcasters' First Amendment rights. The Court said the FCC could modify its indecency regulations if it chooses to do so and courts could rule whether the current or modified regulations are constitutional. The Second Circuit already has said the current indecency regulations are unconstitutionally vague. If indecency regulations are constitutionally acceptable, courts allow broadcasters to air indecent material between 10 p.m. and 6 a.m. local time.

Attempting to give parents control over the television programming their children watch, Congress required set manufacturers to include V-chips. The chips read ratings information television stations, networks and cable systems provide with their programming. ■

Cable Indecency

Cable and broadcast television are very different media in the courts' and the FCC's eyes. Cable comes into a home only if the residents invite it in by paying a monthly fee. Even then, cable customers generally may select the cable networks they want to receive and not subscribe to others. For example, a cable customer might pay for HBO and Showtime or decide not to pay for any premium cable programming. However, radio and broadcast television programs are ubiquitous. They are everywhere—cars, stores, homes, restaurants. Broadcast indecency is channeled into the safe harbor period because children otherwise inadvertently could be exposed to it. The same rationale does not apply to cable television. At least, that is the courts' and the FCC's reasoning for not limiting indecent material on cable networks.

Not everyone agrees cable should be able to carry indecent material. HBO's development in 1975 spurred cable's popularity. Certain movies that HBO showed, and various other cable network content, so offended some state legislators and local officials that by the early 1980s they adopted laws forbidding cable indecency. Courts uniformly rejected these restrictions. For example, a Miami, Fla., ordinance prohibited cable systems from distributing "obscene or indecent" material.[126] A federal appellate court said the restrictions on broadcasting indecent material upheld in the *Pacifica* decision did not apply to cable television. Parents may prevent their children from watching cable television by not subscribing. The court also said the Miami law was overbroad because it did not allow any period when a cable system could transmit indecent material. Courts struck down several similar laws that the Utah legislature and many Utah cities adopted to ban indecent material on cable television.[127] Congress adopted the first federal law regulating cable in 1984 but did not use the statute to limit indecent content on cable television. Rather, the law said only the obvious: cable systems could not transmit obscene material.[128] The 1984 Cable Act's one concession to those concerned about indecent material on cable networks was to require cable system operators to provide lockboxes to customers who requested them. Lockboxes allowed subscribers to block receipt of individual cable channels.[129]

The FCC has not attempted to extend its broadcast indecency regulations to cable television. Responding to complaints about the cable network FX show "Nip/Tuck," the commission stated clearly: "The Commission does not regulate cable indecency. In this regard, the Commission recently stated, 'Indecency regulation is only applied to broadcast services,' not cable."[130]

However, in 1992 Congress decided that indecent cable content required its attention. Legislation adopted that year included three provisions limiting indecent content on cable television. In *Denver Area Educational Telecommunications Consortium, Inc. v. FCC,* the Supreme Court found two of the provisions unconstitutional.[131] The law dealt only with two kinds of cable channels. First, community members, local schools and government agencies may use a cable system's public, educational and government (PEG) access channels. Congress allowed cable operators—though not the government—to ban indecent programming on

PEG access channels. Second, cable systems' leased access channels can be rented by individuals and companies to show programming they want cable subscribers to see. (Both types of access channels are discussed in Chapter 11.) The law also said cable systems—again, not the government—could ban any leased access programming a cable operator believes "describes or depicts sexual or excretory activities or organs in a patently offensive manner." The Supreme Court upheld the leased-access provision. But the Court said cable systems could not prohibit indecent programming on PEG access channels. Nor would the Court allow a requirement that cable systems put all patently offensive—that is, indecent—leased-access programming on one channel and deliver that channel only to subscribers who request it.

The Court's *Denver Area* decision was fractious. Even when a group of justices agreed on a result, they could not agree on a reason for the outcome. Five justices voted to strike down the provision allowing cable operators to ban PEG indecent programming; six justices found the "segregate and block" provision unconstitutional; and seven justices voted to allow bans on leased-access indecent programming. Justice Stephen Breyer wrote the Court's opinion, but five other justices wrote separate opinions.

Justice Breyer questioned Congress' intent to control content. He acknowledged the important reason to control content: protecting children from sexually oriented programming. But even when the purpose of limiting content is extremely important, doing so is rarely constitutionally permitted. Permitting, rather than requiring, cable operators to ban indecent leased access programming is a narrowly drawn way to accomplish Congress' goal, Justice Breyer said. That is not true for PEG programming, however. Cable operators historically have not controlled PEG content, Justice Breyer said. Rather, government officials or nonprofit organizations oversee PEG programming. Congress gave cable operators a right they did not have—namely, the power to censor PEG content. This could eliminate, for example, sex education programming, content meant for marginal political groups or experimental artistic programs, Justice Breyer said.

Justice Breyer said it is unconstitutional to require cable operators to put all indecent leased-access programming onto one channel and then deliver that channel only to subscribers who specifically request it. This is not a narrowly tailored way to protect children from sexually oriented content, Justice Breyer said.

Congress continued its efforts to limit programming indecency on PEG access channels. In the Telecommunications Act of 1996, Congress said cable operators could not exercise editorial control over PEG content, but they "may refuse to transmit any public access program or portion of a public access program which contains obscenity, indecency, or nudity."[132] This provision has yet to be challenged in court.

However, the Supreme Court overturned other sections of the 1996 act dealing with sexually explicit cable programming. Congress required cable operators to scramble the signal of any indecent programming on adult-oriented channels.[133] In part, Congress said, this was to prevent adult programming signals from bleeding into channels that children could see even in homes that did

Points of Law

Censoring the Internet

The U.S. Supreme Court said,

The record demonstrates that the growth of the Internet has been and continues to be phenomenal. As a matter of constitutional tradition, in the absence of evidence to the contrary, we presume that governmental regulation of the content of speech is more likely to interfere with the free exchange of ideas than to encourage it. The interest in encouraging freedom of expression in a democratic society outweighs any theoretical but unproven benefit of censorship.[1]

1. Reno v. ACLU, 521 U.S. 844, 875 (1997).

not subscribe to adult channels. Alternatively, Congress said, cable programmers could offer adult programming only during hours when children are unlikely to be watching. The FCC said the period would be 10 p.m. to 6 a.m.[134]

A unanimous Supreme Court said those provisions of the 1996 act were content-based regulations requiring a strict scrutiny analysis.[135] Protecting children from exposure to sexually explicit programming is a compelling state interest, the Court agreed. However, Congress' method was not the least restrictive approach. Instead, the Court said, cable subscribers may ask cable companies to block channels and may request lockboxes. The availability of these alternatives make the 1996 act's provisions unconstitutional, the Court ruled.

Internet Indecency

Many websites contain sexually explicit images. It has been estimated that 40 million Americans regularly look at pornographic Internet content.[136] It is not surprising that Congress' concern about cable indecency paled next to Congress' attempts to prevent children from seeing sexually explicit material on the Internet. Congress has used two approaches in trying to separate children from indecent Internet content.[137] First, it has limited content, making it illegal to provide children indecent material through the Internet. Courts have found these attempts unconstitutional because, in part, material they prohibit from being sent to children also cannot be seen by adults. There is no technologically feasible way to allow adults but not children to receive Internet transmissions. Second, Congress and some local governments have limited children's access to content by, for example, requiring public and school libraries to block indecent material. The Supreme Court approved this method of preventing children's exposure to sexually explicit Internet content.

Many parents told members of Congress they were angry their children could see indecent material on the Internet—sometimes deliberately, often not. Congress responded by including the Communications Decency Act (CDA) in the Telecommunications Act of 1996.[138] The CDA made it illegal to knowingly transmit "obscene or indecent messages to any recipient under 18 years of age" or to make available "patently offensive messages" to anyone under 18 years old. People could not be convicted of violating the CDA if they either took "good faith" actions to prevent minors from seeing those materials or used procedures the law specified (such as a verified credit card) to confirm a recipient's age.

The Supreme Court rejected the CDA, finding it unconstitutionally overbroad in *Reno v. ACLU.*[139] The Court first said that, unlike broadcasting, the Internet had full First Amendment protection. The Internet is not limited by spectrum scarcity, as is broadcasting, because millions of people are able to use the Internet simultaneously. Also, the Internet is not as intrusive as broadcasting. Families not wanting children to access the Internet at home need not subscribe to an Internet service, the Court said. For these reasons, the Court refused to find the Internet bound by the *Pacifica* case, which involved George Carlin's seven dirty words. Also, *Pacifica* at least allowed indecent material on the air at times children likely were not in the audience. But the CDA completely banned indecent Internet content.

Because the CDA directly restricted speech, the Court used a strict scrutiny analysis. The Court did not deny that Congress had a compelling interest in protecting children from sexually explicit content. But the Court decided the law was too sweeping, not the least restrictive way to achieve the government's goal. The CDA denied adults access to protected speech as a way to prevent minors from being exposed to potentially harmful content, the Court said. The Court noted that there was no technology allowing adults to see Internet material while preventing children from doing so. The Court also said the CDA was overbroad because Congress had not carefully defined the words "indecent" and "offensive." The law made it illegal to provide children with "large amounts of nonpornographic material with serious educational or other value," the Court said.[140]

The Court's decision did not include the CDA's restriction on sending obscene material over the Internet. This limitation remains part of the federal law.

Congress enacted the Child Online Protection Act (COPA) in 1998, intending to correct the CDA's constitutional problems.[141] Courts consistently have found the COPA unconstitutional. The COPA differed from the CDA in two important ways. First, the COPA banned Internet distribution to children of material "harmful to minors," defined in part as being designed to pander to prurient interest, determined by applying contemporary community standards. The CDA more broadly limited obscene, indecent or offensive content. Second, the COPA's restriction on transmitting harmful content applied only to people intending to profit from using the Internet. The law also defined minors as 16 years old and younger, not 17 years old and younger as the CDA did.

Congress' definition of harmful to minors resembled the *Miller* obscenity definition. This meant the COPA affected a narrower range of materials than did the CDA. But the definition focused on materials inappropriate for minors. For instance, the COPA restricted material that "depicts, describes, or represents in a manner patently offensive with respect to minors." This meant the COPA limited adults to accessing materials appropriate for children—just as the CDA did.

Challenges to the COPA stayed in the courts for a decade. First, a federal district court preliminarily stopped the government from enforcing the law.[142] The U.S. Court of Appeals for the Third Circuit affirmed that decision, concluding that the community standards language was overbroad.[143] The U.S. Supreme Court disagreed with the Third Circuit and vacated the decision.[144] In 2003, reviewing the case again, the Third Circuit issued an injunction blocking the COPA's enforcement. The court said there were technological methods of limiting children's access to websites containing inappropriate material and that therefore a sweeping ban on "material harmful to children" was not the least restrictive way to achieve Congress' purpose of preventing minors from being exposed to sexual material on the Internet.[145]

The Supreme Court left the preliminary injunction in place in 2004, saying that blocking and filtering software could effectively limit children's access to harmful material. However, the Court sent the case back to the trial court to update information about Internet technology. Courts must have current information to decide if the COPA limits more speech than necessary to protect children, the Court said. When a content-based speech regulation, such as the COPA, is challenged, the government must show there are no alternatives less restrictive of First Amendment rights. Less restrictive means do exist to limit children's access to Internet pornography, according to the Court. Filters could prevent children from seeing harmful material while allowing adults access to Internet content, the Court said. Also, filters would not chill speech. Websites could include content unacceptable for children but constitutionally protected for adults. Additionally, filters are able to prevent children's access to pornography sent via e-mail and available on websites located in other countries. The COPA applies only to websites located in the United States. A congressionally appointed commission found filtering software to be the most effective means of preventing children from seeing harmful material. For these reasons, it would be difficult for the government to show that the COPA would be more effective and less restrictive than filters, the Supreme Court concluded.[146]

A federal district court in 2007 found that the COPA was not narrowly tailored and not the least restrictive nor most effective way to achieve Congress' compelling interest in protecting children.[147] The government once again appealed the decision.

Hearing the case one more time, the Third Circuit affirmed the district court's decision.[148] Applying strict scrutiny, the appellate court agreed the government had a compelling interest in protecting children from exposure to harmful material on the Internet. But the court said the COPA was not narrowly tailored to achieve that goal. The government failed to show the COPA was a better, less restrictive method of protecting children than using filters that could prevent a computer from receiving certain Internet sites. The court also held that several words and phrases in the law, such as "minor," were vague and not clearly defined. The court referred to its earlier decision, in which it said,

> The type of material that might be considered harmful to a younger minor is vastly different—and encompasses a much greater universe of speech—than material that is harmful to a minor just shy of seventeen years old. Thus, for example, sex education materials may have "serious value" for, and not be "patently offensive" as to, sixteen-year-olds. The same material, however, might well be considered "patently offensive" as to . . . children aged, say, ten to thirteen, and thus meet COPA's standard for material harmful to minors.[149]

In 2009, the Supreme Court refused to hear the government's appeal of the Third Circuit's decision.[150] Eleven years after the COPA's adoption, courts definitively ruled it unconstitutional.

Even before Congress adopted the Child Online Protection Act, it took an indirect route to keeping sexual material off the Internet. The Child Pornography Protection Act (CPPA), adopted in 1996, made it illegal to send or possess digital images of child pornography (children in sexually suggestive or sexually explicit situations).[151] The CPPA applied whether the image was created by computer—"virtual kiddy porn"—or was an actual photograph or film. The law also applied if the image was of a real person who looked like a minor but in fact was 18 years old or older. The law said it is illegal to send or possess an image that "is, or appears to be, of a minor engaging in sexually explicit conduct," or if the image is advertised or distributed in a way "that conveys the impression" that a minor is "engaging in sexually explicit conduct."[152]

The Supreme Court said the CPPA abridged First Amendment rights.[153] In *Ashcroft v. Free Speech Coalition,* the Court said the language "appears to be" and "conveys the impression" was overbroad. The language made it illegal to send or possess images that were not obscene. This would prevent adults from seeing protected content in order to prevent children from being exposed to it. Because the CPPA was a content-based regulation, the Court applied strict scrutiny. It said Congress had a compelling interest in protecting children from being involved in the sex trade. However, the Court said, since computer-generated pictures are outlawed, the CPPA would prohibit child pornography that does not harm an actual child. That also would be true when adults who appear to be children are pictured.

In response, Congress adopted the Prosecutorial Remedies and Other Tools to End the Exploitation of Children Today Act (the Protect Act) of 2003.[154] The Protect Act makes it illegal to provide someone with or request from someone an image that "is indistinguishable from that of a minor" in a sexual situation. This wording differs from the "appears to be" and "conveys the impression" language in the CPPA. In 2008 the Supreme Court found the Protect Act constitutional. The Court said the act did not focus on the material but on the speech—offering or requesting child pornography—that could put the material into distribution. The First Amendment does not protect offers to engage in illegal transactions, the Court said, because offering to give or receive unlawful material has no social value.[155]

The Supreme Court found constitutional at least one congressional attempt to deal with online content. Congress enacted the Children's Internet Protection Act (CIPA) in 2000. This law focused on schools and libraries that receive money from a federal program helping to fund Internet connections and computer equipment purchases. The CIPA would stop money from going to schools and libraries that do not install "technology protection measures" on their computers accessing the Internet. Those schools and libraries wanting to continue receiving federal funds would have to install filtering software that blocks obscenity, child pornography or material "harmful to minors."[156] The Supreme Court held in

United States v. American Library Association that Congress has the right to set conditions for receipt of federal money.[157] The Court said public libraries already choose to purchase or not purchase certain books and other materials. For example, most libraries exclude pornographic material from their print collections, the Court said. Limiting what Internet sites are available on the computers that libraries provide to the public is an equivalent decision. The Court also said requiring adults to ask a librarian to unblock a computer does not infringe on adults' First Amendment rights.

SUMMARY

BECAUSE PARENTS MAY CHOOSE NOT TO SUBSCRIBE to cable television, courts have not allowed the government to ban indecent material from cable. The one exception is that cable system operators may reject public access programs that are obscene or indecent or contain nudity.

The Supreme Court has rejected several congressional attempts to prevent children from seeing sexually oriented material on the Internet. The Court did allow Congress to withhold government funds for computers and Internet connections from public libraries and schools that do not install blocking software on computers available to the public. ∎

Video Games and Media Violence

The Internet's pervasiveness and vast content make it a ready target for citizens and legislators who believe the media should be held responsible if they deliver speech promoting violence. Scholars, politicians and citizens have clamored for legislation and civil remedies to reduce violent crime in America. One solution, they argued, would be to regulate violent content reaching minors through the Internet, television, books, music, video games and movies.[158] Courts rapidly squelched most of these initiatives with rulings that the First Amendment protects violent expression.[159] However, some people argued that specific regulations should limit violent content in video games and Internet sites because the content is directed at and readily accessible to impressionable youngsters. For example, the two teenagers who killed fellow students and a teacher at Columbine High School in Littleton, Colo., in 1999, reportedly were avid players of violent video games, as were the shooters at Virginia Tech, Paducah, Ky., and Sandy Hook Elementary School in Newtown, Conn.[160]

The Supreme Court refused to hear a case in which parents of three murdered girls argued that violent video games, such as "Doom," and websites that reach minors are not constitutionally protected.[161] The lower court had said that although protecting children from violent content is a legitimate government goal, it should be achieved through legislative, not judicial, action.[162]

International Law

Games and Violence in Russia and China

United States judges, scholars and citizens debate whether media violence—including violent video games and online games—causes people to commit violent acts. Incidents in Russia and China may suggest an answer.

In Ufa, a city east of Moscow, a group of 20-something students played an Internet game against older, more experienced gamers. The older group "killed" a student avatar. Days later several members of the two groups met in person and fought. An older gamer was beaten to death. Police arrested a 22-year-old student for the murder. In another case, a Ukrainian gamer visited Moscow to meet his online opponent and beat him to death. In a third incident, an online game player in Petrosavodsk, northeast of St. Petersburg, killed his grandmother when she interrupted his game by asking him to come eat.[1]

In Shanghai, China, Qui Chengwei, an online player, won a "cyber-weapon" called a Dragon Sabre. Qui loaned the virtual weapon to Zhu Huimin who sold it to another player for approximately $870. When Qui discovered the sale, he asked police to intervene. But the police said the weapon was not real, just an imaginary item in a game, and the law did not apply to it. Zhu refused to give Qui a share of the sale price. Qui went to Zhu's home and killed him with a knife. Qui was sentenced to death, a penalty later commuted to prison time.

A Shanghai prosecutor said online games have caused some children to steal money to pay for the games and others to injure or even murder to obtain virtual weapons and equipment. The prosecutor said a few Chinese parents have called online and video games "e-heroin."[2]

1. *Online Game Rivalry Ends with Real Life Murder,* RUSSIA TODAY (Jan. 17, 2008), *available at* http://rt.com/news/online-game-rivalry-ends-with-real-life-murder/.
2. Cao Li, *Death Sentence for Online Gamer,* CHINA DAILY (June 8, 2005), at 3, *available at* http://www.chinadaily.com.cn/english/doc/2005–06/08/content_449494.htm; *Virtual Game, a Double-Edged Sword,* CHINA DAILY (June 22, 2005), *available at* http://www.chinadaily.com.cn/english/doc/2005–06/22/content_453683.htm.

In part, the court suggested the First Amendment protects violent content, although it does not protect obscenity. As a federal appellate court said, the concerns that "animate obscenity laws" and those that cause some people to urge limits on media violence are different.[163] The court said,

> A work is classified as obscene not upon proof that it is likely to affect anyone's conduct, but upon proof that it violates community norms regarding the permissible scope of depictions of sexual or sex-related activity. . . . Obscenity is to many people disgusting, embarrassing, degrading, disturbing, outrageous and insulting, but it generally is not believed to inflict [physical] (as distinct from spiritual) harm.[164]

However, behind moves to prevent children from seeing violent content "is a belief that violent video games cause [physical] harm by engendering aggressive attitudes and behavior, which might lead to violence," the judge said.[165] Courts have not seen that as a sufficient reason to remove First Amendment protection from violent content.

In 2011 the U.S. Supreme Court said video games have communicative content and therefore have First Amendment protection.[166] Courts initially said video games

realWorld Law

Dickens v. The House of the Dead

U.S. Appellate Judge Richard Posner wrote,

Maybe video games are different [from movies or television]. They are, after all, interactive. But this point is superficial, in fact erroneous. All literature (here broadly defined to include movies, television, and the other photographic media, and popular as well as highbrow literature) is interactive; the better it is, the more interactive. Literature when it is successful draws the reader into the story, makes him identify with the characters, invites him to judge them and quarrel with them, to experience their joys and sufferings as the reader's own. Protests from readers caused Dickens to revise *Great Expectations* to give it a happy ending. . . . Most of the video games . . . are stories. Take . . . "The House of the Dead." The player is armed with a gun—most fortunately, because he is being assailed by a seemingly unending succession of hideous axe-wielding zombies, the living dead conjured back to life by voodoo. The zombies have already knocked down and wounded several people, who are pleading pitiably for help; and one of the player's duties is to protect those unfortunates from renewed assaults by the zombies. His main task, however, is self-defense.

Self-defense, protection of others, dread of the "undead," fighting against overwhelming odds—these are all age-old themes of literature, and ones particularly appealing to the young. "The House of the Dead" is not distinguished literature. . . .[1]

---

1. Am. Amusement Machine Ass'n v. Kendrick, 244 F.3d 572, 577–78 (7th Cir.), *cert. denied*, 534 U.S. 994 (2001).

do not inform, that they do not communicate information.[167] In later cases, courts showed uncertainty about video games. "We cannot tell whether the video games at issue here are simply modern day pinball machines or whether they are more sophisticated presentations involving storyline and plot that convey to the user a significant artistic message protected by the First Amendment," one court said.[168]

Brown v. Entertainment Merchants Association settled the issue in 2011. The Court invalidated a California law that banned selling or renting violent video games to minors. Video games express ideas in the same ways movies and books do, the Court said.[169] The Court rejected the argument that the interactivity of playing video games is different from the passive activity of reading or watching movies.[170] While speech categories such as obscenity and incitement are exempt from the general rule that government may not restrict expression because of its content, the Court said government may not legislate new categories of restricted speech simply because society deems them harmful. That includes limiting violent expression, as California did by banning violent video game sales to minors, the Court ruled.

Restricting video game sales and rentals is a content-based regulation requiring a strict scrutiny analysis, the Court said. There has to be a direct correlation between a regulation and its effectiveness in achieving a state's compelling interest. There is little evidence that playing violent video games harms children psychologically or that banning their sale would protect children, the Court ruled. The Court also said the California law is underinclusive because it does not include other violent content, such as Saturday-morning cartoons. And the law is overinclusive, the Court said, because not all parents want violent video games unavailable to their children.

Concerns that violent media content has profound effects on children have not diminished, nor have worries that the mass media deliberately exploit children's fascination with violence rather than imposing effective self-regulation to prevent children's access to inappropriate violent content. A report from the Federal Trade Commission (FTC) titled "Marketing Violent Entertainment to Children," released in 2000, concludes that the motion picture, music recording and video game industries intentionally market violent content to children.[171] The FTC says children under 17 years old may easily buy recordings and video games labeled as inappropriate for children and tickets to R-rated movies, a rating indicating the film is meant for viewers 17 years old and older. Exposure to media violence tends to inure children to violence in society, make them more aggressive in their own behavior, incline them to view violence as a means to solve problems and increase their belief that the world is more violent than it in fact is, the FTC says its review of academic studies shows.

Under pressure from Congress, the FCC reviewed televised violence and its impact on children. The commission's 2007 violence report recognized that scholarly studies disagree about how media violence affects young people.[172] The FCC noted the FTC report and agreed with a 2000 U.S. Surgeon General's report that "'a diverse body of research provides strong evidence that exposure to violence in the media can increase children's aggressive behavior in the short term.'" But, the commission said, it does recognize that "'many questions remain regarding the short- and long-term effects of media violence, especially on violent behavior.'"[173] The commission's primary focus, though, was "that a significant number of health professionals, parents and members of the general public are concerned about television violence and its effects on children."[174]

The FCC did not adopt new regulations responding to those concerns. Rather, it recommended that Congress and the television industry take action. The commission said that devices currently available allowing viewers to block programming so that children could not see it, perhaps based on program ratings, likely will not solve the problem. The V-chip has only limited effectiveness, the FCC said, because fewer than half of television sets have V-chips and few viewers use the V-chips even if they are available in their sets. Similarly, cable television blocking technology is not available in more than half of television sets and is rarely used even when available. However, the commission suggested that more effective and user-friendly systems enabling viewers to block violent television content could be useful. The commission suggested Congress should develop a definition of excessively violent programming that courts could find acceptable under the First Amendment. Also, Congress could consider channeling violent

realWorld Law

Video Game Ratings

Several states have adopted laws preventing the selling or renting of violent video games to minors. But courts have consistently found that the government has failed to prove that playing such games causes psychological harm.

The Entertainment Software Rating Board established by the video game industry applies the following ratings when manufacturers submit video games for the board's consideration:

- EC (Early Childhood): Content is intended for young children

- E (Everyone): Content is generally suitable for all ages. May contain minimal cartoon, fantasy or mild violence and/or infrequent use of mild language.

- E10+ (Everyone 10 and Older): Content is generally suitable for ages 10 and up. May contain more cartoon, fantasy or mild violence, mild language and/or minimal suggestive themes.

- T (Teen): Content is generally suitable for ages 13 and up. May contain violence, suggestive themes, crude humor, minimal blood, simulated gambling and/or infrequent use of strong language.

- M (Mature): Content is generally suitable for ages 17 and up. May contain intense violence, blood and gore, sexual content and/or strong language.

- AO (Adults Only): Content suitable only for adults ages 18 and up. May include prolonged scenes of intense violence, graphic sexual content and/or gambling with real currency.[1]

---

1. ESRB Game Ratings (n.d.), *available at* http://www.esrb.org/ratings/ratings_guide.jsp.

television programming into certain hours when children are less likely to be watching, as is done with indecent programming. The commission urged the television industry to reduce violence in programs children likely will watch. Finally, the FCC suggested that cable and satellite providers could allow subscribers to purchase only certain, more family-friendly channels rather than having that programming included with channels containing violence.

The movie, recording and video game industries have adopted self-regulatory systems for identifying and notifying potential purchasers or their parents of sexual and violent content. The video game industry began the Entertainment Software Rating Board (ESRB) in 1994, in response to congressional moves to impose a ratings system for computer games.[175] The ratings system is voluntary for video game manufacturers, but the ESRB says it has rated more than 10,000 games manufactured by 350 companies.[176] The front of a video game package is to have a label specifying the ESRB's ratings. On the back of video game packages are more detailed descriptions, such as, "Alcohol Reference" (Reference to and/or images of alcoholic beverages), "Blood" (Depictions of blood) and "Sexual Violence" (Depictions of rape or other sexual acts).

The ESRB uses 30 or more of these types of these Content Descriptors, which accompany a game's rating on its package and indicate content that factored into its age rating.[177]

Ratings systems advising parents about violent or sexual content would be unnecessary if the government could ban movies, music recordings and video games containing material inappropriate for children. Of course, the government cannot simply censor movies and recordings, which have had First Amendment protection for decades. However, courts only recently have considered whether video games have constitutional protection.

Is there sufficient empirical evidence to show a causal link between playing violent video games and increased violence in children? The FCC in 2010 cited a study showing "that children who spend more time playing video games are more likely to get into physical fights."[178] However, the U.S. Supreme Court asserted that studies California presented "show at best some correlation between exposure to violent entertainment and minuscule real-world effects, such as children's feeling more aggressive or making louder noises in the few minutes after playing a violent game than after playing a nonviolent game."[179]

SUMMARY

COURTS FIND THE FIRST AMENDMENT protects video games because the games have communicative content. State laws preventing minors from buying or renting violent video games consistently have been found unconstitutional. The video game industry has adopted a voluntary labeling system to alert purchasers and parents about the games' contents. ∎

Cases for Study

Thinking About It

The two case excerpts that follow offer the U.S. Supreme Court's definitions of obscenity and indecency. As you read these case excerpts, keep the following questions in mind:

- Is the *Miller* obscenity definition clear and easily applied?

- The *Miller* obscenity definition remains in use today. Have circumstances—technology, the public's toleration of media content—changed sufficiently that *Miller* no longer is an appropriate definition?

- In *Fox,* does the Supreme Court clearly justify why the law forbids indecency?

- Does the ban on broadcast indecency remain appropriate for the 21st century?

Miller v. California
SUPREME COURT OF THE UNITED STATES
413 U.S. 15 (1973)

CHIEF JUSTICE WARREN BURGER delivered the Court's opinion:

. . . [Miller] conducted a mass mailing campaign to advertise the sale of illustrated books, euphemistically called "adult" material. After a jury trial, he was convicted of . . . a misdemeanor, by knowingly distributing obscene matter [and a California appellate court affirmed]. His conviction was specifically based on his conduct in causing five unsolicited advertising brochures to be sent through the mail in an envelope addressed to a restaurant in Newport Beach, California. The envelope was opened by the manager of the restaurant and his mother. They had not requested the brochures; they complained to the police.

The brochures advertise four books entitled "Intercourse," "Man-Woman," "Sex Orgies Illustrated," and "An Illustrated History of Pornography," and a film entitled "Marital Intercourse." While the brochures contain some descriptive printed material, primarily they consist of pictures and drawings very explicitly depicting men and women in groups of two or more engaging in a variety of sexual activities, with genitals often prominently displayed.

This case involves the application of a State's criminal obscenity statute to a situation in which sexually explicit materials have been thrust by aggressive sales action upon unwilling recipients who had in no way indicated any desire to receive such materials. This Court has recognized that the States have a legitimate interest in prohibiting dissemination or exhibition of obscene material when the mode of dissemination carries with it a significant danger of offending the sensibilities of unwilling recipients or of exposure to juveniles. It is in this context that we are called on to define the standards which must be used to identify obscene material that a State may regulate without infringing on the First Amendment as applicable to the States through the Fourteenth Amendment. . . .

This much has been categorically settled by the Court, that obscene material is unprotected by the First Amendment. We acknowledge, however, the inherent dangers of undertaking to regulate any form of expression. State statutes designed to regulate obscene materials must be carefully limited. As a result, we now confine the permissible scope of such regulation to works which depict or describe sexual conduct. That conduct must be specifically defined by the applicable state law, as written or authoritatively construed. A state offense must also be limited to works which, taken as a whole, appeal to the prurient interest in sex, which portray sexual conduct in a patently offensive way, and which, taken as a whole, do not have serious literary, artistic, political, or scientific value.

The basic guidelines for the trier of fact must be: (a) whether "the average person, applying contemporary community standards" would find that the work, taken as a whole, appeals to the prurient interest; (b) whether the work depicts or describes, in a patently offensive way, sexual conduct specifically defined by the applicable state law; and (c) whether the work, taken as a whole, lacks serious literary, artistic, political, or scientific value. We do not adopt as a constitutional standard the "utterly without redeeming social value" test of *Memoirs v. Massachusetts;* that concept has never commanded the adherence of more than three Justices at one time. If a state law that regulates obscene material is thus limited, as written or construed, the First Amendment values applicable to the States through the Fourteenth Amendment are adequately protected by the ultimate power of appellate courts to conduct an independent review of constitutional claims when necessary.

We emphasize that it is not our function to propose regulatory schemes for the States. That must await their concrete legislative efforts. It is possible, however, to give a few plain examples of what a state statute could define for regulation under part (b) of the standard announced in this opinion:

(a) Patently offensive representations or descriptions of ultimate sexual acts, normal or perverted, actual or simulated.
(b) Patently offensive representations or descriptions of masturbation, excretory functions, and lewd exhibition of the genitals.

Sex and nudity may not be exploited without limit by films or pictures exhibited or sold in places of public accommodation any more than live sex and nudity can be exhibited or sold without limit in such public places. At a minimum, prurient, patently offensive depiction or description of sexual conduct must have serious literary, artistic, political, or scientific value to merit First Amendment protection. For example, medical books for the education of physicians and related personnel necessarily use graphic illustrations and descriptions of human anatomy. In resolving the inevitably sensitive questions of fact and law, we must continue to rely on the jury system, accompanied by the safeguards that judges, rules of evidence, presumption of innocence, and other protective features provide, as we do with rape, murder, and a host of other offenses against society and its individual members.

Mr. Justice Brennan . . . has abandoned his former position and now maintains that no formulation of this Court, the Congress, or the States can adequately distinguish obscene material unprotected by the First Amendment from protected expression. Paradoxically, Mr. Justice Brennan indicates that suppression of unprotected obscene material is permissible to avoid exposure to unconsenting adults, as in this case, and to juveniles, although he gives no indication of how the division between protected and nonprotected materials may be drawn with greater precision for these purposes than for regulation of commercial exposure to consenting adults only. Nor does he indicate where in the Constitution he finds the authority to distinguish between a willing "adult" one month past the state law age of majority and a willing "juvenile" one month younger.

Under the holdings announced today, no one will be subject to prosecution for the sale or exposure of obscene materials unless these materials depict or describe patently offensive "hard core" sexual conduct specifically defined by the regulating state law, as written or construed. We are satisfied that these specific prerequisites will provide fair notice to a dealer in such materials that his public and commercial activities may bring prosecution. If the inability to define regulated materials with ultimate, god-like precision altogether removes the power of the States or the

Congress to regulate, then "hard core" pornography may be exposed without limit to the juvenile, the passerby, and the consenting adult alike, as, indeed, Mr. Justice Douglas contends. . . . In this belief, however, Mr. Justice Douglas now stands alone.

Mr. Justice Brennan also emphasizes "institutional stress" in justification of his change of view. Noting that "the number of obscenity cases on our docket gives ample testimony to the burden that has been placed upon this Court," he quite rightly remarks that the examination of contested materials "is hardly a source of edification to the members of this Court." He also notes, and we agree, that "uncertainty of the standards creates a continuing source of tension between state and federal courts. . . ." "The problem is . . . that one cannot say with certainty that material is obscene until at least five members of this Court, applying inevitably obscure standards, have pronounced it so."

It is certainly true that the absence . . . of a single majority view of this Court as to proper standards for testing obscenity has placed a strain on both state and federal courts. But today, for the first time since *Roth v. United States* was decided in 1957, a majority of this Court has agreed on concrete guidelines to isolate "hard core" pornography from expression protected by the First Amendment. . . .

This may not be an easy road, free from difficulty. But no amount of "fatigue" should lead us to adopt a convenient "institutional" rationale—an absolutist, "anything goes" view of the First Amendment— because it will lighten our burdens. . . .

. . . It is neither realistic nor constitutionally sound to read the First Amendment as requiring that the people of Maine or Mississippi accept public depiction of conduct found tolerable in Las Vegas, or New York City. People in different States vary in their tastes and attitudes, and this diversity is not to be strangled by the absolutism of imposed uniformity. As the Court made clear . . . the primary concern with requiring a jury to apply the standard of "the average person, applying contemporary community standards" is to be certain that, so far as material is not aimed at a deviant group, it will be judged by its impact on an average person,

rather than a particularly susceptible or sensitive person—or indeed a totally insensitive one. We hold that the requirement that the jury evaluate the materials with reference to "contemporary standards of the State of California" serves this protective purpose and is constitutionally adequate.

The dissenting Justices sound the alarm of repression. But, in our view, to equate the free and robust exchange of ideas and political debate with commercial exploitation of obscene material demeans the grand conception of the First Amendment and its high purposes in the historic struggle for freedom. . . . The First Amendment protects works which, taken as a whole, have serious literary, artistic, political, or scientific value, regardless of whether the government or a majority of the people approve of the ideas these works represent. "The protection given speech and press was fashioned to assure unfettered interchange of *ideas* for the bringing about of political and social changes desired by the people." But the public portrayal of hard-core sexual conduct for its own sake, and for the ensuing commercial gain, is a different matter.

There is no evidence, empirical or historical, that the stern 19th century American censorship of public distribution and display of material relating to sex in any way limited or affected expression of serious literary, artistic, political, or scientific ideas. On the contrary, it is beyond any question that the era following Thomas Jefferson to Theodore Roosevelt was an "extraordinarily vigorous period," not just in economics and politics, but in *belles lettres* and in "the outlying fields of social and political philosophies." We do not see the harsh hand of censorship of ideas—good or bad, sound or unsound—and "repression" of political liberty lurking in every state regulation of commercial exploitation of human interest in sex.

Mr. Justice Brennan finds "it is hard to see how state-ordered regimentation of our minds can ever be forestalled." These doleful anticipations assume that courts cannot distinguish commerce in ideas, protected by the First Amendment, from commercial exploitation of obscene material. Moreover, state regulation of hard-core pornography so as to make it unavailable to nonadults, a regulation which Mr. Justice Brennan finds constitutionally permissible, has all the elements of "censorship" for adults; indeed even more rigid enforcement techniques may be called for with such dichotomy of regulation. One can concede that the "sexual revolution" of recent years may have had useful byproducts in striking layers of prudery from a subject long irrationally kept from needed ventilation. But it does not follow that no regulation of patently offensive "hard core" materials is needed or permissible; civilized people do not allow unregulated access to heroin because it is a derivative of medicinal morphine.

In sum, we (a) reaffirm the *Roth* holding that obscene material is not protected by the First Amendment; (b) hold that such material can be regulated by the States, subject to the specific safeguards enunciated above, without a showing that the material is "utterly without redeeming social value"; and (c) hold that obscenity is to be determined by applying "contemporary community standards," not "national standards." The judgment of the Appellate Department of the Superior Court, Orange County, California, is vacated and the case remanded to that court for further proceedings not inconsistent with the First Amendment standards established by this opinion.

Vacated and remanded.

JUSTICE WILLIAM DOUGLAS, dissenting:

Today we leave open the way for California to send a man to prison for distributing brochures that advertise books and a movie under freshly written standards defining obscenity which until today's decision were never the part of any law.

The Court has worked hard to define obscenity and concededly has failed. . . .

Today the Court retreats from the earlier formulations of the constitutional test and undertakes to make new definitions. This effort, like the earlier ones, is earnest and well intentioned. The difficulty is that we do not deal with constitutional terms, since "obscenity" is not mentioned in the Constitution or

Bill of Rights. And the First Amendment makes no such exception from "the press" which it undertakes to protect nor, as I have said on other occasions, is an exception necessarily implied, for there was no recognized exception to the free press at the time the Bill of Rights was adopted which treated "obscene" publications differently from other types of papers, magazines, and books. So there are no constitutional guidelines for deciding what is and what is not "obscene." The Court is at large because we deal with tastes and standards of literature. What shocks me may be sustenance for my neighbor. What causes one person to boil up in rage over one pamphlet or movie may reflect only his neurosis, not shared by others. We deal here with a regime of censorship which, if adopted, should be done by constitutional amendment after full debate by the people.

Obscenity cases usually generate tremendous emotional outbursts. They have no business being in the courts. . . .

The idea that the First Amendment permits government to ban publications that are "offensive" to some people puts an ominous gloss on freedom of the press. That test would make it possible to ban any paper or any journal or magazine in some benighted place. The First Amendment was designed "to invite dispute," to induce "a condition of unrest," to "create dissatisfaction with conditions as they are," and even to stir "people to anger." The idea that the First Amendment permits punishment for ideas that are "offensive" to the particular judge or jury sitting in judgment is astounding. No greater leveler of speech or literature has ever been designed. To give the power to the censor, as we do today, is to make a sharp and radical break with the traditions of a free society. The First Amendment was not fashioned as a vehicle for dispensing tranquilizers to the people. Its prime function was to keep debate open to "offensive" as well as to "staid" people. The tendency throughout history has been to subdue the individual and to exalt the power of government. The use of the standard "offensive" gives authority to government that cuts the very vitals out of the First Amendment. As is intimated by the Court's opinion, the materials before us may be garbage. But so is much of what is said in political campaigns, in the daily press, on TV, or over the radio. By reason of the First Amendment—and solely

because of it—speakers and publishers have not been threatened or subdued because their thoughts and ideas may be "offensive" to some. . . .

FCC v. Fox Television Stations, Inc.
SUPREME COURT OF THE UNITED STATES
132 S. Ct. 2307 (2012)

JUSTICE ANTHONY KENNEDY delivered the Court's opinion:

In FCC v. Fox Television Stations, Inc. (2009) (Fox I), the Court held that the Federal Communication Commission's decision to modify its indecency enforcement regime to regulate so-called fleeting expletives was neither arbitrary nor capricious. The Court then declined to address the constitutionality of the policy, however, because the United States Court of Appeals for the Second Circuit had yet to do so. On remand, the Court of Appeals [in 2010] found the policy was vague and, as a result, unconstitutional. The case now returns to this Court for decision upon the constitutional question.

. . .

[The U.S. Criminal Code] provides that "[w]hoever utters any obscene, indecent, or profane language by means of radio communication shall be fined . . . or imprisoned not more than two years, or both." The Federal Communications Commission (Commission) has been instructed by Congress to enforce [that provision] between the hours of 6 a.m. and 10 p.m. And the Commission has applied its regulations to radio and television broadcasters alike. . . .

This Court first reviewed the Commission's indecency policy in FCC v. Pacifica Foundation (1978). In *Pacifica,* the Commission determined that George Carlin's "Filthy Words" monologue was indecent. It contained "language that describes, in terms patently offensive as measured by contemporary community standards for the broadcast medium, sexual or excretory activities and organs, at times of the day when there is a reasonable risk that children may be in the audience." This Court upheld the Commission's ruling. . . .

In 1987, the Commission determined it was applying the *Pacifica* standard in too narrow a way. It stated that in later cases its definition of indecent language would "appropriately includ[e] a broader range of material than the seven specific words at issue in [the Carlin monologue]." Thus, the Commission indicated it would use the "generic definition of indecency" articulated in its 1975 *Pacifica* order and assess the full context of allegedly indecent broadcasts rather than limiting its regulation to a "comprehensive index . . . of indecent words or pictorial depictions."

Even under this context based approach, the Commission continued to note the important difference between isolated and repeated broadcasts of indecent material. In the context of expletives, the Commission determined "deliberate and repetitive use in a patently offensive manner is a requisite to a finding of indecency." For speech "involving the description or depiction of sexual or excretory functions . . . [t]he mere fact that specific words or phrases are not repeated does not mandate a finding that material that is otherwise patently offensive . . . is not indecent."

In 2001, the Commission issued a policy statement intended "to provide guidance to the broadcast industry regarding [its] caselaw interpreting [the indecency law] and [its] enforcement policies with respect to broadcast indecency." In that document the Commission restated that for material to be indecent it must depict sexual or excretory organs or activities and be patently offensive as measured by contemporary community standards for the broadcast medium. Describing the framework of what it considered patently offensive, the Commission explained that three factors had proved significant:

"(1) [T]he explicitness or graphic nature of the description or depiction of sexual or excretory organs or activities; (2) whether the material dwells on or repeats at length descriptions of sexual or excretory organs or activities; (3) whether the material appears to pander or is used to titillate, or whether the material appears to have been presented for its shock value."

As regards the second of these factors, the Commission explained that "[r]epetition of and persistent focus on sexual or excretory material have been cited consistently as factors that exacerbate the potential offensiveness of broadcasts. In contrast, where sexual or excretory references have been made once or have been passing or fleeting in nature, this characteristic has tended to weigh against a finding of indecency." The Commission then gave examples of material that was not found indecent because it was fleeting and isolated, and contrasted it with fleeting references that were found patently offensive in light of other factors.

It was against this regulatory background that the three incidents of alleged indecency at issue here took place. First, in the 2002 Billboard Music Awards, broadcast by respondent Fox Television Stations, Inc., the singer Cher exclaimed during an unscripted acceptance speech: "I've also had my critics for the last 40 years saying that I was on my way out every year. Right. So f*** 'em." Second, Fox broadcast the Billboard Music Awards again in 2003. There, a person named Nicole Richie made the following unscripted remark while presenting an award: "Have you ever tried to get cow s*** out of a Prada purse? It's not so f***ing simple." The third incident involved an episode of NYPD Blue, a regular television show broadcast by respondent ABC Television Network. The episode broadcast on February 25, 2003, showed the nude buttocks of an adult female character for approximately seven seconds and for a moment the side of her breast. During the scene, in which the character was preparing to take a shower, a child portraying her boyfriend's son entered the bathroom. A moment

of awkwardness followed. The Commission received indecency complaints about all three broadcasts.

After these incidents, but before the Commission issued Notices of Apparent Liability to Fox and ABC, the Commission issued a decision sanctioning NBC for a comment made by the singer Bono during the 2003 Golden Globe Awards. Upon winning the award for Best Original Song, Bono exclaimed: "'This is really, really, f***ing brilliant. Really, really great.'" Reversing a decision by its enforcement bureau, the Commission found the use of the F-word actionably indecent. The Commission held that the word was "one of the most vulgar, graphic and explicit descriptions of sexual activity in the English language," and thus found "any use of that word or a variation, in any context, inherently has a sexual connotation." Turning to the isolated nature of the expletive, the Commission reversed prior rulings that had found fleeting expletives not indecent. The Commission held "the mere fact that specific words or phrases are not sustained or repeated does not mandate a finding that material that is otherwise patently offensive to the broadcast medium is not indecent."

Even though the incidents at issue in these cases took place before the *Golden Globes* Order, the Commission applied its new policy regarding fleeting expletives and fleeting nudity. It found the broadcasts by respondents Fox and ABC to be in violation of this standard.

As to Fox, [in 2006] the Commission found the two Billboard Awards broadcasts indecent. Numerous parties petitioned for a review of the order in the United States Court of Appeals for the Second Circuit. The Court of Appeals granted the Commission's request for a voluntary remand so that it could respond to the parties' objections. In its remand order, the Commission applied its tripartite definition of patently offensive material from its 2001 Order and found that both broadcasts fell well within its scope. As pertains to the constitutional issue in these cases, the Commission noted that under the policy clarified in the *Golden Globes* Order, "categorically requiring repeated use of expletives in order to find material indecent is inconsistent with our general approach to indecency enforcement." Though the Commission deemed Fox should have known Nicole Richie's comments were actionably indecent even prior to the *Golden Globes Order*, it declined to propose a forfeiture in light of the limited nature of the Second Circuit's remand. The Commission acknowledged that "it was not apparent that Fox could be penalized for Cher's comment at the time it was broadcast." And so, as in the Golden Globes case it imposed no penalty for that broadcast.

Fox and various intervenors returned to the United States Court of Appeals for the Second Circuit, raising administrative, statutory, and constitutional challenges to the Commission's indecency regulations. In a 2-to-1 decision, with Judge Leval dissenting, the Court of Appeals found the *Remand* Order arbitrary and capricious because "the FCC has made a 180-degree turn regarding its treatment of 'fleeting expletives' without providing a reasoned explanation justifying the about-face." While noting its skepticism as to whether the Commission's fleeting expletive regime "would pass constitutional muster," the Court of Appeals found it unnecessary to address the issue.

The case came here on certiorari. Citing the Administrative Procedure Act, this Court noted that the Judiciary may set aside agency action that is arbitrary or capricious. In the context of a change in policy (such as the Commission's determination that fleeting expletives could be indecent), the decision held an agency, in the ordinary course, should acknowledge that it is in fact changing its position and "show that there are good reasons for the new policy." There is no need, however, for an agency to provide detailed justifications for every change or to show that the reasons for the new policy are better than the reasons for the old one.

Judged under this standard, the Court in *Fox I* found the Commission's new indecency enforcement policy neither arbitrary nor capricious. The Court noted the Commission had acknowledged breaking new ground in ruling that fleeting and nonliteral expletives could be indecent under the controlling standards; the Court concluded the agency's reasons for expanding the scope of its enforcement activity were rational. Not only was it "certainly reasonable to

determine that it made no sense to distinguish between literal and nonliteral uses of offensive words," but the Court agreed that the Commission's decision to "look at the patent offensiveness of even isolated uses of sexual and excretory words fits with the context-based approach [approved] . . . in *Pacifica*." Given that "[e]ven isolated utterances can . . . constitute harmful 'first blow[s]' to children," the Court held that the Commission could "decide it needed to step away from its old regime where nonrepetitive use of an expletive was *per se* nonactionable." Having found the agency's action to be neither arbitrary nor capricious, the Court remanded for the Court of Appeals to address respondents' First Amendment challenges.

On remand from *Fox I*, the Court of Appeals held the Commission's indecency policy unconstitutionally vague and invalidated it in its entirety. The Court of Appeals found the policy, as expressed in the 2001 Guidance and subsequent Commission decisions, failed to give broadcasters sufficient notice of what would be considered indecent. Surveying a number of Commission adjudications, the court found the Commission was inconsistent as to which words it deemed patently offensive. It also determined that the Commission's presumptive prohibition on the F-word and the S-word was plagued by vagueness because the Commission had on occasion found the fleeting use of those words not indecent provided they occurred during a bona fide news interview or were "demonstrably essential to the nature of an artistic or educational work." The Commission's application of these exceptions, according to the Court of Appeals, left broadcasters guessing whether an expletive would be deemed artistically integral to a program or whether a particular broadcast would be considered a bona fide news interview. The Court of Appeals found the vagueness inherent in the policy had forced broadcasters to "choose between not airing . . . controversial programs [or] risking massive fines or possibly even loss of their licenses." And the court found that there was "ample evidence in the record" that this harsh choice had led to a chill of protected speech.

The procedural history regarding ABC is more brief. On February 19, 2008, the Commission issued a forfeiture order finding the display of the woman's nude buttocks in NYPD Blue was actionably indecent. The Commission determined that, regardless of medical definitions, displays of buttocks fell within the category of displays of sexual or excretory organs because the depiction was "widely associated with sexual arousal and closely associated by most people with excretory activities." The scene was deemed patently offensive as measured by contemporary community standards, and the Commission determined that "[t]he female actor's nudity is presented in a manner that clearly panders to and titillates the audience." Unlike in the Fox case, the Commission imposed a forfeiture of $27,500 on each of the 45 ABC-affiliated stations that aired the indecent episode. In a summary order the United States Court of Appeals for the Second Circuit vacated the forfeiture order, determining that it was bound by its *Fox* decision striking down the entirety of the Commission's indecency policy.

. . . These are the cases before us.

A fundamental principle in our legal system is that laws which regulate persons or entities must give fair notice of conduct that is forbidden or required. This requirement of clarity in regulation is essential to the protections provided by the Due Process Clause of the Fifth Amendment. It requires the invalidation of laws that are impermissibly vague. A conviction or punishment fails to comply with due process if the statute or regulation under which it is obtained "fails to provide a person of ordinary intelligence fair notice of what is prohibited, or is so standardless that it authorizes or encourages seriously discriminatory enforcement." As this Court has explained, a regulation is not vague because it may at times be difficult to prove an incriminating fact but rather because it is unclear as to what fact must be proved.

Even when speech is not at issue, the void for vagueness doctrine addresses at least two connected but discrete due process concerns: first, that regulated parties should know what is required of them so they may act accordingly; second, precision and guidance are necessary so that those enforcing the law do not act in an arbitrary or discriminatory way. When speech is involved, rigorous adherence to those requirements is necessary to ensure that ambiguity does not chill protected speech.

These concerns are implicated here because, at the outset, the broadcasters claim they did not have, and do not have, sufficient notice of what is proscribed. And leaving aside any concerns about facial invalidity, they contend that the lengthy procedural history set forth above shows that the broadcasters did not have fair notice of what was forbidden. Under the 2001 Guidelines in force when the broadcasts occurred, a key consideration was "'whether the material dwell[ed] on or repeat[ed] at length'" the offending description or depiction. In the 2004 *Golden Globes* Order, issued after the broadcasts, the Commission changed course and held that fleeting expletives could be a statutory violation. In the challenged orders now under review the Commission applied the new principle promulgated in the *Golden Globes* Order and determined fleeting expletives and a brief moment of indecency were actionably indecent. This regulatory history, however, makes it apparent that the Commission policy in place at the time of the broadcasts gave no notice to Fox or ABC that a fleeting expletive or a brief shot of nudity could be actionably indecent; yet Fox and ABC were found to be in violation. The Commission's lack of notice to Fox and ABC that its interpretation had changed so the fleeting moments of indecency contained in their broadcasts were a violation of [the indecency law] as interpreted and enforced by the agency "fail[ed] to provide a person of ordinary intelligence fair notice of what is prohibited." This would be true with respect to a regulatory change this abrupt on any subject, but it is surely the case when applied to the regulations in question, regulations that touch upon "sensitive areas of basic First Amendment freedoms."

The Government raises two arguments in response, but neither is persuasive. As for the two fleeting expletives, the Government concedes that "Fox did not have reasonable notice at the time of the broadcasts that the Commission would consider non-repeated expletives indecent." The Government argues, nonetheless, that Fox "cannot establish unconstitutional vagueness on that basis . . . because the Commission did not impose a sanction where Fox lacked such notice." As the Court observed when the case was here three Terms ago, it is true that the Commission declined to impose any forfeiture on Fox, and in its order the Commission claimed that it would not consider the indecent broadcasts either when considering whether to renew stations' licenses or "in any other context." This "policy of forbearance," as the Government calls it, does not suffice to make the issue moot. Though the Commission claims it will not consider the prior indecent broadcasts "in any context," it has the statutory power to take into account "any history of prior offenses" when setting the level of a forfeiture penalty. Just as in the First Amendment context, the due process protection against vague regulations "does not leave [regulated parties] . . . at the mercy of *noblesse oblige*." Given that the Commission found it was "not inequitable to hold Fox responsible for [the 2003 broadcast]," and that it has the statutory authority to use its finding to increase any future penalties, the Government's assurance it will elect not to do so is insufficient to remedy the constitutional violation.

In addition, when combined with the legal consequence described above, reputational injury provides further reason for granting relief to Fox. As respondent CBS points out, findings of wrongdoing can result in harm to a broadcaster's "reputation with viewers and advertisers." This observation is hardly surprising given that the challenged orders, which are contained in the permanent Commission record, describe in strongly disapproving terms the indecent material broadcast by Fox, and Fox's efforts to protect children from being exposed to it. Commission sanctions on broadcasters for indecent material are widely publicized. The challenged orders could have an adverse impact on Fox's reputation that audiences and advertisers alike are entitled to take into account.

With respect to ABC, the Government with good reason does not argue no sanction was imposed. The fine against ABC and its network affiliates for the seven seconds of nudity was nearly $1.24 million. The Government argues instead that ABC had notice that the scene in NYPD Blue would be considered indecent in light of a 1960 decision where the Commission declared that the "televising of nudes might well raise a serious question of programming contrary to [the indecency law]." This argument does not prevail. An isolated and ambiguous statement from a 1960 Commission decision does not suffice for the fair notice required when the Government intends to impose over a $1 million fine for allegedly impermissible speech. . . .

The Commission failed to give Fox or ABC fair notice prior to the broadcasts in question that fleeting expletives and momentary nudity could be found actionably indecent.

Therefore, the Commission's standards as applied to these broadcasts were vague, and the Commission's orders must be set aside.

It is necessary to make three observations about the scope of this decision. First, because the Court resolves these cases on fair notice grounds under the Due Process Clause, it need not address the First Amendment implications of the Commission's indecency policy. It is argued that this Court's ruling in *Pacifica* (and the less rigorous standard of scrutiny it provided for the regulation of broadcasters) should be overruled because the rationale of that case has been overtaken by technological change and the wide availability of multiple other choices for listeners and viewers. The Government for its part maintains that when it licenses a conventional broadcast spectrum, the public may assume that the Government has its own interest in setting certain standards. These arguments need not be addressed here. In light of the Court's holding that the Commission's policy failed to provide fair notice it is unnecessary to reconsider *Pacifica* at this time.

This leads to a second observation. Here, the Court rules that Fox and ABC lacked notice at the time of their broadcasts that the material they were broadcasting could be found actionably indecent under then-existing policies. Given this disposition, it is unnecessary for the Court to address the constitutionality of the current indecency policy as expressed in the *Golden Globes* Order and subsequent adjudications. The Court adheres to its normal practice of declining to decide cases not before it.

Third, this opinion leaves the Commission free to modify its current indecency policy in light of its determination of the public interest and applicable legal requirements. And it leaves the courts free to review the current policy or any modified policy in light of its content and application.

* * *

The judgments of the United States Court of Appeals for the Second Circuit are vacated, and the cases are remanded for further proceedings consistent with the principles set forth in this opinion.

It is so ordered.

Justice Sotomayor took no part in the consideration or decision of these cases.

Chapter 13

If "piracy" means using the creative property of others without their permission . . . then the history of the content industry is a history of piracy. Every important sector of "big media" today—film, records, radio and cable TV—was born of a kind of piracy. . . . There is piracy of copyrighted material. Lots of it. . . . No one should condone it, and the law should stop it.

Lawrence Lessig, Harvard Law School professor[1]

There is a reason this Disneyland statue has Walt Disney holding Mickey Mouse's hand. Disney's copyright forbidding others from using Mickey without permission made Walt a very rich man.

Intellectual Property
Protecting and Using Intangible Creations

Copyright

The Development of U.S.
   Copyright Law
The 1976 Copyright Act
Proving Copyright
   Infringement
Remedies for Copyright
   Infringement
Copyright Infringement
   Defense: Fair Use
Copyright, Computers and
   the Internet
Music Licensing
Music, the Internet and File
   Sharing

Trademarks

Distinctiveness Requirement
Registering a Trademark
Domain Names
Trademark Infringement
Trademark Infringement
   Defenses

Cases for Study

➤ *Golan v. Holder*
➤ *Metro-Goldwyn-*
   Mayer Studios, Inc. v.
   Grokster, Ltd.

Suppose . . .

. . . that a movie is made in England in 1990. If the filmmaker registered the film with the U.S. Copyright Office, copyright protection would last until 70 years after the filmmaker's death. But if the movie were not registered, it would have no copyright protection in the United States. It would be in the public domain. That was the situation until 1994 when Congress gave copyright protection to many foreign works that had been in the public domain. After the congressional action, the movie was protected as if the filmmaker initially had registered it. Should Congress be able to give copyright protection to works that once were in the public domain? Look for the answer to this question when the case of *Golan v. Holder* is discussed later in this chapter, and the case is excerpted at the end of the chapter.

The law protects people's personal property. Stealing someone's car is illegal. Robbing a bank, burglarizing a house or shoplifting a book from a store is illegal. If a person writes a magazine article, it is against the law to take the manuscript without permission. Although the paper may be worth a few dollars, that is not the real concern. The law also protects what is written on the paper—the author's expression of his or her ideas. No one but the author may publish that article unless the writer consents. Nor may the article be made into a movie or used in any other way without the author's permission. The magazine article is not personal property the way a car is. The law calls the article "intangible property." Nonetheless, copyright law gives the article legal protection.

Similarly, trademark law protects creations such as product names, advertising slogans, movie and book titles and cartoon characters. Patent law protects inventions. Patent, trademark and copyright statutes all are categorized as **intellectual property law.** Generally, intellectual property laws—particularly patent and copyright statutes—are intended to encourage creativity. Ensuring that people will benefit financially from their creations encourages them to continue being creative. If people could use others' intellectual creations without permission, there would be no financial incentive to write, paint or invent.

Beginning in the Middle Ages, patent law prevented skilled workers—such as goldsmiths—from using other craftsmen's creations. Congress adopted the United States' current patent law in 1952, giving protection to useful, novel, "nonobvious" processes and inventions.[2] Trademarks also began in the Middle Ages—although it has been suggested that potters 3,500 years ago marked their wares—when members of a guild, an organization of artisans, used unique marks to distinguish their goods from those of other guilds. The Lanham Act, discussed in Chapter 14, is the current U.S. trademark law, intended to prevent consumer confusion about what company supplies particular goods.[3]

intellectual property law The legal category including copyright, trademark and patent law.

Copyright

copyright An exclusive legal right used to protect intellectual creations from unauthorized use.

A **copyright** is an exclusive legal right protecting intellectual creations from unauthorized use. Copyright law attempts a balancing act between the creator's right to restrict the use of his or her work and society's belief that some uses should be allowed without the creator's permission. Achieving the balance has been a difficult task since the United States adopted its first copyright law in 1790.

Copyright law encourages people to create new works by allowing them to profit from their efforts. The profits—and copyright infringement damages—may be considerable. Novelist James Patterson's books—all of them protected by copyright—earn him nearly $100 million a year.[4] Copyright law also stimulates innovation in novels, paintings, motion pictures, newspapers, music.

U.S. copyright law protects the rights of creators of "original works of authorship" to use their creations.[5] The copyright holder has complete control over a work. Effectively, the federal copyright law creates a monopoly allowing the work's creator—the copyright holder—to say who can use the work, for what purpose and for how long. The U.S. Constitution grants creators control over their works for only a "limited

Points of Law

The U.S. Constitution: Copyrights and Patents

The Congress shall have Power . . . [t]o promote the Progress of Science and useful Arts, by securing for limited Times to Authors and Inventors the exclusive Right to their respective Writings and Discoveries.[1]

1. U.S. CONST., art. 1, § 8, cls. 1, 8.

time."[6] Once the limit was 28 years. Today copyright for many works lasts for the creator's life plus 70 more years.

Protecting creators' works was trivial before development of the printing press and subsequent reproduction technologies. Reproducing manuscripts by hand was tedious. No one could steal someone else's work and transcribe enough copies to make the theft worthwhile. But in the 15th century the printing press enabled many copies to be printed cheaply. In England, the monarchy settled the issue of who should profit: Printers would control publication, and the Crown would control printers. Authors might be paid for a manuscript, but then they dropped out of the picture.[7]

Copyright's initial purpose was not to reward creators but to prevent sedition—criticizing the king or queen. The Crown gave a group of printers, called the Stationers' Company, control over printing in mid-16th-century England. Licensed printers received the right to publish the work in perpetuity. The ban on anyone else publishing the work lasted forever.

The license requirement ended in 1694, but the Stationers' Company did not disappear. Rather, it shifted its focus from printers to authors. The first copyright law in England, called the **Statute of Anne** of 1710, protected authors' works[8] and granted authors copyright protection if they registered their works with the government. When the copyright period ended after 14 years, or 28 years if the author renewed the copyright—the work went into the public domain, and anyone could use it without permission. Under the Statute of Anne, authors controlled their creations but often sold their rights to printers as a way of turning their works into ready cash.

The Development of U.S. Copyright Law

The U.S. Constitution followed England's lead, allowing Congress to adopt copyright and patent laws to encourage authors to create new works.[9]

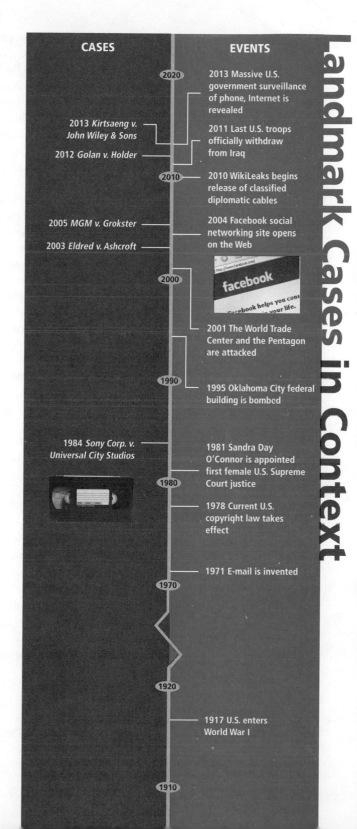

Landmark Cases in Context

CASES

2013 *Kirtsaeng v. John Wiley & Sons*

2012 *Golan v. Holder*

2005 *MGM v. Grokster*

2003 *Eldred v. Ashcroft*

1984 *Sony Corp. v. Universal City Studios*

EVENTS

2013 Massive U.S. government surveillance of phone, Internet is revealed

2011 Last U.S. troops officially withdraw from Iraq

2010 WikiLeaks begins release of classified diplomatic cables

2004 Facebook social networking site opens on the Web

2001 The World Trade Center and the Pentagon are attacked

1995 Oklahoma City federal building is bombed

1981 Sandra Day O'Connor is appointed first female U.S. Supreme Court justice

1978 Current U.S. copyright law takes effect

1971 E-mail is invented

1917 U.S. enters World War I

2020
2010
2000
1990
1980
1970
1920
1910

Statute of Anne The first copyright law, adopted in England in 1710.

Before the Constitution was ratified, 12 of the 13 states had passed their own copyright laws. The first Congress in 1790 adopted a law giving books, maps and charts a 14-year copyright.[10] The U.S. Supreme Court later ruled that the federal law took the place of state statutes and any common-law copyright claims.[11] This decision also applies to later copyright acts, including the current one; the federal law is the country's only copyright statute.

During the 19th century, Congress amended the copyright law to protect musical compositions, photographs and paintings.[12] The 1870 act established the Library of Congress, giving it the power to register copyrights and requiring the deposit with the library of two copies of a copyrighted published work.

In 1866, the Berne Convention for Protection of Literary and Artistic Works was signed by several countries in a step toward protecting works across international borders. However, the United States did not join the Berne treaty. The country was unconcerned with protecting its citizens' works overseas and did not want to protect foreign creators' works in the United States. The **Berne Convention,** though, spurred a major revision of U.S. copyright law in 1909.[13] Among other changes, the law extended copyright protection to 28 years, with a renewal period of another 28 years.

Berne Convention The primary international copyright treaty adopted by many countries in 1886 but by the United States only in 1988.

As the 20th century progressed, entertainment, news, computer and other industries pressured Congress to change the copyright law to accommodate the many technological developments that had occurred since 1909. In response, Congress adopted the Copyright Revision Act of 1976, which took effect Jan. 1, 1978. In 1988, Congress amended the 1976 act in ways that permitted the United States to join the Berne Convention, effective in 1989—nearly 125 years after the treaty's initial adoption.[14]

SUMMARY

INTELLECTUAL PROPERTY LAW INCLUDES COPYRIGHTS, trademarks and patents. The United States brought copyright law from England, included in the Constitution a congressional right to adopt copyright laws and passed its first copyright statute in 1790. Congress comprehensively revised the copyright law in 1870, 1909 and 1976. The United States adopted the major international copyright agreement, the Berne Convention, in 1988, 102 years after the treaty took effect. ■

The 1976 Copyright Act

After two decades of debate and compromise, Congress adopted the current copyright law in 1976. The act, amended several times since, specifies what may be protected by copyright, what rights that protection includes, any restrictions on those rights and the formalities necessary to exercise the rights.

International Law

It's Cool to Be Uncool

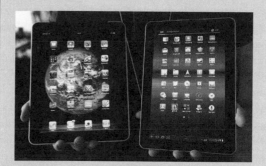

Britain's Court of Appeal ruled the Samsung Galaxy Tab 10.1 tablet, on the right, is an original design and not a copy of Apple's iPad, on the left, because the Galaxy is "not as cool" as the iPad.

Manufacturers naturally want their products to be attractive to consumers. But maybe they would trade that for not losing a copyright infringement lawsuit. Apple sued Samsung in Great Britain, claiming the Samsung Galaxy tablet copied Apple's iPad's design. Not so, ruled Britain's Court of Appeal. The court upheld a lower court decision in which the judge said, "The extreme simplicity of the Apple design is striking," noting its "undecorated flat surfaces, very thin rim and crisp edge." The iPad "is an understated, smooth and simple product," the judge said. But the court said the Galaxy is an original design, not a copy of the iPad, because the Galaxy is "not as cool."[1]

The Supreme Court of the Netherlands in 2013 agreed the Samsung tablet does not infringe on Apple's iPad design. The court said many of Apple's design elements occur in similar products sold by other companies.[2]

1. Associated Press, Apple Loses Copyright Appeal Against Samsung in Britain, N.Y. TIMES, Oct. 19, 2012, at B5.
2. Loek Essers, *Dutch Court: Samsung's Galaxy Tab 10.1 Does Not Infringe on iPad Design*, INFOWORLD (May 31, 2013), *available at* http://gigalaw.com/2013/06/02/dutch-court-says-samsungs-tab-doesnt-infringe-ipad/.

The act was outdated almost immediately. It did not foresee the personal computer, the Internet, MP3 players, satellite-delivered television and radio, wireless transmissions and other new technologies. Technology moves too quickly for the law ever to fully protect media content.

Copyright law also does not completely account for another change. The statute protects creators, but creators usually sell their creations—and accompanying copyrights—to corporations. For example, a writer grants the copyright of his or her novel to a publisher in return for a share of the book's sales revenue. And when people working for corporations create material as part of their employment, the corporation owns the copyright. News and entertainment corporations have come to rely on it to protect their products.[15] In fact, copyright's original purpose of inspiring individuals to create may have become less important than its role in the national and international marketplace. The length of time a copyright lasts is the only important legal difference between an individual and a corporation holding a copyright.

The Works Copyright Protects U.S. copyright law protects a wide variety of works. Realizing that it could not list all possible works eligible for copyright, however, Congress provided two broad criteria, offered some examples and left it to the courts to provide more clarity. The 1976 law says that copyright protection applies to "original works of authorship" that are "fixed in any tangible medium of expression."[16] By authorship, the law does not mean only written works. Rather, Congress used the word "authorship" to include artists, composers, journalists, sculptors and many other creators.

A work must be substantially original to be protected.[17] Copyright law does not define "original." As one court said, "[O]riginality" simply means "a work independently created by its author, one not copied from pre-existing works, and a work that comes from the exercise of the creative powers of the author's mind."[18] Young Zachary Maxwell's documentary entitled "Yuck: A 4th Grader's Short Documentary About School Lunch" qualifies.[19] But a play called "Macbeth II," with 10 words changed from Shakespeare's tragedy, would not be found original. A work does not have to be of high or even average quality to qualify for copyright protection. It just must be a work no one else has created before.

A collection of previously created works can be protected if there is substantial originality in the choice or arrangement of the works.[20] The copyright law refers to this as a "compilation," such as a book consisting of selected magazine articles.[21] The statute grants a copyright to the creation of the compilation, but each work included in the collection retains its own copyright protection. However, a list of names, addresses and telephone numbers is not sufficiently original to have copyright protection. There must be originality or novelty in compiling or organizing facts.[22]

In addition to being original, a work must be fixed in a tangible medium. This means a work must be capable of being seen, "reproduced, or otherwise communicated, either directly or with the aid of a machine or device"—words or pictures on paper, images on videotape, a quilt made of cloth, a statue made of marble, words and music on a CD.[23] A baseball game shown on broadcast television is not fixed in a tangible medium until the broadcast is, for example, saved digitally.

What works are original and fixed in a tangible medium so they may be copyrighted? The 1976 copyright act lists eight categories of eligible works: (1) literary works, (2) musical works, including any accompanying words, (3) dramatic works, including any accompanying music, (4) pantomimes and choreographic works, (5) pictorial, graphic and sculptural works, (6) motion pictures and other audiovisual works, (7) sound recordings and (8) architectural works.[24] These categories are more illustrative than definitive. For example, software can be copyrighted, even though it is not listed among the eight categories. Designs, patterns and shapes also can have copyright protection.

The 1976 statute protects all works eligible for copyright, both published and unpublished.[25] Before the 1976 statute was adopted, unpublished works were protected by state common law, not the federal statute. Common-law protection for unpublished works and protection lasted forever.[26] The new law changed this scheme, giving unpublished creations the same protection as published works.

A work that is not original or is not fixed in a tangible medium cannot be copyrighted. For example, a telephone directory's contents of names, addresses and phone numbers lacked originality, the U.S. Supreme Court ruled. There was insufficient creativity in an alphabetical list.[27] Neither can ideas, history or facts be copyrighted.[28] A news story reporting an automobile accident can receive copyright protection. But the underlying facts—the accident itself—cannot be copyrighted. A reporter's description of the accident is original and is fixed in a tangible medium when typed into a computer. However, the reporter may not successfully claim he or she was first on the scene and therefore no other journalist can write about the accident. Nor may a scholar write a book about a historical incident—even one that has not been described previously—and prevent anyone else from writing about the incident. An author proposed that a German crew member sabotaged the dirigible Hindenburg, causing it to explode and kill 36 people while attempting to dock in Lakehurst, N.J., in 1937.[29] Copyright protected the author's book describing his idea. But neither the facts nor the author's interpretation of the facts can be copyrighted. The author could not prevent a Hollywood studio from making a motion picture based on his idea about why the dirigible exploded.

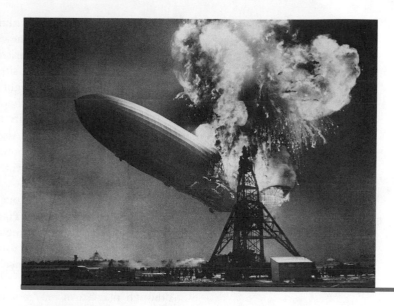

A book's ideas about why the dirigible Hindenburg exploded in midair became the basis of the 1975 movie, "The Hindenburg," but the book's author lost a copyright infringement suit against the film's producer because history and ideas cannot be copyrighted.

Although copyright law does not protect news facts, one mass medium cannot persistently take information from another and present the news as its own. This is called "misappropriation" or "unfair competition." Unfair competition is not a copyright infringement. Instead, it is actionable under the common law of individual states.

Nearly a century ago, the Supreme Court found unfair competition when one news service used information gathered by another.[30] During World War I, British censors would not allow International News Service (INS) journalists to send war reports to the United States. Reporters for The Associated Press (AP), a competing service, were able to get their stories into the country. The INS bought copies of newspapers served by the AP, rewrote the war stories and sent them to INS papers. The AP had not copyrighted its stories, as necessary for protection under the 1909 law. But the AP sued the INS on the common-law basis of unfair competition. The Court agreed with the AP.[31] The INS profited from taking material the AP had developed through its own skill and money, the Court said. Unfair competition also could apply if a radio station consistently rewrites stories from a local newspaper and presents the stories as the station's own reporting.

The INS decision became known as the "hot news" doctrine. Today, courts find misappropriation of news when (1) a news organization spends money to gather news, (2) the information is time sensitive, (3) a competing person or company uses that information without permission or payment and (4) the news organization's ability to gather news is threatened by others' using the information.[32] The issue particularly arises when a website can instantaneously copy information posted on a different site.[33]

The law does not give copyright protection to words and phrases, including advertising slogans and titles of books, movies and television programs. These lack sufficient originality to qualify for copyright protection. However, a trademark can protect these creations. Also, works created by the U.S. government are not eligible for copyright protection.[34] For example, a report issued by the U.S. Department of Justice is not protected by copyright and may be used by anyone without obtaining permission.

Using someone's work without identifying the source may be plagiarism rather than a copyright violation. **Plagiarism** commonly means using others' ideas without attribution. But when someone's work is sufficiently similar to another's creation—copying a novel's plot, using similar fictional characters or replicating another's interpretation of historical facts, for example—plagiarism becomes a copyright law violation.

Although plagiarism may not rise to the level of a copyright violation, it can have serious consequences. For example, Kendra Marr resigned from Politico, a prominent political website, after some of her articles were found to be rewrites of other reporters' work.[35] Jonah Lehrer's publisher stopped distributing his book "Imagine" after learning it contained fabricated Bob Dylan quotations and discontinued selling his next book, "How We Decide," because it contained quotations Lehrer copied from other publications.[36] CNN and Time magazine suspended writer and television host Fareed Zakaria after one of his Time columns copied material from someone else's article.[37] Best-selling authors, including primatologist Jane Goodall, and law school professors have been accused of plagiarism.[38] New York Times reporter Jayson Blair resigned after being charged with plagiarism.[39] The Times' public editor, Margaret Sullivan, wrote in 2013, the 10-year anniversary of Blair's resignation, that Blair "lied and faked and cheated his way through story after story—scores of them, for years. He fabricated sources, plagiarized material from other publications, and pretended to be places he never went. The problem, once fully investigated and made public by The Times itself, brought down not only the reporter but also The Times's executive editor and managing editor."[40]

plagiarism Using another's work or ideas without attribution.

SUMMARY

AN ORIGINAL WORK FIXED IN A TANGIBLE medium may have copyright protection. This includes literary, musical, dramatic, motion picture and many other works. Ideas, history and facts may not be copyrighted. Short phrases, titles and advertising slogans may not be copyrighted. Using information from news reports without permission may be unfair competition. ∎

realWorld Law

Happy Money . . . er, Birthday

Did friends and family sing "Happy Birthday to You" at your last birthday party? If so, did they pay royalties to Warner/Chappell, a division of Time Warner? Two Kentucky kindergarten teachers, Mildred J. and Patty Smith Hill, published the melody for "Happy Birthday" in 1893 and, after legal disputes were settled, copyrighted the music and words in 1935—more than 40 years after composing the song. Warner/Chappell purchased the copyright in 1988 for an estimated $25 million. The company earns $2 million annually in royalties from "Happy Birthday." Because the song is copyrighted, restaurant servers celebrating customers' birthdays often sing something other than "Happy Birthday"—otherwise, the restaurant would have to pay royalties to Time Warner. A documentary film "The Corporation" includes a minute of silence rather than using "Happy Birthday" during a party scene. Otherwise the film producers would have had to pay thousands of dollars in royalties. Steve James paid $5,000 to use the song in the 1994 movie "Hoop Dreams." "Happy Birthday to You" will not enter the public domain until at least the year 2030.[1]

1. *See* Eldred v. Ashcroft, 537 U.S. 186, 262 (2003) (Breyer, J., dissenting); Bonneville International Corp. v. Peters, 347 F.3d 485, 487 n.1 (3d Cir. 2003); Thomas Plotkin & Tarae Howell, *"Fair Is Foul and Foul Is Fair": Have Insurers Loosened the Chokepoint of Copyright and Permitted Fair Use's Breathing Space in Documentary Films?*, 15 CONN. INS. L.J. 407, 416–17 (2009); Robert Brauneis, *Copyright and the World's Most Popular Song*, 56 J. COPYRIGHT SOC'Y U.S.A. 335 (2009); Benjamin Weiser, *Birthday Song's Copyright Leads to a Lawsuit for the Ages*, N.Y. TIMES, June 14, 2013, at A24.

When Copyright Takes Effect An original work automatically is copyrighted from the moment it is created and fixed in a tangible medium. The law gives immediate protection to a news story typed into a computer, a journalist's notes written on a pad of paper, a television reporter's story put on videotape and a filmed Hollywood movie. To obtain copyright protection, the creator needs no more than to fix an original work in a tangible medium. The copyright must be registered, however, before the creator may sue for copyright infringement under the federal law. Registration is discussed later in this chapter.

Copyright Ownership A work's creator owns the work's copyright—with some exceptions.[41] For example, if two people create a work, the copyright is jointly owned. That is, both creators have all the protection a copyright gives and each owns half the work. Joint ownership works the same with three or more creators.

However, when a person creates a work as part of her or his employment, the law gives the copyright to the employer.[42] If a journalist employed full-time by a television station reports a story on the evening news, the story's copyright belongs to the station, not to the reporter. The copyright law calls such a creation a **"work made for hire."**[43]

A work made for hire occurs in only two circumstances. First, an employee preparing a work as part of his or her regular employment will not own the copyright.[44] Instead, the employer will own the copyright. Second, and less common, a work may be for hire if the creator and employer agree to that in writing

work made for hire Work created when working for another person or company. The copyright in a work made for hire belongs to the employer, not the creator.

and if the work is specially ordered or commissioned for use in, for example, a compilation, a motion picture, a textbook or any of several other categories the law specifies.[45]

The U.S. Supreme Court has listed a number of factors for courts to consider in determining whether a person acted as an employee so that the works were made for hire.[46] The case involved a nonprofit organization that asked an artist to create a sculpture. When the artist completed the work, both he and the organization claimed to own the copyright. In *Community for Creative Non-Violence v. Reid*, the Court said the organization would own the copyright only if the sculptor was the organization's employee. Finding in favor of the artist, the Court said several criteria help to determine a person's status as an employee or, instead, an independent contractor: (1) the organization's right to control how the work is accomplished, (2) who owns the equipment used to create the work, (3) where the work took place—at the organization's offices or the artist's studio, (4) who determined the days and hours the artist worked, (5) whether there was a long-term relationship between the two parties, (6) who hired any assistants the artist used and several other factors. The more the company or organization controls the factors, the more the balance tips toward the creator being an employee and the work being made for hire. When the criteria more generally favor the creator, the more likely he or she will be an independent contractor and own the work's copyright.

Under most circumstances, freelance journalists own the copyrights to their work. However, the Court's factors likely mean that a student interning at a television station or other media outlet creates works made for hire when she or he completes assignments from supervisors.

The copyright law allows copyright ownership to be changed by contract. A magazine may agree to purchase a story written by a freelance journalist only if the journalist agrees to transfer the copyright to the magazine. But if a famous newspaper columnist wants to own the copyrights to his or her columns, the newspaper and columnist may sign a contract to that effect. In the absence of a contract, the newspaper would own the copyrights because the columns would be works made for hire.

When a magazine or newspaper reproduces editions in, for example, CD-ROM form, the articles and pictures remain in context. A picture will be seen surrounded by the same pictures or words as in the original publication. The copyright law calls newspapers and magazines "collective works."[47] If a publication has permission to print an article or picture, the law allows it to use the work in any revision of the collective work. Reproduction in CD-ROM form or in a coffee table book, for instance, is a revision under the copyright law. A photographer could not successfully claim copyright infringement when his pictures were included in a CD-ROM set containing each National Geographic magazine from 1888 through 1996, a federal appellate court said. "The Complete National Geographic" contained issues as they originally were published. The pictures, then, remained in context.[48]

realWorld Law

Oz the Copyrighted

The 2013 Disney movie, "'Oz the Great and Powerful," is not a musical. But it is about Dorothy and Oz the wizard, so it has to have the yellow brick road and the ruby slippers, doesn't it? Not unless Disney wanted Warner Brothers to sue for copyright infringement. Warner owns the copyright on the 1939 MGM movie, "The Wizard of Oz." In Disney's movie there is a yellow brick road, but actors do not skip on it and the road changes during the movie—becoming overgrown and with broken bricks, for example. The wicked witch of the west is green, but a different shade than in the 1939 movie. There are Munchkins with strange hair, but the 40 dwarfs cast in the 2013 film are ethnically diverse. No winged monkeys as in the original movie; rather, there are baboons in the new film. And the ruby slippers? Not to be seen in the Disney version. All these changes, and others, are to convince Warner's copyright lawyers that the 2013 film is not substantially similar to the 1939 movie.[1]

1. Brooks Barnes, *We Aren't in the Old Kansas, Toto*, N.Y. Times, Mar. 3, 2013, at AR14.

However, contracts transferring copyrights in freelancer material to a newspaper or magazine did not explicitly transfer control to media organizations when they put their contents online. The media assumed the contracts implicitly allowed online publication under their copyright control of the collection as a whole. The media said they merely were using their copyright in the collection—each complete newspaper containing individual stories—to put the material online. But the U.S. Supreme Court disagreed.[49] In *New York Times Co., Inc. v. Tasini*, the Court said the online publication reproduced and distributed each individual article, not the newspapers as a whole. That is, the Times took articles out of context because the database contained individual articles rather than articles in the context of the original newspaper page. The freelance writers retained their copyrights in the individual articles, the Court said. If a contract between a freelancer and a newspaper did not specifically include online publications, the agreement covered only the initial publication.

SUMMARY

AN ORIGINAL WORK IS COPYRIGHTED FROM THE MOMENT it is fixed in a tangible medium. A work's creator owns the copyright to the work. However, if an employee creates a work, it is a work made for hire. The employer owns the copyright to a work made for hire in the absence of a contract stating otherwise. Courts use several criteria to determine whether a creator was an employee or independent contractor. Freelance journalists usually are considered to be independent contractors and thus own the copyrights to their work. ∎

Copyright Protection The law specifies six exclusive rights copyright holders have in their works:[50]

1. *The right to reproduce the work.* No one may copy a work without the copyright holder's permission. This prevents anyone from copying the original work or copying an authorized reproduction. A court said a jury could find copyright infringement when a luggage store used a computer scanner to copy part of a copyrighted photograph.[51] Without permission from the copyright holder, the store enlarged the scanned photo and displayed it on its walls.

    There are exceptions to this copyright protection. The U.S. Supreme Court allowed home taping of television broadcasts for personal use.[52] Also, Congress amended the copyright act to permit making a single copy of an analog or digital recording for personal use.[53]

    The law also permits broadcasters to make a copy, such as on videotape, if necessary to air the material. This may be to broadcast the program on a delayed basis, for example. The law calls such copies "ephemeral recordings." The recording must be destroyed within six months or placed in archives and not used on the air.[54]

2. *The right to make derivative works.* Without the copyright holder's permission, no one may use a novel as the basis of a play or make a movie from a television program. The play and movie would be derived from works that are protected by copyright. In one case, the entertainer Prince owned a copyright for a symbol used as a visual element in clothing, jewelry and other items. Another person made a guitar closely resembling Prince's symbol. A court said the guitar infringed on Prince's copyright because it was a derivative work based on a copyrighted design.[55]

3. *The right to distribute the work publicly.* The copyright owner determines when a work will be publicly distributed. For example, a federal district court said merely posting photos on Twitter does not allow others to use them without permission.[56] The decision is important as one of the first to consider whether content posted to social media sites may be freely used for commercial purposes. Daniel Morel photographed scenes after the Haiti earthquake in January 2010. He posted these photos to his Twitter account. Without Morel's permission, an employee of Agence France Presse (AFP), an international news agency, sent eight of Morel's photos to the AFP photo desk. Also without permission, The Washington Post used four of Morel's Haiti pictures as part of the Post's online earthquake coverage. Morel sued AFP and the Post for copyright infringement. AFP argued that when Morel posted his photos on Twitter he accepted Twitter's terms of service and those terms automatically granted permission to use the photos. A federal district court disagreed, holding that

Twitter's terms of service do not state or mean that content posted to a Twitter account essentially falls into the public domain. Both AFP and the Post infringed Morel's copyrights, the court ruled.

4. *The right to publicly perform a work.* This right applies to "literary, musical, dramatic, and choreographic works, pantomimes, and motion pictures and other audiovisual works."[57] This restricts anyone from transmitting a movie to the public, for example, without the copyright holder's permission. This seems more obvious than it is. For example, a company named Aereo uses dime-sized antennas to receive broadcast television signals in New York City and other metropolitan areas. Aereo converts the signals "into a video format viewable by computers and mobile devices."[58] Aereo's subscribers then can receive or record the signals through the company's streaming technology. Broadcasters claimed this was an unauthorized public performance, no different than if Aereo received a station's signal and showed the program to hundreds of viewers on a large screen. In 2013 the U.S. Court of Appeals for the Second Circuit disagreed,[59] accepting Aereo's argument that the antennas are leased to individual subscribers so the streaming is a private performance, not a transmission to the public. The court relied in part on an earlier case it decided holding that a cable company did not abridge broadcasters' transmission rights when it allowed customers to record and play back programs using the cable company's hard drives rather than a customer's own device, such as Tivo.[60] The cable company only allowed one customer, not the general public, to see the recorded program, the court concluded.

However, two federal district courts, one in Washington, D.C., and one in California, disagreed with those decisions.[61] They found that companies offering a service similar to Aereo's, did violate broadcasters' transmissions rights. The courts said that even if a service transmitted a program to a single viewer, there were many viewers subscribing to the service. The group of subscribers constituted a public and the Copyright Act requires permission to transmit copyrighted material to the public, the courts said.

5. *The right to publicly display a work.* This applies to "literary, musical, dramatic, and choreographic works, pantomimes," as does the right to publicly perform a work. But this right adds protection for "pictorial, graphic, or sculptural works, including the individual images of a motion picture or other audiovisual work."[62] Under this provision, no one may display a painting, sculpture, photograph or similar work without the copyright owner's permission.

6. *The right to transmit a sound recording, such as a CD, through digital audio means.*[63] This provision requires obtaining permission from a recording company to play one of its recordings via the Internet, satellite

radio or other digital media, including interactive services. Permission is not required to play a recording over a broadcasting station or in live performance.

moral rights Under U.S. copyright law, the rights of certain artists—creators of paintings, drawings, prints, sculptures and art photographs—to require that their names be associated with their works, forbid others from claiming to be creators of the works and to prevent intentional harm to or modification of a work that would harm the artist's reputation.

Additionally, under U.S. copyright law, creators of certain works have what are called **moral rights.** These rights protect a work's integrity and the creator's reputation. Many European countries grant extensive moral rights.[64] For example, print authors may prevent others from falsely attributing works to those authors. Also, no one may use the author's works in ways that would reflect adversely on the author's professional reputation. Some countries forbid even the owner of a copyrighted work—a painting, for example—from deforming or changing it in any way. The Berne Convention, the most important international copyright agreement, also includes a moral rights provision. The treaty protects authors' rights to "object to any distortion, mutilation, or other modification" of their works that would harm their reputations.[65]

When the United States joined the Berne Convention, it had to grant some moral rights to copyright holders, as the treaty required. Congress adopted a very narrow moral rights provision.[66] The right applies only to certain artistic works: paintings, drawings, prints, sculptures or art photographs. The law protects single copies—an original painting or sculpture, for example—or a copy that is one of a limited number of a single work, consecutively numbered and signed by the artist. Creators have two moral rights in these works. First, they may claim authorship of a work; authors may prevent removal of their name from the work and require connection of their name with the work when it is displayed. Also, artists may prevent having their name attached to works they did not create. Second, artists have a right to prevent intentional harm to or modification of a work that would adversely affect their reputations.[67]

Print media works, broadcast programs and motion pictures, among other creations, are not protected by the U.S. copyright law's moral rights provision. This leaves movie directors, for example, without a remedy when they believe their creations are being altered without their permission, such as companies removing offensive language, sexual scenes and violent action from films and selling the edited movies. The studios and directors claimed copyright infringement—that the companies made derivative works without permission by making the films into something other than the original movie.[68] While litigation continued, Congress adopted the Family Movie Act (FMA), part of the Family Entertainment and Copyright Act of 2005.[69] The FMA allows people to purchase and use technology that will filter from a movie the material a viewer does not want to see or hear. Specifically, the law says it is not an infringement to make "imperceptible . . . limited portions of . . . a motion picture . . . for performance in a private home."[70] The FMA does not allow sale of an edited movie without permission of the copyright holder.

The movie directors were concerned with more than derivative works being distributed without permission. They also did not want their films altered in any way. The directors wanted to defend their moral rights, an effort not possible under U.S. copyright law.[71]

Points of Law

Exclusive Rights in Copyrighted Works

The copyright holder with exclusive rights may do the following:

1. Reproduce the copyrighted work

2. Prepare derivative works based upon the copyrighted work

3. Distribute copies of the copyrighted work to the public by sale or other transfer of ownership, or by rental, lease or lending [except CDs and computer software]

4. Perform the copyrighted work publicly in the case of literary, musical, dramatic and choreographic works, pantomimes, and motion pictures and other audiovisual works

5. Display the copyrighted work publicly in the case of literary, musical, dramatic and choreographic works, pantomimes, and pictorial, graphic, or sculptural works, including the individual images of a motion picture or other audiovisual work, and

6. Perform the copyrighted work publicly by means of a digital audio transmission in the case of sound recordings.[1]

1. 17 U.S.C. § 106.

Copyright Law Limitations Some protections are not absolute under U.S. copyright law. For instance, although the law says that only the creator may copy his or her work, the Supreme Court held that individuals may make videotape copies of television programs for their own use.[72] The Court said using a videotape recorder merely to shift the time a program is watched is not a copyright infringement. Congress also allowed individuals to make a copy of a recording for the individual's own use.[73]

Libraries open to the public have a limited right to make photocopies for certain purposes.[74] Libraries may make a copy to respond to an interlibrary loan request or to replace a deteriorating copy of a work, for example.

Though not part of the law, Congress provided guidelines for teachers in not-for-profit educational institutions. A teacher may, no more than twice per term, copy one chapter from a book for the teacher's own use or copy an excerpt of no more than 1,000 words or 10 percent of a book to distribute to a class. The guidelines do not allow students to copy materials.

Copyright owners do not have the right to control individual copies of their works after distribution—with a few exceptions. A person who buys a copy of a novel may give away that book, or sell it, or rent it or throw it away.[75] The author has no right to stop the purchaser from taking any of those actions. This is called the "**first-sale doctrine.**"[76] The copyright law says that once creators have distributed copies of a work, they no longer can regulate what happens to those copies. However, when copyright holders agree to transfer the physical object containing

first-sale doctrine Once a copyright owner sells a copy of a work, the new owner may possess, transfer or otherwise dispose of that copy without the copyright owner's permission.

Emerging Law

Sell That Song?

Tired of that Selena Gomez song you downloaded? Don't know why you downloaded that Stephen King novel? Why not sell them? Because at least one federal court says the sale would violate the law.

Amazon and Apple think you should be able to sell your used digital music and books. In 2013 Amazon obtained and Apple applied for separate patents to enable the exchange of digital music and print material.[1]

But the courts may have intervened. The U.S. Court of Appeals for the Second Circuit ruled that a company called ReDigi infringed Capitol Records' copyrights in its sound recordings.[2] ReDigi allowed people to "sell their legally acquired digital music files, and buy used digital music from others at a fraction of the price currently available on iTunes." Essentially, ReDigi acted as a used digital music store.

The Second Circuit held that when a digital music file moves from one person's computer to another computer the file is reproduced. Because reproduction is one of the rights guaranteed to a copyright owner, ReDigi infringed Capitol's rights under the copyright law, the court said.

The first-sale doctrine, like some other parts of the copyright law, was meant for a pre-digital world. Copyright scholar Jessica Litman says the doctrine allows the owner of a book "to sell, loan, rent or give it away" but does not allow someone receiving a "lawful digital copy to transmit it to someone else."[3] The problem is when a digital copy is sent from one computer to another, the receiving computer makes an additional copy of the document, something the law does not allow.

---

1. David Streitfeld, *Imagining a Swap Meet for E-Books and Music,* N.Y. Times, Mar. 8, 2013, at B1.
2. Capitol Records, LLC v. ReDigi Inc., 2013 U.S. Dist. LEXIS 48043 (S.D.N.Y. Mar. 30, 2013).
3. Jessica Litman, *Billowing White Goo,* 31 Colum. J.L. & Arts 587, 594 (2008).

---

the copyrighted work—the book containing a novel, a DVD containing a movie, a magazine containing articles—they do not transfer any rights in the copyrighted work. The law still restricts copying the novel, making derivative works from a movie and so on. The first-sale doctrine distinguishes between the physical object and the intellectual creation itself. The doctrine does not change the copyright holder's control of the creation, only control of the object containing the creation. Courts and Congress justify the first-sale doctrine based on a preference not to limit what a person can do with her or his own property. Also, copyright law is meant to encourage people to create but also to give the public access to those creations. The first-sale doctrine allows copies to be disseminated less expensively—used books, free libraries, secondhand CDs—than if the copyright holder controlled every copy of his or her creation.

Concerns about people renting computer software or recordings, such as CDs, and then making cheap copies prompted Congress to limit the first-sale doctrine. Congress restricted rentals of recordings without the copyright holder's permission.[77] One federal appellate court ruled that the ban on renting recordings applies only to recordings of musical works but does not include recordings of audiobooks or books on tape.[78] The law also forbids renting computer software. Additionally, the law's moral rights provision limits what owners of artistic works may do with them.

The first-sale doctrine allows the buyer of a book manufactured and purchased in the United States to resell that book. And it allows the buyer of a book manufactured in the United States but bought overseas to resell that book. But can someone lawfully resell a book in the United States if a U.S book publisher manufactured the book overseas? Surprisingly, there was no clear answer until a Thai citizen moved to the United States to study mathematics. He asked his family to purchase foreign-edition English-language textbooks, which cost less in Thailand than they do in the United States, and send them to him. He then sold the books. One book publisher said that violated the U.S. copyright law. In 2013 the U.S. Supreme Court said the first-sale doctrine allowed the purchase of foreign-manufactured books and the sale of them in the United States.[79]

SUMMARY

COPYRIGHT PROTECTS THE CREATOR'S RIGHT to reproduce the work, make derivative works and distribute, perform or display a work. It also protects the right to transmit a sound recording through digital audio means. U.S. law grants creators of artistic works limited moral rights, protecting a work's integrity and the creator's reputation. Individuals may make videotape copies of television programs and audiotape copies of recordings for their own personal use. The first-sale doctrine allows purchasers to dispose as they choose of objects containing copyrighted works, such as books and videotapes. However, CDs and software may not be rented. ■

Copyright Notice Until 1989, copyright could be lost if a published work did not include a copyright notice, such as "© 2015 Jane Doe." To the contrary, international copyright agreements do not require a copyright notice for a work to be protected. When the United States joined the Berne Convention, Congress changed the law so it does not require a copyright notice to be placed on works published on or after March 1, 1989.[80] The 1976 copyright act encourages including a notice, however.[81] For example, an infringer might claim she or he did not know a work was copyrighted because it did not have a copyright notice. If a court accepts that argument, the court could award a small amount in **statutory damages,** damage amounts specified in certain laws. The copyright statute allows a court to award damages even if an infringer does not make a profit from the creator's work.[82]

statutory damages Damages specified in certain laws. Under these laws, copyright being an example, a judge may award statutory damages even if a plaintiff is unable to prove actual damages.

Transferring Copyrights A copyright is a property right. Just like a person's automobile, a copyright can be given away, sold or leased.

Rights protected by copyright can be thought of as a bundle of sticks. Each of the rights includes a number of sticks. For example, an author writes a novel and has the right, among others, to prevent unauthorized copying. If the author sells to a publisher the right—the stick—to reproduce the novel as a hardback book, the author still has all the other copying sticks. The author may sell the paperback copying stick to another publisher. Because the author also has the sticks representing all the other copyright holder's rights, the author may sell to a film studio one of the derivative work's sticks—the right to make a movie from the novel. That still leaves the author with many other sticks. Or the author may choose to sell the whole bundle of sticks to one person or company. Each time the author sells a stick, or the whole bundle of sticks, he or she receives a lump sum payment or, often, a percentage of revenue from sales.

Whoever buys a stick from the author then owns that right unless a contract between the author and the buyer says otherwise. If the buyer wants to sell the right to a third person, the author cannot refuse to allow the sale unless the author has a contractual right to do so.

A copyright does not disappear when the copyright holder dies. The copyright holder may transfer the right to someone else through a will.

The 1976 copyright law recognizes that creators often do not have equal bargaining rights with the large corporations purchasing creators' copyrights. To strike a more equal balance, the law gives creators a termination right.[83] This allows creators, or their heirs, to require the transferred rights be returned 35 to 40 years after the original transfer. This does not apply to works made for hire. For example, in 2013 Victor Willis, the former lead singer of the Village People and lyric writer of the group's hit song "YMCA," reclaimed rights to 33 songs.[84]

Not only may copyright holders completely transfer their rights; they may license or lease rights to another person. A license is a contract giving limited permission to use a stick. For example, a photographer may license a picture to a company for use in an advertising campaign during the year 2015. The photographer has not given up any rights but, rather, retains the copyright on the picture and all the rights protected by the copyright. The agreement may give the company exclusive use of the photograph for advertising during 2015, or the photographer may retain the right to allow others also to use it.

Copyright Duration The Constitution gives Congress the right to adopt copyright and patent laws "for limited times."[85] Lobbying by corporate copyright holders—movie and television program producers, book publishers and others—convinced Congress to stretch the definition of limited times almost to the breaking point.

The 1976 copyright law gave copyright protection for the creator's lifetime plus 50 years after the creator's death with no renewal possible. The Sonny Bono Copyright Term Extension Act of 1998 extended all copyright periods by 20 years. After the Bono Act took effect, the copyright period for works created on or after Jan. 1, 1978, became the author's lifetime plus 70 more years.[86] Works made for hire are protected for 95 years from publication or 120 years from creation, whichever is shorter.[87]

Copyright protection's duration depends on several factors. First, the current law did not affect works created in the United States that were in the **public domain** on Jan. 1, 1978. When the current copyright statute took effect, many works were in the public domain because their copyrights had expired—such as Herman Melville's "Moby-Dick." Also, some works copyrighted under the 1909 law lost protection because their creators failed to renew copyrights.

public domain The sphere that includes material not protected by copyright law and therefore available for use without the creator's permission.

realWorld Law

The Sonny Bono Law

Mickey Mouse as Steamboat Willie in the first Mickey cartoon.

Sonny Bono, formerly an entertainer and singer-actress Cher's first husband, was a member of the U.S. House of Representatives when he died. Congress named the copyright extension act in Bono's honor because Bono believed copyrights should last forever.[1]

Mickey Mouse's copyright protection, originally granted in 1928 when Mickey's first cartoon, "Steamboat Willie," was shown, would have expired in 2003. But the Walt Disney Company, which owns Mickey's copyright, lobbied Congress to make the copyright period longer than the 1976 Copyright Act specified. By one estimate, Disney spent more than $6.3 million persuading members of Congress to change the law. The Copyright Term Extension Act—the Sonny Bono law—protects Mickey's copyright until 2023.[2] Considering that Mickey may be worth more than $3 billion, will the Walt Disney Company be talking with Congress then?[3]

1. *See* 3 Melville B. Nimmer & David Nimmer, Nimmer on Copyright § 9.01 (2013).
2. Laurie Richter, *Reproductive Freedom: Striking a Fair Balance Between Copyright and Other Intellectual Property Protections in Cartoon Characters*, 21 St. Thomas L. Rev. 441, 451–52 (2009).
3. Joseph Menn, *Disney's Rights to Young Mickey Mouse May Be Wrong*, L.A. Times, Aug. 22, 2008, at A1.

The 1976 law also covers unpublished works, formerly given perpetual protection under state common law. The statute replaced common law protection and protected unpublished works for the author's life plus 70 years.

The Supreme Court upheld the Bono Act against claims that it violates the constitutional copyright clause and the First Amendment.[88] In *Eldred v. Ashcroft* the Supreme Court said extending the copyright period is constitutional. The creator's life plus 70 years is a limited time within the meaning of the Constitution's copyright clause, the Court said. The phrase "limited time" does not mean a fixed time. The copyright period may be flexible. Congress could justify extending the copyright period because people live longer now than when earlier laws were in force, the Court said. Also, technology changes—for example, DVDs and other digital media—make copyrighted works last longer.

Congress has the right to determine what "limited" means as long as the copyright period is not forever, the Court said. However, the Court did not define "limited time," nor did it offer a test for determining what period might go beyond "limited."

The Court also rejected First Amendment arguments against the Bono Act. The Constitution's adopters found no tension between the First Amendment and the copyright clause, according to the Court. The current law balances free speech

Points of Law

The Public Domain

Material that no longer is under copyright protection is in the public domain. Material that never was copyrighted in the first place, such as federal government publications, also is in the public domain. Such public domain material, including text, photographs, drawings and other materials, some of which may be found on the Internet, may be used without obtaining permission. Be sure material is not protected before using it without permission. Some public domain material may include works that remain under copyright. And material that no longer is under copyright protection still may be protected by trademark.

Material also may be in the public domain if the creator says it is. The creator may disavow copyright protection and allow anyone to use the material without permission.

and copyright protection concerns. Original expression is protected, but ideas and facts are not. And the fair use defense, discussed later in this chapter, allows the public to use portions of copyrighted works under certain circumstances, the Court said.

Eldred suggested the Supreme Court would give Congress a free hand to adopt whatever copyright laws it wanted. A 2012 decision left little doubt that was the Court's intention. When the United States joined the Berne Convention in 1989 many works created in other countries had fallen into the public domain here but not in their creators' countries.[89] That allowed orchestras on limited budgets and school programs, for example, to perform compositions by 20th-century composers such as Dmitri Shostakovich and Igor Stravinsky without paying a royalty fee. Films Alfred Hitchcock directed in England and Pablo Picasso's paintings also were freely available. In 1994 Congress gave these foreign works copyright protection.[90] Works affected largely were those created between 1923 and 1989 that still were under copyright in the country where created.[91]

Groups directly affected by losing free access to these works sued, arguing Congress' action was unconstitutional. In *Golan v. Holder* the U.S. Supreme Court disagreed.[92] First, the Court said the Constitution's language allows Congress to give copyright protection to works that once were in the public domain. The Court rejected the plaintiffs' claim that allowing Congress to bring works back under copyright would extend protection for an indefinite period. Nothing in the law suggests Congress is moving toward perpetual copyright protection, the Court said. Congress' action did no more than put the United States in the same position as other countries that are parties to the Berne Convention.

Second, the plaintiffs argued that copyright is meant to provide incentives to create new work, and there is no incentive to create works that already exist, specifically the foreign works in the public domain. The Court said Congress might reasonably assert that U.S. copyright law comport with the laws of other Berne members would help create a well-functioning international system and thus inspire new works.

Third, the Court rejected the plaintiffs' argument that their First Amendment rights were abridged because they no longer could perform the newly protected

realWorld Law

Use It for Free

Harvard Law School professor Lawrence Lessig

Law professor Lawrence Lessig, who represented Eric Eldred, the plaintiff in the Supreme Court *Eldred v. Ashcroft* case upholding extension of copyright terms, led development of the Creative Commons, an attempt to make copyrighted material more accessible to those who want to use it in their own creations. Through Creative Commons, copyright holders may license their works in whatever way they choose. As one article explains, "Advocates of Creative Commons hope to reduce the transaction costs inherent in the traditional licensing system. Creative Commons is creating a user-friendly license system that copyright owners can adopt to designate what rights they are willing to give up and under what conditions they are willing to surrender those rights."[1] Creators may register their works with Creative Commons as well as with the U.S. Copyright Office.

1. Lynn M. Forsythe & Deborah J. Kemp, *Creative Commons: For the Common Good?*, 30 U. LA VERNE L. REV. 346, 347–48 (2009).

works. The Court said any work Congress brought under copyright protection remained available, just for a fee. The Court used the example of Sergei Prokofiev's "Peter and the Wolf." Orchestras still can perform the work but have to pay for permission. Also, the Court said, copyright law always has balanced protection for creators against the First Amendment by leaving ideas and facts in the public domain while protecting expression of those ideas and facts. Also, the copyright law allows fair use of protected expression.

The Court emphasized Congress' freedom to broadly interpret the Constitution's copyright clause: "Congress determined that U.S. interests were best served by our full participation in the dominant system of international copyright protection. Those interests include ensuring exemplary compliance with our international obligations, securing greater protection for U.S. authors abroad, and remedying unequal treatment of foreign authors."[93]

Registering a Copyright An original work fixed in a tangible medium has copyright protection from the moment it is created. Registration with the U.S. Copyright Office is not required for a work to be copyrighted.[94] However, if a copyright is infringed upon, the copyright holder cannot sue under the law unless the copyright has been registered.[95]

To register a copyright, the creator must complete and submit the proper form, available at the Copyright Office's website (http://www.copyright.gov). A $35 fee is required to register online, as the Copyright Office prefers. The mail registration fee is $50 or $65, depending on the form used. The registration process also requires submitting two copies of a published work or one copy of an unpublished work.[96] There are provisions for registering online-only works, daily newspapers, feature films and other works. After registering a work, which takes four to six months, the Copyright Office will send a Certificate of Registration to the creator.

An author may wait until after a copyright infringement occurs before registering a copyright and bringing a lawsuit, but this is inadvisable. First, unless registration occurs before the infringement, the author cannot recover statutory damages. Nor can the court require the infringer to pay the author's attorney's fees and court costs.[97] Second, registration is the best proof of when the author created the work.[98] A court will assume that the registration certificate form accurately shows who created the work and when the work was created. If a copyright infringer claims to have created the work first, he or she bears the burden to prove the claim in the face of the registration.

Registering a copyright does not mean the copyright is valid. The Copyright Office does not confirm that each submitted item is original. If a registered copyright is challenged, a court may find that the work does not comply with the requirements necessary to receive copyright protection. Also, the Copyright Office may refuse to register a copyright if it finds the work—such as a book title or advertising slogan—is not eligible for copyright protection.[99]

Federal authorities may bring criminal action against a copyright infringer even if the copyright has not been registered.[100]

Compulsory Copyright Licenses In cable television's infancy, the Supreme Court held that cable did not infringe on anyone's copyright when it retransmitted broadcast station signals to subscribers.[101] The Court said retransmitting broadcast signals was not a performance under the 1909 copyright law and did not require copyright holder permission.

Congress agreed to override the Court's decisions in the 1976 law and adopted a compromise that cable system owners had reached with the producers and broadcasters.[102] That law allows cable operators to retransmit radio and television broadcast signals without obtaining permission in exchange for a compulsory fee based on a percentage of a cable system's annual revenues. The U.S. Copyright Office collects and distributes the fees to copyright holders of the programs and other material broadcast and retransmitted by cable.

Direct broadcast satellite (DBS) services have a similar compulsory license to retransmit broadcast signals.[103] DBS services pay royalties according to the number of their subscribers.

SUMMARY

PROVIDING COPYRIGHT NOTICE IS NOT NECESSARY to retain protection of original material, but applying a notice provides certain rights under the copyright law. Copyrights may be given away, sold or leased.

Copyrights on works created on or after Jan. 1, 1978, last for the creator's life plus 70 years. A work made for hire lasts for 95 years from publication or 120 years from creation, whichever is shorter. Works protected under the 1909 law and still in copyright when the current law took effect are protected for 95 years from the date they first were copyrighted.

A copyright must be registered before a creator may sue for infringement under the copyright law.

A compulsory copyright license allows cable and satellite television providers to retransmit broadcast signals to their subscribers. ■

Proving Copyright Infringement

Using any part of a copyrighted work is infringement unless there is an applicable defense. A copyright owner can sue an infringer for damages, and in some cases the government may bring criminal charges.

To sue for copyright infringement, the plaintiff first must show proof of a valid copyright. A plaintiff must really own the copyright to sue alleged infringers, the U.S. Court of Appeals for the Ninth Circuit emphasized in 2013. Lawyers operating under the name Righthaven had filed more than 250 lawsuits against bloggers who used articles from the newspaper Las Vegas Review-Journal without permission. Righthaven and the Review-Journal owner signed what they called a Strategic Alliance Agreement. The agreement gave Righthaven the right to sue for copyright infringement but no other rights under the copyright law. The appellate court found that insufficient to make Righthaven the copyright owner of the newspaper's articles.[104] Therefore, Righthaven did not have the right to sue for infringement. The Ninth Circuit also ruled that Fox television network does not own the copyrights to commercials inserted in Fox programs.[105] Therefore, Fox could not prove the Dish satellite television company violated Fox's copyright by offering subscribers the "Hopper" device. The "Hopper" allows a subscriber to record prime-time programs and automatically skip all the commercials when playing back the shows.

In addition to a valid copyright, the copyright must be registered prior to bringing a lawsuit. If the copyright holder can prove direct copying, she or he can win the suit if the defendant has no effective defense. More likely, the plaintiff will attempt to show that the infringer had access to the copyrighted work and the two works are substantially similar. To prove that a defendant could have been exposed to the copyrighted material, the plaintiff must show a reasonable possibility of access. Access may be inferred if the work has been widely distributed and the defendant's and plaintiff's works are very similar.[106] In one case, a composer claimed that the theme song to a James Bond film, "The World Is Not Enough," used a four-note sequence from one of his songs. The court said there was no evidence that the Bond theme composer could have had access to the plaintiff's song, which had not been generally distributed.[107]

Some courts employ a two-part, extrinsic/intrinsic test to determine whether works are substantially similar. The objective "extrinsic" component compares

Points of Law

Infringing Copyright

A copyright plaintiff must prove the following:

1. The work used is protected by a valid copyright—meaning it is an original work fixed in a tangible medium.

2. Ownership of the copyright.

3. The valid copyright is registered with the Copyright Office.

4. And either:

   a. There is evidence the defendant directly copied the copyrighted work, or

   b. The infringer had access to the copyrighted work and the two works are substantially similar.

similarities between the two works' expressive qualities. The subjective "intrinsic" element considers whether a reasonable person would judge the two works to be conceptually similar.

The extrinsic component may be straightforward. A woman sued Paramount Pictures claiming the movie "Titanic" was based on movie scripts she developed. A federal district court compared the screenplay and the plaintiff's scripts and said the plots and sequences of events in the two were significantly different. The plaintiff's scripts tell of a whistleblower forced out of the U.S. Air Force in the 1950s who suffers a variety of misfortunes. "Titanic" is a love story between a young socialite and a working-class man that takes place on the British passenger ship before it hits an iceberg and sinks. The court said the moods, characters and dialogues were dissimilar.[108]

The intrinsic component may be as obvious. For example, plaintiffs wrote a Christmas story titled "Santa Paws: The Story of Santa's Dog." More than a decade later, the Disney company created two movies, "Santa Buddies: The Legend of Santa Paws" and "The Search for Santa Paws." A federal district court acknowledged some similarities between the story and the movies: "The plots . . . involve some threat to the Christmas holiday or spirit, which is then saved by a talking Christmas dog . . . [and] feature a dog named 'Paws' 'Santa Paws,' or 'Puppy Paws.' . . . [They] take place, in part, at the North Pole, and all of the works also use an American city or town as a second setting." However, the court held, because the "remaining aspects of the plot surrounding the Christmas dog are entirely dissimilar, . . . no reasonable viewer of the defendants' movies—or reader of their corresponding screenplays—would recognize them as a 'dramatization or picturization' of plaintiffs' short story."[109]

A plaintiff does not have to prove that a copyright infringement was deliberate. Accidental infringement violates the law. A court may reduce statutory damages imposed on a person who unintentionally infringed on another person's copyright and waive statutory damages completely if the innocent infringer works for a nonprofit library or public broadcaster.[110]

Contributory Infringement A plaintiff does not have to prove that the defendant directly infringed on copyright. Showing that the defendant knowingly aided or contributed to copyright infringement is sufficient. Although contributory infringement is not specifically banned in the copyright law, the statute implies that contributory infringement violates the law and courts long have held it actionable.[111]

Contributory infringement may be difficult to prove. Several television program producers sued Sony for making videocassette recorders (VCRs) that allowed viewers to tape copyrighted programs without permission. The producers claimed the VCRs enabled unauthorized copying. The U.S. Supreme Court

realWorld Law

Are These Photos Substantially Similar?

Donald Harney's photograph, on the left, and Sony Pictures' photograph, on the right, bear a remarkable resemblance to each other, or do they?

Some courts analyze substantial similarity in disputed photographs by separating protected elements from those not protected by copyright. For example, Donald Harney took a picture, published in a neighborhood newspaper, of a "blond girl in a pink coat riding piggyback on her father's shoulders as they emerged from a Palm Sunday service in the Beacon Hill section of Boston."[1] A year later the father abducted the girl during a custodial visit. The FBI used Harney's photo in a "wanted" poster. Sony Pictures made a television movie about the abduction that ran on the A&E cable network. The movie included an image "similar in pose and composition to Harney's original [photograph], but different in a number of details."[2] Harney sued for copyright infringement, but in 2013 the U.S. Court of Appeals for the First Circuit ruled there was not substantial similarity between Harney's photo and the picture the movie used.[3]

Noting that photographers "may not copyright the reality of their subject matter," the court ruled that "Harney may not claim exclusive rights to the piggyback . . ., [the father's and daughter's] clothing, the items they carried, or the Church of the Advent shown with bright blue sky behind it."[4] None of these is original with the photographer and therefore cannot be protected by copyright, the court ruled. The court said, "Sony copied little of Harney's original work—only the placement of [the father and daughter] in the photograph—and no jury could conclude that the similarity resulting solely from that copying is substantial."[5]

1. Harney v. Sony Pictures Television, Inc., 704 F.3d 173, 176 (1st Cir. 2013).
2. *Id.*
3. *Id.*
4. *Id.* at 185, 186.
5. *Id.* at 188.

said Sony might have known that viewers used VCRs to tape television programs, but it could be fair use to tape programs to watch later—time shifting. As discussed following, fair use is a defense against a charge of copyright infringement. Sony was not liable because the VCRs could be used for non-infringing purposes, the Court ruled.[112]

A quarter-century after the *Sony v. Universal City Studios* case, Cablevision Systems moved the VCR to computers on the cable system owner's premises. Cablevision customers had to alert the company before a program began and then could watch the recorded program at a later time. A group of movie studios and broadcast and cable networks argued that Cablevision directly infringed on program copyrights by making unauthorized copies on computers and publicly performing the programs when customers later watched them. Nonetheless, the U.S. Court of Appeals for the Second Circuit ruled that the cable customer, rather than Cablevision, copied the program. Cablevision's computers acted as a modern VCR or another kind of TiVo. Because only one customer at one time viewed the program, the program was not publicly performed, "public" being a larger group than just one customer.[113]

Those who benefit financially from copyright infringement also may be liable under copyright law. This might include a store selling pirated DVDs copied without permission of the movies' copyright holders. These are called "vicarious copyright infringers."

Finally, the U.S. Supreme Court established a third type of indirect copyright infringer. These are individuals or companies who induce or encourage others to engage in copyright infringement. In the *Metro-Goldwyn-Mayer Studios, Inc. v. Grokster, Ltd.* decision, discussed further in the music licensing section of this chapter, the Court held that Grokster infringed on the copyright because it knew people used its software to download music files. The Court said it did not matter that the software could be used for legal purposes because Grokster encouraged, or induced, users to infringe on copyrights.[114]

Websites allowing users to illegally download movies violate *Grokster*'s inducement rule, the Ninth Circuit held in 2013.[115] Seven major movie studios showed that the defendant's peer-to-peer file-sharing sites directly helped site users upload copyrighted films, locate specific movies and television programs to upload and burn copyrighted material onto DVDs to play on television sets. The court said this and other evidence showed the defendant encouraged his sites' users to infringe the movie studios' copyrights.

However, embedding a video image on a website is not contributory infringement, a federal appellate court ruled.[116] A gay pornography site sued myVidster, a "social bookmarking" service. MyVidster subscribers can "bookmark" videos uploaded with or without permission to a server computer. The myVidster site finds the embed code and stores it with an image from the video. Then myVidster patrons can select the video, transmitted for viewing from the server computer, without going through any computer controlled by myVidster. The pornography site claimed myVidster contributed to copyright infringement by linking to websites containing illegal copies of the videos. The court disagreed. Just as a newspaper lists theaters where a movie is playing, myVidster is not helping customers either copy or perform the videos, the court said.

Remedies for Copyright Infringement

A copyright infringement suit is a tort action—the copyright holder seeks compensation for the harm the infringer caused.[117] The plaintiff may ask for actual damages.[118] These include income the copyright holder lost and profits the infringer made because of the infringement.

Alternatively, the plaintiff may seek statutory damages. The copyright statute allows a plaintiff to ask for appropriate compensation ranging from $750 to

$30,000.[119] The defendant may ask that a jury rather than a judge decide how much to award in statutory damages.[120] Statutory damage awards depend in part on the defendant's actions. The court may award up to $150,000 in cases of deliberate infringement.[121] Statutory damages may be as little as $200 against an innocent infringer if, for example, the plaintiff did not include a copyright notice and the defendant reasonably did not know the work was protected by copyright.[122]

A judge can award attorney's fees to the winning party in a copyright infringement suit.[123] Even the defendant may receive attorney's fees if the lawsuit had little merit. Despite First Amendment limitations on prior restraints, the copyright law allows a court to impose an injunction on works that infringe copyrights.[124] Also, unauthorized copies of recordings, such as CDs, may be seized and destroyed.[125]

The government can bring criminal charges for copyright infringement even if the infringer did not profit from the infringement as long as the infringer received something of value.[126] The No Electronic Theft Act allows prosecution even in the absence of an infringer's profit motive.[127] In part, Congress wanted to allow criminal prosecution of people downloading numerous copyrighted audio and video works or making copies of copyrighted videodiscs for their own use without permission.

SUMMARY

To PROVE COPYRIGHT INFRINGEMENT, the copyright holder must show (1) he or she has a valid copyright, (2) the work is registered and (3) the defendant either directly copied the work or the defendant had access to the copyrighted work and the two works are substantially similar. Many courts use a two-part test to determine whether works are substantially similar. The courts apply an objective "extrinsic" test and a subjective "intrinsic" test. Other courts ask if an average person would consider the disputed work to have been taken from the original work.

A copyright plaintiff may ask for actual damages or statutory damages. The winning party in a copyright infringement suit may be awarded attorney's fees. ■

Copyright Infringement Defense: Fair Use

A person sued for copyright infringement might claim that the plaintiff did not file within the law's three-year statute of limitations (or five years for criminal charges).[128] Or a defendant may argue that the copyright holder knowingly has abandoned the copyright, placing the work in the public domain.[129] The most common defense, however, is **fair use.**

Courts recognized the fair use defense long before Congress wrote it into the 1976 copyright law.[130] Courts understood that the copyright statutes—from 1790 to the present—give copyright holders the right to forbid any use of their works without permission. But what if an English teacher copies a few paragraphs from a novel for a class discussion? Or a movie reviewer shows 15 seconds

fair use A test courts use to determine whether using another's copyrighted material without permission is legal or an infringement. Also used in trademark infringement cases.

Points of Law

Fair Use Defense

1. For what purpose was the copyrighted work used without permission?

2. What was the nature of the copyrighted work that was used without permission?

3. How much and what portion of the copyrighted work was used without permission?

4. What effect did the unauthorized use have on the copyrighted work's market value?

of a film on television to illustrate a point about the movie? Or a comedian sings a portion of a song's lyrics in a parody? Courts long ago decided that these and similar uses could be fair to the copyright holder and to society. The 1976 copyright act included fair use as a defense.[131]

Fair use is difficult to define. One judge has said that to be fair "the use must be of a character that serves the copyright objective of stimulating productive thought and public instruction without excessively diminishing the incentives for creativity."[132] Deciding whether a use is fair is not an exact science partly because courts do not agree on what a copyright means, whether it grants a narrow group of rights to the copyright holder and allows the public generally to use copyrighted works or confers nearly complete control to the copyright holder with only narrow exceptions for public use.[133]

The 1976 law set out four criteria courts use in balancing the plaintiff's rights to forbid any use of a work without permission and the defendant's right to use a portion of the work under certain circumstances: (1) the purpose and character of the use, (2) the nature of the copyrighted work, (3) the amount and substantiality of the portion used and (4) the effect on the plaintiff's potential market.

In more detail, the following are four criteria.

1. The purpose and character of the use. For what purpose did the defendant use the copyrighted material? In determining the purpose and character of the use, courts consider several factors, including whether the use is for commercial or nonprofit purposes. The law gives examples of uses that would tilt the balance toward a fair use: criticism, comment, news reporting, teaching (including multiple copies for classroom use), scholarship and research. Other uses also may be seen as fair, such as parody.[134]

News reporting may be considered a fair use, but this is not clear. For example, The Nation magazine used 300 to 400 words from President Gerald R. Ford's memoirs without the book publisher's permission. In fact, the publisher had sold Time magazine the exclusive right to run excerpts. The U.S. Supreme Court acknowledged that Ford's thoughts were news, but that alone did not make The Nation's copying fair use.[135]

In a case involving a crude cover version of a popular song, the Supreme Court considered whether a parody changes the work it mocks or merely repeats without permission the copyrighted material.[136] The Court made transformativeness a key part of fair use's first element. The more the parody transforms the work it mimics, the more likely it is a fair use. As the Court said, fair use is more likely to be found if the new work "adds something new, with a further purpose or different character, altering the [copyrighted work] with new expression, meaning, or message."[137] A 2 Live Crew parody of Roy Orbison's song "Oh,

realWorld Law

"South Park": Infringement or Parody?

A federal appellate court found a "South Park" parody to be fair use and not copyright infringement.

Parody often requires using a substantial amount of the original copyrighted work. However, this does not prevent the parody from successfully claiming fair use, the U.S. Court of Appeals for the Seventh Circuit found in 2012.[1] The animated television program "South Park" parodied a video that had gone viral, "What What (In the Butt)." The animated character Butters Stotch, an innocent fourth grader, sings the same sexually explicit lyrics used in the original video while dressed in various costumes. One costume is a version of that worn by the singer in the original.

The video copyright owner sued for copyright infringement, but the court ruled that fair use protected the defendants. Regarding the first part of the fair use test, the court said "South Park's" intent was "to comment on and critique the social phenomenon that is the 'viral video.'" And the program's focus was "one particularly well-known example of such a video. . . . This kind of parodic use has obvious transformative value, which . . . is fair use," the court said. As to the second part of the test, the original video was "creative and expressive . . . [but] parodies almost invariably copy publicly known, expressive works," the court said. "South Park" certainly used a considerable and the most important part of the video. However, "when a parody achieves its intended aim, the amount taken becomes reasonable when the parody does not serve as a market substitute for the work."[2] Here, the portion of "South Park" at issue is clearly a parody that did not take the original video's place. To the contrary, the court said, the "South Park" parody no doubt increased the number of views the original video would get.

1. Brownmark Films, LLC v. Comedy Partners, 682 F.3d 687 (7th Cir. 2012).
2. *Id.* at 693.

Pretty Woman" might be fair use because it did transform the original, the Court said.[138] However, the other fair use factors also must be considered before finally concluding whether the parody infringed on the original song's copyright. The "Oh, Pretty Woman" case suggests that without fair use protection society largely would be without parodies.[139]

Using "a computer program to scrape news articles on the web" and provide excerpts of those stories to website users is not transformative, a federal district court ruled in 2013.[140] Subscribers to a monitoring service named Meltwater identified news topics. Meltwater then found pertinent stories on the Web, including many Associated Press articles, and provided excerpts. AP sued for copyright infringement. The court rejected Meltwater's fair use defense, primarily because Meltwater repackaged or republished a copyrighted work and did not transform the original, the court said. Using the work in a different format—online rather than in a newspaper, for example—also is not transformative. Neither does Meltwater engage in the fair use practices of newsgathering and research, the court said. Its computers automatically found and republished articles without adding any additional commentary or reporting.

2. The nature of the copyrighted work. Focused on the work that is being used without permission, this factor examines whether the copyrighted work is largely creative, such as a feature film, or more informational or functional, like a compilation of court decisions?[141] Courts often find more copyright protection for creative works. Copying portions of factually based materials may tilt the balance toward a fair use.

The question of whether unpublished materials should be especially protected against a fair use defense arose when a court allowed J.D. Salinger, the author of "Catcher in the Rye," to stop distribution of an unauthorized biography including excerpts from his letters.[142] A federal appellate court held that unpublished materials are entitled to more protection than published works. Congress later amended the Copyright Act to clarify that unpublished materials are not necessarily protected if all four fair use factors show copying without permission should be permitted.[143]

3. The amount and substantiality of the portion used. Courts ask two questions with regard to the amount and substantiality factor. First, how much of the copyrighted work was used without permission? Courts may count how many words from a story or seconds from a DVD were used or may consider what percentage of the original was used. Taking 100 words from a 400-page novel is more likely to tilt toward a fair use than quoting 10 words from a 12-word poem.

Copying the entirety of a copyrighted work does not necessarily mean the use was not fair. A group of students sued the company that owns Turnitin, a plagiarism detection service. The students said work they or their teachers submitted for Turnitin to check was archived in the company's computers. The students claimed the archiving effectively copied their work, thus infringing their copyrights. The U.S. Court of Appeals for the Fourth Circuit disagreed.[144] It found Turnitin's archiving to be fair use, although the company copied all of each student paper. The court acknowledged that "as the amount of the copyrighted material that is used increases, the likelihood that the use will constitute a 'fair use' decreases."[145] Here, however, the court balanced the amount used against other fair use factors, particularly the first factor. Turnitin uses each student paper for a limited purpose, that is, to enable students and teachers to expose plagiarism.

Similarly, a federal appellate court said reprinting full pictures of Grateful Dead posters and concert tickets did not preclude finding fair use when the images were scattered throughout a book in collages of images, text and graphic art. The court said the use was transformative because images were shown in reduced size and only a few unauthorized copyrighted works were published among 2,000 images.[146]

Emerging Law

Can Google Own Every Book Ever Printed?

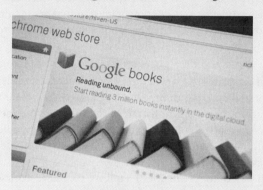

A group of universities contracted with Google to scan nearly 10 million books in their libraries, amounting to approximately 73 percent of the books protected by copyright as well as other items such as photographs. The project also involves "orphan works," material protected by copyright but whose creators are not known or cannot be located. The digital books would be available through the universities' libraries and Google Books.

Several book publishers and the Authors Guild, representing authors whose works would be made into digital books without their permission, sued Google, claiming copyright infringement. The parties settled, but a federal district court rejected the agreement because it "would grant Google significant rights to exploit entire books, without permission of the copyright owners."[1] The publishers then settled again with Google while the authors continued their lawsuit, but lost.

A federal district judge ruled in 2012 that scanning the books amounted to fair use for purposes of preserving the works, making the books available to those with sight impairment and enabling the works to be searched.[2] A transformative use under the first part of the fair use test favors the defendant, the court noted. In this case, "[t]he use to which the works . . . are put is transformative because the copies serve an entirely different purpose than the original works: the purpose is superior search capabilities rather than actual access to copyrighted material. The search capabilities . . . have already given rise to new methods of academic inquiry such as text mining," the court said.[3] Although entire books are being copied, the court said, "entire copies were necessary to fulfill [the] purposes of facilitation of searches and access for print-disabled individuals."[4]

The Authors Guild has appealed the district court's decision.

1. Authors Guild v. Google, Inc., 770 F. Supp. 2d 666, 669 (S.D.N.Y. 2011).
2. Authors Guild, Inc. v. Hathitrust, 902 F. Supp. 445 (S.D.N.Y. 2012).
3. *Id.* at 460.
4. *Id.* at 462.

Not all courts or copyright scholars would agree that reprinting an entire poster, or all of any copyrighted work, would be fair use.[147] But the U.S. Court of Appeals for the Ninth Circuit ruled in 2013 that copying the entirety of every program during prime time is fair use.[148]

Second, what particular portion of the copyrighted work was used and how important was it to the copyrighted work? Quoting from the last page of a mystery novel—the words telling who committed the murder, how and why—would tip the balance toward copyright infringement, not fair use. The balance would tip toward infringement even if only a comparatively few words—but the most important words—were quoted from the mystery novel.

The Supreme Court found this to be an essential point when it rejected The Nation magazine's fair use defense. The magazine used only about 300 words from President Ford's 200,000-word memoirs, but those were the very words explaining why Ford pardoned President Richard Nixon. The Court called this excerpt "essentially the heart of the book."[149] In contrast, college and university professors, film and media studies students and documentary filmmakers generally may use short clips from movie DVDs for criticism, commentary or even to make new, noncommercial videos, the Librarian of Congress ruled.[150]

4. The effect on the plaintiff's potential market. Many courts consider the extent to which the unauthorized copying diminished the copyright holder's likely profits from his or her creation the most important of the four fair use factors. Giving away the end of a mystery novel might mean potential readers would not purchase the book and would have a financial impact on a copyright holder and the incentive to create.

When a Kinko's store responded to professors' requests to make course packets by copying chapters from numerous books without permission, several publishers sued for copyright infringement. A court rejected Kinko's fair use defense.[151] Finding the fourth factor the "single most important" part of the fair use test, the court said,

> [T]he competition for "student dollars" is easily won by Kinko's, which produced 300- to 400-page packets including substantial portions of copyrighted books at a cost of $24 to the student. [One packet] contained excerpts from 20 different books, totaled 324 pages, and cost $21.50. While it is possible that reading the packets whets the appetite of students for more information from the authors, it is more likely that purchase of the packets obviates purchase of the full texts.[152]

The U.S. Supreme Court has said copying a substantial portion of a copyrighted work without permission may prove a "greater likelihood of market harm under the fourth" element of the fair use test.[153]

SUMMARY

THE COPYRIGHT LAW SPECIFIES A THREE-YEAR statute of limitations, or five years for criminal prosecutions.

Fair use, the most common copyright infringement defense, is a four-part balancing test. Courts consider (1) the purpose and character of the use, (2) the nature of the copyrighted work, (3) the amount and substantiality of the portion used and (4) the effect on the plaintiff's potential market. Criticism, news, scholarship and parody tend toward fair use. Using an important part of a work may suggest infringement. Harm to the plaintiff's potential profits may be the most important fair use criterion. ■

Copyright, Computers and the Internet

Copyright infringement can occur on the Internet just as it can in print. Copying pictures from a magazine's website onto another website or into a class paper without permission violates the copyright law, for example.[154] More important, downloading copyrighted music or movies infringes on copyright holders' rights.

But although computers and a rudimentary Internet existed in 1976, they were not part of Congress' thinking when it passed the current copyright law. Since then, Congress and the courts have struggled to apply copyright concepts and laws to these newer technologies.

In 1998 Congress adopted the Digital Millennium Copyright Act (DMCA) in an attempt to bring the Internet and other digital media into the copyright law.[155] The DMCA bans software and hardware that facilitates circumventing copyright protection technology, with certain exceptions.[156] For example, the act forbids software that would disable anti-copying features in a DVD player or software enabling video DVDs to be copied.[157] The DMCA also prohibits removing or changing copyright information, such as the copyright owner's name.[158]

The DMCA also deals with concerns that Internet service providers (ISPs) could lose copyright suits based on content their users put on the ISPs' systems. One court found that an ISP violated the copyright law when its subscribers uploaded and downloaded copyrighted pictures without the ISP's knowledge.[159] Another court said a bulletin board service operator infringed on copyright when its customers used the service to trade copyrighted computer games.[160]

To protect ISPs and video-sharing sites, the DMCA shields them from copyright infringement claims if an ISP removes material that a copyright holder tells the website is posted without permission.[161] This is called a "takedown notice." This protection is available if a website names an agent to receive takedown requests, lets site users know of the site's copyright infringement policy and complies with takedown requests it receives. ISPs must comply with takedown requests that clearly identify the work claimed to infringe copyright and provide the Uniform Resource Locator (URL) of the infringing work.[162] A customer cannot sue the ISP for removing material even if the customer later shows the material did not violate a copyright holder's rights. ISPs that knowingly transmit material that violates copyright are not protected.

The DMCA offers other protection to video-sharing websites. The DMCA protects video-sharing websites from monetary damages when a user, rather than the site, posts copyrighted material without permission. The copyright holder cannot successfully sue if the site operator (1) did not know the content infringed on someone's copyright, (2) did not earn money directly from the posted material and (3) promptly complied with a takedown notice. These takedown protections, or safe harbors, limit video-sharing sites' liability.

The DMCA's safe harbors saved Veoh Networks, an Internet-based video-sharing service, from losing a copyright infringement suit in 2013. Universal Music Group (UMG), one of the world's largest recording companies, sued Veoh over user-uploaded videos that included UMG-copyrighted songs. Veoh had implemented a copyright infringement policy and taken down videos when notified of violations but had not been able to prevent all infringements. Despite failure to notify Veoh of all infringing videos, UMG said Veoh should have known some of its videos infringed copyright. The U.S. Court of Appeals for the Ninth Circuit said the DMCA requires specific notification to Veoh of videos that need to be removed.[163] Absent notification by a copyright owner, Veoh had neither the right nor ability to prevent user posting of videos that infringed copyright, the court said. Simple labeling of "music video" postings was insufficient to show Veoh knew a video infringed UMG's copyright.

The DMCA's safe harbor provision also kept Google-owned YouTube from losing a $1 billion suit filed by Viacom. Viacom owns Paramount Pictures, the CBS television network and several cable networks such as MTV, VH1 and Comedy Central. On remand from a federal appellate court, a district judge in 2013 held that YouTube's removal of 100,000 videos that Viacom said infringed its copyrights did not show YouTube knew it carried Viacom's copyrighted material.[164] Without that knowledge, the safe harbor protected YouTube.

A website or blog containing an embedded copyrighted video does not lose DMCA protection. As long as the video is a link to another site and no copy is maintained, the DMCA applies.[165]

Music Licensing

Copyrighted music is part of many media presentations. Even the print media must be concerned with music copyrights if they print song lyrics or a composition's score.

Obtaining permission to use copyrighted music may involve many steps because there are many copyright holders. Listening to a recording means listening to two copyrighted works. First, the composition: the music and the lyrics. Songs, symphonies and other musical compositions that are original and fixed in a tangible medium have copyright protection. Second, a recorded song is a sound recording: the words and music performed by musicians and embedded into a CD, DVD or another recording medium. But there is more. Third, the CD, DVD or other object containing the sound is called a "phonorecord." Phonorecords have copyright protection. Finally, permission is needed to copy a recorded composition onto film or a DVD. This is called a "synchronization license."

Compositions Because copyright protects compositions, permission is needed to use them. Composers have the right to limit public performances of their works.[166] Consent is required to broadcast or record a song, perform the song live, play a recording containing the song in many restaurants and stores, or use the song in any of numerous other ways. A composer cannot know each time a song, called "musical work" in the copyright act, is performed. Nor can a composer reach contractual agreements with every person who might want to perform the song—even if each of those people wants to seek permission. Instead, music licensing organizations represent music publishers and most composers.

The oldest performing rights organization, ASCAP (American Society of Composers, Authors and Publishers) began in 1914. In 1939, when ASCAP increased the fees broadcasters paid to play compositions on the air, radio stations organized BMI (Broadcast Music, Inc.). SESAC (once called the Society of European Stage Authors and Composers) operates as the third performing rights organization. ASCAP, BMI and SESAC grant licenses (another word for contracts) to people, groups and businesses that permit performance of copyrighted songs for specific purposes. ASCAP, BMI and SESAC most often grant blanket licenses to perform all the songs in their catalogs. They also grant per-program licenses allowing a broadcaster to use music in a particular program. Their licenses are for songs, not for complete works such as musical comedies, operas, operettas and motion picture scores. Permission to use these musical creations comes from the music publishers who produce the printed scores for these works.

In return for the licenses, the groups collect fees from the song users. The fees may be a few hundred dollars annually for a small bar that hosts live musicians to millions of dollars for a major broadcast television network. The three performing rights organizations combined distribute nearly $2 billion annually to their member composers and music publishing companies.[167] The license fees are distributed semiannually to music publishers and composers primarily based on how often their songs are played. ASCAP and BMI are nonprofit organizations, while SESAC, the smallest of the three, is a for-profit. A composer joins just one of the organizations or is represented by a music publisher that belongs to one of them. Thus, a composition is under the auspices of one performing rights organization, and most music users must have agreements with all three groups. The country's largest music publisher, Sony/ATV, no longer uses the performing rights organizations' services. Anyone who wants to use compositions in Sony/ATV's control must negotiate directly with it. Sony/ATV's catalog includes songs by Michael Jackson, Lady Gaga and Taylor Swift, as well as most of the Beatles' songs.

Songwriters who join a performing rights organization do not give up their copyrights. They may grant performance rights themselves, even if they belong to ASCAP, BMI or SESAC. Usually, however, composers allow the organizations to represent them, ensuring that they are paid when their songs are performed.

Performing rights organization representatives visit nightclubs, stores, radio stations and other music users and issue warnings to convince them to obtain licenses. If warnings are not successful, they sue for copyright infringement.[168]

Points of Law

What Does "Perform" Mean?

A congressional report explains that

> a singer is performing when he or she sings a song; a broadcasting network is performing when it transmits his or her performance (whether simultaneously or from records); a local broadcaster is performing when it transmits the network broadcast; a cable television system is performing when it retransmits the broadcast to its subscribers; and any individual is performing whenever he or she plays a phonorecord embodying the performance or communicates the performance by turning on a receiving set.[1]

1. House of Representatives Report No. 1476, 94th Congress, 2d Session 63 (1976).

Congress settled a long-standing dispute. ASCAP and BMI insisted stores have licenses just to turn on a radio and play music, and courts disagreed, even when stores amplified music through a speaker system.[169] In the Fairness in Music Licensing Act of 1998, Congress endorsed a compromise between the performing rights organizations and businesses that established that certain businesses could broadcast music in their stores without a license.[170] The exemption applies to small retail stores and restaurants that charge no admission and do not play the music outside the establishments. Larger establishments with no more than six speakers and four television sets also are exempt. The law applies only to playing music through radio and television sets in businesses. It does not apply to live performances, the playing of recordings or other nonbroadcast uses of copyrighted compositions.

mechanical license Permission to record a composition.

Permission to record a composition obtained from a New York City nonprofit organization, the Harry Fox Agency, is called a **"mechanical license."** When a song's copyright holder allows one recording to be made of a composition, the law grants a compulsory license—also called "statutory license"—to anyone else who wants to make a recording of the song.[171] That is, the composition's copyright holder must allow others to record the song. In return, the song's copyright holder receives compensation based on the number of recordings sold. The compulsory license applies only to individual songs, not to musical comedy scores, movie soundtracks, operas and similar scores. Also, the license does not allow other material to be included in the recording, such as CD-ROMs that include video images or text information. The right to record a composition is separate from the right to publicly perform a song, such as a radio station or a large department store playing a recording of a song.

An ASCAP or BMI license allows broadcast stations to both air compositions and stream them on the station's website. SESAC charges separately for these two rights.[172]

Sound Recordings A sound recording, the series of musical or other sounds recorded on a vinyl disc, a CD, a DVD, an audiotape or some other storage medium,[173] are eligible for copyright protection.[174] A sound recording is not the composition or CD itself. Both have their own copyright protection.

A sound recording of the musical sounds and words must have originality to be given copyright protection. Originality may be found in two elements of a sound recording. First, the performers bring the composition to life. As one judge said, "A musical score in ordinary notation does not determine the entire performance. . . . In the vast number of renditions, the performer has a wide choice, depending on his gifts, and this makes his rendition . . . quite as original" as the composition itself.[175] Second, a record producer may add originality through choosing which sounds to emphasize, editing the recording and making suggestions to the musicians.

The sound recording copyright may be owned by the performers or owned jointly by the musicians and the record producer. A recording company also may own the sound recording copyright because of an employment situation—the producer may work full-time for a recording company—or a contractual agreement between the performers and the recording company.

Sound recording copyright holders have only three rights.[176] First, no one may copy the sound recording without permission. Second, consent is required to make a derivative work based on the sound recording. This right does not preclude cover records—recordings of the same song by other musicians—even if the new recording sounds exactly like the original.[177] Third, the sound recording copyright owner has exclusive right to publicly distribute the recording.

Copyright law prohibits digitally transmitting sound recordings without permission. This does not apply to performing a sound recording live, as a DJ might, or broadcasting it through nondigital means, as an over-the-air radio station does. The law applies only to sound recordings performed through a digital audio transmission, such as by a satellite music service or a radio station streaming its programming on a website.

Interactive services allowing users to choose what artist or song will be played or to know in advance the recordings that will be played must negotiate directly with sound recording copyright holders. In contrast, "noninteractive" services, such as webcasters, that play no more than two songs in a row from the same album and no more than three songs in any four-hour period from the same artist,[178] obtain a statutory license. Pandora Internet radio is an example of a noninteractive service. The license requires all affected copyright owners to grant the licensed permission for established royalties paid by the service and disbursed to the copyright holders. The recording industry established a non-profit group, SoundExchange, to administer the royalties. Users of copyrighted material may negotiate a fee with SoundExchange or, if negotiations fail, pay royalties established every five years by the federal Copyright Royalty Board.[179] Some services, such as Clear Channel, Entercom and Sirius XM, have chosen not to deal with SoundExchange and instead negotiate directly with recording companies.

Outside of the music context, using a small portion of copyrighted material may be considered fair use. Courts even have referred to this as "*de minimis* copying"—that is, copying so little that it is not worth a court's time to hear a copyright infringement case. But "sampling"—using a few notes from one recording on a different recording—could be copyright infringement. Courts differ. The U.S. Court of Appeals for the Sixth Circuit held that any sampling from a sound recording, no matter how small, is infringement.[180] The Ninth Circuit and the 11th Circuit disagree. The Ninth Circuit said using a few notes of a composition is not infringement.[181] The 11th Circuit says even when there is direct evidence of copying, the plaintiff still must prove substantial similarity.[182]

Musicians Artists who perform compositions have few copyright protections. Most musicians—in their roles as musicians—sign away their sound recording copyrights as part of the contracts between the artists and their recording companies. (Some artists even agree to transfer their composition copyrights to recording companies.) In one way, this is not much different from a novelist who transfers her or his copyright to a book publishing company in return for a share of the book's sales revenues. Recording artists receive a share of their recordings' sales revenues—per their contracts with their recording companies. However, many performers and some legal scholars argue that recording company contracts are unfair to recording artists.[183] One complaint is that recording companies require artists to agree that their recordings are works made for hire, giving the company complete control over the recordings. The recording artist Prince "went so far as trading in his name for an unpronounceable symbol to protest his relationship with his label at the time, Warner Brothers. During the rest of his contract with Warner Brothers, [he] took to scribbling the word 'slave' on his face during appearances."[184]

Congress has given performers one right. They have the right to prevent bootleg copies—audio or video recordings—of live musical performances.[185] Making copies of the live recordings and selling or distributing the copies also infringes on the performers' rights.[186]

Phonorecords When a composition is recorded, usually on a CD or another digital device, the recording company has made a phonorecord. Congress first protected the sound recordings contained in records and tapes in a law taking effect in 1972.[187] Previously Congress and courts thought that if the naked eye could not see the work contained in an object, the law could not protect the object.[188] Words could be seen in a book, and drawings could be seen on paper, but the musical sounds the record contained could not be seen and so could not receive copyright protection.

In the 1976 copyright law, Congress said phonorecords—the disc, record, tape or other object containing the sound recording—have copyright protection. It violates copyright to copy, distribute or make adaptations of a phonorecord without permission.[189] In practice, this means a broadcast radio station that simply plays song recordings need only have ASCAP, BMI and SESAC licenses, not recording companies' permission. However, if the station copies the recordings—while taping the radio program that includes the recordings, for example—it then must have the recording companies' permission granted through a "master use license."

Synchronization Rights If a television station uses a recording as background music, in a station promotional spot, for example, one additional permission is required: a synchronization license. Beyond the appropriate ASCAP, BMI or SESAC license and the recording company's permission to copy the sound recording and phonorecord onto videotape, the synchronization license allows the station to synchronize the musical work with the images on videotape. Synchronization rights are needed any time a recorded composition is used in a filmed or videotaped work. Motion picture producers also need a synchronization license to include recorded music in movies.

Synchronization rights belong to the composer and music publisher that publishes and publicizes the song. Synchronization rights must be obtained directly from the music publisher.

International Law

The Beatles' 1960s Recordings Are Safe for Another 20 Years

The European Union (EU) extended copyrights by 20 years on what the United States calls "sound recordings." In 2011 EU legislation increased protection on music recordings from 50 to 70 years. Known as "Cliff's law," after musician Sir Cliff Richard, who campaigned for the law, the extension came just in time for recordings made in the 1960s. The law applies only to performers and recording companies that own copyrights to the recordings. EU copyright law already protected composers who own their copyrights until 70 years after their deaths, as in the United States.[1]

The law covers works still under the 50-year copyright in 2013 when the legislation takes effect. In 2013 Sony Music issued a limited edition compilation of early Bob Dylan recordings that otherwise would have fallen into the public domain. Now the recordings will come under the 20-year extension.[2]

1. Josh Halliday, *Cliff's Law Puts Extra 20 Years on Record Royalties,* GUARDIAN (LONDON), Sept. 13, 2011, at 13.
2. Allan Kozinn, *Sony Issues Dylan CDs to Extend Copyright,* N.Y. TIMES, Jan. 8, 2013, at C1.

Alternatives to Licensing One way to avoid the complexities of music licensing is through companies that hire composers to write songs and hire musicians to record those songs. The companies sell CDs and audiotapes containing the recordings. Because the company owns all the rights—for the compositions, sound recordings, phonorecords and synchronization—it can sell a complete package. These recordings are not of best-selling, well-known songs, but they may offer an easier and less expensive way to obtain music for some purposes. Firms providing these services are variously called "music library companies," "needle-drop shops" or "one-stop shops." Muzak is a well-known music library.

Music, the Internet and File Sharing

It seems like ancient history when Napster first allowed one computer user to reach into another computer to retrieve files containing copyrighted music. Millions of individuals used this peer-to-peer (P2P) network to make unauthorized copies of sound recordings before a federal appellate court agreed with the recording industry that Napster's operation violated the copyright law.[190] Napster's sole purpose was to aid copyright infringement by allowing users to download software and share copyrighted music, according to the court.

Subsequent P2P systems generally avoided the central server scheme Napster used, but the recording industry continued to sue individual downloaders. A federal appellate court affirmed a $222,000 award to the recording industry in a case involving a woman who distributed 24 songs using the KaZaA P2P network. That long-running litigation ended in 2013 when the U.S. Supreme Court refused to hear her appeal.[191] Another federal appellate court upheld a jury's decision ordering a Boston University graduate student to pay $675,000 in damages for illegally downloading and sharing 30 songs.[192]

The recording and movie industries filed a copyright infringement lawsuit against two P2P networks, Grokster and Morpheus, claiming they contributed to copyright infringement by allowing network users to illegally download copyrighted songs and movies. The U.S. Supreme Court agreed and said Grokster and Morpheus promoted and encouraged their users to violate the copyright law.[193] In its unanimous decision the Court said the P2P systems aided in copyright "infringement on a gigantic scale" and that "the probable scope of copyright infringement is staggering."[194] Grokster and Morpheus argued they were no more responsible for copyright infringement than was Sony for making videocassette recorders. Two decades earlier in *Sony v. University City Studios,* the U.S. Supreme Court had ruled that because VCRs had many non-infringing purposes, such as time shifting of a television program, and Sony had not encouraged copyright violations, Sony was not contributing to copyright infringement.[195]

But the Court said the difference between Sony and the file-sharing services is "inducement." Sony may have known VCRs could be used to infringe on copyright, but it did not encourage illegal copying. Grokster and Morpheus, however, aimed their services at former Napster users, did not develop filtering tools to prevent copyright infringement and sold advertising directed to people who were illegally downloading copyrighted digital content, the Court said. All this showed Grokster and Morpheus encouraged or induced their users to illegally download protected content, according to the Court.

In another attempt to limit online theft, the recording and movie industry activated the Copyright Alert System in 2013. Copyright holders will notify five major Internet service providers—Verizon, Comcast, AT&T, Cablevision, and Time Warner—when any of the ISPs' customers engage in illegal downloading using P2P software. The customer then will receive up to six warning notices from the ISP before more stringent action may be taken. A customer's available bandwidth may be limited or a customer may automatically be sent to a website with information about copyright law. The Copyright Alert System may limit the hundreds of thousands of cases, most dismissed or settled, content providers have brought against illegal downloaders.[196]

SUMMARY

USING COPYRIGHTED MUSIC MAY INVOLVE obtaining permission from several sources. Songwriters and music publishers usually have a music licensing organization—ASCAP, BMI or SESAC—represent them. The organizations grant licenses allowing use of compositions. Copyright holders receive compensation from the license fees.

When a composition is performed and recorded on a disc or other medium, the recorded performance is a sound recording. The disc containing the sound recording is a phonorecord. Both sound recordings and phonorecords have copyright protection, including bans on copying them without permission. However, sound recordings may be "performed" without permission. This occurs when a broadcast radio station plays a recording, for example. However, permission must be obtained to play a sound recording through a digital transmission, such as satellite radio.

Additionally, synchronization rights are required to copy a recorded composition onto videotape or film.

Some companies hire songwriters and performers to make sound recordings. These companies will sell CDs of their music and provide all necessary performance, copying and synchronization rights.

The Digital Millennium Copyright Act bans technologies that circumvent copyright protections. The law also protects Internet service providers against copyright suits if the ISP takes down material a copyright holder says is posted without permission.

The recording industry has sued services providing software that allows file sharing when the networks have been used for unauthorized copying of sound recordings. The recording and movie industries have instituted the Copyright Alert System to let notify copyright infringers they are violating the law. ∎

Trademarks

A **trademark** is a word, name, symbol or design used to identify a company's goods and distinguish them from similar products other companies make.[197] A service mark accomplishes the same purpose for services a firm provides. A trade name identifies a particular company rather than the company's product or service. Federal law also protects trade dress, which describes a product's total look, including size, shape, color, texture and graphics. The word "trademark" may be used generally to include all four of these categories. However, the law does not protect trade names or trade dress as completely as it protects trademarks and service marks.

Companies use trademarks to advertise their products and services. Customers use trademarks to ensure they are getting the goods or services from the particular company. Trademarks are valuable. Consider the importance of McDonald's, Nike, Kodak, Kleenex and Coke as trademarks. Reaching for a soft drink, a customer does not want to have to read the small print on a can's label to confirm that a company named Coca-Cola in Atlanta, Ga., licenses the product. A customer simply wants to see the word "Coke" and know it is the product he or she wants. Coca-Cola's trademark is worth millions of dollars.

Trademarks may be considered brand names or logos designed to identify a company's product. The Nike "swoosh" is a well-known logo. But the list of what can be trademarked is lengthy: letters (CBS), numbers (VO-5), domain names (Amazon.com), slogans ("Just do it"), shapes (Coke bottle), colors (Corning Fiberglass pink insulation),[198] sounds (quacking noise made by guides and participants in duck boat tours)[199] and smells ("fresh cut grass" for tennis balls).[200]

trademark A word, name, symbol or design used to identify a company's goods and distinguish them from similar products other companies make.

realWorld Law

Sports Trademarks

Penn State said a high school's logo, on the right, looked too much like the university's panther, on the left, and therefore could be a trademark infringement.

Professional and university sports leagues and teams protect their trademarks because they are worth millions of dollars. The leagues' and teams' logos are used on clothing and other merchandise, in advertising for game tickets and as part of televised sports events. When a T-shirt maker puts the phrase "Who Dat" on shirts, it has used a phrase the National Football League says it has trademarked and is used by New Orleans Saints fans.[1] The words "Super Bowl" and "Olympics" also are trademarks. So are "March Madness" and even "Elite Eight."

Colleges also protect their trademarked logos. The University of Florida ordered a private

K–12 school to stop using an alligator as its mascot because it nearly matched Florida's Gator. The school said it could cost $60,000 to change its logo on everything from uniforms to the gym floor. Penn State told a Texas high school—1,400 miles from the university—its Cougar logo looked too much like Penn State's Nittany Lion. The University of Pittsburgh instructed a Toledo, Ohio, high school to stop using Pitt's trademarked Panther. The university and the high school both used the logo for sports teams and, more generally, to identify the schools. Using a trademark without permission for purposes similar to the trademark owner's use violates federal law.[2]

1. Ken Sugiura & Michael Carvell, *In Brief*, Atl. J-.Const., Jan. 30, 2010, at 1C.
2. Adam Himmelsbach, *Colleges Fight to Keep Logos off High School Playing Fields*, N.Y. Times, Nov. 27, 2010, at A1, A3.

The federal Lanham Act protects trademarks that are eligible for registration with the U.S. Patent and Trademark Office.[201] The law ensures that if a company complies with certain requirements, no other company may use a word, symbol, slogan or other such item that will confuse consumers about who supplies a particular product or service. The Lanham Act also prevents using a mark to falsely suggest a product's source even if the mark is not registered.[202]

Distinctiveness Requirement

Distinctive words, designs or other indicators of a product's or service's origin are eligible for trademark registration.[203] A trademark will be protected only if it is distinctive. The mark must distinguish one company's goods from another's. The word "popcorn" simply tells what the product is, not what company makes it. Act II indicates the popcorn comes from ConAgra. "Act II" is a distinctive term for a certain product, distinguishing it from other manufacturers' popcorn.

A trademark will be protected only if it is distinctive. There is a spectrum of distinctiveness in trademark law. The less unique a mark is—that is, the more broadly descriptive it is—the less likely that it will be eligible for trademark registration.

The most distinctive category is "fanciful marks." These are invented marks, including made-up words. Lexus, Xerox and Exxon are examples of fanciful marks. A court found that Peterbilt and Kenworth are fanciful marks applied to trucks.[204] The trucks' manufacturer sued a website operator who used the words "Peterbilt" and "Kenworth" in the site's address without permission. The court said fanciful marks are the strongest and most distinctive trademarks possible. When a strong mark is infringed on, the court said, it becomes more likely that consumers would be confused. Therefore, the most trademark protection should be applied to fanciful marks, the court concluded.

"Arbitrary marks," the next most distinctive category, are words that have ordinary meanings not applied to the product or service. For example, an apple is a fruit. But Apple is a trademark for computers and other products manufactured by Apple Computer, Inc. A dictionary will define the word "apple" as a fruit, but not as a computer. Numbers and letters arranged in a distinctive order may be arbitrary marks, such as BEBE for clothes[205] or V-8 for vegetable juice.[206]

"Suggestive marks" hint at a product's qualities or imply their manufacturer's business but do not describe what the product is. A suggestive mark requires consumers to use their imaginations to discern the company's exact business.[207] One court said Coppertone, Orange Crush and Playboy are good examples of suggestive marks "because they conjure images of the associated products without directly describing those products."[208] A court held that the word "CarMax" is a suggestive mark for a used car dealership.[209] The word suggests that CarMax is involved in the automobile business but does not say the company sells used cars.

A "descriptive mark" leaves little to a consumer's imagination. The mark describes the product or service and may or may not suggest what company provided it. Many soft drink companies may use the word "refreshing" to describe their products. Generally, commonly used descriptive terms should be available for everyone's use, and they cannot be trademarked.

However, a descriptive mark may be a trademark if it has acquired a distinctive connection to the product for which it is used, or what courts call a "secondary meaning" beyond the word's common meaning. Distinctive, arbitrary and suggestive marks do not require a secondary meaning. To obtain a secondary meaning, the public must associate a word with a product's source or producer, not the product. Courts do not agree on a test for finding a secondary meaning, but the Ninth Circuit's approach is illustrative. It considers: "(1) whether actual purchasers of the product bearing the claimed trademark associate the trademark with the producer; (2) the degree and manner of advertising under the claimed

Points of Law

Confusing?

The Lanham Act says trademark infringement occurs when a mark "is likely to cause confusion, or to cause a mistake, or to deceive as to the affiliation, connection, or association of such person with another person, or as to the origin, sponsorship, or approval of his or her goods, services, or commercial activities by another person. . . ."[1]

1. 15 U.S.C. § 1125(a)(1) (Lanham Act—U.S. trademark law).

realWorld Law

Apple and Its Trademarks

Although Apple co-founder Steve Jobs described himself as a rabid Beatles fan, his company and the Beatles' holding company and record company owner, Apple Corps, fought for 20 years over a McIntosh apple, at least over the image of an apple and the name "Apple." They reached agreement in 2007, but only finalized it in 2012. Now Apple—the computer, iPhone, iPad company—owns the trademark Apple Corps and the apple logo.[1] In 2013 Apple received trademark protection for the minimalist design and layout of its retail stores.[2] A year earlier Apple registered a trademark (technically, a sensory mark) for the startup sound of Mac computers.[3] Apple has trademarks for "There's an App for that," the leaf in the Apple logo[4] and hundreds more words and logos.

1. John Paczkowski, *Beatles' Apple Now Apple's Apple,* ALL THINGS DIGITAL (Oct. 25, 2012), *available at* http://allthingsd.com/20121025/beatles-apple-now-apples-apple/?ak_action.
2. Erin Geiger Smith, *Apple Wins Trademark for Minimalist Design of Its Retail Stores,* SAN JOSE MERCURY NEWS (Jan. 29, 2013), *available at* http://www.reuters.com/article/2013/01/29/us-apple-stores-trademark-idUSBRE90S13X20130129.
3. Josh Lowensohn, *Apple Wins U.S. Trademark for Mac Boot Chime,* CNET (Dec. 12, 2012), *available at* http://news.cnet.com/8301-135793-57558807-37/apple-wins-u.s.-trademark-for-mac-boot-chime.
4. *Apple's Classic Mac Startup Chime Is Now a Registered Trademark,* PATENTLYAPPLE (Dec. 12, 2012), *available at* http://www.patentlyaple.com/patently-apple/2012/12/apples-classic-mac-startup-chime-is-now-a-registered-trademark.html.

trademark; (3) the length and manner of use of the claimed trademark; and (4) whether use of the claimed trademark has been exclusive."[210]

Certain groups of descriptive words, such as geographic terms, have difficulty acquiring a secondary meaning and cannot be a registered trademark if they only describe where the goods or services are made or offered. For example, a court refused to find that the word "Boston" had a secondary meaning in the phrase "Boston Beer."[211] Although the beer is manufactured in Boston, "Boston" means the Massachusetts city and is not connected in the public's mind with that brand of beer, the court said. The court did not allow Boston Beer to be a trademark. But 90 years ago the Supreme Court held "The American Girl" to be an arbitrary trademark for a brand of shoes because it did not suggest the shoes were made in America or even that the product was shoes.[212] A geographic term also cannot be a registered trademark if it is deceptive. For example, a ham processor located in Nebraska cannot use the term "Danish ham" as a trademark for its product.

Similarly, people's names must acquire a secondary meaning to be protected. The first names Steven and Linda, and the last names Jones and Smith, are shared by millions of people and therefore are not distinctive. In one case, Fabrikant & Sons, a jewelry company, trademarked the word "Fabrikant." Several years later, Fabrikant Fine Diamonds began business as a buyer and seller of jewelry. Both companies are located in New York City and both are owned by individuals named Fabrikant. A court ruled that Fabrikant Fine Diamonds had to either stop using the name Fabrikant or use a first name in front of the

International Law

Sounds in Canada

The lion's roar—at least the one beginning and/or ending MGM movies—now is protected in Canada. The Canadian Intellectual Property Office (CIPO) decided in 2012 that sounds can be trademarked. MGM and the CIPO reached an agreement approved by a Federal Court judge, ending MGM's 20-year battle to protect its famous lion's roar in Canada. A lion first appeared in a movie to represent MGM in 1917 and began to roar in 1928.[1]

In the United States, the Supreme Court wrote that a trademark may be "almost anything at all that is capable of carrying meaning."[2] That includes sounds. Perhaps the earliest sound registered in the United States is the NBC chimes, given protection 65 years before Canada recognized that sounds can be trademarked. The MGM lion's roar has long had trademark protection in the United States.

1. *This Sound Is My Sound,* Toronto Star, Apr. 11, 2012, at B3.
2. Qualitex Co. v. Jacobson Prods. Co., 514 U.S. 159, 164 (1995).

word to distinguish it from Fabrikant & Sons.[213] Otherwise the public would be confused, the court said.

Courts often consider three factors to rule in competing name cases. As one court put it, the factors are "(a) the interest of the plaintiff in protecting the good will which has attached to his personal name trademark, (b) the interest of the defendant in using his own name in his business activities and (c) the interest of the public in being free from confusion and deception."[214]

Finally, generic words will not be given trademark protection. A graham cracker manufacturer cannot use the word "cracker" as a trademark, for example. A manufacturer is not allowed to take a word commonly used to describe a product category and use it exclusively for the company's own purpose. For instance, Harley-Davidson could not use the word "hog" as a mark for its motorcycles,[215] nor could a concert promoter obtain a trademark for the term "summer jam" to advertise its summer concerts.[216]

Some marks that once were protected became generic when the public used the mark to mean a category of goods rather than a particular manufacturer's product. Thermos, cellophane, brassiere, aspirin, shredded wheat and monopoly (the board game) all once were protected copyrights that became generic words.[217] Courts ask what a word's primary significance is to the public. If the public thinks of a word as describing a class of goods—a vacuum bottle is a thermos—the word is generic and cannot be a protected mark. If the word primarily means a particular manufacturer—Xerox makes Xerox copying machines—the word will remain a trademark.[218]

Companies can take several steps to prevent a trademark from becoming generic. Among other actions, a company should select a distinctive mark, advertise the goods using both the trademark and the product's generic word (Kleenex facial tissue), use advertisements to educate the public that the product's trademark is not a generic word and use the trademark on several different products.[219]

Registering a Trademark

A history of using a distinctive mark to identify a product can give the mark protection even if it is not registered with the U.S. Patent and Trademark Office (PTO). The first person or company to use the mark owns it. State courts recognize common law rights in marks within the geographic area where the mark is used. It is not necessary to register a mark to give it common-law protection. An owner of a mark protected by common law may use the symbols ™ (trademark) or ˢᴹ (service mark), but these are not recognized by statute.

Federal registration provides a mark more protection than does the common law, however. Registration is for nationwide use and lets competitors know that a company owns the mark. Registration also dates when the mark first was used if another company argues it had a prior interest in the mark. A company may use the statutory symbol for registered marks. The symbol ® or the phrase "Registered U.S. Patent and Trademark Office" is acceptable. If a registered mark is infringed, its owner may sue in federal court. After a company uses a registered mark for five years, there are few grounds on which the registration may be contested, providing nearly complete protection.[220]

A mark must be registered with the PTO to have statutory protection under the Lanham Act.[221] Registering a mark requires submitting an application form, a drawing of the mark and a filing fee to the PTO. If the registration is based on prior use, specimens of the use also must be submitted. Trademark law's complexity means a trademark attorney needs to be involved in registering a mark.

Registering a mark on the Principal Register gives all legal rights to a distinctive mark being used in commerce.[222] The Principal Register also can be used for marks that may be used in the future. However, using the Principal Register to reserve a mark for future use does not allow a federal registration to be issued. The PTO, however, will not register a mark that does not qualify if it is considered immoral or deceptive, includes a flag or other insignia of any country or U.S. state or city, includes a name or other identification of a living person without the individual's consent or is only a descriptive mark without secondary meaning. Descriptive marks go on the Supplemental Register, with their owners hoping to move them to the Principal Register once secondary meaning has been established.[223]

Nor will the PTO register a mark identical to or similar to an existing mark. PTO examiners carefully consider each mark submitted for registration and publicize marks proposed for registration. Any company believing the mark will cause consumer confusion and harm the company's use of a similar mark may object. The PTO resolves objections before approving and registering the mark.

During the sixth year after registration, a mark owner must file an affidavit confirming the mark has been in continued use.[224] Marks registered after Nov. 16, 1989, have a 10-year term. Registrations may be renewed indefinitely.[225]

Domain Names

Congress adapted trademark law to the Internet, but Web addresses, or domain names, have been a particular problem for trademark law. Domain names may be trademarked and protected against infringement, although the domain name suffixes, such as .com or .org, are not considered part of a trademarked domain name.

A cybersquatter is a person who claims domain names that include trademarks or famous people's names. Trademark owners often sued cybersquatters, frequently successfully, and Congress passed the Anticybersquatting Consumer Protection Act (ACPA) to try to stop the practice.[226] The law provides civil and criminal remedies for registering a domain name with the intention of selling it to the trademark owner. The ACPA applies to a domain name identical or confusingly similar to a trademark and to a domain name that disparages or injures a well-known trademark. A defendant must have acted in bad faith to be liable under the statute. Damages can be as high as $100,000.

In one ACPA case, a company named Spider Webs registered hundreds of domain names, including ErnestandJulioGallo.com. The Gallo winery sued. A federal appellate court held the ACPA constitutional and said the unauthorized domain name could injure Gallo's trademark.[227] Spider Webs admitted it registered the domain name hoping the ACPA would be found unconstitutional. That showed bad faith, the appellate court said and upheld a $25,000 damage award and a court order preventing Spider Webs from registering any domain name that used "Gallo" or "Ernest and Julio."

Two companies might have identical or similar trademarks for two different products and the companies' domain names would be the same—chip.com for a computer chip company for a potato chip company. In such a case, one court said trademark law takes precedence over domain registration. The court gave a disputed domain name—moviebuff—to the company that first used the mark.[228] However, if two domain names are similar and both describe the companies' products, courts may allow the firms to continue using the names. For example, the manufacturer of Beanie Babies sued a company using bargainbeanies.com as a domain name. The bargain beanies company sold used beanbag animals. A federal appellate court said preventing a firm from using a domain name describing its business would be like "forbidding a used car dealer who specializes in selling Chevrolets to mention" the car's name in the dealer's advertising.[229] The court allowed both companies to use their domain names.

Trademark Infringement

Valid trademarks are protected by the common law or federal registration. Competing marks that confuse consumers or lessen a competing trademark's value are not permitted.

Anyone may use a protected trademark in a way that is not confusing. Including the words "Pontiac," "Tommy Hilfiger" and "Burger King" in this paragraph is not a trademark infringement. Using marks for informational purposes is a fair use. The First Amendment protects using a competitor's trademark in comparative advertising, courts have ruled.[230] However, a competitor may not alter a mark in a comparative ad. In one case, a competitor to John Deere's lawn tractor business aired a comparative ad that distorted and animated Deere's trademarked deer logo, showing the deer jumping through a hoop that breaks apart, for instance. The ad diminished Deere's logo in consumers' minds, a court ruled.[231]

Trademark infringement occurs when there is a likelihood of confusion.[232] Facebook claimed likelihood of confusion and won a trademark infringement lawsuit against a social networking site named Teachbook. Teachbook aimed its site at teachers, stating that many schools forbid teachers from using Facebook because students might learn teachers' personal information. There was a likelihood of confusion between the two marks because the "Teachbook mark is highly similar to the registered Facebook mark in appearance, sound, meaning, and commercial impression," a federal district court found.[233] Both services offer a similar product through the Internet, the court added.

Similar—even identical—marks may not cause confusion if the goods for which the marks are used are not the same. Wendy's automobile parts may coexist with Wendy's restaurants if a court says consumers would not think the restaurant company also owns the auto parts store.

Courts use a variety of criteria to determine whether consumers likely will be confused by similar marks. These include the marks' similarities, the similarities of products or services for which the marks are used, how consumers purchase the goods (impulse buying or careful consideration), how well known the first-used mark is, actual confusion that can be proved and how long both marks have been used without confusion.[234]

Using a famous trademark in a way that disparages the mark or diminishes its effectiveness is known as "dilution." Dilution may happen in two ways.[235] First, a product name similar to a well-known trademark could make the famous mark less distinctive. Consumers' attention to the famous mark could be distracted by the similar product name. What the law calls "blurring" whittles away a trademark's selling power. Second, a poorly made product using a name similar to a famous trademark could cause consumers to think less of the well-known mark. This is "tarnishment," linking a substandard or unsavory product with the famous mark.[236]

Congress revised federal antidilution in response to a U.S. Supreme Court decision involving an "adult novelties" store in Elizabethtown, Ky. The store initially opened as Victor's Secret. After Victoria's Secret, operating more than 750 retail

realWorld Law

Diluting a Trademark

A federal appellate court used the famous jewelry store Tiffany's name to help explain what the word "dilution" means in trademark law:

> Suppose an upscale restaurant calls itself "Tiffany." There is little danger that the consuming public will think it's dealing with a branch of the Tiffany jewelry store if it patronizes this restaurant. But when consumers next see the name "Tiffany" they may think about both the restaurant and the jewelry store, and if so the efficacy of the name as an identifier of the store will be diminished. . . . So "blurring" is one form of dilution.
>
> Now suppose that the "restaurant" that adopts the name "Tiffany" is actually a striptease joint. Again, and indeed even more certainly than in the previous case, consumers will not think the striptease joint under common ownership with the jewelry store. But because of the inveterate tendency of the human mind to proceed by association, every time they think of the word "Tiffany" their image of the fancy jewelry store will be tarnished by the association of the word with the strip joint. So "tarnishment" is a second form of dilution.[1]

1. Ty, Inc. v. Perryman, 306 F.3d 509, 511 (7th Cir. 2002), *cert. denied,* 538 U.S. 971 (2003).

stores and distributing 400 million catalogs annually, asked the store's owners not to use the name Victor's Secret, the owners called it Victor's Little Secret. Victoria's Secret sued for trademark dilution. The Supreme Court said Victoria's Secret had to show actual dilution of its trademark, which might be difficult for the large corporation to do.[237] The Court said there is "a complete absence of evidence of any lessening of the capacity of the Victoria's Secret mark to identify . . . goods . . . sold in Victoria's Secret stores or advertised in its catalogs."[238]

Congress rejected that approach. Its revised antidilution law requires companies with famous trademarks to show only a likelihood of dilution, not actual dilution of its trademark's effectiveness. But the core of the antidilution law remains the same: A company does not have to prove it is likely consumers will be confused between a famous trademark and a similar product or service name. Rather, the company only has to show another firm's similar mark has diminished the well-known mark's distinctiveness or injured its reputation.

Nearly half the states have antidilution statutes. These laws protect dilution of all marks used in the state, not just the famous marks the federal antidilution law protects.

Several remedies are available for trademark infringement. First, anyone notified of an alleged infringement may stop using the disputed mark voluntarily. Second, a court may issue an order requiring the infringing company to stop using the mark. If a mark owner is able to prove actual consumer confusion, a court may award monetary damages against the infringer.

Trademark Infringement Defenses

The Lanham Act lists nine defenses to a trademark infringement action.[239] Most turn on disputed facts. For example, a defendant might argue that the registered trademark was obtained fraudulently, that the trademark has been abandoned and no longer is in use or that the mark misrepresents a product's origin. A defendant also might claim to have used and registered the mark first.

The Lanham Act also provides a fair use defense.[240] This permits using one company's trademark to describe another company's product. Courts will accept the fair use defense if the defendant used the mark to describe its goods and not as a trademark. Also, the use cannot cause customer confusion. For example, when a computer user accessed a contact lens company's website, competitors' ads popped up. The contacts company sued the firm causing the pop-up ads to appear, claiming trademark infringement. A federal appellate court ruled that the pop-up ad firm did not suggest it supplied goods or services from the contacts company. Therefore, it did not use the trademark in an infringing way. Rather, the pop-up ad firm's use of the contacts company's trademark was fair use.[241]

Referring to the defendant's own product or service by using the plaintiff's mark without permission also may be a fair use. This may be done in comparative advertising, or in other contexts. In one case, two newspapers used the trademarked name of a band, New Kids on the Block, to promote the newspapers' telephone polls about the band. The papers used the band's name to describe the papers' own product: the telephone poll. A court found this a fair use because the band could not be identified without using its trademarked name, and the papers did not suggest that the band endorsed the poll.[242]

The antidilution law also provides a fair use exception. Using a famous trademark for comparative advertising, parody or all forms of news reporting and commentary is not an infringement.[243]

SUMMARY

THE FEDERAL LANHAM ACT PROTECTS trademarks from infringement. The common law protects unregistered marks within the geographic area where they are used. Marks may be words, designs, colors and other devices identifying the source of products or services. A trademark will be protected only if it is distinctive. Distinctiveness ranges from strongly distinctive to merely descriptive and generic. Merely descriptive and generic marks cannot be protected.

A mark must be registered with the U.S. Patent and Trademark Office to have protection under the Lanham Act. Registering is a complex process, and marks may be rejected for a variety of reasons.

Domain names may be registered as trademarks. The federal Anticybersquatting Consumer Protection Act is intended to prevent people from claiming domain names only to sell them to companies or individuals. ∎

Cases for Study

Thinking About It

The U.S. Supreme Court decides few cases concerning copyright law. The following excerpts are from two of the six copyright cases the Court has decided in the 21st century. As you read these case excerpts, keep the following questions in mind:

- Does the U.S. Supreme Court seem to be favoring copyright holders or users of copyrighted material?

- Do you agree with *Golan*'s interpretation of "for a limited time" in the U.S. Constitution's copyright provision? Why or why not?

- Do you agree with the distinction drawn in Grokster between that case and the Sony decision allowing home taping of television programs? Why or why not?

Golan v. Holder
SUPREME COURT OF THE UNITED STATES
132 S. Ct. 873 (2012)

JUSTICE RUTH BADER GINSBURG delivered the Court's opinion:

The Berne Convention for the Protection of Literary and Artistic Works (Berne Convention or Berne), which took effect in 1886, is the principal accord governing international copyright relations. Latecomer to the international copyright regime launched by Berne, the United States joined the Convention in 1989. To perfect U.S. implementation of Berne, and as part of our response to the Uruguay Round of multilateral trade negotiations, Congress, in 1994, gave works enjoying copyright protection abroad the same full protection available to U.S. works. Congress did so in Section 514 of the Uruguay Round Agreements Act (URAA), which grants copyright protection to preexisting works of Berne member countries, protected in their country of origin, but lacking protection in the United States for any of three reasons: The United States did not protect works from the country of origin at the time of publication; the United States did not protect sound recordings fixed before 1972; or

the author had failed to comply with U.S. statutory formalities (formalities Congress no longer requires as prerequisites to copyright protection).

The URAA accords no protection to a foreign work after its full copyright term has expired, causing it to fall into the public domain, whether under the laws of the country of origin or of this country. Works encompassed by Section 514 are granted the protection they would have enjoyed had the United States maintained copyright relations with the author's country or removed formalities incompatible with Berne. Foreign authors, however, gain no credit for the protection they lacked in years prior to Section 514's enactment. They therefore enjoy fewer total years of exclusivity than do their U.S. counterparts. As a consequence of the barriers to U.S. copyright protection prior to the enactment of Section 514, foreign works "restored" to protection by the measure had entered the public domain in this country. To cushion the impact of their placement in protected status, Congress included in Section 514 ameliorating accommodations for parties who had exploited affected works before the URAA was enacted.

Petitioners include orchestra conductors, musicians, publishers, and others who formerly enjoyed free access to works Section 514 removed from the public domain. They maintain that the Constitution's Copyright and Patent Clause and the First Amendment both decree the invalidity of Section 514. Under those prescriptions of our highest law, petitioners assert, a work that has entered the public domain, for whatever reason, must forever remain there.

In accord with the judgment of the Tenth Circuit, we conclude that Section 514 does not transgress constitutional limitations on Congress' authority. Neither the Copyright and Patent Clause nor the First Amendment, we hold, makes the public domain, in any and all cases, a territory that works may never exit. . . .

We first address petitioners' argument that Congress lacked authority, under the Copyright Clause, to enact ß514. The Constitution states that "Congress shall have Power . . . [t]o promote the Progress of Science . . . by securing for limited Times to Authors . . . the exclusive Right to their . . . Writings." Petitioners find in this grant of authority an impenetrable barrier to the extension of copyright protection to authors whose writings, for whatever reason, are in the public domain. We see no such barrier in the text of the Copyright Clause, historical practice, or our precedents.

The text of the Copyright Clause does not exclude application of copyright protection to works in the public domain. Petitioners' contrary argument relies primarily on the Constitution's confinement of a copyright's lifespan to a "limited Tim[e]." "Removing works from the public domain," they contend, "violates the 'limited [t]imes' restriction by turning a fixed and predictable period into one that can be reset or resurrected at any time, even after it expires."

Our decision in *Eldred* is largely dispositive of petitioners' limited-time argument. There we addressed the question whether Congress violated the Copyright Clause when it extended, by 20 years, the terms of existing copyrights. Ruling that Congress acted within constitutional bounds, we declined to infer from the text of the Copyright Clause "the command that a time prescription, once set, becomes forever 'fixed' or 'inalterable.'" "The word 'limited,'" we observed, "does not convey a meaning so constricted." Rather, the term is best understood to mean "confine[d] within certain bounds," ""estrain[ed]," or "circumscribed." The construction petitioners tender closely resembles the definition rejected in *Eldred* and is similarly infirm. . . .

Carried to its logical conclusion, petitioners persist, the Government's position would allow Congress to institute a second "limited" term after the first expires, a third after that, and so on. Thus, as long as Congress legislated in installments, perpetual copyright terms would be achievable. As in *Eldred*, the hypothetical legislative misbehavior petitioners posit is far afield from the case before us. In aligning the United States with other nations bound by the Berne Convention, and thereby according equitable treatment to once disfavored foreign authors, Congress can hardly be charged with a design to move stealthily toward a regime of perpetual copyrights. . . .

Petitioners' ultimate argument as to the Copyright and Patent Clause concerns its initial words. Congress is empowered to "promote the Progress of Science and useful Arts" by enacting systems of copyright and patent protection. Perhaps counterintuitively for the contemporary reader, Congress' copyright authority is tied to the progress of science; its patent authority, to the progress of the useful arts.

The "Progress of Science," petitioners acknowledge, refers broadly to "the creation and spread of knowledge and learning." They nevertheless argue that federal legislation cannot serve the Clause's aim unless the legislation "spur[s] the creation of . . . new works." Because Section 514 deals solely with works already created, petitioners urge, it "provides no plausible incentive to create new works" and is therefore invalid.

The creation of at least one new work, however, is not the sole way Congress may promote knowledge and learning. In *Eldred*, we rejected an argument nearly identical to the one petitioners rehearse. The *Eldred* petitioners urged that the "CTEA's extension of existing copyrights categorically fails to 'promote the Progress of Science,' . . . because it does not stimulate the creation of new works." In response to this argument, we held that the Copyright Clause does not demand that each copyright provision, examined discretely, operate to induce new works. Rather, we explained, the Clause "empowers Congress to determine the intellectual property regimes that, overall, in that body's judgment, will serve the ends of the Clause." And those permissible ends, we held, extended beyond the creation of new works.

Even were we writing on a clean slate, petitioners' argument would be unavailing. Nothing in the text of the Copyright Clause confines the "Progress of Science" exclusively to "incentives for creation." Evidence from the founding, moreover, suggests that inducing *dissemination*—as opposed to creation—was viewed as an appropriate means to promote science. Until 1976, in fact, Congress made "federal copyright contingent on publication, [thereby] providing incentives not primarily for creation," but for dissemination. Our decisions correspondingly recognize that "copyright supplies the economic incentive to create *and disseminate* ideas."

Considered against this backdrop, Section 514 falls comfortably within Congress' authority under the Copyright Clause. Congress rationally could have concluded that adherence to Berne "promotes the diffusion of knowledge." A well-functioning international copyright system would likely encourage the dissemination of existing and future works. Full compliance with Berne, Congress had reason to believe, would expand the foreign markets available to U.S. authors and invigorate protection against piracy of U.S. works abroad, thereby benefitting copyright intensive industries stateside and inducing greater investment in the creative process.

The provision of incentives for the creation of new works is surely an essential means to advance the spread of knowledge and learning. We hold, however, that it is not the sole means Congress may use "[t]o promote the Progress of Science." Congress determined that exemplary adherence to Berne would serve the objectives of the Copyright Clause. We have no warrant to reject the rational judgment Congress made.

We next explain why the First Amendment does not inhibit the restoration authorized by Section 514. To do so, we first recapitulate the relevant part of our

pathmarking decision in *Eldred*. The petitioners in *Eldred*, like those here, argued that Congress had violated not only the "limited Times" prescription of the Copyright Clause. In addition, and independently, the *Eldred* petitioners charged, Congress had offended the First Amendment's freedom of expression guarantee. The CTEA's 20-year enlargement of a copyright's duration, we held in *Eldred*, offended neither provision.

Concerning the First Amendment, we recognized that some restriction on expression is the inherent and intended effect of every grant of copyright. Noting that the "Copyright Clause and the First Amendment were adopted close in time," we observed that the Framers regarded copyright protection not simply as a limit on the manner in which expressive works may be used. They also saw copyright as an "engine of free expression: By establishing a marketable right to the use of one's expression, copyright supplies the economic incentive to create and disseminate ideas."

We then described the "traditional contours" of copyright protection, i.e., the "idea/expression dichotomy" and the "fair use" defense. Both are recognized in our jurisprudence as "built-in First Amendment accommodations."

The idea/expression dichotomy is [part of the U.S. copyright law:] "In no case does copyright protec[t] . . . any idea, procedure, process, system, method of operation, concept, principle, or discovery . . . described, explained, illustrated, or embodied in [the copyrighted] work." "Due to this [idea/expression] distinction, every idea, theory, and fact in a copyrighted work becomes instantly available for public exploitation at the moment of publication"; the author's expression alone gains copyright protection.

The second "traditional contour," the fair use defense, [also is in the copyright law]: "[T]he fair use of a copyrighted work, including such use by reproduction in copies . . ., for purposes such as criticism, comment, news reporting, teaching (including multiple copies for classroom use), scholarship, or research, is not an infringement of copyright." This limitation on exclusivity "allows the public to use not only facts and ideas contained in a copyrighted work, but also [the author's] expression itself in certain circumstances."

Given the "speech-protective purposes and safeguards" embraced by copyright law, we concluded in *Eldred* that there was no call for the heightened review petitioners sought in that case. We reach the same conclusion here. Section 514 leaves undisturbed the "idea/expression" distinction and the "fair use" defense. Moreover, Congress adopted measures to ease the transition from a national scheme to an international copyright regime: It deferred the date from which enforcement runs, and it cushioned the impact of restoration on "reliance parties" who exploited foreign works denied protection before Section 514 took effect.

Petitioners attempt to distinguish their challenge from the one turned away in *Eldred*. First Amendment interests of a higher order are at stake here, petitioners say, because they—unlike their counterparts in *Eldred*—enjoyed "vested rights" in works that had already entered the public domain. The limited rights they retain under copyright law's "built-in safeguards" are, in their view, no substitute for the unlimited use they enjoyed before Section 514's enactment. Nor, petitioners urge, does Section 514's "unprecedented" foray into the public domain possess the historical pedigree that supported the term extension at issue in *Eldred*.

However spun, these contentions depend on an argument we considered and rejected above, namely, that the Constitution renders the public domain largely untouchable by Congress. Petitioners here attempt to achieve under the banner of the First Amendment what they could not win under the Copyright Clause: On their view of the Copyright Clause, the public domain is inviolable; as they read the First Amendment, the public domain is policed through heightened judicial scrutiny of Congress' means and ends. As we have already shown, the text of the Copyright Clause and the historical record scarcely establish that "once a work enters the public domain," Congress cannot permit anyone—"not even the creator—[to] copyright it." And nothing in the historical record, congressional practice, or our own jurisprudence warrants exceptional First Amendment solicitude for copyrighted works that were once in the public domain. Neither this challenge nor that raised in *Eldred*, we stress, allege Congress transgressed a generally applicable First Amendment prohibition; we are not faced, for example, with copyright protection that hinges on the author's viewpoint. . . .

Section 514, we add, does not impose a blanket prohibition on public access. Petitioners protest that fair use and the idea/expression dichotomy "are plainly inadequate to protect the speech and expression rights that Section 514 took from petitioners, or . . . the public"—that is, "the unrestricted right to perform, copy, teach and distribute the *entire* work, for any reason." "Playing a few bars of a Shostakovich symphony," petitioners observe, "is no substitute for performing the entire work."

But Congress has not put petitioners in this bind. The question here, as in *Eldred*, is whether would-be users must pay for their desired use of the author's expression, or else limit their exploitation to "fair use" of that work. Prokofiev's Peter and the Wolf could once be performed free of charge; after Section 514 the right to perform it must be obtained in the marketplace. This is the same marketplace, of course, that exists for the music of Prokofiev's U.S. contemporaries: works of Copland and Bernstein, for example, that enjoy copyright protection, but nevertheless appear regularly in the programs of U.S. concertgoers. . . .

Congress determined that U.S. interests were best served by our full participation in the dominant system of international copyright protection. Those interests include ensuring exemplary compliance with our international obligations, securing greater protection for U.S. authors abroad, and remedying unequal treatment of foreign authors. The judgment Section 514 expresses lies well within the ken of the political branches. It is our obligation, of course, to determine whether the action Congress took, wise or not, encounters any constitutional shoal. For the reasons stated, we are satisfied it does not. The judgment of the Court of Appeals for the Tenth Circuit is therefore affirmed.

Justice Kagan took no part in the consideration or decision of this case.

Metro-Goldwyn-Mayer Studios, Inc. v. Grokster, Ltd.
SUPREME COURT OF THE UNITED STATES
545 U.S. 913 (2005)

JUSTICE DAVID SOUTER delivered the Court's opinion:

The question is under what circumstances the distributor of a product capable of both lawful and unlawful use is liable for acts of copyright infringement by third parties using the product. We hold that one who distributes a device with the object of promoting its use to infringe copyright, as shown by clear expression or other affirmative steps taken to foster infringement, is liable for the resulting acts of infringement by third parties.

Respondents Grokster, Ltd., and StreamCast Networks, Inc., defendants in the trial court, distribute free software products that allow computer users to share electronic files through peer-to-peer networks, so called because users' computers communicate directly with each other, not through central servers. The advantage of peer-to-peer networks over information networks of other types shows up in their substantial and growing popularity. Because they need no central computer server to mediate the exchange of information or files among users, the high-bandwidth communications capacity for a server may be dispensed with, and the need for costly server storage space is eliminated. Since copies of a file (particularly a popular one) are available on many users' computers, file requests and retrievals may be faster than on other types of networks, and since file exchanges do not travel through a server, communications can take place between any computers that remain connected to the network without risk that a glitch in the server will disable the network in its entirety. Given these benefits in security, cost, and efficiency, peer-to-peer networks are employed to store and distribute electronic files by universities, government agencies, corporations, and libraries, among others.

Other users of peer-to-peer networks include individual recipients of Grokster's and StreamCast's software, and although the networks that they enjoy through using the software can be used to share any type of digital file, they have prominently employed those networks in sharing copyrighted music and video files without authorization. A group of copyright holders (MGM for short, but including motion picture studios, recording companies, songwriters, and music publishers) sued Grokster and StreamCast for their users' copyright infringements, alleging that they knowingly and intentionally distributed their software to enable users to reproduce and distribute the copyrighted works in violation of the Copyright Act. MGM sought damages and an injunction.

Discovery during the litigation revealed the way the software worked, the business aims of each defendant company, and the predilections of the users. Grokster's eponymous software employs what is known as FastTrack technology, a protocol developed by others and licensed to Grokster. StreamCast distributes a very similar product except that its software, called Morpheus, relies on what is known as Gnutella technology. A user who downloads and installs either software possesses the protocol to send requests for files directly to the computers of others using software compatible with FastTrack or Gnutella. On the FastTrack network opened by the Grokster software, the user's request goes to a computer given an indexing capacity by the software and designated a supernode, or to some other computer with comparable power and capacity to collect temporary indexes of the files available on the computers of users connected to it. The supernode (or indexing computer) searches its own index and may communicate the search request to other supernodes. If the file is found, the supernode discloses its location to the computer requesting it, and the requesting user can download the file directly from the computer located. The copied file is placed in a designated sharing folder on the requesting user's computer, where it is available for other users to download in turn, along with any other file in that folder.

In the Gnutella network made available by Morpheus, the process is mostly the same, except that in some versions of the Gnutella protocol there are no supernodes. In these versions, peer computers using the protocol communicate directly with each other. When a user enters a search request into the Morpheus software, it sends the request to computers connected with it, which in turn pass the request along to other connected peers. The search results are communicated to the requesting computer, and the user can download desired files directly from peers' computers. As this description indicates, Grokster and StreamCast use no servers to intercept the content of the search requests or to mediate the file transfers conducted by users of the software, there being no central point through which the substance of the communications passes in either direction.

Although Grokster and StreamCast . . . argue that potential noninfringing uses of their software are significant in kind, even if infrequent in practice. Some musical performers, for example, have gained new audiences by distributing their copyrighted works for free across peer-to-peer networks, and some distributors of unprotected content have used peer-to-peer networks to disseminate files, Shakespeare being an example. . . .

. . . MGM's evidence gives reason to think that the vast majority of users' downloads are acts of infringement, and because well over 100 million copies of the software in question are known to have been downloaded, and billions of files are shared across the FastTrack and Gnutella networks each month, the probable scope of copyright infringement is staggering.

Grokster and StreamCast concede the infringement in most downloads, . . . and it is uncontested that they are aware that users employ their software primarily to download copyrighted files, even if the decentralized FastTrack and Gnutella networks fail to reveal which files are being copied, and when. From time to time, moreover, the companies have learned about their users' infringement directly, as from users who have sent e-mail to each company with questions about playing copyrighted movies they had downloaded, to whom the companies have responded with guidance. And MGM notified the companies of 8 million copyrighted files that could be obtained using their software.

Grokster and StreamCast are not, however, merely passive recipients of information about infringing use. The record is replete with evidence that from the moment Grokster and StreamCast began to distribute their free software, each one clearly voiced the objective that recipients use it to download copyrighted works, and each took active steps to encourage infringement.

After the notorious file-sharing service, Napster, was sued by copyright holders for facilitation of copyright infringement, StreamCast gave away a software program of a kind known as OpenNap, designed as compatible with the Napster program and open to Napster users for downloading files from other Napster and OpenNap users' computers. Evidence indicates that "[i]t was always [StreamCast's] intent to use [its OpenNap network] to be able to capture email addresses of [its] initial target market so that [it] could promote [its] StreamCast Morpheus interface to them"; indeed, the OpenNap program was engineered "to leverage Napster's 50 million user base." . . .

. . . StreamCast developed promotional materials to market its service as the best Napster alternative. . . .

The evidence that Grokster sought to capture the market of former Napster users is sparser but revealing, for Grokster launched its own OpenNap system called Swaptor and inserted digital codes into its Web site so that computer users using Web search engines to look for "Napster" or "[f]ree filesharing" would be directed to the Grokster Web site, where they could download the Grokster software. And Grokster's name is an apparent derivative of Napster. . . .

In addition to this evidence of express promotion, marketing, and intent to promote further, the business models employed by Grokster and StreamCast confirm that their principal object was use of their software to download copyrighted works. Grokster and StreamCast receive no revenue from users, who obtain the software itself for nothing. Instead, both companies generate income by selling advertising space, and they stream the advertising to Grokster and Morpheus users while they are employing the programs. As the number of users of each program increases, advertising opportunities become worth more. While there is doubtless some demand for free Shakespeare, the evidence shows that substantive volume is a function of free access to copyrighted work. Users seeking Top 40 songs, for example, or the latest release by Modest Mouse, are certain to be far more numerous than those seeking a free Decameron, and Grokster and StreamCast translated that demand into dollars.

Finally, there is no evidence that either company made an effort to filter copyrighted material from users' downloads or otherwise impede the sharing of copyrighted files. Although Grokster appears to have sent e-mails warning users about infringing content when it received threatening notice from the copyright holders, it never blocked anyone from continuing to use its software to share copyrighted files. StreamCast not only rejected another company's offer of help to monitor infringement, but blocked the Internet Protocol addresses of entities it believed were trying to engage in such monitoring on its networks. . . .

In *Sony Corp. v. Universal City Studios,* this Court addressed a claim that secondary liability for infringement can arise from the very distribution of a commercial product. There, the product, novel at the time, was what we know today as the videocassette recorder or VCR. Copyright holders sued Sony as the manufacturer, claiming it was contributorily liable for infringement that occurred when VCR owners taped copyrighted programs because it supplied the means used to infringe, and it had constructive knowledge that infringement would occur. At the trial on the merits, the evidence showed that the principal use of the VCR was for "time-shifting," or taping a program for later viewing at a more convenient time, which the Court found to be a fair, not an infringing, use. There was no evidence that Sony had expressed an object of bringing about taping in violation of copyright or had taken active steps to increase its profits from unlawful taping. Although Sony's advertisements urged consumers to buy the VCR to "record favorite shows" or "build a library" of recorded programs, neither of these uses was necessarily infringing.

On those facts, with no evidence of stated or indicated intent to promote infringing uses, the only conceivable basis for imposing liability was on a theory of contributory infringement arising from its sale of VCRs to consumers with knowledge that some

would use them to infringe. But because the VCR was "capable of commercially significant noninfringing uses," we held the manufacturer could not be faulted solely on the basis of its distribution. . . .

In sum, where an article is "good for nothing else" but infringement, there is no legitimate public interest in its unlicensed availability, and there is no injustice in presuming or imputing an intent to infringe. Conversely, the doctrine absolves the equivocal conduct of selling an item with substantial lawful as well as unlawful uses, and limits liability to instances of more acute fault than the mere understanding that some of one's products will be misused. It leaves breathing room for innovation and a vigorous commerce. . . .

Sony's rule limits imputing culpable intent as a matter of law from the characteristics or uses of a distributed product. But nothing in *Sony* requires courts to ignore evidence of intent if there is such evidence, and the case was never meant to foreclose rules of fault-based liability derived from the common law. Thus, where evidence goes beyond a product's characteristics or the knowledge that it may be put to infringing uses, and shows statements or actions directed to promoting infringement, *Sony*'s staple-article rule will not preclude liability. . . .

The rule on inducement of infringement as developed in the early cases is no different today. Evidence of "active steps . . . taken to encourage direct infringement," such as advertising an infringing use or instructing how to engage in an infringing use, show an affirmative intent that the product be used to infringe, and a showing that infringement was encouraged overcomes the law's reluctance to find liability when a defendant merely sells a commercial product suitable for some lawful use.

For the same reasons that *Sony* took the staple-article doctrine of patent law as a model for its copyright safe-harbor rule, the inducement rule, too, is a sensible one for copyright. We adopt it here, holding that one who distributes a device with the object of promoting its use to infringe copyright, as shown by clear expression or other affirmative steps taken to foster infringement, is liable for the resulting acts of infringement by third parties. We are, of course, mindful of the need to keep from trenching on regular commerce or discouraging the development of technologies with lawful and unlawful potential. Accordingly, just as *Sony* did not find intentional inducement despite the knowledge of the VCR manufacturer that its device could be used to infringe, mere knowledge of infringing potential or of actual infringing uses would not be enough here to subject a distributor to liability. Nor would ordinary acts incident to product distribution, such as offering customers technical support or product updates, support liability in themselves. The inducement rule, instead, premises liability on purposeful, culpable expression and conduct, and thus does nothing to compromise legitimate commerce or discourage innovation having a lawful promise.

The only apparent question about treating MGM's evidence as sufficient to withstand summary judgment under the theory of inducement goes to the need on MGM's part to adduce evidence that StreamCast and Grokster communicated an inducing message to their software users. The classic instance of inducement is by advertisement or solicitation that broadcasts a message designed to stimulate others to commit violations. MGM claims that such a message is shown here. It is undisputed that StreamCast beamed onto the computer screens of users of Napster-compatible programs ads urging the adoption of its OpenNap program, which was designed, as its name implied, to invite the custom of patrons of Napster, then under attack in the courts for facilitating massive infringement. Those who accepted StreamCast's OpenNap program were offered software to perform the same services, which a factfinder could conclude would readily have been understood in the Napster market as the ability to download copyrighted music files. Grokster distributed an electronic newsletter containing links to articles promoting its software's ability to access popular copyrighted music. And anyone whose Napster or free file-sharing searches turned up a link to Grokster would have understood Grokster to be offering the same file-sharing ability as Napster, and to the same people who probably used Napster for infringing downloads; that would also have been the understanding of anyone offered Grokster's suggestively named Swaptor software, its version of OpenNap. And both companies communicated a clear message by responding affirmatively to requests for help in locating and playing copyrighted materials.

In StreamCast's case, of course, the evidence just described was supplemented by other unequivocal indications of unlawful purpose in the internal communications and advertising designs aimed at Napster users ("When the lights went off at Napster . . . where did the users go?") Whether the messages were communicated is not to the point on this record. The function of the message in the theory of inducement is to prove by a defendant's own statements that his unlawful purpose disqualifies him from claiming protection (and incidentally to point to actual violators likely to be found among those who hear or read the message). Proving that a message was sent out, then, is the preeminent but not exclusive way of showing that active steps were taken with the purpose of bringing about infringing acts, and of showing that infringing acts took place by using the device distributed. Here, the summary judgment record is replete with other evidence that Grokster and StreamCast, unlike the manufacturer and distributor in *Sony,* acted with a purpose to cause copyright violations by use of software suitable for illegal use.

Three features of this evidence of intent are particularly notable. First, each company showed itself to be aiming to satisfy a known source of demand for copyright infringement, the market comprising former Napster users. StreamCast's internal documents made constant reference to Napster, it initially distributed its Morpheus software through an OpenNap program compatible with Napster, it advertised its OpenNap program to Napster users, and its Morpheus software functions as Napster did except that it could be used to distribute more kinds of files, including copyrighted movies and software programs. Grokster's name is apparently derived from Napster, it too initially offered an OpenNap program, its software's function is likewise comparable to Napster's, and it attempted to divert queries for Napster onto its own Web site. Grokster and StreamCast's efforts to supply services to former Napster users, deprived of a mechanism to copy and distribute what were overwhelmingly infringing files, indicate a principal, if not exclusive, intent on the part of each to bring about infringement.

Second, this evidence of unlawful objective is given added significance by MGM's showing that neither company attempted to develop filtering tools or other mechanisms to diminish the infringing activity using their software. While the Ninth Circuit treated the defendants' failure to develop such tools as irrelevant because they lacked an independent duty to monitor their users' activity, we think this evidence underscores Grokster's and StreamCast's intentional facilitation of their users' infringement.

Third, there is a further complement to the direct evidence of unlawful objective. It is useful to recall that StreamCast and Grokster make money by selling advertising space, by directing ads to the screens of computers employing their software. As the record shows, the more the software is used, the more ads are sent out and the greater the advertising revenue becomes. Since the extent of the software's use determines the gain to the distributors, the commercial sense of their enterprise turns on high-volume use, which the record shows is infringing. This evidence alone would not justify an inference of unlawful intent, but viewed in the context of the entire record its import is clear.

The unlawful objective is unmistakable.

In addition to intent to bring about infringement and distribution of a device suitable for infringing use, the inducement theory of course requires evidence of actual infringement by recipients of the device, the software in this case. As the account of the facts indicates, there is evidence of infringement on a gigantic scale, and there is no serious issue of the adequacy of MGM's showing on this point in order to survive the companies' summary judgment requests. Although an exact calculation of infringing use, as a basis for a claim of damages, is subject to dispute, there is no question that the summary judgment evidence is at least adequate to entitle MGM to go forward with claims for damages and equitable relief.

In sum, this case is significantly different from *Sony* and reliance on that case to rule in favor of StreamCast and Grokster was error. *Sony* dealt with a claim of liability based solely on distributing a product with alternative lawful and unlawful uses, with knowledge that some users would follow the unlawful course. The case struck a balance between the interests of protection and innovation by holding that the product's capability of substantial lawful employment should bar the imputation of fault and consequent secondary liability for the unlawful acts of others.

MGM's evidence in this case most obviously addresses a different basis of liability for distributing a product open to alternative uses. Here, evidence of the distributors' words and deeds going beyond distribution as such shows a purpose to cause and profit from third-party acts of copyright infringement. If liability for inducing infringement is ultimately found, it will not be on the basis of presuming or imputing fault, but from inferring a patently illegal objective from statements and actions showing what that objective was.

There is substantial evidence in MGM's favor on all elements of inducement, and summary judgment in favor of Grokster and StreamCast was error. On remand, reconsideration of MGM's motion for summary judgment will be in order.

The judgment of the Court of Appeals is vacated, and the case is remanded for further proceedings consistent with this opinion.

It is so ordered.

Chapter 14

Our question is whether speech which does "no more than propose a commercial transaction," is so removed from any "exposition of ideas" and from "truth, science, morality and arts in general, in its diffusion of liberal sentiments on the administration of Government," that it lacks all protection. Our answer is that it is not. . . . [T]he particular consumer's interest in the free flow of commercial information . . . may be as keen, if not keener by far, than his interest in the day's most urgent political debate.

U.S. Supreme Court Justice Harry Blackmun[1]

Amid litigation losses, the FTC in 2013 backed away from its mandate that half of every cigarette pack carry an image like one of these.

Advertising
When Speech and Commerce Converge

The Evolution of the Commercial Speech Doctrine

Controlled Substances and Activities

Corporate Speech Regulation

Legislative and Agency Advertising Regulation

The Federal Trade Commission

Other Administrative Regulation

Internet Advertising

Cases for Study

➤ *Central Hudson Gas & Electric Corp. v. Public Service Commission of New York*

➤ *Sorrell v. IMS Health Inc.*

Suppose . . .

. . . that a state law prohibits drug marketers and data-mining companies from buying doctor's prescription records from pharmacies. The state says the law helps protect the privacy of doctors and prevent aggressive drug marketing that would distort doctors' choices of which drugs to prescribe. But the law allows access to the prescription records by anyone other than a drug company marketer or the companies that compile data for drug companies. State legislative records show that the law is designed to encourage sales of generic over more costly brand-name drugs.

Does the law regulate commercial activity or commercial speech? If it regulates speech, is it a permissible exercise of government authority or does it unconstitutionally target speech because of government disfavor with its content? Look for answers to these questions when the case of *Sorrell v. IMS Health Inc.*[2] is discussed later in this chapter and excerpted at the chapter's end.

A s the lifeblood for many media organizations, advertising's First Amendment protection is important to journalists and their employers as well as to advertisers. The Supreme Court long excluded advertising, or commercial speech, from First Amendment protection because it advanced profit rather than core free speech values.[3] Although commercial speech has moved from the outer fringe of First Amendment protection, it remains unclear, at best, whether commercial speech enjoys the same level of protection as political speech.

A 1942 U.S. Supreme Court case about a used submarine is the starting point for modern commercial speech doctrine. An entrepreneur named F.J. Chrestensen bought a submarine from the U.S. Navy and docked it at a New York City pier, hoping to attract people for paid tours by distributing handbills. When Chrestensen learned that city law prohibited commercial handbill distribution, he printed a protest of that law on the flipside of the advertisement. When he learned that the inclusion of this "political speech" did not immunize him from prosecution, he filed suit seeking an injunction to bar interference with his leafleting. The injunction was granted and affirmed on appeal. The U.S. Supreme Court, however, reversed.

The Court viewed Chrestensen's handbill as little more than advertising, which it said had no First Amendment protection and was subject to reasonable regulation. Because "the streets are proper places for the exercise of the freedom of communicating information and disseminating opinion," the Court said,[4] states and municipalities may not unduly limit such communication. However, "the Constitution imposes no such restraint on government as respects purely commercial speech."[5] Many, including judges, interpreted the *Valentine v. Chrestensen* to mean that advertising fell outside the scope of First Amendment protection. Over time, the legal status of commercial speech changed.

The Evolution of the Commercial Speech Doctrine

Courts use the term "commercial speech" to mean ads that propose commercial transactions. Other kinds of ads—political, informational or issue ads, for example—generally are specifically labeled as such.

The landmark ruling that gave advertising its push under the First Amendment umbrella was *New York Times Co. v. Sullivan*, the Supreme Court's 1964 libel ruling discussed in Chapter 4. The case involved a paid advertisement for the civil rights movement, and Justice William Brennan's opinion for the Court began to clarify the meaning of *Chrestensen*: "That the Times was paid for publishing the advertisement is as immaterial in this connection as is the fact that newspapers and books are sold."[6] Although in *Chrestensen* the submarine tour handbill did no more than advertise a commercial transaction, in *Sullivan* the ad communicated information, expressed opinions and sought support "on behalf of a movement whose existence and objectives are matters of the highest public interest and concern."[7] The Court categorized this as paid political speech. The Supreme Court further acknowledged First Amendment protection for commercial speech when it affirmed the ability of governments to regulate advertising but suggested that (1) advertising a commercial transaction may serve a First Amendment interest and (2) the interest could outweigh the government's interest in regulating the advertising.[8]

Then, in a case involving a New York-based abortion referral service's paid ads in a Virginia newspaper (a state that made it illegal to encourage or obtain an abortion), the Court ruled that the state could not prohibit the advertisements.[9] By the time the Supreme Court heard the appeal of newspaper publisher Jeffrey Bigelow, its ruling in *Roe v. Wade*[10] had made most abortions legal, and the Court found it difficult to justify criminalizing advertisements for a legal service. Moreover, in *Bigelow v. Virginia,* the Court again found that the ad was not purely commercial speech. Instead, it "did more than simply propose a commercial transaction. It contained factual material of clear 'public interest.'"[11]

The *Bigelow* Court went further. It said, "Our cases . . . clearly establish that speech is not stripped of First Amendment protection merely because it appears in [the] form" of paid commercial advertisements.[12] The fact that the abortion referral service ads had commercial aspects or reflected the advertiser's commercial interests, the Court said, did not erase all First Amendment guarantees. The *Bigelow* Court reiterated that *Chrestensen* did not immunize all statutes regulating commercial advertising from First Amendment challenge.[13] While the Court did not say explicitly that purely commercial speech had First Amendment protection, it said that commercial speech does not automatically lack constitutional protection.

Next the Court considered a Virginia state regulation that prohibited licensed pharmacists from advertising the price of prescription drugs. The rule, intended to maintain professionalism and avoid price wars, prevented publication of information that would inform the public about prescription drug purchasing choices. Reviewing a challenge that the First Amendment entitles prescription drug purchasers to receive pricing and discount information that pharmacists wish to communicate to them through advertising and other promotions, the Supreme Court agreed in *Virginia Board of Pharmacy v. Virginia Citizens Consumer Council* but indicated that the constitutional protection of such commercial speech is far more limited than that afforded to other

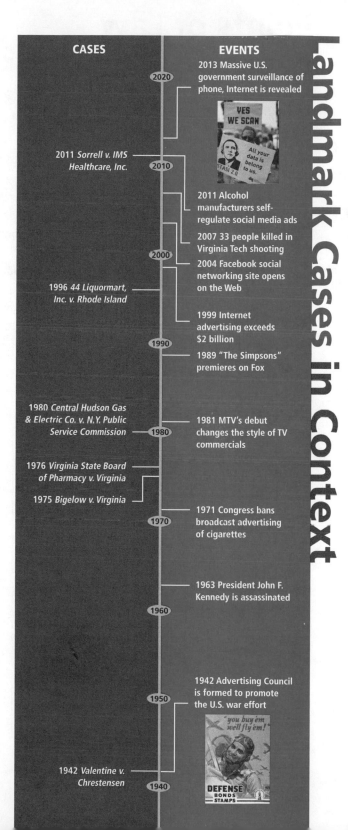

CASES

2011 *Sorrell v. IMS Healthcare, Inc.*

1996 *44 Liquormart, Inc. v. Rhode Island*

1980 *Central Hudson Gas & Electric Co. v. N.Y. Public Service Commission*

1976 *Virginia State Board of Pharmacy v. Virginia*

1975 *Bigelow v. Virginia*

1942 *Valentine v. Chrestensen*

EVENTS

2013 Massive U.S. government surveillance of phone, Internet is revealed

2011 Alcohol manufacturers self-regulate social media ads

2007 33 people killed in Virginia Tech shooting

2004 Facebook social networking site opens on the Web

1999 Internet advertising exceeds $2 billion

1989 "The Simpsons" premieres on Fox

1981 MTV's debut changes the style of TV commercials

1971 Congress bans broadcast advertising of cigarettes

1963 President John F. Kennedy is assassinated

1942 Advertising Council is formed to promote the U.S. war effort

Landmark Cases in Context

Points of Law

The Free Flow of (Commercial) Information

In *Virginia State Board of Pharmacy v. Virginia Citizens Consumer Council*,[1] the U.S. Supreme Court established the following:

- "Freedom of speech" applies both to the speaker and recipient of information.

- "[S]peech does not lose its First Amendment protection because money is spent to project it, as in a paid advertisement."[2]

- Speech that does no more than propose a commercial transaction is not so removed from "any exposition of ideas" that it lacks all protection.

- General public interest in entirely commercial information may be as high as, if not higher than, the interest in the day's most urgent political debate.

- Particularly in a free-enterprise economy, it is a matter of public interest that economic decisions be intelligent and well informed.

- Some forms of commercial speech, such as deceptive or misleading speech, may be regulated.

1. 425 U.S. 748 (1976).
2. *Id.* at 761.

Points of Law

The Commercial Speech Doctrine

- The government may regulate advertising that is false, misleading or deceptive.

- The government may regulate advertising for unlawful goods and services.

Even truthful, honest advertising for legal goods and services may be regulated if the government:

- Shows a substantial state interest justifies the regulation.

- Demonstrates that the regulation directly advances the claimed interest.

- Attempts to achieve a reasonable fit between the claimed interest and the regulation.

categories of speech.[14] It said that untruthful commercial expression could be regulated more readily than falsehood in a political context. Yet the Court did not establish clearly when, exactly, commercial speech could be regulated without offending the First Amendment.

In its 1980 ruling in *Central Hudson Gas & Electric Corp. v. Public Service Commission*, the Court changed that.[15] Amid a nationwide energy crisis, Central Hudson was among the utility companies a New York state regulation prevented from all advertising that encouraged the use of energy. The company sued, arguing that the advertising ban violated its First Amendment rights. To decide the case, the Court developed a test.

The Court reaffirmed that (1) government may ban untruthful and misleading advertising and ads that promote illegal products or services. If an advertisement clears that hurdle, *Central Hudson* said, then a government regulation is constitutional only if (2) a substantial state interest justifies the regulation,

International Law

New EU Tune on Misleading Advertising

The European Commission (EU) in 2012 proposed new rules on misleading and comparative business-to-business practices.[1]

The commission identified the most frequent misleading practices and scams in the European Union as deceit to induce participation in a contract, abusive Internet offers, fake provision of Internet domain names or trademark protection, misleading directory services and other Internet-based frauds. The commission also said current EU regulation did not adequately address the use of competitors' trademarks, comparative product statements and prices in comparative advertising.

In 2005, the European Union adopted regulations[2] somewhat parallel to the U.S. Fair Trade Commission Act[3] that set forth broad regulations against businesses treating consumers unfairly. The EU rules were designed to achieve what it called "maximum harmonization" of business-to-consumer advertising law among EU member states to provide both a high level of consumer protection and to free up internal EU trade. They defined "unfair commercial practices" to include practices in advertising and marketing that are likely to materially distort the economic behavior of the average consumer, including commercial practices that are either misleading or aggressive. Misleading advertising "contains false information and is therefore untruthful or in any way . . . deceives or is likely to deceive the average consumer."[4]

The new rules are necessary to protect the small businesses the commission believes are particularly vulnerable to unfair business-to-business advertising practices. The new rules will take effect in June 2014.[5]

---

1. Misleading Advertising; Unfair Commercial Practices; Consumer Protection Law Directive, *available at* http://ec.europa.eu.
2. Council directive 2005/29.
3. 15 U.S.C §§ 41–58, *as amended*.
4. Council directive 2005/29, art. 6(1).
5. The Directive on Consumer Rights, 2011/83/EC, *available at* http://ec.europa.eu/justice/consumer-marketing/rights-contracts/directive/index_en.htm.

(3) the regulation directly advances that state interest and (4) the regulation employs the least speech-restrictive means possible. Applying this test, the Court found the complete advertising ban imposed on *Central Hudson* to be unconstitutional.

The Court modified the last element of its *Central Hudson* test in *Board of Trustees of the State University of New York v. Fox*.[16] The Supreme Court backed away from its standard that regulation must employ the "least restrictive means" available to the state. Instead, regulation must demonstrate a "reasonable fit" to the state interest. Writing for the Court, Justice Antonin Scalia said that although *Central Hudson* encouraged the least restrictive means standard, that standard was not strictly required. "What our decisions require is a 'fit' between the legislature's ends and the means chosen to accomplish those ends— a fit that is not necessarily perfect, but reasonable," the Court concluded.[17] This revision makes it easier for advertising regulations to pass the test and be ruled constitutional.

The prominent labeling of alcohol content in beer has been the subject of debate and regulation because such labeling may function like advertising to promote consumption of beer and other vice products and activities.

Controlled Substances and Activities

As with other First Amendment areas, controversial commercial speech—such as advertising for "vice" products or advertising to susceptible audiences—is the primary locus for testing the limits of protection for commercial speech. Thus, Supreme Court decisions often determine the constitutional protection for advertising of alcohol, tobacco, drugs, gambling and, more recently, marijuana.

Alcohol Advertising When Coors Brewing Company wanted to print the percentage of alcohol in its beer on the label and in ads, a federal law stood in the way. Coors challenged the law on First Amendment grounds, and the federal government defended the law as a reasonable means to prevent "strength wars" among brewers that might increase beer potency and harm society. Writing for the Supreme Court, Justice Clarence Thomas said that although combating "strength wars" may be a substantial interest, a law banning speech about alcohol content did not achieve that goal, which would be better served by "alternatives that would prove less intrusive to the First Amendment's protections for commercial speech."[18]

Another commercial speech test originated with a Rhode Island law forbidding liquor stores from advertising the price of their products. After the state levied a hefty fine on one liquor store owner who tried to circumvent it by placing the exclamation "Wow" next to certain bargain products in his newspaper ads, he sued. He argued that the First Amendment protected his right to advertise prices. Rhode Island relied on *Central Hudson* to argue that its law advanced the government's substantial interest in promoting temperance. The state claimed that promotion of bargain prices on alcoholic beverages would increase consumption. The U.S. Supreme Court disagreed.[19] The Court said the state had failed to show a causal relationship between its ban on advertising and its promotion of temperance. The Court found the law was unconstitutional.

Tobacco Advertising The Lorillard brothers began advertising their snuff and tobacco products in a New York daily newspaper in 1789. More than a century and a half later, one federal district court upheld the right of government to regulate tobacco advertising, concluding that government could impose regulations to protect minors and others from the lure of tobacco. The court found that the federal Public Health Cigarette Smoking Act, which banned cigarette advertising on broadcast television and radio stations, did not abridge the free speech rights of tobacco companies because they had other outlets in which to advertise.[20] In response, tobacco producers pursued those outlets—print media, billboards and others—with vigor.

In 2001, Lorillard stood before the U.S. Supreme Court to argue that a Massachusetts law restricting its ability to advertise tobacco products was unconstitutional. Massachusetts regulations prohibited outdoor advertising of smokeless tobacco or cigars within 1,000 feet of a school or playground,

Emerging Law

Weed Control?

The legalization of marijuana in several states has prompted new federal and state efforts to adopt regulations similar to those that control the promotion of alcohol products.

Marijuana may be legal for medicinal and other purposes in nearly two dozen states,[1] but the feds and several states are zipping up the bag on marijuana advertising.

In Colorado, which like Washington voted in 2012 to regulate marijuana like alcohol, a 2013 task force urged the state legislature to "prohibit all mass-market campaigns that have a high likelihood of reaching minors (billboards, television, radio, direct mail, etc.)" but to allow "advertising in adult-oriented newspapers and magazines."[2] The city of Boulder, Colo., earlier banned marijuana ads that target young people or recreational users based on the "tone" of the ad.[3]

Although California law permits the sale of marijuana for medicinal purposes, federal law prohibits both its sale and advertising, and federal prosecutors in four California districts said they would target enforcement efforts against media that advertise medical marijuana dispensaries.[4] One prosecutor said she would move to prosecute advertising in print, radio and TV because "it's gone mainstream. Not only is it inappropriate—one has to wonder what kind of message we're sending to our children—it's against the law."[5] The penalty for the first offense of violating the federal law is up to four years in prison (or eight years for someone with a prior felony conviction).[6]

In response, the CEO of one Sacramento newspaper wrote, "I don't see how . . . running medical-marijuana ads is any different from TV stations running massive amounts of commercials for pharmaceutical companies selling drugs."[7]

---

1. The 20 States and One Federal District with Effective Medical Marijuana Laws, Marijuana Policy Project (n.d.) *available at* http://www.mpp.org/assets/pdfs/library/MMJLawsSummary.pdf; States Lead the Way in Loosening Marijuana Laws (Apr. 30, 2013), *available at* http://nugblasters.com/cannabis-medical-benefits/states-lead-the-way-in-loosening-marijuana-laws.
2. Jacob Sullum, *Are Marijuana Ad Restrictions Constitutional?* (Mar. 15, 2012), *available at* http://reason.com/blog/2013/03/15/are-marijuana-ad-restrictions-constituti.
3. Michael Montgomery, Feds to Target Radio, Newspapers for Medical Marijuana Ads, CAL. WATCH (Oct. 12, 2011), *available at* californiawatch.org.
4. *Id.*
5. *Id.*
6. *Id.*
7. *Id.*

restricted point-of-sale promotions on cigarette machines and other self-service displays and required that certain tobacco products be placed out of the consumer's reach. Applying the *Central Hudson* test, the Court found there was a legitimate state interest in regulating tobacco advertising to prevent minors from accessing tobacco products and the regulations would address that interest. However, the rules on outdoor advertising were unconstitutional because the

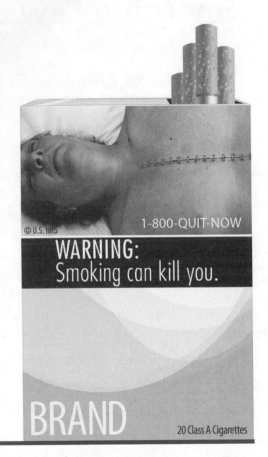

WARNING:
Smoking can kill you.

1-800-QUIT-NOW

© U.S. HHS

BRAND

20 Class A Cigarettes

One of the proposed cigarette-package images abandoned by the federal Food and Drug Administration.

state failed to achieve a reasonable fit between the regulations and the state's legitimate interest, the Court said. However, the other state restrictions on retail sales practices of all tobacco products withstood First Amendment scrutiny because the state's interest was "unrelated to the communication of ideas."[21]

Cartoons came under the realm of government attempts to protect people—particularly children thought to be especially susceptible to advertising—from tobacco promotions after Camel introduced the cartoon character of Joe Camel into its product advertisements in the 1990s. Critics who said Joe Camel would unduly tempt minors were supported when, following the incorporation of Joe Camel, Camel cigarettes' share of the youth market rose from 4 percent to 13 percent.[22]

In response, then-President Bill Clinton instructed the Food and Drug Administration (FDA) to "initiate a broad series of steps all designed to stop sales and marketing of cigarettes and smokeless tobacco to children." A federal district court in North Carolina ruled that the rules fell within the reasonable authority of the FDA,[23] and the tobacco industry settled with all 50 states, ending all use of cartoon characters as well as all billboard and transit ads to promote tobacco products.

Regulators continue to struggle to find the appropriate balance between protecting consumers and protecting tobacco company free speech rights. In 2013, the Food and Drug Administration preempted a much-ballyhooed appeal to the Supreme Court when it announced plans to revise rather than defend its proposed graphic labeling requirements for cigarettes.[24] The U.S. Courts of Appeals for the D.C. and Sixth Circuits disagree on whether the FDA may constitutionally force tobacco companies to "emblazon cigarette packaging with images of people dying from smoking-related disease, mouth and gum damage linked to smoking and other graphic portrayals of the harms of smoking."[25] The Second Circuit Court earlier said FDA authority preempted New York City's law requiring stores to post graphic health warnings next to cash registers and cigarette displays.[26]

Five leading tobacco companies had argued that the mandatory cigarette pack graphics exceeded the FDA's authority to compel commercial speech to protect, inform or educate consumers and instead attempted to advocate a change in behavior. Although smoking is the leading cause of early and preventable death in the United States, according to the Centers for Disease Control, "[t]he government's interest in advocating a message cannot and does not outweigh plaintiff's First Amendment right to not be the government's messenger," one district court wrote.[27] A similar argument has been made to counter government efforts to impose advertising and labeling requirements on "foodstuffs" marketed to children.[28] And the FDA earlier declined to appeal a landmark federal district court ruling that the First Amendment prohibited it from criminalizing truthful promotion of "off-label" uses of prescription drugs.[29]

Congress authorized the FDA to regulate the tobacco industry in 2009,[30] but the images the FDA mandated to fill the top half of cigarette packs were "constitutionally indefensible," First Amendment attorney Floyd Abrams said.[31]

Gambling Advertising When neighboring states differ in their regulation of disfavored activities, such as gambling or lotteries, the Supreme Court may be called in. For example, a radio station owned by Edge Broadcasting challenged a federal law that prohibited it and other North Carolina broadcasters from airing ads for any lottery. The station was located only three miles from the Virginia border, where most of its listeners lived and where the state-licensed lottery sought to buy broadcast advertising. Lotteries were illegal in North Carolina at the time. The U.S. Supreme Court upheld the ban on lottery advertising because states have a right to ban gambling and also have a legitimate subordinate interest in discouraging its promotion.[32] In affirming the challenged law, the Court deferred to Congress' judgment and concluded that

> Congress surely knew that stations in one state could often be heard in another but expressly prevented each and every North Carolina station, including Edge, from carrying lottery ads. Congress plainly made the commonsense judgment that each North Carolina station would have an audience in that state, even if its signal reached elsewhere and that enforcing the statutory restriction would insulate each station's listeners from lottery ads and hence advance the governmental purpose of supporting North Carolina's laws against gambling. This congressional policy of balancing the interests of lottery and nonlottery states is the substantial governmental interest that satisfies *Central Hudson*.[33]

In dissent, Justice John Paul Stevens argued that in a nation with legal lotteries in (at that time) 34 states—and with North Carolina itself then considering adopting a lottery—the government lacked a substantial interest in trying to discourage gambling.[34]

A few years later, a group of New Orleans broadcasters challenged a regulation that banned broadcasters from airing ads for private casino gambling. Here, even though broadcast signals from New Orleans might reach states where casino gambling was unlawful, those signals originated from a state where such gambling was legal. Justice Stevens wrote for a unanimous Court that the regulation failed the *Central Hudson* test because, although the state had a substantial interest in reducing the social costs associated with gambling, the law did not advance that interest.[35] Prohibiting advertising for private casinos while allowing it for others (such as casinos operated by Native American tribes) and allowing advertising for other forms of gambling such as lotteries did not deter but direct gamblers to favored outlets. Moreover, the Court said, the regulation was not as narrowly tailored as it could be.[36]

realWorld Law

Smoke-Filled Rooms and Hazy Standards?

In *Lorillard*, the U.S. Supreme Court ruled that state bans on outdoor advertising of tobacco products near schools and playgrounds must clearly balance the "costs and benefits" of such restrictions on free speech.

The tobacco advertising ruling in *Lorillard Tobacco Co. v. Reilly*[1] suggests a shift in the U.S. Supreme Court's application of the *Central Hudson* commercial speech doctrine. At issue were Massachusetts regulations that prohibited both outdoor and point-of-sale tobacco product advertising within 1,000 feet of a school or playground.

Although the Court's majority agreed that the law passed the first three prongs of the *Central Hudson* test, it said the outdoor rules did not present a reasonable fit to the state interest in reducing tobacco consumption by minors.[2] The Court blamed the Massachusetts attorney general for failure to "carefully calculate the costs and benefits associated with the burden on speech imposed by the regulations."[3] Lorillard claimed the regulations would prohibit its advertising in about 90 percent of the land area in Massachusetts' biggest cities, and the Court said the 1,000-foot perimeter around tobacco ads likely banned the ads in any urban areas with densely clustered schools and playgrounds. In the Court's view, this kind of near-total ban was not the reasonable fit required by *Central Hudson*.

On a related point, the Supreme Court said that "efforts to protect children from exposure to harmful material will undoubtedly have some spillover effect on the free speech rights of adults," and "finding the appropriate balance is no easy matter."[4] Such balancing requires careful consideration of the specific restrictions imposed and their effects, the Court said, but offered no further guidance on how to correctly address the subjective nature of such balancing. As one analyst wrote, "[T]he Court can use the *Central Hudson* test to defeat objectionable legislation without articulating any set of coherent limits for commercial speech doctrine."[5]

1. 533 U.S. 525 (2001).
2. *Id.*
3. *Id.*
4. *Id.*
5. Charles Fischette, *A New Architecture of Commercial Speech Law*, 31 HARV. J.L. & PUB. POL'Y 663, 666–67 (2008).

Prescription Medicines Prescription drugs, like alcohol and tobacco, are highly controlled substances. But in 2012, the Supreme Court declined to apply its commercial speech doctrine to review a Vermont law that prohibited drug marketers and data-mining companies from buying doctor's prescription records from pharmacies for marketing purposes.[37] The state law restricted the sale or disclosure of pharmacy prescription records to brand-name drug marketers in order to protect doctors' privacy and prevent aggressive marketing that might distort doctors' prescribing practices and harm the best interests of patients.[38] Vermont feared aggressive drug-company marketing would quash demand for cheaper generic drugs.

In *Sorrell v. IMS Health Inc.*, the Court said the law violated the First Amendment right of pharmacies by limiting their sale and distribution of information and by prohibiting drug marketers from purchasing the records others could obtain. "The state has burdened a form of protected expression that it found too persuasive. At the same time, the state has left unburdened those speakers whose messages are in accord with its own views," the Supreme Court said. "This the state cannot do."[39]

The Court said it applied strict scrutiny to the law because the restriction of speech was, on its face, both content-based and viewpoint-discriminatory. The law "does not simply have an effect on speech," Justice Anthony Kennedy wrote for the majority. "[It] is directed at certain content and is aimed at particular speakers."

In sharp dissent, three justices said the Court's abandonment of the commercial speech doctrine was but a thinly veiled imposition of its own economic neo-liberalism and liberal capitalism.[40] They concluded that "At best the Court opens a Pandora's box of First Amendment challenges to many ordinary regulatory practices that may only incidentally affect a commercial message. . . . At worst, it reawakens [the] threat of substituting judicial for democratic decision-making where ordinary economic regulation is at issue."[41]

Many said the decision eviscerated well-developed precedent that speech intended solely to generate profits and sales should not receive the full constitutional protection afforded to political, artistic or scientific speech.[42] Sen. Patrick Leahy, chairman of the Senate Judiciary Committee, said the *Sorrell* ruling was "one more example of the Supreme Court using the First Amendment as a tool to bolster the rights of big business at the expense of individual Americans."[43] A year after the decision, another observer said the *Sorrell* decision already had distorted rulings on misappropriation of Michael Jordan's image and limits on tobacco advertising in school zones and on cigarette package labels.[44] It is possible, though, as one Court watcher wrote, that "Vermont simply botched the job of promoting the availability of cheaper, generic drugs by over-reaching."[45]

Advertising by Attorneys Though certainly not advertising for a "vice" product, advertising of lawyers' services has been controversial. State bar associations once prohibited the practice, considering it to be unethical or unprofessional. Judges, many of whom started out as practicing attorneys, have a great interest in whether such bans are permissible. That question reached the Supreme Court when two Arizona lawyers challenged that state bar's advertising ban.[46] The Court rejected the arguments presented by the Arizona Bar Association to defend its regulation but stopped short of granting a blanket First Amendment protection to attorney advertising. "Reasonable" restrictions—for example, those pertaining to false advertising—could survive First Amendment scrutiny, the Court said.[47]

Corporate Speech Regulation

Corporations and businesses sometimes communicate with customers through advertising. Most ads have the clear purpose of enhancing sales. Moreover, it usually is clear that when a corporation "speaks" through advertising, attempts to regulate that speech are subject to the commercial speech doctrine.

But sometimes the distinction between commercial speech and another kind of speech—political, for example—is not clear. What happens when a business claims to have engaged in political speech?

First, the U.S. Supreme Court has upheld the right of corporations to communicate purely political speech. Thus, when a bank wanted to express its viewpoint to influence a voter referendum, the Court affirmed the free speech right of the bank.[48] The Court maintained but narrowed this view over time, providing businesses' political speech with greater protection than it would provide commercial speech.[49]

But what if a corporation wants to communicate about an issue of public importance in a way that would place the corporation in an improved public light and, thereby, potentially increase its sale? This was the situation that led *Nike, Inc. v. Kasky* to reach the U.S. Supreme Court early in the 21st century.[50] Nike faced accusations that workers were abused and subjected to unsafe conditions and worked illegally long hours in the company's overseas plants. Nike responded in the form of press releases and letters to newspapers, university presidents and university athletic directors.

An activist in California, Marc Kasky, filed a claim against Nike, saying its statements were knowingly false. A trial court dismissed the case, but the California Supreme Court reversed, ruling that the speech was commercial and could therefore be punished under state false advertising and unfair competition laws. The court's rationale was threefold: (1) Nike engaged in commerce, (2) the intended audience was largely composed of potential Nike customers and (3) the speech consisted of representations of fact of a commercial nature that were intended to maintain and increase sales of Nike products.[51] The dissenters argued that the speech was a protected political response to claims—themselves protected speech—that Nike mistreated workers.[52]

On appeal to the U.S. Supreme Court, Nike argued that, even if false, its speech was political—part of an important public discussion of overseas factory working conditions—and absolutely protected by the First Amendment. Nike characterized commercial speech as speech involving things such as product pricing or performance characteristics. The Supreme Court failed to resolve the question, instead dismissing the case on the grounds Kasky did not suffer an injury and, therefore, did not have the **standing** required to file a lawsuit. Nike and Kasky later settled the dispute, which reportedly included a Nike payment of $1.5 million to the Fair Labor Association.

Though not a commercial speech case, 2010's *Citizens United v. Federal Election Commission*[53] is worth noting here because it addresses corporate speech regulation. The U.S. Supreme Court ruling, analyzed in Chapters 1 and 3,

standing The position of a plaintiff who has been injured or has been threatened with injury. No person is entitled to challenge the constitutionality of an ordinance or statute unless he or she has the required standing—that is, unless he or she had been affected by the ordinance or statute.

extended the degree to which corporations' speech has First Amendment protection. By including corporate and union funding of politics within protected speech, the Court's decision in *Citizens United* opened the floodgates for First Amendment challenges to regulatory constraints on corporate involvement in political advertising. In 2012, for example, the Federal Election Commission (FEC)—dubbed the "Failure to Enforce Commission" by its critics—said that it would continue to defend rather than revise its controversial rules on "electioneering communications."[54]

The decision came amid ongoing litigation brought by Rep. Chris Van Hollen of Maryland, who argued that the FEC's rules improperly exempt from mandatory disclosure the identities of labor unions and corporations that fund political ads intended to influence voters without explicitly advocating for or against a "clearly identified candidate for federal office."[55] The case involves millions of dollars in corporate and union contributions to political action committees without the express purpose of funding a specific candidate's ads.

A federal district court sided with Van Hollen that Congress intended the FEC to mandate disclosure of all contributors above $1,000, but the Court of Appeals for the D.C. Circuit reversed and remanded for further rulemaking by the FEC. The appeals court did not agree with the lower court that Congress "spoke plainly" about its intention when it imposed new regulations on political advertising by broadcast, cable or satellite companies.[56] Like so many issues in commercial speech, the First Amendment protection for "indirect" corporate political electioneering remains unclear.

SUMMARY

AFTER INITIAL REFUSAL TO GRANT First Amendment protection to commercial speech, the U.S. Supreme Court has acknowledged advertising often contains important information that deserves some constitutional protection. The Court elaborated its commercial speech doctrine and established a framework to determine when an advertising regulation is constitutional in *Central Hudson*. Advertising regulation is constitutional if there is a substantial state interest, the regulation directly advances that interest and there is a reasonable fit between the interest and the regulation. The most noteworthy applications of this test have involved regulation of controversial goods and services, where the Supreme Court seems to be expanding the constitutional protection of commercial speech. ∎

Legislative and Agency Advertising Regulation

Advertising is subject to some regulation on the state level, but the federal government has largely assumed this responsibility because commercial speech often crosses state lines and, therefore, falls under the U.S. Constitution's commerce clause.

realWorld Law

The Jury's Out: Does Advertising Increase Product Demand?

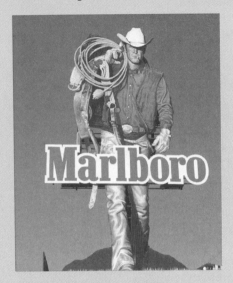

Regulators and lawmakers sometimes target tobacco advertising, with disputes often settled in court.

Advertising is premised on the idea that it increases product demand, and the U.S. Supreme Court reviews advertising regulations with that premise in mind. For example,

- In the *Central Hudson* case, the Court said the utility company would not have contested the advertising ban "unless it believed that promotion would increase sales."[1]

- Reviewing a ban on casino advertising in Puerto Rico, the Court said legislatures ban advertising of disfavored products because they believe advertising "would serve to increase the demand for the product advertised. We think the legislature's belief is a reasonable one."[2]

- Examining restrictions on tobacco advertising, the Court said: "[W]e have acknowledged the theory that product advertising stimulates demand for products, while suppressed advertising may have the opposite effect. . . . [N]umerous studies . . . support this theory in the case of tobacco products."[3]

Those outside the courts are less certain, and policy and empirical studies have produced mixed results. Although the Food and Drug Administration found a correlation between advertising and increased product demand,[4] others in federal government were "not convinced that advertising leads to increased consumption"[5] and hesitated to support advertising bans. On the one hand, a study on cigarette advertising suggests that advertising increases demand.[6] On the other, a study shows advertising has minimal effect on demand and consumption of alcohol, including beer. Alcohol advertising, the study concludes, reallocates brand sales with no effect on total consumption.[7]

Although the scientific jury may be out, courts have accepted the proposition that advertising increases sales and make their rulings with that in mind.

---

1. Central Hudson Gas & Electric Corp. v. New York Public Service Commission, 447 U.S. 557, 569 (1980).
2. Posadas de Puerto Rico Associates v. Tourism Co. of Puerto Rico, 478 U.S. 328, 342 (1986).
3. Lorillard Tobacco Co. v. Reilly, 533 U.S. 525, 557 (2001).
4. *See, e.g.,* Rosalind M. Kendellen, *The Food and Drug Administration Retreats from Patient Package Inserts for Prescription Drugs,* 40 FOOD DRUG COSM. L.J. 172 (1985) (showing the FDA's motivation for establishing a package insert plan for consumers).
5. 1 ANTITRUST & TRADE REG. REP. (BNA) No. 1277, p. 199 (Aug. 7, 1986).
6. Barry J. Seldon & Khosrow Doroodian, *A Simultaneous Model of Cigarette Advertising: Effects on Demand and Industry Response to Public Policy,* 71 REV. ECON. & STAT. 673 (1989).
7. Jon P. Nelson & John R. Moran, Advertising and U.S. Alcoholic Beverage Demand: System-Wide Estimates, 27 APPLIED ECON. 1225 (1995).

Congress first passed the **Lanham Act** in 1938 to prohibit any false or misleading description of goods, services or commercial activities in any forum, including commercial advertising or promotion.[57] Though initially the law was seldom used to curtail advertising practices, it became the foundation for lawsuits as advertising grew and began using new techniques, such as product or price comparisons. For example, truck rental company Jartran's comparative print advertising campaign prompted Lanham Act challenges. Jartran compared its trucks and prices with U-Haul's, using photographs of brand-new, shiny Jartran trucks and beaten-up U-Haul trucks and calculating comparison rates unfairly. In the wake of the ads, U-Haul profits plummeted while Jartran's rose. U-Haul sued, and a federal court ruled that the advertisements violated the Lanham Act by being deliberately false and misleading to consumers.[58]

Lanham Act A federal law that regulates the trademark registration process but that also contains a section permitting business competitors to sue one another for false advertising.

The Federal Trade Commission

In addition to state and federal laws that regulate advertising, executive branch agencies, primarily at the federal level, also regulate commercial speech. Congress established the **Federal Trade Commission (FTC)** in 1914 and expanded its powers in 1938. The commission has five members, nominated by the president and confirmed by the Senate, who serve seven-year terms. The president selects the chair, and no more than three commissioners may be from the same political party.

Federal Trade Commission (FTC) A federal agency created in 1914. Its purpose is to promote free and fair competition in interstate commerce; this includes preventing false and misleading advertising.

Points of Law

False and Misleading?

A Federal Trade Commission Policy Statement establishes the three-part federal definition of false and misleading advertising:

- First, there must be a representation, omission or practice that is likely to mislead the consumer.

- Second, we examine the practice from the perspective of a consumer acting reasonably in the circumstances. If the representation or practice affects or is directed primarily to a particular group, the commission examines reasonableness from the perspective of that group.

- Third, the representation, omission or practice must be a "material" one. The basic question is whether the act or practice is likely to affect the consumer's conduct or decision with regard to a product or service.[1]

---

1. FTC Policy Statement by Chairman James C. Miller III (Oct. 14, 1983), *available at* http://www.ftc.gov/bcp/policystmt/addecept.htm.

The primary function of the FTC is to protect consumers from unfair or deceptive practices by businesses, primarily by regulating advertising and assuring that advertisers substantiate the accuracy of their claims in order for the FTC to detect deception. A division of the FTC's Bureau of Consumer Protection "is the nation's enforcer of federal truth-in-advertising laws."[59] Recently, it has focused on the following:

- Deceptive advertising of fraudulent claims for dietary supplements and weight-loss products
- Misleading Internet marketing practices related to public health issues
- Enforcement strategies for new advertising techniques, such as word-of-mouth marketing
- Advertising of food to children, including its impact on childhood obesity
- Marketing of violent movies, music and electronic games to children
- Alcohol and tobacco marketing

puffery Advertising that exaggerates the merits of products or services in such a way that no reasonable person would take the ad seriously. Usually, puffery is not illegal given that a reasonable person understands the claim is not to be taken literally.

The FTC distinguishes deception from "**puffery**," which it defines as advertising that exaggerates the merits of products or services in such a way that no reasonable person would take the claim seriously. As one former FTC commissioner said,

> The FTC does not pursue subjective claims or puffery—claims like "this is the best hairspray in the world." But if there is an objective component to the claim—such as "more consumers prefer our hairspray to any other" or "our hairspray lasts longer than the most popular brands"—then you need to be sure that the claim is not deceptive and that you have adequate substantiation *before* you make the claim. These requirements apply both to explicit or express claims and to implied claims. Also, a statement that is literally true can have a deceptive implication when considered in the context of the whole advertisement, even if that implication is not the only possible interpretation.[60]

Points of Law

FTC Mechanisms

Preventive Measures	Corrective Measures
• Opinion letters	• Cease and desist orders
• Advisory opinions	• Consent orders
• Industry guides	• Substantiation
• Trade rules	• Litigated orders
• Voluntary compliance	• Corrective advertising
	• Injunctions

The FTC at Work The FTC learns of potentially problematic advertisements through consumer or business complaints, congressional inquiries, news articles or other public debate. Some issues arise directly from advertisers seeking advice to avoid problems. The FTC protects its investigations and those investigated by generally conducting nonpublic inquiries and fact findings.

FTC powers designed either to prevent problematic advertising before it reaches the public or to remedy already public ads are intended to protect the public. But the FTC also works

realWorld Law

Cheat Death or Cease and Desist?

In 2013, the Federal Trade Commission ordered POM Wonderful to "cease and desist" an ad campaign the commission said exaggerated the product's health benefits.

When judges speak, people listen and follow their directions or pay the penalty. At least that seems to be one logic behind POM Wonderful's 2012 ad campaign.[1]

A representative online ad, reprinted in The New York Times, pictured a noose around the neck of a bottle of juice beneath the headline: "Cheat death. POM Wonderful. The Antioxidant Superpower." Below the bottle, the ad continued, "Natural Fruit Product with Health Promoting Characteristics.—FTC Judge," and provided a link to "learn more."[2] Another ad with the headline "Life Support" featured an inverted bottle of POM as an intravenous drip bottle.

The pomegranate juice manufacturer launched the campaign to challenge a Federal Trade Commission judge's ruling that the company materially exaggerated the health benefits of its product. The judge prohibited POM Wonderful from making claims for 20 years that the juice reduces the risk of heart disease and prostate cancer and provides other specific health benefits.

The ad and its accompanying text "plucked" "flattering phrases" from the court's ruling and encouraged readers to "be the judge" but failed to mention the judge's negative comments, according to The New York Times. A representative of the FTC declined to comment on the ruling or the advertisements "because one or both parties are likely to appeal certain aspects of the administrative law judge's initial decision."[3] A company spokesperson said POM Wonderful would run the ads "as long as necessary to inform the public of the truth."[4] POM Wonderful also appealed the FTC order in the U.S. Court of Appeals for the D.C. Circuit on the grounds that it unconstitutionally banned protected speech.[5]

1. Stephanie Strom, *POM Uses Ad to Answer Judge's Order* (May 25, 2012), *available at* http://www.nytimes.com.
2. *Id.*
3. *Id.*
4. *Id.*
5. Riëtte van Laack, *POM Wonderful Petitioners File Appeal Briefs in D.C. Circuit* (Aug. 20, 2013), FDA L. Blog, *available* at http://www.fdalawblog.net/fda_law_blog_hyman_phelps/2013/08/pom-wonderful-petitioners-file-appeal-briefs-in-dc-circuit.html

with advertisers to ensure that they are not inadvertently doing anything improper. FTC measures range from quite informal letters to serious, official legal actions.

Preventive Measures The least formal FTC action is to send an **opinion letter** to an advertiser seeking advice about a potential ad. Advice contained in such letters does not bind the commission in any way, but such letters provide

opinion letter An informal Federal Trade Commission communication providing general advice about advertising techniques.

a quick and efficient means for businesses to avoid problems with possible deception or fraud.

advisory opinion A Federal Trade Commission measure that offers formal guidance on whether a specific advertisement may be false or misleading and how to correct it.

An FTC **advisory opinion** is more official and typically contains more information than an opinion letter. As part of the official public record, advisory opinions hold the FTC accountable. As a consequence, these opinions tend to be both formal and harsh; they often oblige the advertiser to adhere to the opinion provided.

industry guides In advertising, a Federal Trade Commission measure that outlines the FTC's policies concerning a particular category of product or service.

On a less individual level, the FTC issues **industry guides** that outline official policy intended to prevent problems concerning a particular category of product or service. For example, the FTC issued an industry guide updating policies about advertising testimonials and endorsements, especially celebrity endorsements. First, the guide establishes that endorsers may be personally liable for false claims and that the frequently used disclaimer that "reported results may not be typical" will not remove liability from endorsers, advertisers or the media for misleading testimonial ads. "So a radio announcer paid to try a diet plan or some other product and to report about its results on the air needs to be sure not only that his statements are truthful but that the 'results' claimed are in line with what the advertiser can actually prove for the product through clinical study and research. The radio pitchman cannot turn a blind eye to claims that are inherently incredible," the guide establishes.[61]

"Material connections," such as payment for the endorsement, must be disclosed. Third, the guide warns "new media," specifically bloggers, social media and viral campaigners, that they also are subject to FTC enforcement action, as are "nontraditional" advertising endorsers, such as "on-air DJ's."[62]

trade regulation rule A broadly worded statement by the Federal Trade Commission that outlines advertising requirements for a particular trade.

Another measure the FTC may use to deal with deceptive advertising is the **trade regulation rule.** Like industry guides, these rules are broad and target an entire trade. They differ from guides in that they mandate rather than suggest a particular practice. Through trade regulation rules, the FTC can deal with an entire group of advertisers rather than taking separate action against each one individually. Individual advertisers, however, may challenge the rules to the commission and appeal any FTC decision in court.

voluntary compliance The general Federal Trade Commission practice to allow advertisers to follow FTC rules and correct violations before the commission takes action.

The FTC also oversees advertiser **voluntary compliance** with rules and regulations and advertiser response to consumer complaints. Thus, the commission generally asks advertisers to respond to complaints it believes have merit before initiating its own corrective measures.

cease and desist order An administrative agency order prohibiting a person or business from continuing a particular course of conduct.

Corrective Measures If an advertiser fails to voluntarily comply with regulatory directives, the FTC then may begin corrective measures. The commission takes an official, public action through a **consent order**, which may contain, for example, a **cease and desist order** requiring an advertiser to stop particular practices. A consent order also may be referred to as a "consent agreement" because representatives of both the advertiser and the FTC sign it, agreeing to its terms. In one such order, the FTC made public its agreement with American Nationwide Mortgage Co. in response to its direct mail ad campaign that stated, "30-Year Fixed. 1.95%." However, a fine-print, virtually illegible footnote to the ad stated, "4.981% Annual Percentage Rate," and a fine-print disclosure on the reverse

consent order An agreement between the Federal Trade Commission and an advertiser stipulating the terms that must be followed to address problematic advertising; also called a consent agreement.

realWorld Law

Advertisers Beware!

Skechers became another shoe manufacturer to run afoul of ramped-up federal enforcement efforts and fines intended to stop manufacturers from making exaggerated product claims.

In 2012, Skechers followed Reebok into the Federal Trade Commission's doghouse when the FTC ordered it to reimburse consumers $40 million for deceptive claims that its shoes would shape you up and help you shed pounds.

The FTC said Skechers had deceived consumers with claims that some of its shoes could tone legs, tighten buttocks and slim you up "without setting foot in the gym."[1] One endorsement ad featured reportedly independent chiropractor studies, which the FTC said the spouse of a Skechers executive conducted.[2] Among its other findings, the FTC said Skechers "cherry-picked results and failed to substantiate" many of its claims. In the previous year, Reebok agreed to refund consumers $25 million for false claims about its EasyTone sneakers.[3]

The American Association of Advertising Agencies (the 4As) in 2011 also warned its members that they needed to assure that they did not discriminate when placing ads with broadcast stations.[4] The policy followed a directive from the Federal Communications Commission (FCC) that required broadcasters to prevent advertising buyers and sellers from discriminating against minority-formatted stations.[5] The FCC rule was designed to avoid the "no urban, no Spanish" policies of some advertisers. The FCC applauded the 4A's rule as an important complement to its own anti-discrimination policy, which is enforced through the broadcast license renewal process.[6]

1. Anahad O'Connor, *A Toning Shoe Settlement for Skechers* (May 17, 2012), *available at* http://www.nytimes.com.
2. *Id.*
3. *Id.*
4. David Oxenford, *As Adopt Antidiscrimination in Advertising Policy—Should Help Broadcasters Comply With Requirements for Antidiscrimination Provisions in Advertising Agreements* (Oct. 27, 2011) available at http://www.broadcastlawblog.com.
5. FCC Enforcement Advisory (Oct. 3, 2011), *available at* http://hraunfoss.fcc.gov/edocs_public/attachmatch/DA-11–500A1.pdf.
6. Michael D. Berg, *License Renewal Quiz Gets a Bit Tougher,* TVNews Check (Apr. 13, 2012), *available at* http://www.tvnewscheck.com/article/58708/license-renewal-quiz-gets-a-bit-tougher.

side of the ad stated: "Initial Annual Percentage Rate (APR) for a 30-year mortgage loan with 80% loan to value is 4.981%. Rate is fixed for 12 months and adjusts upward 7.5% of the payment amount annually for the first ten years of the loan."[63] In the order, the commission and the mortgage company agreed to discontinue the advertisement because it failed to adequately disclose the true terms of the mortgage offer.

A consent order is for settlement purposes only. It does not constitute an admission of guilt by the advertiser. While some advertisers may be reluctant to

litigated order A Federal
Trade Commission order filed
in administrative court and
enforceable by the courts whose
violation can result in penalties,
including fines of up to $10,000
per day.

sign such an agreement, there are practical reasons to do so. Failure to sign may generate negative publicity and FTC imposition of severe penalties. In 2010, for example, the FTC issued an agreement containing a consent order with Rite Aid Corporation. The FTC concluded that Rite Aid pharmacies failed to provide their advertised protection of prescription drug customers' privacy by discarding materials that contained personal information in unsecured, publicly accessible trash containers. The FTC's order contained specific corrective measures for Rite Aid and fined the company $1 million.[64]

Though it is usually advantageous to sign a consent order and follow its directives, advertisers may fail to do so, prompting the FTC to issue a **litigated order.** The FTC files its litigated orders in an administrative court. If the court affirms the order, the advertiser may appeal to a federal court. Failure to follow the stipulations of an order upheld by the courts can result in fines of up to $10,000 per day. In one early litigated action that contributed significantly to validating the FTC's authority, the commission ordered Geritol to cease and desist its advertising claims that its vitamin and iron tonic cured "iron poor blood" and increased users' vitality. The commission found the claims misleading because it said fatigue stems from issues Geritol does not address. After the company failed to discontinue the ads, the FTC fined Geritol's manufacturer, the J.B. Williams Company. The company appealed, ultimately lost and was required to pay a $280,000 fine.[65]

More recently, the promoters of CortiSlim and CortiStress, dietary supplements advertised for weight loss and disease prevention, respectively, agreed to pay the FTC $4.5 million in cash and other assets for their roles in false or unsubstantiated product claims and deceptively formatted infomercials.[66]

substantiation The authority of
the Federal Trade Commission to
demand that an advertiser prove its
advertised claims.

Substantiation is a tool vital to the FTC's work and can be part of its corrective measures. Substantiation empowers the commission to demand that an advertiser prove its claims with "competent and reliable evidence."[67]

The FTC's demand to "prove it" was central to its case against Tropicana's Healthy Heart orange juice. In both television and print, Tropicana advertised that drinking three or more glasses per day of its product would increase levels of "good" cholesterol and lower blood pressure. The FTC said the clinical study Tropicana cited when asked to substantiate its claims was insufficient.[68] The FTC found the ads false or misleading and ordered Tropicana to stop making the claims.

If an advertiser fails to confirm its advertised assertions, the FTC may also order **corrective advertising** that requires the advertiser to correct erroneous claims through new ad campaigns and/or other kinds of information distribution.

corrective advertising The
Federal Trade Commission power
to require an advertiser to advertise
or otherwise distribute information
to correct false or misleading
advertisement claims.

The FTC used its corrective advertising power 40 years ago against Listerine mouthwash manufacturer Warner-Lambert. The FTC found that Listerine ads had misled the public for more than half a century by claiming that the product helped prevent colds and sore throats. The commission decided corrective advertising was called for, and a federal appeals court ruled the FTC's mandate of corrective advertising did not violate the First Amendment.[69] The court reasoned that "Listerine's advertisements play[ed] a substantial role in creating or reinforcing in the public's mind a false belief about the product. . . . [that would] linger on after the false advertising ceases."[70] The court concluded that the approximately one year of required corrective advertising was not "an unreasonably long time in which to correct a hundred years of cold claims."[71] Warner-Lambert spent $10 million on those ads.

In what some believe is the first such action since Warner-Lambert, the FTC issued a litigated corrective advertising order for unsubstantiated superiority claims in advertisements and packaging for Doan's analgesic products.[72] The commission said it based its requirement of corrective action on substantial evidence in six areas: amount of deception, materiality of deceptive claims, consumer belief measurement, linkage of ad claims to consumer beliefs, lingering effects estimation and remedy calibration.[73] The order required the Doan's manufacturers to pay their average annual advertising budged on ads that would run for a minimum of one year stating that Doan's was not better at relieving back pain than other analgesics.[74]

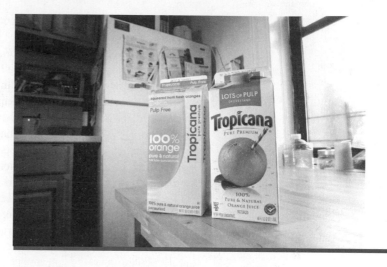

The Federal Trade Commission put the squeeze on Tropicana Products, Inc., for claims the orange juice company made in advertising.

The FTC also can seek a court injunction or restraining order to stop advertising that is not only false or misleading but also may cause immediate harm. In general these orders stop the advertising until a full hearing takes place. In 2010, for example, the FTC sought permanent injunctions against companies accused of making unsubstantiated claims to lure consumers into paying thousands of dollars in up-front fees but failing to reduce credit card debts as promised. According to the FTC, the defendants made deceptive claims via websites and television and radio ads that consumers who enrolled in their programs could eliminate 30 to 60 percent of their credit card debt and be out of debt in 18 to 36 months. One operation claimed to use "secret programs most credit card companies won't tell you about."[75]

SUMMARY

The regulation of advertising begins with legislative action. In 1914, Congress established the Federal Trade Commission, giving it authority to regulate advertising, and in 1938 it passed the Lanham Act, which defines unfair and deceptive advertising. Although other agencies are involved, the FTC is the primary advertising regulator. The commission uses several measures to police advertising, some preventive and some corrective. Advertisers who believe the FTC unjustly sanctions them appeal FTC rulings in federal court. ■

Other Administrative Regulation

The Federal Communications Commission has the authority to deal with problematic broadcast advertising. The Food and Drug Administration may also regulate advertising for products within its area of expertise, at least indirectly. After Congress passed the Family Smoking Prevention and Tobacco Control Act,[76] the FDA used its new power to issue an Enforcement Action Plan that restricted promotion and advertising of tobacco products. The 2010 action plan detailed how the FDA would implement its authority, including targeting of advertising, especially ads directed at minorities and minors.[77]

In 2013, a landmark federal district court ruling suggested limits to the FDA's power over advertising.[78] The FDA declined to appeal its holding that the First Amendment prohibited the agency from criminalizing truthful promotion of "off-label" uses of prescription drugs.

Internet Advertising

Internet advertising comprises a significant proportion of advertising because advertisers view it as cost effective. Although a state-of-the-art interactive website may cost a substantial sum to produce, an Internet ad may reach hundreds of thousands of consumers nationally, and even more internationally. Internet techniques also gather user activity data useful to marketers. Controversial

realWorld Law

In the Amazon Jungle: Third-Party Liability

A 2010 ruling in New York signaled that "third-party liability" may not exist in the world of Internet advertising. The case involved Amazon, Google and several online companies.

Sellify, the parent company of online marketer OneQuality, complained when the Amazon-affiliated advertiser Cutting Edge Designs purchased keywords from Google so that warnings like "Beware of the SCAM Artist" would pop up with searches for keywords such as "onequality.com." Sellify demanded that Amazon remove Cutting Edge's ads.

Amazon did not have the ability to remove the ads of its affiliates but issued a warning to Cutting Edge. When there was no response, Amazon terminated its affiliation with Cutting Edge. Meanwhile, Sellify sued Amazon, claiming the retail giant was responsible for the problem ads. The New York court dismissed the case and held that Amazon could not be held liable for the actions of a third party (Cutting Edge) it had simply partnered with but did not control. The court said that granting permission to third parties to link to its website did not make Amazon responsible for the actions of Cutting Edge, which was not acting as Amazon's authorized agent.[1]

1. Sellify, Inc. v. Amazon.com, Inc., 2010 U.S. Dist. LEXIS 118173 (S.D.N.Y. Nov. 4, 2010).

Emerging Law

Piling on Unwanted Texts

Sometimes, simply sending a text or e-mail is unfair and deceptive, according to the Federal Trade Commission.

Responding to a complaint against a "mind-boggling" number of commercial texts and e-mails marketing a mortgage alteration and audit service, the Federal Trade Commission ruled that the texts amounted to an unfair and deceptive practice because they (1) were sent without prior explicit permission and (2) were annoying, frustrating and paid for by the recipients.[1] The marketing also misleadingly suggested government affiliation, the FTC said, because it provided a URL that contained "gov," called itself "official" and featured an American flag.[2] The FTC order, which permanently prohibited all unauthorized and unsolicited commercial texts to cellphones subject to forfeitures of $16,500 and fines of $1,500 for each violation, seemed to pile on existing Federal Communication Commission rules that prohibit unauthorized en mass automated messages ("spam") to cellphones and mandate a recipient opt-out mechanism (see Chapter 11 for related coverage).[3]

1. Ronald G. London, *FTC Settlement Ups Ante on Ned for Prior Express Consent to Lawfully Text-Message,* PRIVACY & SECURITY L. BLOG (Sept. 30, 2011), *available at* http://www.dwt.com.
2. *Id.*
3. *Id.*

data-mining methods also enable advertisers to target ads to consumer interests. Online advertisements offer consumers more detailed product and company information than traditional print or broadcast advertisements. They also offer convenient, immediate purchases, saving time and money.

The instantaneous nature of Internet advertising and purchasing also provides fertile ground for fraud and unwanted ads. The FTC monitors illegal advertising on the Internet and enforces laws against online fraud. The commission issued its first consent decree for deceptive online advertising after a service placed advertisements on the Internet advising consumers to take illegal steps to repair their credit records.[79] The action required the advertiser to provide consumer compensation, cease misrepresentations and to cooperate in FTC investigations of the sellers of the credit program materials.

In 2013, new FTC Chair Edith Ramirez told advertisers that the industry needed to give consumers "effective and meaningful privacy protection" by providing them with an easy, Internet-wide "Do Not Track" option.[80] For several years, the FTC has said that because the mechanism to target advertising is invisible—accomplished with "cookies" that reveal consumer website visits—consumers should have a way to control it.[81] Although some Internet browsers, such as Internet Explorer 9,[82] enable users to block cookies, the FTC wants a simpler, more global solution for consumers.

Some believe the FTC should take action to resolve consumer complaints about unsolicited, unwanted e-mail, or spam advertising. In response to estimates that spam constituted up to 65 percent of all e-mail, public pressure increased for the government to address the problem. The federal Controlling the Assault of Non-Solicited Pornography and Marketing (CAN-SPAM) Act[83] empowers Internet service providers, state attorneys general and federal agencies to pursue spammers in federal courts with criminal and civil penalties. The law prohibits the use of false header information in commercial e-mail and requires unsolicited messages to include opt-out instructions. It also provides protection against spam containing unmarked pornographic material. Penalties for violations include up to five years' imprisonment and fines of up to $6 million. Subsequent FTC rules strengthen its enforcement policies.[84]

Most states have their own anti-spam laws.[85] In Virginia, where laws target unsolicited commercial bulk e-mails,[86] Jeremy Jaynes, a man once considered one of the world's most prolific spammers,[87] was charged with violating the law after he sent more than 55,000 unsolicited e-mails to subscribers of America Online. The Virginia Supreme Court overturned lower court rulings upholding Jaynes' conviction. The court said the law's prohibition on false routing information was overbroad and facially unconstitutional because it infringed the First Amendment right to engage in anonymous speech by targeting not only unsolicited commercial bulk e-mails but "the anonymous transmission of all unsolicited bulk e-mails including those containing political, religious or other speech protected by the First Amendment to the United States Constitution."[88] The U.S. Supreme Court declined to review the decision.[89]

The Eighth Circuit Court in 2013 addressed a similar problem related to fax advertisements. The Telephone Consumer Protection Act requires all unsolicited faxed ads to include instructions on how to opt out of future ads.[90] Deferring to the FCC's interpretation of its rules, the appeals court said the opt-out provision applied even to faxes for which the recipient had consented because the rule was intended to prevent recipients' limited consent from becoming global and permanent.[91] The decision returned the case to the trial court where the sender faced a multimillion-dollar class action suit for neglecting to include opt-out language in faxes for which the recipient had given prior explicit consent.

SUMMARY

THE GROWTH OF THE INTERNET HAS MEANT a growth in advertising on the medium. As with other media, the government monitors Internet advertising. The Federal Trade Commission and federal and state legislators have dealt with improper advertising practices online. Congress enacted the CAN-SPAM Act to help prevent unsolicited e-mail messages. A majority of states also have anti-spam laws, though a section of at least one, Virginia's, has been ruled unconstitutional. ∎

Cases for Study

Thinking About It

The two case excerpts that follow address the regulation of commercial speech and whether specific regulations are consistent with the First Amendment. The first is the U.S. Supreme Court case that established the test for answering that question. In the second case, the U.S. Supreme Court declines to apply that test and shifts toward the scrutiny it employs in "pure" speech cases. As you read these case excerpts, keep the following questions in mind:

- What are the circumstances surrounding each case?
- Specifically what type of speech is involved and in what ways is it intermingled with commerce?
- What is the nature of the regulations being challenged?
- What is the state interest in each case? Are those interests legitimate?
- How does the Court's review in *Sorrell* differ from the test established by *Central Hudson?* What implications does this shift have for First Amendment protection of commercial speech?

Central Hudson Gas & Electric Corp. v. Public Service Commission of New York
SUPREME COURT OF THE UNITED STATES
447 U.S. 557 (1980)

JUSTICE LEWIS POWELL delivered the Court's opinion:

This case presents the question whether a regulation of the Public Service Commission of the State of New York violates the First and Fourteenth Amendments because it completely bans promotional advertising by an electrical utility.

In December, 1973, the Commission, appellee here, ordered electric utilities in New York State to cease all advertising that "promot[es] the use of electricity." The order was based on the Commission's finding that "the interconnected utility system in New York State does not have sufficient fuel stocks or sources of supply to continue furnishing all customer demands for the 1973–1974 winter."

Three years later, when the fuel shortage had eased, the Commission requested comments from the public on its proposal to continue the ban on promotional advertising. Central Hudson Gas & Electric Corp., the appellant in this case, opposed the ban on First Amendment grounds. After reviewing the public comments, the Commission extended the prohibition in a Policy Statement issued on February 25, 1977.

The Policy Statement divided advertising expenses "into two broad categories: promotional—advertising intended to stimulate the purchase of utility services . . . and institutional and informational, a broad category inclusive of all advertising not clearly intended to promote sales." The Commission declared all promotional advertising contrary to the national policy of conserving energy. It acknowledged that the ban is not a perfect vehicle for conserving energy. For example, the Commission's order prohibits promotional advertising to develop consumption during periods when demand for electricity is low. By limiting growth in "off-peak" consumption, the ban limits the "beneficial side effects" of such growth in terms of more efficient use of existing powerplants. And since oil dealers are not under the Commission's jurisdiction and thus remain free to advertise, it was recognized that the ban can achieve only "piecemeal conservationism." Still, the Commission adopted the restriction because it was deemed likely to "result in some dampening of unnecessary growth" in energy consumption.

The Commission's order explicitly permitted "informational" advertising designed to encourage "shifts of consumption" from peak demand times to periods of low electricity demand. Informational advertising would not seek to increase aggregate consumption, but would invite a leveling of demand throughout any given 24-hour period. The agency offered to review "specific proposals by the companies for specifically described [advertising] programs that meet these criteria."

When it rejected requests for rehearing on the Policy Statement, the Commission supplemented its rationale for the advertising ban. The agency observed that additional electricity probably would be more expensive to produce than existing output. Because electricity rates in New York were not then based on marginal cost, the Commission feared that additional power would be priced below the actual cost of generation. The additional electricity would be subsidized by all consumers through generally higher rates. The state agency also thought that promotional advertising would give "misleading signals" to the public by appearing to encourage energy consumption at a time when conservation is needed. . . .

The Commission's order restricts only commercial speech, that is, expression related solely to the economic interests of the speaker and its audience. The First Amendment, as applied to the States through the Fourteenth Amendment, protects commercial speech from unwarranted governmental regulation. Commercial expression not only serves the economic interest of the speaker, but also assists consumers and furthers the societal interest in the fullest possible dissemination of information. In applying the First Amendment to this area, we have rejected the "highly paternalistic"

view that government has complete power to suppress or regulate commercial speech. . . .

Nevertheless, our decisions have recognized "the 'commonsense' distinction between speech proposing a commercial transaction, which occurs in an area traditionally subject to government regulation, and other varieties of speech." . . . The Constitution therefore accords a lesser protection to commercial speech than to other constitutionally guaranteed expression. The protection available for particular commercial expression turns on the nature both of the expression and of the governmental interests served by its regulation.

The First Amendment's concern for commercial speech is based on the informational function of advertising. Consequently, there can be no constitutional objection to the suppression of commercial messages that do not accurately inform the public about lawful activity. The government may ban forms of communication more likely to deceive the public than to inform it, or commercial speech related to illegal activity.

If the communication is neither misleading nor related to unlawful activity, the government's power is more circumscribed. The State must assert a substantial interest to be achieved by restrictions on commercial speech. Moreover, the regulatory technique must be in proportion to that interest. The limitation on expression must be designed carefully to achieve the State's goal. Compliance with this requirement may be measured by two criteria. First, the restriction must directly advance the state interest involved; the regulation may not be sustained if it provides only ineffective or remote support for the government's purpose. Second, if the governmental interest could be served as well by a more limited restriction on commercial speech, the excessive restrictions cannot survive. . . .

The second criterion recognizes that the First Amendment mandates that speech restrictions be "narrowly drawn." The regulatory technique may extend only as far as the interest it serves. The State cannot regulate speech that poses no danger to the asserted state interest, nor can it completely suppress information when narrower restrictions on expression would serve its interest as well. . . .

In this case, the Commission's prohibition acts directly against the promotional activities of Central Hudson, and, to the extent the limitations are unnecessary to serve the State's interest, they are invalid. . . .

In commercial speech cases, then, a four-part analysis has developed. At the outset, we must determine whether the expression is protected by the First Amendment. For commercial speech to come within that provision, it at least must concern lawful activity and not be misleading. Next, we ask whether the asserted governmental interest is substantial. If both inquiries yield positive answers, we must determine whether the regulation directly advances the governmental interest asserted, and whether it is not more extensive than is necessary to serve that interest.

We now apply this four-step analysis for commercial speech to the Commission's arguments in support of its ban on promotional advertising.

The Commission does not claim that the expression at issue either is inaccurate or relates to unlawful activity. Yet the New York Court of Appeals questioned whether Central Hudson's advertising is protected commercial speech. Because appellant holds a monopoly over the sale of electricity in its service area, the state court suggested that the Commission's order restricts no commercial speech of any worth. The court stated that advertising in a "noncompetitive market" could not improve the decisionmaking of consumers. The court saw no constitutional problem with barring commercial speech that it viewed as conveying little useful information.

This reasoning falls short of establishing that appellant's advertising is not commercial speech protected by the First Amendment. Monopoly over the supply of a product provides no protection from competition with substitutes for that product. . . .

Even in monopoly markets, the suppression of advertising reduces the information available for consumer decisions and thereby defeats the purpose of the First Amendment. The New York court's argument appears to assume that the providers of a monopoly service or product are willing to pay for wholly ineffective advertising. Most businesses—even regulated monopolies—are unlikely to underwrite promotional

advertising that is of no interest or use to consumers. Indeed, a monopoly enterprise legitimately may wish to inform the public that it has developed new services or terms of doing business. A consumer may need information to aid his decision whether or not to use the monopoly service at all, or how much of the service he should purchase. In the absence of factors that would distort the decision to advertise, we may assume that the willingness of a business to promote its products reflects a belief that consumers are interested in the advertising. Since no such extraordinary conditions have been identified in this case, appellant's monopoly position does not alter the First Amendment's protection for its commercial speech.

The Commission offers two state interests as justifications for the ban on promotional advertising. The first concerns energy conservation. Any increase in demand for electricity—during peak or off-peak periods—means greater consumption of energy. The Commission argues, and the New York court agreed, that the State's interest in conserving energy is sufficient to support suppression of advertising designed to increase consumption of electricity. In view of our country's dependence on energy resources beyond our control, no one can doubt the importance of energy conservation. Plainly, therefore, the state interest asserted is substantial.

The Commission also argues that promotional advertising will aggravate inequities caused by the failure to base the utilities' rates on marginal cost. The utilities argued to the Commission that if they could promote the use of electricity in periods of low demand, they would improve their utilization of generating capacity. The Commission responded that promotion of off-peak consumption also would increase consumption during peak periods. If peak demand were to rise, the absence of marginal cost rates would mean that the rates charged for the additional power would not reflect the true costs of expanding production. Instead, the extra costs would be borne by all consumers through higher overall rates. Without promotional advertising, the Commission stated, this inequitable turn of events would be less likely to occur. The choice among rate structures involves difficult and important questions of economic supply and distributional fairness. The State's concern that rates be fair and efficient represents a clear and substantial governmental interest.

Next, we focus on the relationship between the State's interests and the advertising ban. Under this criterion, the Commission's laudable concern over the equity and efficiency of appellant's rates does not provide a constitutionally adequate reason for restricting protected speech. The link between the advertising prohibition and appellant's rate structure is, at most, tenuous. The impact of promotional advertising on the equity of appellant's rates is highly speculative. Advertising to increase off-peak usage would have to increase peak usage, while other factors that directly affect the fairness and efficiency of appellant's rates remained constant. Such conditional and remote eventualities simply cannot justify silencing appellant's promotional advertising.

In contrast, the State's interest in energy conservation is directly advanced by the Commission order at issue here. There is an immediate connection between advertising and demand for electricity. Central Hudson would not contest the advertising ban unless it believed that promotion would increase its sales. Thus, we find a direct link between the state interest in conservation and the Commission's order.

We come finally to the critical inquiry in this case: whether the Commission's complete suppression of speech ordinarily protected by the First Amendment is no more extensive than necessary to further the State's interest in energy conservation. The Commission's order reaches all promotional advertising, regardless of the impact of the touted service on overall energy use. But the energy conservation rationale, as important as it is, cannot justify suppressing information about electric devices or services that would cause no net increase in total energy use. In addition, no showing has been made that a more limited restriction on the content of promotional advertising would not serve adequately the State's interests.

Appellant insists that, but for the ban, it would advertise products and services that use energy efficiently. These include the "heat pump," which both parties acknowledge to be a major improvement in electric heating, and the use of electric heat as a "backup" to solar and other heat sources. Although the Commission has questioned the efficiency of electric heating before this Court, neither the Commission's Policy Statement nor its order denying rehearing made findings on this issue. In the absence of authoritative findings to the contrary, we must credit as within the realm of possibility the claim that electric heat can be an efficient alternative in some circumstances.

The Commission's order prevents appellant from promoting electric services that would reduce energy use by diverting demand from less efficient sources, or that would consume roughly the same amount of energy as do alternative sources. In neither situation would the utility's advertising endanger conservation or mislead the public. To the extent that the Commission's order suppresses speech that in no way impairs the State's interest in energy conservation, the Commission's order violates the First and Fourteenth Amendments, and must be invalidated.

The Commission also has not demonstrated that its interest in conservation cannot be protected adequately by more limited regulation of appellant's commercial expression. To further its policy of conservation, the Commission could attempt to restrict the format and content of Central Hudson's advertising. It might, for example, require that the advertisements include information about the relative efficiency and expense of the offered service, both under current conditions and for the foreseeable future. In the absence of a showing that more limited speech regulation would be ineffective, we cannot approve the complete suppression of Central Hudson's advertising.

Our decision today in no way disparages the national interest in energy conservation. We accept without reservation the argument that conservation, as well as the development of alternative energy sources, is an imperative national goal. Administrative bodies empowered to regulate electric utilities have the authority—and indeed the duty—to take appropriate action to further this goal. When, however, such action involves the suppression of speech, the First and Fourteenth Amendments require that the restriction be no more extensive than is necessary to serve the state interest. In this case, the record before us fails to show that the total ban on promotional advertising meets this requirement.

Accordingly, the judgment of the New York Court of Appeals is

Reversed. . . .

JUSTICE WILLIAM REHNQUIST, dissenting:

The Court today invalidates an order issued by the New York Public Service Commission designed to promote a policy that has been declared to be of critical national concern. The order was issued by the Commission in 1973 in response to the Mideastern oil embargo crisis. It prohibits electric corporations "from promoting the use of electricity through the use of advertising, subsidy payments . . . or employee incentives." Although the immediate crisis created by the oil embargo has subsided, the ban on promotional advertising remains in effect. The regulation was re-examined by the New York Public Service Commission in 1977. Its constitutionality was subsequently upheld by the New York Court of Appeals, which concluded that the paramount national interest in energy conservation justified its retention.

The Court's asserted justification for invalidating the New York law is the public interest discerned by the Court to underlie the First Amendment in the free flow of commercial information. Prior to this Court's recent decision in *Virginia Pharmacy Board v. Virginia Citizens Consumer Council,* however, commercial speech was afforded no protection under the First Amendment whatsoever. Given what seems to me full recognition of the holding of *Virginia Pharmacy Board* that commercial speech is entitled to some degree of First Amendment protection, I think the Court is nonetheless incorrect in invalidating the carefully considered state ban on promotional advertising in light of pressing national and state energy needs. . . .

This Court has previously recognized that, although commercial speech may be entitled to First Amendment protection, that protection is not as extensive as that accorded to the advocacy of ideas. . . . We have not discarded the 'common-sense' distinction between speech proposing a commercial transaction, which occurs in an area traditionally subject to

government regulation, and other varieties of speech. To require a parity of constitutional protection for commercial and noncommercial speech alike could invite dilution, simply by a leveling process, of the force of the Amendment's guarantee with respect to the latter kind of speech. Rather than subject the First Amendment to such a devitalization, we instead have afforded commercial speech a limited measure of protection, commensurate with its subordinate position in the scale of First Amendment values, while allowing modes of regulation that might be impermissible in the realm of noncommercial expression."

The Court's decision today fails to give due deference to this subordinate position of commercial speech. The Court in so doing returns to the bygone era . . . in which it was common practice for this Court to strike down economic regulations adopted by a State based on the Court's own notions of the most appropriate means for the State to implement its considered policies.

I had thought by now it had become well established that a State has broad discretion in imposing economic regulations. . . . The State of New York has determined here that economic realities require the grant of monopoly status to public utilities in order to distribute efficiently the services they provide, and in granting utilities such status it has made them subject to an extensive regulatory scheme. When the State adopted this scheme and when its Public Service Commission issued its initial ban on promotional advertising in 1973, commercial speech had not been held to fall within the scope of the First Amendment at all. . . .

The Court today holds not only that commercial speech is entitled to First Amendment protection, but also that when it is protected a State may not regulate it unless its reason for doing so amounts to a "substantial" governmental interest, its regulation "directly advances" that interest, and its manner of regulation is "not more extensive than necessary" to serve the interest. The test adopted by the Court thus elevates the protection accorded commercial speech that falls within the scope of the First Amendment to a level that is virtually indistinguishable from that of noncommercial speech. . . .

An ostensible justification for striking down New York's ban on promotional advertising is that this Court has previously "rejected the 'highly paternalistic' view that government has complete power to suppress or regulate commercial speech. '[P]eople will perceive their own best interests if only they are well enough informed and . . . the best means to that end is to open the channels of communication, rather than to close them. . . .'" Whatever the merits of this view, I think the Court has carried its logic too far here. . . .

While it is true that an important objective of the First Amendment is to foster the free flow of information, identification of speech that falls within its protection is not aided by the metaphorical reference to a "marketplace of ideas." There is no reason for believing that the marketplace of ideas is free from market imperfections any more than there is to believe that the invisible hand will always lead to optimum economic decisions in the commercial market. . . . Indeed, many types of speech have been held to fall outside the scope of the First Amendment, thereby subject to governmental regulation, despite this Court's references to a marketplace of ideas. . . .

I remain of the view that the Court unlocked a Pandora's Box when it "elevated" commercial speech to the level of traditional political speech by according it First Amendment protection in *Virginia Pharmacy Board v. Virginia Citizens Consumer Council.* The line between "commercial speech," and the kind of speech that those who drafted the First Amendment had in mind may not be a technically or intellectually easy one to draw, but it surely produced far fewer problems than has the development of judicial doctrine in this area since *Virginia Pharmacy Board.* . . .

The notion that more speech is the remedy to expose falsehood and fallacies is wholly out of place in the commercial bazaar, where if applied logically the remedy of one who was defrauded would be merely a statement, available upon request, reciting the Latin maxim *"caveat emptor."* But since "fraudulent speech" in this area is to be remediable under *Virginia Pharmacy Board,* the remedy of one defrauded is a lawsuit or an agency proceeding based on common-law notions of fraud that are separated by a world of

difference from the realm of politics and government. What time, legal decisions, and common sense have so widely severed, I declined to join in *Virginia Pharmacy Board,* and regret now to see the Court reaping the seeds that it there sowed. For in a democracy, the economic is subordinate to the political, a lesson that our ancestors learned long ago, and that our descendants will undoubtedly have to relearn many years hence.

The Court concedes that the state interest in energy conservation is plainly substantial, as is the State's concern that its rates be fair and efficient. It also concedes that there is a direct link between the Commission's ban on promotional advertising and the State's interest in conservation. The Court nonetheless strikes down the ban on promotional advertising because the Commission has failed to demonstrate, under the final part of the Court's four-part test, that its regulation is no more extensive than necessary to serve the State's interest. In reaching this conclusion, the Court conjures up potential advertisements that a utility might make that conceivably would result in net energy savings. The Court does not indicate that the New York Public Service Commission has in fact construed its ban on "promotional" advertising to preclude the dissemination of information that clearly would result in a net energy savings, nor does it even suggest that the Commission has been confronted with and rejected such an advertising proposal. The final part of the Court's test thus leaves room for so many hypothetical "better" ways that any ingenious lawyer will surely seize on one of them to secure the invalidation of what the state agency actually did. . . .

Ordinarily it is the role of the State Public Service Commission to make factual determinations concerning whether a device or service will result in a net energy savings and, if so, whether and to what extent state law permits dissemination of information about the device or service. Otherwise, as here, this Court will have no factual basis for its assertions. And the State will never have an opportunity to consider the issue and thus to construe its law in a manner consistent with the Federal Constitution. . . .

It is, in my view, inappropriate for the Court to invalidate the State's ban on commercial advertising here, based on its speculation that in some cases the advertising may result in a net savings in electrical energy use, and in the cases in which it is clear a net energy savings would result from utility advertising, the Public Service Commission would apply its ban so as to proscribe such advertising. Even assuming that

the Court's speculation is correct, I do not think it follows that facial invalidation of the ban is the appropriate course. . . .

For the foregoing reasons, I would affirm the judgment of the New York Court of Appeals.

Sorrell v. IMS Health Inc.
SUPREME COURT OF THE UNITED STATES
131 S. Ct. 2653 (2011)

JUSTICE ANTHONY KENNEDY delivered the Court's opinion:
. . . Pharmaceutical manufacturers promote their drugs to doctors through a process called "detailing." This often involves a scheduled visit to a doctor's office to persuade the doctor to prescribe a particular pharmaceutical. Detailers bring drug samples as well as medical studies that explain the "details" and potential advantages of various prescription drugs. Interested physicians listen, ask questions, and receive followup data. Salespersons can be more effective when they know the background and purchasing preferences of their clientele, and pharmaceutical salespersons are no exception. Knowledge of a physician's prescription practices—called "prescriber-identifying information"—enables a detailer better to ascertain which doctors are likely to be interested in a particular drug and how best to present a particular sales message. Detailing is an expensive undertaking, so pharmaceutical companies most often use it to promote high-profit brand-name drugs protected by patent. Once a brand-name drug's patent expires, less expensive bioequivalent generic alternatives are manufactured and sold.

Pharmacies, as a matter of business routine and federal law, receive prescriber-identifying information when processing prescriptions. Many pharmacies sell this information to "data miners," firms that analyze prescriber-identifying information and produce reports on prescriber behavior. Data miners lease these reports to pharmaceutical manufacturers subject to nondisclosure agreements. Detailers, who represent

the manufacturers, then use the reports to refine their marketing tactics and increase sales.

In 2007, Vermont enacted the Prescription Confidentiality Law. The measure is also referred to as Act 80. It has several components. The central provision of the present case is § 4631(d).

A health insurer, a self-insured employer, an electronic transmission intermediary, a pharmacy, or other similar entity shall not sell, license, or exchange for value regulated records containing prescriber-identifiable information, nor permit the use of regulated records containing prescriber-identifiable information for marketing or promoting a prescription drug, unless the prescriber consents. . . . Pharmaceutical manufacturers and pharmaceutical marketers shall not use prescriber-identifiable information for marketing or promoting a prescription drug unless the prescriber consents. . . .

The quoted provision has three component parts. The provision begins by prohibiting pharmacies, health insurers, and similar entities from selling prescriber-identifying information, absent the prescriber's consent. The parties here dispute whether this clause applies to all sales or only to sales for marketing. The provision then goes on to prohibit pharmacies, health insurers, and similar entities from allowing prescriber-identifying information to be used for marketing, unless the prescriber consents. This prohibition in effect bars pharmacies from disclosing the information for marketing purposes. Finally, the provision's second sentence bars pharmaceutical manufacturers and pharmaceutical marketers from using prescriber-identifying information for marketing, again absent the prescriber's consent. The Vermont attorney general may pursue civil remedies against violators.

Separate statutory provisions elaborate the scope of the prohibitions. . . . "Marketing" is defined to include "advertising, promotion, or any activity" that is "used to influence sales or the market share of a prescription drug." § 4631(d) further provides that Vermont's Department of Health must allow "a prescriber to give consent for his or her identifying information to be used for the purposes" identified. . . . Finally, the Act's prohibitions on sale, disclosure, and use are subject to a list of exceptions. For example, prescriber-identifying information may be disseminated or used for "health care research"; to enforce "compliance" with health insurance formularies, or preferred drug lists; for "care management educational communications provided to" patients on such matters as "treatment options"; for law enforcement operations; and for purposes "otherwise provided by law."

Act 80 also authorized funds for an "evidence-based prescription drug education program" designed to provide doctors and others with "information and education on the therapeutic and cost-effective utilization of prescription drugs." An express aim of the program is to advise prescribers "about commonly used brand-name drugs for which the patent has expired" or will soon expire. Similar efforts to promote the use of generic pharmaceuticals are sometimes referred to as "counter-detailing." The counter-detailer's recommended substitute may be an older, less expensive drug and not a bioequivalent of the brand-name drug the physician might otherwise prescribe. Like the pharmaceutical manufacturers whose efforts they hope to resist, counterdetailers in some states use prescriber-identifying information to increase their effectiveness. States themselves may supply the prescriber-identifying information used in these programs. . . .

Act 80 was accompanied by legislative findings. Vermont found, for example, that the "goals of marketing programs are often in conflict with the goals of the state" and that the "marketplace for ideas on medicine safety and effectiveness is frequently one-sided in that brand-name companies invest in expensive pharmaceutical marketing campaigns to doctors. Detailing, in the legislature's view, caused doctors to make decisions based on "incomplete and biased information." Because they "are unable to take the time to research the quickly changing pharmaceutical market," Vermont doctors "rely on information provided by pharmaceutical representatives." The legislature further found that detailing increases the cost of health care and health insurance; encourages hasty and excessive reliance on brand-name drugs, before the profession has observed their effectiveness as compared with older and less expensive generic alternatives; and fosters disruptive and repeated marketing visits tantamount to harassment. . . . Use of prescriber-identifying data also helps detailers shape their messages by "tailoring" their "presentations to individual prescriber styles, preferences, and attitudes."

The present case involves two consolidated suits. One was brought by three Vermont data miners, the other by an association of pharmaceutical manufacturers that produce brand-name drugs. . . . Contending that § 4631(d) violates their First Amendment rights as incorporated by the Fourteenth Amendment, the respondents sought declaratory and injunctive relief. . . .

After a bench trial, the United States District Court for the District of Vermont denied relief. The District Court found that "[p]harmaceutical manufacturers are essentially the only paying customers of the data vendor industry" and that, because detailing unpatented generic drugs is not "cost-effective," pharmaceutical sales representatives "detail only branded drugs." . . . The United States Court of Appeals for the 2nd Circuit reversed and remanded. It held that § 4631(d) violates the First Amendment by burdening the speech of pharmaceutical marketers and data miners without an adequate justification. . . . The decision of the 2nd Circuit is in conflict with decisions of the United States Court of Appeals for the 1st Circuit concerning similar legislation enacted by Maine and New Hampshire. Recognizing a division of authority regarding the constitutionality of state statutes, this Court granted certiorari.

The beginning point is the text of § 4631(d). In the proceedings below, Vermont stated that the first sentence . . . prohibits pharmacies and other regulated entities from selling or disseminating prescriber-identifying information for marketing. The information, in other words, could be sold or given away for purposes other than marketing. . . . At oral argument in this Court, however, the state for the first time advanced an alternative reading . . . namely, that pharmacies, health insurers, and similar entities may not sell prescriber-identifying information for any purpose, subject to the statutory exceptions set out [in the law]. It might be argued that the state's newfound interpretation comes too late in the day. . . . For the state to change its position is particularly troubling in a First Amendment case, where plaintiffs have a special interest in obtaining a prompt adjudication of their rights, despite potential ambiguities of state law.

In any event, § 4631(d) cannot be sustained even under the interpretation the state now adopts. As a consequence this Court can assume that the opening clause . . . prohibits pharmacies, health insurers, and similar entities from selling prescriber-identifying information, subject to the statutory exceptions set out . . . Under that reading, pharmacies may sell the information to private or academic researchers, but not, for example, to pharmaceutical marketers. There is no dispute as to the remainder of § 4631. It prohibits pharmacies, health insurers, and similar entities from disclosing or otherwise allowing prescriber-identifying information to be used for marketing. And it bars pharmaceutical manufacturers and detailers from using the information for marketing. The questions now are whether § 4631(d) must be tested by heightened judicial scrutiny and, if so, whether the state can justify the law.

On its face, Vermont's law enacts content- and speaker-based restrictions on the sale, disclosure, and use of prescriber-identifying information. The provision first forbids sale subject to exceptions based in large part on the content of a purchaser's speech. For example, those who wish to engage in certain "educational communications," may purchase the information. The measure then bars any disclosure when recipient speakers will use the information for marketing. Finally, the provision's second sentence prohibits pharmaceutical manufacturers from using the information for marketing. The statute thus disfavors marketing, that is, speech with a particular content. More than that, the statute disfavors specific speakers, namely pharmaceutical manufacturers. As a result of these content- and speaker-based rules, detailers cannot obtain prescriber-identifying information, even though the information may be purchased or acquired by other speakers with diverse purposes and viewpoints. Detailers are likewise barred from using the information for marketing, even though the information may be used by a wide range of other speakers. For example, it appears that Vermont could supply academic organizations with prescriber-identifying information to use in countering the messages of brand-name pharmaceutical manufacturers and in promoting the prescription of generic drugs. But § 4631(d) leaves detailers no means of purchasing, acquiring, or using prescriber-identifying information. The law on its face burdens disfavored speech by disfavored speakers.

Any doubt that § 4631(d) imposes an aimed, content-based burden on detailers is dispelled by the record and by formal legislative findings. As the District Court noted, "[p]harmaceutical manufacturers are essentially the only paying customers of the data vendor industry"; and the almost invariable rule is that detailing by pharmaceutical manufacturers is in support of brand-name drugs. Vermont's law thus has the effect of preventing detailers—and only detailers—from communicating with physicians in an effective and informative manner. Formal legislative findings accompanying § 4631(d) confirm that the law's express purpose and practical effect are to diminish the effectiveness of marketing by manufacturers of brand-name drugs. . . . The legislature designed § 4631(d) to target those speakers and their messages for disfavored treatment. "In its practical operation," Vermont's law "goes even beyond mere content discrimination, to actual viewpoint discrimination." Given the legislature's expressed statement of purpose, it is apparent that § 4631(d) imposes burdens that are based on the content of speech and that are aimed at a particular viewpoint.

Act 80 is designed to impose a specific, content-based burden on protected expression. It follows that heightened judicial scrutiny is warranted. The Court has recognized that the "distinction between laws burdening and laws banning speech is but a matter of degree" and that the "Government's content-based burdens must satisfy the same rigorous scrutiny as its content-based bans."

The First Amendment requires heightened scrutiny whenever the government creates "a regulation of speech because of disagreement with the message it conveys." . . . Even if the hypothetical measure on its face appeared neutral as to content and speaker, its purpose to suppress speech and its unjustified burdens on expression would render it unconstitutional. Commercial speech is no exception. A "consumer's concern for the free flow of commercial speech often may be far keener than his concern for urgent political dialogue." That reality has great relevance in the fields of medicine and public health, where information can save lives.

The State argues that heightened judicial scrutiny is unwarranted because its law is a mere commercial regulation. It is true that restrictions on protected expression are distinct from restrictions on economic activity or, more generally, on nonexpressive conduct. It is also true that the First Amendment does not prevent restrictions directed at commerce or conduct from imposing incidental burdens on speech. . . . But § 4631(d) imposes more than an incidental burden on protected expression. Both on its face and in its practical operation, Vermont's law imposes a burden based on the content of speech and the identity of the speaker. While the burdened speech results from an economic motive, so too does a great deal of vital expression. Vermont's law does not simply have an effect on speech, but is directed at certain content and is aimed at particular speakers. . . .

Vermont further argues that § 4631(d) regulates not speech but simply access to information. Prescriber-identifying information was generated in compliance with a legal mandate, the state argues, and so could be considered a kind of governmental information. . . . An individual's right to speak is implicated when information he or she possesses is subjected to "restraints on the way in which the information might be used" or disseminated. . . . It is true that the respondents here . . . do not themselves possess information whose disclosure has been curtailed. That information, however, is in the hands of pharmacies and other private entities. There is no question that the "threat of prosecution . . . hangs over their heads." . . . [R]estrictions on the disclosure of government-held information can facilitate or burden the expression of potential recipients and so transgress the First Amendment. Vermont's law imposes a content- and speaker-based burden on respondents' own speech. That consideration . . . requires heightened judicial scrutiny.

The state also contends that heightened judicial scrutiny is unwarranted in this case because sales, transfer, and use of prescriber-identifying information are conduct, not speech. Consistent with that submission, the United States Court of Appeals for the 1st Circuit has characterized prescriber-identifying information as a mere "commodity" with no greater entitlement to First Amendment protection than "beef jerky. " In contrast the courts below concluded that a prohibition on the sale of prescriber-identifying information is a content-based rule akin to a ban on the sale of cookbooks, laboratory results, or train schedules.

This Court has held that the creation and dissemination of information are speech within the meaning of the First Amendment. Facts, after all, are the beginning point for much of the speech that is most essential to advance human knowledge and to conduct human affairs. There is thus a strong argument that prescriber-identifying information is speech for First Amendment purposes.

The state asks for an exception to the rule that information is speech, but there is no need to consider that request in this case. The state has imposed content- and speaker-based restrictions on the availability and use of prescriber-identifying information. So long as they do not engage in marketing, many speakers can obtain and use the information. But detailers cannot. Vermont's statute could be compared with a law prohibiting trade magazines from purchasing or using ink. Like that hypothetical law, § 4631(d) imposes a speaker- and content-based burden on protected expression, and that circumstance is sufficient to justify application of heightened scrutiny. As a consequence, this case can be resolved even assuming, as the state argues, that prescriber-identifying information is a mere commodity.

In the ordinary case it is all but dispositive to conclude that a law is content-based and, in practice, viewpoint-discriminatory. The state argues that a different analysis applies here because, assuming § 4631(d) burdens speech at all, it at most burdens only commercial speech. As in previous cases, however, the outcome is the same whether a special commercial speech inquiry or a stricter form of judicial scrutiny is applied. For the same reason there is no need to determine whether all speech hampered by § 4631(d) is commercial, as our cases have used that term. Cf.

Under a commercial speech inquiry, it is the state's burden to justify its content-based law as consistent with the First Amendment. To sustain the targeted, content-based burden § 4631(d) imposes on protected expression, the state must show at least that the statute directly advances a substantial governmental interest and that the measure is drawn to achieve that interest. There must be a "fit between the legislature's ends and the means chosen to accomplish those ends." As in other contexts, these standards ensure not only that the state's interests are proportional to the resulting burdens placed on speech but also that the law does not seek to suppress a disfavored message.

The state's asserted justifications for § 4631(d) come under two general headings. First, the state contends that its law is necessary to protect medical privacy, including physician confidentiality, avoidance of harassment, and the integrity of the doctor-patient relationship. Second, the state argues that § 4631(d) is integral to the achievement of policy objectives—namely, improved public health and reduced health-care costs. Neither justification withstands scrutiny.

Vermont argues that its physicians have a "reasonable expectation" that their prescriber-identifying information "will not be used for purposes other than . . . filling and processing" prescriptions. It may be assumed that, for many reasons, physicians have an interest in keeping their prescription decisions confidential. But § 4631(d) is not drawn to serve that interest. Under Vermont's law, pharmacies may share prescriber-identifying information with anyone for any reason save one: They must not allow the information to be used for marketing. Exceptions further allow pharmacies to sell prescriber-identifying information for certain purposes, including "health care research." § 4631(e). And the measure permits insurers, researchers, journalists, the state itself, and others to use the information. . . .

Perhaps the state could have addressed physician confidentiality through "a more coherent policy." . . . But the state did not enact a statute with that purpose or design. Instead, Vermont made prescriber-identifying information available to an almost limitless audience. The explicit structure of the statute allows the information to be studied and used by all but a narrow class of disfavored speakers. Given the information's widespread availability and many permissible uses, the state's asserted interest in physician confidentiality does not justify the burden that § 4631(d) places on protected expression.

The State points out that it allows doctors to forgo the advantages of § 4631(d) by consenting to the sale, disclosure, and use of their prescriber-identifying information. See § 4631(c)(1). . . . Vermont has given its doctors a contrived choice: Either consent, which will allow your prescriber-identifying information to be disseminated and used without constraint; or, withhold consent, which will allow your information to be used by those speakers whose message the state supports. Section 4631(d) may offer a limited degree of privacy, but only on terms favorable to the speech the state prefers. . . . [T]he state has conditioned privacy on acceptance of a content-based rule that is not drawn to serve the state's asserted interest. To obtain the limited privacy allowed by § 4631(d), Vermont physicians are forced to acquiesce in the state's goal of burdening disfavored speech by disfavored speakers.

. . . Rules that burden protected expression may not be sustained when the options provided by the state are too narrow to advance legitimate interests or too broad to protect speech. As already explained, § 4631(d) permits extensive use of prescriber-identifying information and so does not advance the state's asserted interest in physician confidentiality. The limited range of available privacy options instead reflects the state's impermissible purpose to burden disfavored speech.

The state also contends that § 4631(d) protects doctors from "harassing sales behaviors." "Some doctors in Vermont are experiencing an undesired increase in the aggressiveness of pharmaceutical sales representatives," the Vermont Legislature found, "and a few have reported that they felt coerced and harassed." It is doubtful that concern for "a few" physicians who may have "felt coerced and harassed" by pharmaceutical marketers can sustain a broad content-based rule like § 4631(d). Many are those who must endure speech they do not like, but that is a necessary cost of freedom. In any event the State offers no explanation why remedies other than content-based rules would be inadequate. Physicians can, and often do, simply decline to meet with detailers, including detailers who use prescriber-identifying information. Doctors who wish to forgo detailing altogether are free to give "No Solicitation" or "No Detailing" instructions to their office managers or to receptionists at their places of work. . . .

Vermont argues that detailers' use of prescriber-identifying information undermines the doctor-patient relationship by allowing detailers to influence treatment decisions. According to the state, "unwanted pressure occurs" when doctors learn that their prescription decisions are being "monitored" by detailers. Some physicians accuse detailers of "spying" or of engaging in "underhanded" conduct in order to "subvert" prescription decisions. And Vermont claims that detailing makes people "anxious" about whether doctors have their patients' best interests at heart. But the state does not explain why detailers' use of prescriber-identifying information is more likely to prompt these objections than many other uses permitted by § 4631(d). In any event, this asserted interest is contrary to basic First Amendment principles. Speech remains protected even when it may "stir people to action," "move them to tears," or "inflict great pain." The more benign and, many would say, beneficial speech of pharmaceutical marketing is also entitled to the protection of the First Amendment. If pharmaceutical marketing affects treatment decisions, it does so because doctors find it persuasive. Absent circumstances far from those presented here, the fear that speech might persuade provides no lawful basis for quieting it.

The state contends that § 4631(d) advances important public policy goals by lowering the costs of medical services and promoting public health. If prescriber-identifying information were available for use by detailers, the state contends, then detailing would be effective in promoting brand-name drugs that are more expensive and less safe than generic alternatives. This logic is set out at length in the legislative findings accompanying § 4631(d). Yet at oral argument here, the state declined to acknowledge that § 4631(d)'s objective purpose and practical effect were to inhibit detailing and alter doctors' prescription decisions. The state's reluctance to embrace its own legislature's rationale reflects the vulnerability of its position.

While Vermont's stated policy goals may be proper, § 4631(d) does not advance them in a permissible way. As the Court of Appeals noted, the "state's own explanation of how" § 4631(d) "advances its interests cannot be said to be direct." The state seeks to achieve its policy objectives through the indirect means of restraining certain speech by certain speakers—that is, by diminishing detailers' ability to influence prescription decisions. Those who seek to censor or burden free expression often assert that disfavored speech has adverse effects. But the "fear that people would make bad decisions if given truthful information" cannot justify content-based burdens on speech. These precepts apply with full force when the audience, in this case prescribing physicians, consists of "sophisticated and experienced" consumers.

As Vermont's legislative findings acknowledge, the premise of § 4631(d) is that the force of speech can justify the government's attempts to stifle it.

Indeed the state defends the law by insisting that "pharmaceutical marketing has a strong influence on doctors' prescribing practices." This reasoning is incompatible with the First Amendment. In an attempt to reverse a disfavored trend in public opinion, a state could not ban campaigning with slogans, picketing with signs, or marching during the daytime. Likewise the state may not seek to remove a popular but disfavored product from the marketplace by prohibiting truthful, nonmisleading advertisements that contain impressive endorsements or catchy jingles. That the state finds expression too persuasive does not permit it to quiet the speech or to burden its messengers.

The defect in Vermont's law is made clear by the fact that many listeners find detailing instructive. Indeed the record demonstrates that some Vermont doctors view targeted detailing based on prescriber-identifying information as "very helpful" because it allows detailers to shape their messages to each doctor's practice. Even the United States, which appeared here in support of Vermont, took care to dispute the state's "unwarranted view that the dangers of [n]ew drugs outweigh their benefits to patients." There are divergent views regarding detailing and the prescription of brand-name drugs. Under the Constitution, resolution of that debate must result from free and uninhibited speech. . . . The choice "between the dangers of suppressing information, and the dangers of its misuse if it is freely available" is one that "the First Amendment makes for us."

Vermont may be displeased that detailers who use prescriber-identifying information are effective in promoting brand-name drugs. The state can express that view through its own speech. But a state's failure to persuade does not allow it to hamstring the opposition. The state may not burden the speech of others in order to tilt public debate in a preferred direction. "The commercial marketplace, like other spheres of our social and cultural life, provides a forum where ideas and information flourish. Some of the ideas and information are vital, some of slight worth. But the general rule is that the speaker and the audience, not the government, assess the value of the information presented."

It is true that content-based restrictions on protected expression are sometimes permissible, and that principle applies to commercial speech. Indeed the government's legitimate interest in protecting consumers from "commercial harms" explains "why commercial speech can be subject to greater governmental regulation than noncommercial speech." Here, however, Vermont has not shown that its law has a neutral justification. The state nowhere contends that detailing is false or misleading within the meaning of this Court's First Amendment precedents. Nor does the state argue that the provision challenged here will prevent false or misleading speech. The state's interest in burdening the speech of detailers instead turns on nothing more than a difference of opinion.

* * *

The capacity of technology to find and publish personal information, including records required by the government, presents serious and unresolved issues with respect to personal privacy and the dignity it seeks to secure. In considering how to protect those interests, however, the state cannot engage in content-based discrimination to advance its own side of a debate.

If Vermont's statute provided that prescriber-identifying information could not be sold or disclosed except in narrow circumstances then the state might have a stronger position. Here, however, the state gives possessors of the information broad discretion and wide latitude in disclosing the information, while at the same time restricting the information's use by some speakers and for some purposes, even while the state itself can use the information to counter the speech it seeks to suppress. Privacy is a concept too integral to the person and a right too essential to freedom to allow its manipulation to support just those ideas the government prefers.

When it enacted § 4631(d), the Vermont Legislature found that the "marketplace for ideas on medicine safety and effectiveness is frequently one-sided in that brand name companies invest in expensive pharmaceutical marketing campaigns to doctors." "The goals of marketing programs," the legislature said, "are often in conflict with the goals of the state." The text of § 4631(d), associated legislative findings, and the record developed in the District Court establish that Vermont enacted its law for this end. The state has burdened a form of protected expression that it found too persuasive. At the same time, the state has left unburdened those speakers whose messages are in accord with its own views. This the state cannot do.

The judgment of the Court of Appeals is affirmed.

It is so ordered.

JUSTICE STEPHEN BREYER, with whom JUSTICE RUTH BADER GINSBURG and JUSTICE ELENA KAGAN join, dissenting.

The Vermont statute before us adversely affects expression in one, and only one, way. It deprives pharmaceutical and data-mining companies of data, collected pursuant to the government's regulatory mandate, that could help pharmaceutical companies create better sales messages. In my view, this effect on expression is inextricably related to a lawful governmental effort to regulate a commercial enterprise. The First Amendment does not require courts to apply a special "heightened" standard of review when reviewing such an effort. And, in any event, the statute meets the First Amendment standard this Court has previously applied when the government seeks to regulate commercial speech. For any or all of these reasons, the Court should uphold the statute as constitutional.

Endnotes

Chapter 1

The Rule of Law

1. Powell v. McCormack, 395 U.S. 486, 506 (1969) (citing Kilbourn v. Thompson, 103 U.S. 168, 199 (1881)).

2. Austin v. Michigan Chamber of Commerce, 494 U.S. 652 (1990); McConnell v. Federal Election Commission, 540 U.S. 93 (2003).

3. 2 U.S.C. § 441b (McCain–Feingold Act).

4. Federal Election Commission v. Wisconsin Right to Life, 551 U.S. 449, 534 (2007) (Souter, J., dissenting).

5. Citizens United v. Federal Elections Comm'n, 530 F. Supp. 2d 274 (D.D.C. 2008).

6. 588 U.S. 50 (2010).

7. *See* Dr. Seuss, The Lorax (1971). (Dr. Seuss is Theodore Seuss Geisel's pseudonym.)

8. Hedges v. Obama, No. 12 Civ. 331, 2012 WL 1721124 (S.D.N.Y. May 16, 2012) (order granting preliminary injunction).

9. Pub. L. No. 112-81, 125 Stat. 1298 (Dec. 31, 2011).

10. In re Hedges v. Obama, 133 S. Ct. 1307 (2013) (application to vacate stay denied).

11. Linda Greenhouse, *2,691 Decisions*, N.Y. Times, July 13, 2008, at WK1.

12. 5 U.S. 137, 177 (1803).

13. *See, e.g.,* Keeton v. Hustler Magazine, Inc., 465 U.S. 770 (1984) (overturning lower court ruling dismissing libel suit filed by resident of New York against Ohio corporation in New Hampshire court). *See also* New York Times v. Sullivan, 376 U.S. 254 (1964) (in which trial and first appeal were heard in Alabama courts).

14. Sherwin-Williams Co. v. Holmes County, 343 F.3d 383 (5th Cir. 2003); *see also In re* Condor Insurance Limited, 601 F.3d 319 (5th Cir. 2010).

15. Young v. New Haven Advocate, 315 F.3d 256, 261 (4th Cir. 2002), *cert. denied,* 538 U.S. 1035 (2003).

16. 28 U.S.C. § 1292(a)(1).

17. U.S. Const. art. III, § 1.

18. John P. Avlon, *Is Elena Kagan a Liberal—or a Centrist?*, CNN Opinion, June 30, 2010, *available at* http://www.cnn.com/2010/OPINION/06/29/avlon.kagan.centrist/index.html.

19. *Analysis: Justice Kagan—Giving Liberals a Rhetorical Lift*, Thompson Reuters News & Insignt, Feb. 23, 2013, *available at* http://newsandinsight.thomsonreuters.com/Legal/News/2012/04_-_April/Analysis__Justice_Kagan—Giving_liberals_a_rhetorical_lift/.

20. The Volokh Conspiracy, *available at* http://www.volokh.com/posts/1212602633.shtml (posted Aug. 3, 2008).

21. 5 U.S. 137 (1803).

22. *See, e.g.,* Gregory A. Caldeira & John R. Wright, *The Discuss List: Agenda Building in the Supreme Court*, 24 Law & Society Rev. 807 (1990).

23. Lisa McElroy, *Citizens United v. TEC in Plain English*, SCOTUS Blog, Jan. 22, 2010, *available at* http://www.scotusblog.com/2010/01/citizens-united-v-fcc-in-plain-english/.

24. Adam Liptak, *Justices, 5–4, Reject Corporate Spending Limit*, N.Y. Times, Jan. 21, 2010, *available at* http://www.nytimes.com/2010/01/22/us/politics/22scotus.html.

25. Glenn Greenwald, *What the Supreme Court Got Right*, Salon, Jan. 22, 2010, *available at* http://www.salon.com/news/opinion/glenn_greenwald/2010/01/22/citizens_united.

26. Samuel D. Warren & Louis D. Brandeis, *The Right to Privacy*, 4 Harv. L. Rev. 193 (1890).

27. *See, e.g.,* David Ardia, *Free Speech Savior or Shield for Scoundrels? An Empirical Study of Intermediary Immunity Under Section 230*, Citizen Media Law Project Blog, June 30, 2010, *available at* http://www.citmedialaw.org/blog.

28. Aktepe v. United States, 105 F.3d 1400, 1402 (11th Cir. 1997) (citing Japan Whaling Ass'n v. American Cetacean Soc., 478 U.S. 221, 230 (1986)).

29. Stephanie Condon, *After 148 Years, Mississippi Finally Ratifies 13th Amendment,* CBS News, Feb. 18, 2013, *available at* http://www.cbsnews.com/8301–250_162–57569880/after-148-years-mississippi-finally-ratifies-13th-amendment-which-banned-slavery/.

30. Susan Dente Ross, *Access and New Media Technology: Teleconferencing, Telecommuting, and Public Access,* *in* Access Denied: Freedom of Information in the Information Age 65–85 (Charles Davis & Sig Splichal eds., 2000).

31. U.S. Const. art. VI, ¶2.

32. *See* Dept. of Justice v. Reporters Comm. for Freedom of the Press, 489 U.S. 749 (1989).

33. *See, e.g.,* Red Lion Broadcasting Co. v. FCC, 395 U.S. 367 (1969); Miami Herald Pub. Co. v. Tornillo, 418 U.S. 241 (1974).

34. Agostini v. Felton, 521 U.S. 203 (1997) (reversing Aguilar v. Felton, 473 U.S. 402 (1985)).

35. Nike v. Kasky, 539 U.S. 654 (2003).

36. Nikebiz.com, *The Inside Story Press Release: Nike Inc. and Kasky Announce Settlement of Kasky v. Nike First Amendment Case, available at* http://www.nike.com/nikebiz/news/pressrelease.jhtml?year=2003&month=09&letter=f (posted Sept. 2003).

37. Mourning v. Family Publishing Service, 411 U.S. 356, 382 (1973). *See also* Adickes v. Kress & Co., 389 U.S. 144, 157 (1970); United States v. Diebold, Inc., 369 U.S. 654, 655 (1979).

38. *See* Anderson v. Liberty Lobby, Inc., 477 U.S. 242 (1986).

39. Stephen B. Burbank, *Vanishing Trials and Summary Judgment in Federal Civil Cases: Drifting Toward Bethlehem or Gomorrah?* 1 J. Empirical Leg. Studies 591 (2004).

40. Washington Post Co. v. Keogh, 365 F.2d 965, 968 (D.C. Cir. 1966).

41. *See* New York Times v. Sullivan, 376 U.S. 254 (1964).

42. *See, e.g.,* 44 Liquormart v. Rhode Island, 517 U.S. 484 (1996).

43. *See New York Times,* 376 U.S. 254.

44. *See, e.g.,* Dan Eggen & T.W. Farnam, *More Setbacks for Campaign Finance Rules,* Wash. Post, July 15, 2010, at A17; Green Party of Connecticut v. Garfield, 2010 U.S. App. LEXIS 14248 (2d Cir. July 13, 2010); Long Beach Area Chamber of Commerce v. City of Long Beach, 603 F.3d 684 (9th Cir. 2010); SpeechNow.org v. Federal Election Comm'n, 599 F.3d 686 (D.C. Cir. 2010); Citizens United v. Federal Election Comm'n, 588 U.S. 50 (2010).

45. *Connecticut Campaign Finance Decisions from Second Circuit: Green Party v Garfield,* Constitutional Law Prof Blog, July 13, 2010, *available at* http://lawprofessors.typepad.com/conlaw/2010/07/connecticut-campaign-finance-decisions-from-second-circuit-green-party-v-garfield.html.

46. Michael Cummins, Citizens United *and the Roberts Court,* Campaign for Liberty, June 30, 2010, *available at* http://www.campaignforliberty.com/article.php?view=978.

47. Damon W. Root, *Citizens United, Stare Decisis, and the Chicago Gun Case,* Reason, Jan. 22, 2010, *available at* http://reason.com/blog/2010/01/22/citizens-united-stare-decisis.

48. 5 U.S. 137 (1803).

Chapter 2

The First Amendment

1. John Trenchard & Thomas Gordon, Cato's Letters No. 15, at 110 (Ronald Hamowy ed., Liberty Fund 1995) (1755).

2. Gitlow v. New York, 268 U.S. 652 (1925).

3. Note that even Justice Hugo Black, viewed as nearly a First Amendment absolutist, acknowledged that the authors of the First Amendment accepted some restraints on speech.

4. *See* Jonathan Peters, *WikiLeaks, the First Amendment, and the Press,* Harv. L. and Pol'y Rev., Apr. 18, 2011, *available at* http://hlpronline.com; Bland v. Roberts, 857 F. Supp. 2d 599 (E.D. Va. 2012).

5. Potter Stewart, *Or of the Press,* 26 Hastings L.J. 631 (1975); David A. Anderson, *The Origins of the Press Clause,* 30 UCLA L. Rev. 455 (1983); M. Ethan Katsh, *Rights, Camera, Action: Cyberspatial Settings and the First Amendment,* 104 Yale L.J. 1681 (1995).

6. *See* Texas v. Johnson, 491 U.S. 397 (1989) (striking down conviction for flag burning).

7. Adam Liptak, *Study Challenges Supreme Court's Image as Defender of Free Speech,* N.Y. Times, Jan. 8, 2012, at A21 (citing Monica Youn, The Roberts Court's Free Speech Double Standard (2012)).

8. Brompton Bldg., LLC v. Yelp!, 2013 Ill. App. Unpub. LEXIS 145 (Jan. 31, 2013).

9. United States v. Stevens, 559 U.S. 460 (2010).

10. 315 U.S. 568, 571–72 (1942).

11. United States v. Alvarez, 132 S. Ct. 2537 (2012).

12. 18 U.S.C. § 704(b).

13. John Milton, *Areopagitica* (1st ed. n.p. 1644) in GREAT BOOKS OF THE WESTERN WORLD 409 (1952).

14. JOHN LOCKE, THE SECOND TREATISE OF CIVIL GOVERNMENT (1690).

15. JEAN-JACQUES ROUSSEAU, THE SOCIAL CONTRACT (1762).

16. 4 WILLIAM BLACKSTONE, COMMENTARIES 151–52 (London: 1769).

17. *Id.*

18. FREDERICK S. SIEBERT, FREEDOM OF THE PRESS IN ENGLAND 1476–1776, at 10 (1952); LEONARD LEVY, LEGACY OF SUPPRESSION (1960).

19. *See, e.g.,* LEONARD LEVY, LEGACY OF SUPPRESSION (1960); LEONARD LEVY, EMERGENCE OF A FREE PRESS (1985). *But see* ZECHARIAH CHAFEE, FREE SPEECH IN THE UNITED STATES 2 (1941) (arguing First Amendment was designed to eliminate law of sedition forever).

20. *See* JAMES MORTON SMITH, FREEDOM'S FETTERS (1956).

21. *See* New York Times v. Sullivan, 376 U.S. 254 (1964).

22. *See, e.g.,* JOHN STUART MILL, ON LIBERTY (1859); ALEXANDER MEIKLEJOHN, FREE SPEECH AND ITS RELATION TO SELF-GOVERNMENT (1948); THOMAS I. EMERSON, THE SYSTEM OF FREE EXPRESSION (1970); CASS SUNSTEIN, DEMOCRACY AND THE PROBLEM OF FREE SPEECH (1993).

23. *See, e.g.,* Vincent Blasi, *The Checking Value in First Amendment Theory,* 1977 AM. B. FOUND. RES. J. 521 (1977).

24. 376 U.S. 254 (1964).

25. *See, e.g.,* CATHARINE MacKINNON, FEMINISM UNMODIFIED, DISCOURSES ON LIFE AND LAW (1987); WORDS THAT WOUND: CRITICAL RACE THEORY, ASSAULTIVE SPEECH, AND THE FIRST AMENDMENT (Mari J. Matsuda et al. eds., 1993).

26. *See, e.g.,* LEE C. BOLLINGER, THE TOLERANT SOCIETY: FREEDOM OF SPEECH AND EXTREMIST SPEECH IN AMERICA (1986).

27. *See, e.g.,* C. Edwin Baker, *Scope of the First Amendment Freedom of Speech,* 25 UCLA L. REV. 964 (1978).

28. 395 U.S. 367 (1969).

29. *Id.* at 387, 389.

30. 418 U.S. 241, 256 (1974).

31. *Id.*

32. ITHIEL DE SOLA POOL, TECHNOLOGIES OF FREEDOM (1983).

33. *See* Lovell v. Griffin, 303 U.S. 444, 452 (1938); Burstyn v. Wilson, 343 U.S. 495 (1952).

34. Kovacs v. Cooper, 336 U.S. 77, 97 (1949) (Jackson, J., concurring).

35. Minneapolis Star & Tribune Co. v. Minnesota Comm'r of Revenue, 460 U.S. 575, 585 (1983).

36. *See, e.g.,* Red Lion Broadcasting Co. v. FCC, 395 U.S. 367 (1969).

37. *See, e.g.,* Turner Broadcasting Sys. Inc. v. FCC, 512 U.S. 622 (1994); Turner Broadcasting Sys. Inc. v. FCC, 530 U.S. 180 (1997).

38. Project for Excellence in Journalism of the Columbia University Graduate School of Journalism, Overview: *The State of the News Media 2005, An Annual Report on American Journalism, available at* http://www.journalism .org.

39. *Id.*

40. *Id.*

41. Timothy Karr, *Big Media: The Real Elephant in the Garden,* Aug. 27, 2004, *available at* http://www.Media Channel.org.

42. *Id.*

43. Project for Excellence in Journalism of the Columbia University Graduate School of Journalism, *Journalist Survey, The State of the News Media 2004, An Annual Report on American Journalism, available at* http://www. journalism.org.

44. 283 U.S. 697 (1931).

45. *Id.*

46. 403 U.S. 713 (1971).

47. *Id.* at 714.

48. Nebraska Press Ass'n v. Stuart, 427 U.S. 539, 559 (1976).

49. New York Times v. Jascalevich, 439 U.S. 1317 (1978); Nebraska Press Ass'n v. Stuart, 427 U.S. 539 (1976).

50. CBS v. Davis, 510 U.S. 1315 (1994) (Blackmun, J., Circuit Justice).

51. Miami Herald Publ'g Co. v. Mc1ntosh, 340 So. 2d 904, 910 (Fla. 1977).

52. CBS, 510 U.S. at 1320

53. Barclays v. TheFlyontheWall.com, 700 F. Supp. 2d 310 (S.D.N.Y. 2010).

54. Barclays v. TheFlyontheWall.com, 650 F.3d 876 (2d Cir. 2011).

55. Sam Bayard, *New Hampshire Supreme Court Rules Website Covered by State Reporter's Privilege*, CITIZEN MEDIA LAW PROJECT, May 6, 2010, *available at* http://www.citmedialaw.org.

56. *Summary:* The Mortgage Specialists v. Implode-Explode Heavy Industries, CITIZEN MEDIA LAW PROJECT, Apr. 1, 2009, *available at* http://www.citmedialaw.org.

57. *Court Order*, Apex Technology v. Doe, N.J. Sup. Ct., Dec. 23, 2009, *available at* http://www.programmersguild.org.

58. Immigrations and Customs Enforcement, *European Law Enforcement Agencies and Europol Seize 132 Domain Names Selling Counterfeit Merchandise in "Project Cyber Monday 3" and "Project Transatlantic" Operations*, Nov. 26, 2012, *available at* http://www.ice.gov.

59. *Operation In Our Sites Protects American Online Shoppers, Cracks Down on Counterfeiters; ICE-Led IPR Center Seizes 150 Website Domains Selling Counterfeit and Pirated Merchandise*, Nov. 28, 2011, *available at* http://www.ice.gov.

60. *Id.*

61. Mike Masnick, *List of Sites Challenging Domain Seizures*, LEGAL ISSUES, June 13, 2011, *available at* http://www.techdirt.com.

62. Mike Masnick, *As Expected, ICE Seizes 313 Websites in Its Role as the NFL's Private Police Force*, LEGAL ISSUES, Jan. 31, 2013, *available at* http://www.techdirt.com.

63. Agatha M. Cole, *ICE Domain Name Seizures Threaten Due Process and First Amendment Rights*, FREE FUTURE, June 20, 2012, *available at* http://www.aclu.org.

64. *Julius Baer Bank and Trust v. WikiLeaks*, CITIZEN MEDIA LAW PROJECT, Feb. 18, 2008, *available at* http://www.citmedialaw.org.

65. Hill v. Colorado, 530 U.S. 703 (2000).

66. Burson v. Freeman, 504 U.S. 191 (1992).

67. 502 U.S. 105 (1991).

68. *Id.*

69. United States v. O'Brien, 391 U.S. 367 (1968).

70. *Id.*

71. Ward v. Rock Against Racism, 491 U.S. 781 (1989). *See also* Matthew D. Bunker & Emily Erickson,

The Jurisprudence of Precision: Contrast Space and Narrow Tailoring in First Amendment Doctrine, 6 COMM. L. & POL'Y 259 (2001).

72. Forsyth County, Ga. v. The Nationalist Movement, 505 U.S. 123 (1992).

73. Virginia v. Black, 538 U.S. 343, 365 (2003).

74. Meyer v. Grant, 486 U.S. 414 (1988).

75. *See, e.g.,* Buckley v. Valeo, 424 U.S. 1 (1976).

76. Sarah Kessler, *Reporter Put on Leave After Refusing to Remove Facebook Post*, MASHABLE SOCIAL MEDIA, June 14, 2012, *available at* http://www.mashable.com.

77. Nelson v. McClatchy, 936 P.2d 1123 (Wash. 1997).

78. 558 U.S. 50 (2010).

79. 424 U.S. 1 (1976).

80. *2012 Election Spending Will Reach $6 Billion, Center for Responsive Politics Predicts*, *available at* http://www.opensecrets.org.

81. Republican Nat'l Comm. v. FEC, 130 S. Ct. 3543 (2010).

82. SpeechNow.org v. FEC, 599 F.3d 686 (D.D.C.), *cert. denied*, 131 S. Ct. 553 (2010).

83. Emily's List v. FEC, 581 F.3d 1 (D.D.C. 2009).

84. Ysura v. Pocatello Educ. Ass'n., 555 U.S. 353 (2010).

85. Randall v. Sorrell, 548 U.S. 230 (2006).

86. Nixon v. Shrink Missouri Government PAC, 528 U.S. 377 (2000).

87. White House, Office of the Press Secretary, *Ensuring Responsible Spending of Recovery Act Funds*, Memo for the Heads of Executive Departments and Agencies, March 20, 2009.

88. McIntyre v. Ohio Election Commission, 514 U.S. 334, 357 (1995).

89. *See* Talley v. California, 362 U.S. 60 (1960); Buckley v. American Const'l Law Found., 525 U.S. 182 (1999); Watchtower v. Stratton, 536 U.S. 150 (2002).

90. Doe v. Reed, 130 S. Ct. 2811 (2010).

91. Doe v. Reed, 823 F. Supp. 2d 1195 (W.D. Wash. 2011).

92. 555 U.S. 460 (2009).

93. *Id.*

94. *Id.* at 481.

95. *See, e.g.,* Perry v. Sindermann, 408 U.S. 593 (1972). For discussion of parallel treatment of public school students, see Chapter 3 and Tinker v. Des Moines Independent Community School Dist., 393 U.S. 503 (1969).

96. *See, e.g.,* Pickering v. Board of Education, 391 U.S. 563 (1968); Snepp v. United States, 444 U.S. 507 (1980); Toni M. Massaro, *Significant Silences: Freedom of Speech in the Public Sector Workplace,* 61 S. CAL. L. REV. 1 (1987); SISSELA BOK, SECRETS (1993). *But see* DANIEL N. HOFFMAN, GOVERNMENTAL SECRECY AND THE FOUNDING FATHERS: A STUDY IN CONSTITUTIONAL CONTROLS (1981); Benjamin S. DuVal, Jr., *The Occasions of Secrecy,* 47 U. PITT. L. REV. 579 (1986); Seth F. Kreimer, *Sunlight Secrets and Scarlet Letters: The Tension Between Privacy and Disclosure in Constitutional Law,* 140 U. PA. L. REV. 1 (1991); Kermit L. Hall, *The Virulence of the National Appetite for Bogus Revelation,* 56 MD. L. REV. 1 (1997); FREEDOM AT RISK: SECRECY, CENSORSHIP, AND REPRESSION IN THE 1980s (Richard O. Curry ed., 1998).

97. *See, e.g.,* United Pub. Workers of Am. v. Mitchell, 330 U.S. 75 (1947); U.S. Civil Serv. Comm'n v. Nat'l Ass'n of Letter Carriers, 413 U.S. 548 (1973).

98. Garcetti v. Ceballos, 547 U.S. 410 (2006).

99. Tom Schoenberg, *Facebook Tells Court "Like" Feature Vital to Free Speech,* May 16, 2013, *available at* http://www.bloomberg.com/news/2013–05–16/facebook-s-like-faces-free-speech-test-in-u-s-court.html.

100. 547 U.S. 410 (2006).

101. Connick v. Myers, 461 U.S. 138, 146–47 (1983).

102. Garcetti, 547 U.S. at 422.

103. Borough of Duryea v. Guarnieri, 131 S. Ct. 2488 (2011).

104. Hague v. Committee for Industrial Organization, 307 U.S. 496, 515 (1939).

105. *See, e.g.,* Susan Dente Ross, *An Apologia to Radical Dissent and a Supreme Court Test to Protect It,* 7 COMM. L. & POL'Y 401 (2002); Ronald J. Krotoszynski, Jr., *Essay: Celebrating Selma: The Importance of Context in Public Forum Analysis,* 104 YALE L.J. 1411 (1995).

106. *See, e.g.,* Skokie v. Nat'l Socialist Party of America, 439 U.S. 916 (1978); Hess v. Indiana, 414 U.S. 105 (1973); Brown v. Louisiana, 383 U.S. 131 (1966); Edwards v. South Carolina, 371 U.S. 229 (1963); NAACP v. Claiborne Hardware Co., 458 U.S. 886 (1982); Gregory v. City of Chicago, 394 U.S. 111 (1969); Grayned v. Rockford, 408 U.S. 104 (1972).

107. Snyder v. Phelps, 131 S. Ct. 1207 (2011).

108. Grayned v. Rockford, 408 U.S. 104, 116 (1972); Perry Educ. Ass'n v. Perry Local Educators' Ass'n, 460 U.S. 37 (1983).

109. *See, e.g.,* Hague v. Comm. for Industrial Org., 307 U.S. 496 (1939).

110. *See, e.g.,* Greer v. Spock, 424 U.S. 828 (1976).

111. *See, e.g.,* United States v. Albertini, 472 U.S. 675 (1985); Los Angeles City Council v. Taxpayers for Vincent, 466 U.S. 789 (1984); United States v. Kokinda, 497 U.S. 720 (1990).

112. *See, e.g.,* Adderley v. Florida, 385 U.S. 39 (1966).

113. *See, e.g.,* Frisby v. Schultz, 487 U.S. 474 (1988); Madsen v. Women's Health Center, Inc., 512 U.S. 753 (1994). *But see* Scheidler v. Nat'l Organization for Women, 537 U.S. 393 (2003) (removing civil injunction on anti-abortion protesters and rejecting claim that their protests constituted illegal extortion and racketeering).

114. Reichle v. Howards, 132 S. Ct. 2088 (2012).

115. Marcavage v. City of New York, 689 F.3d 98 (2d Cir. 2012).

116. *See, e.g.,* Amalgamated Food Employees Union v. Logan Valley Plaza, Inc., 391 U.S. 308 (1968); Hudgens v. National Labor Relations Board, 424 U.S. 507 (1976); Prune Yard Shopping Center v. Robins, 447 U.S. 74 (1980). *But see* Lloyd Corp., Ltd. v. Tanner, 407 U.S. 551 (1972).

117. *Prune Yard Shopping Center,* 447 U.S. 74.

118. *Id.* at 82 (footnote omitted).

119. *Id.* at 83 (footnote omitted).

120. *See also* Troy Ltd. v. Renna, 727 F.2d 287 (3d Cir. 1984); Flynn v. City of Cambridge, 383 Mass. 152 (1981); State v. Shack, 58 N.J. 297 (1971).

121. Glickman v. Wileman Bros. & Elliott, 521 U.S. 457, 505 n.2 (1997) (Souter, J., dissenting).

122. *See, e.g.,* David F. Freedman, *Press Passes and Trespasses: Newsgathering on Private Property,* 84 COLUM. L. REV. 1298 (1984).

123. *See, e.g.,* Bd. of Regents of the Univ. of Wis. v. Southworth, 529 U.S. 217 (2000); Rosenberger v. Rector & Visitors of the Univ. of Virginia, 515 U.S. 819 (1995).

124. *See, e.g.,* Grosjean v. Am. Press Co., 297 U.S. 233 (1936); Minneapolis Star & Tribune Co. v. Minnesota Commiss'r of Revenue, 460 U.S. 575 (1983); Arkansas Writers' Project v. Ragland, 481 U.S. 221 (1987). *But see* Leathers v. Medlock, 499 U.S. 439 (1991).

125. Nat'l Endowment for the Arts v. Finley, 524 U.S. 569 (1998).

126. Island Trees Union Free School Dist. Board of Ed. v. Pico, 457 U.S. 853 (1982).

127. Wooley v. Maynard, 430 U.S. 705, 714 (1977).

128. *See, e.g.*, Boy Scouts of America v. Dale, 530 U.S. 640 (2000).

129. Hurley v. Irish-American Gay, Lesbian and Bisexual Group of Boston, 515 U.S. 557, 575 (1995).

Chapter 3

Speech Distinctions

1. Schenck v. United States, 249 U.S. 47, 52 (1919).

2. 491 U.S. 397 (1989).

3. Margaret A. Blanchard, Revolutionary Sparks 489 (1992); Margaret A. Blanchard, *"Why Can't We Ever Learn?" Cycles of Stability, Stress and Freedom of Expression in United States History,* 7 Comm. L. & Pol'y 347 (2002); Martin E. Halstuk, *Policy of Secrecy—Pattern of Deception: What Federalist Leaders Thought About a Public Right to Know,* 1794–98, 7 Comm. L. & Pol'y 51 (2002); Susan D. Ross, *An Apologia to Radical Dissent and a Supreme Court Test to Protect It,* 7 Comm. L. & Pol'y 401 (2002).

4. Vincent Blasi, *The Pathological Perspective and the First Amendment,* 85 Colum. L. Rev. 449, 450 (1985).

5. ACLU Press Release, *PATRIOT Act Fears Are Stifling Free Speech, ACLU Says in Challenge to Law* (Nov. 3, 2003), *available at* http://www.aclu.org/safefree/patriot/18418prs20031103.html.

6. Holder v. Humanitarian Law Project, 130 S. Ct. 2705 (2010).

7. Office of the Coordinator for Counterterrorism, *Foreign Terrorist Organizations,* U.S. Department of State, Jan. 19, 2010, *available at* http://www.state.gov/s/ct/rls/other/des/123085.htm.

8. *Humanitarian Law Project*, 130 S. Ct. at 2727, 2728.

9. *Id.* at 2720.

10. *Id.* at 2731.

11. The Uniting and Strengthening America by Providing Appropriate Tools Required to Intercept and Obstruct Terrorism Act of 2001, Pub. L. No. 107–56, 115 Stat. 272; USA PATRIOT Improvement and Reauthorization Act of 2005, 18 U.S.C. §2709, Pub. L. No. 109–177, 120 Stat. 192 (2006).

12. Nancy Kranich, Commentary: *The Impact of the USA PATRIOT Act on Free Expression,* Aug. 27, 2003, *available at* http://www.fepproject.org/commentaries/patriotact.html.

13. Foreign Intelligence Surveillance Act Amendments Act (FISA), Pub. L. 110–261 (July 10, 2008). In 2012, Congress reauthorized FISA through 2017. *See FISA Amendments Act Reauthorization Act of 2012,* govtrack.us, Dec. 28, 2012, *available at* http://www.govtrack.us/congress/votes/112–2012/s236.

14. William H. Rehnquist, All the Laws But One 224 (1998).

15. Kleindienst v. Mandel, 408 U.S. 753, 773 (1972) (Douglas, J., dissenting).

16. Chaplinsky v. New Hampshire, 315 U.S. 568, 572 (1942).

17. Schenck v. United States, 249 U.S. 47, 52 (1919).

18. *Id.*

19. *Id.*

20. Frohwerk v. United States, 249 U.S. 204 (1919).

21. *Id.* at 208–09.

22. Debs v. United States, 249 U.S. 211 (1919).

23. Abrams v. United States, 250 U.S. 626 (1919).

24. *Id.* at 628 (Holmes, J., dissenting).

25. *Id.* at 630.

26. Dennis v. United States, 341 U.S. 494 (1951); Scales v. United States, 367 U.S. 203 (1961). *See also* Whitney v. California, 274 U.S. 357 (1927); Kent Greenawalt, *Speech and Crime,* 1980 Am. B. Found. Res. J. 645 (1980).

27. Gitlow v. New York, 268 U.S. 652 (1925).

28. *Id.* at 667.

29. *Id.* at 669.

30. *Id.* at 673 (Holmes, J., dissenting).

31. *Id.* at 666.

32. Whitney v. California, 274 U.S. 357 (1927).

33. *Id.* at 377–78 (Brandeis, J., concurring).

34. *Id.* at 379 (emphasis added).

35. Am. Communications Ass'n v. Douds, 339 U.S. 382, 448–49 (1950) (Black, J., dissenting).

36. Dennis v. United States, 341 U.S. 494 (1951); Kunz v. New York, 340 U.S. 290, 300 (1951); Yates v. United States, 354 U.S. 298 (1957).

37. *See* Liezl Irene Pangilinan, Note: *"When a Nation Is at War": A Context-Dependent Theory of Free Speech for the Regulation of Weapon Recipes,* 22 Cardozo Arts & Ent. L.J. 683 (2004).

38. 395 U.S. 444 (1969).

39. *Id.* at 447.

40. *Id.* at 448.

41. Cohen v. California, 403 U.S. 15 (1971).

42. Martin H. Redish, *Advocacy of Unlawful Conduct and the First Amendment: In Defense of Clear and Present Danger,* 70 Cal. L. Rev. 1159, 1162 (1982).

43. Gitlow v. New York, 268 U.S. 652, 673 (1925).

44. 315 U.S. 568 (1942).

45. *Id.* at 571–72.

46. Terminiello v. Chicago, 337 U.S. 1, 4 (1949) (emphasis added).

47. *Id.*

48. *Id.*

49. *See, e.g.,* Gooding v. Wilson, 405 U.S. 518 (1972).

50. Stahl v. City of St. Louis, 687 F.3d (8th Cir. 2012).

51. *Id.*

52. R.A.V. v. City of St. Paul, 505 U.S. 377 (1992).

53. 130 S. Ct. 1577 (2010).

54. Brown v. EMA, 131 S. Ct. 2729 (2011).

55. *Id.*

56. 538 U.S. 343 (2003).

57. *Id.* at 394.

58. *See* Watts v. United States, 394 U.S. 705 (1969).

59. United States v. Baker, 890 F. Supp. 1375 (S.D. Mich. 1995).

60. *Id.* at 1382.

61. *Id.* at 1385.

62. *Id.* at 1390 (footnote omitted).

63. Planned Parenthood v. American Coalition of Life Activists, 290 F.3d 1058 (9th Cir. 2002), *cert. denied,* 593 U.S. 958 (2003).

64. United States v. O'Brien, 391 U.S. 367, 376 (1968).

65. Tinker v. Des Moines Indep. Community School Dist., 393 U.S. 503, 505 (1969).

66. United States v. O'Brien, 391 U.S. 367 (1968).

67. 491 U.S. 397 (1989). The Supreme Court has said symbolic speech exists and warrants First Amendment protection when (1) speech and action combine, (2) there is an intent to convey a message, and (3) witnesses are likely to understand that message.

68. *Id.* at 414.

69. Hess v. Indiana, 414 U.S. 105 (1973).

70. Mark C. Rahdert, Point of View: *The Roberts Court and Academic Freedom,* Chronicle Higher Educ., July 27, 2007, *available at* http://chronicle.com/forums/index.

71. *See, e.g.,* Board of Regents v. Southworth, 529 U.S. 217 (2000); Rosenberger v. Rector of the Univ. of Va., 515 U.S. 819 (1995).

72. Board of Regents v. Southworth, 529 U.S. 217, 234 n.7 (2000).

73. Widmar v. Vincent, 454 U.S. 263, 274 (1981).

74. Bethel School Dist. v. Fraser, 478 U.S. 675, 683 (1986). *See also* Edwards v. Aguillard, 482 U.S. 578, 583 (1987).

75. Tinker v. Des Moines Indep. Community School Dist., 393 U.S. 503 (1969).

76. Erwin Chemerinsky, *Students Do Leave Their First Amendment Rights at the Schoolhouse Gates: What's Left of* Tinker? 48 Drake L. Rev. 527 (2000).

77. Tinker v. Des Moines Indep. Comty. Sch. Dist., 393 U.S. 503, 508 (1969).

78. *Id.* at 509.

79. *Id.*

80. *Id.* at 506.

81. Grayned v. Rockford, 408 U.S. 104 (1972).

82. 551 U.S. 393 (2007).

83. *Id.* at 410.

84. *Id.* at 2649 (Stevens, J. dissenting).

85. 393 U.S. 503 (1969).

86. D.J.M. v. Hannibal Pub. Sch. Dist. #60, 647 F.3d 754 (8th Cir. 2011).

87. *Id.*

88. Kowalski v. Berkeley County Schools, 652 F.3d 565 (4th Cir. 2011), *cert. denied,* 132 S. Ct. 1095 (2012).

89. Doninger v. Niehoff, 527 F.3d 41 (2d Cir. 2008).

90. Snyder v. Blue Mountain School District, 650 F.3d 915 (3d Cir. 2011) (en banc), *cert. denied,* 132 S. Ct. 1097 (2012); Layshock v. Hermitage School District, 593 F.3d 249 (3d Cir. 2010)), *cert. denied,* 132 S. Ct. 1097 (2012).

91. *Third Circuit Applies* Tinker *to Off-Campus Speech,* 125 Harv. L. Rev. 1064 (2012), *available at* http://www. harvardlawreview.org.

92. 816 N.W.2d 509 (Minn. 2012).

93. Emily Gurnon, *Amanda Tatro Dies,* June 26, 2012, *available at* http://TwinCities.com.

94. Bd. of Educ., Island Trees Union Free School Dist. v. Pico 457 U.S. 853 (1982).

95. *Id.* at 857.

96. *Id.* at 868.

97. *Id.* at 870.

98. 478 U.S. 675 (1986).

99. *Id.*

100. Hazelwood v. Kuhlmeier, 484 U.S. 260 (1988).

101. *Id.* at 271.

102. *Id.* at 270–71.

103. *Id.* at 270.

104. *Id.* at 273 n.7.

105. Parents Family and Friends of Lesbians and Gays v. Camdenton R-111 School District, 853 F. Supp. 2d 888 (W.D. Mo. 2012).

106. Michael Winerip, *School District Told to Replace Web Filter Blocking Pro-Gay Sites,* N.Y. Times, March 26, 2012, *available at* http://www.nytimes.com.

107. Lawrence v. Texas, 539 U.S. 538 (2003).

108. Wooley v. Maynard, 430 U.S. 705, 714 (1977) (Burger, C.J.).

109. West Virginia State Bd. of Educ. v. Barnette, 319 U.S. 624 (1943).

110. Ambach v. Norwick, 441 U.S. 68 (1979).

111. *See, e.g.,* Epperson v. Arkansas, 393 U.S. 97 (1968); Edwards v. Aguillard, 482 U.S. 578 (1987); Pickering v. Bd. of Educ., 391 U.S. 563 (1968).

112. West Virginia State Bd. of Educ. v. Barnette, 319 U.S. 624, 633 (1943).

113. *Id.* at 642.

114. *Id.*

115. *See, e.g.,* Abood v. Detroit Bd. of Educ., 431 U.S. 209 (1977).

116. Rosenberger v. Rector, 515 U.S. 819, 833 (1995).

117. *See, e.g.,* Bd. of Regents of the Univ. of Wis. v. Southworth, 529 U.S. 217 (2000); Rosenberger v. Rector and Visitors of the Univ. of Va., 515 U.S. 819 (1995).

118. *Southworth,* 529 U.S. at 239 (Souter, J., concurring).

119. Papish v. Bd. of Curators of the Univ. of Mo., 410 U.S. 667, 670 (1973).

120. *Id.; see also Southworth,* 529 U.S. at 233.

121. *Southworth,* 529 U.S. at 242-43 (Souter, J., dissenting).

122. Note that the Court said this public forum also enhanced the university's curricular goals, but public forum analysis typically protects precisely those types of speech that would not be embraced by the government agency providing the forum.

123. 130 S. Ct. 2971 (2010).

124. *Id.* at 2991.

125. Tinker v. Des Moines Indep. Cmt. Sch. Dist., 393 U.S. 503, 506 (1969).

126. 130 S. Ct. at 3000 (Alito, J., dissenting).

127. Greg Lukianoff, *Feigning Free Speech on Campus,* N.Y. Times, Oct. 25, 2012, *available at* http://www.nytimes .com.

128. Tatro v. Univ. of Minn., 816 N.W.2d 509 (Minn. 2012).

129. *Id.*

130. Tinker v. Des Moines Indep. Community School Dist., 393 U.S. 503, 506 (1969).

131. Hazelwood v. Kuhlmeier, 478 U.S. 675 (1986).

132. OSU Student Alliance v. Ray, 699 F.3d 1053 (9th Cir. 2012).

133. Kincaid v. Gibson, 236 F.3d 342 (6th Cir. 2001) (en banc).

134. Hosty v. Carter, 412 F.3d 731 (7th Cir. 2005), *cert. denied,* 546 U.S. 1169 (2006).

135. Richard Perez-Pena, *Editors Quit at University of Georgia,* N.Y. Times, Aug. 17, 2012, *available at* http:// www.nytimes.com.

136. Alexis Steven, *Editors Rejoin UGA Student Newspaper,* Aug. 20, 2012, *available at* http://www.ajc.com.

137. *Michele Nagar Fired for Diversity's Sake,* July 22, 2004, *available at* http://www.campusreportonline.net/main/ articles .php?id=139.

138. *SPJ Members Issue Resolution Condemning Kansas Adviser's Firing,* Oct. 6, 2004, available at http://www .splc.org; *SPLC Condemns Kansas State's "Bizarre" Interpretation of the First Amendment,* July 21, 2004, available at http://www.splc.org/newsflash.

139. *Johnson Fired from Position of Director, Collegian Adviser,* Kan. St. Collegian, May 11, 2004, at 1.

140. *Newspaper Content Analysis Given in Reasons Not to Reappoint Collegian Adviser*, Kan. St. Collegian, May 18, 2004, *available at* http://www.kstatecollegian .com/ article.php?a=2141.

141. *See* Lane v. Simon, 2005 U.S. Dist. LEXIS 11330 (D. Kan. 2005), *vacated and remanded*, 2007 U.S. App. LEXIS 17814 (10th Cir., July 26, 2007).

142. *Id.*

143. *See, e.g.,* Dinesh D'Souza, Illiberal Education: The Politics of Race and Sex on Campus (1992).

144. *See, e.g.,* The Price We Pay: The Case Against Racist Speech, Hate Propaganda, and Pornography (Laura Lederer & Richard Delgado eds., 1994).

145. *See, e.g.,* Andrew Altman, *Liberalism and Campus Hate Speech,* in Campus Wars: Multiculturalism and the Politics of Difference (John Arthur & Amy Shapiro eds., 1993).

146. *See, e.g.,* Doe v. Univ. of Mich., 721 F. Supp. 852 (E.D. Mich. 1989); UWM Post v. Univ. of Wis. Bd. of Regents, 774 F. Supp. 1163 (E.D. Wis. 1991); Dambrot v. Central Mich. Univ., 839 F. Supp. 477 (E.D. Mich. 1993).

147. Doe v. Univ. of Mich., 721 F. Supp. 852, 864 (E. D. Mich. 1989).

148. Arati R. Korwar, War of Words: Speech Codes at Public Colleges and Universities (1994); Jon B. Gould, *The Precedent That Wasn't: College Hate Speech Codes and the Two Faces of Legal Compliance,* 35 Law & Soc'y Rev. 345 (2001).

149. Greg Lukianoff, *Spotlight on Speech Codes 2013: The State of Free Speech on Our Nation's Campuses,* The Foundation for Individual Rights in Education, *available at* http://www.thefire.org.

Chapter 4

Libel: The Plaintiff's Case

1. New York Times v. Sullivan, 376 U.S. 254, 270–72 (1964).

2. *See, e.g., Diane Leenheer Zimmerman, Defamation in Fiction: Real People in Fiction: Cautionary Words About Troublesome Old Torts Poured into New Jugs,* 51 Brooklyn L. Rev. 355 (1985).

3. Milkovich v. Lorain Journal Co., 497 U.S. 1, 22 (1990) (Rehnquist, C.J.).

4. Rosenblatt v. Baer, 383 U.S. 75, 86 (1966).

5. Dun & Bradstreet, Inc. v. Greenmoss Builders, Inc., 472 U.S. 749, 757 (1985).

6. *See* Gavin Clark, Famous Libel and Slander Cases of History (1950).

7. M. Lindsay Kaplan, The Culture of Slander in Early Modern England 9 (1997).

8. *See, e.g.,* Norman L. Rosenberg, Protecting the Best Men: An Interpretive History of the Law of Libel (1986).

9. Van Vechten Veeder, *The History and Theory of the Law of Defamation,* 3 Colum. L. Rev. 546, 565 (1903) (quoting De Libellis Famois, 5 Co. Rep. 125 (1606)).

10. *Id.*

11. J.H. Baker, An Introduction to English Legal History 506 (3d ed. 1990).

12. 4 William Blackstone, Commentaries 152 (1979).

13. *Id.*

14. Milkovich v. Lorain Journal Co., 497 U.S. 1, 12 (1990) (Rehnquist, C.J.).

15. The Sedition Act of 1798, ch. 74, 1 Stat. 596 (1798).

16. John Marshall, *Report of the Minority on the Virginia Resolutions,* 6 J. House of Delegates (Va.) 93–95 (Jan. 22, 1799), *reprinted in* 5 The Founders' Constitution 136–38 (Philip B. Kurland & Ralph Lerner eds., 1987).

17. *Id.* at 138.

18. James Madison, *The Virginia Report of 1799–1800, Touching the Alien and Sedition Laws, reprinted in* The Founders' Constitution 141–42 (1986).

19. The expression "SLAPP" was initially coined by two University of Denver professors. *See* Penelope Canan & George W. Pring, *Studying Strategic Lawsuits Against Public Participation: Mixing Quantitative and Qualitative Approaches,* 22 Law & Soc'y Rev. 385 (1988).

20. *See, e.g.,* Cal. Code Civ. Proc. § 425.16 (stating, in part, "The Legislature finds and declares that there has been a disturbing increase in lawsuits brought primarily to chill the valid exercise of the constitutional rights of freedom of speech and petition for the redress of grievances. The Legislature finds and declares that it is in the public interest to encourage continued participation in matters of public significance, and that this participation should not be chilled through abuse of the judicial process. . . .

A cause of action against a person arising from any act of that person in furtherance of the person's right of petition or free speech under the United States or California Constitution in connection with a public issue shall be subject to a special motion to strike, unless the court determines that the plaintiff has established that there is a probability that the plaintiff will prevail on the claim.").

21. Reporters Committee for Freedom of the Press (Mar. 19, 2010), *available at* http://www.rcfp.org/browse-media-law-resources/news/washington-strengthens-state-anti-slapp-protections.

22. *New Developments 2012*, MLRC BULLETIN, Dec. 2012, at 49; *see, e.g.,* Sandholm v. Kuecker, 962 N.E.2d 418 (2012).

23. *See, e.g.,* Whitney v. California, 274 U.S. 357, 374–77 (1927) (Brandeis, J., concurring) ("The best answer for bad speech is more speech.").

24. Admission Consultants, Inc. v. Google, Inc., N.Y.L.J., Dec. 8, 2008, p. 17, col. 1 (Sup. Ct., N.Y. Co.).

25. *New Developments 2012*, MLRC BULLETIN, Dec. 2012, at 65; *see, e.g.,* Martin v. Daily News, LP, 35 Misc. 3d 1210A (N.Y. Sup. 2012).

26. Lunney v. Prodigy Services Co., 94 N.Y.2d 242, 249 (1999).

27. Cubby, Inc. v. CompuServe, Inc., 776 F. Supp. 135 (S.D.N.Y. 1991) (holding that the ISP is not responsible for content posted).

28. Stratton Oakmont v. Prodigy Servs. Co., 23 Med. L. Rep. 1794 (N.Y. Sup. Ct., May 24, 1995) (holding that because Prodigy claimed to monitor its content, the ISP is placed in the role of publisher).

29. Zeran v. America Online, Inc., 129 F.3d 327, 330 (4th Cir. 1997).

30. Blumenthal v. Drudge, 992 F. Supp. 44 (D.D.C. 1998).

31. Dimeo v. Max, 433 F. Supp. 2d 523 (E.D. Pa. 2006).

32. *Id.* at 529 (Dalzel, J.).

33. McIntyre v. Ohio Elections Commission, 514 U.S. 334, 357 (1995).

34. *In re* Verizon Internet Services, Inc., 257 F. Supp. 2d 244 (D.D.C. 2003).

35. Enterline v. Pocono Medical Ctr., 751 F. Supp. 2d 782, 786 (M.D. Pa., 2008).

36. Restatement (Second) of Torts § 564A cmt. b (1976).

37. Neiman-Marcus v. Lait, 13 F.R.D. 311, 316 (S.D.N.Y. 1952).

38. Carter-Clark v. Random House, Inc., 768 N.Y.S.2d 290, 293 (N.Y. Sup. Ct. 2003).

39. *See* Restatement (Second) of Torts § 559 (1997).

40. *See* W. PAGE KEETON ET AL., PROSSER AND KEETON ON THE LAW OF TORTS § 111, at 773–78 (5th ed. 1984).

41. *See* Restatement (Second) of Torts § 559 cmt. e.

42. *See, e.g.,* Kimmerle v. New York Evening Journal, Inc., 262 N.Y. 99 (1933).

43. Yonaty v. Mincolla, N.Y.S. 2d 774 (N.Y. App. 2012).

44. Burke v. Gregg, 55 A.3d 212 (R.I. 2012).

45. *New Developments 2012*, MLRC BULLETIN, Dec. 2012, at 51.

46. Kaelin v. Globe Communications, 162 F.3d 1036 (9th Cir. 1998).

47. *Id.* at 1042.

48. Knutt v. Metro Int'l, 938 N.Y.S.2d 134 (N.Y. App. Div. 2012).

49. Cochran v. NYP Holdings, Inc., 58 F. Supp. 2d 1113, 1121 (C.D. Cal. 1998).

50. Bose Corp. v. Consumers Union, 466 U.S. 485, 487 (1984).

51. Auvil v. CBS, 836 F. Supp. 740 (E.D. Wash. 1993).

52. Auvil v. CBS, 67 F. 3d 816 (9th Cir. 1995).

53. Philadelphia Newspapers, Inc. v. Hepps, 474 U.S. 767, 776–77 (1986).

54. Masson v. New Yorker Magazine, Inc., 501 U.S. 496, 516–17 (1991).

55. Dolcefino and KTRK Television v. Turner, 987 S.W. 2d 100, 109 (Tex. Ct. App. 1998).

56. Yeakey v. Hearst Communcations, Inc., 234 P.3d 332 (Wash. App. 2010).

57. Stevens v. Iowa Newspapers, Inc., 728 N.W.2d 823 (Iowa 2007).

58. 376 U.S. 254 (1964).

59. *See, e.g.,* Harry Kalven, Jr., *The New York Times Case: A Note on "The Central Meaning of the First Amendment,"* 1964 SUP. CT. REV. 191.

60. New York Times v. Sullivan, 376 U.S. 254, 272 (1964).

61. *Id.* at 270.

62. *Id.* at 266.

63. *Id.* at 279.

64. *Id.* at 270.

65. *Id.* at 278.

66. *See, e.g.,* Lawrence Friedman, American Law in the 20th Century 341 (2002).

67. Goldwater v. Ginsburg, 414 F.2d 324 (2d Cir. 1969), *cert. denied,* 396 U.S. 1049 (1970).

68. Masson v. New Yorker Magazine, Inc., 501 U.S. 496, 517 (1991).

69. Curtis Publishing Co. v. Butts, 388 U.S. 130, 158 (1967).

70. Associated Press v. Walker, 388 U.S. 130, 140 (1967).

71. *Id.* at 157–59.

72. St. Amant v. Thompson, 390 U.S. 727, 731 (1968).

73. Herbert v. Lando, 441 U.S. 153 (1979).

74. Harte-Hanks Communications, Inc. v. Connaughton, 491 U.S. 657 (1989).

75. Rosenblatt v. Baer, 383 U.S. 75, 85 (1966).

76. *Id.* at 86.

77. *Id.* at 87.

78. 388 U.S. 130, 163 (1967) (Warren, C.J., concurring).

79. *Id.* at 163–64.

80. Gertz v. Robert Welch, Inc., 418 U.S. 323, 345 (1974).

81. *Id.*

82. *Id.* at 344.

83. *Id.* at 345.

84. Curtis Publishing Co. v. Butts and Associated Press v. Walker, 388 U.S. 130, 163 (1967).

85. Wolston v. Reader's Digest Ass'n, 443 U.S. 157 (1979).

86. Time, Inc. v. Firestone, 424 U.S. 448 (1976).

87. Hutchinson v. Proxmire, 443 U.S. 111 (1979).

88. *Id.* at 135.

89. Chuy v. Philadelphia Eagles Football Club, 431 F. Supp. 254, 276 (E.D. Pa. 1977).

90. Renner v. Donsbach, 749 F. Supp. 987 (W.D. Mo. 1990).

91. *See, e.g.,* Williams v. Pasma, 656 P.2d 212 (Mont. 1982).

92. Gertz v. Robert Welch, Inc., 418 U.S. 323, 351 (1974).

93. *Id.* at 345.

94. Tillman v. Freedom of Information Commission, 2008 Conn. Super. LEXIS 2120, *25 (Aug. 15, 2008).

95. Dun & Bradstreet v. Greenmoss Builders, Inc., 472 U.S. 749 (1985).

96. *Id.* at 783.

97. *Id.* at 774.

98. *See, e.g.,* Brad Snyder, *Protecting the Media from Excessive Damages: The Nineteenth-Century Origins of Remittitur and Its Modern Application in Food Lion,* 24 Vt. L. Rev. 299, 325 (2000) ("The Sullivan case is a classic example of how punitive damages can inhibit the freedom of the press.").

99. *See* Gertz v. Robert Welch, Inc., 418 U.S. 323, 349 (1974) (endorsing the compensation of private individuals for injury to reputation for actual damages, but holding "that the States may not permit recovery of presumed or punitive damages, at least when liability is not based on a showing of knowledge of falsity or reckless disregard for the truth").

100. Randall P. Bezanson et al., Libel Law and the Press: Myth and Reality 79 (1987).

101. *New Developments 2012,* MLRC Bulletin, Dec. 2012, at 63.

102. *See, e.g.,* Lyndon F. Bittle, Comment: *Punitive Damages and the Eighth Amendment: An Analytical Framework for Determining Excessiveness,* 75 Calif. L. Rev. 1433 (1987); David Crump, *Evidence, Economics, and Ethics: What Information Should Jurors Be Given to Determine the Amount of a Punitive-Damage Award?* 57 Md. L. Rev. 174 (1998); Susan M. Gilles, *Taking First Amendment Procedure Seriously: An Analysis of Process in Libel Litigation,* 58 Ohio St. L.J. 1753 (1998); Lisa Litwiller, *Has the Supreme Court Sounded the Death Knell for Jury Assessed Punitive Damages? A Critical Re-Examination of the American Jury,* 36 U.S.F.L. Rev. 411 (2002); Victor E. Schwartz, Mark A. Behrens & Joseph P. Mastrosimone, *Reining in Punitive Damages "Run Wild": Proposals for Reform by Courts and Legislatures,* 65 Brooklyn L. Rev. 1003 (1999); William W. Van Alstyne, *Defamation and the First Amendment: New Perspectives: Reputation, Compensation, and Proof: First Amendment Limitations on Recovery from the Press—an Extended Comment on "The Anderson Solution,"* 25 Wm. & Mary L. Rev. 793 (1984).

103. *See, e.g.,* Brown & Williamson v. Jacobsen, 827 F.2d 1119 (7th Cir. 1987).

Chapter 5

Libel: Defenses and Privileges

1. Gertz v. Robert Welch, Inc., 418 U.S. 323, 339–40 (1974).

2. Moreno v. Crookston Times and McDaniel, 30 Med. L. Rep. 1208 (Minn. 2002).

3. Hurst v. Capital Cities Media, Inc., 754 N.E.2d 429 (Ill. App. 2001).

4. Weimer v. Rankin, 790 P.2d 347 (Ida. 1990).

5. DMC Plumbing and Remodeling, LLC v. Fox News Network, LLC, et al., No. 12-cv-12867, 2012 U.S. Dist. LEXIS 167318 (E.D. Mich. Nov. 26, 2012); *New Developments 2012*, MLRC Bulletin, Dec. 2012, at 60–61.

6. Milligan v. U.S., 670 F. 3d 686, 698 (6th Cir. 2012).

7. *New Developments 2012*, MLRC Bulletin, Dec. 2012, at 61.

8. *But see, e.g.,* Lee v. Dong-A Ilbo, 849 F.2d 876 (4th Cir. 1988) (ruling that the privilege does not extend to official reports issued by governments other than those in the United States).

9. Cowley v. Pulsifer, 137 Mass. 392, 394 (1884).

10. Liquori v. Republican Co., 396 N.E.2d 726, 728 (Mass. App. 1979).

11. Salzano v. North Jersey Media Group, 201 N.J. 500, 520 (2010).

12. Piscatelli v. Smith, 35 A.3d 1140 (2012).

13. McIntosh v. The Detroit News, Inc., 2009 Mich. App. LEXIS 128 (Jan. 22, 2009).

14. Moldea v. New York Times, 793 F. Supp. 335, 337 (D.D.C. 1992).

15. Moldea v. New York Times, 22 F.3d 310, 315 (D.C. Cir. 1994).

16. 1 Fowler V. Harper & Fleming James, Jr., Law of Torts § 5.28, at 456 (1956).

17. *See* Restatement of Torts § 606 (1938).

18. Restatement (Second) of Torts (1977) § 566, cmt. a.

19. Milkovich v. Lorain Journal Co., 497 U.S. 1, 14 (1990) (Rehnquist, C.J.).

20. *See* Gertz v. Robert Welch, Inc., 418 U.S. 323, 339–40 (1974).

21. Citizen Publishing Co. v. U.S., 394 U.S. 131, 139–40 (1969).

22. Whitney v. California, 274 U.S. 354, 375 (1927) (Brandeis, J., concurring).

23. New York Times v. Sullivan, 376 U.S. 254 (1964).

24. *Id.*

25. Ollman v. Evans, 750 F.2d 970 (D.C. Cir. 1984).

26. *Id.*

27. Janklow v. Newsweek, 788 F.2d 1300, 1305 (8th Cir. 1986).

28. Spelson v. CBS, Inc., 581 F. Supp. 1195 (N.D. Ill. 1984); Anderson v. Liberty Lobby, Inc., 746 F.2d 1563 (D.C. Cir. 1984), *aff'd on other grounds,* 477 U.S. 242 (1986); Henderson v. Times Mirror Co., 669 F. Supp. 356 (D. Colo. 1987); Dow v. New Haven Indep., Inc., 549 A.2d 683 (Conn. 1987).

29. Gertz v. Robert Welch, Inc., 418 U.S. 323, 339 (1974).

30. Milkovich v. Lorrain Journal Co., 497 U.S. 1, 4 (1990).

31. *Id.* at 1.

32. *Id.* at 18.

33. *Id.*

34. *Id.* at 21.

35. *New Developments 2012*, MLRC Bulletin, Dec. 2012, at 52.

36. *Id.*

37. *Id.; see also* Redmond v. Gawker Media LLC, 2012 Cal. App. Unpub. LEXIS 5879 (Cal. App. Aug. 10, 2012) (unpublished).

38. *Id.*

39. John v. Tribune Co., 24 Ill. 2d 437, 442 (1962).

40. Madison v. Frazier, 539 F.3d 646, 654 (7th Cir. 2008).

41. Missner v. Clifford, 393 Ill. App. 3d 751 (2009).

42. *See* Robert D. Sack, Sack on Defamation: Libel, Slander, and Related Problems 2–68–2–69 (1999, rev. 2008) (citations omitted).

43. Couloute v. Ryncarz, et al., No. 11 CV 5986, 2012 U.S. Dist. LEXIS 20534 (S.D.N.Y. Feb. 15, 2012).

44. Madsen v. Buie, 454 So. 2d 727, 729 (Fla. Dist. Ct. App. 1984).

45. Wampler v. Higgins, 752 N.E.2d 962 (Ohio 2001).

46. Hustler Magazine v. Falwell, 485 U.S. 46 (1988).

47. Greenbelt Cooperative Publishers Association, Inc. v. Bressler, 398 U.S. 6, 7–8 (1970).

48. *Id.* at 14.

49. Old Dominion Branch No, 496, Nat'l Assn. of Letter Carriers v. Austin, 418 U.S. 264 (1974).

50. *Id.* at 268.

51. *Id.* at 285–86.

52. Knievel v. ESPN, Inc., 223 F. Supp. 2d 1173, 1180 (2002).

53. Silberman v. Georges, 456 N.Y.S.2d 395 (1982).

54. New Times, Inc. v. Isaacks, 91 S.W.3d 844, 850 (Tex. 2002).

55. New Times, Inc. v. Isaacks, 146 S.W.3d 144 (Tex. 2004), *cert. denied,* 545 U.S. 1105 (2005).

56. Edwards v. National Audubon Society, 556 F.2d 113 (2d Cir. 1977) (ruling that "when a responsible, prominent organization . . . makes serious charges against a public figure, the First Amendment protects the accurate and disinterested reporting of those charges, regardless of the reporter's private views of their validity. . . . We do not believe that the press may be required under the First Amendment to suppress newsworthy statements merely because it has serious doubts regarding their truth."). *Id.* at 120.

57. Dan Laidman, *When the Slander Is the Story: The Neutral Report Privilege in Theory and Practice,* 17 UCLA ENT. L. REV. 74, 76 (2010).

58. McKinney v. Avery Journal, Inc., 393 S.E.2d 295 (N.C. 1990).

59. Auvil v. CBS, 140 F.R.D. 450 (E.D. Wash. 1991).

60. *See* Firth v. State of New York, 775 N.E.2d 463 (N.Y. 2002), which outlines the principles of applying the single-publication rule to the Internet and which is often used as a precedent to support similar cases in other states and in the federal court system.

61. Cardillo v. Doubleday Co., Inc., 518 F.2d 638 (2d Cir. 1975) (ruling that the passages of a book whose authors wrote that a habitual criminal was involved in various other criminal activities did not constitute actual malice).

62. Liberty Lobby, Inc. v. Anderson, 746 F.2d 1563 (D.C. Cir. 1984), *rev'd on other grounds,* 477 U.S. 242 (1986).

63. *Id.* at 1568.

64. *Id.*

65. Logan v. District of Columbia, 447 F. Supp. 1328 (D.D.C. 1978).

66. Masson v. New Yorker Magazine, Inc., 501 U.S. 496, 523 (1991).

67. Mourning v. Family Publ'ns. Serv., 411 U.S. 356, 382 (1973). *See also* Adickes v. Kress & Co., 389 U.S. 144, 157 (1970); U.S. v. Diebold, Inc., 369 U.S. 654, 655 (1979).

68. *See* Anderson v. Liberty Lobby, Inc., 477 U.S. 242 (1986).

69. Washington Post Co. v. Keogh, 365 F.2d 965, 968 (D.C. Cir. 1966).

70. Hutchinson v. Proxmire, 443 U.S. 111, 120 n.9 (1979).

71. Anderson v. Liberty Lobby, Inc., 477 U.S. 242, 244, 256 (1986).

72. *See, e.g.,* Hustler Magazine, Inc., 465 U.S. 770 (1984) (overturning a lower court ruling dismissing a libel suit filed by a resident of New York against an Ohio corporation in a New Hampshire court). *See also* New York Times v. Sullivan, 376 U.S. 254 (1964) (where the trial and first appeal were heard in Alabama courts).

73. Young v. New Haven Advocate, 315 F.3d 256, 261 (4th Cir. 2002), *cert. denied,* 538 U.S. 1035 (2003).

74. *Id.* at 263.

75. *Id.*

76. 47 U.S.C. §§ 230 (c)(1), (e)(3).

77. *Legal Guide for Bloggers, Section 230 Protections,* ELECTRONIC FRONTIER FOUNDATION, *available at* https://www.eff.org/issues/bloggers/legal/liability/230.

78. *Id.*

79. Batzel v. Smith, 333 F. 3d. 1018 (9th Cir., 2008).

80. Although this was not a libel case (the underlying right of publicity is discussed in Chapter 6), the court's ruling broadly applied to how Section 230 is used by services like Facebook to defend libel and privacy claims.

81. Fraley et al. v. Facebook, Inc., 830 F.Supp. 2d 801-802 (N.D. Cal., 2011).

82. *New Developments 2012,* MLRC BULLETIN, Dec. 2012, at 48; *See also* Jones v. Dirty World Entertainment Recordings LLC 2013 U.S. Dist. Lexis 113031 (2013); Jones v. Dirty World Entertainment Recordings LLC (E.D. Ky. Jan. 10, 2012)

83. John C. Martin, *The Role of Retraction in Defamation Suits,* 1993 U. CHI. LEGAL F. 293, 294 (1993).

84. Two states' retraction statutes apply only to newspapers. *See* Minn. Stat. Ann. 548.06 (1987); S.D. Codified Laws 20–11–7 (1995). Two others include media other than newspapers but exclude radio and television. *See* Wis. Stat. 895.05 (1998); Okla. Stat. tit. 12, 1446a.

85. Dennis Hale, *The Impact of State Prohibitions of Punitive Damages on Libel Litigation: An Empirical Analysis,* 5 VAND. J. ENT. L. & PRAC. 96, 100 (2003).

86. Boswell v. Phoenix Newspapers, Inc., 730 P.2d 186 (Ariz. 1986).

87. ARIZ. REV. STAT. §§ 12–653.02 and 12.653.03.

88. ARIZ. CONST., art. 18, § 6.

89. Early v. Toledo Blade, 720 N.E.2d. 107 (Ohio Ct. App. 1998).

90. Dolcefino and KTRK Television, Inc. v. Turner, 987 S.W. 2d 100 (Tex. 1998).

91. In its entirety, the column reads as follows:

Yesterday in the Franklin County Common Pleas Court, judge Paul Martin overturned an Ohio High School Athletic Assn. decision to suspend the Maple Heights wrestling team from this year's state tournament.

It's not final yet—the judge granted Maple only a temporary injunction against the ruling—but unless the judge acts much more quickly than he did in this decision (he has been deliberating since a Nov. 8 hearing) the temporary injunction will allow Maple to compete in the tournament and make any further discussion meaningless.

But there is something much more important involved here than whether Maple was denied due process by the OHSAA, the basis of the temporary injunction.

When a person takes on a job in a school, whether it be as a teacher, coach, administrator or even maintenance worker, it is well to remember that his primary job is that of educator.

There is scarcely a person concerned with school who doesn't leave his mark in some way on the young people who pass his way—many are the lessons taken away from school by students which weren't learned from a lesson plan or out of a book. They come from personal experiences with and observations of their superiors and peers, from watching actions and reactions.

Such a lesson was learned (or relearned) yesterday by the student body of Maple Heights High School, and by anyone who attended the Maple-Mentor wrestling meet of last Feb. 8.

A lesson which, sadly, in view of the events of the past year, is well they learned early.

It is simply this: If you get in a jam, lie your way out.

If you're successful enough, and powerful enough, and can sound sincere enough, you stand an excellent chance of making the lie stand up, regardless of what really happened.

The teachers responsible were mainly head Maple wrestling coach, Mike Milkovich, and former superintendent of schools H. Donald Scott.

Last winter they were faced with a difficult situation. Milkovich's ranting from the side of the mat and egging the crowd on against the meet official and the opposing team backfired during a meet with Greater Cleveland Conference rival Metor [sic], and resulted in first the Maple Heights team, then many of the partisan crowd attacking the Mentor squad in a brawl which sent four Mentor wrestlers to the hospital.

Naturally, when Mentor protested to the governing body of high school sports, the OHSAA, the two men were called on the carpet to account for the incident.

But they declined to walk into the hearing and face up to their responsibilities, as one would hope a coach of Milkovich's accomplishments and reputation would do, and one would certainly expect from a man with the responsible poisition [sic] of superintendent of schools.

Instead they chose to come to the hearing and misrepresent the things that happened to the OHSAA Board of Control, attempting not only to convince the board of their own innocence, but, incredibly, shift the blame of the affair to Mentor.

I was among the 2,000-plus witnesses of the meet at which the trouble broke out, and I also attended the hearing before the OHSAA, so I was in a unique position of being the only non-involved party to observe both the meet itself and the Milkovich-Scott version presented to the board.

Any resemblance between the two occurrances [sic] is purely coincidental.

To anyone who was at the meet, it need only be said that the Maple coach's wild gestures during the events leading up to the brawl were passed off by the two as 'shrugs,' and that Milkovich claimed he was 'Powerless to control the crowd' before the melee.

Fortunately, it seemed at the time, the Milkovich-Scott version of the incident presented to the board of control had enough contradictions and obvious untruths so that the six board members were able to see through it.

Probably as much in distasteful reaction to the chicanery of the two officials as in displeasure over the actual incident, the board then voted to suspend Maple from this year's tournament and to put Maple Heights, and both Milkovich and his son, Mike Jr. (the Maple Jaycee coach), on two-year probation.

But unfortunately, by the time the hearing before Judge Martin rolled around, Milkovich and Scott apparently had their version of the incident polished and reconstructed, and the judge apparently believed them.

"I can say that some of the stories told to the judge sounded pretty darned unfamiliar," said Dr. Harold Meyer, commissioner of the OHSAA, who attended the hearing. 'It certainly sounded different from what they told us.'

Nevertheless, the judge bought their story, and ruled in their favor.

Anyone who attended the meet, whether he be from Maple Heights, Mentor, or impartial observer, knows in his heart that Milkovich and Scott lied at the hearing after each having given his solemn oath to tell the truth.

But they got away with it.

Is that the kind of lesson we want our young people learning from their high school administrators and coaches?

I think not.

Chapter 6

Protecting Privacy

1. Jennifer Martinez, *Internet Firms Grilled on Privacy*, L.A. TIMES, July 28, 2010, at B6.

2. United States v. Jones, 132 S. Ct. 945, 956 (2012) (Sotomayor, J., concurring).

3. U.S. CONST. amend. IV.

4. U.S. CONST. amend. III.

5. Barton Gellman & Laura Poitras, *U.S., British Intelligence Mining Data from Nine U.S. Internet Companies in Broad Secret Program*, WASH. POST (June 7, 2013), *available at* http://www.washingtonpost.com/investigations/us-intelligence-mining-data-from-nine-us-internet-companies-in-broad-secret-program/2013/06/06/3a0c0da8-cebf-11e2-8845-d970ccb04497_story.html.

6. Julia Angwin, *The Web's New Gold Mine: Your Secrets*, WALL ST. J. (July 30, 2010), *available at* http://online.wsj.com/article/; Julia Angwin & Tom McGinty, *Sites Feed Personal Details to New Tracking Industry*, WALL ST. J. (July 30, 2010), *available at* http://online.wsj.com/article/; Jennifer Valentino-DeVries, *Lawsuit Tackles Files That "Re-Spawn" Tracking Cookies*, WALL ST. J. (July 30, 2010), *available at* http://blogs.wsj.com/digits/2010/07/30/.

7. *See, e.g., In re* Doubleclick Inc. Privacy Litation, 154 F. Supp. 2d 497 (S.D.N.Y. 2001).

8. Jordan Robertson, *What Your Phone App Doesn't Say: It's Watching*, SAN JOSE MERCURY NEWS (July 30, 2010), *available at* https://advance.lexis.com/GoToContentView?requestid=440dbd6c-f591-6e1b-e7be-40c6b5931869&crid=32d39741-2819-6d42-9176-2577875dfeb0.

9. Alex Fitzpatrick, *Google Fined $7 Million in Street View Privacy Settlement*, MASHABLE.COM (Mar. 12, 2013), *available at* http://mashable.com/2013/03/12/google-street-view-settlement/.

10. Associated Press, *Financial Info. on Celebs, Officials Leaked Online*, POLITICO.COM (Mar. 12, 2013), *available at* http://www.politico.com/story/2013/03/financial-info-on-celebs-officials-leaked-online-88740.html.

11. Ostergren v. Cuccinelli, 615 F.3d 263 (4th Cir. 2010).

12. Jessica Rich, Federal Trade Commission, Deputy Director of Consumer Protection, *Protecting Youths in an Online World*, testimony before U.S. Senate Committee on Commerce, Science and Transportation, Subcommittee on Consumer Protection, Product Safety, and Insurance (July 15, 2010), *available at* http://www.ftc.gov/os/testimony/os/testimony/100715toopatestimony.pdf.

13. Declan McCullagh, *FTC Says Current Privacy Laws Aren't Working*, CNET NEWS (June 22, 2010), *available at* http://news.cnet.com/8301-13578_3-20008422-38.html.

14. Lorrie Faith Cranor, *A Guide to Facebook's Privacy Options*, WALL ST. J. (Mar. 10, 2013), *available at* http://online.wsj.com/article/SB10001424127887324880504578300312528424302.html; *see also* Nick Bilton, *Price of Facebook Privacy? Start Clicking*, N.Y. TIMES, May 13, 2010, at B8.

15. Federal Trade Commission, *FTC Issues Final Commission Report on Protecting Consumer Privacy* (Mar. 26, 2012), *available at* http://ftc.gov/opa/2012/03/privacyframework.shtm.

16. City of Ontario v. Quon, 130 S. Ct. 2619 (2010).

17. O'Conner v. Ortega, 480 U.S. 709 (1987).

18. Ray Lewis, Comment: *Employee E-mail Privacy Still Unemployed: What the United States Can Learn from the United Kingdom*, 67 LA. L. REV. 959 (2007).

19. Smyth v. Pillsbury Co., 914 F. Supp. 97, 101 (E.D. Pa. 1996).

20. 50 U.S.C. §§ 1804(a)(7)(B), 1823(a)(B) (2003).

21. United States v. Jones, 132 S. Ct. 945 (2012).

22. Katz v. United States, 389 U.S. 360 (1967) (Harlan, J. concurring).

23. Daniel T. Pesciotta, *I'm Not Dead Yet: Katz, Jones, and the Fourth Amendment in the 21st Century*, 63 CASE W. RES. 187, 198 (2012).

24. United States v. Jones, 132 S. Ct. 919 (2012).

25. Florida v. Jardines, 133 S. Ct. 1409 (2013).

26. Pesciotta, *supra* note 23 at 213.

27. 18 U.S.C. §§ 2701–2712.

28. Rebecca DiLeonardo, *Federal Appeals Court Rules Data Stored on Cell Phones Not Protected*, JURIST (Dec. 13, 2012), *available at* http://jurist.org/paperchase/2012/12/federal-appeals-court-rules-data-stored-on-cell-phones-not-protected.php.

29. Jennifer Valentino-DeVries, *Judges Questioned Use of Cellphone Tracking Devices*, WALL ST. J. (Mar. 27, 2013), *available at* http://blogs.wsj.com/digits/2013/03/27/judges-question-use-of-cellphone-tracking-devices/.

30. Joel Stashenko, *Judge Denies Right to Privacy in "Ping" of Cell Phone Location*, N.Y.L.J. (Feb. 21, 2013), *available at* http://www.law.com/jsp/lawtechnologynews/PubArticleLTN.jsp?id=1361430854252&slret urn=20130305183341.

31. Brendan Sasso, *Lawmakers Push Bill to Limit GPS Tracking*, HILL (Mar. 21, 2013), *available at* http://thehill.com/blogs/hillicon-valley/technology/289575-lawmakers-push-bill-to-limit-gps-tracking.

32. *Id.*

33. The "First Amendment has a penumbra where privacy is protected from governmental intrusion." Griswold v. Connecticut, 381 U.S. 479, 482 (1965).

34. *Griswold*, 381 U.S. 479.

35. U.S. CONST. amend. V.

36. *Griswold*, 381 U.S. 479.

37. Eisenstadt v. Baird, 405 U.S. 438 (1972).

38. Roe v. Wade, 410 U.S. 113 (1973).

39. Lawrence v. Texas, 539 U.S. 538 (2003).

40. Jeffery A. Smith, *Moral Guardians and the Origins of the Right to Privacy*, 10 JOURNALISM & COMM. MONOGRAPHS 65 (2008).

41. Samuel D. Warren & Louis D. Brandeis, *The Right to Privacy*, 4 HARV. L. REV. 193 (1890).

42. Warren and Brandeis rested their contention on an English case, Prince Albert v. Strange, 64 Eng. Rep. 293 (V.C.

1848), on appeal, 64 Eng. Rep. 293 (1849). But not until 2001 did English courts explicitly recognize a right to privacy. See Douglas v. Hello! Ltd., [2001] W.L.R. 992, 1033, para. 110 ("We have reached a point at which it can be said with confidence that the law recognizes and will appropriately protect a right of personal privacy.") (per Sedley, L.J.).

43. *See* DON R. PEMBER, PRIVACY AND THE PRESS (1972).

44. William L. Prosser, *Privacy*, 48 CAL. L. REV. 383 (1960).

45. MEDIA LAW RESOURCE CENTER, MEDIA PRIVACY AND RELATED LAW SURVEY 2012–2013 (2012).

46. RESTATEMENT (SECOND) OF TORTS § 652I.

47. *See, e.g.,* RESTATEMENT (THIRD) OF UNFAIR COMPETITION § 46 cmt. d (right of publicity limited to "natural persons").

48. RESTATEMENT (SECOND) OF TORTS § 652E cmt. b, illus. 1.

49. Spahn v. Julian Messner, 233 N.E.2d 840 (N.Y. 1967).

50. MEDIA LAW RESOURCE CENTER, MEDIA PRIVACY AND RELATED LAW SURVEY 2012–2013 (2012). Colorado, Florida, Massachusetts, Minnesota, New York, North Carolina, South Carolina, Texas, Virginia and Wisconsin reject false light.

51. Solano v. Playgirl, Inc., 292 F.3d 1078, 1082 (9th Cir.), *cert. denied*, 537 U.S. 1029 (2002).

52. *See* RESTATEMENT (SECOND) OF TORTS § 652E.

53. *Id.* at § 652I cmt. c.

54. *Id.* at § 652D cmt. a.

55. *See, e.g.,* Solano v. Playgirl Inc., 292 F.3d 1078 (9th Cir.), *cert. denied*, 537 U.S. 1029 (2002).

56. *See, e.g., id.*

57. *See, e.g.,* Eberhardt v. Morgan Stanley Dean Witter Trust FSB, 2001 U.S. Dist. LEXIS 1090 (N.D. Ill. 2001).

58. Brauer v. Globe Newspaper Co., 217 N.E.2d 736 (1966).

59. Howard v. Antilla, 294 F.3d 244 (1st Cir. 2002).

60. Peterson v. Grisham, 594 F.3d 723 (10th Cir. 2010).

61. Moriarty v. Greene, 732 N.E.2d 730 (Ill. App. Ct. 2000).

62. Fanelle v. LoJack Corp., 2000 U.S. Dist. LEXIS 17767 (E.D. Pa. 2000).

63. Kelson v. Spin Publications, Inc., 1988 U.S. Dist. LEXIS 4675 (D. Md. 1988).

64. Peoples Bank & Trust Co. v. Globe International, 978 F.2d 1065 (8th Cir. 1992), *on remand*, Mitchell v. Globe

International Publications, Inc., 817 F. Supp. 72 (W.D. Ark.), *cert. denied,* 510 U.S. 931 (1993).

65. Time, Inc. v. Hill, 385 U.S. 374 (1967).

66. State courts or federal courts applying state law to follow *Gertz* rather than *Hill* and *Cantrell,* thus not requiring private false light plaintiffs to prove actual malice, include Alabama, Delaware, Kansas, Utah, West Virginia and the District of Columbia. MEDIA LAW RESOURCE CENTER, MEDIA PRIVACY AND RELATED LAW 2012–2013 (2012).

67. State courts or federal courts applying state law to follow *Hill* and *Cantrell* rather than *Gertz,* thus requiring private false light plaintiffs to prove actual malice, include Arkansas, California, Connecticut, Florida, Georgia, Illinois, Indiana, Iowa, Kentucky, Maine, Michigan, Mississippi, Montana, Nebraska, Nevada, New Jersey, Oklahoma, Oregon, Pennsylvania, Tennessee and Washington. *Id.* at 788–90.

68. *See* HARVEY L. ZUCKMAN ET AL., MODERN COMMUNICATIONS LAW 357–61 (1999).

69. *See id.* at 360–61 (1999).

70. *E.g.,* Veilleux v. NBC, 206 F.3d 92, 134 (1st Cir. 2000), said opinion could be a false light defense, while Boese v. Paramount Pictures Corp., 952 F. Supp. 550, 558–59 (N.D. Ill. 1996), said opinion is not a false light defense.

71. *See* ZUCKMAN ET AL., *supra* note 68, at 351–52 (1999).

72. Hilton v. Hallmark Cards, 599 F.3d 894, 899 (9th Cir. 2010).

73. MEDIA LAW RESOURCE CENTER, MEDIA PRIVACY AND RELATED LAW 2012–2013 (2012).

74. RESTATEMENT (THIRD) OF UNFAIR COMPETITION § 46.

75. Some states, such as Georgia, New Jersey and Utah, and the U.S. Court of Appeals for the Second Circuit have decided by common law that the right of publicity survives after death. Statutes in 10 states say the same. Some states, such as Illinois and Ohio, and the U.S. Courts of Appeals for the Sixth and Seventh Circuits, say by common law that the right of publicity ends when a person dies. Five states agree by statute: Arizona, Massachusetts, New York, Rhode Island and Wisconsin.

76. By statute: California, Florida, Illinois, Indiana, Kentucky, Nebraska, Nevada, Ohio, Oklahoma, Pennsylvania, Tennessee, Texas, Virginia, Washington. By common law: Connecticut, Georgia, Michigan, New Jersey, Utah. J. THOMAS MCCARTHY, THE RIGHTS OF PUBLICITY AND PRIVACY §§ 9:20–9:39 (2013).

77. *Id.* § 9:18. For example, Virginia limits the right of publicity to 20 years after a person's death, Indiana and Oklahoma allow the right to last 100 years after a person's death, and Nebraska has no stated duration. *Id.*

78. *New Developments 2012,* MLRC BULLETIN, Dec. 2012, 68–71.

79. Milton H. Greene Archives v. Marilyn Monroe LLC, 692 F. 3d 983 (9th Cir. 2012).

80. Hebrew University of Jerusalem v. General Motors LLC, 40 Media L. Rep. 2449 (C.D. Cal 2012).

81. N.Y. Civil Rights Law §§ 50–51.

82. Haelan Laboratories, Inc. v. Topps Chewing Gum, Inc., 202 F.2d 866 (2d Cir. 1953).

83. *See* MCCARTHY, *supra* note 76, §§ 1:27, 4:7.

84. *See, e.g.,* Dalbec v. Gentleman's Companion, Inc., 828 F.2d 921 (2d Cir. 1987).

85. Shamsky v. Garan, Inc., 632 N.Y.S.2d 930, 934 (Supp. 1995).

86. *See* MCCARTHY, *supra* note 76, § 3:7.

87. Abdul-Jabbar v. General Motors Corp., 85 F.3d 407 (9th Cir. 1996).

88. Prudhomme v. The Procter & Gamble Co., 800 F. Supp. 390 (E.D. La. 1992).

89. Tin Pan Apple, Inc. v. Miller Brewing Co., 737 F. Supp. 826 (S.D.N.Y. 1990).

90. Midler v. Ford Motor Co., 849 F.2d 460 (9th Cir. 1988). A federal district court denied Midler punitive damages, but the jury awarded $400,000 in compensatory damages. The Ninth Circuit affirmed. Midler v. Young & Rubicam, Inc., 944 F.2d 909 (9th Cir. 1991), *cert. denied,* 503 U.S. 951 (1992).

91. White v. Samsung Electronics America, Inc., 971 F.2d 1395 (9th Cir. 1992), *cert. denied,* 508 U.S. 951 (1993).

92. William L. Prosser, *Privacy,* 48 CAL. L. REV. 383, 401 n.155 (1960).

93. Wendt v. Host International, Inc., 125 F.3d 806 (9th Cir. 1997), *cert. denied,* 531 U.S. 811 (2000).

94. *Norm and Cliff Cheered by Lawsuit,* CHI. TRIB., June 22, 2001, at C2.

95. *See, e.g.,* Cardtoons, L.C. v. Major League Baseball Players Assoc., 95 F.3d 959 (10th Cir. 1996).

96. McCarthy, *supra* note 76, § 4:46.

97. The Romantics v. Activision Pub., Inc., 574 F. Supp. 2d 758 (E.D. Mich. 2008).

98. Restatement (Third) of Unfair Competition § 49 cmt. d.

99. ETW Corp. v. Jireh Publishing, Inc., 332 F.3d 915, 924 (6th Cir. 2003).

100. Messenger v. Gruner + Jahn Printing & Publishing, 727 N.E.2d 549 (N.Y. 2000, 208 F.3d 122 (2d Cir. 2000) (vacating district court decision based on New York Court of Appeals decision), *cert. denied,* 531 U.S. 818 (2000).

101. Toffoloni v. LFP Pub. Group, 572 F.3d 1201 (11th Cir. 2009).

102. C.B.C. Distribution and Marketing, Inc. v. Major League Baseball Advanced Media, L.P., 505 F.3d 818 (8th Cir. 2007), *cert. denied,* 553 U.S. 1090 (2008).

103. *See* Mark S. Lee, *Agents of Chaos: Judicial Confusion in Defining the Right of Publicity-Free Speech Interface,* 23 Loyola L.A. Ent. L. Rev. 471, 488 (2003).

104. Haelan Laboratories, Inc. v. Topps Chewing Gum, Inc., 202 F.2d 866, 868 (2d Cir.), *cert. denied,* 346 U.S. 816 (1953).

105. Cardtoons, L.C. v. Major League Baseball Players Association, 95 F.3d 959, 962 (10th Cir. 1996).

106. *Id.* at 969.

107. *Id.* at 976.

108. Factors Etc., Inc. v. Pro Arts, Inc., 579 F.2d 215 (2d Cir. 1978); Brinkley v. Casablancas, 438 N.Y.S.2d 1004 (App. Div. 1981); Titan Sports, Inc. v. Comics World Corp., 870 F.2d 85 (2d Cir. 1989).

109. Paulsen v. Personality Posters, Inc., 299 N.Y.S.2d 501 (Sup. Ct. 1968); Montana v. San Jose Mercury News, Inc., 40 Cal. Rptr. 2d 639 (Ct. App. 1995).

110. The Hollywood Reporter, *Lindsay Lohan Loses Lawsuit Against Pitbull Over Hit Song* (Feb. 21, 2013), *available at* http://www.hollywoodreporter.com/thr-esq/lindsay-lohan-loses-lawsuit-pitbull-423228.

111. Rogers v. Grimaldi, 875 F.2d 994, 999 (2d Cir. 1989).

112. Mattel, Inc. v. MCA Records, Inc., 296 F.3d 894 (9th Cir. 2002), *cert. denied,* 537 U.S. 1171 (2003).

113. Parks v. LaFace Records, 329 F.3d 437, 442 (6th Cir. 2003), *cert. denied,* 540 U.S. 1074 (2003).

114. *See* Campbell v. Acuff-Rose Music, 510 U.S. 569 (1994); Pierre N. Leval, *Toward a Fair Use Standard,* 103 Harv. L. Rev. 1105, 1111 (1990).

115. Comedy III Productions, Inc. v. Gary Saderup, Inc., 106 Cal. Rptr. 2d 126 (Cal. 2001).

116. For a thorough and critical discussion of the Three Stooges decision, see F. Jay Daugherty, *All the World's Not a Stooge: The "Transformativeness" Test for Analyzing a First Amendment Defense to a Right of Publicity Claim Against Distribution of a Work of Art,* 27 Col. J. L. & Arts 1 (2003).

117. Comedy III Productions, Inc., 106 Cal. Rptr. 2d at 140.

118. Winter v. DC Comics, 69 P.3d 473 (Cal. 2003).

119. *Id.* at 478 (*quoting* Comedy III Prods., Inc. v. Gary Saderup, Inc., 106 Cal. Rptr. 2d at 140 (2001)).

120. ETW Corp. v. Jireh Publishing, Inc., 332 F.3d 915 (6th Cir. 2003).

121. Doe v. TCI Cablevision, 110 S.W.3d 363 (Mo. 2003), *on remand,* Doe v. McFarlane, 207 S.W.3d 52 (Mo. Ct. App. 2006).

122. Seale v. Gramercy Pictures, 949 F. Supp. 331 (E.D. Pa. 1996), *aff'd without opinion,* 156 F.3d 1225 (3d Cir. 1998).

123. Rosemont Enterprises, Inc. v. Random House, Inc., 294 N.Y.S.2d 122 (Sup. 1968), *judgment aff'd,* 301 N.Y.S.2d 948 (App. Div. 1969).

124. *See, e.g.,* Tyne v. Time Warner Entertainment Co., 336 F.3d 1286 (11th Cir. 2003).

125. Guglielmi v. Spelling-Goldberg Productions, 603 P.2d 454 (1979); Taylor v. National Broadcasting Co., Inc. 22 Media L. Rep. 2433 (Cal. Supp. 1994).

126. Booth v. Curtis Publishing Co., 223 N.Y.S.2d 737 (N.Y. Sup. Ct.), *aff'd,* 228 N.Y.S.2d 468 (1962).

127. Cher v. Forum International, 692 F.2d 634 (9th Cir.), *cert. denied,* 462 U.S. 1120 (1983).

128. Schifano v. Greene Country Greyhound Park, Inc., 624 So. 2d (Ala. 1993).

129. Netzer v. Continuity Graphic Associates, Inc., 963 F. Supp. 1308 (S.D.N.Y. 1997).

130. Pooley v. National Hole-in-One Association, 89 F. Supp. 2d 1108 (D. Ariz. 2000).

131. Restatement (Second) of Torts § 652B.

132. Media Law Resource Center, Media Privacy and Related Law Survey 2012–2013 (2012).

133. Webb v. CBS Broadcasting Inc., 2009 U.S. Dist. LEXIS 38597, at *9 (N.D. Ill., May 7, 2009).

134. *See, e.g.*, Broughton v. McClatchy Newspapers, Inc., 588 S.E.2d 20 (N.C. App. 2003).

135. Boring v. Google Inc., 362 Fed. Appx. 273, *cert. denied*, 131 S. Ct. 150 (2010).

136. Hill v. Colorado, 530 U.S. 703 (2000).

137. Cal. Civ. Code § 1708.8.

138. Shulman v. Group W Productions, Inc., 74 Cal. Rptr. 2d 843, *opinion modified*, 1998 Cal. LEXIS 4846 (Cal. 1998).

139. United States v. Maldonado-Norat, 122 F. Supp. 2d 264 (D.P.R. 2000).

140. Le Mistral, Inc. v. Columbia Broadcasting System, 402 N.Y.S.2d 815 (1978).

141. Medical Laboratory Management Consultants v. American Broadcasting Cos., Inc., 306 F.3d 806, 819 (9th Cir. 2002).

142. Belluomo v. KAKE TV & Radio, Inc., 596 P.2d 832 (Kan. App. 1979).

143. Machleder v. Diaz, 538 F. Supp. 1364 (S.D.N.Y. 1982).

144. Desnick v. American Broadcasting Companies, 44 F.3d 1345 (7th Cir. 1995).

145. Carter v. Superior Court of San Diego County, 2002 Cal. App. Unpub. LEXIS 5017 (Ct. App. 2002).

146. Dietemann v. Time, Inc., 449 F.2d 245, 249 (9th Cir. 1971).

147. *Id.*

148. *See* John J. Walsh et al., *The Constitutionality of Consequential Damages for Publication of Ill-Gotten Information*, 4 Wm. & Mary Bill Rts. J. 1111, 1137–40 (1996).

149. Medical Laboratory Management Consultants v. American Broadcasting Companies, Inc., 30 F. Supp. 2d 1182 (D. Ariz. 1998), *aff'd on other grounds*, 306 F.3d 806 (9th Cir. 2002).

150. Sanders v. American Broadcasting Companies, 978 P.2d 67, 74 (Cal. 1999).

151. Restatement (Second) of Torts § 652D.

152. Michaels v. Internet Entertainment Group, 5 F. Supp. 2d 823, 842 (C.D. Cal. 1998).

153. Brents v. Morgan, 299 S.W. 967 (Ky. Ct. App. 1927).

154. Media Law Resource Center, Media Privacy and Related Law Survey 2012–2013 (2012). Four states have rejected the tort—Nebraska, New York, North Carolina and Virginia.

155. *See, e.g.*, Jones v. U.S. Child Support Recovery, 961 F. Supp. 1518 (D. Utah 1997). A debt collection agency sent a WANTED poster to the employer of a divorced parent who was behind on child support payments.

156. *See, e.g.*, Y.G. v. Jewish Hospital of St. Louis, 795 S.W.2d 488 (Mo. Ct. App. 1990). A couple, pregnant with triplets after an in vitro fertilization process, were invited to and attended a social gathering for couples who were part of a hospital's in vitro program. The hospital promised there would be no publicity. However, a television station reporting team was at the gathering, photographing and trying to interview the couple. The couple's pictures were part of the station's television report. The couple had not told anyone they were part of the in vitro program.

157. *See, e.g.*, Baugh v. CBS, Inc., 828 F. Supp. 745 (N.D. Cal. 1993). Without permission, a television program taped and showed the aftermath of a domestic violence incident.

158. *See, e.g.*, Michaels v. Internet Entertainment Group, 5 F. Supp. 2d 823, 842 (C.D. Cal. 1998). Musician Bret Michaels brought a private facts suit against an Internet adult entertainment company for distributing a videotape showing Michaels and actress Pamela Anderson Lee having sex. Michaels and Lee made the tape, which an unknown person apparently stole and sold to the Internet company.

159. Daly v. Viacom, Inc., 238 F. Supp. 2d 1118 (N.D. Cal. 2002).

160. Zieve v. Hairston, 598 S.E.2d 25 (Ga. App. 2004).

161. See Robert C. Post, *The Social Foundations of Privacy: Community and Self in the Common Law Tort*, 77 Cal. L. Rev. 957, 983–984 (1989).

162. Restatement (Second) of Torts § 652D cmt. c.

163. *See* M.G. v. Time Warner, Inc., 107 Cal. Rptr. 2d 504, 511 (Cal. App. 2001).

164. Sandler v. Calcagni, 565 F. Supp. 2d 184 (D. Me. 2008).

165. Restatement (Second) of Torts § 652D cmts. g, h.

166. The Restatement also adopted the test. *Id.* cmt. h.

167. Virgil v. Time, Inc., 527 F.2d 1122 (9th Cir. 1975), *cert. denied*, 425 U.S. 998 (1976).

168. Virgil v. Sports Illustrated, Inc., 424 F. Supp. 1286 (S.D. Cal. 1976).

169. Michaels v. Internet Entertainment Group, Inc., 5 F. Supp. 2d 823 (C.D. Cal. 1998).

170. Diaz v. Oakland Tribune, 188 Cal. Rptr. 762 (1983).

171. RESTATEMENT (SECOND) OF TORTS § 652D, requires the private facts to be disseminated "to the public at large, or to so many persons that the matter must be regarded as substantially certain to become one of public knowledge."

172. *See* Patrick J. McNulty, *The Public Disclosure of Private Facts: There Is Life After* Florida Star, 50 DRAKE L. REV. 93, 100 (2001).

173. See Beaumont v. Brown, 257 N.W.2d 522, 531 (Mich. 1977), *overruled in part on other grounds,* Bradley v. Saranac Board of Education, 565 N.W.2d 650 (1997).

174. Johnson v. K Mart Corp., 723 N.E.2d 1192 (Ill. Ct. App. 2000).

175. Florida Star v. B.J.F., 491 U.S. 524, 541 (1989).

176. *See id.* at 536–37.

177. 491 U.S. 524 (1989).

178. 420 U.S. 469 (1975).

179. Oklahoma Publishing Co. v. District Court, 430 U.S. 308 (1977).

180. Smith v. Daily Mail, 443 U.S. 97 (1979).

181. 532 U.S. 514 (2001).

182. *See, e.g.,* Carafano v. Metrosplash, 207 F. Supp. 2d 1055 (C.D. Cal. 2002), *aff'd on other grounds,* 339 F.3d 1119 (9th Cir. 2003).

183. *See, e.g.,* United States v. Smith, 992 F. Supp. 743 (D.N.J. 1998).

184. *See, e.g.,* Doe v. New York City, 15 F.3d 264 (2d Cir. 1994).

185. *See* Green v. Chicago Tribune Co., 675 N.E.2d 249 (Ill. App. Ct. 1996), *appeal denied,* 679 N.E.2d 379 (Ill. 1997).

186. Sidis v. F-R Publishing Corp., 113 F.2d 806 (2d Cir.), *cert. denied,* 311 U.S. 711 (1940).

Chapter 7

Emotional Distress and Physical Harm

1. Bruce W. Sanford & Bruce D. Brown, *Hit Man's Miss Hit,* 27 N. KY. L. REV. 69, 71 (2000).

2. A jury awarded McDonald's drive-through customer Sheila Liebeck $2.7 million in punitive damages after she spilled hot coffee onto her lap. An appellate court reduced the award to $480,000. *See* Andrew Tilghman, *Lawsuit Juries Harder to Find,* HOUS. CHRON., Feb. 14, 2004, at A1.

3. RESTATEMENT (SECOND) OF TORTS § 46 (1965) cmt. j.

4. *See, e.g.,* Gouin v. Gouin, 249 F. Supp. 2d 62 (D. Mass. 2003).

5. *See* Charles E. Cantu, *An Essay on the Tort of Negligent Infliction of Emotional Distress in Texas: Stop Saying It Does Not Exist,* 33 ST. MARY'S L.J. 455, 458 (2002).

6. Cox Newspaper L.P. v. Wooten, 59 S.W.3d 717 (Tex. Ct. App. 2001).

7. Idema v. Wager, 29 Fed. Appx. 676 (2d Cir. 2002).

8. *See, e.g.,* Nancy Levit, *Ethereal Torts,* 61 GEO. WASH. L. REV. 136 (1992).

9. *Id.*

10. RESTATEMENT (SECOND) OF TORTS § 46 (1965).

11. *See, e.g.,* Covey v. Detroit Lakes Publishing Co., 490 N.W.2d 138, 144 (Minn. Ct. App. 1992).

12. *See* Pierce v. Clarion Ledger, 236 Fed. Appx. 887, 889 (5th Cir. 2007).

13. RESTATEMENT (SECOND) OF TORTS § 46 (1965).

14. *Id.* cmt. d.

15. *Id.*

16. Lin v. Rohm & Haas Co., 293 F. Supp. 2d 505, 522 (E.D. Pa. 2003), *quoting* Hunger v. Grand Cent. Sanitation, 670 A.2d 173, 177 (Pa. Super. Ct. 1996).

17. Showler v. Harper's Magazine Foundation, 222 Fed. Appx. 755 (10th Cir.), *cert. denied,* 552 U.S. 825 (2007).

18. Alvarado v. KOB-TV, L.L.C., 493 F.3d 1210, 1222 (10th Cir. 2007).

19. Hatfill v. New York Times, 532 F.3d 312 (4th Cir.), *cert. denied,* 555 U.S. 1085 (2008).

20. *See* Scott Shane & Eric Lichtblau, *New Details on F.B.I.'s False Start in Anthrax Case,* N.Y. TIMES, Nov. 26, 2008, at A23.

21. Best v. Malec, 2010 U.S. Dist. LEXIS 58996 (N.D. Ill., June 11, 2010).

22. Armstrong v. H & C Communications, 575 So. 2d 280 (Fla. App. 1991).

23. *Id.* at 281.

24. *Id.* at 282.

25. *Id.*

26. KOVR-TV, Inc. v. Superior Court, 37 Cal. Rptr. 2d 431 (Cal. App. 1995).

27. Roach v. Stern, 675 N.Y.S.2d 133 (1998).

28. Estate of Duckett v. Cable News Network, 2008 U.S. Dist. LEXIS 88667 (M.D. Fla., July 31, 2008), *quoting* Williams v. City of Minneola, 575 So. 2d 683, 691 (Fla. Ct. App. 1991).

29. RESTATEMENT (SECOND) OF TORTS § 46(1) (1965).

30. Catsouras v. Department of California Highway Patrol, 181 Cal. App. 4th 856 (Cal. App. Ct. 2010.

31. 376 U.S. 254 (1964).

32. Hustler Magazine, Inc. v. Falwell, 485 U.S. 46 (1988).

33. *See* RODNEY SMOLLA, SMOLLA AND NIMMER ON FREEDOM OF SPEECH § 24.10 (2012). *See also* RODNEY A. SMOLLA, JERRY FALWELL V. LARRY FLYNT: THE FIRST AMENDMENT ON TRIAL (1988).

34. Falwell v. Flynt, 797 F.2d 1270 (4th Cir.), *rehearing en banc denied,* 805 F.2d 484 (4th Cir. 1986).

35. Hustler Magazine, Inc. v. Falwell, 485 U.S. 46 (1988).

36. Snyder v. Phelps, 131 S. Ct. 1207, 1214 (2011).

37. *Id.* at 1217.

38. Snyder v. Phelps, 580 F.3d 206 (4th Cir. Md. 2009).

39. *Snyder,* 131 S. Ct. at 1215.

40. *Id.* at 1211 (*quoting* Connick v. Myers, 461 U.S. 138, 146 (1983)).

41. The Honoring America's Veterans and Caring for Camp Lejeune Families Act, 38 U.S.C. § 101.

42. Timothy L. Allsup, "United States v. Cassidy: *The Federal Interstate Stalking Statute and Freedom of Speech,*" 13 N.C. J.L. & TECH. ON. 227, 227 (2012).

43. 18 U.S.C. § 2261A(1).

44. United States v. Cassidy, 814 F. Supp. 2d 574 (D. Md. 2011).

45. United States v. Sayer, 2012 U.S. Dist. LEXIS 67684, *5 (D. Maine, May 15, 2012).

46. *Id.*

47. *Id.* at *10.

48. *See also* United States v. Petrovic, 701 F.3d 849 (8th Cir. 2012).

49. *See* RonNell Anderson Jones & Lyrissa Barnett Lidslay, *Recent Developments in the Law of Social Media Communications, in* 3 COMM. L. IN THE DIGITAL AGE 2012, at 17, 121–50 (2012).

50. States without a cyberharassment law are Alaska, Indiana, Kansas, Louisiana, Maine, Nebraska and New Mexico. *Id.*

51. *See, e.g.,* Neilson v. Union Bank of Cal., N.A., 290 F. Supp. 2d 1101, 1142 (C.D. Calif. 2003).

52. *See, e.g.,* Dowty v. Riggs, 385 S.W.3d 117 (Ark. 2010).

53. *See, e.g.,* Nelson v. Harrah's Entertainment Inc., 2008 U.S. Dist. LEXIS 46524 (N.D. Ill., June 13, 2008).

54. *See* Camper v. Minor, 915 S.W.2d 437, 440 (Tenn. 1996).

55. *Id.*

56. *See, e.g.,* Boyles v. Kerr, 855 S.W.2d 593 (Tex. 1993).

57. *See, e.g.,* Johnson v. Ruark Obstetrics and Gynecology Associates, 395 S.E.2d 85 (N.C. 1990).

58. RESTATEMENT (SECOND) OF TORTS § 436A (1965).

59. Doe v. American Broadcasting Companies, Inc., 543 N.Y.S.2d 455 (N.Y. App.), *appeal dismissed,* 549 N.E.2d 480 (N.Y. 1989).

60. Sleem v. Yale University, 843 F. Supp. 57 (M.D.N.C. 1993).

61. Hyde v. City of Columbia, 637 S.W.2d 251 (Mo. Ct. App. 1982).

62. Times-Mirror Co. v. Superior Court, 244 Cal. Rptr. 556 (Cal. Ct. App. 1988).

63. *See* Dave Itzkoff, *Scholar Finds Flaws in Work by Archenemy of Comics,* N.Y. TIMES, Feb. 20, 2013, at C1.

64. FED. TRADE COMM'N, VIOLENCE IN MEDIA REPORT i–ii (2000).

65. FED. TRADE COMM'N, MARKETING VIOLENT ENTERTAINMENT TO CHILDREN: A SIXTH FOLLOW-UP REVIEW OF INDUSTRY PRACTICES IN THE MOTION PICTURE, MUSIC RECORDING & ELECTRONIC GAME INDUSTRIES i (Dec. 2009).

66. Am. Acad. of Pediatrics, *Family Life: TV Violence* (2013) *available at* http://www.healthychildren.org/English/family-life/Media/Pages/TV-Violence.aspx.

67. *Sunday Dialogue: Mayhem on Our Screens,* N.Y. TIMES, Jan. 27, 2013, at SR2; Tracy Reilly, *The "Spiritual Temperature" of Contemporary Popular Music: An Alternative to the Legal Regulation of Death-Metal and Gangsta-Rap Lyrics,* 11 VAND. J. ENT. & TECH. L. 335 (2009).

68. *See generally* John Charles Kunich, *Shock Torts Reloaded,* 6 APPALACHIAN J.L. 1 (2006); John Charles Kunich,

Natural Born Copycat Killers and the Law of Shock Torts, 78 WASH. U.L.Q. 1157 (2000).

69. *See, e.g.,* Ty Burr, *An Uncertain Line Between Fantasy's Lure, Nightmare,* BOSTON GLOBE, July 21, 2012, at A1 (James Holmes); Nolan Finley, *Missing the Real Lessons from Arizona,* DETROIT NEWS, Jan. 20, 2011, at B1 (Jared Loughner); Marc Fisher, Robert O'Harrow, Peter Finn, *Lanza's Isolated Life Stymies Investigators,* WASH. POST, Dec. 23, 2012, at A1 (Adam Lanza).

70. Zamora v. Columbia Broadcasting System, 480 F. Supp. 199, 200 (S.D. Fla. 1979).

71. *Id.* at 201, 205.

72. Olivia N. v. National Broadcasting Co., 126 Cal. App. 3d 488 (1981).

73. Sanders v. Acclaim Entertainment, Inc., 188 F. Supp. 2d 1264 (D. Colo. 2002).

74. James v. Meow Media, Inc., 300 F.3d 683 (6th Cir. 2002), *cert. denied,* 537 U.S. 1159 (2003).

75. *Id.* at 693.

76. Eimann v. Soldier of Fortune Magazine, Inc., 880 F.2d 830, 832 (5th Cir. 1989), *cert. denied,* 493 U.S. 1024 (1990).

77. Norwood v. Soldier of Fortune, Inc., 651 F. Supp. 1397 (W.D. Ark. 1987).

78. *Id.* at 1403.

79. Eimann v. Soldier of Fortune Magazine, Inc., 880 F.2d 830, 834 (5th Cir. 1989), *cert. denied,* 493 U.S. 1024 (1990).

80. *Id.* at 834.

81. Braun v. Soldier of Fortune Magazine, Inc., 968 F.2d 1110 (11th Cir. 1992), *cert. denied,* 506 U.S. 1071 (1993).

82. *Id.* at 1115.

83. Winter v. G. P. Putnam's Sons, 938 F.2d 1033 (9th Cir. 1991).

84. McCollum v. CBS, Inc., 249 Cal. Rptr. 187 (Cal. App. 1988).

85. *See* April M. Perry, Comment: *Guilt by Saturation: Media Liability for Third-Party Violence and the Availability Heuristic,* 97 NW. U.L. REV. 1045, 1055–56 (2003).

86. Watters v. TSR, Inc., 904 F.2d 378 (6th Cir. 1990).

87. David A. Anderson, *Incitement and Tort Law,* 37 WAKE FOREST L. REV. 957 (2002).

88. 395 U.S. 444, 447 (1969) (per curiam).

89. 414 U.S. 105 (1973) (per curiam).

90. Anderson, *supra* note 87 at 957, 985.

91. Byers v. Edmundson, 712 So. 2d 681 (La. App. 1998), *cert. denied,* 526 U.S. 1005 (1999).

92. Byers v. Edmundson, 826 So. 2d 551 (La. App. 2002).

93. Herceg v. Hustler Magazine, 814 F.2d 1017 (5th Cir. 1987), *cert. denied,* 485 U.S. 959 (1988).

94. Yakubowicz v. Paramount Pictures Corp., 536 N.E.2d 1067 (Mass. 1989).

95. Rice v. Paladin Enterprises, Inc., 128 F.3d 233 (4th Cir. 1997), *cert. denied,* 523 U.S. 1074 (1998).

96. *Id.* at 244.

97. Martin Garbus, *State of the Union for the Law of the New Millennium, the Internet, and the First Amendment,* 1999 ANN. SURV. AM. L. 169, 173–74.

98. Wilson v. Midway Games, Inc., 198 F. Supp. 2d 167 (D. Conn. 2002).

99. Weirum v. RKO General, Inc., 123 Cal. Rptr. 468 (1975).

100. 47 U.S.C. §§ 230 (c)(1), (e)(3).

101. Doe v. MySpace, Inc., 528 F.3d 413 (5th Cir.), *cert. denied,* 129 S. Ct. 600 (2008).

102. Doe II v. MySpace Inc., 175 Cal. App. 4th 561 (Calif. Ct. App. 2009), *rev. denied,* 2009 Cal. LEXIS 10656 (Calif., Oct. 14, 2009).

103. Doe IX v. MySpace, Inc., 629 F. Supp. 2d 663 (E.D. Tex. 2009).

104. Fair Housing Council of San Fernando Valley v. Roommates.com, LLC, 521 F.3d 1157 (9th Cir. 2008).

105. *See, e.g.,* GW Equity LLC v. Xcentric Ventures LLC, 2009 U.S. Dist. LEXIS 1445 (N.D. Tex., Jan. 9 2009).

106. Gibson v. Craigslist, Inc., 2009 U.S. Dist. LEXIS 53246 (S.D.N.Y., June 15, 2009).

107. Barnes v. Yahoo!, Inc., 570 F.3d 1096 (9th Cir. 2009), *on remand,* 2009 U.S. Dist. LEXIS 116274 (D. Or., Dec. 8, 2009).

108. Wildmon v. Berwick Universal Pictures, 803 F. Supp. 1167 (D. Miss. 1992), *aff'd without opinion,* 979 F.2d 21 (5th Cir. 1992).

109. Savage v. Pacific Gas and Electric Co., 26 Cal. Rptr. 2d 305 (Cal. Ct. App. 1993).

110. Caine v. Duke Communications, International, 24 MEDIA L. REP. 1187 (C.D. Calif. 1995).

111. Nemet Chevrolet Ltd. v. ConsumerAffairs.com Inc., 591 F.3d 250 (4th Cir. 2009).

112. Doe 2 v. Associated Press, 331 F.3d 417 (4th Cir. 2003).

Chapter 8

Newsgathering

1. Branzburg v. Hayes, 408 U.S. 665, 728 (1972).

2. See, e.g., Matthew D. Bunker, Sigman L. Splichal & Sheree Martin, *Triggering the First Amendment: Newsgathering Torts and Press Freedom*, 4 Comm. L. & Pol'y 273 (1999); Erwin Chemerinsky, *Protect the Press: A First Amendment Standard for Safeguarding Aggressive Newsgathering*, 33 U. Rich. L. Rev. 1143 (2000).

3. Branzburg v. Hayes, 408 U.S. 665, 684 (1972).

4. *Id.* at 681.

5. Chemerinsky, *supra* note 2 at 1143, 1145.

6. *Id.* at 1158.

7. Potter Stewart, *Or of the Press*, 26 Hastings L.J. 631, 636 (1975).

8. See, e.g., Cohen v. Cowles Media Co., 501 U.S. 663, 669 (1991) ("generally applicable laws do not offend the First Amendment simply because their enforcement against the press has incidental effects on its ability to gather and report the news").

9. Matthew D. Bunker, Sigman L. Splichal & Sheree Martin, *Triggering the First Amendment: Newsgathering Torts and Press Freedom*, 4 Comm. L. & Pol'y 273, 296–97 (1999).

10. Pell v. Procunier, 417 U.S. 817 (1974) (emphasis added).

11. Huchins v. KQED, 438 U.S. 1 (1978).

12. See Pell v. Procunier, 417 U.S. 817; Saxbe v. Washington Post, 417 U.S. 843 (1974).

13. Channel 10, Inc. v. Gunnarson, 337 F. Supp. 634 (D. Minn. 1972).

14. Glik v. Cunniffe, 655 F.3d 78 (1st Cir. 2011).

15. See Lilly Chapa, *Justice Issues Letter Supporting Photojournalist Arrested for Taking Pictures of Police*, Reporters Comm. for Freedom of the Press News (Mar. 7, 2013), *available at* http://www.rcfp.org/browse-media-law-resources/news/justice-issues-letter-supporting-photojournalist-arrested-taking-pic.

16. American Civil Liberties Union of Illinois v. Alvarez, 679 F.3d 583 (7th Cir.), *cert. denied,* 133 S. Ct. 651 (2012).

17. Beacon Journal Publishing Co., Inc. v. Blackwell, 389 F.3d 683 (6th Cir. 2004).

18. PG Publishing Co. v. Aichele, 705 F.3d 91 (3d Cir.), *cert. denied*, 2013 U.S. LEXIS 4192 (June 3, 2013).

19. Richmond Newspapers, Inc. v. Virginia, 448 U.S. 555 (1980); Globe Newspaper Co. v. Superior Court for Norfolk County, 457 U.S. 596 (1982); Press-Enterprise Co. v. Superior Court of California for Riverside County, 478 U.S. 1 (1986).

20. Leigh v. Salazar, 677 F.3d 892 (9th Cir. 2012).

21. See Reporter's Committee for Freedom of the Press, *Department of Defense Memo: Interaction with the Media* (July 2, 2010), *available at* http://www.rcfp.org/newsitems/docs/20100910_105806_dod_memo_2.pdf.

22. See, e.g., Thom Shanker, *Defense Secretary Tightens Rules for Military's Contact with News Media*, N.Y. Times, July 3, 2010, at A7.

23. Gina Lubrano, *Who Paid for the Media in Iraq?*, San Diego Union-Tribune, June 23, 2003, at B-7. See also Jack Shafer, *Full Metal Junket: The Myth of the Objective War Correspondent*, Slate (Mar. 5, 2003), *available at* http://slate.msn.com/id/2079703.

24. See, e.g., Miller v. NBC, 232 Cal. Rptr. 668, 677 (Cal. Ct. App. 1986): "The essence of the cause of action for trespass is an 'unauthorized entry' onto the land of another."

25. Thomas S. Leatherbury & Travis R. Wimberly, *2012 Update: Developments in the Law of Newsgathering Liability, in* 3 Comm. L. in the Digital Age 2012, at 598–99 (2012).

26. Miller v. NBC, 232 Cal. Rptr. 668, 682 (Cal. Ct. App. 1986).

27. *Id.* at 683.

28. *Id.* at 684 (*quoting* Dietemann v. Time, Inc., 449 F.2d 245, 249 (1971)).

29. *Id.*

30. "At trial, Paul Berger was acquitted of federal charges of violating laws protecting eagles and found guilty of misdemeanor use of a pesticide." Nancy L. Trueblood, Comment: *Curbing the Media: Should Reporters Pay When Police Ride-Alongs Violate Privacy?*, 84 Marq. L. Rev. 541, 560 n.131 (2000).

31. Berger v. Hanlon, 129 F.3d 505 (9th Cir. 1997), *withdrawn,* 188 F.3d 1155 (9th Cir. 1999) (affirming the district court's decision in part, reversing in part, and remanding in part, complying with the Supreme Court's opinion in Hanlon v. Berger, 526 U.S. 808 (1999)). See Trueblood, *supra* note 30 at 541, 560.

32. Hanlon v. Berger, 526 U.S. 808 (1999).

33. 129 F.3d 505, 510 (9th Cir. 1997).

34. *Obituaries*, St. Petersburg (Fla.) Times, Apr. 20, 2003, at 21A.

35. Wilson v. Layne, 526 U.S. 603, 607 (1999).

36. *Id.* at 611 (1999).

37. *Id.*

38. *Id.* at 613.

39. *Id.*

40. *Id.*

41. *Id.* at 614.

42. *See, e.g.,* Shulman v. Group W Productions, Inc., 955 P.2d 469 (Cal. 1998) (ruling that outfitting a nurse with a wireless microphone then videotaping her rescue of two people in an overturned automobile at the bottom of an embankment, then broadcasting the tape, constituted intrusion).

43. Greg Braxton, *Producers Say Ruling Won't Affect Shows; "COPS" and Others Claim Privacy Issues Are Already Addressed*, L.A. Times, May 26, 1999, at F4.

44. Galella v. Onassis, 353 F. Supp. 196 (S.D.N.Y. 1972).

45. Galella v. Onassis, 487 F.2d 986 (2d Cir. 1973).

46. Wolfson v. Lewis, 924 F. Supp. 1413 (E.D. Pa. 1996).

47. Cal Civ. Code § 1708.8.

48. *See* Clay Calvert & Robert D. Richards, *The Irony of News Coverage: How the Media Harm Their Own First Amendment Rights,* 24 Hastings Comm. & Ent. L.J. 215, 218 (2002) (stating that the federal anti-paparazzi legislation was not passed "because no further Diana-like tragedies have occurred, and because it turned out that the initial media-created perception that members of the paparazzi were culpable for Diana's death was simply wrong"). *See also* Andrew D. Morton, *Much Ado About Newsgathering: Personal Privacy, Law Enforcement, and the Law of Unintended Consequences for Anti-Paparazzi Legislation,* 147 U. Pa. L. Rev. 1435 (1999).

49. *See generally* Jane Kirtley, *It's the Process, Stupid: Newsgathering Is the New Target,* Colum. Jour. Rev. (Sept./Oct. 2000). "New and more intrusive methods of newsgathering, often involving electronic equipment such as video cameras and recording devices, became commonplace. Reporters and their editors, eager to feed the appetite of a voyeuristic public, assumed that the First Amendment would allow them to do anything they wished to get a story. They couldn't have been more wrong." *Id.*

50. Food Lion, Inc. v. Capital Cities, Inc./ABC, 964 F. Supp. 956, 959 (M.D. N.C. 1997).

51. *Id.* "The duty of loyalty recognized in this case requires an employee to use her efforts, while working, for the service of her employer. The jury found that each of the producers violated this duty by failing to make a good faith effort toward performing the job requirements of her employer Food Lion as a result of the time and attention she was devoting to her investigation for ABC and by performing specific acts on behalf of ABC which proximately resulted in damage to Food Lion." *Id.*

52. *Id.*

53. *Id.*

54. See, e.g., Russ W. Baker, *Damning Undercover Tactics as "Fraud": Can Reporters Lie About Who They Are? The Food Lion Jury Says No,* Colum. Jour. Rev. 28 (Mar./Apr. 1997); Russ W. Baker, *Truth, Lies, and Videotape: "PrimeTime" Live and the Hidden Camera,* Colum. Jour. Rev. 25 (July/Aug. 1993); Neil Hickey, *Climate of Change: Everybody Is More Careful Than They Used to Be,* Colum. Jour. Rev. 52 (Sept./Oct. 2000); Jane Kirtley, *Don't Pop That Cork: The Food Lion Verdict Was Hardly a Total Victory for the News Media,* Amer. Jour. Rev 84, (Jan./Feb. 2000); Jim Moccou, *Newsgathering Tactics on Trial,* Editor & Publisher, Dec. 18, 1999, at 18.

55. Food Lion, Inc. v. Capital Cities, Inc./ABC, 194 F.3d 505, 526 (4th Cir. 1999) (Niemeyer, J., dissenting).

56. According to one of the attorneys involved, ABC's bill from one of the law firms handling the appeal only was in the "six figures" (personal communication).

57. *Hidden Cameras, Hard Choices,* "Primetime Live" (Feb. 12, 1997). After the trial portion of the case, ABC's "Primetime Live" broadcast interviews with members of the jury. One juror said that on a scale of 1 to 10, with 10 being the worst, ABC's wrongdoing was a 10. "Because the—the girls were telling stories to get into a man's personal business, and they even made up stories to get in." This same juror said she wanted the punitive damages levied against ABC to be $1 billion. *Id.*

58. Special Force Ministries v. WCCO Television, 584 N.W. 2d 789 (Minn. 1998).

59. Veilleux v. NBC, 8 F. Supp. 2d 23, 30 (D. Me. 1998).

60. Veilleux v. NBC, 206 F.3d 92, 105 (1st Cir. 2000).

61. Nancy Garland, *Settlement Reached in "Dateline" Suit,* Bangor Daily News, Sept. 1, 2000.

62. Cohen v. Cowles Media, 501 U.S. 663 (1991).

63. Cohen v. Cowles Media, 479 N.W.2d 387 (Minn. 1992).

64. RonNell Anderson Jones & Lyrissa Barnett Lidsky, *Recent Developments in the Law of Social Media Communications, in* 3 COMM. L. IN THE DIGITAL AGE 2012, at 75, 85 (2012).

65. *See* Reporters Committee for Freedom of the Press, *A Practical Guide to Taping Phone Calls and In-Person Conversations in the 50 States and D.C.* (2012), *available at* http://www.rcfp.org/taping. This section draws from the Reporters Committee's excellent guide to state and federal recording laws.

66. Calif. Penal Code § 632.

67. *Id.* at § 632(a).

68. John Schwartz, *Report Uncovers No Voting Fraud by ACORN,* N.Y. TIMES, Dec. 24, 2009, at A15.

69. Vera v. O'Keefe, 2012 U.S. Dist. LEXIS 112406 (S.D. Cal. Aug. 9, 2012).

70. 18 U.S.C. § 2510(1).

71. *See, e.g.,* Rafe Needleman & Felisa Yang, *Internet Calling: What It Is,* CNET.COM (May 6, 2005), *available at* http://reviews.cnet.com/4520-9140_7-5131539-1.html; *Howstuffworks: How VoIP Works* (n.d.), *available at* http://computer.howstuffworks.com/ip-telephony.htm.

72. 18 U.S.C. § 2510 (2002) (defining the "aural transfer" that occurs in wire communication as "a transfer containing the human voice at any point between and including the point of origin and the point of reception.").

73. 18 U.S.C. §§ 2701–2711 (2000).

74. Eric Koester, *VoIP Goes the Bad Guy: Understanding the Legal Impact of the Use of Voice over IP Communications in Cases of NSA Warrantless Eavesdropping,* 24 J. MARSHALL J. COMPUTER & INFO. L. 227, 234 (2006).

75. See Reporters Committee for Freedom of the Press, *A Practical Guide to Taping Phone Calls and In-Person Conversations in the 50 States and D.C.* (2012), *available at* http://www.rcfp.org/taping.

76. *Id.*

77. *Id.*

78. 18 U.S.C. § 2511(2)(d).

79. *See* Use of Recording Devices in Connection with Telephone Service, 2 F.C.C.R. 502 (1986).

80. See *id.*

81. 47 C.F.R. § 73.1206.

82. Bartnicki v. Vopper, 532 U.S. 514, 518–19 (2001).

83. 18 U.S.C. § 2511(1)(c).

84. *Id.* at 527 (citation omitted).

85. *Id.* at 534, 535.

86 *Id.* at 525.

87. Declan McCullagh, *IRS Claims It Can Read Your E-mail Without a Warrant,* CNET NEWS (Apr. 10, 2013), *available at* http://news.cnet.com/8301–13578_3–57578839–38/irs-claims-it-can-read-your-e-mail-without-a-warrant/.

88. United States v. Warshak, 631 F.3d 266 (6th Cir. 2010).

89. Jessup-Morgan v. America Online, Inc., 20 F. Supp. 2d 1105 (E.D. Mich. 1998).

90. 18 U.S.C. §§ 2510(2), 2511(1)(a), (c), (d).

91. Bowens v. Aftermath Entertainment, 254 F. Supp. 2d 629 (E.D. Mich. 2003), *summary judgment granted,* 364 F. Supp. 2d 641 (E.D. Mich. 2005)().

92. Sigma Delta Chi v. Speaker, Maryland House of Delegates, 310 A.2d 156 (Ct. App. Md. 1973).

93. *Id.* at 8.

94. *See also* RONALD L. GOLDFARB, TV OR NOT TV, TELEVISION JUSTICE, AND THE COURTS 56–95 (1998).

95. City of Oak Creek v. Ah King, 436 N.W.2d 285 (Wis. 1989).

96. 20 U.S.C. § 1232g. (The nickname "Buckley Act" refers to the U.S. senator who introduced the bill, James Buckley of New York.)

97. *See* 34 C.F.R. § 99.3.

98. Red & Black Publishing Co. v. Board of Regents, Univ. of Georgia, 427 S.E.2d 257 (Ga. 1993); John Doe v. Red & Black Publishing Co., 437 S.E.2d 474 (Ga. 1993).

99. Red & Black Publishing Co., 427 S.E.2d 257.

100. United States v. Miami University, 294 F.3d 797 (6th Cir. 2002).

101. 18 U.S.C. §§ 2721–2725.

102. Reno v. Condon, 528 U.S. 141 (2000).

103. 18 U.S.C. § 1801.

104. Letter from James Madison to W. T. Barry (Aug. 4, 1822), in 9 THE WRITINGS OF JAMES MADISON, 1819–1836, at 103 (Galliard Hunt ed. 1910).

105. *See, e.g.,* SHANNON E. MARTIN, FREEDOM OF INFORMATION: THE NEWS THE MEDIA USE (2008).

106. Dep't of the Air Force v. Rose, 425 U.S. 352, 361 (1976).

107. *See e.g.*, Mark Carreau, *Another Shuttle, Another Breach*, Houston Chron., July 9, 2003, at A1; Lee Hockstader, *Release of Challenger Tape Ordered*, Wash. Post, July 30, 1988, at A8; John Schwartz & Matthew L. Wald, *Earlier Shuttle Flight Had Gas Enter Wing on Return*, N.Y. Times, July 9, 2003, at A14; Ralph Vartabedian, *E-Mail to Columbia Discounted Danger*, L. A. Times, July 1, 2003, at A12.

108. 5 U.S.C. § 552(f)(1).

109. *See* Kissinger v. Reporters Comm. for Freedom of the Press, 445 U.S. 136, 156 (1980). *But cf.* United States v. Clarridge, 811 F. Supp. 697 (D.D.C. 1992) (holding that the Tower Commission was an "agency" for purposes of 18 U.S.C. § 1001). Compare Meyer v. Bush, 981 F.2d 1288 (D.C. Cir. 1993) (holding that FOIA does not reach President's Task Force on Regulatory Relief, comprising vice president and certain cabinet members) and National Security Archive v. Archivist of the United States, 909 F.2d 541 (D.C. Cir. 1990) (holding that FOIA does not reach Office of Counsel to President) and Rushforth v. Council of Economic Advisers, 762 F.2d 1038 (D.C. Cir. 1985) (holding that FOIA does not reach CEA) and Pacific Legal Found. v. Council on Envtl. Quality, 636 F.2d 1259 (D.C. Cir. 1980) (holding that FOIA does not reach CEQ) with Energy Research Found. v. Defense Nuclear Facilities Safety Bd., 917 F.2d 581 (D.C. Cir. 1990) (holding that Board is agency for purposes of FOIA and Sunshine Act). The Sunshine Act incorporates the FOIA's definition of "agency."

110. Goland v. CIA, 607 F.2d 339, 345 (D.C. Cir. 1978). In Forsham v. Harris, 445 U.S. 169, 178 (1980), the Supreme Court declared that Congress "did not provide any definition of 'agency records.'"

111. *Forsham*, 445 U.S. at 183.

112. *Id.* at 178.

113. *Id.* at 184.

114. Washington Post v. U.S. Dep't of State, 632 F. Supp. 607 (1986).

115. Note: *A Control Test for Determining "Agency Record" Status Under the Freedom of Information Act*, 85 Colum. L. Rev. 611, 616 (1985).

116. See, e.g., Note: *The Definition of "Agency Records" Under the Freedom of Information Act*, 31 Stan. L. Rev. 1093, 1093 (1979); Note: *What Is a Record? Two Approaches to the Freedom of Information Act's Threshold Requirement*, 1978 B.Y.U. L. Rev. 408, 408; Nichols v. United States, 325 F. Supp. 130, 134 (D. Kan. 1971), *aff'd on other grounds*, 460 F.2d 671 (10th Cir.), *cert. denied*, 409 U.S. 966 (1972).

117. Goland v. CIA, 607 F.2d 339 (D.C. Cir. 1978).

118. *Id.* at 347.

119. Reporters Committee for Freedom of the Press, *How to Use the Federal FOIA Act* (n.d.), *available at* http://www.rcfp.org/foiact/index.html.

120. Reporters Committee for Freedom of the Press, *FOI Letter Generator* (n.d.), *available at* http://www.rcfp.org/foi_letter/generate.php.

121. David Cuillier, Honey v. Vinegar: Testing Compliance-Gaining Theories in the Context of Freedom of Information Laws, 15 Comm. L & Pol'y 203–29 (2010).

122. David Cuillier & Charles N. Davis, The Art of Access: Strategies for Acquiring Public Records (2010). *See also* http://www.theartofaccess.com.

123. Citizens for Responsibility and Ethics in Washington v. Fed. Election Comm'n, 711 F.3d 180 (D.C. Cir. 2013).

124. Reporters Committee for Freedom of the Press, *Citizens Group Wins FOIA Battle with Nuclear Agency* (n.d.), *available at* http://www.rcfp.org/newsitems/index.php?i=4891.

125. ACLU v. Central Intelligence Agency, 2013 U.S. App. LEXIS 5166 (D.C. Cir. Mar. 15, 2013).

126. *See* Memorandum for Heads of All Federal Departments and Agencies (Oct. 12, 2001) from Atty. Gen. John Ashcroft, *available at* http://www.usdoj.gov/foia/011012.htm: "I encourage your agency to carefully consider the protection of all such values and interests when making disclosure determinations under the FOIA. Any discretionary decision by your agency to disclose information protected under the FOIA should be made only after full and deliberate consideration of the institutional, commercial, and personal privacy interests that could be implicated by disclosure of the information. . . . When you carefully consider FOIA requests and decide to withhold records, in whole or in part, you can be assured that the Department of Justice will defend your decisions unless they lack a sound legal basis or present an unwarranted risk of adverse impact on the ability of other agencies to protect other important records."

127. New Attorney General FOIA Memorandum Issued (Oct. 15, 2001), *available at* http://www.fas.org/sgp/foia/ashcroft.html.

128. *See, e.g.*, Mark Fitzgerald, *The War of Fog in D.C.*, Editor & Publisher, Apr. 7, 2003, at 16.

129. *See, e.g.*, Brett Strohs, *Protecting the Homeland by Exemption: Why the Critical Infrastructure Information*

Act of 2002 Will Degrade the Freedom of Information Act, 2002 Duke L. & Tech. Rev. 18 (2002).

130. Memorandum for the Heads of Executive Departments and Agencies, White House news release (Jan. 23, 2009), *available at* http://www.whitehouse.gov/the_press_office/FreedomofInformationAct.

131. See, e.g., David Carr, *Blurred Line Between Espionage and Truth,* N.Y. Times, Feb. 27, 2012, at B1.

132. *US Agencies Are Still Slow to Open Files,* Boston Globe, Mar. 15, 2010, at 2.

133. *See* Exec. Order No. 12958, § 4.2 (b), *available at* http://www.fas.org/sgp/bush/drafteo.html.

134. Cent. Intelligence Agency v. Sims, 471 U.S. 159, 183 (1985).

135. Am. Civil Liberties Union v. U.S. Dep't of Justice, 681 F.3d 61 (2d Cir. 2012).

136. Dep't of the Air Force v. Rose, 425 U.S. 352, 369–70 (1976).

137. Milner v. Dep't of Navy, 131 S. Ct. 1259 (2011).

138. Chrysler v. Brown, 441 U.S. 281, 292 (1979).

139. Russell v. Dep't of the Air Force, 682 F.2d 1045, 1048 (D.C. Cir. 1982).

140. Dep't of the Interior and Bureau of Indian Affairs v. Klamath Water Users Protective Association, 532 U.S. 1, 7 (2001) (*quoting* Dep't of Air Force v. Rose, 425 U.S. 352, 361 (1976)).

141. Cochrane v. United States, 770 F.2d 949, 956 (11th Cir. 1985).

142. *See* U.S. Dep't of Justice v. Reporters Comm. for Freedom of the Press, 489 U.S. 749 (1989).

143. Fed. Communications Comm'n v. AT&T, 131 S. Ct. 1177 (2011).

144. Dep't of Justice v. Reporters Comm. for Freedom of the Press, 489 U.S. 749, 765 (1989).

145. Nat'l Archives and Records Admin. v. Favish, 541 U.S. 157 (2004).

146. *Id.* at 173.

147. Dep't of Justice v. Reporters Comm. for Freedom of the Press, 489 U.S. 749, 773 (1989).

148. Federal Communications Comm'n v. AT&T Inc., 131 S. Ct. 1177 (2011).

149. Electronic Freedom of Information Act Amendments of 1996, Pub. L. No. 104-231, § 1–12, 110 Stat. 3048 (1996).

150. General Accounting Office Briefing to the Senate Committee on Governmental Affairs, Government Paperwork Elimination Act (Aug. 8, 2001), *available at* http://www.gao.gov/new.items/d011100.pdf. *See also* Electronic Government: Selection and Implementation of the Office of Management and Budget's 24 Initiatives, GAO-03–229 (Nov. 22, 2002).

151. TPS, Inc. v. Dep't of Defense, 330 F.3d 1191 (9th Cir. 2003).

152. *See, e.g.,* Arkansas Freedom of Information Act, *available at* http://www.foiarkansas.com/1010/1010foia.html.

153. Electronic Records: Management and Preservation Pose Challenges, GAO-03–936T (July 8, 2003).

154. Some studies indicate that FOIA use is very low among journalists. *See, e.g.,* Heritage Foundation, *Media Center Study Finds Little FOIA Use by Journalists* (Dec. 1, 2001), *available at* http://www.heritage.org/Research/Reports/2001/12/Media-Center-Study-Finds-Little-FOIA-Use-by-Journalists (showing that only 5% of FOIA requests came from journalists).

155. Haw. HB 2002, § 2.

156. Del. Code Ann. tit. 29, § 10001.

157. 5 Ill. Comp. Stat. 140/1–1.

158. T.C.A. § 10–7–301 (6).

159. Shabazz v. Campbell, 63 S.W.3d 776 (Tenn. Ct. App. 2001).

160. Daxton R. "Chip" Stewart, *Let the Sunshine In, or Else: An Examination of the "Teeth" of State and Federal Open Meetings and Open Records Laws,* 15 Comm. L. & Pol'y 265, 307–8 (2010).

161. 5 Ill. Comp. Stat. § 140/1–1.

162. They are Arkansas, Connecticut, Maine, Missouri, North Dakota, South Carolina and Virginia.

163. The Michigan Open Meetings Act and Freedom of Information Act, *available at* http://www.legislature.mi.gov/documents/Publications/OpenMtgsFreedom.pdf.

Chapter 9

Reporter's Privilege

1. Branzburg v. Hayes, 408 U.S. 665, 709–10 (1972).

2. Record at 1279, Cohen v. Cowles Media Co. (No. 90–634) (testimony of Bernard Casserly, characterizing the use of confidential sources as "a way of life in the profession of journalism").

3. *See, e.g.,* Brief of Petitioner, Cohen v. Cowles Media Co., 501 U.S. 663 (1990). One of the best known examples of investigative journalism, The Washington Post's uncovering of the Watergate scandal, was driven by a confidential source the reporters dubbed "Deep Throat." *See* Bob Woodward, The Secret Man: The Story of Watergate's Deep Throat (2005).

4. Record at 694, Cohen v. Cowles Media Co., 501 U.S. 663 (testimony of Arnold Ismach).

5. United States v. Bryan, 339 U.S. 323, 331 (1950).

6. Branzburg v. Hayes, 408 U.S. 665, 710 (1972) (Powell, J., concurring).

7. *See, e.g.,* Nathan Swinton, *Privileging a Privilege: Should the Reporter's Privilege Enjoy the Same Respect as the Attorney-Client Privilege?,* 19 Geo. J. Legal Ethics 979 (2006).

8. *See generally* David Rudenstine, *A Reporter Keeping Confidences: More Important Than Ever,* 29 Cardozo L. Rev. 1431 (2008).

9. 408 U.S. 665, 710 (1972).

10. *Id.* at 674.

11. *Id.* at 709.

12. *Id.* at 710.

13. *Id.* at 725.

14. *Id.*

15. *Id., quoting* Time, Inc. v. Hill, 385 U.S. 374, 389 (1967).

16. *Id.* at 712.

17. *Id.* at 739.

18. *Id.* at 743.

19. *See, e.g.,* United States v. Lloyd, 71 F.3d 1256 (7th Cir. 1995) (finding that a district court did not abuse discretion in quashing subpoena in criminal case); LaRouche v. NBC, 780 F.2d 1134 (4th Cir. 1986) (finding that a lower court correctly applied privilege when it quashed subpoenas for journalists in libel case); United States v. Caporale, 806 F.2d 1487 (11th Cir. 1986) (recognizing qualified privilege in criminal case); Zerilli v. Smith, 656 F.2d 705 (D.C. Cir. 1981) (recognizing existence of federal privilege in a civil case in which journalists were not parties); Miller v. Transamerican Press, Inc., 621 F.2d 721 (5th Cir. 1980) (finding that journalists have a First Amendment privilege, although it is not absolute); United States v. Cuthbertson, 630 F.2d 139 (3d Cir. 1980) (stating that federal privilege exists in both civil and criminal cases); Silkwood v. Kerr-McGee, 563 F.2d 433 (10th Cir. 1977) (recognizing

privilege and finding that documentary filmmaker could assert it); Cervantes v. Time, Inc., 464 F.2d 986 (8th Cir. 1972) (determining that a magazine could assert privilege in a libel case); Bursey v. United States, 466 F.2d 1059 (9th Cir. 1972) (finding that newspaper employees could assert privilege to quash grand jury subpoenas); Baker v. F & F Investment Co., 470 F.2d 778 (2d Cir. 1972) (recognizing privilege in civil case).

20. Grand Jury Proceedings, 810 F.2d 580 (6th Cir. 1987).

21. Peck v. City of Boston (*In re* Slack), 768 F. Supp. 2d 189 (D.D.C. 2011).

22. Keefe v. City of Minneapolis v. Star Tribune Media Co., 2012 U.S. Dist. LEXIS 187017, at *12–*13 (D. Minn. May 25, 2012).

23. United States v. Sterling, 2013 U.S. App. LEXIS 14646 (4th Cir. July 19, 2013); *see also* Charlie Savage, *Court Tells Reporter to Testify in Case of Leaked C.I.A. Data,* N.Y. Times, July 19, 2013, at A1.

24. *See Paying the Price: A Recent Census of Reporters Jailed or Fined for Refusing to Testify* (n.d.), *available at* http://www.rcfp.org/jail.html. *See also* Edmond J. Bartnett, *Columnist Loses in Contempt Case,* N.Y. Times, Oct. 1, 1958, at 30 (explaining the jailing of reporter Marie Torre for refusing to disclose a source of information); Ross E. Milloy, *Writer Who Was Jailed in Notes Dispute Is Freed,* N.Y. Times, Jan. 5, 2002, at A8 (detailing Leggett's incarceration and release).

25. Chevron Corp. v. Berlinger, 629 F.3d 297 (2d Cir. 2011).

26. *In re* McCray, 2013 U.S. Dist. LEXIS 22688 (S.D. N.Y. Feb. 19, 2013).

27. *In re* McCray, 2013 U.S. Dist. LEXIS 31142, at *10 (S.D. N.Y. March 5, 2013).

28. Grand Jury Subpoena (Josh Wolf), 201 Fed. Appx. 430 (9th Cir. 2006).

29. Jesse McKinley, *8-Month Jail Term Ends as Maker of Video Turns Over a Copy,* N.Y. Times, Apr. 4, 2007, at A9.

30. *In re* Grand Jury Subpoenas, No. 01–20745 (5th Cir. Aug. 17, 2001) (unpublished) (per curiam), *cert. denied,* 535 U.S. 1011 (2002).

31. *Id.* at 4.

32. *Id.* at 8–9.

33. Matera v. Superior Court, 825 P.2d 971 (Ariz. Ct. App. 1992).

34. Branzburg v. Hayes, 408 U.S. 665, 706 (1972).

35. *In re* John Doe Grand Jury Investigation, 410 Mass. 596, 598 (1991).

36. Castellani v. Scranton Times, 956 A.2d 937 (Pa. 2008) (emphasis added).

37. Minn. Stat. Ann. § 595.023.

38. Obsidian Financial Group v. Cox, 2011 U.S. Dist. LEXIS 137548 (D. Ore. Nov. 30, 2011).

39. *Id.* at *13.

40. Obsidian Financial Group v. Cox, 2012 U.S. Dist. LEXIS 43125, at *20 (D. Ore. Mar. 27, 2012).

41. Too Much Media v. Hale, 993 A.2d 845 (N.J. App. Div. 2010).

42. Too Much Media v. Hale, 20 A.3d 364, 382 (2011).

43. Lipsky v. Durant, No. 11–0798 (Tex. Dist. Ct. May 15, 2012).

44. Johns-Byrne Co. v. TechnoBuffalo, No. 2011-L-009161 (Ill. Cir. Ct. Jan. 13, 2012); *see* James C. Goodale et al., *Reporter's Privilege—Recent Developments 2011–2012, in* 2 Comm. L. in the Digital Age 2012, at 25–26 (2012).

45. United States v. Nixon, 418 U.S. 683 (1974).

46. 28 C.F.R. § 50.10.

47. United States v. Cotterman, 709 F.3d 952 (9th Cir. 2013).

48. Zurcher v. Stanford Daily, 436 U.S. 547, 563–64 (1978).

49. *Invading the Newsroom,* N.Y. Times, July 29, 1980, at A14.

50. 42 U.S.C. § 2000aa.

51. Charlie Savage, *Holder Tightens Rules on Getting Reporters' Data,* N.Y. Times (July 12, 2013), *available at* http://www.nytimes.com/2013/07/13/us/holder-to-tighten-rules-for-obtaining-reporters-data.html?_r=1&.

52. *Id.*

Chapter 10

The Media and the Courts

1. *See, e.g.,* Dylan Stableford, *CNN Criticized for Steubenville Verdict Coverage,* Yahoo! News (Mar. 18, 2013), *available at* news.yahoo.com.

2. Sheppard v. Maxwell, 384 U.S. 333, 362 (1966).

3. *See, e.g.,* CNN iReport (n.d.), *available at* http://ireport.cnn.com/search/ireports?q=drew+peterson.

4. Jamie Stengle, *Randy Travis DUI: Country Music Star enters Guilty Drunk Driving Plea,* Huffington Post (Jan. 13, 2013), *available at* huffingtonpost.com.

5. *See, e.g.,* Kimberly Gross & Sean Aday, *The Scary World in Your Living Room and Neighborhood: Using Local Broadcast News, Neighborhood Crime Rates, and Personal Experience to Test Agenda Setting and Cultivation,* 53 J. Comm. 411 (2003); Meredith Diane Lett et al., *Examining Effects of Television News Violence on College Students Through Cultivation Theory,* 21 Comm. Res. Rep. 39 (2004); Daniel Romer et al., *Television News and the Cultivation of Fear of Crime,* 53 J. Comm. 88 (2003).

6. Estes v. Texas, 381 U.S. 532 (1965).

7. The Pulitzer Prizes, 1963 Winners, *available at* http://www.pulitzer.org/awards/1963.

8. Patton v. Yount, 467 U.S. 1025 (1984).

9. Sheppard v. Maxwell, 384 U.S. 333 (1966).

10. *Id.* at 340.

11. Interactive Media Lab, *Sheppard v. Maxwell* (1966), College of Journalism and Communications, University of Florida, *available at* http://iml.jou.ufl.edu/projects/Spring01/Woell/Sheppard.html.

12. *News Media Barred from Hearing in Slaying of NFL Player* (Apr. 7, 2011), *available at* http://www.ap.com.

13. Claire S.H. Lim, J.M. Snyder & David Stromberg, *Media Influence on Courts: Evidence from Civil Case Adjudication* (2010), *available at* http://www.economics.cornell.edu/csl228/Media_paper_2010.pdf.

14. Jon Bruschke & William Loges, Free Press vs. Fair Trials: Examining Publicity's Role in Trial Outcomes (2004).

15. Vincent Carroll, *Overreacting to Pretrial Publicity,* Denv. Post (Aug. 19, 2012), *available at* http://www.denverpost.com/ci_21331048/overreacting-pretrial-publicity?IADID=.

16. Mu'Min v. Virginia, 500 U.S. 415 (1991).

17. Batson v. Kentucky, 476 U.S. 79 (1986); J.E.B. v. Alabama, 511 U.S. 127 (1994).

18. *See, e.g.,* Don J. DeBenedictis, *The National Verdict,* A.B.A. J., Oct. 1994, at 52, 54 (citing poll finding 86 percent of those people questioned thought media had some effect on trial fairness); Edith Greene, *Media Effects on Jurors,* 14 Law & Human Behav. 439, 448 (1990).

19. United States v. Koubriti, 305 F. Supp. 2d 723 (E.D. Mich. 2003).

20. *See, e.g.,* United States v. Shryock, 342 F.3d 948 (9th Cir. 2003), *cert. denied,* 541 U.S. 965 (2004).

21. Tex. Crim. Proc. Code Ann. § 35.29 (1994).

22. United States v. Wecht, 537 F.3d 222 (3d Cir. 2008); United States v. Blagojevich, 612 F.3d 558 (7th Cir. 2010).

23. United States v. Blagojevich, 614 F.3d 287 (7th Cir. 2010).

24. Capperton v. Massey, 556 U.S. 868, 870 (2009).

25. *Id.*

26. Sheppard v. Maxwell, 384 U.S. 333, 342 (1966).

27. Republican Party of Minn. v. White, 536 U.S. 765 (2002).

28. *Id.* at 787.

29. Gannett v. DePasquale, 433 U.S. 368 (1979).

30. *Id.* at 378.

31. 433 U.S. 368, 383 (1979).

32. *Id.* at 415, 423.

33. 448 U.S. 555 (1980).

34. *Id.* at 569.

35. *Id.* at 581.

36. *Id.* at 575.

37. Rapid City Journal v. Delaney, 804 N.W.2d 388 (S.D. 2011).

38. Globe Newspaper v. Superior Court, 457 U.S. 596 (1982).

39. *Id.* at 606.

40. Press-Enterprise (I) v. Superior Court, 464 U.S. 501 (1984); Press-Enterprise (II) v. Superior Court, 478 U.S. 1 (1986).

41. Press-Enterprise (II) v. Superior Court, 478 U.S. 1, 9 (1986).

42. N.Y. Civil Liberties Union v. N.Y. City Transit Auth., 684 F.3d 286 (2d Cir. 2012); North Jersey Media Group v. Ashcroft, 308 F.3d 198 (3d Cir. 2003); Detroit Free Press v. Ashcroft, 303 F.3d 681 (6th Cir. 2002); Leigh v Salazar, 677 F.3d 892 (9th Cir. 2012).

43. Presley v. Georgia, 558 U.S. 209 (2010).

44. *Id.* at 214.

45. *Id.* at 215.

46. *Id.*

47. *See, e.g., In re* Globe Newspaper Co., 920 F.2d 88 (1st Cir. 1990).

48. Press-Enterprise (I) v. Superior Court, 464 U.S. 501, 510 (1984).

49. ABC Inc. v. Stewart, 360 F.3d 90 (2d Cir. 2004).

50. Hollingsworth v. Perry, 558 U.S. 183 (2010).

51. Lisa Leff, *Court Won't Order California Officials to Appeal Ruling That Struck Down Gay Marriage Ban,* L.A. Times (Sept. 8, 2010), *available at* http://www.latimes.com/sns-ap-us-gay-marriage-tria1,0,3059623.story.

52. AMD v. INTEL Antitrust Litigation (n.d.), *available at* http://are.berkeley.edu/~sberto/AMDIntel.pdf.

53. *In re* Intel Corp. Microprocessor Antitrust Litigation, Consolidated Action: Motion to Intervene for Purpose of Unsealing Judicial Records and for Partial Reassignment, C.A. No. 05–441-JJF (D. Del. Aug. 21, 2008).

54. AMD v. Intel Corp., 2006 U.S. Dist. LEXIS 72722 (D. Del. Sept. 26, 2006).

55. Intel Corp. v. AMD, 524 U.S. 241 (2004).

56. Greg Sandoval & Declan McCullagh, *Judge Seals Courtroom in MPAA DVD-Copying Case,* CNET News (Apr.24, 2009), *available at* http://news.cnet.com/8301–13578_3–10227195–38.html. *See also* RealNetworks Response to RealDVD Preliminary Injunction Ruling (Aug. 11, 2009), *available at* http://www.realnetworks.com/pressroom/releases/2009/realdvd_initial_ruling.aspx.

57. Bill Rosenblatt, *MPAA Wins Settlement in RealDVD Case* (Mar. 4, 2010), *available at* http://copyrightandtechnology.com/2010/03/04/mpaa-wins-settlement-in-realdvd-case/.

58. Butterworth v. Smith, 494 U.S. 624 (1990).

59. Multimedia Holdings Corp. v. Circuit Court of Fla., 544 U.S. 1301 (2005); *Justice Kennedy Denies Application for Stay in Prior Restraint Case; First Coast News v. Circuit Court of Florida, St. Johns County,* Media Law Prof Blog (Apr. 25, 2005), available at http://lawprofessors.typepad.com/media_law_prof_blog/2005/04/justice_kennedy.html.

60. *Id.*

61. Multimedia Holdings Corp. v. Circuit Court of Fla., 544 U.S. 1301, 1304 (2005).

62. Kent v. United States, 383 U.S. 541, 556 (1966).

63. *In re* Gault, 387 U.S. 1, 33, 36–37 (1967).

64. Smith v. Daily Mail, 443 U.S. 97, 107 (1979).

65. Kristen Rasmussen, *Access to Juvenile Justice,* Reporters Committee for Freedom of the Press (2012), *available at* http://www.rcfp.org/rcfp/orders/docs/SJAJJ.pdf.

66. Kristin N. Henning, *Eroding Confidentiality in Delinquency Proceedings: Should Schools and Public Housing Authorities Be Notified?* 79 N.Y.U. L. Rev. 520 (2004). States that presumptively close juvenile proceedings are Alabama, Alaska, the District of Columbia, Illinois, Kentucky, Massachusetts, Mississippi, New Jersey, New York, Oklahoma, Rhode Island, South

Carolina, Tennessee, Vermont, West Virginia, Wisconsin and Wyoming.

67. W.M. Horne, *The Movement to Open Juvenile Courts: Realizing the Significance of Public Discourse in First Amendment Analysis*, 39 Ind. L. J. 659 (2012); Robert E. Shepherd, *Collateral Consequences of Juvenile Proceedings: Part II, Media Exposure*, 15:3 Crim. J. Mag. (2000), available at http://www.abanet.org/crimjust/juvjus/cjmcollconseq1.html; Barbara White Stack, *The Trend Toward Opening Juvenile Court Is Now Gaining Momentum* (Sept. 23, 2001), *available at* http://old.post-gazette.com.

68. John Diedrich, *Bill Would Open Juvenile Court Records* (Feb. 4, 2012), *available at* www.jsonline.com; *Group Sues over L.A. Judge's Decision to Open Juvenile Courts* (Feb. 7, 2012), *available at* latimesblogs.latimes.com.

69. Kristin N. Henning, *Eroding Confidentiality in Delinquency Proceedings: Should Schools and Public Housing Authorities Be Notified?* 79 N.Y.U. L. Rev. 520 (2004). States with presumptively open proceedings are Arizona, Arkansas, Colorado, Florida, Iowa, Kansas, Maryland, Michigan, Montana, Nevada, New Mexico, North Carolina, Ohio, and Washington. States with open proceedings for children over a certain age or charged with certain offenses are California, Delaware, Georgia, Hawaii, Idaho, Indiana, Louisiana, Maine, Minnesota, Missouri, North Dakota, Pennsylvania, South Dakota, Texas, Utah and Virginia.

70. Juvenile Courts and Juvenile Offenders, Juvenile Justice Act of 1977, Rev. Code Wash. (ARCW) § 13.40.140.

71. New World Communications of Ohio, Inc. v. Geauga County Court of Common Pleas, Juvenile Division, 734 N.E.2d 1214 (Ohio 2000).

72. *Id.*

73. Commonwealth v. Barnes, 963 N.E.2d 1156 (Mass. 2012).

74. Kristen Rasmussen, *Access to Juvenile Justice*, Reporters Committee for Freedom of the Press (2012), *available at* http://www.rcfp.org/rcfp/orders/docs/SJAJJ.pdf; *e.g.,* Howard Snyder & Melissa Sickmund, *Juvenile Offenders and Victims: 2006 National Report*, Nat'l Center for Juv. Just. & U.S. Dept. of Justice, Office of Juv. Just. & Delinquency Prevention (Mar. 2006), *available at* http://www.ojjdp.ncjrs.gov/ojstatbb/nr2006/.

75. For a summary of these statutes, *see* American Prosecutors Research Institute, Rape Shield Laws, *available at* http://www.arte-sana.com/articles/rape_shield_laws_us.pdf.

76. Nat'l Dist. Att'ys Assoc., *Rape Shield Summary Chart* (Jan. 2010), *available at* http://www.ndaa.org/ncpa_state_statutes.html.

77. *See, e.g.,* Colorado Rape Shield Law § 18–3–407 (2)(a).

78. Ariz. Rev. Stat. § 13–1421.

79. Mu'Min v. Virginia, 501 U.S. 1269 (1991).

80. *Id.*

81. Butterworth v. Smith, 494 U.S. 624 (1990).

82. Chuck Murphy, *Good Intentions, Bad Results in Judge's Gag Order*, Denv. Post, Aug. 5, 2012, at 18-A.

83. Jeremy P. Meyer & Kurtis Lee, *Judge Expands Gag Order in Shooting Case to Include University*, July 27, 2012, Denv. Post, at 6-A.

84. Sheppard v. Maxwell, 384 U.S. 333, 350, 362 (1966).

85. 427 U.S. 539 (1976).

86. United States v. Noriega, 917 F.2d 1543 (11th Cir. 1990).

87. United States v. CNN, 865 F. Supp. 1459 (S.D. Fla. 1994).

88. United States v. Noriega, 752 F. Supp. 1032 (S.D. Fla. 1990).

89. Phil Kloer, *On Television, CNN Retreats, Airs Admission of Guilt*, Atl. J.-Const., Dec. 20, 1994, at D8.

90. Seattle Times v. Rhinehart, 467 U.S. 20 (1984).

91. Chandler v. Florida, 449 U.S. 560 (1981).

92. C. Danielle Vinson & John S. Ertter, *Entertainment or Education: How Do Media Cover the Courts?* 7 Harv. Int'l J. Press/Politics 80 (2002).

93. The participating courts are Middle District of Alabama, Northern District of California, Southern District of Florida, District of Guam, Northern District of Illinois, Southern District of Iowa, District of Kansas, District of Massachusetts, Eastern District of Missouri, District of Nebraska, Northern District of Ohio, Southern District of Ohio, Western District of Tennessee, Western District of Washington.

94. *See, e.g.,* Perry v. Brown, 667 F.3d 1078 (9th Cir. 2012).

95. *Id.*

96. *See* Electronic Access to the Courts, Sup. Ct. R. 1:19 (Mass. 2012), *available at* http://www.mass.gov/courts/sjc/docs/final-sjc-rule-119.pdf.

97. Sup. Ct. R. 10–8 & 10–9 (S.D. 2011).

98. Ill. Code of Judicial Conduct, Rule 63 (A) (7).

99. 735 Ill. Code Civil Procedure 5/Art. VII, Part 7, § 8–701, Broadcast or Televised Testimony.

100. *See* Rule 2.450, Rules of Judicial Administration, Florida Rules of Court (2008); Florida v. Palm Beach Newspapers, 395 So. 2d 544 (1981).

101. Re: *WLBT-TV*, 905 So. 2d 1196, 1199 (Miss. 2005).

102. Nathan Braverman et al., *Report of the Committee to Study Extended Media Coverage of Criminal Trial Proceedings in Maryland,* Feb. 1, 2008.

103. James Podgers, *Social Media Is New Norm, But Courts Still Grappling with Whether to Let Cameras In,* ABA J. (Aug. 8, 2010), *available at* http://www.abajournal.com/news/article/social_media_is_norm_but_courts_still_grappling_with_whether_to_let_cameras/.

104.

	Video	Audio or Webcast
Alabama	Some	No
Alaska	Yes	No
Arizona	Yes	Yes
Arkansas	Some	Yes
California	Yes	Yes
Colorado	Yes	Yes
Connecticut	Yes	No
Delaware	No	Yes
D.C.	No	Yes
Florida	Yes	Yes
Georgia	Yes	No
Hawaii	Yes	Yes
Idaho	Yes	No
Illinois	No	Yes
Indiana	No	Yes
Iowa	Yes	Yes
Kansas	Yes	Yes
Kentucky	Yes	Yes
Louisiana	No	Yes
Maine	Yes	Yes
Maryland	No	Yes
Massachusetts	Yes	Yes
Michigan	Yes	Yes
Minnesota	Some	Yes
Mississippi	Yes	Yes
Missouri	Yes	Yes
Montana	Yes	No
Nebraska	Yes	No
Nevada	Yes	Yes
New Hampshire	Yes	Yes
New Jersey	Yes	Yes
New Mexico	Yes	No
New York	Some	Yes
North Carolina	Yes	No
North Dakota	Yes	Yes
Ohio	Yes	Yes
Oklahoma	No rules	No
Oregon	Yes	Yes
Pennsylvania	Some	No
Rhode Island	Some	No
South Carolina	Yes	No
South Dakota	Some	Yes
Tennessee	Yes	No
Texas	Some	Yes
Utah	Some	Yes
Vermont	Yes	Yes
Virginia	Yes	Yes
Washington	Yes	No
West Virginia	Yes	Yes
Wisconsin	Yes	Yes
Wyoming	Yes	No

105. *See, e.g.,* Associated Press, *Kan. Reporter Gets OK to Use Twitter to Cover Federal Gang Trial* (Mar. 6, 2009), *available at* http://www.firstamendmentcenter.org/news.aspxid=21329&SearchString=media.

106. Dana Liebelson, *Judge Approves Web Coverage of Hearing,* Reporters Comm. for Freedom of the Press News (Jan. 16, 2009), *available at* http://www.rcfp.org/newsitems/index.php?i=9903.

107. Associated Press, *1st Circuit Won't Allow Song-Swapping Hearing to Be Webcast* (Apr. 17, 2009), *available at* http://www.firstamendmentcenter.org/news.aspxid=21491&SearchString=media; RIAA v. Tenenbaum Verdict, Law & Fin. Mgmt. Channel (Aug. 10, 2009), *available at* http://lawfinancechannel.squarespace.com/law-finance-channel/2009/8/10/riaa-v-tenenbaum-verdict.html.

108. Greg Sandoval, *RIAA Suffers Big Setback in Tenenbaum Case*, CNET NEWS (July 9, 2010), *available at* http://news.cnet.com/8301–31001_3–20010164–261.html.

109. Am. Assoc. for Justice, *Texts and "Tweets" by Jurors, Lawyers Pose Courtroom Conundrums*, 45:8 TRIAL NEWS & TRENDS (Aug. 2009), *available at* http://www.justice.org/cps/rde/xchg/justice/hs.xsl/10049.htm.

110. Laurie Sullivan, *Courtroom Bans on Social Media Spreading Across United States*, ONLINE MEDIA DAILY (Mar. 10, 2010), *available at* http://www.firstamendmentcoalition.org/2010/03/courtroom-bans-on-social-media-spreading-across-united-states/.

111. Federated Pub., Inc. v. Kurtz, 615 P.2d 440 (Wash. 1980).

112. Federated Pub., Inc. v. Swedberg, 633 P.2d 74 (Wash. 1981), *cert. denied*, 456 U.S. 984 (1982).

113. 435 U.S. 589 (1978).

114. *Id.* at 608–11.

115. United States v. Dimora, 862 F. Supp. 2d 697 (N.D. Ohio 2012).

116. President Barack Obama, Exec. Order: Review and Disposition of Individuals Detained at the Guantanamo Bay Naval Base and Closure of Detention Facilities (Jan. 22, 2009), *available at* http://www.whitehouse.gov/the_press_office/ClosureOfGuantanamoDetentionFacilities.

117. Ginnie Graham, *Courts Keeping Cases Secret*, TULSA WORLD (Aug. 10, 2008), *available at* http://www.tulsaworld.com/news/article.aspx?articleID–20080810_11_A1_hDistr562350.

118. Doe v. C.A.R.S. Protection Plus Inc., 543 F.3d 178 (3d Cir.), *cert. denied*, 555 U.S. 1013 (2008).

119. Kathleen Cullinan, *Newspaper Asks Supreme Court to Review Secret Docket*, REPORTERS COMMITTEE FOR FREEDOM OF THE PRESS NEWS (Oct. 14, 2008), *available at* http://www.rcfp.org.

120. Doe, 543 F.3d at 179.

121. Robert Timothy Reagan et al., Sealed Settlement Agreements in Federal District Court (Federal Judicial Center) (2009).

122. United States v. Reynolds, 345 U.S. 1 (1953).

123. Josh Gerstein, *State Secrets Showdown Looms* (Apr. 21, 2013), *available at* http://www.politico.com/blogs/under-the-radar/2013/04/state-secrets-showdown-looms-162193.html.

124. *The State Secrets Privilege*, ELECTRONIC FRONTIER FOUND. (Dec. 4, 2012), *available at* https://www.eff.org/nsa-spying/state-secrets-privilege.

125. Open the Government, *2008 Secrecy Report Card* (n.d.), *available at* http://www.openthegovernment.org/otg/SecrecyReportCard08.pdf.

126. Gerstein, *supra* note 122.

127. Glenn Greenwald, *Obama Wins the Right to Invoke 'State Secrets' to Protect Bush Crimes*, SALON (Sept. 8, 2010), *available at* http://www.salon.com/news/opinion/glenn_greenwald/2010/09/08/obama.

128. Charlie Savage, *Court Dismisses a Case Asserting Torture by CIA*, N.Y. TIMES (Sept. 8, 2010), *available at* http://www.nytimes.com/2010/09/09/us/09secrets.html?_r=1&hp.

129. *In re* Sealed Case, 494 F.3d 139 (App. D.C. 2007).

130. Florida Star v. B.J.F., 491 U.S. 524 (1989).

131. *Id.*

132. IND. CODE § 5–15–3–3, § 5–14–3–4.

133. KAN. STAT. ANN. § 45–217(e)(2)(A).

134. *See* Nast v. Michels, 730 P.2d 54 (Wash. 1986).

135. State ex rel. Cincinnati Enquirer v. Winkler, 805 N.E.2d 1094 (Ohio 2004).

136. Copeland v. Copeland, 966 So. 2d 1040 (La. 2007).

137. Alan Carlson & Martha Wade Steketee, *Public Access to Court Records: Implementing the* CCJ/COSCA Guidelines *Final Project Report* (2005), *available at* http://www.ncsconline.org/WC/Publications/Res_PriPub_PubAccCrtRcrds_FinalRpt.pdf; Martha Wade Steketee & Alan Carlson, *Developing CCJ/COSCA Guidelines for Public Access to Court Records: A National Project to Assist State Courts*, at vi (State Justice Institute) (Oct. 18, 2002), *available at* http://www.courtaccess.org/modelpolicy/18Oct2002FinalReport.pdf.

138. U.S. Courts, Judicial Privacy Policy Page: Privacy Policy (n.d.), *available at* http://www.privacy.uscourts.gov/b4amend.htm.

139. *A Quiet Revolution in the Courts: Electronic Access to State Court Records* (Aug. 2002), *available at* https://www.cdt.org/publications/020821courtrecords.shtml.

140. Privacy/Public Access to Court Records, State Links, *available at* http://www.ncsc.org/topics/access-and-fairness/privacy-public-access-to-court-records/state-links.aspx.

141. C. Danielle Vinson & John S. Ertter, *Entertainment or Education: How Do Media Cover the Courts?* 7 HARV. INT'L J. PRESS/POLITICS 80 (2002).

142. Beth Givens, *Public Records on the Internet: The Privacy Dilemma*, PRIVACY RIGHTS CLEARINGHOUSE (Apr. 19, 2002), *available at* http://www.privacyrights.org/ar/onlinepubrecs.htm.

143. Samuel Warren & Louis D. Brandeis, *The Right to Privacy*, 4 HARV. L. REV. 193 (1890).

144. Final Report Minn. Sup. Ct Advisory Committee and Order on Rules of Public Access to Records of the Judicial Branch. Minn Court Rules: Record Access Rules Order No. C4–85–1848, Minn. Statutes.

145. Developing CCJ/COSCA Guidelines for Public Access to Court Records: A National Project to Assist State Courts, State Justice Institute (Oct. 18, 2002), available at http://www.courtaccess.org/modelpolicy/18Oct2002FinalRepo rt.pdf.

146. Department of Justice v. Reporters Committee, 489 U.S. 749 (1989).

147. General Rule 31, adopted Oct. 7, 2004, by the Washington Supreme Court. *See* http://www.courts.wa.gov/newsinfo/?fa=newsinfo.pressdetail&newsid=484.

Chapter 11

Electronic Media Regulation

1. Julius Genachowski, *Prepared Remarks of FCC Chairman Julius Genachowski, Technology Transitions Policy Task Force Workshop*, FEDERAL COMMUNICATIONS COMMISSION, Mar. 18, 2013, *available at*: http://www.fcc.gov/document/genachowski-remarks-technology-transitions-policy-task-force.

2. Pub. L. 262, 36 Stat. 629.

3. *See* THOMAS G. KRATTENMAKER, TELECOMMUNICATIONS LAW AND POLICY 3–4 (1994).

4. Pub. L. 264, 27 Stat. 302.

5. United States v. Zenith Radio Corp., 12 F.2d 614 (N.D. Ill. 1926).

6. *Id.*

7. Pub. L. 69–632, ch. 169, 44 Stat. 1162.

8. Fed. Radio Comm'n v. Nelson Bros., 289 U.S. 266 (1933).

9. Ch. 652, 48 Stat. 1064.

10. Pub. L. No. 98–549, 98 Stat. 2779.

11. 47 U.S.C. §§ 151, 303(g); *see* Nat'l Ass'n of Broadcasters v. FCC, 740 F.2d 1190 (D.C. Cir. 1984).

12. Mike M. Ahlers, *RIP Excessively Loud TV Commercials*, CNN.COM, Dec. 13, 2012, *available at:* http://www.cnn.com/2012/12/13/showbiz/tv-ad-volume

13. 47 U.S.C. § 153(6).

14. 47 U.S.C. § 605.

15. Joseph Burstyn, Inc. v. Wilson, 343 U.S. 495, 503 (1952).

16. National Broadcasting Co. v. FCC, 319 U.S. 190 (1943).

17. 395 U.S. 367 (1969).

18. Miami Herald Publ'g Co. v. Tornillo, 418 U.S. 241 (1974).

19. 319 U.S. 190 (1943).

20. FCC v. League of Women Voters, 468 U.S. 364, 376 n.11 (1984).

21. Amrita Khalid, *Google CEO: Internet Hampered by 'Outdated' Laws*, THE HILL.COM, May 15, 2013, *available at:* http://thehill.com/blogs/hillicon-valley/technology/300033-google-ceo-internet-hampered-by-outdated-laws.

22. FCC v. Pacifica Found., 438 U.S. 726 (1978).

23. *See* Robinson v. American Broadcasting Co., 441 F.2d 1396, 1399 (6th Cir. 1971).

24. *See, e.g.,* 47 U.S.C. §§ 302(a), 307(d), 309(a) and 316(a).

25. 47 U.S.C. § 326.

26. 47 U.S.C. § 315.

27. *See, e.g.,* 47 C.F.R. 73.1940.

28. Paramount Pictures Corp., 3 F.C.C.R. 245, 246 (Mass Media Bureau 1988).

29. *Id.*

30. Time-Telepictures Television, 17 F.C.C.R. 16273 (2002).

31. Multimedia Entm't Inc., 9 F.C.C.R. 2811 (Political Programming Branch 1994).

32. Infinity Broadcasting, 18 F.C.C.R. 18603 (Media Bureau 2003).

33. Arkansas Educational Television Comm'n v. Forbes, 523 U.S. 666 (1998).

34. 47 U.S.C. § 315(b).

35. 47 U.S.C. §§ 317, 507.

36. Becker v. FCC, 95 F.3d 75 (D.C. Cir. 1996).

37. Farmers Educ. and Cooperative Union v. WDAY, Inc., 360 U.S. 525 (1959).

38. 47 U.S.C. § 312(a)(7).

39. CBS v. FCC, 453 U.S. 367 (1981).

40. *Id.* at 387–88.

41. Radio-Television News Dir. Ass'n v. FCC, 229 F.3d 269 (D.C. Cir. 2000).

42. 47 U.S.C. § 399.

43. Federal Communications Commission v. League of Women Voters, 468 U.S. 364 (1984).

44. 47 U.S.C. § 315(3e)(1).

45. McConnell v. Federal Election Comm'n, 540 U.S. 93 (2003) (ruling on challenges to Pub. L. No. 107–155, 116 Stat. 81).

46. 26 U.S.C. § 527.

47. *Top Individual Contributors to Federally Focused 527 Organizations, 2012 Election Cycle,* OpenSecrets.org, *available at* http://www.opensecrets.org/527s/527indivs.php

48. Kate Phillips, *Settlements Including Fines Are Reached in Election Finance Cases of Three Groups,* N.Y. Times, Dec. 14, 2006, at A38.

49. Children's Television Act, Pub. L. 101–437, 104 Stat. 996.

50. 47 C.F.R. § 73.520, 73.671.

51. Children's Television Programming, 6 F.C.C.R. 7199 (1990).

52. Children's Television Programming, 6 F.C.C.R. 2111 (1991); Children's Television Programming, 6 F.C.C.R. 5093 (1991).

53. Children's Television Programming; Revision of Programming Policies for Television Broadcast Stations, 11 F.C.C.R. 10660 (1996).

54. 47 C.F.R. § 73.671(c)(5).

55. 21 F.C.C.R. 1106519 (2006); F.C.C.R. 22943 (2004).

56. Children's Television Report and Policy Statement, 50 FCC 2d 1, 13–14 (1974).

57. Children's Television Programming; Revision of Programming Policies for Television Broadcast Stations, 11 F.C.C.R. 10660, 10730 (1996).

58. 47 C.F.R. § 73.1217.

59. Ch. 287, 37 Stat. 302, 308.

60. Ch. 169, 44 Stat. 1162, 1172.

61. 47 U.S.C. § 325(a).

62. *See* Justin Levine, *A History and Analysis of the Federal Communications Commission's Response to Radio Broadcast Hoaxes,* 52 Fed. Comm. L.J. 273, 277–79 (2000); Hadley Cantril, The Invasion from Mars (1940).

63. *See, e.g.,* Tim Crook, *The Psychological Power of Radio* (n.d.), *available at* http://www.irdp.co.uk/hoax.htm.

64. *See* Justin Levine, *A History and Analysis of the Federal Communications Commission's Response to Radio Broadcast Hoaxes,* 52 Fed. Comm. L.J. 273, 280–87 (2000).

65. 47 C.F.R. § 73.1217.

66. *See* Levine, *supra* note 64, at 313.

67. Great Lakes Broadcasting, 3 F.R.C. Ann. Rep. 34 (1929).

68. Editorializing by Broadcast Licensees, 13 F.C.C. 1246 (1949).

69. *Id.* at 1257–58.

70. Red Lion Broadcasting Co. v. FCC, 395 U.S. 367, 391 (1969).

71. Miami Herald Pub. Co. v. Tornillo, 418 U.S. 241 (1974).

72. Syracuse Peace Council, 2 F.C.C.R. 5043 (1987).

73. Syracuse Peace Council v. FCC, 867 F.2d 654 (D.C. Cir.1989), *cert. denied,* 493 U.S. 1019 (1990).

74. Radio-Television News Directors Ass'n v. FCC, 229 F.3d 269 (D.C. Cir. 2000).

75. 47 U.S.C. § 399; FCC v. League of Women Voters, 468 U.S. 364 (1984).

76. 47 U.S.C. § 317.

77. 47 U.S.C. § 508.

78. 47 C.F.R. § 73.1212.

79. *See* Devin Kosar, Note: *Payola: Can Pay-for-Play Be Practically Enforced?,* 23 St. John's J.L. Comm. 211, 220–22 (2008).

80. *See* Chuck Philips, *Clear Channel Fined Just $8,000 by FCC for Payola Violation,* L.A. Times, Oct. 20, 2000, at C1.

81. *See* Jeff Leeds & Louise Story, *Radio Payoffs Are Described as Sony Settles,* N.Y. Times, July 26, 2005, at A1.

82. *See, e.g.,* Citadel Broadcasting Corp., 22 F.C.C.R 7856 (2007).

83. Univision Radio, Inc., 2010 FCC LEXIS 4600 (July 26, 2010).

84. *See* Clay Calvert, *What Is News? The FCC and the New Battle over the Regulation of Video News Releases,* 16 CommLaw Conspectus 361, 370 (2008).

85. Sonshine Family Television, Inc., 22 F.C.C.R. 18686 (2007).

86. Comcast Corp., 22 F.C.C.R. 17474 (2007); 22 F.C.C.R. 17030 (2007).

87. Use of Video News Releases by Broadcast Licensees and Cable Operators, 20 F.C.C.R. 8593 (2005).

88. Sponsorship Identification Rules and Embedded Advertising, Notice of Inquiry and Notice of Proposed Rule Making, 23 F.C.C.R. 10682 (2008).

89. 47 U.S.C. § 301.

90. 47 U.S.C. § 309(j); 47 C.F.R. §§ 73.5000–73.5009; Competitive Bidding Order, 13 F.C.C.R. 15920 (1998).

91. 47 U.S.C. §§ 308(b), 319(a).

92. 47 U.S.C. § 310(b).

93. 47 U.S.C. § 308(b).

94. *See* Character Qualifications in Broadcast Licensing, 5 F.C.C.R. 3252 (1990); Character Qualifications in Broadcast Licensing, 102 F.C.C.2d 1179 (1986).

95. 47 U.S.C. § 308(b).

96. 47 C.F.R. § 73.3555(a).

97. 47 C.F.R. § 73.3555(e); Consolidated Appropriations Act of 2004, Pub. L. No. 108–199, § 629, 118 Stat. 3, 99.

98. 47 C.F.R. § 73.3555(b); Review of the Commission's Regulations Governing Television Broadcasting, 14 F.C.C.R. 12903, 12907–8 (1999).

99. 47 C.F.R. § 73.3555(c).

100. Consolidated Appropriations Act of 2004, Pub. L. 108–199, § 629, 118 Stat. 3, 86ff.

101. 2006 Quadrennial Review, 23 F.C.C.R. 2010 (2008).

102. Katy Bachman, *Another Delay in FCC Media Ownership Rules Proceeding: Regs on Hold Pending Impact Study on Minority Ownership,* Adweek, Feb. 26, 2013, *available at:* http://www.adweek.com/news/television/another-delay-fcc-media-ownership-rules-proceeding-147571

103. *See, e.g.,* Metro Broadcasting, Inc. v. FCC, 497 U.S. 547 (1990).

104. *See, e.g.,* Adarand Constructors, Inc. v. Pena, 515 U.S. 20 (1995); Lamprecht v. Federal Communications Commission, 958 F.2d 382 (D.C. Cir. 1992).

105. Promoting Diversification of Ownership in the Broadcasting Services, 23 F.C.C.R. 5922 (2007).

106. 2002 Biennial Regulatory Review, 18 F.C.C.R. 13620, 13627 (2003), *aff'd in part and remanded in part,* Prometheus Radio Project. v. Federal Communications Commission, 373 F.3d 372 (2004), *cert. denied,* 545 U.S. 1123 (2005).

107. *See, e.g.,* Fox Television Stations, Inc., FCC 08–277 (Dec. 22, 2008).

108. 2010 Quadrennial Regulatory Review, FCC 12–1667 (Nov. 14, 2012).

109. 47 U.S.C. § 399B.

110. 47 U.S.C. § 399b(a).

111. Commission Policy Concerning the Noncommercial Nature of Educational Broadcasting Stations, 7 F.C.C.R. 827 (1992).

112. *See* Minority Television Project, Inc., 19 F.C.C.R. 25116 (2004).

113. 47 U.S.C. § 396(g)(1)(A).

114. Accuracy in Media, Inc. v. FCC, 521 F.2d 288 (D.C. Cir. 1975), *cert. denied,* 425 U.S. 934 (1976).

115. FCC v. League of Women Voters of California, 468 U.S. 364 (1984).

116. *Id.* at 402.

117. National Farmworkers Service Center, Inc., 25 F.C.C.R. 7486, 7488 (2010).

118. Reexamination of the Comparative Standards for Noncommercial Educational Applicants, 16 F.C.C.R. 5074 (2001), *aff'd,* American Family Ass'n v. FCC, 365 F.3d 1156 (D.C. Cir. 2004); 47 C.F.R. § 73.7003.

119. *See* James C. Goodale, All About Cable § 1.02 (2011).

120. Frontier Broadcasting Co., 24 F.C.C. 251 (1959).

121. Carter Mountain Transmission Corp., 32 F.C.C. 459 (1962), *aff'd,* 321 F.2d 359 (D.C. Cir. 1963), *cert. denied,* 375 U.S. 951 (1963).

122. United States v. Southwestern Cable Co., 392 U.S. 157 (1968).

123. 47 U.S.C. § 224.

124. Am. Elec. Power Serv. Corp. v. FCC, 708 F.3d 183 (D.C. Cir. 2103).

125. Pub. L. No. 98–549, 98 Stat. 2779.

126. Pub. L. No. 102–385, 106 Stat. 1460.

127. Pub. L. No. 104–104, 110 Stat. 56.

128. Turner Broadcasting System v. FCC, 512 U.S. 622 (1994).

129. Denver Area Educational Telecommunications Consortium, Inc. v. FCC, 518 U.S. 727 (1996) (plurality opinion).

130. *See* United States v. Playboy Entertainment Group, Inc., 529 U.S. 803 (2000).

131. 512 U.S. 622 (1994).

132. Turner Broadcasting System v. FCC, 520 U.S. 180 (1997).

133. 518 U.S. 727 (1996) (plurality opinion).

134. *Id.* at 743.

135. 529 U.S. 803 (2000).

136. 47 U.S.C. § 561.

137. 47 U.S.C. § 542.

138. 47 U.S.C. § 544.

139. 47 U.S.C. § 546.

140. 47 U.S.C. § 537(e).

141. Alliance for Community Media v. FCC, 529 F.3d 763 (6th Cir. 2008), *cert. denied,* 557 U.S. 904 (2009).

142. Nat'l Cable & Telecommunications Ass'n v. FCC, 567 F.3d 659 (D.C. Cir. 2009).

143. Implementation of Section 621(a)(1), 22 F.C.C.R. 5101 (2007).

144. Comcast Corp. v. FCC, 579 F.3d 1 (D.C.Cir. 2009); 240 F.3d 1126 (D.C. Cir. 2001).

145. 47 U.S.C. § 533(a).

146. 47 U.S.C. §§ 571, 573.

147. Implementation of the Child Safe Viewing Act; Examination of Parental Control Technologies for Video or Audio Programming, 24 F.C.C.R. 11413, 11438 (2009).

148. 47 U.S.C. §§ 534 (commercial stations), 535 (noncommercial stations).

149. 520 U.S. 180 (1997).

150. 391 U.S. 367 (1968).

151. Cablevision Sys. Corp. v. FCC, 570 F.3d 83 (2d Cir. 2009), *cert. denied,* 130 S. Ct. 3275 (2010).

152. 47 U.S.C. § 531.

153. *See, e.g.,* Denver Area Educational Telecommunications Consortium, Inc. v. FCC, 518 U.S. 727, 761–62 (1996).

154. Time Warner Entertainment Co. v. FCC, 93 F.3d 957 (D.C. Cir. 1996).

155. 47 U.S.C. § 532.

156. 47 U.S.C. §§ 531(e) (public access), 532(c)(2) (leased access).

157. 47 C.F.R. §§ 76.92, 76.94.

158. 47 C.F.R. § 76.5(j).

159. 47 C.F.R. § 76.101.

160. 47 C.F.R. § 76.111.

161. 47 U.S.C. § 548(b).

162. 47 C.F.R. § 76.1001.

163. Development of Competition and Diversity in Video Programming Distribution and Carriage, 8 F.C.C.R. 3359 (1993).

164. Cablevision Sys. Corp. v. FCC, 597 F.3d 1306 (D.C. Cir. 2010).

165. 47 U.S.C. § 533(f)(1)(B).

166. 47 C.F.R. § 76.504.

167. 47 U.S.C. § 551.

168. Annual Assessment of the Status of Competition in the Market for the Delivery of Video Programming, 26 F.C.C.R. 14091 (2012).

169. National Association of Broadcasters v. FCC, 740 F.2d 1190 (D.C. Cir. 1984).

170. Pub. L. No. 102–385, § 25, 106 Stat. 1460.

171. Daniels Cablevision, Inc. v. United States, 835 F. Supp. 1 (D.D.C. 1993).

172. Application of Network Non-Duplication, Syndicated Exclusivity, and Sports Blackout Rules to Satellite Retransmissions of Broadcast Signals, 15 F.C.C.R. 21688 (2000), modified by 17 F.C.C.R. 20693 (2002).

173. Direct Broadcast Satellite Public Interest Obligations, 13 F.C.C.R. 23254 (1998); 47 C.F.R. § 100.5.

174. Direct Broadcast Satellite Public Interest Obligations, 19 F.C.C.R. 5647 (2004).

175. Satellite Home Viewer Improvement Act, Pub. L. No. 106–113, § 1001–1012, 113 Stat. 1501. The act was upheld in Satellite Broadcasting and Communications Association v. FCC, 275 F.3d 337 (4th Cir. 2001), *cert. denied,* 536 U.S. 922 (2002).

176. Satellite Television Extension & Localism Act of 2010 (STELA), Pub. L. 111–175, 124 Stat. 1218.

177. Carriage of Digital Television Broadcast Signals, 23 F.C.C.R. 5352 (2008).

178. *See* Broadcast Signal Carriage Issues, 16 F.C.C.R. 16544 (2001); Good Faith Negotiation and Exclusivity, 16 F.C.C.R. 15599 (2001); Broadcast Signal Carriage Issues, Retransmission Consent Issues, 16 F.C.C.R. 1918 (2000).

179. *See* Katie Hafner & Matthew Lyon, Where Wizards Stay Up Late: The Origins of the Internet 103–36 (1996).

180. *See Internet Corporation for Assigned Names and Numbers,* n.d., *available at* http://icann.org/; ICANN Watch, *ICANN for Beginners,* n.d., *available at* http://www.icannwatch.org/icann4beginners.shtml.

181. Appropriate Framework for Broadband Access to the Internet over Wireline Facilities, 20 F.C.C.R. 148653 (2005).

182. 47 U.S.C. § 154(i).

183. United States v. Southwestern Cable Co., 392 U.S. 157 (1969); United States v. Midwest Video Corp., 406 U.S. 649 (1972) (*Midwest I*); United States v. Midwest Video Corp., 440 U.S. 689 (1979) (*Midwest II*).

184. National Cable & Telecommunications Assoc. v. Brand X Internet Services, 545 U.S. 967 (2005).

185. 47 U.S.C. §§ 201–209, 251(a)(1).

186. High-Speed Access to the Internet over Cable and Other Facilities, 17 F.C.C.R. 4798 (2002).

187. Broadband Industry Practices, 223 F.C.C.R. 13028 (2008).

188. Comcast Corp. v. FCC, 600 F.3d 642, 644 (D.C. Cir. 2010).

189. In the Matter of Preserving the Open Internet, 25 F.C.C.R 17905 (2010).

190. Edward Wyatt, *A Ruling Could Support F.C.C.'s Net Neutrality Defense,* N.Y. Times, May 20, 2013, *available at:* http://bits.blogs.nytimes.com/2013/05/20/aid-for-f-c-c-in-defending-its-net-neutrality-rules/

191. Arlington v. FCC, 2013 U.S. Lexis 3838 (May 20, 2013), http://www.supremecourt.gov/opinions/12pdf/11–1545_1b7d.pdf

192. *Wyatt, supra* note 190.

193. Reno v. American Civil Liberties Union, 521 U.S. 844 (1997).

194. Pub. L. No. 104–104, Title V, §§ 501–561, 110 Stat. 56, 133–43 (codified at 18 U.S.C. §§ 1462, 1465, 2422 and at scattered sections of 47 U.S.C.).

195. Reno v. ACLU, 521 U.S. at 869.

196. *Id.* at 853.

197. *Id.* at 870.

198. Miller v. California, 413 U.S. 15 (1973).

Chapter 12

Obscenity, Indecency and Violence

1. Jacobellis v. Ohio, 378 U.S. 184, 197 (1964) (Stewart, J., concurring).

2. Erznoznik v. City of Jacksonville, 422 U.S. 205 (1975).

3. Cohen v. California, 403 U.S. 15 (1971).

4. *See* Margaret A. Blanchard, Revolutionary Sparks: Freedom of Expression in Modern America (1992).

5. An Act for the Suppression of Trade in, and Circulation of, Obscene Literature and Articles of Immoral Use, ch. 258, § 2, 17 Stat. 598, 599 (1873).

6. Congress amended the Comstock Act in 1876. Amendment to the Comstock Act, ch. 186, § 1, 19 Stat. 90.

7. L.R. 3 Q.B. 360, 371 (1868).

8. United States v. One Book Called "Ulysses," 5 F. Supp. 182, 184, 185 (S.D.N.Y. 1933), *aff'd sub nom.* United States v. One Book Entitled "Ulysses" by James Joyce, 72 F.2d 705 (2d Cir. 1934).

9. 18 U.S.C. §§ 1460–1470.

10. 18 U.S.C. §§ 1470, 2252B; 47 U.S.C. §§ 223(d), 231.

11. Roth v. United States, 354 U.S. 476, 489 (1957).

12. Miller v. California, 413 U.S. 15 (1973).

13. *Id.* at 22.

14. *Roth,* 354 U.S. at 487 n.20.

15. Smith v. United States, 431 U.S. 291, 305 (1977); Hamling v. United States, 418 U.S. 87, 104–5 (1974).

16. Jacobellis v. Ohio, 378 U.S. 184 (1964).

17. Ward v. Illinois, 431 U.S. 767 (1977).

18. Mishkin v. New York, 383 U.S. 502, 508–9 (1966).

19. United States v. Thomas, 74 F.3d 701 (6th Cir.), *cert. denied,* 519 U.S. 820 (1996).

20. Ashcroft v. ACLU, 535 U.S. 564, 597 (2002) (Kennedy, J., concurring in the judgment).

21. *Id.* at 590 (Breyer, J., concurring in part and concurring in the judgment).

22. *Id.* at 586–89 (O'Connor, J., concurring in part and concurring in the judgment).

23. United States v. Kilbride, 584 F.3d 1240 (9th Cir. 2009).

24. United States v. Little, 365 Fed. Appx. 159 (11th Cir. 2010).

25. Miller v. California, 413 U.S. 15, 25 (1973).

26. Jenkins v. Georgia, 418 U.S. 153 (1974).

27. Ward v. Illinois, 431 U.S. 767 (1977).

28. *Jenkins*, 418 U.S. at 160.

29. *Id.*

30. A Book Named John Cleland's Memoirs of a Woman of Pleasure v. Attorney Gen. of Mass., 383 U.S. 413 (1996).

31. Pope v. Illinois, 481 U.S. 497 (1987).

32. Luke Records, Inc. v. Navarro, 960 F.2d 134 (11th Cir.), *cert. denied*, 506 U.S. 1022 (1992).

33. Butler v. Michigan, 352 U.S. 380, 383 (1957).

34. *Id.*

35. Ginsberg v. New York, 390 U.S. 629 (1968).

36. 18 U.S.C. § 2256(8).

37. Jennifer A.L. Sheldon-Sherman, *Rethinking Restitution in Cases of Child Pornography Possession*, 17 LEWIS & CLARK L. REV. 215, 223 (2013) (citations omitted).

38. 458 U.S. 747 (1982).

39. *Id.* at 758.

40. 18 U.S.C. §§ 2251(a), 2252(b)(4), 2256(8).

41. 18 U.S.C. § 2256(2)(A).

42. John A. Humbach, *"Sexting" and the First Amendment*, 37 HASTINGS CONST. L.Q. 433, 446 (2010).

43. United States v. Knox, 32 F.3d 733, 737 (3d Cir. 1994), *cert. denied*, 513 U.S. 1109 (1995).

44. *Id.*

45. United States v. Matthews, 209 F.3d 338, 345 (4th Cir.), *cert. denied*, 531 U.S. 910 (2000).

46. Erica Goode, *Life Sentence for Possession of Child Pornography Spurs Debate over Severity*, N.Y. TIMES, Nov. 5, 2011, at A9.

47. Ashcroft v. Free Speech Coalition, 535 U.S. 234 (2002).

48. United States v. Hotaling, 634 F.3d 725 (2d Cir.), *cert. denied*, 132 S. Ct. 843 (2011).

49. New Hampshire v. Zidel, 940 A.2d 255 (N.H. 2008).

50. 18 U.S.C. § 2259.

51. *See* Emily Bazelon, *Money Is No Cure*, N.Y. TIMES, Jan. 27, 2013, §8 (Magazine), at 22.

52. United States v. Monzel, 641 F.3d 528 (D.C. Cir.), *cert. denied*, 132 S. Ct. 756 (2011); United States v. Kearney,

672 F.3d 81 (1st Cir. 2012), *cert. dismissed*, 133 S. Ct. 1521 (2013); United States v. Aumais, 656 F.3d 147 (2d Cir. 2011); United States v. Crandon, 173 F.3d 122 (3d Cir.), *cert. denied*, 528 U.S. 855 (1999); United States v. Burgess, 684 F.3d 445 (4th Cir.), *cert. denied*, 133 S. Ct. 490 (2012); United States v. Evers, 669 F.3d 645 (6th Cir. 2012); United States v. Laraneta, 700 F.3d 983 (7th Cir. 2012); United States v. Fast, 709 F.3d 712 (8th Cir. 2013); United States v. Kennedy, 643 F.3d 1251 (9th Cir. 2011); United States v. McGarity, 669 F.3d 1218 (11th Cir.), *cert. denied*, 133 S. Ct. 378 (2012).

53. *In re* Amy Unknown, 701 F.3d 749 (5th Cir. 2012) (*en banc*), *cert. granted sub nom*, Paroline v. United States, 2013 U.S. LEXIS 4943 (June 27, 2013).

54. *See* Joanna R. Lampe, Note: *A Victimless Sex Crime: The Case for Decriminalizing Consensual Teen Sexting*, 46 U. MICH. J.L. REFORM 703 (2013).

55. *The Nat'l Campaign to Prevent Teen and Unplanned Pregnancy, Sex and Tech: Results from a Survey of Teens and Young Adults 1 (2008), available at* http://www.thenationalcampaign.org/sextech/.

56. John A. Humbach, *"Sexting" and the First Amendment*, 37 HASTINGS CONST. L.Q. 433, 438 (2010).

57. Mary Graw Leary, *Sexting or Self-Produced Child Pornography? The Dialog Continues—Structured Prosecutorial Discretion Within a Multidisciplinary Response*, 17 VA. J. SOC. POL'Y & L. 486 (2010).

58. A.H. v. State, 949 So. 2d 234 (Fla. Dist. Ct. App. 2007).

59. Osborne v. Ohio. 495 U.S. 103 (1990).

60. *See* John A. Humbach, *'Sexting' and the First Amendment*, 37 HASTINGS CONST. L.Q. 433, 434 (2010).

61. Miller v. Mitchell, 598 F.3d 139 (3d Cir. 2010); *see* Catherine Arcabascio, *Sexting and Teenagers: OMG R U Going 2 Jail???*, 16 RICH. J.L. & TECH. 10 (2010).

62. Nathan Koppel & Ashby Jones, *Are "Sext" Messages a Teenage Felony or Folly*, WALL ST. J., Aug. 25, 2010, at D1.

63. Stanley v. Georgia, 394 U.S. 557 (1969).

64. *Id.* at 568.

65. 18 U.S.C. § 2252A; Osborne v. Ohio, 495 U.S. 103 (1990).

66. *Osborne*, 495 U.S. 103.

67. Joseph Burstyn, Inc., v. Wilson, 343 U.S. 495 (1952).

68. Times Film Corp. v. City of Chicago, 365 U.S. 43 (1961).

69. Freedman v. Maryland, 380 U.S. 51 (1965).

70. Pub. L. No. 91-452, 84 Stat. 922 (1970), codified at 18 U.S.C. §§ 1961–1968 (as amended by USA-Patriot Act of 2001, Pub. L. No. 107-56, § 813, 115 Stat. 272, 382).

71. *See* Teresa Bryan et al., *Racketeer Influenced and Corrupt Organizations,* 40 Am. Crim. L. Rev. 987 (2003).

72. Alexander v. United States, 509 U.S. 544 (1993).

73. 18 U.S.C. § 1464; 47 C.F.R. § 73.3999.

74. 18 U.S.C. § 1464.

75. FCC v. Pacifica Found., 438 U.S. 726, 739 (1978).

76. *Id.* at 740.

77. *Id.* at 727.

78. Enforcement of Prohibitions Against Broad. Indecency, 8 F.C.C.R. 704, 705 n.10 (1993).

79. 423 U.S. 15 (1973).

80. *See, e.g.,* Cohen v. California, 403 U.S. 15 (1971).

81. FCC v. Fox Television Stations, Inc., 132 S. Ct. 2307 (2012).

82. *See* Fox Television Stations, Inc. v. FCC, 613 F.3d 317 (2d Cir. 2010), *vacated by, remanded by,* Fox Television Stations, 132 S. Ct. 2307.

83. Pub. L. 69-632, ch. 169, § 29, 44 Stat. 1162 (1927); ch. 652, § 326, 48 Stat. 1064 (1934).

84. 18 U.S.C. § 1464.

85. 47 U.S.C. § 503(b)(1)(D).

86. *See, e.g.,* Sable Communications of California, Inc. v. FCC, 492 U.S. 115, 126 (1989).

87. 47 U.S.C. § 326.

88. *See, e.g.,* Application of The Jack Straw Memorial Foundation for Renewal of the License of Station KRAB-FM, Seattle, Wash., 21 Rad. Reg. 2d (P&F) 505 (1971).

89. Sonderling Broad. Corp., 41 F.C.C.2d 777, 782 (1973), *aff'd,* Illinois Citizens Comm. for Broad. v. FCC, 515 F.2d 397 (D.C. Cir. 1974).

90. Pacifica Found., 56 F.C.C.2d 94 (1975) (the words, as listed in the FCC's decision, are "shit, piss, fuck, cunt, cocksucker, motherfucker, and tits").

91. Citizen's Complaint Against Pacifica Found. Station WBAI (FM), N.Y, N.Y., 56 F.C.C.2d 94 (1975).

92. FCC v. Pacifica Found., 438 U.S. 726, 750 (1978).

93. *Id.*

94. 438 U.S. 726.

95. Pacifica Found., 2 F.C.C.R. 2698, 2699 (1987).

96. *In re* Infinity Broad. Corp. of Penna., 2 F.C.C.R. 2705 (1987); *In re* Pacifica Found., 2 F.C.C.R. 2698 (1987); *In re* Regents of the Univ. of Cal., 2 F.C.C.R. 2703 (1987); New Indecency Enforcement Standards to Be Applied to All Broad. & Amateur Radio Licensees, 2 F.C.C.R. 2726 (1987).

97. 2 F.C.C.R. 2726 (1987). The D.C. Circuit upheld the FCC's more expansive indecency definition. Action for Children's Television v. FCC, 852 F.2d 1332 (D.C. Cir. 1988) (ACT I).

98. 438 U.S. at 772.

99. *In re* Indus. Guidance on the Comm'n's Case Law Interpreting 18 U.S.C. § 1464 & Enforcement Policies Regarding Broad. Indecency, 16 F.C.C.R. 7999, 8002–3 (2001).

100. *In re* Complaints Against Various Broad. Licensees Regarding Their Airing of the "Golden Globe Awards" Program, 19 F.C.C.R. 4975 (2004).

101. *In re* Complaints Regarding Various Television Broad. Between Feb. 2, 2002 & Mar. 8, 2005, 21 F.C.C.R. 2664 (2006).

102. *See* Fox Television Stations, Inc. v. FCC, 613 F.3d 317, 324 (2d Cir. 2010), *vacated by, remanded by* FCC v. Fox Television Stations, Inc., 132 S. Ct. 2307 (2012).

103. FCC v. Fox Television Stations, Inc., 556 U.S. 502 (2009).

104. *In re* Complaints Against Various Television Licensees Regarding Their Broadcast on Nov. 11, 2004, of the ABC Television Network's Presentation of the Film "Saving Private Ryan," 20 F.C.C.R. 4507 (2005).

105. FCC v. Fox Television Stations, Inc., 132 S. Ct. 2307 (2012).

106. Fox Television Stations, Inc. v. FCC, 613 F.3d 317, 322 (2d Cir. 2010), *vacated by, remanded by* 132 S. Ct. 2307 (2012).

107. Complaints Against Various Television Licensees Concerning Their Feb. 1, 2004, Broad. of the Super Bowl XXXVIII, 19 F.C.C.R. 19230 (2004).

108. CBS Corp. v. FCC, 535 F.3d 167, 174 (3d Cir. 2008), *vacated and remanded,* 556 U.S. 1218 (2009).

109. 556 U.S. 1218 (2009).

110. CBS Corp. v. FCC, 663 F.3d 122 (3d Cir. 2011), *cert. denied,* 132 S. Ct. 2677 (2012).

111. FCC v. Fox Television Stations, Inc., 132 S. Ct. 2307, 2320 (2012).

112. Jonathan Make, *FCC Asks If It Should Stick With Policy of Not Pursuing Fleeting Indecency*, COMM. DAILY, Apr. 2, 2013.

113. 47 C.F.R. § 73.3999.

114. Action for Children's Television v. FCC, 58 F.3d 654 (D.C. Cir. 1995) (*en banc*), *cert. denied*, 516 U.S. 1043 (1996) *(ACT III)*.

115. New Indecency Enforcement Standards to Be Applied to All Broad. & Amateur Radio Licensees, 2 F.C.C.R. 2726 (1987).

116. Action for Children's Television v. FCC, 852 F.2d 1332 (D.C. Cir. 1988) *(ACT I)*.

117. Pub. L. No. 100-459, § 608, 102 Stat. 2186, 2228.

118. Enforcement of Prohibitions Against Broad. Indecency in 18 U.S.C. § 1464, 5 F.C.C.R. 5297 (1990).

119. Action for Children's Television v. FCC, 932 F.2d 1504 (D.C. Cir. 1991) *(ACT II)*, *cert. denied*, 503 U.S. 913 (1992).

120. Public Telecommunications Act of 1992, Pub. L. No. 102-356, § 16(a), 106 Stat. 949.

121. Enforcement of Prohibitions Against Broad. Indecency in 18 U.S.C. § 1464, 8 F.C.C.R. 704 (1993).

122. Action for Children's Television v. FCC, 58 F.3d 654 (D.C. Cir. 1995), *cert. denied*, 516 U.S. 1043 (1996) *(ACT III)*.

123. Federal Communications Commission, *FCC V-Chip Task Force Releases Updated Survey on the Encoding of Video Programming*, 2000 FCC LEXIS 143 (2000).

124. Implementation of Section 551 of the Telecommunications Act of 1996; Video Programming Ratings, 13 F.C.C.R. 8232, 8237 (1998).

125. *See Classification and Rating Administration, Questions & Answers: Everything You Always Wanted to Know about the Movie Rating System* (n.d.), *available at* http://www.mpaa.org/ratings/what-each-rating-means.

126. Cruz v. Ferre, 755 F.2d 1415 (11th Cir. 1985), citing FCC v. Pacifica Found., 438 U.S. 726 (1978).

127. *See, e.g.*, Community Television of Utah, Inc. v. Roy City, 555 F. Supp. 1164 (D. Utah 1982); Home Box Office, Inc. v. Wilkinson, 531 F. Supp. 987 (D. Utah 1982).

128. 47 U.S.C. § 532(h) (franchising authorities may prohibit leased access programming that is "obscene or is in conflict with community standards in that it is lewd, lascivious, filthy or indecent, or is otherwise unprotected by the Constitution of the United States"); 47 U.S.C. § 544(d)(i) (franchising authorities may require a franchise to prohibit obscene or "otherwise unprotected" programming); 47 U.S.C. § 558 (franchising authorities may enforce state or local laws forbidding obscenity and "other similar laws").

129. 47 U.S.C. § 544(d)(2).

130. Various Complaints Against the Cable/Satellite Television Program "Nip/Tuck," 20 F.C.C.R. 4255, 4255 (2005), *quoting* Violent Television Programming and Its Impact on Children, Notice of Inquiry, 19 F.C.C.R. 14394, 14403 (2004).

131. Denver Area Educ. Telecomm. Consortium, Inc. v. FCC, 518 U.S. 727 (1996) (ruling on Pub. L. No. 102-385, § 10, 106 Stat. 1486).

132. 47 U.S.C. § 531(e).

133. Telecommunications Act of 1996, Pub. L. 104-104, §§ 504, 505, 110 Stat. 136.

134. Implementation of Section 505 of the Telecommunications Act of 1996, 12 F.C.C.R. 5212 (1997).

135. United States v. Playboy Enter., Inc., 529 U.S. 803 (2000).

136. Dan Thang Dang, *Cell Phone the Newest Frontier for Porn*, BALTIMORE SUN, Feb. 19, 2004, at 9D.

137. *See generally* Amitai Etzioni, *Do Children Have the Same First Amendment Rights as Adults? On Protecting Children from Speech*, 79 CHI.-KENT L. REV. 3 (2004).

138. Pub. L. No. 104-104, § 502, 110 Stat. 56 (1996) (codified at 47 U.S.C. §§ 223(a)(1)(B)(ii), 223(d)).

139. 521 U.S. 844 (1997).

140. *Id.* at 877.

141. Pub. L. No. 105-277, §§ 1401–1406, 112 Stat. 1681 (codified at 47 U.S.C. § 231).

142. ACLU v. Reno, 31 F. Supp. 2d 473 (E.D. Pa. 1999).

143. ACLU v. Reno, 217 F.3d 162 (3d Cir. 2000).

144. Ashcroft v. ACLU, 535 U.S. 564 (2002).

145. ACLU v. Ashcroft, 322 F.3d 240 (3d Cir. 2003).

146. Ashcroft v. ACLU, 542 U.S. 656 (2004).

147. ACLU v. Gonzales, 478 F. Supp. 2d 775 (E.D. Pa. 2007).

148. ACLU v. Mukasey, 534 F.3d 181 (3d Cir. 2008), *cert. denied*, 555 U.S. 1137 (2009).

149. ACLU v. Ashcroft, 322 F.3d 240, 268 (3d Cir. 2003).

150. Mukasey v. ACLU, 555 U.S. 1137 (2009).

151. Pub. L. 104-208, 110 Stat. 3009.

152. 18 U.S.C. § 2256(8)(B), (D).

153. Ashcroft v. Free Speech Coalition, 535 U.S. 234 (2002).

154. Pub. L. 108-21, §§ 102–601, 117 Stat. 650.

155. United States v. Williams, 553 U.S. 285 (2008).

156. Pub. L. No. 106-554, 114 Stat. 2763A-335 (2000).

157. 539 U.S. 194 (2003).

158. *See, e.g.,* Amitai Etzioni, *Porn Blocking Law Should Be Scrapped,* BROWARD DAILY BUS. REV., Mar. 19, 2003, at A7; James v. Meow Media, 300 F.3d 683 (6th Cir. 2002), *cert. denied,* 537 U.S. 1159 (2003).

159. *See, e.g.,* Am. Amusement Machine Ass'n v. Kendrick, 244 F.3d 572 (7th Cir.), *cert. denied,* 534 U.S. 994 (2001).

160. *See* N.R. Kleinfield et al., *Newtown Killer's Obsessions, in Chilling Detail,* N.Y. TIMES, Mar. 29, 2013, at A1; Timothy Dylan Reeves, Note: *Tort Liability for Manufacturers of Violent Video Games: A Situational Discussion of the Causation Calamity,* 60 ALA. L. REV. 519, 520 n.7 (2009).

161. James v. Meow Media, 300 F.3d 683 (6th Cir. 2001), *cert. denied,* 537 U.S. 1159 (2003).

162. James v. Meow Media, Inc., 90 F. Supp. 2d 798 (W.D. Ky. 2000).

163. Am. Amusement Machine Ass' v. Kendrick, 244 F.3d 572, 575 (7th Cir.), *cert. denied,* 534 U.S. 994 (2001).

164. *Id.* at 574.

165. *Id.* at 575.

166. Brown v. Enm't Merchants Ass'n, 131 S. Ct. 2729 (2011).

167. *See, e.g.,* America's Best Family Showplace Corp. v. New York City, 536 F. Supp. 170, 172 (E.D.N.Y. 1982).

168. Rothner v. City of Chicago, 929 F.2d 297, 303 (7th Cir. 1991).

169. *Brown,* 131 S. Ct. at 2733.

170. *Id.* at 2737–38; *see, e.g.,* Timothy Dylan Reeves, Note: *Tort Liability for Manufacturers of Violent Video Games: A Situational Discussion of the Causation Calamity,* 60 ALA. L. REV. 519, 522 (2009) ("The interactive nature of violent video games has a disturbing effect.").

171. FEDERAL TRADE COMMISSION, MARKETING VIOLENT ENTERTAINMENT TO CHILDREN: A REVIEW OF SELF-REGULATION AND INDUSTRY PRACTICES IN THE MOTION PICTURE, MUSIC RECORDING & ELECTRONIC GAME INDUSTRIES (2000).

172. 22 F.C.C.R. 7929 (2007).

173. *Id.* at 7938, quoting YOUTH VIOLENCE: A REPORT OF THE SURGEON GENERAL (2001), at Appendix 4-B.

174. *Id.* at 7938.

175. See William Li, Note: *Unbaking the Adolescent Cake: The Constitutional Implications of Imposing Tort Liability on Publishers of Violent Video Games,* 45 ARIZ. L. REV. 467 (2003).

176. *About ESRB* (n.d.), *available at* http://www.esrb.org/about/index.jsp.

177. *ESRB Game Ratings* (n.d.), *available at* http://www.esrb.org/ratings/ratings_guide.jsp.

178. Empowering Parents and Protecting Children in an Evolving Media Landscape, 24 F.C.C.R. 13171, 13181 (2010).

179. *Brown,* 131 S. Ct. at 2738.

Chapter 13

Intellectual Property

1. LAWRENCE LESSIG, FREE CULTURE 53, 62 (2004).

2. 35 U.S.C. §§ 101–103, 112.

3. 15 U.S.C. §§ 1051–1127.

4. *The Celebrity 100,* FORBES, June 4, 2012, at 86.

5. 17 U.S.C. § 102(a).

6. U.S. CONST., art. I, § 8, cl. 8.

7. *Id.*

8. 8 Anne, C. 19 (1710).

9. U.S. CONST., art. I, § 8, cl. 8.

10. Act of May 31, 1790, ch. 15, 1 Stat. 124.

11. Wheaton v. Peters, 33 U.S. 590 (1834).

12. Act of Feb. 3, 1831, 4 Stat. 436 (musical compositions); Copyright Act of 1865, 13 Stat. 540 (photographs); Act of July 8, 1870, 16 Stat. 212 (paintings).

13. Pub. L. No. 60-349, 35 Stat. 1075.

14. Berne Convention Implementation Act of 1988, Pub. L. 100-568, 102 Stat. 2853.

15. 17 I. Fred Koenigsberg, Commentary: *Overview of Title 17, Copyrights,* 17 NAT'L INST. TRIAL ADVOC. 101 (2010).

16. 18 U.S.C. § 102(a).

17. *See* Burrow-Giles Lithographic Co. v. Sarony, 111 U.S. 53 (1884).

18. Boisson v. Banian, Ltd., 273 F.3d 262, 268 (2d Cir. 2001).

19. U.S. Copyright Office, Congressman Goodlatte Addresses Creators and Copyright Office at World IP Day Event, Apr. 24, 2013.

20. *See, e.g., id.;* American Dental Association v. Delta Dental Plans Association, 126 F.3d 977 (7th Cir. 1997).

21. 17 U.S.C. § 103.

22. Feist Publications, Inc. v. Rural Telephone Service Co., Inc., 499 U.S. 340 (1991).

23. 17 U.S.C. § 102(a).

24 *Id.*

25. 17 U.S.C. § 301.

26. *See* Wheaton v. Peters, 33 U.S. 591 (1834).

27. *Feist,* 499 U.S. at 340.

28. *See* 17 U.S.C. § 102(b).

29. Hoehling v. Universal City Studios, Inc., 618 F.2d 972 (2d Cir. 1980), *cert. denied,* 449 U.S. 841 (1980).

30. Int'l News Serv. v. Associated Press, 248 U.S. 215 (1918).

31. *Id.*

32. Nat'l Basketball Ass'n v. Motorola, Inc., 105 F.3d 841, 845 (2d Cir. 1997).

33. *See, e.g.,* Barclays Capital Inc. v. Theflyonthewall.com, Inc., 700 F. Supp. 2d 310 (S.D.N.Y. 2010).

34. 17 U.S.C. § 105.

35. John F. Harris & Jim VandeHei, *Editors' Note,* POLITICO (Oct. 13, 2013), *available at* http://www.politico.com/news/stories/1011/65940.html.

36. Leslie Kaufman, *Publisher Pulls a 2nd Book by Lehrer, "How We Decide,"* N.Y. TIMES, Mar. 2, 2013, at B2.

37. Christine Haughney, *Time and CNN Reinstate Journalist After Review,* N.Y. TIMES, Aug. 17, 2012, at B2.

38. *See* Ralph Blumenthal & Sarah Lyall, *Repeat Accusations of Plagiarism Taint Prolific Biographer,* N.Y. TIMES, Sept. 21, 1999, at A1; Leslie Kaufman, *Goodall Book Delayed after Copying Is Found,* N.Y. TIMES, Mar. 26, 2013, at C3; Sara Rimer, *When Plagiarism's Shadow Falls on Admired Scholars,* N.Y. TIMES, Nov. 24, 2004, at B9; Jacques Steinberg, *New Book Includes Passages from Others,* N.Y. TIMES, May 31, 2003, at B9.

39. JAYSON BLAIR, BURNING DOWN MY MASTER'S HOUSE: MY LIFE AT THE NEW YORK TIMES (2004).

40. Margaret Sullivan, *Repairing the Credibility Cracks,* N.Y. TIMES, May 5, 2013, at SR12.

41. 17 U.S.C. § 201(a).

42. 17 U.S.C. § 201(b).

43. 17 U.S.C. §§ 101, 201.

44. Community for Creative Non-Violence v. Reid, 490 U.S. 730 (1989).

45. 17 U.S.C. § 101.

46. *Community for Creative Non-Violence,* 490 U.S. at 730.

47. 17 U.S.C. § 201(c).

48. Greenberg v. Nat'l Geographic Soc'y, 533 F.3d 1244 (11th Cir.), *cert. denied,* 555 U.S. 1070 (2008).

49. 533 U.S. 483 (2001).

50. 17 U.S.C. § 106.

51. Silberman v. Innovative Luggage, Inc., 2003 U.S. Dist. LEXIS 5420 (S.D.N.Y. Apr. 3, 2003).

52. Sony Corp. of America v. Universal City Studios, Inc., 464 U.S. 417 (1984).

53. Audio Home Recording Act of 1992, Pub. L. No. 102-563, 106 Stat. 4244 (codified at 17 U.S.C. §§ 1001–1010).

54. 17 U.S.C. § 112(a).

55. Pickett v. Prince, 207 F.3d 402 (7th Cir. 2000).

56. Agence France Presse v. Morel, 2013 U.S. Dist. LEXIS 5636 (S.D.N.Y. Jan. 14, 2013).

57. 17 U.S.C. § 106(4).

58. Fox TV Stations, Inc. v. FilmOn X, 2013 U.S. Dist. LEXIS 126543 at *10 (D.D.C. Sept. 5, 2013).

59. WNET v. Aereo, Inc., 712 F.3d 676 (2d Cir. 2013).

60. Cartoon Network, LP v. CSC Holdings, Inc. (Cablevision), 536 F.3d 121 (2d Cir. 2008).

61. Fox Television Systems, Inc. v. BarryDriller Content Systems, 915 F. Supp. 2d 1138 (C.D. Cal. 2012); *FilmOn X,* 2013 U.S. Dist. LEXIS 126543.

62. 17 U.S.C. § 106.

63. Digital Performance Right in Sound Recordings Act, Pub. L. No. 104-39, 109 Stat. 336, *as amended by* Digital Millennium Copyright Act, Pub. L. 105-304, 112 Stat. 2860.

64. *See* 4 MELVILLE NIMMER & DAVID NIMMER, NIMMER ON COPYRIGHT § 8D.01[A] (2013).

65. Berne Convention, art. 6bis(1).

66. Visual Artists Rights Act, Pub. L. No. 101-650, § 601, 104 Stat. 5089.

67. 17 U.S.C. § 106A.

68. Clean Flicks of Colo., LLC v. Soderbergh, 433 F. Supp. 2d 1236 (D. Colo. 2006).

69. Pub. L. No. 109-9, 119 Stat. 218 (2005) (codified at 17 U.S.C. §§ 408, 506(a) and 18 U.S.C. § 2319).

70. 17 U.S.C. § 110(11).

71. See Jacob Armstrong, *FECA Matter: An Epic Copyright Infringement Trial, Congressional Interference, and the Diminution of Moral Rights in the United States of America,* 7 J. Marshall Rev. Intell. Prop. L. 376 (2008).

72. Sony Corp. of America v. Universal City Studios, Inc., 464 U.S. 417 (1984).

73. 17 U.S.C. § 1008.

74. 17 U.S.C. § 108.

75. 17 U.S.C. § 109(a).

76. The Supreme Court provides a brief history and interpretation of the first-sale doctrine in Quality King Distributors, Inc. v. L'Anza Research Int'l, Inc., 523 U.S. 135 (1998).

77. 17 U.S.C. § 109(b)(1)(A); Computer Software Rental Amendments, Pub. L. No. 101-650, tit. viii, 104 Stat. 5089, 5134–35; Record Rental Amendment of 1984, Pub. L. No. 98-450, 98 Stat. 1727.

78. Brilliance Audio, Inc. v. Haights Cross Communications, Inc., 474 F.3d 365 (6th Cir. 2007).

79. Kirtsaeng v. John Wiley & Sons, Inc., 133 S. Ct. 1351 (2013).

80. Berne Convention Implementation Act of 1988, Pub. L. 100-568, 102 Stat. 2853.

81. 17 U.S.C. § 401.

82. 17 U.S.C. § 401(c).

83. 17 U.S.C. §§ 203(a), 304(c).

84. Larry Rohter, *Copyright Victory, 35 Years Later,* N.Y. Times, Sept. 11, 2013, at C1.

85. U.S. Const. art I, § 8, cl. 8.

86. 17 U.S.C. § 302(a).

87. 17 U.S.C. § 302(c).

88. 537 U.S. 186 (2003).

89. This was "due to (i) failure to comply with copyright formalities, (ii) lack of subject matter protection, or (iii) lack of national eligibility due to the absence of copyright relations with the" United States. Davis Wright Tremaine, *Golan v. Holder and the Controversial New Efforts to Update IP Law for the Internet Age* (2012), *available at* http://www.medialawmonitor.com/2012/03/golan-v-holder-and-the-controversial-new-efforts-to-update-ip-law-for-the-internet-age.

90. 17 U.S.C. § 104A.

91. *Davis Wright Tremaine, supra* note 89.

92. Golan v. Holder, 132 S. Ct. 873 (2012).

93. *Id.* at 861.

94. 17 U.S.C. § 408(a).

95. 17 U.S.C. § 411(a).

96. 17 U.S.C. §§ 407, 408(b); 37 C.F.R. § 201.3.

97. 17 U.S.C. § 412.

98. 17 U.S.C. § 410(c).

99. 37 C.F.R. § 202.1.

100. 17 U.S.C. § 411.

101. Teleprompter Corp. v. Columbia Broad. Sys., 415 U.S. 394 (1974); Fortnightly Corp. v. United Artists Television, Inc., 392 U.S. 390 (1968).

102. 17 U.S.C. § 111.

103. 17 U.S.C. § 119; Satellite Home Viewer Improvement Act of 1999, Pub. L. No. 106-113, §§ 1001–1012, 113 Stat. 1501.

104. Righthaven LLC v. Hoehn, 716 F.3d 1166 (9th Cir. 2013).

105. Fox Broadcasting Co., Inc. v. Dish Network L.L.C., 723 F.3d 1067 (9th Cir. 2013).

106. *See, e.g.,* Cottrill v. Spears, 87 Fed. Appx. 803 (3d Cir. 2004), *amended,* 2004 U.S. App. LEXIS 10773 (3d Cir. June 2, 2004).

107. Fogerty v. MGM Group Holdings Corp., 379 F.3d 348 (6th Cir. 2004), *cert. denied,* 543 U.S. 1120 (2005).

108. Princess Samantha Kennedy v. Paramount Pictures Corp., 2013 U.S. Dist. LEXIS 43882 (S.D. Cal. Mar. 27, 2013).

109. Harter v. Disney Enter., Inc., 2012 U.S. Dist. LEXIS 134409 (E.D. Mo. Sept. 20, 2012).

110. 17 U.S.C. § 504(c).

111. *See, e.g.,* Kalem Co. v. Harper Bros., 222 U.S. 55 (1911) (producer of infringing film violated copyright law although movie theaters, not producer, showed film to public); 17 U.S.C. §§ 106, 501(a).

112. Sony Corp. of America v. Universal City Studios, Inc., 464 U.S. 417 (1984).

113. Cartoon Network LP v. CSC Holdings, 536 F.3d 121 (2d Cir. 2008), *cert. denied,* 557 U.S. 946 (2009).

114. Metro-Goldwyn-Mayer Studios, Inc. v. Grokster Ltd., 545 U.S. 913 (2005).

115. Columbia Pictures Indus., Inc. v. Fung, 710 F.3d 1020 (9th Cir. 2013).

116. Flava Works, Inc. v. Gunter, 689 F.3d 754 (7th Cir. 2012).

117. *See* 17 U.S.C. § 501(b).

118. 17 U.S.C. § 504(b).

119. 17 U.S.C. § 504(c)(1); *See* Digital Theft Deterrence and Copyright Damages Improvement Act, Pub. L. No. 106-160, 113 Stat. 1774.

120. Feltner v. Columbia Pictures Television, Inc., 523 U.S. 340 (1998).

121. 17 U.S.C. § 504(c)(2).

122. *Id.*

123. 17 U.S.C. § 505; *See* Fogerty v. Fantasy, Inc., 510 U.S. 517 (1994).

124. 17 U.S.C. § 502.

125. 17 U.S.C. § 509.

126. 17 U.S.C. §506; 17 U.S.C. § 101 (definition of "financial gain").

127. Pub. L. No. 105-147, 111 Stat. 2678.

128. 17 U.S.C. § 507.

129. *See, e.g.,* Dam Things from Denmark v. Russ Barrie & Co., 290 F.3d 548, 560 (3d Cir. 2002).

130. *See* Pierre N. Leval, *Toward a Fair Use Standard,* 103 HARV. L. REV. 1105, 1105 (1990).

131. 17 U.S.C. § 107.

132. Leval, *supra* note 125, at 1110.

133. *See, e.g.,* Jessica Litman, *Billowing White Goo,* 31 COLUM. J.L. & ARTS 587, 596 (2008).

134. Campbell v. Acuff-Rose Music, Inc., 510 U.S. 569, 578 (1994).

135. Harper & Row Publishers, Inc. v. Nation Enter., 471 U.S. 539 (1985).

136. *See* 4 MELVILLE NIMMER & DAVID NIMMER, NIMMER ON COPYRIGHT § 13.05[A][1] (2013).

137. *Campbell,* 510 U.S. at 579.

138. *Id.* at 569.

139. See NIMMER & NIMMER, *supra note* 136, at § 13.05[C][1].

140. Associated Press v. Meltwater U.S. Holdings, Inc., 2013 U.S. Dist. LEXIS 39573 (S.D.N.Y. Mar. 21, 2013).

141. *See* NIMMER & NIMMER, *supra* note 136, at § 13.05[A][2].

142. Salinger v. Random House, Inc., 811 F.2d 90 (2d Cir. 1987), *cert. denied,* 484 U.S. 890 (1988).

143. 17 U.S.C. § 107; Pub. L. No. 102-492, 106 Stat. 3145.

144. A.V. v. iParadigms, LLC, 562 F.3d 630 (4th Cir. 2009).

145. *Id.* at 642.

146. Bill Graham Archives v. Dorling Kindersley Ltd., 448 F.3d 605 (2d Cir. 2006).

147. *See, e.g.,* Paul Goldstein, *Fair Use in Context,* 31 COLUM. J.L. & ARTS 433, 442 (2008).

148. Fox Broadcasting Co., Inc. v. Dish Network L.L.C., 723 F.3d 1067 (9th Cir. 2013).

149. Harper & Row, Publishers, Inc. v. Nation Enter., 471 U.S. 539, 566 (1985).

150. Benny Evangelista, *Consumers Can Now Pass Go, Collect Any App,* S.F. CHRON., July 27, 2010, at D1.

151. Basic Books, Inc. v. Kinko's Graphics Corp., 758 F. Supp. 1522 (S.D.N.Y. 1991).

152. *Id.* at 1534.

153. Campbell v. Acuff-Rose Music, Inc., 510 U.S. 569, 587 (1994).

154. *See, e.g.,* Playboy Enter., Inc. v. Russ Hardenburgh, Inc., 982 F. Supp. 503 (N.D. Ohio 1997).

155. Pub. L. 105-304, 112 Stat. 2860.

156. 17 U.S.C. § 1201.

157. *See, e.g.,* 321 Studios v. Metro Goldwyn Mayer Studios, Inc., 307 F. Supp. 2d 1085 (N.D. Cal. 2004).

158. 17 U.S.C. § 1202.

159. Playboy Enter., Inc. v. Frena, 839 F. Supp. 1552 (M.D. Fla. 1993).

160. Sega Enter., Ltd. v. Maphia, 857 F. Supp. 679 (N.D. Cal. 1994).

161. 17 U.S.C. § 512(c).

162. Perfect 10, Inc. v. Google, Inc., 2010 U.S. Dist. LEXIS 75071 (C.D. Cal., July 26, 2010), aff'd, 653 F.3d 976 (9th Cir. 2011), cert. denied, 132 S. Ct. 1713 (2012).

163. UMG Recordings, Inc. v. Veoh Networks, Inc., 718 F.3d 1006 (9th Cir. 2013); see also Io Group, Inc. v. Veoh Networks, Inc., 586 F. Supp. 2d 1132 (N.D. Cal. 2008).

164. Viacom Int'l, Inc. v. YouTube, Inc., 2013 U.S. Dist. LEXIS 56646 (S.D.N.Y. Apr. 18, 2013), on remand from, Viacom Int'l Inc. v. YouTube, Inc., 676 F.3d 19 (2d Cir. 2012); see Meg James, YouTube Prevails in Viacom Copyright Suit, L.A. TIMES, Apr. 19, 2013, at B3.

165. Perfect 10, Inc. v. Amazon.com, 508 F.3d 1146, 1160–61 (9th Cir. 2007).

166. 17 U.S.C. § 106(4).

167. John Bowe, The Copyright Enforcers, N.Y. TIMES, Aug. 8, 2010, §6 (Magazine), at 38. [BB 16.5(a)]

168. Id.

169. See, e.g., Twentieth Century Music Corp. v. Aiken, 422 U.S. 151 (1975); Edison Stores v. BMI, 954 F.2d 1419 (8th Cir. 1992).

170. Pub. L. 105-298, § 201, 112 Stat. 2827 (1998).

171. 17 U.S.C. § 115.

172. David Oxenford, Steps to Legal Streaming (Aug. 2010), available at http://www.broadcastlawblog.com.

173. 17 U.S.C. § 101.

174. 17 U.S.C. § 102(a)(7).

175. Capitol Records, Inc. v. Mercury Records Corp., 221 F.2d 657, 664 (2d Cir. 1955) (L. Hand, J., dissenting).

176. 17 U.S.C. § 114(b).

177. See, e.g., Lieb v. Topstone Indus., Inc., 788 F.2d 151, 153 (3d Cir. 1986).

178. 17 U.S.C. § 114(j)(13); see Arista Records, LLC v. Launch Media, Inc., 578 F.3d 148 (2d Cir. 2009), cert. denied, 559 U.S. 929 (2010).

179. See Oxenford, supra note 166.

180. Bridgeport Music, Inc. v. Dimension Films, 410 F.3d 792 (6th Cir. 2005).

181. Newton v. Diamond, 388 F.3d 1189 (9th Cir. 2004), cert. denied, 545 U.S. 1114 (2005).

182. See Saregama India Ltd. v. Mosley, 687 F. Supp. 2d 1325, 1339 (S.D. Fla. 2009), citing Leigh v. Warner Bros., Inc, 212 F.3d 1210, 1214 (11th Cir. 2000).

183. See, e.g., Scott T. Okamoto, Comment: Musical Sound Recordings as Works Made for Hire: Money for Nothing and Tracks for Free, 37 U.S.F.L. REV. 783 (2003).

184. Phillip W. Hall, Jr., Smells Like Slavery: Unconscionability in Recording Industry Contracts, 25 HASTINGS COMM. & ENT. L.J. 189, 190 (2002).

185. 18 U.S.C. § 2319A. See United States v. Moghadam, 175 F.3d 1269 (11th Cir. 1999).

186. 17 U.S.C. § 1101.

187. Sound Recording Amendment, Pub. L. 92-140, 85 Stat. 391 (1971).

188. See White-Smith Music Publ'g Co. v. Apollo Co., 209 U.S. 1 (1908).

189. 17 U.S.C. § 106(1), (2), (3).

190. A&M Records, Inc. v. Napster, Inc. 239 F.3d 1004 (9th Cir. 2001).

191. Capitol Records, Inc. v. Thomas-Rasset, 692 F.3d 899 (8th Cir. 2012), cert. denied, 133 S. Ct. 1584 (2013).

192. Sony BMG Music Ent. v. Tenenbaum, 660 F.3d 487 (1st Cir. 2011), cert. denied, 132 S. Ct. 2431 (2012).

193. Metro-Goldwyn-Mayer Studios, Inc. v. Grokster Ltd., 545 U.S. 913 (2005).

194. Id. at 922, 940.

195. Sony Corp. of America v. Universal City Studios, Inc. 464 U.S. 417 (1984).

196. Adrianne Jeffries, "Education" over Lawsuits, VERGE (Feb. 25, 2013), available at http://www.theverge.com/2013/2/25/4026194/infamous-six-strike-anti-piracy-program-barks-harder-than-it-bites.

197. 15 U.S.C. § 1127.

198. Qualitex Co. v. Jacobson Products Co., Inc., 514 U.S. 159 (1995).

199. Ride the Ducks, LLC v. Duck Boat Tours, Inc., 2005 U.S. Dist. LEXIS 4422 (E.D. Pa. Mar. 21, 2005), aff'd, 138 Fed. Appx. 431 (3d Cir. Pa. 2005).

200. See ANNE GILSON LALONDE, GILSON ON TRADEMARKS § 10A.09[5] (2013).

201. 15 U.S.C. § 1051 et seq.

202. 15 U.S.C. § 1125(a).

203. 15 U.S.C. § 1052.

204. PACCAR, Inc. v. TeleScanTechnologies, L.L.C., 319 F.3d 243 (6th Cir. 2003).

205. Bebe Stores, Inc. v. May Dep't Stores Int'l, 313 F.3d 1056 (8th Cir. 2002) (per curiam).

206. Standard Brands, Inc. v. Smidler, 151 F.2d 34 (2d Cir. 1945).

207. *See* Anne Gilson LaLonde, Gilson on Trademarks § 2.04[1] (2013).

208. Sara Lee Corp. v. Kayser-Roth Corp., 81 F.3d 455, 464 (4th Cir. 1996).

209. Circuit City Stores Inc. v. CarMax Inc., 165 F.3d 1047 (6th Cir. 1999).

210. Japan Telecom, Inc. v. Japan Telecom of America, Inc., 287 F.3d 866, 873 (9th Cir. 2002).

211. Boston Beer Co., L.P. v. Slesar Bros. Brewing Co., Inc., 9 F.3d 175 (1st Cir. 1993).

212. Hamilton-Brown Shoe Co. v. Wolf Bros. & Co., 240 U.S. 251 (1918).

213. M. Fabrikant & Sons, Ltd. v. Fabrikant Fine Diamonds, Inc., 17 F. Supp. 2d 249 (S.D.N.Y. 1998).

214. Anne Gilson LaLonde, Gilson on Trademarks § 2.08[1] (2013).

215. Harley-Davidson, Inc. v. Grottanelli, 164 F.3d 806 (2d Cir. 1999).

216. Small Bus. Assistance Corp. v. Clear Channel Broad., Inc., 210 F.3d 278 (5th Cir. 2000).

217. *See* Sung In, Note: *Death of a Trademark: Genericide in the Digital Age*, 21 Rev. Litig. 159 (2002).

218. See, e.g., George K. Chamberlin, *Annotation: When Does Product Mark Become Generic Term or "Common Descriptive Name" So as to Warrant Cancellation of Registration of Mark*, 55 A.L.R. Fed. 241 (2004).

219. *See* Anne Gilson LaLonde, Gilson on Trademarks § 2.02[6] (2013).

220. 15 U.S.C. § 1115(a), (b).

221. 15 U.S.C. § 1051.

222. 15 U.S.C. §§ 1052, 1072, 1115.

223. 15 U.S.C. § 1091.

224. 15 U.S.C. § 1058.

225. 15 U.S.C. § 1059.

226. Pub. L. 106-113, 113 Stat. 1536.

227. E. & J. Gallo Winery v. Spider Webs Ltd., 286 F.3d 270 (5th Cir. 2002).

228. Brookfield Communications, Inc. v. West Coast Ent. Corp., 174 F.3d 1036 (9th Cir. 1999).

229. Ty, Inc. v. Perryman, 306 F.3d 509, 513 (7th Cir. 2002), *cert. denied,* 538 U.S. 971 (2003).

230. *See, e.g.,* Triangle Publ'ns v. Knight-Ridder Newspaper, Inc., 626 F.2d 1171 (5th Cir. 1978).

231. Deere & Co. v. MTD Products, Inc., 41 F.3d 39 (2d Cir. 1994).

232. 15 U.S.C. § 1114(1).

233. Facebook, Inc. v. Teachbook.com LLC, 819 F. Supp. 2d 764, 781 (N.D. Ill. 2011).

234. *See* Applicant of E. I. DuPont de Nemours & Co., 476 F.2d 1357, 1361 (C.C.P.A. 1973).

235. 15 U.S.C. §§ 1125(c), 1127.

236. Anne Gilson LaLonde, Gilson on Trademarks § 5A.01[5], [6] (2013).

237. Moseley v. V Secret Catalogue, Inc., 537 U.S. 418 (2003).

238. *Id.* at 434.

239. 15 U.S.C. § 1115(b).

240. 15 U.S.C. § 115(b)(4).

241. 1–800 Contacts, Inc. v. WhenU.com, Inc., 414 F.3d 400 (2d Cir.), *cert. denied*, 546 U.S. 1033 (2005).

242. New Kids on the Block v. News American Publ'g, Inc., 971 F.2d 302 (9th Cir. 1992).

243. 15 U.S.C. § 1125(c)(3).

Chapter 14

Advertising

1. Va. State Bd. of Pharmacy v. Va. Citizens Consumer Council, 425 U.S. 748, 762, 763, 764 (1976).

2. 131 S. Ct. 2653 (2011).

3. *See, e.g.,* Alexander Meiklejohn, Free Speech and Its Relation to Self-Government (1948).

4. Valentine v. Chrestensen, 316 U.S. 52, 54 (1942).

5. *Id.*

6. New York Times v. Sullivan, 376 U.S. 254, 266 (1964).

7. *Id.*

8. Pittsburgh Press Co. v. Pittsburgh Comm'n on Human Relations, 413 U.S. 376, 389 (1973).

9. Bigelow v. Virginia, 421 U.S. 809 (1975).

10. Roe v. Wade, 412 U.S. 113 (1973).

11. *Bigelow*, 421 U.S. at 809, 822.

12. *Id.* at 817.

13. *Id.* at 820.

14. Va Bd. of Pharmacy v. Va. Citizens Consumer Council, Inc., 425 U.S. 748 (1976).

15. 447 U.S. 557 (1980).

16. 492 U.S. 469 (1989).

17. *Id.* at 480.

18. Rubin v. Coors Brewing Co., 514 U.S. 476, 490 (1995).

19. 44 Liquormart, Inc. v. Rhode Island, 517 U.S. 484, 507 (1996).

20. Capital Broad. Co. v. Mitchell, 333 F. Supp. 582 (D.D.C. 1971).

21. Lorillard Tobacco Co. v. Reilly, 533 U.S. 525, 569 (2001).

22. *Id.* at 558.

23. Coyne Beahm, Inc. v. FDA, 966 F. Supp. 1374 (M.D.N.C. 1997).

24. Steven Reinberg, *U.S. Abandons Effort to Place Graphic Labeling on Cigarettes*, HEALTHDAY (Mar. 20, 2013), *available at* http://health.usnews.com.

25. Discount Tobacco City & Lottery Co. v. United States, 674 F.3d 509 (6th Cir. 2012); *contra* R.J. Reynolds Tobacco Co. v. Food & Drug Admin., 696 F.3d 1205 (D.C. Cir. 2012); *cert. den'd* (2013).

26. 94th St. Grocery Corp. v. New York City Bd. of Health, 685 F.3d 174 (2nd Cir. 2012).

27. Stephanie Strom, *U.S. Judge Rejects Gruesome Cigarette Labels*, N.Y. TIMES (Feb. 29, 2012), *available at* http://www.nytimes.com.

28. Mark Bittman, *The Right to Sell Kids Junk* (Mar. 27, 2012), *available at* http://markbittman.com.

29. United States v. Caronia, 703 F.3d 149 (2d Cir. 2012).

30. Family Smoking Prevention and Tobacco Control Act (FSPTCA), Pub. L. No. 111-31, 123 Stat. 1776 (2009).

31. Steven Reinberg, *U.S. Abandons Effort to Place Graphic Labeling on Cigarettes* HEALTHDAY(Mar. 20, 2013), *available at* http://health.usnews.com.

32. United States v. Edge Broad., 509 U.S. 418 (1993).

33. *Id.* at 428.

34. *Id.* at 441.

35. Greater New Orleans Broad. Ass'n., Inc. v. United States, 527 U.S. 173 (1999).

36. *Id.*

37. Sorrell v. IMS Health Inc., 131 S. Ct. 2653 (2011).

38. Vt. Stat. Ann., Tit. 18, § 4631 (Supp. 2010).

39. *Sorrell*, 131 S. Ct. at 2672.

40. *Id.*

41. *Id.* at 2685.

42. *One Year Later: The Consequences of Sorrell v. IMS Health Inc.*, JUSTICE WATCH (July 2, 2012), *available at* http://afjjusticewatch.blogspot.com.

43. *Id.*

44. *Id.*

45. Lyle Denniston, *Like Ships Passing in the Night . . . ,* COMMENT. & ANALYSIS (JUNE 23, 2011), *available at* http://www.scotusblog.com.

46. *See, e.g.,* Bates v. State Bar of Ariz., 433 U.S. 350 (1977). "We recognize, of course, and commend the spirit of public service with which the profession of law is practiced and to which it is dedicated. The present Members of this Court, licensed attorneys all, could not feel otherwise and we would have reason to pause if we felt that our decision today would undercut that spirit." *Id.* at 368.

47. *Id.*

48. First Nat'l Bank of Boston v. Bellotti, 435 U.S. 765 (1978).

49. *See, e.g.,* FEC v. Nat'l Right to Work Comm., 459 U.S. 197 (1982); FEC v. Nat'l Conservative Political Action Comm., 470 U.S. 480 (1985); FEC v. Massachusetts Citizens for Life, Inc., 479 U.S. 238 (1986); and Austin v. Mich. State Chamber of Commerce, 494 U.S. 652 (1990).

50. Nike, Inc. v. Kasky, 539 U.S. 654 (2003).

51. Kasky v. Nike, Inc., 45 P.3d 243, 258 (Cal. 2002).

52. *Id.* at 263.

53. 130 S. Ct. 876 (2010).

54. Keenan Steiner, *With Court Case Looming, FED Has Trouble Deciding How to Say It Can't Decide*, SUNLIGHT FOUND. REPORTING GROUP (Mar. 8, 2013), *available at* http://reporting.sunlightfoundation.com.

55. Van Hollen v. FEC, 851 F. Supp. 2d 69 (D.D.C. Mar. 30, 2012); Ctr. for Individual Freedom v. Van Hollen, 694 F.3d 108 (D.C. Cir. Sept. 18, 2012).

56. Van Hollen v. FEC (May 1, 2013), *available at* http://www.fec.gov.

57. 15 U.S.C. 1125, § 43 (a)(1)(A)(B).

58. U-Haul Int'l, Inc. v. Jartran, Inc., 793 F.2d 1034 (9th Cir. 1986).

59. The Division of Advertising Practices (n.d.), *available at* http://consumerprotection.uslegal.com.

60. Roscoe B. Starek, III, *Myths and Half-Truths About Deceptive Advertising,* address to the National Infomercial Marketing Association (Oct. 15, 1996), *available at* http://www.ftc.gov/speeches/starek/nima96d4.htm.

61. *Id.*

62. *Three Home Loan Advertisers Settle FTC Charges; Failed to Disclose Key Loan Terms in Ads* (Jan. 8, 2009), *available at* http://www.ftc.gov/opa/2009/01/anm.shtm.

63. *Id.*

64. *Rite Aid Settles FTC Charges That It Failed to Protect Medical and Financial Privacy of Customers and Employees* (July 27, 2010), *available at* http://www.ftc.gov/opa/2010/07/riteaid.shtm.

65. U.S. v. Williams, Co., 498 F.2d 414 (2d Cir. 1975).

66. *Three Cortislim Defendants to Give Up $4.5 Million in Cash and Other Assets* (Sept. 21, 2005), *available at* http://www.ftc.gov/opa/2005/09/windowrock.shtm.

67. Lesley Fair, *Substantiation: The Science of Compliance* (n.d.), *available at* http://business.ftc.gov/documents/substantiation-science-compliance.

68. In the Matter of Tropicana Products, Inc., Federal Trade Commission Complaint, Docket No. C-4145 (2005), *available at* http://www.ftc.gov/os/caselist/0423154/050825comp0423154.pdf.

69. Warner-Lambert Co. v. FTC, 562 F.2d 749 (1977), *cert. denied,* 435 U.S. 950 (1978).

70. *Id.* at 762.

71. *Id.* at 764.

72. Michael B. Mazis, *FTC v. Novartis: The Return of Corrective Advertising?* 20 J. Pub. Pol'y & Market'g 114 (2001).

73. *Id.*

74. Novartis Corp., FTC Mod. Order, Docket 9279 (July 2, 1999), *available at* http://ftc.gov/os/adjpro/d9279/omodpfradamafs990702.pdf.

75. *FTC Charges Marketers with Making Unsubstantiated Claims That They Could Eliminate Consumers' Debt* (Dec. 2, 2010), *available at* http://www.ftc.gov/opa/2010/12/ffdc.shtm.

76. Family Smoking Prevention and Tobacco Control Act (FSPTCA), Pub. L. No. 111-31, 123 Stat. 1776 (2009).

77. *Enforcement Action Plan for Promotion and Advertising Restrictions* (Oct. 2010), *available at* http://www.fda.govdownloads/TobaccoProducts/GuidanceComplianceRegulatoryInformation/UCM227882.pdf.

78. United States v. Caronia, 703 F.3d 149 (2d Cir. 2012).

79. FTC v. Corzine, No. Civ.-S-94–1446 (E.D. Ca. 1994).

80. Jessica Guynn, *FTC Calls on Online Ad Industry to Agree on Do-not-Track Standard,* L.A. Times (Apr. 17, 2013), *available at* http://www.latimes.com/business/technology/la-fi-tn-ftc-online-ad-industry-do-not-track-20130417,0,5397711.story.

81. *FTC Testifies on Do Not Track Legislation* (Dec. 2, 2010), *available at* http://www.ftc.gov/opa/2010/12/dnttestimony.shtm).

82. *Microsoft Adds "Do Not Track" Option to Internet Explorer 9,* NPR (Dec. 8, 2010), *available at* http://www.npr.org/blogs/alltechconsidered/2010/12/09/131914019/microsoft-ads-do-not-track-option-to-internet-explorer-9.

83. 15 U.S.C. §§ 7701–7713 (2004).

84. *FTC Approves New Rule Provision Under the CAN-SPAM Act* (May 12, 2008), *available at* http://www.ftc.govopa/2008/05/canspam.shtm.

85. These states are Alaska, Arizona, Arkansas, California, Colorado, Connecticut, Delaware, Florida, Georgia, Idaho, Illinois, Indiana, Iowa, Kansas, Louisiana, Maine, Maryland, Michigan, Minnesota, Missouri, Nevada, New Mexico, North Carolina, North Dakota, Ohio, Oklahoma, Pennsylvania, Rhode Island, South Dakota, Tennessee, Texas, Utah, Virginia, Washington, West Virginia, Wisconsin and Wyoming.

86. Va. Code Ann. § 18.2–152.3:1.

87. *See Virginia: Spam Law Struck Down on Grounds of Free Speech,* N.Y. Times, Sept. 13, 2008, at A17.

88. Jaynes v. Commonwealth of Virginia, 276 Va. 443, 464 (2008), *cert. denied,* 129 S. Ct. 1670 (2009).

89. Virginia v. Jaynes, 129 S. Ct. 1670 (2009).

90. 47 U.S.C. § 227(b)(1)(A) (1991).

91. Nack v. Walburg, No. 11–1460 (8th Cir. May 21, 2013) *available* at http://law.justia.com/cases/federal/appellate-courts/ca8/11–1460/11–1460–2013–05–21.html.

Glossary

absolute privilege A complete exemption from liability for the speaking or publishing of defamatory words of and concerning another because the statement was made within the performance of duty such as in judicial or political contexts.

actual malice In libel law, a statement made knowing it is false or with reckless disregard for its truth.

ad hoc balancing Making decisions according to the specific facts of the case under review rather than more general principles.

administrative law The orders, rules and regulations promulgated by executive branch administrative agencies to carry out their delegated duties.

admonitions Judges' instructions to jurors warning them to avoid potentially prejudicial communications.

advisory opinion A Federal Trade Commission measure that offers formal guidance on whether a specific advertisement may be false or misleading and how to correct it.

affirm To ratify, uphold or approve a lower court ruling.

all-purpose public figure In libel law, a person who occupies a position of such persuasive power and influence as to be deemed a public figure for all purposes. Public figure libel plaintiffs are required to prove actual malice.

amicus brief A submission to the court from an amicus curiae, or "friend of the court," an interested individual or organization who is not a party in the case.

amicus curiae, or "friend of the court" An interested individual or organization that is not a party in the case.

appellant The party making the appeal; also called the petitioner.

appellee The party against whom an appeal is made.

appropriation Using a person's name, picture, likeness, voice or identity for commercial or trade purposes without permission.

artistic relevance test A test to determine whether the use of a celebrity's name, picture, likeness, voice or identity is relevant to a disputed work's artistic purpose. It is used in cases regarding the infringement of a celebrity's right of publicity.

as applied A phrase referring to interpretation of a statute on the basis of actual effects on the parties.

B

Berne Convention The primary international copyright treaty adopted by many countries in 1886 but by the United States only in 1988.

black-letter law Formally enacted, written law that is available in legal reporters or other documents.

bootstrapping In libel law, the forbidden practice of a defendant claiming that the plaintiff is a public figure solely on the basis of the statement that is the reason for the lawsuit.

burden of proof The requirement for a party to a case to demonstrate one or more claims by the presentation of evidence. In libel law, for example, the plaintiff has the burden of proof.

C

categorical balancing A judge's or court's practice of deciding cases by weighing different broad categories, such as political speech, against other categories of interests, such as privacy, to create rules that may be applied in later cases with similar facts.

cease and desist order An administrative agency order prohibiting a person or business from continuing a particular course of conduct.

child pornography Any image showing children in sexual or sexually explicit situations.

chilling effect   The discouragement of a constitutional right, especially free speech, by any practice that creates uncertainty about the proper exercise of that right.

civil contempt   Acts, generally outside the courtroom, that defy court orders or obstruct court proceedings, such as failure to comply with a subpoena to appear in court; sometimes called "indirect contempt."

clear and present danger   Doctrine establishing that restrictions on First Amendment rights will be upheld if they are necessary to prevent an extremely serious and imminent harm.

commercialization   The appropriation tort used to protect people who want privacy.

common law   Unwritten, judge-made law consisting of rules and principles developed through custom and precedent.

Communications Decency Act (CDA)   The part of the 1996 Telecommunications Act that largely attempted to regulate Internet content. The CDA was successfully challenged in *Reno v. ACLU* (1997).

compelling interest   A government interest of the highest order, an interest the government is required to protect.

concurring opinion   A separate opinion of a minority of the court or a single judge or justice agreeing with the majority opinion but applying different reasoning or legal principles.

conditional (or qualified) privilege   An exemption from liability for repeating defamatory words of and concerning another because the original statement was made within the performance of duty such as in judicial or political contexts; usually claimed by journalists who report statements made in absolutely privileged situations; this privilege is conditional (or qualified) on the premise that the reporting is fair and accurate.

consent order   An agreement between the Federal Trade Commission and an advertiser stipulating the terms that must be followed to address problematic advertising; also called a consent agreement.

constitutional law   The set of laws that establish the nature, functions and limits of government.

contempt of court   Any act that is judged to hinder or obstruct a court in its administration of justice. For example, journalists may be cited for contempt of court for refusing to disclose information.

content-based laws   Laws enacted because of the message, the subject matter or the ideas expressed in the regulated speech.

content-neutral laws   Laws that incidentally and unintentionally affect speech as they advance other important government interests.

continuance   Postponement of a trial to a later time.

copyright   An exclusive legal right used to protect intellectual creations from unauthorized use.

corrective advertising   The Federal Trade Commission power to require an advertiser to advertise or otherwise distribute information to correct false or misleading advertisement claims.

criminal contempt   Conduct in or near a court that willfully disregards, disobeys or interferes with the court's authority; sometimes called "direct contempt."

D

damages   Monetary compensation that may be recovered in court by any person who has suffered loss or injury. Damages may be compensatory for actual loss or punitive as punishment for outrageous conduct.

defamation   A false communication that harms another's reputation and subjects him or her to ridicule and scorn; incorporates both libel and slander.

defendant   The party accused of violating a law, or the party being sued in a civil lawsuit.

deference   A policy by which courts give weight to the judgment of expert administrative agencies or of legislative policies and strategies.

demurrer   A request that a court dismiss a case on the grounds that although the claims are true they are insufficient to warrant a judgment against the defendant.

de novo   Literally, "anew" or "over again." On appeal, the court may review the facts de novo rather than simply reviewing the legal posture and process of the case.

deposition   Testimony by a witness conducted outside a courtroom and intended to be used in preparation for trial.

designated public forum   Government spaces or buildings that are available for public use (within limits).

discovery   The pretrial process of gathering evidence and facts. The word also may refer to the specific items of evidence that are uncovered.

discretion   The authority to determine the proper outcome.

dissenting opinion   A separate opinion of a minority of the court or a single judge or justice disagreeing with the result reached by the majority and challenging the majority's reasoning or legal basis of the decision.

distinguish from precedent   To justify an outcome in a case by asserting that differences between that case and preceding cases outweigh any similarities.

doctrines   Principles or theories of law (e.g., the doctrine of content neutrality).

Driver's Privacy Protection Act   Federal legislation that prohibits states from disclosing personal information that drivers submit in order to obtain drivers' licenses.

due process   Fair legal proceedings. Due process is guaranteed by the Fifth and Fourteenth Amendments to the U.S. Constitution.

E

Electronic Freedom of Information Act (EFOIA)   A 1996 amendment to the Freedom of Information Act (FOIA) that updates the act by including electronically stored information and subjecting it to the FOIA's provisions.

emotional distress   Serious mental anguish.

en banc   Literally, "on the bench" but now meaning "in full court." The judges of a circuit court of appeals will sit en banc to decide important or controversial cases.

equity law   Law created by judges to apply general principles of ethics and fairness, rather than specific legal rules, to determine the proper remedy for legal harm.

establishment clause   The portion of the First Amendment that prohibits government from setting up an official religion or passing laws that favor a specific religious doctrine.

executive orders   Orders from a government executive, such as the president, a governor or a mayor, that have the force of law.

experience and logic test   A doctrine that evaluates both the history and the current role the openness of a specific process plays in assuring its credibility and to determine whether it is presumptively open.

F

facial challenges   A broad legal claim based on the argument that the challenged law or government policy can never operate in compliance with the Constitution.

facial meaning   The surface, apparent or obvious meaning of a legal text.

fact finder   In a trial, a judge or the jury determining which facts presented in evidence are accurate.

fair comment and criticism   A common law privilege that protects critics from lawsuits brought by individuals in the public eye.

fair report privilege   A privilege claimed by journalists who report events on the basis of official records. The report must fairly and accurately reflect the content of the records; this is the condition that sometimes leads to this privilege being called "conditional privilege."

fair use   A test courts use to determine whether using another's copyrighted material without permission is fair or an infringement. Also used in trademark infringement cases.

false light   A privacy tort that involves making a person seem in the public eye to be someone he or she is not. Several states do not allow false light suits.

Family Educational Rights and Privacy Act (FERPA)   A federal law that protects the privacy of student education records. The law applies to all schools that receive funds under an applicable program of the U.S. Department of Education; FERPA gives parents certain rights with respect to their children's school records; these rights transfer to the student when he or she reaches the age of 18 or attends a school beyond the high school level.

Federal Communications Commission (FCC)   An independent U.S. government agency, directly responsible to Congress, charged with regulating interstate and international communications by radio, television, wire, satellite and cable. The FCC was established by the Communications Act of 1934; its jurisdiction covers the 50 states, the District of Columbia and U.S. possessions.

Federal Radio Commission (FRC)   A federal agency established by the Federal Radio Act in 1927 to oversee radio broadcasting. The FRC was succeeded by the Federal Communications Commission in 1934.

Federal Trade Commission (FTC) A federal agency created in 1914. Its purpose is to promote free and fair competition in interstate commerce; this includes preventing false and misleading advertising.

federalism A principle according to which the states are related to yet independent of each other and are related to yet independent of the federal government.

fiduciary relationship A legal duty or responsibility one party owes to another when the parties are in certain relationships with each other.

fighting words Words not protected by the First Amendment because they cause immediate harm or illegal acts.

first-sale doctrine Once a copyright owner sells a copy of a work, the new owner may possess, transfer or otherwise dispose of that copy without the copyright owner's permission.

for-cause challenge In the context of jury selection, the ability of attorneys to remove a potential juror for a reason the law finds sufficient, as opposed to a peremptory challenge.

forum shopping A plaintiff choosing a court in which to sue because he or she believes the court will rule in the plaintiff's favor.

franchise A contract or agreement between a government, usually a city, and a cable system operator.

franchise fees The charges cable companies pay to franchising authorities for the right to use public rights-of-way.

franchising authority The governmental unit granting a franchise to a cable system operator; usually a city, but may also be a state or county.

Freedom of Information Act (FOIA) The 1966 act that requires records held by federal government agencies to be made available to the public, provided that the information sought does not fall within one of nine exempted categories.

G

gag orders A nonlegal term used to describe court orders that prohibit publication or discussion of specific materials.

generally applicable law A law that is enforced evenly, across the board. Within First Amendment contexts, it is the idea that the freedom of the press clause does not exempt journalists and news organizations from obeying laws.

Government in the Sunshine Act Sometimes referred to as the Federal Open Meetings Law, an act passed in 1976 that mandates that meetings of federal government agencies be open to the public unless all or some part of a meeting is exempted according to exceptions outlined in the law.

grand jury A group summoned to hear the state's evidence in criminal cases and decide whether a crime was committed and whether charges should be filed; grand juries do not determine guilt. A grand jury may be convened on the county, state or federal level; with 12 to 23 members, grand juries are usually larger than trial juries.

H

habeas corpus A court order requiring the government to present a detained person to the court and to show legal grounds for the person's detention.

hate speech A category of speech that includes name-calling and pointed criticism that demeans others on the basis of race, color, gender, ethnicity, religion, national origin, disability, intellect or the like.

Hicklin rule A rule taken from a mid-19th-century English case and used in the United States until the mid-20th century that defines material as obscene if it tends to corrupt children.

Health Insurance Portability and Accountability Act (HIPAA) A federal law protecting against health professionals and institutions revealing individuals' private medical records.

holding The decision or ruling of a court.

I

impanel To select and seat a jury.

important government interest An interest of the government that is substantial or significant (i.e., more than merely convenient or reasonable) but not compelling.

incorporation The Fourteenth Amendment concept that most of the Bill of Rights applies equally to the states.

indecency A narrow legal term referring to sexual expression inappropriate for children on broadcast radio and television.

industry guides In advertising, a Federal Trade Commission measure that outlines the FTC's policies concerning a particular category of product or service.

injunction   A court order prohibiting a person or organization from doing some specified act.

innocent construction   Allegedly libelous words that are capable of being interpreted, or construed, to have an innocent meaning are not libelous, so long as that interpretation is a reasonable one.

intellectual property law   The legal category including copyright, trademark and patent law.

intentional infliction of emotional distress   Extreme and outrageous intentional or reckless conduct causing plaintiffs severe emotional harm; public official and public figure plaintiff also must show actual malice on defendant's part.

intermediate scrutiny   A standard applied by the courts to the review of laws that implicate core constitutional values; also called heightened review.

intrusion upon seclusion   Physically or technologically disturbing another's reasonable expectation of privacy.

involuntary public figure   In libel law, a person who does not necessarily thrust himself or herself into public controversies voluntarily but is drawn into a given issue.

J

judicial review   The power of the courts to determine the meaning of the language of the Constitution and to assure that no laws violate constitutional dictates.

jurisdiction   The geographic or topical area of responsibility and authority of a court.

L

Lanham Act   A federal law that regulates the trademark registration process but that also contains a section permitting business competitors to sue one another for false advertising.

laws of general application   Laws such as tax and equal employment laws that fall within the express power of government. Laws of general application are generally reviewed under minimum scrutiny.

legislative history   Congressional reports and records containing discussions about proposed legislation.

libel per quod   A statement whose injurious nature requires proof.

libel per se   A statement whose injurious nature is apparent and requires no further proof.

libel-proof plaintiff   A plaintiff whose reputation is deemed to be so damaged already that additional false statements of and concerning him or her cannot cause further harm.

limited-purpose public figure   In libel law, those plaintiffs who have attained public figure status within a narrow set of circumstances by thrusting themselves to the forefront of particular public controversies in order to influence the resolution of the issues involved; this kind of public figure is more common than the all-purpose public figure.

litigated order   A Federal Trade Commission order filed in administrative court and enforceable by the courts whose violation can result in penalties, including fines of up to $10,000 per day.

lowest unit rate   The maximum rate a broadcaster or cable system may charge a politician for advertising time during the 45 days before primary elections and the 60 days before general elections.

M

mechanical license   Permission to record a composition.

memorandum order   An order announcing the vote of the Supreme Court without providing an opinion.

modify precedent   To change or revise rather than follow or reject precedent.

moot   Term used to describe a case in which the issues presented are no longer "live" or in which the matter in dispute has already been resolved; a case is not moot if it is susceptible to repetition but evades review.

moral rights   Under U.S. copyright law, the rights of certain artists—creators of paintings, drawings, prints, sculptures and art photographs—to require that their name be associated with their works, forbid others from claiming to be creators of the works and prevent intentional harm to or modification of a work that would harm the artist's reputation.

motion to dismiss   A request to a court for a complaint to be rejected because it does not state a claim that can be remedied by law or because it is legally lacking in some other way.

N

negligence   Generally, the failure to exercise reasonable or ordinary care. In libel law, negligence is usually the minimum level of fault a plaintiff must prove in order to receive damages.

negligent infliction of emotional distress   Owing a duty to a plaintiff, breaching that duty and causing the plaintiff severe emotional harm.

neutral reportage   In libel law, a defense accepted in some jurisdictions that says when an accusation is made by a responsible and prominent organization, reporting that accusation is protected by the First Amendment even when it turns out the accusation was false and libelous.

nonduplication rules   FCC regulations requiring cable systems not to carry certain programming that is available through local broadcast stations.

nonpublic forum   Government-held property that is not available for public speech and assembly purposes.

Notice of Proposed Rule Making   A notice issued by the FCC announcing that the commission is considering changing certain of its regulations or adopting new rules.

O

O'Brien test   A three-part test used to determine whether a content-neutral law is constitutional.

opinion letter   An informal Federal Trade Commission communication providing general advice about advertising techniques.

originalists   Supreme Court justices who interpret the Constitution according to the perceived intent of its framers.

original intent   The perceived intent of the framers of the First Amendment that guides contemporary First Amendment application and interpretation.

original jurisdiction   The authority to consider a case at its inception, as contrasted with appellate jurisdiction.

overbroad law   Violates the principles of precision and specificity in legislation.

overrule   To reverse the ruling of a lower court.

overturn precedent   To reject the fundamental premise of a precedent.

P

patently offensive   Term describing material with hard-core sexual conduct.

PEG access channels   Channels that cable systems set aside for public, educational and government use.

per curiam opinion   An unsigned opinion by the court as a whole.

peremptory challenge   During jury selection, a challenge in which an attorney rejects a juror without showing a reason. Attorneys have the right to eliminate a limited number of jurors through peremptory challenges.

plagiarism   Using another's work or ideas without attribution.

plaintiff   The party who files a complaint; the one who sues.

political questions   Questions the courts will not review because they either fall outside the jurisdiction of the court or are incapable of judicial resolution; an issue that can and should be handled more appropriately by another branch of government.

pornography   A vague—not legally precise—term for sexually oriented material.

precedent   Case judgment that establishes binding authority and guiding principles for cases to follow on closely analogous questions of law within the court's jurisdiction.

predominant use test   In a right-of-publicity lawsuit, a test to determine whether the defendant used the plaintiff's name or picture more for commercial purposes or protected expression.

prior restraint   Action taken by the government to prohibit publication of a specific document or text before it is distributed to the public; a policy that requires government approval before publication.

private facts   The tort under which media are sued for publishing highly embarrassing private information that is not newsworthy or lawfully obtained from a public record.

private figure   In libel law, a plaintiff who cannot be categorized as either a public figure or public official. Generally, a private figure is not required to prove actual malice in order to recover damages but merely negligence on the part of the defendant.

probable cause   The standard of evidence needed for an arrest or to issue a search warrant. More than mere suspicion, it is a showing through reasonably trustworthy information that a crime has been or is being committed.

promissory estoppel   A legal doctrine requiring liability when a clear and unambiguous promise is made and is relied on and injury results from the breaking of the promise.

proximate cause   Determining whether it is reasonable to conclude the defendant's actions led to the plaintiff's injury.

prurient interest   Lustful thoughts or sexual desires.

public domain The sphere that includes material not protected by copyright law and therefore available for use without the creator's permission.

public figure   In libel law, a plaintiff who is in the public spotlight, usually voluntarily, and must prove the defendant acted with actual malice in order to win damages.

public forum   Government property held for use by the public, usually for purposes of exercising rights of speech and assembly.

public record   A government record, particularly one that is publicly available.

puffery   Advertising that exaggerates the merits of products or services in such a way that no reasonable person would take the ad seriously. Usually, puffery is not illegal given that a reasonable person understands the claim is not to be taken literally.

Q

quash   To nullify or annul, as in quashing a subpoena.

R

radio frequencies   The part of the electromagnetic spectrum used to send information, such as voice and pictures.

rational review   A standard of judicial review that assumes the constitutionality of reasonable legislative or administrative enactments and applies minimum scrutiny to their review.

reasonable person   The law's version of an average person.

reckless   Word used to describe actions taken with no consideration of the legal harms that might result.

remand   To send a case back to a lower court for further action.

reporter's privilege   The concept that reporters can keep information such as source identity confidential. The idea is that the reporter–source relationship is similar to doctor–patient and lawyer–client relationships.

restraining order   A court order forbidding an individual or group of individuals from doing a specified act until a hearing can be conducted.

retraction statutes   In libel law, state laws that limit the damages a plaintiff may receive if the defendant had issued a retraction of the material at issue. Retraction statutes are meant to discourage the punishment of any good-faith effort of admitting a mistake.

retransmission consent   Part of the federal cable television law allowing broadcast television stations to negotiate.

ride-along   A term given to the practice of journalists and other private citizens accompanying government officials—usually those in law enforcement or other emergency response personnel—as they carry out their duties.

right of publicity   The appropriation tort protecting a celebrity's right to have his or her name, picture, likeness, voice and identity used for commercial or trade purposes only with permission.

rule of law   The framework of a society in which pre-established norms and procedures provide for consistent, neutral decision making.

S

safe harbor policy   An FCC policy designating 10 p.m. to 6 a.m. as a time when broadcast radio and television stations may air indecent material without violating federal law or FCC regulations.

search warrant   A written order issued by a judge, directed to a law enforcement officer, authorizing the search and seizure of any property for which there is reason to believe it will serve as evidence in a criminal investigation.

Sedition Act of 1798 Federal legislation under which anyone "opposing or resisting any law of the United States, or any act of the President of the United States" could be imprisoned for up to two years. The act also made it illegal to "write, print, utter, or publish" anything that criticized the president or Congress. The act ultimately was seen as a direct violation of the First Amendment and expired in 1801.

seditious libel Communication meant to incite people to change the government; criticism of the government.

sequestration The isolation of jurors to avoid prejudice from publicity in a sensational trial.

serious social value Material cannot be found obscene if it has serious literary, artistic, political or scientific value determined using national, not local, standards.

shield laws State laws that protect journalists from being found in contempt of court for refusing to reveal a source.

single-publication rule A rule that limits libel victims to only one cause of action even with multiple publications of the libel, common in the mass media and on websites.

slander per se A spoken statement whose injurious nature is apparent and requires no further proof.

SLAPP (strategic lawsuits against public participation) Lawsuits whose purpose is to harass critics into silence, often to suppress those critics' First Amendment rights.

sound-alike Someone whose voice sounds like another person's voice. Sound-alikes may not be used for commercial or trade purposes without permission or a disclaimer.

spectrum scarcity The limitation that arises because only a certain number of broadcast radio and television stations in a geographical area may use the spectrum without causing interference with other stations' signals. Spectrum scarcity is the primary reason courts give for allowing Congress and the FCC to regulate broadcasters.

standing The position of a plaintiff who has been injured or has been threatened with injury. No person is entitled to challenge the constitutionality of an ordinance or statute unless he or she has the required standing—that is, unless he or she had been affected by the ordinance or statute.

stare decisis Literally, "stand by the previous decision."

Statute of Anne The first copyright law, adopted in England in 1710.

statutory construction The review of statutes in which courts determine the meaning and application of statutes. Courts tend to engage in strict construction, which narrowly defines laws to their clear letter and intent.

statutory damages Damages specified in certain laws. Under these laws, copyright being an example, a judge may award statutory damages even if a plaintiff is unable to prove actual damages.

statutory law Written law formally enacted by city, county, state and federal legislative bodies.

strict liability Liability without fault; liability for any and all harms, foreseeable or unforeseen, which result from a product or an action.

strict scrutiny A test for determining the constitutionality of laws restricting speech, under which the government must show it employs the least restrictive means available to directly advance a compelling interest.

subpoena A command for someone to testify in court.

substantiation The authority of the Federal Trade Commission to demand that an advertiser prove its advertised claims.

summary judgment The quick resolution of a legal dispute in which a judge summarily decides certain points and issues a judgment dismissing the case.

summons A notice asking an individual to appear at a court. Potential jurors receive such a summons.

symbolic expression Action that warrants First Amendment protection because its primary purpose is to express ideas.

T

textualists Judges—in particular, Supreme Court justices—who rely exclusively on a careful reading of legal texts to determine the meaning of the law.

time/place/manner (TPM) laws A First Amendment concept that laws regulating the conditions of speech are more acceptable than those regulating content; also, the laws that regulate these conditions.

tort A private or civil wrong for which a court can provide remedy in the form of damages.

tortious newsgathering The use of reporting techniques that are wrongful and unlawful and for which the victim may obtain damages in court.

trademark A word, name, symbol or design used to identify a company's goods and distinguish them from similar products other companies make.

trade regulation rule A broadly worded statement by the Federal Trade Commission that outlines advertising requirements for a particular trade.

traditional public forum Lands designed for public use and historically used for public gathering, discussion and association (e.g., public streets, sidewalks and parks). Free speech is protected in these areas.

transformativeness test A test to determine whether a creator has transformed a person's name, picture, likeness, voice or identity for artistic purposes. If so, the person cannot win a right-of-publicity suit against the creator.

true threat Speech directed toward one or more specific individuals with the intent of causing listeners to fear for their safety.

U

underinclusive A First Amendment doctrine that disfavors narrow laws that target a subset of a recognized category for discriminatory treatment.

USA Patriot Act The Uniting and Strengthening America by Providing Appropriate Tools Required to Intercept and Obstruct Terrorism Act of 2001. Passed in the wake of the Sept. 11, 2001, attacks, the act was designed to give law enforcement agencies greater authority to combat terrorism.

V

vague laws Laws that either fail to define their terms or use such general language that neither citizens nor judges know with certainty what the laws permit or punish.

variable obscenity The concept that sexually oriented material would not meet the definition of obscenity if distributed to adults but would be found obscene if distributed to minors.

venire Literally, "to come" or "to appear"; the term used for the location from which a court draws its pool of potential jurors, who must then appear in court for voir dire., A change of venire means a change of the location from which potential jurors are drawn.

venue The locality of a lawsuit and of the court hearing the suit. Thus, a change of venue means a relocation of a trial.

viewpoint-based discrimination Government censorship or punishment of expression based on the ideas or attitudes expressed. Courts will apply a strict scrutiny test to determine whether the government acted constitutionally.

voir dire Literally, "to speak the truth"; the questioning of prospective jurors to assess their suitability.

voluntary compliance The general Federal Trade Commission practice to allow advertisers to follow FTC rules and correct violations before the commission takes action.

W

work made for hire Work created when working for another person or company. The copyright in a work made for hire belongs to the employer, not the creator.

Wiretap Act A federal law initially passed in 1968 to protect the privacy of phone calls and other oral conversations that makes it illegal to intercept, record, disseminate or use a private communication without one party's permission. The law allows the government to bring criminal charges and those whose privacy was violated to sue for civil damages.

writ of certiorari A petition for review by the Supreme Court of the United States; *certiorari* means "to be informed of."

Z

Zapple rule A political broadcasting rule that allows a candidate's supporters equal opportunity to use broadcast stations if the candidate's opponents' supporters use the stations.

Recommended Readings

1. The Rule of Law

Amar, Akhil Reed. America's Unwritten Constitution: The Precedents and Principles We Live By. New York: Basic Books (2012).

Bingham, Tom. The Rule of Law. New York & London: Penguin Global (2010).

Cass, Ronald A. The Rule of Law in America. Baltimore: Johns Hopkins University Press (2001).

Clouatre, Douglas. Presidents and Their Justices. Lanham, Md.: University Press of America (2011).

Nichols, John & Robert W. McChesney. Dollarocracy: How Money and the Media Election Complex Is Destroying America. New York: Nation Books (2013).

Raz, Joseph. The Authority of Law. New York: Oxford University Press (1979).

Scarry, Elaine. Rule of Law, Misrule of Men. Cambridge, Mass.: MIT Press (2010).

Tamanaha, Brian Z. Law as a Means to an End: Threat to the Rule of Law. New York: Cambridge University Press (2006).

Toobin, Jeffrey. The Nine: Inside the Secret World of the Supreme Court. New York: Doubleday (2007).

2. The First Amendment

Amar, Akhil Reed. The Bill of Rights: Creation and Reconstruction. New Haven, Conn.: Yale University Press (2000).

Barbas, Samantha. Creating the Public Forum, 44 AKRON L. REV. 809 (2011).

Bunker, Matthew D. *Originalism 2.0 Meets the First Amendment: The "New Originalism," Interpretive Methodology and Freedom of Expression,* 17 COMM. L. & POL'Y 329 (2012).

Chafee, Zechariah. Free Speech in the United States. Cambridge, Mass.: Harvard University Press (1941).

Fish, Stanley. There's No Such Thing as Free Speech, and It's a Good Thing, Too. New York: Oxford University Press (1994).

Pasley, Jeffrey L. "The Tyranny of Printers": Newspaper Politics in the Early American Republic. Charlottesville, Va.: University of Virginia Press (2001).

Redish, Martin. The Adversary First Amendment: Free Expression and the Foundations of American Democracy. Stanford, Cal.: Stanford University Press (2013).

Rudenstine, David. The Day the Presses Stopped: A History of the Pentagon Papers Case. Berkeley, Cal.: University of California Press (1996).

Sunstein, Cass R. A Constitution of Many Minds: Why the Founding Document Doesn't Mean What It Meant Before. Princeton, N.J.: Princeton University Press (2009).

3. Speech Distinctions

Abrams, Floyd. Friend of the Court: On the Front Lines with the First Amendment. New Haven, Conn.: Yale University Press (2013).

Bollinger, Lee C. & Geoffrey R. Stone (eds.). Eternally Vigilant: Free Speech in the Modern Era. Chicago: University of Chicago Press (2002).

Cohen-Almagor, Raphael. The Scope of Tolerance: Studies on the Costs of Free Expression and Freedom of the Press. New York: Routledge (2006).

Finan, Christopher M. From the Palmer Raids to the Patriot Act: A History of the Fight for Free Speech in America. Boston: Beacon Press (2007).

Freeberg, Ernest. Democracy's Prisoner: Eugene V. Debs, the Great War, and the Right to Dissent. Cambridge, Mass.: Harvard University Press (2008).

Lewis, Anthony. Freedom for the Thought That We Hate: A Biography of the First Amendment. New York: Basic Books (2010).

Martin, Robert W.T. Government by Dissent: Protest, Resistance and Radical Democratic Thought in the Early American Republic. New York: New York University Press (2013).

Shiell, Timothy. Campus Hate Speech on Trial. Lawrence, Kan.: University Press of Kansas (2d ed. 2009).

Stone, Geoffrey R. Perilous Times: Free Speech in Wartime from the Sedition Act of 1798 to the War on Terrorism. New York: W.W. Norton (2004).

4. Libel: The Plaintiff's Case

Bernstein Ellen., Libel Tourism's Final Boarding Call, 20 SETON HALL J. SPORTS & ENT. L. 205 (2010).

Forde, Kathy Roberts. Literary Journalism on Trial: *Masson v. New Yorker* and the First Amendment. Amherst, Mass.: University of Massachusetts Press (2008).

Lewis, Anthony. Make No Law: The *Sullivan* Case and the First Amendment. New York: Random House (1991).

McNamara, Lawrence. Reputation and Defamation. New York: Oxford University Press (2007).

Milo, Dario. Defamation and Freedom of Speech. New York: Oxford University Press (2008).

Sack, Robert D. Sack on Defamation: Libel, Slander, and Related Problems. New York: Practicing Law Institute (4th ed. 2010).

Schachter, Madeleine & Joel Kurtzberg. Law of Internet Speech. Durham, N.C.: Carolina Academic Press (3d ed. 2008).

Smolla, Rodney A. The Law of Defamation. St. Paul, Minn.: West Group (2d ed. 2010).

Solove, Daniel J. The Future of Reputation: Gossip, Rumor, and Privacy on the Internet. New Haven, Conn.: Yale University Press (2007).

5. Libel: Defenses and Privileges

Ehrenfeld, Rachel. *A Legal Thriller in London*, NEWSWEEK, June 7, 2010, at 12.

Elder, David A. Truth, *Accuracy and "Neutral Reportage": Beheading the Media Jabberwock's Attempts to Circumvent* New York Times v. Sullivan, 9 VAND. J. ENT. & TECH. L. 551 (2007).

Kirchmeier, Jeffrey L. *The Illusion of the Fact-Opinion Distinction in Defamation Law*, 39 CASE W. RES. 867 (1989).

Laidman, Dan. *When the Slander Is the Story: The Neutral Report Privilege in Theory and Practice*, 17 UCLA ENT. L. REV. 74 (2010).

Rothfeld, Charles. *The Surprising Case Against Punitive Damages in Libel Suits Against Public Figures*, 19 YALE L. & POL'Y REV. 165 (2000).

Sack, Robert D. *Protection of Opinion Under the First Amendment*, 100 COLUM. L. REV. 294 (2000).

6. Protecting Privacy

Cate, Fred H. The Privacy Problem: A Broader View of Information Privacy and the Costs and Consequences of Protecting It. Nashville, Tenn.: First Amendment Center (2003).

Friedman, Lawrence M. Guarding Life's Dark Secrets: Legal and Social Controls over Reputation, Propriety, and Privacy. Stanford, Cal.: Stanford University Press (2007).

Jasper, Margaret C. Privacy and the Internet: Your Expectations and Rights Under the Law. New York: Oxford University Press (2009).

Klosek, Jacqueline. The War on Privacy. Westport, Conn.: Praeger (2007).

Osorio, Andrew. Note, *Twilight: The Fading of False Light Invasion of Privacy*, 66 N.Y.U. ANN. SURV. AM. L. 173 (2010).

Rosen, Jeffrey. The Unwanted Gaze: The Destruction of Privacy in America. New York: Random House (2000).

Solove, Daniel J. Privacy, Information, and Technology. New York: Aspen Pub. (2009).

Solove, Daniel J. Understanding Privacy. Cambridge, Mass.: Harvard University Press (2008).

7. Emotional Distress and Physical Harm

Anderson, David A. *Incitement and Tort Law*, 37 WAKE FOREST L. REV. 957 (2002).

Cullen, Dave. Columbine. New York: Twelve (2009).

Hsiou, Melody. Comment: *Harsh Reality: When Producers and Networks Should Be Liable for Negligence and Intentional Infliction of Emotional Distress*, 23 SETON HALL J. SPORTS & ENT. L. 187 (2013).

Jaffe, Elizabeth M. *Sticks and Stones May Break My Bones but Extreme and Outrageous Conduct Will Never Hurt Me: The Demise of Intentional Infliction of Emotional Distress Claims in the Aftermath of Snyder v. Phelps,* 57 WAYNE L. REV. 473 (2011).

Kunich, John Charles. *Shock Torts Reloaded,* 6 APPALACHIAN J.L. 1 (2006).

Levinson, Rosalie Berger. *Targeted Hate Speech and the First Amendment: How the Supreme Court Should Have Decided Snyder,* 46 SUFFOLK U.L. REV. 45 (2013).

Smolla, Rodney. Deliberate Intent: A Lawyer Tells the True Story of Murder by the Book. New York: Crown Pub. (1999).

Smolla, Rodney. *Jerry Falwell v. Larry Flynt:* The First Amendment on Trial. New York: St. Martin's Press (1988).

Volokh, Eugene. *Freedom of Speech and the Intentional Infliction of Emotional Distress Tort,* 2010 CARDOZO L. REV. DE NOVO 300.

8. Newsgathering

Bean, Hamilton. Open Source Information and the Reshaping of U.S. Intelligence. Santa Barbara, Cal.: Praeger Pub. (2011).

Bezanson, Randall P. How Free Can the Press Be? Urbana, Ill.: University of Illinois Press (2003).

Birkinshaw, Patrick. Freedom of Information: The Law, the Practice, and the Ideal. New York: Cambridge University Press (4th ed. 2010).

Bishop, Cheryl Ann. Access to Information as a Human Right. El Paso, Tex.: LFB Scholarly Pub. (2012).

Cuillier, David & Charles N. Davis. The Art of Access: Strategies for Acquiring Public Records. Washington, D.C.: CQ Press (2011).

Jeffreys-Jones, Rhodri. In Spies We Trust: The Story of Western Intelligence. New York: Oxford University Press (2013).

Klosek, Jacqueline. The Right to Know: Your Guide to Using and Defending Freedom of Information Law in the United States. Santa Barbara, Cal.: Praeger/ABC-CLIO (2009).

Montgomery, Bruce P. The Bush-Cheney Administration's Assault on Open Government. Westport, Conn.: Praeger Pub. (2008).

Stefanick, Lorna. Controlling Knowledge: Freedom of Information and Privacy Protection in a Networked World. Vancouver, British Columbia: UBC Press (2011).

Stewart, Daxton R. *Let the Sunshine In, or Else: An Examination of the "Teeth" of State and Federal Open Meetings and Open Records Laws,* 15 COMM. L. & POL'Y 265 (2010).

9. Reporter's Privilege

Clark, Kellie C. & David Barnette. *The Application of the Reporter's Privilege and the Espionage Act to Wikileaks,* 37 DAYTON L. REV. 165 (2012).

Eliason, Randall D. *The Problems with the Reporter's Privilege,* 57 AM. U.L. REV. 1341 (2008).

Jones, RonNell Andersen. *Rethinking Reporter's Privilege,* 111 MICH. L. REV. 1221 (2013).

Kirtley, Jane E. *Mask, Shield, and Sword: Should the Journalist's Privilege Protect the Identity of Anonymous Posters to News Media Websites?,* 94 MINN. L. REV. 1478 (2010).

Pearlstine, Norman. Off the Record: The Press, the Government, and the War over Anonymous Sources. New York: Farrar, Straus and Giroux (2007).

Pracene, Ulan C. (ed.). Journalists, Shield Laws, and the First Amendment: Is the Fourth Estate Under Attack? New York: Novinka Books (2005).

Rudenstine, David. *A Reporter Keeping Confidences: More Important Than Ever,* 29 CARDOZO L. REV. 1431 (2008).

Toland, Carol J. Comment: Internet Journalists and the Reporter's Privilege: Providing Protection for Online Periodicals, 57 KAN. L. REV. 461 (2009).

Ugland, Erik. *The New Abridged Reporter's Privilege: Policies, Principles, and Pathological Perspectives,* 71 OHIO ST. L.J. 1 (2010).

U.S Senate. Reporters' Privilege Legislation: Preserving Effective Federal Law Enforcement. Washington, D.C. BiblioGov Project (2010).

10. The Media and the Courts

Alexander, S. L. Media and American Courts: A Reference Handbook. Santa Barbara, Cal.: ABC-CLIO (2004).

Bruschke, Jon & William E. Loges. Free Press vs. Fair Trials: Examining Publicity's Role in Trial Outcomes. New York: Routledge (2003).

Bybee, Keith (ed.). Bench Press: The Collision of Courts, Politics and the Media. Stanford, Cal.: Stanford University Press (2007).

Davis, Richard. Justices and Journalists: The U.S. Supreme Court and the Media. New York: Cambridge University Press (2011).

Fox, Richard & Robert W. Van Sickel. Tabloid Justice: Criminal Justice in an Age of Media Frenzy. Boulder, Colo.: L. Rienner (2001).

Giles, Robert & Robert W. Snyder (eds.). Covering the Courts: Free Press, Fair Trials & Journalistic Performance. New Brunswick, N.J.: Transaction Pub. (1999).

Phillipson, Gavin. Trial by Media: The Betrayal of the First Amendment's Purpose, 71 LAW & CONTEMP. PROB. 15 (2008).

Scherer, Mark R. Rights in Balance: Free Press, Fair Trial, and Nebraska Press Association v. Stuart. Lubbock, Tex.: Texas Tech University Press (2008).

Youm, Kyu Ho. Cameras in the Courtroom in the Twenty-First Century: The U.S. Supreme Court Learning From Abroad?, 2012 B.Y.U.L. REV. 1989 (2012).

11. Electronic Media Regulation

Black, Sharon K. Telecommunications Law in the Internet Age. San Francisco: Morgan Kaufmann Pub. (2002).

Carter, T. Barton, et al. The First Amendment and the Fifth Estate: Regulation of Electronic Mass Media. New York: Foundation Press (7th ed. 2008).

Creech, Kenneth. Electronic Media Law and Regulation. Boston: Focal Press (5th ed. 2007).

Dominick, Joseph R., et al. Broadcasting, Cable, the Internet, and Beyond: An Introduction to Modern Electronic Media. Boston: McGraw Hill (6th ed. 2008).

Lipschultz, Jeremy Harris. Free Expression in the Age of the Internet: Social and Legal Boundaries. Boulder, Colo.: Westview Press (2000).

Scott, Michael D. Scott on Multimedia Law. New York: Aspen Pub. (2008).

Slotten, Hugh Richard. Radio's Hidden Voice: The Origins of Public Broadcasting in the United States. Urbana, Ill.: University of Illinois Press (2009).

Sterling, Christopher N. & John Michael Kittross. Stay Tuned: A History of American Broadcasting. Mahwah, N.J.: Lawrence Erlbaum Associates (3d ed. 2002).

Travis, Hannibal. The FCC's New Theory of the First Amendment, 51 SANTA CLARA L. REV. 417 (2011).

12. Obscenity, Indecency and Violence

Collins, Ronald K.L. & David M. Skover. The Trials of Lenny Bruce: The Fall and Rise of an American Icon. Naperville, Ill.: Sourcebooks MediaFusion (2002).

Corcos, Christine A. George Carlin, Constitutional Law Scholar, 37 STETSON L. REV. 899 (2008).

Fairman, Christopher M. Fuck: Word Taboo and Protecting Our First Amendment Liberties. Naperville, Ill.: Sphinx Pub. (2009).

Heins, Marjorie. Not in Front of the Children: "Indecency," Censorship and the Innocence of Youth. New Brunswick, N.J.: Rutgers University Press (2007).

Jasper, Margaret C. The Law of Obscenity and Pornography. New York: Oxford University Press (2009).

Lambert, Josh Nathaniel. Unclean Lips: Jews, Obscenity, and American Culture. New York: New York University Press (2013).

Lipschultz, Jeremy Harris. Broadcast and Internet Indecency: Defining Free Speech. New York: Routledge/Taylor & Francis (2008).

MacKinnon, Catharine A. Women's Lives, Men's Laws. Cambridge, Mass.: Belknap Press of Harvard University Press (2005).

Potter, Rachel & David Bradshaw (eds.). Prudes on the Prowl: Fiction and Obscenity in England, 1850 to the Present Day. New York: Oxford University Press (2013).

Strub, Whitney. Obscenity Rules: Roth v. United States and the Long Struggle over Sexual Expression. Lawrence, Kan.: University Press of Kansas (2013).

Strub, Whitney. Perversion for Profit: The Politics of Pornography and the Rise of the New Right. New York: Columbia University Press (2013).

Wood, Janice Ruth. The Struggle for Free Speech in the United States, 1872–1915: Edward Bliss Foote, Edward Bond Foote, and Anti-Comstock Operations. New York: Routledge (2008).

13. Intellectual Property

Bently, Lionel, Uma Suthersanen & Paul Torremans (eds.). Global Copyright: Three Hundred Years Since the Statute of Anne, from 1709 to Cyberspace. Northampton, Mass.: Edward Elgar Pub. (2010).

Cvetkovski, Trajce. Copyright and Popular Media: Liberal Villains and Technological Change. Basingstoke, U.K.: Palgrave Macmillan (2013).

Fishman, Stephen. Copyright and the Public Domain. New York: Law Journal Press (2009).

Goldstein, Paul. Copyright's Highway. Stanford, Cal.: Stanford University Press (rev. ed. 2003).

Hilty, Reto M. & Nérisson, Sylvie. Balancing Copyright: A Survey of National Approaches. New York: Springer Pub. (2012).

Johns, Adrian. Piracy: The Intellectual Property Wars from Gutenberg to Gates. Chicago: University of Chicago Press (2009).

Krikorian, Gaëlle, & Amy Kapczynski, eds. Access to Knowledge in the Age of Intellectual Property. New York: Zone Books (2010).

Leaffer, Marshall A. Understanding Copyright Law. New Providence, N.J.: LexisNexis (5th ed. 2010).

Netanel, Neil. Copyright's Paradox. New York: Oxford University Press (2008).

Tehranian, John. Infringement Nation: Copyright 2.0 and You. New York: Oxford University Press (2011).

14. Advertising

Baker, C. Edwin. Nike v. Kasky and the Modern Commercial Speech Doctrine: Paternalism, Politics, and Citizen Freedom: The Commercial Speech Quandary in Nike, 54 CASE W. RES. 1161 (2004).

Bennigson, Tom. Nike Revisited: Can Commercial Corporations Engage in Non-Commercial Speech? 39 CONN. L. REV. 379 (2006).

Bhagwat, Ashutosh. A Brief History of the Commercial Speech Doctrine (With Some Implications for Tobacco Regulation), 2 HASTINGS SCI. & TECH. L.J. 103 (2010).

Fischette, Charles. A New Architecture of Commercial Speech Law, 31 HARV. J.L. & PUB. POL'Y 663 (2008).

Klasmeier, Coleen & Martin H. Redish. Off-Label Prescription Advertising, the FDA and the First Amendment: A Study in the Values of Commercial Speech Protection, 37 AM. J. L. AND MED. 315 (2011).

Kuhne, Cecil C. III. Testing the Outer Limits of Commercial Speech: Its First Amendment Implications, 23 REV. LITIGATION 607 (2004).

Moore, Roy L. Advertising and Public Relations Law. New York: Routledge (2011).

Ortiz, Nicholas A. Consumer Speech and the Constitutional Limits of FTC Regulations of "New Media," 2010 COLUM. BUS. L. REV. 936.

Piety, Tamarra R. Brandishing the First Amendment: Commercial Expression in America. Ann Arbor, Mich.: University of Michigan Press (2013).

Photo Credits

1. The Rule of Law

Page 2: © AP Photo/Steven Senne
Page 5: © iStockphoto.com/EdStock; © GL Archive/Alamy
Page 6: © Bill Losh/The Image Bank/Getty Images
Page 7: © SHANNON STAPLETON/Reuters/Corbis
Page 14: Justices Roberts, Thomas, Ginsburg, Breyer, Alito, Sotomayor, and Kagan: Steve Petteway, Collection of the Supreme Court of the United States
Page 18: Wikimedia Commons
Page 22: © AP Photo/The White House
Page 23: The National Archives
Page 28: © AP Photo/Carolyn Kaster, File

2. The First Amendment

Page 50: © EDUARDO MUNOZ/Reuters/Corbis
Page 52: ©AP Photo/Lefteris Pitarakis
Page 53: AP Photo/Charles Tasnadi, File; © Archive Pics/Alamy
Page 55: AP Photo/Dennis Cook
Page 59: © Rex Features via AP Images
Page 62: © AP Photo/Paul Sakuma
Page 66: AFP/Getty Images
Page 67: © AP Photo
Page 74: © Ann Heisenfelt/AP/Corbis
Page 79: © iStockphoto.com/RomanOkopny
Page 83: © Joseph Reid/Alamy

3. Speech Distinctions

Page 100: Getty Images
Page 103: © iStockphoto.com/CribbVisuals; Michael Ochs Archives/Getty Images
Page 105: © Reuters/CORBIS
Page 106: ©AP Photo/The Miami Herald, Michelle Kanaar
Page 107: {US-PD} Wikimedia Commons
Page 110: AP Photo/The Miami Herald, Michelle Kanaar

Page 116: © AP Photo/Mary Altaffer, File
Page 124: © Bettmann/CORBIS
Page 131: © ALEX GALLARDO/Reuters/Corbis
Page 133: Reprinted with permission by Evan Stichler

4. Libel: The Plaintiff's Case

Page 142: © Bettmann/CORBIS
Page 145: AP Photo/Haraz N. Ghanbari; © iStockphoto.com/pearleye
Page 146: Getty Images
Page 147: Reprinted with permission of ThreatenedGlobal Voicesonline.org
Page 149: NBCU Photo Bank via Getty Images
Page 154: Getty Images
Page 161: PA Photo/MJ Schear
Page 166: Originally published in the New York Times March 29, 1960
Page 169: Photo by Kim Komenich/Time Pictures/Getty Images
Page 173: Time & Life Pictures/Getty Images

5. Libel: Defenses and Privileges

Page 188: © iStockphoto.com/franckreporter
Page 191: © iStockphoto.com/jcarillet; US Department of Defense
Page 193: State Historical Society of Iowa, Iowa City—Ms178 Orville and Jane Rennie Collection
Page 194: Bloomberg via Getty Images
Page 199: © AP Photo/Henry Griffin
Page 201: Reprinted with permission of Trip Advisor, LLC
Page 207: Reprinted with permission of Rachel Ehrenfeld
Page 209: © Sam Sharpe/The Sharpe Image/Corbis

6. Protecting Privacy

Page 226: Colin Anderson

Page 229: © iStockphoto.com/danhowl; © Thomas J. O'Halloran, U.S. News & World Reports

Page 230: Reprinted with permission by Dow Jones and Company, Inc.

Page 231: © AP Photo/J. Scott Applewhite, File

Page 234: © iStockphoto.com/alexsl

Page 239: © AP Photo/Tina Fineberg

Page 246: Getty Images

Page 248: © Jeff Chiu/AP/Corbis

Page 249: Getty Images

Page 252: © Bettmann/CORBIS

Page 254: © William Philpott/Reuters/Corbis

Page 255: © AP Photo/Isaac Brekken, File

Page 256: Reprinted by permission of Jireh Publishing and Rock Rush, www.RickRushArt.com

7. Emotional Distress and Physical Harm

Page 284: © Martin H. Simon/Corbis

Page 287: Library of Congress Prints and Photographs Division Washington, D.C. 20540 USA

Page 290: NBC via Getty Images

Page 292: Getty Images

Page 293: © JASON DECROW/AP/Corbis

Page 296: Hustler magazine, LFP Publishing Group, LLC

Page 302: Getty Images

Page 308: © Ted Soqui/Corbis

8. Newsgathering

Page 324: BAVARIA.

Page 327: © iStockphoto.com/Fentino; Courtesy of JSC Digital Image Collection, NASA

Page 331: Getty Images

Page 334: © Bettmann/CORBIS

Page 338: © Kathy deWitt/Alamy

Page 349: © GARY CAMERON/Reuters/Corbis

Page 357: Memo excerpt from, "Interrogation of al Qaeda operative" by Jay S. Bybee, Assistant Attorney General, OLC to John Rizzo, Acting General Counsel of the Central Intelligence Agency. August 1, 2002. Can be found online at http://www.fas.org/irp/agency/doj/olc/zubaydah.pdf

Page 359: © iStockphoto.com/EdStock

Page 363: © Mike Stewart/Sygma/Corbis

Page 365: © AP Photo, File

Page 370: © iStockphoto.com/winhorse

9. Reporter's Privilege

Page 382: © AP Photo/Benjamin Sklar

Page 385: George Doyle/Stockbyte/Thinkstock; Kay Nietfeld/picture-alliance/dpa/AP Images

Page 386: © CORBIS

Page 392: Getty Images

10. The Media and the Courts

Page 418: © AP Photo/Keith Srakocic, Pool

Page 420: © AP Photo/Ferd Kaufman

Page 421: © ©iStockphoto.com/danhowl; © iStockphoto.com/MathieuViennet

Page 422: © AP Photo/Elise Amendola

Page 425: © imagebroker/Alamy

Page 430: © AP Photo/Janet Hamlin

Page 445: © AP Photo/J. Scott Applewhite

Page 446: © Justin Sullivan/Staff/Getty Imgaes News/Getty Images

Page 447: © www.CartoonStock.com

Page 449: © AP Photo/Janet Hamlin

Page 454: © AP Photo/ThoughtWorks, Pernille Ironside, File

11. Electronic Media Regulation

Page 474: © AP Photo/Susan Walsh

Page 476: © Hulton Archive/Stringer/Getty Images

Page 477: © iStockphoto.com/mjbs; Image reprinted by permission of Keith Greenhalgh

Page 479: © AFP/Getty Images

Page 480: © iStockphoto.com/alexsl

Page 483: Courtesy of the Advanced Light Source, Berkeley Lab

Page 487: © AP Photo/Romney Presidential Campaign

Page 490: © AP Photo/Dario Lopez-Mills

Page 492: © Tibrina Hobson/Contributor/Getty Images Entertainment/Getty Images

Page 494: © iStockphoto.com/becky rockwood

Page 498: © AP Photo/Kathleen Beall

Page 502: © iStockphoto.com/EdStock

Page 511: © Bloomberg/Contributor/Getty Images

12. Obscenity, Indecency and Violence

Page 526: © Michael Caulfield Archive/Wire Image/ Getty Images

Page 528: © Larry Lee Photography/CORBIS

Page 529: US Department of Defense

Page 531: © Bettmann/CORBIS

Page 536: © John Springer Collection/CORBIS

Page 542: The National Campaign to Prevent Teen and Unplanned Pregnancy

Page 547: © Deborah Feingold/Corbis

Page 549: © AP Photo/Ron Edmonds, File

Page 564: © AP Photo/Paul Sakuma

13. Intellectual Property

Page 576: © AFP/Getty Images

Page 579: © iStockphoto.com/LongHa2006; © iStockphoto .com/pearleye

Page 581: © Jo Yong hak/Reuters/Corbis

Page 583: © Bettmann/CORBIS

Page 595: © AF archive/Alamy

Page 597: © FADI ALASSAAD/X01928/Reuters/Corbis

Page 601: Harney v. Sony Pictures Television, Inc., 704 F.3d 173, 176 (1st Cir. 2013).

Page 605: © AF archive/Alamy

Page 607: © Jonathan Fickies/Bloomberg/Getty Images

Page 615: © iStockphoto.com/Martin Wahlborg

Page 618: © AP Photo/Gene J. Puskar. Logo reprinted by permission of Buna Independent School District.

Page 621: © Moviestore collection Ltd/Alamy

14. Advertising

Page 636: © REUTERS/Ho New

Page 639: Kay Nietfeld/picture-alliance/dpa/AP Images; © ClassicStock/Alamy

Page 642: © Jeff Morgan 01/Alamy

Page 643: © Mario Anzuoni/Reuters/Corbis

Page 644: © REUTERS/Ho New

Page 646: © Chuck Franklin/Alamy

Page 650: © Carl & Ann Purcell/CORBIS

Page 653: © POM Wonderful

Page 655: © Skechers

Page 657: © David Brabyn/Corbis

Page 659: © Reprinted by permission of Isabella Piccininni

Text Credits

4. Libel: The Plaintiff's Case

Page 167: 105w from pp. 215–217 from "Oxford Guide to United States Supreme Court Decisions" edited by Hall, Kermit L. (2001). By permission of Oxford University Press, Inc.

Page 167: Supreme Court Review excerpt of Harry Kalven Jr., "Case: A Note on 'The Central Meaning of the First Amendment.'" The New York Times, (1964) Supreme Court Review, 191. Reprinted with permission by University of Chicago Press.

6. Protecting Privacy

Page 255: Gina Reif Ilardi, First Amendment v. The Right of Publicity: The Game Is On!, METROPOLITAN CORPORATE COUNSEL, Aug. 20, 2012

7. Emotional Distress and Physical Harm

Page 294: SPEAKING OUR MINDS: CONVERSATIONS WITH THE PEOPLE BEHIND LANDMARK FIRST AMENDMENT CASES by Joseph Russomanno. Copyright 2002 by Taylor & Francis Group LLC - Books. Reproduced with permission of Taylor & Francis Group LLC - Books in the format Other book via Copyright Clearance Center.

8. Newsgathering

Page 326: Potter Stewart, *Or of the Press*, 26 Hastings L.J. 631, 636 (1975)

Page 338: Stephen Castle & Alan Cowell, Britain: Newspapers Protest New Press Rules, N.Y. TIMES, March 20, 2013, at A6

Page 349: Margaret Sullivan, The Danger of Suppressing the Leaks, N.Y. TIMES, March 10, 2013, at SR12

9. Reporter's Privilege

Page 400: SPEAKING OUR MINDS: CONVERSATIONS WITH THE PEOPLE BEHIND LANDMARK FIRST AMENDMENT CASES by Joseph Russomanno. Copyright 2002 by Taylor & Francis Group LLC - Books. Reproduced with permission of Taylor & Francis Group LLC - Books in the format Other book via Copyright Clearance Center.

10. The Media and the Courts

Page 449: Media Law Resource Center, Newsgathering Committee Defense Counsel Section (2010) available at http://www.medialaw.org/Content/NavigationMenu/Member_Resources/Litigation_Resources/Litigation_Resources.html.

12. Obscenity, Indecency and Violence

Page 530: VIRGINIA LAW REVIEW by Nadine Strossen. Copyright 1993 by Virginia Law Review. Reproduced with permission of Virginia Law Review in the format Other book via Copyright Clearance Center.

Page 564: The ESRB ratings are trademarks of the Entertainment Software Association.

Case Index

Page numbers in **bold** indicate excerpted cases. Boxes and notes are indicated by *b* or *n* following the page numbers. Alphabetization is letter-by-letter (e.g., "Newton" precedes "New York City").

A

A&M Records, Inc. v. Napster, 720*n* 190
Abbott v. State, 119*b*
ABC Inc. v. Stewart, 704*n* 49
Abdul-Jabbar v. General Motors Corp., 691*n* 87
Abood v. Detroit Bd. of Educ., 682*n* 115
A Book Named John Cleland's Memoirs of a Woman of Pleasure v. Attorney Gen. of Mass., 713*n* 30
Abrams v. United States, 109, 680*n* 23
Accuracy in Media, Inc. v. FCC, 710*n* 114
ACLU; Reno v., 477*b*, 514, 529*b*, 556
ACLU v. Ashcroft, 715*n* 145, 715*n* 149
ACLU v. Central Intelligence Agency, 700*n* 125
ACLU v. Department of Defense, 365*b*
ACLU v. Gonzales, 715*n* 147
ACLU v. Mukasey, 715*n* 148
ACLU v. Reno, 715*n* 142–143
Action for Children's Television v. FCC, 714*n* 97, 715*n* 114, 715*n* 116, 715*n* 119, 715*n* 122
Adarand Constructors, Inc. v. Pena, 710*n* 104
Adderley v. Florida, 679*n* 112
Adickes v. Kress & Co., 676*n* 37, 687*n* 67
Admission Consultants, Inc. v. Google, Inc., 684*n* 24
Agence France Presse v. Morel, 717*n* 56
Agostini v. Felton, 676*n* 34
Aguilar v. Felton, 676*n* 34
A.H. v. State, 713*n* 58
Aktepe v. United States, 675*n* 28
Albertini; United States v., 679*n* 111
Alexander v. United States, 714*n* 72
Alliance for Community Media v. FCC, 711*n* 141
Alvarado v. KOB-TV, L.L.C., 694*n* 18
Alvarez; United States v., 55, 677*n* 11
Am. Amusement Machine Ass'n v. Kendrick, 716*n* 159, 716*n* 163
Am. Civil Liberties Union v. U.S. Dep't of Justice, 701*n* 135

Am. Communications Ass'n v. Douds, 680*n* 35
Am. Elec. Power Serv. Corp. v. FCC, 710*n* 124
Amalgamated Food Employees Union v. Logan Valley Plaza, Inc., 679*n* 116
Ambach v. Norwick, 682*n* 110
AMD v. INTEL Antitrust Litigation, 704*n* 52, 704*n* 54
American Amusement Machine Association v. Kendrick, 562*b*
American Broadcasting Cos., Inc.; Doe v., 695*n* 59
American Broadcasting Cos., Inc. v. Aereo, Inc., 507*b*
American Civil Liberties Union of Illinois v. Alvarez, 697*n* 16
American Dental Association v. Delta Dental Plans Association, 717*n* 20
American Family Ass'n v. FCC, 710*n* 118
American Freedom Def. Initiative v. Metro. Transp. Auth., 83*b*
American Library Association; United States v., 560
America's Best Family Showplace Corp. v. New York City, 716*n* 167
Amy Unknown, *In re,* 713*n* 53
Anderson v. Liberty Lobby, Inc., 676*n* 38, 686*n* 28, 687*n* 68, 687*n* 71
Anonymous Online Speakers, *In re* v. U.S. District Court, 79*b*
Apex Technology v. Doe, 678*n* 57
Arista Records, LLC v. Launch Media, Inc., 720*n* 178
Arkansas Writers' Project v. Ragland, 679*n* 124
Arlington v. FCC, 514, 712*n* 191
Armstrong v. H & C Communications, 694*n* 22
Ashcroft v. ACLU, 712*n* 20, 715*n* 144, 715*n* 146, 715*n* 149
Ashcroft v. Free Speech Coalition, 529*b*, 559, 713*n* 47, 716*n* 153
Ashcroft v. Iqbal, 209*b*
Ashwander v. TVA, 44
Associated Press; Doe 2 v., 696*n* 112
Associated Press v. Canterbury, 368*b*
Associated Press v. Meltwater U.S. Holdings, Inc., 719*n* 140
Associated Press v. Walker, 145*b*, 172, 184, 685*n* 70, 685*n* 84
Aumais; United States v., 713*n* 52
Austin v. Michigan Chamber of Commerce, 41–46, 675*n* 2, 722*n* 49

Authors Guild v. Google, Inc., 607*b*
Authors Guild v. Hathitrust, 607*b*
Auvil v. CBS, 684*n* 51–52, 687*n* 59
A.V. v. iParadigms, LLC, 719*n* 144

B

B. J. F. v. Florida Star, 229*b*, 269–270
Baker; United States v., 681*n* 59
Baker v. F & F Investment Co., 702*n* 19
Barclays Capital Inc. v. TheFlyontheWall.com, Inc., 678*n* 53–54, 717*n* 33
Barnes v. Yahoo!, Inc., 696*n* 107
Bartnicki v. Vopper, 75*b*, 271, 327*b*, 343–344, 699*n* 82
Basic Books, Inc. v. Kinko's Graphics Corp., 719*n* 151
Bates v. State Bar of Ariz., 722*n* 46
Batson v. Kentucky, 703*n* 17
Batzel v. Smith, 687*n* 79
Baugh v. CBS, Inc., 693*n* 157
Bd. of Educ., Island Trees Union Free School Dist. v. Pico, 682*n* 94
Beacon Journal Publishing Co., Inc. v. Blackwell, 697*n* 17
Beaumont v. Brown, 694*n* 173
Bebe Stores, Inc. v. May Dep't Stores Int'l, 721*n* 205
Becker v. FCC, 708*n* 36
Bell Atlantic Corp. v. Twombly, 209*b*
Belluomo v. KAKE TV & Radio, Inc., 693*n* 142
Berger v. Hanlon, 697*n* 31
Best v. Malec, 694*n* 21
Bethel Sch. Dist. v. Fraser, 123*b*, 127, 681*n* 74
Bigelow v. Virginia, 639*b*, 722*n* 9
Bill Graham Archives v. Dorling Kindersley Ltd., 719*n* 146
Blagojevich; United States v., 704*n* 22–23
Bland v. Roberts, 62*b*, 80, 676*n* 4
Bloom v. Illinois, 387*b*
Blumenthal v. Drudge, 684*n* 30
Board of Regents of the University of Wisconsin v. Southworth, 123*b*, 679*n* 123, 681*n* 71–72, 682*n* 117–118
Board of Trustees of the State University of New York v. Fox, 641
Boese v. Paramount Pictures Corp., 691*n* 70
Boisson v. Banian, Ltd., 717*n* 18
Bonneville International Corp. v. Peters, 585*b*
Booth v. Curtis Publishing Co., 692*n* 126
Boring v. Google Inc., 693*n* 135
Borough of v. *See n ame of party*
Bose Corp v. Consumers Union, 684*n* 50

Boston Beer Co., L.P. v. Slesar Bros. Brewing Co., Inc., 721*n* 211
Boswell v. Phoenix Newspapers, Inc., 688*n* 86
Bowens v. Aftermath Entertainment, 699*n* 91
Boyles v. Kerr, 695*n* 56
Boy Scouts of America v. Dale, 680*n* 128
Bradley v. Saranac Board of Education, 694*n* 173
Brandenburg v. Ohio, 103*b*, 110–111*b*, 123*b*, 287*b*, 306, 307*b*, 309, 310*b*
Branzburg v. Hayes, 383, 385, 385*b*, 388, 393*b*, **404–416**, 697*n* 1, 697*n* 3, 701*n* 1, 702*n* 6, 702*n* 34
Brauer v. Globe Newspaper Co., 690*n* 58
Braun v. Soldier of Fortune Magazine, 304, 696*n* 81
Brents v. Morgan, 693*n* 153
Bridgeport Music, Inc. v. Dimension Films, 720*n* 180
Brilliance Audio, Inc. v. Haights Cross Communications, Inc., 718*n* 78
Brinkley v. Casablancas, 692*n* 108
Brompton Bldg., LLC v. Yelp!, 79*b*, 676*n* 8
Brookfield Communications, Inc. v. West Coast Ent. Corp., 721*n* 228
Broughton v. McClatchy Newspapers, Inc., 693*n* 134
Brown & Williamson v. Jacobsen, 685*n* 103
Brownmark Films, LCC v. Comedy Partners, 605*b*
Brown v. Entertainment Merchants Association, 103, 116, 529*b*, 562, 681*n* 54, 716*n* 166, 716*n* 169, 716*n* 179
Brown v. Louisiana, 679*n* 106
Bryan; United States v., 413, 702*n* 5
Buckley v. American Const'l Law Found., 678*n* 89
Buckley v. Valeo, 77, 678*n* 75
Burgess; United States v., 713*n* 52
Burke v. Gregg, 684*n* 44
Burrow-Giles Lithographic Co. v. Sarony, 717*n* 17
Bursey v. United States, 702*n* 19
Burson v. Freeman, 678*n* 66
Burstyn v. Wilson, 677*n* 33
Butler; Regina v., 530*b*
Butler v. Michigan, 713*n* 33
Butterworth v. Smith, 704*n* 58, 705*n* 81
Byers v. Edmundson, 696*n* 91–92

C

Cablevision Sys. Corp. v. FCC, 711*n* 151, 711*n* 164
Cahil; Doe v., 155*b*, 156*b*
Caine v. Duke Communications, International, 696*n* 110
Caldwell v. United States, 405, 413, 415
California v. Paparazzi, 335*b*

Campbell v. Acuff-Rose Music, Inc., 295*b*, 692*n* 114, 719*n* 134, 719*n* 153

Camper v. Minor, 695*n* 54

Cantrell v. Forest City Publishing Co., 241–242

Capital Broad. Co. v. Mitchell, 722*n* 20

Capitol Records, Inc. v. Mercury Records Corp., 720*n* 175

Capitol Records, Inc. v. Thomas-Rasset, 720*n* 191

Capitol Records, LLC v. ReDigi Inc., 592*b*

Caporale; United States v., 702*n* 19

Capperton v. Massey, 704*n* 24

Carafano v. Metrosplash, 694*n* 182

Cardillo v. Doubleday Co., Inc., 687*n* 61

Cardtoons, L.C. v. Major League Baseball Players Assoc., 691*n* 95, 692*n* 105

Caronia; United States v., 722*n* 29, 723*n* 78

C.A.R.S. Protection Plus, Inc.; Doe v., 453, 707*n* 118, 707*n* 120

Carter-Clark v. Random House, Inc., 684*n* 38

Carter v. Superior Court of San Diego County, 693*n* 145

Cartoon Network, LP v. CSC Holdings, Inc., 507*b*, 717*n* 60, 719*n* 113

Cassidy; United States v., 695*n* 44

Castellani v. Scranton Times, 703*n* 36

Catsouras v. Department of California Highway Patrol, 695*n* 30

C.B.C. Distribution and Marketing, Inc. v. Major League Baseball Advanced Media, L.P., 692*n* 102

CBS v. Davis, 677*n* 50, 677*n* 52

CBS v. FCC, 709*n* 39, 714*n* 108, 714*n* 110

Cent. Intelligence Agency v. Sims, 701*n* 134

Central Hudson Gas & Electric Corp. v. New York Public Service Commission, 639*b*, 640–641, 642, 643, 645, 646*b*, 650*b*, **661–667**

Cervantes v. Time, Inc., 702*n* 19

Chandler v. Florida, 442, 705*n* 91

Channel 10, Inc. v. Gunnarson, 697*n* 13

Chaplinsky v. New Hampshire, 53*b*, 54, 112, 118*b*, 680*n* 16

Cher v. Forum International, 692*n* 127

Chevron Corp. v. Berlinger, 702*n* 25

Christian Legal Society v. Martinez, 130, 134*b*

Chrysler v. Brown, 361, 701*n* 138

Chuy v. Philadelphia Eagles Football Club, 685*n* 89

Cincinnati Enquirer, State ex rel. v. Winkler, 707*n* 135

Circuit City Stores Inc. v. CarMax Inc., 721*n* 209

Citizen Publishing Co. v. United States, 686*n* 21

Citizens United v. Federal Election Commission, 3, 5*b*, 7*b*, 18, 19, **40–46**, 77, 78*b*, 648–649, 675*n* 5

City of v. *See n ame of party*

Clarridge; United States v., 700*n* 109

Clean Flicks of Colo., LLC v. Soderbergh, 718*n* 68

CNN; United States v., 705*n* 86

Cochrane v. United States, 701*n* 141

Cochran v. NYP Holdings, Inc., 684*n* 49

Cohen v. California, 112, 681*n* 41, 712*n* 3, 714*n* 80

Cohen v. Cowles Media Co., 314, 385*b*, 399–400*b*, **416–417**, 697*n* 8, 698*n* 62, 699*n* 63, 701*n* 2, 702*n* 3–4

Columbia Pictures Indus., Inc. v. Fung, 719*n* 115

Comcast Corp. v. FCC, 711*n* 144, 712*n* 188

Comedy III Productions, Inc. v. Gary Saderup, Inc., 692*n* 115, 692*n* 117, 692*n* 119

Commonwealth v. Barnes, 705*n* 73

Community for Creative Non-Violence v. Reid, 586, 717*n* 44, 717*n* 46

Community Television of Utah, Inc. v. Roy City, 715*n* 127

Complaints Against Various Broad. Licensees Regarding Their Airing of the "Golden Globe Awards" Program, *In re*, 714*n* 100

Complaints Against Various Television Licensees Concerning Their Feb. 1, 2004, Broad. of the Super Bowl XXXVIII, *In re*, 714*n* 107

Complaints Against Various Television Licensees Regarding Their Broadcast on Nov. 11, 2004, of the ABC Television Network's Presentation of the Film "Saving Private Ryan," *In re*, 714*n* 104

Complaints Regarding Various Television Broad. Between Feb. 2, 2002 & Mar. 8, 2005, *In re*, 714*n* 101

Condor Insurance Limited, *In re*, 675*n* 14

Connick v. Myers, 679*n* 101, 695*n* 40

Conradt v. NBC Universal, 290*b*

Convertino v. U.S. Department of Justice, 368*b*

Copeland v. Copeland, 707*n* 136

Cortrill v. Spears, 718*n* 106

Cotterman; United States v., 703*n* 47

Couloute v. Ryncarz, et al., 686*n* 43

Covey v. Detroit Lakes Publishing Co., 694*n* 11

Cowley v. Pulsifer, 686*n* 9

Cox Broadcasting Corp. v. Cohn, 229*b*, 270

Cox Newspaper L.P. v. Wooten, 694*n* 6

Cox v. Louisiana, 85*b*

Coyne Beahm, Inc. v. FDA, 722*n* 23

Crandon; United States v., 713*n* 52

Cruz v. Ferre, 715*n* 126

Ctr. for Individual Freedom v. Van Hollen, 722*n* 55

Cubby, Inc. v. CompuServe, Inc., 684*n* 27

Curtis Publishing Co. v. Butts, 145*b*, 172, 183, 184, 685*n* 69, 685*n* 84

Cuthbertson; United States v., 702*n* 19

D

Daly v. Viacom, Inc., 693*n* 159

Dambrot v. Central Mich. Univ., 683*n* 146

Dam Things from Denmark v. Russ Barrie & Co., 719*n* 129

Daniels Cablevision, Inc. v. United States, 711*n* 171

Debs v. United States, 680*n* 22

Deere & Co. v. MTD Products, Inc., 721*n* 231

Dendrite International, Inc. v. John Doe No. 3, 155*b*, 156*b*

Dennis v. United States, 680*n* 26, 680*n* 36

Denver Area Educational Telecommunications Consortium, Inc. v. FCC, 85*b*, 503, 529*b*, 554–555, 711*n* 129, 711*n* 153, 715*n* 131

Department of Justice v. Reporters Committee for Freedom of the Press, 34, 327*b*, 363, **376–381**, 457, 676*n* 32, 701*n* 142, 701*n* 144, 701*n* 147, 708*n* 146

Dep't of the Air Force v. Rose, 699*n* 106, 701*n* 136, 701*n* 140

Dep't of the Interior and Bureau of Indian Affairs v. Klamath Water Users Protective Association, 701*n* 140

Desnick v. American Broadcasting Companies, 693*n* 144

Detroit Free Press v. Ashcroft, 704*n* 42

Diaz v. Oakland Tribune, 694*n* 170

Dickens v. The House of the Dead, 562*b*

Diebold; United States v., 676*n* 37, 687*n* 67

Dietemann v. Time, Inc., 693*n* 146, 697*n* 28

Dimeo v. Max, 684*n* 31

Dimora; United States v., 707*n* 115

Discount Tobacco City & Lottery Co. v. United States, 722*n* 25

D.J.M. v. Hannibal Pub. Sch. Dist. #60, 681*n* 86

DMC Plumbing and Remodeling, LLC v. Fox News Network, LLC, et al., 686*n* 5

Doe v. *See n ame of opposin g party*

Dolcefino and KTRK Television, Inc. v. Turner, 684*n* 55, 688*n* 90

Domville v. State, 425*b*

Doninger v. Niehoff, 681*n* 88

Doubleclick Inc. v. Privacy Litigation, *In re,* 689*n* 7

Douglas v. Hello! Ltd., 690*n* 42

Dowty v. Riggs, 695*n* 52

Dow v. New Haven Indep., Inc., 686*n* 28

Drew; United States v., 308*b*

Dun & Bradstreet, Inc. v. Greenmoss Builders, Inc., 321–322, 683*n* 5, 685*n* 95

Duryea; Borough of v. Guarnieri, 81, 679*n* 103

E

E. & J. Gallo Winery v. Spider Webs Ltd., 721*n* 227

Early v. Toledo Blade, 688*n* 89

Eberhardt v. Morgan Stanley Dean Witter Trust FSB, 690*n* 57

Edge Broad.; United States v., 722*n* 32

Edison Stores v. BMI, 720*n* 169

Edwards v. Aguillard, 681*n* 74, 682*n* 111

Edwards v. National Audubon Society, 191*b*, 205*b*, 687*n* 56

Edwards v. South Carolina, 679*n* 106

Eimann v. Soldier of Fortune Magazine, 304, 696*n* 76, 696*n* 79

Eisenstadt v. Baird, 690*n* 37

Eldred v. Ashcroft, 579*b*, 585*b*, 595–597, 597*b*, 628–630

Emily's List v. FEC, 678*n* 83

Energy Research Found. v. Defense Nuclear Facilities Safety B., 700*n* 109

Enterline v. Pocono Medical Ctr., 684*n* 35

Epperson v. Arkansas, 682*n* 111

Erznoznik v. City of Jacksonville, 712*n* 2

Estate of Duckett v. Cable News Network, 695*n* 28

Estes v. Texas, 420–421, 703*n* 6

ETW Corp. v. Jireh Publishing, Inc., 692*n* 99, 692*n* 120

Euclid v. Ambler Realty Co., 548*b*

Evers; United States v., 713*n* 52

F

Facebook, Inc. v. Teachbook.com LLC, 721*n* 233

Factors Etc., Inc. v. Pro Arts, I nc., 692*n* 108

Fair Housing Council of San Fernando Valley v. Roommates. com, 696*n* 104

Falwell v. Flynt, 695*n* 34

Fanelle v. LoJack Corp., 690*n* 62

Farmers Educ. and Cooperative Union v. WDAY, Inc., 709*n* 37

Fast; United States v., 713*n* 52

FCC v. AT&T, 327*b*

FCC v. League of Women Voters, 708*n* 20, 709*n* 43, 709*n* 75, 710*n* 115

FCC v. Pacifica Foundation, 529*b*, 547–548, 548*b*, 554, 557, 570, 574, 708*n* 22, 714*n* 75, 714*n* 92, 714*n* 96, 715*n* 126

FEC v. Massachusetts Citizens for Life, Inc., 722*n* 49

FEC v. Nat'l Conservative Political Action Comm., 722*n* 49

FEC v. Nat'l Right to Work Comm., 722*n* 49

Fed. Communications Comm'n v. AT&T, 701*n* 143, 701*n* 148

Fed. Radio Comm'n v. Nelson Bros., 708*n* 8

Federal Communications Commission v. Fox Television Stations, Inc., 527, 529*b*, 550, 551, **570–575**, 714*n* 105, 714*n* 111, 714*n* 81–82, 714*n* 102–103

Federal Election Commission v. *See n ame of opposin g party*

Federated Pub., Inc. v. Kurtz, 707*n* 111

Federated Pub., Inc. v. Swedberg, 707*n* 112

Feist Publications, Inc. v. Rural Telephone Service Co., 717*n* 22

Feltner v. Columbia Pictures Television, Inc., 719*n* 120

Ferber v. New York, 539

First Nat'l Bank of Boston v. Bellotti, 722*n* 48

Firth v. State of New York, 687*n* 60

Flava Works, Inc. v. Gunter, 719*n* 116

Florida Star v. B.J.F., 455, 694*n* 175, 707*n* 130

Florida v. Jardines, 233, 690*n* 25

Florida v. Palm Beach Newspapers, 706*n* 100

Flynn v. City of Cambridge, 679*n* 120

Fogerty v. Fantasy, Inc., 719*n* 123

Fogerty v. MGM Group Holdings Corp., 718*n* 107

Food Lion, Inc. v. Capital Cities, Inc./ABC, 336, 698*n* 50, 698*n* 55

Forsham v. Harris, 700*n* 110–111

Forsyth County, Ga. v. The Nationalist Movement, 678*n* 72

Fortnightly Corp. v. United Artists Television, Inc., 718*n* 101

44 Liquormart Inc. v. Rhode Island, 639*b*, 722*n* 19

Fox Broadcasting Co., Inc. v. Dish Network L.L.C., 718*n* 105, 719*n* 148

Fox Television Stations, Inc. v. BarryDriller Content Systems, 717*n* 61

Fox Television Stations, Inc. v. FCC, 498*b*, 714*n* 102, 714*n* 106

Fox TV Stations, Inc. v. FilmOn X, 717*n* 58

Fraley v. Facebook, 248*b*, 687*n* 81

Freedman v. Maryland, 714*n* 69

Frisby v. Schultz, 85*b*, 322, 679*n* 113

Frohwerk v. United States, 680*n* 20

FTC v. Corzine, 723*n* 79

G

Galella v. Onassis, 698*n* 44–45

Gannett v. DePasquale, 421*b*, 429, 431, 704*n* 29

Garcetti v. Ceballos, 80, 679*n* 98, 679*n* 102

Gault, *In re*, 704*n* 63

Gertz v. Robert Welch, Inc., 145*b*, 173, 174, 176*b*, **182–187**, 191*b*, 217, 219, 223, 242, 685*n* 80, 685*n* 92, 685*n* 99, 686*n* 1, 686*n* 20, 686*n* 29

Gibson v. Craigslist, Inc., 696*n* 106

Ginsberg v. New York, 538, 713*n* 35

Gitlow v. New York, 103*b*, 109, 676*n* 2, 680*n* 27, 681*n* 43

Glickman v. Wileman Bros. & Elliott, 679*n* 121

Glik v. Cunniffe, 697*n* 14

Globe Newspaper Co. v. Superior Court for Norfolk County, 431, 697*n* 19, 704*n* 38, 704*n* 47

Goland v. CIA, 700*n* 110, 700*n* 117

Golan v. Holder, 577, 579*b*, 596, **627–630**, 718*n* 92

Goldwater v. Ginsburg, 685*n* 67

Gooding v. Wilson, 681*n* 49

Gouin v. Gouin, 694*n* 4

Grace; United States v., 85*b*

Grand Jury Proceedings, 702*n* 20

Grand Jury Subpoena (Josh Wolf), 702*n* 28

Grand Jury Subpoena (Miller), *In re*, 389*b*

Grand Jury Subpoenas, *In re*, 702*n* 30

Grayned v. Rockford, 679*n* 106, 679*n* 108, 681*n* 81

Greater New Orleans Broad. Ass'n, Inc. v. United States, 722*n* 35

Greenbelt Cooperative Publishers Association, Inc. v. Bressler, 686*n* 47

Greenberg v. Nat'l Geographic Soc'y, 717*n* 48

Green Party of Connecticut v. Garfield, 676*n* 44

Green v. Chicago Tribune Co., 694*n* 185

Greer v. Spock, 679*n* 110

Gregory v. City of Chicago, 679*n* 106

Griswold v. Connecticut, 690*n* 36, 690*n* 33–34

Grosjean v. Am. Press Co., 679*n* 124

Guglielmi v. Spelling-Goldberg Productions, 692*n* 125

GW Equity LLC v. Xcentric Ventures LLS, 696*n* 105

H

Habush v. Cannon, 245*b*

Haelan Laboratories, Inc. v. Topps Chewing Gum, Inc., 691*n* 82, 692*n* 104

Hague v. Committee for Industrial Organization, 679*n* 104, 679*n* 109

Hamilton-Brown Shoe Co. v. Wolf Bros. & Co., 721*n* 212

Hamling v. United States, 712*n* 15

Hanlon v. Berger, 330*b*, 332, 697*n* 31–32

Harley-Davidson, Inc. v. Grottanelli, 721*n* 215

Harney v. Sony Pictures Television, Inc., 601*b*

Harper & Row Publishers, Inc. v. Nation Enter., 719*n* 135, 719*n* 149

Harte-Hanks Communications, Inc. v. Connaughton, 685*n* 74

Harter v. Disney Enter., Inc., 718*n* 109

Hart v. Electronic Arts, Inc., 255*b*

Hatfill v. New York Times, 694*n* 19

Hazelwood v. Kuhlmeier, 103*b*, 123*b*, 128, 131, 132, 133, 682*n* 100, 682*n* 131

Hebrew University of Jerusalem v. General Motors LLC, 691*n* 80

Hedges v. Obama, 675*n* 8, 675*n* 10

Henderson v. Times Mirror Co., 686*n* 28

Herbert v. Lando, 685*n* 73

Herceg v. Hustler Magazine, 696*n* 93

Hess v. Indiana, 287*b*, 306, 307, 309, 679*n* 106, 681*n* 69

Hickling; Regina v., 531–532

Hill v. Colorado, 74, 261, 678*n* 65, 693*n* 136

Hilton v. Hallmark Cards, 691*n* 72

Hoehling v. Universal City Studios, Inc., 717*n* 29

Holder v. Humanitarian Law Project (HLP), 103, 680*n* 6, 680*n* 8

Hollingsworth v. Perry, 704*n* 50

Home Box Office, Inc. v. Wilkinson, 715*n* 127

Hosty v. Carter, 682*n* 134

Hotaling; United States v., 713*n* 48

Howard v. Antilla, 690*n* 59

Howell Education Association v. Howell Board of Education, 368*b*

Huchins v. KQED, 697*n* 11

Hudgens v. National Labor Relations Board, 679*n* 116

Hunger v. Grand Cent. Sanitation, 694*n* 16

Hurley v. Irish-American Gay, Lesbian and Bisexual Group of Boston, 680*n* 129

Hurst v. Capital Cities Media, Inc., 686*n* 3

Hustler Magazine v. Falwell, 200, 287*b*, 294*b*, 295, 297, **317–319**, 686*n* 46, 695*n* 32, 695*n* 35

Hutchinson v. Proxmire, 685*n* 87, 687*n* 70

Hyde v. City of Columbia, 695*n* 61

I

Idema v. Wager, 694*n* 7

Illinois Citizens Comm. for Broad. v. FCC, 714*n* 89

Indiana Newspapers Inc. v. Junior Achievement of Central Indiana, Inc., 398*b*

Infinity Broad. Corp. of Penna., *In re*, 714*n* 96

In re. See n ame of party

Intel Corp. v. AMD, 704*n* 55

In the Matter of. *See* name of party

Int'l News Serv. v. Associated Press, 717*n* 30

Io Group, Inc. v. Veoh Networks, Inc., 720*n* 163

Island Trees Union Free School Dist. Board of Ed. v. Pico, 680*n* 126

J

Jacobellis v. Ohio, 712*n* 1, 712*n* 16

James B. Beam Distilling Co. v. Georgia, 19*b*

James v. Meow Media, Inc., 696*n* 74, 716*n* 158, 716*n* 161–162

Janklow v. Newsweek, 686*n* 27

Japan Telecom, Inc. v. Japan Telecom of America, Inc., 721*n* 210

Jaynes v. Commonwealth of Virginia, 723*n* 88

J.E.B. v. Alabama, 703*n* 17

Jenkins v. Georgia, 713*n* 26, 713*n* 28

Jessup-Morgan v. America Online, Inc., 699*n* 89

John Doe Grand Jury Investigation, *In re*, 703*n* 35

Johns-Byrne Co. v. TechnoBuffalo, 703*n* 44

Johnson v. K Mart Corp., 694*n* 174

Johnson v. Ruark Obstetrics and Gynecology Associates, 695*n* 57

John v. Tribune Co., 686*n* 39

Jones; United States v., 227, 229*b*, 233, 235, **278–283**, 689*n* 2, 689*n* 21, 690*n* 24

Jones v. Dirty World Entertainment Recordings LLC, 687*n* 82

Jones v. U.S. Child Support Recovery, 693*n* 155

Joseph Burstyn, Inc. v. Wilson, 708*n* 15, 713*n* 67

K

Kaelin v. Globe Communications, 684*n* 46

Kalem Co. v. Harper Bros., 719*n* 111

Kasky v. Nike, 722*n* 51

Katz v. United States, 229*b*, 233, 235*b*, 276, 279–280, 690*n* 22

Kearney; United States v., 713*n* 52

Keefe v. City of Minneapolis v. Star Tribune Media Co., 702*n* 22

Keeton v. Hustler Magazine, Inc., 675*n* 13

Keller v. Electronic Arts, Inc., 255*b*

Kelson v. Spin Publications, Inc., 690*n* 62

Kennedy; United States v., 713*n* 52

Kent v. United States v., 704*n* 62

Kilbourn v. Thompson, 675*n* 1

Kilbride; United States v., 535*b*, 713*n* 23

Kimmerle v. New York Evening Journal, Inc., 684*n* 42

Kincaid v. Gibson, 682*n* 133

Kirtsaeng v. John Wiley & Sons, 579*b*, 718*n* 79

Kissinger v. Reporters Comm. for Freedom of the Press, 700*n* 109

Kleindienst v. Mandel, 680*n* 15

Knievel v. ESPN, Inc., 687*n* 52

Knox; United States v., 713*n* 43

Knutt v. Metro Int'l, 684*n* 48

Kokinda; United States v., 85*b*, 679*n* 111

Koubriti; United States v., 703*n* 19

Kovacs v. Cooper, 677n 34
KOVR-TV, Inc. v. Superior Court, 695n 26
Kowalski v. Berkeley County Schools, 681n 88
Kunz v. New York, 680n 36

L

Ladue; City of v. Gilleo, 75b
Lake v. City of Phoenix, 370b
Lamprecht v. Federal Communications Commission, 710n 104
Lane v. Simon, 683n 141
Laraneta; United States v., 713n 52
LaRouche v. NBC, 702n 19
Lawrence v. Texas, 682n 107, 690n 39
Layshock v. Hermitage School District, 681n 90
Leathers v. Medlock, 679n 124
Lee v. Dong-A Ilbo, 686n 8
Leigh v. Salazar, 697n 20, 704n 42
Leigh v. Warner Bros., Inc., 720n 182
Le Mistral, Inc. v. Columbia Broadcasting System, 693n 140
Lemon v. Kurtzman, 123b
Liberty Lobby, Inc. v. Anderson, 687n 62
Lieb v. Topstone Indus., Inc., 720n 177
Lin v. Rohm & Haas Co., 694n 16
Lipsky v. Durant, 703n 43
Liquori v. Republican Co., 686n 10
Liquormart v. Rhode Island, 676n 42
Little; United States v., 713n 24
Lloyd; United States v., 702n 19
Lloyd Corp., Ltd. v. Tanner, 679n 116
Logan v. District of Columbia, 687n 65
Long Beach Area Chamber of Commerce v. City of Long Beach, 676n 44
Lorillard Tobacco Co. v. Reilly, 646b, 650b, 722n 21
Los Angeles City Council v. Taxpayers for Vincent, 679n 111
Lovell v. Griffin, 677n 33
Luke Records, Inc. v. Navarro, 713n 32
Lunney v. Prodigy Services Co., 684n 26

M

M. Fabrikant & Sons, Ltd. v. Fabrikant Fine Diamonds, Inc., 721n 213
Machleder v. Diaz, 693n 143
Madison v. Frazier, 686n 40

Madsen v. Buie, 686n 44
Madsen v. Women's Health Center, Inc., 85b, 118b, 322–323, 679n 113
Maldonado-Norat; United States v., 693n 139
Marbury v. Madison, 5b, 6, 18, 38–39, **46–49**
Marcavage v. City of New York, 679n 115
Martin v. Daily News, LP, 684n 25
Masson v. New Yorker Magazine, Inc., 145b, 169b, 191b, 684n 54, 685n 68, 687n 66
Matera v. Superior Court, 702n 33
Mattel, Inc. v. MCA Records, Inc., 692n 112
Matthews; United States v., 713n 45
Mayfield v. National Association for Stock Car Auto Racing, 209b
McCollum v. CBS, Inc., 696n 84
McConnell v. Federal Election Commission, 44–46, 78b, 675n 2, 709n 45
McCray, In re, 702n 26–27
McFarlane; Doe v., 692n 121
McGarity; United States v., 713n 52
McIntosh v. The Detroit News, Inc., 686n 13
McIntyre v. Ohio Election Commission, 678n 88, 684n 33
McKinney v. Avery Journal, Inc., 687n 58
Medical Laboratory Management Consultants v. American Broadcasting Cos., Inc., 693n 141, 693n 149
Memoirs v. Massachusetts, 567
Messenger v. Gruner + Jahn Printing & Publishing, 692n 100
Metro Broadcasting, Inc. v. FCC, 710n 103
Metro-Goldwyn-Mayer Studios, Inc. v. Grokster, Ltd., 579b, 602, **631–635**, 719n 114, 720n 193
Meyer v. Bush, 700n 109
Meyer v. Grant, 678n 74
M.G. v. Time Warner, Inc., 693n 163
Miami Herald Publishing Co. v. McIntosh, 677n 51
Miami Herald Publishing Co. v. Tornillo, 53b, 63, 482, 676n 33, 708n 18, 709n 71
Miami University; United States v., 699n 100
Michaels v. Internet Entertainment Group, 693n 152, 693n 158, 694n 169
Midler v. Ford Motor Co., 691n 90
Midler v. Young & Rubicam, Inc., 691n 90
Midwest Video Corp. (Midwest I); United States v., 712n 183
Midwest Video Corp. (Midwest II); United States v., 712n 183
Milkovich v. Lorain Journal Co., 189, 191b, 197, **221–225**, 683n 3, 683n 14, 686n 19, 686n 30
Milk Wagon Drivers Union of Chicago v. Meadowmoor Dairies, 118b

Miller v. California, *528b, 529b, 533–539, 533b, 537b, 545, 557,* **566–570,** *712n* 12, *712n* 198, *713n* 25

Miller v. Mitchell, *713n* 61

Miller v. NBC, *697n* 24, *697n* 26

Miller v. Transamerican Press, Inc., *702n* 19

Miller v. United States, *385b, 389b*

Milligan, Ex parte, *107b*

Milligan v. United States, *686n* 6

Milner v. Dept. of Navy, *327b, 701n* 137

Milton H. Greene Archives v. Marilyn Monroe LLC, *691n* 79

Mink v. Knox, *146b*

Minneapolis Star & Tribune Co. v. Minnesota Comm'r of Revenue, *677n* 35, *679n* 124

Mishkin v. New York, *712n* 18

Missner v. Clifford, *686n* 41

Mitchell v. Globe International Publications, Inc., *690n* 64

Moghadam; United States v., *720n* 185

Moldea v. New York Times, *686n* 14–15

Montana v. San Jose Mercury News, Inc., *692n* 109

Monzel; United States v., *713n* 52

Moreno v. Crookston Times and McDaniel, *686n* 2

Moriarty v. Greene, *690n* 61

Morse v. Frederick, 124, *134b*

Mosely v. V Secret Catalogue, Inc., *721n* 237

Mourning v. Family Publishing Service, *676n* 37, *687n* 67

Mukasey v. ACLU, *715n* 150

Multimedia Holdings Corp. v. Circuit Court of Florida, *421b, 704n* 59–61

Mu'Min v. Virginia, 438, *703n* 16, *705n* 79

Musumeci v. U.S. Dep't of Homeland Security, *345b*

MySpace, Inc.; Doe IX v., *696n* 103

MySpace, Inc.; Doe v., *696n* 101–102

N

NAACP v. Claiborne Hardware Co., *679n* 106

NAACP v. United States, *118b*

Nack v. Walburg, *723n* 91

Naked Cowboy v. CBS, *249b*

Nast v. Michels, *707n* 134

National Archives and Records Administration v. Favish, *327b, 701n* 145

National Association of Broadcasters v. FCC, *711n* 169

National Broadcasting Co. v. FCC, 482, *708n* 16

National Cable & Telecommunications Assoc. v. Brand X Internet Services, *712n* 184

National Security Archive v. Archivist of the United States, *700n* 109

Nat'l Ass'n of Broadcasters v. FCC, *708n* 11

Nat'l Basketball Ass'n v. Motorola, Inc., *717n* 32

Nat'l Cable & Telecommunications Ass'n v. FCC, *711n* 142

Nat'l Endowment for the Arts v. Finley, *679n* 125

NBC v. United States, *477b*

Near v. Minnesota, *53b,* 65–66, *68b,* **89–97**

Nebraska Press Ass'n v. Stuart, *67b,* 421, 439, *439b,* 451, *677n* 48–49

Neilson v. Union Bank of Cal., N.A., *695n* 51

Neiman-Marcus v. Lait, *684n* 37

Nelson v. Harrah's Entertainment Inc., *695n* 53

Nelson v. McClatchy, 76, *678n* 77

Nemet Chevrolet Ltd. v. Consumer Affairs.com, Inc., *696n* 111

Netzer v. Continuity Graphic Associates, Inc., *692n* 129

New Hampshire v. Zidel, *713n* 49

New Kids on the Block v. News American Publ'g, Inc., *721n* 242

New Times, Inc. v. Isaacks, *687n* 54–55

Newton v. Diamond, *720n* 181

New World Communications of Ohio, Inc. v. Geauga County Court of Common Pleas, Juvenile Division, *705n* 71

New York City; Doe v., *694n* 184

New York Times Co. v. National Aeronautics and Space Administration, *362b*

New York Times Co. v. Sullivan, *5b,* 60, 143, *145b,* 164–165, *167b*–168, 169, 171, 172, 173, 174, *176b,* 178, **180–182,** 183–184, 185, 186–187, 191, 195, 198, 208, 222, 296, 318, 638, *675n* 13, *676n* 41, *676n* 43, *677n* 21, *683n* 1, *684n* 60, *686n* 23, *687n* 72, *721n* 6

New York Times Co. v. Tasini, 587

New York Times Co. v. United States, 49, *53b,* 67, 89, **97–99**

New York Times v. Jascalevich, *677n* 49

Nike, Inc. v. Kasky, 648, *676n* 35, *722n* 50

94th St. Grocery Corp. v. New York City Bd.of Health, *722n* 26

Nixon; United States v., *703n* 45

Nixon v. Shrink Missouri Government PAC, *678n* 86

Nixon v. Warner Communications, 452

Noriega; United States v., *705n* 86, *705n* 88

North Jersey Media Group v. Ashcroft, *704n* 42

Norwood v. Soldier of Fortune Magazine, 304, *696n* 77

N.Y. Civil Liberties Union v. N.Y. City Transit Auth., *704n* 42

O

Oak Creek, City of v. Ah King, *699n* 95

O'Brien; United States v., *53b,* 73, *74b,* 121, 508, *678n* 69, *681n* 64, *681n* 66

Obsidian Finance Group, LLC v. Cox, 175*b*, 703*n* 38–40

O'Connor v. Ortega, 275, 276, 689*n* 17

Oklahoma Publishing Co. v. District Court, 694*n* 179

Old Dominion Branch No. 496, Nat'l Assn of Letter Carriers v. Austin, 687*n* 49

Olivia N. v. National Broadcasting Co., 696*n* 72

Ollman v. Evans, 191*b*, 196, 197, 199*b*, 200, **216–221**, 223, 686*n* 25

Olmstead v. United States, 279

One Book Called "Ulysses"; United States v., 712*n* 8

One Book Called "Ulysses" by James Joyce; United States v., 712*n* 8

1–800 Contacts, Inc. v. WhenU.com, Inc., 721*n* 241

O'Neill v. City of Shoreline, 370*b*

Ontario, City of v. Quon, 229*b*, 232, **273–277**, 689*n* 11

Osborne v. Ohio, 713*n* 59, 713*n* 65–66

Ostergren v. Cuccinelli, 689*n* 11

OSU Student Alliance v. Ray, 682*n* 132

P

PACCAR, Inc. v. TeleScan Technologies, L.L.C., 720*n* 204

Pacific Legal Found. v. Council on Envt. Quality, 700*n* 109

Papish v. Board of Curators of the University of Missouri, 129, 682*n* 119

Parents Family and Friends of Lesbians and Gays v. Camdenton R-111 School District, 682*n* 105

Parks v. LaFace Records, 692*n* 113

Paroline v. United States, 713*n* 53

Patterson v. Colorado, 94

Patton v. Yount, 703*n* 8

Paulsen v. Personality Posters, Inc., 692*n* 109

Payton v. New York, 375

Peck v. City of Boston (*In re* Slack), 702*n* 21

Pell v. Procunier, 697*n* 10, 697*n* 12

Pennekamp v. Florida, 5*b*, 387*b*

Peoples Bank & Trust Co. v. Globe International, 690*n* 64

Perfect 10, Inc. v. Google, Inc., 720*n* 162, 720*n* 165

Perry Educ. Ass'n v. Perry local Educators' Ass'n, 679*n* 108

Perry v. Brown, 705*n* 94

Perry v. Sindermann, 678*n* 95

Peterson v. Grisham, 690*n* 60

Petrovic; United States v., 695*n* 48

PG Publishing Co. v. Aichele, 697*n* 18

Philadelphia Newspapers, Inc. v. Hepps, 684*n* 53

Pickering v. Board of Education, 679*n* 96, 682*n* 111

Pickett v. Prince, 717*n* 55

Pierce v. Clarion Ledger, 694*n* 12

Piscatelli v. Smith, 686*n* 11

Pittsburgh Press Co. v. Pittsburgh Comm'n on Human Relations, 722*n* 8

Planned Parenthood v. American Coalition of Life Activists, 681*n* 63

Playboy Enter., Inc. v. Frena, 719*n* 159

Playboy Enter., Inc. v. Russ Hardenburgh, Inc., 719*n* 154

Playboy Entertainment Enterprises, Inc.; United States v., 477*b*, 503, 711*n* 130, 715*n* 135

Pleasant Grove City v. Summum, 80

Pooley v. National Hole-in-One Association, 692*n* 130

Pope v. Illinois, 537, 713*n* 31

Posadas de Puerto Rico Associates v. Tourism Co. of Puerto Rico, 650*b*

Powell v. McCormack, 675*n* 1

Preserving the Open Internet, In the Matter of, 712*n* 189

Presley v. Georgia, 432, 704*n* 43

Press-Enterprise (II) v. Riverside Co. Superior Court, 432, 432*b*, 433*b*, 455, 704*n* 48, 704*n* 40–41

Press-Enterprise (I) v. Riverside Co. Superior Court, 421*b*, 455, 704*n* 40

Press-Enterprise v. Riverside Co. Superior Court of California for Riverside County, 697*n* 19

Prince Albert v. Strange, 690*n* 42

Princess Samantha Kennedy v. Paramount Pictures Corp., 718*n* 108

Prometheus Radio Project v. Federal Communications Commission, 710*n* 106

Prudhomme v. The Procter & Gamble Co., 691*n* 88

Prune Yard Shopping Center v. Robins, 86, 679*n* 116–117

Q

Qualitex Co. v. Jacobson Prods. Co., Inc., 621*b*, 720*n* 198

Quality King Distributors, Inc. v. L'Anza Research Int'l, Inc., 718*n* 76

Quigley Corp v. Karkus, 425*b*

R

Radio-Television News Directors Ass'n v. FCC, 709*n* 41, 709*n* 74

Randall v. Sorrell, 678*n* 85

Rapid City Journal v. Delaney, 704*n* 37

RAV v. City of St. Paul, 79*b*, 103*b*, 114, 118*b*, 681*n* 52

Red & Black Publishing Co.; John Doe v., 699*n* 98

Red & Black Publishing Co. v. Board of Regents, Univ. of Georgia, 699*n* 98–99
Red Lion Broadcasting Co. v. Federal Communications Commission, 53*b*, 62, 475, 477*b*, 482, 494–495, **516–521**, 524, 676*n* 33, 677*n* 36, 709*n* 70
Redmond v. Gawker Media LLC, 686*n* 37
Reed; Doe v., 678*n* 90–91
Regents of the Univ. of Cal., *In re,* 714*n* 96
Regina v. Butler, 530*b*
Regina v. Hickling, 531–532
Reichle v. Howards, 84, 679*n* 114
Renner v. Donsbach, 685*n* 90
Reno v. ACLU, 477*b*, 514, 529*b*, 556, 712*n* 193, 712*n* 195
Reno v. Condon, 699*n* 102
Republican Nat'l Comm. v. FEC, 678*n* 81
Republican Party of Minn. v. White, 704*n* 27
Reynolds; United States v., 707*n* 122
Rice v. Paladin Enterprises, Inc., 287*b*, 310*b*, 696*n* 95
Richmond Newspapers v. Virginia, 421*b*, 431, 432*b*, 467–473, 697*n* 19
Ride the Ducks, LLC v. Duck Boat Tours, Inc., 720*n* 199
Righthaven LLC v. Hoehn, 718*n* 104
Riley v. National Federation of the Blind of North Carolina, 75*b*
R.J. Reynolds Tobacco Co. v. Food & Drug Admin., 722*n* 25
Roach v. Stern, 695*n* 27
Robinson v. American Broadcasting Co., 708*n* 23
Roe v. Wade, 639, 690*n* 38, 722*n* 10
Rogers v. Grimaldi, 253–254, 256, 692*n* 111
Rosemont Enterprises, Inc. v. Random House, Inc., 692*n* 123
Rosenberger v. Rector & Visitors of the Univ. of Virginia, 679*n* 123, 681*n* 71, 682*n* 116–117
Rosenblatt v. Baer, 683*n* 4, 685*n* 75
Rothner v. City of Chicago, 716*n* 168
Roth v. United States, 532, 533, 568, 569, 712*n* 11, 712*n* 14
Rubin v. Coors Brewing Co., 722*n* 18
Rushforth v. Council of Economic Advisers, 700*n* 109
Russell v. Dep't of the Air Force, 701*n* 139

S

Sable Communications of California, Inc. v. FCC, 714*n* 86
Salinger v. Random House, Inc., 719*n* 142
Salzano v. North Jersey Media Group, 686*n* 11
Sanders v. Acclaim Entertainment, Inc., 696*n* 73
Sanders v. American Broadcasting Companies, 693*n* 150
Sandholm v. Kuecker, 684*n* 22
San Diego v. Roe, 321

Sandler v. Calcagni, 693*n* 164
Saragama India Ltd. v. Mosley, 720*n* 182
Sara Lee Corp. v. Kayser-Roth Corp., 721*n* 208
Savage v. Pacific Gas and Electric Co., 696*n* 109
Saxbe v. Washington Post, 697*n* 12
Sayer; United States v., 695*n* 45
Scales v. United States, 680*n* 26
Schatz v. Republican State Leadership Committee, 209*b*
Scheidler v. Nat'l Organization for Women, 679*n* 113
Schenck v. United States, 108, 680*n* 1, 680*n* 17
Schifano v. Greene Country Greyhound Park, Inc., 692*n* 128
Schneider v. New Jersey, 85*b*
Sealed Case, *In re,* 707*n* 129
Seale v. Gramercy Pictures, 692*n* 122
Search King v. Google Technology, 62*b*
Seaton d/b/a Grand Resort Hotel & Convention Ctr. v. Tripadvisor, 201*b*
Seattle Times v. Rhinehart, 705*n* 90
Sega Enter., Ltd. v. Maphia, 719*n* 160
Sellify, Inc. v. Amazon.com, Inc., 658*b*
Shabazz v. Campbell, 701*n* 159
Shack; State v., 679*n* 120
Shamsky v. Garan, Inc., 691*n* 85
Sheppard v. Maxwell, 419, 421–424, 421*b*, 426, 438, 450, **459–466**, 703*n* 2, 703*n* 9, 704*n* 26, 705*n* 84
Sherwin-Williams Co. v. Holmes County, 675*n* 14
Showler v. Harper's Magazine Foundation, 694*n* 17
Shryock; United States v., 703*n* 19
Shulman v. Group W Productions, Inc., 693*n* 138, 698*n* 42
Sidis v. F-R Publishing Corp., 694*n* 186
Sigma Delta Chi v. Speaker, Maryland House of Delegates, 699*n* 92
Silberman v. Georges, 687*n* 53
Silberman v. Innovative Luggage, Inc., 717*n* 51
Silkwood v. Kerr-McGee, 702*n* 19
Simon & Schuster v. Crime Victims Board, 72
Skokie v. Nat'l Socialist Part of America, 679*n* 106
Sleem v. Yale University, 695*n* 60
Small Bus. Assistance Corp. v. Clear Channel Broad., Inc., 721*n* 216
Smith; United States v., 694*n* 183, 712*n* 15
Smith v. Daily Mail, 694*n* 180, 704*n* 64
Smyth v. Pillsbury Co., 689*n* 19
Snepp v. United States, 679*n* 96
Snyder v. Blue Mountain School District, 681*n* 90
Snyder v. Phelps, 79*b*, 82, 285, 287*b*, 295, 297, **319–323**, 695*n* 36–40
Soboroff; State v., 119*b*
Solano v. Playgirl, Inc., 690*n* 51, 690*n* 55

Sondik v. Kimmel, 249*b*

Sony BMG Music Ent. v. Tenenbaum, 720*n* 192

Sony Corp. v. Universal City Studios, Inc., 579*b*, 601, 616, 633–635, 717*n* 52, 720*n* 195

Sorrell v. IMS Healthcare, Inc., 637, 639*b*, 647, **667–674,** 722*n* 37

Southwestern Cable Co.; United States v., 710*n* 122, 712*n* 183

Spahn v. Julian Messner, 690*n* 49

Special Force Ministries v. WCCO Television, 698*n* 58

SpeechNow.org v. Federal Election Comm'n, 676*n* 44, 678*n* 82

Spelson v. CBS, Inc., 686*n* 28

St. Amant v. Thompson, 685*n* 72

Stahl v. City of St. Louis, 681*n* 50

Standard Brands, Inc. v. Smidler, 721*n* 206

Stanley v. Georgia, 542*b*, 713*n* 63

State ex rel. *See* name of party

Sterling; United States v., 702*n* 23

Stevens; United States v., 8*b*, 116, 677*n* 9

Stevens v. Iowa Newspapers, Inc., 684*n* 57

Stratton Oakmont v. Prodigy Servs. Co., 684*n* 28

Sweezy v. New Hampshire, 414

Syracuse Peace Council v. FCC, 709*n* 73

T

Talley v. California, 678*n* 89

Tatro v. University of Minnesota, 126, 682*n* 128

Taylor v. National Broadcasting Co., Inc., 692*n* 125

TCI Cablevision; Doe v., 692*n* 121

Teleprompter Corp. v. Columbia Broad. Sys., 718*n* 101

Terminiello v. Chicago, 113, 681*n* 46

Texas Beef Group v. Oprah Winfrey, 161*b*

Texas v. Johnson, 5*b*, 121, **136–138,** 676*n* 6

The Romantics v. Activision Pub., Inc., 692*n* 97

Thomas; United States v., 712*n* 19

Thornhill v. Alabama, 85*b*

321 Studios v. Metro Goldwyn Mayer Studios, Inc., 719*n* 157

Tillman v. Freedom of Information Commission, 685*n* 94

Time, Inc. v. Firestone, 685*n* 86

Time Inc. v. Hill, 229*b*, 241–242, 385*b*, 691*n* 65, 702*n* 15

Times Film Corp. v. City of Chicago, 713*n* 68

Times-Mirror Co. v. Superior Court, 695*n* 62

Time Warner Entertainment Co. v. FCC, 711*n* 154

Tinker v. Des Moines Independent Community School District, 103*b*, 123*b*–126, 130, 131, **138–141,** 678*n* 95, 681*n* 65, 681*n* 75, 681*n* 77, 682*n* 125, 682*n* 130

Tin Pan Apple, Inc. v. Miller Brewing Co., 691*n* 89

Titan Sports, Inc. v. Comics World Corp., 692*n* 108

Toffoloni v. LFP Pub. Group, 692*n* 101

Too Much Media v. Hale, 703*n* 41–42

TPS, Inc. v. Dep't of Defense, 701*n* 151

Treasury Employee v. Von Raab, 275

Triangle Publ'ns v. Knight-Ridder Newspaper, Inc., 721*n* 230

Tropicana Products, Inc., In the Matter of, 723*n* 68

Troy Ltd. v. Renna, 679*n* 120

Turner Broadcasting Sys. Inc. v. FCC, 75*b*, 477*b*, 502–503, 508, **521–525,** 677*n* 37, 711*n* 128, 711*n* 132

Twentieth Century Music Corp. v. Aiken, 720*n* 169

Ty, Inc. v. Perryman, 625*b*, 721*n* 229

Tyne v. Time Warner Entertainment Co., 692*n* 124

U

U-Haul Int'l, Inc. v. Jartran, Inc., 723*n* 58

UMG Recordings, Inc. v. Veoh Networks, Inc., 720*n* 163

United Pub. Workers of Am. v. Mitchell, 679*n* 97

United States v. *See* name of opposing party

Univ. of Michigan; Doe v., 683*n* 146–147

Universal Communications Systems, Inc. v. Lycos, Inc., 153*b*

U.S. Civil Serv. Comm'n v. Nat'l Ass'n of Letter Carriers, 679*n* 97

UWM Post v. Univ. of Wis. Bd. of Regents, 683*n* 146

V

Va. State Bd. of Pharmacy v. Va. Citizens Consumer Council, 721*n* 1, 722*n* 14

Valentine v. Chrestensen, 638, 639, 721*n* 4

Van Hollen v. FEC, 722*n* 55–56

Veilleux v. NBC, 691*n* 70, 698*n* 59–60

Vera v. O'Keefe, 699*n* 69

Verizon Internet Services, Inc., In re, 684*n* 34

Viacom Int'l, Inc. v. YouTube, Inc., 720*n* 164

Virgil v. Sports Illustrated, Inc., 693*n* 168

Virgil v. Time, Inc., 693*n* 167

Virginia State Board of Pharmacy v. Virginia Citizens Consumer Council, 639*b*, 640*b*, 665–666

Virginia v. Black, 79*b*, 117–118*b*, 678*n* 73

Virginia v. Jaynes, 723*n* 89

W

Wampler v. Higgins, 686*n* 45

Ward v. Illinois, 712*n* 17, 713*n* 27

Ward v. Rock Against Racism, 74*b*, 678*n* 71

Warner-Lambert Co. v. FTC, 723*n* 69

Warshak; United States v., 699*n* 88

Washington Post Co. v. Keogh, 676*n* 40, 687*n* 69

Washington Post v. U.S. Dep't of State, 700*n* 114

Watchtower v. Stratton, 678*n* 89

Watters v. TSR, Inc., 696*n* 86

Watts v. United States, 118*b*, 681*n* 58

Webb v. CBS Broadcasting Inc., 693*n* 133

Wecht; United States v., 704*n* 22

Weimer v. Rankin, 686*n* 4

Weirum v. RKO General, Inc., 696*n* 99

Wendt v. Host International, Inc., 691*n* 93

West Virginia State Bd. of Educ. v. Barnette, 682*n* 109, 682*n* 112

Wheaton v. Peters, 716*n* 11, 717*n* 26

White-Smith Music Publ'g Co. v. Apollo Co., 720*n* 188

White v. Samsung Electronics America, Inc., 691*n* 91

Whitney v. California, 110, 680*n* 26, 680*n* 32, 684*n* 23, 686*n* 22

Widmar v. Vincent, 681*n* 73

Wildmon v. Berwick Universal Pictures, 696*n* 108

Williams; United States v., 716*n* 155, 723*n* 65

Williams v. City of Minneola, 695*n* 28

Williams v. Pasma, 685*n* 91

Wilson v. Layne, 325, 327*b*, 332*b*, 333, **373–376**, 698*n* 35

Wilson v. Midway Games, Inc., 696*n* 98

Winter v. DC Comics, 692*n* 118

Winter v. G.P. Putnam's Sons, 696*n* 83

Wisconsin Right to Life, Inc.; Federal Election Commission v., 57, 675*n* 4

WLBT-TV, *In re*, 706*n* 101

WNET v. Aereo, Inc., 507*b*, 717*n* 59

Wolfson v. Lewis, 698*n* 46

Wolston v. Reader's Digest Ass'n, 685*n* 85

Wooley v. Maynard, 680*n* 127, 682*n* 108

Y

Yakubowicz v. Paramount Pictures Corp., 696*n* 94

Yates v. United States, 680*n* 36

Yeakey v. Hearst Communications, Inc., 684*n* 56

Y.G. v. Jewish Hospital of St. Louis, 693*n* 156

Yonaty v. Mincolla, 684*n* 43

Young v. New Haven Advocate, 675*n* 15, 687*n* 73

Ysura v. Pocatello Educ. Ass'n, 678*n* 84

Z

Zamora v. Columbia Broad. Sys., 301, 696*n* 70

Zenith Radio Corp.; United States v., 708*n* 5

Zeran v. America Online, 145*b*, 153*b*, 684*n* 29

Zerilli v. Smith, 702*n* 19

Zieve v. Hairston, 693*n* 160

Zurcher v. Stanford Daily, 385*b*, 402–403, 703*n* 48

Subject Index

Page numbers in *italics* denote photos/illustrations. Boxes, maps, figures and notes are indicated by *b, m, f* and *n* respectively, following page numbers. Alphabetization is letter-by-letter (e.g., "Courtroom" precedes "Court system").

A

Abbott, Walter C., Jr., 119*b*
ABC News, 335–337
Abdul-Jabbar, Kareem, 246, *246*
Abrams, Floyd, 645
Abrams, Jacob, 109
Absolute privilege, 192
Abu Ghraib, 365*b*
Access to Private Property Trespass, 330
Access to trials
    court closure challenges, 430*b*, 441
    court closure justification, 432–435
    court closure to protect juveniles, 435–437,
        437*m*, 444*m*
    court closure to protect sexual assault victims, 437–438
    electronic, 441–450, 442*f*, 445*b*, 446*b*, 447*b*,
        448*m*, 449*b*
    gags to limit extrajudicial discussion, 438–441,
        439*b*, 440*b*
    generally, 429
    juror bias, 434*b*
    open court proceedings, 432*b*
    Press-Enterprise test, 431, 432*b*
    presumption of open trials, 429–432
Actual damages, 178
Actual malice
    intentional infliction of emotional distress, 293–297
    libel, 165, 168–178, 168*b*
Adams, John, 38, 59
Ad hoc balancing, 54
Administrative law, 21
Administrative Procedure Act (APA), 377, 478, 572
Administrative rules, 27–29
Advanced Micro Devices (AMD), 434
Advertising, 636–674
    appropriation, 257

appropriation and keyword advertising, 245*b*
*Central Hudson Gas & Electric Co. v. N.Y. Public Service
    Commission,* 639*f*, 661–667
commercial speech doctrine, 638–649, 640*b*, 642, 643,
    644, 646*b*
false and misleading, 651*b*
generally, 637–638
international law, 641*b*
Internet regulation, 658–660, 658*b*, 659*b*
legislative and agency advertising regulation, 649–657, 650*b*,
    651*b*, 652*b*, 653*b*, 655*b*, 657
political broadcasting regulation, 483–489, 485*b*, 487
Sorrell v. IMS Healthcare, Inc., 639*f*, 667–674
Advisory opinion, 654
A&E, 290, 492*b*
Aereo, 507*b*, 589
Aereokiller LLC, 507*b*
Affirm, defined, 14
Agence France Presse (AFP), 588
Agency memos, Freedom of Information Act and, 361
Alcindor, Ferdinand Lewis ("Lew"), 246, *246*
Alcohol advertising, 642, *642*
Alito, Samuel
    First Amendment, 80
    privacy and, 281–283
    rule of law, 13, 13*b*, 14*b*, 14*f*, 16, 40
    speech distinctions, 116, 130
All-purpose public figures, 173
Amazon, 658*b*
American Academy of Pediatrics, 301
American Association of Advertising Agencies, 655*b*
American Bar Association, 4*b*, 6
American Birds, 205*b*
American Civil Liberties Union (ACLU), 80, 328, 344,
    356, 430*b*
American Coalition of Life Activists (ACLA), 118–119
American Library Association, 128

American Nationwide Mortgage Company, 654–655

American Opinion, 182–183

American Political Science Association, 221

American Society of Composers, Authors and Publishers (ASCAP), 611–612, 614

American Society of Newspaper Editors, 351

America Online (AOL), 152, 344

Amicus brief, 13

Amicus curiae, 13

Anderson, David, 306

Angie's List, 194*b*

Animal Crush Video Prohibition Act, 116

Ann-Margret, 536

Anonymous (hacktivist group), 66*b*

Anonymous speech
   First Amendment and, 78–79, 79*b*
   libel and, 153–157, 155–156*b*

Anticybersquatting Consumer Protection Act (ACPA), 623, 626

Anti-SLAPP protection, 148–149, 148*b*, 149*b*

Appeal process, 15*f*

Appellants, 32

Appellees, 32–33

Apple, 581*b*, 619, 620*b*

Appropriation
   commercialization and right of publicity torts, 244–246, 244*b*, 249*b*, 256, 256
   commercial use and keyword advertising, 245*b*
   defenses, 247*b*, 250–258, 252
   defined, 243
   generally, 237*b*, 243
   plaintiff's cases, 246, 246–250, 248*b*

Aqua, 253

"Arbitrary marks," 619

Arch Wireless Operating Company, 273–274

Aristotle, 4

Arizona Constitution, 213

Artistic relevance test, 253

Ashcroft, John, 358, 424

Assange, Julian, 52*b*, 392*b*

Assaults, on speech, 111–120, 113*b*, 115*b*, 118*b*, 119*b*

Associated Press (AP), 170, 316, 339, 583

Association of Community Organizations for Reform Now (ACORN), 340–341

Astaire, Fred, 253

AT&T, 616

Attorneys, advertising by, 647

Authority for Television on Demand (ATVOD) (UK), 539*b*

Authors Guild, 607*b*

B

Ballot issues, regulation and, 489

Barnes, Cynthia, 313

Beanie Babies, 623

Beasley, Carole, 463

Beeson, Ann, 103

Bench-bar-press guidelines, 450–452

Bergen, Candice, 536, *536*

Berger, Paul, 332, 697*n* 30

Berne Convention for Protection of Literary and Artistic Works, 580, 590, 627

Best, Eran, 290–291

Beyoncé, 229

Biden, Joe, 229

Bigelow, Jeffrey, 639

Bildt, Carl, 59*b*

Billings Gazette, 398*b*

Bill of Rights, 23*b*, 24

Bills, process of becoming laws, 24*b*

Binalshibh, Ramzi, 449*b*

Bin Attash, Walid, 449*b*

Bipartisan Campaign Reform Act of 2002 (BCRA), 15, 41, 45–46, 76–77, 489

B.J.F. (rape victim), 269–270

Black, Hugo, 97–98, 110, 140–141

Black, Robert, 304

Black, Sandra, 304

Black-letter law, 21

Blackmun, Harry, 99, 430–431, 451, 472

Black Panther Party, 257

Blackstone, William, 58, 60, 94, 146, 374

Blair, Jayson, 584

Blogging, libel and, 176*b*

Bold and the Beautiful, The (television program), 249*b*

Bonds, Barry, 252

Bono, 548, *549*, 550, 571

Bono, Sonny, 595*b*

Book banning, schools and, 126–128

Booth, Shirley, 257

Bootstrapping, 174

Bork, Robert, 199*b*, 219–220

Bose Corporation, 160

Boyle, Paul, 392*b*

Branch Davidians, 311*b*

Branches of federal government, defined, 22*b*

Brandeis, Louis, 44, 110, 195, 236–237, 456

Brandenburg, Clarence, 110

Brandenburg test, 110–111, 111*b*

Branzburg, Paul, 385
Branzburg v. Hayes, 385–388, 386*f*, 393*b*, 404–416
Breach of contract, 313–314, 314*b*
Brennan, William J.
    advertising, 638
    First Amendment and, 59, 98
    libel, 165, 171, 173, 178, 180–182, 195
    media and the courts, 471–472
    obscenity, indecency, and violence, 567–569
    reporter's privilege, 411–416
    speech distinctions, 121, 136–137
Breyer, Stephen G.
    advertising, 674
    electronic media regulation, *502, 503*
    media and the courts, 446*b*
    newsgathering and, 344
    obscenity, indecency, and violence, 535, 555
    privacy and, 281–283
    rule of law, 13, 13*b*, 14*b*, 14*f*, 16, 42–46
Brinkley, Christie, 252
British Broadcasting Company (BBC), 154*b*
Broadcast Music Inc. (BMI), 611–612, 614
Broadcast regulation
    broadcast licensing, 497–499
    children's programming, 490, 490–493
    generally, 481
    on hoaxes, 493–495, 494*b*
    indecency and, 526, 545–553, 547*b*, 548*b*, 549, 552*b*
    noncommercial, 499–500
    program and advertising regulation, 483–489, 485*b*, 487
    public interest standard, 483
    reality television, 492*b*
    reasons for, 481–483
    sponsorship identification, 495–496
    television program ratings, 552–553, 552*b*
Brunskill, Frank W., 90
Bryant, Paul "Bear," 169
"Bullying" subpoenas, 32*b*
Burck, Robert John, 249*b*
Burden of proof
    defined, 150
    as deterrent, in libel cases, 163*b*
    for libel cases, 150
Bureau of Consumer Protection, 652
Burger, Warren, 99, 431, 467–470, 566–570
Burnett, George, 170
Burns, Ken, 390
Bush, George W., 21, 489

Businesses, libel and reputation of, 160
Butts, Wally, 169

C

Cable Act of 1984, 554
Cable Communications Policy Act of 1984, 502, 509
Cable Television Consumer Protection and Competition Act of 1992, 502, 511, 521–522
Cable television regulation
    cable franchising, 504–505
    cable ownership, 505
    cable programming, 506–511
    development of cable television, 500–502
    First Amendment and, *502*, 502–503
    generally, 500
    indecency and, 554–556
Cablevision Systems, 508, 601–602, 616
California, on libel, 683–684*nn* 20
California Anti-SLAPP Project, 149*b*
California Highway Patrol, 292
California Newspaper Publishers Association, 335*b*
Camdenton (Missouri) High School, 128
Camel (cigarettes), 644
Cameras in courtrooms. *See* Electronic access to trials
Cameras in the Courtroom Act of 2011, 446*b*
Campagna, Don, 422*b*
Campaign finance, 76–78, 78*b*
Campari Liqueur, 294–295, 317
Campus Security Act (Clery Act), 347
Canada
    intellectual property law, 621*b*
    obscenity law, 530*b*
    trademarks, 621*b*
Canadian Charter of Rights and Freedoms, 530*b*
Canadian Intellectual Property Office (CIPO), 621*b*
Cantrell, Margaret, 241–242
Cantrell, Melvin, 241
Carlin, George, 546, 547–548, 547*b*, 548*b*
CarMax, 619
Carneal, Michael, 303
Carr, David, 176*b*
Carroll, Jill, *330*
Carter, Jimmy, 488
Case briefs, 37–39
Case law, reading, 35–37
Case process, 29–34
    civil lawsuits, 30–33, 30*f*

criminal cases, 29, 33–34
generally, 29–30, 33–34
summary judgment, 33
Categorical balancing, 55
CATV, 501
CBS News, 68
CBS Television Network, 488
Cease and desist orders, 654
Ceballos, Richard, 81
Censorship, political advertising and, 487–488. *See also*
Obscenity and indecency
Center for Responsive Politics (CRP), 77
Centers for Disease Control, 644
*Central Hudson Gas & Electric Co. v. N.Y. Public Service
Commission,* 639f, 661–667
Central Intelligence Agency (CIA), 66b, 356, 389, 453, 455
Central Park Five (movie), 390
Challenger (space shuttle), 324, 361b, 362b
Chaplinsky, Walter, 112–113
Chapman, Mark David, 311b
Chemerinsky, Erwin, 131b
Cheney, Dick, 84
Cher, 257, 549, 550, 571
Cherry Sisters, 193
Child Online Protection Act (COPA), 557–559
Child pornography, 538–542, 539b
Child Pornography Protection Act (CPPA), 540, 559
Children's Internet Protection Act (CIPA), 559
Children's Television Act, 490, 490, 490–493
Chilling effect, 105
China, video games in, 561b
Chisholm, Shirley, 229b
Chrestensen, F. J., 638
Christian Legal Society (CLS), 130
Chronicle of Higher Education, 348
Chrysler Corporation, 360
Citations, for legal cases, 34–35
Citizens United v. Federal Elections Commission, 2, 3, 5f, 7b,
40–46, 77, 648–649
City of Ontario v. Quon, 227f, 273–277
Civil contempt, 385b
Civil lawsuits, 30–33, 30f
Clark, Tom, 459–466
Clear and present danger, 108–110
Clear Channel Communications, 65, 495, 613
Cleveland Plain Dealer, 241–242
"Cliff's law," 615b
Clinton, Bill, 363
Clinton, Hillary, 3, 229, 363

CNN, 292, 439–440, 504, 584
Coalition of Journalists for Open Government (CJOG), 355b
Coca-Cola, 617
Codes, speech, 134
Cohen, Dan, 399, 400, 400b, 416–417
Cohen, Paul Robert, 112
Cohen v. Cowles Media, 386f, 399–400, 400b, 416–417
Colgate, Samuel, 530
Colleges, campus speech and, 128–133, 134b. *See also* Speech
distinctions; *individual names of colleges*
Colorado Springs Gazette, 76
Columbine High School, Littleton, Colorado, 303
Comcast Corporation, 496, 513, 616
"Commentaries on the Law of England" (Blackstone),
58, 146, 374
Commercialization, 244–246, 244b
Commercial speech doctrine
advertising by attorneys, 647
commercial speech, defined, 638
controlled substances and activities, 636, 642, 642–647,
643, 644, 646b
corporate speech regulation, 648–649
free flow of commercial information, 640b
generally, 638–641, 640b
Common law, 21, 26–27
Communications Act of 1934
electronic media regulation, 478, 481, 485, 492b, 496, 499,
500, 512, 518
obscenity, indecency, and violence, 544–545, 546
rule of law, 29
Communications Assistance for Law Enforcement Act
(CALEA), 234b
Communications Decency Act (CDA) of 1996
electronic media regulation, 515
emotional distress, 312–313
libel, 151–152, 153b, 154b, 211, 215
obscenity, indecency, and violence, 556
privacy, 265b
rule of law, 25
Communist Labor Party, 110
"Community standards," obscenity and, 532–535, 535b
Compelled speech, 87–88
Compelling interest, 72
Compositions, musical, 610–612
Computer Fraud and Abuse Act (CFAA), 308b
Computer records, Freedom of Information Act and,
366–367
Comstock, Anthony, 530, 531b, 531b
Comstock Act, 531, 532

Concurring opinion, 14, 15

Conditional privilege, 192

Conference of Chief Justices, 456

Conference of State Court Administrators, 456

Confidentiality, breaking promises of, 399–400

Congressional Record, 351

Connecticut Decency Act, 265b

ConnectU, 434

Conradt, Louis, 290b

Consent
  consent orders, 654
  First Amendment and appropriation, 257–258
  intrusion and, 261–262

Considine, Robert, 463

Constitutional law, generally, 21

Consumer Reports, 160

Consumer reviews, 194b

Contempt of court, 387b, 395b

Content-based laws, 71 72

Content-neutral laws, 70, 72–73

Continuance, 428

Contracts
  breach of, 313–314
  defined, 314b

Contributory infringement, 600–601

Controlled substances/activities, advertising regulation,
    636, 642, 642–647, 643, 644, 646b

Controlling the Assault of Non-Solicited Pornography and
    Marketing (CAN-SPAM) Act, 660

Cook, Fred J., 517

Coors Brewing Company, 642

Coppertone, 619

Copyright
  computers and Internet, 609–610
  Copyright Act (1976), 580–587
  defined, 578
  development of, 579–580
  generally, 578–579
  infringement, defense (fair use), 603–608, 604b, 605b
  infringement, proving, 599–603, 600b, 601b
  music licensing, 610–615, 611b, 615b
  notice, 593–599
  protection, 583b, 585b, 588–593, 591b, 592b, 595b, 607b
  public domain and, 251–252, 594–597, 596b

Copyright Alert System, 616, 617

Copyright Revision Act of 1976, 580

Copyright Royalty Board, 613

Coroners and Justice 2009 (UK), 146b

Corporate speech regulation, 648–649

Corporation for Public Broadcasting (CPB), 499

Corrective advertising, 656

Cortislim, 656

Cortistress, 656

Cosby, William, 58

Court records, access to, 451b, 452–458, 454b

Court system, 8–18
  appeal process, 15f
  federal court and state court systems, compared,
      9f, 10–11t
  generally, 8–9, 17–18
  jurisdiction, 9–12, 9b
  trial courts, 12
  U.S. Circuit Courts of Appeal, 12f, 13–15
  U.S. Supreme Court, 14f, 15–17

Covert recording, 339–346, 340b, 341b, 342m, 345b

Cox, Crystal, 176b

Craigslist, 312–313

Creative Commons, 597b

Crime reporting, crime rate and, 422b

Criminal cases
  Colorado on criminal libel, 146b
  generally, 29, 33–34

Criminal contempt, 387b

Cutting Edge Designs, 658b

Cyberbullying, 308b

Cyber Intelligence Sharing and Protection Act
    (CISPA), 234b

Cybersecurity, executive order on, 28b

Cyberstalking, 297–298

D

Dajaz1.com, 70

Dalglish, Lucy, 32b

Damages
  actual damages, 178
  appropriation, 250
  libel, 147, 178–179
  presumed damages, 178–179
  punitive damages, 179
  special damages, 178
  statutory damages, 593

David (Michelangelo), 527

Davis, Charles G., 90

Davis, David, 107b

Davis, Jake, 66b

Debs, Eugene, 109

Defamation
    international law on libel tourism and U.K. Defamation
        Bill 2013, 207b
    as libel case element (U.S.), 58, 161b, 188
Defamation Bill (U.K.), 207b
Defendants, 30
Defenses
    appropriation, 247b, 250–258, 252
    copyright infringement (fair use), 603–608, 604b, 605b
    false light, 242
    intrusion, 261–263
    neutral reportage defense, 203–204, 204b, 205b
    shield laws, 397–398
    trademark infringement, 626
    wire service defense, 204, 204b
    See also Libel defenses and privileges
Deference, 28
Demurrer, 31
Dendrite test, 156b
De novo, 13
DePasquale, Daniel, 429
Deposition, 171
"Descriptive marks," 619
Designated public forums, 83
Desnick, J. H., 262
Detroit News, 193
Diadiun, J. Theodore, 221–225
Diana, Princess, 261, 335
Diaz, Antonio, 268
Diaz, Toni, 268
DiCaprio, Leonardo, 302
Digital Millenium Copyright Act (DMCA), 609–610, 617
Diller, Barry, 507b
Direct broadcast satellites, regulation of, 483f, 511, 511–512
Disclosure, 352
Discovery, 31
Discretion, 5, 6
Disney, Walt, 576
Dissenting opinion, 14, 15
Distinctiveness, trademark and, 618–622
Distinguish from precedent, defined, 27
Distributors, libel and, 152–153, 153b
Doan's, 657
Dockets, court, 452–453
Doctrines, 21
Dodge, William, Jr., 530
Domain names, 623
Douglas, William, 97–98, 386, 569–570
Dowler, Milly, 338b

Drew, Lori, 308b, 308b
Drew, Sarah, 308b, 308b
Driver's Privacy Protection Act of 1994, 348–350, 350
Drudge, Matt, 152
Drug Enforcement Administration, 454
Duckett, Melinda, 292
Due process, 13
Duke, Steven, 274–275
Duty of due care, 299

E

Edge Broadcasting, 645
Editorials, broadcast, 489
Education, speech in the schools and, 122–135, 123b, 124,
    131b, 133, 134b
Ehrenfeld, Rachel, 207b
E/I (educate and inform), 491
Einstein, Albert, 245
Eldred, Eric, 597b
Elections, First Amendment and, 76–78, 78b
Electronic access to trials
    broadcasting and recording, 442–443
    cameras in courtrooms, 444–446
    cameras in courtrooms, federal courts, 442f, 445b, 446b
    Cameras in the Courtroom Act of 2011, 446b
    electronic access to court records, 456–457
    generally, 441
    new technologies, 447–450, 447b, 449b
    video, audio, webcasts of state courtrooms, 448m
Electronic Arts (EA), 255b
Electronic Communications Privacy Act (ECPA), 231b,
    343–344
Electronic Freedom of Information Act of 1996 (EFOIA), 353,
    366–367, 376
Electronic Frontier Foundation, 234b
Electronic media regulation, 474–525
    broadcast regulation, 481–500, 483f, 485b, 487, 490, 491b,
        492b, 494b, 498b
    cable television regulation, 500–511, 502, 507b
    direct broadcast satellites, 483f, 511, 511–512
    FCC and, 475–481, 479b, 480b
    generally, 474–478
    Internet regulation, 512–515
    Red Lion v. FCC, 477f, 516–521
    Turner Broadcasting v. FCC, 477f, 502–503, 521–525
Elizabeth II (Queen of England), 207b
Elliott, Christopher, 32b

Ellsberg, Daniel, 67, 349*b*

E-mail
  advertising and, 659*b*
  as public record, 368*b*

Emergency Alert System, 494*b*

Eminem, 344

Emotional distress and physical harm, 284–323
  breach of contract, 313–314, 314*b*
  Communications Decency Act (CDA), 312–313
  emotional distress, defined, 286
  fraudulent misrepresentation, 315–316
  generally, 285–286
  Hustler Magazine v. Falwell, 287*f*, 294*b*, 317–319
  incitement, 306–311, 307*b*, 308*b*, 310*b*, 311*b*
  intentional infliction of emotional distress, 288–298, 289*b*, 290*b*, 292, 293*b*, 294*b*, 295*b*, 296*f*
  interference with economic advantage, 314–315
  lawsuit development and, 286–288
  negligent infliction of emotional distress, 298–301, 299*b*
  physical harm, 301–306, 302, 305*b*
  Snyder v. Phelps, 287*f*, 319–323

En banc, 13

EndRevengePorn.com, 265*b*

Enforcement Action Plan, 658

Entercom, 613

Entertainment Merchants Association (EMA), 116

Entertainment Software Rating Board (ESRB), 564–565, 564*b*

Equity law, 21, 26

ErnestandJulioGallo.com, 623

Eshelman, Fred, 489

Espionage Act of 1917, 349*b*

ESPN, 502, 504

Estes, Billy Sol, *420*, 421

Eszterhas, Joe, 241–242

European Union (EU)
  on advertising, 641*b*
  on sound recordings, 615*b*, 641*b*

Evans, Rowland, Jr., 199*b*, 216–221

Executive orders, 21, 28*b*, 29

Experience and logic test, 431–432

Extreme Fast Food, 249*b*

Exxon, 619

F

Fabrikant & Sons, 620–621

Fabrikant Fine Diamonds, 620

Facebook, 62*b*, 80, 211, 230, 230*f*, 248*b*, 425*b*, 434

Face-to-face recording, 340–341

Facial challenges, 8*b*

Facial meaning, 25

Fact finder, 239

Fact magazine, 168

Fair comment and criticism, *193,* 193–195, 194*b*

Fair Labor Association, 648

Fairness doctrine, 494–495

Fairness in Music Licensing Act of 1998, 612

Fair report privilege, 190–193, 190*b*

Fair trial
  access to court records, 451*b*, 452–458, 454*b*
  access to trials, 429–441, 430*b*, 432*b*, 433*b*, 434*b*, 437*m*, 439*b*, 440*b*
  electronic access to trials, 441–450, 442*f*, 444*m*, 445*b*, 446*b*, 447*b*, 448*m*, 449*b*
  prejudicial speech, remedies, 426–429
  prejudicial speech and, *420,* 420–426, 425*b*

Fair use, 603–608, 604*b*, 605*b*

False light, 237–243, 237*b*, 238*b*

False pretenses, 262–263

Falsity, 162–165, 163*b*

Falwell, Jerry, 294–295, 294*b*, 296, 317–319

Family Educational Rights and Privacy Act (FERPA), 347–348

Family Movie Act (FMA), 590

Family Smoking Prevention and Tobacco Control Act, 658

"Fanciful marks," 619

Faneuil Hall, Boston, 388

FastTrack, 631

Fat Boys, The, 247

Fault (libel cases), 164–168

Favish, Allan, 363, 364

FCC v. Fox Television Stations, 529*f*, 570–575

Federal Advisory Committee Act (FACA), 368–369

Federal Bureau of Investigation (FBI), 228, 289, 363, 457

Federal Communications Commission (FCC)
  administrative law, 21
  advertising, 659*b*
  defined, 475
  electronic media regulation, 478–481, 483, 485*b*, 490–491, 494, 497–501, 505–506
  electronic media regulation and Internet, 512–515
  First Amendment, 62
  newsgathering, 341*b*, 343
  rule of law, 21, 27

Federal courts
  cameras in, 442*f*, 445*b*, 446*b* (*See also* Media and the courts)

shield laws and options for protection of confidential sources, 394*b*

state court systems compared to, 9*f,* 10–11*t*

Federal Election Commission (FEC), 77, 489, 649

Federalism, 22

Federal Judicial Center, 440*b,* 453

Federal meetings, access to, 367–372

Federal Open Meetings Law, 368, 371*b*

Federal Radio Act of 1927, 545

Federal Radio Commission (FRC), 476, 477–478, 517

Federal Rules of Civil Procedure, 397, 443

Federal Trade Commission (FTC)
    advertising, *636,* 651–657, 651*b,* 659*b*
    defined, 651
    FTC mechanisms, 652*b*
    obscenity, indecency, and violence, 563
    privacy, 229, 301
    rule of law, 21
    on video games, *100*

Fellini, Federico, 253

"Female Forces," 290–291

Fiction, identification in, 158

Fiduciary relationship, 315–316

Fighting words, 112–113, 113*b,* 115*b*

File sharing, 615–616

Finding the law, 34–39
    case briefs, 37–39
    reading case law, 35–37
    research resources, 34–35

Finkelstein, Howard, 239

FIRAC (Facts, Issue, Rule of Law, Analysis and Conclusion), 37–38

First Amendment, 50–99
    cable television and, 502–503
    compelled speech, 87–88
    court scrutiny and, 71–75, 72*b,* 74*b,* 75*b*
    generally, *50,* 51–53, 52*b*
    Internet access and international law, 66*b*
    Internet's First Amendment status, 514–515
    interpreting, 53–56, 55*b*
    media emergence, convergence and consolidation, 64–65
    Near v. Minnesota, 53*f,* 89–97
    New York Times v. United States, 53*f,* 97–99
    origins of, 56–59
    political speech, 76–81, 78*b,* 79*b*
    prior restraint and, 65–70, 67*b,* 68*b*
    privacy and, 252–257, 269–272
    public and nonpublic forums, 81–87, 83*b,* 85*b*
    speech, defined, 62*b*

UN on freedom of expression and information, 59*b*
    values, 60–63, 61*b*
    WikiLeaks and, 69*b*
    See also Emotional distress and physical harm; Libel; Libel defenses and privileges; Media and the courts; Newsgathering; Obscenity and indecency; Reporter's privilege; Speech distinctions

First Amendment Center, 149*b*

First-sale doctrine, 591–592

527 groups, 489

Flag burning, as symbolic speech, 121

Florida Star, 270

Flynt, Larry, 294–295, 294*b*

Folgers, 247

Food and Drug Administration (FDA), 644, 650*b,* 658

Food Channel, 508

Food Lion, 335–337, 336*b*

For-cause challenge, 427

Ford, Gerald R., 604, 608

Ford Motor Company, 247

Foreign Intelligence Surveillance Court, 452

Foreseeability, 303–305

Fortas, Abe, 138–140

Forum shopping, 11

Foster, Lisa, *363*

Foster, Vincent, 363, *363*

Fowler, Mark, 483

Fox Broadcasting, 66*b*

Fraley, Angel, 211, 248*b*

Franchise fees, 504

Franchises, 504

Franchising authority, 504

Frank, Jerome, 245

Franklin, Benjamin, 156

Fraser, Matthew, 127

Fraud
    fraudulent misrepresentation, 315–316
    newsgathering and, 335–328

Frederick, Joseph, 124

Freedom Communications, 76

Freedom of Information Act (FOIA), 347, 351–364, 365*b,* 367, 370, 457
    access to federal records, 351–356
    defined, 351
    examples, 357*b,* 361–362
    exemptions, 356–365, 356*b*
    generally, 350, 351*b*
    government responsiveness to, 355
    open-government laws, 351

Privacy Act and, 347
rule of law, 27
Free Expression Policy Project (FEPP), 105
Free Press Act of 2012, 149*b*
Free Press Underground, 129
Free speech. *See* First Amendment
Free Speech Clause, 80
Friendly, Henry, 223–224
Frischling, Steve, 32*b*
Frohwerk, Jacob, 108
Furchtgott-Roth, Harold, 115*b*

G

Galella, Ron, 334
Gambling advertising, 645
Gaston Gazette (North Carolina), 398*b*
Gates, Robert, 329
Gay-Straight Alliance Network, 128
Genachowski, Julius, 479, 479*b*, 480*b*, 498
General Accounting Office, 366
General Electric, 65
Generally applicable law, 400
Generic words, trademarking and, 621–622
Geolocation Privacy and Surveillance Act (GPSA), 235
Geological data, Freedom of Information Act and, 365
Gerber, Sam, 459–461
Geritol, 656
Gertz, Elmer, 173, *173*, 182–187
Gertz v. Robert Welch, Inc., 143*f*, 173, *173*, 176*b*, 182–187
Gibson, Calvin, 312
Gibson, Mel, 229
Ginsburg, Ralph, 168
Ginsburg, Ruth Bader
   advertising, 674
   intellectual property, 627–630
   obscenity, indecency, and violence, 535
   privacy and, 281–283
   rule of law, 13, 13*b*, 14*b*, 14*f*, 16, 42–46
   speech distinctions, 130
Gitlow, Benjamin, 109
Gizmodo, 197–198
Glomar Explorer, 356
Gnutella, 631
GoDaddy, 265*b*
Golan v. Holder, 579*f*, 627–630
Goldman, Ronald, 160
Goldwater, Barry, 168, 517

Goodall, Jane, 584
Good faith, 155*b*
Google, 62*b*, 79*b*, 106*b*, 228, 607*b*, 658*b*
Google Maps, 147*m*, 260
Government in the Sunshine Act, 368
Government land, press access to, 329
Government speakers, First Amendment and, 78–79, 79*b*
Grace, Nancy, 292, *292*
Grand jury, 30
Grand Resort and Convention Center, 201*b*
Gray, Larry, 304
Greenhouse, Linda, 6
Grisham, John, 239, *240*
Grokster, 602, 616, 631–635
Group identification, libel and, 157–158
Guardian (U.K.), 154*b*, 228, *338b*
Gun violence, electronic media regulation and, 491*b*

H

Hacking
   of Emergency Alert System (EAS), 494*b*
   hacktivism, 66*b*
   newsgathering and, 338*b*
Hallmark Cards, 243
Hamilton, Andrew, 58
Hand, Learned, 181
Hansen, Chris, 290*b*, *290b*
"Happy Birthday to You" (song), 585*b*
Harassment, newsgathering and, 334–335
Hargis, Billy James, 517
Harlan, John Marshall, II, 99, 141, 170, 233, 279
Harley-Davidson, 621
Harney, Donald, 601*b*
Harper's, 289, 318
Harris, Eric, 303
Harry Fox Agency, 612
Hart, Ryan, 255*b*
Hate speech, 114, 115*b*
Hatfill, Steven J., 289, 395*b*
Hayes, Susan, 461
Hazelwood (Missouri) East High School, 127
Health Insurance Portability and Accountability Act (HIPAA), 348
Hearn, John Wayne, 304
Henry VIII (King of England), 56
Hess, Gregory, 306
Hester, David, 492*b*
Hicklin rule, 531–532

Hill, Henry, 72
Hill, Mildred J., 585*b*
Hill, Patty Smith, 585*b*
Hillary: The Movie, 41
Hilton, Paris, 229, 243
Hinckley, John W., 311*b*
Hindenburg (dirigible), 583, 583
Hiss, Alger, 517
Hit Man: A Technical Manual for Independent Contractors
     (book), 310
Hoaxes, electronic media regulation on, 493
Holder, Eric, 403
Holding, 36
Holiday, 257
Holmes, James Egan, 302, 438
Holmes, Oliver Wendell, 106*b*, 108, 109, 192
Home Box Office (HBO), 501, 553
Homeland Security Act, 358
Hoover, J. Edgar, 517
"Hopper" device, 599
Horn, Lawrence, 310*b*
Horn, Mildred, 310*b*
House of the Dead, The (video game), 562*b*
Howard, Robert, 239
Hughes, Charles, 89–97
Hughes, Howard, 257, 356
Hustler, 251, 307–308
Hustler Magazine v. Falwell, 287*f*, 294*b*, 317–319
Hypertext Markup Language (HTML), 541

Ice Cube, 344
Identification (libel cases), 157–162
Identity, appropriation of, 247–250
Ideology, court system and, 13*b*
Images, harmful, 116–117
Immigrations and Customs Enforcement (ICE), 69
Impanel, defined, 427
Implication, libel and, 163–164
Important government interest, 73
Incitement
     Brandenburg test, 110–111, 111*b*
     emotional distress and physical harm, 306–311, 307*b*, 308*b*,
          310*b*, 311*b*
Incorporation doctrine, 109
Indecency
     broadcast, 526, 545–553, 547*b*, 548*b*, 549, 552*b*

     cable television, 554–556
     defined, 530
     generally, 544–545
     Internet, 535*b*, 556–560, 556*b*
     See also Obscenity and indecency
Indiana Open Records Law, 455
Industry guides (FTC), 654
Injunction, 67
Innocence of Muslims (movie), 106*b*
Innuendo, libel and, 163–164
Intellectual property, 576–635
     copyright, computers and Internet, 609–610
     copyright, development, 579–580
     copyright, generally, 578–579
     copyright, infringement defense (fair use), 603–608, 604*b*,
          605*b*
     copyright, music licensing, 610–615, 611*b*, 615*b*
     copyright, proving infringement, 599–603, 600*b*, 601*b*
     Copyright Act (1976), 580–587
     copyright and Creative Commons, 597*b*
     copyright notice, 593–599
     copyright protection, 583*b*, 585*b*, 588–593, 591*b*, 592*b*,
          595*b*, 607*b*
     generally, 577–578
     Golan v. Holder, 579*f*, 627–630
     intellectual property law, defined, 578
     international law, 581*b*, 621*b*
     MGM v. Grokster, 579*f*, 631–635
     public domain, 251–252, 594–597, 596*b*
     trademark, 611–626, 618*b*, 619*b*, 620*b*
     U.S. Constitution on, 578*b*
Intentional infliction of emotional distress, 286, 288–298
     actual malice, 293–297
     cyberstalking, 297–298
     defined, 286
     examples, 290*b*, 294*b*, 296*f*
     generally, 288–289
     intentional or reckless action, 292–293
     outrageousness, 289–292
     parody *versus* satire, 295*b*
     plaintiff's case, 289*b*
Intentional infliction of emotional distress (IIED), 293*b*,
     295–296
Intermediate scrutiny, 73, 74*b*, 75*b*
International agency rules, Freedom of Information Act and,
     359–360
International law
     advertising, 641*b*
     child pornography, 539*b*

electronic media regulation, 498*b*
intellectual property, 581*b*, 615*b*, 621*b*
libel, 146*b*, 147*m*
libel defenses and privileges, 207*b*
obscenity, 530*b*
trademarks, 621*b*
video games, 561*b*
International News Service (INS), 583
Internet
advertising regulation, 658–660, 658*b*, 659*b*
appropriation and keyword advertising, 245*b*
copyright and, 609–610
cyberbullying, 308*b*
Cyber Intelligence Sharing and Protection Act (CISPA), 234*b*
cybersecurity executive order, 28*b*
cyberstalking, 297–298
free speech issues, 66*b*
indecency and, 535*b*, 556–560, 556*b*
Internet service providers (ISPs) and ECPA, 344–346
libel and Internet service providers (ISPs), 156–157
libel issues of consumer reviews and criticism online, 194*b*
regulation, 512–515
shield laws and websites, 395–397
for television programming, 507*b*
Internet Corporation for Assigned Names and Numbers (ICANN), 512
Interstate Stalking Statute, 297–298
Intimate facts, 265–266
Intrusion
defenses, 261–263
generally, 237*b*, 259–264, 261*b*
intrusion upon seclusion, 259
methods of, 259–260
on private property, 260–261
reasonable person, 259
by trespass, 261*b*
Involuntary public figures, 175
Iqbal standard, 209*b*
Isaacman, Allan, 294*b*
IsAnybodyUp, 265*b*

J

Jackson, Janet, 550
James, Steve, 585*b*
Jartran, 651
Jaynes, Jeremy, 660
Jay-Z, 229

J.B. Williams Company, 656
Jefferson, Thomas, 38
Jehovah's Witnesses, 128
Jobs, Steve, 620*b*
"Joe Camel" (cartoon character), advertising and, 644
John Birch Society, 182
John Deere, 624
Johnson, Gregory Lee, 101, 121
Johnson, Marlene, 416–417
Johnson, Ron, 133
Jones, Antoine, 278–281
Jones, John, 224
Jordan, Michael, 647
Journalists
as defined by shield laws, 394
journalist's privilege (*See* Reporter's privilege)
libel and journalistic responsibility, 169*b* (*See also* Libel; Libel case elements)
See also Media and the courts; Newsgathering; *individual names of journalists; individual names of media outlets*
JSTOR (database), 454*b*
Judicial review, 18–20, 19*b*. See also Content-based laws; Content-neutral laws; Rational review
Judiciary Act of 1789, 38, 39
Jurisdiction
defined, 9
libel defenses and privileges, 210, 210*b*
rule of law and court system, 9–12, 9*b*
Jurors
admonition of, 428
bias of, 434*b*
jury selection, 427
selection of, 427
sequestration of, 428
Justice Management Institute, 456

K

Kaelin, Brian "Kato," 160
Kagan, Elena
advertising, 674
privacy, 281–283
rule of law, 13, 13*b*, 14*b*, 14*f*, 16
Kalven, Harry, Jr., 167*b*, 168
Kansas, on shield laws, 396*b*
Kansas State University, 133
Kardashian, Kim, 229
Karnas, Jerry, *110*

Kasky, Mark, 31, 648
KaZaA, 449, 615
Keller, Sam, 255*b*
Kennedy, Anthony
    advertising, 647, 667–674
    electronic media regulation, 521–525
    First Amendment, 55
    libel, 169
    media and the courts, 435, 446*b*
    obscenity, indecency, and violence, 535, 570–575
    privacy and, 273–277
    rule of law, 13, 13*b*, 14*b*, 14*f*, 16, 40–46
    speech distinctions, 137
Kennedy, Jamie, 293*b*
Kentucky State University, 132
Kenworth, 619
Kerry, John, 489
Keyword advertising, 245*b*
Kimmel, Jimmy, 249*b*
Kinko's, 608
Kiriakou, John, 349*b*
Kirtley, Jane, 430*b*
Klebold, Dylan, 303
Kleenex, 622
Kmart, 269
Knowledge of falsity, 168–169
Krawczyski, John, 154*b*
Kristof, Nicholas, 289
Krumholz, Sheila, 77
Ku Klux Klan (KKK), 110, 117
Kurdistan Workers Party (PKK), 103
Kutcher, Ashton, 229 291*b*, 293*b*
Kyle, John, 149*b*

L

Langballe, Jesper, 115*b*
Langley, John, 334
Lanham Act
    advertising and, 651–657
    trademark and, 578, 618, 619*b*, 622, 626
Lanza, Adam, 302
Las Vegas Review-Journal, 599
Lawfully obtained information, 270–271
Laws of general application, 86
Leach, George E., 90
Leahy, Patrick, *231b*, 647
Lee, Pamela Anderson, 268, 693*n* 158

Legal research. *See* Sources of the law
LegalTrac, 35
Leggett, Vanessa, 391
Legitimate public concern, 267–268
Lehrer, Jonah, 584
Leno, Jay, 294*b*
Lessig, Lawrence, 597*b*, 597*b*
Letterman, David, 294*b*
Letters to the editor, 200
LexisNexis, 34, 35
Lexus, 619
Libel, 144–187
    anonymous speech and, 153–157, 155–156*b*
    anti-SLAPP protection, 148–149, 148*b*, 149*b*
    blogging and, 176*b*
    contemporary issues, 149–150
    defined, 145*b*
    elements of plaintiff's case, 150–179 (*See also* Libel case
        elements)
    generally, 143–144
    Gertz v. Robert Welch, Inc., 143*f*, 173, *173*, 176*b*, 182–187
    history of, 144–149, 145*f*, 148*b*
    international law issues, 146*b*, 147*m*
    journalistic responsibility and, 169*b*
    New York Times Co. v. Sullivan, 144, 164–173, 166*b*, 167*b*,
        176*b*, 180–182, 638
    public figures, 173–177, 174*b*
    reckless disregard, 171*b*
    slander *versus,* 144*b*
    See also Libel defenses and privileges
Libel case elements
    actual malice, 165, 168–178, 168*b*
    burden of proof for libel cases, 150
    damages, 147, 178–179
    defamation, 58, 161*b*, 188
    falsity, 162–165, 163*b*
    fault, 164–168
    identification, 157–162
    publication, 151–157, 153*b*, 154*b*
    statement of fact, 150–151
Libel defenses and privileges, 188–225
    fair comment and criticism, *193,* 193–195, 194*b*
    fair report privilege, 190–193, 190*b*
    generally, 189–190
    international law on libel tourism and U.K. Defamation Bill
        2013, 207*b*
    jurisdiction, 210, 210*b*
    libel-proof plaintiffs, 206–208
    Milkovich v. Lorain Journal Co., 191*f,* 221–225

motion to dismiss and, 209*b*

neutral reportage, 203–204, 204*b*, 205*b*

Ollman v. Evans, 191*f*, 199*b*, 216–221

opinion, 195–203, 196*b*, 199*b*, 201*b*

responsible reporting, 214

retractions, 212–213

Section 230 immunity, 211–212

single-publication rule, 204–205

statutes of limitation, 212, 213*m*

statutes of limitations, 212

summary judgment, 208–210

wire service defense, 204, 204*b*

Libel per quod, 159

Libel per se, 158–159

Libel-proof plaintiffs, 206–208

Liberty (Oregon State University), 132

Library of Congress, 580

Licensing, broadcast, 497

Licensing Act, 57

Liebeck, Sheila, 694*n* 2

Life, 262

Likeness, appropriation of, 246–247

Limited-purpose public figures, 173–175

Listerine, 656

Litigated orders, 656

Litman, Jessica, 592*b*

Little, Paul, 535

Locke, John, 57, 60

Locy, Toni, 395*b*

Lohan, Lindsey, 253

LoJack Corporation, 240

London, Jack, 202

Lorain Journal Company, 222

Lorillard brothers, 642

Los Angeles Times, 76

Loughner, Jared, 302

Love, Courtney, 154*b*

Lowest unit rate, 487

LulzSec, 66*b*

M

Madden, 255*b*

Madison, James, 38, 94, 95, 147, 181, 184, 351

Major League Baseball, 252

Malcolm, Janet, 168, 169*b*

Manning, Bradley, 349*b*, 349*b*

Manson, Charles, 311*b*

Marbury, William, 38

Marbury v. Madison, 5*f*, 18, 38–39, 46–49

Marconi, Guglielmo, 476, 476

Mardis, Dylan J., 125

Marijuana advertising, 643*b*

Marlboro (cigarettes), 650*b*

Marr, Kendra, 584

Marriage Equality Act (New York), 159

Marshall, John, 38, 46–49, 147

Marshall, Thurgood, 411–416, 471–472

Martin, Paul, 688–689*nn* 91

Martin, Trayvon, 447*b*

Maryland State Board of Censors, 543

Masson, Jeffrey, 168, 169*b*

"Masters of August, The" (Rush), 256, 256*b*

Matera, Dary, 391

Mattel, 253

Maxwell, Zachary, 582

Mayfield, Jeremy, 209*b*

Maynard, George, 87

McAlpine, Alistair, 154*b*

McChrystal, Stanley, 329

McDonald's, 285

McGraw, Phil, 161*b*

McMahon, Patrick, 274

Mechanical license, 612

Media and the courts, 418–473

access to court records, 451*b*, 452–458, 454*b*

access to trials, 429–441, 430*b*, 432*b*, 433*b*, 434*b*, 437*m*, 439*b*, 440*b*, 444*m*

bench-bar-press guidelines, 450–452

crime reporting and crime rate, 422*b*

electronic access to trials, 441–450, 442*f*, 445*b*, 446*b*, 447*b*, 448*m*, 449*b*

fair trial and prejudicial speech, 420, 420–426, 425*b*

generally, 419–420

remedies to prejudice, 426–429

Richmond Newspapers v. Virginia, 421*f*, 466–473

Sheppard v. Maxwell, 421–423, 421*f*, 459–466

Media Law Resource Center, 449*b*

Media Libel Survey, 179

Medical records, access to, 348

Medico, Charles, 378–381

Meier, Megan, 308*b*

Meltwater, 605

Melville, Herman, 594

Memorandum order, 17

MGM, 621*b*, 621*b*

MGM v. Grokster, 579*f*, 631–635

Miami Herald, 423
Michaels, Bret, 268, 693*n* 158
Michelangelo, 527
"Mickey Mouse" (cartoon character), intellectual property
    laws and, 595, 595*b*
Midler, Bette, 247
Military sites, press access to, 329–334, *330*
Milkovich, Michael, 197, 221–225
Milkovich v. Lorain Journal Co., 191*f,* 221–225
Miller, Judith, 389*b,* 390
Miller, Marvin, 533*b*
Miller (beer), 247
Miller v. California, 528*b,* 529*f,* 533*b,* 537*b,* 566–570
Milligan, Lambden P., 107*b*
Milton, John, 57, 59
Minneapolis Journal, 90
Minneapolis Star and Tribune, 416–417
Minneapolis Tribune, 90
Misrepresentation, newsgathering and, 335–328, 336*b*
Mitchell, Nellie, 241
Modify precedent, 27
Mohammed, Khalid Sheik, 430*b*
Monroe, Marilyn, 245
Montana, Joe, 253
Moot, 16
Moral Majority, 294
Moral rights, 590
Morel, Daniel, 588
Morgan, J. P., 530
Morpheus, 616, 631–635
Morse, Deborah, 124–125
Motion Picture Association of America (MPAA), 434, 553
Motion to dismiss, 31, 209*b*
MoveOn, 489
MTV, 502
Murdoch, Rupert, 338*b,* 498*b,* 498*b*
Music licensing, 610–615, 611*b,* 615*b*
Must-carry rules, 506–508
Musumeci, Antonio, 345*b*
Muzak, 615
MySpace, 312

N

Naked Cowboy, 249*b*
Name, appropriation of, *246,* 246–247
Names, trademarking, 620–621
Napster, 615

NASCAR, 209*b*
Nast, Thomas, 318
Nation, 604, 607
National Aeronautics and Space Administration, 361*b*
National Association of Broadcasters, 485*b,* 553
National Association of Theater Owners, 553
National Audubon Society, 205*b*
National Cable Television Association, 553
National Center for Juvenile Justice, 437
National Center for State Courts, 456
National Collegiate Athletic Association (NCAA), 255*b*
National Defense Authorization Act, 5
National Endowment for the Arts (NEA), 86–87
National Examiner, 160
National Football League, 69, 509
National Lawyers Guild, 183
National Nuclear Security Administration (NNSA), 355
National Public Radio (NPR), 499
National Religious Broadcasters (NRB), 115*b*
National Science Foundation, 491*b*
National security
    executive order on cybersecurity, 28*b*
    Freedom of Information Act and, 359
    speech distinctions, 102–108, 104*b,* 105*f,* 106*b,* 107*b*
National Security Agency, 228, 234*b*
NBA Live, 255*b*
NBC, 65, 290*b*
Near, Jay, 66
Near v. Minnesota, 53*f,* 89–97
Nebraska Bar/Press Guidelines, 439
Negligence, 175–177
Negligent infliction of emotional distress, 286, 298–303, 299*b*
Neiman-Marcus, 157
Nelson, Sandra, 76
Net neutrality, 513–514
Neutral reportage, 203–204, 204*b,* 205*b*
New Kids on the Block, 626
News Corporation, 338*b,* 498*b*
Newsgathering, 324–381
    access to federal meetings, 367–372, 368*b,* 370*b,* 371*b*
    access to property, 327–334, *330, 331b, 333b*
    covert recording, 339–346, 340*b,* 341*b,* 342*m,* 345*b*
    denying access to records, 346–350, 349*b*
    generally, 325–327
    newsgathering pitfalls, *334,* 334–339, 335*b,* 336*b,* 338*b*
    newsgathering protections, 350–367, 351*b,* 355*b,* 356*b,*
        357*f,* 359, 362*b,* 363, 365*b*
    *U.S. Dept. of Justice v. Reporters Committee for Freedom of
        the Press,* 327*f,* 376–381

Wilson v. Layne, 327f, 331, 332–334, 332b, 333b, 373–376
  See also Reporter's privilege
News of the World, 338b
Newsroom searches, 401–402
Newsworthiness, 250–251, 263
New venire, 427
New York City Metropolitan Transportation Authority
    (MTA), 83b
New Yorker, 168, 339
New York Times
  First Amendment, 97–98
  intellectual property, 584
  libel, 164–165, 166f, 172, 180, 193, 205b
  newsgathering, 324, 361b
  reporter's privilege, 389b
  rule of law, 26
New York Times Co. v. Sullivan, 144, 164–173, 166b, 167b,
    176b, 180–182, 638
New York Times v. United States, 53f, 97–99
Nichols, Mike, 536
Nicholson, Jack, 536, 536
Nickelodeon, 504
Nielsen, 509
Nike, 31, 648
Nixon, Richard, 53b, 145b, 241, 452, 608
No Child Left Behind, 496
No Electronic Theft Act, 603
Nolan, Rick, 7
Noncommercial broadcasting, regulation and, 499–500
Noncovert recording, 345–346
Nonduplication rules, 509
Nonpublic forums
  defined, 84
  public forums *versus,* 81–87, 83b, 85b
  Supreme Court on, 85b
Noriega, Manuel, 439
Norwood, Norman, 304
Notice of Proposed Rule Making, 479
Novak, Robert, 199b, 216–221
Nuccio, Richard, 182
NYPD Blue, 573, 574

O

Obama, Barack
  electronic media regulation, 474
  libel and, 145b
  media and the courts, 452, 453

newsgathering and, 359
rule of law, 7, 28b
O'Bannon, Ed, 255b, 255b
O'Brien, David Paul, 72–73, 121
O'Brien test, 73
Obscenity and indecency, 526–575
  FCC v. Fox Television Stations, 529f, 570–575
  generally, 527–529, 528
  indecency, broadcast, 526, 545–553, 547b, 548b, 549, 552b
  indecency, cable, 554–556
  indecency, defined, 530
  indecency, generally, 544–545
  indecency, Internet, 535b, 556–560, 556b
  Miller v. California, 528b, 529f, 533b, 537b, 566–570
  obscenity, current definition, 532–538, 536, 542f
  obscenity, history, 529–532, 530b, 531b
  obscenity, in Canada, 530b
  obscenity, in U.K., 539b
  obscenity, law enforcement, 538–544
  violence in media and, 560–565, 561b, 562b, 564b
Obsidian Finance Group, 176b
Occupy DC, 74b
"Occupy the Courts" event, 2
Occupy Wall Street movement, 7b, 50, 74b, 103b
O'Connor, Sandra Day
  First Amendment, 78b
  libel and, 145b, 162
  obscenity, indecency, and violence, 535
  speech distinctions and, 103b, 116, 137–138
Offensive speech, 112
Office of Communications (Ofcom) (UK), 539b
Ohio High School Athletic Association (OHSAA), 222
Ollman, Bertell, 199b, 216–221
Ollman v. Evans
  case, 191f, 199b, 216–221
  Ollman test, 196–197, 196b
Olson, Floyd B., 90
O'Mara, Mark, 447b
Onassis, Jacqueline Kennedy, 334, 334
OneQuality, 658b
"On its face," 8b
Online search engines, for legal research, 35
Open Government Act, 351
Open-records laws, 455–456
Open the Government, 454
Operation Gunsmoke, 373
Opinion, libel and, 195–203, 196b, 199b, 201b
Opinion letters (FTC), 653–654
Orange Crush, 619

Orbison, Roy, 604
Oregon State University (OSU), 132
Oren, Michael, 131*b*
Organization for Economic Co-Operation and Development (OECD), 59*b*
Original intent, 54
Originalists, 20
Original jurisidiction, 15, 16
"Orphan works," 607*b*
Osbourne, Ozzy, 305
Outkast, 253
Outrageousness, 289–292
Overbroad laws, 5, 6
Overrule, 15
Oversight Monitoring Board, 553
Overturn precedent, defined, 27
"Ox the Great and Powerful" (movie), 587*b*

P

Padrick, Kevin, 176*b*
Page, Larry, 482
Paladin Press, 309
Papish, Barbara, 129
Paramount Pictures, 308–309, 600
Parents Against Tired Truckers (PATT), 337
Parker, Chief Justice, 95
Parks, Rosa, 253–254, *254*
Parody, 200–203
Parody, satire *versus*, 295*b*
Passage of time, 272
Passolt, Melvin C., 90
Patently offensive, defined, 536–537
Patterson, James, 578
Payola, 495
PEG access channels, 509
Pennsylvania State University, 618*b*
Pentagon Papers, 67, 69*b*, 344
People Can Change, 128
Per curiam opinion, 17
Peremptory challenges, 32
Perez, Jane, 194*b*
Performance, musical, 611*b*, 613–614
Perry, James, 309, 310*b*
Personal privacy, Freedom of Information Act and, 361–262
Perverted Justice, 290*b*
Peterbilt, 619

Petitions
    First Amendment and, 85–86
    "We the People" website, 22*b*
Phelps, Fred, 295, 319–323
Phonorecords, copyright and, 614
Physical harm, 301–306, *302, 305b*. *See also* Emotional distress and physical harm
Pitbull, 253
Plagiarism, 584
Plaintiffs
    appropriation, *246*, 246–250, 248*b*
    defined, 30
    effect of potential market of, 608 (*See also* Copyright)
    false light cases, 238–242, 238*b*
    intentional infliction of emotional distress, 289*b*
    libel-proof plaintiffs, 206–208
    See also Libel case elements
Playboy, 539*b*, 619
Pocan, Mark, 7
Pole rules, 501
Political broadcasting, regulation of, 483–489, 485*b*, *487*
Political questions, 21
Political speech, 76–81, 78*b*, 79*b*
Politico, 584
Polling places, press access to, 328
POM Wonderful, 653*b*, 653*b*
Pooley, Dan, 258
Pope, Zazi, 311*b*
Pornography
    censorship and, 530*b*
    child pornography, 538–542, 539*b*
    defined, 530
    See also Obscenity and indecency
Posner, Richard, 425, 562*b*
Post-Newsweek, 423
Powell, Lewis
    advertising, 661–665
    libel, 195
    libel and, 173, 182–187
    newsgathering and, 325
    reporter's privilege, 386, 388, 411
Precedent, 6
Predominant use test, 256–257
Prejudicial speech, fair trial and, *420*, 420–429, 425*b*
Prescription medicines, advertising of, 646–647
Presley, Elvis, *103b*, 252
Press-Enterprise test, 433*b*
Presumed damages, 178–179
Primary Colors (novel), 158

Prince, 588

Principal Register, 622

Prior restraint
defined, 57–58
generally, 65–70, 67*b*, 68*b*
Near v. Minnesota, 53*f*, 89–97

Privacy, 226–283
appropriation, 237*b*, 243–259, 244*b*, 245*b*, 246, 247*b*, 248*b*, 249*b*, 252, 254, 255*b*, 256
City of Ontario v. Quon, 227*f*, 273–277
Communications Assistance for Law Enforcement Act (CALEA), 234*b*
Electronic Communications Privacy Act (ECPA), 231*b*
false light, 237–243, 237*b*, 238*b*
generally, 226, 227–232, 230*f*
intrusion, 237*b*, 259–264, 261*b*
privacy law development, 236–237
private facts, 237*b*, 264–272, 264*b*, 265*b*
sources of protection for, 235–236
United States v. Jones, 227*f*, 278–283
U.S. Constitution on, 235*b*
U.S. Supreme Court on, 232–235
See also Newsgathering

Privacy Act of 1974, 347, 379

Privacy Protection Act, 402–403

Private facts, 237*b*, 264–272, 264*b*, 265*b*

Private figures, 175

Private property, as public forum, 84–86

Privilege. *See* Reporter's privilege

Probable cause, 29–30

Professional Golfers' Association Masters Tournament, 256, 256*b*

Promissory estoppel, 399

Property, press access to, 327–334, 330, 331*b*, 333*b*

Prosecutorial Remedies and Other Tools to End the Exploitation of Children Today Act (The Protect Act), 559

Prosser, Dean, 247

Prosser, William, 236–237

Proximate cause, 305, 305*b*

Prudhomme, Paul, 247

Prune Yard Shopping Center, 85–86

Prurient interest, 532–533

Public Access to Court Electronic Records (PACER), 456

Publication (libel cases), 151–157, 153*b*, 154*b*

Public Broadcasting Act, 500

Public Broadcasting Service (PBS), 66*b*, 499

Public Citizen, 194*b*

Public Disclosure Act (Washington State), 455

Public domain, 251–252, 594–597, 596*b*

Public figures
all-purpose, 173
defined, 172–173
involuntary, 175
limited-purpose, 174*b*
losing status of, 175
private figures *versus*, 175

Public forums
defined, 82
designated, 83
nonpublic forums, defined, 84
nonpublic forums *versus*, 81–87, 83*b*, 85*b*
traditional, 82, 85*b*

Public Health Cigarette Smoking Act, 642

Public interest standard, 483

Publicity, privacy and, 268–269

Public property, press access to, 327–334

Public record, 269, 271

Public Service Commission of the State of New York, 661–667

Public significance, 269–270

Puffery, 652

Punitive damages, 179

Q

Qualified privilege, 192

Quash, defined, 384

Qui Chengwei, 561*b*

Quon, Jeff, 273–277

R

Racketeer Influenced and Corrupt Organizations Act (RICO), 543–544

Radio Act of 1912, 476, 493

Radio Act of 1927, 477, 483, 493, 518

Rambis, Kurt, 154*b*

Ramirez, Edith, 659

Ratings
Entertainment Software Rating Board (ESRB), 564–565, 564*b*
Motion Picture Association of America (MPAA), 434
Nielsen, 509
television broadcast regulation, 552–553, 552*b*

Rational review, 71

Ratzenberger, John, 248

RealDVD, 434

Reality television programs
  electronic media regulation and, 492*b*
  emotional distress and, 293*b*

Reasonable person, 259

Reckless acts, 286, 292–293

Reckless disregard, 169–171, 171*b*

Recording, copyright infringement and, 600–601. *See also* Copyright

Recording, of conversations, 341–346, 341*b*, 342*m*

Recording Industry of America, 69

Recordkeeping, broadcast, 489

Records (court)
  denying access to press, 346–350, 349*b*
  Freedom of Information Act and, 362–364

Records (student), access to, 347–348

Recovery Act of 2009, 78

Red and Black (University of Georgia), 133, *133*

ReDigi, 592*b*

Redish, Martin, 104*b*

Red Lion v. FCC, 477*f,* 516–521

Reebok, 655*b*

Reese, Chuck, *133*

Regulation
  corporate speech regulation, 648–649
  Internet advertising, 658–660, 658*b,* 659*b*
  legislative and agency advertising regulation, 649–657, 650*b,* 651*b,* 652*b,* 653*b,* 655*b,* 657
  See also Advertising

Rehnquist, William H.
  advertising, 665–667
  emotional distress, 317–319
  libel, 143–144, 197, 221–225
  media and the courts, 444, 472–473
  newsgathering, 373–376
  speech distinctions and, 106, 137–138

Religion
  First Amendment and, 83*b,* 87
  speech distinctions and, 106*b,* 128–129, 131*b*

Remand, defined, 14, 16

Reporters Committee for Freedom of the Press (RCFP), 32*b,* 149*b,* 354, 363, 378, 437, 438

Reporter's privilege, 382–417
  Branzburg v. Hayes, 385–388, 386*f,* 393*b,* 404–416
  breaking promises of confidentiality, 399–400
  Cohen v. Cowles Media, 386*f,* 399–400, 400*b,* 416–417
  contempt of court and, 387*b*
  defined, 384–385
  generally, 383–384

post-*Branzburg,* 388–391, 389*b*
  search warrants, 401–403
  shield laws, 391–399, 392*b,* 393*b,* 394*b,* 395*b,* 396*b,* 398*b*
  test of, 386*b*

Report on Editorializing by Broadcast Licensees, 517

Report on the Virginia Resolutions of 1798, 184

Republication, 151–152

Research. *See* Sources of the law

Responsible reporting, 214

Restraining order, 438

Retractions, 212–213

Retransmission consent, 506–508

"Revenge porn," 265*b*

Review, granted by U.S. Supreme Court, 16

Rhetorical hyperbole, 200–203, 201*b*

Rich, Jessica, 689*n* 12

Richard, Cliff, 615*b*

Richie, Nicole, 549, 571, 572

Richmond Newspapers v. Virginia, 421*f,* 466–473

Ride-alongs, 331, 332–334, 332*b,* 333*b*

RightChange.com, 489

Righthaven, 599

Right of publicity, 244–246, 244*b,* 249*b,* 252–257, 255*b,* 256

Risen, James, 389–390

Rite Aid Corporation, 656

Ritter, Carol, 429

Roberts, John
  emotional distress, 319–323
  media and the courts, 445*b*
  newsgathering, 364
  rule of law, 13, 13*b,* 14*b,* 14*f,* 16, 40
  speech distinctions, 116, 125

Rockefeller, Jay, 491*b*

Rogers, Ginger, 253

Rojadirector.com, 69

Roman Catholic Church, 56

Romantics, 249

Romney, Mitt, *487*

Roosevelt, Franklin D., 13, 13*b*

Rosetta Stone, 211, 248*b*

Rousseau, Jean-Jacques, 57, 60

Rule of law, 2–51
  case process, 29–34, 30*f,* 32*b*
  Citizens United v. Federal Elections Commission, 2, 3, 5*f,* 7*b,* 40–46, 77, 648–649
  court system, 8–18, 9*b,* 9*f,* 10–11*t,* 12*f,* 13*b,* 14*f,* 15*f,* 18
  defined, 4
  facial challenges, 8*b*
  finding the law, 34–39

generally, 3–8
instant petitions, 22*b*
judicial review, 18–20, 19*b*
landmark cases in context, 5*f*
Marbury v. Madison, 5*f, 18,* 38–39, 46–49
ranking of U.S. rule of law, 4*b*
sources of the law, 20–29, 20*b,* 22*b,* 23*b,* 24*f,* 28*b*
transnational rules of justice, 6*b*
Rule of Law Initiative, 6
Rush, Rick, 256, 256*b*
Russia, video games in, 561*b*

S

Safe harbor policy, 551
Salinger, J. D., 606
Salisbury, Bill, 400*b*
Samsung Electronics, 247, 581*b*
Sanders, William, 303
Sandy Hook (Connecticut) Elementary School, 491*b*
Satire, 200–203, 295*b*
Saturday Evening Post, 169–170
Saturday Press (Minneapolis, Minnesota), 66, 90–91
Savage, Michael, 304
Scalia, Antonin
    advertising, 641
    libel, 156, 199*b,* 220–221
    privacy and, 278–280
    rule of law, 13, 13*b,* 14*b,* 14*f,* 19, 19*b*
    speech distinctions, 117
Scharf, Lloyd, 273–277
Schenck, Charles, 108
Schumer, Charles, 392*b*
Sci-Fi Channel, 293*b*
Scott, H. Don, 222–225
Scotusblog, 176*b*
Scrutiny. *See* Intermediate scrutiny; Strict scrutiny
Seale, Bobby, 257
Search warrants, 331*b,* 401–403
Seattle Post-Intelligencer, 163
Section 315 (Communications Act), 484, 485–486,
    488–489, 516
Section 230 immunity, 211–212
Sedition Act of 1798, 58, 59, 147–148, 167*b*
Seditious libel, 58
Sellify, 658*b*
Serious social value, 537
Sexting, 541–542, 542*f*

Shakespeare, William, 582
Sheppard, Marilyn, 459–460
Sheppard, Sam, 422–423, 459–466
Sheppard v. Maxwell, 421–423, 421*f,* 459–466
Shield laws
    contempt of court and, 395*b*
    defenses, 397–398
    defined, 391
    generally, 391–394, 399
    information covered by, 394–395
    journalists defined by, 394
    Kansas on, 396*b*
    options for protection of confidential sources, 394*b*
    websites and, 395–397
    West Virginia on, 393*b*
    WikiLeaks and, 392*b*
Shotke, Officer, 460
Simon & Schuster, 72
Simorangkir, Dawn, 154*b*
Simpson, Nicole Brown, 160
Simpson, O. J., 160
Single-publication rule, 204–205
SiriusXM, *511,* 613
Skechers, 655*b,* 655*b*
Slander, libel *versus,* 144*b*
SLAPP (strategic lawsuits against public participation),
    148–149, 148*b,* 149*b*
SLAPS test, 537*b*
Smolla, Rodney, 333*b*
Snoop Dogg, 344–345
Snowden, Edward J., 349*b*
Snyder, Albaert, 296–297
Snyder, Matthew, 319–323
Snyder v. Phelps, 287*f,* 319–323
Soboroff, Jeffrey, 119*b*
Social media
    electronic access to trials, 447–450, 447*b,* 449*b*
    as newsgathering sources, 338–339
Society for the Suppression of Vice, 530, 531*b*
Society of European Stage Authors and Composers (SESAC),
    611, 614
Society of Professional Journalists (SPJ), 133, 351, 440*b*
Socrates, 144
Soldier of Fortune, 303–305
Sonny Bono Copyright Term Extension Act of 1998, 594,
    595, 595*b*
Sony/ATV, 611
Sony Pictures, 66*b,* 601*b*
Sorrell v. IMS Healthcare, Inc., 639*f,* 667–674

Sotomayor, Sonia
  First Amendment, 42–46
  media and the courts Amendment, 446b
  rule of law, 13, 13b, 14b, 14f, 16
Sound-alikes, 247
SoundExchange, 613
Sound recordings, copyright and, 612–613
Sources of the law, 20–29
  administrative rules, 27–29
  common law, 26–27
  equity law, 26
  executive orders, 28b, 29
  generally, 20–21, 20b
  how bills become law, 24b
  statutes, 24–25
  three branches of federal government and, 22b
  U.S. Constitution and state constitutions, 21–25, 23b
Souter, David, 3, 80, 129, 445b, 535, 631–635
South Park (television program), 605b, 605b
Spahn, Warren, 238, 240
Special damages, 178
Spectrum scarcity, 482
Speech distinctions, 100–141
  court tests to protect disruptive speech, 108–111, 111b
  generally, 101–102
  national security and tranquility, 102–108, 104b, 105f,
      106b, 107b
  speech assaults, 111–120, 113b, 115b, 118b, 119b
  speech in the schools, 122–135, 123b, 124, 131b,
      133, 134b
  symbolic speech, 120–122
  Texas v. Johnson, 136–138
  Tinker v. Des Moines, 103f, 124, 138–141
Spider Webs, 623
Sponsorship identification
  broadcast systems, 495–496
  political advertising and, 487
Spooner, William, 154b
Sports, trademark and, 618b
Sports Illustrated, 267
St. Paul Pioneer Press, 400b, 416
Stahl, Donald, 113
Standards for Privacy of Individually Identifiable Health
    Information, 348
Standing, 648
Stanford Daily (Stanford University), 401–402
Stanford University, 401
Star Chamber (England), 145, 148b
Stare decisis, 6, 26–27, 42
Starr, Kenneth, 199b, 216–220

Statement of fact, 150–151
State secrets, 453–455
States/state courts
  advertising, 723n 85
  federal courts compared to, 9f, 10–11t
  open court proceedings and children, 705n 69
  open-meetings laws, 371–372, 371b
  open-records laws, 369–371, 370b
  on right of publicity, 691n 75
  shield laws and options for protection of confidential
      sources, 394b
  state constitutions as source of law, 21–25
  video, audio, webcasts of, 448m (See also Media and
      the courts)
  See also individual names of U.S. states
Stationers' Company (England), 579
Statute of Anne of 1710 (England), 579, 580
Statutes, generally, 24–25
Statutes of limitation, 212, 213m
Statutory construction, 24, 25
Statutory damages, 593
Statutory exemptions, 360
Statutory law, 21
Stern, Howard, 291–292
Steubenville (Ohio), rape trial in, 418
Stevens, John Paul
  advertising, 645
  electronic media regulation, 515
  First Amendment, 77
  media and the courts, 470
  newsgathering, 363, 376–381
  rule of law, 16, 40–46
  speech distinctions, 125, 138
Stevens, Robert J., 116
Stewart, Martha, 433
Stewart, Potter
  First Amendment, 53, 55b, 56, 99
  media and the courts, 429, 472
  newsgathering, 326
  obscenity, indecency, and violence, 527
  reporter's privilege, 386, 411–416
Stolen Valor Act, 55–56
Storage Wars (television program), 492b
Stored Communications Act, 234, 341
Streamcast, 631–635
Strict liability, 30–31
Strictly Broadband, 539b
Strict scrutiny, 71–72, 72b
Strossen, Nadine, 530b
Student Press Law Center, 133

Student records, access to, 347–348
Subpoena, 31
Substantial truth, 162–163
Substantiation, 656
"Suggestive marks," 619
Sullivan, L. B., *144, 164–165,* 180
Sullivan, Margaret, 584
Sulzberger, Arthur, Jr., 389*b*
Summary judgment, 33, 208–210
Summons, 427
Sun (supermarket tabloid), 241
Supplemental Register, 622
Swartz, Aaron, *454b, 454b*
Swift Boat Veterans for Truth, 489
Sylvester, William, 438
Symbolic expression, 73
Symbolic speech, 120–122
Synchronization rights, copyright and, 614–615

T

Tate, Sharon, 311*b*
Tatro, Amanda, 130–131
Taylor, Elizabeth, 257
Taylor, Sean, 423
Teachbook, 624
Telecommunications Act of 1996, 25, 29, 312, 502, 513, 514, 556
Telephone Consumer Protection Act, 660
Texas Beef Group, 161*b*
Texas v. Johnson, 136–138
Texts
  advertising and, 659*b*
  sexting, 541–542, 542*f*
  text threats, 119
Textualists, 20
Texxxan.com, 265*b*
TheFlyontheWall.com, 68
Thomas, Clarence
  advertising, 642
  rule of law, 13, 13*b,* 14*b,* 14*f,* 16
  speech distinctions, 117
Threatened Voices, 147*m*
Threats, 117–120, 121*b*
Three Stooges, 254
Tiffany, 625*b*
Timberlake, Justin, *550*
Time, Inc., 241
Time Crisis II, *100*

Time (magazine), 584, 604
Time/place/manner (TPM) laws, 72–73
Time Warner, 509, *585b,* 616
Tinker, Lorena, *124*
Tinker, Mary Beth, *124*
Tinker, Paul, *124*
Tinker v. Des Moines, 103*f,* 123–126, *124,* 138–141
Titanic (ship), 476
Tobacco advertising, *636,* 642–645, *644,* 646*b*
Torre, Marie, 702*n* 24
Tortious newsgathering, 334–335
Torts, 30
Trade libel, 160–162
Trademark, 611–626
  defined, 617
  diluting, 625*b*
  distinctiveness requirement, 618–622
  domain names, 623
  examples, 618*b,* 620*b*
  generally, 617–618
  infringement, 624–625
  infringement defenses, 626
  Lanham Act, 578, 618, 619*b,* 622m 626
  registering, 622–623
Trade regulation rule, 654
Trade secrets, Freedom of Information Act and, 360–361
Traditional public forums, 82, 85*b*
Transformativeness test, 254
Transportation Safety Administration, 232
Transportation Security Administration, 32*b*
Transportation Security Administration (TSA), 32*b*
Travel Channel, 249*b*
Travis, Randy, 420
Trial Behavior Consulting, 32
TripAdvisor.com, 201*b*
Tropicana, 656, 657
True threat, 117
Tryon, barrett, 76
Tsarnaev, Tamerlan, 422*b*
Tulsa World, 453
Turner Broadcasting v. FCC, 477*f,* 502–503, 521–525
Turnitin, 606
Twain, Mark, 156
Tweed, William M. "Boss," 318
21st Century Communications and Video Accessibility Act of 2010, 474
Twistelli, Anthony "Tony Twist," 256
Twitter, 79*b,* 588–589
Twobly standard, 209*b*
2 Live Crew, 537, 604

U

U-Haul, 651
Underinclusive, defined, 114
Uniform Code of Military Justice, 349*b*
United Kingdom
  copyright law, 581*b*
  intellectual property law, 615
  seditious libel, 146*b*
  U.K. Defamation Bill 2013, 207*b*
United Nations
  Human Rights Committee, 207*b*
  Human Rights Council, 59*b*
  rule of law, 6
  transnational rules of justice and, 6*b*
United States v. Jones, 227*f*, 278–283
Universal Declaration of Human Rights, 20
Universal Music Group (UMG), 609–610
Universal Pictures, 65
University of Florida, 618*b*
University of Maryland, 199*b*, 216
University of Mississippi, 170
University of Pittsburgh, 618*b*
Uruguay Round Agreements Act (URAA), 627
U.S. Air Force, 66*b*
U.S. Bureau of Land Management, 329, 432
U.S. Circuit Courts of Appeal, 12*f*, 13–15
U.S. Constitution
  Bill of Rights, 23*b*, 24
  on copyrights and patents, 578*b* (*See also* Intellectual
    property)
  on federal court system, 10
  Fourth Amendment, 227–228 (*See also* Privacy)
  on privacy, 235*b* (*See also* Privacy)
  rule of law, 6
  Sixth Amendment, 420, 429–432, 441 (*See also* Media and
    the courts)
  state constitutions and, 21–25
  See also First Amendment
U.S. Copyright Office, 597–598
U.S. Department of Defense, 66*b*, 67, 330, 365*b*
U.S. Department of Education (DOE), 347
U.S. Department of Homeland Security, 21, 32
U.S. Department of Justice, 328, 403
*U.S. Dept. of Justice v. Reporters Committee for Freedom of
  the Press*, 327*f*, 376–381
U.S. Fair Trade Commission Act, 641*b*
U.S. Fish and Wildlife Service, 332
U.S. Healthcare, 334
U.S. Marshals Service, 192

U.S. Park Police, 363
U.S. Patent and Trademark Office (PTO), 622
U.S. Supreme Court
  First Amendment and court scrutiny, 71–75, 72*b*, 74*b*, 75*b*
    (*See also* First Amendment)
  libel, 144 (*See also* Libel)
  on privacy, 232–235 (*See also* Privacy)
  rule of law and court system, 14*f*, 15–17
  speech distinctions and court tests to protect disruptive
    speech, 108–111, 111*b* (*See also* Speech distinctions)
  See also First Amendment; Libel; Libel defenses and
    privileges; *individual names of cases*
USA Network, 65
USA Patriot Act, 105, 232, 235, 347
USA Today, 496
Use rule (Section 315), 484, 485–486, 488–489, 516

V

Vague laws, 4–5, 8
Valentino, Rudolph, 257
Van Hollen, Chris, 649
Variable obscenity, 538
V-chip, 552–553, 552*b*
Veilleux, Raymond, 337
Vendors, libel and, 152–153, 153*b*
Venire, 31
Venue, 31, 427
Venus de Milo (sculpture), *528*
Veoh Networks, 609–610
Verizon, 156
Viacom, 610
Victor's Secret, 624–625
Video games
  incitement and emotional distress, 307*b*
  interactivity of, 562*b*
  ratings, 564*b*
  Russia and China on, 561*b*
  speech distinctions, *100*, 116–117
  violence in, 560–565
Video news releases (VNRs), 495–496
Video Voyeurism Prevention Act, 350
Vidster, 602
Viewpoint-based discrimination, 114
Village People, 594
Violence
  media regulation and, 491*b*
  in video games, 560–565
  See also Obscenity and indecency

Virgil, Mike, 267
Voice, appropriation of, 247
Voir dire, 31
Volokh, Eugene, 62b, 176b
Voluntary compliance, 654
Voyeurism, video, 350

W

Walker, Edwin, 170
Wall Street Journal, 228
Walt Disney Company, 576, 595b
Ward, Claire, 146b
Warner Brothers, 587b, 614
Warner/Chappell, 585b
Warner-Lambert, 656–657
"War of the Worlds" (radio broadcast), 493
Warren, Earl, 172
Warren, Samuel, 236–237, 456
Washington, George, 318
Washington Post, 26, 97–98, 199b, 228, 338–339, 588
Websites, for legal research, 35
Weir, Dominic, 266
Welles, Orson, 493
Wells, H. G., 493
Wendt, George, 248
Westboro Baptist Church (Topeka, Kansas), 284, 295–297,
    319–323
West Virginia, on shield laws, 393b
"We the People" website, 22b
White, Byron
    electronic media regulation, 516–521
    First Amendment and, 99
    libel and, 169b
    reporter's privilege, 386, 388, 394, 400, 402, 404–410,
        416–417
    speech distinctions and, 137–138, 140–141
White, Vanna, 247–249
Whitney, Anita, 110
Whitney, Wheelock, 416–417
Wichita Eagle, 396b
Wi-Fi, 480b
Wi-fi networks, FCC and, 480b
WikiLeaks, 52b, 53b, 69b, 70, 392b
Wildmon, Donald, 314
Williams, Armstrong, 496
Willis, Victor, 594
Wilson, Charles, 373–376
Wilson, Dominic, 373–376

Wilson, Geraldine, 373–376
Wilson v. Layne, 327f, 331, 332–334, 332b, 333b,
    373–376
Winfrey, Oprah, 161b
Winter, Edgar, 256
Winter, Johnny, 256
"Wire" conversations, recording, 341–345, 341b, 342m
Wireless Ship Act of 1910, 476
Wire service defense, 204, 204b
Wiretap Act, 341
Withstand motion to dismiss, 155b
Withstand summary judgment motion, 155b
Wolf, Chris, 79b
Wolf, Frank, 491b
Wolf, Josh, 382, 390
Woods, Tiger, 256, 256b
Work made for hire, 585–587
World Justice Project (American Bar Association), 4b
World Trade Center, 105
Writ of certiorari, 15, 16

X

Xerox, 619, 621
XM Radio, 511

Y

Yahoo!, 313
Yale University, 300
Yelp!, 54, 149b, 194b
Young, Andre, 344–345
Young and Modern, 251
Young Men's Christian Association (YMCA), 530
YouTube, 610

Z

Zacchini, Hugo, 251, 252
Zakaria, Fareed, 584
Zamora, Ronny, 302
Zapple rule, 489
Zenger, John Peter, 58
Zeran, Kenneth, 153b
Zhu Huimin, 561b
Zimmerman, George, 447b

⑨SAGE researchmethods

The essential online tool for researchers from the world's leading methods publisher

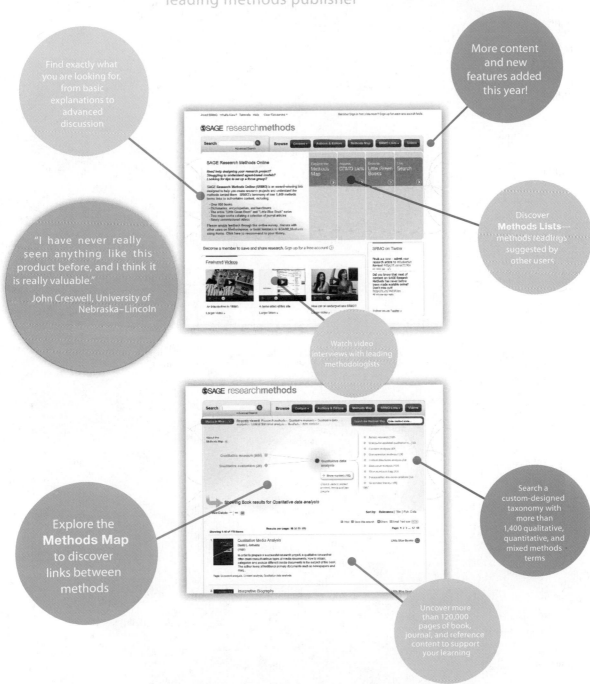

Find exactly what you are looking for, from basic explanations to advanced discussion

More content and new features added this year!

Discover **Methods Lists**— methods readings suggested by other users

"I have never really seen anything like this product before, and I think it is really valuable."

John Creswell, University of Nebraska–Lincoln

Watch video interviews with leading methodologists

Explore the **Methods Map** to discover links between methods

Search a custom-designed taxonomy with more than 1,400 qualitative, quantitative, and mixed methods terms

Uncover more than 120,000 pages of book, journal, and reference content to support your learning

Find out more at
www.sageresearchmethods.com